JOACHIM SMET, O. CARM.

THE MIRROR OF CARMEL

A Brief History of the Carmelite Order

CARMELITE MEDIA

This book is a digest of *The Carmelites*, Darien, IL, 1976-1988, 4 v. in 5.

Footnotes have been omitted. The reader interested in sources may refer to the unabridged original.

The title recalls a classic work in the historiography of the Carmelite Order: the *Speculum carmelitanum* (1686).

Edited by William J. Harry, O. Carm.

Carmelite Media
8501 Bailey Road
Darien, Illinois 60561

Phone: 1-630-971-0724
Email: publications@carmelnet.org
Website: carmelites.info/publications

Printed Book: ISBN: 978-1-936742-01-1
eBook: ISBN: 978-1-936742-03-5

For Martha

Aurelian. I can't remember everything.
Besides, it happened years ago,
And all of it's so tied with history,
So unintelligible,
Unless you know in great detail
Our origin, our rise, and then our move to Europe.
If once we had a man to gather all the facts
And lay them down in one straight line,
Well, then we'd know.

Gervase Toelle, O. Carm., *The Mantle of Elias*

TABLE OF CONTENTS

PART I: The Origins to the Council of Trent

Conclusion

Part One

THE ORIGINS TO THE COUNCIL OF TRENT

Chapter 1

The Hermits of Mount Carmel

"Every Order taketh its name either from a place or from a saint," writes John Baconthorpe, 14th century English Carmelite; "from a place, like the Cistercians who are called after Citeaux, and our Order after Carmel." As a matter of fact, it is to Mount Carmel, a mountain in Palestine on the Bay of Haifa, that the Carmelite Order traces its origin. The date of its origin, the subject of an age-old controversy, can now be ascertained with relative accuracy.

The Latin Kingdom of Jerusalem

During the 12th century, the crusaders established in Syria and Palestine the Latin Kingdom of Jerusalem, a feudal state consisting of subordinate units under the King of Jerusalem. The kingdom at its apogee extended over all of Palestine, but even at the zenith of Frankish power, the conquerors' hold on the land remained a tenuous one.

Jacques de Vitry, bishop of Acre from 1216 to 1228, describes in glowing terms the flowering of the Latin Church consequent upon the conquest of Palestine: "Pilgrims full of zeal for God, and religious men, flocked into the Holy Land, attracted by the sweet savour of the holy and venerable places. Old churches were repaired, and new ones were built; by the bounty of princes and the alms of the faithful, monasteries of regular monks were built in fitting places; parish priests and all things appertaining to the service and worship of God, were properly and suitably established everywhere."

The Patriarchate of Jerusalem was set up with metropolitan sees in Tyre, Caesarea, Nazareth, and Petra. The Canons Regular of St. Augustine were introduced into the most important churches in Jerusalem and, most likely, into all or most cathedral chapters. With regard to the monastic picture, De Vitry's description is a bit overdrawn. In all of Palestine there were only four Benedictine monasteries of men together with an equal number of women and two Premonstratensian monasteries. That there were Cistercian monks in Palestine, as sometimes alleged, remains questionable.

The Eremitical Life in Palestine

De Vitry makes special mention of the eremitical life in Palestine: "Holy men renounced the world, and, according to their various affections and wishes and their religious fervor, chose places to dwell in suitable to their object and devotion. Some, especially attracted by the Lord's example, chose that desirable wilderness called Quarantena, wherein our Lord fasted for forty days after his baptism (Mt. 4), therein to dwell as hermits and served God most valiantly in humble cells. Others, in imitation of the holy anchorite, the prophet Elijah, led solitary lives on Mount Carmel, especially on that part thereof which overhangs the city of Porphyria, now called Haifa, near the well called Elijah's Well, not far from the Convent of St. Margaret the Virgin, where in little comb-like cells, those bees of the Lord laid up sweet spiritual honey."

Palestine with Egypt was the classic land of the solitary life, hallowed by the memory of Hilarion, Cariton, Euthymius, Saba, Theodosius, and other valiant warriors of Christ. De Vitry testifies to the presence of western hermits in Quarantena, a mountain northeast of Jericho near the Jordan. The Valley of Jehosaphat, beneath the southern walls of Jerusalem, was a flourishing center of hermits, some of whom, according to the testimony of the pilgrim Theodoric (ca. 1172), were under the jurisdiction of the Benedictine abbey of St. Mary of the Valley of Jehosaphat. Mount Tabor was another refuge of hermits, who like those in the Valley of Jehosaphat, may have been connected with the Benedictine monastery there. Galilee, the native land of the Savior, also attracted the hermits. "Others of these religious men," De Vitry writes, "went to that wilderness near the Sea of Galilee where the Lord often preached... Here they chose their solitary dwellings, some of them on the plain, where there was much hay from dried grass; others on the neighboring mount, to which the Lord was wont to go apart to pray." Not all hermits lived in caves in the mountains; some inhabited the plains, living in grass huts.

The Horns of Hattin

The victory of Saladin at Hattin in 1187 put the quietus on religious life, cenobitical and eremitical, in Palestine. After that disaster, the only city left in Christian hands was Tyre. Subsequent crusades painfully won back some of the lost territory, mostly along the coast. The patriarch of Jerusalem fixed his residence in Acre. Fugitives from the monasteries settled there and in Tyre. The 13th century brought new Orders, including the Mendicants: the Franciscans with houses eventually in Acre, Tyre, and Sidon; and the Dominicans and Friars of the Sack with convents in Acre.

The Hermits of Mount Carmel

After Hattin, the eremitical life in the open countryside became difficult, if not impossible, for Latins. One place remained where hermits might follow their vocation undisturbed: Mount Carmel until the end of the kingdom lay within the sphere of Frankish power.

Carmel offered an ideal setting for retirement and reflection. Its rugged slopes, dense with vegetation; its remote valleys and wide views over the blue Mediterranean or the hills of Galilee, beckon to prayer and contemplation.

De Vitry would seem to indicate that western hermits settled on Mount Carmel from the beginning of the Frankish conquest of Palestine, yet indisputable evidence occurs only in the 13th century.

Two earlier references must be discarded. In 1163, the Spanish rabbi, Benjamin of Tudela, saw near the cave of Elijah a church built by two Christians and dedicated to the prophet. About the year 1174, John Phocas, a Greek monk from Patmos, found a group of monks near the same cave. The cave of Elijah, known as *el-chadr* (the "Green One") situated at the northernmost tip of the promontory at the base of the mountain, is quite distinct from the fountain of Elijah mentioned by De Vitry. Moreover, it is not even certain that Benjamin is referring to religious. The monks noted by Phocas were probably Greeks.

The first appearance of western hermits on Mt. Carmel in 13th century literature, the fact that other eremitical locations were now under Moslem control, suggest that refugees from other parts of Palestine found a haven on Carmel. Perhaps it is not all imagination that leads the early chroniclers of the Carmelite Order to claim for Carmel the other deserts in Palestine and Antioch.

The Frankish hermits settled around the fountain of Elijah in the *wadi 'ain es-siah*, a valley opening toward the sea on the western flank of Carmel, about two miles south of the promontory. The perennial fountain of Elijah offered a yearlong source of water. Fig, granate, and olive trees added variety to their diet. Below them lay the calm expanse of the sea. In this quiet valley, the hermits, bees of the Lord in their comb-like cells, "laid up spiritual honey."

In time, the hermits approached the papal legate and patriarch of Jerusalem, Albert of Vercelli, then resident in Acre, to set down their way of life in the form of a rule.

The Rule of St. Albert

Born in the diocese of Parma, Albert joined the canons regular of Mortara. "A man outstanding for his life, learning, and reputation," as the author of the *Gesta Innocentii III* put it, Albert ruled the diocese of Vercelli for twenty years and was frequently called on by the popes to carry out delicate diplomatic missions in the north of Italy. He composed a Rule for the Humiliati. In the Holy Land, where he arrived in 1206, he dedicated himself as legate to the much needed work of promoting harmony among the feuding Christian princes. On September 14, 1214, during a procession in the Church of the Holy Cross in Acre, Albert was assassinated.

The Rule of St. Albert is perhaps the least known of existing medieval rules. "Many are the ways," Albert begins, "the holy Fathers have instituted for following Christ and serving him faithfully with a pure heart and good conscience." The "following of Christ" should here be given the special connotation it no doubt had for the inhabitants of the Holy Land, of literally tracing Christ's footsteps on earth and a faithful vigil in his native land.

The *formula vitae* outlined by the patriarch echoes the style of life of the oriental monks in the *laurae* of Palestine. The hermits obey a superior, but their relations are not determined in every detail. It was a loose relationship of reverence on the part of the subject (ch. 18) and of service on the part of the prior (ch. 17). Each hermit had his own cell apart from the others (ch. 3), where he was to remain, meditating day and night on the law of the Lord and watching in prayer (ch. 7). Common penitential practices, fasting and prayer, are prescribed (ch. 12, 16). The hermits came together daily for Mass in the oratory in the midst of the cells; in ancient times, the hermits of the laurae met only once a week, on Saturday or Sunday, for Mass and an instruction by the *hegumenos*.

The hermits of Carmel probably did not recite the canonical office. For the hermit his psalter was enough, and he knew it by heart.

To continual prayer are added two other elements of classical eremitical life: poverty and manual labor for the purpose of earning one's daily bread (ch. 9, 15). Chapter 14 describes the spiritual armor of the *militia christiana*, the hermit's hand to hand encounter with Satan in the solitude of the wilderness. This passage, which outlines Christian combat in terms of a knight's gear, takes on special poignancy when we reflect that it was addressed to men living in the shadow of the scimitar.

The Rule does not prescribe the form of habit, but from a contemporary drawing we know that it was a habit of undyed wool, consisting of a tunic with belt, scapular and hood, over which was worn a mantle of seven white and dark vertical stripes.

From the account of a French pilgrim, written about 1231, we know that the oratory in the midst of the cells, prescribed by the Rule, was dedicated to the Blessed Virgin: "On the slope of this same mountain is a very fair place and delicious, where is a little church of our Lady." In time, the hermits of Mount Carmel became known as the "Brothers of Our Lady of Mount Carmel." As early as 1252 the term occurs in papal documents, so it probably already enjoyed popular usage. From this tiny mustard seed grew the wide-spreading tree of the Marian devotion of the Order.

Elijah, Founder of Religious Life

The site chosen for the hermitage, the fountain of Elijah, is worthy of note, for it was to have a profound influence on the charism of the Order. The memory of the prophets Elijah and Elisha attached to various localities in the Palestine of the crusades is very striking. Among the places associated with Elijah is Mount Carmel. Hardly a pilgrim who passed this imposing land mass on the road from Acre to Jerusalem failed to inform his readers that this was the abode of the prophet Elijah. In the case of the hermits, Carmel had an added attraction in that Elijah was considered in patristic writings and in the eremitical literature of the times to be the model and founder of the solitary way of life.

No less an authority than St. Anthony declares that "the ascetic should model his life as in a mirror after the example of the great Elijah."

"Every vocation has its leader," writes St. Jerome. "Bishops and priests have the apostles and apostolic men as models... We, however, have proposed for emulation our Pauls, Anthonys, Julians, Macarios and - if I may have recourse to the authority of Holy Writ - our leader Elijah, our Elisha, our sons of the prophets, who dwelt in the fields and solitary places and pitched their tents by the waters of the Jordan."

The hermits who settled on Carmel would not have had to come to Palestine to learn of this tradition, for it was also current among the hermits of Western Europe. The *Regula Solitariorum* states: "Many have often wondered who was the first hermit. Some go back in history and say the eremitical life had its origin in St. Elijah and John; others say St. Anthony was the first example of this way of life."

"This way of life," St. Peter Damian attests, "to go back to the earliest examples, was begun by Elijah in the Old Testament. Elisha increased the band of disciples and developed the way of life. In the New Testament, Paul and Anthony are considered their equivalents."

The hermits of Carmel must certainly have been aware of the peculiar appropriateness of the place they chose. They must also have been conscious of continuing the life Elijah had inaugurated in that very place.

Later Developments

During the second decade of the century the hermits of Carmel sought to solidify their juridical status. In 1226, they obtained confirmation of their "norm of living" from Pope Honorius III.

April of 1229 brought several privileges and decisions from Pope Gregory IX. On April 9, he placed the hermitage on Carmel under the protection of the Holy See and granted permission for divine service to be held there behind closed doors in time of interdict. Papal protection at the time entailed the right of direct appeal and was the first stage toward exemption.

On April 5, the prior of the hermitage on Mount Carmel was given power to dispense repentant apostates from censures, "because it would be too difficult to refer such cases to the Holy See in parts beyond the sea."

In the bull of April 6, Gregory forbids the hermitage to possess "places or possessions, that is, houses or revenues." The decision is sometimes interpreted as a first step toward mendicancy on the part of the Order, but such poverty was practiced by other eremitical communities, such as Grandmont. As a matter of fact, the pope adduces the contemplative character of the hermits' life as the reason why they should not have possessions, "lest those who, ascending the mountain to pray with the Lord, have washed their feet, should again soil them." The monasteries of Palestine were supported by revenues coming from Europe. Perhaps the hermitage on Carmel had been offered such stable support, which was now prohibited by the pope.

In the same document, the pope decreed that the prior of the hermitage was to obtain office only through the consent of the "*majoris et sanioris partis*" of the brethren.

The Prior of Mount Carmel

The historiography of the Order has its origin in Europe in the fourteenth century. What happened before that is not recorded. Consequently, the period when the eremitical life obtained, and Mount Carmel was the center of gravity remains lost in the mists of legendry. It was nonetheless real.

Lists of priors general were compiled by John Trissa, of the province of Narbonne (d. 1363) and John Grossi, of the province of Toulouse (d. ca. 1434), himself a prior general. These are supplemented by lists of general chapters by the same Trissa and Sibert de Beka, provincial of Germany (d. 1332).

Trissa begins his list of general chapters with that held in Messina in 1259; de Beka with Toulouse, 1264. The first prior general Trissa records is Ralph (d. 1274). Grossi begins his list with an otherwise unknown Alan, "though several others preceded him."

A 14th century catalog of saints lists the first three priors general of the Order: Berthold, Brocard, to whom the Rule is said to have been directed, and Cyril. All three are said to have died and been buried on Mount Carmel. They are generally considered to be legendary figures - perhaps because of the hagiographical nature of the information about them. But why invent these particular persons with these particular names?

The other 13th century priors general after Alan with probable dates of their term of office were Godfrey, 1247-1254, St. Simon Stock, 1254-1266, Nicholas of France, 1266-1271, Ralph Fryston 1271- , Peter of Millau, -1294, Raymond of Ile, 1294-1297.

With the expansion of the Order in the West, the priors of Mount Carmel ceased ruling the Order. It is not known when this occurred; perhaps Nicholas the Frenchman, who lived on Cyprus, is the last to do so.

Chapter 2

From East to West

While the hermitage on Carmel was stabilizing itself and growing from within, forces were at work without, which would eventually lead to its destruction. The third decade of the century, spanned by the ten-year truce negotiated by Frederick II in 1229, was not marked by any major recurrence of hostilities between Saracen and Christian.

Nevertheless, the hermits must have suffered disturbance, for it is at this period that a number of them decided to return or migrate to the West. A religious foundation in the open countryside was always prey to raids by bands of bedouins or other hostile groups. "The inroads of the pagans," Innocent IV was to write later, "have driven our beloved sons, the hermits of Mount Carmel, to betake themselves, not without great affliction of spirit, to parts across the sea."

Migration to the West

According to the Dominican, Vincent of Beauvais (d. 1264), the Carmelites migrated to Europe in 1238. This date need not be taken as anything more than approximate, nor the migration as a single event that took place in one year.

The foundation of the Carmelites in Valenciennes made as early as 1235 is doubtful. Foundations were made in Messina in Sicily, Aylesford and Hulne in England (1242), and Les Aygalades near Marseilles in Provence. It was probably at this time, too, that the Carmelites crossed to Cyprus, to Fortamia (today probably Karmi, near Nicosia) - a less drastic removal from the Holy Land. The island had been in Frankish hands since Richard the Lion-Hearted had wrested it from the control of Isaac Ducas Comnenus in 1191.

The Mitigation of the Rule, 1247

Only a decade after a portion of the Carmelites had fled to Europe, we find them considering a modification of their *formula vitae*. This document, drawn up for a single hermitage, no longer suited their worldwide circumstances. The first foundations had indeed been made in remote places, but we soon see the hermits settling in more populated areas. This involved, too, a more cenobitical lifestyle. In 1247, accordingly, the Carmelites sent envoys to Pope Innocent IV, then residing at Lyons, requesting "that he deign to clarify and correct certain doubts and mitigate certain severities" in the Rule of St. Albert. The pope charged Cardinal Hugh of St. Cher and William, Bishop of Anterados (Tartous), both Dominicans, with the task and upon its completion, on October 1, 1247, issued his letter, *Quae honorem*, modifying the Carmelite Rule.

The most notable changes are: foundations need no longer be made in desert places only, meals are to be taken in common, the recitation of the canonical office is imposed, the time of silence is confined between compline and prime, the abstinence is mitigated in favor of those travelling and begging their way.

The revision of the Rule of 1247 is sometimes said to have made an active order of the Carmelites, but the obligation to remain in the cell and pray, together with other eremitical elements, remains in force. Only in the 15th century did the Carmelites cease to be hermits, though in theory, not in practice.

Not long thereafter, we find the Carmelites requesting the papal privileges. In 1252, Innocent IV gave them permission to have churches with a belfry and one bell - the sign of a public church - and a cemetery for their own use. In Innocent IV granted the prior general the right of bestowing faculties on his subjects for preaching and hearing confessions. In 1262, Urban IV allowed them to bury laymen in their cemeteries provided the canonical portion of the parish priest was satisfied.

These faculties are compatible with the eremitical life - preaching and spiritual direction are known occupations of hermits - but they no doubt served to draw the Carmelites into the active life.

The *Fiery Arrow*

The prior general, Nicholas of France, has left an account (1270) of his visitation of the Order. Named by its author *The Fiery Arrow*, it is indeed a burning indictment of the Order. The move away from the desert, he finds, has brought disastrous consequences. Nicholas does not so much object to preaching, hearing confessions, and counseling as to the inept manner this ministry is carried out by the "stepsons" of the Order. Two by two, these roam the streets, day and night, not to minister to widows and orphans but to flirt with silly girls, beguines, nuns, and highborn ladies. The Rule prescribes separate cells, not contiguous ones. The separate cells have been exchanged for a common house. Contemplation is impossible amid the noise and confusion. The Carmelites must return to the desert.

No doubt the picture is a bit overdrawn. The contemplative life still survived in the more remote houses. There were still "true sons," whom Nicholas calls upon to oppose the "stepsons."

The Second Council of Lyons, 1274

A great number of mendicant orders rose in imitation of the Franciscans and Dominicans: Crosiers, Friars of the Sack, Friars of the Blessed Virgin, Friars of the Penitence of the Martyrs, Apostolic Friars, etc. The opposition to the mendicants, especially to these small proliferating groups, found voice at the Second Council of Lyons of 1274.

The Fourth Council of the Lateran of 1215 had forbidden the founding of new orders; in the future, prospective founders were to adopt one of the existing rules. This council renewed the prohibition of 1215 and furthermore forbade all mendicant orders to take new candidates with a view to their extinction. Exception was made for the Franciscans and Dominicans in view of their evident service to the Church. The Carmelites, here ranked among the mendicants, and Augustinians who antedated 1215 were allowed to continue until the Holy See determined otherwise. Only in 1298 did Pope Boniface VIII remove the restriction of 1274. During that limbo the growth of the Order suffered considerably.

In 1317, Pope John XXII granted the Carmelites full exemption from episcopal jurisdiction. In 1326, the same long-lived pope extended the *super cathedram* to the Order, thereby making it partaker of all the privileges and exemptions of the Franciscans and Dominicans.

The Evolution of the Constitutions

The spread of the Order involved adequate legislation. The internal organization of the Order grew out of the legislation called "constitutions," enacted in general meetings, or "chapters." The Carmelite legislation was modeled after that of the Dominicans, in turn influenced by the Cistercians and Premonstratensians.

Government is carried on along three levels: local, provincial, and general. Each convent is presided over by a prior, assisted in his duties by three councilors. Houses with at least twenty-four members also have a sub-prior. Once a week, conventual chapter is held, and faults are confessed and corrected. The conventual chapter elects the councilors, a *socius* of the prior to the provincial chapter and a vicar to rule the convent when the prior is absent (if the convent has no sub-prior).

Convents in a given country or region constitute a province, presided over by a prior provincial. The annual (the modern practice of triennial provincial chapters dates from the constitutions of 1586) provincial chapter is attended by the provincial and the priors, each with his *socius*.

The entire Order is presided over by the prior general, elected at the general chapter. The prior general and the priors provincial, each with two *socii*, have a seat in the general chapter. The business of the chapter is carried out by the prior general and the definitors elected in the provinces. The frequency of the general chapter is not specified; it was probably held every three years in accordance with the general law of the Church (c. 8, X, III, 35).

The decisions of the general chapters were periodically collected into systematic bodies of laws, called constitutions. They must early have begun to be drawn up. The mitigation of the Rule in 1247 had been requested by a general chapter. In 1256, Pope Alexander IV already mentions constitutions of the Order. Other collections are said to have been made in the chapters of 1266, 1271, 1274, 1281, 1294, 1297, and 1306. Those of 1281 and 1294 have survived. Of the 13th century, no acts of provincial chapters are known today.

The monastic orders originally had only monks of equal status, although some were also priests. In time, notably among the Cistercians, servants in the monastery were accepted as associates who performed the needed manual labor. Among the mendicants, the lay brother was an equal in the community, but without the privilege of voting or being elected to office, since they were usually uneducated. Originally, the Carmelite lay brothers also had this right, and were only deprived of it in 1281.

The Second Half of the 13th Century

With the adaptation of the mendicant way of life, the Order experienced an unparalleled growth. By the end of the century, it numbered about 150 houses divided into 12 provinces: The Holy Land, Sicily, England, Provence, Tuscany, Francia, Lower Germany, Lombardy, Aquitaine, Spain, Upper Germany, and Scotland/Ireland.

In the Province of the Holy Land, besides Mount Carmel, convents were founded in Tyre (before 1254) and Acre (before 1261). After the fall of the Kingdom of Jerusalem in 1291, the Province of the Holy Land survived on Cyprus. Besides, the original foundation of Fortamia (1238), the Order is known to have had houses in Limassol, Paphos, Famagusta, and Nicosia, but when they were founded is not known.

The Province of Sicily included southern Italy; the rest of the peninsula formed one province of Italy. At an unknown date it was divided into the Provinces of Lombardy and Tuscany.

By 1294 the Province of Scotland/Ireland had been separated from England.

Some time before 1270, when a provincial of Aquitaine is mentioned in the records, that province was separated from Provence. The rest of modern France and the County of Flanders formed the Province of Francia.

The constitutions of 1281 list only one province of Germany. It was probably divided into Upper and Lower the same time as the Province of England.

The general chapter held in London in 1254 decreed the foundation of houses in Spain. In the constitutions of 1281, Spain appears last in the list of provinces, so it was probably erected shortly before.

Marian Devotion

The years of the Order's early expansion in Europe also witnessed the growth and shaping of its devotion to Our Lady. Everywhere they dedicated their churches to the Blessed Virgin.

Not surprisingly, their churches featured Marian confraternities (not to be confused with later scapular confraternities). The confraternity of Our Lady of Mount Carmel of Toulouse in 1267 numbered 5,000 men and women. *Laudesi*, Marian hymn-singers, occur in Florence (1280), Siena (1289), and Cambridge (ca. 1300).

At this time, the Hermits of Mount Carmel become the Brothers of Our Lady of Mount Carmel. This name, which probably originated in popular usage, now becomes the subject of conscious reflection on the part of the Order. In the age of scholasticism the name of a thing denoted its essence. The constitutions of 1294 direct that "whenever anyone asks about our Order or its name, the name of the Blessed Virgin is to be given it." Bishops and the Holy See itself granted indulgences to its use. The idea gains ground that the Order was founded in honor of Mary. A bull of Clement V, March 5, 1311, to cite but one example, begins, "Your holy Order, divinely instituted in honor of the blessed Mary, the glorious Virgin...."

Perhaps the change of the mantle, the sign of our Order, is to be placed in this context of its name. The distinctive striped mantle worn by the Carmelites became in Europe the occasion of derision and hindered youth from entering the Order. At the general chapter of 1287, accordingly, the striped mantle was exchanged for a white one, which in time became a symbol for Our Lady's purity. It may not have been entirely coincidental that shortly before this, in 1274, a mendicant order with a Marian title and white mantle, the Friars of the Blessed Virgin, or Pied Friars, had been suppressed, thus clearing the way for the decision of the general chapter.

St. Simon Stock, prior general from 1254 to 1266, who used earnestly to recommend the needs of the Order to Our Lady (in fact, the Mendicant privileges of the Order were acquired at this time) was favored with a vision of the Virgin, who held the scapular of the Order in her hands and announced, "This is the privilege for you and yours; whoever dies in it will be saved." Later, the scapular of Our Lady of Mount Carmel was to become an important means of promoting devotion to Mary in the Church.

Saints of Carmel

The Order produced a number of men outstanding for sanctity of life, whom it honors as saints: Sts. Simon Stock, Albert of Sicily, Angelus the Martyr, Avertanus, Bl. Franco of Sienna. Little is known of these early saints, but Albert and Angelus were widely venerated and have been the subject of portraits by eminent artists.

Chapter 3

Carmel in the Late Middle Ages

The general chapter of Bruges in 1297 elected Gerard of Bologna, the first Carmelite doctor at the University of Paris. This event marks the end of an era and foreshadows the coming age. Thirteenth century Carmel was predominantly eremitical; all its generals had been hermits. The generals of the coming age are doctors of theology and often retire to bishoprics.

During three quarters of this century the papacy resided at Avignon. The convent at Avignon, established by 1263, became the residence of the prior general. Some of the pomp of the princely court of Avignon wore off on the hermits of Mount Carmel.

The care of souls undertaken by the Carmelites required a theological training at the universities. In fact, the constitutions of 1281 already show the beginnings of study at the University of Paris. By the end of the 14th century, the Order had houses of study, or *studia*, affiliated with all the great centers of learning of Europe. The intellectual formation of its members enabled the Order to enter more profoundly into the life of the times, to share in current events, and to contribute to the dialogue over religious problems of the day.

Some Disputed Questions

In the first quarter of the 14th century the powerful Franciscan Order and the Church itself were torn by the question of the theological implications of the evangelical life popularized by St. Francis. As mendicants, the Carmelites were drawn into the debate. Theologians who contributed to the controversy were Gerard of Bologna, Augier de Spuento, and especially Guy Terreni, who advised Pope John XXII on the question of the orthodoxy of the extremist Franciscan Spirituals and wrote his work, *De perfectione vitae*, about evangelical poverty.

In the perennial friction between emperor and pope the Franciscan Spirituals endorsed the cause of Louis of Bavaria. Both Guy Terreni and the Carmelite theologian and provincial of Germany, Sibert de Beka, were among those who advised John XXII on the orthodoxy of Marsilius of Padua's famous *Defensor pacis*.

Two noteworthy antagonists of mendicantism among the secular clergy were Jean de Pouilly, professor at the Sorbonne (d. 1330), and Richard FitzRalph, archbishop of Armagh (d. 1360). Whether the Carmelites took part in the debate of the mendicants with Pouilly at Avignon is not known. Pope John XXII condemned Pouilly's teachings in 1321. Richard FitzRalph attacked religious poverty in his work, *De pauperie Salvatoris*, in which he contended that Christ had never practiced voluntary poverty and that one cannot prudently take upon oneself the burden of voluntary poverty. In 1357, he was summoned before a consistory at which the superiors general of the mendicant orders were also present. The office of prior general of the Carmelites was vacant due to the death of Raymond de Grasse a few months previously. The provincial of Aquitaine, John Ulet, wrote a treatise, *Contra propositionem Armachani*, now lost, which may bear some relation with this debate.

In England, the Carmelites were among the foremost antagonists of Wyclifism, or Lollardy. John Wyclif, a doctor of Oxford (d. 1384), attacked the possessions of the Church, taught that dominion is founded on grace, and denied transubstantiation. John Cunningham (d. 1399) for years engaged him in academic debate. Richard of Maidstone (d. 1396) debated the subject of poverty with John Ashwardby, vicar of St. Mary's, and a Wyclif sympathizer. A number of Carmelites took part in 1382 in the Blackfriars Synod in London, which condemned twenty-four propositions of Wyclif. Peter Stokes, the most mordant of Wyclif's opponents, whom he called the "white dog," (the reference is to the Carmelite white mantle; the white-robed Dominicans were called *Domini cani*, dogs of the Lord) was given the task of seeing that the Synod's decision was published in Oxford. He was vigorously supported by his provincial, Stephen Patrington.

Patrington's successor as provincial, Thomas Netter, of Saffron Walden, (d. 1430), whom M. de la Taille calls "the only great theologian of the 15th century," wrote the final word in his monumental work against Lollardy, his *Doctinale antiquitatum fidei catholicae ecclesiae.*

The Western Schism (1378-1417)

In the two score years straddling the 14th and 15th centuries, occurred the disastrous schism of the West, dividing members of religious orders as well as society generally. On the whole, the orders conformed to the allegiance of the countries in which they were situated. Pope and anti-pope wooed the religious orders, vying with each other in granting privileges and exemptions, much to the prejudice of observance.

Bernard Oller, the prior general at the outbreak of the schism, adhered to the Avignon pope, Clement VII; he was followed by Raymond Vaquer (1383-1388), and John Grossi (1388-1411). In 1381, the followers of the Roman pope, Urban VI, elected Michael Aiguani general; his successors were John of Rho (1387-1404) and Matthew Aiguani, brother of Michael (1405-1411).

Both Carmelite priors general and their theologians attended the Council of Pisa (1409). Eminent among the latter was Thomas Netter of Walden. At a general chapter held in Bologna in 1411, the Order was reunited under one prior general, John Grossi.

Carmelites who are known to have concerned themselves with the question of the schism are John Golein, prior of the Place Maubert, who was active on behalf of Clement at the University of Paris. At the request of the king of Catalonia, Francis Martí proposed a plan for the solution of the schism, involving the concession by each claimant of his putative powers to the other. The procurator general of the Order, Michelino de Novara, preaching before the pope on the Carmelite day in Advent, 1401, was so indiscreet as to rebuke the pope for delaying putting an end to the schism and ended up in jail. Thereafter, Gregory XII insisted on seeing beforehand the text of sermons preached in his presence.

The Black Death (1348-1349)

During the 14th century the Order continued to grow, but at a considerably slower pace. By the end of the century, there were about three hundred houses, as many again as in the previous century, but it took twice as long to do it. A certain letup was to be expected after the first fervor had passed. There were other causes:

the fact that the Order came to maturity in a waning society was one. The Black Death was another.

This grim reaper, which in the years 1348 to 1349 harvested, some say, as much as half the population of Europe, claimed its share of the mendicant orders; their apostolate among city dwellers made them particularly vulnerable.

Surprisingly, little information is available about this striking phenomenon, still less about its effect on the Carmelites. At the general chapter in 1348, two hundred friars perished during the sessions or while traveling to and from the meeting. The convent in Avignon lost 66 members; the necrology of Florence lists more than a 100 dead in the Tuscan province during these years. The convent in London lost 24 members in one year of the plague. Papal dispensations from the full course of studies for the doctorate had to be requested on account of the shortage of masters due to the plague.

The Hundred Years War

The dynastic quarrel between England and France known as the Hundred Years War (1337-1453) led to the invasion of France and its devastation. Edward III conducted a campaign through Normandy to Flanders, culminating in the slaughter of the French nobility at Crécy (1346) and the siege and capture of Calais. From his duchy in Guyenne, the Black Prince struck deep into the Midi and in 1356 inflicted another severe defeat on the French at Poitiers, capturing their king, John II, into the bargain. The peace of Brétigny (1360) only released bands of unemployed mercenaries, "companies," on the defenseless populace.

About a third of the Carmelite houses in France were destroyed. Of the seven French provinces, Gascony and Narbonne lost half of their houses. Toulouse lost two of its four houses. Francia lost eight houses, Provence three. Calais was joined to the English Province and remained such until the Reformation.

The Carmelite chronicler, Jean de Venette, provides a glimpse of the convent in the Place Maubert in Paris in 1360, when the populace of the faubourg moved into the city before the English advance. "I myself saw priests of ten country parishes communicating their people and keeping Easter in various chapels or any spot they could find in the monastery of the Carmelite friars at Paris."

Expansion in the 14th Century

In spite of the disasters of the 14th century the Order continued to grow, adding new foundations and dividing into new provinces.

The general chapter of 1303 instituted an independent Province of Ireland, not without the opposition of the English provincial, William Ludlington, who ended up in the papal prison of Sant'Angelo in Rome. Scotland, which had been joined to England, became autonomous in 1324, after the country had won independence under Bruce.

In Italy, in 1333, the Province of Tuscany was separated from that of Rome, which extended south to the end of the peninsula. The same year, Bologna was separated from Lombardy and became the Province of Bologna, which included the famous *studium* of Bologna.

In spite of the Hundred Years' War, the Order in France nearly doubled its houses (90), and at the same time its historic seven provinces took shape. In 1321, Narbonne originated from Provence. Toulouse was constituted in 1342. In 1358, Gascony was separated from Aquitaine. The division of Touraine from Francia, made in the Avignon chapter of 1384, was confirmed by the chapter that united the Order in 1411.

In the first half of the 14th century, the two German provinces, in the troubled times of Louis of Bavaria, were several times united and separated, to be definitively separated in 1348. The Lower German province comprised the Low Countries and the Rhineland. The vast Upper German province, eventually to be in turn divided, extended from Eastern Germany into Austria, Bohemia, and Hungary.

During the first third of this century, there still remained only one province in Spain, still partly under Moorish domination. In 1339, the vicariate of Majorca was created, to become a province in 1342. When the Kingdom of Aragon recaptured the islands, the Balearic houses were joined to those in Catalonia to become in 1354 the province of Catalonia. In 1416, the province of Spain was divided into Castile and Aragon, Castile retaining the traditional precedence of the province of Spain.

Two outstanding saints, both celebrated by artists of note, date from this time: Peter Thomas, papal legate to the Levant and Latin patriarch of Constantinople, and Andrew Corsini, bishop of Fiesole near Florence.

The earliest Carmelite bishops known at present are Henry Jonghen and Gratiadeus, suffragans of Cologne (1304) and Aquileia (1310) respectively.

Chapter 4

Intellectual Life in the 14th Century

The Carmelites were already at least a century in existence before they began to develop an intellectual and literary tradition. Unlike the Dominicans, learning does not lie at the roots of their origins. "The primitive dwellers on Mount Carmel were simple hermits," explains John of Hildesheim (d. 1375), "unlettered, poor, they possessed no parchments, nor were they writers. They were accustomed to pray rather than to write." The growth of the intellectual life of the Carmelites is the result of their apostolic activity and more specifically of their entry into the universities.

Carmelite Scholasticism

The Carmelites were the last of the mendicants to enter the schools and they arrived when the golden age of scholasticism was already drawing to a close. The philosophical systems, each with its firmly entrenched exponents, were already well defined, so it was difficult for a Carmelite doctor to head a distinctive school. Nevertheless, the Order did produce a number of distinguished doctors.

To name a few, the earliest of the Paris doctors, Gerard of Bologna (d. 1317) graduated when such great figures of scholasticism as Giles of Rome, Henry of Ghent, and Godfrey de Fontaines still graced the podium. An eclectic, Gerard follows no consistent line, though he seems to prefer the extreme intellectualism of Godfrey of Fontaines. His works, all unedited, include *Quaestiones ordinariae*, *Quodlibeta*, and a *Summa*, the opening *quaestiones* of which Paul de Vooght, O.S.B., regards as the first systematic treatise on the methodology of theology.

Guy Terreni of Perpignan (d. 1342) may be counted among such outstanding 14th century scholastics as Hervé Natalis, Durandus of San Porciano, and Peter Auréole. In the period immediately preceding the nominalism of William of Ockham, together with John de Pouilly, Terreni was the principal exponent of the extreme Aristotelianism inaugurated by Godfrey of Fontaines. His unpublished works are *Commentarii in libros Sententiarum, Quodlibeta I-VI, Quaestiones ordinariae de Verbo I-XII, Quaestiones disputatae I-XIII, Commentarius super decretum*, and commentaries on various books of Aristotle. His *Summa de heresibus* saw two editions: Paris, 1528, and Cologne, 1631.

John Baconthorpe (d. 1348), the most important scholastic the Order produced, has been compared to Duns Scotus; both in fact are characterized by a critical rather than a constructive spirit. His method is synthetic, not in the sense that he attempts an eclectic solution, but that he seeks a solution above and beyond the opinions of others which eminently contains them. Besides such standard theological works as *Commentarii in libros I-V Sententiarum, Quaestiones canonicae, Quodlibeta I-III*, his works include commentaries on various books of sacred scripture, Aristotle, Augustine, and Anselm.

Michael Aiguani (d. 1400), apart from the offices he held in the Order, spent his long life at the university, writing and lecturing; his works reveal a good teacher rather than an original thinker. He revives some early scholastic theories; for instance Peter Lombard's doctrine on the power of the keys. His works are *Lectura sententiarum* (Milan, 1510, and Venice, 1622), *Tractatus conceptionis Virginis Mariae*,

Informatio cuiuslibet peccatoris, Dictionarium sacrum, Lectura super psalterio (often printed), besides commentaries on other books of the Bible, and various *tabulae*, or indices to works of other authors.

Historical and Polemical Works

Apart from scholastic writings, Carmelite authors occupied themselves mainly with three areas of concern, often contested by outsiders: the origin of the Order, its approval by the popes, and its Marian title. The historical content of these writings is meager and mostly taken from such well-known medieval sources as Peter Comestor, Jacques de Vitry, Vincent of Beauvais, O.P., and Stephen of Salignac, O.P., but they are important for the internal growth of the Order.

From the beginning, the Carmelites were concerned with establishing their credentials in a hostile Europe. The constitutions opened with a statement, the *Rubrica prima*, in its earliest known form of 1281 probably written before 1247, an official statement about the origin of the Order. It is the tiny seed from which issued over the centuries the luxuriant growth of the Elijan legend:

> We declare, bearing testimony to the truth, that from the time when the prophets Elijah and Elisha dwelt devoutly on Mount Carmel, holy fathers, both of the Old and New Testaments, whom the contemplation of heavenly things drew to the solitude of the same mountain, have without doubt led praiseworthy lives there by the fountain of Elijah in holy penitence unceasingly and successfully maintained.
>
> It was these same successors whom Albert the patriarch of Jerusalem in the time of Innocent III united into a community, writing a rule for them which Pope Honorius, successor of the same Innocent, and many of their successors, approving this Order, most devoutly confirmed by their charters. In the profession of this Rule, we, their followers, serve the Lord in diverse parts of the world, even to the present day.

John Baconthorpe wrote four short tracts, *Speculum de institutione Ordinis* and *Compendium historiarum et iurium* are juridical; his *Tractatus super regulam* and *Laus religionis Carmelitanae* may be described as allegorical exegesis.

In his *Speculum* (1337) John de Chemineto attempts to impose some sort of reason on the various rules so far imposed on the Carmelites. He also first specifically calls Elijah "founder" of the Order (ch. 1).

Writers in the second half of the century include John de Venette, William of Conventry, John of Hildesheim, Bernard Oller, and John Grossi.

The ultimate elaboration of all this is Philip Ribot's *De institutione et peculiaribus gestis Carmelitarum*, written late in his life, which ended in 1391. Following but expanding preceding accounts, Ribot presents the history of the Order from Elijah to the migration to Europe under guise of editing and commenting on four alleged ancient works:

1. The *Book of the First Monks*, supposed to have been written in Greek in 412 by John, 44th bishop of Jerusalem.
2. The *Epistle of Cyril*, supposed to have been written by Cyril, alleged prior general from 1221 to 1224.

3. Sibert de Beka, *De consideratis super Carmelitarum regula*, explains the changes made in the Rule in 1247.

4. The *Chronicon* of William of Sanvico, provincial of the Holy Land.

An ocean of ink has been spilled over the question of the authenticity of Ribot's work; lately the considered judgment of students is that these works do not antedate their publication by Ribot. They do not begin to influence Carmelite historiography until the end of the 14th century.

The Marian Content of Early Carmelite Writings

The chronicles and treatises in defense of the Order also concern themselves with the Order's title (and consequently with its Marian character) and in other contexts contain reflections on the role of Mary in Carmelite life.

The tract, *De inceptione Ordinis*, contributes the detail that the chapel on Mount Carmel was dedicated to Mary. It is also found in the *Rubrica prima* in the version of the 1324 constitutions, although it may already have occurred in earlier versions.

Baconthorpe is so concerned with the Virgin Mary in his writings that he may be considered the first of the Order's "Marian" authors. His *Speculum de institutione Ordinis pro veneratione Beatae Mariae*, the complete title of which already betrays its contents, is the first attempt to unite the Elijan and Marian traditions of the Order. His *Laus religionis carmelitanae*, which is also largely concerned with Mary, for the first time in Carmelite literature associates Mary with the little cloud seen by Elijah on Carmel (Bk. I, ch. 9). His *Tractatus super regulam* sees the life of Mary as the source for the various prescriptions of the Rule.

For John de Chemineto, Elijah, Elisha, and many of the sons of the prophets resemble Mary because they practiced virginity.

In all this literature Mary is principally regarded as patroness, the feudal *domina loci*, the source of favor, the saint in whose honor the Order exists. In his *Informatio*, Bernard Oller examines the nature of this patronage at some length. Nevertheless, the concept of Mary as mother, later to become so popular in the Order, is not lacking. Imitation of Mary is the keynote of the period, as especially appears from Baconthorpe's commentary on the Rule and the *Book of the First Monks*.

The Immaculate Conception of the Blessed Virgin was held in special honor. The feast seems to have been introduced into the liturgy in 1306. By a custom already in use in Baconthorpe's day, the general curia at Avignon solemnly celebrated the feast with a sermon preached before the cardinals. Richard FitzRalph, later to fall out with the mendicants, preached the sermon in 1342 and 1349.

About a score of 14th century Carmelite writers treated the question of the Immaculate Conception. All except Gerard of Bologna, Guy Terreni and Paul of Perugia defended the privilege. Baconthorpe changed from an opponent to a protagonist of the doctrine- "*un des plus importants triomphes de l'Immaculée Conception en ce siècle*," according to Paul Doncoeur, S.J. Also worthy of note are the treatises on the Immaculate Conception by Michael Aiguani and Francis Marti.

Devotional Works

The early chronicles not only contain elements of Marian devotion and doctrine, but to a certain extent also qualify as literature of devotion, written as they are to inspire, direct, and convince as well as inform. At the same time, these "histories" with their insistence on the prophetic origins of Carmel kept alive the contemplative ideal of the Order. It was probably this single factor of historical preoccupation with their origins that in the case of the Carmelites fostered the consciousness of the contemplative ideal. While Carmel launched full sail on the sea of apostolic activity, its spiritual literature remained that of the desert.

Ribot's *Book of the First Monks*, is a work of primary importance in shaping the spirit of the Order. Its opening chapters constitute a treatise on "the manner (*forma*) of attaining prophetic perfection and the end of eremitical monastic life." This life has a twofold end, one which we attain by our own labor and virtuous actions aided by divine grace, and consists in offering God a holy heart free from all actual stain of sin. The other end of this life is bestowed on us by the free gift of God, and consists in tasting somewhat in our hearts and experiencing in our minds, not only after death, but already in this mortal life, the power of God's presence and the sweetness of heavenly glory. This second end refers to mystical experience, which therefore becomes a goal of Carmelite life. The author expands his theme in the form of a gloss on the text: "Depart from here and turn eastward, and hide yourself by the brook Cherith, that is east of the Jordan. You shall drink from the brook, and I have commanded the ravens to feed you there." (1 Kgs. 17: 3-4).

Thus, one century after Nicholas of France launched his *Fiery Arrow*, the Order is once more presented with the eremitical ideal. This time it caused no alarm, because it was presented under guise of an historical document. Nevertheless, it was obviously meant to be more than a mere museum piece. As a matter of fact, the *Book of the First Monks* has been accepted as describing the fundamental spirit of the Order and has enjoyed great prestige through the centuries.

The 14th century was the golden age of English mysticism. The Order there produced no outstanding writers, but one finds the Carmelites intimately involved in the movement. Richard Misyn, bachelor of Oxford and prior of Lincoln, who for a while lived as a hermit, englished Richard Rolle's *Incendium amoris* and *Emendatio vitae* at the request of the anchoress Margaret Heslyngton. Thomas Fishlawe made a Latin version of Walter Hilton's *Scale of Perfection*. The popular devotional work, *Le merure*, was similarly set into Latin by an unknown Carmelite.

Carmelites figure in the *Book of Margery Kempe*. Robert Southfield (d. 1414), of Norwich convent, is described as a man given to prayer and penance, but of cheerful countenance and attractive manner and speech. It was to seek his counsel, as well as Dame Julian's concerning the rather strange spiritual phenomena she was experiencing, that Margery came to Norwich. "Jesu, mercy and gramercy," exclaimed the holy friar after he had heard her story; "sister, dread not your manner of living, for it is the Holy Ghost working plenteously his grace in your soul."

Her regular spiritual adviser was another Carmelite, Master Aleyn of Lynn, who was her constant support and comfort in the many trials of her bizarre career. When a stone and piece of beam fell from the roof of the church on her head and back without causing her bodily harm, Master Aleyn, "desiring the work of God to be magnified," carefully weighed the stone and beam, which one of the keepers of the church was on the point of putting into the fire. When a famous preaching friar would not allow Margery to attend his sermon because of her uncontrollable habit of weeping and crying aloud on such occasions, Master Aleyn interceded for her, visited the preacher, "and sent for wine to cheer him with." In the end, the provincial forbade Aleyn to have anything further to do with the strange mystic, much to her sorrow. Lynn wrote a treatise, *In stimulum amoris*, now lost.

To the Dominican mystical school in Germany belonged the Carmelite, Henry Hane (fl. end of 13th cent.). Summaries of three of his sermons in the Thuringian dialect have been preserved in the collection, *Paradisus animae intelligentis*. He shows the influence of Master Eckhart, but avoids his more hardy expressions.

Sibert de Beka acted on a commission of the mendicant orders which condemned the works of Eckhart (1327).

Michael Aiguani's *Dictionarium sacrum* (1386-1389) and commentaries contain much devotional matter. In commentating scripture, he refers to Nicholas de Lira for the literal sense and confines himself to dogmatic and devotional reflection. His most significant work is his much printed *Commentary on the Psalms*, considered by H. Denifle, O.P., *"ein der grössten Erklärungen über die Psalmen, die nach meiner Kenntnis je geschrieben worden sind."* The Anglican J. M. Neale calls it "on the whole, the best of those that have been contributed to the treasury of the Church."

Literary Works

The early years of the Order's intellectual life produced several literary figures of note.

The earliest example of a writer on secular themes is Robert Baston, who was present at the battle of Bannockburn (1314) and celebrated it in 131 lines of rather pedestrian verse.

Guido da Pisa wrote *Fiori d'Italia*, meant to be a history in seven books of Italy from the earliest times to the fall of the empire in the West, but he got only as far as the coming of Aeneas to Italy. This last part, a prose summary of Virgil's *Aeneid*, separated from the rest, became a schoolroom classic still in print, much prized for its purity of style and diction. He also left a commentary on Dante's *Inferno* not without interest for Dante studies.

John Fillous (or Fillons), of Venette, wrote a Latin chronicle of events in the kingdom of France, 1340-1368, which A. Colville calls, "one of the most significant historical documents of the 14th century." Strikingly different is Venette's long (40,000 lines) and banal poem in French on the Three Marys (1357).

The *History of the Three Magi* by John of Hildesheim (d. 1375), a synthesis of legends about the Magi with interesting stories about the lands and customs of the Orient, was a medieval best seller and was translated into many languages. Goethe was struck by its naive charm and revived its vogue in modern times.

Chapter 5

Religious Decline and First Movements of Reform

During the 15th century, the life of the Order was intimately linked to the frequent general councils attended by the major superiors and the best talent of the Order. The religious trends of the time find echoes in the Order: the desire of autonomy, anti-papalism, the desperate sense of the need for reform and the inability to effect it. Particularly, the Order reflected the decline of religious fervor in the Church.

Carmelites at the General Councils

There is no record that the prior general, John Grossi, attended the Council of Pavia-Sienna (1423-1424). In his declining years, he seems to have been confined to his native southern France, but he sent Thomas Netter. Other English and Italian theologians are also known to have been present.

Grossi's successors, Bartholomew Roqual, Natale Bencesi, and John Facy attended the Council of Basle-Ferrara-Florence (1431-1445), in which papal supremacy eventually triumphed over conciliarism. Noteworthy among Carmelite theologians at the council are John Kenynghale, who features in the debate with the Hussites, Jerome of Castellaccio, and Giles of Byedborch.

Basle wrote another chapter in the perennial mendicant-secular debate. The opponent of the mendicants, Philip Norris, canon of the cathedral of Dublin, was condemned for his doctrines by Eugene IV. This phase of the quarrel climaxed in the *Mare magnum* (1476) of Sixtus IV, former Conventual Franciscan, which excessively extended the mendicant privileges. It was unsuccessfully attacked by the bishops at the 5th Lateran Council (1512-1517). In 1516, Leo X attenuated the more extreme privileges of the mendicants.

Decline of Religious Fervor

Religious fervor had already begun to decline in the second half of the 14th century; the laxity which is only too apparent in the 15th century, the Age of the Renaissance, is but an acute form of old diseases.

From the middle of the century, general chapters begin to invoke sanctions against the neglect of the divine office. The chapter of 1354 complains that silence after complin, "alas, is observed very little." Eating and drinking in the rooms, even by large companies, had to be legislated against.

Perhaps the most serious defect was the violation of poverty. Religious were permitted to keep money and other personal effects and to buy their own cells from the convent. Doctors of theology, who could keep their earnings from teaching and preaching, lived much more comfortably than the "simple" friars, who suffered want, when the community could not support them. Conventuality, or the attachment of each religious to the convent of his profession, became the rule after 1430.

Second Mitigation of the Carmelite Rule

At the general chapter of 1430 the Holy See was requested to modify the Carmelite Rule, specifically with regard to the obligation of solitude and perpetual abstinence from meat. The severity of the Rule, the petition read, was too great for human frailty or physical strength to bear; it discouraged vocations and occasioned remissness. In 1432, Eugene IV authorized Carmelites to eat meat three days a week and at suitable times to walk about in the church, the cloister, and adjacent places. Subsequent dispensations limited abstinence to Wednesdays, Fridays, and Saturdays and extended the regulation of fast and abstinence to the provincials.

The mitigation of 1432 brought the Rule up to date with the actual lifestyle of the Order, which was anything but eremitical. However, it came at a time when the reform of the Order was finally getting under way and was at once rejected by the participants in the movement. The general chapter of 1440 imposed the mitigated Rule; there may be some connection between this decree and the erection of the reform of Mantua into a Congregation in 1442.

The Mantuan Congregation

In the first decade of the 15th century, a movement of reform originated in the Tuscan province. Originator of the reform was Jacobo di Alberto, prior of the convent of Le Selve near Florence, first mentioned as "a house of observance" at the provincial chapter of 1413, which confirmed its special constitutions. Jacobo's successor was Bl. Angelus Mazzinghi (d. 1438), who was also the first to make profession in the reform. Mantua and Geronde in Switzerland were added to the observance, when the Breton, Thomas Connecte, visited Italy with his followers, who likewise joined the reform.

In 1442, Eugene IV constituted these three convents a Congregation under the immediate jurisdiction of the prior general, whose powers, for that matter, were strictly limited.

The reform stressed silence and cloister and the common life. The mitigation of Eugene IV regarding abstinence was not accepted. The Mantuan friars wore a habit of rough undyed wool.

In the Lower German province, John Ubach was not alone in renouncing all privileges for life (1435). The prior of Enghien, John Inguen, did the same, "from a motive of holy reformation." Mörs was a reformed house, probably since its foundation. Priors and members of both houses were to play important roles in the reform the prior general, John Soreth, was soon to inaugurate.

In the Upper German province, Heilbronn was founded under the aegis of reform (1451).

Chapter 6

Blessed John Soreth (c. 1395-1471)

The general chapter of 1451 elected Blessed John Soreth, one of the great priors general in the history of the Order.

Born in Caen around 1395, he entered the Order there and went on to study at the University of Paris. From 1440 until his election as prior general, he was provincial of Francia. He was one of those persons in the 15th century alive to the need for renewal in the Church. Through him, Carmel joined the general movement of reform in religious Orders and society.

The Callistine Observance

Soreth's design for the renewal of the Order was twofold: where he found good will he established fully reformed houses; elsewhere, he tried to eliminate abuses and raise the standard of observance.

He appointed a vicar to head the movement already in progress in Mörs and Enghien and with their priors to draw up statutes for his reform. These were promulgated at the general chapter in Paris in 1456 and confirmed by Pope Callixtus III the following year, thus acquiring the name, "Callixtine," as distinct from the "Eugenian," or Mantuan Reform.

In a solemn ceremony which inaugurated the reform of a convent, members renounced temporal goods, privileges, and exemptions. All ate at a common table. Visiting both in and outside the convent was restricted. Sufficiently mature candidates underwent a term of postulancy. Reformed convents could elect their own priors, provincials could not remove or add members to such convents without their consent.

Soreth met with his greatest success in the Lower German province (Belgium, Holland, the Rhineland). Information on other provinces is lacking, but his reform is known to have made some conquests in the provinces of Upper Germany, Francia, and Sicily. A product of the reform in Sicily is Bl. Aloysius Rabatà.

The Reform of the Conventuals

Soreth did not impose his reform on the conventuals but he was implacable in eliminating abuses and insisting on the religious observance they had vowed. He obliged those with benefices to renounce them and return to the convent. He appealed to ordinaries to have offenders imprisoned.

The constitutions of the Order had not been overhauled for a century and were a hodgepodge of capitular decrees. Not the least of Soreth's services to the improvement of religious life was to present the Order with an orderly, updated code of laws which remained in force until 1586 and in some of its expressions continued down to modern times.

The Carmelite Women

Another important feature of Soreth's reform was the institution of cloistered Carmelite nuns.

From earliest times, in Italy especially, women associated themselves with the Order in varying degrees. The *conversae* professed the three vows taken by the friars and submitted to the superiors of the Order. One authority, Fr. Claudio Catena, holds that the vows were solemn, and the *conversae* were nuns in the modern sense of the word. Other women took only one or other of the vows or simple vows and sometimes formed communities without cloister. They were variously called *mantellates*, *pinzocchere* (Italy), and *beatas* (Spain). Confraternity members participated in the spiritual benefits of the Order in exchange for material ones.

Bl. Joan of Toulouse, an anchoress attached to the Carmelite church there early in the 15th century, may probably be classed as a *conversa*.

In 1452, by the bull *Cum nulla*, Nicholas V bestowed papal authorization for receiving women into the Carmelite Order. It was actually the prior of Florence, Bartholomew Masi, who fetched the bull from Rome on behalf of the *pinzocchere* aggregated to the convent, but he is not to be personally credited with the bull; only the prior general could have obtained a privilege applicable to the whole Order.

Soreth was personally involved in the foundation of several cloistered monasteries in the Low Countries. His friend, Bl. Frances d'Amboise, duchess of Brittany, introduced his nuns into her domains and herself joined them.

The monastery of St. Mary of the Angels in Florence, Italy, was founded in 1454, but only later accepted cloister and the obligation of the choral office. Besides Florence, Parma, Reggio Emilia, Brescia, Mantua, Ferrara numbered monasteries under the care of the Mantuan Congregation. Examples of saintly nuns are Bl. Archangela Girlani and Bl. Joan Scopelli.

Bl. John Soreth never personally visited Spain and his reforming efforts did not extend there. After 1452, a number of communities were formed, not all of them cloistered. The *beaterio* of Avila, famous for its most illustrious member, Teresa de Ahumada y Cepeda, was founded in 1479.

Chapter 7

Carmel on the Eve of the Protestant Reformation

At the death of Bl. John Soreth in 1471, the effort at renewal of the Order came to a virtual standstill. His successors, Christopher Martignoni (1472-1481), Ponce Rainaud (1482-1503), Peter Terrasse (1503-1511), and Bernardine Landucci (1517-1523) failed to carry forward his program. Bl. Baptist of Mantua (1513-1517), elected against his better judgement, was too old and infirm to accomplish much.

Martignoni, of the Mantuan Congregation, had been elected with a view to reform, but he proved a disappointment, almost immediately becoming embroiled with his former confreres over the color of the habit. His attempt to impose on the Congregation the black habit of the Order eventually failed. He also reapportioned the provinces of Italy, creating twelve where there had been five (1472). In 1473, the province of Bologna was absorbed into the Mantuan Congregation.

The Reform of Albi

It is not surprising that an attempt at reforming the Order at this time should originate outside it.

Louis d'Amboise, reforming bishop of Albi, replaced the community of Albi with poor students from John Standonck's Collège Montaigu in Paris and imported Eligius Denis, of the Mantuan Congregation, to initiate them into Carmelite life (1499). After Melun had accepted reform, the legate *a latere*, Cardinal George d'Amboise, like his brother, Louis, a dedicated promoter of reform, established the Congregation of Albi (1502).

In 1503, the cardinal also undertook the reform of the *studium* of Paris in the Place Maubert through Louis de Lire, who emerges as the leader of the reform. The community elected the Fleming, James Dassoneville, as prior. The general chapter held in Piacenza the same year forbade De Lire to reform convents without authorization by the prior general. When he was unable to impose his authority during a visitation of Paris in 1503, Terrasse excommunicated De Lire and Dassoneville and withdrew the faculty and students from the college, thus leaving the great house of studies to the reformers, a severe blow to the Order.

In the Mantuan, the reform met with a sympathetic reception. When Pope Leo X gave apostolic approval to the Congregation and absolved De Lire from censure (1513), Bl. Baptist not only did not object but warmly approved the pope's decision.

In 1517, the Congregation possessed itself of the *studium* of Toulouse, like Paris an important center of learning of the Order. Landucci's efforts to regain it met with failure and he ended up, in 1519, giving the reformers a free hand with regard to any convents that needed renewal. As a matter of fact, the Congregation had no further growth. Landucci's successor, the great reforming general Nicholas Audet, also proved a friend and in 1532 gave it official recognition.

The Reform of Albi produced many men of learning and virtue. Among the latter, one might mention John de Campo, whom Durandus de Fraccinis had fetched from Ghent. Known as "the father of the reform," he gave much edification by his

life of prayer and patience in illness. The fact that so many members came from
the Flemish houses of the Francia province would lead one to think that Soreth's
reform still retained its vitality.

Monte Oliveto

Contemporary with the Reform of Albi is the foundation of the hermitage of
Monte Oliveto near Genoa. Sometimes known as the "Reform of Monte Oliveto,"
it was simply an autonomous house of the Order. Its founder was Hugh Marengo,
of the Mantuan Congregation, who envisioned a hermitage according to the original
Carmelite way of life. When his proposal was rejected by the Congregation, he went
ahead on his own. In 1516, the Congregation expelled him, but the same year, he
obtained papal approval of his hermitage and was appointed its vicar apostolic,
independent of the prior general.

In connection with religious fervor at this time mention might be made of Bl.
Jacobinus of Crevacuore (alias, de Canepaciis), of the convent of Vercelli in the
Lombardy province. A lay brother, he functioned as porter and was esteemed for
his charity to the poor and spirit of work and prayer. He died in 1508, a victim of
the plague.

New Provinces in the 15th Century

In 1411, the convents in Bohemia, Poland, Prussia, Hungary, Saxony, and
Thuringia were separated from Upper Germany with the name, province of
Bohemia. The provincial was Arnold of Sehnsen, one of the outstanding scholastics
the Order in Germany produced. In 1440, the houses that survived the Hussite wars
were again divided between Upper Germany and the newly created province of
Saxony. In 1462, the province of Poland and Bohemia was erected. The province
of Denmark dates from the same year.

In 1416, the province of Aragon was divided from that of Spain, thereafter
called Castile. Andalusia (Betica) was separated from Castile in 1498 and underwent
rapid growth.

Bl. John Soreth undertook the reform of the Spanish provinces through his
vicars, but neither their efforts nor those of the famous reforming cardinal, Francis
Ximénez de Cisneros, had much effect. General chapters scheduled to meet in
Spain were repeatedly deflected to Italy. The Spanish court became disillusioned
with the indifference of popes and religious superiors and ended by themselves
taking needed reform in hand.

The province of Portugal, which appears for the first time at the general chapter
of 1425, owes its existence to St. Nun'Alvares Pareira, national hero of Portugal.
He built a convent in Lisbon for the Carmelites and later himself entered the Order
as a *semifrater* (a sort of lay brother). With the 13th century foundation in Moura it
constituted the new province, to which Colares and Vidigueira were added in the
15th century.

Spiritual Writings and Devotion of the 15th Century

North of the Alps, the spiritual life was characterized by the *devotio moderna*,
especially in the Low Countries, where its propagandists, the Brothers of

the Common Life, flourished. A reaction to the intellectualism of medieval scholasticism, it stressed a simple life of prayer and asceticism.

As a reformer interested in observance, Bl. John Soreth's writing took the form of a commentary on the Rule, *Expositio paraenetica* (Paris, 1625). Another commentary was the unpublished *Lucerna fratrum* by Matthias Fabri (d. after 1497).

In Belgium, John van Paeschen (1449-1539) wrote his *Devote maniere om op gheestelijck pelgrimagie te trecken* (Devout Manner of Making a Pilgrimage in Spirit), the earliest example of the present form of the Stations of the Cross.

Meditation remained a private exercise in the Order, except in the province of Portugal and among the Mantuan nuns.

The practice of the Mantuan nuns may have been due to influence from the North, for Italy, too, had its *devotio moderna*, "Italian style," which took the form of "contemplation and devotion," a short period of meditation after the liturgy. A representative of this spirituality was Louis Pittori, called *il Bigo*, who is known to have been in contact around 1490 with Mary Magdalene Petrata, of the monastery of Ferrara.

Baptist of Mantua, remembered mostly for his poetry, is a representative of the Italian *devotio moderna* and should be classed among Carmelite spiritual writers of the period by virtue of his prose works, *De vita beata* (1463) and *De patientia* (1486). The latter is the fruit of reflection and discussion of scripture texts by a circle of friends grouped around Charles Anthony Fantuzzi. In John Francis della Mirandola, too, the Mantuan and *il Bigo* had a mutual friend.

The ministry to the cloistered nuns constituted another source of spiritual literature. Bl. Frances d'Amboise's conferences have come down to us. It was probably for sisters or lay persons affiliated with the Order that Nicholas Calciuri (d. 1466) of the Mantuan Congregation wrote *Vita fratrum del Sancto Monte Carmelo* (Roma, 1957). Thomas of Limburg, chaplain of the sisters of Namur (1476-1487) left *Exhortations*, or conferences. For the sisters, too, he translated in the Liège dialect lives of saints and the *Book of the First Monks*. It was translated into English by Thomas Scrope, of Bradley, who lived many years as a solitary before being made bishop of Dromore in Ireland. From a Spanish translation made for the nuns of Avila, St. Teresa first learned of the eremitical origins of Carmel and dreamed of returning to that way of life.

Marian Writings and Devotion

Among writers on the Virgin Mary at this time, Baldwin Leers (d. 1483), prior of Arras, made a collection of the favors and graces Mary obtained for the Carmelites, *Collectaneum exemplorum et miraculorum*. More important is *De patronatu et patrocinio Beatae Virginis Mariae*, by Arnold Bostius, a first synthesis of the Order's devotion to Mary, which did much to call attention to the vision of St. Simon Stock. Others who wrote about St. Simon and his vision were Giles Smet (Faber, d. 1506), Monaldus de Rosariis (d. 1508), Roland Bouchier (d. 1540).

About this time, too, there appeared the spurious "Sabbatine Bull," according to which Our Lady appeared to Pope John XXII in 1322 promising assistance on the Saturday after death to wearers of the Carmelite habit. It probably originated in Sicily around 1430. It was to play an important role in the devotion of the scapular of Mount Carmel.

The earliest reference to the patronal feast of the Order, the *Commemoratio solemnis Sanctae Mariae*, occurred in 1386. Generally celebrated on July 17, later on July 16, the feast probably originated in England and during the 15th century spread to the continent.

Chapter 8

Carmel and the Renaissance

The Italian Renaissance one associates with painting, sculpture, and the cult of ancient Roman and Greek art, literature, and philosophy. North of the Alps philological and religious preoccupations prevail. The Renaissance spirit as shared by the Carmelites shows these local differences.

The Carmine of Florence

If Florence was the scene of the rebirth of art, the Carmine was very much a part of it. In 1422, the great Gothic church, begun in 1268, was solemnly consecrated. Masaccio, "the creator of painting" in Stendhal's phrase, recorded the colorful event in a fresco in the cloister, his *Sagra*, since destroyed. The church displayed on its walls and in its chapels the work of some of the outstanding artists of the Gothic period: Bicci di Lorenzo and his son, Neri; Agnolo Gaddi (d. 1396); Spinello of Arezzo (d. 1410), whose frescos in the chapel of St. John the Baptist were attributed, after Vasari, to Giotto; and Gherardo Starnina.

The most noteworthy is the Brancacci Chapel, dedicated to St. Peter the Apostle. In 1425, Masolino began to decorate its walls with episodes from the apostle's life and was joined a couple of years later by his pupil, Masaccio. The series, left unfinished at Masaccio's death at the age of twenty-seven, was completed many years later, in 1484, by Filippino Lippi. "This chapel," Vasari wrote, "has indeed become a school of art for the most celebrated sculptors and painters, who have constantly gone there to study."

Fra Filippo Lippi (1406-1469)

The Carmine's most illustrious, if not most pious, son, Filippo Lippi, needs no introduction. The offspring of humble parents, Filippo and his older brother John were taken in as boys by the community of the Carmine. Filippo was professed in 1421, probably at the earliest permissible age of fifteen, and in due course was ordained a priest. An early work, called the *Reform of the Carmelite Rule*, for want of a better name, a fresco in the cloister, shows the influence of his master, Masaccio, but the figures are more realistic, proletarian, and give notice that Humanism is under way.

During the 40's, Lippi is Florence's leading painter. No need here to discuss his *oeuvre*, about which an extensive literature exists. Mention might be made of *Our Lady of Humility* of the Trivulzio Collection (Milan, Museo del Castello), "among the most astonishing creations of Italian painting;" *Madonna and Child*, 1437 (Corneto Tarquinio, Museo Nazionale); the altarpiece for the Barbadori Chapel in the Church of the Santo Spirito (Paris, Louvre), "with which the history of Florentine altarpieces enters on a new chapter;" the *Coronation of the Virgin* for the high altar of the Church of Sant'Ambrogio (Florence, Uffizi Galleries), and his *Annunciation* (Florence, Church of San Lorenzo); the *tondo* depicting the Virgin and Child and scenes from her birth (Florence, Pitti Palace), the forerunner of Botticelli's *Magnificat* and Raphael's *Madonna della Sedia*. From 1452 to 1464, Fra Filippo worked on frescos in the duomo of Prato, at the same time filling commissions in Prato, Florence, and elsewhere. Among them are some of his most famous paintings, such as the Virgin before a landscape with two angels (Florence, Uffizi Galleries).

During this period occurs his well-known involvement with the Augustinian nun, Lucretia Buti, by whom he had Filippino as well as a daughter, Alexandria. Despite his contentious and far from exemplary life, Lippi does not seem to have been particularly addicted to the sins of the flesh, and his lasting love for Lucretia Buti in his mature years should be judged a serious relationship.

With the Carmelite, Fra Diamante di Feo, Lippi in 1466 had begun decorating the apse of the cathedral of Spoleto, when he was interrupted by death. He appears on his sarcophagus clothed with the Carmelite habit, and his confreres in Florence dutifully entered the date of his death in the conventual necrology.

Italian Humanists

An early figure in the field of letters was John Andrew Ferabos, of Verona, poet, and translator into Italian of Arentino's Latin version of Phalaris' *Letters* (Copinger 4736). He was also active in early humanist circles in Paris.

John Crastone, of Piacenza, compiled a *Lexicon secundumm alphabetum* (Hain 5812) and *Vocabulista* (Hain 5816), pioneer works of Greek lexicography. He also translated into Latin Constantine Lascaris' grammar, *Compendium octo orationis partium* (Hain 9921, 1922), and published a Greek and Latin psalter (Hain 13454).

Humanist interest in Roman antiquities is represented by Michael Fabrizio Ferrarini (d. 1492), who made a collection of inscriptions much consulted by scholars. He also wrote *Significatio litterarum antiquarum Valerii Probi* (Hain 13377), a work on Probus' explanation of Roman abbreviations.

Bl. Baptist Spagnoli, of Mantua (1447-1516)

The most important literary figure the Order produced during the Renaissance was Bl. Baptist Spagnoli of Mantua. He studied grammar under George Tifernate and George Merula in Mantua, later philosophy under Paul Bagelardi in Padua. In 1463, he entered the novitiate of the Mantuan Congregation at Ferrara, was ordained a priest in 1470, and five years later obtained the doctorate in theology at the University of Bologna.

After acquiring his degree, Baptist resolved to devote himself to the Muse, but in fact much of his life was occupied in the affairs of the Congregation. He served six terms as vicar general and during that time won the right to the grey habit for the Congregation (1484), acquired the convent of San Crisogono in Rome (1486), and obtained the custody of the Holy House of Loreto (1489).

Nevertheless, the Mantuan found time to write an enormous amount of verse which has undergone hundreds of editions. Most famous are his *Eclogues*, composed before he entered Carmel. Longer works include *Sylvae*, *De calamitatibus temporum*, *Parthenices VI*, *Alphonsus*, *Fasti*. The two short moralistic pieces, *Contra poetas impudice loquentes* and *De morte contemnenda* enjoyed wide popularity. *De vita beata* and *De patientia* are in prose.

The Mantuan was highly esteemed by his contemporaries, who considered him a second Virgil. His *Eclogues* particularly were taught in school in many countries: in Dean Colet's in London and in Charles Hoole's in Rotherham, in Jacob Wimpheling's in Germany. Samuel Johnson testifies that the Mantuan was read in the schools of England into the 18th century. Luther had been taught him. St. Peter Canisius recommended him. In Italy, the Mantuan was less cultivated, and knowledgeable Latinists had little regard for his style.

The Mantuan has left echoes in other authors, in Spenser, Milton, Shakespeare, Tasso, to mention only the most important.

Bostius and the Northern Renaissance

The Order in the North produced no artists or scholars of the stature of the best of those found in Italy. Nevertheless, there were not lacking in the North diligent practitioners of humanistic letters.

The Belgian Carmelite, Arnold Bostius, himself wrote little, but through his voluminous correspondence, phrased in elegant Latin, kept in touch with the humanist circle in the Order and placed it in contact with the larger movement outside. His correspondents included the Mantuan and Hermolaus Barbarus in Italy; Erasmus, the Fernand brothers, Gaguin, and Badius in France; Beyssel and Trithemius in Germany, as well as members of the Order, whom he encouraged in the pursuit of the new learning. In polished Latin, he traded views concerning writers, criticized the work of friends, exchanged poems, encouraged new talent. The Carmelite historian, Benedict Zimmermann, O.C.D., calls him the pivot of the humanist movement in the Order and designates the half century, 1475-1525, the "Age of Bostius."

One of Bostius' interests was the defense of the doctrine of the Immaculate Conception, again the object of battle in theological lists. He interested friends like the Trinitarian Robert Gaguin, the printer Josse Badius Ascensius, the Benedictine John Trithemius, and the Carmelites John Oudewater (alias, Palaeonydorus), Philip Kersebele, and James Keymolanus to compose works on the Immaculate Conception and the Virgin's parents, Joachim and Anne, and against the Dominicans, Vincent Bandello and Wiegand Wirt. It was at Bostius' suggestion that Erasmus wrote a poem on St. Anne.

In connection with humanism in the North, mention should be made of Lawrence Bureau (alias, Burelli, d. 1504), who wrote elegies on illustrious Carmelites, and John Minnegod (alias, Diophylax, d. 1527) author of an acrostic on the gospel of St. John.

Humanism and Theology

Scholasticism continued to reign in the theological faculties of the universities. During the 15th century, an attempt was made to inspire loyalty to Carmelite doctors - perhaps an expression of the Renaissance thirst for glory. The general chapters of 1416, 1430, and 1510 recommended the Carmelite doctors to teachers, and in fact Baconthorpe, Aiguani, and Terreni now appeared in print. Yet, if any school can be said to be favored by Carmelite doctors at this time it was Scotism.

An interesting example of humanist thought is Mantuan's *Opus aureum in Thomistas* (1492), according to P. O. Kristeller, "the most eloquent and detailed attack against St. Thomas and the Thomists to come down to us from humanist circles of the 15th century." Written in careful Latin with frequent classical allusions, it insists on the preeminence of the *Bible* and the Fathers over St. Thomas. The influence of Marsilio Ficino and Mantuan's friend, Pico della Mirandola, is discernable.

In the Low Countries, the Carmelites continued to favor scholasticism. Erasmus counted some of his bitterest enemies among them, especially Nicholas Baechem, of Egmond (Egmondanus, d. 1526), Inquisitor of the Netherlands, whom he nicknamed "the Camel."

In Denmark, on the other hand, the *sinceriora studia* flourished among the Carmelites. The Order there had only recently arrived, dating from the 15th century, and probably shared in the fervor Soreth had inspired. A center of Christian humanism was the Carmelite College in Copenhagen, endowed in 1517 by King Christian II. Its regent was Paul Helie, champion of Catholicism in later battles with Protestantism, but suspected by his co-religionists because of his attacks on scholasticism and his scriptural approach to theology.

Carmelite Musicians in the 15th Century

Necrologies and provincial acts of the 14th century already mention cantors and organists, but it is only in the 15th century that the Order begins producing composers and theoreticians of music, profane as well as sacred, some of them of more than local importance.

Bartolino of Padua (d. 1410), known to have been a Carmelite from one of the manuscript collections of his compositions, composed ballads and madrigals in the style of the *Ars Nova* of Italy.

The Englishman, John Hothby (d. 1487), wrote theoretical works, some of them recently edited.

John Bonadies (Gutentach? d. 1500), teacher of Franchino Gaffurio, compiled *Regulae cantus*, an anthology of musical theory, which contains a *Kyrie* of his own composition.

Chapter 9

Nicholas Audet (1481-1562)

Before he died, the prior general, Bernardine Landucci, had transferred the site of the next general chapter from Lyons to Naples. Pope Adrian VI in 1523 bestowed the vicarship on Nicholas Audet, provincial of the Holy Land. The general chapter of Venice, 1524, duly elected Audet prior general. Born on Cyprus of lesser French nobility, Nicholas followed his older brother John into the Order in Famagusta and made his studies in Nicosia. Since 1489, Cyprus had been under Venetian control, and relations between the provinces of the Holy Land and Venice were very close. Audet joined the Venetian province and studied at Padua and Parma. When the provincial of the Holy Land, John of Cyprus, perished in a shipwreck, returning from the general chapter of 1513, Baptist of Mantua named Audet his successor.

Audet brought to his office a breath of the Holy Land, cradle of the Order. He became one of the great generals of the Order. His term of office, 1524-1562, providentially was the lengthiest of any prior general in the history of the Order, except John Grossi, if one counts the time he ruled the Avignon faction during the Western Schism. With Audet, the renewal of the Order, which had languished since the death of John Soreth, again became a reality.

Even while still vicar general, Audet had seen the need of reform and had drawn up a detailed plan for its implementation, which he gave the title *Isagogicon*. The general chapter gave it its approval and itself drew up a series of decrees called *Caput unicum*.

Articles of Reform

"The reform of the Order," the *Caput unicum* begins, "First and foremost concerns, as is fitting, divine worship, to be treated with great devotion and solemnity, especially the divine office, which should be celebrated more gravely and seriously, as befits reformed friars of the regular observance." In his visitations, Audet, in fact, was to lay great stress on worship. Priests who could not read or knew no Latin were told to be given instruction. Novices and students were to be taught the divine office and other services. The restoration of the liturgy was one of Audet's achievements. He caused the liturgical books of the Order to be revised and published: the breviary (1542, 1543), the ordinal (1544), the missal (1551). Audet's ordinal adheres closely to Sibert de Beka's and shows no influence of the changes occurring in the Roman Rite at the time.

"The foundation of the reform is the common life." But while the perfect observance of the common life is the ideal, the chapter, facing up to reality, recognizes various degrees in its realization. In every province there should be some "completely reformed" houses in which the reformed friars renounced all ownership, even the usufruct of mobile goods. All income from Masses, confession, etc., pertains to the community. In other houses, "for those who are being introduced to the reform for the first time," usufruct of hereditary possessions is tolerated with permission of the prior general, as well as earnings from teaching, preaching, etc.

The chapter does not recognize reformed and non-reformed houses, but distinguishes between reformed and less reformed houses. From now on, the Order is considered to stand under the sign of reform; no house is immune from some degree of renewal. The material of the habit, if not the color, is to be the same for reformed and less reformed friars and should be inexpensive *sargia*. Neither is there a difference between the two kinds of houses in the matter of cloister, silence, and the observance of fast and abstinence.

The chapter strips of privileges all who arrived at degrees since the chapter of Rome (1513) by any other way than the stony path of study. Houses with ten priests are to support a regent who is to lecture daily on the *Bible* in a manner intelligible to the simple, though he should be able to compete in public disputation to the credit of the Order. All are obliged to attend the lectures. Houses with eight priests should maintain a student in the arts.

These decrees, and others of the *Isagogicon* regarding initial and ongoing formation, are by no means unprecedented, but their implementation became one of the prior general's serious concerns during his visitation of the Order. Everywhere he went he took care that the traditional *studia* of the Order were provided with lecturers and students. Particularly in Italy he revived the schools. The promotion of studies is another of Audet's important achievements. If the Carmelites in any way made a creditable showing at the Council of Trent, it was largely due to him; the presence with him at the Council of so many learned Carmelites must have caused him the keenest satisfaction.

Other ordinances of the *Isagogicon* and *Caput unicum*, too many to mention here, among other things revoke permissions to remain outside the cloister, abolish perpetual priorates, forbid the sale of offices and academic degrees, impose attendance in choir and refectory, limit occasions for leaving the convent.

The chapter decreed a new edition of the constitutions. The edition of 1524 reproduced the texts of the *Isagogicon*, the *Caput unicum*, and the constitutions of Bl. John Soreth, the latter to be read in the light of the first two.

The Visitation of Italy

After the general chapter Audet set out on visitation to implement its decrees. The years 1524 to 1527 he spent visiting Italy. In the North, he visited Venice, Romagna, Tuscany, and Lombardy. He had no luck trying to tame the Carmine of Florence. He visited the province of Naples (Terra di Lavoro) and perhaps Puglia. He had his greatest success in Sicily. At the provincial chapter of Catania, 1527, Trapani, Palermo, Sciacca, Siracusa, Catania, and Messina are designated as reformed.

Audet was occupied with this chapter when the sack of Rome began, May 1, 1527. Traspontina, situated within the fortifications of Castel Sant'Angelo, was temporarily spared, but San Martino felt the full fury of the invasion. During the siege of the castle, Traspontina had hindered the deployment of the artillery, so Clement VII began to press the Carmelites to move, but the prior general managed to have a final decision deferred. Later, Audet renovated the convent and established a flourishing *studium*, where he spent the last decade of his life.

The Visitation Outside Italy

Late in 1529, Audet made Octavian Sangalli, of Soncino, his vicar for Italy and crossed over into France. In a letter to Theodoric de Gouda, provincial of

Lower Germany, April 5, 1530, Audet reports his progress. Gascony and Toulouse were completely reformed, as well as most of Aquitaine, and many convents of Narbonne. Thereafter, he visited the province of Touraine, as well as the monasteries of Nantes and Vannes, the constitutions of which he approved. The next six months he visitated the Congregation of Albi. Its members, unlike those of the Mantuan Congregation later on, had no difficulty in acknowledging the prior general's jurisdiction over them. Audet even chose them as his *socius* in the visitation of the other provinces.

He held the chapter of the province of Francia at Bruges in January of 1531; the monastery of Our Lady of Sion there he took under his immediate jurisdiction. At the chapter of Lower Germany, he marked the whole province for the observance. Due to the unsettled condition of the Upper Germany province, Audet could not visit it, but he had an interview with its provincial, Andrew Stoss, in Cologne. Writing again to Theodoric from Bourges on August 1, 1531, Audet reports the reform of Touraine. His last act before retiring beyond the Alps was the reform of Provence.

He had spent more than three years in France and Germany and had reduced over one hundred houses to observance.

Spain once more failed to attract the personal ministrations of a reforming general. Audet sent Salvatus de Quercu and Peter Vareriis as his vicars. In Castile, a number of houses were reformed, among them Salamanca, Moraleja, and Toledo. In 1530, the two visitators convened a chapter of the Catalan province at Barcelona, and decreed various measures of reform. Aragon with its principal convents of Zaragoza and Valencia were also visited. The perennial factions in Andalusia frustrated Quercu's efforts.

Perhaps the vicars' services were not required in Portugal. There, in 1529, the papal legate had appointed the provincial, Balthasar Limpo, reformer of the province, who seems to have been successful.

The prior general also sent vicars to the British Isles and Denmark. James Calco achieved nothing in Scotland. Perhaps it was Theodoric de Gouda that Audet sent to Denmark.

The Quarrel with the Mantuan Congregation

Having completed his visitation and reform of the provinces, Audet, on May 18, 1532, summoned a general chapter at Padua, which reelected him and took further initiatives in the matter of reform.

To complete his initial work of reform Audet set out to visitate the Mantuan Congregation. He had become familiar with the Mantuan way of life during his studies at Parma, and his brother John had been a member of the congregation. Late in 1524, he had visited Mantua, Ferrara, Florence, and Viterbo, and for part of the journey had had as his companion John Baptist Granelli, vicar general of the congregation. With the years, the congregation had fallen into the same bad habits, especially regarding possessions, as had the unreformed part of the Order. Audet considered it his responsibility as superior to remedy these defects also. But before he could do so he would have to attack the barrier of papal privileges behind which the congregation was entrenched.

He proposed a six-point plan to regulate his relationship to the congregation:

1) all are to make profession in the name of the prior general, 2) the congregation shall observe all decrees of the general chapters for the *totaliter reformati*, 3) the congregation may not make decrees which contradict those of the general chapters, 4) ceremonies are to be conducted according to the liturgical books of the Order, 5) the vicar may not grant his subjects permission to remain outside the Order, 6) the congregation shall grant hospitality to Carmelites travelling with permission of their superiors.

The Mantuans predictably were not about to surrender their precious privileges. A long drawn-out suit before the Rota ensued, the details of which need not detain us here. Suffice it to say that the quarrel ended in a stalemate, and on March 22, 1538, was finally settled outside of court. The general is recognized as the true head of the Order in whose name all make profession. He has the right to visitate, but under such restrictive conditions as practically to nullify his effectiveness.

The Later Years

Audet did not bother to visitate the congregation and in the opinion of his biographer, Adrian Staring, thereafter prosecuted reform with less energy: "He did not request any more papal faculties; apparently he had permanently lost confidence in papal legal procedures."

For the remainder of his life Audet did not leave Italy except to attend the Council of Trent. In the thirty years after 1532 he convened only two more general chapters, in 1539 and 1548.

After 1532 he ranged far and wide over the Italian peninsula, personally or through vicars confirming his reform. He spent much time in the Carmine of Naples, "which," in his own words, "among the convents of Italy holds almost the first place" and which he had placed under his direct jurisdiction. In Naples, he approved the constitutions of the monastery of Santa Croce di Lucca. There, too, he made the acquaintance of Jerome Seripando, general of the Augustinians, and this great churchman became his fast friend. After the chapter of 1539, Audet is to be found mostly in Venice, where he was also close to Trent.

Some time after 1550, Audet drew up a report on the state of the Order, probably for the cardinal protector. Of the 30 provinces six, with 120 convents, have been destroyed by the Lutherans. The best provinces are found outside Italy with many houses of study, students, and monasteries of nuns. In Italy, there are seven provinces with about 120 convents. Abroad, Lower Germany, Francia, Narbonne, Castile, and Portugal belong to the observance. The rest are reformed or disposed to reform. Italy also has some reformed provinces and some disposed to reform, but the degree of observance differs from place to place. Every province, however, has some completely reformed or observant houses.

Audet and the General Reform of Religious

In 1553, Pope Julius III appointed a committee to draw up a general program for the reform of religious orders. Among others, it was submitted to Audet for comment. "The Carmelite general," Hubert Jedin, historian of Trent, remarks, "who had labored for thirty years in the cause of religious reform had the right to be heard in these matters."

Audet's approach to the problems of reform is realistic, his criticism of the program moderate. He saw no reason why boys of fourteen could not be received as oblates in well-regulated convents with a novitiate. Requests for dispensation from vows on the grounds of ignorance and coercion should be carefully examined, and the word of apostates not taken lightly. Above all, they should not be awarded benefices. The word *proprietarius* should be used with caution; circumstances should be taken into consideration. Religious not of observant congregations should not be lumped together under the category of conventuals, or unreformed. Visitations by apostolic commissars are financially burdensome to small convents (a tactful reference to the notorious venality of papal visitators). The primitive Rule should not be imposed, as the committee wished to do, on those who have made profession according to a Rule mitigated by the Holy See.

But where Audet did the greatest service was the reform of the papal curia itself. Nothing more effectively frustrated reform than the irresponsible concession of dispensations by venal curial officials. The Penitentiary, papal legates and nuncios, the *Segnatura*, and the Secretariat for Briefs dispensed permissions to remain outside the Order, to transfer to a less strict order (the Canons Regular of St. Augustine was a favorite), confer academic degrees, and absolve apostates. By buying a position in the following of a cardinal one could withdraw from obedience to the Order and be free to accept a benefice.

The religious superiors cooperated with the commissions appointed by Paul III, especially by calling attention to abuses. Audet, as senior in age among the religious superiors, seems to have been the soul of their common action for reform of the curia. Theodoric de Gouda, provincial of Lower Germany, kept Audet informed of the malpractice of papal officials in Germany, and Audet saw to it that his letters were widely read in Rome by prelates, cardinals, and the pope himself.

In the 50's complaints against curial abuses began to have their effect. Julius III carried out some reform, but it took the draconian methods of Paul IV to put an end to the greatest abuses. His bull of July 22, 1558, eliminated transfers to other orders except to the Carthusians and Camaldolese. For these there were less volunteers. Apostolic briefs were to pass through the cardinal protector and the procurator of the Order. Reasons alleged for the request were to be investigated. Under Paul IV and his successors the *Segnatura* and the Penitentiary were reformed.

So at the end of his life Audet witnessed the end of one of the greatest evils against which he and other superiors had battled for almost forty years. He died on December 6 or 7, 1562.

Chapter 10

The German Provinces During the Protestant Reformation

While the Order in the Latinate countries was making a belated effort at betterment, in more northerly Europe it was not accorded this grace. The wave of Protestantism rolled over the provinces of Saxony, England, Ireland, Scotland, and Denmark. Lower and Upper Germany sustained severe losses. The eastern portions of the latter also suffered from the incursions of the Turks. Poland, too, at this time was diminished.

The image of religious life had already been considerably tarnished in the skirmishes of the humanists, led by Erasmus, with the scholastics. Luther also found many sympathizers among the humanists in his attacks on Rome. His "Opinion on Monastic Orders" (1521), the logical consequence of his doctrine on good works and justification, theologically eliminated the justification for the religious state in Christian life. Many religious, already weak in their vocation, needed no further incentive to propel them out the monastery door. Few candidates were to be found to take their places. Municipal magistrates took over the depopulated or deserted premises. Lessening of alms from the diminishing Catholic population threatened the continued existence of the surviving houses, unable to meet their financial obligations.

The Province of Saxony

The province of Saxony, situated in the homeland of Luther, early succumbed to the Reformation.

Jena and Hettstedt suffered materially during the peasant uprising in 1525. The same year the prior of Hettstedt, John Glockman, surrendered the convent to the grafs of Mansfield, attesting that religious life was not based on holy writ, but clearly the contrary. That year also, the community of Pössneck yielded its convent to the municipality; the prior, Henry Kaiser, and eight of the brethren embraced Lutheranism. Three others remained steadfast to the old faith and left. Striegau ceased to exist in 1539. Stettin is mentioned the last time in 1541. In 1551, the cathedral chapter of Magdeburg ceded the convent of Querfurt to the city. In 1543, the prior of Dahme witnessed a Lutheran wedding, so not much Catholic life could have been left in the convent. In 1564, Sigismund, first Lutheran archbishop of Magdeburg, turned the convent over to the municipal council.

The principal convent of the province in Magdeburg was torn down in 1550 to make way for a bastion in the fortifications of the city. During the 20's, Valentine of Magdeburg was the most vehement opponent of Protestantism. Audet recommends him in a letter to Theodoric de Gouda in 1534. A Protestant satirical poem celebrates a redheaded Carmelite, "full of beer and wine," probably Valentine, who challenged a Lutheran preacher in Magdeburg's St. George Hospital.

The last known provincial was John Campen, mentioned in a document of 1522. He had held office since at least 1510. The general chapters of 1575 and 1580 placed Saxony under Upper Germany. The general chapter of 1593 established the custom of supplying titular provincials for provinces lost through the Reformation.

Bohemia and Poland

The province of Bohemia and Poland suffered severely in the political and religious disturbances at this time. All the Bohemian houses (Prague, Tachov, Rabstein, and Chiesch) were lost, most of them probably in the Peasants' War. In the Polish half of the province, Lwów fell to the Turks; Rastemburg, Krisborg, and Priwitz also ceased to exist. In 1562, Danzig, Cracow, Bygoszcz, Poznan, and Wilno still survived.

During this time, the general chapters made no attempt to name provincials for this province. So little was known about it that its two components came to be considered separate provinces. The chapter of 1575 left the provinces of Denmark and Bohemia to whatever course was best under the circumstances, not excluding annexation to Upper Germany. The chapter of 1580 recommended that a rector be placed over Denmark and Bohemia. When the office of titular provincial was created by the chapter of 1593, Bohemia received a titular provincial, James Ramirez, of the Neapolitan province, regent of Naples; while Master Stanislaus of Cracow was confirmed as actual provincial of Poland. In effect, the Order gained a titular provincial for Bohemia, a province which before that had not existed independently.

The two German provinces outlived the rise of Protestantism, but in a greatly reduced and weakened state, especially Upper Germany. In the first quarter of the 16th century, this province numbered twenty-six houses, counting four in Hungary. Of these, only about half, much diminished in personnel, resisted the storms of the age. According to Daniel of the Virgin Mary, only forty friars eventually remained - perhaps not an inaccurate estimate. Even this remnant might not have survived, had not the province been blessed with a capable and energetic leader.

Andrew Stoss, Provincial of Upper Germany

Andrew, son of the famous sculptor, Veit Stoss, was born around 1477 in Nürnberg and entered the Order there. He studied philosophy in Cracow (1502), theology in Vienna (1508), and canon law in Ingolstadt (1517). At the latter university, he made the acquaintance of the Dominican, John Eck.

When the office of prior of the convent of Nürnberg fell vacant in 1520, Stoss, proposed by the senate (*Rat*), was duly elected by the community. By this time, the city was definitely inclining toward the doctrines of the Wittenberg friar. The senate and some of the most influential citizens, specifically the group around the humanist, Willibald Pirkheimer, which included Christopher Scheurl, Lazarus Spengler, Casper Nutzel, and Albrecht Dürer, frequented the pulpit of John Staupitz at the Augustinian church and came to accept Luther's teachings. Other heterodox pulpits were St. Lawrence's, St. Sebald's, and the Hospital of the Holy Cross. Scheurl introduced Luther's theses to Nürnberg, and Nutzel translated them into German. Enthusiasm for Luther increased through personal contact during his visit en route to Augsburg in 1518.

The Nürnberg Colloquy

The Diets held in Nürnberg in 1522/3 and 1524 were powerless against the Lutheran trend in the city. That of 1524 proposed a German synod at Speyer to arrive at a peaceful solution. For Franconia, Margrave Casimir of Brandenburg-

Anspach prepared twenty-three articles as a basis for the reports of the theologians. At Nürnberg the senate on August 24, 1524, divided the religious institutions into three groups, each of which was to present a common report: the parish churches and the hospital; the Benedictines of St. Giles, the Carthusians, and Augustinians; and the Dominicans, Franciscans, and Carmelites. The last was the only Catholic group. The friars' report, apparently composed by Stoss, ignored Casimir's articles, refused to debate the new teachings which were only old heresies, and declared debate useless with those who claimed to be inspired by the Holy Spirit. Even if they reached an agreement, would Rome accept it?

The senate was determined to put an end to the opposition of the friars. The friars were eventually constrained to agree to "a friendly colloquy," which took the form of a solemn session of the senate under the chairmanship of Christopher Scheurl before an audience of about five hundred persons. Speakers were to answer according to God's word, not according to the pope, councils, church fathers or canon law. Stoss objected that Scheurl required nothing less than the abandonment of tradition as a source of doctrine and of canon law as a norm of conduct. The other friars took a less intransigent stand, and the colloquy was able to continue, but as the days passed, the friars saw they had made a mistake in allowing themselves to be drawn into discussion under such unpropitious circumstances. They boycotted the final session which was to hammer out a definite formula.

The wrath of the senate was not long in making itself felt. The friars of the three Catholic orders were forbidden to preach or hear confessions. The Dominican and Franciscan nunneries were assigned evangelical chaplains, but the superior of the latter, Charity Pirkheimer, Willibald's sister, a cultured woman in the finest humanistic tradition, stood fast in the Catholic faith. Stoss was given three days to leave town. Not long after, the remaining Carmelite community turned the convent over to the city.

Defense of the Faith in Bamberg

In 1528, Stoss became prior in Bamberg. The following year, he was elected provincial, his predecessor, John Reuther, having been made bishop of Würzburg. Stoss retained the office of prior of Bamberg until his death.

In Bamberg, too, Lutheranism had made considerable progress. In Stoss' own community, Eucharius Ott, friend of the popular evangelical preacher, John Schwanhauer, drew large crowds to the Carmelite church in the marketplace with his sermons; sermons, incidently, which have been blamed for the insurrection of the peasants in the area.

Perhaps the sobering experience of the Peasants' War made the bishop of Bamberg, Weigand von Redwitz (1522-1556), take a second look at Luther's teachings. During the Nürnberg Diet of 1522/3, he had never missed a Sunday sermon from the evangelical pulpit of St. Sebald's. Nürnberg, the most important city in his diocese, had converted to Lutheranism without let or hindrance on his part. His chapter included several zealous converts to Lutheranism.

With time, however, the bishop began to take a determined stand against the Reform. Stoss' biographer, Reinhold Schaffer, attributes his change of attitude and policy to the Carmelite's influence and does not hesitate to state, "Without doubt

it is mainly to Stoss' credit that Catholicism was saved in the diocese of Bamberg."
Von Redwitz certainly trusted his judgment in full and called upon his services on
important occasions. The Carmelite provincial accompanied him to the Diet of
Augsburg in 1530 and was among the *confutatores* who prepared the refutation of
the Lutheran Confession. In 1537, Von Redwitz sent Stoss to represent him at the
aborted council scheduled to meet at Mantua in 1537.

Efforts to Save the Province

Stoss' tough intransigent attitude stood him in good stead in his work as provincial
of wresting convents from the clutches of princes and municipal authorities. His
daybook, in which he carefully registered copies of letters, visitation reports,
accounts, notes on events in the Order, etc., tells the story of his discouraging life
and death struggle to save his convents. For ten years, in spite of indifferent health,
Stoss travelled incessantly over insecure roads through his widespread province.

No need here to chronicle in detail his laborious years. His difficulties were
partly financial; in this respect Vogelsburg, Nördlingen, Weissenburg, and Vienna
seem to have been especially problematic houses, often requiring his presence to
float loans or sell community property to salvage the foundation. The authorities
in Nördlingen would not allow Stoss to import friars from elsewhere. Eventually,
this convent and Weissenburg were lost to the Order. Vienna's problems came from
the mismanagement of the prior, John Stockelsteiner. All Stoss' efforts to salvage
this *studium* of the Order were ultimately in vain. In 1568, Maximilian II bestowed
it on the deserving Jesuits.

A second difficulty was the tendency of secular authorities to seize the convents,
especially in localities that tended to Lutheranism. In Heilbronn, the senate did not
take over the convent, ruined during the Peasants' War, but forbade all Catholic
services. The imperial town of Esslingen was won for the Reform by Ambrose
Blarer, the Mass was abolished, and the old services forbidden. In 1532, the prior,
Bernard Rueff, fled with the convent's seal, documents, and valuables. He later
embraced Lutheranism and became pastor in Bonlanden near Stuttgart. Under
its prior, John Frosch, the convent of St. Anne in Augsburg became a center of
evangelical teaching. Urban Regius and Stephen Agricola took up residence in the
convent. Frosch was a friend of Luther, who accepted his hospitality when he
came to Augsburg for his meeting with Cajetan in 1518. In 1525, Frosch laid aside
the habit and took a wife. Other members of the community also followed his
example. In 1534, the five remaining friars made over the convent to the Hospital
of the Holy Spirit.

But his own brethren were the provincial's biggest problem. Certainly little is to
be said for the quality of Carmelite life in those regions. All except Stoss seemed
strangely indifferent to or unaware of the fact that their house was coming down
around their ears. Most of the pulpits in the province were empty, and Stoss had the
greatest difficulty convincing his subjects to undertake this ministry performed with
such alacrity and effect by the evangelical preachers. There was the same reluctance
to fill posts of responsibility and lack of trustworthiness in some who did. Michael
Schwanfelder, prior of Schweinfurt, had to be removed from office for holding out
money. Evidently no one in the community could be trusted, because Stoss had to

hand over the convent's valuables to the senate for safekeeping. John Stockelsteiner, prior of Vienna, disappeared after wasting community goods. Finally, the alacrity with which so many abandoned the old faith shows that behind the general inertia lay a lack of conviction.

Andrew Stoss lived during a sad hour for the Church and faced many disappointments, yet he cherished a sublime faith and trust in God. "There are twelve hours to the day and twelve hours to the night," he wrote to the senate of Rottenburg; "God will bestow his grace and will not permit the barque of Peter to founder, nor religious orders to be extirpated." To the community in Vienna he wrote these serene words: "Neither you nor I can do more than God wishes and the times permit."

Stoss' immediate successors were Eucharius Ott (1540-1556?), George Rab (1547-1558), Leonard Gamann (1558-1569). Fourteen of the twenty-six convents of Upper Germany had succumbed to the pressure of the times: Esslingen, Augsburg, Nördlingen, Nürnberg, Weissenburg, Schweinfurt, Sparneck, Neustadt am Kulm, Vienna, Gösling. The four Hungarian houses (Budapest, Priwitz, Epperjes, Pecs) fell victim to the Turks after the battle of Mohacs (1526).

The Lower German Province

The Lower German province, embracing the Netherlands and the Rhineland with its center in "Holy Cologne," the Rome of the North, was less exposed to the new doctrines. This is not to say that it was entirely out of danger. Membership had fallen off for the usual reasons - apostasy, the lure of benefices, apostolic dispensations - and few candidates presented themselves to take the place of the departed. In 1530, of the German houses, besides Cologne, Frankfurt with seven members was the best staffed; the others had five or less. In that region, too, the convents in Strasburg, Kassel, Marienau, Spangenberg, Ath, and Husen had been lost to the Order, and most of their members had apostatized.

During these critical times, fortunately, the province was led by men of outstanding ability and dedication to the Catholic faith. Theodoric von Gouda, whose term of office corresponded in time to that of Andrew Stoss in the other province (1527-1539), was a member of the conservative theology faculty of Cologne and a champion of orthodoxy. He cooperated fully with Audet in the reform of the province; in spite of the weaknesses already noted, the general chapter of Padua, 1532, enrolled Lower Germany among the reformed provinces of the Order. After the brief term (1540-1541) of Martin Cuyper, prior of Mechelen, soon elected coadjutor bishop of Cambrai, Theodoric was succeeded by Eberhard Billick, a man destined not only to defend the Carmelite Order but the Catholic faith as well.

Eberhard Billick and Cologne

Eberhard Billick (d. 1557) came of a family of Cologne which had given many members to the Order. He was professed in 1514 and upon ordination functioned as first lector in the *studium* of Cologne. Elected prior in 1536, he received his doctorate at the university in 1540. The chapter of 1542 elected him provincial.

At the time, he was already involved in the affairs of the archdiocese, where the familiar signs of the disintegration of the Catholic establishment were beginning to manifest themselves. Archbishop Hermann von Wied, a worldly prelate, given to the joys of the chase, was attracted to the new doctrines. Several of his councilors were of the Lutheran persuasion. His court preacher and confessor, a Franciscan, preached "the pure teaching of the gospel" to large congregations. Through his councilman, Peter Medmann, who had been won over by Melanchthon, Von Wied was brought into contact with the latter. In 1540, he met the Strassburg reformer, Martin Bucer, and the same year permitted him to begin his ministry in the cathedral of Bonn.

Bucer's preaching at Bonn aroused the opposition of the cathedral chapter, the lower clergy, and the senate of Cologne, who demanded his removal. In 1543, the cathedral chapter composed a paper, *Sententia delictorum de vocatione Martini Buceri*, which elicited a reply from Bucer, *Was im Namen des Heiligen Evangeli unseres Herren Jesu Christi jetztundt zu Bonn im Stift Collen gelehret und gepredigt wurdt*. This in turn occasioned a rebuttal by the university and clergy of Cologne, actually composed by Billick, *Iudicium cleri et universitatis Coloniensis de doctrina et vocatione Martini Buceri ad Bonnam* (Cologne, C. Gennep, 1543). "The poet of the piece," Melanchthon wrote to the Wittenberg theologian, Casper Cruciger, on May 23, "is a well-fed Carmelite, a priest of Bacchus and Venus. The vilifications are taken from the plays of Plautus, which this Carmelite seems to enjoy more than the psalms."

The *Iudicium cleri* won replies from Melanchthon and Bucer. John Oldendorp, of the University of Marburg, former professor of law in Cologne, wrote three tracts against the Cologne theologians, two of them dealing with Billick's work. Billick defended himself against all these attacks with his *Iudicii universitatis et cleri Coloniensis adversus calumnias Philippi Melanchthonis, Martini Buceri, Oldendorpii et eorum asseclarum defensio* (Cologne, C. Gennep, 1545), which enjoyed wide dissemination, undergoing a French edition (Paris, C. Guillard, 1545).

At the Landtag of Bonn in July, 1543, Archbishop von Wied presented his plan for the reform of his diocese along evangelical lines, composed by Bucer, Melanchthon, and other Lutheran divines. The clergy rejected it and published their comments under the title, *Christliche und Catholische Gegenberichtung eyns Erwirdigen Dhomcapittels zu Coellen wider das Buch der gnanter Reformation* (Cologne, C. Gennep, 1544), composed by the famous controversialist, John Gropper, but representing the reflections of a committee, of which Billick was one. The *Gegenberichtung* belongs, by reason of its solid contents, to the best polemical literature of the time. Billick's Latin translation, *Antididagma, seu christianae et catholicae religionis propugnatio* (Cologne, C. Gennep, 1544), made it available to a wider readership.

Matters now came to a head in the quarrel of the archbishop with the clergy and magistrates. On October 9, 1544, the cathedral chapter, clergy, and university made a public appeal to pope and emperor. Von Wied sought support among the Protestant princes. On June 27, 1545, the emperor granted letters of protection to those who had made the appeal to pope and emperor. On July 10, the archbishop appealed to a German national synod and ignored a summons from Charles V and Pope Paul III. On April 16, 1546, the pope excommunicated Hermann von Wied and declared his coadjutor, Adolf von Schauenburg, administrator of the diocese. Gropper and Billick were appointed to examine his orthodoxy.

The appeal to the emperor proved effective, because Charles was finally able to concern himself with German affairs and was winning his first victories over the Protestant Schmalkaldic League. John von Isenburg and Billick were dispatched to meet the emperor and secure his support for the enforcement of the papal ban. After an adventurous journey through the Schmalkaldic lines, the two emissaries successfully completed their mission. At the Landtag of Cologne, January 24, 1547, two imperial representatives presided over the installation of Schauenburg. Von Wied publicly renounced office.

The struggle to keep Cologne Catholic was no tempest in a teapot, and Billick's role in that struggle was far from inconsequential. "Had his (Bucer's) attempt to introduce a reform into the Archdiocese of Cologne under Bishop von Wied met with success," writes the church historian, John P. Dolan, "it may have changed the entire course of the Reformation in Germany."

Billick and Religious Colloquies

Eberhard Billick also took part in some of the colloquies between Catholic and Protestant theologians Charles V sponsored in the hope of promoting Christian unity in his realms, after the central council of Mantua failed to meet.

John Gropper and Billick were among the representatives Hermann von Wied sent to the colloquy of Hagenau-Worms-Regensburg, 1540-1541. Billick took part in the session held by the Catholic delegates in the Dominican convent in Worms but did not appear at the colloquy itself. In Regensburg, according to John Eck, he disapproved of the contents of the Interim and opposed the "secret counsels of certain persons." Unsubstantiated sources claim that Billick worked on a revision of the Augsburg Confession at the request of the legate, John Morone.

During the height of the troubles in Cologne, Billick received an imperial summons to the colloquy of Regensburg in 1546. He had little faith in these attempts to reconcile Protestant and Catholic ideas, as he frankly stated in a letter to the papal nuncio, Jerome Verallo, of November 27, 1545. The Catholic debaters, besides Billick, were the imperial court chaplain, Peter Malvenda, a Spaniard; John Hofmeister, Augustinian provincial; and John Cochläus, noted controversialist. The Protestant theologians were Martin Bucer, George Major, Erhard Schnepf, and John Brenz.

Bucer wrote to Philip of Hesse, March 15, 1546, "Malvenda has aspirations of becoming something in Spain and that through the imperial confessor (Peter de Soto)... The Carmelite from Cologne is, after Gropper, the most poisonous and chief tool of the Cologne tyranny against Christ, our Lord... The Augustinian from Colmar is younger, bolder, and eloquent in German, but more able at dancing with nuns (as he did here last Shrove Tuesday) than at disputation... Cochläus is an old pitiable child, barks weakly, and bites hardly at all, so that even his fellow debaters are ashamed of him."

When the discussions got under way, Malvenda and Billick expounded the Catholic doctrine on justification. "Malvenda, it is true, is singing the old song of the scholastics concerning justification," Brenz wrote to Melanchthon, "but at least he speaks in a respectable manner; Billick on the contrary, thinks Malvenda's speech has not prickles enough and is a very devil, for he twists the best and plainest words for one." The colloquy broke up after ten days without accomplishing anything.

Billick sent his account of the proceedings, a letter to the citizens of Cologne, April 30, 1546, to the prior general, Nicholas Audet, at the Council of Trent. An Italian translation is preserved in the archive of the Order in Rome. Billick's letters got around. On December 13, 1545, the day the council opened, the papal nuncio in France, Jerome Dandino, sent one to Cardinal Marcellus Cervini, requesting him to keep the information confidential, lest the writer be jeopardized. Billick later published *De ratione summovendi praesentis temporis dissidia* (Cologne, C. Gennep, 1557).

At the emperor's behest, Billick appeared at the Diet of Augsburg in 1547, which resulted in the Interim of 1548, but he almost immediately fell ill and did not recover until Christmas. Nevertheless, he took part in the work as one of a committee of five. He incorporated his ideas in a position paper, dated October 26, 1547, *Consilium de pace stabilienda et Ecclesia reformanda*. Charles limited the Interim to the Protestant States; for Catholics he issued a *Formula reformationis*, the text of which, according to his publisher, Casper Gennep, was Billick's.

The archbishop of Cologne did not attend the Reichstag of 1555, so Billick had no part in the Peace of Augsburg, though he recorded his dissatisfaction with that famous arrangement in his treatise, *De ratione summovendi praesentis temporis dissidia* (Cologne, C. Gennep, 1557). After the declaration of peace, Protestant activity in Cologne resumed, but determined action by authorities in the end prevailed. A Protestant pasquil nailed to the doors of churches occasioned Billick's last salvo, *Cacopasquili. . . confutatio* (Cologne, C. Gennep, n. d.).

Eberhard Billick, Provincial

It seemed to Billick that his services to the emperor led him to neglect his duties as provincial, but in fact at the various diets he was able personally to approach the princes and delegates of the cities in which the Order's houses were threatened. Influential friends of the emperor lent their support. In writing to magistrates at home, Billick was able to use imperial messengers to lend force to his demands.

Billick never succeeded in recovering the houses already lost when he took office in 1542, but at least while Charles V was victorious over Protestant princes, he managed to fend off secular control over threatened houses in Mörs, Kreuznach, Weinheim, Speyer, Hirschhorn, and Frankfurt. However, after the defeat of the imperial forces at Innsbruck in 1552, Billick was left without resources, and the province also suffered materially from the war.

In his efforts to salvage the province, Billick stood firm on the legal property rights of the Order. In this he was largely successful. Although the province suffered a serious diminution of personnel, relatively few houses were lost. He was unsuccessful in obtaining the reconstruction of the convent in Düren, torn down by imperial troops in the defense of the town. Mörs was sold to Maurice of Nassau in 1614. Kreuznach, Hirschhorn, and Weinheim remained in Protestant hands, but the Order never relinquished its rights and later, around 1625, managed to repossess them. Husen, too, the community of which had embraced Lutheranism, was reopened in 1694.

Chapter 11

Protestantism in Other Provinces

The Carmelite Order played a paradoxical role in the Danish Reformation: it contributed outstanding leaders both to the Protestant and Catholic sides of the debate. On the one hand, it produced Paul Helie, in the words of his biographer, Ludwig Schmitt, S.J., "the only noteworthy champion of the Church." On the other hand, as the historian, E. H. Dunkley, writes, the Carmelite Order, as "preeminently the learned Order in the Denmark of the early 16th century... contributed more to the Reformation movement in that country than any other community."

Paul Helie and King Christian II

Paul Helie was born around 1480 in Varberg, in the province of Halland, of a Danish father and a Swedish mother, and it is most likely there that at an early age he entered the Order. There also, or in Landskrona or Helsingør, he made his studies. An early work, *De simoniaca pravitate* (Copenhagen, 1517), already shows the frank criticism of the faults of the Church which characterized his career.

In 1519, the provincial chapter at Landskrona appointed Helie first regent of the new *studium* in Copenhagen. In 1522, he was elected provincial. In that capacity *"Paulus Dacus"* attended the general chapter at Padua in 1532 under the prior general, Nicholas Audet.

Under Lector Paul, the Carmelite *studium* in Copenhagen became a center of the humanistic *sinceriora studia*, the scriptural, patristic approach to theology. He had no quarrel with scholastics other than with those who saw no other approach to revelation.

Like Erasmus, Helie was attracted by the evangelical character of Protestantism. He knew the early works of Luther. He was on friendly terms with Matthias Gabler, of Stuttgart, who had acquired a bachelor's degree in Wittenberg in 1519, and who taught Greek at the university of Copenhagen. Among Helie's students may have been the German priest, Martin Reinhard, of the diocese of Würzburg, who subsequently became royal chaplain and brought the doctrines of Luther to the court of Denmark. But, no more than Erasmus, was he willing to follow Luther in his radical revision of Catholic belief. On being asked, he left no doubt in the mind of King Christian II as to his opinion of Luther's teachings. (Neither did he mince words about the King's relationship with his Dutch mistress, Duveke).

But Christian's days were numbered. His attempt to limit the power of the nobles and bishops alienated these classes, and his arbitrary and bloodthirsty acts of tyranny gave plausibility to their cause. In April of 1523, he fled to The Netherlands, and the throne was offered to his uncle, the duke of Schleswig-Holstein, who became Frederick I.

"Name, if you can," Helie wrote to Peter Ivarsen, canon of Lund, November 3, 1524, "among those who with braggart words boast of having done everything, even one who by speech and pen has opposed the King's violence with such outspokenness as I." Helie's activity against Christian included a Latin translation of the complaints against the king, circulated among the bishops, and a lengthy commentary in Danish on the act of deposition. C. T. Engelstoft conjectures that

Helie composed in Danish the original list of complaints against Christian which was later incorporated into the electoral charter of Frederick.

The Church Under Frederick I

In his electoral charter (*Handfaestning*), drawn up at the assembly of notables (*Herredag*) at Roskilde, August 3, 1523, Frederick was required to promise among other things not to allow heretics to preach or teach in the realm. Other stipulations, however, were designed to eliminate dependence on Rome. The bishops' dream of a national Danish church free of Lutheranism was illusory. Perhaps, too, Lutheranism would have been less attractive, if their own witness to Catholicism had been more credible.

Frederick's sympathy for Lutheranism soon became apparent. His court neglected the Church abstinence and received communion under both species. In May of 1526, Helie was summoned to preach before the king and, although he spoke with reserve, *mediocri libertate*, he left under insults and threats of the soldiery. The encounter convinced Frederick that the Carmelite was not the Lutheran he was rumored to be.

It was perhaps as a result of this experience that Helie in 1526 wrote his first polemic tract in Danish, *A Christian Instruction on Lutheranism*, which attacks Luther's characteristic doctrines on good works, freedom of the will, the sacraments, the infallibility of the Church, and her jurisdictional power. In Sweden, it evoked a rebuttal from Olaf Petersen, secretary of the council of Stockholm (Stockholm, 1527).

Helie's first polemic to survive and the earliest in Danish literature is his *Answer* to John Mikkelsen's comments in a Danish translation of the New Testament (Rostock, Brothers of the Common Life, 1527). It was printed in Wittenberg in 1524, and Mikkelsen did the apostolic letters, prefacing them with an introduction. It was Mikkelsen's contribution which formed the object of Helie's attack, never subsequently equalled, according to Chr. Bruun, for polemic incisiveness and power. Later editions of the translation omitted Mikkelsen's offending comments.

At the Herretag held in Odense in December, 1526, it was decided that in the future the archbishop of Lund, not the pope, would confirm Danish bishops. The tax paid to Rome on such occasions would instead be paid into the royal treasury. The bishops pressed the king to desist from authorizing preachers contrary to their authority. Frederick in 1526 had granted letters of protection and authority to preach in Viborg to John Tausen, former Hospitaller of St. John, and to George Sadolin, who joined Tausen in Viborg and opened a school which became a training ground for Lutheran ministers. The bishops could not bring themselves to make the material concessions demanded by the nobles and so failed to win their support, even though the latter were predominantly Catholic.

Although Lector Paul was an outstanding and able opponent of the new teachings, he was not trusted by his own co-religionists because of his frank criticism of the Church and his supposed leanings toward Lutheranism. In 1527, the Jutland bishops invited John Eck and John Cochlaeus to Denmark to defend the Catholic faith, but without result. "The journey is very long, and the people are said to be barbarous," the fastidious Erasmus wrote to Cochlaeus on August 25.

On the other hand, the Lutherans were disappointed in their expectations, when, after all, Helie turned against them.

The Malmö Book

In Malmö, the ex-priest, Nicholas Mortensen, armed with letters of protection from the king against Archbishop Aage Sparre, conducted evangelical services. The houses of the local religious, Franciscans and Brothers of the Holy Spirit, were confiscated by the local authorities. The town was completely won over to the Reformation and soon became the Wittenberg of Denmark. In 1530, the *Malmö Book* appeared, describing the course of the Reformation there, the new doctrines, and the order of divine worship.

Helie lost no time in replying to this work, which in effect constituted a full dress presentation of the new doctrines. His *Against the Malmö Book* readily admits what is amiss in the current practice of Christianity, but defends the basic Catholic doctrines. Unfortunately, it was never printed and thus was not available to challenge the *Malmö Book* in the public forum.

Author of the *Malmö Book* is generally considered to be the ex-Carmelite, Peter Laurentsen, of Naestved, one of Helie's former students. He was living in the Carmelite convent of Assens, when in 1527 he laid aside the habit. He joined Mortensen in Malmö, married his sister, Anne, and was named lecturer in scripture at the school for Lutheran clergy, to which King Frederick accorded approval in 1530. Laurentsen wrote extensively on behalf of the new doctrines. He was a member of the commission which in 1537 drew up the *Church Ordinance*, the constitution of the Danish Church.

Another former Carmelite and student of Helie was Francis Wormordsen, of Halland. He came to Malmö in 1529, married, and rose to prominence in the Lutheran Church. In 1537, he was ordained superintendent (bishop) of Lund by John Bugenhagen, pastor of Wittenberg, whom Frederick had imported for his coronation. Wormordsen also collaborated on the Church Ordinance of 1537 and later supplemented it with a manual for divine service, *Haandbog* (1539), a predecessor of Peter Palladius' *Alterbogen* (1556), the definitive book of prayer of the Danish Church. Wormordsen's translation of the psalter was likewise supplanted by the *Bible* in Danish of Christiern Pedersen, who says about previous psalters in Danish that "all complain that they cannot understand them."

It was Lector Paul's lifelong regret that so many of the students whom he had introduced to humanist studies abandoned the old faith for Lutheranism.

The Copenhagen Confession

On July 2, 1530, a Herredag met in Copenhagen at the royal summons for the purpose of healing the religious differences in the kingdom. Besides about 30 nobles, the archbishop, six bishops, and a few religious and canons, there appeared "Master Tausen and his company," numbering more than 20 evangelical preachers from every province in the land. The reformers defined their doctrinal position in a statement consisting of 43 articles, the *"Copenhagen Confession,"* which became the creed of the Danish Protestant Church, corresponding to the Augsburg Confession of German Lutheranism and Zwingli's *Fidei Ratio* and *Confessio Tetrapolitana*. The

Danish confession is a quite independent composition, formerly attributed to Tausen, but recently awarded to Peter Laurentsen as the author.

The Catholic theologians, who included several foreigners, presented a list in Danish of 27 errors attributed to the reformers. Helie is generally thought to be the author of this list. The reformers wrote a *Reply* to the 27 accusations and added 12 of their own against the bishops. The debate remained in literary form only; the Catholic party saw the inadvisability of a public debate witnessed by the people. These had been thoroughly aroused against the bishops and clergy by the fiery sermons of the preachers. One of the targets of their oratory was Lector Paul, who now received the nickname, "Vendekaabe" (Turncoat). Without an armed escort the streets were unsafe for him and the other Catholic theologians.

The End of the Danish Province

The Herredag of 1530 ended without the condemnation of Protestantism the bishops had hoped for. During the following years Catholicism rapidly lost ground. Helie continued to support its desperate cause. His many polemical works cannot be considered here; the critical edition of his writings comprises seven volumes.

After Frederick's death in 1533, the elective office of king fell open, and the nobles again assumed power. It was an opportunity for the Catholic cause. The Catholic majority managed to pass the restrictions against heresy Frederick had always sidestepped and entrusted the bishops with the appointment of preachers. Tausen was called on the carpet to answer charges brought forward by Lector Paul, was banished from Copenhagen, but soon recalled by Bishop Joachim Ronnov. In the war of succession, the Protestant, Christian III, was victorious, and the fate of Catholicism in Denmark was sealed.

The dissolution of the ten convents of the province of Denmark had already begun during the reign of Frederick I. In 1529, the convent of Assens was lost to the Lutherans through the apostasy of Peter Laurentsen. The convent of Landskrona was ceded to the citizenry by the king in 1530. Due to straitened circumstances, the Carmelites of Aarhus turned their property over to Bishop Ove Bilde (1531). The king bestowed Skelskør on his councilor, John Urne (1532). Driven by poverty, the Carmelites of Saeby turned their house over to the municipality (1536). The fate of the remaining houses was no doubt similar. The convent and church of Helsingør and the church of Saeby survive.

The Order in Denmark cannot long have outlived the disestablishment of the episcopacy by Christian III in 1536 and the *Church Ordinance of 1537*, which practically abolished the Mendicant Orders. Probably the last provincial was Anders Christensen, of whom there is record in 1538. The general chapter of 1539, no doubt for lack of other information, still lists "Paul the Dane" as provincial of Denmark.

Helie's ultimate fate is unknown. He was at work on a Latin chronicle of events in Denmark between 1448 and 1534, called the *Skiby Chronicle*, from the town in which it was found in 1650 behind the altar of the church. The book ends in mid-sentence of a description of the Swedish siege of Helie's native Varberg.

The English Province

Since the days of the Lollards, the Carmelites produced no figure of note. The last foundation had been made in the middle of the 14th century, and although the number of houses remained the same - thirty-nine - the number of religious greatly declined in the century before the dissolution of the monasteries. None of the Order's reforms penetrated to England; had they done so, the English province might have shown some of the spirit of the German and Danish provinces. Here the provincial led the way in apostasy.

The English Church Separated from Rome

The steps by which King Henry VIII separated the Church in England from Rome were accomplished by a series of laws, the most important of which were the Succession Act and the Act of Supremacy, passed in 1534 under penalty of treason, by which the king was recognized "as the supreme and only head of the Church of England," and which acknowledged the validity of Henry's marriage to Anne Boleyn and the right of their offspring to succession to the throne.

Henry required the assent of his subjects to these claims under oath. John Hilsey, Dominican provincial, and George Browne, Augustinian provincial, were appointed visitators of the friars to administer the oath. With the exception of the Observant Franciscans all went smoothly. On June 21, 1534, Hilsey wrote from Exeter that he had "not found any religious persons who have utterly refused the oath of obedience, although some have sworn to it with an evil will and slenderly taken it."

Perhaps a few Carmelites were among those who had "slenderly taken it." On May 22, 1537, William Gibson and John Pecock were charged at Norwich with plotting insurrection and were sentenced to life imprisonment.

On June 10, 1537, one Francis Turpin informed against the Carmelite Robert Austin, who in a sermon in St. Bride's Church in Fleet Street had omitted the King's title as supreme head of the English Church and had not preached against "the usurped power of the bishop of Rome." Austin was arrested, but his subsequent fate is unknown.

Lawrence Cook, prior of Doncaster, was accused of aiding the rebels during the Pilgrimage of Grace. Imprisoned in the Tower and at Newgate, he was condemned by an act of attainder a few days before the fall of Cromwell. He was pardoned on October 2, 1540, but there is some doubt as to whether he escaped execution.

The King's Marriages

Upon the death of the incumbent, Henry, in 1532 appointed to the see of Canterbury, Thomas Cranmer, of overt Lutheran sympathies, who had taken a wife. Cranmer quickly expedited the King's "great matter." In 1533, he found Henry's marriage with Catherine of Aragon null and void, declared his marriage with Anne Boleyn valid, and crowned her queen. Pope Clement VII finally made up his mind and the same year excommunicated Cranmer and the king as well, unless he gave up Anne and returned to his lawful wife.

Several Carmelites were involved in the matter of the King's divorce. In 1531, the provincial, John Bird, had written a treatise in its favor. With Bishop Fox and Thomas Bedyll, he went on a mission from the king to Catherine to try to dissuade her from using the title of queen, "which nevertheless she would not do." After the King's supremacy in spiritual matters had been decreed, Henry in 1535 made

Bird "general" of the Carmelites in England, Wales, and Ireland. In the campaign of propaganda which Henry unleashed in 1534 to undermine the pope's authority, Bird was assigned as preacher for Easter of 1537. At the dissolution of the religious orders, Bird received the bishopric of Penrith, later that of Bangor. He showed equal zeal on behalf of Henry's marriage with Anne of Cleves. In 1539, he went on the mission to Germany, where Cromwell wrote him to obtain a "picture of the lady." At the convocation of that year, as bishop of Bangor, he subscribed to the divorce of Henry from Anne. Under Mary he recanted, repudiated his wife, and was appointed suffragan to Bishop Edmund Bonner of London. He died in 1558.

Two other Carmelites, adventurers and opportunists from abroad, fished in the muddied waters of Henry's marital affairs. James Calco, of Lodi, onetime prior of Traspontina in Rome and doctor of Paris, busied himself with the question of the divorce while on visitation of the Order in the British Isles. He obtained a judgment favorable to Henry from the theologians of the University of Paris. He has been credited with an anonymous pamphlet in Latin and English, *Gravissimae atque exactissimae illustrissimarum totius Italiae ac Galliae academiarum censurae* (London, 1550). In England, he taught at various universities, pensioned by the king. He also wrote against the primacy of the pope. The general chapter of 1532 declared him an apostate and excommunicate for supporting the "odious cause of the divorce of the Most Serene King of England" and ordered his capture, but Calco died of the pest the following year. He was buried, censures and all, in the Carmelite church in London.

John Baptist Pallavicini, of a noble Genoese family, entered the Mantuan Congregation in 1514. He became one of the most famous preachers in Italy but repeatedly fell under suspicion of heresy. He was a member of the theology faculty of Bologna and bestirred himself on behalf of Henry's divorce there and at the University of Ferrara. In 1534, he wrote from the French court congratulating Henry on having cast off the Roman yoke and reassured him as to his own orthodoxy with regard to the Eucharist, but the following year the fickle friar turned about face, attacked the English king and the book which his ambassador, Stephen Gardiner, had written against the jurisdiction of the pope.

Good use was made in official propaganda in England of the support given the King's suit at the universities.

The End of the English Province

As spiritual head of the English Church, King Henry inherited the supervision of religious orders. The result of his solicitude was the disappearance of these orders during the years 1538-1539.

Visitator for the friars was Richard Ingworth, ex-Dominican, and currently bishop of Dover. He was assisted in some parts by Dr. John London.

The Carmelite *studium* of Oxford was surrendered to London in July of 1538. The house was in a ruinous condition, and the prior was in the process of liquidating its meager assets when the visitator arrived. The buildings were pulled down or sold. In 1596, the refectory supplied stones for the enlargement of the library of St. John's College.

In Cambridge, Cromwell on August 10, commissioned George Deye, provost of King's College, and William Maye, master of Queen's College, and others to receive the Carmelite house for the King's use and to inventory its possessions. Maye eventually came into possession of the property and in turn sold it to Queen's College. Some windows of the Carmelite house survive in its library.

On November 10, John Gibbys, prior, and twelve other friars surrendered the Carmelite house in London. The site of Whitefriars retained the right of sanctuary into the 18th century and is the subject of numerous allusions in literature. Today, a small vaulted room, possibly the undercroft of the prior's lodging, remains in a building off Fleet Street.

On December 13, Ingworth arrived in Canterbury after receiving the Carmelite house at Aylesford into the King's hands. Cromwell made the property available to the poet, Sir Thomas Wyatt. Under Queen Elizabeth it passed to Sir John Sedley, of Southfleet. Charles Sedley, the poet, was born at Aylesford in 1639. The house returned into the possession of the Carmelites in 1949.

No record exists of the suppression of Hulne, the earliest Carmelite foundation in England. Ingworth was in the North early in 1539 and apparently received it then. Extensive but uninhabited remains of the buildings are still standing.

Records of the dissolution of the Carmelite houses provide information on the number of inmates for 21 of the 39 convents. The average membership was eight friars. This would place the number of Carmelites in the English province at 309 at the time of its suppression. This figure would not include the friars who left before the final hour sounded.

Ingworth, after all, wrote what may be the most moving word on the vanished province of the English Carmelites. Arriving at the convent of Sele on the feast of Our Lady of Mount Carmel, July 16, 1538, he found no one at home and the doors lying open. "No prior there," he noted, "nor none to serve God."

John Bale, 1495-1563

The most noteworthy English Carmelite of the time converted to Protestantism. He turned into a bitter foe of the old faith, but at least his story is not one of time-serving or passive acquiescence to a political situation. He converted to continental Protestantism and stuck by his convictions amid the shifting fortunes of the time at great personal sacrifice.

John Bale was born at Cove, Suffolk, and entered the Order at Norwich. In 1514, he entered Cambridge, when Erasmus was still teaching Greek there. Lutheranism found a sympathetic hearing at Cambridge, and Bale had as fellow-students men whose names are writ large across the pages of Reformation history: Thomas Cranmer, Stephen Gardiner, Hugh Latimer, Matthew Parker, and others. No doubt at this time Bale first imbibed his Protestant convictions, together with other Carmelites like John Bird and John Barret. After studies abroad in Toulouse and Louvain, he returned to Cambridge. In 1532, he received the doctorate conferred by the Order.

Not long after completing his studies Bale left the Order, at the same time taking a wife, Dorothy, who stood by him through all the storms and misfortunes of his career. He found a patron in Thomas Cromwell, who used his talents as a playwright for propaganda against Rome. His friend, John Leland, antiquarian of the realm, persuaded him to continue his researches into Carmelite bibliography, begun while he was in the Order.

After Cromwell was beheaded in 1540, Bale fled to the continent. He came into contact with Melanchthon, Conrad Gesner, and others, gaining a name as a redoubtable religious pamphleteer. He also continued his antiquarian researches; his first catalog of English writers, the *Summarium*, appeared in Wesel in 1548. The same year he returned to England, where he shared the hospitality of the Duchess of Richmond with John Foxe, the martyrologist. Edward VI named him bishop of Ossory in Ireland (1553), but at Mary's accession he had to flee, in the process losing his library consisting of two wagon loads of manuscripts and incunabula.

At Frankfurt, Bale joined the English Protestant colony, but for most of his second exile he lived in Basle near his printer, John Oporinus, who published his second catalog of English writers, the *Catalogue* (2 v., 1557-1559). He also carried on his pamphleteering, meeting such Protestant writers as Conrad Gesner, Henry Bullinger, John Junius, and Josiah Simler. He became the friend of Matthias Flacius Illyricus, the Centuriator, and supplied him with information.

After the death of Queen Mary, Bale, old and worn by labors, returned to England. In 1559, Queen Elizabeth granted him a prebend in the cathedral of Canterbury, a small reward in his opinion for all his efforts. Yet, with his hoary hairs, in the words of Barnaby Googe, he did "persist to turn the painful book." At the time of his death, he was working on a chronicle of England and for this purpose trying to recover his library.

As a controversialist, "bilious Bale" created a genre of martyr literature later followed by Foxe. His plays stand between the medieval moralities and Elizabethan drama. Finally, Bale has been called "the first historian of English literature." He is the only source for many English writers of the 16th century. His manuscript notes on Carmelite history are preserved in the British Museum in London and the Bodleian Library in Oxford.

Ireland and Scotland

Henry VIII was king of Ireland as well as England and Wales, and so his religious policy applied to both islands. The Parliament of 1536 passed all his legislation for Ireland. Nevertheless, the king was not able to impose his authority here in the same degree as in England. Outside the Pale, English influence was limited. In remoter regions, religious houses sometimes continued to exist in spite of the act of dissolution.

A few convents were suppressed in the years 1538-1539, but by 1540 all those in the Pale and in lands under English control, numbering almost a score, had disappeared. Especially after the accession of Queen Elizabeth, religious houses were more and more confined to the west and northwest of the island. After the battle of Kinsale in 1601, even these were lost.

The Irish Carmelites on the whole remained loyal to the old faith. R. Dudley-Edwards notes the irony of the fact that the suppression of religious houses only loosed their inmates on the countryside, where they even more effectively continued their opposition to the religious policies of the crown.

In his account of the state of the Order in 1531, Audet says about Ireland that it "has many convents and friars, but because of distance the province is little or almost not known. The provincial is an old man of sound doctrine." The general chapter of 1532 names a certain "Master John of Ireland as provincial. Mahon McSweeney, of Rathmullen, Co. Donegal, attended the general chapter of 1575. The obituary of the convent of San Martino ai Monti in Rome notes that on July 30, 1591, "Fr. Hugh of Ireland died in peace and was buried in the grave of our religious. He was very old. Let us pray for him."

The Kingdom of Scotland under James V, for the time being, remained Catholic. The Scottish provincial, William Stobbe, and his *socius*, William Lindsay, attended the general chapter in 1539. John Cristeson, of Aberdeen, occurs as provincial at the general chapter of 1548. He is the last known to have held office. In the second half of the century Scotland not only cast off the yoke of Rome but adopted the Calvinism of John Knox.

Protestantism in Italy

"In the '30's," writes Gottfried Buschbell, "it seemed as though in Italy also the religious, who almost exclusively occupied the pulpits and confessionals there, would become the heralds of Protestant propaganda." We have already mentioned James Calco and John Baptist Pallavicini in connection with the divorce of Henry VIII.

Pallavicini was repeatedly cited and imprisoned for heresy. He took refuge under the patronage of Margaret of Parma and again ended up in prison for his involvement in the question of the validity of her marriage. He is last heard of in 1545, serving a life's sentence at Ostia.

The Mantuan Congregation produced a staunch defender of the Catholic faith in John Mary Verrato (d 1563) of Ferrara. He took the Carmelite habit in 1506 and acquired the doctorate at Bologna in 1533; his diploma was signed by John Baptist Pallavicini! His numerous works, published in seven volumes (Venice, 1571), include many concerned with controverted doctrines of the time, notably his *Disputationes adversus Lutheranos*, which underwent a number of editions.

Lutheranism gained little ground in Italy due to the decisive action of ecclesiastical authorities, especially after the institution of the Roman Inquisition in 1543. Bishop John Matthew Giberti, of Verona, noted Catholic reformer, consulted Elisha de Azzalis (d. 1572), prior and regent of the Carmelite *studium* of Padua, and dean of the theology faculty of the university there, regarding the orthodoxy of certain priests.

The Order itself also began to take measures against heresy. The general chapter of 1548 instructed all provincials and priors to punish with loss of vote and, if necessary, imprisonment any subject found to be in any way tainted with heresy. On November 12 of that year, Audet sent a circular letter to the whole Order ordering a search to be made within three days for any books contrary to the Catholic faith. Such books were to be publicly burned and their owners imprisoned until the next general chapter. No one should be permitted to preach, unless he were steadfast in the Catholic faith. Suspicion of heresy alone was enough to disqualify a preacher.

In Spain, the Inquisition acted so vigorously that heretical doctrines were unable to take root.

Chapter 12

Carmelites at the Council of Trent

On December 13, 1545, the long-desired ecumenical council finally met at Trent. During the years of stormy controversy, men of all stripes had appealed to it: some looked for an authoritative decision on the questions that divided men's minds; others sought to elude immediate judgment by authority. Originally needed for the reform of Christian morals, the council was now faced with the task of reassessing doctrine in the face of the Protestant challenge. Carmelites, too, had a part in this important assembly which set the tone of Catholic faith and morals for centuries to come. Their part was a modest one, but they were represented at all twenty-five sessions of the council, save one, faithfully "supporting many labors for the defense of the Catholic faith." As far as can be determined, about forty Carmelites participated in the council, among them a prior general and four bishops.

The procession that wended its way into the cathedral of Trent at 9:30 on that morning of December 13, 1545, to begin the momentous council comprised four cardinals, four archbishops, 21 bishops and five generals of the Mendicant Orders (Franciscan Conventuals and Observants, Augustinians, Carmelites and Servites). A modest beginning, but a beginning at last.

The first meetings were dedicated to determining the order of procedure. The work of the council proceeded in three stages. The congregations of theologians discussed the questions to be treated and so to provide the bishops with needed information. The general congregations consisted of the "Fathers" or prelates with a right to vote; at these meetings the prelates presented their vote on the matters under discussion. The Fathers were subdivided into three *classes*, who held particular congregations to formulate the decrees. Audet was a member of the third *classis* under Cardinal Reginald Pole, an exile from England for his refusal to take the oath of supremacy. (These *classes* were abandoned as too cumbersome in May, 1546.) The completed decrees were voted on in solemn sessions in the church of St. Vigilius, the cathedral of Trent. Unlike the councils of the 15th century, Trent limited the vote to bishops, generals of Orders, and representatives of monastic congregations. Each general of an Order was entitled to bring two theologians.

On December 20, Anthony Marinari, provincial of Puglia, preached before the assembled Fathers. With great eloquence and command of scripture he discoursed on law, faith, and the freedom of the children of God. Angelo Massarelli, secretary to the council, wrote words of extravagant praise in his diary: "Master Anthony... gave such an excellent account of himself that he was commended and honored by all beyond any who have so far spoken in that place, for his doctrine, art, piety, and religion." Ercole Severoli, promoter of the council, judged the sermon "learned and brilliant." Not all his hearers were to be similarly impressed by Marinari's later discourses.

Session Three: Scripture and Tradition

The third session of the council, beginning February 4, 1546, treated of scripture and tradition. There is extant a treatise of Audet, probably presented at the particular congregation of Pole on February 11th, in which the Carmelite general defends the canonicity of the deutero-canonical books of the New and Old Testament. Nevertheless, he shared the minority opinion of Cervini, Pole, Madruzzo, Seripando, and others, that a distinction of the degree of authority in the various books should be made. On April 1st, he voted with the minority for having doubtful passages of Scripture clearly indicated. He wanted the apocrypha excluded, the names of the authors of the books included. He also favored condemning heretics.

In the debate over tradition, Audet on April 1st approved of limiting the notion of tradition to apostolic traditions, of not specifying particular traditions, of accepting scripture and tradition "with equal loving adhesion" (*pari pietatis affectu*) and of anathematizing those who "violated" tradition. The latter expression (*violaverit*) was softened in the final form of the decree.

The council had decided to handle simultaneously questions of doctrine and morals. Beginning with the particular congregations of March 1st, the assembly accordingly treated of the abuses against scripture and their punishment. Audet prepared a treatise, *Six Abuses in Scripture*, which reveals familiarity with scriptural science as it stood at that time and the influence of humanism. He prefers the Vulgate by reason of its authority acquired by long use in the Church. The basic errors for him were that the Bible was allotted the place of the Church, and individual interpretation was preferred to the authoritative exposition of the Church.

In the general congregation of April 3rd, Audet opposed the intransigent attitude of Cardinal Peter Pacheco, who rejected all editions of the Bible other than the Vulgate, and the view of Christopher Madruzzo, Prince-Bishop of Trent, who wanted to include vernacular translations. He held the opinion adopted in the decree that the Vulgate be accepted as official without prejudice to the authority of the Septuagint or other editions that might help to throw light on the Vulgate. Further, he did not want the errors of the Vulgate noted, though they should be corrected; he approved interpretation only according to the mind of the Church and the Fathers, wanted sanctions against printers who published the Bible without ecclesiastical approval and favored the intervention of the Inquisition.

In connection with the decree on scripture, the Fathers, in session 4, applied themselves to the matter of biblical study and preaching. Here the question of the exemption of the mendicants arose. The bishops wanted greater control over the religious; extremists among them denied them all rights to the ministry. It was probably for the particular congregation of April 13th that Audet prepared his *Tractatus de praedicatoribus*. Audet was not present, and it was read by the bishop of Fano, Peter Bertano.

On the question of the divine right of episcopal jurisdiction, the Carmelite general held a strictly curial point of view: bishops as well as mendicant preachers owed their jurisdiction to the pope. The final decree, approved in the solemn session of June 17th, allowed regulars to preach in their own churches; to preach outside them required the permission of the local bishop. In cases of scandal, the bishop could forbid regulars the pulpit; in cases of heresy bishops were given faculties to intervene as delegated by the Holy See. Thus religious were subjected to the bishops in the ministry, but the former retained their exemption and right to punish their own. This did not entirely satisfy the bishops, who returned to the subject in session 7 (1547). There they were given the right to visitate even exempt churches and to take steps against vagabond religious, but only as authorized by the Holy See. Religious privileges were thus at least externally retained. In these discussions, both in the particular and general congregations, which so affected the interest of the Order, Audet, needless to say, took an active part.

In session 4, the council debated the doctrine of original sin. Audet did not get back to Trent until the discussion of the final formula, June 14th. He voted for the decree as formulated, with the reservations expressed by Cardinal Pole, Bishop Peter Bertano, and Bishop Cornelius Musso, namely that the phrase, "God hates nothing in the reborn," be modified to allow for sin in man after baptism. He supported Pacheco in favor of the Immaculate Conception, but did not want the question debated. He accepted the explanations of the council that it did not intend to include the Virgin Mary in the universal taint of original sin.

Session Six: Justification

The doctrine of justification, Trent's most formidable task and its most important accomplishment, was formulated in the sixth session. On June 30, a schema for the debate received the approval of the council fathers, among them Audet. It presented the problem in terms of three stages in the process of justification: 1) conversion of the infidel to faith; 2) the preservation and increase of justice in the just person; 3) reacquisition of justice once lost through sin.

On July 13, Audet read his *votum* on the first case or stage of justification; on July 23 his *vota* on the second and third stages. Like all his *vota*, these are characterized by exactness and clarity. He carefully states the question to be discussed, then answers it clearly. Such orderly methodology is not a common thing among the council fathers. This is not the place to analyze in detail Audet's conception of justification, which has already been adequately done elsewhere. Audet follows Cardinal Pole's advice to avoid technical expressions and the terminology of the schools. His *vota* are strongly biblical and patristic and in this respect compare favorably with some other *vota* in the council. Soundly orthodox, they nevertheless give evidence of original insights. The striking similarity between the *votum* of the Carmelite general on the third stage of justification and the first formulation of the conciliar decree proposed on July 24 has been noticed, and there is no reason to deny the dependence of the latter on Audet.

Due to the outbreak of the Schmalkaldic War, debate did not begin until August 13th. Audet, like most of the others, found the formula too lengthy. After this, he was again ill and did not return to the congregations until that of November 29th, which discussed twofold justification and the certainty of grace. For Audet, only one justification, an interior one, was necessary. Concupiscence and the *fomes peccati* were not sinful.

During most of December, Audet was again absent due to illness. His sickness seems to have been kidney stones. He was able to be present only at the general congregations of December 6 and 7, which discussed the third formulation of the decree. Although named to the new commission of theologians on December 10, he had no part in the final formulation. He voted his approval at the general congregation of January 11, 1547, and the solemn congregation of the 13th.

Meanwhile a second Carmelite had joined the ranks of the council Fathers: Balthasar Limpo, Bishop of Porto, who arrived on November 18, 1546. Although he was the first Portuguese bishop to arrive at the council and would remain the only one during its first phase, he did not enjoy the powers of envoy of the king. His qualifications recommended him for the small but influential committee of theologian-bishops formed in December to expedite the final formulation of the decree. In this group, we find the bishop of Porto making well-taken points in the discussion on the decree in its final stages of formulation.

The Certainty of the State of Grace

One of the most hotly debated questions connected with justification was that of the certainty of the state of grace. Aside from the Lutheran position that certainty of one's salvation is essential to righteousness, there was a difference of opinion between Scotists and Thomists as to the degree of certainty obtainable in this matter.

On August 13th, Audet joined those who urged that the problem be well weighed before a decision against any kind of certainty be reached. Understandably, he did not want John Baconthorpe, one of the Order's scholastic lights, condemned. He also wrote a letter to the legates presiding over the council refuting the arguments of Cardinal Peter Pacheco against certainty. He asked permission to explain "very modestly" his viewpoint in the coming congregation or, better, to take the baths at Abano Terme near Padua, as his doctor urged, whence he could submit his opinion in writing. In any case, he was absent on August 28th, when it was decided against the imperial party to condemn only the Lutheran doctrine and avoid discussing the theories of the schools. His *votum*, today Codex 614 in the library of the Gregorian University in Rome, may have been read on this occasion.

The second redaction of the decree submitted to the general congregation of September 23th, from which Audet was again absent, left the possibility of certainty open. On October 15th, the question was again opened. Most were for some sort of certainty. It was probably at this time that Audet composed his second tract, in which he develops his solution in greater detail, supporting it with scriptural and patristic texts. Certainty is not *de fide*, but follows from faith and from moral certainty regarding inner experience.

Balthasar Limpo spoke on the question of the certitude of grace on November 29th, at the very end of the discussion. He shared the floor at that session with the prior general of the Carmelites; together they spoke for three hours. Limpo's *votum* exists only in Massarelli's garbled notes. Limpo seems, like the three Portuguese theologians, to have denied certitude of grace. In the general congregation of December 17th, the council voted a final time to confine itself to a condemnation of Luther's certitude of salvation. Limpo was one of sixteen prelates of the imperial party who supported Cardinal Pacheco, when he insisted to the end that all certainty should be excluded.

In his *votum* of November 29th, Limpo also treated the question of the loss of faith through sin. Luciano degli Ottoni, abbot of Pomposa near Ferrara, in criticism of chapter 15 of the decree had declared that faith is lost together with justice. The next day, he explained to raised eyebrows that he had meant faith informed by charity. Of subsequent speakers, Seripando and Limpo provided the most effective refutations.

Episcopal Residence

Contemporarily with the complicated question of justification, the council was wrestling with a delicate problem of human interest, namely episcopal residence. Connected with the failure of bishops to reside in their sees was the evil of accumulation of benefices.

The discussion of episcopal residence was bristling with difficulties and constituted a threat to the very existence of the council, already very tenuous. In effect, the council fathers were being asked to decree their own radical moral betterment and to sacrifice attractive financial advantages. Moreover, it was only too painfully evident that the worst offenders in the matter of absenteeism and accumulation of benefices were to be found in the Roman Curia. Even if the council decreed reforms, their acceptance by Rome would remain doubtful. Until Rome showed some willingness to reform, the credibility gap at Trent would continue to yawn wide. The delicate task of the legates was to see that things did not move too fast at Trent, while they encouraged signs of life in Rome. The reforms painfully hammered out for approval in the 6th and 7th sessions by no means met the needs of the problem or satisfied the desire for reform. Episcopal residence occupied the fathers down to the end of the council.

The question of residence cut across national lines, but the imperial party, especially the bishops from the Iberian peninsula, pushed the cause of reform. Less exposed to Protestantism, reform of morals, not heresy, was their special concern. The bishop of Porto was the Carmelite most involved in this vital question for the future of the Church.

Limpo held the extreme views of Cardinal Pacheco and the imperialists, though his position was also dictated by personal conviction and previous policy as bishop of Porto. He averred that the obligation of residence was of divine law and included cardinals as well. These and other severe views he proposed in the preliminary discussions on December 30, 1546, and upon their being rejected opposed the publication of any decree. His critique of the actual decree, published in the 6th session, January 13, 1547, was accordingly negative. In the same vein were his comments, delivered on February 3 and 28, on the second decree published in the 7th session, March 3.

Session Seven: The Sacraments

After the 6th session, the council began a discussion of the sacraments of the Church, another doctrine endangered by Protestantism. Audet's health continued poor and he was often absent from the congregation. On February 21, 1547, Massarelli read his *votum* on the sacraments in general, Baptism, and Confirmation. Audet was present at the 7th session, March 3, when the decrees on these subjects were solemnly approved,

Limpo, too, shared in the preparation of these decrees or canons, delivering his *vota* on February 10-11, 26, and March 1. In the first meeting of the general congregation on March 8 Limpo spoke to Massarelli's list of errors on the Eucharist.

The Council Transferred to Bologna

The 7th session was hardly concluded and the discussion of the sacraments resumed, when the existence of the council was threatened by the plague. The legate, Cervini, felt he could not oblige the council Fathers to remain in Trent, when it was threatened by plague, but refused to allow the council to be suspended. At session 8 on March 11, 1547, the Fathers voted for translation to Bologna. Balthasar Limpo, the only Carmelite present, rose to say, "What I am concerned about is not whether we should stay or go, but the unity of the council." He voted for translation only on the condition that the fact of the epidemic be established. In spite of pressure by the imperial party, Limpo persisted in his determination to move to Bologna.

The move of the council to Italian territory made even more remote the chance of Protestant participation.

Carmelites at Trent, 1545-1547

According to Massarelli's list 104 theologians were involved in the first period of the council at Trent. All of them were not always present at the same time, and their number varied considerably from congregation to congregation. The first of the theologians' congregations, which the bishops attended as spectators, was held on February 20, 1546. Fifteen Carmelite theologians are known to have participated in the first period of Trent, never more than five or six at a time.

Noteworthy among them is Anthony Marinari (d. 1570). He entered the Order at Grottaglie (Taranto). Regent at Venice and Rome, he was twice provincial of Puglia, 1538-1548, 1551-1568; in between he functioned as procurator general of the Order. He was a preacher to Bona Sforza, widow of King Sigismund of Poland, who resided in Bari from 1548 until her death in 1558. He wrote *Consonantia Iesu et prophetarum* (Venice, 1540), which enjoyed a number of editions, and an unpublished *Expositio in epistolam Pauli ad Romanos* (1569) which would be interesting to examine in view of the leaning toward Lutheranism ascribed to him by some.

Marinari was among those who anticipated the opening of the council, arriving on August 11, 1545. He attended sessions 1-5, 15-16. Of his theological activity at Trent only his opinion on justification, delivered at the theologians' congregation, June 26, 1546, was recorded, but his sermons won him considerable notoriety.

A council is a liturgical act; Trent, presided over by the papal legates, followed the custom of the *capella papalis* which featured sermons by members of the mendicant orders on the Sundays of Advent and Lent. The Carmelites were assigned the 4th Sunday in both seasons. The first period of the Council at Trent included two Advent and one Lenten seasons.

We have already noted the success of Marinari's sermon for the 4th Sunday of Advent, December 20, 1545. He was also assigned the following sermon in the series for *Laetare* Sunday, April 4, 1546. His topic was that of good works, and some of his expressions disturbed his more sensitive hearers. The great Dominican theologian, Dominic de Soto (*qui scit Sotum scit totum*), accused him of heresy. Marinari successfully defended himself before Cardinal Pedro Pacheco, Juan Quintana, jurist of the Spanish crown, and Diego de Alaba y Esquivel, Bishop of Astorga. Paolo Sarpi, the anti-papal historian of Trent, found in Marinari material for his notion that there were crypto-Lutherans among the theologians of Trent. He ascribes to him a number of Lutheran doctrines. Marinari is supposed to have delivered a *votum* on tradition at the first congregation of theologians on February 20, 1546, in which he defends the Protestant principle of *scriptura sola* and which earned him a stinging rebuke from Cardinal Pole. For none of this is there any trace in the sources.

The Carmelite sermon for Advent of 1546 (December 19) was preached by Louis of Siena, otherwise not identified.

No Carmelite was more faithful in attendance at the council than Vincent di Leone who was present at thirteen sessions and contributed many well weighed opinions. He taught at the university of Catania and became its dean in 1528. In 1533, he is among the doctors Audet was collecting for his new *studium* at Traspontina in Rome. In that year and in 1535, Di Leone represented the Order against the Mantuan Congregation in some of the phases of the process before the Rota. In 1539, he became provincial of the Roman province. At the council he is designated as "vicar of Palermo."

Di Leone arrived in Trent, August, 1545, and participated in all but the last of the eight sessions of this period. Among the thirty-four theologians who spoke in the six congregations on justification, June 22-28, were Anthony Marinari and Vincent di Leone. The *vota* of only five of these theologians remain today; Di Leone's fortunately is one of them. His opinion on the question of twofold justice, delivered October 15, is also extant. Di Leone also contributed to the discussions on the sacraments in general (Jan. 25, 1547) and the Eucharist (February 7, 1547).

With few exceptions the Carmelite theologians in the first period of Trent were Italians. Spain and Germany sent no one, unless Albert de Sicli was German. In the protocol of the council, he is designated both as German and as French. He was already present at Trent in May of 1545, but seems to have participated only in session 4. Frenchmen present in the first period of Trent were William Proe Gothlingus (session 6) and Nicholas Taborel of Troyes (sessions 6 and 7). His *vota* on justification and on certitude of grace show that he denied a twofold justification and admitted some sort of certitude of grace. He also contributed to the debate on the sacraments in general (January 24, 1547) and on the Eucharist (February 12, 1547).

Carmelite Attendance in Bologna

Carmelite attendance at Bologna, from session 9 of the council, April 21, 1547, until its suspension, February 16, 1548, was sparse. It was Lent, and the theologians at first were probably all occupied with preaching. The convent at Bologna belonged to the Mantuan Congregation, where members of the Order, including the prior general, would not have been welcome. Eventually the absence of representatives of the Order may have begun to appear suspicious, a criticism of the transfer to Bologna. Shortly after September 2, 1547, Audet left Venice for Bologna. On September 15, Bishop Limpo also arrived from Venice.

Audet's health continued poor. He was present at the general congregations of September 14 and 19, but failed to attend the rest. On September 24, Massarelli read his *votum* on the sacrament of matrimony.

Bishop Limpo missed a number of congregations. He presented his views on the sacrament of matrimony, September 22, and on baptism and confirmation, September 27. On November 28, he was appointed in the place of the bishop of Bitonto to the deputation for the catechism. In the congregations from December 9, 1547 to January 9, 1548, he contributed to the debate on Matrimony, Penance, and Orders as well as on problems concerned with the political situation of the council. On February 27, he was present at a general congregation a last time, and seems to have criticized Pope Paul III for transferring the council and for the slow progress of proceedings. After his return to Portugal, he became archbishop of Braga and primate of Portugal in 1550, retaining the office until his death in 1558.

The Mantuan Congregation had not participated in the first eight sessions of the council, but with the transfer to Bologna it sent Anthony Ricci, of Novellara (d. 1571). Ricci with Octavian of Soncino produced the *Constitutions of the Mantuan Congregation* (1540) and was three times vicar general. In 1542, he joined the faculty of theology of the university of Bologna. At the council he attended session 10 (June 2, 1547) and presented opinions in the theologians' congregations on purgatory (June 25), indulgences (July 7), and the sacrifice of the Mass (August 4). Ricci wrote a tract, *De jurisdictione prelati*, on episcopal residence, never published. His *vota* delivered at the council have been preserved and will eventually be published in the Goerres edition of the Council of Trent.

The Council Returns to Trent

The council reconvened at Trent on May 1, 1551, under the new pope, Julius III. Poor health again kept Audet in Rome, but Vincent di Leone arrived back on April 29 in the company of the legates and took his seat among the Fathers of the council as bishop of Bosa. He was present at all six sessions of this period (sessions 11-16) and delivered opinions in the general congregations regarding the Eucharist (September 28, October 7, 1551), the safe-conduct for the Protestants to the council (October 10), penance and extreme unction (November 14, 21 and 23) and holy orders and the sacrifice of the Mass (January 10, 1552).

Di Leone brought as his theologian Desiderio Mazzapica di San Martino (d. 1593), a native of Palermo. He was present at sessions 12-16. In the theologians' congregations he delivered his *votum* on the eucharist (September 16) and on penance (October 30).

This period of the council is distinguished by the presence of German Carmelites. Eberhard Billick arrived on October 10, 1551, in the company of Adolph von Schauenburg, archbishop of Cologne. He took part in sessions 13 to 16 and spoke in the theologians' congregations on penance and extreme unction (October 26, 1551), on the sacrifice of the Mass (December 15) and on holy orders (December 21).

"The fathers meet daily with incredible zeal," he wrote on Christmas Eve to Casper Doroler, prior of Cologne; "controverted dogmas are pondered and discussed from morning till night, with scarcely time for meals. Greater diligence could not be exercised, even if our adversaries were here. Only the adversaries are missing, and their absence gives us pain." Great as is his admiration for the dogmatic work of the council, he regrets that the reformation of morals is not given equal attention. Reform of morals is the theme of the sermon he preached at the council on New Year's Day, 1552. Like Gropper, Billick seems to have made an impression in the congregations of the council; in a letter to Andrew Masio, Vulmarus Bernaerts speaks of them as *theologi praecipui*.

Billick notes with pride that the University of Cologne is second only to Salamanca in the number of its representatives. Other bishops had resolved to use Cologne as a model for the reform of their dioceses. On December 14, the university appointed Billick, Gropper, and the Carmelite Alexander Blanckaert to secure from the council the ratification and increase of its privileges, but before this could be achieved the council broke up under the threat of war.

The Flemish Carmelite Alexander Blanckaert (*Candidus*, d. 1555) was present at the council as representative of the Regent of the Netherlands, Mary of Austria, widow of Louis II of Hungary and sister of Emperor Charles V; he also represented the university of Cologne. Billick summoned him to Cologne, where he took an active part in the religious controversies then raging. He accompanied Billick as his secretary to the colloquy of Regensburg in 1546. In 1550, after acquiring the doctor's degree, he joined the faculty of the university of Cologne. His works include a refutation of Calvin's attack on relics, *Judicium Joannis Calvini de sanctorum reliquiis* (Cologne, Casper Gennep, 1551) and a translation of the Bible into Flemish (Cologne, Casper Gennep, 1547). Blanckaert arrived at Trent on September 26, 1551, and attended sessions 13 to 16, contributing *vota* on penance (October 23) and on holy orders (December 12). He preached twice, on October 25 and on the regular Carmelite day, December 20, the 4th Sunday of Advent.

Billick's secretary at Trent was Jodocus of Haarlem. His notes on the activities of Billick and Blanckaert at the council remain unpublished.

Only five Carmelite theologians appear in the protocol of the 2nd period of the council. On April 28, 1552, after Maurice of Saxony had joined the French king in war with the emperor, the council hastily suspended its activities.

Carmelites in the Final Period at Trent

When the council opened at Trent for the third and final time on January 18, 1562, Audet was 80 years old and bore, besides his physical infirmities, the burden of old age. However, he did not consider himself absolved from his responsibilities, as he declared to Peter Rees, provincial of Upper Germany: "We have not wished to neglect the usual duty of our Order, which has always been prompt to obey, when it was a question of placing itself at the service of the Church of God, represented in the holy council." Being hindered by old age from personally attending the council, Audet appointed John Stephen Facini his representative. By papal bull of November 9, 1561, Facini was invested with the powers of the prior general at the council, including the right of a definitive vote. On November 29, he was admitted to the council.

John Stephen Facini (d. 1572), professor of theology at the University of Padua, equalled Di Leone in time spent at the council, attending in all thirteen sessions. He had been on hand in May of 1545, before the council opened, and attended sessions 1-3 and 5 of its first period. As vicar for the prior general he was present at all nine sessions of the last period (sessions 17-25). He presented opinions in the general congregations on the index of forbidden books (February

12, 1562), on the safe conduct to the council for Protestants (March 2, 1562), on the duty of episcopal residence (April 17 and 20, 1562; January 18, 1563), on the form of receiving communion (July 4, 10, and 14, 1562), on holy orders and their abuse (December 9, 1562; June 16; July 12, 1563), on marriage (July 31, August 23; September 10, 1563), on the reform of religious (November 27, 1563), on the reform of the clergy (November 7, 1563). Facini preached on the feast of the Assumption, 1563.

Two Carmelite bishops appeared for the first time amid the fathers of the council. Diego de León (d. 1589), suffragan of Siponto, was the only Spanish Carmelite to attend Trent. A doctor of theology, he is said to have composed a Hebrew grammar and Greek dictionary, never published. Diego arrived in Trent July 5, 1561. He was present at the last five sessions (21-25) and in the general congregations delivered opinions on the Eucharist, the sacrifice of the Mass, communion under both species for laymen, holy orders, marriage, the duty of episcopal residence, and reform of the Church.

Mantuans at Trent

Julius Soperchio (d. 1585), bishop of Accia in Corsica, while at the council, on January 30, 1563, was transferred to the see of Caorle and made suffragan to John Trivisano, patriarch of Venice. Soperchio arrived in Trent on August 11, 1561, before the opening of the third period of the council and attended all the sessions (17-25). In the general congregations, he presented *vota* on the index, the safe-conduct for Protestants, the duty of episcopal residence, the Eucharist, the sacrifice of the Mass, communion under both species for the laity, holy orders, marriage, the reform of the clergy and regulars. He preached on Sexagesima Sunday February 1, 1562.

The Mantuan Congregation participated more fully in this last period of the council. Lucretius Tiraboschi (d. 1583), acquired the doctorate in theology at Bologna in 1549 and taught there. He accompanied John Jerome Trivisano, patriarch of Venice, to the council and was present at sessions 19-23. He contributed opinions at the theologians' congregations on the use of the Eucharist, the sacrifice of the Mass and Holy Orders. His sermon on the 4th Sunday of Lent, 1563, was published at Brescia (G. B. Bozola, 1563). He is the author of a commentary on the psalms (Venice, 1572), (his commentary on psalm 118 had already appeared as *Ethica Spiritus Sancti*, Brescia, 1566) and *Rationes textus hebraici et editionis Vulgatae* (Venice, 1572).

The bishop of Cremona, Nicholas Sfrondati, brought Theodore Masi to Trent as his theologian and advisor. The reforming bishop seems to have made use of the Mantuan Carmelites. Masi acquired the doctorate (1557) and taught at Bologna. He was present at sessions 17-21 and 23; although not mentioned among those present at the last two sessions, his bishop was there, and theologians are not listed in the protocol of these sessions. He participated in the theologians' congregations on June 19, 1562, concerning the use of the Eucharist and on September 24, 1562, concerning holy orders. He preached twice at the council: on the 4th Sunday of Lent, March 8, 1562, and on the 18th Sunday after Pentecost, September 20, 1562. His Lenten sermon was published at Brescia in 1567 (*apud Ludovicum Sabiensem*).

Silvester of Mantua attended the council as confessor and advisor to the cardinal of Mantua, Ercole Gonzaga. He was present at sessions 17-20 and 23. He preached on the 2nd Sunday after Pentecost, May 31, 1562.

Among the eight Carmelite theologians who participated in this final period of the council were two Frenchmen, both of whom, however, had settled in Italy. Taborel is back as a theologian for the prior general, participating in sessions 19-20 and 23. Erard Charpentier, of Rheims (d. 1578), also appears in session 23 as the general's theologian.

The other theologian of the general, Lawrence Laureto, of Venice (1534-1598), was a young man of twenty-seven, destined for an illustrious career. He preached on the 4th Sunday of Advent, December 21, 1561, (published *Roma, apud Antonium Bladium*, 1561), on the 12th Sunday after Pentecost, August 9, 1562, and on the 4th Sunday of Advent, December 20. He was present at sessions 20, 22 and 23. He presented *vota* at the theologians' congregations concerning the Eucharist (June 20, 1562) and Holy Orders (October 2). His career lay principally in the years after the council. He taught theology at Cremona, Venice, Padua, and Rome (at Traspontina and at the pontifical university, the Sapienza). He was provincial of Venice and of Rome. In 1587, he became procurator general of the Order. In 1591, he was made bishop of Adria and suffragan to the patriarch of Venice.

Desiderio Mazzapica, now regent in Palermo, returned to Trent, this time as one of the theologians sent by Philip II of Spain. He was commissioned on July 9, 1562, when the king praised him for the way he carried out his commission at the council in the time of Julius III. Mazzapica is not listed among the participants at the solemn sessions, but the protocol of the council shows that on February 4, 1563, he was enlisted among the theologians who were to study the sacrament of marriage; on March 15, he presented his opinion.

The Council Draws to an End

In spite of infirmity and old age, Audet's interest in the council remained unabated. The question as to whether episcopal residence was a matter of divine or merely ecclesiastical right again arose in the third period of the council and took a more serious turn, when after September 7, 1562, the debate broadened into the question as to whether the office of bishop itself was of divine origin. At play here were episcopalistic and Gallican convictions and scholastic-canonical views on the primacy. Someone sent a paper on the question to Audet and requested his opinion. Audet's reply, addressed to an unknown bishop, was submitted to the secretary of the council on November 2, to be incorporated into the acts. Audet distinguishes the power of orders, jurisdiction, and administration. Only the power of episcopal orders is *jure divino*.

Facini spoke at the general congregation of December 9, 1562. His *votum* has points of resemblance to Audet's, with which he was no doubt familiar, but in some respects is closer to the opinions of the Jesuit general, Diego Laynez, who on October 2 had made the famous distinction between the *potestas ordinis*, which bishops had directly from God, and the *potestas jurisdictionis* deriving indirectly from God through the pope.

On the second day of the 25th and final session, December 4, 1563, three Carmelites placed their signatures, *definiens subscripsi*, to the acts of the momentous

Council of Trent: Julius Soperchio, bishop of Caorle, the 118th bishop to sign; Diego de León, bishop of Columbria, 136th bishop to sign; and John Stephen Facini, vice-general of the Carmelite Order.

In the Goerres edition of the acts of the council, Ehses, following one manuscript, omits the word *definiens* from Facini's signature. Yet other equally authentic manuscripts include the word. Moreover, the bull of November 9, 1561, expressly granted Facini the power of expressing a definitive opinion at the council. Audet's death in the previous year did not affect Facini's standing, for John Baptist Rossi, Audet's successor, remained a vicar general until his election as prior general in 1564. Even after Audet's death, Facini continued to sit among the generals of religious orders, never among their procurators.

The Reform of Religious

In the 25th session on December 3, the single decree, *De regularibus*, comprising 22 chapters, was solemnly promulgated. The hand of the bishops is considerably strengthened, especially in the ministry of souls. On the other hand, bishops often are to exercise their supervision only as delegated by the Holy See. In this way, the papacy did not entirely renounce the protection of its bodyguards, the Mendicants.

For present purposes, the following details may be noted. Religious shall observe the rules of their institutes; superiors by means of chapters and canonical visits are to see to the faithful observance of the rules (ch. 1). Religious are to possess no goods, moveable or immobile; usufruct of immobile goods is also forbidden to individuals (ch. 2). All convents, except those of the Capuchins and Friars Minor of the Observance, may possess immobile goods. Convents should not have more members than are able to be supported from their incomes. Permission of the bishop is required to found new houses (ch. 3). No religious without the permission of his superior may enter the service of a prelate, prince, university, community, or other person or place. Religious may not leave their convents, even to visit their superiors, without due permission (ch. 4). The constitution, *Periculoso* of Boniface VIII is renewed, thereby obliging all nuns to the cloister. Once professed, they may not leave the monastery for any reason, even for a brief time, without the bishop's permission. No one may enter the monastery without permission of the bishop or competent authority (ch. 5). Election of superiors must take place by secret vote. Votes of absentees may not be supplied (ch. 6). Constitutions of nuns should provide for at least monthly confession and communion. Two or three times a year an extraordinary confessor should hear the confessions of all (ch. 10). Exempt religious who commit a notorious crime outside the convent shall on request of the bishop be punished by their superior, who must inform the bishop afterwards; otherwise the delinquents shall be deprived of their office by the superior and punished by the bishop (ch. 14). The minimum age of profession for men and women religious is sixteen years completed. A year of trial should precede profession (ch. 15). Women religious may not be clothed with the habit before the age of twelve (ch. 17). Those who force anyone to enter a religious order or hinder them from doing so are liable to excommunication (ch. 18). The *commenda* is abolished (ch. 21).

On May 29, 1566, the constitution, *Circa pastoralis*, of Pius V elaborated the point of cloister of religious women. All nuns of whatever order, even though not so obliged by their rule, are hereafter bound to perpetual cloister. Tertiaries, or penitents, if they have solemn vows, are likewise obliged to cloister. If they have no solemn vows, they are to be urged to take them and submit to cloister. Those who will not live with vows and cloister are forbidden to receive new candidates.

The Tridentine decree on religious presented a minimal program of reform; it was rather a sanation and confirmation of existing customs. Yet it represented a firm step ahead on the road to renewal. It finally provided a common law for religious. It rescued religious life from the suffocating morass of privileges and dispensations, papal and otherwise. Nevertheless, it seemed to some a rather tame result for all the clamor that had gone before. Among those who felt that Trent did not go far enough was Philip II of Spain.

Part Two

THE POST-TRIDENTINE PERIOD
1550-1600

Chapter I

Rossi and Saint Teresa

Not the least significant feature of the great restoration of Catholic life that followed the Council of Trent was the revival of the religious orders. New orders fitting the spirit and needs of the time were founded, old orders were renewed. None of these manifestations was more vital and brilliant than that of the Carmelites; unfortunately, pouring the wine of the new spirit into the old bottle of Carmel had the effect predicted by the scriptures in such cases. The new shoot of St. Teresa's reform, transplanted from the ancient trunk of Carmel - to mix a metaphor - sprang to luxuriant growth; it was not until the 17th century that the old Carmel experienced a similar rebirth.

After the long and fruitful rule of Nicholas Audet, who led the Order during the difficult times of the rise of Protestantism, the Carmelites were blessed with another outstanding leader to guide and inspire them in the task of renewal imposed by Trent. At the death of Audet, Pope Pius IV on December 16, 1562, named John Baptist Rossi vicar general of the Order, until a general chapter could be convened.

John Baptist Rossi

The choice was a happy one, for as St. Teresa later put it, Rossi was "a most outstanding person in the Order, and very rightly so." A descendant of the Rossi of Parma, Counts of San Secondo, John Baptist was born in 1507 at Ravenna and entered the Order there. He studied the arts at Siena under the distinguished mathematician and astrologer, Julian Ristori, and theology at Padua, where John Stephen Facini was regent. Subsequently, he was regent at Naples and Siena.

Before being appointed vicar general, Rossi had had a distinguished career. In 1546, he was named procurator general of the Order and began lecturing at the University of Rome, the "Sapienza," commenting on the gospel of St. Mark. Paul III admitted him to the group of theologians who disputed theological questions at his table; he also participated in the consultations on the Council of Trent held before the same pontiff. He preached in the papal chapel and in various churches of Rome. As prior of San Martino, beginning in 1548, he became the friend of Cardinal Diomedes Carafa, nephew of Paul IV, a frequent visitor at the Carmelite convent, whom Rossi assisted in the hour of death; also a friend of Cardinal Vitelozzo Vitelli and Cardinal James du Puy, protector of the Order, who employed Rossi as his theological consulter. Paul IV enlisted Rossi in the Roman Inquisition.

The General Chapter of 1564

When the general chapter opened on Pentecost Sunday, May 21, 1564, five hundred Carmelites gathered in Rome for the occasion. Fifteen provincials and their *socii* brought the total of definitors to forty-two. Besides these, there were doctors of theology and preachers to partake in the public disputations and preach the indulgence granted by the pope for the occasion. Sermons were delivered not only in the churches of the Order - San Martino, Traspontina, San Giuliano—but in the vernacular in the national churches of the city.

The election was held the first day by secret ballot according to the new prescriptions of Trent, Balthasar Nieto, provincial of Andalusia, announcing the votes in a loud voice. John Baptist Rossi emerged the choice of the chapter, *nemine penitus discrepante*. Carmelites went in procession from San Martino to the Vatican to present their new general to Pope Pius IV. As the procession crossed the bridge of Sant'Angelo, the cannons of the castle, on orders from the pope, sent out a salvo in honor of the Carmelite general. In St. Peter's Basilica, the cardinal protector, Charles Borromeo, had the Holy Shroud of Veronica exposed for veneration by the Carmelites. During dinner at Traspontina, the *schola* of Castel Sant'Angelo provided music.

It was a royal send-off for the Counter-Reformation in the Carmelite Order. Behind the festivities lay the serious business of implementing the decrees of the Council of Trent. Under the presidency of John Baptist Rossi, the chapter in the spirit of Trent issued a number of decrees concerning divine cult, the government and administration of the convents, and reform.

With regard to the important matter of poverty and the common life, the chapter forbids ownership by individuals of immobile goods (lands, pastures, vineyards, houses, etc.). Superiors may grant the use of mobile goods, not in superfluity but in a measure sufficient for needs: "Our religious should understand that the things they are given to use are not their own but belong to the community." The permission of the superior is required before any goods may be used, as ordained by the Council of Trent. The money the brethren acquire is to be kept in a common box. Subsequent events show that, although the friars deposited their money in this box, they retained exclusive use of it.

No friar or nun may leave a cell to another in a will, no matter how much effort was spent in furnishing and decorating it. "Primary" graduates and ex-provincials should be given the best rooms, "because in every family and even more in every republic there is order and a diversity of degree."

The chapter abandons Audet's distinction between "completely reformed" and "less reformed" houses. It rejects the division of the Order into observants and conventuals and declares all houses to be observant: "Let the brethren of our Order know that the said Order never labored under the name of conventuality: it was ever in flourishing observance, though sometimes some of its members or convents failed to achieve this ideal. The Order always lived under obedience to one head, partook of a common refectory, shared all things in common (meager as they might be). Therefore, our brethren should in no way declare themselves to be conventuals, but, of the observance of the provinces, as is most clearly apparent from the indults of many popes, especially Clement VII."

Rossi's reforming effort was aimed at bringing about a sincere dedication to religious life within the framework of existing obligations. He did not try to raise the ideal or propose a "primitive" way of life. The perhaps deliberately vague directives of Trent regarding poverty were benignly interpreted. The perfect common life; that is, the unconditional sharing of all goods in common, was nowhere imposed. The old system of privilege remained basically intact. Rossi unstintingly devoted his not inconsiderable talents and ability to urging upon the brethren in season and out of season a life in keeping with their commitments.

Philip II and the General Chapter of 1564

From the beginning of his reign (1556) the Most Catholic King Philip II of Spain had at heart the reform of the religious orders in his realms. Trent had entrusted the reform of religious orders to their superiors, but Philip had little faith in a solution that had brought so little result in the past.

His plans for the reform of the orders included the Carmelites. From Michael de Carranza, provincial of Aragon, the king learned of the existence of vicars general in the Order - those of the Mantuan and Albi Congregations. He now proposed to the general chapter the permanent appointment by the prior general of a Spaniard as vicar general for Spain with the title and plenipotential powers of reformer.

The institution of a vicar in Spain which such sweeping prerogatives would, as in the case of Mantua and Albi, effectually cut off the prior general from any real influence in Philip's realm.

Rossi managed to refuse the king without alienating him. Spain would have its vicar general, elected by the five provinces (including Portugal), if the prior general did not personally visit the peninsula within two years. To facilitate communication between Rome and Madrid, the chapter appointed a procurator general to the Spanish court, Desiderio Mazzapica, who had been king's theologian at Trent.

Whatever else is to be said of Philip's interference in Carmelite affairs, it brought action deferred for centuries. This time, Spain held priority in the itinerary of the prior general. Nevertheless, affairs kept Rossi in Italy until April, 1566.

The question of the relocation of Traspontina at this time reached a crisis. Church and convent were in the way of the completion of the octagonal outworks of Castel Sant'Angelo. The Carmelites thought the question of a new site was still pending, when to their amazement, workers began demolishing their church. Rossi managed to have operations suspended, and Pope Pius IV granted the Carmelites a site nearer the Vatican in the Borgo Pio, the new suburb he was constructing between the Leonine city and the castle. Pius V, on February 18, 1566, authorized the construction of a new church. In March, the general assisted at the laying of the first stone, but construction did not begin until 1569.

On February 24, 1566, Rossi obtained faculties from Pius V, creating him apostolic commissary with full powers to visitate and reform the whole Order, including the congregations. In view of the jurisdictional conflict to follow, his quality as apostolic commissary, which even cardinals and legates *a latere* are called upon to respect, is worth special attention.

Sometime after April 18, the prior general finally set out from Rome for the visitation of Spain and Portugal. He traveled by mule, sometimes on horseback, accompanied by his secretary, Nicholas Rouhier (Rotarius), Valerius Montoni, bursar of the curia, and a *socius* - during the years 1566 to 1568, the Sicilian, Bartholomew Ragusio; from 1572 to 1576, the Portuguese, Jerome Tostado. Approaching a city or town, he would be met by a committee of lay and ecclesiastical notables and conducted to the Carmelite convent.

The Incorporation of Monte Oliveto

While in the area of Genoa, Rossi journeyed to nearby Multedo to visit the convent of Monte Oliveto. For fifty years, since its foundation, this community had lived on the fringe of the Carmelite family without contact either with the Mantuan Congregation or the Order. Now Trent required hermits to adopt an approved Rule and submit to the superior of an established order. On November 24, 1564, the newly elected Rossi had written to the hermits of Monte Oliveto, inviting them to make their profession in his hands and place themselves under his immediate jurisdiction. (By the terms of its foundation the hermitage was already under jurisdiction of the prior general, but this evidently had been forgotten or neglected.) The hermits in any case agreed, and on March 30, 1565, Rossi had received them under his obedience and protection. Appearing now in person, the prior general began his visitation on April 29, 1566, but for some reason, possibly favorable sailing conditions, interrupted it to resume it on his return. There were about twenty hermits in the community.

After his visit, Rossi and his party travelled by sea from Genoa to Savona, thence by land, passing the Spanish frontier at Salces near Perpignan. He proceeded directly to Madrid, arriving, on June 10, 1566, just within the date agreed on. The purpose of the visit was not purely social; Rossi needed His Catholic Majesty's *placet* to be able to use his apostolic faculties in Spain. The encounter passed without incident. "I have been to kiss the hand of His Majesty," Rossi wrote to St. Charles Borromeo, "and he heard me most courteously."

Rossi's Manner of Visitating

At the door of the church, the prior general would be met by the community in procession according to the ceremonial of the Order.

In the choir, all would approach to kiss his hand in token of filial obedience. After resting a while in the quarters reserved for him, Rossi summoned the community to the chapter room to hear a spiritual conference, sometimes of considerable length. (The chapter at Genoa in 1568 lasted from 2:00 until 7:00 p.m.) He usually ended with an explanation of his plan of reform, insisting particularly on dress and footwear as a sign of the reform. At times, he would then and there call in a barber to shave off beards. After all had been made to promise formally to tell the whole truth, each friar was interviewed concerning private ownership, choir, divine cult, silence, recollection, peace and brotherly love, care of the sick, administration of the goods of the convent, observance of fasts and abstinence, conduct of superiors and officials, the education of novices and students, etc. Meanwhile, his associates examined the accounts of the convent and went through the cells, confiscating objects contrary to the religious spirit; musical instruments like the lyre, barbiton and lute, and every sort of arms. Collars and cuffs not of wool were cut from shirts, ornaments from birettas. Those found possessed of incomes or benefices were called upon to renounce them publicly before a notary summoned for this purpose. When he had fully ascertained conditions in the convent, Rossi drew up decrees which he had read in the refectory by the secretary. If legal action had to be taken against any religious, Rossi himself acted as judge and executioner, himself wielding the scourge, when this form of punishment was prescribed by law. He did not hesitate to apply the severest sanctions: expulsion from the Order and condemnation to the galleys. The times called for decisive measures, and he punished misdemeanor when proved. But he was just, merciful before repentance, quick to acknowledge merit and goodness. He did not supersede his powers nor overrule the authority of his inferiors.

For the most part, Rossi preferred to remain aloof. He ate in his rooms, except at the beginning and end of the visitation and on feast days. On the principal feast days, he offered community Mass, distributed Communion and preached before and after Mass. He would remain several weeks in the houses of study, showing special concern for the progress of the students. He tried particularly to win these future superiors, lecturers, and masters to the idea of reform. In the general *studia*, he would gather the students in his room after dinner or supper and preside at disputations on philosophical and theological questions.

The Visitation of Andalusia

On the eve of Rossi's visit the four provinces of Spain (Castile, Aragon, Catalonia, Andalusia) together numbered forty-eight convents with about 550 religious. Under Audet Castile had been reformed, some progress had been made in Aragon and Catalonia, but Andalusia, torn by rival factions, had effectively resisted all efforts at renewal. Now the nine convents of Castile had little more than 100 members. Provincial since 1560 was Angel de Salazar. Aragon had ten houses with 112 members; Catalonia thirteen houses with 85 members. The largest province was Andalusia with sixteen convents and 250 friars.

At the time, there were twelve monasteries or *beaterios* in Spain. In the province of Andalusia there were Ecija, Granada, Seville, Antequera, Aracena, Paterna del Campo, Osuna. The province of Aragon had a monastery in Valencia. Castile had *beaterios* at Avila, Fontiveros and Piedrahita. After consultation with St. Teresa, Mary of Jesus (Yepes) had founded the monastery of La Imagen at Alcalá de Henares under the jurisdiction of the bishop (1563).

Rossi began his visitation of Andalusia with the convent of Jaén, on July 28, 1566. He visited ten of the most important houses of friars. The three monasteries visited by the prior general - Ecija, Seville and Antequera - by this time had adopted the cloister according to the decrees of Trent, and so, too, perhaps had the other monasteries in the province.

In three months, more than 150 friars and an equal number of nuns passed before the visitator. Surprisingly, Rossi did not visit the college at Osuna, which the general chapter had ordered improved. He may have sent one of his companions.

Most of Andalusia's troubles were due to the three Nieto brothers, Casper, Balthasar, and Melchior, whose only resemblance to the holy Magi was their names. "When we came to Andalusia," Rossi later declared, "we strongly rebuked these three brothers for their petulant and libidinous conduct by which they had each befouled themselves." Casper was provincial and favored his brothers. Balthasar, aged 42 at the time, had been a Franciscan, but was admitted to the Carmelite Order by his brother, the provincial, who in 1565 made him his vicar. While stationed in Utrera, Balthasar assaulted the prior, Michael de Ulloa; corrected by Rossi, he replied with an insolent letter. He gave occasion to many rumors about his moral life.

The most unsavory of the three was Melchior. One witness, Fray Cristóbal de Vargas, a partisan of the Nietos, describes him as "without morals (*un hombre perdido*), a destroyer of convents." According to Fray Diego de León, *pesquinos* appeared on walls in Ecija about his relations with a certain woman. The prioress of Ecija, Doña María Ponce de León, characterizes him as *loco*. He was prior in various houses before becoming prior of Ecija, from which office also he had to be removed.

On August 25, 1565, in the convent of Ecija, Melchior attacked the visitator,

Desiderio Mazzapica, struck him in the face, leaving a mark, seized and tore his capuche and threw him to the ground. Casper threw himself on his brother, crying that he had committed an injury to the Order, had him put in irons and dispatched him to Seville. En route, in the convent of Carmona, Balthasar got into the cell where his brother was being detained, provided him with a sword and himself with another cleric and layman, all armed, helped him to escape. The priors of a number of houses, partisans of the Nietos, provided him with asylum. He also received support from influential laymen, including Don Gómez Suárez de Figueroa, Lord of Zafara, native place of the Nietos.

Casper Nieto kept himself in power with the help of supporters, principal among them, John de Mora, prior of Seville. If frequently repeated complaints are to be believed, the ruling caste treated their subjects despotically and tyrannically, "like captives and black slaves," lived comfortably themselves, while communities wanted the necessities. In Utrera, each friar bought his own wine for meals. The students were neglected spiritually and materially. More than once, priors are accused of punishing students physically. In Granada, the students were afraid to buy brooms, because the prior, Gabriel de la Peñuela, would use them on them. The sick were neglected.

Visitations tend to bring out the negative aspects of religious life. The province, Rossi recorded, had "masters of theology and fathers well deserving of the Order, most attached to obedience, whose minds are not a little disturbed by these disputes." It was not easy for Rossi to arrive at the truth from the conflicting testimonies – laudatory of Nieto's partisans, fiercely resentful of those he had alienated. Nevertheless, the general picture emerged clearly enough.

The Chapter of Andalusia, 1566

On September 22, 1566, the provincial chapter opened in the Casa Grande of Seville with a great affluence of friars and the usual pomp, processions, sermons, and public disputations. Rossi excluded John de Mora, "a tyrant and a person of ill fame," and other Nieto supporters from candidacy for provincial, presenting instead a slate of six names of his choice. John de la Quadra, a neutral in the warring factions, was elected and immediately confirmed by the prior general. Michael de Ulloa, a protagonist of reform, became prior of the important convent of Seville; John de Mora moved to Utrera. Casper Nieto was made prior of Castro del Rio, an insignificant house. Rossi was indulgent to these two; he even provided Nieto with a patent praising his services to the province, "so that he might live in peace and to the honor of the divine majesty."

All defamatory papers relating to the past were burned, "to preserve the public honor of that province." Balthasar, for aiding and abetting his brother Melchior, got three years' exile in Castile or Portugal with privation of place, voice, and grades. Before leaving, he spent eighteen days in irons and was administered the discipline on naked shoulders by the prior general himself. Later, his exile was commuted to confinement in the convent and town of Utrera and again, at the intervention of illustrious persons, to Jaén or Gibraleón. Melchior, still at large, was declared apostate, rebellious, contumacious, and excommunicated and condemned to three years in his majesty's galleys. Superiors of the provinces are ordered to have him captured by the secular arm. Influential friends interceded on behalf of the Nieto brothers - the provisor of Cordoba, the nobles of Ecija, the marquis of Priego, the lord inquisitors of Seville, the marquis of Valderas, and other nobles of the court, but Rossi would not relent.

Diego de Castro, who had provided Melchior with a white cloak, was deprived of his grade and exiled to Aracena, "a mountain place." He also received discipline at the chapter. Gabriel de la Peñuela received a number of penances for offenses proved against him. Many malefactors were punished. A certain John de la Magdalena, convicted of living with a prostitute for more than six years, was condemned to the galleys. All in all, Rossi considered that he had acted with restraint; while seeking to remove the causes of dissent, he did not wish to give anyone reason to complain of excessive punishment.

At the end of the chapter Rossi published *Institutiones et ordinationes*, printed before he left Seville (Sevilla, Juan Gutierrez, 1566). A blueprint for the reform of the province, it is practically a complete body of constitutions with directives listed under the headings of divine cult, studies and students, the observance of the regular life, the care of the sick, the preservation of peace, the rule and administration of convents, the office of provincial, novices and professed, nuns.

Rossi's *Institutiones* in printed form provided each member of the Andalusian province with a handy code of laws, detailed and adapted to the particular needs of the province. Rossi's visitation had been thorough, his action prudent. Andalusia had finally received the sort of spiritual attention and leadership it had long lacked. There is no doubt that under other circumstances the visitation would have borne good and lasting fruit.

The Visitation of Portugal

On November 2, 1566, the prior general set out from Seville to visit Portugal. Portugal now numbered nine friaries. In 1541, a *beaterio* in Beja had been aggregated to the Order. Two sisters came from Castile to inaugurate the foundation. Beja gave rise to foundations in Lagos (1558) and Tentugal (1565).

Before the general chapter, Rossi, as vicar general, had had a conflict of jurisdiction with the Cardinal Infante, Henry, over rights of visitation. But if the prior general had any misgivings about his reception in Portugal, he was soon reassured. The thirteen-year old King Sebastian, the Cardinal Infante Don Henry and Queen Catalina sent courtiers to the Lisbon convent to welcome the prior general from Rome. "Not only was I not hindered," he wrote to Charles Borromeo, protector of the Order, "but I was shown favor and could do what I desired, reforming and reducing all to the regular life; although," he adds, "this province is very exemplary as regards the common life and of great observance."

In 1551, the convent at Lisbon counted seventy members; at the time of Rossi's visit there were probably more. The general found nothing to censure, much to praise. When I was there," he later recalled, "I experienced great joy at your service of God, honorable ways inside and outside the convent, perfect silence in the designated places, merciful correction of the erring, cleanliness in the sacristy, modesty in everything and at much else worthy of no little praise."

On December 13, Rossi opened the provincial chapter. Louis da Luz, one of those presented by the general and favored by Don Henry, was elected provincial. He was thought to be a natural son of King John III and had been appointed visitor of the province by Don Henry in 1563. At the end of the chapter the decrees of reform were printed (Lisbon, Manuel João, 1567). No copy is known.

Esteem for the learned Carmelite general was not lessened by the sermons he preached on two occasions before the king, queen, and nobles of the realm. "Because the king did not well understand our language," he wrote to Borromeo, "I used a mixture of Spanish and Italian, so that they understood me and were satisfied."

The Visitation of Castile

On January 23, 1567, Rossi left Lisbon to begin the visitation of the province of Castile. His first stop was the interprovincial house of studies in Salamanca. Rossi found there four students of theology and seven of the arts. They were all to distinguish themselves in their later careers. One of them, John of St. Matthias, of Fontiveros, a third year student of the arts, with permission of his superiors was following the primitive Rule and was considering becoming a Carthusian. He was, of course, St. John of the Cross. Unfortunately, the account of the visitation of Salamanca is wanting, but one early biographer of St. John, Alonzo of the Mother of God, states that the young friar made an impression on the prior general, who in later years remembered the encounter at Salamanca.

Rossi entrusted the visitation of Toledo, the principal house of the province, to Mariano di Leone, successor of Desiderio Mazzapica as procurator of the Order at the court, and like him a Sicilian.

On February 12, Rossi began the visitation of the *beaterio* in Piedrahita. The sisters wore the white veil and took the three vows of religion, but were not cloistered. Like many sisters in Spain, they felt they should not be bound by Trent to a cloister they did not profess, nor did Rossi press the point. "Certainly these nuns have embraced the three vows of religion with fervor," Rossi concludes, "excellent morals prevail among them, they dedicate themselves to divine cult with great diligence and integrally keep the cloister." At this time, Rossi apparently was unaware of Pius V's legislation of the previous May 29, which put an end to all discussion. Back in Italy, in May or June, 1568, Rossi revoked all dispensations from cloister granted in Spain.

The Incarnation at Avila

Rossi arrived in Avila on February 16 or 17. The Carmelite friary lay along the north wall of the city. Almost opposite it was the monastery of the Incarnation. According to his custom, facilitated by the proximity of the two houses, Rossi alternated interviews with the friars and nuns; only the visitation of the nuns remains, and this includes the interviews of only about half of the 180 members of the monastery. Yet these amply suffice to provide an insight into life in the monastery in which St. Teresa passed twenty-seven years of her life. In assessing the results of Rossi's visitation, one must bear in mind that the Incarnation was a *beaterio*, not a cloistered monastery.

The prioress was Doña Frances de Briceño. From the visitation account it is immediately apparent that the monastery was in serious economic straits. The income was inadequate to meet the needs of the community, property had to be sold and debts incurred. Very little could be provided in the common refectory, and the sick lacked adequate care. To make matters worse, the monastery had to provide for a certain number of hangers-on — relatives and friends of the nuns, as well as a few children. About twenty nuns asked the prior general for permission to have rents and to retain alms and money, as in fact they had been doing hitherto. Cells were bought and sold, goods left to relatives by testament. On the other hand, a certain amount of luxury and frivolity of dress were not wanting.

The Incarnation had also become a haven for the daughters of nobility, the *señores doñas*, whose dowries permitted them more spacious quarters with a small hallway, kitchen and sitting-room with alcove, in which to entertain relatives and friends. There was a noticeable tension between the "ladies" and the sisters who slept in the common dormitory. Even in the choir, the ladies insisted on the first places instead of observing the order of profession. A number of ladies asked permission to retain their maids. Doña Aldonza de Valderrabano requested "to be allowed to keep her black slave girl." The comings and goings of the maid servants caused no little distraction in the monastery.

The nuns took advantage of the presence of the apostolic visitator to obtain permission to visit relatives; the motive of such visits was mostly economic: to obtain financial help from their families.

The many confessors who served the monastery added to the busy scene. Besides the two Carmelites from the nearby friary, about ten priests, secular and religious of other orders, appear in the partial account of the visitation. They include clerics of the highest caliber such as Julian of Avila.

It is not surprising that in this complex society the common life would be affected. Rossi was asked for dispensations from the common refectory, from the fasts, or simply from all common acts. Of the ninety nuns interviewed, forty asked to be dispensed from office in choir.

The populous Incarnation, the largest Carmelite nunnery in Spain, its innocent and bustling existence, dedicated to the grim business of survival, seems ill suited to a life of prayer and reflection. Yet the monastery numbered many dedicated religious, some of whom were to form the nucleus of the reform of St. Teresa. From numerous testimonies, it is evident that peace, harmony, good morals, fervent devotion reigned in the Incarnation. The sisters themselves were aware of and deplored their shortcomings, many of them beyond their control.

Rossi's provisions for the reform of the Incarnation have not survived. It is known that he tried to alleviate the problem of poverty by forbidding the acceptance of more nuns. In time, this remedy, plus the exodus to the reform of St. Teresa, had its effect. In the next twenty-five years, the number of nuns of the black veil was reduced to half.

"Some Affairs of the Order" at the Court

For a reason not entirely clear, Rossi interrupted his visitation of the Castilian province to return to Madrid, where we find him on March 17, 1567. In a letter to Borromeo of the twenty-second, he simply states that he had come to treat some affairs of the Order. He had audiences with King Philip, Queen Isabelle, Prince Charles, Fray Bernard de Fresnada, and other notables at the court.

It may be that the situation in Andalusia brought Rossi to the court. The peace he hoped he had established in Andalusia proved illusory; the Nieto party had not waited for him to cross the Portuguese border to counterattack. The ousted group claimed that the chapter had not been free, accused the prior general of venality, and called for a visitation by the king. Focus of the trouble was Utrera, where John de Mora was prior, and Christopher de Vargas, another Nieto partisan, was sub-prior. Balthasar did not bother to perform the penance imposed on him, sat at the prior's table as though he still had precedence, and left the convent at will. At Castro del Rio, Caspar Nieto formented opposition to the prior general and his visitation. The provincial, John de la Quadra, presented Rossi with a formal complaint against Mora and other rebellious subjects. The prior general, on March 21, "in our hospice in Madrid," cited Caspar Nieto and Mora, "the stronger ones in controversy," to appear before him at Avila by mid-April.

Shortly afterwards, on April 5, Rossi got rid of Melchior Nieto, changing his sentence to the triremes to expulsion from the Order with the obligation of entering another. Melchior subsequently became a Third Order Franciscan.

The whole while that Rossi was at court, Philip II, serenely indifferent to the Carmelite apostolic visitator and reformer, was pursuing his own plans for the reform of the religious orders in Spain, Carmelites among them. He had finally found a sympathetic, if not wholly pliant collaborator in the Dominican pope, St. Pius V, who on December 2, 1566, issued the *Maxime cuperemus*, entrusting the reform of religious orders to the bishops. These, with the aid of an observant provincial and religious, were to reduce all conventuals to observance. On December 12, followed *Cum gravissimis de causis*, applying the same measures to nuns.

Next, Philip turned his attention to the reform of orders that had no observance, among which he classed the Carmelites. On March 17, 1567 - the very time Rossi was at the court - Requeséns wrote to the king that things looked good for the royal plan. As a matter of fact, on April 16, appeared the brief, *Superibus mensibus*, instructing the bishops personally or through delegates to reform the Carmelites, Trinitarians, and Mercedarians. For this work, they were to avail themselves of the assistance of two observant Dominicans.

The king's action set aside religious exemption and the decree of the Council of Trent, entrusting reform to religious superiors. The Carmelite general chapter of 1564 had laid claim to the title of observant and had denounced conventuality. It was in the interest of observance that the prior general by apostolic delegation and with the leave of the king was visiting the Spanish Carmelite houses. Mercifully, *Superioribus mensibus* still lay in the womb of the future during Rossi's visit to Madrid. Later, he was to blame the Andalusian insurgents for bringing the visitation of the bishops on the Order, but this arrangement was only part of Philip's large design. The Carmelites' clamor against the Italian visitator may only have helped convince the king, if that were necessary, of the correctness of his course of action.

The Chapter of Castile, 1567

From Madrid, Rossi continued his visitation of the Castilian province, visiting San Pablo de la Moraleja, Medina del Campo, and Valladolid. At Fontiveros, he visited the *beaterio* of the Mother of God. The community numbered forty-five sisters, but only five interviews remain. The cloister here resembled that of Piedrahita and Avila: women and girls lived in the monastery with the same inconvenience to regular life, which, however, was found to be satisfactory.

On April 12, 1567, the provincial chapter of Castile began. Voters at the chapter numbered about twenty. Only the nominations to office are known. The new provincial turned out to be the sixty-eight-year old Alonso González, in the past active for the reform of the province. The foundation of a college at Alcalá de Henares was approved. Toledo, Avila, and San Pablo de la Moraleja were named novitiates.

As in Andalusia and Portugal, Rossi no doubt published decrees of reform in Castile, but no copy is known to exist. After his visitation of the province in 1571, the Dominican Peter Fernández claimed only to summarize and to translate into Castilian Rossi's decrees of reform. Authorities disagree concerning the degree to which Fernández may have departed from his model.

"The province on the whole is in good state," Rossi concluded, "though there are some disorders." He may have been referring to shortcomings in administration on the part of priors who did not keep proper records or share responsibility with the designated officials. Castile had accepted the reform of Audet and as a consequence had suffered a drastic reduction in membership. The province had no *studia* of its own; it managed to muster only two masters of theology and four candidates for the doctorate (*presentati*) for the chapter. In short, the province was small, but to present the level of religious observance as unsatisfactory or downright decadent, as has been done, is inaccurate.

It was probably during the chapter that the bishop of Avila, Don Alvaro de Mendoza, told the prior general of a monastery of nuns under his jurisdiction, which followed the primitive Rule of Carmel. Strangely, during the visitation the sisters of the Incarnation had hardly mentioned the new house which had been founded four years previously by one of their members and which had roused such opposition at the time. Rossi no doubt knew about the foundation of San José, but he waited for the bishop to broach the subject. Foundress of San José was Doña Teresa de Ahumada.

Doña Teresa de Ahumada y Cepeda

This is not the place to tell the story of St. Teresa, one of the most remarkable women of all time; it has been told with incomparable verve by herself and has been the subject of innumerable biographies.

Teresa de Ahumada y Cepeda was born March 28, 1515, at Avila, probably at the family's country estate in the neighboring village of Gotarrendura. She was the third child of the second marriage of Don Alonso Sánchez de Cepeda with Doña Beatrix de Ahumada.

Doña Teresa entered the monastery of the Incarnation on All Saints Day, 1535; there her life was similar to that of the other wealthy ladies. She had her rooms where she could converse with her friends. She was permitted to leave the monastery for her health and for other sufficient reasons.

She led a devout and exemplary life, but was not at ease and longed for greater intimacy with God. A mystical experience she had before an image of Christ during Lent of 1554 and a reading of St. Augustine's *Confessions* turned her life around, and she began to dedicate herself seriously to contemplation. Directed by a series of Jesuit confessors, she made rapid progress in mystical prayer and experienced visions and raptures.

At this point, her thoughts turned to a place of greater solitude. "I wanted to leave this place and go and take my dowry to another convent, much more strictly enclosed than the one I was then in, which I had heard remarkably well spoken of. It belonged to my own Order and was a long way away... But my confessor never allowed me to go."

One day early in the Fall of 1560, a group of friends and relatives were gathered as usual in the cell of St. Teresa, and the conversation turned to the way of life in the monastery. The topic may have come up in connection with the austere life led by the Discalced Franciscan nuns St. Peter of Alcantara had just founded. "Half in jest," writes Teresa's niece, Maria de Ocampo, they began to plan "how to reform the Rule observed in that monastery... and to found monasteries after the manner of hermitages, like the original one kept at the beginning of this Rule, which our holy fathers of old founded." (Teresa and the other sisters would have been fully informed of the life of the "holy fathers of old" from the *Book of the First Monks*, of which the Incarnation possessed a Spanish translation, extant today.) Maria offered to contribute 1000 ducats to the project. Some objected that they could not go to a hermitage, but that they should found a small monastery with a few nuns where they might all go to do penance. To Doña Guiomar, who arrived late, Teresa laughingly explained: "These young ladies were saying a short while ago that we should found a small monastery after the manner of the Discalced Nuns of St. Francis." Doña Guiomar volunteered to help as much as she could with so holy a work.

A Convent Called St. Joseph's

At the time nothing definite was decided, but soon Teresa began to be urged by the Lord in prayer to put the plan into action and to inform her confessor to this effect. Her confessor, the Jesuit, Balthasar Alvarez, told her to talk the matter over with her superior and do what he advised. St. Peter of Alcantara advised her to go ahead with her plan. Eventually it was Doña Guiomar who approached the provincial of Castile, Angel de Salazar, proposing the idea as her own. The provincial, "who is well-disposed to the religious orders," readily gave his consent. Prospective revenues were discussed and it was agreed that the number of nuns in the convent ought never to exceed thirteen."

A storm of opposition arose at the news of a prospective new monastery; the provincial withdrew his permission and Teresa's confessor forbade her to have anything to do with the project. The opposition was due, no doubt, to reluctance on the part of the authorities of the town to have another monastery to support. However, the Dominicans of the town came to her support, and Peter Ibáñez, "the most learned man in the place," in whom she had confided, fully approved her spirit in his well-known *Dictamen*. Alvarez also relented.

It was now agreed to proceed in secret without the permission of the provincial. Doña Guiomar and Father Ibáñez wrote to Rome for apostolic faculties to found a Carmelite monastery. St. Peter of Alcantara apparently also had a hand in the arrangements. The new foundation was to be placed under the jurisdiction of the bishop. St. Teresa writes that the Lord "told me to send to Rome, and to follow a certain procedure, which he also described to me." A small house was purchased in the name of Teresa's brother-in-law, Don John de Ovalle, the husband of her sister Joanne.

In early July, 1562, the very evening of her return to Avila from Toledo, where the provincial had sent her to comfort the newly widowed Dona Louisa de la Cerda, Teresa received the rescript from the Apostolic Penitentiary authorizing the foundation of a Carmelite monastery under the jurisdiction of the bishop of Avila. Dated February 7, 1562, it was addressed to Doña Guiomar de Ulloa and her mother, Doña Aldonza de Guzmán. Since it did not specify that it should be founded in absolute poverty, another rescript with this provision was acquired under the date December 5, 1562. Teresa was also delighted to find at hand in Avila her old friend, Fray Peter of Alcantara. It was he who overcame the misgivings of the bishop, Don Álvaro de Mendoza, about founding the house in poverty, and who persuaded him to accept it under his jurisdiction.

A sickness of her brother-in-law, John de Ovalle, who was living alone in the house destined for the monastery, provided Teresa with an excuse for staying there to attend him; at the same time she could oversee last-minute preparations for the opening of the monastery. On August 24, 1562, four women took the habit: Antonia de Henao (of the Holy Spirit), a penitent of St. Peter of Alcantara; Maria de la Paz (of the Cross), a serving girl of Doña Guiomar de Ulloa; Ursula de Revilla (of the Saints), a protege of Gaspar Daza; Maria de Avila (of St. Joseph), sister of Julian de Avila. With Teresa were two nuns of the Incarnation, her cousins Inés and Anna de Tapia. Gaspar Daza, as representative of the bishop, received the vows of the candidates, offered Mass and reserved the Sacrament. "So, with the full weight of authority this convent of our most glorious father, Saint Joseph, was founded in the year 1562." But the "full weight of authority," one might note, had been obtained in a rather surreptitious manner.

Peter Ibáñez, who returned to Avila around mid-December, 1562, persuaded Bishop Mendoza to obtain permission for Teresa and some companions to live at St. Joseph's to initiate the divine office and to instruct the novices. Four nuns from the Incarnation, Anne Dávila, Anne Gómez, Mary Ordóñez, and the novice, Isabel de la Peña, accompanied her. Teresa made Anne Dávila prioress and Anne Gómez subprioress. Early in 1563, the bishop made Teresa prioress. The sisters dropped their family names, and Teresa de Ahumada became Teresa of Jesus. On August 22, 1563, Salazar gave permission to Teresa and three companions from the Incarnation to remain in St. Joseph's for one year. (Anne Dávila had returned to the Incarnation.) At the end of this period, Teresa asked the papal nuncio, Alexander Crivelli, permission, to be confirmed by the provincial, to transfer definitively from the Incarnation to St. Joseph's.

Teresa's Ideal of the Carmelite Life

In founding St. Joseph's Teresa professed to observe the "first" or "primitive" Rule, in contrast to the Rule "according to the bull of mitigation." Teresa's "first Rule" was in reality the mitigated Rule of 1247: "We observe the Rule of Our Lady of Carmel, and we keep it without mitigation, in the form drawn up by Fray Hugo, Cardinal of Santa Sabina, and given in the year 1248 [sic], in the fifth year of the pontificate of Pope Innocent IV."

In any case, Teresa's concern was to undertake the life of prayer in solitude which was the essence of the life on Mount Carmel. "This will always be the aim of our nuns - to be alone with Him only." Thus does she sum up the story of the foundation of St. Joseph's. She taught the sisters at St. Joseph's: "The whole style of life which we profess to live is not only to be nuns but to be solitaries." Again in the *Interior Castle* she tells them: "All of us who wear this sacred habit of Carmel are called to prayer and contemplation - because that was the first principle of our Order and because we are descended from the line of those holy Fathers of ours from Mount Carmel who sought this treasure, this precious pearl of which we speak (contemplation), in such great solitude and with such great contempt for the world."

Teresa's new foundation was meant to present "a picture, however imperfect, of our Order as it had been in its early days," but the tiny monastery of St. Joseph's in Avila - in reality a reconverted private house - was no hermitage. The sisters lived in a close relationship from which all distinctions of class and rank were eliminated. If Teresa limited her communities to thirteen sisters to avoid financial difficulties and consequent relaxation of poverty and the common life resulting from large numbers, this limitation also had the effect of creating an intimate family atmosphere. A happy innovation that contributed effectively to a close community spirit was the recreation period.

Into this closely-knit community, Teresa paradoxically infused the spirit of prayer in solitude proper to the eremitical life. Strict enclosure was imposed. The sisters kept to their rooms as much as possible. Prayer other than liturgical, spiritual reading, and work were carried out in solitude. Another characteristic of Teresa's foundation fitted the eremitical pattern: austerity. The sisters wore woolen habits and sandals, their rooms contained only the poorest and barest necessities. Total abstinence from meat, an ancient monastic tradition, was observed.

In her work of founding reformed Carmelite monasteries, Teresa did not lay claim to originality: "I am not asking anything new of you, my daughters - only that we should hold to our profession." She may be said to have realized her goal of restoring the observance of the Rule of 1247 - the eremitical-cenobitical life.

To promote her work Teresa wrote her classic books. Without pretension she lavished the treasures of her mystical experience and religious genius on the handful of "poor orphans" she had collected in her little monastery. Hardly had she completed her "big book," her autobiography, than at the insistence of the Dominican Dominic Bañez, she began her "little book," the *Way of Perfection*, in which she undertakes to set down for her sisters "certain things about prayer" (ca. 1565). The *Interior Castle* (1577), the product of her mature years, completes St. Teresa's incomparable trilogy.

Launching the Reform

When the prior general of the Order appeared in Avila, Teresa was understandably uneasy. "I was afraid of two things," she candidly admits, "first that the general might be angry with me.... secondly, that he might make me go back to the convent of the Incarnation." Nevertheless, it was she who took the first step toward an understanding. "I arranged for him to come to Saint Joseph's and the bishop was pleased that he should be shown all the respect which was paid to his own person. I told him my story quite truthfully and simply, for, whatever the consequences, I am always inclined to deal in that way with prelates, as they are in the place of

God, and also with confessors, for otherwise I should not think my soul was safe. And so I told him about my soul, and about almost the whole of my life, wicked as it has been."

Teresa's fears proved to be groundless. "The general is such a servant of His (the Lord's), and so discreet and learned, that he regarded the work as good, and, for the rest, showed me not the least displeasure.... He comforted me greatly and assured me that he would not order me to leave." The juridical gist of Rossi's conversations with Teresa is not clear. According to Julian de Avila, Rossi challenged the bishop's jurisdiction over St. Joseph's on the grounds that he, Rossi, had not been consulted. However, there is no record of such a challenge, and St. Joseph's remained under the bishop until August 2, 1577.

Apparently all the prior general did was to point out to Teresa that although St. Joseph's was subject to the bishop of Avila, she did not on this account cease to be a Carmelite. First of all, he straightened out the matter of the nuns' profession; after his visit they began to make profession in his name, not that of the bishop. Secondly, he immediately grasped the significance for the Order of what was going on at St. Joseph's. He took Teresa's work under his immediate jurisdiction and made plans for its propagation. In other words, as a result of Rossi's initiative what might be called the "observance of Avila" became the Teresian reform.

Without being asked, Rossi issued letters patent of April 27, 1567, by which he authorized her to found an unspecified number of monasteries of the Order in Castile. The nuns, whose number in each monastery is not to exceed twenty-five, are to follow the "first Rule" and wear habits of grey *xerga*. The monasteries are to be under the immediate jurisdiction of the prior general and immune from interference by provincials. For each monastery to be founded, two nuns from the Incarnation might volunteer. Later Rossi wrote, urging her to found as many monasteries as she had hairs on her head.

Without the prior general's patronage and leadership, Teresa's dream of reviving the Order's primitive way of life might have remained confined within the crenelated walls of the City of the Cavaliers.

The Teresian Friars

If Teresa was to extend her reform, she would need friars to direct her nuns. According to St. Teresa, it was the bishop of Avila, Don Alonso de Mendoza, who first approached the general for a license to found in his diocese a few convents of "discalced friars of the Primitive Rule," but Rossi put him off for the time being. After he had left Avila, Teresa herself wrote, making the same request and adducing as a motive "what a service it would be to Our Lady to whom he was most devoted." Rossi could not refuse his daughter, when she appealed to his love of the Virgin.

Rossi's patent is dated from Barcelona, August 10, 1567. Desirous that all friars and nuns of the Order be as "mirrors, lamps, burning torches and shining stars to light and guide wayfarers in this world and should speak with God in prayer and unite themselves to him in meditation," the prior general acceded to the request to found "some houses of friars of our Order in which Mass will be said, divine office recited and chanted, prayers, meditations and other spiritual exercises engaged in, so that they be called and actually be houses or monasteries of contemplative

Carmelites; the latter should also help their neighbor when occasion arises." They are to observe "the old Constitutions" (Soreth's, revised by Audet and Rossi himself) and be subject to the provincial, and Fray Angel de Salazar, prior of Avila, and are to receive two houses "of our profession, our obedience and our habit, in the form which will be specified and declared in our acts."

The letters reflect a solemn appeal for unity, "for it is not our intention to give occasion to hellish quarrels, but to promote the perfection of Carmelite religious life." The contemplative Carmelites are "to live perpetually united to the obedience of the province of Castile, and if at any time any friar under pretext of living in greater perfection should seek to separate himself from the province by the favor of princes and with briefs and other concessions of Rome, we pronounce and declare them men moved and tempted by the evil spirit, authors of seditions, quarrels, contentions and ambitions to the deceit and loss of their souls."

Plainly, Rossi was captivated by his vivacious daughter and did everything in his power to smooth her way. Teresa on her part conceived for him a deep regard and warm affection that survived the storms of later misunderstandings. "He showed me very real and genuine kindness: whenever he could be free he would come here to talk of spiritual things, and, as he was one to whom the Lord must have granted great favors, it made us very happy to hear him on this subject." It was with a sense of loss that St. Teresa bade him good-bye on his last visit. "I was very sorry when I saw our father general returning to Rome; I had conceived a great love for him and felt very much deserted when he left."

Chapter 2

The Discalced Reform

Caspar Nieto and John de Mora, the chief troublemakers in the Andalusian province failed to appear in Avila by mid-May, 1567, to account for their rebelliousness, as ordered by the prior general. Instead, the latter found himself called on the carpet at Madrid. Casper Nieto and John de Mora had gone to the court to lodge a complaint against him and his visitation of the province and had been received by the king. It was the "recourse to force," the appeal to the royal council against ecclesiastical authorities.

The prior general had no difficulty exculpating himself and was able to continue his visitation, having first, however, by letter of May 21, 1567, instituted an official investigation into the conduct of Nieto and Mora, to be sent to the procurator of the Order at the court, Mariano di Leone, no doubt with a view to prosecuting the case after his departure.

The brief, *Superioribus mensibus*, of April 16, 1567, which was to entrust the reform of the Carmelites to the bishops, had not yet reached Madrid, but its imminent arrival was awaited. All Rossi could do was to continue his visitation and prepare as best he could for the "reform of the king."

The Visitation of Aragon and Catalonia

Rossi visited few houses in these provinces. On June 7, 1567, the Aragonese chapter opened at Valencia. Four reformers of the province were elected. The provincial, John Nadal, had his term of office prolonged to consolidate reform. The chapter members promised to extirpate from the province not only the name but all customs and practices of conventuality, "especially after having heard from the Most Reverend Father of the Order that the Carmelite Order has never admitted conventuality, as he demonstrated in effect from the Rule and constitutions, although occasionally, due to evil times and negligence and lack of care on the part of superiors, the ways of some became lax."

The chapter of Valencia also published *Instituta* (Valencia, Juan May, 1567), for the most part identical with the decrees of Seville.

The chapter of the Catalan province opened on August 3. John Montaner was elected provincial. Together with the provincial, Jerome Tostado, prior of Barcelona, was named reformer general of the province. Here, too, decrees of reform were published, though no copy has survived, and conventuality was renounced.

Rossi left Barcelona to return to Italy on September 8, 1567. The prior general's feelings on leaving Spain must have been mixed. His efforts at pacifying Andalusia had failed completely; moreover, the recalcitrant Andalusians had discredited him in Madrid and given the king's council an excuse to interfere in the affairs of the Order. Over the Spanish provinces hung the threat of the king's reform under the jurisdiction of the bishops. On the other hand, Rossi had everywhere inspired the brethren to renewed dedication to their vocation and in his person had reestablished lines of communication between Spain and Rome.

Most consoling of all was the renascence of Carmelite life in the little house of St. Joseph under Mother Teresa of Jesus. "I give infinite thanks to the divine

Majesty," Rossi later wrote, "for the great favor bestowed on this Order by the diligence and goodness of our Reverend Mother Teresa of Jesus. She profits the Order more than all the Carmelite friars in Spain." He had at once properly evaluated the significance of Teresa's vision and had made sure, or so he thought, that this vital force would from the very outset be injected into the body of the Order and renew its members.

The King's Reform

Meanwhile preparations for the king's reform went forward with utmost secrecy. A memorandum dated August 30, 1567, outlined the procedure to be followed by the bishops who received their faculties early in September. They were not to change the habit, Rule or constitutions of the three Orders concerned, but only eliminate abuses. To each Carmelite, Trinitarian, and Mercedarian convent in his diocese the local bishop was to assign his vicar or other suitable ecclesiastic. Likewise, for each house the Dominican provincial was to supply two of his friars. The visitators were to be accompanied by the secular arm, to which they could appeal in case of resistance. The friars and nuns could not allege that they had already been reformed: this was a new reform decreed by the pope. On October 5, the visitation was to begin simultaneously in all convents and monasteries of the realm. Since property was the worst abuse, the visitators were to pounce on the guilty ones before they could hide or otherwise dispose of their ill-gotten goods.

Philip was to learn that all the king's horses and all the king's men could not put religious life together again. His reform, which lasted from 1567 to 1569, brought no measurable improvement to the orders concerned. Visitators unfamiliar with the ideals, customs, and obligations of a religious order were unsuitable for reforming it. The situation was worsened by the fact that Philip decided to dispense with the services of the Dominicans, so that the visitation was carried out exclusively by diocesan clergy and laymen.

In a report to the Holy See, Rossi gives an account of his visitation of Spain and that of the king, and asks that the latter be revoked. He lists some of the complaints that reached his ears. In a letter of June 2, 1569, he countermanded the measures taken by the king's reformers in Andalusia, where his efforts at reform had been nullified and former malefactors returned to power.

The Visitation by Dominicans

At this point, Pius V decided to remove the visitation from the hands of the bishops and entrust it to the Observant Dominicans. Perhaps the laments of the superiors general finally had their effect, or the Dominican pope resolved to terminate an arrangement he never really liked. On January 31, 1570, he formally revoked the brief *Superioribus mensibus*, which had instituted Philip's reform.

Dominican visitators were assigned to the Carmelites: Peter Fernández for Castile, Francis Vargas for Andalusia, and Michael Hebrera for Aragon and Catalonia.

Fernández' faculties, dated August 20, 1569, and valid for four years, enabled him to take charge of the reports of the episcopal visitation and implement their directives. The Dominican may re-visitate houses if necessary. Further, he has the power to punish superiors (vicars general, provincials and priors) and any other religious found guilty of misdemeanors. He is to reduce the term of office of superiors to three years, may appoint superiors even outside the chapters, convene and preside at provincial chapters, depose superiors without process, make statutes, regulations, and ordinances and change existing ones. He should increase the size of communities and suppress houses unable to support twelve members and unite such houses and their perquisites to other houses. Further, he may move religious from house to house and province to province, assist superiors in their offices or depute others from the Dominican and Carmelite Orders for this task. Such deputies may live in Carmelite convents. Fernández may visit, correct and reform Carmelite convents and command, correct, and punish superiors and their subjects. He may perform all acts necessary for the visitation, correction, and reform of head and members of all houses of friars and nuns; if such acts require greater faculties than are herein expressly stated, these are granted. Finally, he may take other Dominicans or Carmelites as his associates or subdelegate his powers.

The same faculties were extended to Vargas and Hebrera.

On November 1, 1569, "since much may happen beyond the commission of the pope," Rossi appointed twenty commissaries to defend the rights of the Order in Spain, instructing them how to conduct themselves in the new visitation. The prior general instructs his commissaries first to ask for a copy of the apostolic brief of the visitators. If the visitators wish to make constitutions already found in the legislation of the Order, they are to be shown these laws, "lest it appear to anyone that our Carmelite Order has so far existed without institutions and a Rule." The commissaries should allow no directives contrary to the Order's legislation for reform or permit the privileges granted to the Order by the Holy See to be infringed. Those under censure of the prior general are not to be absolved. The Order is to be judged according to the mitigated Rule and the old constitutions (Soreth's, revised by Audet and Rossi himself). If the apostolic letters of the visitators contain very wide powers to make changes beyond the matter of reform, the commissaries are to accept them in respectful silence.

Obviously Rossi does not consider that their faculties for reform give the visitators a *carte blanche* to do as they please, or that his own faculties as apostolic visitator and the rights of the Order bestowed by the Holy See have ceased to exist. Much of the controversy to follow was due to the interpretation the authorities in question put on the powers conceded them by the Holy See.

The Book of Foundations

Rossi was still in Spain when Teresa bestirred herself to carry out his wish that she found more houses in the pattern of St. Joseph's in Avila. In the spring of 1567 she was 52 years old and in poor health. She had written her "big book," her autobiography; she was about to begin a new book, the book of her foundations, the book of the "*monja andariega*—the wandering nun," as the papal nuncio, Nicholas Ormaneto, was to call her. The rest of her life was spent in ceaseless journeying up and down Spain, multiplying and confirming her monasteries.

"Here was a poor discalced nun, without help from anywhere, except from the Lord, loaded down with patents and good wishes but devoid of all possibility of making them effective." In these straits Teresa turned to her old friends, the Jesuits, specifically to her former confessor, Balthasar Alvarez, now rector in Medina del Campo, a prosperous trade center some fifty miles northwest of Avila. Alvarez helped to obtain consent for a foundation in poverty from the town magistrates and the bishop. Fray Antonio de Heredia, prior of the Carmelite convent of St. Anne at Medina, acquired a house that could eventually be bought. Teresa took with her for the new foundation two nuns from St. Joseph's, her niece, Mary Baptist, and Anna of the Angels, and four from the Incarnation, all cousins: Agnes of Jesus, Anne of the Incarnation, Isabelle of the Cross, and Teresa del Pilar. The house on arrival proved to be in a very dilapidated condition, but the next morning, the feast of the Assumption, 1567, after a few makeshift arrangements Mass was offered for the first time, the nuns assisting through the chinks in the door opposite the altar.

Teresa kept the prior general informed of everything. "The Reverend Mother Teresa of Jesus has written us about the whole affair," Rossi wrote to the sisters at Medina on January 8, 1569, "the great honor in which you are held in that city and its great satisfaction at your presence. I give infinite thanks to the divine Majesty for the great favor bestowed on this Order by the diligence and goodness of our Reverend Mother Teresa of Jesus. She profits the Order more than all the Carmelite friars of Spain. God grant her many years of life. I admonish all to obey the above mentioned Teresa as a true superior and a jewel to be much valued as precious and a friend of God."

The prior general showed the same interest and satisfaction with regard to Teresa's later foundations. "He wrote to me about every house that we founded, saying it gave him the keenest pleasure that the foundations in question were being made. Really the greatest relief I had in all my trials was to see what joy this gave him, for I felt that in affording it to him I was serving Our Lord, as he was my superior, and, quite apart from this, I have a great love for him."

On May 15, 1569, Rossi appointed the provincial of Castile, Fray Alonso González, his commissary for the nuns professing the first Rule. González was given this commission independently of his office as provincial and he was to exercise it "not according to your own will, nor according to the mitigated Rule, but, as stated, according to the injunctions of the first Rule and our constitutions insofar as they are not contrary to the aforesaid Rule."

On April 6, 1571, the prior general renewed his faculties to Teresa of April 27, 1567, this time without any limit of place in which she might found houses. Rossi called Teresa "our vicegerent for founding monasteries of nuns." Teresa testifies: "I have all possible freedom, from both the general and the provincial, to receive postulants, to move nuns from one house to another, and to help any one house from the funds of others. She insists that "these foundations were made, not only with a license from our most reverend Father General but under an express command subsequently given."

Teresa, laboring up to the end of her life, founded nunneries in Avila (1562), Medina del Campo (1567), Malagón (1568), Valladolid (1568), Toledo (1569), Pastrana (1569), Salamanca (1570), Alba de Tormes (1571), Segovia (1574), Beas (1575), Seville (1575), Caravaca (1576), Villanueva de la Jara (1580), Palencia (1580), Soria (1581), Granada (1582), and Burgos (1582).

Among the novelties of Teresa's foundations were their homogeneity, coherence, and drive to multiply. With the clearly defined ideals formulated by their saintly and dynamic foundress and their close spirit of cooperation, spiritual and material, they contrasted with the monasteries of the old Order, each of which grew out of local circumstances, possessed its own customs and ordinances, and showed little inclination to expand. The closest administrative parallel to the Teresian nunneries at the time were those of the Mantuan Congregation.

The Discalced Friars: Duruelo

With her second foundation a reality, Teresa began to give serious thought to acquiring some contemplative friars. She mentioned her problem to the prior of Medina, Fray Anthony de Heredia, who offered to be the first to join her reform. She thought he was joking, but he told her that he had made up his mind to become a Carthusian. Teresa did not think he had "sufficient spirituality." They agreed that he should undergo a year of trial.

Shortly afterwards St. Teresa was introduced to a young Carmelite studying at Salamanca, Fray John of St. Matthias. About him Teresa had no doubts and convinced him that he did not have to become a Carthusian to be a contemplative. "When I saw that I had two friars to make a beginning with," she concludes, "the thing seemed to me settled, although I was still not quite satisfied with the prior."

John de Yepes was born at Fontiveros, June 24, 1542. His father, Gonzalo de Yepes, came of a noble family, but he had been disowned when he married a girl beneath his rank, Catalina Alvarez. Gonzalo took up his wife's trade of weaving, but died soon after John's birth, after which Catalina was obliged to support her three sons by her own labor. In 1551, Catalina moved to Medina del Campo, a large town with better chances for finding work. There, in 1563, John entered the Carmelite convent of St. Anne, taking the name John of St. Matthias. The following year, he was sent to the Carmelite *studium* at Salamanca and from 1564 to 1568 attended the famous university, then experiencing a period of flourishing activity. After Rossi's visit to the college in 1567, John was ordained a priest.

In June of 1568, when St. Teresa was back at St. Joseph's in Avila, a gentleman of that town, Don Raphael Mejía, offered her a small house he owned in Duruelo, a hamlet on the road to Medina del Campo. The provincial, Alonso González, granted permission for a foundation at Duruelo.

On November 28, 1568, the first convent of contemplative friars was formally opened. The provincial offered Mass and received the profession according to the Rule of 1247 of Anthony of Jesus (Heredia), John of the Cross and Joseph of Christ, a deacon and member of the convent of Medina. From the provincial, too, the friars received the discalced habit of rough undyed wool and discarded their shoes. Thus, Teresa, in spite of her misgivings about the province of Castile, ended by founding there the friars to initiate her ideal of Carmelite life.

At Duruelo, constitutions were already observed, which in revised form (1576) eventually became the constitutions of the Discalced Carmelites. Adapted from the legislation already observed by the nuns, they were drawn up at Medina del Campo by Teresa, John of the Cross, and Anthony of Jesus. Anthony sent a copy of the part concerning "the division of time" to the prior general for his approval.

In 1570, the community of Duruelo moved to Mancera de Abajo, a village about 3 miles away. The provincial and other friars of the province accompanied their barefooted brethren in solemn procession to Mancera on the feast of St. Barbara, June 11.

Pastrana

Meanwhile a second convent of contemplative friars had been founded at Pastrana. Teresa was about to found a nunnery there, sponsored by the princess of Eboli, wife of Ruy Gómez de Silva, one of the most powerful men in Spain, when she was introduced to a hermit named Mariano Azaro.

Azaro was born in 1510 at Bitonto in the Kingdom of Naples. A fellow student of the future Gregory XIII, he was proficient in theology, canon law, mathematics, and engineering. He was sent on a mission to the court of Poland, serving for a while Catherine of Austria, consort of King Sigismund of Poland. He became a Knight Hospitaller of St. John and fought under Philip II against the French at the battle of St. Quentin (1557). Philip employed him on a project to make the Guadalquivir navigable between Cordova and Seville. He decided to leave the world and entered the hermitage of El Tardón in the Sierra Morena. When Teresa met him, Mariano was engaged by Philip on a canal to bring the waters of the Tagus to Aranjuez.

Azaro was accompanied by John Narducci (d. 1616), a Neapolitan whom he had known in Italy and had met again at El Tardón. Narducci had studied painting under Claude Coello and under his later name in the reform, John de la Miseria, is remembered for his portrait of St. Teresa.

Teresa had no difficulty in convincing Mariano to transfer to the Carmelite Order, the Rule of which prescribed the same way of life as that observed in El Tardón. Ruy Gomez had offered Mariano a hermitage at Pastrana; Mariano now presented this to Teresa, and he and Narducci agreed to enter the Order there. Teresa obtained authorization for her second house of friars from Fray Alonso Gonzalez and Angel de Salazar, provincial. On July 13, 1569, Anthony of Jesus officially opened the hermitage of St. Peter.

Fray Mariano was to become one of the leaders of the discalced reform, also one of the most active agents for secession from the Order. Within the reform he favored the contemplative life and de-emphasis of the ministry.

Pastrana became the novitiate for the friars of the first Rule. The candidates who presented themselves included members of the Order, among them Balthasar Nieto, who had survived a series of censures and at the time was a member of the community of Valderas. He took the name Balthasar of Jesus and was prior of Pastrana from 1570 to 1575, although he did not renounce the mitigation until the latter year. Balthasar is certainly an enigmatic character. After his malodorous career in the Order, he becomes an exemplary member of the reform.

In all things that do not concern the stricter life, Rossi wrote on August 8, 1570, the contemplatives are to be subject to the provincial who may visitate and correct them in their own houses. He may not transfer them to houses of the province. Priors of contemplative houses and their *socii* have the right to participate in provincial chapters. Each community is not to have more than twenty members. No more contemplative houses are to be founded.

In spite of this ban on further expansion, a house of studies for the Discalced in the university town of Alcalá de Henares was almost immediately opened. According to one witness, Mary of St. Joseph, Rossi himself authorized the foundation at the request of the prince of Eboli, Ruy Gómez. It was inaugurated on November 1, 1570, with Balthasar of Jesus as superior.

The college at Alcalá became an important center of study for the Discalced; the *Complutenses* was the philosophical counterpart of the *Salmanticenses*, the prestigious theological *summa* produced by their college at Salamanca.

Before he lost control of the movement, Rossi issued six more patents for Discalced foundations, of which three were realized: Altomira (1571), La Roda (1571), Almodóvar del Campo (1574).

Peter Fernández in Castile

In the province of Castile, the apostolic visitation by the Dominicans went forward without a hitch. Fernández tactfully carried out his responsibilities within the normal legislative channels of the Order.

On September 23, 1571, Fernández, having completed his visitation of the province, summoned a chapter at San Pablo de la Moraleja and published "acts and ordinances... with the counsel and consent of the Very Reverend Father Provincial and definitors of the provincial chapter." His purpose, the apostolic commissary declares, is "not to make new laws but to call to mind and emphasize some of those which the Most Reverend General made and to put them in a form which all can read and understand, since not all know Latin."

Fernández and Teresa

It is not clear when the Dominican visitator first met St. Teresa. In the course of the transactions for the foundation at Medina del Campo (1567), he felt obliged to come to her defense against a certain religious who compared her to the spurious mystic of Cordoba, Magdalena de la Cruz.

On July 13, 1571, before witnesses Teresa and Agnes of Jesus renounced the mitigation. On October 6, Fernández accepted the renunciations and assigned Teresa conventuality at Salamanca. This does not mean that she was required to live there. At the time she was prioress of Medina.

The reason for this ceremony becomes apparent from the "acts or constitutions" which Fernández issued for the Discalced nuns. Only fragments remain of the text which is dated Medina, September 2, 1571. The Dominican confirms Rossi's decision that the nuns should remain under the jurisdiction of the prior general. The visitator of the nuns should be a friar of the primitive Rule. He should visit the monasteries once a year, may make directives but may not change the constitutions. (The constitutions of the nuns will be considered later.) Nuns may join the Discalced without renouncing the mitigation, but they may not be superiors unless they do. Communities without possessions are to be limited to thirteen or fourteen nuns; those with incomes may have twenty. Since the reform is new and has few persons experienced in government, prioresses may be reelected. To spare the friars distraction and continual coming and going, the ordinary chaplain of the monastery should be a diocesan priest. The chaplain may also be confessor, but the prioress may call in suitable religious to confess the nuns, even outside the three times allowed by the Council of Trent.

In these constitutions, the result no doubt of close collaboration between the apostolic visitator and the mother foundress, the basic juridical structures of the institution of Discalced nuns, embodying the freedoms Teresa deemed essential, are already present.

Teresa did not long remain in Medina. A visit to the Incarnation convinced Fernández that the leadership of Teresa in material and spiritual matters was required. In agreement with the definitory of the provincial chapter of September 23, 1571, he appointed Teresa prioress. On October 6, the new provincial, Angel de Salazar, introduced her into the monastery in spite of the vehement protests of the nuns. Teresa soon won them over by her unruffled manner, her love, and concern. She also managed to find solutions to the most pressing economic and spiritual problems of the monastery.

No little credit for the changed atmosphere at the Incarnation must go to St. John of the Cross. Teresa was dissatisfied with the quality of the spiritual guidance of the confessors supplied by the Carmelite convent of Avila and determined to have them replaced by her own friars. She appealed to Fernández, who after some hesitation acquiesced. Teresa was particularly pleased with one of the confessors. On September 27, 1572, she reported to her sister Joan: "This Discalced Father who is confessor is doing a great deal of good: his name is Fray John of the Cross."

At first, John stayed at the friary of Avila; later he moved to a small house close to the Incarnation. He remained confessor at the Incarnation until his clamorous removal in 1577. During this time, for a nun of the Incarnation, Anne Mary of Jesus, he made his famous drawing of the crucified Christ which inspired the masterpiece of Salvador Dali. These years, too, constituted the longest period that John and Teresa were together, and the two saints acted as powerful spiritual catalysts on each other. On November 18, 1572, St. Teresa attained the mystical marriage.

Evidently Fernández did not feel that he could - or should - require the general's vicar of the nuns to be a Discalced friar. Teresa did not hit it off as well with González as she had with Father General.

Fernández used the Discalced friars to reform the convents of the province. In view of the Incarnation, he was especially solicitous for the friary at Avila. "I stayed here almost a fortnight," he wrote to the Duchess of Alba, January 22, 1573, "to organize the convent of friars, so that it should be a help, and not a hindrance, to the monastery of nuns. I have brought a number of discalced friars here, not because I want the community to become Discalced, but so that it may be governed according to their laws; if they keep these, they will be holy."

At Toledo, too, as appears from the same letter, Fernández placed Discalced in charge. To organize the growing number of Discalced houses in Castile, he made Balthasar of Jesus vicar provincial.

The Dominican visitation of Castile may be said to be a success. The reform of the province was peacefully progressing. The Incarnation had been permanently reformed, as Angel de Salazar was to attest many years later. The houses of the Discalced friars and nuns had multiplied; the former, still attached to the province, were harmoniously developing a needed internal structure.

Vargas in Andalusia

On September 9, 1571, the nuncio, John Baptist Castagna, could report to the secretary of Pope Pius V, Jerome Rusticucci, that the visitors of the Carmelites had finished visiting the houses and were ready to convene chapters in a month.

The visit by Hebrera of Aragon and Catalonia seems to have come off without a hitch.

In Andalusia things had not gone so well. The Dominican visitator, Francis Vargas, who had the unenviable task of reforming the province, supported the faction disapproved of by Rossi, as had the king's reformers; he, too, failed to quell the fires of dissension.

On October 26, Vargas reported to the prior general on the chapter he had held two days previously. The Dominican visitator contented himself with emphasizing certain reform decrees of the prior general. He continued the use of the deposit box. Permissions to leave the convent should be granted only once a week.

At this point, Vargas decided that the only solution to his problem was the discalced reform of Castile. On April 28, 1573, he delegated Balthasar of Jesus, of the province of Castile, with his powers over the Discalced houses founded or to be founded in Andalusia. He could name and depose priors and receive novices, provided these were not of the province, in which case permission of the provincial was required. The appointment had in view two convents to be founded in Granada and La Peñuela. Nieto founded Los Mártires in Granada on May 19. The following June 29, La Peñuela was founded by Gabriel of the Conception (de la Peñuela), one of the friars punished by Rossi at the provincial chapter of Seville in 1566.

Balthasar did not choose to exercise his prerogatives personally, perhaps because the memory of his past was still green in those parts. He returned to Pastrana, where he was prior, and on August 4, 1573, entrusted with the task of visitator of the Discalced in Andalusia a young friar fresh from the novitiate, Jerome Gracián. Thus enters on the scene one destined to play a leading role in the history of the reform, a sign of contradiction fated for conflict with the Order and the reform.

Jerome Gracián (1545-1614) was born at Valladolid, one of fifteen children of Diego Gracián and Juana Dantisco. Don Diego was a secretary to the king, Doña Juana the natural daughter of the Polish ambassador. Two of Jerome's brothers, Anthony and Thomas, followed their father in the king's service as secretaries, a career for which Jerome, too, was destined, but after obtaining the master's degree in arts at Alcalá, he was ordained to the priesthood in 1570. He owed his spiritual formation to the Jesuits and thought of joining them, but he never returned from a visit to the Carmelite novitiate at Pastrana. His novitiate, during which he had the spiritual charge of the nuns at Pastrana and heard confessions in the village and environs, was followed by profession, April 25, 1573.

Gracián now took over the leadership of the Discalced reform. He was a gentle, charming, and courtly person, but quite lacking in prudence and a knowledge of ecclesiastical law. His concept of his office of apostolic commissary and visitator, later conferred on him, was that all things were permitted him in the name of reform. Gracián, Mariano Azaro, John of Jesus Roca, none of them with any previous experience of Carmelite life, turned the Discalced movement down a separate path.

To leave his province in order to carry out his commission, Gracián had to practice a slight deception on his superior, Fray Angel de Salazar. Mariano received permission to go to Seville with an unspecified companion to see to certain personal affairs. Thereupon, in September, 1573, he and Gracián travelled to Seville for a meeting with Vargas. When he discovered he had been tricked, Salazar ordered his two subjects to return to Pastrana, but Vargas overrode him.

On October 17, Gracián restored San Juan del Puerto to the Andalusian province;

the attempt to make of it a Discalced foundation had failed. On January 5. 1574, Gracián opened a new house for the Discalced in Seville (Los Remedios).

The Discalced now had three houses in Andalusia: Granada, La Peñuela, Seville. Gracián once composed a memorandum to show that an apostolic visitator could found houses in Andalusia. With characteristic fondness for numbering the sequence of his thoughts, he musters eleven arguments to prove his point. His approach is logical rather than juridical, though his syllogisms are not always above exception. Some samples: "The 3rd (reason): the visitator has higher faculties than the general in all that pertains to the good of the Order. The general can grant permission to found the said houses; therefore so can the visitator. The 4th: the visitator can place primitive friars in mitigated convents for their reform; therefore, he can place houses in the province for the good of the whole province... The 7th: although the brief does not explicitly grant permission to found houses of primitives, it is enough that general authorization be given to do what is most suitable for the reform and well being of the Order. For, tell me, what is more perfect: to increase the number of primitives or mitigated friars?"

In a letter to the prior general that has not survived, Gracián described his activities in Seville. Rossi failed to be impressed. "You are scarcely a novice," he wrote, April 26, 1574; "without knowledge of the institutions of the Order you may easily be led along ways and paths that are not good. I believe actions take their goodness from circumstances, and that the intention is not enough. Your intention is according to God, but because you act against obedience and your conscience is burdened with sanctions and censures, I think you are not acting in the service of God. I am afraid that beneath the pretext of laudable zeal there lie suspicions and contention. God will provide the remedy for violence. I will do what pertains to my office and I will not do what is improper."

With this shot across the bows, contact between Gracián and Rossi seems to have ended.

Nicholas Ormaneto, Reformer of Carmel

Meanwhile the new pope, Gregory XIII, was wondering what had become of the visitation of the Carmelites in Spain. The current nuncio, Nicholas Ormaneto, upon looking into the matter and learning of the misdeeds of the Andalusians, gave it as his opinion that the visitation should be continued there, though he did not feel that Vargas was the man for the job. The Dominican, in fact, had no more stomach for reforming Carmelites. Eventually, on September 22, 1574, Ormaneto appointed Vargas and Gracián in *solidum* apostolic visitators of Andalusia.

By this time, however, on August 13, 1574, Gregory XIII had declared the Dominican visitation ended and ordained that henceforth the Order should be visited by the prior general and his delegates. On October 10, Ormaneto wrote to the Holy See inquiring whether this affected his own faculties as nuncio to visit and reform religious Orders in Spain. On December 16, he was assured by the papal secretary, Ptolemy Galli, that the recall of the Dominican visitators did not affect his powers to visit and reform religious orders.

The Veronese Nicholas Ormaneto had already played an important role in Tridentine reform. He had acted in close collaboration with and enjoyed the highest esteem of some of the most prominent figures in Catholic reform. A disciple of

John Matthew Giberti (1495-1543), noted reforming bishop of Verona before the Council of Trent, he was carefully selected as his vicar general to initiate reform in his archdiocese of Milan by none other than St. Charles Borromeo, the very incarnation of the Counter Reformation. St. Pius V conferred on Ormaneto the unprecedented office of "reformer of Rome" with the Herculean task of cleaning out the Augean stable of the eternal city, not excluding the papal court itself. He could therefore be counted on, as nuncio in Spain, to have a personal interest and more than usual tenacity in pursuing religious reform.

That reform, however, no longer emanated immediately from Rome, but had local Spanish origins, even though "apostolic," and depended on the initiative of the nuncio in office.

Teresa in Andalusia

Teresa was delighted with the progress of her spiritual sons in Andalusia. On May 14, 1574, the saint wrote to Mary Baptist Cepeda y Ocampo, prioress of Valladolid: "Oh, if you could see the to-do that is going on – secretly of course – in favor of the Discalced! It is something one ought to praise the Lord for, and it has all been aroused by the Fathers who went to Andalusia, Gracián and Mariano. My pleasure is greatly tempered by the distress it will cause the Father General, for whom I have such affection: on the other hand, I can see that our position was getting hopeless."

Although Gracián had been in correspondence with St. Teresa even before his entrance into the Order, the two did not meet until April, 1575, at the monastery of Beas, which Teresa had recently founded. It is an interesting insight into the femininity of St. Teresa that this personable but imprudent young man should have so completely captivated her. Their attachment must be ranked among the classic friendships of saints of the opposite sex. Gracián told her the story of his life. "It may seem an improper thing," Teresa later reflected, "that he should have spoken to me in such detail about his soul."

On the other hand, Teresa opened her heart to him. "She communicated her spirit to me." Gracián recalled, "without concealing anything, and I declared all my interior to her in the same way; and there we agreed always to work together in all our affairs." To Teresa it seemed that she had finally found the leader her movement among the friars had always lacked. Still under the spell of their first meeting, Teresa wrote to Agnes of Jesus, prioress of Medina, on May 13: "Oh, Mother, how much I have wished you were with me during these last few days! I must tell you that, without exaggeration, I think they have been the best days in my life. For over three weeks, we have had Father Master Gracián here; and, much as I have had to do with him, I assure you I have not yet fully realized his worth. To me, he is perfect, and better for our needs than anyone else we could have asked God to send us. What your Reverence and all the nuns must do now is to beg His Majesty to give him to us as a superior. If that happens, I can take a rest from governing these houses, for anyone so perfect and yet so gentle, I have never seen. May God have him in His keeping, and preserve him; I would not have missed seeing him and having to do with him for anything in the world." As a result of a vision, Teresa made a vow of obedience to Gracián.

From now on, Teresa's impressions of the feud between the Order and the

Reform are filtered through the mind of Gracián and are consequently one-sided and unfavorable to the Order. Nevertheless, she never quite overcame an uneasiness at the turn her movement had taken in relation to the prior general.

On May 29, 1575, Teresa made a foundation of nuns in Seville and duly reported it to the prior general. Beyond a visit from Michael de Ulloa, the prior of Seville and a defender of the Order, who asked to see her patents, the Carmelites of the city caused her no trouble, even though the Order already had a monastery there, the Incarnation.

Rossi himself was trying to reach "his daughter." He penned letters in October, 1574, and January, 1575, which showed up simultaneously at Seville on June 17. In them, the prior general had evidently expressed his displeasure with Gracián and Mariano whom he considered disobedient and with the acceptance among the contemplatives of Gabriel de la Peñuela; the Discalced houses in Andalusia would have to be closed. Teresa's answer on the following day is characterized by the Teresian scholar, E. Allison Peers, as "one of the most striking in the entire collection" of her letters.

"Every day," Teresa begins, "a special prayer for your Reverence is said in choir, and, apart from that, all the sisters are careful to pray for you, since they are aware how much I love you. They, too, knowing no other father, have a great love for your Reverence, which is not surprising, for you are all we have in the world. They are all very happy, and so they never cease to be grateful to your Reverence, since it is to you that the Reform owes its beginning." She goes on to protest the loyalty and good intentions of her Discalced friars. (We already know what Rossi thought of Gracián's good intentions.)

As to closing the Discalced houses in Andalusia, Teresa in her forthright manner reads the general a lesson in *Realpolitik*. "It may be that the whole Order is reformed already, but people certainly do not think so here: they consider every one of our friars, without exception, as saints. And they do in fact lead good lives, are extremely recollected, and are much given to prayer... They stand very well with the king, and the archbishop here says they are the only real friars there are. Now if your Reverence drives them out of the Reform - assuming you do not want them there - you must believe me that, even if you have all the right in the world on your side, people will not look at it like that."

Her final suggestion is a saint's and eminently correct, but perhaps not possible, given the state of men's minds: "I beg you to commend the matter to His Majesty, and, like a true father, forget the past, and remember that you are a servant of the Virgin and that she will be offended if you cease to help those who, by the sweat of their brow, seek the increase of the Order." The expansion of the Discalced reform in an atmosphere of unity and harmony did not lie entirely in the general's hands – nor in Teresa's.

Even as Teresa wrote these wise words the general chapter at Piacenza had passed into history.

Chapter 3

"An Intolerable Kind of Feud"

The general chapter which convened at Piacenza, May 22, 1575, lost no time addressing itself to the question of the Discalced friars in Andalusia.

The General Chapter of Piacenza and the Discalced

The brief of August 13, 1574, recalling the Dominican visitors, was read, followed by another, dated April 15, 1575, the purpose of which was to invest the acts of the chapter with apostolic authority. This brief specified that those who had been made superiors against the general statutes and obedience due to superiors of the Order, who had accepted or lived in convents or places prohibited by the same superiors, should be removed; to this end all opportune remedies were to be applied in order to restore obedience without the right of appeal. Archbishops, papal nuncios, legates *a latere* were obliged to aid the general in the implementation of its decrees.

At the opening of the chapter, so important for the Order in Spain, of the Spanish definitors only the Catalans were at hand. The provincial of Andalusia, Master Augustine Suárez, and his *socius*, arrived on June 8. The definitor for Castile arrived after the chapter was over, but approved and signed the acts. The Aragonese failed to appear. Since no fresh information on developments in Spain was available, the chapter confined itself to reaffirming the position the prior general had so far taken: those who have opened houses against the will of the general are deposed from office without the right of appeal. The convents at Granada, Seville and La Peñuela are to be abandoned within three days. The authorities indicated in the papal brief are called on to implement these decisions. Those concerned who do not obey are cited to appear within three months. Mariano Azaro and Balthasar Nieto are to be expelled from the Order if they remain obdurate.

The Castilian definitor, Martin Garcías, brought letters from his province and provincial. Though the chapter was over, the definitors were still at hand and these delegated the prior general to provide for the situation as revealed by the letters from Castile. Rossi's directives, which are the general chapter's, forbid the contemplative fathers to form a province or congregation separate from the province of Castile. Alphonse González is confirmed as delegate for the nuns of the first Rule, and Angel de Salazar, provincial of Castile, is to examine their confessors. The friars and nuns of the primitive Rule are to follow the Order's liturgy with regard to the chants of the office and Mass. They are not to go completely barefoot, "since nowhere in the Rule is such a thing prescribed." They are not to be called "discalced," but "contemplatives" or "primitives."

These and other directives were not intended to suppress the primitives, but to confine them within the Order. "We protest before God and men," Rossi declared in the post-chapter decrees, "that we have always had the one desire to grant them every favor, grace and benefit, if only they consulted the interests of peace, tranquility, concord and friendship, remaining faithful to obedience." Given the information at hand, the decision of the chapter was inevitable, but in the reality of the situation its attitude was too unyielding and was bound to exacerbate the conflict.

One decision of the chapter was not published but communicated to the person concerned by the provincial, Angel de Salazar: Mother Teresa of Jesus was not to leave her monastery. She accepted the will of her superiors, though not without a sense of hurt. "It has never been realized here," the saint pointed out to Rossi in February, 1576, "nor is it realized now, that the Council, or the *Motu proprio*, deprives superiors of the right to send nuns to particular houses for the good of the Order." The decree of the chapter has not survived; it has generally been interpreted as a penance, but the situation had considerably changed since Pius V's legislation, imposing cloister on all nuns. Ormaneto himself, as will be seen, disapproved of Teresa's travels. Later, under their own superiors the Discalced nunneries were due for some painful adjustment to the new rigid concepts of cloister.

Gracián's Visitation of Andalusia

On August 3, 1575, Ormaneto named Gracián commissary and reformer of the Carmelites in Andalusia and of the primitives in Castile, "apostolic letters granted to the Carmelite Order and its superiors, persons and general chapters in general, in particular or otherwise to the contrary notwithstanding." After the recall of the Dominican visitation, the general chapter of Piacenza had confirmed Augustine Suárez as provincial of Andalusia and had decreed that the friars of the first Rule were to remain under the provincial of Castile.

Teresa, who had been reassured in a vision, encouraged Gracián to begin his task of visitator of the Andalusian province. On November 21, 1575, the feast of the Presentation, he accordingly began with the Casa Grande in Seville. When he presented his credentials, the friars raised a tumult, locked the doors of the convent and at first would not let him leave. Gracián thought they were going to lay violent hands on him. Some one ran to tell Teresa he was dead. A shudder of excitement thrilled through the Discalced nunneries. In thanksgiving for Gracián's alleged escape, Teresa thereafter had her nuns celebrate the Presentation with special solemnity.

Dramatics aside, the community of Seville at first refused to acknowledge Ormaneto's authority and Gracián's patents, but in the end capitulated.

The visitation of the friary of Seville took place from February 21 to April 1. The visitator laid the axe to the root of private possessions in whatever form. Inventory was made of all the belongings and furnishings of the house, including the cells, and all was declared common property. Similarly, all books in the convent (over 1,000) were collected into one room, designated the library, for the use of all. A common supply room was established, to which the friars were to have recourse for their needs, even the most insignificant. The *depositum* was abolished. Gracián revoked all permissions for friars to live outside the convent on their properties and to receive rents.

The community should not exceed forty members and ten guests, the number which the income of the house could support, supplying all wants. (In overpopulated houses the budget could manage only the most urgent needs: *vestiarium*, bread, wine, oil; for the rest individuals were expected to forage on their own.)

Permissions to leave the house should be granted only in cases of grave necessity and rarely. (The legislation of the Order permitted religious to leave the house twice a week).

Seville was declared the only novitiate in the province. The novices had been living together in one large room, but Gracián had separate cells made according to the Rule. He himself took personal charge of the novices.

Two half hours of meditation were introduced. At the king's request for prayer, Gracián instituted perpetual adoration, all Carmelite houses, Discalced or Calced, in Castile and Andalusia taking turns.

Gracián deposed the provincial from office, as "the head of the band (that caused all) of these disturbances," and kept the reins of government in his own hands.

Gracian's measures of reform, no doubt encouraged by the king and Ormaneto, were aimed at introducing the perfect common life, upon which Trent had not insisted. Gracián's bloated concept of his prerogatives as visitator caused him to function without reference to the legislation of the Order and the consequent limits to the obligations of its members.

But how seriously Gracián went about his reformer's task is a moot question. He seems to have many about him, left and right, indifferent to his chances of success. "I was charged with the visitation and reform of the Calced Carmelites of Andalusia," he wrote in his autobiographical *Pilgrimage of Anastasius*, "in which I was engaged for four or five years, although my principal intention was to carry through the foundations of the Discalced, because the Calced were opposing us, and we could better defend ourselves by keeping them subject than by having them rule us."

"Tostado Will See to It"

It was not to be expected that the Carmelites would submit gracefully to the nuncio's high-handed action, nor was the prior general about to allow the rights of the Order to be trampled. He petitioned Pope Gregory XIII to forbid Ormaneto to interfere in the visitation of the Carmelite houses in Spain or to allow the Discalced to visitate, but admit the ordinary visitator who had gone there for that purpose. To the pope, in fact, as his secretary, Ptolemy Galli, pointed out to Ormaneto, it seemed "right that their ordinances, constitutions, and privileges be preserved. Since what is explained in the said petition is true," Galli goes on to say, "His Holiness wishes that Your Lordship in the best manner possible remove all occasions for complaint."

The visitator to whom the prior general alludes is Jerome Tostado (1523- 1582). He was born in Lisbon, where he made his vows in 1545. He is said to have acquired his doctorate at Paris and was afterwards invited to lecture in the province of Catalonia. When Rossi visited Barcelona in 1567, he was prior there. The general added the office of reformer general of Catalonia. Tostado was among the defenders of the Order appointed by Rossi in 1569. He accompanied the prior general on his visitations in Italy, 1572-1575, and was his *socius* at the general chapter of Piacenza. On December 10, 1575, Rossi appointed him visitator, reformer, and commissary general of the Spanish provinces. In May, 1576, Tostado was elected provincial of Catalonia. On November 18, 1581 Gregory XIII confirmed him as visitator and reformer of Spain, but Tostado died at Naples, February 24, 1582.

The career of this friar speaks for itself. His long association with Rossi, the confidence he shared with him, made Tostado the ideal choice as his representative. His task was a hopeless one, and his mission was a failure before it started. He was preceded by the rumor that he had come to destroy the reform. To Teresa - and through her to the general reading public since - he is the *bête noire* of the reform, "the sole cause" of its ills.

Tostado arrived on August 5, 1576; by August 29 he was already on his way out of Andalusia. Ormaneto advised Tostado to postpone his visit of Andalusia and to pass on to Portugal.

"God has delivered us from Tostado!" Teresa exclaimed.

Tostado's patents did not apply to Portugal, but apparently he had subsequently received a commission for that province. On September 30, 1576, he presided at the chapter "and contributed much to its peaceful realization."

The Abortive Discalced Province

Meanwhile, in letters patent of August 3, 1576, Gracian created a separate province and congregation of Discalced Carmelites, consisting of the Discalced friaries and nunneries in Castile and Andalusia, as well as those to be founded in the future. He confirmed the three Discalced friaries in Andalusia, "since the faculties of apostolic visitors are greater than those of the Most Reverend Father General" (as if the prior general were no apostolic visitator). Friars and nuns are to keep the same constitutions and manner of living; that is, the directives laid down by the Dominican visitators and himself. The Discalced are immediately subject to the prior general, who alone may visitate and then only in company with a Discalced friar. If he cannot personally visit, he may delegate only a Discalced who must be accompanied by the Discalced provincial. The Discalced may not transfer to the old Order under pain of apostasy. Priors and their *socii* are to meet in chapter at Almodóvar de Campo on August 26 to elect a provincial and definitors.

The chapter of Almodóvar met in due course under the presidency of Jerome Gracián. Present were the priors of the nine Discalced houses and their *socii*: Mancera, Pastrana, Alcalá, Altomira, La Roda, Granada, La Peñuela, Seville, Almodóvar. Gracián deferred the election of a provincial, as he explained to the assembled members of the chapter in a letter dated September 1, 1576, because he was still apostolic commissary and visitator, and another head or provincial would be a source of confusion in the province. The moment his commission lapsed through revocation or absence or death of the nuncio, the first definitor, Anthony of Jesus, should convene a chapter to elect a provincial, who for this first time would not require confirmation by the prior general. Thus, of his own initiative, Gracián separated the reform from the provinces and placed himself at its head.

St. Teresa was elated with the results of the chapter of Almodóvar. "The Fathers have come back from it in the highest spirits," she wrote to Gracián from Toledo on September 20, 1576. Evidently the high-spirited Fathers had not bothered to tell the Mother of their attempt to erect a province. "I was also very glad," she writes in the same letter, "that the plan for getting our Father General to have us made into a separate province is being pursued in every possible way, for it is an intolerable kind of feud when one is on bad terms with one's superior."

Later, when she was evidently fully appraised of the goings on in Almodóvar, she consulted with Fray Peter Fernández. "He thinks the commissaries cannot make us into a separate province or nominate definitors, unless they have more authority now than they had before," she wrote to Mariano on February 16, 1577.

Ormaneto Under Fire

The reform of the religious orders in Spain was Ormaneto's personal devotion, catered to by the Holy See with increasing reluctance. "His Beatitude," Galli wrote on September 19, 1576, "is kept so busy listening to and answering the complaints that many religious orders in Spain are continually making... that, to tell the truth, he is being caused too much inconvenience... His Beatitude wants you to proceed less drastically, so that (religious) have no more reason to run here and cry out the way they do. Don't say that His Holiness needn't listen to such complaints, because his office won't allow it; besides, the complaints are such that they cannot always be said to be wrong."

The following January 15, Galli again wrote to Ormaneto: many Carmelites have left Spain for Rome and do nothing but complain about Gracián, the commissary deputized by him. The pope has never liked the idea that one Order be visited by members of another order or Rule. He orders his nuncio to suspend Gracián's authority for the time being and to give complete liberty to Tostado, who being of the same Rule, will be better informed of the ordinances and needs of the Carmelites and consequently more apt to reform them. If the visit does not produce the desired fruit, Ormaneto is to report to the pope who will issue further instructions.

In October of 1576, Gracián had resumed his visitation of the province of Andalusia. On April 6, 1577, he was able to announce to Ormaneto that he had visited almost all the houses of the province and listed the decrees of reform to be published at the provincial chapter.

At this critical moment Ormaneto died, June 18, after an illness of ten days, without settling the question of the Carmelite visitation. Certainly he left nothing in writing about this matter. His instructions from Rome had been to suspend Gracián's faculties and to allow Tostado to visitate.

Ormaneto was a holy man, as St. Teresa recognized, but he was severe and unbending. The fracas between the Order and the Reform was in large measure due to his concept of his responsibility for religious observance in Spain and his insistence on using the Discalced for visitation.

In spite of previous protestations, Gracián now proved curiously reluctant to surrender his powers. He denied that Ormaneto had altered his status. The opinion was sought of theologians and lawyers at Alcalá, Madrid, and Toledo. They concluded that Gracián's patents continued to be valid *re non integra* - as long as the business for which they had been granted was not finished. The president of the royal council, Bishop Diego de Covarrubias, a loyal friend of the Discalced, told Gracián to continue his commission. Gracián continued to visitate the Discalced friaries in Castile.

Gracián versus Tostado

With the arrival of the new nuncio, Philip Sega, on August 29, 1577, the policy of the nunciature in Madrid suffered a sea change.

On October 14, Sega received his instructions from Rome: "With regard to the business of the friars, His Beatitude says that he intends that their charge be left to the officers appointed by their generals for their reform and for all that may be necessary to reduce the religious to a life conformable to their profession and obligations. This they will be more easily able to do, since they are assisted and armed with the authority of His Beatitude by means of special briefs." Only if the superiors are negligent of their duty or prove insufficient for their task is the nuncio to interfere and then only with the consent of the king. Without the king's consent nothing is to be undertaken.

The nuncio forbade Gracián to visitate any more. Gracián went first to Alcalá then to Pastrana where he lived in a cave. He improved the time by directing memoranda to the king, in which he pointed out "the great disadvantages that accrue to the religious Orders of Spain, when nuncios issue briefs contrary to the ordinances of their superiors." This "beatific candor," to borrow Silverio de Santa Teresa's phrase, needless to say, did little to endear the former visitator to the nuncio. "I considered myself as good as dead," Gracián later recalled with the exaggeration that was wont to strike terror into the heart of St. Teresa, "and feared I might be burned at the stake."

As to Tostado's status during the next months, Francis of St. Mary states that on November 5, 1577, the royal council forbade him to visitate in Andalusia and Castile. He was recognized in the convents of the provinces and there surreptitiously exercised his authority - as the Discalced did not fail to tattle to the court.

Trouble in Avila

At the Incarnation of Avila, three years had passed since Teresa's successful superiority, and many of the nuns were anxious to have her back. On October 7, 1577, the election of prioress was held under the presidency of the provincial of Castile, John Gutiérrez de la Magdalena. Before the balloting, Gutiérrez let it be known that candidates outside the community were ineligible. In spite of this instruction, most of the nuns voted for Teresa. Their ballots were declared null, and the choice of the remaining ones, Doña Juana del Aguila, became prioress. When the pro-Teresian nuns insisted that their candidate had been validly elected and refused to acknowledge Doña Juana as prioress, the provincial excommunicated them. Tostado upheld the provincial's conduct of the election.

All this did not take place without heated passion on both sides. The Discalced side of the controversy is well known to posterity, especially through the agile pen of St. Teresa, but today after the smoke of battle has cleared somewhat, it may be safely said that the provincial was within his rights.

When the royal council ordered the provincial to absolve the nuns from excommunication, on instructions from Tostado he complied, signifying his eagerness to obey the king, his "natural Lord." Ignoring an appeal of the nuns to the royal council, of his own accord he granted the absolution. The nuns continued to object to the election, but in this they received no support: the validity of the election was not in question.

The provincial deputed Ferdinand Maldonado, prior of Toledo, to absolve the nuns, December 2-3, 1577. At the same time, he was commissioned to remove the Discalced confessors from the monastery. It is generally said that he was under orders from Tostado, but there is no reason why the provincial could not have decided this measure on his own authority.

The Dominican visitator, Fernández, had placed Discalced friars at the Incarnation as confessors with great spiritual profit for the nuns. Later, Ormaneto suggested to Gracián founding a house in Avila for confessors. "It never seemed to me to be good," he wrote on November 11, 1575, "to have two or three friars in a house attached or not attached to a monastery." Another matter he would like to mention: he does not like the way Mother Teresa, saint though she is, goes about founding and visiting monasteries. Religious women should stay in their monasteries and not travel about; that is the job of their superiors. However, the nuncio does not want his commissary to mention this opinion to a soul, as he does not wish to hurt "this good and holy Mother."

Not long after this, the prior of Avila, Alonso Valdemoro, created a commotion by removing the Discalced confessors, John of the Cross and Germain of St. Matthias, from the Incarnation, but Ormaneto ordered them restored. Now that Gracián's faculties had been suspended, another attempt could be made to remove the Discalced confessors from the Incarnation. Since the Discalced had created their own province, it was unlikely that John and Germain would obey Gutiérrez, so they were forcibly removed. St. John was imprisoned in Toledo until his escape in August, 1578. Germain was confined at San Pablo de la Moraleja: he escaped in March. (Conventual jails were notoriously insecure.) Teresa immediately wrote to the king in great distress, pleading that he command the Carmelites to set free their prisoners. "I would rather see them among the Moors, for they might well show them more pity." Philip did not interfere.

The importance of this distressful incident has been blown up out of all proportion. Biographers and novelists have spared neither imagination nor descriptive skill on the story of St. John's imprisonment and treatment in prison. As a matter of fact, little first hand information is available. Not all the punishments applicable by law are to be presumed to have been inflicted on the prisoners. Imprisonment, flogging, fasting on bread and water were standard penalties in religious orders of the time, Discalced as well as others.

The provincial had a right to change confessors; he evidently felt that Calced friars were more suited to the needs of the Incarnation, which belonged to the old Order. John remained curiously aloof from the battle between the Order and the Reform, but his actions leave no doubt as to where he thought his duty lay.

One bright ray in this dark picture: in his prison cell in the convent of Toledo St. John of the Cross composed a number of poems including most of the *Spiritual Canticle* and the *Dark Night*.

Sega Takes the Initiative

In May, 1578, Tostado passed on to Aragon and Catalonia, which the king allowed him to visitate. His departure was the signal for Gracián to return to the scene. The new president of the royal council, Anthony Maurice Pazos y Figueros, ordered him to resume the visitation; on June 19, he obtained for Gracián the king's consent to use the secular arm.

Gracián was now in desperate straits. Neither pope nor nuncio would have any part of his apostolic powers. He was operating only on the strength of the royal mandate.

The nuncio, who had forbidden Gracián to visitate, could hardly overlook the contravention of his command. On July 23, 1578, he formally deprived Gracián of his commission, ordering him under pain of excommunication to present himself within six days and surrender all documents concerning his visitations and reforms. Mincing no words, the nuncio declares that Gracián was led by a spirit of presumption and arrogance in continuing to exercise his faculties after Ormaneto's death, even after he had been expressly forbidden under censure to do so, "to the detriment of your honor and your soul and to the prejudice and scandal of the whole Order."

Teresa was shocked by the nuncio's tone, when she was served with his letter on August 9. Realist that she was, she set about at once to mend her fences: the next day, she sent the chaplain of St. Joseph's, Julian de Avila, to Madrid to make an act of obeisance and to beg the nuncio not to put the Discalced under the provincials. At the same time, she composed a memorandum, to be distributed among "various people" in Madrid, justifying Gracián's conduct and showing "the injustice of the brief's harsh treatment of him."

The intervention of influential friends had its effect. The king's council sequestered Gracián's papers in order to review Sega's action, but the nuncio eventually succeeded in gaining possession of them. His decree of July 23 went unchallenged. Next, he set about investigating "the life of this Gracián and the manner of living of these Discalced... to see what manner of man he is, what sort of religious these are, what Rule they profess, in what manner they are governed, since they object to being governed by the Calced."

At this moment, Gracián's time bomb, set in 1576, unfortunately exploded. As arranged then, at the lapse of Gracián's commission, Anthony of Jesus, first definitor of the alleged Discalced province, convened a chapter at Almodóvar, October 9, 1578, to elect a provincial. Anthony himself emerged as provincial.

Sega's reply, on October 16, was to declare the whole procedure null and void and to forbid Anthony under pain of excommunication to act as provincial. He furthermore placed the Discalced friars and nuns under the jurisdiction of the provincials of Castile and Andalusia, Diego de Cardenas and John Gutiérrez de la Magdalena.

Besides Antonio, Gregory Nazianzen, Mariano Azaro, and Gabriel of the Assumption were placed under arrest in various convents. Gracián was confined to the Carmen of Madrid.

The Discalced Reunited to the Provinces

To assist him in his investigation of Fray Jerome Gracián and the Discalced, Sega, at his own request to the king, received the services of Don Louis Manrique, royal chaplain; Hernando Castillo, Dominican; and Lawrence de Villavicencio, Augustinian. Gracián was required to answer fifteen objections to his conduct of the visitation.

To the accusation that he did not frequent refectory and choir, Gracián answered rather weakly that he had been afraid he would be poisoned and had no time to go to choir; besides he could not sing. He had not abstained from meat because he was ill. He had made no decrees which were not in conformity to the councils and the primitive Rule; he admitted going against the Order's legislation which was lax. He had founded houses in Andalusia with authorization of the apostolic visitor, Francis Vargas. If anyone claimed Vargas did not have the power, that was his business; it was not the subject's place to judge the superior's authority. Ormaneto had ordered him to continue his visitation in spite of the general chapter of 1575, confirmed by the pope; indeed had expressly ruled it out in his patents.

As to his continuing the visitation after the nuncio's prohibition, he did not recall Sega's forbidding it under censure. When the president of the royal council, Pazos, had ordered him to proceed, he had thought he had the power to do so. He had divided the province and held the chapter on orders from Ormaneto who had told Fray Mariano orally "to hold the chapter and the rest."

Sega issued his verdict on December 20, 1578. He absolved Gracián from all censures, but deprived him *in perpetuum* of the office of reformer, sent him to the convent of Alcalá, imposed penances of fasts and scourgings and forbade him to write or receive letters, especially from nuns, or otherwise interfere in the affairs of the Order.

The nuncio now had the reins of authority firmly in hand. Although he was never able to obtain recognition for the visitor from Rome, he did manage to bring Gracián to heel and to insert the Discalced into the normal administrative channels of the Order. His constant purpose was not to "undo" the reform, as its members somewhat hysterically claimed, but to put a stop to "the noise of the friars," to bring calm to the troubled waters of religious reform in Spain. His subjection of the Discalced to the provincials, as he had written to Cardinal Philip Buoncompagni on November 13, 1578, was "provisional, until otherwise determined." In fact, on April 1, 1579, Sega withdrew the Discalced from the jurisdiction of the provincials and placed them under a special vicar general, Angel de Salazar, prior of Valladolid.

By this time, John Baptist Rossi, "the spiritual father of the Order," had died in Rome, September 4, 1578. A devout and learned man, deeply committed to reform, it had been his fate to run afoul of the great reforming movement which had risen in the Order, corresponding to the new spiritual force at work everywhere in the Church. In the parlor of St. Joseph's at Ávila, St. Teresa's vision of Carmel had found sympathetic resonance in his soul. "I was intensely grieved at the news which I received about our Father General," Teresa wrote to Gracián. "I feel deeply moved by it. On the day I heard it, I wept and wept – I could do nothing else – and I felt very much distressed at all the trouble we have caused him, which he certainly did not deserve: if we had gone to him about the matter everything would have been smoothed out. God forgive the person who has continually put obstacles in the way: for, though you had little confidence in my suggestion, I could have come to an understanding with your Paternity."

To the end, Teresa remained the obedient daughter of the prior general. This constant loyalty to its head may be taken to mean that Teresa's desire was to maintain the unity of the Order.

Chapter 4

Gracián and Doria

The question of an independent province was a different matter. Not long after she found in Fray Jerome Gracián a leader for her reform, St. Teresa began urging separation from "those of the cloth." The erection of a separate province had become a necessity.

The Discalced Appeal to Rome

With Gracián *hors de combat*, Teresa in May of 1579 set on foot her own negotiations. John of Jesus (Roca) and Diego of the Trinity donned secular clothes and assumed the names John Bullón and Diego de Heredia respectively. They embarked from Alicante in mid-May, 1579. The Discalced nuns, organized by St. Teresa, supplied the money for their journey and sojourn to Rome. Teresa also helped support Peter of the Angels, previously dispatched to Rome by Gracián, the delegations working simultaneously. Another negotiator for St. Teresa was Canon Diego de Montoya, of Avila, agent for the Inquisition in Rome, "who has been fighting for our lives."

Peter of the Angels defected to the old Observance, of which he had originally been a member. "Words cannot describe the treachery committed against the saint and her sons," comments the Discalced historian, Silverio of St. Teresa. John of Jesus and Diego of the Trinity, posing as Spanish gentlemen, spent a year in Rome winning influential friends for the reform and urging the erection of a Discalced province.

In the end, it was not this cloak and dagger caper that won the day. On July 15, 1579, Philip Sega and his commission reported to the king on the second phase of their investigation – the manner of living of the Discalced. St. Teresa's sons and daughters passed this test with flying colors, and for their benefit and for the sake of peace the nuncio recommended to the Holy See the erection of a separate province of Discalced friars and nuns. On June 22, 1580, Pope Gregory XIII in his brief, *Pia consideratione*, acceded to the request of King Philip II and the Discalced, "who were the object of a number of molestations and hindrances disturbing to their institute from the friars... called mitigated," and erected a separate province of Discalced friars and nuns. They were to be immediately subject to the prior general who had the right to visitate only in person or through a Discalced delegate. The provincial required the confirmation of the general. Only the permission of the provincial was needed to found new houses. Recourse to the pope or the cardinal protector is expressly declared to be licit.

The Discalced had not won consent to all their requests, but their province was given privileges above the common, and in fact was already a congregation.

The Chapter of Alcalá, 1581

At King Philip's request, Gregory XIII, on November 20, 1580, named the Dominican John de las Cuevas president of the forthcoming Discalced chapter.

St. Teresa, who was keeping a close watch over events, now that her work was reaching its consummation, did not scruple to make known to the president her preferences on the choice of a provincial. Gracián – "there is no one like my Father Gracián" – was of course her first choice, followed by Nicholas of Jesus and Mary Doria, and John of Jesus Roca. Roca, she admits, she added to the list only so that she might not seem to be limiting her choice. Anthony of Jesus definitely would not do.

Gracián, was, in fact, elected provincial. At the provincial chapter of Alcalá, March 3, 1581, Gracián received eleven out of twenty votes; Anthony of Jesus, seven – not exactly a landslide, considering Gracián's outstanding role in the growth of the reform and Teresa's enthusiastic endorsement of him and disapproval of Anthony. The four definitors were respectively Nicholas of Jesus and Mary, Anthony of Jesus, John of the Cross, and Gabriel of the Assumption. The chapter decreed special suffrages for the king in token of their gratitude, as indeed they had reason to do.

Caffardi confirmed the new provincial, June 29, 1582.

An important task of the chapter was to provide legislation for the reform. As apostolic commissary for the Discalced in Castile and Andalusia, Gracián in 1575 or 1576 had composed constitutions or ordinances for the friars, who up to then had been governed by the constitutions of Duruelo approved by Rossi. Gracián's constitutions consist of fifteen brief chapters and presume the general legislation of the Order in so far as it is not contrary to the "primitive" Rule.

The constitutions now issued by the chapter for the friars (Alcalá, H. Ramírez, 1581) form a complete body of legislation, at least at the provincial level, and replace the constitutions of the Order, of which they preserve Soreth's basic structure of five parts and many juridical elements not affecting the reformed way of life. They canonize characteristic elements of the Teresian reform: confinement to the cell, liturgical and mental prayer, silence, austerity in dress, perpetual abstinence from meat, common life of poverty, manual labor, study.

Only a few kinds of apostolate are admitted: preaching, catechesis, hearing confessions. The care of parishes is forbidden; missions are not yet contemplated.

Another concern of the chapter was the legislation of the nuns. On May 7, 1576, Jerome Gracián, "provincial and apostolic visitator," had issued a decree designed to organize the life of the Discalced nuns. They were to follow the constitutions made by the prior general and Pedro Fernández. The former had ordained that the visitator of the nuns should be a friar of the primitive Rule, if possible. Since such friars were now to be had in abundance, Gracián forbade the nuns under pain of rebellion to admit a Calced visitator. The chapter now undertook to issue definitive constitutions for the nuns.

In the weeks before the chapter, St. Teresa engaged in a brisk exchange of letters with Gracián about this business so vital to her. Suggestions for modifications, carefully censored by the mother foundress, were sent from all the monasteries. The chapter retained the nuns' constitutions intact with only a few additions and modifications of a stylistic and juridical nature. Teresa's comments were also generally followed.

The sisters were placed under the direct jurisdiction of the provincial, thus eliminating interference by the local prior. Communities without income were limited to thirteen or fourteen nuns; those with income to twenty. Teresa preferred all houses to have income, but the chapter decided to recommend poverty when possible. There was to be no difference in life-style in the two sorts of houses. The chaplain, chosen by the prioress and provincial in consultation, should be a secular priest. He could also be confessor (not recommended by Teresa). The prioress was free to call in other confessors besides the ordinary one. The same freedom applies to preachers. She did not need permission from the provincial. This structure, unusual in an age of male chauvinism, gave the nuns needed freedom. The constitutions of Alcalá were printed in Salamanca by the heirs of Matthias Gast, 1581.

The new province numbered twelve friaries and twelve nunneries with almost four hundred friars and two hundred nuns.

Teresa could now sing her *Nunc dimittis*; her life's work was secured. "Now, Calced and Discalced alike," she wrote after the chapter, "we are all at peace, and no one hinders us in Our Lord's service."

But the troubles of the reform were not yet at an end. Times were coming when the battles with the fathers of the cloth would seem child's play. Teresa, however, was to be spared the internecine wars which would have wounded her mother's heart even more deeply. This marvelous woman, so heavenly yet so human, died on October 4, 1582.

Nicholas of Jesus and Mary Doria

Recent years had seen the rise of a man who was now to challenge Gracián's leadership and ideas. Nicholas Doria (1539-1594), the scion of a merchant family of Genoa, settled in 1570 in Seville, trading center of the Indies. He had amassed a comfortable fortune when he decided to embrace the ecclesiastical state. After studies at the Dominican College of St. Thomas in Seville, he took priestly orders. He came to know Fray Mariano, a fellow Italian, at the Discalced convent of Los Remedios. Even as a priest, his talent for business continued to serve him. He saved from the hands of creditors the palace of the archbishop of Seville, Don Christopher Rojas y Sandoval, who became his grateful friend as a result. He likewise gave valued advice to Philip II on financial matters. The foundress herself knew and esteemed him for his virtue and sound sense. Eventually, he joined the Discalced reform, pronouncing his vows on March 25, 1578.

A mature man of affairs, his talents were immediately put to use; within months of profession he became superior at Los Remedios. As such, on December 1, 1578, he wrote a letter of filial submission in answer to Caffardi's announcement of Rossi's death and his own appointment as vicar general of the Order. By this diplomatic gesture – the sort of thing Teresa had been urging for years, which Gracián had never had the sense to make – Doria made himself spokesman for the reform at a time when it lacked a head, Gracián being in disgrace with the nuncio. His letter, allegedly written on behalf of the Seville community, was signed by friars from other houses as well, among them John of the Cross, vicar of El Calvario.

Teresa hoped Doria would become Gracián's right hand; the two men complemented each other in temperament and talent. In a letter to Gracián, July 7, 1579, she praises Doria's talents and virtue and recommends cooperating with him. Teresa's dream of close collaboration between Gracián and Doria was doomed to disappointment. Doria was one of many who felt that Gracián's conduct was not in keeping with the contemplative and penitential character of the reform.

Jerome Gracián, Provincial, 1581-1585

Gracián's policy as provincial was expansionist and activist and little in keeping with the tone of the new constitutions; his brief term of office was plagued by dissent. He was by no means as acceptable to the friars as he was to the nuns, with whom from the start he was accused of being too familiar.

On October 14, 1581, a foundation was made in Portugal at Lisbon. The Prudent King, who had recently added Portugal to his extensive realms, made no difficulties over a foundation by Spaniards under his loyal friend, Fray Mariano. A monastery of nuns under Mary of St. Joseph followed in 1585.

In Lisbon, the focus of Portugal's colonial enterprises, with its marvelous estuary opening on worlds beyond the sea, Gracián's imagination took fire at the prospect of converting the heathen. He had no time, he claimed, to notify the prior general, but he consulted with Doria, Roca, Azaro, and the Valladolid community. As a result, after a couple of unsuccessful starts, a party of Discalced missionaries, which left Lisbon on April 10, 1584, arrived safely in the Congo and initiated the Discalced mission in Africa.

The provincial held office for four years, but the chapter met every two years, when the definitors were elected. The chapter which convened at Almodóvar, May 1, 1583, elected as definitors John of Jesus Roca, Mariano Azaro, Augustine of the Kings, and Ambrose of St. Peter. It altered the constitutions in the matter of the election of priors and ordained that these should be elected by the provincial rather than the conventual chapter.

When the time came for the accusation of faults, Doria, according to the historian, Francis of St. Mary, faced Gracián with the allegation that he had "destroyed the Order by his easy ways and lack of rectitude in government." Nicholas' eloquence so inflamed the minds of the others that they wanted to depose the provincial then and there, but Doria restored calm, and the chapter was satisfied to make a decree limiting Gracián's preaching engagements which caused him to be absent from choir and community acts.

During his second term, Gracián continued to expand the Discalced missionary effort. In Lisbon, he met the Friar Minor, Martin Ignatius de Loyola, recently returned from the Far East. This veteran missionary and relative of the founder of the Society of Jesus, turned Gracián's attention to China. On April 9, 1585, Gracián and Loyola signed an agreement, *Vínculo de hermandad misionera*, for the mutual collaboration of their Orders "for the conversion of pagans in Ethiopia (Africa), the kingdoms of China, the Philippines, and other parts of the East and West Indies." This remarkable document, which betrays an open-mindedness and lack of self-interest unique in the competitive business of the missions of religious orders, was undoubtedly the work of Gracián.

Before the provincial could realize his plan, the chapter opened in Lisbon, May 11, 1585. Nicholas Doria received all votes save two as provincial. The new definitors were respectively Jerome Gracián, John of the Cross, Gregory Nazianzen, and John Baptist "el Rondeño." Doria was away in Italy engaged in making a foundation in his native Genoa, so the chapter was adjourned pending his return.

Gracián used the interval to launch his missionary enterprise, availing himself of his position as first definitor and vicar in the absence of the provincial. A common missionary trajectory to China, ever since Columbus had mistaken Cuba for Japan, was over Mexico and the Philippines. On May 13, 1585, Gracián obtained royal patents for Fray John of the Mother of God and eleven other friars to cross the sea to the Indies. On July 11, the courageous little band set sail for Mexico, where they made a successful settlement.

Gracián's precipitous entry into the mission field is typical of the way he did the right things the wrong way – or as St. Teresa affectionately chided him, swam against the stream. Many friars felt that missionary activity could not be reconciled with the contemplative vocation of the Carmelite. Gracián must have known that the newly elected provincial was one of these. Under Doria, the missionary effort of the Spanish Discalced was doomed to wither on the vine.

That Gracián's provincialate had been riddled with quarrels and opposition appears from the "Apology and Defense" of his office against calumniators. The principal accusations against him were that he was remiss in correcting faults, with the result that the Order was being ruined, that he spent too much time in preaching and study to the neglect of his duties as provincial, that he was too attentive to the nuns. The airing of these complaints at the chapter shows little judgement on Gracián's part, but he could never resist the temptation to justify himself.

Nicholas Doria, Provincial, 1585-1588

On December 1, 1584, Nicholas Doria had founded the first Discalced house outside Spain in his native city of Genoa. From this seed the other houses in Italy and Europe and the missions in the East were to spring.

On his return from Genoa, Doria reconvened the chapter at Pastrana, October 17, 1585. Under Gracián the province had come to number nineteen friaries in Spain, Italy, Africa and Mexico, as well as twenty nunneries. The province was divided into four vicariates, each in charge of a definitor dependent on the provincial: Old Castile, New Castile, Andalusia, and Portugal. St. John of the Cross was given the care of Andalusia; Jerome Gracián, of Portugal. Genoa, Africa and Mexico remained under the jurisdiction of the provincial. The four vicars and the provincial constituted the diet or *consulta*, which met annually and carried on the business of the province.

Thus originated the famous *consulta*, source of much controversy in the future. Its critics objected to the decisive vote of the consultors, as a result of which the province was ruled by a commission not a single person, while it was precisely this feature that appealed to Doria and was doggedly defended by him.

Unforgettable was the fiery exhortation to observance of the new provincial. The reform, Doria declared, had departed from its pristine fervor and had started down the broad and easy path of laxity. He served notice that observance was to be the concern of his provincialate. The dead wood, he assured his spellbound listeners, would be pruned from the tree of Carmel. He also touched on the matter of excessive freedom between friars and nuns; he decried the freedom the nuns had to choose confessors according to their own whims.

"So loud were the roars of the noble cub of Carmel, now become a strong lion," writes the admiring Francis of St. Mary, historian of the Reform, "that not only the flock and the pastures trembled, but the shepherds as well."

"Even after my death," Doria declaimed, "my bones, clashing together in the tomb, will cry out: observance, observance."

Gracián tied a knot in the lion's tail by circulating a tract entitled *Apology for Charity Against Some Who Under Color of Observance of the Law Cause Charity to Grow Cold and Disturb Religious Orders.*

A meeting of the definitory beginning August 13, 1586, resulted in several important decisions confirmed by Sixtus V, September 20. The independence of the Discalced province was confirmed, the Discalced were given permission to adopt the Roman breviary and to have a procurator in Rome. John of Jesus Roca became the first procurator.

Gracián Under a Cloud

Relations between Gracián and Doria worsened after the provincial chapter of Pastrana in 1585, which created the *consulta*. From now on, Jerome was to carry on a relentless opposition to the government which he felt was replacing the spirit of simplicity and love Teresa had left to her heirs in Carmel by external formality. To the austere Doria, Gracián was simply rationalizing an easygoing way of life that could not abide the contemplative and penitential character of the Order.

In Portugal, Gracián persevered in his zeal for the missions, producing a little treatise, *Estímulo de la propagación de la fe* (Lisbon, Andrés Lobato, 1586), often reprinted and translated, the first missiological work by a Carmelite. Carried away by enthusiasm, the author showed that missionary work was not alien to the reformed way of Carmelite life and referred to those who would not send laborers into the missions as "demons in the flesh who prefer to remain in Spain and live off the alms of the faithful." Perhaps for this reason he did not deem it advisable to obtain permission for publication.

In fact, under Doria the opinion of the "super-hermits" prevailed, and missionary activity slacked off. The Congo mission was discontinued. The Mexican enterprise endured and became a province, but the friars abandoned the *doctrinas*, or missions to the natives, and plans to expand into New Mexico.

On April 18, 1587, the provincial chapter met in Valladolid. Jerome Gracián was made vicar of Mexico. On July 23, he received his orders to depart for his vicariate with nine other friars, but it turned out that no fleet sailed that year for fear of Drake. Not long afterwards, Gracián appears in the diocese of Jaén to found a friary in Úbeda. He also made himself useful to the bishop, Don Francisco Sarmiento.

Actually he had been sent there by Augustine of the Kings, vicar provincial of Andalusia, as much to get him away from the nuns of Seville as to use his help in Jaén. It would take some doing, Augustine wrote to Doria, to get him away from Seville, due to the influence of Don Pedro Cerezo, wealthy friend of Gracián, and others. The two had spent a few nights in the church of the nuns. In the chapter, nothing had been done about Gracián's frequenting the monasteries, Augustine wrote to Doria, because his departure for the Indies was imminent, but now that his departure had been postponed for a year, he had shown no improvement. After Augustine's letter, Doria decided to get the *consulta*'s consent to call Gracián to order.

On October 18, Elias of St. Martin, first definitor, was dispatched to Gracián at Úbeda with a list of ten allegations against him, to which he was requested to reply. The list criticizes Gracián's frequent and late visits to the monasteries in Seville and Lisbon, and the nuns' pampering him with special food and linens. Besides, he is accused of ordinarily eating meat, wearing linen, sleeping on a mattress, and using sheets of serge on the excuse of ill health.

Gracián replied to the accusations in detail, not so much denying many of them as justifying his conduct.

On November 28, 1587, the provincial and his councilors sent Gracián a formal admonition. Whatever happened in the past, the *consulta* commands him for the future to lead the common life in clothing and cell, to remain at home, to exercise prudence in visiting the nuns, no matter how beneficial these visits are considered to be. He is reminded that the nuns are no longer his charge, and he should not meddle in their affairs any more than the province wishes.

Encouraged perhaps by the mild tone of the *consulta*'s admonition, Gracián on May 2, 1588, wrote a letter of humble submission. He acknowledges that he has been guilty of carelessness out of simplicity of nature not maliciousness. He urges the provincial to enforce prudent visiting of the nuns and the equal observance of the regular life by all. He expresses willingness to resign as vicar of Mexico, if Doria thinks it best. He asks to be assigned to a convent where without any responsibilities he can devote himself to prayer and study. He is willing to renounce active and passive voice.

Thus, it looked as though Doria had at last won the battle of reducing Gracián to the ranks. On May 12, the *consulta* ordered Jerome to Seville before leaving for Mexico and assigned six priests, two professed clerics and one laybrother as his companions.

The Discalced Congregation

With the growth of the Discalced reform, the division into provinces and the erection of a congregation was simply a matter of time. On July 10, 1587, by his brief *Cum de statu*, Sixtus V raised the Discalced reform to the status of a congregation headed by a vicar general who had all the powers over the congregation the prior general had over the entire Order. The *consulta* remained, but whereas it had previously been composed of the vicars provincial, it now constituted a body over and above the provincials.

Doria used the occasion to obtain papal confirmation of the *consulta*.

The chapter to implement the brief, *Cum de statu*, met in Madrid on June 19, 1588. Nicholas Doria was elected first vicar general of the new congregation. Definitors were respectively: John of the Cross, Augustine of the Kings, Anthony of Jesus, Elias of Saint Martin. The six members of the *consulta* were: John of the Cross, Anthony of Jesus, Mariano Azaro, John Baptist "*el Andaluz*", Louis of St. Gregory, Bartholomew of Jesus. Five provincials were elected for the five newly constituted provinces: John Baptist "*el Remendado*" for Old Castile, Elias of St. Martin for New Castile, Augustine of the Kings for Andalusia, Gregory of Nazianzen for Portugal, John of Jesus Roca for Aragon. In the future, the local priors were to attend only the provincial chapters, though they continued to be elected by the chapter of the congregation or by the *consulta*, when there was no chapter. The *consulta* in fact carried out most of the day by day business of the congregation, leaving very little to the discretion of the provinces. The vicar general was elected for six years, the other officials for three.

Two decrees of the chapter Doria considered so important that he obtained apostolic confirmation for them from the nuncio: all matters are decided collegially by the *consulta*, which also governs the nuns in the same manner.

On the eve of the chapter, June 17, the *consulta* replied to Jerome's letter of submission of May 2, ordering it implemented in every detail, except that as an alternative to withdrawing to a house for recollection he might go to Mexico, but no longer as vicar.

The same day, June 17, 1588, the nuncio, Caesar Speziano, no doubt at Doria's request, added the weight of apostolic authority. He ordered Jerome to lead the same regular life as the others in matters of clothing, food, cell, and leaving the convent. Gracián was forbidden to treat with persons outside the Order or to write to them without permission of his superiors, as the constitutions ordain. He should not air his complaints to laymen, but to his superiors or to him, the nuncio.

In what was evidently intended as a gesture of good will, Doria on June 2 made Graciàn his *socius*. Protesting himself Graciàn's brother in all things, Nicholas declared himself desirous of reciprocating Graciàn's act, when he had become first provincial.

But Teresa's good friend, Teutonio de Braganza, archbishop of Evora, urgently wanted Graciàn in his diocese. Archduke and Cardinal Albert, governor of Portugal, also asked him to return to Lisbon. Through the king, these worthies put pressure on Doria, who a week after appointing Gracián his *socius* found himself on June 27 signing patents ordering him to report to Evora.

Gracián in Portugal

At Evora, Gracián escalated his attack on the government of the congregation. On November 2, 1588, he appealed to the king against Doria. The devil, he stated, had invented three ways to destroy the charity, sincerity, and simplicity which hitherto characterized the Discalced brotherhood. The first way was through "a new government in the form of a republic" imposed by a Genoese friar. Secondly, the vicar general was arranging to meet with the Calced to elect a prior general according to his own taste, "which is the total destruction of the Discalced Congregation." (Jerome seems to be alluding here to preparations for a general chapter which for some reason did not eventuate. No general chapter had been held since 1580, and none would be held until 1593, when Doria's choice was Michael Carranza.) Finally, Gracián claimed that Doria had punished and discredited persons who did not agree with his government. He asked the king, "as the protector and true refuge of religion after God" to appoint one or two persons to examine Doria's government, its laws, and all that had been done in its name.

Doria, alerted to Gracián's attack, did not wait for the king to invite a reply. In an undated letter, he defended his system of government in detail. On February 20, 1589, Fray Nicholas was officially notified by the royal chaplain, García de Loaysa, of the king's satisfaction with the laws and mode of governing decreed by the chapter of Madrid.

Early in 1589 Jerome returned to Lisbon, summoned there by the Cardinal Archduke Albert, Philip II's twenty-five year old nephew and governor of Portugal. Lisbon before and during the raid of Sir Francis Drake, May, 1589, offered ample opportunity for Gracián's apostolic fervor. He did much good work preaching, hearing soldiers' confessions, founding a refuge for fallen women, who were especially numerous and without means in the war-torn city.

The Cardinal Archduke also found Fray Jerome useful for political ends. The spirit of Nun'Alvares Pereira was still very much alive in the Carmo of Lisbon. Don Antonio numbered many sympathizers in the Carmelite community of one hundred friars, in Gracián's phrase "perhaps the most restless in the kingdom." The prior, Antonio Calderón, was placed under arrest by the Spaniards, another friar had been one of Don Antonio's captains, others had broken bread with him. It was rumored that six thousand arquebuses were hidden in the fort-like Carmo, against which the artillery of the castle across the valley was constantly trained.

Archduke Albert entrusted Gracián with the "reform" of the Carmo. The scope was purely political, Jerome assured Michael de Carranza, vicar general for Spain and Portugal, who appeared on the scene; he did not concern himself with the regular observance of the friars, "for in this no province of the whole Order of Calced Carmelites exceeds them." The rumor about the weapons proved unfounded. Gracián sent to other convents some of the more politically dangerous members of the community. During the battle, the Portuguese friars were locked in an upper dormitory, while the convent was occupied by two thousand destitute refugees. Gracián and his Discalced friars went about hearing the confessions of soldiers. After the battle, he sallied forth with a company of arquebusiers to identify the dead — "since I knew the Castilian soldiers" — so that the Catholics could be buried and the heretics burned. Three hundred Catholics were placed face up with their arms crossed; eight hundred Lutherans were turned face down, "looking at hell, where their souls were burning."

All this was far removed from the studious and prayerful retirement which Gracián had elected and to which he had been consigned. Doria tried in vain to get him back to Spain. As appears from a letter of the king, November 28, 1589, Nicholas had asked Philip three months previously to recall Jerome to Spain. The Prudent King took no further action at the moment, perhaps because he found Gracián useful in Portugal. Jerome remained in Lisbon for another year and a half.

It seems to have been around this time that Gracián appealed to the pope against the rule of the *consulta*. Authorized by Cardinal Albert and the protector of the Order, he dispatched to Rome a loyal supporter, Peter of the Purification, living in Genoa. Peter's trip may have been made in connection with the nuns' recourse to Rome.

The Revolt of the Nuns

Doria felt constrained to explain once more the workings of the *consulta* and the question of the reelection of prioresses. This he did in a circular letter to the congregation, January 24, 1590. Gracián countered with a rebuttal.

In Madrid, the prestigious Anne of Jesus, prioress of the important monastery in that city, had been won to the cause against the *consulta*. She was one of St. Teresa's most distinguished daughters. Comparing her to St. Teresa, Báñez declared that she was in no way inferior in supernatural gifts and in natural gifts had the advantage. St. John of the Cross dedicated his *Spiritual Canticle* to her. After functioning as prioress in a number of monasteries in Spain, she went on to found the Order in France and the Low Countries. Anne collaborated with the noted Augustinian humanist, Louis de León, in producing the *editio princeps* of St. Teresa's works (Salamanca, G.

Foquel, 1588).

In August of 1588, the *consulta* had authorized the monastery to reprint the nuns' constitutions. They appeared the same year (Madrid, Pedro Madrigal, 1588). According to Mary of the Incarnation (Yolante de Salazar), lady-in-waiting to Empress Maria, sister of Philip II, who had entered the Order in 1586, Anne had wrung from Nicholas the admission that it would be a good thing to obtain papal confirmation of the nuns' constitutions. This was not yet authorization to do so, nor above all to request changes in the government of the congregation.

Sent secretly to Rome, Barnaby del Mármol succeeded in obtaining from Pope Sixtus V his brief, *Salvatoris*, June 5, 1590. It contained all that the nuns' hearts desired. The constitutions of Alcalá with slight changes received papal approval. The pope, moreover, recalled the power of the chapter and the vicar to change the constitutions and revoked changes already made. He placed the nuns directly under the jurisdiction of the vicar general who every three years was to depute a commissary general having voice and place in the chapter after the vicar general. He prohibited provincials, councilors and bishops from interfering in the affairs of the nuns. Finally, he instructed bishops to defend the interests of the nuns when they appealed.

It was no accident that Sixtus in a brief of June 21 should appoint as executors of the papal brief Gracián's friend, Archbishop Teutonio de Braganza, and Anne's friend, Fray Louis de León. Within a month of receiving their commission, they were to convene a chapter of the congregation, publish the papal brief and elect a commissary general for nuns.

Before the brief reached Spain, Doria, on June 10, 1590, convened an extraordinary chapter in Madrid. The purpose of the meeting, among other things, was to publish new constitutions (Madrid, Pedro Madrigal, 1590). These canonized such disputed points as the decisive vote of the consultors, the governance of the nuns by the *consulta*, etc. Nicholas thus consolidated his innovations, which were now the law of the congregation.

The chapter also considered the case of Jerome Gracián. In view of letters he had written to certain nuns and laymen, the chapter decreed that no friar or nun should write to him without permission of the *consulta*, nor should they write to anyone else about his affairs. All letters and papers regarding him are also to be turned over to the *consulta*.

Gracián for his part wrote a detailed criticism of the constitutions of the chapter.

At the time of the chapter, Doria had not yet heard of the existence of the sisters' papal brief, but on August 21, 1590, he addressed them a circular letter, stating that he was constrained either to appeal against the brief with hurt to many or relinquish the care of the nuns.

Gracián, too, wrote to the nuns, "for it is good that they know the reasons they have in their favor."

The efforts of Louis de León, acting also for Braganza, to convoke a chapter and elect a commissary of the nuns proved unavailing.

Both sides appealed to the king. The monastery of Madrid appointed the Mármol brothers its procurators. Louis de León also remained in the breach.

Doria's threat to abandon them struck consternation into the camp of the nuns. It is not known how many monasteries had rallied to "the captain of the prioresses." As time went on, the friars increased pressure on the monasteries to abandon Anne and her cause. Among eminent personages who remained faithful to the regime was Bl. Anne of St. Bartholomew, companion of Teresa.

On January 26, 1591, the committee entrusted with the case under the Count de Barajas was able to report to the king. The Discalced friars should not renounce the care of the nuns. Anne of Jesus, one of two or three nuns who had "raised this dust," should be given to understand that her duty lay in obedience to superiors. She should desist from urging the implementation of the brief which will not be admitted. The same holds for Mary of St. Joseph, about whom the king should write to the Lord Cardinal Archduke. Dr. Mármol and his brother should also be told to give up their efforts. One of them who is rumored about to leave again for Rome to obtain confirmation of the brief should be refused a passport. The *asistente* or regent of Seville should likewise caution Peter Cerezo, who provided funds for obtaining the brief. Louis de León should be told to attend to his job of provincial of the Augustinians. Finally, the king should instruct his ambassador in Rome, the Count de Olivares, to persuade the pope to revoke his brief.

Doria Wins His Case

The year 1590 witnessed the reign of three popes: Sixtus V died on August 27; Urban VII ruled from September 15-27, followed on December 5 by Gregory XIV. The latter on April 25, 1591, issued his brief, *Quoniam non ignoramus*. With regard to the burning issues, the provincials were given charge of the nuns as well as the friars, with powers to correct all except the most grave faults specified in the constitutions. The office of commissary was specifically abolished. Prioresses could not be immediately reelected, nor could they choose confessors, but provincials were reminded in the words of the Council of Trent to provide an abundance of confessors.

Obviously, it was a compromise devised by the Roman curia. The nuns did not realize their dream of being under one head as in the idyllic days of Gracián's rule. Still they had escaped the cold impersonal bureaucracy of the *consulta* and could treat on a personal basis with the provincials. The *consulta* had had its tail bobbed, but at least the commissary was no more.

There remained the culprits to be punished. Any other course to the severe Doria would have been dereliction of duty: this had been a fault for which he had reproved Gracián. It was not so much that the rebels had appealed to the Holy See; they had gone about it the wrong way (*subreptitie et obreptitie*). Anne of Jesus was deprived of active and passive voice, confined to a cell and denied Communion except monthly for three years.

The prioress of Madrid, Mary of the Nativity, was deposed. A new prioress, Mary of St. Jerome, cousin of St. Teresa, and the lay sister, Bl. Anne of St. Bartholomew, were imported from Avila, which in the words of Bl. Anne "had not taken part in any revolt, and matters had remained in the state in which the saint had left them."

Fray Louis de León, at Anne's encouragement finished the commentary on Job he had begun in 1578 and dedicated it to her - an appropriate gift, and she no doubt made abundant use of it.

Mary of St. Joseph's part in the affair is not clear. As prioress of Seville and later of Lisbon, she was known to be a close friend of Gracián and shared his disapproval of the *consulta*. In August of 1588, she had been required to answer a questionnaire similar to Gracián's and had been forbidden to correspond with him. She now was deprived of vote for two years and sentenced to one year in a locked cell; she was not permitted to communicate with others by written or spoken word or to assist at Mass except Sundays. She was allowed to confess and communicate once a month.

With the controversy settled, Doria produced his constitutions, the term of half a dozen years' evolution. Separate editions appeared for the friars (Madrid, Peter Madrigal, 1592) and the nuns (Madrid, Peter Gómez, 1592). Oddly enough, Doria's constitutions for the nuns was a Spanish translation of the Latin text published in Gregory's brief. Thus was lost the spontaneity and freshness of expression of the Teresian constitutions of 1588. The latter, at the initiative of Cardinal Pierre de Bérulle, were adopted by the monasteries in France and Belgium.

Gracián in Disgrace

Gracián finished his visitation of the Carmo of Lisbon, May 14, 1591. His services were no longer required. On June 3, the vicar general ordered Fray Jerome to report within twenty-five days to the Discalced convent in Madrid. Exactly twenty-five days later Jerome walked in the door, "like a desperado without humility or resignation," Gregory of the Holy Angel disapprovingly recorded.

The king added two judges to the bench: Francis de Segovia, Jeronimite prior of Madrid, and Francis Muñoz, rector of the Dominican College of St. Thomas. The unanimous opinion of the judges was read on February 17, 1592. Fray Jerome Gracián was declared guilty of sixty proven charges, most of which he admitted, "of excess in his conduct with the nuns as well as excessive familiarity with one of them (Mary of St. Joseph?), laxity and defect in the regular observance of his profession and of other faults for which our Order was on the point of being destroyed." He had also sown discord in the Order and against his superiors. For these faults he had been repeatedly but vainly corrected and now he refused to accept sentencing and punishment. As incorrigible, he was accordingly expelled from the Order (*Constitutiones*, 1592, pt. 3, ch. 8, par. 6, no. 1).

Before communicating the sentence to Jerome, Gregory urged him to reconsider. By way of answer Gracián silently cast off his capuce. After sentencing, his monastic tonsure was removed and he was given the garb of a secular priest, "new and of very good quality," and sent on his way.

It was a shocking disgrace and an incredible end for the favorite of St. Teresa and collaborator with her in the establishment of the Discalced friars.

Subsequently, all Gracian's efforts to be reinstated and readmitted to the Reform proved in vain. However, current opinion is that Gracian was unjustly condemned, and he has been officially re-instated and readmitted into the Order of Discalced Carmelites.

The difficulty with this interpretation of the case is that it makes the first superiors of the Teresian reform appear to be unjust and revengeful individuals.

There is an explanation, however, which solves the problem and saves the goodwill of all concerned: Jerome lacked a contemplative vocation, at least as it is expressed in prayer, silence, and solitude – Teresa's ideal of the Carmelite charisma.

"They would have buried me in some convent," he later wrote, "where I would have had no other occupation but to confess an occasional *beata* and to follow the choir." Hardly a sentence St. John of the Cross would have written. Jerome should have persevered in his attraction to the Jesuits.

It is not known that Gracian had many supporters among the friars; his friends are mostly to be found among the nuns, the nobility, and the wealthy. His neglect of the austere requirements of the contemplative life and his dogged opposition to the superiors of the reform made it imperative that he should disappear from the scene.

The rest of Gracián's extraordinary career can be briefly summed up. He travelled to Rome to make a fruitless appeal to the pope to be reinstated. Later, he had the bad luck to be captured by Turkish pirates and spent two years in captivity in Tunis.

In the end, his old enemies, the Calced, took him back into their ranks. He comforted himself with the reflection that after all he was returning to the profession he had originally made to the prior general, that the Rule, which is the essence of the Order, was the same for both Orders, and that the constitutions of the Discalced had been altered in a way that made it impossible for him to observe them. "I clearly perceived,' he wrote, "that the perfection I so much desired did not consist only in external and corporal austerity." The twelve signs of charity St. Paul "names can be acquired in the habit of the Calced as well as in other Orders, though they do not go bare foot." He concludes: "Having returned to the Calced, I have experienced greater peace, and they have treated me with greater love, honor, and charity than when I was with the Discalced." Nevertheless, his heart remained in the reform founded by his beloved Mother Teresa.

Gracián spent his last years in Flanders, where his old patron, Archduke Albert, was now regent. He died in the Carmelite convent of Brussels, September 21, 1614.

St. John of the Cross

Little has been said in this narrative about St. John of the Cross for the simple reason that he hardly enters into the external course of events. "I cannot think why that saint is so unfortunate that no one remembers him," Teresa once exclaimed. Attempts to make St. John the "Father of the Reform" and "first Discalced Carmelite" are based on the dictates of the heart rather than on sober fact.

Not that he was insignificant. To say nothing of the influence of his writings, St. John was undoubtedly held in high esteem by his contemporaries for his role as one of the first members of the reform, his strength of character, and the authority of his unquestioned sanctity. He was several times elected prior and from the first functioned as definitor and consultor. He was very much a part of the institution Gracian so vehemently decried.

Apart from the more than thirty extant letters, mostly dating from the last years of the saint's life, primary sources contemporary to events are scarce. Knowledge of St. John's life rests mainly on early biographies and the processes of beatification and canonization. These yield a rich harvest of *fioretti*, which contain much information but have to be treated with greater caution than has generally been done.

There is little hard evidence for Doria's alleged "persecution" of St. John. On the other hand, John cannot be shown to have been particularly favorable to Gracián and his ideas. Fray John Evangelist, beloved disciple of the saint, recalled forty years later that St. John began to avoid the meetings of the *consulta* at the end of his term of office, when that body was discussing Gracián's case, not out of sympathy for Jerome, but because the affairs of the Order were being broadcast outside it. "Now that the prey has been flushed," John is supposed to have said, "we should run it to ground without help from anyone else." Among the friends whom Gracián claimed Doria favored unfairly were Augustine of the Kings and John of the Cross. John would also have qualified for Gracián's criticism that Doria accumulated offices on his favorites.

As to Gracián's ideas of Carmelite spirituality, there is a passage in the *Spiritual Canticle B* that would appear to be a shoe to fit his foot: "Let those, then, that are great actives, that think to girdle the world with their outward works and their preachings, take note that they would bring far more profit to the Church and be far more pleasing to God (apart from the good example which they would give of themselves) if they spent even half this time in abiding with God in prayer."

At the chapter of 1591, St. John retired from office as definitor and consulter. Gregory of the Holy Angel, elected to the *consulta* at the chapter, recalled in 1627 that John had been left without office so that he could not be elected commissary of the nuns. At least in one detail Gregory's memory played him false: the commissary did not have to be a superior. Moreover, John, like the other definitors and consultors, was not eligible for re-election to the same office (*Constitutiones*, 1590, ch. 10, n. 2).

In spite of his close relationship to Anne of Jesus, John of the Cross, as a member of the *consulta*, almost certainly did not approve of the surreptitious acquisition of the papal brief. Under its prioress, Mary of the Incarnation (Bracamonte), Segovia, where St. John was confessor, remained loyal to Doria.

One thing is certain. As John wrote to Anne of Jesus (Jimena), July 6, 1591, Doria wanted him to continue in charge of Segovia, but the saint wanted urgently to remain without office. Apparently, he managed to persuade the vicar general to leave him free.

Evidently by this date John's assignment to Mexico – a curious episode – had already been cancelled. The saint's first biographer, Joseph of Jesus and Mary Quiroga, states that the definitory on June 25, 1591, ordered John to Mexico with twelve companions. Two years after the appearance of Quiroga's book, John Evangelist in 1630 informed Jerome of St. Joseph that he could not recall any such decree. Nevertheless, when Jerome published his biography of St. John in 1641, he verbally quoted the book of acts, June 2 (not June 25), 1591, to the effect that the chapter accepted St. John's offer to go to Mexico with eleven others. John commissioned John of St. Anne, his companion, to gather volunteers in Andalusia. When John of St. Anne later reported to St. John the completion of his task, the latter answered after much delay, "that the expedition to the Indies had fallen through, and that he had gone to La Peñuela to embark for better Indies."

There is about all this something that does not ring true. For St. John of the Cross at this point in his life to embark on the apostolic life of a missionary flies in the face of all that is characteristic of him as a profound contemplative and dedicated solitary. If the chapter at which he was present assigned him to Mexico on June 2 (or June 25), why was he concerned on July 6 about being put in charge of Segovia? It is hardly likely that it was a question of a temporary assignment, as has been opined. For some reason, the decree may have been a dead letter from the start: Fray John Evangelist had never heard of it. If so, why had John of St. Anne proceeded with the rounding-up of volunteers? In fact, it is odd that the *consulta* did not itself name the friars who were to go to the Indies, as they had done in the case of Gracian's assignment to Mexico.

At the time of the chapter, St. John was a very sick man; he had only months to live. He was eventually assigned to the remote convent of La Peñuela in the province of Andalusia - not his favorite place on earth - where his old companion in the foundation of the reform, Anthony of Jesus, had been elected provincial. There he happily devoted himself to solitary prayer. But the saint of the cross was not to be left off so easily.

In Madrid, Gracián's trial was in progress. Fray Diego Evangelista, newly elected member of the *consulta* who was investigating Gracián's case, thought he had struck a scent leading to John of the Cross, like Gracián much involved in the direction of nuns. There followed the usual cross examinations and signed statements. The nuns complained that Diego distorted and falsified their testimony. Diego's zeal was misplaced and yielded no results. Besides, John was no Gracián; he did not rush to his own defense and would have accepted punishment without a word. "Son, let this not grieve you," the saint is supposed to have written to John of St. Anne, "for I am quite prepared to amend my ways in all wherein I have strayed and to be obedient, whatsoever penance they give me." It was a sad note on which to end his life.

History has not been kind to Diego Evangelista, but unlike ourselves he did not know he was dealing with a saint. He should be given credit for being sincere, if unwise. "He was young, of little prudence and choleric," a contemporary, Ferdinand of the Mother of God, remembered. In 1594, Diego was elected provincial of Andalusia, but died on the way to his province, aged 34.

St. John of the Cross died at Úbeda, December 14, 1591. It is an irony of history, not often noted, that both St. Teresa and St. John of the Cross lived and died as members of the old Carmel. The Discalced reform had not yet become a separate Order. This final step was not long in coming.

The Order of Discalced Carmelites

At the general chapter of Cremona, which convened on June 6, 1593, the Discalced Congregation was represented by its vicar general, Nicholas Doria, his two *socii* and three provincials with their *socii*. Doria's candidate for prior general, and Philip II's as well, was Michael de Carranza. Carranza, as a matter of fact, was present at the chapter by special mandate of Clement VIII. Carranza (d. 1607) was certainly a worthy candidate for the Order's highest office, and in the light of the tragic career of John Stephen Chizzola, who was actually elected, it is a pity that Philip II's wishes for once were not honored by the Order. One of the outstanding Carmelites of all Spain, Carranza earned the king's esteem for his zeal for reform. He would have suited the mood of Clement VIII. Anne of Jesus refers to Carranza as "a great friend of our Discalced friars."

The general chapter of Cremona of 1593 is mostly remembered for the division of the Order. John Baptist, procurator of the Discalced Congregation, proposed the complete independence of the Congregation from the Order, to be confirmed by the pope. By secret vote the chapter agreed on the condition *sine qua non* that the Discalced would not accept houses in places where the Order was already represented. On December 20, 1593, Clement VIII in his constitution, *Pastoralis officii*, confirmed the decree of the chapter and erected the Order of Discalced Carmelites under a preposite general.

Doria was nominated to this office until the first general chapter of the new Order, but on May 9, 1594, the Lion of Carmel passed to his reward. It is to be hoped that his bones in fact found rest in the tomb. With blind stubbornness he battled the most brilliant and imaginative spirits of the reform; this was one time the bull won the *corrida*.

Doria was skilled at manipulating the law and never transgressed anyone's legal rights. Had he, instead of Gracián, been in charge of the Discalced from the start, the separation of the reform from the Order might equally have taken place, but it would have been brought about with less hysterics.

In any case the rift in the unity of Carmel, inevitable under the circumstances, can only be regretted.

Chapter 5

Rossi and the Provinces Outside the Iberian Peninsula

On his return from the visitation of Spain, 1566-1567, John Baptist Rossi planned to visit the provinces of France. He crossed the border, passed through Narbonne and reached Montpellier on his way to Paris before he was persuaded to renounce his project. The roads were unsafe, the convents en route were in ruins or hardly habitable, and the French provinces could not defray the expenses of his journey. The latter consideration offered no difficulties, for the prior general had prudently come provided with money. Nevertheless, he turned his steps back to Italy, "not without tears."

The cause, of course, for the disrupted condition of the country was the state of war brought about by the religious differences between Catholicism and Calvinism. The first half of the century had witnessed great losses to the Order through the rise of Lutheranism and the schism of the Church in England. In the latter half of the century, similar havoc was wrought by Calvinism in the Carmelite provinces of France and the Low Countries. In these areas, Rossi's zeal for carrying out the reform of the Order was utterly frustrated.

The Religious Wars in France

The Massacre of Vassy, March 1, 1562, when members of the suite of the Duke of Guise killed a number of Huguenots meeting illegally for worship, touched off a series of eight wars (1562-1563, 1567, 1568-1570, 1572-1573, 1575-1576, 1577, 1580, 1585-1598). During these terrible years, marked by the assassination of the leaders of both sides and by wholesale massacre and pillage, churches and religious houses were special targets for rapine by soldiery and religious fanatics. One estimate places the number of priests killed at five thousand and thirty-five, of whom six hundred and seventy-seven were Dominicans, Carmelites and Augustinians. Material and moral damage was incalculable.

The effect of all this on the religious orders was predictable. "Almost all the religious orders have strayed from the strait and narrow path," the nuncio, Alexander de Medici, reported. "Their members are dissolute, evil-mannered, sordid, filthy, lazy. The Rule is nowhere observed except among the Carthusians." In the case of the Carmelites, as of other religious orders, with so many convents destroyed or damaged, religious were often forced to live for many years in temporary quarters, to the detriment of regular life. Convents were too poor to provide the necessities of life to its members, who were obliged to forage for themselves. The spirit of poverty and common life suffered accordingly.

The province of Narbonne at this time numbered twenty convents. Of these, thirteen were at one time or other pillaged or destroyed, their inmates driven away or slain. Gex, only two leagues from Geneva, fell to the Calvinists from Berne as early as 1536. During the war of 1562, the convents in Montpellier, Lyon, Nimes, Le Puy, Mende, Millau, Moulins, Chomérac, and Tournon fell into the hands of the Huguenots. Bagnols and Lunel succumbed to the troubles in 1567.

At Lunel, the friars were killed and their bodies thrown into a pit. At Gex, the friars were killed, the convent and church burned, the library destroyed. In 1561, the

Huguenots of Montpellier, taking advantage of the greater freedom granted them after the death of Francis II under the regency of Catherine de' Medici, pillaged the cathedral of St. Peter and other churches and convents in the city. More than two hundred priests and religious died that day. At the Carmelite church near St. Peter's, all the friars at hand were killed, the statues broken, altars overturned, the tombs profaned, and the church set on fire. Some of the friars managed to escape in secular clothing. At Nîmes, during the Michaelmas Massacre of 1567, the superiors of the four Mendicant Orders in the city were among seventy-two Catholics killed together with the bishop, Bernard d'Elbène. When the soldiers of Captain Merle overran Mende in 1586, a venerable old Carmelite, Jean de Joyeuse, was tortured in his private parts, but survived the ordeal to live another five years.

The province of Provence suffered less severely. Of its nineteen convents nine were affected by the wars: St. Hilaire, Orange, St. André d'Estoublon, Pinet, Beauvoir, Vienne, Le Luc, St. Marcellin, and Pont Beauvoisin. Dates of destruction are not ascertainable in every case.

At Le Luc, Somerset had five Carmelite friars dismembered alive.

Of the ten convents of Aquitaine, all except Limoges and Mortemart were damaged or destroyed: Montauban, St. Antonin, Lauzerte, La Rochefoucauld, La Châtre in the war of 1562; Aurillac in that of 1568-1570; Figeac in that of 1575-1576; Cahors in 1580.

The convent of St. Antonin was pillaged by the army of Duras in 1562. The friars returned after the peace, only to fall victims to the violence which broke out in 1572. The fanatical populace butchered the twelve inmates of the convent in the most brutal fashion. Some were burned alive after suffering horrible outrages, others were drowned in the river, the rest killed by the sword in the Royal Tower or thrown from a high window. The Huguenot army of Duras entered the city of Figeac, December 23-24, 1576. They pillaged the churches and convents and slew many religious and priests. Two Carmelites were buried up to their necks, and their tormentors pretended to play quoits with their heads, until death brought them merciful release.

Only Bondon, Pont-l'Abbé, and Angers remained relatively unscathed of the sixteen houses in the province of Touraine. La Rochelle, Vivonne, Aulnay, Loudun, Orléans, and Ploermel were leveled to the ground. Poitiers, Tours, and Hennebont were seriously damaged. Dol was transformed into a fortification. Nantes, Rennes, and St.-Pol-de-Léon issued from the troubles of the times in various stages of dilapidation.

Henry II had already ordered part of the Carmelite convent of La Rochelle torn down in the interests of the defense of the town. Giles Croseol, vicar of the convent, appealed in vain against the royal order (1556). When the Huguenots took over the town the religious of the city fled. During the first war (1562) the Carmelite convents and churches of Tours, Poitiers, Vivonne, Angers, and Orléans in various ways felt the effects of Huguenot occupation. Loudun and Aulnay were destroyed in 1568. At Aulnay the whole community with two exceptions was massacred. Some of the friars were shot, others thrown from a tower into the river. Among those killed was Stephen Jamois, doctor in theology and zealous preacher, who was on a visit from his native convent of La Rochelle. A certain Friar Jubert converted to Calvinism, later married and practiced the trade of carpenter. Friar

Foulon managed to escape alive. In the last war, that of the "Three Henrys," the convent of Rennes (1589) was partially, those of Hennebont (1590), and Ploermel (1592) completely razed to make way for fortifications. The Carmelite convent of Ploermel was architecturally the gem of the region of Morbihan. When Henry IV heard of its destruction, he is reported to have said that it would have been better to tear down the town.

A report in 1670 on the state of the province of Gascony by Mark of the Nativity lists only four of the seventeen houses as unharmed by the troubles of the previous century: Bordeaux, Dax, Aiguillon, Pavie, Bergerac, and Jonzac were destroyed in the first war (1562), Sauveterre in the second (1567). Most of the damage occurred during the third war (1568 1570) and the campaigns of Montgomery, leader of the army of Queen Joan of Navarre, when Agen, Condom, Tarbes, Lectoure, Trie, Rabastens, Langon, and Castillon were put to fire and the sword. Mark provides no information on the fate of Bayonne and Tonneins.

During his visit in 1604, the prior general, Henry Silvio, contrary to Mark's account reported Aiguillon still in a ruinous state as the result of the ravages of the heretics.

Less information is at present available on the provinces of Toulouse and Francia.

The province of Toulouse, the smallest in France, numbered seven houses: Castelnaudary, Castelsarrasin, Pamiers, Narbonne, Carcassonne, Béziers, and Montréal. Pamiers was already plundered by Calvinists in 1555, completely destroyed in 1608. Béziers was demolished in 1562, Montréal in 1594.

During most of the 16th century, Francia numbered eighteen convents, including seven in modern Belgium and the Netherlands. Montreuil was demolished during a siege in 1537. In 1562, the Carmelites of Caen were expelled from their convent, which with the church was sacked. They were able to return the following year. The Carmelite convent at Pont-Audemer was torn down for the sake of fortification.

The Congregation of Albi, which had been reported in a flourishing state by the prior general, Nicholas Audet, in 1531, received the *coup de grâce* in the second half of the century. The congregation consisted of four houses: Paris, Albi, Melun, and Toulouse. In 1568, the Carmelite church and convent in Albi were demolished for the defense of the city. The convent of Melun was set afire in 1590 by the army of Henry IV at the approach of the Duke of Parma, Alexander Farnese. During the battle between Catholics and Huguenots, May 12-16, 1562, for possession of the city of Toulouse, the Carmelite convent fortunately remained in Catholic hands.

As a result of all this destruction and the loss of libraries and archives involved, one need not look for much information on Carmel in France before the 16th century.

Rossi and the Order in France

Faced with conditions north of the Alps, Rossi did not despair of elevating the religious spirit of the Carmelites there. He did what he could through commissaries.

Writing from Avignon en route to Italy from Spain, Rossi on September 23, 1567, named Bartholomew Esprit his vicar for the visitation and reform of the French provinces. "It would have been a great pleasure," he writes, "to perform and carry out by our own efforts and presence the task we are now forced to impose on you; namely, to devote yourself to the reform of all the provinces and houses beyond these mountains, as we did in the provinces of Portugal and Spain." Esprit was especially to visit the *studium* of Paris and exorcise the differences between the Order and the Congregation of Albi. The same day, the prior general confirmed Esprit's election as provincial of Narbonne: "Above all, we enjoin on you the duty of introducing reform, first as our constitutions urge and require, then as contained in the enclosed summary of some statutes of our reform, which we regret not to have carried out personally and in due form."

The *studium* of Paris, administered by the decadent Congregation of Albi, was a special concern of the priors general, for the sad state into which it had fallen affected the provinces of the whole Order that wished to send students there. The general chapter of 1564, which had elected Rossi, had made a number of decrees for the benefit of the *studium* in the Place Maubert, but the outbreak of the second war of religion, occasioned by the unsuccessful attempt of the Huguenots to possess themselves of the royal family at Monceaux-en-Brie, prevented Esprit from visiting the Place Maubert.

In a letter to Esprit of March 1, 1569, Rossi noted that the Albi Carmelites had done nothing to implement the wishes of the general chapter. He appointed Esprit his commissary to bring this about. This time Esprit had no better luck, as the observants would not listen to him and asked him to leave.

In a letter of March 1, 1569, Rossi commissioned Esprit to reform the convent of Besançon in the province of Francia. He was also to provide a master of theology in "the college of the most illustrious family de Granvelle." This work of reform was being urged on the Carmelites by "most distinguished men, very deserving of our religion, highly placed in the church."

The one to do the urging was Cardinal Anthony Perrenot de Granvelle, former counsellor of Margaret of Parma, governess of the Netherlands, and archbishop of Mechelen, who from 1565 to 1579 served Philip II in Rome and Naples. Rossi speaks of him with the highest regard.

On December 19, 1569, Rossi wrote to the provincial of Francia, Adrian Tonnelier: "As I already indicated to your Reverend Paternity, the most illustrious Lord Cardinal Granvelle often complained to us of the shameful deeds (*flagitiis*) of several individuals, and when we heard of their infamy (*turpitudines*) from him, we were covered with the greatest shame. He threatened to reform that convent (Besançon) through an apostolic visitator, or to withdraw it entirely from our society."

Bartholomew Esprit, sent by Rossi to visitate Besançon, had found that Lector John L'Abbé, of Reims, "had set himself to destroy the convent, utterly besmirching his honor." Summoned to Besançon to give an account of his administration, L'Abbé had failed to appear.

Another black sheep of Besançon was Charles Godard, accused of "having perpetrated certain evil deeds (*scelera*) to the disgrace of our Order" at Châlon. Such actions were deplorable, "especially in these unhappy times, in which everyone should restrain himself within the bounds of the regular life." Godard pleaded innocent, and Rossi accepted his appeal for a hearing before his commissary, Bartholomew Esprit. Besançon was destined to become one of the first convents of the reform.

The prior general was also concerned with the improvement of conditions in the province of Provence. There, he had appointed Claude Bernard vicar provincial in an effort to establish peace in the province. Bernard in turn named Eleazar de la Porte as his assistant. When this appointment also met with resistance, Rossi on August, 10, 1570, confirmed it and enjoined obedience on all. The following year, Bernard was elected provincial. He is said to have been dedicated to solitude and contemplation. At his death, Esprit named John Renohard vicar until a provincial chapter could be convened, an appointment Rossi confirmed May 16, 1574. In his letter, the prior general expresses his frustration at the obstacles created by the religious troubles of the times.

The zealous prior general clung to his hope of penetrating the French border. A measure of his concern for the French provinces and the *studium* of Paris is to be found in his decision to convoke the next general chapter in Paris, the first time one had been held there since 1456. The date May 24, 1572, was designated for the convocation of the chapter, and Rossi set out well in advance, accompanied by several Italian provincials and their associates, but circumstances frustrated his effort. He contented himself with naming delegates for reform. This time Bartholomew Esprit was given Jacques Maistret as an associate.

On June 1, 1572, these officials published new statutes regulating the rights and obligations of the faculty and students at Paris. The new statutes, agreed to also by the superiors of Albi, do not seem to have brought improvement.

In 1573, or 1574, in a double-pronged maneuver, Rossi included Albi in his attack on the congregation of Mantua. He asked Gregory XIII to unite the houses of Albi to the provinces, or failing that, to return the *studium* of Paris to the Order. The prior general's request went unheard, at least as far as Albi was concerned. On June 8, 1574, the pope reappointed Esprit and Maistret as commissaries, this time including in their prerogatives the *studium* of Toulouse.

In 1571, Rossi sent Maistret to visitate the province of Toulouse. Like Esprit a member of the province of Narbonne, Maistret also acted as vicar over a group of convents in his province, possibly an aggregation of reformed houses.

Religious Troubles in the Netherlands

In modern Belgium, the province of Francia had houses in Bruges, Ypres, Ghent, Liège, Aalst (Alost), and Marche. In the modern Netherlands, it counted Flushing (Vlissingen). The convents in the Eastern half of Belgium – Brussels, Mechelen (Malines), Tienen (Tillemont), Enghien, Geraardsbergen (Grammont), Antwerp – belonged to the Lower German province, which also included Haarlem, Schoonhoven, Woudsend, Ylst, Alkmaar, Utrecht, Appingen, Ath in the Netherlands.

Lutheranism made little progress in the Low Countries. Although Anabaptism gained a certain number of adherents, it was Calvinism that eventually swept over the land with the violence and destruction that marked its path through France.

In the northern provinces of the Low Countries, where Protestantism prevailed, the Order lost all its houses.

When Lutheranism began to make strides in the Duchy of Oldenburg, the Carmelites were driven from their convent of Ath (Atens) in East Frisia (1522). This foundation had been in existence only since 1505. A second convent in East

Frisia at Appingen was lost in 1530, when Enno, Count of East Frisia, bestowed it on the Dominican nuns; these in turn were expelled by the Lutherans in 1545. The earliest known Carmelite victim of the religious differences was Adrian Martinszoon, who lost his life in Friesland in 1549.

In 1572, William van der Marck, Lord of Lumey, leader of the *watergeuzen*, who took Den Briel, seized the Zeeland town of Flushing. The troops, decked out in the vestments of plundered churches, carried out the usual vandalism. The Carmelite prior, Gregory Waters (Aquarius) and members of the community fled first to Middleburg, then to Bruges. One of the community, William Haze, became prior of Ypres, to be driven from that city also by the heretics. While preaching at Poperingen, he was wounded by *geuzen*. He survived the attack but died as a result shortly afterwards in 1578.

In the province of Holland, the Order had foundations in Alkmaar, Haarlem, and Schoonhoven. The Carmelites were driven from Alkmaar, when the city was taken by Fox in 1572. The last prior, Peter Winckel, later became regent of studies at Louvain (1582-1594). Haarlem felt the rage of the *beeldenstorm* of August, 1566. It subscribed to the Pacification of Ghent, 1577, but the following year, on the feast of Corpus Christi, May 26, during the procession of the sacrament, the troops under a French leader from Orange, invaded the religious houses and drove from the city the clergy and religious gathered in the cathedral of St. Bavon with their bishop, Govert of Mierlo. In his visitation book, the provincial, John Mayer, lists the last nine friars to be professed at Schoonhoven, which he visited for the last time in 1571. Lumey took the town in October, 1572, with the usual plunder and proscription of priests and religious. Some Carmelites seem to have lingered on until 1578, when the prior, Henry of Schoonhoven, fled to Utrecht.

Utrecht proved to be no safe haven. In 1529, the Carmelites of Utrecht had been assigned the parish of St. Nicholas in exchange for their original location needed for purposes of defense. In 1566, church and convent underwent the scourge of the *beeldenstorm*. In 1577, the troops of the States of Holland took Utrecht. The following year, clergy and religious were banished as adherents of Don Juan. Nevertheless, some religious lingered on in secular dress. After the Union of Utrecht, a petition of the magistrates in June 10, 1579, requested the banishment of, among others, two Brothers of Our Lady one from Antwerp and one from Schoonhoven – Andrew Hubertzoon, assistant pastor, and Henry of Schoonhoven. The pastor of St. Nicholas, Hubert Willemzoon, stayed on and died in Utrecht in 1585.

Woudsend and Ylst lay in West Frisia. The Carmelites were expelled from Woudsend in 1580. Ylst was sacked by the *geuzen* in 1572. Eight years later, the Carmelites were banished and their goods put up for public sale.

The nunnery at Haarlem shared the fate of the friary there. The monastery was completely destroyed in December, 1579. When Lumey took Rotterdam in 1572, the Carmelite nuns fled; their monastery was torn down in 1578.

Religious Troubles in Belgium

Although the Catholic faith prevailed in the southern provinces, all the houses of the Order there suffered the scourge of the religious wars. Besides the "wonder year" of 1566, the years 1572-1584, between the campaign of William of Orange and the final ascendancy of Alexander Farnese, were particularly difficult.

The year 1578 saw the destruction or alienation of the convents of Enghien, Geraardsbergen, Antwerp, Ghent, Bruges, and Ypres.

During the *beeldenstorm* of 1566, the Carmelite convent and church of Valenciennes were sacked. In the troubles of the ensuing years, several members of this convent lost their lives. In 1566, John Cordeau, zealous preacher and catechist, was killed in the marketplace by heretics. Amandus Clemens, indefatigable in teaching Christian doctrine and hearing confessions, was killed in 1567 on the bridge of Nero. During the plunder of the church in 1572, the sacristan, Peter Bonner, lost his life in an attempt to save the Blessed Sacrament and the statues in the church.

Orange took over Brussels in 1578, when Don Juan retired to Namen. The Carmelites were forced to share their church and convent with the Calvinists, but on April 23, 1581, they were shown the gates of the city. The prior was Lawrence Cuyper, a religious of high moral quality and author of spiritual writings. Cuyper was taken in chains to Bergen-op-Zoom. The Catholics of that town raised the money for his release. At the death of the provincial, Peter Wolf, Cuyper was appointed in his place by the prior general, John Baptist Caffardi, since it was impossible to hold a chapter (1581). In this capacity, Cuyper took up residence in Cologne. In 1589, while on a visitation at Geraardsbergen, he was again taken prisoner by Protestants. This time, the province raised the ransom.

At Ypres, several Carmelites lost their lives. Friar Basil, a deacon, was beheaded and his body exposed in a field. Henry Turch, a zealous preacher, wounded by a bullet and his arm broken, was left tied to a tree. He survived, but was later mortally wounded while on *terminus* at Nieuwpoort. A third victim, Giles Coussaert, was indefatigable in his efforts at preserving the faith and keeping the citizenry loyal to the Catholic king.

The provincial, Peter Wolf, zealous for reform, was killed in the marketplace of Mechelen on April 8, 1580, during one of the times the city changed hands between the warring parties. The same day, the sub-prior, Gerard de Hondt, was killed in the convent of the Carmelites.

Rossi and the Order in the Low Countries and Germany

Rossi's efforts at reform of the French provinces through delegates produced no noticeable results. He had slightly better luck in the Low Countries. There he was able to bring about the reform of the houses in Brabant.

In a letter written from Naples, August 22, 1571, to John Mayer, provincial of Lower Germany, he speaks of reports he would rather not believe: "We may not omit to mention that we have been informed that those responsible for reform and regular life have almost all turned their backs, indulging night and day in the delights of the table, in drinking, and (God forbid) in the lust of fornication, especially at Antwerp. From all this the name of our Reverend Master Provincial has not been wanting. Were this to be true, our heart would be seized with the greatest sorrow and sadness. At present, under inspiration from God we merely apply our finger to the ulcer (if there be any)."

John Mayer was provincial of Lower Germany from 1562 to 1576. The book of his annual visitations was still preserved in the convent of Antwerp in the 18th century. The Lower German province also counted nine houses in the Rhineland.

As in the case of his native Besançon, Cardinal Granvelle was again probably the source of information on conditions in Antwerp and the Lower German province. Upon his recommendation, Rossi, on December 5, 1572, appointed Jean de Cartigny his commissary and visitator of the Lower German province. The duty of religious, Rossi wrote, "is to draw the minds of the faithful to the practice of virtue, salutary discipline, and the service of God. Now, however, we have been given to understand by the testimony of trustworthy persons that our Carmelite religious of the Lower German province do exactly the opposite, especially in the territory subject to the diocese of Mechelen. Truly a very great distress seized our mind, for our Carmelite society there formerly rejoiced, exulted, and gloried in the regular life, holy customs and the untainted observance of our Rule." Rossi also gives his previous approval to an associate whom the cardinal is to appoint. The two commissaries are to reform especially the convents of Brussels and Antwerp.

In letters patent of July 16, 1573, Rossi states that he had named his commissaries and visitators Martin Cuyper, Carmelite suffragan bishop of Cambrai, and Master Jean de Cartigny. When Cuyper died, Rossi had issued new patents for Cartigny and asked Granvelle, "my most revered Lord and very deserving of the Carmelite society," to name a second commissary and visitator. But since the visitation tarried, Rossi gave his visitators a month to carry out their commission, after which period their faculties were declared lapsed, and he would appoint others, possibly from outside the Order. Meanwhile, he deposed Henry Willem from his office as prior of Brussels. He directed Peter Wolf, prior of Mechelen, to preside at a new election, to be conducted according to the recent norms of the Council of Trent. The choice of candidates was limited by Rossi to Stephen of Enghien and Josse Sproch. Wolf and the two visitators were also to carry out the reform of Antwerp.

The following September 12, Rossi named Peter Wolf and Philip Ertricius, prior of Tienen, commissaries and visitators of the Lower German province. Cartigny had asked to be relieved of his commission, because of advanced age and chronic arthritis (*arteticum morbum*).

In letters patent of October 3, Rossi describes the difficulty he had experienced in finding apt candidates for the role of commissary and visitator. When the bishops complained to him about the conduct of his religious, he did not know what course to take, because he knew of no observant friar. The ancient directive of the general chapters by which provincials were required to submit a report on their provinces had in the case of Flanders been completely neglected. Decisions were made without the knowledge of the prior general: candidates were promoted to theological degrees, the sites of the *studia* were changed, almost all matters were arranged without regard to law. To remedy all this, Rossi confirms and amplifies his previous patents to Wolf and Ertricius, instructing them to visit and reform all the houses of the Lower German province. All the religious are to be obliged to attend choir, day and night, and to offer Mass devoutly. The vice of ownership is to be totally abolished, so that not even the smell of it remains. The needs of the friars are to be seen to. Every effort is to be made to eliminate drunkenness, frequenting taverns, gluttony, theft, fornication. No quarter is to be given to those guilty of crimes or homosexuality (*nefario vitio*). Inside and outside the convents the greatest probity of life is to prevail, the cloister is to be maintained inviolate, silence uninterrupted, conduct incorrupt, garments rough. Studies at Cologne and Louvain are to be restored, if lapsed, and should be discontinued at Trier and Mainz, provided the first two colleges do not suffer thereby. Each house should have a well-instructed friar to teach grammar and the rudiments, elucidate moral *casus* and comment on the fourth book of *Sentences* and Walden, just published at Venice. In brief, Rossi provided his visitators with a short checklist of the chief points in his reform.

On December 28 Rossi issued further instructions to Wolf, who now had his complete confidence. The problem of the Lower German province he declares to be internal – a striking statement, considering the rampant warfare in those parts. "The province suffers from our own religious in such a way that the sources of evil can be openly seen in our own houses." Rossi was pleased to hear that Master Peter had begun to exercise the faculties granted him. In order to facilitate his visitator's task, even if he functions alone, Rossi forbids the provincial, John Mayer, from visiting the province meanwhile. He declares all the friars in all the convents subject to his visitator and his colleague. No chapter is to be celebrated until further notice. "Since nothing is so repugnant and opposed to the essence of our profession as the vice of property," Rossi especially emphasizes that all possessions, money, and deeds to property, are to be placed in the community chest, to be used, not for current expenses, but for the other needs of the friars, so that in the words of the council the religious have nothing superfluous, but lack nothing they need. If expedient, the burses of the province's nations of Holland and Brabant are to be applied to Louvain, those of the other two nations to Cologne. Finally Wolf is to visit and reform Aalst (province of Francia) in the diocese of Mechelen, of which Cardinal Granvelle complains.

The prior general's faith in Wolf was not misplaced. The latter was keenly aware of the contradiction to the Christian commitment of the lives of many of the clergy, whose scarlet sins he castigated with the vehemence of a Calvinist hedge-preacher. His sympathy with Baius designates him as a man of severe morals. He was in any case an exemplary religious, who lived in community and faithfully attended the divine office. He succeeded in reforming the Belgian houses of the Lower German province: Mechelen, Brussels, Antwerp, Tienen, Enghien, and Geraardsbergen.

Rossi sent Wolf a special invitation to the general chapter of 1575, in spite of the fact that the provincial and his *socii* had a right to be there, "for no injury is done to anyone, if new means are adopted in special cases and needs which arise." The general chapter which convened on May 22 directed that the above named reformed houses should remain under the authority of Wolf. The rest of the province was committed to the provincial. In separate patents dated June 12, Rossi appointed Wolf his vicar over Mechelen, which he took under his immediate jurisdiction.

The general chapter further ordered each of the provinces of France, Spain, and Italy to send two masters of theology to Upper and Lower Germany, to lecture in theology and philosophy, conduct cases of conscience and otherwise oversee the observance of the Rule and constitutions. This invasion of forty doctors, needless to say, never took place.

Wolf succeeded Mayer as provincial, 1576. Wolf's untimely death in the embattled marketplace of Mechelen (1580) removed a potent force for renewal in the province.

The Belgian houses under the jurisdiction of the province of Francia (Bruges,

Ypres, Ghent, Liège, Valenciennes, Aalst, Marche) regrettably had no Peter Wolf, though as mentioned above, Wolf had been commissioned to reform Aalst.

A letter of the prior general, October 12, 1573, reveals a disconcerting state of affairs in Ghent. Rossi laments the alienation by unauthorized persons of the property of the convent. Tin (*stannum*) receptacles had been sold, silver chalices, gilded ciboria, and a silver cross had been alienated, as well as fields, meadows, houses, incomes, and other goods pertaining to the community. "All that remains," the prior general cries, "is the unbridled licence of the religious of that convent, neglect of divine things, abandon of the cloister, meretricious living, cells open to prostitutes, free access for every sort of cupidity." The goods that were alienated belonged to the patrimony of Peter, those who committed this deed acted like thieves, are bound to restitution, and have fallen under excommunication. Rossi further declares them deprived of active and passive voice and perpetually ineligible for office and forbids any further alienation of the convent's goods. The goods already disposed of should be recovered.

At the provincial synod held at Louvain, May 19, 1574, the bishops of Ypres, Bruges, and Ghent requested of Rossi the services of Peter Wolf for the reform of the houses in Flanders, because the French visitators appeared too seldom to have much effect. Wolf does not seem to have been given this commission. Instead, the general chapter of the following year commanded the provincial of Francia, Simon Pignart, absent from the chapter, to reform his province, especially Besançon, Ghent, Liège, Ypres, Namur, and Bruges, as well as the nunneries dependent on the province. Alienation of community property was to be prohibited, alienated property restored, and guilty parties punished. At this time, Francia had in its territory the nunneries of Bruges, Liège, Huy, and Namur.

Of Ghent at least it is known that observance improved after the religious troubles abated. As prior, Leo DuLay, revered for his holy life, worked to renew the spiritual life of his community. Greatly dedicated to prayer, he actually died kneeling at his *prie-dieu* in the act of prayer, October 4, 1600. It was no accident that Ghent became the center of the reform of the province that was about to begin.

Rossi and the Upper German Province

During this period communications between Rome and the Upper German province were very tenuous. Between 1532 and 1609, the province sent a representative only to the general chapter of 1593. Provincials after George Raab were: Leonard Gamman (1558-1569), John Neff (1569-1573), Jacob Ochsenhardt (1573-1584), Sebastian Fluck (1584-1587), George Sattler (1587-1603). In the eleven houses of the province material and spiritual resources were low.

The definitory of the general chapter of 1564 confirmed Master Leonard Gamman as provincial, adding that it considered him "worthy of every laurel crown because of his perseverance amid so many dangers of the faith and controversies."

It was at the insistence of Pope Gregory XIII that the general chapter of 1575 was moved to do something about conditions in Upper Germany. The chapter urged John Mayer, provincial of Lower Germany, to visit the sister province as soon as possible, "to restore to holy reform the religious of all our convents of Upper Germany, so that they abstain from unbridled license inside and outside the convent, from an unbecoming way of life, and from all vice of ownership. They should eat in the refectory and take their meals moderately and in silence. The absurd habit of revelling and remaining a long time at table should be eliminated and utterly rejected. Let the regular life give off its good odor inside and outside the convent. Men of letters, modest and religious, should be given office. The definitors implore Father General to send religious of learning and good morals from the provinces of France, Italy, and Spain, as our Most Holy Lord, Pope Gregory XIII, and the most illustrious Lord Cardinals ordained and proposed to the prior general."

On June 13, 1575, Rossi provided Mayer with letters patent for his commission, adding as his assistant Peter Wolf, vicar general, in whom he had greater faith. The two are known to have visited at least Straubing. They do not seem to have visited Bamberg.

Monte Oliveto Revisited

Frustrated in his attempts to visit the Order north of the Alps. John Baptist Rossi spent the rest of his life in Italy, where he continued to work untiringly for the betterment of the Order. On his return from Spain, he lingered in the north of Italy from October 6, 1567, to May 30, 1568. He visited the provinces of Lombardy, Venice, Romagna, and Tuscany.

On October 19-21, 1567, Rossi resumed his visitation of the convent of Monte Oliveto, interrupted by his departure for Spain. The *scrutinium* of his visit, containing his interrogations of seventeen friars, is extant. It appears that the community observed a life of prayer, abstinence, and perfect poverty according to their profession. The care of the parish left nothing to be desired. Prior at the time was Jerome Brussato. A discordant note is struck by John Baptist Cella, whom the prior general transferred to a house in the province of Lombardy because he did not live according to the observance and had struck the prior. Likewise John Paul Centurioni on the testimony of practically all the members of the community greatly disturbed the peace. After a visit to the Inquisitor at Genoa, Rossi removed Centurioni to Cremona. The general suspected his orthodoxy because of certain indiscreet statements he had made. The inquisitor gave Centurioni a clean bill of health, and Rossi later permitted him to return to Monte Oliveto, provided the others would have him.

Some outstanding friars of Monte Oliveto around this time: Fra Celso da Serro in 1528 received permission to live as a hermit in a remote shrine. Andrew of St. Blaise (d. 1562) and Onofrio Mambrello (d. 1592) were remembered for their lives of penance and prayer. The Genoese nobleman, Angelo Castiglione, was a renowned preacher whose sermons have been published. He entered Monte Oliveto in 1525 and became prior in 1538. Twenty years later he transferred to the Mantuan Congregation. In the 18th century some letters of his to St. Charles Borromeo were still extant. Jerome Bersotto was skilled in ancient languages. Albert Oneto was a woodcarver.

Rossi in Italy

As he had done in the provinces of the Iberian peninsula, Rossi published a *Compendium constitutionum* (Venice, 1568) for the benefit of the Italian provinces. The prior general wished that "these exhortations of ours," "this compendium of reform" should be observed until an amended edition of Soreth's constitutions could be published. Actually, the *Compendium* is more than a dry pandect of laws.

Beginning with the statement that "the first and foremost interest" of the Carmelite "is to make every effort to remain day and night united in spirit to God the Father in prayer, contemplation and uninterrupted love," the little book resembles more a spiritual treatise, presenting the ideal Carmelite in every action of his daily life and in the fulfillment of the offices he may be called on to carry out in the community.

The device of the "deposit box" (*arca depositi*) is fully explained in the *Compendium*. The deposit box is to be kept in the chest with the three locks (*arca trium clavium*), which contained property deeds and other valuables of the community. Individual friars may deposit there whatever they acquire through preaching, lecturing, shriving, and other personal efforts, or through gifts from relatives and friends. If a friar is transferred to another convent, his money goes with him. Although these moneys belong to the community, they should be kept apart for the needs of the individuals who acquired them and should be surrendered on request without delay.

The *Compendium constitutionum* provides a clear picture of the financial administration of the convents and the practice of poverty. There are three kinds of goods: 1) stable, or certain goods: pastures, vineyards, gardens, houses, and rents accruing from these; 2) goods deriving from the free gift of the faithful: questing (begging tours), funerals, offerings, masses, and other religious services; 3) goods acquired by individual initiative: preaching, lectures, confessions, honest labor, gifts from friends and relatives. All three classes of goods belong to the community. Incomes from the first two are to be applied to common needs, such as grain, wine, oil, wood, salt, doctors' and barbers' fees, laundry, furniture, etc. The third class of goods is to be used to satisfy individual needs.

Rossi justified his device of the deposit box by the fact that the incomes of many communities were not sufficient to alleviate the needs of its members. Yet the poverty of the communities was more often than not induced by selfish concern and insensitivity to the common good. The deposit box was a need of the times and another halting step in the direction of true community living, but it did not exorcise the private way of life that characterizes conventuality.

As elsewhere, Rossi did not attempt to set up houses of perfect observance. He tried to elevate all to a certain level of religious perfection consistent with reality. He inculcated a spirit of recollection and prayer, of study, zeal for souls, and detachment from material things. Much of his effort went into making the friars look like religious, ordering beards to be shaved, birettas given up, fancy additions to the habit such as buttons, cuffs, etc., removed. Everywhere he proceeded against the vice of ownership, but he was content if the *depositum* was observed.

The three years from June 1568 to June 1571, as appears from the headings of his letters, the prior general remained in Rome.

The Loss of the Province of the Holy Land

Rossi experienced the sorrow of witnessing the extinction of the Order's most revered province at the hands of the enemy that pressed the other flank of the Church. In 1570-1571, during the reign of Selim II, the Turks took Cyprus from the Venetians and put an end to the Order's first province, the Holy Land. In 1550, Nicholas Audet, himself a Cypriot, reported the existence of two convents and three "places" in the province of the Holy Land, all on Cyprus. The two convents were in Famagusta and Nicosia. It is not likely that many Carmelites survived the siege of these two towns. During the fall of Nicosia (1570) there is a brief glimpse of the provincial attempting to persuade a group of peasants to make a stand against the enemy in the city square. This may have been Master Nicholas Robustus, named provincial by the general chapter of 1564 with the proviso that he be confirmed by the prior general after three years.

In his will, Nicholas Audet had left 2,000 *scudi* in the bank of the Foscareni for the convent of Famagusta and another 1,000 in the bank of the Delfini for Nicosia. On October 14, 1576, Pope Gregory XIII ordered these sums applied to the construction of Traspontina.

The general chapter of 1575 decreed that the province of the Holy Land, the most ancient in the Order and the first in precedence, should be revived on Crete or some other Venetian possession in the Near East. There should always be a provincial of the Holy Land, appointed by the prior general.

The General Chapter of Piacenza, 1575

After eleven years, Rossi finally managed to convene another general chapter at Piacenza, May 22, 1575. He had visited as many provinces as it was physically possible to reach and he was now in a position to prescribe measures for the improvement of the Order based on personal experience. The chapter published a great many decrees of reform.

"Since obedience is the root and foundation of our profession," the chapter prescribes the inviolable observance of the ordinances made by the forefathers which do not contravene the council.

"By apostolic authority, as founded in the apostolic letters of the Most Holy Father Gregory XIII, all fathers of the provinces and of the Mantuan and Albi Congregations are ordered to strive efficaciously and proceed toward all that pertains to the salvation of souls, the edification of the Christian people, and the praise of almighty God. By the same authority all are to observe the rules of our profession and salutary reform; most of all, Carmelites in all convents are to live without property and the use of property according to our Rule and the sacred Council of Trent; neither should they fail to carry out the reformation drawn up and promulgated for Italy." Those who love the regular life and reform are to be given office, "so that health may be diffused from the head to the members." The prior general will depose priors who oppose reform.

The houses of study on both sides of the Alps are to be properly administered, discreet religious, eager for learning, are to be placed in charge, students with talent should not be hindered from making progress in science.

All provincials are to reform the convents under their jurisdiction; if they fail in this, the prior general may remove them from office. Directives for visitation and other instructions are provided.

"The Reverend Definitors desire that all Carmelites be disposed to, faithful to, and retain in their inmost hearts the doctrine of the Roman, Catholic, Symbolic, and Apostolic Church, nor ever deviate from it. They should instruct other Christians in a Catholic manner and if occasion arises, even with danger to life and the shedding of blood, refute, trample under foot, overthrow, and totally root out all heresy." As shown above, by the grace of God there were not lacking Carmelites capable of giving this ultimate witness to their faith.

Rossi and the Mantuan Congregation

A remarkable feature of the general chapter was the unprecedented presence of representatives of the Mantuan Congregation. At this time, the Congregation numbered 42 houses scattered through northern and central Italy. Of these, 12 had been added since Bl. Baptist's death (1516): Mantua, Le Selve, Ferrara, Lucca, Brescia, Reggio Emilia, Parma, Bologna, Ripa d'Albino, San Felice, Modena, Trino, Novellara, Kevere, Bergamo, Genoa, Gorlago, Bariano, Rome, Sutri, Morrocco, Fermo, Camurana, Milano, Casal Monferrato, Florence, Viconovo, Sora, Pistoia, Acquapendente, Frassino (1517), San Giacomo a Zibito (1517), Viterbo (1517), Venice (1518), Castellina (1521), Collalto (San Salvatore 1524), Sali (1526), Soncino (1530), Anghiari (1548), Macerata (15661, Rai (1567), Monterubiano (1573). The Congregation also had monasteries of nuns at Parma, Reggio Emilia, Brescia, Ferrara, Mantua, Trino, Florence, Sutri, Vinovo, Albino, and Bologna. The reforming general could not overlook this significant body of houses in his determination to renew Carmelite life in Italy.

The struggle to establish hegemony over the Mantuan Congregation by Rossi's predecessor, Nicholas Audet, had ended in the *Concordia*, or agreement of 1538, which recognized the prior general as head of the whole Order and granted him the right to visitate the Congregation, but under such restrictions that Audet never bothered to act out the charade.

After his election in 1564, when requesting faculties as apostolic visitator of the Order, Rossi attempted to obtain confirmation of the brief of Clement VII, *Romanus pontifex*, 1532, revoking the privileges of the Congregation. The cardinal protector of the Order, St. Charles Borromeo, did not think it wise to raise the specific issue of the Congregation's privileges, and when Rossi's faculties appeared, they spoke of his right to visitate the Congregations of Albi and Mantua only in general terms.

Now, after completing to the best of his ability the task of reforming the provinces of the Order and before convening a general chapter, Rossi once again attempted to normalize the relations between the Order and the Congregations of Albi and Mantua, especially the latter.

In an appeal to Pope Gregory XIII, 1573-1574, the prior general complained of the lack of obedience of these two groups and of the unrest they caused. Rossi's suggestions in regard to Albi have already been considered. As to Mantua, he appeals against the concordat made by the procurators of the Order and the Congregation, which was never accepted by the Order. The Congregation defended the *Concordia*, claiming it had never been challenged and therefore, if for no other reason, had force by prescription.

When Gregory XIII's brief *Quaecumque* appeared on November 3, 1574, it was a compromise. The privileges of the Congregation were not revoked, but the *Concordia* was, and the relations between the two groups of Carmelites were clearly defined under twelve headings. The election of the vicar general was to be confirmed by the prior general within three months, otherwise the vicar was to be considered apostolically confirmed. Chapters of the Congregation should not be called chapters of the Order or of the Observance, nor should vicars general be called vicars general of the Order but of the Congregation. The prior general could preside at the chapters of the Congregation. The vicar general and the Congregation, like the provinces, were subject to the prior general, with due regard for the privileges of Eugene IV. Profession was to be made to the prior general. The vicar general and a *socius* were obliged to attend the general chapters of the Order and had active and passive voice. The vicar general and members of the Congregation were to observe the general statutes of the Order and the decrees of the general chapters concerning the state of life, regular observance, and uniformity of divine cult insofar as allowed by the constitutions of the Congregation and its stricter customs. The prior general should not relax the stricter laws and laudable customs of the Congregation. He could personally visitate the houses of the Congregation after he had celebrated his first general chapter and thereafter every four years. In more serious matters, he should consult prudent members of the Congregation. He might delegate the administration of punishment, which should remain within the convent. On visitation, which should not last longer than a year, he could take along four or five persons and their mounts. He could not transfer members of the Congregation or introduce those of the provinces. The prior general was to be solemnly received on visitation. He could not reserve a room to himself in any house of the Congregation.

Gregory's *motu proprio* put an end to the diplomatic impasse caused by the dubious validity of the *Concordia* and clearly defined the relationship of the Order and the Congregation. Nevertheless, it did not bring peace. The independence of the Congregation was impossible to reconcile with its duty to obey the prior general and the general laws of the Order.

The prior general lost no time in availing himself of the powers granted to him by the pope. He presided at the chapter of the Congregation which met at Bologna, May 2, 1575, and elected Lucrezio Tiraboschi vicar general, who was duly confirmed by Rossi. The chapter decreed that those with academic degrees were obliged to attend choir, except when actually lecturing. The vicar general should not license anyone to preach who had not completed the course *"in litteris speculativis."*

After the general chapter at Piacenza Rossi set out to visitate the Congregation. As was his custom in visiting the provinces, he published *Regulae et institutiones* for the Congregation. These add no obligations beyond those binding on the Order in general; in fact, reminding the Mantuans that the pope obliged them to follow the general legislation of the Order and the decrees of the general chapters, Rossi tried particularly to produce uniformity of usage among all Carmelites in Italy.

After the chapter of the Congregation in 1577 Rossi lived only another year. A fall from his mule in 1576, when he was 68 years old, certainly was not calculated to prolong his life.

Chapter 6

Caffardi and Chizzola: an Interlude

Under the next two priors general there is a slackening in the pace of reform set by Audet and Rossi. John Baptist Caffardi indeed continued to apply the norms devised by Rossi but with less vigor. But if Caffardi did not greatly stir the waters, his term of office is marked by a number of positive achievements characteristic of a time of peace. John Stephen Chizzola had the opportunity of riding the crest of the reforming zeal of Pope Clement VIII to introduce the perfect common life into the Order, but his brief life ended in tragedy.

John Baptist Caffardi (d. 1592) was born at Civitella and entered the Order in Siena. He acquired the doctorate at the university of Padua and taught in the Order's *studia* in Florence, Pisa, Siena, and at the Sapienza in Rome. In 1572, he became provincial of Tuscany. In 1578, Pope Gregory XIII named him vicar general. The general chapter of 1580 chose him as prior general.

More than four hundred white-robed friars, walking modestly in pairs, proceeded to the Vatican to receive the blessing of Pope Gregory XIII and to hear his exhortation on behalf of study and the election of wise superiors.

The definitors of the chapter ordered the appointment of vicars general for reform in Spain, France, and other provinces beyond the Alps, "because there are many who indulge their senses and conduct their lives not according to our laws but according to their own ways of thinking."

Likewise, procurators general to the courts of Spain and France were instituted, "who are to perform the same function as the procurator general in the Roman curia."

The Constitutions of 1586

An important decree of the chapter was that requiring a new edition of the constitutions conforming to the Council of Trent. Caffardi's constitutions were printed in Rome by Francis Zanetti, 1586. The Order's legislation was still that of Soreth revised by Audet (1524), supplemented by the latter's *Isagogicon* and the *Caput unicum* of the general chapter of Venice, 1524. The slender, elegantly printed volume produced by Caffardi incorporates these sources into one body of laws, further updated according to Rossi's reform and the decrees of the Council of Trent. The elimination of most of the abbreviations, relics of the age before printing, makes the book easy to read and gives it a modern appearance. The long paragraphs of the Soreth-Audet edition are subdivided, the many typographical errors mostly eliminated.

Michael de Carranza, vicar general for Spain and Portugal, at Caffardi's behest later published another edition of the constitutions (Valencia, apud Petrum Patricium, 1590).

In Caffardi's as in Audet's constitutions, Soreth's durable legislation lives on in revised form. The five-fold classification of the laws is retained, though in Caffardi's edition part four (punishments) and five (elections) of Soreth's change places. The new legislation is created by accretion; regulations are multiplied, reflecting the exteriorization of life. The chapter on the divine office (pt. 1, ch. 3) is expanded with regulations from the *Isagogicon* of Audet and the Tridentine legislation. All priests are obliged to offer Mass (n. 30) and recite the canonical hours daily (n. 34). The Blessed Sacrament must be changed weekly and preserved in gold-plated silver vessels (n. 32).

References to reformed houses no longer appear in these constitutions. The entire Order is considered to be reduced to observance. From the *Isagogicon* a chapter is added on the proper conduct of the brethren outside the convent (pt. 1, ch. 7). No one may leave the convent more than twice a week and then with a companion (n. 2) and wearing the white mantle of the Order (n. 3). The friars are not to visit monasteries of nuns (n. 5), tarry in shops and offices, or be too familiar with seculars (nn. 8-9). The same *Isagogicon* supplies additional material for the chapter on the instruction of novices (pt. 1, ch. 14, nn. 5-11) and a new chapter on professed students (pt. 1, n. 15). The professed are to remain under training and segregation in charge of a master of professed until the subdiaconate (n. 2) and are to be instructed daily in letters and virtue. (Formation and studies will be considered below.)

With regard to the administration of the Order, new chapters are added on the offices of vicar general and commissary general, which had recently come into frequent use (pt. 2, ch. 4). Another new chapter is devoted to the solemn reception of the prior general (pt. 2, ch. 7).

"Superiors may permit the use of mobile goods in such a way that in the appurtenances of the religious nothing is superfluous and nothing that is necessary is wanting. Religious should realize that these appurtenances are not their own, but are provided for their use from the goods of the community" (pt. 3, ch. 11, no. 5). The Tridentine principle, already enunciated in the general chapter of 1564, was realized in fact by the deposit box, a device, as we have seen, by which individuals still had exclusive use of money acquired by their own initiative (n. 3). There is no longer talk, as in Soreth's constitutions, of acquiring or constructing one's own cell. The cells of the brethren are to be simply furnished in keeping with the vow of poverty (pt. 1, ch. 6, n. 2).

Another new and important feature is the special chapter on nuns, incongruously inserted at the end of the section on misdemeanors (pt. 3, ch. 12). In part, it reflects the legislation of the Mantuan Congregation; noteworthy is the directive concerning an hour's meditation in common, taken literally from this source (n. 6).

Provincial chapters are to be held every three years (instead of annually) on the third Sunday after Easter (pt. 4, ch. 10, n. 1). Provincials may not be reelected for six years (pt. 4, ch. 15, n. 3). The general chapter of 1580 had specified a lapse of ten years.

Part 5, on the punishment of misdemeanors, is greatly expanded. The most particular actions of daily life are minutely cataloged, and to each is assigned a penance according as they are to be avoided or performed. Three new chapters are added concerning deposition, suspension, and inability for office (ch. 8-10); four others on apostates, rebels, conspirators, and proprietors (ch. 12-15). Significantly, heresy is singled out for special legislation (pt. 3, ch. 7, nn. 1-3).

Caffardi's reform of the liturgy will be discussed in another context.

The Suppression of the Congregation of Albi

The reform of Albi had greatly declined since the days of Nicholas Audet, when it constituted a dedicated and learned elite, hopeful of raising the level of religious life in the French provinces through control of the general *studium* of the Order in the Place Maubert in Paris. Before the general chapter of 1580, the vicar general of the Congregation, Eloi Charron, let it be known that he could not attend, because he could not afford the expense of the journey. The Congregation numbered only three houses, all in dire financial straits. Charron requested that the chapter name minor officials for Paris, since there was no one able for these functions in the community itself. A visitation ordered by Caffardi while he was still vicar general confirmed the sad state of affairs in the Place Maubert. Caffardi's delegates, Peter Dumas, regent of Paris, and Arnold Richard, prior of Moulins, listened to complaints of the students regarding the observants in charge of the college. According to the students, the Albi Carmelites failed to attend choir, wasted their time in gaming, frequenting taverns, and gossiping. Funds were wasted or sequestered, the fabric of the buildings was neglected, the students were mistreated and not consulted about the charges they were required to pay.

Dumas and Richard attended the general chapter of 1580, which appointed Didier Buffet Caffardi's vicar for the French provinces and the *studium* of Paris. Henceforward, all the priests in the college (and not only the members of the Albi Congregation) were to have a vote in the affairs of the college, except in the election of the prior, who was to be appointed by the prior general. Caffardi named Arnold Richard prior. Peter Dumas was confirmed in the office of regent of studies. Choice of officials in the Place Maubert was not to be limited to members of the community; all the convents of France could supply candidates.

In spite of the intervention of the general chapter in the affairs of the Paris *studium*, the Albi Carmelites in February, 1581, elected a new prior, John Commenault, former vicar of the Congregation. In July, Didier Buffet, armed with a warrant from the Parliament of Paris, carried out a visitation of the Place Maubert. His report to the nuncio at Paris, John Baptist Castelli, dated August 2, 1581, reveals that the congregation counted only twelve friars in the community; of these, only two, Eloi Charron, master, and Guy Le Roux, bachelor, had degrees. The rest were not able to hold offices of responsibility or to teach in a house of study. The divine services and the Rule were neglected, finances maladministered, the fabric of the college left in disrepair.

Charron was the only member of the Congregation willing to yield in the matter of its prerogatives. On August 4, 1581, he wrote to the prior general, urging that capable personnel be sent from the provinces; three days later he informed the Parliament that the prior and subprior wanted to resign on account of illness, and that it would be desirable, at least temporarily, to grant active and passive voice to the bachelors of the provinces. When two councilors of the Parliament, James Viole and Theobald Leseur, presented themselves on September 28 to look into the matter, Charron changed his mind about the vote; Commenault also showed no inclination to resign. The councilors decided that the case of the bachelors' vote should be written up and presented to Rome for a decision.

Gregory XIII sent the dossier of documents back to Paris to be examined by the Privy Council (*Conseil d'Etat*). On May 8, 1583, Peter d'Epinac, archbishop of Lyon, in charge of the case, made his report to the Council, which recommended to the king that the pope be asked to put an end to the quarrels of the Carmelites. The answer was the *Pastoralis officii* of Gregory XIII, May 1, 1584, which suppressed the Congregation and restored its convents to the provinces of the Order. The Congregation consists of only three houses, the pope writes, with hardly thirty members, "of whom many are youths ignorant of letters, inclined to crime, inept for the duties of religious life." Paris was placed under the immediate jurisdiction of the general. All priests professed four years who resided in the college enjoyed the right to vote, the community, presided over by the vicar general or a delegate from Rome, was to elect the prior, who in turn was to be confirmed by the prior general. Other functionaries of the college could be chosen from any convent in France.

On July 29, 1584, Caffardi confirmed Didier Buffet in his office of vicar general for France and made Peter Dumas his assistant. On October 27, these two officials convoked the community of the Place Maubert in the refectory and received the submission of the Congregation of Albi to the papal brief. In January, 1585, Buffet published new statutes for the *studium* of Paris.

In spite of this edifying gesture, the Albi Congregation was far from giving up the ghost. As though nothing had happened, Commenault continued to act as prior of Paris. On February 12, 1585, Buffet appealed to the Parliament for the removal of Commenault, but he made himself a *persona non grata* with that august body by ignoring their order to return documents he had taken from the Observants. On August 23, the Parliament ordered the Congregation of Albi to continue.

On June 3, 1586, Caffardi appointed Anthony Brelucque procurator for the Order at the French court with the special commission of enforcing the suppression of the Congregation of Albi. On August 7, Brelucque, supported by the new nuncio, Fabio Frangipani, presented his petition to the council, which replied on January 22, 1587, proposing that before dissolving the Congregation of Albi the pope be requested to institute a reform by the bishops of the whole Order in France. In a letter to the pope, Henry III added his authority to the council's plea for a reform of the French Carmel. Sixtus V, however, let the king know that he wanted his predecessor's letter put into effect. Consequently, on instruction from the council Cardinal Philip de Lenoncourt and Renaud de Beaune, archbishop of Bourges, accompanied by the nuncio, Francis Morosini, on August 10, visited the Place Maubert. John Commenault resigned as prior. Anastasius Cochelet, of the convent of Reims, was elected in his place. Thus, the Order reaffirmed its authority in the *studium* of Paris, but the Congregation of Albi continued to exist.

During his term of office, Caffardi visited the provinces outside Italy through commissaries. His visitors for Spain were Angel Salazar and Jerome Hurtado. For France, he appointed John Stephen Chizzola and Jerome Aleotto, August 2, 1588. They were to visit all the French provinces to bring about the reform requested by the privy council of the realm and obtain information on the Order in England, Ireland, Scotland, the Low Countries, Germany, and Poland. No sooner had the news gotten out than Guy Le Roux, procurator of the Congregation, paid a visit to Henry III at Blois and secured royal protection for the Congregation (October 10). However, the Roman visitor with Anthony Brelucque set the king right on the matter of the Congregation. On November 10, Henry summoned Le Roux before the privy council. The latter, on January 27, 1589, ordered Albi united to the Order.

The war between the League and Henry III made it impossible for Chizzola and

Aleotto to carry out the visitation of the provinces. They contented themselves with drawing up "constitutions and articles for the reformation and general reunion of all the convents of France" (Paris, Jean Le Blanc, 1590), which they published in the refectory of the college in the Place Maubert, April 22, 1589. In the visitation that followed, Commenault and Le Roux were exiled from Paris and the provinces of Francia, Toulouse, and Aquitaine (where the Congregation had houses). Another member of the Congregation, Simon Fileul, was condemned to a year's imprisonment. Thereupon, the two visitors, in view of the uncertainty of the times, returned to Rome.

After the departure of the Roman visitors, Commenault and Le Roux reappeared in Paris to appeal again to Parliament. These were the turbulent days of the march on Paris of Henry III and Henry of Navarre, of the assassination of the king by the Dominican James Clement, and the retirement of Navarre into Normandy. The appeal of the Congregation, made on September 9, 1598, was rejected, and the constitutions of Chizzola and Aleotto were ordered registered. Another blow to the Congregation was the loss of the convent of Melun, torn down on September 20, 1590, in the course of the fortification of the town against the threat of attack by the Spaniards under the Duke of Parma, Alexander Farnese.

At the accession of Henry IV, the Albi Congregation returned to power. On April, 27, 1594, the Parliament, purged of *ligueurs*, issued a warrant for the election of Simon Fileul as prior of the Place Maubert to replace Anastasius Cochelet, "who," it was noted, "is not of the said Congregation." The new vicar general for the French provinces, Noel de Sens, was unable to dislodge him. In 1597, Fileul was succeeded by Charles Dubois, also of the Congregation.

The Congregation of Albi now consisted of a few friars in possession of the *studium* of Paris; the other convents of the reform together with their members had been absorbed into the provinces of the Order. Incredibly, at this eleventh hour, Guy Le Roux journeyed to Italy and on June 20, 1598, succeeded in obtaining from Clement VIII, in temporary residence at Ferrara, a new confirmation of the Congregation. Returning to Paris, Le Roux turned out of doors the vicar general for the French provinces, William Champcherieux. On July 1, 1599, the pope revoked his approval of the previous year, which Le Roux, "led only by the spirit of ambition and suppressing the truth of the matter, had otherwise surreptitiously extorted." After another long legal battle, this document was accepted by the Parliament, July 20, 1602. On October 23, the new prior general, Henry Silvio, on visit to the provinces of France, arrived at the Place Maubert. At the end of his visit, he gave the college a new prior in the person of Edmund Matherot of the province of Narbonne; as subprior and councilors he appointed former members of the Congregation.

Thus, after a death struggle lasting a score of years, the Congregation of Albi was finally laid to rest. Its energetic resistance to suppression, favored by the circumstances of the times as well as by the fact that former members of the reform went on to fill posts of responsibility in the provinces, suggest that the Congregation may not have been as decadent as alleged in the brief of Gregory XIII of 1584. The reluctance of the Parliament to dissolve the reform, if something better were not forthcoming, may indicate that at least the friars of the observance were no worse than those of the provinces. The decline of the Congregation may be attributed to two causes: it concentrated its principal energies on the reform of the Place Maubert, like all international *studia* with their huge and heterogenous communities, a hard nut to crack. Secondly, the religious wars of France effectively checked the progress of reform after its first expansion.

Caffardi in Italy

Caffardi did not leave Italy and was content to urge observance at the level of existing norms without striving for a more perfect common life.

On December 26, 1578, while yet vicar general, he sent a circular letter to the Italian provincials. The divine cult is to be carried out with due reverence. There should be frequent confession and chapter of faults. Woolen shirts (*camiciae*) should be worn under the habit. No one should leave the convent without a companion and the permission of the prior. Only confessors or deputies of the provincial may visit nunneries of any kind. On visitation, provincials should diligently inquire into the matter of possessions, and all should be obliged to reveal what they possess. Any undeclared goods discovered are to be seized and applied to the construction of the curial convent of Traspontina.

In 1579, still vicar general, Caffardi toured most of the Italian provinces, presiding at their chapters. He drew up "constitutions made in his solemn visitation of the provinces" with chapters on the choir, sacristy, clothing, fasting, care of the sick, the refectory, shaving, birettas and sandals, silence, modesty, and houses of study.

In 1581, he convened the chapter of the province of Naples.

The following year, he visited the Mantuan Congregation. The visit passed without incident and seems to have been in every respect a success. He published the brief *Decreta* (Florentiae, F. Tosi, 1582), treating the divine office, common life and clothing, proper conduct inside and outside the convent, the spiritual care of the nuns. For a reasonable cause, Caffardi allows Matins to be recited later, provided they are finished by dawn. He also permits graduates to wear birettas (forbidden by Rossi). Perpetual silence is to be observed in the refectory. A half hour meditation is to be made twice a day, "and we wish that the novices especially be instructed in this manner of prayer." A number of decrees concern the novices. Finally, the prior general orders the constitutions of the Congregation to be revised according to the Council of Trent and urges all to harmony and peace. He had been instrumental in mediating several quarrels within the Congregation.

Caffardi presided at the chapters of the Congregation in 1582 and 1584. At the latter, the term of office of the vicar general was changed from two to three years. Between 1596 and 1670, the two-year term was again in practice.

In 1587, Caffardi presided at the chapters of Romandiola and Tuscany, the next year, at that of Naples. This seems to have been the extent of his activity as visitator.

John Stephen Chizzola

At the death of Caffardi in 1592, Pope Clement VIII on April 8, appointed John Stephen Chizzola vicar general of the Order, at the time procurator general. Chizzola was born at Riparoli and entered the Order in Cremona. A brother, John Peter (d. 1593), was a member of the Mantuan Congregation. Lector at Pavia in 1579, John Stephen took part in the disputations at the general chapter of 1580.

He was provincial of the Roman province in 1588, when he accompanied Caffardi on a visit to the province of Naples. On August 2, 1588, Caffardi appointed him together with Jerome Aleotto commissary and visitor of France. On February 14, 1591, Caffardi made him procurator of the Order. At the same time, he taught at the Sapienza in Rome. Shortly after being made vicar general, Chizzola left Rome to visit Sicily.

When he made Chizzola vicar general of the Order, Ippolito Aldobrandini himself had only recently, on January 30, become Clement VIII. From the outset, he made one of the goals of his pontificate the reform of religious orders, convinced that "from them depends the welfare and reform of all Christianity." Into this effort, the pope poured all the energy of his vigorous nature. He was determined once and for all to make the religious orders live up to their commitments. His legislation became the foundation of modern religious life as it was lived until the Second Vatican Council. Clement's decrees as proclaimed by the priors general became the *magna carta* of the 17th century reform movement which finally introduced into the Order true common life and a return to the contemplative ideal of the Order. Chizzola was given the opportunity to become the instrument of this renewal, but he failed. It remained for his successor to carry out this historic task.

Clement VIII and the Reform of the Orders

For Clement to want a thing done was to do it himself. His notorious reluctance to share responsibility is nowhere better illustrated than in his reform of religious. In spite of his many preoccupations as pope and of recurring attacks of gout, he personally undertook the visitation of churches and religious houses of Rome as the first step in a program for the universal reform of religious. On March 16, 1592, he held a meeting of all superiors general in the house of Cardinal Aldobrandini, at which with harsh words he made known his determination to suppress small houses not able to support twelve religious and to visit infidelity to religious obligations with the same rigor he had inflicted on the notorious bandit, Mark di Sciarra. The prior general of the Carmelites, John Baptist Caffardi, who was soon to die at Siena on April 3, was probably not present at this meeting, but the Order would have been represented by its procurator, John Stephen Chizzola.

On March 21, the pope issued a decree forbidding religious to procure academic degrees or dignities through influence and on April 1, he commanded the execution of his ban on small convents. These measures were only later applied to the Carmelite Order. On December 1, the decree for the suppression of small houses was conceded to the Order at Chizzola's own request. On May 21, 1593, Clement's *motu proprio* forbade the obtaining of degrees and privileges through influential persons outside the Order. On May 29, he forbade under severe penalties the removal of books from Carmelite libraries. It is not clear what provoked this prohibition, but it was to assume drastic significance for Chizzola later on. Equally decisive for Chizzola's fate was Clement's prohibition to religious, on December 26, 1592, to confer gifts of any sort.

Meanwhile, on June 8, 1592, Clement announced his intention to carry out a personal visitation of the churches and religious houses of Rome, since it was proper that in the matter of reform the see of Peter should set the example. On June 14, he fittingly began the visitation of the churches with St. John Lateran, then followed Mary Major's and St. Peter's.

On August 7, it was the turn of religious, when he visited the Conventual Franciscans and their church and convent of the Twelve Apostles. "The pontiff spoke in a sharper manner than ever before," a commentator notes, "but there were those who said he could not have found sufficiently sharp and harsh words." The pope followed the same procedure in all his visitations. First, he inspected the altars and chapels of the church. Then he gathered the community in the sacristy or some other suitable place and in severest terms exhorted all to reform. After Mass, he visited the convent, cell by cell, eliminating anything contrary to religious poverty. Food went back to the kitchen, money to the common chest, jewels and other valuables to hospitals and asylums, secular books to the flames. Generally, windows opening up on the street were ordered walled up, balconies torn down. Any religious from other houses found in Rome without reason were sent packing. At the end of his visit, the pope united the community and promulgated provisional decrees of reform. This process sometimes could not be accomplished in one visit, and the pope would return another day, often without warning.

On September 17, the pope again convened the generals and procurators. "We have visited a few places," he told them, "and we have encountered such great misdeeds and enormities and, with regard to the care of nuns, such grave exorbitances and excesses that Turks would speak of them with less shame - matters about which we cannot speak calmly." After noting that he had observed very little improvement since he began his visits, he unceremoniously ordered his hearers to implement his measures for reform without further ado. "In no manner will we rest in this matter nor will we suffer the church of God to live with religious orders so perverted and corrupt. It is not up to you to make excuses but to act." Superiors were to prepare separate lists of exemplary and incorrigible subjects and were to delegate three or four large convents in each province where religious observance could be perfectly maintained. A contemporary report concludes, "He protested before the superiors, `I will require the blood of your brothers from your hands.' The pope left without another word, and the generals and procurators withdrew from the place without uttering a word in reply, astonished and lost in thought." Chizzola would have been present at this meeting as vicar general of the Carmelites; he should have taken the pope's words to heart.

On October 26, Clement unexpectedly visited the Servites of San Marcello. His opening sermon was one of the most severe he ever gave. "If we had been told that it was difficult to persuade assassins of the street and men wrapped up and submerged in the world to life in a good and Christian fashion, it would have been difficult to believe; but that it would prove difficult and almost impossible so to persuade religious persons, who besides what they have renounced in baptism have also renounced their own wills by their profession, we confess we would have found most difficult to believe." He accused the friars of very serious shortcomings and offered them the choice of voluntarily improving their lives or being forced to do so.

Clement continued his visits to the religious houses of Rome until early in 1600 and indeed never entirely abandoned his practice of dropping in on them, much to the discomfiture of their inmates.

Eventually, Clement's famous "general decrees," *Nullus omnino*, for the reform of religious, June 25, 1599, proved to be almost identical with the decrees he had first formulated for the Conventual Franciscans of the Twelve Apostles, the Servites of San Marcello and other convents of Rome.

The general decrees oblige all, including the superior general, to attend choir regularly. Exceptions are: superiors when their duties actually require their presence elsewhere, lecturers and preachers on the days they are engaged in their functions, the sick and those legitimately excused for purposes of study. In each religious house, a lecture on scripture or casuistry, followed by discussion, is to be held twice a week, and all are obliged to attend. All income, even that acquired by personal initiative, is to go indiscriminately into the common fund for the needs of all. Superiors as well as subjects are to eat at a common table. Superiors are to keep accounts and are not to administer community goods; this task is to be entrusted to three religious who are to make a monthly report. No convent is to have more members than can be supported from its incomes. No lecturer or preacher may enjoy the privileges of his rank unless he actually lectures or preaches. Only the general may grant permission to have a fellow religious as assistant or servant, who must be at least twenty-five years old and preferably a laybrother. Perpetual cloister is to be observed; the door should be guarded by a porter, who may not permit anyone to leave, unless he has a companion and permission from the superior. No one should leave the house without a reason; before leaving and on returning, each religious should request the blessing of the superior. General permissions to go out are forbidden. The superior should have a key to all rooms in order to visit them. At night, a light should be kept burning in the sleeping quarters of the convent. Clothing and furnishings are to be uniform and in keeping with poverty. Each religious should have a separate cell adjacent to the others, simply furnished with bed and table. Walls should be without ornament. There are to be no stoves in the cells. Windows opening on streets and houses are to be blocked. There should be an infirmary for the sick. In the future, no one may be given permission to live outside the convent. No one may receive the habit except in houses designated in each province by the Holy See. Superiors are to enforce the papal constitution forbidding gifts by religious and prescribing the forms of hospitality. Procuring votes is forbidden.

The directives of the Council of Trent regarding elections are to be observed. In each province, there are to be three examiners of preachers, confessors, and lectors. A weekly conference on religious discipline is recommended. A list of daily assignments should be posted in a public place. "We admonish superiors in the Lord to be mindful of the account they will be called on to make on the last day of the flock committed to their care. Therefore, they should watch with the greatest care that whatever is prudently and piously prescribed in their rules and constitutions concerning mental prayer, silence, fasts, chapter of faults, and other spiritual exercises be scrupulously observed in every detail."

Here obviously Clement VIII is imposing on the religious orders in the Church the perfect common life, a step urged by some reformers at Trent, which the council shrank from taking, at least specifically.

Chizzola's Decrees of Reform

In this fervid atmosphere of reform, the vicar general, back from Sicily, prepared for the coming general chapter of the Order. He drew up a plan of reform to be submitted to the chapter for discussion and approval. As appears from the introduction of the printed edition of the plan, as well as from references in the text, Chizzola had the advice and encouragement of the pope.

The two hundred and eighty-seven reforming decrees are divided into eleven chapters dealing with divine services, religious poverty, proper conduct within and outside the convent, the administration of temporal goods, care of the sick, training of novices, pastoral activities, office of the provincial, houses of study and their curriculum. Such a division of material had its precedents in similar collections by Audet and Rossi. To these chapters are added thirty special statutes for Spain and Portugal. In the thoroughgoing spirit of Clement VIII, life is regulated in the minutest detail, such as, for instance, the number of times the holy water stoups are to be cleaned (ch. 1, no. 20).

As in the general decrees of Clement VIII, attendance in choir is compulsory for all except teachers who are actually lecturing, preachers on the day they must deliver their sermon, the sick and those who have been in the Order fifty years (ch. 1, no. 1). Leaving the house is even more restricted than in the Constitutions. Rossi had already decreed that the brethren were to be allowed to leave the house only once a week, but for deserving cases a dispensation for twice a week might be allowed. Now the brethren without exception are allowed outside the convent only once a week (ch. 4, n. 1).

A significant innovation is the prescription of half an hour's meditation made in common twice a day (ch. 1, no. 10). Thus, this spiritual exercise of Counter-Reformation spirituality entered into the practice of the Order.

With regard to poverty, the principle is enunciated: "Our religious are permitted the use of mobile goods allowed by the sacred council, which is uncertain and *facti*, not certain nor *iuris*, because religious are dependent on the will of the superior" (ch. 2, n. 2). For the rest, Chizzola takes over literally Rossi's legislation as found in the *Compendium constitutionum* for Italy. He may have had some doubts as to whether the practice of the deposit box was reconcilable with Clement VIII's current reform, which specified that earnings of individual religious were to be handed over to the superior and "mixed up" (*confundantur*) with the other incomes of the convent for the common good, so he took pains to secure the opinion of the learned professors of the Roman College. After making all due distinctions, Fr. John Azor, S.J., on May 10, 1593, gave it as his opinion that as long as the prior was free by law and custom to dispose of money kept in an individual's name, such a practice was not contrary to religious poverty.

An important directive of Chizzola's plan of reform was the establishment in Rome of the general archive. Provincial archives were also to be erected in all the provinces (ch. 5, n. 10).

In the schools, the doctrine of St. Thomas is prescribed: "Regents will profess the doctrine and method of St. Thomas in philosophy as well as in theology; they may use whatever commentators they wish... However, they should not omit to cite the opinion of our doctors, John Baconthorpe and Michael Aiguani in philosophy as well as theology; where there is need... with regard to dogma, they should prefer the doctrine of Thomas Waldensis to all others" (ch. 10, n. 19). The choice of these particular doctors is obvious: they were the only ones ever published.

The general chapter met at Cremona on June 6, 1593. Chizzola had previously obtained permission from the Congregation of the Council to represent suppressed provinces by titular provincials, and this practice, which lasted down to recent times, was implemented here for the first time.

Chizzola had not yet turned thirty-five, when he was elected prior general. "He was young and carefree," as one contemporary put it. His youth and inexperience go a long way to explain his brief and tragic career.

The chapter approved Chizzola's reform decrees, which were published under the title, *Constitutiones et decreta pro reformandis bonarum litterarum studiis quam pro reparanda vitae regularis observantia* (Cremona, apud Christophorum Draconium, 1593). However, they were almost immediately outdated in several aspects by Clement VIII's more stringent requirements for the common life.

The Apostolic Visitation of Traspontina

On February 5, 1594, Clement VIII's reformers visited the church and convent of Traspontina, headquarters of the Order. Here as elsewhere, the pope applied his general decrees with certain modifications. All are to attend choir and conventual Mass. Only those administering the sacraments are excused from choir. As already decreed by the general chapter, a half hour meditation is to be made twice a day, and for this exercise meditation books are to be used. Some part of the day is to be spent in the reading of spiritual books; the less educated may use books in the vernacular, "those who cannot read at all should learn the excellent doctrine of love from the book of the cross of Christ." Once a week, a sermon is to be delivered on prayer, religious discipline, and the observance of the Rule and constitutions. In the matter of poverty, the strict norm of the general decrees (nn. 3-7) is adhered to. All - even the prior general - are obliged to the common table. The general is to keep an account book. In the future, he is not to grant titles of honor, such as *fratres emeriti*, etc., and those granted in the past are revoked. No master is to have a member of the Order as a *socius* to serve him. To the general decrees about leaving the convent the pope in the case of the Carmelites adds the obligation of wearing the white mantle and the restriction of leaving only once or at most twice a week. Those found outside the convent without a companion, even with the prior's permission, are to be condemned to three years in the triremes. The same punishment is ordered for the porter who knowingly allows anyone to leave the convent without a companion and the permission of the superior. The constitutions of the Order, in so far as they do not contradict these decrees, are to be inviolably followed.

Clement VIII's visitation of the generalate of the Order was to become the model of reform throughout the Order.

The Visitation of Spain and Portugal

Shortly after the visitation of Traspontina, Chizzola left for Spain. In 1588, with Jerome Aleotto he had visited France. There, Henry IV had since established his authority and with it peace, but Chizzola decided to visit Spain first; France, Germany, and the other provinces would come later. On March 5, 1594, Clement VIII bestowed on him faculties as commissary and visitor apostolic. Through the cardinal protector of the Order, Dominic Pinelli, the pope further instructed him to limit his entourage to four persons, to wear a habit of rough serge without ornaments and undergarments of wool, to ride a mule while travelling, and to go about town on foot with a single companion, to offer or at least hear Mass, and assist in choir when possible, to eat the same food as the rest in the common refectory, to keep down expenses, not to confer academic degrees contrary to the decree of the chapter of Cremona, not to accept gifts, but to make the visitation for the honor of God and the service of religion without regard to gain.

The prior general was accompanied on his visitation by the Sicilian Alfio Mattioli, procurator general, and the youthful Benedict Sivori, his secretary and a member of his own province of Lombardy. Two other Sicilians, Andrew de Castro, chaplain, and Andrew Caracapa, completed the party. In Spain, Fray Ferdinand Suárez, procurator of the Order at the court, accompanied the general at the request of the king.

On March 31, 1594, the prior general and his party set out from Rome for Spain. On June 24, after an audience with Philip II, he began the visitation of the Carmelite convent in Madrid, where he settled the disputed election of the provincial.

The province of Castile had expanded since the visit of Rossi, when St. Teresa claimed it was dying out. It now numbered 15 convents with about 300 religious. Chizzola promulgated much the same decrees in all the convents of Spain and Portugal: a consideration of these will be left for the end of the visitation. After Madrid, Chizzola visited Toledo, the friary and nunnery of Avila, the nunnery of Piedrahita, Salamanca, Medina del Campo, and Valladolid. Here the chapter met on September 18, 1594. Peter Royuela was elected provincial; Ambrose de Valderrama became prior of Valladolid.

After the chapter, Chizzola interrupted his labors to travel to Galicia and satisfy his devotion at the famous shrine of Santiago de Compostella. The trip required almost a month: he left Valladolid on October 2; it was not until October 28 that he arrived in Coimbra to begin the visitation of Portugal.

Chizzola proceeded by way of Torres Novas to Lisbon. The prior general seems to have remained in Lisbon, while Alfio Mattioli made an excursion southeast to visit Evora, Vidigueira, Beja, and Moura. At Beja, there was a monastery of nuns, but it was not visited.

The provincial chapter convened January 15, 1595. John de Costa was elected provincial.

It was almost a month later that the prior general began the visitation of Andalusia, graveyard of visitators. On February 15, 1595, he arrived at Gibraleón to begin the visit. Over San Juan del Puerto, Trigueros, Aracena, Villalba, and Escena he arrived on February 26 at Seville with its community of over 90 friars. There he also visited the monasteries of the Incarnation and of St. Anne. From Seville, on March 28, he took an excursion south to Jerez. Setting out again from Seville on April 17, he visited Carmona, the friary and nunnery of Ecija, Cordova, Castro del Rio, Granada, Jaén, Alhama, the nunnery of Antequera, the college of Osuna, and the friary and nunnery of Utrera.

Reform Decrees for Spain and Portugal

From Chizzola's record of the visitation, little can be deduced concerning the spiritual state of the provinces he visited. He does not record individual interviews.

He had drawn up a list of thirty-six questions regarding religious observance and the fulfillment of duty by superiors and officials. These were apparently filled out in writing by the brethren. In each case, the prior general lists the members, material assets, and accounts of the convent, adding decrees for reform. Even the latter are not always included, or a note is made to the effect that they are the same as those made for Toledo. Chizzola's method was simply to apply to each convent his reform decrees approved by the general chapter, but modified in view of Clement VIII's requirements. Other decrees grew out of special conditions in Spain and Portugal. The result was his *Decreta pro conservanda et amplificanda vitae regularis observantia necnon pro gubernandi uniformitate in Hispaniae et Lusitaniae provinciis Ordinis Carmelitarum inducenda* (Sevilla, 1595). Chizzola's important legislation regarding novices and professed will be considered below.

Upon consultation with Mattioli, Suárez, and the provincials of Spain, the prior general also added a body of legislation for the nuns of Spain, *Decreta pro vita regulari sanctimonialium Ordinis Carmelitarum amplificanda* (1593). The 178 decrees are divided into nine chapters, treating the divine office, community life, cloister, reception of novices, election of officers, education of girls, chaplains and confessors, administration of temporal goods, chapter of faults. A tenth chapter lists faults and their punishment. Ceremonies for clothing novices, making vows, and imposing the veil end the volume. These constitutions, the first of their kind in Spain, undoubtedly filled a real need. To persons not versed in canon law they provided brief and practical guidelines to cloistered contemplative life, updated according to the Council of Trent and developments within the Order itself.

Chizzola issued his decrees for the friars and nuns from Seville in 1595, on September 14 and 26 respectively, but he had long ago suspended his visitation. For over a year, he had been continuously astride his mule, crossing the provinces of Spain and Portugal, tarrying hardly a day in most convents. He was young, but his health seems to have been precarious. Several times, his secretary, Benedict Sivori, records "fevers" of the *Reverendissimo*. He was sometimes absent from choir due to "indisposition"; he suffered from asthma, which occasionally kept him from offering Mass. He determined not to travel during the heat of summer, for the previous year, it had brought about a rash (*rospilla*) on his face. The doctor had counseled a rest in the country. For ten days, he was the guest in the home of the Genoese Marc Anthony Terilli, a relative of Sivori. He returned to Seville for a month, but the doctor again urged him to leave the city. This time, the Marquis of Alcalá lent him his country estate, called La Florida. There he remained two months until September 16.

Chizzola Accused

Meantime, in the Casa Grande at Seville murmurs began to be heard against the general living like a lord in a country house. No one really knew what was going on behind the walls of La Florida, but there were not lacking those who let their imaginations supply the facts. Then in the oppressive heat of the Andalusian summer, the storm broke.

On August 25, 1595, the provincial of Andalusia, Jerome Ferrer, and another friar, Ildefonsus de Salinas, aged twenty-seven, lector of Arts in Seville, presented themselves before the nuncio in Madrid and made charges of a most serious nature against the prior general. Fray Ildephonsus, or Alphonsus, made the same accusations in a letter to the pope. According to these two gentlemen, the general was the ruin of the province. Before his visit, at least a small number of priests attended choir, now only four or five joined the novices and professed students for office. The general himself never attended choir and only occasionally assisted at Mass, pontificating like a bishop or cardinal. Before, some mental prayer was made in common, now none. Before, silence, penitence, charity, and modesty were practiced, not any longer. Before, the brethren left the convent by turn once or twice a week, now all are to be found daily wandering about the streets morning and afternoon. Before, all except prelates ate at a common table, now all except a few dine sumptuously in their rooms like the general during Lent as well as Eastertide at great expense. Before, the young treated the priests with greater respect, now they are quarrelsome, proud, luxurious, greedy, and clothed with every sort of vice. Before, offices were sold secretly, now openly for 30, 50, and 100 gold pieces. Before the chapter of Cremona, those with degrees were few; after it, there were first 40 now almost 60 graduates. Before, the general granted patents for degrees, now such patents bestowed on the young and ignorant, dispensations from choir, patents of conventuality, etc., are granted for 15 or 20 gold pieces. Before, concubines were used with discretion and in secrecy, now the general, priors, and others speak with women in churches and chapels, eat with them openly, and - it must be stated - fornicate with them. The general and his secretary have been taking their delight and fornicating with concubines in a country house outside Seville since the Feast of Corpus Christi, to the scandal of nobility and people alike. Ecclesiastical authorities, judges, and police have considered arresting them, but have refrained for the good name of the Order. The general and his secretary can be seen in town in a coach or riding mules, followed by his servant, Sidonius, and three others, dressed in multicolored livery. The general himself wears fine clothes and linens. Before, gambling was indulged in secretly, now the general, priors, and doctors lose or win 200 or 300 gold pieces at games. Before, virtue was rewarded, vice punished, now the opposite is the case. Before, the pope's *motu proprio* about giving gifts was observed, now it is not remembered in the wildest dreams; with both hands the brethren shower on the general gifts of gold, silver, books, bills of exchange, etc., to the extent that he has filled more chests than ten carts can carry. Before, few spent the night in the homes of laypeople, now young religious and others stay in such places by the month. Before, our nuns lived at least mediocre lives of virtue, now they live openly like prostitutes.

The nuncio might have been expected to give little ear to these ravings, yet he began a process which was to cost Chizzola his office and perhaps indirectly his life.

The Interrogation by the Nuncio

On August 31, 1595, Gaetani sent Chizzola an ominous note, summoning him immediately to Madrid "for a few important matters I have to discuss with your Most Reverend Paternity." Chizzola did not appear in Madrid until October 10. Meanwhile, the nuncio lost no time in reporting the general of the Carmelites to Rome. On September 9 – before he gave Chizzola a chance to defend himself, as the latter bitterly complained – he wrote to the pope's nephew, Cardinal Peter

Aldobrandini, secretary of state, that the apostolic visitor "by the example of his dissolute life, avarice, extortion, and consequent misgovernment is scandalizing many in the province of Andalusia." The reaction of Clement VIII to such news can easily be imagined. He instructed his nuncio in Spain to investigate the rumors, and if they proved well-founded to suspend the general from office and to send him to Rome. Master Alfio Mattioli was to take his place.

From October 11-28, Gaetani interrogated the general, his secretary, and other members of his entourage. In the presence of only his auditor, Paul Beni, in order to avoid notoriety, Gaetani questioned Chizzola on the matter of accepting gifts, attendance at divine office, Mass and community meals, relations with women, conferring of degrees, offices and privileges, expenses occurred during the visit, correction of offenses.

In the matter of gifts, it eventuated that Chizzola had accepted certain presents, such as pieces of porcelain and of *benzaar*, vases of balm and oil, and other objects from the Indies. He had also collected a number of books not available in Italy. The prior of Ecija, Francis de León, was said to have given him the works of St. Thomas to the value of 100 *scudi*, but Chizzola claimed he bought them for 30 *scudi*. He also claimed he had accepted the gifts before the appearance of Clement VIII's bull forbidding presents by religious. Although the pope had issued this prohibition during the first year of his visitation of Rome, his bull *Religiosae congregationis* did not appear until June 19, 1594, after Chizzola had left Italy. Some accused Chizzola of saying that the bull was not to be obeyed. The bull, as a matter of fact, aroused much opposition, especially in Spain, where at a meeting in October of 1594, the Spanish religious with the exception of the Jesuits agreed that the bull was impracticable. In Spain, it was customary for religious to bestow gifts on friends and illustrious persons, and for this reason they were allowed to keep gifts and money in their rooms. The religious asked the nuncio to petition the pope for the abrogation of the bull but earned only a rebuke from Gaetani, who let them know that they were bound to obey no matter what the consequences.

A curious gift not mentioned by Chizzola's accusers was a black slave boy, John, twelve years of age, given him in Lisbon by the Carmelite bishop of Cabo Verde, Peter Brandão. Sivori had bought himself one by the name of Diego, nine years old.

At Seville, Chizzola seems seldom if ever to have appeared in choir and refectory. His excuses of ill health and other reasons failed to convince.

The general was also accused of promising the priorates of certain convents before the office fell vacant, of bestowing degrees on unsuitable candidates and of granting privileges derogatory to the common life, such as exceptions from attending choir. These accusations were claimed to be of matters "public and notorious." Chizzola effectively countered them by challenging his accusers to produce the alleged patents. He likewise denied incurring excessive expenses during the visitation and he gave the nuncio a full account of the punishments meted out to refute the accusation that he had failed to punish evildoers and to take measures against infractions of religious discipline. He was able to point to the reforming decrees for friars and nuns then in the course of being printed in Seville. He was especially accused of failing to punish Francis de León, accused of a long-standing affair with a married woman, the sister of one of the friars, apparently Peter of the Mother of God, and of promising to make him provincial of Andalusia. Francis was alleged to have given him books and other presents, as well as a valuable pen to Sivori.

In any case, Chizzola declared he had to err on the side of leniency in the interests of prudence. At this point, he in his turn unburdens himself of some rather negative judgments on the spiritual state of the Spanish provinces, especially Andalusia. He had found many disorders, "because here the superiors are not fathers, as they should be and is proper in religious orders, nor wards of community goods, but lords and absolute rulers - I should rather say, tyrants, who govern not according to our laws but despotically and arbitrarily, according to their own caprice without regard for the constitutions." In all the provinces, the priors personally dispose of community funds. They accept Mass stipends and other money without accounting to the sacristan or *clavarii*. They sell the staples of the community - oil, wine, and grain - without telling the *clavarii*, they undertake construction without consulting the community. They keep the account books in their rooms and make whatever entries they please, practicing extortion on the brethren and exacting obedience contrary to justice. Government is in the hands of a small clique who succeed each other in office in the various convents. They never go to choir, seldom read Mass, and are almost always away from home. They seldom eat in refectory and when they do, they want a double portion. Those with academic degrees, especially, dine out with two or three friends and spend more than the whole convent. Many superiors impose taxes without permission of the Holy See and without necessity, others liquidate the assets of the community and the inheritances of the brethren and spend stipends before the Masses are read. In all the convents, card playing is common. There is a great deal of complaint about relations with women, especially in Andalusia and Seville. Meat is eaten in the refectory on days forbidden by the Church. "Most important of all, the general concludes, "in all these provinces I found endless discord and enmity, all because of an inordinate ambition for the offices of provincial and prior and for other dignities. As soon as I arrived in a province, disputing parties would fly to me with memorials against each other, mixing a thousand lies with one truth, and the more investigations I initiated and the further I progressed in the trials, the more blood became heated and quarrels multiplied."

Chizzola Accused of Adultery

The most serious accusation against the prior general was adultery. While the nuncio was interrogating the prior general and his companions in Madrid, the cardinal of Seville, Roderick de Castro, was carrying on his own investigation. He stopped after hearing the "four principal friars of the convent of Seville," because the general's actions, he said, were evidently public knowledge. This interrogation is not available, but another hearing of sixty witnesses, later held from November 17, 1595, to January 18, 1596, by a canon of Seville, John Hurtado, leaves no doubt that the convent of Seville was the hotbed of the rumors and accusations about the general's morals. It was said that he was staying at the home of Marina de Grado, mother of Fray Francis Sarmiento. The general's name was linked with Francis' sister, Doña Bernardina, "twenty-four years old and quite beautiful," the wife of John Baptist Gualtero. The general is supposed to have brought her to La Florida for immoral purposes. When Chizzola finally returned to Seville from La Florida, he was unable to ride and had to be carried in a litter; the rumor went around that he had contracted syphilis. In all the testimony, there is little evidence for allegations made. Salinas, the author of the whole affair, prefaces his testimony with the amazing admission that what he has to say is hearsay only.

The most damning evidence came not from the Andalusians, but from the two Sicilians in the general's company. Andrew de Castro, the general's chaplain, at first made no accusations, but on being examined a second time, declared that he had arrived at La Florida twenty days after the general, and that all the time he was there, Doña Bernardina had slept and eaten with the general, while Sivori slept with another woman, called Mary, whose husband was in the Indies. Andrew Caracapa testified that De Castro had told him Mary had been preceded by Leonarda, and that Mary had brought with her another woman, who had offered herself to him, but that he had refused. De Castro also told Caracapa another story about the general in Granada. Opposite Chizzola's window was that of a very beautiful woman. He entered her house, but came out, his face on fire. The husband of the woman had returned and threatened his life. Later, during the trial in Rome, Chizzola's lawyer tried to discredit De Castro, who, he said, had been under investigation by the general on suspicion of having had a child by a certain widow.

The general denied that Doña Bernardina had ever been to La Florida. He had spoken to her about five times, but always in church and in company of her mother and other women. He was at a disadvantage in that during the whole of his interrogation he remained in the dark concerning the exact nature of the accusations against him and could only reply to questions put him.

Not all the friars of Seville testified against the general. Fray Ferdinand Suárez, commissary general for Spain, admitted he had heard the friars of the convent talking about women at La Florida but had never held it as a fact. He esteemed as honorable the women alleged to be involved. With regard to the booty the general allegedly shipped to Italy, he stated that "it was all noise." Fray Peter Marquez, novice master, stated he did not believe the rumors and added that "the reformation of the province consisted in the reformation of its heads; they should have peace and love among each other, for the others are obedient and submissive." Gaetani received a letter signed by many Andalusian friars in praise of the general, but he discounted it because the provincial and others claimed it had been forced.

Chizzola's secretary, Benedict Sivori, was accused of accepting gifts and exacting excessive taxes for patents, of carrying a brace of pistols, and of familiarity with an unmarried woman, Leonarda, twenty-five years of age. Andrew Carapaca testified that on one occasion he and Sivori had spent the day at the home of Leonarda and her mother, had stayed for dinner and siesta afterward, and had left only in the evening. He claimed that Sivori confessed to him that he had had relations with Leonarda at her home and in La Florida.

Mattioli Placed in Charge

Until he received instructions from Rome, Gaetani, on October 29, 1595, ordered Chizzola to employ his secretary, Ambrose Vallejo, lector at the university of Salamanca, in place of Sivori, who was to retire to Avila. Chizzola was to betake himself to Toledo and from there carry on the duties of his office. The nuncio forbade him to do anything without the authorization of his *socius*, Alfio Mattioli, of whom he had excellent reports.

Chizzola took all this in very poor grace, especially his subjection to Mattioli, whom he accused of being "the head of the whole conspiracy against me." He did not recognize the nuncio's authority over him, an apostolic commissary, and refused to obey him. He was convinced that Gaetani was prejudiced in his disfavor and looked for justice from Rome. As a matter of fact, the nuncio's preliminary reports to Aldobrandini before all the evidence was in, as well as his subsequent correspondence, manifests great readiness to believe in Chizzola's guilt. The general of the Carmelites enjoyed the favor of the cardinal protector of the Order, Dominic Pinelli, but theirs was not a winning team; the influential nuncio had the ear of the reforming pope through his nephew, Peter Aldobrandini.

Only on December 9 did Gaetani notify Chizzola of the pope's mandate, communicated by Aldobrandini on October 23, recalling him to Rome. Mattioli, as Gaetani had suggested, was to remain behind to take care of unfinished business. Chizzola had been in Barcelona since December 11, awaiting the departure of the galleys for Italy, when he received the nuncio's communication on December 20. Gaetani would have liked to try the case in Spain. Philip II instructed his ambassadors in Rome to make sure justice was done.

The final lot of the ill-starred Sivori is not known. He died on his feast day, March 21, 1596, at Perpignan. He evidently never reached Italy.

Master Alfio Mattioli continued the visitation of the Spanish provinces at the behest of the nuncio, who was concerned lest the king take the occasion to appoint Dominicans or Discalced Carmelite visitors. In consultation with Don García de Loaysa, the confessor of the king, and his majesty himself, Gaetani drew up "a brief reform," based on the decrees of Clement VIII, "a reform which Cardinal Sega had made when he was nuncia," and the constitutions of the general chapter of Cremona.

Mattioli received the apostolic confirmation requested by Gaetani. He visited Catalonia, Aragon, and Andalusia. "He reduced the affairs of this latter province to such a state," Gaetani wrote to Aldobrandini on June 28, 1597, "that to my great consolation I see for the most part remedied the scandal and laxity caused by the indulgence and bad example of the general." The chapter of Andalusia was presided over by the archbishop of Granada, appointed by the nuncio.

The nuncio has the highest esteem for Alfio Mattioli. "This friar," he wrote to Aldobrandini on October 24, 1597, when Mattioli was on the point of returning to Italy, "is an outstanding religious. Here he has done admirably whatever he was commissioned to do, without respect of persons, or passion, or any prejudice. He is learned, prudent, of good presence, incorrupt, and most observant of the Rule of his Order." In other quarters, enthusiasm for Mattioli was less, "because they wrongly blame him for the general's downfall." To Gaetani's annoyance, Mattioli, absent in Spain, was not named to the vicarship general, the plum customarily bestowed on the procurator general and the final rung in the ladder to the supreme office of the Order. The vicarship was bestowed on Henry Silvio by Clement VIII *motu proprio* on August 17, 1596. Silvio, in turn, on November 21, 1597, appointed Basil Angusciolo procurator general, thus ending Mattioli's career. Chizzola was no doubt wrong in accusing Mattioli of conspiring against him, yet statements by Mattioli are sometimes found at the bottom of conclusions arrived at by more incendiary spirits. It was not necessary for him to be Chizzola's enemy; it was bad enough that he was his friend.

Trial and Sentence

Meanwhile, on June 1, 1596, the unfortunate Chizzola had arrived in Rome. About a month later, the record of the inquest arrived from Spain and the trial could begin. Clement VIII with his customary passion for detail insisted on examining the record personally. Chizzola was suspended from office and on August 4 imprisoned in Castel Sant'Angelo next to Traspontina. A young friar, Bartholomew Franceschini, of the province of Romandiola, charitably volunteered to share his imprisonment and care for his needs. Letters arrived from leading members and superiors of Portugal and all the provinces of Spain except Andalusia, attesting to the general's conduct of the visitation. Chizzola's defense more or less followed the lines pursued in his original interrogation: some points he admitted but attempted to attenuate, others he denied outright. On August 18, 1597, sentence was passed. After listing his transgressions - accepting and bestowing gifts, adultery, disobeying the pope's express instructions (regarding the number of *socii* during the visitation, offering Mass daily if possible, frequenting choir and refectory) and failure to keep accounts as required by the acts of the visitation of Traspontina - the court declared the prior general guilty of transgressing the orders of the pope, the sacred constitutions and regular observance, and of adultery. He was condemned to two years of detention in a monastery in Sicily. He was to give an account of his resources as general and apply the value of the gifts received from his own subjects to the construction of Traspontina.

On August 26, Chizzola was released from prison. On September 20, 1597, he left Rome for Trapani. He did not long survive his disgrace, dying there a broken man on November 24, 1599. His early death suggests that in fact he suffered from chronic ill health.

In the present state of knowledge of the case, it would be hazardous to attempt a definitive conclusion, at least with regard to the most serious charge of adultery. Although Chizzola seems to have been rather easygoing, it would appear unlikely that a man of his station could so grievously forget his obligations. The friars of Seville were obviously speaking from hearsay, but the evidence of Andrew de Castro is disconcerting. Yet, if he was as dissolute as he is accused of being, his word need not be taken seriously. Of the other charges Chizzola was no doubt guilty. It was his misfortune to have his slackness coincide with the reforming zeal of Clement VIII. He was a casualty of the initiative of the Holy See in the matter of religious reform.

Implacable to the end, Gaetani expressed his satisfaction to Albobrandini: "All have been edified at the justice His Beatitude rendered in the case of the general. It will serve as an incentive to the heads of religious Orders to comport themselves in their offices with the prudence and exemplary life required of them." Exemplary life and prudence were two elements lacking in Chizzola. His remiss ways, his readiness to excuse himself from the common life no longer sufficed and would not be forgiven in the church of the Counter-Reformation. His lack of prudence exposed him to the attacks of the invidious. Gaetani laid his finger on a vital error of the general when he noted that Chizzola had paid too little heed to the pope's instructions before he left for Spain. Gaetani made another canny observation to his fellow Italian, Pinelli: "He failed to gauge properly the mood of these Spanish friars, who led him to the edge of the precipice and then gave him a push."

Chapter 7

Carmelite Missions in South America

By the bull *Omnimodo*, May 9, 1522, Pope Adrian VI authorized the mendicant orders to evangelize the Indies. The post-Tridentine age saw the development of the missionary apostolate of the Order, an essential dimension of the Christian spirit, so far lacking in the life of the Order. In this work, the provinces of the Iberian peninsula led the way, especially Portugal and Andalusia, the two provinces of which the windows opened on the Western sea. Unfortunately, as far as the Carmelites were concerned, the Prudent King exercised a careful control over the flow of missionaries to his realms beyond the sea. His motive seems to have been not to multiply orders in the new world and to carry on the work of evangelization with the orders already established there. This was not a hard and fast rule: subsequently, one or two other orders were admitted to the Indies. When the Carmelites finally made a concerted effort to obtain permission for the Order to work in the missions, it was too late; the gates of the Indies were closed.

Early Carmelite Missionaries

The earliest Carmelite in the Indies of whom there is record is Gregory de Santa Maria, of Seville, who in 1527 made his way to Yucatán, apparently as chaplain to the expedition of Francis Montejo.

In 1535, the Dominican bishop, Thomas Berlenga of Darien, Panama, asked Emperor Charles V to permit religious to found houses without authorization of the crown. Berlenga had already turned away the Carmelites and the Trinitarians.

As early as 1562, the Carmelites had made a foundation in Cartagena (Cartago), New Granada, but had abandoned it due to a lack of financial resources.

The Franciscan Peter de Aguado records the presence of two Carmelites in New Granada around 1560: a certain Fray Barnabas had a little church, where "remaining in prayer like Moses, he petitioned God for the life of his people and for victory." Fray Anthony de León in the company of Don Anthony of Toledo, *alcade* of Mariquita, is shown preaching to the Indians through interpreters.

John Baptist Rossi and the Missions

Among the many services Rossi performed for the Order is the promotion of the missions. This great Marian devotee combined his love of Mary with interest in the propagation of the faith. He wanted the Order to spread to the New World, "for great is the protection of the Most Blessed Virgin Mother Mary, merciful patroness of men and women. By the help of this protection all the faithful are rescued, and quickly raised up, and freed from all sufferings, hardships, and sorrows." Moreover, Rossi insisted that convents be founded, where regular observance could be maintained; he gave no licenses to wandering friars. He also laid down the condition that proper permissions be obtained of king and bishop.

Already in 1563, when he was still vicar general, Rossi appointed Francis Ruiz of Seville his commissary general with the mandate of founding convents and churches dedicated to Our Lady of Mount Carmel in the newly found provinces of Spain. Ruiz' jurisdiction was limited to members of the Andalusian province.

During his visitation of Spain, Rossi, on October 12, 1566, at Seville, granted permission at the request of eminent gentlemen to Fray Sebastian de Herrera, of Seville, to remain in New Spain and New Galicia until 1570. From Valencia, on July 8, 1567, Rossi appointed his procurators Master Anthony de Villafuerte, a Castilian but a member of the Andalusian province, and another friar of his choice to claim the property of Francis Sosa, of Mexico City, formerly a cleric, now a member of the Order. Villafuerte was confessor to the cardinal archbishop of Toledo, Caspar Quiroga, friend and admirer of St. Teresa. On November 12, 1567, Rossi granted patents to Diego Obregón and Augustine dos Santos, of the province of Castile, to remain in the Indies three years. The illustrious ladies, Jane and Marianne Anríquez, would obtain royal patents for Obregón, who was to make every effort to found a house and church in honor of Our Lady of Mount Carmel; in fact, this was Rossi's motive for granting permission. John de Madrid was a Mexican Augustinian who had transferred to the Carmelite Order; on September 16, 1568, Rossi granted him permission to return to Mexico City for two years to support his mother there. On March 14, 1569, Anthony de Lima, of the province of Portugal, received permission to remain in Santo Domingo for a year. In 1573, Rossi made Augustine Montero, of Valladolid, his vicar with powers to found houses in the region of the Rio de la Plata. Montero either did not go or else remained only a brief time, for the next year Rossi gave him patents to reside in Valladolid; if the superior caused difficulties, he could found a new convent in Castile or with the king's leave, in the Indies. In 1573, Fray Alfonso de Molina is found searching for the volcano of Masaya in Nicaragua. The Dominican Reginald de Lizzáraga (d. 1615) relates that when Francis de Toledo, viceroy of Peru, 1567-1581, wondered that the savage and hostile Chiriguanes knew how to make the sign of the cross, he explained that they had been taught by a Carmelite missionary who spent some years among them and built churches in honor of the Virgin Mary. They did not harm him and listened willingly when he dissuaded them from cannibalism and incest. Rossi was probably referring to the Antilles when in 1574 he granted permission to Fray Lope Suárez, of the province of Portugal, to remain in "the islands of his Catholic Majesty" for a year. Two years previously, Fray Lope had been granted patents to become a chaplain "on some trireme or ship of his imperial Majesty."

In 1570, Rossi laments that he still has not managed to make a permanent foundation of the Order in the New World. "From the day that we heard that the other orders of mendicants had crossed over to the Indies of his Catholic Majesty," he wrote in patents of November 14, 1570, "and that in those regions many convents and churches for divine worship had been given to the religious of those orders and daily multiplied to the glory of God and the salvation of souls, we have been moved and led by a great desire to the honor of the divine Majesty and the ornament and splendor of the most Blessed Virgin Mary, Mother of God and Mistress of this our Order of Mount Carmel, to cross over and transplant our religious there, so that just as in the East the white mantle of Carmel's beauty and the name and devotion of the Virgin Mother of God flourish, so in the West the same grace and protection may shine forth and be diffused to the great consolation and joy of the devout. This was the reason and cause why we gave patents to a number of Carmelite friars journeying to the Indies, to erect houses and churches under the name and title of the Most Holy Mother of God of Mount Carmel, having first obtained permission to cross over from the Catholic king or his ministers, and taking into account the manner of erecting monasteries promulgated by the Council of Trent. But many, after they had received patents constituting them vicars general (we did not give them all at the same time, but successively to whomever should first erect a house and church of our Order with the permission of superiors, or take possession of a place built for divine worship), deceived us, wandering about here and there against the obedience of their profession to the great scandal of the devout." Rossi thereupon canceled all patents for vicars general he had so far issued and made his vicar whomever had made or would make a permanent foundation. He excepted Diego Molina, to whom he gave a year's grace to found a convent in Guatemala. Fray Diego was an ex-Augustinian whom Rossi had permitted to be professed immediately on transferring to the Order, in order to set out for the Indies. "Since those who had previously arrived in India did so furtively, we name you vicar general; you are to construct a convent in the city of Guatemala, and all the convents of that province shall be subject to you. If any of the religious who are there refuse to obey, they are to embark on the first ships crossing to Spain." It may have been Fray Diego who was responsible for the chapel dedicated to Our Lady of Mount Carmel noted by Fuentes y Guzmán in Guatemala City in the 17th century.

The Vicariate of New Granada

As a matter of fact, the previous year, 1569, a Carmelite house had been founded in the New World. Fray Gonzales Ramírez, of the province of Andalusia, had succeeded in establishing a house and church dedicated to Our Lady of Mount Carmel in Santa Fe de Bogotá, New Granada. According to the Franciscan, Fray Peter Simón, the foundation had been made by two Carmelites, one of them called Barnabas Cabrera, on land owned by Captain John de Céspedes, who also sponsored them. Perhaps the Fray Barnabas, whom, as we saw, Aguado places in New Granada is to be put in this context.

In any case, Rossi made Ramírez vicar general of New Granada on March 12, 1572. The following year, Ramírez returned to Spain to recruit more friars. Rossi on April 14, 1573, made him vicar general of all the Indies and authorized him to collect ten or twelve friars from all the provinces. "In treating of these matters, the Reverend Vicar General will try to find a way to carry out his task gradually, discreetly, and without commotion." The prior general urged the provincial of Andalusia to give ready cooperation to Ramírez, who was to reside in the convent of Seville. Lastly, Rossi authorized his vicar to accept an "abbey" on the island of Jamaica in the territory of the Duke of Veragua. On May 7, Ramírez obtained from Pope Gregory XIII the confirmation of the privileges of the Order for the foundation in Santa Fe and for any other foundation made in the Indies. Ramírez was apparently in Seville when he obtained the general's permission, May 16, 1573, for Beatrice de Guzmán to enter the Incarnation there.

It finally looked as though the Carmelites would be established in the Indies and take their place alongside the other mendicants in this mission field, but in the end this promising beginning failed. The dean of the diocese, *sede vacante*, opposed the foundation, alleging that it had been made without the authorization of the crown. Moreover, according to Fray Peter Simón, the Carmelites had settled on the site of the Franciscans. In 1573, the Franciscan Luis Zapata de Cárdenas became the second bishop of Santa Fe. On October 11, 1575, the *Consejo de Indias* ordered the establishment closed. Ramírez returned to Europe. On May 26, 1576, Rossi renewed the patents for vicar general of the Indies he had granted Ramírez on April 14, 1573. "But if it happens that the business of the Indies is completely finished," Ramírez is given the right to live in Seville, Valencia, or any other Spanish convent of his choice. He is to have Fray Blaise of the Cross as his *socius*, whether he goes to the Indies or remains in Spain. "If he does not receive permission of his Catholic Majesty to go to the Indies to carry out his business there, he is absolutely to abstain from it." Finally, Rossi decreed that after outstanding debts had been liquidated, whatever incomes Ramírez had realized should be applied to Traspontina, where Ramírez had made his vows. He was to give a full account to the general's vicar in Spain, Jerome Tostado.

Salazar, Lobbyist for the Missions

The Spanish crown carefully supervised- and financed- the propagation of the faith in the Indies. It was a policy Philip II inherited. Already in 1533, only the three mendicant orders of Dominicans, Franciscans, and Augustinians were considered for the evangelization of the Indies – a concept confirmed in 1560. In 1566, the Jesuits were authorized to send missionaries. In 1572, Philip instructed his ambassador in Rome to persuade the pope to forbid all other orders in the Indies, except the Dominicans, Franciscans, Augustinians, and Jesuits, to receive novices with a view to extinguishing them there. The four orders favored by the king had the most members and had proven their worth in the early days of the conquest. They themselves were not disposed to share the new possibilities for expansion with other orders. The civil authorities, too, often opposed sending more friars than the small developing Spanish communities could support. As subsequent events proved, the king was not entirely indisposed, given good reasons, to admit other orders to the Indies.

The Italian general in far-off unfriendly Rome was not the person most likely to succeed in winning a place for the Order in the mission fields of his Catholic Majesty. What was needed was a lobby by a reputable person or persons in the Spanish court. This tactic was finally but belatedly tried by the respected Angel de Salazar, appointed vicar general for Spain by John Baptist Caffardi in 1582. On February 15, 1586, he presented a petition to the *Consejo de Indias* to the effect that "although his Order is one of the four mendicant orders and the other three are established in the Indies, up to the present his own Order has not passed over. With the same good intention as the others, they have desired and desire to serve Our Lord and Your Majesty in the conversion and instruction of the natives and in preaching the gospel and for this purpose to send religious to those parts to found houses and to become instructed in this work. In Seville, they have a number of religious, well lettered and skilled in preaching, of good lives and example... The Order could have founded monasteries in the Indies from the beginning of their discovery, since it as well as the other mendicant orders has been granted so many graces and privileges with a view to their work in the apostolic exercise of conversion, teaching, and preaching to that idolatrous people without knowledge of the true God. Since then, members of the Mercedarian Order and of the Company of Jesus have gone, and his Order has not been called as they were. A beginning could be made to their participation in so holy and great a work by sending up to twenty or twenty-four [Carmelites] to Peru with orders to found a house or monastery."

An undated petition of Salazar refers to an earlier one, possibly that of February 15, 1586, repeating substantially the same arguments.

It would seem that Philip II was not entirely unfavorable to Salazar's request, but that the opposition came from beyond the sea. On April 21, 1586, Salazar's petition was forwarded to the *audiencia* of Guatemala with the request that the king be advised as to the need for more religious or additional Orders. The answer was negative. The same request was sent to Quito and the Philippines with presumably the same results.

Prospects of a permanent foundation came from Peru. The same year, 1586, Salazar sent Fray John de Valenzuela to round up all the brethren wandering around Peru without benefit of patents from their religious superiors. Valenzuela actually succeeded in collecting a group of Carmelites in Los Reyes (Lima) who were lodged in the house of Dr. Arteaga, *oidor* of the *audiencia real*. On May 4, 1592, the municipal council wrote to the king requesting a permanent foundation of Carmelites. This effort, too, met with ultimate failure, for Fray Anthony Vázquez de Espinosa found no convent of his Order at the time of his visit to Lima in 1619. The Carmelites were back again at the end of the 17th century, when they opposed the coming of their Discalced brothers in 1690. Fray Michael of the Mother of God declared that the Calced had more seculars and servants than friars in their convent.

Opposition to the original attempt at a foundation in Lima probably came from the viceroy of Peru, Don Ferdinand Torres y Portugal, Count of Villar. In reply to what may have been another petition of Salazar to the king the count replied on April 25, 1588: "Again Your Majesty instructs me to inform you whether it would be advisable for the Carmelite Order to pass over to these realms. It seems to me no, unless it be the Discalced, for if these were to come, it would be very fruitful." As early as 1584, the count had suggested to the king calling the Discalced Carmelites to the Indies.

The following year, 1585, Jerome Gracián requested and readily obtained permission from the king for the Discalced province to send twelve friars to Mexico. Through St. Teresa, Mariano Azaro, and Gracián himself, the reform was well-known to the king and his ministers, who had the highest regard for the exemplary life of its members. The entry of the Discalced into the mission was the coup de grâce to Salazar's efforts, for he could no longer use the argument that the Carmelites were the only Mendicants not represented in the Indies. On September 19, 1588, the king established the principle that only Discalced Carmelites might pass over to the Indies.

Thus was finally realized Rossi's dream of translating Our Lady's Order to the Indies. Regrettably, the Spanish Carmelites were committed to a role of restricted activity to the missions.

Other Carmelites in Spanish America

In spite of the fact that the Order was not permitted to make a permanent foundation in Spanish America, individual Carmelites continued to make their way there. Not all who crossed the seas were driven by thirst for souls. Some saw in the Indies a welcome haven where they could carry on their irregular lives with less interference from authority.

The extent of the activity of the Carmelites in Spanish America is a matter that remains to be investigated. Some facts, however, are known.

John Baptist Caffardi granted patents for the Indies to John de Magdalena (1579), John and Francis Nieto (1586) and Diego Velázquez (1586). In 1581, the Carmelite John de Mexia is found in the company of the Dominican bishop of Tucumán, Francis de Vitoria. In 1584, Melchior de Portes was given permission by the king to cross over to Peru to collect an estate (*hacienda*). Francis de Villafuerte, of Madrid, taught at the university of Mexico City, where he died in 1608. In 1590, the king ordered the Viceroy, Anthony de Mendoza, to collect the Carmelites and Trinitarians found in Quito without proper permission. The viceroy protested the difficulty of the task, for these friars "are scattered in the most remote parts of these realms, some are very rich, others favored by the bishops." Three years later he repeated the order. In 1600, the prior general, Henry Silvio, granted faculties to Master Louis Ruiz Cavallero, procurator general in Spain, to erect houses in the Indies, clothe candidates in the habit, and recover goods of friars deceased there for the construction of Traspontina.

Under the successors of Philip II (d. 1598) the search for renegade Carmelites continued. In 1600, Philip III requested Archbishop Toribio Mogrovejo to seek out Carmelites having estates (*haciendas*) and assist the viceroy in sending them home. In 1611, the king instructed the Marqués de Montesclaros to send back to Spain all Carmelites found without authorization. In 1617, the prior general, Sebastian Fantoni, wrote to Fray Angel de León, vicar general of Peru and New Spain, to round up stray Carmelites and to take possession of the property of those who had died. The property was to be applied to the construction of Traspontina. Fantoni wondered that he had not heard from Fray Angel, especially since he knew that the late Diego Reinel, of the province of Catalonia, had left property. On October 24, 1640, all Carmelites found without permission in Guadalajara and Zacatecas were ordered to be sent back to Spain. In 1633, their convents had been ordered torn down, but the *audiencia* had protected the friars who had been remiss in presenting their licenses.

In 1642, the prior general, Theodore Straccio, granted a license to Master Ambrose Rocca to go to the West Indies, if His Catholic Majesty consented. The general chapter of 1645 instructed the procurator general in Spain to obtain permission from the king or his council for Carmelites to go to the West or East Indies. In 1655, John de la Plata, of Seville, is found in Concepción de el Viejo, Nicaragua, where he assured the Franciscans that their statue of the Virgin had been donated by St. Teresa. Fray John wrote a history of the Carmelites (Seville, 1639) and a work against John IV of Portugal (Alcala, 1641).

Anthony Vázquez de Espinosa

Certainly the most celebrated Carmelite missioner in Spanish America is Fray Anthony Vázquez de Espinosa. Born in Castilleja de la Cuesta, he entered the Order in Seville. After teaching theology for six years, he set out for the Indies and for fourteen years travelled extensively throughout New Spain, Honduras, Nicaragua, and Peru. Of a decidedly scientific and practical bent, Fray Anthony found time in the midst of his missionary labors to take careful note of all he saw and heard that might be of use to his earthly majesty as well as his divine Lord. He returned to Spain in 1622 and settled near the court in Madrid to record and publish his experiences. He was preparing to return to the Indies when he died in 1630.

Besides a number of short tracts and memorials on Spanish America, Fray Anthony wrote *Compendium and Description of the West Indies*. This voluminous work dropped out of sight until 1930, the third centenary of the author's death, when Charles Upson Clark discovered it, part in printer's proofs, part in manuscript, in the Vatican Library. "Even with a delay of three hundred years in its publication," writes Dr. Clark, "it is not to be considered for a moment as merely a historical curiosity." Fray Anthony's work is a "description of the West Indies," an informed itinerary providing a mine of information on geography, botany, and anthropology. The minute account of Spanish and ecclesiastical administration makes the book indispensable to the study of Spanish American history. Vázquez exposes the abuse of the Indian, but he is no blind critic of Spanish rule in America.

The Carmelite friar mentions in Cumaná, New Andalusia, a shrine to Our Lady of Mount Carmel with a hospital for the poor, and Carmelite convents in Belém and São Luis in the region of the River Marañon. In Lima, he notes the Confraternity of La Caridad, which has among its good works "an admirable hospital for poor sick women and a refuge and seminary beyond compare for impecunious young ladies and girls; they wear the Carmelite habit, with dark gray gowns and white sashes, and the shield and insignia of the Virgin; they have a Directress in charge of them. Here they are educated in great virtue and in retirement; they leave this school and nursery, or planting ground, to get married or become nuns; and this noble hospital gives them the dowry for that. I certify that in the presence of that nobility and beautiful display of sanctity, under the most holy habit of the Virgin Our Lady, when I was in that city it seemed to me the greatest thing in the world."

Also in Lima is "the retreat and convent of the Carmelite Order, of the Glorious Virgin St. Teresa, glory of our Spain, with the title of St. Joseph; it was founded by Domingo Gómez de Silva and Catalina Mariá, his wife" for the education of girls. "They wear the Carmelite habit and keep the Carmelite Rule, and this sacred Order is much sought after in this devout city. The daughters of leading persons are educated in this retreat in great virtue and isolation and continual choral practice, more than if they were Barefoot Nuns. It was originally established a league out from the city on the road leading to Callão, with the shield and arms of *Nuestra Señora del Carmen*; then they moved into the city, where there is also another Carmelite convent next to Santa Clara and very popular with the people." Fray Anthony is familiar with the foundations of the Discalced in Mexico and speaks highly of them. San Sebastián of Mexico City "has over eighty friars, who keep with perfect strictness the original Rule of our glorious Father St. Albert. Here there have been, and are, many acknowledged saints, and for their noble example and virtue they are reverenced and respected by the whole city. They have an excellent church with cloisters and very strict dormitories and a garden for their recreation." Of St. Teresa this perceptive friar says, "She was like a Spanish apostle and had the courage of a man."

The *Compendio* was "a veritable Baedeker," but Fray Anthony was more than a tourist: he did not forget the main reason why he had come to the Indies. He confided to his friend, Don Luis de Paredes, "I preached more than two thousand sermons, instructed and baptized more than three thousand Indians, and I administered the sacraments to them. In the highlands of Arica, I indoctrinated eighteen villages (*poplaciones*); I reduced the Indians in them to the service of God and His Majesty, teaching them Christian doctrine and good conduct. In order to understand them and hear their confessions, I learned the Aymará language in little more than a month and by this means I did a great deal of good in that country and to those new believers. I did the same in the provinces of New Spain and Honduras."

At the conclusion of his study, Dr. Clark characterizes Fray Anthony as "one of the noblest and ablest of those scores of thousands who carried Spanish civilization and ideals to the New World."

Carmelite Bishops in Spanish America

Although the Spanish crown did not permit the Carmelites to go to America as missionaries, it sometimes nominated them as bishops there. Some Carmelite bishops in Spanish America were: Ambrose de Vallejo (Popayán,1619; Santo Domingo, 1628; Trujillo, 1631), Peter de Carranza (Buenos Aires, 1620), John Alphonse de Solis (Puerto Rico, 1636), Ferdinand Lobo (Puerto Rico, 1649), Matthew Panduro y Villafane (Popayán, 1696; La Paz, 1714), John de Llamas (Panama, 1714), Bernard Serrada y Vilastre (Panama, 1721; Cuzco, 1725). Bishop Serrada brought with him to Panama his confreres, Fray John de Villarreal and Fray Michael de los Angeles Menchaca.

Carmelite Missions in Brazil

The Carmelites had no difficulty establishing themselves in Brazil, the Cinderella to Portugal's India. They were preceded there only by the Friars Minor and the Jesuits. It was the interval of the Cardinal-King Henry's reign, between King Sebastian's mysterious death (1578) and Philip II's annexation of Portugal (1580), dominated by the question of the succession. The Carmo of Lisbon, too, went to work in a more businesslike fashion than the Casa Grande of Seville. When Henry in 1579 was preparing an expedition under Frutuoso Barbosa to colonize Paraíba, he applied to the Carmelites of Lisbon for missionaries. The newly-elected provincial, Damian da Costa, had not yet been confirmed by Rome, and the first definitor of the chapter, John Caiado, was in charge. On January 26, 1580, Caiado appointed Dominic Freire, Albert of St. Mary, Bernard Pimentel, and Antonio Pinheiro, "all men of approved religious life, professed priests of our Order, to accompany the said captain [Barbosa] on a voyage to build the city of Paraíba, there to found a monastery of the same Order under the title of Our Lady of Victory, and not only in that land, but also in Pernambuco and in all places offered them, such a course being of advantage to the service of God, the souls of our fellow man and the good of religion." Frei Dominic was named vicar with powers, too, to grant letters of confraternity "to all who request them with piety and devotion."

At the time, nothing came of the attempt at colonization; Barbosa returned to Portugal, but the Carmelites remained behind in Pernambuco. The provincial chapter of 1583 confirmed the foundation made in connection with the chapel of St. Anthony in Olinda. In 1586, Frei Damian Cordeiro and three companions arrived in Brazil to settle in Bahia on a large tract of land which included the chapel of Our Lady of Mercy. In 1588, Peter Viana returned from Portugal with more recruits and the title of commissary of the Carmelites in Brazil. The following year, he accepted the administration of the chapel of Our Lady of Grace and extensive property for a convent in Santos. In 1590, the Carmelites received more than a league of land for a convent of the Order in Rio de Janeiro.

The Vicariate of Brazil

The provincial chapter of Portugal of 1595, presided over by the prior general, John Stephen Chizzola, erected the vice-province of Brazil and drew up statutes for its proper administration. John de Seixas was elected first vicar provincial, to be succeeded in three years by Bartholomew da Silva. The priors of the four Brazilian convents were named: Bartholomew de Evora, Pernambuco (Olinda); Jerome de Carvalho, Bahia; Peter Viana, Rio de Janeiro; Anthony de Alfama, St. Vincent's (Santos). In 1600, the prior general, Henry Silvio, decreed that the vicar should reside in Bahia, the most centrally located convent. Because of the great distances between houses and the difficulty of communication, local communities were given the power to elect their priors. In 1596, Olinda, later Bahia, became houses of study. One of the professors at Bahia, Ignatius of Jesus and Mary, produced an enlarged edition of the *Doutrina Christiã ordenada a maneira de dialogo para ensinar os minimos* (Lisbon, Miguel Manescal, 1678) of Cardinal Marcello Durazzo, nuncio to Portugal, which underwent a number of reprintings.

By 1606, São Paolo (1596) and Paraiba had been added, and the vicariate numbered ninety-nine members. By 1635, this number had risen to two hundred, and convents had been founded in Angra dos Reis, Sergipe, Mogí das Cruzes, São Luis (Maranhão), and Belém (Pará).

An early casualty of the Portuguese missionary effort occurred in 1619. Frei Louis do Rosario, of the Lisbon convent, set out for the Indies on the same ship with Martin de Souza de Sampaio, governor of the captaincy of Pernambuco. The Portuguese were captured by a Dutch ship bound for the East Indies, and Frei Louis was among forty persons thrown overboard. He had in his arms a statue of Our Lady of Mercy and managed to keep afloat while he comforted his companions. When he clutched at the side of a boat, one of the Dutchmen lopped off his hand with an ax. He was finally dispatched by gunfire.

The same year, Anthony of the Incarnation, prior of Olinda, was poisoned by a person whose evil life he had reproved.

The Brazilian vicariate began to press for independence. As the procurator, Sebastian dos Anjos, pointed out in 1635, the vicariate had a sufficient number of experienced and learned friars to warrant self-government; its membership was largely recruited in Brazil. In 1640, the Brazilian province of St. Elias was in fact erected with Francis do Rosario as first provincial, but the Portuguese government (it was the year of the revolt from Spain) canceled the arrangement. Instead, the Order in Brazil was divided into the vicariates of the State of Brazil with nine houses and the State of Maranhão with three.

In 1643, the prior general, Theodore Straccio, sent Louis of the Purification (de Mertola) to visit the vicariate of Brazil as his commissary and visitator general.

Mertola, former novice master in Lisbon, eloquent preacher and author of a number of religious biographies and a polemical work against the Jews, was known for his virtuous and exemplary life. "I marvel greatly," he wrote to the Brazilian friars, March 4, 1644, "at the lack of care in these parts, the small importance attributed to the things that lead to perfection." He singled out for special criticism ambition for office, neglect of religious poverty, lack of qualifications on the part of confessors. He concluded: "Let us try to be poor and live the common life, obedient, free from ambition, which is the cause of all evil. To arrive at perfection the best means are recollection, prayer, the reading of good books, honestly occupying the hours of day and night, and practicing great devotion to Our Lady and the passion of Christ." Frei Louis had brought to Brazil most of his library of books on spiritual theology, sermons, dogmatic theology, philosophy, pastoral theology, and canon and civil law; these he left behind in the convent of Bahia.

The Order suffered from the war with the Dutch, but by 1675 new convents had been erected in Recife and Goiana. The vicariate of Brazil numbered one hundred and eighty-six friars; Maranhão sixty.

The Vicariates of Rio de Janeiro and Bahia-Pernambuco

In 1685, the vast vicariate of Brazil was divided in two. The vicariate of Rio de Janeiro was allotted the convents of Rio de Janeiro, São Paulo, Santos, Angra dos Reis, Mogí das Cruzes, and Vitória do Espírito Santo (1685). The Vicariate of Bahia and Pernambuco comprised Olinda, São Cristóvão, Paraiba, Recife, Goiana, Bahia (modern Salvador), and Rio Real. In 1715, the vicariate of Bahia numbered 218 religious, Rio de Janeiro 163, not counting novices and 25 absent from their convents in Portugal.

Finally, on April 20, 1720, Pope Clement XI erected the two autonomous provinces of Bahia-Pernambuco and Rio de Janeiro.

After this initial development, the Order did not add many foundations in Brazil. Although the Carmelites had no apparent difficulty establishing themselves in the overseas possessions of Portugal, restriction of the evangelization of the Indians to certain orders existed there as well as in Spanish America. For a century, their apostolate was largely confined to ministering to the Europeans in the towns, catechizing, and teaching school. They had contact only with the Indians serving in the houses and on the farms of the whites.

On August 17, 1687, King Peter II authorized the Carmelites to administer *aldeias*, or native villages, and to indoctrinate the Indians.

A few details on the missions of the Bahia-Pernambuco vicariate are known. Frei Joseph of Jesus and Mary in 1690 travelled nine hundred leagues to the Rio San Francisco. There Frei Anthony da Piedade founded the mission of Japaratubá. Frei John of the Trinity worked among the Indians there during an epidemic of smallpox. The Carmelites were also active along the Rio Real. They founded the mission of Siri; around 1733, Manuel da Esperança was active there. In 1741, John V, "the most faithful king," assigned the convents which had embraced reform missions in the Baia da Traição and at Preguiça in the captaincy of Paraiba and at Gramació in the captaincy of Rio Grande do Norte.

Information on the missionary activity of the Rio vicariate, if any, is not available at present.

The Vicariate of Maranhão

An arduous missionary activity was carried out by the third Carmelite vicariate of Maranhão in northern Brazil. The State of Maranhão developed more or less without relation to the rest of Brazil. Due to adverse currents and winds, it was easier to communicate with Portugal than Bahia and more southerly parts of Brazil. As a result, Maranhão remained the most Portuguese part of the colony. The Carmelite vicariate of Maranhão reflected this general geographical and political situation. It never achieved the status of an autonomous province; its vicars continued to be elected at the triennial chapters of the province of Portugal and ruled without benefit of definitors.

When Alexander de Moura set out to drive the French out of São Luis in Maranhão, two Carmelites, Andrew of the Nativity and Cosmas of the Annunciation, from Olinda, accompanied his troops as chaplains. After the surrender of the French on November 4, 1615, Moura gave the Carmelites a site for a convent. Frei Andrew became the first prior. In a report of March 7, 1623, to the new Congregation for the Propagation of the Faith, the prior general, Sebastian Fantoni, mentions this development. The previous year, he relates, the provincial of Portugal had written him about the discovery of a new land, great and rich, called Maranhão. The captain general had taken with him Carmelite friars of the province of Brazil who had converted more than one hundred and forty thousand souls (!) and had founded a convent. The captain general had sent a report of all this to the king's council and had requested that more Carmelites be sent. In view of having acted as chaplains to Alexander de Moura, the Carmelites in 1618 requested the exclusive privilege of performing this function for the troops garrisoned in Maranhão.

In 1624, Francis of the Purification was named commissary. Frei Francis had crossed the sea with the laybrother Gonzalo of the Mother of God in the same ship with the first governor of Maranhão, Francis Coelho de Carvalho. Both friars had spent some time in the contemplative convent of Collares near Lisbon before volunteering for the missions. Frei Gonzalo's reputation for sanctity preceded him to the New World, for the governor had been greatly impressed by him during the journey. In São Luis, the brother continued to live a life of solitude and prayer and was greatly esteemed by the people. After his death in 1654, an inquest was held into his life and reputation for miracles (1661).

In 1638, São Luis became a house of studies with Louis de Miranda as first lecturer. In 1624, a second convent was founded at Belém in Pará. The pioneer, Andrew of the Nativity, became the first prior. In time, Belém superseded São Luis as the principal house of the vicariate and the domicile of the vicar. In 1698, the house of studies was transferred to Belém. On June 25, 1727, Benedict XIII authorized the vicariate of Maranhão to grant the doctorate to its students.

Among the professors of the *studium* of Belém were Bartholomew do Pilar, future bishop of the new diocese of Belém, who in 1702 received his doctoral insignia in Lisbon from Cardinal Michael Conti, later Innocent XIII; Anthony da Piedade, vicar provincial of Maranhão and governor of the diocese of Belém, founder of the *aldeia* of Japaratubá; Ignatius of the Conception, author of *Consultationes de jurisdictione spirituali, suscitata lite inter canonicos et rectores dioecesis Paraensis* (Lisbon, Miguel Rodríguez, 1741) and vicar provincial, who in 1728 drew up missionary statutes for the vicariate; Peter of St. Elisha, who wrote *Relationem de situ ac inventione civitatis Paraensis et de epidemia qua plures Indorum in ipsa obierunt* (Lisbon, Pedro [Ferreira, 1749). His manuscript *Cursus philosophici* is preserved in the National Library of Lisbon.

Former students at Belém include Andrew da Piedade who as prior enriched his alma mater with a library of 2,600 volumes; Manuel da Cruz was its librarian. Anthony de Araujo drew up statutes: *Statuta pro bono regimine studiorum in Vicaria Carmelitarum Maranhonensis Status* (Lisbon, Miguel Rodríguez, 1747). Joseph of the Nativity, novice master, prior and vicar provincial, composed a *Directorium pro recitando divino officio* (Lisbon, Pedro Ferreira).

The Carmelite and Mercedarian students, travelling overland to Bahia in 1711 to be ordained, fell into the hands of the Anapuru Indians and were put to death. Onofre of St. Angelus was the first priest to sing his first Mass in Belém. A native of São Luis, he entered the Carmelite Order there in 1636 and crossed over to Portugal to be ordained. His priestly ministry was destined to be short-lived. Travelling by canoe to a farm of the convent of Belém, he was drowned on June 10, 1644, at a place called Comedia dos Peixes Bois.

In 1639, Frei Andrew of the Nativity was named the first vicar of the new vicariate of Maranhão. Frei Joseph of St. Teresa, the first novice of Maranhão, fluent in the native language, was instrumental in acquiring a foundation in 1647 at Tapuitapera (Alcantara). In 1675, the vicariate numbered 60 members: 30 at São Luis, 18 at Belém, six at Gurupá and six at Tapuitapera. During the 18th century a hospice was erected at Ponta do Bonfim (1718) and a convent at Vigia (1737).

The Carmelites of Maranhão and Pará did not undertake the evangelization of the Indian until the end of the seventeenth century. This activity was reserved by the Conselho Ultramarino to the Franciscans and Jesuits. "The Carmelites," the mission procurator of the Company wrote in 1663, "are distinguished for religious observance and virtue, but it is not the purpose of their institute to engage in missionary work." In any case, lack of sufficient personnel probably kept them from seriously considering missionary work. In 1704, the vicar provincial, Victorian Pimentel, lamented that the vicariate had only twenty-four priests, a number constantly threatened by the high mortality rate due to the climate and by the temptation to return to the mother province to which the vicariate was closely attached.

The Mission Along the Rio Negro and Los Solimões

In 1693, the *Conselho Ultramarino* at the insistence of the *câmara* of Pará proceeded to re-allot the mission territories of the Amazon and to open the field to new orders. Unaccounted for in the new distribution of the Franciscan and Jesuit missions was the vast and remote region of the River Negro and the Solimões. The Portuguese crown was especially anxious to place missionaries there, because the Jesuit, Samuel Fritz, had extended his missionary forays down the Amazon from the Napo to the Negro and was claiming the whole area for Spain. The Carmelites were now charged with the evangelization of the territory of the Negro and the Solimões.

Early in 1697, the vicar provincial, Manuel da Esperança, with Sebastian da Purificação inaugurated the Carmelite mission along the Solimões. Frei Manuel eventually fell seriously ill and was forced to return. His successor as vicar, Joseph de Lima, sent Frei John William and Francis of St. Anastasius. The latter was killed

by natives in the *aldeia* of Manutá. In 1701, another friar, Francis Xavier was killed
by the Coxigueras Indians in the islands of the Solimões.

In 1702, the vicar, Victorian Pimentel, visited the Carmelite missions along
the Negro and the Solimões and left an interesting and informative account of
his journey. The purpose of his trip was to come to an understanding with Fritz
through a personal encounter, but on this score his long and tiring effort was
without result. The territorial dispute between the Spanish and Portuguese and
their respective missionaries was not settled until the Portuguese in 1711 erected a
fort in this outpost of their possessions. That the present-day boundary of Brazil
includes this area is in no small part due to the Carmelites.

The method of the missionaries was to collect the natives into villages, or
aldeias, in order to instruct and domesticate them. Near the mouth of the Amazon,
large farms were organized and worked by the Indians who thereby supported
the missionary effort and learned the skills of agriculture. A bitter struggle for
the temporal control of the *aldeias* sprang up between secular and ecclesiastical
authorities, finally won by the latter in 1681. Laymen accused the clergy of using
the Indians to enrich themselves; on the other hand, the villages were convenient
targets for the raids of slavers who were spared the trouble of seeking their victims
in remote areas of the jungle.

Acts for the administration of the missions were drawn up by the vicar, Ignatius
of the Conception, in 1728. The missioners should not fail to bring his white
mantle, not only to edify the Indians, but also that he might be buried in it when
he died. He should wear it when preaching on Sundays and feastdays. He should
not be seen without his habit. Laymen of evil custom should not be permitted
into the villages; no layman should have dominion over the Indians. The Blessed
Sacrament should not be exposed in the remoter villages, where there is danger of
raids by savage Indians. In their sermons, the missioners should not show kerchiefs
(*sudarios*) improperly painted to the Indians "in whom the faith enters by the eyes
rather than the ears." Without fail, the missionary should daily instruct the boys
and girls of the village, trying as much as possible to instill in them a love for the
mysteries they are taught. The children should learn Portuguese, according to the
letter of the current year from the king, whom God preserve. Adult Indians should
not be baptized until they are taught the articles of faith and renounce the errors of
paganism. The villagers should be obliged to confess once a year, and for this reason
the sacrament of penance should be thoroughly explained to them in instructions
on Sundays and holidays, when all should attend Mass. The missionary should not
leave the mission except to go to confession himself, to procure the spiritual good
of another or to receive care in grave illness. Under pain of excommunication no
missionary may obtain the sale or purchase of Indians. "No Indian of the *aldeias*
may act as guide or interpreter for seculars who illicitly enter the wilderness of the
mission for piece contracts, since such negotiations arc forbidden by the king and
are usually accompanied by violence, death, bitterness (*amarracões*) and assaults."
The missioners should not consent to the sale of Indians in their presence, lest the
transaction be justified by that circumstance. Missionaries should not hold contracts.
The canoes sent out for the support of the mission are to be turned over to the
mission procurator, who will note their contents in the presence of the *clavarii* of the
convent. The missionary leaving the mission may not take with him what has been

earned for the mission by the labor of the Indians. On the death of a missionary, his companion is to make an inventory and may dispose of nothing. The temporal administration of the missions was in charge of a procurator appointed by the vicar general.

In patents of October 21, 1737, the vicar general, Anthony de Araujo, urges Andrew da Piedade whom he appoints mission procurator, "to attend in this occupation more to the increase and credit of the missions, so much recommended by His Majesty, whom God preserve, than to the interest and particular advantage of the missionaries." He is not to condone slavery: the masters of the canoes are to be men of good behavior and laudable habits. He is exempt from the *tabella* of daily tasks in the community and is granted two Masses a week for expenses.

The story of Frei Dominic of St. Teresa, as told by the vicar, Francis of St. Elijah, will serve to illustrate the work of the Carmelite missioners in Maranhão and Pará. On September 18, 1734, Frei Dominic of St. Teresa received his mandate for the mission of St. Paul among the Cambebas, the remotest frontier of the Portuguese Amazon. It took him three months to cover the eight hundred leagues from Belém to his mission, which he found abandoned and in ruins, its inhabitants "scattered and wandering in the midst of the wilderness, like a herd without a pastor, in spite of the fact that this mission was one of the oldest on the River Solimões and therefore should be the most tamed and domesticated." Frei Dominic set about building new houses and a church, to which he devoted great care in spite of the primitive conditions. He sent all the way to Portugal for a statue of Our Lady of Mount Carmel; on the gospel side of the chapel he placed St. Paul, patron of the mission, on the epistle side St. Ephigenia. The natives made vestments. He devoted himself completely to the material and spiritual needs of the Indians, caring for them in their illnesses, bleeding the poor creatures according to the best medical techniques of the times.

For eleven years, he devoted himself to their betterment, instructing them three times a day. Every evening the Indians sang terce of Our Lady with a procession through the village on Sunday. He taught them the celebration of the Eucharist according to the Carmelite rite, carried out with chant on Sundays. He settled more than four hundred Indians in the *aldeia*, which seemed like a primitive Christian community.

He founded another village dedicated to St. Peter for the Tocunas, Maieninas, and Tomanas tribes and placed a white man in charge of instruction. Here, too, he built houses, spending more than three thousand cruzados. He baptized four hundred persons.

Near the mission of Our Lady of Guadalupe of Turuquatube he founded the settlement of St. Joseph of the Tocunas, collecting three hundred savages from the wilderness. Finally, he resettled his mission on another site after it was threatened by floods.

No accurate information is available on the number and identity of the many missions administered by the Carmelites in Maranhão. Due to the lack of missionaries and the inconstancy of the natives many *aldeias* had only an ephemeral existence. In 1722, they are said to number fifteen; in 1751, eighteen.

Missionaries protected the Indians against the rapacious white man. Thus, at Belém around 1745 Frei Andrew da Piedade was instrumental in freeing slaves from the houses and farms where they were forced to work against their will. On the other hand, the missionaries in Maranhão were given permission by the government to use the Indians of their *aldeias* on their farms, provided they treated them as free men and paid them salaries. In 1727, the convents of São Luis and Belém were each authorized to import one hundred Indian couples to replace the victims of smallpox, provided the Indians were properly ransomed and willing to live under the administration and doctrine of the religious.

With regard to the epidemics which decimated the Indians, it is interesting to note that during his journey down the Amazon in 1735, Charles Marie de la Condamine saw a Carmelite friar inoculating his Indian pupils for smallpox. Frei Joseph da Madalena is known to have been practicing variolation at that time.

Mention has already been made of some Carmelites who lost their lives in the service of the gospel. On September 24, 1757, Frei Raymund of St. Elisha, missioner in the *aldeia* of Camará (a.k.a, Caboquena) on the Rio Negro, was assassinated by mutinous Indians from another Carmelite mission of Dari under a certain Dominic. Matthias of St. Bonaventure (Diniz) was killed by Indians on the left bank of the Amazon on the site of present São Paolo de Oliveira.

Carmelite bishops during this period were Francis de Lima (d. 1704) named bishop of Maranhão in 1691, but before he took possession of his see, transferred to Pernambuco, 1695; Bartholomew do Pilar (1667-1733), named bishop of Belém in 1717. The Portuguese Manuel of St. Catharine, brother of Frei Joseph de Lima, was provisor and governor of the diocese of Pernambuco before becoming bishop of Angola, Africa, in 1719. Fabian dos Reis, vicar provincial of Brazil, became bishop of Cochim in 1668 and was transferred to the see of Cabo Verde in 1671.

Chapter 8

The Carmelite Nuns and the Confratres

In the 16th century, the various forms of Carmelite life besides the friars (men in solemn vows) developed into the types we know today: cloistered nuns, third order secular (lay Carmelites), and the scapular confraternity. The congregations of active sisters (third order regular) are mainly a development of recent times.

At the time of the Council of Trent, nuns (*moniales*) were religious women who professed the three solemn vows of religion according to an approved rule. In his constitution *Periculoso* (1290), Boniface VIII had determined that solemn vows implied cloister, but this law was by no means universally observed. Tertiaries (sisters who professed a third order rule), not having solemn vows, were not obliged to cloister. Neither necessarily were those who, either out of devotion or by papal indult, made solemn vows along with their profession of a third order rule. Even monasteries of nuns in the strict sense, which had never since time immemorial observed cloister, were considered by theologians and canon lawyers to have a *ius acquisitum*, or to be tolerated by authorities.

The fathers of Trent on their way out the door at the end of the council renewed Boniface's *Periculoso* without concerning themselves with particular problems of its application to the varied forms of life observed by religious women at the time (*De regularibus*, sess. 25, ch. 5). As a result, the matter of cloister became one of the disputed questions of the day. The generals of the mendicant orders opposed introducing the cloister where it had not been specifically promised, though they agreed that it might be well to enforce it in the future. Such was Rossi's answer to a question of the Congregation of the Council in 1565.

Pope Pius V by his constitution *Circa pastoralis*, May 29, 1566, put an end to discussion. Nuns by virtue of their profession were obliged to cloister, whatever the tenor of their rules or whatever immemorial customs they enjoyed. The same applied to tertiaries living in community with solemn vows. Tertiaries without solemn vows (simple vows) were forbidden to receive novices in the future and so were condemned to extinction. In other words, in the post-Tridentine church all religious women were to be cloistered. This severe measure must be seen in the context of an age in which immorality in houses of religious women was a serious problem.

Predictably, there was opposition to the decree. Sisters who had entered open monasteries had done so without any intention of committing themselves to cloister. Even where good will existed, urgent social and economic factors sometimes militated against the imposition of the cloister. Some monasteries, notably in the Republic of Venice, traditionally and expressly existed as a solution for the nobility for disposing of extra daughters. These women bore their lot with the best grace possible; to ask them to undertake a rigorous penitential regime was adding insult to injury. Mendicant communities especially could not survive without the possibility of leaving the monastery to beg or otherwise acquire funds.

Not all ecclesiastics were as cooperative as St. Charles Borromeo and his vicar general, Nicholas Ormaneto, whose activities were alluded to above. Trent had given bishops the power of discretion in determining legitimate reasons for leaving the monastery, which some prelates used quite freely. But Pius V, convinced that the key to reform of feminine institutions was the cloister, was not to be outmaneuvered. His bull, *Decori et honestati,* January 24, 1570, restricted the reasons for leaving the cloister to fire, pestilence, and leprosy. Gregory XIII proved no more accommodating. He appointed apostolic visitators to oversee the enforcement of cloister, a move that panicked lagging superiors general into immediate compliance. The *Circa pastoralis* had already attempted to overcome the economic difficulties of monasteries by ordaining that begging could be done by non-professed lay sisters (*conversae*); where these were lacking, professed sisters could be used (par.5). But this solution contradicted the Tridentine principle that solemn vows implied cloister. Gregory XIII, *Deo sacris virginibus,* December 30, 1572, ordered professed *conversae* back to the monasteries as soon as their support was assured. On the other hand, he ordained that the alms collected for the poor of dioceses should be shared with impoverished monasteries. These measures often proved inadequate, but the doors of the monasteries remained closed.

The Carmelite Nuns in the 16th Century

Under the influence of the bull *Cum nulla* of 1452, we saw, women who had made profession of the Carmelite Rule and had been living at home (*conversae*) began to group themselves into communities to form monasteries of cloistered nuns. In Spain and Italy, the communities more gradually took on all the characteristics of cloistered nunneries.

During his visitation of the nuns in Spain, Rossi did not insist on cloister where it had not been vowed, in keeping with his opinion expressed to the Congregation of the Council, but on returning to Rome in 1568 and learning of the pope's decision, he revoked all permissions to leave the cloister in Spain. To the chronic economic crisis of the monasteries he applied the ordinance of the Council (sess. 25, *De regularibus,* ch. 3): limiting the population of the monasteries to that able to be supported by their incomes.

The monasteries existing in Spain and Portugal at the time of Rossi's visit were listed above. Shortly after, the province of Aragon added a second monastery in Valencia (St. Anne, 1567) and another in Onteniente (1575). In 1580, Andalusia made a foundation in Utrera. In 1594, the community of Paterna, which Jerome Gracián had tried to reform, returned to Seville, but not to the Incarnation whence it had originated; instead it made a second Sevillan foundation under the title of St. Anne. At the time of the Discalced secession (1593), the Order possessed 32 Teresian monasteries.

The rise of Calvinism marked the end of the monasteries in the northern provinces of the Low Countries at Rotterdam (1572) and Haarlem (1578). Nieukerk, too, ceased to exist in 1590, and Vilvoorde was damaged by fire (1578). Rossi's interest in the Order in the impenetrable north included correspondence with the monastery in Bruges. "He (Matthew de Lalande)," the prior general wrote on December 26, 1577, "wrote me many favorable things, praising your way of life, manners, peace and tranquillity, religious fervor, divine cult, excellent reputation among the people; he admired your observance of poverty."

Besides Bruges and Vilvoorde, Guelders, Huy, Liège, and Namur survived. Due directly or indirectly to the initiative of Bl. John Soreth, these were monasteries of cloistered nuns in the strict sense. The same is true of the two French nunneries in Nantes and Vannes. The losses in these regions were not recouped with new foundations. Given the times, this is hardly surprising.

From 1503, the Carmelites of Cologne were confessors at a beguinage founded in the Butgasse, 1304. In 1549, the prior, Caspar Doroler, composed a rule or statutes, according to which three vows were taken. The beguines, or sisters, attended weekday Mass in the friary church; on Sundays, they frequented the parish church of St. Maurice. In 1565, Rossi admitted them to the habit of the Order and vows at the hands of the provincial, John Mayer, thus constituting them tertiaries regular of the Carmelite Order. They did not evolve into cloistered nuns until a century later.

In Italy, the Order had two houses of sisters in Florence. By 1520, when it passed under the jurisdiction of the archbishop, St. Mary of the Angels had become a cloistered monastery. The monastery of the Annunciation (Nunziatina) accepted the obligations of choir and cloister in 1517. The Mantuan Congregation added a third monastery in Florence, St. Barnabas (1508).

Besides St. Barnabas in Florence, the Mantuan Congregation at the beginning of the 16th century counted nunneries in Parma, Reggio, Brescia, Ferrara, Mantua, and Trino. Parma observed constitutions compiled by Thomas di Caravaggio before 1481, which show it to be a monastery of cloistered nuns. This legislation was adopted in Mantua, Ferrara, and St. Barnabas and St. Mary of the Angels in Florence. Constitutions for the monastery at Mantua were written and translated by Angelus of Genoa, former confessor of Bl. Joan Scopelli (1494). A copy of constitutions at present preserved at Osimo may have been originally observed in Reggio Emilia. They too prescribe the cloister.

In the course of the century, the Mantuan Congregation doubled the number of its monasteries. Sutri was founded in 1515. In 1525, sisters from Brescia helped initiate a foundation in Albino. In 1537, the Augustinian monastery of St. Lucy in Ferrara took the Carmelite Rule under the Mantuan Congregation. A third monastery of the Congregation in Ferrara came about in 1542, when a group of *convertite*, whom Anthony Ricci of Novellara had converted from a life of sin, decided to initiate a cloistered life. A similar case occurred in Bologna, where a number of fallen women, converted by the Lenten sermons of John Baptist Frumenti of Milan, took the Carmelite habit in 1561. Two nuns came from Ferrara to initiate them into cloistered living, when they were aggregated to the Congregation in 1582.

The Mantuan Congregation was undoubtedly responsible for the most flourishing growth of Carmelite nuns in Italy, but monasteries also rose in other provinces there. In Naples, the distinguished monastery of the Holy Cross of Lucca was founded in 1534 by the pious Ippolito Giunta, a native of Mantua, but at the time a member of the Carmine Maggiore. The foundation was made possible by the munificence of Andrew Sbarra and his wife Cremona Spinelli, citizens of Lucca.

Cremona herself took the habit in the monastery she helped found. The great reforming legislator of the Order himself, Nicholas Audet, drew up constitutions and statutes (1538); the former, however, are only a *cento* of the more general principles of the Rule of St. Clara. The prior general placed the monastery directly under his jurisdiction and imposed strict cloister. Rossi also visited the monastery and left statutes and ordinances (1563). The prince of Cellamare, who had four daughters in the monastery, lavishly embellished it and its chapel (1588). The monastery was destroyed during the secularization of the last century, but Benedetto Croce managed to save the chapel, a jewel of Counter-Reformation art. In the course of the 16th century, the Holy Cross of Lucca gave rise to monasteries in Putignano (1552) and Castellamare (1560). Other foundations followed, last but not least, Allentown, Pennsylvania. (1931). By 1600, the monastery of the Holy Cross numbered eighty nuns.

A monastery is known to have existed in Caulonia in Calabria, but its date of foundation is uncertain. In Sicily, the Order acquired two nunneries in Palermo. In 1531, the friary there won a ten-year legal battle with Sister Sigismonda Xarrat, Poor Clare, over the possession of a former hospital, but ceded it to her on condition that she establish a Carmelite monastery. She complied and became first prioress of St. Anthony at Porta Termini. At the time, Palermo already had a Carmelite monastery, St. Mary of Valverde, which had belonged to the Belgian congregation of that name since the thirteenth century. It is not known when it became Carmelite. The monastery of St. Anthony had a brief existence. Chizzola suppressed it in 1597, when it had not yet accepted cloister. A third Sicilian monastery at Messina also arose from the conversion at an unknown date of Sisters of the Congregation of Valverde to the Carmelite Rule.

In the province of Lombardy, there was a monastery in Milan, but around 1567 it was suppressed by the archbishop. Novi was suppressed by Caffardi in 1578 for failure to introduce the cloister. Pontecurone also got into trouble over the cloister, when the minions of the bishop of Tortona came upon Fra Theodore of Piacenza and a companion, Angelus, leaving the monastery early in the morning, after spending the night in a guest house within the monastery precincts (1574). Submitted to torture, Fra Theodore was shown to be innocent of any dishonest actions; nonetheless, he was punished for entering the monastery grounds. There is some doubt whether the Lombardy province ever had a monastery in Cremona. St. Mary of the Angels in Pavia was founded around the beginning of the century.

Our Lady of Hope in Venice was not a cloistered monastery, but a group of tertiaries regular with vows, who may perhaps be traced to a confraternity of *laudesi*, or hymn-singers, known to be in existence in 1300. They survived Chizzola's prohibition in 1593 to accept new candidates.

Thus, at the end of the century, there were twenty-three monasteries in Italy.

The Order took a hard knock, May 28, 1599, when Clement VIII withdrew the monasteries from its jurisdiction and put them in the care of the bishops. The pope states no reason for his *motu proprio*, but it was no doubt intended as a reforming action to alleviate moral conditions in the monasteries which in various parts of Italy were a source of grave concern. In the case of the Carmelite nunneries, at least, it was a needless precaution.

The prior general, John Baptist Caffardi, who had added an unprecedented chapter on the charge of nuns to the friars' constitutions (1586), also drew up constitutions for all Carmelite nuns: *Ordinazioni per le monache carmelitane* (Firenze, Francesco Tossi, 1582). If these ordinances, of which no copy has been found, are the same as the ms. *Constitutioni* preserved in the Holy Cross of Lucca, they were an adaptation of the friars' constitutions to the nuns. Caffardi thus confirms the principle established in the beginning by Bl. John Soreth: the profession of the brothers and sisters of Our Lady of Mt. Carmel is one and the same, and the regulations guiding their lives need vary only as dictated by differences of sex.

The cloistered Carmelite nun of the 16th century realized in a special way the contemplative ideal of the Order. After Trent all nuns were cloistered, but this style of life particularly suited Carmel's vocation to prayer, solitude, silence, and penitence. The prayer of the Carmelite nuns still centered around the liturgy, the Eucharist, and the Hours, which were solemnized in chant, but in Italy, in the Constitutions of the Mantuan nuns and in those of Caffardi, private interiorized prayer in the form of meditation made its appearance, bringing with it a simplification of the performance of the liturgy. St. Teresa ordered the whole office recited without chant, to allow more time for meditation, a novelty of which Rossi strongly disapproved.

The Carmelite nun also revived another feature of the Rule: manual labor. In the Carmels of the old Order work was done in common to the accompaniment of spiritual reading, hymn singing, devout colloquies, nor was a time for reasonable recreation excluded.

The Carmelite nun admirably personified and practiced the Order's distinctive devotion to Mary. Bl. John Soreth's eagerness to promote the Carmelite sisterhood was inspired by the consideration that Our Lady lacked a counterpart to the Carmelite friar. Mary's purity and virginity, Marian characteristics specially dear to the Order, were most aptly witnessed to by the Carmelite nun, who also very fittingly wore the white mantle, the special symbol of these virtues. Monasteries were often dedicated to the mysteries of the Redemption in which Mary played a particular role.

The nuns reflected in their lives the apostolic dimension of the Carmelite vocation. The contemplative life is by nature apostolic, for anyone who claims to love God and hates his neighbor is a liar. The cloistered nun prays and sacrifices on behalf of embattled humanity. In the monastery of St. Mary of the Angels in Florence, Sister Mary Magdalen de' Pazzi was deeply concerned about a contemporary problem, the reform of the Church.

St. Mary Magdalen de' Pazzi

Italy at this time produced one of the greatest saints of the Order and one of its most exalted mystics. St. Mary Magdalen de' Pazzi was born of the noble Florentine family of the Pazzi and was baptized Catherine on April 2, 1566, in the baptistery of the Duomo, the "*bel San Giovanni?*" of Dante, with its exquisite bronze doors by Ghiberti. She was educated by the *Cavaleresse* of Malta. Even as a girl, she was attracted to prayer, solitude, and penance. She had a deep devotion to the Eucharist and made her first Communion at the age of ten. Shortly thereafter, she made a vow of virginity. She was directed by the Jesuits, whose church in the Via de' Martelli the Pazzis attended. When she was nine, Father Andrew Rossi taught her to meditate, using the recently published *Instruction and Admonitions for Meditating the Passion of Christ* by Caspar Luarte, S.J. She brought her little book with her when she entered the Carmelite monastery, where it is still preserved. The accounts of her later mystical experiences show that she never wholly abandoned these girlhood habits of prayer. Her reading included the gospels, "which always gave her more pleasure than any other book," Louis de Granada, Fulvio Androzzi, S.J., and the *Soliloquies* of pseudo-Augustine.

In 1583, Catherine was received as a novice in the monastery of St. Mary of the

Angels in Florence, taking the name of Sister Mary Magdalen. Her profession had to be anticipated due to illness, a fever accompanied by violent coughing, which placed her life in danger. The sudden cure was followed by a state of ecstasy which lasted forty days. In that state, the infirmarian saw that "her face was most beautiful, her skin rosy ... She did not seem to be the person illness had made thin and deathly pale." For forty days, every morning after Mass Sister Mary Magdalen fell into an ecstasy lasting two hours. At other times, she experienced "excesses of love." In the morning ecstasies, she remained rigid and motionless; at other times, she moved gracefully about the room, following the course of her vision in pantomime. When her visions concerned some sorrowful theme, she perspired freely and uttered cries and groans "capable of moving stones to pity." The love of God, the ingratitude of men, judgment, religious life, the Blessed Virgin, the saints are the subjects of her ecstasies. At times, a labyrinthine symbolism is evolved; at other times, the visions concern abstruse and impenetrable mysteries. "I saw God all glorious in himself," she states of her vision of June 25, 1584. "I remained in this consideration about an hour in so far as I could judge, when I returned to myself, but what I tasted in that abstraction of mind I could not say, since I could not understand what was shown to me." But her mysticism is by no means abstract; her revelations come to her through an intimate relationship with Christ. In most cases, the saint has hardly received Holy Communion when Jesus appears to her in bodily form. "After Communion I saw Jesus all beautiful. He caressed me lovingly and gave my soul a kiss of holy peace."

"I seemed to see Jesus all loving at the right hand of the Father, and his eyes were so beautiful, I could never describe their beauty." Jesus then goes on to teach her some truth, or the entire "consideration" is taken up with loving union with her divine Bridegroom.

Sister Mary Magdalen's mystical experiences, accompanied by striking external phenomena continued into the year 1585. The iron curtain of material reality that hides the world of the spirit seemed to take on a gossamer transparency. The periods of community prayer – Mass, divine office, meditation – invariably triggered an "excess of mind," but even at other times - in the refectory, during recreation, in the laundry, in bed - she would fall into trances lasting for hours. On May 2, 1585, at the time the ecstasies were most frequent, the mistress of novices, Mother Evangelista del Giocondo, wrote: "For some time now, the experiences of this blessed soul are so continual and frequent that we can hardly find a free moment to speak to her, as she is constantly in a state of elevation of mind." Beginning on the afternoon of Holy Thursday, April 19, 1585, Sister Mary Magdalen entered into an ecstasy which lasted twenty-six hours. She passed from room to room of the monastery, re-enacting the sufferings of Christ. "She did not seem to walk, but rather to be carried, such was the lightness and speed of her step." At the crucifixion she stood for an hour and a half with arms extended. From May 7-9, she engaged in three colloquies with each of the persons of the Blessed Trinity. The colloquy with the Father lasted twenty-four hours, beginning on the evening of May 8. When she spoke in the person of the Father, it was "with majesty and grandeur." Her part was delivered in "a humble and submissive manner." At one point, apparently wrapt into heaven, "she began to circle the room in a dance, making curtsies and steps with such dexterity and grace that she seemed to be, not a creature, but an angel from heaven." Pentecost, 1585, marked the climax of this period. For eight days, from June 8-16, except for a few hours daily, Sister Mary Magdalen was in a continual trance. Seven times, at Terce, she received the Holy Spirit under various forms. In dialogues with the Holy Trinity she received high intelligences regarding the mystery of God and experienced in her person the meaning of divine union.

This time of spiritual consolations was followed by "the lion's den," a five-year period of "the greatest trial and affliction of spirit," beginning Trinity Sunday, June 16, 1585. Gone was the sense of joy in God's presence. Her whole life seemed a mistake and a trick of the devil. She despaired of salvation. She was severely tempted against chastity. She underwent doubts about her vocation. She still occasionally experienced ecstasies, but they brought little comfort and at times were very painful. A child of the 16th century, the classic age of demonology, the saint felt that she had been abandoned to the power of the devil. Evil spirits caused her to fall down stairs, beat her, bit her, seemed to be sawing her limb from limb. Their cries rang continually in her ears, so that she seemed to be blaspheming rather than reciting the psalms. She was tempted to run away from the monastery, to commit suicide.

At the same time, Jesus was urging her to reform the Church and her own community. A dozen letters exist today, dating from July 25 to September 4, 1586, dictated by the saint in ecstasy and directed to Pope Sixtus V, the cardinals of the Roman Curia, Cardinal Alessandro de' Medici, archbishop of Florence, and to the superiors in Florence of the religious Orders destined to assist in reform: the Jesuits, Dominicans, and Minims. These letters, to quote one authority, "compare favorably for feeling and content with the best of St. Catherine of Siena." It is doubtful whether they reached their destinations, though the addressees living in Florence probably came to know their contents. The saint also wrote privately on the theme of reform to her former confessor, Peter Blanca, S.J., a Sister Veronica of Corbona, and St. Catherine de' Ricci. The latter's cautious reply, advising her Carmelite sister to consult her spiritual director, is still preserved in the archive of St. Mary of the Angels. Saint Mary Magdalen was also influential in bringing about a greater austerity in the lives of the sisters, changes which were incorporated in the constitutions of the monastery of 1610. Thus, the monastery of St. Mary of the Angels of Florence considers itself a distinct expression of the Carmelite ideal.

On the feast of Pentecost, June 10, 1590, in a joyous vision of the saints, Sister Mary Magdalen was freed from "the lions' den." From this time forward, her ecstasies occur less frequently. Often she had requested of God the cessation of the embarrassing mystical gifts which set her apart from others. Yet she did not remain entirely free of them. During Holy Week of 1592, she again experienced the Passion, this time more painfully than in 1585. On May 3 of the same year, occurred the seizure during which, overwhelmed by the thought that God was not loved, she ran about the house ringing the bells, summoning all to love Love. "O Love," she cried, "you make me die and yet I live." Her ecstasies only ceased with her last illness, beginning in 1604.

But if Sister Mary Magdalen de' Pazzi was canonized, it was not for her ecstasies, but for perfection of love, manifested in fidelity to daily duty and sincere dedication to the needs of others. As in her girlhood, she liked to help with household chores. She rose early to light the fire in the kitchen or laundry and spent hours cooking and washing. She was devoted to the aged and infirm; she would have dearly loved to be infirmarian. From 1595 to 1598, she was in charge of the junior professed.

In 1598, she was elected novice mistress; in 1604, sub-prioress.

It is in her continued relations with her family and the world outside that St. Mary Magdalen becomes most real and human. The score of her personal letters that remain give the impression that the saint was a frequent correspondent and encourage the hope that a continued search may unearth more. They are addressed to her family, other religious, and old friends among the Cavaleresse of San Giovannino. With her father and her brother Geri, she is the nun of the family, reminding them of their religious duties. When she inquires about her nephew Paul, who she heard was ailing, when she asks Geri to send her a bit of nutmeg, the misty image of the exalted mystic suddenly comes into sharper focus.

In 1604, Sister Mary Magdalen took to her bed with the illness that was to be her last. For some time, she had been suffering hemorrhages, fever, coughing spells. Violent headaches accompanied her other symptoms, and she could not partake of much-needed nourishment. "In the home of charity," she wryly observed, "I am dying of hunger." In an age when bodies were worn out at forty, her teeth gave out, and severe toothaches added to her pains. She no longer experienced the mystic flights that lifted her above sensations of pleasure and pain. There remained only suffering and with this she was content. "To suffer, not to die," is the motto attributed to St. Mary Magdalen de' Pazzi. If she did not actually utter these words, they express her spirit. "All the wonder," writes one modern biographer, "all the sublimity of her last years on earth consist in her invincible patience, her perfect serenity, her longing to suffer." She died on May 25, 1607. Her last words admirably sum up the continuous act of praise which was her life: "*Benedictus Deus* – Blessed be God!"

While in ecstasy St. Mary Magdalen often described her visions aloud and gave utterance to reflections on the spiritual life. Her sisters copied down her words, adding descriptions of her actions and outward aspect. This compilation in four manuscript volumes constitutes her "works" and at the same time is her biography. Obviously, we have here not a systematic treatise on mystical theology, but "the story of a soul." Its central theme is Jesus Christ, mystery of God and salvation of humanity, whose activity is seen in close relationship to that of the Holy Spirit. Other themes to which the saint often returns are the mystery of the Church and religious life. St. Mary Magdalen's doctrine is enshrined in rich symbolism and striking mystical experience. It still lies in the current of the Middle Ages, while presaging the dawning period of the Baroque.

Third Order and Scapular Confraternity

The apostolate or activity of the Carmelite Order was as varied in previous centuries as it is now. It consisted in offering the Eucharist and administrating the sacraments to the faithful in the friary churches, in teaching, preaching, and studying theology, philosophy and (in lesser measure) the arts and sciences. Individuals undertook special apostolates such as chaplaincies to nuns, nobles, armies, galleys, etc. Beginning with the 16th century, the Carmelites initiated missions in the New World. No small amount of their interest and effort went to the spiritual guidance and care of the numerous faithful who in the spirit of the times to a greater or less degree sought identification with religious life. We have already seen that from earliest times women took vows in the Order (*conversae*), and that these in the second half of the fifteenth century sometimes formed communities to become cloistered

Carmelite nuns (the second Order). Other forms of aggregation gave rise to what today are the third Order secular and the scapular confraternity.

The names "first, second and third Order," deriving from the *Humiliati*, whose structure they accurately describe, were current among the mendicant orders, but apply only imperfectly to the Carmelites with a monastic tradition of affiliation. The Carmelite brothers and sisters professed the same Rule and so were one Order. Besides the brothers and sisters of Carmel, there were *confratres* and *consorores*, general terms that cover various types of aggregation to the Order.

Among these were the non-professed *conversae* called *mantellates, pinzocchere, beatas*. They followed a rule or statutes suitable to their condition and might even take the three vows, though these remained private or "simple," because not made according to the rule of an approved order. An Italian rule, of probable Venetian origin, *Regola de le sorelle* (1482) has come down to us. Bl. John Soreth wrote a *Troisieme regle des Carmes pour les soeurs familieres du Tierce Ordre et autres* (1455). The habit of these was the white mantle.

The general term, *confratres*, also had a specific application to persons whose relationship to the Order was more or less remote. They were organized into confraternities, of men as well as of women, under the title of Our Lady, for the purpose of participating in the spiritual benefits of the Order. Rules of confraternities at Ferrara (1432), Brescia (1453), and Bologna have been found. Otherwise, the existence of such groups is testified to by the ritual for their reception found in the constitutions, ordinal and missals of the time. The religious obligations assumed by these confraternities (fasts and abstinence, prayer, confession and communion, visits to church, alms, scourging, silence, modesty in attire) made them resemble a third Order rather than a confraternity. Lowest in the scale of commitments and affiliation with the Order were those who were only given letters of confraternity which entitled them to a share in the spiritual goods of the Order in view of some benefit bestowed.

Just as the professed *conversae* – at least in Italy and Spain – in the course of the sixteenth century evolved into cloistered nuns, the *confratres* also underwent change. On the one hand, the *mantellates* had their commitment reduced to the two vows of obedience and chastity according to one's state in life (1587) and in time became tertiaries in name and reality. On the other hand, the confraternities evolved into the scapular confraternity. Two factors contributed to this development: the gradual disuse of the mantle as the distinctive garb of the *confratres* and the diffusion at the beginning of the sixteenth century of the *Sanctorale* and the Sabbatine bull.

The story of St. Simon Stock found in the fourteenth century sanctorals relates the vision of the Virgin to the saint and her promise that whoever dies wearing the scapular of the Order will be saved from hell fire. The fifteenth century writers, Nicholas Calciuri (d. 1466), Peter Bruyne (fl. 1474), Baldwin Leers (d. 1483), Arnold Bostius (d. 1499), Giles de Smet (d. 1506) and John Palaeonydorus (d. 1507), spread the account of the miraculous power of the scapular. They also related another vision of the Virgin in reference to the Carmelite habit, that of Pope John XXII.

The Sabbatine Bull

The vision of St. Simon focused the devotion to Our Lady of Mount Carmel on the scapular of the Order, but the phenomenal growth of the devotion of the scapular was due to the "Sabbatine" bull. This document appeared on the scene in the first half of the fifteenth century. It purports to be a confirmation by Alexander V, December 7, 1409, of a bull of John XXII, dated March 3, 1322, and directed to the prior general, brothers, sisters, and members of the confraternity of the Carmelite Order. Pope John relates a vision in which the Virgin promised, among other things, that she would free all members of the confraternity of the Order from Purgatory the Saturday after their death: "And on the day on which they depart from this world and complete their course to Purgatory, I, their mother, will graciously descend on the Saturday after their death and will free whomever I find in Purgatory and will lead them to the holy mountain of eternal life." To be eligible for this favor, confraternity members must recite the canonical hours, or, if they cannot read, must fast on the days prescribed by the Church and abstain from meat on Wednesdays and Saturdays, except on Christmas day.

Apart from the rather unusual contents of the bull of John XXII – a pope describing an appearance to him of the Virgin – there is no trace of the document either in the papal registers or in original copies. The earliest certain documentary evidence for the Sabbatine bull consists of a notarized copy made in Agrigento, Sicily, August 6, 1430, allegedly of another notarized copy executed in Mallorca, January 2, 1421. The Mallorca copy, as well as the bulls it claims to authenticate, offer insuperable diplomatic difficulties. In all likelihood, the Sabbatine bull originated in Sicily in the fifteenth century, probably inspired by the confirmation by Clement V, August 30, 1309, of the bull of Nicholas IV, August 17, 1289, approving the Rule of the Franciscan Third Order.

The general chapter of 1517 recommended that steps be taken to have the Sabbatine bull recognized by the Holy See. An appeal was made to Pope Leo X, but he died in 1521 before doing anything about it. Nicholas Audet obtained from Clement VII the bull *Ex clementi*, August 12,1530. In this document, the pope does not reproduce the text of the bull of Pope John, as might be expected, but only its content, which he "renews and confirms." Moreover, the intervention of the Virgin is reported in very cautious terms: "The most glorious mother of God, Mary ever virgin, will assist the souls of confraternity members, brothers and sisters, after their death by her continuous intercession, merciful prayers, and special protection." There is no mention of the descent of the Virgin into Purgatory on Saturday.

The generals, beginning with Audet, now add the "Sabbatine" privilege with the obligation of wearing the scapular to the spiritual benefits listed in their letters of confraternity. Such letters are among the oldest documents relative to the Order; priors general from time immemorial were accustomed to grant participation in the spiritual goods of the Order to benefactors and other particularly deserving persons. When the priors general began to grant the Sabbatine privilege to the laity and at the same time bestowed their letters of confraternity on increasingly large numbers of the faithful, the way was paved for the confraternity of the scapular of Mount Carmel, which was to replace all the other confraternities of the Order.

John Baptist Rossi, that fervent devotee of the Virgin, played a decisive role in this development. During his visitation of Spain and Portugal (1566-1567), as he himself declared, he distributed around two hundred thousand scapulars and letters of confraternity. He also obtained from Pope Gregory XIII a more specific statement of the Sabbatine privilege. His brief, *Ut laudes*, September 18, 1577, confirms the indulgences granted by popes to the Order in the past and goes on to state: "The same John XXII published, corroborated and confirmed [the favor] for the souls who are in Purgatory and wore the habit of this Order or entered the confraternity or were inscribed in the number of its members in honor of the same Blessed Mary, Mother of God, to be aided on the Saturday after their death by [her] continuous intercession, merciful prayers, merits and special protection."

The constitutions of the Order published by John Baptist Caffardi in 1586 included the blessing of the habit in the ritual for conferring confraternity with the Order. The decrees of the general chapter of 1593 prescribed a monthly procession in honor of Our Lady of Mount Carmel with a sermon "in which the preacher shall explain the indulgences, graces, privileges and faculties granted to our Order, brothers and confraternity members." In 1604, Clement VIII drew up rules for erecting confraternities, which the Council of Trent had subjected to the jurisdiction of the bishops. Paul V, in 1606, enriched the confraternity of Our Lady of Mount Carmel with many indulgences and placed its patronal feast on July 16. Carmelite confraternities could now be erected anywhere in the world, not only in places where the Order had a convent, as was formerly the case. The general chapter of 1609 chose July 16 as the principal feast of the Order. The same year the Discalced obtained the breviary lessons, *"Cum sacra Pentecostes die,"* approved by Cardinal Robert Bellarmine, which emphasize the vision of St. Simon Stock and the Sabbatine privilege. For the time being, the Order was unable to obtain these lessons. Finally, the prior general, Theodore Straccio, issued the official *Manner of Instituting the Confraternity of the Holy Scapular in Carmelite Convents and Churches* (Zaragoza, 1633). When the scapular confraternity had thus fully developed, the letters of confraternity of the priors general resumed their original form.

The Confraternity of the Scapular

The devotion of the scapular of Carmel struck a sympathetic cord in the post-Tridentine Church and fitted the mood of a conscious and orthodox use of indulgences in reaction to the Lutheran attack. Joseph Falcone writes at this time: "In our days, Spain is outstanding; there is not a house in that land in which the habit of Carmel is not worn, in order to obtain the infinite Carmelite indulgences. Both daughters of King Philip of Spain and all his courtiers wore Our Lady of Mount Carmel's habit or "patience" and the long, wide one at that, as worn by the friars of the Order. It was given to them personally by the Most Reverend General, John Baptist Rossi of Ravenna. Does not all of Spain and Portugal seem to be one great Carmelite convent? In Italy, especially in Sicily, in the Kingdom of Naples, and in Lombardy, there are an infinite number of confraternity members who meet frequently with great devotion. At Piacenza, more than ten thousand members are inscribed in the register of the confraternity: men, women, laymen, and religious of other orders, secular priests, and nuns of diverse orders. Upper and Lower Germany has an infinite number of confraternity members, but because of the doomed heretics many fell away. France had the most members of the whole Order, but today it is oppressed by sacramentary enemies."

Just at this moment of triumph the confraternity of the scapular suffered a setback. In 1603, the inquisitor of Portugal had placed on the index, pending correction, a book listing the privileges of the Carmelite Order; in 1609 he outlawed all books mentioning the Sabbatine privilege. In reply to his report, Rome approved the decision with regard to the book of privileges and forbade the Carmelites to speak of their indulgences in the pulpit or elsewhere. When the inquisitor tried to implement these instructions, public scandal was so great that he was obliged to make an exception for the scapular. The Carmelites of Portugal dispatched to Rome two friars, John of St. Thomas, regent of Coimbra, and George Godinez, to appeal to the pope. The result of a protracted study by the Sacred Congregation of the Inquisition was the decree of January 20, 1613. The Carmelite Fathers are permitted to preach that the faithful may devoutly believe that the Blessed Virgin by her continuous intercession, merciful prayers, merits, and special protection will assist the souls of deceased brothers and members of the confraternity, especially on Saturday, the day which the church dedicates to the Blessed Virgin. The conditions for trusting in such a favor are that the recipients die in the state of grace, wear the Carmelite habit, observe chastity according to their state in life, and recite the little office of the Blessed Virgin; if they cannot recite it, they are to observe the Church fasts and abstain from meat on Wednesdays and Saturdays, unless Christmas falls on those days. The decree further forbids representing the Virgin descending into Purgatory to free souls. It was accompanied by a private instruction to the Carmelites: "The Carmelite Fathers. . . shall not mention the Sabbatine bull, in order that the term may be forgotten . . . because it is not entirely clear up to the present that John XXII specified Saturday in the way the Carmelite Fathers understand it, or any other particular day."

This "most wise decree," as Benedict XIV called it, imposed some necessary reserve on a subject that could easily get out of hand. The cocoon of legend was discarded, and there remained the sound Marian doctrine of the scapular devotion. The decree of 1613, constantly called to mind by succeeding popes, continued to regulate teaching and practice with regard to the scapular devotion down to the present day.

Certainly the interposition of ecclesiastical authority did not dampen popular enthusiasm. In Rome, the confraternity of San Martino ai Monti at the time numbered around forty-two thousand members; that of San Crisogono of the Mantuan Congregation, twenty thousand. San Crisogono's was the oldest scapular confraternity in Rome. It was the custom to invite popes on their election to enroll there. In 1610, there were sixteen thousand confraternity members in Lisbon; by 1613, their number had reached twenty-three thousand.

According to Francis Potel, Master Angelo, the prior of San Martino ai Monti, inscribed more than three thousand persons in the scapular confraternity. Potel himself enrolled more than one hundred persons the day the confraternity was erected at Arras. Francis Voersio stated in 1613 that few in the Kingdom of Naples did not wear the scapular. Francis Mondini claimed at least seventy-five thousand members for the confraternity of Venice in 1675. Authors witness to the large number of the faithful who abstained from meat on Wednesdays in Naples, Cologne, Messina, and Venice. At Cologne, there was a special fish market on Wednesdays for this reason. On being told that the royal exchequer was losing more than thirty thousand *scudi* annually because of the abstinence required by the Sabbatine privilege, Philip III of Spain is said to have replied: "I would rather have my subjects devoted to the Virgin than an increase in my income."

Chapter 9

The Spiritual and Intellectual Life of the Order

Catholicism in the second half of the sixteenth century lay in the immediate shadow of the Council of Trent. It was concerned with the task of overcoming the ignorance and moral decrepitude of the declining Middle Ages. A spur to this endeavor was the competition provided by the new large non-Catholic Christian community in the West: Protestantism in the first vigor of its youth.

Post-tridentine devotion stresses an enlightened faith, orthodoxy, the art of living and dying in a Christian manner. After the frequently superstitious and irreverent celebration of the Eucharist and the sacraments in the late Middle Ages, the liturgical revival centered on the reform of ritual and dignified, devout cultic action. The attacks of Protestantism on Catholic worship brought reaffirmation of traditional ways cleansed of dross. The spirit of the times did not invoke the communal aspect of the liturgy. Personal, private prayer became the most satisfying expression of devotion. Instruction, orthodoxy in devotion were a concern. Methods of meditating were developed and propagated.

The unity which had characterized religious life in the Middle Ages brought all actions of the day under "*vacare Deo*." Prayer had consisted of the liturgy, oral prayer, and the *lectio divina* and had formed a whole with study and work. Now, in the world that had given birth to Protestantism, the immediate personal relationship with God was keenly felt. Prayer came to mean mental prayer or contemplation. Moreover, new religious orders were founded with the active apostolate as their goal. For them, prayer served the practical function of energizing action which lay outside prayer and to a certain extent militated against it. The old religious orders did not escape the influence of this dialectic.

Meditation in Common

The general chapter of 1564 which elected John Baptist Rossi reminded the brethren of their obligation of personal prayer: "After our religious have finished the day and night office let them not succumb to idleness and sluggishness, but let them devote themselves to some interest such as letters, meditation or prayer, or manual labor." Those exempt from choir should dedicate themselves to study, meditation, or prayer in their rooms.

In Spain particularly meditation was held in honor, so it comes as no surprise that the Carmelites began to practice it. (Of all unlikely people, Gaspar Nieto, returning from the chapter to Andalusia confirmed in his office of provincial and reformer, introduced the practice of an hour's meditation in common, although how far this directive was actually enforced is not known. In 1576, as already noted, Jerome Gracián ordered a half hour's meditation to be made twice a day in the Casa Grande of Seville and probably in the rest of the province.

In 1571, the Dominican visitator, Peter Fernández, introduced a quarter of an hour of meditation twice daily in the province of Castile, perhaps confirming an ordinance of Rossi in 1566.

The provincial chapter of Aragon in 1572 ordained that novices and professed clerics should remain for a time in prayer before the Blessed Sacrament at Complin time and priests should join them for their edification. The chapter of 1585, presided over by Angel de Salazar, imposed a quarter of an hour of prayer twice a day, "mental or vocal, as the Spirit suggests to each." Two years later, the chapter under Michael Carranza extended the time of mental prayer to an hour and a half a day. Carranza also prescribed the practice in Portugal in 1591, where, for that matter, it had been already decreed in the days of the Holy Constable.

In Italy, the practice of meditation was longer in coming. Rossi did not impose it there. In 1583, John Baptist Caffardi introduced two half hours of mental prayer a day in the province of Sicily; he may have done likewise in the other provinces of Italy. The previous year, he had made the same provision for the friars of the Mantuan Congregation. The nuns of the Congregation — at least in some monasteries — had been making meditation in common since 1481. Their constitutions of 1540 impose it on all. The monastery of Our Lady of the Angels in Florence had similar legislation. Due to the variety of legislation in Carmelite monasteries, it is difficult to form an idea of practice among the nuns. In French monasteries meditation in common was not prescribed.

The general chapter of 1593 for the first time imposed meditation on the whole Order. A half hour was to be made after prime and vespers. Although the obligation remained, due to the decrees of reform for religious of Clement VIII, the constitutions of that part of the Order which did not follow the Stricter Observance never prescribed meditation until observance was unified under the constitutions of 1902.

The Revision of the Liturgy

The general chapter of 1580 also ordered the liturgical books revised. In 1568, Pope Pius V had imposed on the Church in the West the Roman rite as reformed by the Tridentine commission. Exception was made for rites which had been in existence two hundred years; the Carmelite rite thus escaped extinction. Nevertheless, the Order, like the Church, felt the need to reform its liturgy, and in the course of this process the rite underwent the influence of the strong Romanizing trend of the time. The general chapter of 1564 under John Baptist Rossi assigned two "reformers," to each convent, who were to reduce all to uniformity. It also decreed the reform of the breviary, to bring order in the reigning confusion of texts, and the unification of the chant, "for it is not reasonable that the members of one Order having the same name, Rule and superiors should differ in their chants and rites." Finally a catalog or calendar of saints was ordered drawn up with the caution not to remove the offices of saints that had been celebrated a long time. Rossi, in fact, issued a missal (Venice, apud Iuntas, 1574) which incorporated many features of the Roman rite. The following year, he issued a breviary prepared by James Maistret, prior of Lyon (Paris, apud Joannem Stratium, 1575). The breviary, however, proved unsatisfactory, and after the general chapter of 1575, Caffardi entrusted Honorius Francis de Turcis with its reform. The result of his labors (Venice, apud Iuntas, 1579) failed equally to meet demands.

The general chapter of 1580 returned to the subject of liturgical reform. The general appointed a commission to straighten out the rubrical discrepancies in the missals and breviaries. Furthermore, the chapter decreed that "breviaries and missals, constitutions, a perpetual calendar, and books of chant and for funerals be as soon as possible printed at the expense of the Order, corrected and restored to a more attractive form." Caffardi's breviary appeared in 1585 (Rome, Francis Zannetti), his missal in 1587 (Rome, James Tornerio). He had taken care to request papal approval of the breviary, granted by Gregory XIII, August 4, 1584. The brief, printed in all subsequent breviaries, requires apostolic approval for further changes and thus obviates the rubrics of the ordinal. It should be noted that this apostolic approval did not include the missal. Another centralizing factor is found in the brief of Gregory XIII, of September 27, 1584, which reserves to the prior general the right to publish Carmelite breviaries and missals. In Caffardi's breviary and missal, as the pope notes, doubtful and apocryphal writings are eliminated, uncertain texts of the Fathers removed, scriptural passages in the antiphons and the ordinary of the Mass underwent changes. The sanctoral — even in respect to Carmelite saints — was drastically reduced. The manner of indicating the rank of feasts was changed. In spite of all these alterations, Fr. Zimmerman felt justified in writing: "It is only right to say that the liturgy corrected in this way was entirely worthy of the pope's praise; with good taste one cannot sufficiently admire the special traits of the old rite were retained and an important and venerable monument of medieval Christian piety was preserved, while avoiding the errors that had been introduced and had disfigured the purity of the style and the gravity of the diction."

At this time, the Discalced petitioned the Holy See for the Roman rite. Their motive is not known; in granting their request, September 20, 1586, Sixtus V mentions no reasons for the change. Some writers allege that Doria took the occasion to widen the breach between the Order and the reform. Others claim that the Discalced were weary of the constant changes made in the rite and the resultant confusion. St. Teresa objected to changes made in the office by the general chapter of 1580 and wanted the new Discalced constitutions to specify that "we are not bound to observe all these changes but may say the office as we do now."

To the sanctoral of the Roman rite the Discalced added the feasts of the saints celebrated in the Order before Caffardi's decimations, and so ironically they observed more Carmelite feasts than the practitioners of the Carmelite rite. In 1610, the old feasts of the Carmelite saints were restored, but without proper texts. The previous year, the Discalced had obtained proper feasts of the Order revised by Cardinal Robert Bellarmine. The Order repeatedly tried to obtain these feasts with their proper lessons, as appears, for instance, from the resolutions passed by the general chapters of 1620 and 1625. The Carmelites gazed with particular longing on the office of the Solemn Commemoration of the Blessed Virgin with octave and proper lessons, featuring the *"Cum sacra Pentecostes die,"* lesson, which emphasized the scapular devotion. In 1635, the prior general, Theodore Straccio, even offered to abandon the Carmelite rite, with the exception of the recitation of the *Salve Regina* after Mass, provided the Order would be granted the proper offices of its saints. Only in 1672 were these finally acquired.

The Carmelites had the good taste not to avail themselves of the dubious ministrations of the humanist revisors of the hymns of the Roman breviary (1632). *Accessit latinitas, recessit pietas.* The medieval hymns were retained unspoiled in the Carmelite breviary.

The changes wrought in the breviary and missal required a new edition of the ordinal of Sibert de Beka. About 1610, the Spaniard, Cyril de las Heras, commissioned by the prior general, Henry Silvio, prepared a new ordinal or ceremonial. This seems to be the work which the chapter of 1613 ordered examined by a commission with a view to publication. In 1616, the new ceremonial, edited by Peter de los Apóstoles, of the province of Andalusia, appeared (Roma, G. Faciotto, 1616). For order, clarity, and accuracy it compares favorably with any ceremonial produced in the seventeenth century. However, it departed in several respects from the reformed breviary and missal and adopted a number of rubrics from the Roman rite, especially in the Mass.

As a result of the post-Tridentine changes, though the Carmelites still had their own rite, it was no longer correct (if it ever was) to speak of it as the rite of the Holy Sepulchre.

Spiritual Writers of Spain

Up to this point, the spiritual writing produced by the Order was sparse and of somewhat limited interest. In the sixteenth century this activity gathers momentum, the number of Carmelite spiritual writers increases and the range of interest broadens. There is yet no question of a "school," that is, a concentration of interest around a specific aspect of the spiritual life and a characteristic interpretation of its problems. Carmelite writing reflects the spiritual interests of the age.

If Spain dominated sixteenth century devotion and mysticism, it was Carmel that contributed St. Teresa of Avila and St. John of the Cross. It is questionable how far the Order can claim credit for them as writers. Before their time, the Order had not produced a mystical literature comparable to that of monasticism or the other mendicant orders. The two saints bloom like unexpected exotic flowers in the desert of Carmel. They wrote, of course, out of their Carmelite experience; in so far as they depend on literary tradition, the Order had little to offer them. From St. Teresa herself we learn the role played in her life of prayer by the works of the Franciscans, Francis d'Osuna (d. 1540) and Bernardine de Laredo (1482-1540), nor is the influence of the *Spiritual Exercises* through her Jesuit directors to be overlooked. Of the Order's literature the *Book of the First Monks* inflamed her desire for the contemplative life. There is much disagreement about the literary sources of St. John of the Cross; they are probably to be sought outside Spain, especially among the Rheno-Flemish mystics.

The contribution of St. Teresa of Avila and of St. John of the Cross to the literature of Christian mysticism cannot be treated here even in the most summary fashion. Much has already been written on this subject; moreover, after the separation of the Discalced from the Order, the works of these two great Carmelites influenced the Order hardly more than those of other writers. At the same time, the great figures of St. Teresa and St. John cast into shadow the lesser writers the Order produced. These latter remain for the most part yet to be studied, and little more can be done here than list their names.

In the atmosphere of renewal brought about by the reforming efforts of Audet and Rossi, the Spanish provinces began to produce a spiritual literature of considerable interest. James Montañés of the province of Aragon entered the Order in his native Valencia in 1539. Distinguished more for simplicity and piety than for learning, he did not attend the university. He filled the office of prior in various convents; he was prior of Pamplona when he died in 1577. In the Valencian language, Montañés produced a *Mirror for Living Well and a Help for Dying* (Valencia, 1559), which the author himself translated into Castilian and extensively revised (Madrid, Francisco Sanchez, 1573). In a second work, *Mirror and Art of Dying Well* (Valencia, Juan Navarro, 1565), Montañés rewrote the second part of his previous book, adding a detailed narration of the passion and death of our Lord. *The Mirror for Living Well* shows a concern over death, not as a morbid fixation, but as the end of the journey of life. The way of this journey is Jesus Christ. The author recommends mortification of the passions, love of Christ (the Eucharist) and of his mother, and perseverance in good works. To priests preparing for celebrating Mass Montañés suggests a half hour meditation. *The Mirror and Art of Dying Well* is meant to assist and inspire hope in the dying and to urge priests to help them. Montañés' little books are characterized by the Christocentricity of the *Devotio moderna* and of Carmelite spirituality. Writing in a simple manner for humble folk, the author does not hesitate to lead his readers along the path of contemplation. The numerous editions of the two books show that they succeeded in reaching the audience intended for them.

Michael Alphonse Carranza (1527-1606) was one of the outstanding Carmelites in Spain. He entered the Order in his native Valencia, obtained the doctorate in theology and taught at the universities of Huesca and Valencia. As secretary, he accompanied the vicar general, Damian de León, sent by Nicholas Audet in 1552 to reform the Spanish provinces. Elected provincial of Aragon in 1561, he filled this office three times. For many years, he served as apostolic visitator in Spain and Portugal, promoting the practice of methodical meditation and religious observance. A friend of Nicholas Doria, he opposed the separation of the Discalced from the Order and is said to have wept when this came about at the general chapter of 1593. At that meeting he was named vicar general for Spain with the approval of Philip II who esteemed him highly.

Besides editions of other writers' spiritual writings, Carranza wrote *Way to Heaven Divided into Seven Journeys for the Days of the Week* (Valencia, Juan Crisóstomo Garriz, 1601), *The First Part of a Catechism and Doctrine for Religious* (Valencia, Juan Crisóstomo Garriz, 1605). Carranza also alludes to his *Christian Cavalier* and a commentary on the *Prima secundae* of St. Thomas.

Juan Sanz, 1557-1608

Carranza was the novice master of Juan Sanz (1557-1608), the most significant Spanish Carmelite writer of the period. In his life and writings Sanz passes beyond the beginnings of the spiritual life to the realms of mysticism. Born in Onteniente (Valencia), he entered the Order at Játiva and obtained the doctorate in theology at the university of Valencia in 1586. He filled such important posts as professor of theology in Valencia, novice master, prior of Valencia and finally provincial of Aragon (1603-1606). He was a friend of the saintly archbishop of Valencia, John de Ribera, who esteemed him for his virtue and learning. He was much sought after as a preacher and spiritual director. Fray John was much given to penance and prayer, at which he spent three hours a day throughout his busy life.

Sanz wrote a *Spiritual Alphabet*, of which the early editions have been lost, but which was reprinted during his lifetime by John Pinto de Victoria. Only a few of

Sanz's letters of spiritual counsel, preserved for the most part in Pinto's *Life*, have survived. Other unpublished and apparently lost works include *A Bouquet of the Spouse of God* (a directory of nuns) and *The Seven Words of the Savior*.

Sanz's writings reveal a rich doctrine of prayer. The end of the spiritual life is the love of God, which finds its complete expression in contemplative union. This union is eminently affective and is brought about by the Holy Spirit through the gift of piety. The most efficacious means to union with God is prayer, which Sanz divides into intellective (meditation) and affective. The latter receives his closest attention and comprises aspiration, repose, and suspension. In this highest degree of the prayer of suspension, the humanity of Christ gives place to the immediate experience of the Holy Trinity. Sanz is to be ranked among the writers of the age who especially promoted the prayer of aspiration. To this form of prayer he applied the time-honored technique of the alphabet, or acrostic. Sanz's *Alphabet*, moreover, is in poetic form of a high order, combining beauty of expression with eloquence and profundity of sentiment altogether worthy of the golden age of Spanish literature.

Other Spanish spiritual writers of the Order include Diego Velázquez, of Medina del Campo, who published the two-volume *Queen of Heaven* (Medina del Campo, Francisco del Canto, 1580), a popular exposition of the principal mysteries of the life of the Blessed Virgin, based on an allegorical interpretation of scripture. Other devotional works, *The Life and Excellencies of Our Savior* and *The Contempt of Death*, apparently were never printed.

Diego Sánchez de la Camara, like St. Teresa a native of Avila but her junior, wrote a book on the passion of Christ (Madrid, Querino Gerardo, 1589). The Catalan Michael Pedrolo who died in 1608, aged thirty-six, took advantage of a current interest to entitle his book *Discovery of the Treasure and Riches God Has Hidden in the Indies of his Divine Body and Blood* (Barcelona, Onofrio Anglada, 1608).

Other writers produced works of devotion which seem to have remained in manuscript, the whereabouts of which are unknown at present. Diego de Casanate (d. 1557) wrote a commentary on the Rule consisting of two tracts. Casanate was provincial of Aragon and suffragan bishop of Zaragoza. Peter Rivas of Zaragoza (d. 1577) went to the Low Countries as confessor and secretary of Charles V. His works have somber titles: *The Small Number of the Elect*, *The Difficult Road to Heaven*, and *Help for the Souls in Purgatory*. Martin de Acuña, of the province of Andalusia, theologian to Peter Girón, duke of Osuna and viceroy of Naples, bishop of Lipari (1585), left a large manuscript volume, *The Art of Divine Love*. Vicente de Torregrosa gave a son, Thomas of the Nativity (d. 1592) to the Discalced reform. In 1576, he himself entered the Discalced convent in Seville with the name, Vincent de la Paz, but later transferred to the Calced Carmelites in the same city. He left four spiritual works, the titles of which are not known.

In Portugal, Simon Coelho (1514-1606) entered the Order in Lisbon and acquired the doctorate in Italy at Siena. He served as prior in Moura and Lisbon and as provincial, 1584-1588. He is remembered for his piety and devotion to Our Lady, especially her rosary. Among his works are *Compendio das chronicas da ordem de N. S. do Carmo* (Lisboa, Antonio Gonsalvez, 1572) and an unpublished *Dialogue on the Active and Contemplative Life*. Jerome Britto (d. 1583), of Lisbon, left unpublished *Exercises in Honor of the Virgin Mary*. Roderic d'Ornelas, also of

Lisbon, flourished in the middle of the century. He left a manuscript work on *The Garments of Mary*.

Spiritual Writers in the Low Countries

One of the Order's most notable mystical writers was Francis Amelry (fl. 1550). Fallen into oblivion, he was recently restored to deserved recognition by the Jesuit Fathers of the Ruusbroec Society in Antwerp. Although little is known about him beyond the fact that he had the baccalaureate in theology and was prior of Ypres, the freshness and intimacy of his writings say much about him as an humble but strong and noble spirit, sensitive to the divine love present in the world. He is a skillful writer, and the nobility of his theme lifts him to realms of lyricism and literary expression of a high order. Fr. A. Ampe, S.J., aptly calls him "the noble singer of love." Of a dozen or so spiritual tracts, two have been published in recent times. Under the title in Flemish *The Power of God's Love* (Tielt, 1949) Lodewijk Moereels edited seven letters of spiritual direction to a devout person living in the world who "would like to love." *A Dialog between the Soul and Scripture* Moereels issued as *The Soul in Love* (Tielt, 1950). It was translated into Latin (Coloniae, 1605) by the canon regular Anthony van Hemert, also known in the history of Flemish spirituality.

Jean de Cartigny (d. 1580?), of Valenciennes, received the doctorate in 1554 and served as regent and prior of Brussels. Among Cartigny's works is a *Latin Paraphrase of the Seven Penitential Psalms in Elegaic* (Brussels, Kon. Bibl., Ms. 12003-4, ff. 1-9) of which a French version was published in his *Le chevalier errant* (Antwerp, J. Bellerus, 1595). It was only at the insistence of friends, Cartigny wrote to the Carmelite bishop, Martin Cuyper, that he published his *Four Last Ends of Man* (Antwerp, J. Bellerus, 1558). The book is a detailed treatment of this well-worn theme and seems to have found favor with his contemporaries, for it was translated into French and reprinted several times. In some of these editions, Cartigny appears side by side with the Dominican Louis de Granada and Giles Toparius. The French edition contains his *Lament of the Lost Soul with its Body*, a six-hundred line poem of indifferent quality. The Duke of Osuna possessed a manuscript containing three related tracts by Cartigny on the *Correct Manner of Confessing*, the *Correct Manner of Praying*, and the *Manner of Disposing Oneself for Holy Mass* (Madrid, Biblioteca Nacional, Ms. 11258). Cartigny's principal work, the *Voyage of the Wandering Knight*, will be considered later in this chapter.

Lawrence Cuyper (d. 1594) was related to the Carmelite Bishop, Martin Cuyper. Born in Geraardsbergen in West Flanders, he studied at Louvain and Cologne, receiving the doctorate at the latter university in 1573. Prior of Geraardsbergen and Brussels, provincial (1581), theologian and councilor to John Venderville, bishop of Tournai, Cuyper suffered imprisonment during the religious disturbances of the time. He found opportunity, nevertheless, to carry on a considerable literary activity. Among his writings are a volume of twenty-four sermons on the *Four Last Ends* (Cologne, M. Cholinus, 1583), *Paraclesis for the Waging of Spiritual Warfare* (Cologne, M. Cholinus, 1583), and a *Life of St. Anne* (Antwerp, J. Bellerus, 1591, etc.). The beginning of the spiritual life is faith, Cuyper writes, which in turn is divided into belief in God's revelation, belief in his existence, and the faith which is expressed through hope and love. Love, or charity, finds expression in the eight beatitudes, each of which is practiced in three stages. The *Paraclesis* is addressed to Henry von Reuschenburg and the German knights. The evils of the times are not to be ascribed to external causes, such as political circumstances, but are to be combated with the spiritual arms of chastity, humility and mortification, patience and fortitude, justice, holy thoughts, avoiding evil and doing good, charity.

Adrian Hecquet (d. 1580), doctor of theology from Cologne and long-time prior of Arras, was a prolific writer. Much of his work is concerned with religious controversy, but he also produced works of devotion, like *The Repose of the Soul* (Antwerp, G. Simonis, 1557), *The Form of Perfect Penitence* (Antwerp, G. Simonis, 159), *The Ordinary of the True Christian* (Paris, 1576?). Another controversialist, the turbulent Peter Wolf (d. 1580) left a *Book of Virginal Purity* (Brussels, Kon. Bibl., Ms. 4322-4324).

Spiritual Writers of France

French Carmelites during this century of religious turmoil were concerned mostly with preaching and controversy. There is little sign of the explosion of spiritual writing that was to occur in the 17th century. Julian de Rosoy wrote the *Reliques of the Sinful Soul*, a commentary on the *"De Profundis"* (Paris, Jean André, 1542). Julian Guingant, of the Congregation of Albi, wrote *A Remedy for the Sinful Soul*, which fell under censure of the University of Paris in 1544. He received the doctorate there in 1547. He died at Beauvais during a Lenten sermon around 1555. John de Montay left an unpublished life of Bl. Frances of Amboise (1548), which became the main source for the early printed biographies. Louis Gendron, doctor of Paris (1586), provincial of Touraine (1593-1596), spent his last years as vicar of the nuns at Vannes. He wrote about the Eucharist and the three Marys. Peter Courtain (d. 1599), of the province of Provence, doctor of Paris (1581), published several collections of sermons, among them, *A Mixture of Delicacies of the Most Sacred Body and Blood of Christ with the Eight Beatitudes* (Paris, A. Beysius, 1585).

The German provinces, engaged in the struggle for survival, at this time produced no spiritual writers of note.

Spiritual Writers of Italy

In Italy, the Mantuan Congregation contributed some writers of devotional literature. Albert Mary Valesnieri, of Ferrara, wrote twenty *Lectures on the High and Ineffable Mysteries of the Mass* (Milano, G.B. de' Ponte, 1567), a spiritual and symbolical explanation of the parts and rubrics of the Mass. Anthony Ricci, of Novellara (d. 1571), doctor of theology at Bologna, several times vicar general of the Congregation and theologian at the Council of Trent, wrote *A Method of Preparing the Soul for Death* (Ferrara, 1565). Another theologian at Trent, Lucrezio Tiraboschi, wrote *Ethics of the Holy Spirit in the Psalms of the Canonical Hours* (Brescia, 1566), a commentary on Psalm 118, later included in his *Explanation of All the Psalms* (Venice, apud Zannetum 1572). In the interests of promoting mental prayer in the Congregation, the vicar general, Virgil Bentivogli, in 1596 published a manner of making it which seems lost.

In the Italian provinces outside the Mantuan Congregation, the provincial of Tuscany, Nicholas Aurifico Bonfigli (d. 1601?), rendered a service to the devout by publishing editions and anthologies of the writings of the Fathers and of writers like Louis de Granada. He himself wrote a tract on the passion of Christ (Venice, 1568), a *Mirror for Nuns* (Florence, 1591), and *Praise of Mount Calvary*. Elisha Venturini, of the Romandiola province, a doctor of the university of Padua, wrote *The Common Lot of Pilgrim Man* (1599).

Perhaps the most interesting spiritual writer among the Italian Carmelites of this period is Christopher Silvestrani Brenzone (d. 1608), of Verona. He taught theology at Venice, Florence, and Pisa, and was widely active as a preacher. His numerous writings include various devotional works, among them his *Spiritual Portrait* (2nd ed., Ravenna, Cesare Cazazza and Francesco Tebaldini Comp, 1585), a guide to religious perfection. Strikingly, the ideal the author proposes is the solitary life. The virtues needed to arrive at this goal are quiet, poverty, humility, obedience, patience, prayer, and silence. With regard to prayer, he remarks that he "does not attempt to write a treatise on prayer, but only a brief method of making it."

In discussing the time of prayer, Silvestrani describes the sixteenth century friar's day: in the morning, prayer, divine office, Mass, and lectures; at dinner time, prayers of grace, spiritual reading during the meal, prayers for benefactors. Immediately afterwards, follow discussions of the morning's lectures or other useful questions. Then all go to their cells "to apply themselves to contemplation." In the evening, there is examen of conscience and evening prayer. Silence, necessary to contemplation and meditation, is strongly recommended. As an example of uninterrupted prayer, the author cites Master Augustine Vaghistelli, who never abandoned "the spiritual enterprise" in spite of his duties as provincial of Tuscany and vicar general. In his cell, the friar should remain alone, passing his time in spiritual reading, prayer, and study. Silvestrani provides an interesting insight into the lives of the fervent friars of the sixteenth century. However, his peculiar telegraphic style and passion for outlines and tables make his books difficult to read.

Preachers of the Sixteenth Century

Although the Carmelites, unlike the Dominicans, were not founded to preach, they share this apostolate with the other mendicant orders and have on occasion distinguished themselves in the pulpit. Many of the controversialists mentioned in connection with Protestantism were eminent preachers.

Also worthy of note was Sebastian Avezzani (d. 1580), of Cesena in the province of Romagna, doctor and teacher of theology and twice provincial (1571-1574, 1580). To a life of study he joined a fruitful career of preaching. His published sermons include *Homiletic Digressions on Sacred Scripture* (Venice, G. A. Valvassori, 1569) and sermons on the incarnation, birth and resurrection of the Lord.

Thomas Beauxamis (d. 1589), polemicist, preached at the courts of Catherine de Medici, Charles IX, and Henry III. William Chaudière, printer of Paris, published his *Homilies for the Gospels of Lent* (1567, 2 v.), *Homilies on the Mass, Passion, and Resurrection of the Lord* (1570), *Twenty-eight Homilies of the Prophet Habakkuk* (1578), the first two of which underwent several printings. Anselm Stöckl made an interesting anthology of prayers culled from Beauxamis' Lenten sermons: *Enchiridion Quadragesimale precationum diariarum* (München, A. Berg, 1585).

Martin Peraza (d. 1604) held the chair of sacred scripture at the university of Zaragoza and Salamanca and also carried out a busy apostolate of preaching. Besides *Sermons for Lent and the Resurrection* (Salamanca, A. Tabernier y A. Renaut, 1604) and *Sermons for Advent and the Saints* (Zaragoza, A. Tavano, 1600), which enjoyed several printings, he left another two manuscript volumes of Lenten sermons and a volume of sermons on Our Lady. "The oratorical style of Martin Peraza," Miguel Garciá Herrero writes, "is that of the good era: facility, simplicity, liveliness; emotional warmth in the dialog form of which he makes frequent use."

Dionysius Jubero (d. 1612), elected provincial of Castile in 1604, taught at the University of Salamanca. His *Sermons for the Sundays after Pentecost* (Salamanca, A. Tabernier, 1612) were printed several times.

Preachers, according to the constitutions of 1586, should be examined and approved by the prior general or provincial. Besides, since the Council of Trent, they needed the "blessing" of the bishop to preach in Carmelite churches and his licence to preach elsewhere. Stipends for preaching belong to the community, not the individual, though we have seen that this does not exclude their being reserved to the needs of the preacher earning them. Even when preaching in Carmelite churches, preachers should follow the pericope of the Roman missal. Preachers should not propound fanciful prophecies or novel opinions unlikely to edify their hearers, or engage in controversy with other preachers. In sermons on Saturdays of Lent, they should introduce a Marian theme. Neither should they neglect the saints of the Order, nor "the antiquity and greatness of the Order and the scapular confraternity and its indulgences" (*Constitutiones et decreta*, Cremona, 1593, pt. 1, ch. 10).

Studies, 1550-1600

The Council of Trent, in establishing (or reviving) the diocesan seminary or cathedral school (sess. 23, *De reformatione*, can. 18), at last found the remedy that was to heal the long-festering sore of clerical ignorance and immorality. The mendicants, who since the Middle Ages had enjoyed an enviable educational program, saw their preeminence in learning eroded, if not eliminated. Possessed of a well-tried system, they were slow to adopt the new methods of centralization of the various stages in clerical formation, and as in other aspects of Tridentine reform, it sometimes took a papal push to make them move. While the curriculum at the doctoral level was effective, the education of the "simple" friar remained haphazard.

Audet's *Isagogicon* (1524) had found its way into Caffardi's constitutions (1586), which contained a new chapter, *De professis* (pt. 1, ch. 15). The formation of young religious remained the responsibility of the individual convent, but certain seminary-like structures began to take form. Each convent was to have a grammarian – a lay person, if not a friar, – to teach novices and other youths the rudiments (pt. 1, ch. 18, n. 1). The novitiate was to be strictly enclosed (pt. 1, ch.14, n.5, 8, 11).

An important innovation the constitutions inherited from Audet was the provision for the formation of professed clerics. From profession to the subdiaconate, these were to live separately under a master of professed (*magister professorum*), who was to supervise their continuing spiritual as well as intellectual development (pt. 1, ch.15). The master of professed was a new office: the traditional master of students (*magister studentium*) was simply a bachelor of theology obliged to teach philosophy for a year before continuing toward the doctorate (pt. 1, ch. 17, n. 6).

Chizzola's *Decreta* (Seville, 1595), compiled under the influence of Clement VIII, ordered the establishment of one central novitiate and house of professed in each province (two if necessary), where alone in the future novices and professed might be accepted and trained. In other words, the Carmelite seminary was created. A knowledge of Latin was required for admission to the novitiate. Each novitiate should have two masters, one for spiritual instruction, one to teach grammar and rhetoric. The novices were to make a half hour of meditation twice a day in their oratory, and the master was to instruct them in the art of mental prayer. The novices' cells and their furnishings were prescribed. Once a month the novices were permitted to recreate under supervision of their master in some place within the precincts of the convent. Professed not yet in Orders should observe a similar regime (ch. 17). Although these regulations were intended for Spain and Portugal, they represent what was soon to be the law throughout the Church.

In a series of decrees issued at the end of this century and the beginning of the next, Clement VIII regulated the conduct of novitiates, prohibiting the reception of novices by individual convents and limiting it to certain observant houses approved by the Holy See.

Little formal education was required for ordination as such; courses in philosophy and theology were reserved for select clerics destined to become lectors, bachelors, and doctors. Audet asked a speaking knowledge of Latin and grammar for promotion to orders (*Isagogicon*, ch. 1, n. 4; ch. 8; n. 5). The constitutions ordained that clerics should be able to read and sing and should be "sufficiently instructed in the ecclesiastical office" before profession (pt. 1, ch. 13, n. 4). A cleric who fails to learn to read after two years of instruction should be reduced to the state of *conversus* (pt. 1, ch. 14, n. 13). Chizzola required a knowledge of Latin for admission to the novitiate.

According to the constitutions, the continuing education of the ordinary friar, at least in houses with eight priests, was provided by a lector who daily read cases of conscience. "If need be, let them also use the vernacular, so that the brethren may learn, especially the simple ones, and this sort of lecture may be of profit." Convents with twelve priests were to have a regent with a doctor's degree able to teach the arts and theology and to represent the Order with honor on public occasions. For the benefit of all, he was to lecture daily on sacred scripture or cases of conscience "in such a way that they not only be of spiritual profit (to their hearers) but also delight them. Where they (the regents) deem it advisable, they may use the vernacular, and their lectures should be so clear and evident as to be understood and remembered by all" (pt. 1, ch. 18, n. 2-3).

A more advanced age for ordination, examinations for faculties to confess, and other conditions were steps toward a more informed clergy. The Franciscan John Wild (1495-1554), George Witzel (1501-1573), and John Holthusius of Kempen, among others, composed manuals or catechisms of information useful for priests and candidates to ordination. These with the *Expositio in canonem Missae* of Bl. Odo, bishop of Cambrai (d. 1113), Nicholas Aurifico, indefatigable editor and translator, collected into a little volume, *Examen ordinandorum* (Venice, 1568), many times printed in Italy and Germany.

The course of higher studies was traditionally described in three chapters of the constitutions: "On Studies and Students in General," "On Special Studies," "On the Prerogatives of Doctors" (pt. 1, ch. 17-19).

In the chapter on studies in general, the eighteen general *studia* of Soreth increased to twenty-five: Rome, Paris, Toulouse, Padua, Pavia, Naples, Florence, Siena, Pisa, Turin, Cremona, Ravenna, Catania, Trapani, Catalonia, Salamanca, Alcalá, Lérida, Coimbra, London, Cologne, Avignon, Perpignan, Bordeaux, Angers (pt. 1, ch. 17, n. 1). Four *studia* were dropped: Bologna and Ferrara, which belonged to the Mantuan Congregation, Montpellier and Vienna. The latter had been abandoned in the course of the Reformation and in 1568 was given to the Jesuits by Maximilian II. Eleven Italian and Spanish *studia* were added: Rome (which now preceded Paris), Naples, Pisa, Turin, Cremona, Ravenna, Trapani, Salamanca, Alcalá, Lerida, Coimbra. Some *studia* (for instance, London) were obviously retained in the fond hope that they might be revived. On the other hand, the general chapters made promotions to houses of study other than the official general *studia*. Increasingly, graduate studies became the business of the provinces and nations. By the end of the sixteenth century the general chapters had ceased assigning regents and students to individual *studia*.

The general *studia* should be continuously provided with regents, lectors of the arts, and apt pupils. All provinces had the right to send students, but the permission of the prior general was required in each case. Convents need not provide for their students beyond six years. Every convent with eight friars should maintain one student at a general *studium*. Without permission of the general, students should not be sent outside the province for *Logica Vetus*, nor outside Italy, nor promoted *pro forma simplici*. Disagreeable, quarrelsome, or otherwise unacceptable persons should not be recommended for studies. Students were not to return to their provinces before completing their courses, unless authorized by the prior general or – in ultramontane provinces – by the provincial or vicar general. Those promoted to read the *Sentences* also needed the general's permission to proceed to the license or doctorate. The bachelor reading the *Sentences* was to remain another year to teach natural philosophy or ethics. The schedule of lectures in logic, philosophy, and theology was from the Nativity of the Blessed Virgin (September 8) to the octave of the Epiphany (January 13) and from the octave of Easter to the Feast of Sts. Peter and Paul (June 29). Lectures were suspended during Lent to allow both teachers and pupils to preach. Provincial chapters should assign masters, bachelors, and lectors to their posts. No one was to be considered a lector, bachelor, or master, even after completing their courses, unless declared so (*ordinatus*) by the prior general and actually engaged in lecturing. *Cursores* (students of philosophy) are not graduates. No one may lecture publicly (i.e., outside the convent) or publish books without authorization of the general or the general chapter. Masters are eligible for the offices of regent, lecturer, preacher, prior, provincial, visitator, procurator general, *socius* of the general or the provincial; they should leave minor offices such as bursar, sacristan, etc. to the "simple" friars. Students who have shown no progress after three years should be recalled to their convents, "lest they continue to occupy the place of others" (ch. 17).

Chapter 18 on special studies, that is, studies outside the general *studia*, underwent the greatest change. Here Caffardi placed Audet's provisions for daily instruction in the convents laid down in his *Isagogicon*, ch. 1, n. 5-6, and described above.

With regard to the privileges of graduates (ch. 19) masters and bachelors of Paris had precedence over those of other universities. Similarly, masters who had completed a course of studies at a university preceded those promoted by the prior general or granted the doctor's insignia by a university without following the courses. Masters in theology had voice and place in provincial chapters. Graduates and fathers venerable for age and probity were to be revered by the rest of the brethren. No friar, even a master or a prior, might retain a secular servant; this privilege was reserved to the procurator general and the prior general. Those engaged in graduate studies were exempt from common assignments. Simple students were dispensed from compline and prime except on Saturdays and feasts. Students were permitted to leave the convent to attend lectures outside. Bachelors and licentiates were to attend daily Mass and vespers and take turns at Matins on Sundays. The same applied to masters under fifty years of age. All were obliged to offer Mass daily on request of the sacristan. Lectors and *biblici* enjoyed the same exemptions, but were liable to common assignments. All were obliged to attend religious processions, including those for the dead.

In order not to concentrate all privilege on the intellectual element in the Order, a system of exemption was devised to reward other types of merit. Friars who had led lives of distinguished probity and merit or had particularly benefited the Order were divided (in descending order) into *benemeriti, emeriti* and *patres honoris*. Much ingenuity was expended on improvising an order of precedence for all these privileged persons.

The general chapter of 1593 designated Rome (St. Martin's), Pavia, Padua, Naples, and Trapani as general *studia*. Candidates for the *studia* were to be examined and approved in provincial chapters, a procedure even the prior general could not pretermit. Honorary titles were reduced to two: *patres jubilei* (forty-five years of profession) and *patres honoris*. All that was required obviously was that one successfully survive the innumerable plagues and other disasters that menaced longevity in those times. Clement VIII abolished even these honors.

Chizzola's reforming decrees enlarged extensively on these decisions of the chapter (*Constitutiones* 1593, ch. 10). Each *studium* was to accommodate four regents and twenty-four students. Regents should follow St. Thomas in theology and philosophy; students in philosophy should also read Francis of Toledo, Averroes, and John of Janduno. Regents should not neglect the opinion of John Baconthorpe and Michael Aiguani. Daily there were to be two lectures in philosophy and one in theology. The books of Aristotle to be read during the four years of philosophy were specified (*De physico auditu, De caelo* and *De generatione, De anima, Metaphysica*). One part of the *Summa* of St. Thomas was to be covered during each of the four years of theology. A brief summary of the preceding lecture should precede each day's lesson. Students should write down the lectures; regents accordingly should lecture in a way to make this possible and should repeat if necessary. The prior general was to grant the degree of *cursoratus* after the student had completed four years of philosophy and passed an examination of all of philosophy by the regents. The lectorate followed four years of theology and examinations as in philosophy. The baccalaureate and magisterium were conferred after the candidate had either lectured for four years on all of philosophy or had held disputations at least once a year for four years on the four parts of the *Summa* of St. Thomas. Masters were to receive the laureate within a year.

Besides the general *studia*, Chizzola prescribed "minor colleges" in the provinces for the instruction of the professed and other youths in rhetoric and logic. For both types of institution, he describes in detail the methodology of instruction and course content, adding a list of *quaestiones* taken from the four parts of the *Summa* of St. Thomas (*Constitutiones* 1593, ch. 11).

Chizzola's decrees in effect applied mainly to Italy. As the general chapter of 1598 pointed out, France and Spain, as well as Cologne and Louvain, preferred customs of their own.

Houses of Study in Italy

In northern Italy, the venerable *studia* of Padua, Pavia, Florence, Siena, and Pisa maintained their traditional role of preeminence. After the Carmelites established themselves at Turin in 1526, Piedmont acquired a distinguished general *studium*.

In Rome, the new Traspontina remained the seat of the curia and its *studium*. Construction on the church at the new site was begun in 1569. The work of the architects, Sallustio Peruzzi and Ottavio Mascherino, the church was inaugurated by John Baptist Caffardi in 1587. Construction continued during the seventeenth century under Francesco Peperello and his *capomastro*, Simone Broggi. The convent was completed in 1615.

From the middle of the century, Carmelites also taught at the University of Rome, called the Sapienza. There they held the chair of metaphysics. The general chapter of 1660 granted the professors at the Sapienza the same voting rights as the procurators general.

Although it was not unusual for southern Carmelites to travel north for studies, the south was not lacking in *studia*, some of which experienced growth at this time. The Carmine Maggiore of Naples had been constituted a general *studium* in 1333, but the general chapter of 1513 had to order studies reconstituted there. After Audet placed Naples under the jurisdiction of the prior general (1524), studies flourished there uninterruptedly. Catania had been appointed a *studium* for the arts in 1399 and a general *studium* in 1447, but the previously mentioned general chapter of 1513 also had to order studies revived here. After Audet took the place in hand, promotions are regularly made by the general chapters. The general chapter of 1575 ordered Trapani to initiate courses in logic and philosophy. Caffardi's constitutions of 1586 name Trapani among the general *studia* of the Order. Beginning with the general chapter of 1645, the prior of Trapani enjoys *de jure* voice.

The constitutions of the Mantuan Congregation of 1540 list Bologna as its general *studium*. Complete theological faculties are also maintained at Ferrara, Mantua, and Brescia. In other convents, there should be lectors and students "according to possibility and need" (ch. 15, n. 1). The constitutions of 1602 name three "*studia ordinata*": Bologna, Mantua, and Ferrara. Brescia was reduced to the status of the other houses which rated only a lector (ch. 16, n. 1 & 12).

The *studium* at Mantua was authorized to grant the doctorate by Sixtus V in 1587. It was called the Academia Felicia after the pope's baptismal name.

Houses of Study in Spain and Portugal

On the Iberian peninsula serious growth in studies dates from the second half of the sixteenth century.

Barcelona in Catalonia was declared a general *studium* in 1333, but it was to Lérida in that province that the general chapters of the 15th century made promotions. The constitutions of 1586 first listed Lérida among the general *studia* of the Order. General chapters regularly made promotions to Perpignan from 1456 to 1510. Soreth's constitutions (1462) included it among the general *studia* of the Order and it remained such, though dormant, until modern times.

Although constituted a general *studium* in 1379, Valencia in the province of Aragon did not appear in the list of *studia* in the constitutions and developed only much later. The general chapter of 1564 prescribed a college for grammar, logic and rhetoric there. The provincial chapter of 1569 made Valencia a theologate with two regents, which all the students of the province were to attend. In 1572, the Dominican visitator apostolic, Michel de Hebrera, confirmed this decision, prescribing a four-year course on the *Sentences*. The general chapter ordered that Huesca should have a regent who could preside in the university there, if need be. Students were to come from Zaragoza, Calatayud, Pamplona, and Játiva (1575).

The general chapter of 1482 mentioned a *studium* at Salamanca in Castile. In 1548, it became a *studium* for the whole Iberian peninsula. The provincial chapter of 1567 approved the foundation of a college at Alcalá de Henares. The general chapter of 1575 ordained that only theology was to be taught at Salamanca, except to students of other provinces; Alcalá was to specialize in philosophy with the same exception. The constitutions of 1586 included Salamanca and Alcalá among the general *studia* of the Order.

The general chapter of 1564 ordered the province of Andalusia to renovate the convent of Osuna for studies. In his *Institutiones et ordinationes* (Seville, 1566), published after his visitation of the province, Rossi decreed that Seville and Ecija were to maintain regents who should lecture twice daily: once in Latin on philosophy or theology or whatever their audience could absorb, once in the vernacular on cases of conscience. No student should be sent to Osuna, unless he had grammar and minor logic. Students who had followed the arts and theology at Seville, Ecija, and Gibraleón were equal to those who had studied at other universities and might continue to graduate studies. The general chapter of 1575 decreed that the arts and theology should be taught at Osuna and Seville.

Portugal had its house of studies at Coimbra, founded in 1543 by the Carmelite bishop-elect of Porto, Balthasar Limpo. The general chapter of 1548 approved the contract between him and Nicholas Audet signed at the Council of Trent. Limpo also drew up statutes for the college. It was to accommodate fifteen students and a regent of studies. The course consisted of three years of philosophy and five years of theology. In the last year, a course of canon law was also offered, and students might also learn Greek, Hebrew, or some other science. The bishop likewise provided a schedule of the day. In 1571, the college was incorporated into the university of Coimbra. Frei Amador Arrais, Carmelite bishop of Portalegre, resigned his see in 1596 and took up residence in the college where he had formerly taught. He added a church (1597) and cloister (1600) which increased the capacity of the college to thirty students. Coimbra appears as a general *studium* in the constitutions of 1586.

Oddly, the prestigious convent of Lisbon was not a *studium*. The general chapter of 1564 ordered Lisbon, "which is so illustrious," to provide masters to teach the young elegance in speech. The following chapter of 1575 finally established Lisbon as a *studium* for the arts and theology.

Chizzola laid down special regulations for studies in the Iberian peninsula (*Constitutiones* 1595, ch. 9). He centralized studies, appointing two theologates for each province: Salamanca and Alcalá in Castile, Osuna and Cordova in Andalusia, Coimbra and Evora in Portugal. Besides Barcelona and Lérida, Catalonia was allowed a third *studium* on the island of Majorca. The provincial chapter of Aragon was to choose a second *studium* besides Huesca. The chapters of each province should also assign convents for the arts and philosophy and examine and approve candidates for study. Only the prior general could expel a student. Each Spanish province was allowed only twelve masters and twelve bachelors; Portugal, eight masters and six bachelors.

In presenting graduates for confirmation by the prior general, bachelors should give proof of having successfully completed all philosophy and theology in a Carmelite college or approved university, of having lectured in all philosophy in the same colleges, of having defended conclusions in an approved university or the provincial chapter, of being twenty-eight years of age and professed ten years. Full particulars regarding times, persons, places, and circumstances were to be supplied. *Praesentati* should have read theology for four years, be thirty-two years of age, have acquired the baccalaureate, and be presented by the province. The master's degree required the baccalaureate and the *praesentatura* and three years of preaching or reading cases of conscience by deputation of the provincial chapter. Where proper colleges were lacking, students might acquire the doctorate after completing their courses in philosophy and theology by teaching the arts or theology for ten years in an approved university near a convent of the Order. Twenty years of profession were also required.

Ultramontane Houses of Study

Rossi had lost contact with the Order in the Low Countries and Germany. In a letter to Peter Wolf of October 3, 1573, he complains that in the Lower German province candidates are promoted to theological degrees and the sites of the *studia* changed without proper authorization. If necessary, studies are to be restored in Cologne and Louvain; the *studia* at Trier and Mainz should be closed. Each house of the province should have a well-instructed friar to teach grammar, explain cases of conscience and comment on the fourth book of the *Sentences* and "our Thomas of Walden." The general chapter of 1575 once more promoted students to Cologne and Louvain and ordered Mainz, Trier, Enghien, and Utrecht to be provided with regents and students. Utrecht at the time was in the last stages of dissolution.

Cologne was the only German general *studium* listed in the constitutions. Vienna in the Upper German province, constituted as a *studium* in 1385 and listed in Soreth's constitutions of 1462, ceased to exist during the Protestant Reformation.

During Soreth's term of office especially the general chapters made promotions to many *studia* in all the provinces of France. His constitutions (1462) listed Paris, Toulouse, Montpellier, Bordeaux, and Angers as general *studia*. Except for the substitution of Avignon for Montpellier in Caffardi's constitutions (1586), this list remained unaltered until the twentieth century.

With the suppression of the Congregation of Albi, the *studium* of Paris once more became the patrimony of the Order, but never regained its ancient splendor.

Due also to political conditions, it remained in effect a national *studium* for France, though its privileges continued unabated. Directly answerable to the prior general but remote from his control, the incorrigible faculty and students of the Place Maubert to a large extent managed to remain immune from Tridentine reform.

The general chapter of 1564 under Rossi urged Rheims in the province of Francia to organize a *studium*. Toulouse should not refuse students from other convents of the province. The *studium* of Avignon was confirmed and if necessary reconstituted. In 1575, Francia was again urged to establish a *studium* at Rheims. The provincial and definitors were ordered to provide grammarians, secular or regular, in the convents. Regents were assigned to Avignon and Aix in Provence. The provincial or chapter of Touraine should provide a regent at Nantes. Obviously, studies in France of the religious wars were in no flourishing condition.

Carmelites not only attended and taught at the *studia* of the Order but also at the universities. This period produced no summarists or authors of complete courses of theology or philosophy, at least not in published form. Controversy and orthodoxy were the main concern of Carmelite theologians at this time. Outstanding figures were mentioned in connection with Protestantism and the Council of Trent.

Belles Lettres

Certain Carmelite writings on religious themes are better classed as literary works for their graciousness of form and expression. The great mystics, St. Teresa and St. John of the Cross, also head the list in this category, especially the latter who ranks very high on Parnassus as well as in paradise. Other Carmelites left works which have remained a joy to their countrymen.

Spain at this time was in the words of Menéndez Pelayo "a nation of armed theologians," who "joined to the science of theology and to the fire of love of God elegance of form and style." No one perhaps in any literature superseded St. John of the Cross in this fine art, but others, among them Peter de Padilla, also excelled.

Padilla was not a figure of the first magnitude in his time, but it should be remembered that the stage held Cervantes and Lope de Vega. Born at Linares (Jaén) in 1543, Padilla was by virtue of his *Treasury of Various Poems* (1580), *Pastoral Eclogues* (1582), and *Romancero* (1583), already a recognized poet, when at the age of forty-two he became a Carmelite in 1584. After this event, Padilla wrote only religious poetry. His *Spiritual Garden* appeared in 1585; two years later, he published *Grandeurs and Excellencies of Our Lady*. His *Bouquet of Spiritual Flowers* ran into trouble with the Inquisition and has not been heard of since. The National Library at Madrid contains his manuscript works, *Canticle of the Creation of the World* and *Spiritual Stanzas*. Padilla spent his life in Madrid. Padilla's contemporaries are loud in their praise of him, among them no less authorities than his friend Cervantes and Lope de Vega. Padilla's *Treasury* is among the books selected by the curé for Don Quixote's library. Modern critics are more reserved. Padilla's poetry is distinguished more for purity of diction and correctness of style than for inspiration and fire.

In his *Dialogues*, Amador Arrais (d. 1600) bestowed on Portugal one of its enduring classics. He was born in Beja, entered the Carmelite Order at Lisbon in 1545, and the following year made his profession at Coimbra, the first to do so in the new college. He received the doctorate at Lérida (Portuguese not uncommonly studied in Catalonia), later taught at the university and the monastery of the Holy Cross of the Augustinian canons in Coimbra. A popular orator, he became court preacher under King Sebastian. Cardinal Henry chose him with Teutonio Braganza, St. Teresa's friend, as his coadjutor in the diocese of Evora (1578) as well as his chief almoner. In the latter capacity, he was able to provide much help to the needy. Named bishop of Portalegre in 1581, he became the image of the enlightened prelate, especially in his concern for the poor and the instruction of the clergy, founding a seminary, convoking a synod, composing statutes for the diocese, embellishing his cathedral. After a difference with his chapter, Arrais retired to the Carmelite college in Coimbra, where he devoted his declining years to the revision of his *Dialogues*, which had been printed at Coimbra in 1589 by the noted Anthony de Mariz. In the second, posthumously published edition (Coimbra, Diego Gomes de Loureiro, 1604) the seven dialogues have become ten and the whole text has been extensively revised and polished.

In a work which he declares was initiated by his brother, John, Arrais discusses political, social and religious themes of contemporary or transcendental interest. His vast erudition, drawing on the scriptures, classical authors, and the Fathers, does not burden a clear and straightforward expression of thought. "A treasury of excellent prose" is the judgment of Aubrey Bell.

The religious writings of Jean de Cartigny have already been considered. By far his most successful work was his *Voyage of the Wandering Knight* (Antwerp, J. Bellerus, 1557), a chivalric allegory which underwent many editions and translations from the original French into English, German, Flemish, Welsh, and Latin. Cartigny was especially well received in England and was known to later practitioners of the genre, such as Stephen Batman and Paul Bunyan. Edmund Spenser used Cartigny's work for Book One of his *Fairy Queen*. Told in the first person, the story is interesting and well-paced. However, it is more than a tale of chivalry. It is the story of everyman's pilgrimage through suffering, brought on by folly, to ultimate union with God. Though it shows traces of William Deguileville's *Pilgrimage of Man*, it most closely reflects the thought of St. Bernard whose *De pugna spirituali* combines the parable of the prodigal son with the theme of man's pilgrimage through the purgative, illuminative, and unitive ways. Much of *The Wandering Knight* is devoted to an exposition of the virtues and the spiritual life, skillfully woven into the narrative.

Carmelite Historians

Interest in history, stimulated by the Renaissance, is to a certain extent reflected in the Order. No very significant works were written, but certain titles that often appear in Carmelite historiography should be averted to.

Baptist de Cathaneis (d. 1532) published the *Speculum carmelitanum* (Venice, 1507), thus making widely available in print an essential source of Carmelite history, legend, and devotion. Provincial of Venice, Cathaneis is praised for having left to his native convent at his death many books for the library, five chasubles, silken copes for the sacristy, one veil, an annual income of fourteen ducats, and many other goods.

Joseph Falcone (d. 1597), of Piacenza, wrote *La cronica carmelitana* (Piacenza, G. Bazachi, 1595). Of least interest are the largely legendary sections dealing with the history of the Order and of its saints (the longest section). An account of learned and illustrious members of the Order, some of them near in time to the author, is the most useful.

Among the many publications of Nicholas Aurifico is a *Historia carmelitana* (Genoa, Biblioteca Universitaria, Ms. E. IV. 21).

Peter Licht (Latin: Lucius), of Brussels, fled the religious troubles of his native land and found asylum in Florence. Back in Belgium after order had been restored, he died in 1603 of the pestilence contracted in the course of caring for the sick. He wrote *Compendio historico carmelitano* (Firenze, Heredi di J. Giunti, 1595), shorter than Falcone's book and like it much concerned with legendary matters. However, in an informal, more personal style it continues the history of the Order up to the author's day. With its account of the vision of St. Simon Stock, the Sabbatine bull, and the indulgences of the Order it filled a useful function in its time. His short *Carmelitana bibliotheca* (Florentiae, apud G. Marescottum, 1593), a revision of Trithemius' list, earns for Licht a place among Carmelite bibliographers. John Bale's much more important role has already been considered.

For Portuguese readers, Simon Coelho (1514-1600) wrote *Compendio das crónicas da Ordem de Nossa Senhora do Carmo* (Lisbon, A. Conzalez, 1572).

In the wider field of secular history, Roverus Pontanus (Flemish: Bruck, d. 1567), of Brussels, wrote *Rerum memorabilium iam inde ab anno 1500 ad annum 60 in republica christiana gestarum libri quinque* (Coloniae Agrippinae, 1560), purported to be a Catholic rectification of Sleidanus' *Commentaries*.

Carmelite Musicians

The most important Carmelite musician of this period was Matthew Flecha, of the province of Aragon. He studied under the foremost composers of his time: Bartholomew Escabédo, Anthony de Cabezón, and Francis Soto. From 1543, he was attached to the court of the Infanta Maria in Castile; from 1564, to the court of the Empress Maria in Vienna. At Venice in 1568, A. Gardano published madrigals by Flecha, "chaplain of the Lady Empress and musician of the imperial majesty." From the court at Prague in 1581, Flecha published three works: *Liber de musica de punto, Divinarum completarum psalmi, lectio brevis et Salve Regina,* and *Las Ensaladas.* The last is a collection of his uncle's compositions, revised and enlarged by works of his own and of others. It has been issued in a modern edition by H. Anglés (Barcelona, 1955). Flecha died in 1604.

In the Mantuan Congregation, Julius Pellini made a collection of Sunday Masses in five voices by various composers (Milan, M. Tini, 1592). Vincent Neriti was in charge of music in the Carmelite churches of Mantua and Salò. Among other compositions, he published two volumes of *Magnificats* (Venice, A. Gardano, 1593 and 1600) and three volumes of *canzonette* for four voices (Venice, A. Gardano, 1593, 1595 and 1599). Theodore Bachino, of Mantua, was chaplain of the imperial chapel in the court of Rudolph II (1594). Back in Mantua the following year, he became a cantor of the ducal chapel. He is the author of a book of theory *De musica*, not yet found

Carmelites and the New Science

The Order produced several individuals who figured notably in the scientific circles of the time.

Julian Ristori (1492-1556) of Prato obtained his doctorate at Pisa. He taught and filled various offices in the Order, becoming provincial of Tuscany (1530-1538). In 1543, Cosimo dei Medici conferred on him the chair of astronomy of Pisa. In 1550, he was incorporated in the university of Florence and became its dean three years later. He assisted Michelangelo in the construction of the defenses of the city during the siege of 1530. His writings include a commentary on the *Almagest* of Ptolemy and a *Lectura super Ptolomaei quadripartitum.*

Francis Giuntini (1522-1590) was a pupil of Ristori. A native of Florence, he entered the Order there and obtained his doctorate in 1554. He left the Order, migrated to France and embraced Protestantism. Eventually, he was reconciled to the Church and became the almoner of Henry III. His works were collected under the title, *Speculum astrologiae* (2 v.).

Paul Anthony Foscarini (d. 1616) was born in Montalto in Calabria and filled various posts in the province of Calabria, including that of provincial. He is remembered for his *Lettera sopra la mobilità della terra* (Napoli, 1615), in which seventeen years before the *Dialoghi* of Galileo he argues that the heliocentric system was not contrary to scripture.

Julius Cesar Vanini (1585-1619) was born at Taurisano (Lecce), entered the Order at Naples, studied at Naples and Padua. At Naples, among his Carmelite teachers was Bartholomew Argoto. He obtained a doctorate in law at Naples in 1606. At one time or another, he travelled in Germany and the Low Countries. Vanini was a philosopher of nature, not a scientist, yet he was an interested observer of natural phenomena, and some of his ideas on the transformation of animal life are striking, in view of Darwin's later theories. Vanini got into trouble with the authorities of the Order; he speaks of injustice done to him by the prior general, Henry Silvio. He fled to England with a fellow Carmelite, Fra Maria Giovanni Battista, where he abjured his faith and became the guest of the archbishop of Canterbury (1612-1614). His English hosts soon discovered that his conversion had been a matter of convenience, and he ended up in the Tower. Released, he passed over to France. For a while, he practised medicine to support himself. At Toulouse, as a heretic and atheist he was burned at the stake, February 19, 1619, at 34 years of age. His chief writings, the cause of his execution, were the *Amphitheatre of Eternal Providence* (1615) and *Dialogues* (1616).

Part Three

The Catholic Reformation, 1600-1750
(Section I)

Chapter I

The Central Administration of the Order

"In the latter part of the 16th century," writes Leopold Willaert, S.J., "the (Catholic) Restoration, hindered by political disorders and by wars, rapine, and ruin, made only painful progress; contrariwise, in the first half of the 17th century it assumed in many countries an extension and profundity that make it a golden age of monastic and conventual life."

This analysis certainly describes the case of the Carmelites. The brilliant reform initiated by St. Teresa, already jealously Spanish, after her death separated completely from the Order, leaving the latter the task of mounting anew the effort at betterment. This second birth took place in the beginning of the 17th century. It makes sense, therefore, to date the Catholic Reformation in the Carmelite Order from the year 1600.

The post-Tridentine papacy, aided by the new institutions of the Roman Curia (Congregations, Tribunals, Offices), warmly accepted the mandate of the council to implement its decrees. The newly reformed papacy led and coordinated the vast energy of the Catholic Renaissance that now miraculously came into being. Thus, the marked centralization that from now on would characterize the Church, originated in the exigencies of renewal. Whereas the efforts of the great reforming generals of the past - Blessed John Soreth, Nicholas Audet, John Baptist Rossi - often hindered rather than aided by a time-serving Roman Curia, were nurtured by personal spiritual resources, the new generals had only to implement the directives of a revitalized papacy, had only to allow themselves to be borne along by the current of the times. Nevertheless, some generals showed greater personal commitment to the work of renewal. But it was at the level of the individual convent and province that the charism of Carmel was rediscovered.

The years 1600 to 1750 span two very different periods of history. By the end of the 17th century both Catholic and Protestant fervor had cooled and the secularization of society had set in. Yet the new ideas of scientists and philosophers had little apparent resonance in the interior life of the Order. Scholastic philosophy and theology retained their seats of honor in the schools. Habits of devotion and spirituality remained those which had revitalized Catholic life after the Council of Trent. The acts of the last chapters of the French provinces on the eve of the Revolution differ not a whit from all that went before. The general chapters likewise do not reflect the changed secular world (though the chapter of 1750 forbade the use of wigs). In the case of the Carmelites, therefore, there is some justification for treating the 17th century and the first half of the 18th as all of a piece.

Henry Silvio, Reformer of the Order

After the shambles of the Chizzola administration, it was imperative that the Order get back on the track of reform and repair its image before the Holy See.

Henry Silvio was born in 1556 at Mezzovico in the diocese of Como and entered the Order at Asti in 1574. He acquired the doctorate at the University of Genoa in 1587. He was regent of studies in Pavia, when Chizzola called him to Rome in 1592 to be prior to Traspontina. Here he also functioned as regent of studies and supplied for Mattioli in the chair of Metaphysics at the Sapienza. After Chizzola's imprisonment, Clement VIII, on August 17, 1596, made Silvio vicar general of the Order.

At the pope's behest, Silvio convoked the general chapter in Rome on the feast of Pentecost, May 10, 1598. Not surprisingly, he emerged prior general.

On April 28, 1598, Clement VIII had decreed that thereafter the general of the Order was to be elected, not for life, but for a term of five years, after which he could not be reelected until another five years had lapsed. In effect, Silvio remained in office until his death, by virtue of papal dispensations. In 1618, Paul V set the general's term of office at six years, a practice that remained in force thereafter.

The chapter confirmed the right of the prior of Traspontina to vote, not only in the election of the prior general, but also in the definitory of the chapter. The same right was granted for the first time to the priors of Paris and Naples. The prior of Traspontina had already taken his place in the definitories of the chapters of 1524, 1575, 1580, and 1593.

The principal task of the chapter was to apply the religious reform of Clement VIII to the Carmelite Order. For the most part the reforming decrees of the chapter are simply the decrees issued by the pope on the occasion of the visitation of Traspontina in 1594.

Shortly after the chapter, Silvio set out to visitate the Order. Silvio, in fact, visited every province of the Order, besides the Mantuan Congregation and the convent of Monte Oliveto - an unprecedented achievement for a prior general, though the Carmelite world had shrunk considerably since the Reformation. North of the Alps, the Order lay in material and spiritual ruin after the storms of the Protestant Reformation. On the Iberian peninsula, the ghost of Chizzola had to be laid to rest. Everywhere Silvio brought the program of renewal of religious life of the Catholic Reformation.

The Visitation of the Ultramontane Provinces

On April 27, 1602, Silvio left Rome for the visitation of the ultramontane provinces. He arrived in Paris on October 23, and after a visit to the king, began the visitation of the great *studium* of the Order, which had not seen a prior general since Peter Terrasse had visited it a century earlier. Silvio proceeded with due deliberation, remaining three months and issuing a lengthy and detailed list of decrees of reform, divided into seven chapters on the divine office, observance of poverty, clothing, cloister, novices and professed clerics, regents and students, the administration of goods.

On January 23, 1603, the prior general continued the visitation of the province of Francia at Rouen and moved on to Belgium, where he celebrated the chapter at Ghent on April 25, 1603.

Making his way across Belgium, a few leagues out of Cologne, on the edge of a wood, the prior general and his companions fell into the hands of eight stray Dutch soldiers who demanded a ransom of 500 gold *scudi*. The provincial of Lower Germany, Master William Hatting, who had been accompanying the general, was sent on to Cologne to collect the money. In spite of fearsome threats, no one was harmed, except Hatting's servant, Conrad, who got a beating. On payment of the money, the general and his party were sent on their way and reached Cologne the same day with all their possessions intact except the silver ornaments on the harnesses of the horses. Later, Silvio taxed the Italian and Spanish provinces 600 *scudi* to recoup his losses.

Continuing his journey, the prior general visited without interruption the houses of Upper Germany and Poland. In Poland he visited only Cracow and Poznan, opening the provincial chapter on November 7, 1603. He returned to visit more convents of Upper Germany, holding the provincial chapter at Rottenburg, beginning December 15.

"On December 18, 1603," his secretary, Francis Voersio, wrote, "the Most Reverend Father and his companions left Rottenburg and after a wretched journey over mountains and streams, through rain and cold, continually on horseback for seven days, rising three or four hours before dawn and continuing two or three hours after sunset, they arrived late on Christmas Eve at Besançon, where there is a convent belonging to the province of Narbonne."

There followed the visitation of Narbonne, Provence, Toulouse, Aquitaine, Gascony, Touraine. On May 2, 1604, Silvio held the provincial chapter of Aquitaine at Albi; on May 9, of Toulouse at Toulouse; on May 23 of Gascony at Bordeaux; on June 20, and of Touraine at Nantes. Early in July, Silvio was back in Paris; on August 29 he opened the chapter of Lombardy at Asti.

The following year, the prior general spent in Italy, but on October 7, 1605, accompanied by his faithful secretary, Francis Voersio, and a Genoese lay brother, Peter, he set out for the Iberian peninsula. After a visit to the shrine of Loreto, he travelled north to Genoa, where on November 20 he embarked on the galley of the Duke of Savoy. The ship lay by at Nice to pick up the Duke's ambassador to Spain, and the Carmelite prior general spent the interval of waiting to visitate the convent of the Order in Nice. Setting sail once more, the ship arrived at Barcelona on December 29. On January 30, Silvio had an audience with King Philip III.

The general began his Spanish visitation on March 14, 1606, in the Andalusian convent of Jaén. On April 30, he held the provincial chapter at Seville and issued his decrees of reform. As the customary starting point for the generals' visitations, Andalusia absorbed the brunt of their reforming zeal; other provinces were visited less thoroughly. Silvio followed the usual route: after Andalusia he visited Portugal; here he issued a series of decrees, but did not celebrate a chapter. The chapter of the Castilian province opened at San Pablo de la Moraleja on July 15. "The same decrees were left," the secretary notes in the visitation book, "as those for the province of Andalusia, except the ones concerning studies, because they (the Castilians) have special decrees. He (the general) also confirmed certain other decrees, which he had published for this province in the year of our Lord 1599."

The general visited only two or three houses in the provinces of Aragon and Catalonia. The chapter of Aragon opened at Zaragoza on August 27. To promote harmony in the province, Silvio ordered that the provincial should be chosen alternatively from the kingdoms of Aragon and Valencia, and that the other officials should be similarly distributed. The Catalan chapter opened at Barcelona on September 21. On November 21, the general is still at Barcelona; on December 14, he is in Turin.

The Duke of Savoy, Charles Emmanuel I, the Great, did not fail to report the arrival of the Carmelite prior general to the pope. "He is truly a man of religious sentiment, doctrine and prudence, most acceptable to Us," wrote Pope Paul V in his reply of April 23, 1607 – words that seem to go beyond mere chancery protocol. When the duke requested that Silvio be confirmed in office for life, Paul on October 6 politely declined, informing him that such privileges were no longer allowed. Nevertheless, he promised to do what he could to meet his request, and as we have seen Silvio remained prior general for the rest of his life, dispensed after each term of office by the pope.

"It has finally pleased the Lord God," Voersio noted on February 9, 1607, "after much tribulation and weariness undergone in the visitation of Spain and in the traveling involved, to return us safe and sound to this city of Rome." The years since Silvio's election had indeed been intensely busy ones. In 1609, he celebrated a general chapter at Rome, but he did not leave Italy again. He had been designated bishop of Ivrea and ambassador of the Duke of Savoy to the Holy See, when he died, September 14, 1612.

The Nature of Silvio's Reform

The general's method of visitation was the same in each house of the Order. He began with a meticulous inspection of the church and sacristy to make sure that altars, furnishings, vestments and linens were in proper order, a not superfluous precaution at the time. He gathered the community, generally in the sacristy, to open the visitation with a discourse on religious observance and the method of making mental prayer - a practice he introduced everywhere in obedience to the directives of Clement VIII. His conferences, unfortunately, have not come down to us. Next he visited the rooms of the friars. Any superfluous articles of furniture or clothing were ordered removed and consigned to a common storeroom. Once there, such possessions were no longer considered belonging to an individual, but were to be destined for use by anyone in need of them. A detailed inventory of community income and goods, mobile and immobile, was recorded in the general's visitation book. His interest in these matters was not motivated by a mean concern for material goods; the proper keeping of records and accountability of superiors and officials were commonly neglected, with disastrous effect on the economy of the houses.

The religious and moral state of the Order is not immediately apparent from Silvio's visitation books. He did not record the interviews held with individual members of the convents he visited. Occasionally Silvio records penalties - sometimes severe, such as condemnation to the galleys - for misdeeds, mostly unspecified. He compiled a stereotyped list of reforming decrees which he applied more or less mechanically to each house. Basically, these directives revolved around three concerns: prayer, cloister, and the common life.

No one – including doctors of theology (not actually lecturing) and superiors – was any longer excused from divine office in choir. Here the general could afford to be adamant, because he had no choice but to implement the commands of Clement VIII. Also emanating from the pope was the requirement of daily mental prayer. This was a new and unfamiliar requirement, and Silvio was at pains to instruct the communities in the art of methodical meditation. "Daily after Compline and Matins," he told the community of Milan, to take but one instance, "all the brethren will engage in mental prayer for half an hour, as follows: after the hour glass has been set down in the middle of the choir at a half hour, the antiphon, "Come, Holy Spirit," will be recited. Then a portion of some meditation will be read from Peter Alcantara, Granada, or some other pious writer. At the end of half an hour, 'Praise the Lord, all ye people' will be recited with the oration, 'Receive, most merciful God'."

Silvio also recommended that each friar have a book from which he could learn how to make mental prayer. Spiritual writers of the Order, especially in Italy and Spain, were beginning to produce a literature on mental prayer. This trend answered a current need and in turn was stimulated by the general's insistence on the practice of meditation. He commissioned Jerome Gracián, now a member of the Observance, to write what in effect was a directory of the spiritual life, which in its translation by Anthony Bovio (*Della disciplina regolare*, Venice, 1600) enjoyed a wide vogue in the Italian provinces.

A whole series of decrees was designed to discourage idle gadding about and to keep the brethren at home. A porter was to be placed at the main door, also a list of the names of the brethren, so that their comings and goings could be recorded. At the evening Angelus bell, the porter was to bring the key of the convent door to the prior's room. Except for a serious reason, no friar should be out after dark. No one was to go out at any time without a companion or without the white mantle of the Order. (The constitutions of the Order already severely restricted the number of times one might leave the house.) The friars should not loiter about the church or entrance to the convent. Only those called to hear confessions were permitted in church. Within the house, young religious should not enter others' rooms, or permit others to enter theirs; after night silence, priests were not to enter each others' rooms. No boys were to be allowed in the dormitory area. Windows looking out on the street or on private dwellings were to be screened in such a way that no one could look in.

Silvio imposed the observance of the perfect common life, eliminating all private possessions. Any clothing or mobile goods not needed for daily use were to be turned over to the common room for use by all. The *vestiarium*, or allowance for clothing, was not to be paid in money. Individual friars should not spend money; all purchases were to be made through the bursar (*expenditor*). Any money received was to be turned over within twenty-four hours. Preachers and confessors were not permitted to keep their stipends.

Silvio was the first prior general since Audet to attempt to impose the perfect common life, and while his predecessors had been satisfied to realize this ideal in only a part of the Order, in certain reformed houses, Silvio sought to elevate the whole Order to perfect observance without any intermediate steps. The reduction of all religious orders to "observance" had been proposed at the Council of Trent, but had been set aside as impracticable. The redoubtable Clement VIII revived the policy, and it fell to Silvio to bring the Carmelite Order into line.

Reform was thus the keynote of Silvio's generalate. It is questionable, however, how effective his blitzes into the provinces were, but at least he officially set the Order's sights on an ideal and he met with success wherever he found good will. His generalate may be considered the preamble to the reforms that took place in the second half of the 17th century.

In his biography of the prior general published in 1613, Voersio provided the first general statistics on the Carmelite Order. He lists 692 convents with 12,151 friars. His figure for the membership of the Order seems a bit bloated and ought to be reduced by about a quarter. The number of Carmelites in the second half of the 17th century, when vocations had greatly increased, has been conservatively estimated at 10,000.

Sebastian Fantoni and Gregory Canal, 1613-1631

Henry Silvio was succeeded by Sebastian Fantoni (1550-1623), elected at the general chapter of 1613. Born in Palestrina, Fantoni belonged to the Roman province. He acquired the doctorate in theology and taught at the Sapienza in Rome. He also distinguished himself as a preacher in important pulpits of Italy. In 1604, he was elected provincial of his province. On the death of Silvio, Pope Paul V named him vicar general of the Order.

Beginning with the chapter of 1613, provincials, except in special cases, were no longer instituted or confirmed at general chapters.

During his first term of office Fantoni visited the Italian provinces, including, of course, the Carmine of Naples, subject to the priors general. He re-issued the liturgical books of the Order, especially the *Caeremoniale* (Rome, 1616) which remained in force into the 20th century. (It has already been discussed in connection with the revision of the liturgy in the 16th century.) He liked to retire to his native convent of Palestrina, which he restored in 1613 and embellished with a valuable library, which exists today.

Immediately after his re-election in 1620, Fantoni again visited the Carmine of Naples with its *grancie*, or dependencies, as well as some of the houses of the province of Terra di Lavoro.

In 1622, occurred the canonization of Teresa of Avila, the first Carmelite saint to be formally canonized. Other canonizations followed: St. Andrew Corsini (1629), St. Mary Magdalen de' Pazzi (1669), St. John of the Cross (1726). All these occasions were celebrated throughout the Carmelite world with true Counter-Reformation *brio*.

Although Fantoni did not actively promote Silvio's program of reform, he gave willing support to the efforts at renewal which began to be made in the provinces of France and in the Sicilian province of St. Albert.

On Fantoni's death, the general chapter of 1625 elected as prior general Gregory Canal, a Venetian noble, born in 1563. He became provincial of Venice and in 1620 procurator general of the Order.

At the same chapter of 1625, Trapani in the Sicilian province of St. Angelus asked that its priors be granted the right to vote in general chapters, "because it was the most famous of all the convents in that province." The decision was left to the newly-elected prior general, who evidently granted the requested right, for the prior of Trapani appears among the definitors of the next general chapter of 1645 and thereafter.

Canal's generalate is memorable for the publication of new constitutions. Caffardi's constitutions of 1586 had been upstaged by the reforming legislation of Clement VIII and Urban VIII. When the chapter of 1625 requested Canal to appoint a commission to revise the constitutions, he named John Stephen Barberi (procurator general), Theodore Straccio, Dominic Campanella, Julius Fratta, and

John Baptist Lezana for the task. The result of their labors was the *Constitutiones* (Roma, 1626). Reprinted in 1721 and 1766, these constitutions remained the legislation of the Order until the 20th century.

Canal does not seem personally to have visited any of the provinces of the Order; for this purpose he occasionally used the services of his procurator general, Theodore Straccio. He supported the reform which arose at this time in the province of Belgium. He continued his predecessor's policy of support for reform in France, Belgium and Sicily.

Theodore Straccio, 1632-1642

In Canal's successor, Theodore Straccio, the Order once again had an outstanding general, tireless on behalf of the ideals of Carmel. Unlike Soreth or Silvio, he was not a traveling general, but he kept in touch with the minutest details in the daily lives of his subjects through a voluminous correspondence. His "familiar" letters alone fill almost 4,000 pages of his registers. They provide a valuable picture of life in the Order, especially in Italy, in the third decade of the 17th century.

Straccio's career as general is unique in the sense that he was not elected to office and he never held a general chapter. Moreover, as prior general he did not leave Italy, or apparently even Rome, as all his letters are addressed from there, though ironically he died outside Rome. He was in a sense a phantom general, present only through his perceptive and expressive correspondence. Perhaps his age had something to do with his immobility: he was 65 when appointed general and he governed the Order a decade.

Theodore Straccio was born in 1567 at San Giuliano and entered the Order at Cremona. He obtained the doctorate at the general chapter of 1593. Elected provincial of Romagna in 1606, he was confirmed for a second term at the general chapter of 1609, but he resigned. At the general chapter of 1613 under Sebastian Fantoni, he was elected procurator general of the Order. In 1626, Straccio became regent of studies and commissary general of the Carmine in Naples.

On Canal's death, Pope Urban VIII strangely did not make vicar the procurator general, John Michael Rossi, formerly provincial of Naples, whom he had confirmed in office, November 9, 1630; instead he named Straccio, July 28, 1631. The following September 13, the pope confirmed him in office for another year, because it had not been possible to convoke a general chapter due to the pestilence. Another prolongation of the vicar's term was granted April 27, 1632, for the same reason and in order to enable him to carry out visitations. Finally, on December 23 of that year, Urban took the unusual step of appointing Straccio prior general. In 1637, Urban confirmed Straccio in office for another six years, this time "to save the great expense involved in the celebration of a general chapter for the election of a new prior general." Straccio had reached Piperno near Terracina on his way to visitate the Carmine of Naples when he died December 23, 1642. His body was returned to San Martino ai Monti in Rome, 1648.

Straccio did not attempt to continue Silvio's efforts to reduce the whole Order to the perfect common life, no doubt because by this time a strong movement of reform had sprung up independent of central authority. Like the prior general, John Baptist Rossi, he contented himself with the attenuated form of common life represented by the deposit box. In fact, to assure that the brethren might have a quiet conscience with regard to the salvation of their souls, on February 6, 1634, he obtained for the Order the bull granted by Urban VIII to the Conventual Franciscans, authorizing the use of the *depositum*. At the same time, he inquired of the Congregation for the Interpretation of the Council of Trent whether religious might possess mobile and immobile goods with the permission of the superior and on December 2 received an answer in the negative.

On the other hand, the reform movement in the Order found a strong support in Theodore Straccio. In Italy, he may be considered practically the founder of the reform of Santa Maria della Vita in Naples; he also kept a close watch over the beginnings of reform in the Piedmont area of his native province of Lombardy and tightened the bonds with the Order of the reform of Monte Santo in the Sicilian province of St. Albert. During his visit to Spain as procurator general (1617), he attempted to set up a house of observance in every province. North of the Alps, reform was progressing in the French provinces besides Touraine, where it flourished to the greatest extent. He was particularly interested in Aquitaine and its reformer, John Tuaut, whom he summoned to Rome to reform Traspontina.

The prior general saw the need of organizing these scattered manifestations of renewal and of containing them in the Order. He set out to unite all reformed convents under a uniform set of laws and for this purpose engaged the services of Tuaut to compose constitutions based on a copy of the Touraine statutes provided by the provincial, Archangel of St. Luke. Straccio's constitutions were published with the title, *Regula et constitutiones fratrum Beatae Dei Genitricis Mariae de Monte Carmelo Antiquae Observantiae* (Cahors, Jean Dalvy, 1637).

Straccio's constitutions were observed by the province of Belgium until 1641; by Aquitaine until 1654. In Italy, not to speak of Spain and Portugal, Straccio's constitutions had no luck at all.

In 1636, Straccio was happy to announce that he had obtained from Pope Urban VIII the title, "of the Ancient Observance," for the Order.

At Straccio's unexpected death, Pope Urban VIII made Albert Massari vicar general, May 8, 1642. Massari was born in 1585 at Medicina, a town in the province of Romagna that produced four priors general. He entered the Carmelite convent there at the age of fifteen. Summoned to Rome, he became pastor of Traspontina. In 1639, he was elected provincial of his native province. He lisped noticeably, a defect that limited his effectiveness in public. Nevertheless, when it still proved impossible to convene a chapter because of war and pestilence, the pope made him prior general, August 5, 1643. He died the following October 29, aged 48.

In 1645, after two decades, it at last became possible to convene a general chapter. Massari was succeeded by another native of Medicina, Leo Bonfigli, born in 1599. He received the doctorate at Florence in 1621 and was elected provincial of Romagna in 1627. Pope Urban VIII named him vicar general of the Order on December 18, 1643. The general chapter which Bonfigli convened at Traspontina on June 2, 1645, duly elected him prior general.

The Stricter Observance

The general chapter of 1645 was one of the most crucial in the history of the Order.

By that date, the movement of reform had spread throughout the Order in

Europe, but its coat was as variegated as Joseph's. Straccio's attempt to unite and organize reform had failed: his constitutions of 1637 found favor only in Aquitaine and Belgium. The French provinces were influenced by the powerful example of Touraine and its papally approved statutes. South of the Alps and the Pyrenees, reforms, with the exceptions of Monte Santo, were principally concerned with the restoration of the common life.

Noting that the Order was actually being governed by several bodies of law, all approved by the Holy See, the chapter asked the question: should the Order be governed by one set of constitutions or by two? A vote favored the adoption of double legislation. There could be no question of suppressing the reforms of the Order. In effect, the chapter was asking whether the whole Order was willing to embrace reform. The answer, in brief, was no.

Thereupon, the chapter commissioned the provincials of provinces with reform to agree on uniform legislation applicable throughout the Order. They decided that the constitutions approved by Urban VIII, February 16, 1639, for the province of Touraine, were best suited for the purpose and appointed Andrew of St. Francis, provincial of Aquitaine, and Leo of St. John, provincial of Touraine - the two completely reformed provinces with printed laws - to compose an appendix harmonizing the differences arising from the discussion at the chapter and after approval by the pope to incorporate it into the constitutions which were to bear the title *Constitutiones Strictioris Observantiae pro Reformatis in Ordine Carmelitarum*.

In his brief, *Universalis ecclesiae*, September 20, 1645, Pope Innocent X approved the articles prepared by the two provincials. On January 27, 1646, Bonfigli presented the new constitutions to those concerned. They appeared without imprint under the title *Regula et Constitutiones Fratrum Beatae Dei Genitricis et Virginis Mariae de Monte Carmeli Strictioris Observantiae pro Conventibus Reformatis*. Actually the volume was issued in 1646, printed apparently by J. Guillemot at Paris.

Through the new constitutions the reform movement received a powerful stimulus. The contemplative spirit and perfect common life of the Touraine reform became the patrimony of the whole Order. Provinces yet to be reformed had available tried structures, the fruit of mature experience. Each province could add "municipal" regulations according to individual need.

Although the Order was henceforth governed by two sets of legislation of equal juridical validity, it should be noted that the constitutions of the Stricter Observance applied only at the provincial level. The general governance of the Order was still regulated by the old constitutions. Likewise, although only the Stricter Observance received official recognition as the reform of the Order, some reformed provinces of Southern Europe continued to withhold their allegiance.

By confining reform to the provincial level, the Order prevented Congregations from being formed and a subsequent division of the Order.

The chapter also undertook to improve the condition of religious life in the unreformed provinces. Every province of the Order should have at least one reformed convent. The vow of poverty was declared "the basis and foundation of all evangelical and religious perfection," and the perfect common life decreed by the Council of Trent and the popes, especially Clement VIII and Urban VIII, was imposed on all. Nevertheless, the chapter admitted that either because of the poverty of the convents or the shortcomings of superiors or subjects this ideal could not be everywhere realized. In such cases, "forced by unavoidable necessity, we tolerate and permit the use of the deposit box."

After the chapter, Bonfigli set out to visit Sicily, but died in the course of his visit at Mazara in the province of St. Angelus, January 20, 1647. The vicar general, Ippolito Sessoldi, convened the chapter at Traspontina on May 30, 1648, but without any prospect of being elected prior general, since the previous chapter of 1645 had deprived vicars of passive voice. This office fell to John Anthony Filippini in a tight race with Matthew Orlandi. On the third ballot, Filippini inched out his opponent 43 to 41.

Filippini was a Roman, born in the eternal city in 1598. He entered the Order at Florence. His studies for the doctorate were carried out in Pavia (philosophy), Huesca, Zaragoza, Naples and Rome - a cosmopolitan education reminiscent of the Middle Ages. After teaching philosophy in Palestrina, he became prior of San Martino ai Monti in Rome and restored convent and church, especially the latter, which he made into one of the noteworthy churches of Rome. In recognition of his accomplishment, Pope Urban VIII made him perpetual prior of San Martino. Filippini produced a description of his beloved church (Romae, typis Andreae Fey, 1639). Mention might also be made of his lives of St. Angelus (Rome, 1640) and Bl. Francis of Siena (Rome, 1624). As provincial of the Roman province, he similarly restored the nearby convent of St. Julian. Among the eminent offices he filled was that of theologian to the Duke of Mantua, Charles Gonzaga III.

The chapter of 1648 occupied itself with the promotion of the Stricter Observance. Gabriel of the Annunciation, prior of Ghent, was named commissary general for the reform of Upper and Lower Germany. Leo of St. John, commissary for France, and Urban of the Ascension, provincial of Touraine, were instructed to send friars to assist with the reform of Poland.

The growth of reform in France had produced considerable friction there. On instruction from the chapter, the provincials and procurators of the provinces not yet entirely reformed (Narbonne, Francia, Provence, Toulouse, and Gascony) produced nineteen articles designed to facilitate the smooth transition to reform. After the chapter, on September 29, Filippini issued a revised and amplified text of twenty-eight articles to be observed not only in France but throughout the Order.

The "Articles" of Filippini

The more important provisions of the Articles included the following: enrollment in reform occurs after a year's trial and profession. A convent begins to enjoy the privileges of reform immediately on the promulgation of the reformed constitutions, but after a year, the community must promise observance by means of an authentic document to be preserved in the chest with three keys. If this is not done after three months, the convent is not to be considered reformed. When the Stricter Observance is introduced into a convent, those who do not wish to join it are to be sent to the provincial for re-assignment, the aged and infirm being excepted. Once admitted to observance, a convent or individual may not return to the unreformed state. In every province not yet completely reformed, at least two of the definitors should be reformed, otherwise the elections of the chapter are null and void. Reception or profession outside reformed houses are similarly invalid. In case of scandal or some other extraordinary circumstance, reform may be introduced into a convent even without consent of the majority. A non-reformed provincial should be accompanied by a reformed *socius* on visitation. At least one of the two *socii* to the general chapter should be reformed. Reformed friars should not be sent to non-reformed houses for studies. Studies should not be instituted in novitiates. Lectors for the reformed should be members of the Stricter Observance. Presidents of provincial chapters should be reformed, or at least favorable to it.

Filippini's Articles became the blueprint for the establishment and growth of reform in the Order. With the constitutions of the Stricter Observance they formed the twin pillars upon which future reform was based. Still, Filippini's Articles did not plug up all the holes in a complex jurisdictional structure, and it was still possible for a baulky provincial to frustrate reform, as experience was to prove.

In a circular letter of August 2, 1649, to all members of the Order, Filippini painted an enthusiastic picture of the progress of the Stricter Observance.

In France, the Order is once more coming to life. Before reform, Aquitaine and Touraine numbered scarcely 150 members; now there are about 1,200, not to speak of the fragrance of piety and learning with which the Stricter Observance is filling all France. In Belgium, the many convents are so filled with excellent religious that workers have been sent to introduce reform into both German provinces. He had made the Belgian, Gabriel of the Annunciation, visitator, the general reports, together with Fr. Antoninus, of the Touraine province, who had laid the foundation of the Stricter Observance at Trier two years previously. The devil at first unleashed his fury against this good work, but after six months peace reigned once more, and Aachen and Trier had been reformed in the Lower German province, Bamberg and Würzburg in Upper Germany, with the enthusiastic approval of the Electors of Mainz, Cologne, and Trier, and of the Prince-Bishop of Bamberg, as well as other princes and cities, who constantly requested reformed religious, especially for the conversion or confusion of the heretics. Now all is in readiness for reform to spread into Bohemia and Poland. In Italy, too, the Stricter Observance has made a beginning. Besides the entire province of Monte Santo, there is the Reform of Turin, which after a stormy start is now at peace and ready to spread to other houses. The seed of reform planted at Naples and in Sicily is reported to be growing daily. The Spanish fathers, late to try the new, and wisely so, are strong in perseverance once they begin. The Stricter Observance flourishes in some of the convents of Andalusia, and it is hoped that it will spread from there to other provinces.

The zealous prior general concludes his letter by exhorting all to open their hearts to God, who invites them to fulfill their religious vocation. "This is the one thing necessary for Carmelites. This is our work, this is our task to which the glory of God, the honor of the Church, and our salvation call us."

The Visitation of John Anthony Filippini

On April 16, 1651, Filippini set out from Rome to visit the Transalpine provinces. Of his visit, there remains only a diary in the form of a travelogue kept by his companions, Gabriel of St. Joseph and Francis Scannapieco – the latter unmercifully mangling the Belgian and German place names. About the business of the visitation little information is provided. The general and his companions travelled through France, Belgium, and Germany, holding chapters in the provinces of Narbonne, Provence, Touraine, Belgium, Upper and Lower Germany. In Paris, at the Place Maubert, besides visitating the *studium*, Filippini held a meeting of all the provincials of France, "in which decrees were made for the good government of the Maubertine convent and the universal benefit of the Stricter Observance in France."

Filippini returned to Italy by the Brenner Pass, travelling down the eastern coast of the peninsula and visiting the houses of the provinces of Venice, Romagna, and Rome. "On the 18th day of this month (September, 1652)," his secretary notes, "the Most Reverend Father General returned from the visitation of the provinces of France, Belgium, Germany, and Italy with great praise, honor, and utility to the Order, so that the name of John Anthony Filippini will always be remembered in the Order." Certainly Filippini was one of the active and effective generals of the Order. At the general chapter of Rome, 1654, Filippini laid down his office. He retired to his beloved San Martino, where he died August 7, 1657.

Filippini was succeeded by Mario Venturini (1590-1676), born in Siena of noble family. He obtained the doctorate and became provincial of Tuscany. He was related on his mother's side to Cardinal Fabio Chigi, whom he enrolled in the scapular at Traspontina before the cardinal entered the conclave which elected him Alexander VII.

The chapter confirmed the existence of a double legislature for the Order and made further provisions for the benefit of the Stricter Observance, which was recognized as the only reform in the Order.

The chapter of 1660 retired Venturini from office, as was now becoming the rule, since Pope Paul V had set the term of the office of prior general at six years (1618).

The new prior general was Jerome Ari (1603-1667), a native of Asti, the town which had also produced Henry Silvio. Ari's previous career had been mainly academic; he had taught in Italy's most important *studia* at Pavia, Trapani, and Naples. He also became prior of his native Asti and provincial of Lombardy. Filippini made him procurator general in 1648 and sent him to visitate Sicily, Calabria, and Romagna.

This chapter of 1660 established the institution of four assistants general. Another novelty introduced by the chapter was the granting of voice at general chapters to the professor of Metaphysics at the University of Rome, known as the Sapienza.

The Visitation of Jerome Ari

In Jerome Ari, the Order had another active prior general. Besides Italy, he visited France, Belgium, Germany, and Spain. He was particularly apt for pacifying authorities, secular and ecclesiastical, and for extinguishing the inflamed spirits of the brethren. Nevertheless, he was capable of issuing stern reprimands. He aided the cause of reform, particularly by mediating quarrels. In the non-reformed provinces he was content to improve observance and enforce the observance of the deposit box.

One of Ari's first acts as general was to visitate the Mantuan Congregation. He was engaged in this work from September, 1660, until March, 1661, at the same time visiting the provinces of Venice and Lombardy. The first half of 1662 he spent in the Naples area. He managed to liberate the Carmine of a garrison of soldiers, which had been stationed there for more than a decade, much to the detriment of religious life.

On November 25, 1662, the prior general left Rome to visit the ultramontane provinces. Travelling over Paris, which he sought to dispose for the reform he intended to finalize on his return, he first visited Belgium, where on April 19, 1663, he divided the province into the Flandro-Belgian and Gallo-Belgian provinces. He convoked the chapter of the Flandro-Belgian province at Brussels, June 29, 1663; of the Gallo-Belgian province at Valenciennes, July 13. In the course of the Belgian visitation, Ari also visited Cologne and Aachen, but for some reason did not penetrate further into Germany.

From July 27 to September 27, Ari was at the Place Maubert in Paris, which he placed under the Stricter Observance, publishing eighty-four reforming decrees. Next, he visited the province of Touraine. At a general congregation convoked at Rennes, October 13, he settled the dispute over the alternative between Bretons and French.

Apart from his itinerary, Ari's activities in France are not recorded in his visitation book by his Italian secretary, Sebastian Fantoni Castrucci; his French secretary, Albert of St. Joseph kept a separate register, which unfortunately is not at hand.

Passing through the convents of the province of Gascony, Ari crossed the Pyrenees between Bayonne and Pamplona, December 17-21. In Spain, he visited the provinces of Castile, Andalusia, Aragon, and Catalonia, holding chapters and congregations in all of them. From Catalonia, he passed back into Southern France, Aug. 12-14, 1664, where he visited and held chapters in the provinces of Gascony, Toulouse, and Narbonne.

Back in Italy, he held a chapter in the province of Lombardy before proceeding to Rome, which he finally entered, March 25, 1665. But even here the tireless visitator did not tarry long. After the chapter of the province of Rome, he was soon again in the south, holding chapters of the provinces of Naples, Monte Santo, and Santa Maria della Vita. On June 5, he was back in Rome, but his term of office was almost ended. He laid down his office at the general chapter of 1666 and retired to his native Asti, where he died the following year.

His successor, Matthew Orlandi (1610-1695) was born at Carini in Sicily. He did not make his profession in the convent of his native town, but at Palermo, for the curious motive, alleged by one biographer, "to escape the fury of one whose dog he had accidentally killed." After acquiring the doctorate in Rome, he served as regent in Naples, Florence, and Rome. He produced a commentary on the first three parts of the *Summa* (2 v., Rome, 1650, 1653). Pope Alexander VII made him consultor to the Congregation of the Propagation of the Faith. The same pope named him procurator general of the Order at the death of John Baptist Lezana in 1659. At the general chapter of the following year, he exchanged this office for a four-year term of office as provincial of the Roman province. In that period, at his own expense he restored St. Julian's in Rome, adding six rooms to the dormitory. In 1664, Alexander granted him the use of three of these rooms during his lifetime. At the general chapter of 1666, Orlandi was narrowly elected prior general. The procurator general, Paul of St. Ignatius, of the reformed Piedmont province, received 52 votes to his 58.

The same chapter declared Sts. Joachim and Anne patrons of the Order. In 1680, St. Joseph was adopted as primary protector of the Order; in 1756, Gabriel the Archangel as secondary protector.

Orlandi's Visitation of France, 1668-1669

In 1668, King Louis XIV of France, his kingdom once more at peace after the difference with Spain over the Netherlands, requested a visitation by the prior general of the Carmelite convents in his realms. On December 7, the general was in Paris, having passed through Lyon and Moulins. In the province of Touraine he visited Orléans, Tours, Nantes, Vannes, Ploermel, Rennes, and Angers, holding the chapter at Tours. While in Tours, on March 19, 1669, he commissioned Mark of the Nativity to visitate Narbonne and Gascony. In Aquitaine, Orlandi visited Mortemart, Limoges, Cahors, Montauban, leaving the convents he could not visit to a commissary. Of the province of Toulouse he visited Toulouse, Carcassonne and Beziers. Finally, in Provence he visited Montpellier, Arles, Marseilles, and Avignon. He departed from Avignon on September 5 and arrived at Turin, back in Italy, on the 14th. He tarried there until October 23, due to a dislocated arm. Travelling over Milan, Bologna, Florence and Siena, where he celebrated the provincial chapter of Tuscany, he arrived in Rome, April 27, 1670.

No doubt Orlandi visited more houses than those listed above. His itinerary can be known only through the inscriptions of the letters patent he issued along the way; if he kept a visitation book, it has not come down to us. At the end of his visitation, on August 29, 1669, a week before his departure for Italy, Orlandi issued from Avignon letters patent containing sixty-eight decrees for the betterment of the Order in France. "We passed through the provinces and convents and found that the reform begun in the province of Touraine around the beginning of this century had been happily propagated to other provinces." Evidently the degree to which reform had succeeded varied from province to province, for the prior general speaks of "totally reformed provinces" (n. 42) and "convents recently reformed" (n. 28). Orlandi's decrees are based on the constitutions of the Stricter Observance, on which he does not pretend to improve: "We have merely chosen a few points from them which (we considered) were necessary to reform, to be most diligently kept in the convents reformed during our visit and in others where they were less accurately kept."

Another purpose of the general's visit to France was to determine the financial condition of the Order's provinces there, reduce communities to a size commensurate with their incomes, and eliminate houses that had little reason to exist. At the outset of his visitation, on March 1, 1669, Orlandi forbade the reception of novices in France until further notice. From Turin, on September 22, he published his project for the reduction of the communities in keeping with their means. He suppressed eighteen houses, mostly foundations which had failed to recover from the damage wrought by the religious troubles a century previously. At the time of his visit to France he counted 1,692 religious in 122 convents.

Orlandi was in France - fittingly, in the nunnery of Ploermel - when on April 28, 1669, the Order's illustrious sister, Mary Magdalen de' Pazzi, was canonized by Pope

Clement IX. The pope died on December 9, and it was left to his successor, Clement X, to issue the bull of canonization, May 11, 1670. The Order bore the expense of the canonization, 22,000 *scudi*. The beatification of the saint had taken place in an atmosphere of considerably lower temperature. The nuns of the monastery of St. Mary of the Angels in Florence jealously guarded their independence from the Order; they were equally disinclined to acknowledge any relationship with the Discalced. The bull of beatification of St. Mary Magdalen, May 8, 1626, did not even mention that she was a Carmelite. The solemnities of the occasion took place, not at Traspontina, but at the church of St. John of the Florentines, a stone's throw away. In these circumstances, the prior general, Gregory Canal, travelled to Florence (Canossa) in November and received permission of the nuns to offer Mass on the tomb of Bl. Mary Magdalen. Afterwards he spoke with the prioress, Mother Mary Grace de' Pazzi, her niece, and apparently was able to reassure her, for thereafter there was greater harmony, if not unity, between the monastery and the Order.

The expense of the canonization being alleged as a reason for not holding a general chapter, Clement X, on June 13, 1670, confirmed Orlandi in office for another six years, but before the end of this term made him bishop of Cefalù in Sicily, June 27, 1674. The sixty-four year old Carmelite was only beginning a second career; he ruled the diocese another dozen years, dying November 13, 1685.

The Priors General, 1675-1700

Orlandi's successor, Francis Scannapieco, is remarkable for owing all his promotions to papal indult. He was born in Rome in 1617 and was a master of theology; apart from this, the usual sources provide no information about his early career. In 1659, Pope Alexander VII made him provincial of the Roman province, but he resigned at the general chapter of 1660, so that the pope could confer this office on Matthew Orlandi. In recompense, presumably, Alexander the following year made him prior of San Martino ai Monti, an office he held until June 23, 1674, when Pope Clement X named him prior general. The popes adduce no motives for this interference in the normal procedures of the Order for providing offices.

On April 16, 1676, Scannapieco obtained apostolic faculties for visitation, but he had not proceeded far in his visitation when illness forced him to return to Rome. There he lingered for two months before he died, August 30. The suspicion of poisoning that sometimes accompanied unexplainable death in this case was taken seriously by the protector of the Order, Cardinal Paluzzi Altieri degli Albertoni, who ordered an autopsy. The report of the surgeons which eliminated the cause of death by poisoning was made public, in order to allay all rumor.

This time, the machinery set up in 1648 for providing a vicar general ground into motion. The choice of the qualified electors, gathered at Traspontina on November 18, 1676, fell on Emilio Giacomelli, procurator general.

Giacomelli belonged to the province of Romagna and was born in 1607 at Medicina, cradle of priors general. Although he served as provincial of Romagna, 1650-1653, Giacomelli spent most of his life in Rome, in the service of the Order. Secretary of several priors general, he was procurator general from 1670 until his election as vicar general.

To Giacomelli goes the merit of finally convoking a general chapter at Traspontina, June 1, 1680. The law that made Giacomelli vicar ruled out his election as prior general. That distinction fell to the procurator general, Ferdinand Tartaglia, by a large majority of votes. After so long a lapse of time, the general chapter had many matters to consider, and its protocol, one of the lengthiest until modern times, ran to 214 decrees. The acts were published as a separate booklet of 87 pages (Romae, typis Reverendae Camerae Apostolicae, 1680). As the newly-elected prior general explained in its preface, "the one purpose of the legislators was to stress the old laws and to refrain from making new ones, as long as the old ones were able to provide a remedy for present ills." The publication was intended to be a sort of appendix to the constitutions.

To the separate edition of the acts Tartaglia also prefaced a letter, dated December 2, 1680, imposing on every member of the Order the annual ten day retreat, to be made in the cell, if no other place was available.

The chapter of 1680 definitively determined that local priors should be elected by the definitory of the province, not the conventual chapter. Traditionally each convent, at least the larger ones, had elected its prior. However, in reformed provinces priors were elected by the definitory, and the system was gradually seen to be preferable.

According to the current constitutions of 1626 the term of office of priors was three years, after which they could not be re-elected until another three years had lapsed (pt. 4, ch. 19, nos. 4 and 5). The general chapter of 1564 which abolished perpetual priorates confined the term of office to three years; that of 1575 forbade immediate re-election.

The constitutions also limited the provincial's term to three years and required a lapse of six years before re-election (pt. 4, ch. 15, no. 3). The general chapter of 1513 had restricted the provincial's term to six years, at least in Italy. Four years later Pope Leo X set the term at three years.

After the chapter, Giacomelli retired to his birthplace, Medicina, where he died in 1687.

Ferdinand Tartaglia, another native of Medicina, was born in 1626. He was provincial of Romagna from 1662 to 1665. In Rome, he had a distinguished career: professor at the Sapienza, consultor of the Congregation of Rites, prior of Traspontina, where he delivered the panegyric on the occasion of the canonization of St. Mary Magdalen de' Pazzi. He preached in many important cities in Italy. In 1678, he became procurator general.

But the Order continued to have bad luck with its generals. After visiting the Roman province and the Carmine of Naples, he crossed over to Sicily, became ill and died at Catania, March 1, 1682, though not before publishing sixteen *ordinationes* (Palermo, 1681) for the betterment of religious observance.

A month later, the electors of a vicar general once again met at Traspontina and chose the procurator general, Angelus Monsignani. He issued from the election, not as vicar, but as prior general. The chapter of 1680 had decided that since the vicar enjoyed all the prerogatives of the prior general, he should also bear his title. Yet all this bother went for nought; the ingenious engine for electing generals never functioned again. All the priors general, with one exception, happily enjoyed excellent health during their *sexennia*. In that case and in the few instances of assumption to the episcopacy, the Holy See reverted to its old habit of filling vacancies by papal *fiat*.

Angelus Monsignani was born at Forlì in 1628, another prior general of the Romagna province. He entered the novitiate at Ravenna in 1643 and crowned his studies with the doctorate in 1655. He was provincial from 1665 to 1668. In 1672, he became secretary of the Order. Two years later, when he became bishop of Cefalù, Orlandi took him along as vicar general of the diocese. At the general chapter of 1680, Angelus was made procurator general. Elected prior general in 1682, he finished Tartaglia's term of office. After the chapter of 1686, which he convoked, he returned to Forlì, dying there in 1697. A speaker of considerable ability, he preached nineteen Lenten courses, besides other sermons in various places. Except for a sojourn in his native province in 1684 for reasons of health, Monsignani does not seem to have left Rome.

The chapter of 1686 elected Paul of St. Ignatius, of the reformed province of Piedmont. It is not clear how he came to be chosen, for he was not even present at the chapter and for many years had been living in retirement. Evidently the favorite, feted in his room the night before by his supporters as already elected, was Francis La Guzza, second *socius* of the Sicilian province of St. Albert. In fact, La Guzza provided the only competition, gaining 40 votes to Paul's 62.

Paul Gambaldi was born in 1614 in Sobrico in the diocese of Asti. He made his novitiate at Turin under Dominic of St. Mary, leading spirit of reform in the province of Lombardy, of whom he became the trusted collaborator. Paul succeeded his mentor as provincial of Lombardy in 1658. Two years later, Jerome Ari, also of the Lombardy province, called him to Rome as procurator general. Dominic, who at the time was novice master at San Martino ai Monti, may have had something to do with the appointment. Paul's sermons before Alexander VII in the papal chapel were published in Rome in 1662. At the end of Ari's term in 1666, Paul returned to his province and the convent of Pino, which Ari had added to the reform five years previously. He restored convent and church and lived there in prayer and retirement, until elected to lead the Order. After his term of office in 1692, he remained on at San Martino ai Monti another dozen years, dying there at the age of 90 in 1704.

A Spanish Prior General

For almost two centuries the Order had been ruled by Italian priors general. The last non-Italian had been the Catalan, Peter Terrasse (1503-1513), unless one considers Nicholas Audet (1524-1562) a Cypriot. This Italian hegemony may have been due to the custom of the popes of naming as vicar the procurators general who were predominantly Italian and in turn named by the priors general. On the other hand, the Italian generals of the 17th century were almost all unanimously elected. In the instances to the contrary, competition came from another Italian. Perhaps the explanation is to be sought in the political situation, in concern for the liberty of the Order under a subject of one of the two Catholic superpowers, Spain and France. In the 18th century, Spaniards and Frenchmen are at times to be found at the head of the Order.

John Feijóo González de Villalobos was born in 1644, probably, as his name suggests, at Villalobos. He entered the Order at Medina del Campo and studied at Salamanca and Valladolid; at the latter university he held the vesperal chair of theology. There, too, he preached the funeral oration for Queen Maria Louisa, March

28, 1689. He attended the general chapter of 1686 as second *socius* of Castile. On January 28, 1692, Innocent XII appointed him provincial of the Sicilian province of St. Angelus. The election of the provincials of both provinces had been contested. Feijóo's successful mediation of this dispute may explain his election as prior general at the chapter which opened on May 15. In any case, it is known that Charles II of Spain urged his election. This patronage no doubt prejudiced the chances of the only other serious contender for the office, another Spaniard, Andrew Caperó, of the province of Aragon, who gained 32 votes to Feijóo's 66.

Now that Spain finally had a prior general, it was only fitting that he should visit the peninsula. Unfortunately no account of his visit, 1693-1694, has come down to us. Extant acts of provincial chapters over which he presided show his interest in promoting the tenuous reform movements in the various provinces.

Two achievements of Feijóo appeared more significant and commendable at the time than perhaps they do now. In 1693, he obtained from King Charles II, "the Bewitched," the title of grandee of Spain for Carmelite priors general (Dominicans and Franciscans already had it) with the privilege of remaining with head uncovered in the royal presence. Feijóo is also credited with obtaining from the Inquisition of Toledo the condemnation of fourteen volumes of the *Acta Sanctorum*, in which the Bollandists treat historical questions concerning the Carmelite Order (November 14, 1695). The Inquisitions of Aragon, Madrid, Castile, and Portugal followed suit (1695-1696).

At the end of his term of office in 1698, Feijóo returned to Spain. In 1702 he became bishop of Gaudix and died February 10, 1706.

The Priors General, 1700-1750

The other priors general of this period need not detain us long.

The generalate of Charles Philibert Barberi, a studious sort of person, was uneventful in every way. Son of a noted physician of Turin, John Anthony Barberi, he was born in 1652 at Racconigi in the Piedmont province and entered the Order in 1668. At the age of twenty-two, Charles Philibert was already a professor at the University of Turin and theologian of Charles Emmanuel II, Duke of Savoy. In Rome, he joined the faculty of the Sapienza. His opening lecture in the chair of Metaphysics was published (Romae, apud Dominicum Antonium Herculanum, 1689). As lector of the Sapienza, he attended the general chapters of 1692 and 1698. At the latter he was barely elected prior general. At the end of his term of office in 1704 Barberi returned to his chair in the Sapienza, occupying it until his death in 1722 at the age of 70.

In Angelus Cambolas the French once more had a countryman at the head of the Order. One has to go back to the early Renaissance, to Ponce Raynaud (1481-1503), to find another. Cambolas had behind him a most distinguished career. He had been much involved in the French reform movement, though at an administrative rather than an inspirational level. Innocent XII, in conferring on him the title *"Reverendissimus"* (the title of the prior general) with all its perquisites (1692), sums up Cambolas' accomplishments: preacher in the more celebrated cathedrals of France for twenty years, provincial of Toulouse three times, commissary and visitator general eleven times, prior of Paris and commissary general there four times, procurator general for six years. Cambolas came from an illustrious family in Toulouse and had made his studies in the province of Touraine. Elected prior general in 1704, he retired to Toulouse after his *sexennium* and died there in 1716.

The chapter of 1704 issued important legislation on studies, to be considered later.

In 1710, Andrew Caperó is again a contender. In 1698, he had become assistant general for the provinces of Spain and Portugal, in 1704 procurator general. He was prominent in the reform movement of his native province of Aragon and was held in high repute. He was in every respect a worthy candidate for the highest office in the Order and might have been elected were it not for the interference of King John V of Portugal, who formally protested his candidature and threatened to forbid the Portuguese Carmelites to obey him if elected. No doubt the War of the Spanish Succession at this time explains the royal displeasure at the prospects of a Spanish prior general. Notwithstanding, Caperó received 38 votes to the 45 of the actual victor of the election. The latter, Peter Thomas Sánchez, in spite of his name, was a Sicilian, born in Licata, province of St. Angelus, in 1662. He was another schoolman who taught first in Sicily, then in Rome at Traspontina and the Sapienza. His chair at the Sapienza earned him voice in general chapters. He was elected prior general in 1710. After his six year term of office, he returned to teaching in the Eternal City, but died at Licata during a visit to his native place, September 27, 1720.

Charles Cornaccioli bore a noble name in the city of Milan, where he was born in 1668. He studied philosophy at the Carmine of Naples and theology in Milan. He was prior at Milan and Traspontina and provincial of Lombardy. He attended various general chapters and was finally elected prior general in 1716. After six years, he taught at the Sapienza before being made bishop of Bobbio in 1726. At his death in 1737, Joachim Pontalti, later himself prior general, preached the panegyric. It was published with that of Anthony Francis Abanni, canon of the cathedral of Bobbio (Mediolani, typis Petri Antonii Frigerii, 1737).

Licata again bestowed a prior general on the Order in Caspar Pizzolanti, born there in 1674. He taught theology at Traspontina and was attending the general chapter of 1722 as titular provincial of Saxony when he was elected prior general, defeating the Portuguese contender, Emmanuel Ferreira, by a vote of 53 to 43. Made bishop of Cervia in 1727, Pizzolanti remained in office as prior general until he could convoke the general chapter the following year.

Pizzolanti scored two triumphs, to be considered below. Under his generalate the statue of Elijah the prophet was placed in St. Peter's Basilica among the founders of religious Orders, and the liturgical office of Our Lady of Mount Carmel was extended to the universal Church.

Anthony Joseph Aimé Feydeau was little more than a papal interlude among the priors general. Born in 1658 of a titled family of Moulins, he donned the Carmelite habit at Dijon in the province of Narbonne. He was prior in a number of the larger houses of the province, finally of the Place Maubert in Paris. He wrote a genealogical history of the Conti family, for which Innocent XIII (Conti) sent him a gold medal. A treatise in defense of the bull *Unigenitus* earned him a summons to Rome from Benedict XIII in 1724 and the procuratorship. At the general definitory meeting held in place of a chapter in 1728, Benedict named him prior general and appointed his council as well, including a procurator general, Lawrence Fornari. Two years later, Clement XII created Feydeau bishop of Digne. He ruled the diocese until his death in 1741.

The Order being once more without a prior general, Clement XII appointed James Albert Cavina vicar. When he had been made procurator, Fornari, of the Lombardy province, was in Milan, since the Peace of Rastadt (1714) an Austrian possession, and was hindered from corresponding with Rome. The pope accordingly provided a new procurator in the person of Cavina. This friar was born in 1673 in Massalombarda in the Romagna province and joined the Order at Imola in 1689. Regent in the more important *studia* of Italy, Padua, Siena, Bologna, he was also a distinguished preacher. Having convened the chapter of 1731 to elect a new general, he retired to Imola, where he restored convent and church, contributing 1,000 *scudi* of his private means to this undertaking. He died there in 1749.

The chapter of 1731 elected Louis Benzoni, born in 1675 of a titled Milanese family. He had no particularly brilliant career, but served in the Roman curia and was handily elected prior general. He visitated the Italian provinces. After his term of office, he retired to his native convent of Milan, crowned with the title of bishop of Elusa *in partibus infidelium* (1737). He died in 1758.

At the chapter of 1738, Nicholas Ricchiuti became prior general. He was born in 1674 at Grottaglie in Puglia and entered the Order in 1691. In 1720, he became provincial of Puglia, afterwards prior of Traspontina. In the chapter of 1731, Benzoni named him *socius* general (assistant general) for Italy. When the procurator general, Elisha Monsignani, died in 1737, Ricchiuti took his place. After only four years as prior general, Ricchiuti resigned in 1742 for reasons of health and retired to Grottaglie where he died in 1747.

As circumstances would have it, Aloysius Laghi enjoyed an unusually long term of office - fourteen years. Another member of the Romagna province, he was born at Imola in 1691. He made his vows at Ancona in 1707, but later transferred filiation to his native Imola. He acquired the usual doctorate in theology and eventually at Lugo and Bologna became theologian of Cardinal Prosper Lambertini, later Benedict XIV. In 1738, Clement XII made Laghi provincial of Romagna. Ricchiuti appointed him assistant for Italy in 1741. When Ricchiuti resigned, Benedict XIV named Laghi vicar general and personally presided at the general chapter of 1744, which, of course, elected Laghi general. Benedict also took in hand the protectorship of the Order. His opening address at the chapter appeared in Rome in an elegant edition by John Mary Salvioni.

The Sicilian delegates were unable to attend the chapter because of the plague in Messina which carried off most of the community there. The Neapolitan delegates were held in quarantine for forty days at Terracina, frontier of the Papal States, before they were released.

At the general chapter of 1750, Laghi was granted passive voice by mandate of the pope at the request of two anonymous petitioners. In spite of this papal hint, Laghi only narrowly defeated the procurator general, Arsène Duilhè, 65-55. At the end of his second term in 1756, Laghi returned to Imola and died there two years later. On his native convent he bestowed ornaments, vestments and other valuables to the amount of 10,000 *scudi*, as well as a field estimated at 5,000 *scudi*.

Joachim Maria Pontalti was born in 1709 at Verona in the Republic of Venice. It was James Cavina who attracted him to the Order and brought him to Imola. After studies in Rome, he returned north to teach at Ronciglione, Milan, and Imola. At this last place, he also taught the humanities at the university. Meanwhile, he carried on an active and fruitful preaching apostolate. At Venice, he became consultor of the Inquisition, synodal examiner, and censor of books. Present at the general chapter of 1756 as *socius* of the Venetian province, he was elected prior general. Bonaventure Blanciotti, who was there, ascribes the election to the sole influence of God's grace. If so, the victory was hard won, for the procurator general, Emmanuel Barrera y Narvaez, of the province of Andalusia, received 61 votes to Pontalti's 66.

Pontalti visited a number of Italian provinces, also the Mantuan Congregation. In 1761, before the end of his term of office, Clement XIII named him bishop of Hvar in Dalmatia. At the same time, Pontalti remained prior general and as such presided at the general chapter of 1762. Meanwhile, his ex-rival, Emmanuel Barrera, had acquired the title of "apostolic" prior general and a seat in the chapter. The distinction availed him little; Mariano Ventimiglia defeated him 61 to 44. Nor was this the end of Barrera's bad luck. Embarking from Genoa, he, a lay brother assigned to serve him, and two other Andalusian priests were captured by Turkish pirates. Taken first to Sale in Morocco, Barrera died while being transferred to Fez. Another of the unfortunates died shortly after arriving back in Rome. After peace was established between Spain and Morocco in 1766, the other two survivors were able to return to their homeland.

It would seem that Pontalti was expected actually to take up residence in Hvar and administer the diocese. Whether it was because, as the biographer of the priors general, Mariano Ventimiglia, avers, that he could not overcome the language barrier, or some other reason, Pontalti resigned his see and in 1767 was given the titular bishopric of Ascalon in Palestine. With that distinction, he retired to San Martino ai Monti, where he died in 1772.

When Cato was asked why no statue of him had ever been erected, he replied, according to Plutarch, that he would prefer to have to explain why none had been erected than why one had been. With this classical tag, Mariano Ventimiglia modestly excuses himself from providing a biography of himself in his *Chronological History of the Priors General of the Carmelite Order*. Others have supplied the lack.

Mariano Ventimiglia was born in 1703 at Vatolla (Salerno) and received the habit in the Carmine of Naples. He taught philosophy and theology at Piacenza and Naples. In 1743, he was made prior of the Carmine by royal mandate (we are in the age of absolute monarchs). He distinguished himself as a preacher. In 1758, he was elected provincial of the Neapolitan province, but the following year became assistant general for Italy. After his term as prior general, 1762-1768, he retired to Naples, living another score of years until 1790.

Obviously, the days of the great priors general were past. During the eighteenth century, the colorless figures succeed each other at six year intervals with monotonous regularity. Perhaps the brevity of their terms of office had something to do with it. That and the generally flaccid condition of Catholicism in the Age of the Enlightenment.

Chapter 2

The Reform of Touraine

Out of the ashes of a France morally and materially devastated by religious wars, miraculously rose the phoenix of Catholic renewal, the most striking feature of which was, in Bremond's classic phrase, "the mystical invasion." In the generally unreassuring condition of Catholic life, there was to be found a small but dedicated "devout milieu," the focus of an intense religious renaissance. The source of the fervor of these devout persons lay particularly in the cultivation of prayer and the interior life. This spiritual *élite* was recruited especially among the secular clergy at the Sorbonne and among the new religious orders recently arrived in France, the Jesuits (1552) and the Capuchins (1573). Among monastic orders, the Feuillants (reformed Cistercians) and Carthusians distinguished themselves. Nor were members of the laity lacking.

One of the most important centers of the Catholic revival was the salon of Madame Barbe Acarie (1566-1618), wife, mother, and mystic, who was to be instrumental in introducing the Discalced Carmelite nuns into France (1604). She herself became a Carmelite, Mary of the Incarnation, beatified in 1791. The hotel Acarie was frequented by some of the most illustrious figures in the movement: the Capuchin, Benet of Canfield; Andrew Duval, doctor of the Sorbonne; John Quintanadoine de Bretigny; Mme. Acarie's cousin and later cardinal, Pierre de Bérulle; and St. Francis de Sales.

It was in this devout milieu that some of the leaders of Carmel's renewal received inspiration and encouragement.

Peter Behourt, 1564-1633

The province of Touraine had developed little after its foundation in 1384 with 10 convents and not at all after the middle of the 15th century. To the original houses, La Rochelle, Angers, Tours, Ploermel, Nantes, Orléans, Loudun, St.-Pol-de-Léon, Poitiers, and Pont-l'Abbé, were added Hennebont (1389), Vivonne (1397), Dol (1403), Bondon (Vannes, 1424), and Rennes (1449). Aulnay was transferred to Touraine from Aquitaine in 1457.

It was in the youngest house in the province that the reform began. Its initiator was Peter Behourt. Born at Moulins in 1564, he entered the Order at Rennes at 18 years of age. "From the time I entered the Order," Peter wrote many years later, "I have always chosen, desired, and hoped for the restoration to a better state of the whole province." He found a kindred spirit in the young sub-prior, Peter Le Maignan, but at the latter's premature death in 1587, he was left alone with his ideals.

Upon completion of his studies at Paris and Angers in 1588, Peter became prior in a number of houses of the province. He was prized for his honesty and efficiency as an administrator of the mostly ruinous convents of the province, but his efforts to restore observance were little heeded. The unsettled times offered no favorable climate for renewal. Nevertheless, he influenced a number of younger members of the province, who became the nucleus of the future reform.

As prior of Rennes, Behourt sent two promising young friars, William Guerchois and Peter Pleumelet, to complete their studies in Paris. At Angers, he won over to his ideals two newly ordained priests, Louis Perrin and Philip Thibault, and a deacon, Francis Odiau, whom he similarly dispatched to Paris. Of two postulants, he sent Matthew Pinault first to Dol under the tutelage of the prior, Giles Kronays, afterwards to Paris; Mathurin Aubron took the habit at Rennes and remained under the personal direction of Behourt. In this way, a small group of reform-minded students was formed in Paris, the scene of the new mystical revival.

In 1599, Behourt became prior of Ploermel. Here he was joined by his disciples, Guerchois and Pleumelet, and after seeking the advice of Andrew Duval, professor at the University of Paris, the three friars made a formal declaration before God, renouncing all personal property and agreeing to have all things in common. This was the first official act of the reform.

Philip Thibault, 1572-1638

Meanwhile, at Paris the notion of reform was also maturing. Here, too, one man stood out as leader. Philip Thibault was born in 1572 at Brain-sur-Allone near Saumur. When he was eight years of age, his parents brought him to the Carmelite convent of Angers to be educated for the ministry. Until his profession in 1588, Philip was the ward of John de Launay, only a few years his senior, but destined to become provincial (1599-1602) and for many years chaplain of the Carmelite nuns of Nazareth monastery (Vannes). Through the generosity of a wealthy woman of Angers, Philip was able to attend the University of Paris. After the arts course, he studied philosophy under Master James Rampont, a gifted young friar, who later remained in contact with Thibault with regard to the reform of his own province of Francia. On completing three years of theology, Thibault was ordained a priest (1597). During the first half of 1598, Thibault was at Angers, where, as we have seen, he met Behourt.

At Paris, Thibault came to know the leaders of the contemporary spiritual revival. It was no doubt at the university that he became friends with Andrew Duval. Duval in any case introduced him to Dom Richard Beaucousin, who became his spiritual director. Thibault also frequented the monastery of the Feuillants. In later years, Thibault was in touch with other important personages in the French mystical movement: the Jesuit, Peter Coton, confessor of Henry IV; Cardinal Peter de Bérulle, Philip Cospéan, at this time still a student at the Sorbonne and an habitué of the salon of Madame Acarie. It was no doubt from the period of his student years that these friendships date.

On Duval's advice, Thibault with his friend Odiau spent the second half of 1598 and the first half of 1599 at the Jesuit College in Pont-à-Mousson. Duval probably prescribed this course of action to give Thibault a chance to make a Jesuit retreat and decide his future, for the young Carmelite was undergoing a crisis in his vocation. At Paris, he had become acquainted with the new orders like the Jesuits and Capuchins, old orders reformed like the Feuillants or yet in full fervor like the Carthusians. There he found a vibrant spiritual life, the new methods of practicing mental prayer, and exciting interest in the ways of the ascetical and mystical life. It all contrasted rather sadly with the relaxation and even corruption he found in his own institute.

The Reform Takes Shape

In January, 1603, Silvio appeared in Paris on his long-awaited visitation. He published 95 decrees; based on the apostolic visitation of Traspontina, these decrees imposed the perfect common life on the community of the Place Maubert.

The prior general postponed his visitation of the French provinces until he had visited Belgium, Germany, and Poland. Of Touraine he visited the friaries of Poitiers, Loudun, Angers, Nantes, Tours and the nunneries of Ploermel and Nantes. He convened the provincial chapter at Nantes, June 18, 1604. His decrees for the province were published as *Decreta ad reformationem et restaurationem vitae regularis observantiae* (Agen, 1604).

Rennes and Poitiers were designated novitiates by the chapter. Behourt became prior of Rennes with Guerchois and Pleumelet as sub-prior and sacristan respectively. Thus, one of the novitiates of the province was placed in charge of reform-minded friars. Those who felt differently betook themselves elsewhere. The community comprised, besides the prior, William Guerchois, Peter Pleumelet, Peter Deniart, Mathurin Aubron, Briand Goullier, Julian Legendre, Mames Godet and a certain Bienassis whose given name is not known.

At Paris, Silvio named Louis Charpentier prior and vicar general for France, and Thibault sacristan and regent of philosophy. In the latter office, Thibault could bring his influence and ideas to bear on promising young friars of many provinces. These included Francis Odiau, his close friend and like him from Angers, Noel de Mardeaux, and Matthew Pinault from Dol, Anthony Raulin from Bourges, Anthony du Puis from Avignon and John Docquet from Rheims.

In 1607, Louis Charpentier became prior of Rennes. During a visit there the previous year, he had made the declaration renouncing personal possessions. Behourt was back in Rennes and remained there as an ordinary member of the community until his death in 1633. He had done yeoman service in the cause of reform, but he was rigid and lacked the vision to insert the renewal of Carmel into the vital spiritual forces of the times.

On February 1, 1608, Philip Thibault joined the community of Rennes as sub-prior and novice master. In a ceremony on April 21, preceded by the new Forty Hours' Devotion (Thibault's suggestion), the friars renewed their profession, adding the phrase "*cum abdicatione proprietatis.*" They bound themselves not to recede from the reform, renounced the privileges attached to academic degrees, agreed to use the simple form of address "Father," dated precedence only from the date of profession. Those who applied to the reform were required to undergo a new novitiate. After the novitiate in the reform, surnames were replaced by a second saint's name. Participants were: Louis Charpentier, Peter Behourt, Philip Thibault, William Guerchois, Francis Odiau, Noel de Mardeaux, Peter Deniart, Anthony du Puis, Mathurinus Aubron. Later, Matthew Pinault, Charles of St. Agatha, and Michael of the Ave Maria added their signatures. In an enthusiastic letter to the prior general Charpentier described the event.

Nevertheless, the house was not at peace. As the provincial, Christopher Le Roy, pointed out to the general in a letter of October 8, 1607, there were serious differences among the leaders concerning the direction the reform should take. Charpentier was satisfied with the restoration of the common life, Behourt favored certain practices of the Discalced, while Thibault wanted to incorporate the forms of spirituality current in the French revival to which he was closely linked. Charpentier objected to the novices being taught the new methodical meditation Thibault had learned from the Jesuits and Carthusians. With a couple of followers Thibault returned to Paris. However, the community was inclined to his views, so when the opportunity to become prior of Angers presented itself, Charpentier accepted the post and proposed Thibault as his successor. On July 30, 1608, the community of Rennes unanimously elected Thibault prior. The reform was finally united under one leader committed to the new ways.

Brother John of St. Samson, 1571-1636

When Thibault was elected prior of Rennes a second time in 1611, he took pains to enroll in the reform a laybrother whose reputation for holiness was spreading throughout the province.

John du Moulin was born in Sens and was blind, due to medication applied to his eyes when he was three years old. Orphaned at the age of ten, he was taken into the crowded and lively household of his maternal uncle, Zacharias d'Aix. At school, John's main interests were the Latin and the French poets, especially Ronsard, and music. He became proficient in the organ and just about any contemporary musical instrument.

Through the reading of spiritual books John became attracted to the interior life. He had read to him the lives of the saints, the *Imitation of Christ*, the *Institutions* of Tauler and also, it would seem, the life of St. Catherine by Peter Crespet (1543-1594), prior of the Celestines of Sens. But his favorite was *Le mantelet de l'Epoux*, by the Flemish Franciscan, Frans Vervoort. This book, which he came to know practically by heart, awakened in him the love of the cross that characterized his life. For mental prayer John used Louis de Granada and Anthony de Guevara's *Livre du Mont Calvaire*.

At the Carmelite church in the Place Maubert, where he daily attended Mass, John struck up a friendship with Matthew Pinault. Together they read Tauler, Herp, Ruysbroeck, *La perle evangelique*, Thomas Deschamps' *Jardin des contemptatifs*, Gerson and Denis the Areopagite. Other friars soon joined the two friends in Pinault's room, and so John contributed to the formation of the group which would congregate at Rennes to establish the Observance there. On the other hand, John found his vocation and in 1606 was accepted for the novitiate in Dol.

He made his profession on June 26, 1607, adding to his baptismal name the patron saint of Dol.

In 1612, Brother John moved to Rennes and began his year of probation before renewal of vows in the reform. Brother John spent the rest of his life in Rennes and became the unofficial spiritual director of generations of novices recommended to him for counsel in the ways of the spirit. Nor was his influence confined to them alone. Marie de' Medicis added him to her collection of holy men whose prayers and unheeded advice she enlisted on behalf of her machiavellian politics. He took part in the controversy over the *Chapelet secret*, condemned by the Sorbonne in 1633. There is a letter of his, severe in tone, to its author, Mother Agnes Arnauld of Port Royal. John also interested himself in the case of the diabolical possession of the nuns of Loudun. Many devout and illustrious persons found their way to Rennes to visit the blind mystic in the Carmelite convent.

Brother John's spiritual writings will be considered below.

The Spread of the Observance of Rennes

Charpentier's transfer to Angers issued in the acquisition of a second convent for the reform. This house enjoyed the worst reputation in the province. During the civil wars, a certain John Richoust reigned as prior. His apartments took up a quarter of the convent, to which under pretext of belonging to the Congregation of Albi he welcomed any friar who wished to escape monastic discipline. On October 12, 1582, the provincial, Didier Richard, described conditions at Angers to the prior general, Caffardi: "Since he (Richoust) has been prior, a thousand scandals have occurred there. Prostitutes publicly came and went in the convent. Quarrels and contentions frequently occurred. Not only did he not settle them, he even stirred up others to brawling, so that some were seriously wounded with swords. They moved the quarrels of the convent into the crossroads and involved seculars. They were to be found running about the streets at night like assassins." The situation seems to have altered little in the meantime. Only the previous year, on May 31, 1607, Charpentier had written to Silvio, asking him to remove five of the more disreputable members of the community. "They are in such a state that honest citizens forbid their wives and families to visit our church, because this convent is a veritable brothel. These religious do not fear God, for they blaspheme him daily and are so shameless that their whores are present before them in church during divine office." This report of Charpentier's was no doubt excessively pessimistic. Angers was the convent in which Thibault had been reared from boyhood. Later, he recalled that he had been edified by the spirit of prayer and the sense of duty of some of the friars, especially the older ones.

Charpentier took advantage of the absence of the provincial, Christopher Le Roy, at the general chapter of 1609 to introduce a strict regime into the undisciplined house. He ordered all under pain of excommunication to surrender their personal goods within three days. He re-established the cloister, appointed a porter to maintain surveillance at the door, and required all to lead the common life without benefit of privileges.

On May 13, 1610, Charpentier, Thibault, Behourt, Odiau, and Deniart met at Angers to lay out a uniform way of life for the two houses of what may now be called the Observance of Rennes. The resolutions of this congregation, or meeting, of 1610 mark the beginning of the special legislation of the reform.

The special practices of the Observance brought it into conflict with the provincial, Christopher Le Roy, who objected to changes being made in the way of life without his authorization; the reformers themselves sometimes pretended to exaggerated rights. Le Roy actually was an exemplary religious. Before his contacts with Rennes he had already produced a book of prayers taken from the works of St. Teresa, *Le Jardin des Prieres de Ste. Therese dans les Fetes de la Vierge* (Paris, 1604), a book that reveals an interest in the reform of St. Teresa, besides being an early French *Teresianum*. Born at Pattay, 12 miles from Orléans, Le Roy entered the Order at Nantes. He returned there to teach at the university after obtaining his doctorate in 1604. His term as provincial from 1607 to 1611 marks his only aberration from the paths of academe. From 1620 until his death in 1636, he functioned as vicar and confessor of the nuns at Nantes. (The nuns had the right to choose their own vicar, and they usually chose a friar with a reputation for learning and piety.) In his capacity of vicar, Le Roy produced *Les sainctes ardeurs de la Mere Francoise d'Amboise* (Paris, 1621), the first published biography of Bl. Frances, with a series of meditations. Shortly before his death, appeared another work of devotion, *Le sacré bocage de l'ame* (Paris, 1626).

The provincial chapter of 1611 brought a measure of mutual understanding. Philip Thibault was elected a definitor. The province undertook to better itself through "*Declarationes pro observantia.*" The reformers agreed to obey the general and provincial. They were obliged only to the constitutions and the decrees of Silvio, but in cases of doubt the priors of Rennes and Angers had the right to decide. The same priors could transfer their subjects from one convent to another without permission from the provincial. In conclusion, the assembled fathers encouraged the reformed friars to persevere in their good resolutions.

In 1614, the Observance made its first foundation at Chalain.

The same year, Loudun, recovered for the Order, opted for the reform. Its prior, Louis Perrin, like Peter Behourt, had long battled single-handed to improve observance, and now after ten years of hard work his convent was for the most part reconstructed. On the occasion of its adoption into the Observance, the second congregation of the reform was held there. Ten reformed friars were assigned to Loudun. The convents of the reform undertook to assist each other mutually. Authorization by a council was required for any new undertaking. The administration of the three convents (Rennes, Angers, Loudun) would be subject to inspection by a committee of examiners (*discrets*) and bursars. Dress should be uniform. The provincial was to be asked to name a vicar for the reform, and Louis Perrin was proposed for the office. Finally, the friars of the reform resolved to send their theology students to the Jesuit College at La Flèche. The provincial refused his consent to educate students outside the Order, nor did he appoint a vicar.

The reformers now sent a delegation to Rome to obtain approval of the Observance. Mathurinus Aubron, Francis Odiau, and Peter Deniart met with a sympathetic reception from the new prior general, Sebastian Fantoni, and his procurator, Theodore Straccio. By decree of January 20, 1616, Fantoni authorized sending the theology students of the reform to the Jesuit college at La Flèche, even though the Order had no house there. Other privileges included recognition of Rennes, Angers and Loudun as reformed houses of the Order, the right to transfer friars from one house to another, the right (to be used sparingly) to excommunicate those who had illicit possessions, the right of the convents to choose their own priors.

The reform of the province increased in momentum. On October 19, 1617, the provincial, Peter Maillard, agreed to appoint a vicar for the reform and named Matthew Pinault. The same year, Dol entered the fold. The local bishop, Anthony de Revol, and his successors became benefactors of the convent and helped with its material restoration.

The citizens of Ploermel, too, obtained a reformed community for the convent they had rebuilt.

The provincial chapter held at Pont-l'Abbé in 1618 elected Thibault provincial. Fantoni had written Maillard suggesting him for the post. With a reformed friar at its head, the province would be given every encouragement to improve materially and spiritually, while the Observance of Rennes could develop unhampered. The chapter acceded to the request of the citizens of Quintin for a reformed convent. Peter Deniart was named procurator to implement the foundation, which was inaugurated on April 26, 1620.

On August 28, 1619, at Chalain, Thibault convened a congregation of the reform, which now numbered six houses: Rennes, Angers, Loudun, Dol, Ploermel, and Chalain. The assembled fathers agreed that it would be better for the vicar provincial to be elected than to be appointed by the provincial. Four definitors were elected to assist him. The rest of the meeting was devoted to an examination of the suggestions sent by the members of the convents for the betterment of observance. At the end, Francis Odiau was elected vicar. A foundation at Le Guildo in the diocese of St. Malo was approved, pending ratification by the provincial chapter.

Except as a last resort, Thibault did not use his position to force the Rennes Observance on unreformed convents, even after Fantoni, unsolicited, had on January 15, 1620, obtained from Paul V a bull appointing him apostolic commissary general for the reform of the Order in France. Hennebont was one of the houses reformed in this way. After Behourt had failed to eliminate abuses, Thibault had Master Cyril Pennec elected prior, dispersed incorrigible offenders to other convents and replaced them by reformed friars (1620).

During Thibault's visit to Nantes in 1620, the prior, Christopher Le Roy, resigned his office, and Thibault replaced him with Francis Odiau, calling in two other reformed friars as regents of theology. Some of the community elected to transfer to other houses; the rest conformed to the Observance.

At Poitiers, the prior, Peter Chalumeau, had maintained himself in office for twenty years, even during his term as provincial. He put up a stiff resistance to the visitation by Thibault and refused to admit the prior, Nicholas Chasteau, elected by the chapter of Ploermel, 1622. When Chalumeau was paralyzed by a stroke, Providence itself seemed to have taken a hand in the affair. Luke of St. Anthony was brought from Loudun as regent of philosophy, accompanied by fourteen students.

The General Chapter of 1620

At the general chapter of 1620, Archangel of St. Luke, second *socius* for Touraine, proposed eleven headings, or points, to the general for his approval. The convents of Rennes, Angers, Loudun, Dol, Ploermel, Hennebont, Nantes, and Chalain were declared of the Observance of Rennes. No convent of the province is to be considered observant, unless declared so by the prior general, and unless it follows the *Exercitia* of the Observance of Rennes. All priors of the Observance of Rennes with a *socius* designated by their community are to meet yearly. This annual congregation will be presided over by the superior of the Observance, or in his default by the senior among the priors. A vicar provincial shall be elected, who without prejudice to the rights of the provincial or other superiors, will visitate the reformed communities and take care that the religious live devoutly and tranquilly in the continual exercise of mortification and prayer, and that not only individuals but also communities live in perfect community of goods. No professed member of the Order may be admitted to the Observance of Rennes without a year's probation, renewal of vows and commitment of self and possessions to the community in deed and in writing. All members of the Observance of Rennes are to renew their vows each year in the presence of the Blessed Sacrament exposed, after the Forty Hours' Devotion.

On June 15, the eleven points were approved by Fantoni's new procurator general, Gregory Canal, and the French definitors at the chapter: Philip Picquelin (Narbonne), John Masqueret (Francia), Ghislain Lucas (Belgium), John Bourgoin (prior of Paris), John Tuaut (Aquitaine), John Anthony Fezay (Provence), Philip Thibault (Touraine). Fantoni added his approval the next day.

The Brown Habit of Carmel

The habit worn by the reformed friars triggered a controversy in the French provinces which was aired at the chapter.

The constitutions of the time continued to repeat Soreth's ordinance that tunics be *"griseus*, black, or at least tending to black" (*Constitutiones*, 1586, p. 26). The general chapter of 1532 specified that griseus should he worn in Italy; in the rest of the Order, black. The general chapter of 1564 allowed Sicily to wear black.

In the definitory of this chapter, the proposal was made that it would be fitting for all members of the Order to wear habits of the same color. The chapter made no decree to this effect, but on June 30, 1620, Fantoni wrote a letter, urging the French provincials quietly to persuade (*suaviter disponant*) their subjects to adopt the color *griseus*. Anyone who would do so would have the merit of obedience. However, in the case of the province of Touraine, the general left no choice; on November 4, 1621, he instructed the coming provincial chapter to adopt "the one and only color *griseus*, that is, native, without dye of any sort."

At the next general chapter of 1625, complaints about the changes they had made in the color and form of the habit were brought against Touraine and Aquitaine by John Bourgoin, provincial of Francia; Ghislain Lucas, provincial of Belgium; Bernard Berard, provincial of Narbonne; John Louis Durace, provincial of Provence; William Champcheurieux, prior of Paris. The chapter held fast to Fantoni's arrangement: those who wore *griseus* were not to be disturbed; those who wore black were exhorted in the Lord to change, though they were not compelled to do so. In form, the habit was to conform to the constitutions, the provisions of which were reiterated.

The line of battle was not drawn only between reformed and unreformed. Both Bourgoin and Berard favored reform in their provinces. Louis Perrin wrote an apology for the color black. The opposite opinion was proposed by Leo of St. John in his *Typus seu pictura vestis religiosae* (Paris, J. Cottereau, 1625).

When Straccio visited the Iberian peninsula in 1617, *griseus* was worn there, but by 1634 the black habit had become the rule, and on September 11, he ordered the former practice restored. *Griseus*, he noted in his letter, was worn in Italy, Poland, and in all reformed convents of France and Belgium. A month previously Straccio had ordered the Belgian province to adopt *griseus*.

In the 17th century, *griseus*, whatever had been its hue in the Middle Ages, signified dark brown, the color which in the form of dyed cloth has prevailed in modern times.

The Reform of Touraine

Before long the Observance of Rennes had spread throughout the entire province. In some cases, as at Aulnay (1623), Vivonne (1629), and La Rochelle (1633) it was a question of reclaiming foundations which had lain abandoned since the civil wars. At Pont l'Abbé, pestilence had reduced the community to two half-dead friars. To nurse the survivors, reformed friars were summoned, among them a vicar to replace the deceased prior until the next chapter of 1629. At Orléans, Charpentier, plagued by sickness and old age, resigned his priorate in 1631 and was replaced by a reformed friar. He rejoined the Observance, retired to Rennes, took the name Louis of St. Anne, and died in 1640.

At the request of the bishop, Sebastian de Rosmadec, reformed friars were sent to Bondon in 1624, but reform was only achieved under the prior, Denis of the Resurrection. St. Pol was restored in 1618 by Peter Maillard. The chapter of 1629 authorized the introduction of reform. This was brought about by Nicodemus of the Holy Cross, elected prior in 1635. Fifteen reformed friars were sent to Tours in 1615. In 1633, the community elected a reformed friar, Hilary of St. John, as prior. It was not until 1646 that reform became final.

Besides the restoration and reform of the sixteen original convents of the province, nine new foundations were made: Chalain, Le Guildo, Quintin (already mentioned), Josselin (1624), Auray (1627), Paris and its dependency Basses Loges (1631), La Flèche (1629-1631), La Flocellière (1617-1642). Leo of St. John, whose long-standing desire was to establish a house in Paris, *"extra quam magnum nihil,"* to use his own expression, was responsible for acquiring the convent of the Brothers of Charity of Notre Dame in the rue des Billettes (hence the convent's name: Les Billettes). The property called Les Basses Loges in the forest of Fontainebleu at first afforded a refuge in the country from the crowded city. Later it became a "desert," or contemplative house of the province.

To the nunneries at Nantes and Vannes in the territory of the province of Touraine, Philip Thibault added that of the Holy Sepulchre at Rennes (1622) and of Bethlehem at Ploermel (1627).

When the congregation of the reform was held at Chalain in 1633, all the convents of the province had been associated to the reform. The office of vicar provincial for the reform was abolished as superfluous. The Observance of Rennes had become the Reform of Touraine.

The relative smoothness with which the reform spread through the province was no doubt due to the fact that the reins of government since 1618 had been in the hands of the reformed. Philip Thibault, elected provincial in 1618, was succeeded by his disciple, Matthew Pinault, in 1622. Re-elected in 1626, Thibault was followed by Bernard of St. Magdalen (1629), Archangelus of St. Luke (1632), and Leo of St. John (1635).

The Spirit of the Reform of Touraine

At the same time, the reform developed its own legislation, *Statuta fratrum Beatae Dei Genitricis et Virginis Mariae de Monte Carmeli pro conventibus reformatis provinciae Turonensis* (Paris, Jean Guillemot, 1639).

The statutes of Touraine in various contexts refer to the nature of the Carmelite spirit. In connection with the founding of hermitages, they speak of "the practice of divine contemplation and the love of holy solitude, formerly the only part of our sacred Order, now its principal (*potissima*) part" (pt. 1, ch. 2, no. 1). Candidates should have carefully explained to them "the primary end of our institute, namely, meditating day and night on the law of the Lord" (pt. 1, ch. 3, no. 6). With regard to mental prayer, the statutes "profess that the first and principal (*potissimam*) part of our institute consists in prayer and contemplation" (pt. ch. 14, no. 1). Again, "for our Carmelite forefathers dwelling in deserts and solitude one thing was necessary: to attend upon (*vacare*) God by the continual exercise of contemplation." But since the Carmelites have been called by the popes to the active ministry, "the nature (*ratio*) of our institute requires that to mystical theology, which is the best part for Carmelites, we should add the assiduous study of letters and the sciences" (pt. 1, ch. 21, no. 1).

The statutes are divided into four parts, treating in turn religious life, the offices of the local community, elections and misdemeanors. These parts correspond to those of the general constitutions of the Order, but their content and spirit are quite different. The law in all its particulars is concerned with spiritual values, with the interior life of the individual friar and the community.

The traditional first chapter of part 1, "On the Acceptance of Places," now stresses the quality of community life. The members of a new foundation should be carefully chosen; it should be abandoned if with time perfect observance proves impracticable. Controls are placed over building costs and planning to ensure the practice of poverty and equal accommodations for all. An extra chapter, "On a Place of Solitude and Hermits," is added, "in order that this primitive institute may flourish perennially among us" (pt. 1, ch. 2, no. 1).

In the four chapters dealing with the formation of young members, special attention is directed to the fostering of religious ideals. The careful selection of candidates becomes a separate chapter. One house of the province is to be designated as a novitiate, of which the plan and schedule are laid down. The novice master should teach his charges how to meditate, to converse interiorly with God and other spiritual exercises as prescribed in the directory for novices. Novices "should be imbued with zeal for the divine office, to be celebrated with the ancient majesty of the Order" (pt. 1, ch. 5, no. 9).

Profession is made in the province, not in a particular house, and the professed friar may be assigned to any house by superiors (pt. 1, ch. 5, no. 16). Since "the rest of the life of each religious depends on the first years after profession" (pt. 1, ch. 6, no. 1), the newly professed are not to be dispersed throughout the province but should be sent to a convent designated as a seminary. During the first of two years they should continue spiritual exercises; thereafter they may engage in study for a year, especially the humanities, before starting philosophy and theology.

An important statement is added to the chapter on laybrothers: "We declare that our laybrothers are truly and properly religious and enjoy the same privileges of the forum and the canon as the clerics. They are not to be called servants but brothers, and are to be loved and honored by the clerics" (pt. 1, ch. 7, no. 2).

A chapter on community life is a significant addition. Anyone who does not participate in the common life is deprived of voice and place and is *ipso facto* ineligible for office. No one, no matter what his status or office, is exempt from choir, except lecturers and preachers actually engaged as such. The superior may assign the most menial tasks, such as helping in the kitchen and sweeping the house, to any member of the community. To be absent from community activities for any length of time - for instance, to preach a Lenten course - permission of the provincial is required. Honorary titles, such as Master and Doctor, are proscribed. To witness to the mortified nature of religious life, the discipline (penitential flogging) shall be taken in common (pt. 1, ch. 9).

Special chapters on the three vows are another innovation. The chapter on poverty (pt. 1, ch. 10) explicitly excludes the deposit box. "In order that every occasion or kind of private possession may be utterly eradicated from our houses, we strictly forbid that there should be instituted in them a common place, called a *depositum*, in which are kept money or other things with a note or the name of a private religious for his own use" (no. 14). No friar is to consider what is given him for his use as his own, not even the most insignificant thing, such as a rosary, picture, etc. (no. 3). Articles needed for daily use are kept in a common storeroom to be distributed with charity by the superior. When no longer needed, things should be returned to the storeroom (no. 2). The very words "mine" and "thine" are proscribed; religious should use the possessive pronouns "our" and "your" (no. 6). The cells should resemble that of the prophet Elisha; their meager furnishings are specified in detail (no. 7). Cells should be interchanged at least once a year (no. 8).

Not only individuals but communities should have things in common. The wealthier convents should help the poor ones (pt. 1, ch. 10, no. 18). A provincial fund is set up for financing new foundations or reconstructing ruined convents. Stipends earned by preachers of Advent and Lenten courses and the money brought into the Order by novices are to be paid into this fund (nos. 19-20). These were important steps toward breaking down the deeply ingrained concept of conventuality.

To the usual chapter on divine office (oral prayer) the statutes add another on mental prayer (pt. 1, ch. 14). Not that the reform neglected liturgical prayer: its houses were distinguished for its ceremonies. "Besides the continual internal preoccupation with God which all should practise according to their ability and the inspiration of the Holy Spirit, all should make meditation in common twice a day, in periods of one hour and of a half hour (nos. 2-3). Also prescribed are daily reading of scripture in the solitude of the cell, an annual ten-day retreat, examination of conscience three times a day, renewal of vows once a year - in short all the modern practices of piety (nos. 6-9).

With regard to silence (pt. 1, ch. 15), the statutes forbid speaking without permission or a just cause (no. 1). Some form of manual work in silence is also recommended (no. 4).

Besides the chapter in the constitutions on conduct outside the convent, the statutes add another on proper behavior within the house (pt. 1, ch. 18).

Religious observance in the houses of study was as grave a concern for the reform as the pursuit of learning, hence an extra chapter on this subject (pt. 1, ch. 21). At first, the reformers had pondered abolishing doctoral studies altogether. In 1628, Gregory Canal sent patents to this effect, but left it up to Thibault to publish them. In a typical compromise, Thibault allowed reformed students to be promoted on rare occasions, but they were required to renounce all privileges of graduates (pt. 1, ch. 9, no. 10). Certainly, the province of Touraine honored this restriction; subsequently only two members of the province were licensed at the University of Paris. A later amendment allowed reformed provinces to make their own decisions regarding academic degrees and their privileges. The provincial was not required to have a doctorate, as stipulated in the constitutions of the Order (pt. 3, ch. 5, no. 2).

In part 2, separate chapters are devoted to offices which take on greater importance in communities observing the strict common life: the porter, the custodian of linens and clothing, the tailor, personnel in charge of the refectory, the cook, the infirmarian (ch. 12-16). New posts are: the procurator to the parliaments of Paris and Brittany (ch. 8) and the monitor, a sort of troubleshooter between the prior and his subjects (ch. 5).

A by-product of the practice of poverty in the reform was a revolution in library administration (pt. 2, ch. 11). The constitutions of the Order strictly forbade books to be removed from the library (pt. 2, ch. 12, no. 1), a prohibition reinforced in 1593 by Pope Clement VIII. Individual friars, especially lecturers, had their own books which were among the most prized of their possessions. The Touraine statutes forbade the ownership of books by individuals, who on the other hand were allowed to take books from the library to their rooms (no. 2). Already in 1616 Rennes and Angers had obtained a papal dispensation to this effect.

The reform, in fact, effected a complete renewal of the religious spirit in the province. Its houses became centers of fervent prayer and dedicated apostolate. Its friars were sought after by the populace as preachers, confessors, counselors. Municipalities wanted their own convent of this sort of religious. Other provinces of the Order in France as well as in other countries begged for Touraine friars to teach them their way of life. The reform produced many men with profound experience of the interior life and in spite of an early mistrust of academic learning a rich literature of devotion.

In 1627, the year after his reelection as provincial, Thibault became vicar of the nuns of Nazareth at Vannes. He visitated the Place Maubert in 1630 and 1634. He presided at the provincial chapter of Francia, held at Meldun in 1631, and received the unanimous consent of the capitulars for the reform of the province. The reformer of Carmel also labored for the betterment of religious life outside his own Order. He died in the hospice of the monastery of Nazareth, January 24, 1636.

With a minimum of friction Thibault had brought about the renewal of his province, at the same time maintaining communion with the Order. In this, he was aided by his temperament, for he was a man of peace and measured prudence. "More unity, less perfection," was his motto. He refused to resort to force to bring about reform and rejected offers to extend the Observance to houses and provinces not sufficiently disposed to amendment. At times, his diffidence seems almost excessive. He was reticent about his interior life and left no writings: his words were written on the fleshy tablets of human hearts.

Chapter 3

The Stricter Observance in Aquitaine, Narbonne, and Francia

Sometimes the name of Touraine is applied to the entire reform movement of the Order in the 17th century and subsequently. Actually, this title applies only to the province of Touraine. It is true that the Touraine reform was the most successful and provided a model to other provinces. Yet in actuality reform was a provincial concern and proceeded independently in each province with varying degrees of success. To speak of the reform movement as the Reform of Touraine after 1645, when the Stricter Observance was instituted, is anachronistic.

Due to the powerful influence and example of Touraine, it was inevitable that reform should spread to the other provinces of France, but except in the case of Aquitaine the process was drawn out, painful, and for a long time only partial. The attrition was due to the fact that the reformers remained loyally attached to their provinces and did not secede, as would have been the easier course. As a result, they achieved their purpose, though at times only imperfectly: the renewal of the Order in France, spiritually and materially.

The Province of Aquitaine

The province of Aquitaine had maintained the same number of houses since the last quarter of the 14th century: Albi, Cahors, Limoges, Figeac, Montauban, St. Antonin, Lauzerte, La Rochefoucauld, Mortemart, Aurillac, La Châtre, and the hermitage of St. Louis in the forest of Valence. During the 17th century, a last convent was acquired at Pleaux (1639).

The reform of Aquitaine was independent of that of Touraine and contemporary to it. It took place almost simultaneously with that of Touraine and was one of the most successful. Here, too, success was due to the efforts of one leader, though of quite a different sort from Thibault.

John Tuaut, was born in Aurillac, took his doctorate at the University of Cahors. He describes conditions in the province before he began his reforming activity. "Religious life was almost totally relaxed (*depravata*). There had been no provincial chapters or visitations from about 1560 to 1597, when Master Raymond l'Eglise, royal professor at the University of Cahors, had ruled his province with the title of vicar general. Most of the twelve convents of which the province was composed were inhabited by three or four friars, who as a rule served the neighboring parishes and lived more among seculars than in the monastery. Persons of all sorts and of both sexes had free access to the convents. Household work was committed to women domestics. The Blessed Sacrament was nowhere reserved, the divine office was hardly ever recited in choir. Among the forty or fifty friars who composed the province when I took the habit, scarcely two or three were to be found who had anything to say in the pulpit or who knew Latin. If there remained a shadow of religious life in the province, it was to be found in a faint degree at Albi which still retained some remainder of the reform which had originated there."

In 1612, Tuaut undertook the reform of the convent of La Châtre, but his efforts made only modest progress. He had greater success in improving the material conditions of the community, managing between 1613 and 1616 to restore church and convent. After the ravages of the religious wars, the renewal of religious life involved the restoration of religious buildings. It was useless to pretend to religious life in common without this premise.

Tuaut was considering entering the Carthusian Order, when he was elected provincial at the chapter held at Figeac, 1617. He decided to use his new position to resume his efforts at reform, improving the time by restoring and enlarging his native convent of Aurillac, 1618-1629. He got his opportunity in 1619 with the death of Master Peter La Cousture, who had been immovably entrenched in the priorates of Limoges and Mortemart. Tuaut settled the novitiate in Limoges, peopled it with reformed friars from La Châtre and removed those unwilling to reform. Promising young men applied for admittance, and within a year the novices numbered more than twenty.

It was at this time that Tuaut met Philip Thibault at Loudun to ask for two friars from Touraine to introduce the Observance of Rennes into his province. Thibault demurred, but two years later, in 1621, consented to train two friars from Aquitaine in the novitiate of Rennes. They were Louis of the Virgin (Tardien) and Angelus of St. Elijah (de Guilhemet).

In 1620, Tuaut attended the general chapter held in Rome, accompanied by Ponce Druhle and Eugene Corthiade as his *socii*.

Tuaut set the case of Mortemart before the general chapter. This convent had an unenviable record for observance, or rather the lack thereof. The friars of this house pretended that the prior was elected for life, that they could not be transferred, and that by virtue of a bull of John XXII of 1331 they were not accountable to canonical visitators for the administration of the convent.

The general chapter charged the procurator general to take due steps to have the bull, if it ever existed, annulled. The prior general, Sebastian Fantoni, commissioned Tuaut to remove all friars from Mortemart and to introduce the common life as observed at Limoges, Aurillac, and La Châtre. Tuaut carried out his commission, removing the recalcitrants and replacing them with friars favorable to reform. These elected Ponce Druhle as prior, but shortly thereafter he was elected provincial at the chapter held at Mortemart, 1621. Tuaut became prior of Limoges.

In 1600, the provincial, Anthony Nozières, had managed to recover the convent of La Rochefoucauld from the Calvinists. He placed there as prior over one or two inmates Hugh Bories. On his death, August 22, 1622, the provincial Druhle agreed with Tuaut that the time was ripe for reforming the convent. Tuaut lost no time in establishing twelve reformed friars there. The reconstruction of the convent followed.

At the chapter held at La Rochefoucauld in 1624, Louis of the Virgin was elected provincial. The unreformed houses, Albi, Cahors, Lauzerte, Montauban, and Figeac formed a block. Leaders of the opposition were John Labarde, John Petriny, and Arnold de l'Eglise (de Ecclesiis). Petriny (1580-1658) was held in high respect as court preacher and strong opponent of the Calvinists, against whom he wrote *Ministrophthorie, ou renversement des ministres* (Tournon, Claude Michel, 1619).

Tuaut, who had been named prior of La Rochefoucauld, persuaded the provincial to name him to the priorship of Lauzerte, vacated when Francis of Jesus and Mary became prior of Albi. Since the destruction of the convent by the Huguenots in 1560, the community had lived in a house near the parish church of

St. Bartholomew. Tuaut immediately undertook the construction of a convent. He also prevailed on Louis, after winning over the bishop to the project, to introduce reformed friars into Cahors, where Arnold de l'Eglise was prior. Louis confided the task to Angelus of St. Elias, who sorely disappointed the trust placed in him by defecting to Calvinism and marrying. Tuaut himself introduced the reformed friars into the convent on August 3, 1626, over the opposition of the citizenry, who supported the prior. The provincial, Fr. Louis, died there the following year.

At the chapter held at Limoges in 1628, Tuaut was again elected provincial. Arnold de l'Eglise was successfully ousted from the priorship of Cahors, a post he had held for 35 years. Previously, Arnold's uncles, John and Raymond, had entrenched themselves in the job for forty years. With the reform, the convent was also restored.

On February 14, 1622, the prior general, Sebastian Fantoni had granted Tuaut letters as commissary for the restoration of St. Antonin and Montauban, destroyed by heretics about sixty years earlier. St. Antonin was only a hospice with five or six friars in residence.

In August, 1631, Tuaut opened a hospice at Montauban, destroyed in the religious troubles in 1560, until a convent could be erected. The following year, Albi, reduced in numbers by pestilence, was taken over by the reformed.

By 1635, only Figeac remained unreformed, but – the report of that year stated – the community was small and could be reformed whenever the provincial desired.

The vicar general of the Order, Theodore Straccio, wanted to keep the reins of reform in his own hands and did not greatly appreciate the independent spirit of Touraine. He favored the reform of Aquitaine and planned to use it for the reform of the Order.

Become prior general, Straccio, on August 30, 1631, appointed Tuaut prior of Traspontina and charged him with the reform of the Roman convent and also with the preparation of constitutions for all reformed convents of the Order. At the conclusion of the latter task, which had retained him in Traspontina after his term of office, Tuaut, in the words of the house chronicler, "tearfully departed from Rome." He took with him a copy of the new constitutions, which were accepted by the province at the Aquitaine chapter of April 13, 1636, presided over by Tuaut himself. They were printed with the title *Regula et constitutiones fratrum Beatae Dei Genitricis Mariae de Monte Carmelo Antiquae Observantiae* (Cahors, Jean Dalvy, 1637).

On his return to the province, Tuaut became prior of Albi, where he began the restoration of the convent in June of 1636. He was also made vicar general of the diocese of Albi by Bishop Caspar d'Aillon du Lude and produced statutes and a ritual. In 1641, he resigned as provincial, because he had been constituted vicar of the Carmelite nuns of Nazareth near Vannes. He died in his native Aurillac, 1653.

Singlehanded, he had raised his province from the ruins of the religious wars to a condition of religious fervor.

During his visitation of France in 1663-1664 the prior general, Jerome Ari, left a precious list of the names of the 151 members of the province. The houses numbered 13: Albi, Cahors, Figeac, Limoges, St. Antonin, Montauban, Mortemart, La Rochefoucauld, Aurillac, La Châtre, the hermitage of St. Louis, Pleaux, Lauzerte. There were 91 priests, 21 professed clerics, 31 brothers, 8 novices. No masters are listed.

Aquitaine enjoyed a reputation for observance second only to Touraine. Its friars were often called upon to visitate and assist in the reform of other provinces inside and outside France.

The Province of Narbonne

At the beginning of the 17th century, the province of Narbonne numbered twenty-one convents: Montpellier, Bagnols, Nîmes, Millau, Clermont, Mende, Lyon, Besançon, Lodève, Lunel, Le Puy, Châlon, Tournon, Gex, Moulins, Semur, Dijon, Chomérac, Clairvaux, Geronde, Hautvillars; but Chomérac and Hautvillars, destroyed or abandoned during the civil wars, were not subsequently repossessed. Saint Jean de Losne (1623) and Pagny-le-Château (1628) were added in the course of the century.

In 1604, Silvio visited Besançon, Dijon (where he admired the "excellent" library founded by the recently deceased Didier Buffet), Châlon, Lyon, and Tournon, houses later prominent in the process of renewal. They had also been spared during the religious wars. Silvio did not hold a chapter of the province, contenting himself with publishing his reform decrees at Lyon.

Narbonne, like the rest of the French provinces still to be considered, had no single leader to guide and organize reform, which consequently proceeded at a slower pace and less effectively. At first, a number of names emerge, associated with a few convents, later the nucleus of renewal.

Towards the end of 1618, the civil authorities and the bishop of Châlon, as well as Robert Berthelot, the Carmelite auxiliary of Lyon, solicited the help of Philip Thibault in the reform of Châlon. The Touraine reformer eventually sent Francis Odiau and Ignatius of St. Francis, who remained some time with good effect. Thibault himself, on his way to the general chapter of 1620 stopped at Châlon to encourage the reformers. The prior of Châlon at this time was Stephen Molin.

On February 17, 1621, Fantoni accepted Châlon among the reformed houses of the Order, appointed the prior, now Andrew Bouttier, his commissary, and authorized the use of the formulas and dress of Rennes, as had been the practice thus far.

Andrew Bouttier was born at Crevant in 1594, entered the Order in Clermont, and received the doctor's title in the University of Paris in 1618. Since 1614 he had been prior of Clermont. On June 12, 1623, Fantoni appointed him his commissary for the reform of Dijon, at the same time warning him not to change the form of the mantle and tunic. Châlon and Dijon carried on a brisk correspondence with the reformers of Touraine. Bouttier wanted to base the reform of Narbonne on the statutes of Touraine rather than the constitutions of Straccio.

Bouttier was also long associated with his native convent of Clermont, which probably owed its high level of observance to this circumstance. Another member of the Clermont community, who no doubt contributed to raising the quality of religious life there, was Andrew Blanchard, founder of the desert of Graville, to be considered later.

As appears from the letter of Berthelot, Le Puy at this time was also experiencing a rebirth of spiritual fervor. Its prior in 1618 was Vitalis Entier (d. 1627), author of *The Awakening or Resurrection of the Carmelites* (Le Puy, 1622), which described the renovation of the convent after its destruction by the Calvinists and which contained "a discourse . . . to all the good Fathers and Brothers of the Order, exhorting them to persevere in their resolve to live under a holy Rule."

Bouttier presided over the provincial chapter of 1634 as the commissary of the prior general. In 1640, Bouttier became provincial, but shortly after the conclusion of his term of office died at Craponne in 1643. The populace revered him as a saint.

Less is known about the life of another prominent figure in the reform of Narbonne. In 1620, Bernard Berard succeeded Philip Picquelin as provincial. In this capacity, he travelled to Rome for the general chapter of 1625. Among other decisions, the chapter decreed that Strict Observance should be introduced into the provinces of Narbonne, Francia, and Belgium, the provincials of which had shown themselves willing to accept it.

Berard probably should be credited with the excellent observance of a fifth house, Besançon. He had been prior there from 1614 until he became provincial in 1620. Afterwards he returned again as prior in 1626 and spent the remainder of his days there, until his death not long before 1634. On May 19, 1635, Straccio confirmed the faculty granted to Master John Cuissot to receive novices at Besançon.

Philip Picquelin (d. 1637), a native of Semur and doctor of Paris (1594), was another promotor of reform. He was prior in the Place Maubert when the Discalced Carmelites applied for a foundation in Paris, and not only did not oppose the request, but offered the reformed friars lodging. During his terms as provincial (1602, 1618, 1626, 1629), he consistently worked for the reform of the province. Moulins probably owes its reform to him. He was prior there from 1610-1626, sometimes retaining this office even as provincial. In the latter part of his life, after 1626, he lived in his native Semur, another house that appears among those reformed.

Another member of the Narbonne province who was early interested in the reform, not only of his own province but of all the French provinces, was Robert Berthelot (d. 1630), since 1601 suffragan bishop of Lyon. Professed in the convent of Lyon in 1579, he obtained his doctorate at Paris in 1594 and was elected provincial in 1598. Chizzola made him procurator of the Order for France (1593); Silvio appointed him visitator of Aquitaine, Toulouse, and Provence (1599). He cooperated with the establishment of the Discalced Carmelites in Lyon (1617). He assisted St. Francis de Sales at his death in 1622. Even after his elevation to the episcopate, he continued to live in the Carmelite convent of Lyon with a vote in its chapters. He kept in touch with Philip Thibault, whom he may have come to know through Andrew Duval, a graduate with him from the University of Paris. He had originally urged Thibault to send religious to Châlon.

Stephen Molin should probably also be ranked among the reforming spirits of the province. He was prior, as we have seen, of Châlon at the time of its reform.

The Reformed Vicariate of Narbonne

In 1628, the prior general, Gregory Canal, authorized Châlon, Dijon, and the other reformed friars in the province to elect a vicar provincial as well as priors. The following year, Canal appointed Picquelin vicar provincial for reform. It is not clear what powers the vicar had. Apparently, he was not independent of the provincial and in fact was not regularly elected.

On September 12, 1642, Albert Massari, vicar general after the death of Theodore Straccio, appointed the prior of Chalôn, Celestine of St. Ignatius (Soleil), his commissary over the reformed houses of Châlon, Dijon, and Semur and at the same time established his perquisites and those of the reform. Massari's action was confirmed by Urban VIII, February 24, 1644.

The provincial chapter of 1647 allowed Dijon, Châlon, Clermont, and Semur to observe the constitutions of the Strict Observance decreed by the general chapter of 1645.

On August 15, 1647, Leo of St. John, apostolic visitator in France, delegated Lezin of St. Scholastica, of the Touraine province, to visit Narbonne. Beginning his visit with Châlon, Lezin made a number of decrees for the government of the province and designated Chalon, Dijon, and Le Puy respectively as novitiate, seminary for professed and house of study. In 1648, Lezin attended the general chapter as first *socius* for Touraine, and on June 27 the newly-elected Filippini made him vicar provincial of Narbonne.

The provincial chapter of 1649, presided over by Lezin, accepted the constitutions of the Stricter Observance, but the convents under Lezin were regulated by the articles of Filippini.

The following October 18, at the request of the prior, Claude Hugonet, Filippini placed Clermont under the constitutions of the Stricter Observance and his articles for the promotion of reform.

In 1651, Filippini appeared in person to visitate the province. He visited Lyon, Châlon, Dijon, and Semur. At the provincial chapter held in Lyon, Paul Lombard was elected provincial. The entire province was placed under the constitutions of the Stricter Observance. After the chapter, Filippini brought all the young professed and novices from Lyon to Châlon to be formed in the Stricter Observance. Châlon was to be the only novitiate in the province.

By 1656, the last unreformed convent, Moulins, was declared reformed.

However, the reform of the province had occurred on paper more than in reality. Convents had been too readily declared reformed without due regard to the genuine conversion of individual members. Many members of the province had indeed accepted the reform and put it into practice in their personal lives, others were not so committed. Hence there arose the anomaly of a province in which all declared themselves reformed, and yet in which many of the old abuses, privileges and exemptions from common life, private use of money, neglect of prayer, etc., continued to flourish. Here the wisdom of Thibault's policy in Touraine of proceeding slowly with reform becomes evident.

The Reformed Status of the Province in Doubt

In spite of the claim that all convents of the province had been reformed, the real status of reform continued to plague the province of Narbonne.

In effect, only a few convents were truly reformed. When Dijon and Clermont challenged the reformed status of the province, the prior general, on June 1, 1668, gave them a vicar provincial in the person of Prosper of St. Margaret. A member of the province of Touraine, Prosper had been imported by Filippini in 1651 to assist in the reform of Narbonne. For twenty-five years he labored in the service of the province, lecturing in philosophy and theology and filling posts of responsibility until his death in 1680 at the age of 70.

As a result of a visitation by Mark of the Nativity in 1669, Châlon, Clermont, Dijon, and Besançon were given a vicar provincial, directly responsible to the prior general. Lodève was added as a novitiate. On July 3, 1670, the priors and their *socii* of Châlon, Dijon, and Clermont met at Dijon and elected John of the Cross vicar provincial of the reform. Among other decisions, the reformers renounced degrees and their privileges.

The province, which considered itself reformed, saw no need for an independent vicariate of reformed houses and constantly opposed it. They imported provincials from reformed provinces who were not too demanding but gave the patent of reform to the province.

For many years, the reform remained confined to five convents. (The reform of Lodève proved impracticable, but in 1672 in the wake of clamorous scandals Moulins was reformed.) The points of friction were many: election of priors, transfer of religious, control of the novitiate and houses of study, privileges of the doctorate, claims to the reformed status by members of the province. Yet despite the resultant discord, it was well for the province that the vicariate had been established. The level of religious practice in the province was not high, and there was little prospect that it would better itself with time. Also by remaining within the province rather than separating from it, the reform achieved its purpose, which was the betterment of the province.

During these turbulent years, the province was blessed with a capable and durable novice master, Eusebius of St. John (d. 1728). A member of the convent of Dijon, he was appointed to the office by Mark of the Nativity with a special dispensation, since he was only twenty-three years old, and served for twenty-seven years. During his long lifetime - he died in his nineties - he was five times elected prior to Dijon, twice vicar provincial of the reform, four times provincial. He was known for his piety rather than learning, but he had the knack of leadership, instilling in his charges reverence and love. In 1741, his spiritual conferences were still preserved in manuscript in the convent of Dijon.

After the solemn induction of reform into the large and dissolute convent of Lyon in 1684, the pace of affiliation with the reform accelerated. At the chapter of 1699, the entire province was declared reformed, and the office of vicar was abolished. This time no one challenged the claim.

The Carmelite Houses in Switzerland

On November 4, 1624, Gregory Canal made Angelus Le Fort, of the Belgian convent of Valenciennes, commissary general of the Swiss convent of Geronde, currently belonging to the province of Narbonne. Le Fort was authorized to take with him friars from Narbonne or another province and proceed to the reform of the convent.

Reform had been introduced into Valenciennes by Philip Thibault only two months previously, and Le Fort, in fact, may have been fleeing its austerity. The bishop of Sion, Hildebrand Jost, had long had his eye on the incomes of the scandal-ridden Carmelite convent for a prospective seminary. He was soon complaining to the Congregation of the Propagation of the Faith about Le Fort's ignorance, debauchery, and drunkenness. He even had him in his prison for a while.

Whereas Straccio withdrew his appointment of John Baptist of St. Rocco as prior of Besançon, February 11, 1640, he maintained his commission as commissary for Geronde and Clairvaux. By 1645, Narbonne had abandoned Geronde. The general chapter of that year ordered its recovery and the introduction of the reform of Piedmont. The province of Lombardy wanted no part of it, so the general chapter of 1654 tried to give Geronde back to Narbonne, but without any luck.

The other Carmelite convent in Switzerland, Sainte Catherine de Jorat, in the diocese of Lausanne, founded in 1497, did not survive the Wars of Religion.

The Province of Francia

At the time of its separation from Belgium in 1597, the province of Francia retained ten convents: Metz, Liège, Montreuil, Rouen, Pont Audemer, Caen, Rheims, Bourges, Baccarat, St. Amand. In the course of the 17th century, other houses were added: Melun (1605, inherited from the defunct reform of Albi), Arras and St. Pol (1641, returned to the province from Belgium), Wégimont (1647), Landrecies (1657), Pont-a-Mousson (1657), Verviers (1661), Lucheux (1661), Ardres (1664). Hospices were also acquired at Berneuil (1688) and Dunkerque (1737).

After 1641, the province was divided into four "nations" – Francia, Normandy, Picardy, and Lorraine – which did not always live in harmony. The definitors were elected from each of these regions. After the reform had taken root, two of the definitors were required to be reformed.

Dependent on the province of Francia were six nunneries: Liège, Huy, Dinant, Charleville, Rochefort (1629), Fumay (1632). Ciney, founded in 1629, passed over to the Discalced in 1649.

On his way to Belgium from Paris in 1603, Silvio visited Maincy, Rouen, Pont-Audemer, Caen, Montreuil, Arras and Liège (with its nunnery at Huy). Everywhere, Silvio published his decrees on behalf of the common life and revival of liturgical prayer, but he did not tarry to hold a chapter.

In 1607, the provincial, Jean Petit, sent a dismal report to Silvio: "I found one great evil in almost all the houses, namely, that the brethren are more intent on liberty and pleasure than on piety and religion. This evil is so rooted in some houses that it can be eliminated only with the greatest difficulty. To maintain and further support this state of affairs, those are elected priors who are of a sort to insure the free enjoyment of pleasure." He concludes by urging Silvio to authorize the coming provincial chapter to nullify local elections and to appoint priors untainted by selfish interests.

Early Development of Reform

The general chapter of 1625 instructed the prior general, Gregory Canal, to carry through the reform of well-disposed provinces such as Narbonne, Francia and Belgium. It was after this date, as a matter of fact, that reform took permanent root in the province of Francia, though there were earlier ineffectual efforts.

Progress was made under the provincialate of Albert de Saulcy (1598-1640), a native of Liège and doctor of Paris. He was elected provincial in 1632 at the chapter of Melun presided over by Philip Thibault. The following chapter of 1635, presided over by Ignatius of St. Francis, reformer of Chalon, granted him a second term, because he was the most apt "to promote and establish the reform already begun in the province."

The centers of reform, which were also rivals, were Caen for the French houses and Liège for the bishopric-principality of Liège.

In 1678, the community of Caen stated with pride: "It was not in several, even in a few convents that the Stricter Observance originated in the province, but in Caen alone. From there, after it had matured in Liège and Montreuil, joined by Arras, it spread to Rheims and Metz and finally to the other convents. For this reason, Caen in the province of Francia has the same motive for rejoicing as Rennes in Touraine, and other convents in other provinces."

Whatever is to be said of this boast of being the Rennes of Francia, the statement by the Caen community is useful for tracing the itinerary of reform in the province.

Caen was of all the houses of Francia the closest geographically to Touraine and was conscious of having received the spirit of reform from this source. In 1609, Bishop Robert Berthelot wrote to Philip Thibault urging him to send his religious there, but Thibault had only begun his work and was in no position to help others. In 1629, he sent Ignatius of St. Francis who successfully reformed Caen and became vicar of the reform in the province.

Philosophy and theology were taught at Caen by two other members of the province of Touraine, Daniel of St. Joseph (1601-1666) and Paulinus of the Epiphany (d. 1667). The former, nephew of the mayor (*praesul*) of St. Malo, was distinguished for learning. Besides at Caen he taught at Traspontina in Rome and became the provincial of Touraine in 1651. At the end of his life, he retired to the solitude of Le Guildo. Daniel published several works, the most noteworthy being *Disputationes in Summam theologicam D. Thomae* (Caen, Joachim Massienne, 1649).

Ignatius of St. Francis presided at the provincial chapter of 1635, which made Caen the only novitiate in the province. The novitiate at Caen played an important role in the reform of the province; over the years its alumni were a leaven that raised the religious spirit throughout the province. The prior general, Theodore Straccio, on October 10, 1637, took care to have the designation of Caen as only novitiate of the province confirmed by Urban VIII.

The reform of Montreuil followed on that of Caen. In 1640, Straccio appointed Cyprian of St. Denis, member of the Touraine province and prior of Caen, commissary general of Caen and Montreuil.

The following year, Cyprian presided at the provincial chapter, at which the bull of Urban VIII, confirming the novitiate at Caen, was promulgated. At the same chapter, two new convents, Arras and St. Pol, appear, united to the province by Straccio, October 18, 1640. Arras had belonged to the province before the erection of the Belgian province in 1597 and was one of the first houses to embrace reform in that province (see below). St. Pol, too, was probably reformed, for the provincial chapter of 1649 appointed the vicar provincial for reform, Matthias de la Couronne, elected that year, to preside at the election of a prior by the communities of Liège and St. Pol.

Rheims probably owes its reformation to John Bourgoin (d. 1652). Bourgoin was a native of Rheims and its prior, as well as prior of Paris and provincial for three terms. At the provincial chapter of 1641, he refused the priorate of Melun unless it accepted the reform of Caen. The prior general, John Anthony Filippini, appointed Bourgoin to preside over the provincial chapter of 1649, at which his "articles," promulgated by the general chapter of the previous year, were to be read and their implementation urged.

In 1664, Rheims is first mentioned as a novitiate of the province along with Caen. In the years that followed, together with Metz and Caen, it often housed the novices.

Beginning in 1618, the prior of Metz, Nicholas Rampont, former teacher of Thibault, persistently requested help from his erstwhile pupil, but without result. Even Bérulle's authoritative voice echoed in the void. Under Master Peter Collignon, Metz accepted reform. On November 4, 1629, the community promised regular observance and adopted the habit of the reform. The provincial chapter of that year requested Philip Thibault to be commissary for the reform of the convent. The community asked the prior general, Gregory Canal, to take the reform under his protection and proposed the usual exchange of friars with Touraine. In 1632, at the request of the "Most Christian Queen," Straccio confirmed Collignon in the office of the prior of Metz. But all these efforts produced no permanent results, for in 1661 Metz again requested reform.

In 1630 the community of Baccarat, at loggerheads with its prior, expressed a desire for the reform of Metz under its prior Collignon.

The provincial chapter of 1668, obeying a formal precept of the prior general and the expressed will of the Most Christian King, decreed that the Stricter Observance be observed at Metz, Caen, Rheims, Arras "and elsewhere." Rouen, Bourges, St. Amand, and Pont Audemer were to follow the constitutions of the Order scrupulously, especially with regard to poverty – an allusion undoubtedly to the deposit box.

As early as 1608, the prior of Rouen, Stephen Gueroult, wrote to Philip Thibault, expressing his desire to reform his convent and offering to send Master John Masqueret and another priest to Rennes to learn its observances. When Masqueret became prior, he succeeded in 1629 in obtaining the services of Matthew Pinault and Christopher of St. Joseph for the reform of Rouen. Masqueret, (d. 1642), a native of Rouen and doctor of Paris (1606), was the author of several books, among them a work in defense of the Eucharist against heretics (Rouen, Charles Osmont, 1639).

But Masqueret's work did not last. The general chapter of 1666 took steps against the designation of Rouen as a novitiate by Pope Urban VIII. The bull was presumed surreptitious, as Rouen was unreformed. In 1674, the convent consented to reform on condition that certain "articles" be honored. Presented by the prior, Stephen Tuboeuf, these consisted of a list of privileges of the non-reformed members of the community, which were to remain intact.

The one responsible for the introduction of reform in Rouen was Matthew de Gaugy. Yet, this time also reform failed to be permanent.

In 1669, the community of St. Amand asked for a reformed prior, but the chapter of 1671 elected Peter Persac and postponed the reform for three years. The convent was still unreformed in 1677, when the bishop of Bourges requested its reform.

The Controversy Over Liège

In a circular letter to the French provinces, August 2, 1649, Filippini reports the progress of reform in Francia, at the same time alluding to the discord which impeded it: "In the province of Francia, disturbed by so many tempests, a friar of great merit and truly favorable to reform, Francis Masson, has just been elected. In order that diversity of nationality and distance between convents may not do harm to reform, two vicar provincials have been elected. One will have charge of the reformed convents in France; the other, of those in the principality of Liège."

The reform was introduced into his native convent of Liège by Albert de Saulcy in 1632. A promoter of reform there was Matthias de la Couronne, another native of Liège. In 1640, he was commissioned to visitate the Belgian province. At the provincial chapter of Rheims, 1649, he was elected vicar for the reformed.

Liège became a novitiate in 1637, shortly after Caen.

A rivalry existed between the reformed communities of Liège and Caen. The Liègeois were not welcome at Caen, a situation exacerbated by the distance between the outposts of the province in the chronic state of war between France and Spain in the 17th century.

An attempt to unite the Liège convent with the Belgian province became a tug of war which involved secular and ecclesiastical authorities and two decrees of the Congregation for Bishops and Religious, the details of which need not concern us here. Suffice it to say that Liège remained attached to the province of Francia.

The Final Stages of Reform

In 1667, Verviers was declared the novitiate for the convents in the principality of Liège.

In 1678, the province attempted to regain control of the novitiate which Caen continued to hold jealously in its charge. For a number of years the provincial chapter had exercised its prerogative of designating convents for the novitiate of the province, but had never removed it from Caen. Eventually, the case was settled out of court. Pope Innocent XI, approached by the cardinal protector of the Order, let it be known that he did not want the novitiate removed from Caen.

The provincial chapter of 1681 declared that the novitiate should circulate among the four nations of the province and not remain in any one place more than six years, but although this and similar sentiments were expressed in subsequent chapters, the novitiate for the French territory continued to alternate between Metz and Rheims and was never moved from Caen.

In 1680, Pont Audemer accepted reform, after the bishop of Lisieux threatened to turn the convent over to the Discalced. In 1684, since only Bourges remained unreformed, the province was declared in effect reformed. In 1688, this last sheep entered the fold.

The reformed province of Francia retained academic degrees, but renounced their privileges.

Except for the jealousy of Caen over the novitiate and rivalry with Liège, the reform of Francia came about peacefully enough and must be considered one of the most successful.

Chapter 4

The Stricter Observance in Provence, Toulouse, and Gascony

The Province of Provence

The province of Provence comprised the region of southern France east of the Rhône. In the 17th century, it numbered 21 convents: Avignon, St. Hilaire, Les Aygalades, St. André d'Estoublon, Marseilles, Aix, Apt, Manosque, Nice, Orange, Arles, Pinet, Le Luc, La Rochette, Pont Beauvoisin, Beauvoir, Vienne, St. Marcellin, Pertuis, St. Roch de Mazargue (1644), Notre Dame des Lumières (1664). Nice passed over to the province of Piedmont in 1674.

The houses of the province were located in Provence, Dauphine, Savoy, and the papal County of Avignon: political divisions that were reflected in the harmony of the province.

Silvio arrived at the door of the convent of Marseilles at noon of March 1, 1604, and lost no time in making a clean sweep of the place. For introducing women into their rooms for immoral purposes, Anthony Sier, Anthony Argemme, John Molinet, and Bernardine Citerne were banished from the city and told not to return, under penalty of the triremes for three years. Card-playing with seculars in the convent and in taverns and "many other scandals" were corrected. The prior, Betin Guiton, aged 70, was deposed for allowing such conduct to take place. Noel Ferrens was also expelled and a certain Bartholomew Bompard - not a member of the community - was told not to show his face again in Marseilles. Before the purge, the community had numbered ten priests, two clerics, and two novices. Other friars were imported to replace those banished.

Besides Marseilles, Silvio visited Vienne, Pinet, St. Marcellin, Beauvoir, Avignon, St. Hilaire, Aix, Les Aygalades, and Arles. At Vienne, he found three priests, one of them belonging to the convent of Pinet, and two novices, all living "in direst poverty" (*miserrime*). The convent had been almost completely destroyed by the heretics, and there remained only some houses and the church. At Pinet, the convent was "quite ancient and beautiful, but in the country," where three priests lived, two of them with the name Claude Guillaud. He gave the Guillauds permission to serve in a parish, provided part of their earnings went to the repair of the church. Convent and church of St. Marcellin had been destroyed by heretics, but the church was under repair. Of the community of four priests, one cleric, and one novice, only the cleric belonged to the convent. Beauvoir had been levelled to the ground, but in order to maintain claim on the property donated in the past by the kings of France, a prior and another religious lived in a rented house in town until a convent could be built. St. Hilaire had been "most ancient and beautiful," but, situated in the open country, it had suffered much from thieves and vagabonds before being destroyed by heretics. The community had rented a house in Minerva, a well-fortified town in the papal county of Avignon, and intended to build a church. The convent of Les Aygalades, which, the prior general does not fail to note, had been founded by King Louis of France, was "excellently situated and quite good," but it had lost all its incomes during the wars. Now only the prior, Mark Mater, and a laybrother lived there. The convent of Arles was "quite good, but because of the old age and inertia of the friars in an almost ruinous state." The community consisted of seven priests, one cleric and four novices. Silvio made no decrees here, because the observance was satisfactory and because he intended to convene a provincial chapter in this house. However, the chapter does not seem to have materialized.

Early efforts at reform in Marseille and Arles brought no lasting results. Arles was finally reformed in 1655 at the request of the officials of the city.

The Reform of Avignon

In the 30's, the focus of reform was Avignon. On March 2, 1635, the prior general, Theodore Straccio, commissioned Prosper of St. Louis, one of the pioneers of the reform of Touraine, to erect a novitiate at Avignon. Angelus Le Blanc, the provincial, asked the prior general to declare Avignon a reformed convent under his new constitutions for reform, according to which the novices would make profession. Straccio granted this permission on December 12, 1636. The provincial chapter held at Beauvoir in 1637 under the presidency of John Tuaut, reformer of Aquitaine, returned Le Blanc as prior of Avignon. On May 24, 1637, in the presence of John Tuaut as the general's commissary and of Matthew Audoly, provincial elect, Le Blanc solemnly promised to observe the reformed constitutions. On June 20, 1637, Pope Urban VIII confirmed Avignon as a novitiate. In 1640, Straccio sent decrees to Antoninus of St. John, prior of Avignon, for the benefit of the reform which was coming of age there under his leadership.

The promise to observe the reformed constitutions at the provincial chapter of 1637 was repeated by John Avon, prior of St. Hilaire, which Tuaut designated as the hermitage of the province. Situated on a hill overlooking the valley of the river Calavon tributary of the Durance, St. Hilaire was ideally located for a contemplative house, but in fact the community was insignificant and apart from its remoteness had little resemblance to a hermitage.

The Reform of Aix

Next in importance to Avignon as a center of reform was the convent of Aix. The history of its reform dates back as early as that of Avignon, for in 1638 at Straccio's request Aix was declared a second novitiate by Urban VIII. In 1640, Straccio appointed a certain Father Cyprian visitator, reformer, and commissary general of Aix.

In 1647, the province of Touraine sent reinforcements for the effort at reform. Victor of St. Francis became prior of Aix and vicar provincial for reform at the behest of the prior general, Leo Bonfigli. At the same time, Touraine lent Albert of St. Stephen as novice master at Avignon, Maurilius of St. Michael, and John of the Nativity.

Another Touraine friar working at Aix was Severinus of St. Peter, who taught philosophy there. In an open letter to the province of Touraine, 1649, the optimistic Filippini expresses his indebtedness on behalf of Severinus' efforts at reform. "In the province of Provence," he writes, "there is complete peace, and in the midst of this peace there is a fervent novitiate at Avignon, a well-filled house of young professed at Aix, and at the head of each of these houses a friar of your province. The provincial (Angelus Picholin) is well-disposed toward the reform and anticipates gradually bringing all the other houses to reform."

Two years later, Filippini appeared in the province on visitation. He visited only

La Rochette and Pont Beauvoisin before convening the chapter at Vienne, June 14. Arles was added to the reform and Severinus was placed there as commissary general. "Throughout the chapter," the visitation book continues, "the Most Reverend Father often reminded the delegates of the obligation of religious to join the Stricter Observance. He spoke with such fervor and success that all became enthusiastic for reform and agreed on such measures as were most favorable for the Stricter Observance. Four of the outstanding masters of the province spontaneously asked to be admitted to reformed houses, and in fact were admitted. The province was left in a condition that would enable the Stricter Observance to make spontaneous progress."

For the time being, Avignon, Aix, and possibly St. Hilaire remained the only reformed houses. In 1654, Venturini forbade the former two houses to accept deserters from reform or friars not professed in the reform without his written authorization.

The same year, Venturini commissioned Victor of St. Francis to reform St. Marcellin, but the convent had to wait another decade for its reform. The provincial chapter of 1665 ordered the reform of St. Marcellin. It was carried out by Maurice of the Nativity. The following chapter of 1667 declared St. Marcellin officially reformed.

On September 4, 1660, the prior general, Jerome Ari, declared Pertuis reformed.

The Reformed Vicariate of Provence

On June 2, 1659, Venturini appointed Victor of St. Francis vicar provincial for the reformed houses of Provence. This act was the signal for the outbreak of a heated controversy. Matthew Audoly, elected provincial a second time, refused to acknowledge Victor's authority in the province. Appealing to the coming general chapter, he challenged the very office of vicar provincial, claiming among other things that the articles of Filippini ceased to bind after his death.

Audoly found a supporter in the prior of Aix, Jerome Vigne, but the general council, on November 21, 1661, supported the office of vicar for reform.

Victor of St. Francis attended the chapter of Provence which convened at Aix, April 30, 1662, but thereafter retired to his province and, one hopes, to more peaceful days.

On July 15, Ari named as Victor's successor Michael of the Holy Spirit. After Michael, no other vicar seems to have been placed in charge of the reformed houses of the province.

Further Development of Reform

About this time, La Rochette was reformed by Laurence of the Assumption. The prior general, Jerome Ari, describes it as being such, when he passed through it and Pont Beauvoisin on his way north from Italy in January, 1663. It was while the general was in France that the reform-minded provincial, Antoninus Gayon, renewed his profession according to the constitutions of the Stricter Observance at the intermediate congregation of October 21, 1663.

Since Ari's first visit, Pont Beauvoisin had on February 16, 1664, been admitted to the reform. In spite of the euphoria experienced by the prior general and the community at this event, the reform did not last. A decade later (1675) Laurence of the Assumption again introduced the reform into Pont Beauvoisin.

In 1664, Michael of the Holy Spirit obtained a foundation for the Order in connection with the chapel of Notre Dame des Lumières near St. Hilaire. It was the community of St. Hilaire that told him of the miraculous cure of a man at the ruined chapel of Our Lady in the neighborhood. As a result of the miracle the people had rebuilt the chapel. His interest aroused, Michael arranged for the Carmelites to take over its care (1664) and founded a reformed house, confirmed by the general chapter of 1666. Michael wrote a book about the place, *Le pelegrinage de Notre-Dame-des-Lumières* (Lyons, Jean Grégoire, 1666).

Manosque was declared reformed by Ari in 1665. Already in 1634 the town councilors had requested its reform. Reform was finally introduced in 1664 under the prior, Anthony Daunier.

The provincial chapter of 1665 discussed the reformed status of Daunier, elected prior of the reformed convent of Arles. It was agreed that both Daunier and the convent of Manosque had fulfilled all the conditions for entering the reform and needed only the official declaration of the prior general to that effect.

The provincial chapter of 1665 resolved to petition the prior general to obtain papal authorization for a novitiate in the north of the province. The students could not accustom themselves to the heat and the seasoning in the food of the south. Until Vienne could be reformed the novitiate was assigned to the reformed convent of La Rochette. Meanwhile, three reformed friars were to be sent to Vienne to initiate the reform. St. Marcellin and Pinet were also ordered reformed. The general chapter of 1666 approved the petition for a second novitiate.

The provincial chapter of 1667 declared Vienne and St. Marcellin reformed. The provincial-elect, Raymond Rostagny, likewise entered the reform.

After the chapter of 1667, the province seems to have neglected the prescribed formal procedures for the reform of houses. In the course of time, the province came to consider itself completely reformed, and the chapter of 1667 was assigned as the year when this nirvana had been achieved. Actually, by this date only a little more than half of the province had been reformed. The vicar provincialship had been prematurely abandoned. The province placed itself under the constitutions of the Stricter Observance and considered itself reformed, but an authentic renewal had not taken place in all the houses. The province also labored under a special difficulty: it comprised a large number of houses, but except for four or five none had more than five members. Not only was it difficult to find suitable superiors for so many convents, but the small number of their members made community life difficult to achieve.

A Call for Reform, 1679

A sense of malaise with the spiritual state of the province manifested itself several times in the course of the subsequent history of the province.

In 1679, Marseilles, Avignon, Aix, and Arles united in a protest against the spiritual and material state of the province. Their respective priors, Anthony Daunier, Fulgentius of the Trinity, Charles of the Mother of God, and Benedict of St. Philip, on January 10 appealed to the vicar general of the Order, Emilio Giacomelli, against the administration of the provincial, Martin of St. Catherine, which they alleged was sapping the strength of observance in the province.

Eventually, these complaints were expanded into a list of 35 accusations, brought to Rome by Brocard of St. Nicholas, one of the principal protagonists in the controversy over the vicar provincial a decade earlier, and Gabriel Nallys, of Avignon. The provincial later sent a point-by-point refutation of the 35 accusations of Daunier and his confederates. In the end, the interested parties settled their differences among themselves and signed a peace agreement, December 21, 1679.

Later Litigation

In 1695, the cry for reform again went up, this time from the convents of Vienne and Pinet. Prior of Vienne was Honoré of St. Joseph (Brunet). One of the rebels of 1679, Fulgentius of the Trinity, was now prior of Pinet. Another leader in the movement was Jacques Rhedonet, a student at Paris. They called for a visitation by a commissary general and the introduction of reform.

The focus of their attack was the provincial chapter of 1667, which introduced elections of priors by the definitory, and the confirmatory brief of Clement X of 1671. After almost a year of litigation, the reformers lost their case by an arrêt of the royal council, April 17, 1697.

The provincial chapter had by no means calmed spirits at Vienne. The new prior was Peter of St. John, but it was the subprior, Joseph Marie of St. Joseph (Poncet) who took up the banner of reform. On December 8, 1697, Joseph Marie appealed to the prior general, John Feijóo de Villalobos against the recent provincial chapter. The matter came up at the general chapter which convened, May 18, 1698. The newly elected prior general, Charles Philibert Barberi, sent a commissary to France, John Baptist Savey, who extracted from Joseph Marie a retraction of his accusations and submission to the prior general.

Like its sister province of Narbonne, Provence made more than one attempt to renew its spiritual vigor, not sufficiently restored the first time, but such efforts were too weak to issue in permanent results. The would-be reformers lacked the moral strength for their task. The battles were fought in the courtroom rather than in the arena of the spirit. The hey-day of reform was past. Nevertheless, the province professed reform and was periodically called to account with more or less effective results.

The Province of Toulouse

The province of Toulouse, the smallest in France, was composed mainly of transplants from other provinces. To the original four houses, Toulouse, Castelnaudary, Castelsarrasin, and Pamiers, separated in 1342 from Aquitaine to found the province, the general chapter of 1532 added Narbonne, Carcassonne, Béziers and Montréal, separated from the province of Narbonne. In the 17th century, the province of Catalonia contributed Perpignan and Ceret in the County of Roussillon, when that territory was added to the French crown. St.-Paul-de-Lamiette, founded in 1344, never entirely regained status as a full-fledged house after its devastation by the Huguenots.

During the 16th century, the principal house of the province and important center of studies, Toulouse, had been taken over by the Congregation of Albi. When it returned in 1592 at the dissolution of the Congregation, the province once more had a head on its shoulders.

In an account of a visitation in 1594, the provincial, John Callac, former member of the Congregation of Albi, reports the existence of six houses, some of them not visited for 20 years. They number about seven to ten members and are so burdened with debt they hardly manage to provide the necessities of life. Of reform, Callac declares, there is little evidence. He asks the prior general, John Stephen Chizzola, to command that proceeds from preaching, confessing, and questing be deposited in the common fund according to the Rule.

In 1604, Henry Silvio visited Béziers, Narbonne, Carcassonne, Montréal, Castelnaudary, Toulouse, and Castelsarrasin. Béziers was "extremely poor, because it had been almost destroyed by heretics." Narbonne was "quite well off" but poorly built and was being reconstructed. Montréal was also being rebuilt, after having been burned by heretics. Castelnaudary was "quite good." Formerly, it had been outstanding, now it was being gradually restored. On May 9, the prior general convened the provincial chapter at Toulouse and published his decrees of reform.

Early Efforts at Reform

The reform of Béziers was brought about through the efforts of the bishop and magistrates of the town. In 1642, the latter intervened with the prior general to prevent the removal of reformed friars from the convent. In 1639, four students of Béziers, Albert of St. Stephen, Vitalis of St. Franco, John of St. Albert, and John of the Nativity, had asked permission of Straccio to make their novitiate at Rennes. The provincial chapter of 1643 approved their affiliation with Touraine, granted March 17, 1642.

The convent at Narbonne seems also to have been reformed. In 1643, the Spanish laybrother, Francis of the Cross, on his strange pilgrimage carrying a large cross to the Holy Land, passed through Narbonne. There he was told that in France the Order was reformed. Thereupon, Francis took a scissors and shortened his mantle to comply with the usage of the place. The piece of the holy brother's mantle was treasured as a relic.

The provincial chapter of 1643 declared that the province adhered to the constitutions of 1625 and the decrees of Clement VIII. However, when the general chapter of 1645 decreed that the constitutions of the Stricter Observance be drawn up, the provincial of Toulouse, Gaspar Pillore, requested them for his province.

The Reform of the Convent of Toulouse

The reform of the province began in earnest in 1648. That year the provincial of Touraine, Leo of St. John, answered the request of the parliament of Toulouse for friars to reform the Carmelite convent of that city. Among the friars sent, Prosper of St. Louis became prior, Dominic of St. Catherine, novice master; Julian of St. Claude, sacristan; and Isaac of St. Teresa, preacher. Saturninus of the Visitation, later involved in the province of Narbonne, was also sent at this time.

On September 3, 1648, the prior general, John Anthony Filippini, named Prosper of St. Louis vicar provincial for the reform of the province of Toulouse. The following year, on August 16, he declared the convent of Toulouse reformed.

The provincial, Michael de Mandeville, was to remove all friars who did not wish to join the reform.

In 1657, John of the Nativity, one of the friars of Béziers who had been affiliated in Touraine, was elected provincial.

In 1664, Jerome Ari visited Perpignan, Narbonne, Carcassonne, Castelnaudary, Toulouse, Castelsarrasin, and Béziers, where he held the provincial chapter. Unfortunately, his visitation book describes only his itinerary, though it offers some statistics on the province. There are nine convents: Toulouse, Narbonne, Perpignan, Carcassonne, Castelnaudary, Castelsarrasin, Béziers, Pamiers, Montréal. Members total 144: 81 priests, 18 professed clerics, 32 brothers, 11 novice clerics, 2 novice brothers.

When the prior general Matthew Orlandi visited the province in 1669, Castelnaudary, Montréal, Pamiers, and Carcassonne claimed to be reformed for twenty-two years.

The Quality of Observance

The province seems never to have formally fulfilled the conditions for being officially declared totally reformed, though with time it came to be recognized as such. It was governed by the constitutions of the Stricter Observance, but not all houses had been effectively reformed. As a result, the quality of religious renewal was a bit spotty.

Antoninus Gayon, provincial of Provence, who visitated the province in 1682, presents a very flattering account of conditions. Toulouse numbers only ten houses, but they are filled with outstanding religious. "In all of France," he reports to the prior general, "there is scarcely another province in which discipline is more flourishing in matters of morals, piety and study."

On the other hand, at the provincial chapter of 1685, the prior of Toulouse, Dominic of St. John the Baptist, describes the province as utterly relaxed and claims that there is hardly a shadow of reform in convents which abusively enjoy the name and prerogatives of reform. He calls for the designation of a house for those who wish to observe the law in very truth, lest the spirit of the Order be utterly extinguished, as, alas, is the case of the younger members of the province, who after being properly trained in the novitiate, after one or two months imitate the relaxation they see about them. He wants only those to be elected provincial or priors who not only profess the Constitutions of the Stricter Observance, but also put them into practice. In a letter of May 30, to the prior general, Angelus Monsignani, Dominic explains, "Our province was prematurely declared reformed, when not even half the religious observed the constitutions (of the reform)."

Together with Eustace of St. Joseph, Ambrose of St. Agnes, and Joseph of St. Anne, Dominic petitioned the general chapter of 1686 for a convent where they might observe the primitive Rule after the manner of the reform of Monte Santo, but they received only a rebuke for their pains. The chapter found the petition satirical, defamatory, injurious, temerarious, and imprudent. The petitioners were warned to speak and write of their superiors with greater modesty and reverence.

Although these friars did not obtain their request, the prior general, Paul of St. Ignatius, in 1688 sent a message to the following chapter of the province of Toulouse through his commissary, Saturninus of the Visitation, who presided at the assembly, that it was his desire that the province which had formerly been declared reformed by general chapters should in truth conduct itself as such before God and should sincerely eliminate abuses. He commanded the religious to observe the constitutions of the reform they professed. The definitory noted that most abuses had been pointed out by Orlandi during his apostolic visitation (1669) and ordered his decrees reprinted, read in all the houses and observed. The chapter of 1699 again renewed and confirmed the decrees of Orlandi.

In 1714, the prior general, Peter Thomas Sanchez, ordered the Stricter Observance again introduced into the province. Let us hope with better success than in the past.

Toulouse admitted academic degrees, but renounced their privileges.

The Province of Gascony

After the beginning of the 16th century, the province of Gascony, which occupied the southwestern corner of France, added no new foundations to the seventeen of which it was already composed: Bordeaux, Agen, Bayonne, Condom, Lectoure, Dax, Castillon, Aiguillon, Tarbes, Marmande (transferred here from Tonnain in 1629), Langon, Pavie, Bergerac, Trie, Sauveterre, Rabastens, and Jonzac.

Silvio's visit of Gascony was very cursory. On the way from Toulouse to Bordeaux by the River Garonne, he inspected the churches at Aiguillon and Langon. In both places, the convents lay in ruins as a result of the wars.

At Bordeaux with its 12 priests, 7 clerics and 4 novices, he found little to correct. The friars responded with alacrity to the customary invitation to submit inventories of their possessions.

The general's secretary did not fail to make a note concerning St. Simon Stock. "The body of St. Simon Stock is contained intact in a painted casket, set in an elevated position in a special chapel. This saint is held in the greatest veneration in the city, and his office is said in our convent on May 16. It is true that because of wars and devastation by heretics of the convent, which was built 500 years ago, first outside the city, then transferred to its present location inside the city, as can be most clearly shown, there are no writings or documents concerning this saint who was our general, and the relics are venerated only by tradition. There are still in this province religious of 85 and 90 years of age who testify that the aforementioned relics were always venerated and held to be those of St. Simon Stock. A duplex office was composed in his honor, as can be proved by the very ancient choral books which contain the proper office of St. Simon, all in chant."

The provincial chapter was convened at Bordeaux, May 23, 1604. Voters numbered 22. The prior general dispensed from the requirement of sending *socii* from the convents because of the lack of religious. He also permitted the reelection of Master Philip Borruste, who had already served as provincial for more than four years, because he was the only master of theology in the province and had acquitted himself well of his responsibilities in the past.

In a letter of Borruste to Silvio written two years later, we have a rare example of an account of the results of his visitation. "I must admit," Borruste wrote, "that the reform you charge us with is not being completely implemented, but arrangements are gradually being made for it to be observed in every detail. We cannot yet build a novitiate, but the money for its construction has been laid aside, so that, God willing, it will be built within a year." It would already have been built, Borruste adds, had not the plague been raging in Bordeaux for two years.

John Cheron, 1628

The provincial chapter of 1624, which elected John Durban provincial, urged all to engage seriously in reform and the renunciation of property. Durban promised to devote himself heart and soul to this task. Such sentiments were greatly encouraged by the presence of the reforming cardinal of Bordeaux, Francis d'Escoubleau de Sourdis, who exhorted the capitulars to undertake a reform similar to that of Angers. Afterwards, De Sourdis urged the vicar general of the Order, Gregory Canal, to send a commissary as soon as possible. The good king, Louis XIII, desired the reform of the religious of his realm for the confusion of heretics. As a matter of fact, the first definitor, John Cheron, shortly journeyed to Poitiers to request the statutes and a sample habit of the observance of Rennes for the convent of Bordeaux.

John Cheron (1596-1673) played an important role in the reform of the province. He entered the Order in his native Bordeaux in 1611. He taught theology at the *studium* of the Order in Bordeaux, was prior there and three times provincial. He distinguished himself as a theologian, preacher, and spiritual writer.

Cheron was elected provincial the first time in 1628. During his term of office, the reform was introduced into Bordeaux, Jonzac, Langon, and Marmande. At the end of his term of office, the prior general, Theodore Straccio, on November 15, 1632, placed him over these houses as vicar with powers to accept volunteers for reform and to remove others.

Cheron, now prior of Bordeaux, drew up statutes of reform, according to which the community renewed profession on February 15, 1633. Within the next two months, Langon, Marmande, Castillon, Aiguillon, and Jonzac followed suit. It was as provincial also that Cheron accepted Straccio's reformed constitutions in 1640 and those of the Stricter Observance in 1647. The provincial chapter of 1640, it might be noted, was presided over by John Tuaut.

On his return by sea from the general chapter of 1648, Cheron was captured by Turkish pirates and taken to Tunis. In brief, the newly elected prior general, John Anthony Filippini, placed Nicolas Jossé in charge of the province during Cheron's absence. The provincial chapter held in May, 1650, elected Jossé provincial. Cheron, who had been released in April, went to Rome to protest the chapter held without him. The drawn out legal process, involving the Congregation for Bishops and Religious, priors general, general chapters, and various claimants finally ended in 1655, when all concerned allowed the delegate of the prior general, Mattias of St. John, of the Touraine province, to name Maur of the Child Jesus provincial.

The religious life of the province of Gascony benefited greatly by the presence of the Touraine friar. Novice master from 1648 to 1651, he was four times elected prior of Bordeaux and three times provincial, besides functioning on the council of the province.

During his visitation, Jerome Ari on his way to Spain from Touraine in December, 1663, visited Jonzac, Bordeaux, Dax, Bayonne, and Agen. At Bordeaux, he ordered the relics of Simon Stock enclosed in a beautiful silver casket, which had been prepared for this purpose, so that it could not be opened again.

Returning from Spain, Ari convoked the provincial chapter at Agen in September, 1664. Since he had seen so little of the province, the prior general requested a list of houses and members. The seventeen houses listed above had 138 members. Of these, 91 were priests, 15 professed clerics, 17 laybrothers and 15 novices.

The Visitation of Mark of the Nativity, 1669

On his visitation in 1669, the prior general, Matthew Orlandi, delegated Mark of the Nativity to visitate Gascony. Mark had just finished his visitation of Narbonne, and it was from Bordeaux in December of 1669 that he issued his *Declarationes et decreta* that caused such a *furore* in that province. It is significant that although he found fault with many things, he did not consider it necessary to undertake a new effort at establishing true reform, as he did in Narbonne. "The whole province is reformed," he reported to Orlandi on April 15, 1670, "and has the essentials of reform: perfect community of goods, rare converse with seculars, especially in the large convents, sufficiently exact obedience, observance of the fasts and other exercises of the religious profession." This happy state of affairs is unfortunately not equally true of the small houses which number no fewer than 12 of the 17 convents of the province. Bordeaux has 40 friars, Bayonne 14, Dax 17, Tarbes 12, Agen 8, Condom 6, Lectoure 5, the rest 3 or 4. The lack of personnel results in poverty of the houses.

"In small convents," Mark reports, "often no one is in charge of the door, women enter carelessly and wander about, silence is not observed, at the single serving in the refectory the brethren seated on both sides of the table are accustomed to talk after a brief reading, while a layman serves the food. In many cases, the chapter is rarely held, there is no fixed hour for rising, books for chant are lacking and the office is recited without a pause by two friars, seculars are invited for drinks more often than is proper."

In his last visitation, the provincial made a number of decrees against "this almost secular way of life," and Mark added a few more. "What will be the result God knows, but little fruit is hoped for, because the nature of small houses is such that, at least for a long time, the brethren can scarcely live in any other manner." To remedy the situation, Mark suggests uniting five small houses with those nearest to them: Rabastens with Trie, Bergerac with Marmande, Aiguillon with Agen, Pavie with Lectoure, Jonzac with Langon, Sauveterre with Bayonne or Dax.

Mark lists 246 friars in the province, whereas Orlandi in a report on the Order in France made at Turin, September 22, 1669, at the end of his visit to France credits Gascony with only 229 members. Moreover, according to him, no convent had less than nine or ten members. This may be a theoretic distribution to be realized after the suppression he decreed for Rabastens, Sauveterre, and the hermitage of Lormont. (Lormont which was dependent on Bordeaux, will be discussed later.) On the other hand, in the summary at the end of his report Orlandi allows Gascony only 156 members.

Mark also notes a spirit of avarice and lack of fraternal charity, especially on the part of superiors. There are two rival parties in the province.

Finally, Mark makes some allusion to the progress of reform in the province. In the case of Bayonne, he refers to "these last years, since the reform was introduced." At Dax, "where the reform was introduced and then extinguished, it is now revived and flourishing by transferring the friars." He dates the reform of Tarbes at 1651. In Pavie, "the reform is recent and still weak."

Two doctors of theology still remain from former times, and the province has no inclination to promote others, at least with privileges. In 1688, the province accepted academic degrees, provided the Constitutions were faithfully followed and promotions were only "very rarely" made. The chapter of 1691 agreed to provide stable members by affiliation to the Place Maubert. The Carmelites had traditionally contributed professors to the University of Bordeaux.

The chapter of 1672, under the presidency of Albert of St. Peter, of the province of Aquitaine, noting that the plurality of novitiates had been abolished, assigned the novitiate to Bordeaux. It also inaugurated seminaries for the continued spiritual formation of the professed. The chapter of 1678 accepted "the *Directorium* of the Reverend Father Mark of the Nativity of the Blessed Virgin" and recommended its practice throughout the province. The chapter of 1685 urged the faithful observance of the Constitutions of the Stricter Observance, "which our province professes."

One receives the impression that Gascony was one of the more effectively reformed provinces.

Chapter 5

The Stricter Observance in Belgium and Germany

With the exception of the province of Touraine, the renewal of the Order in the 17th century was nowhere more thorough than in Belgium.

The reorganization of the Order in Belgium at the end of the previous century resulted in a more manageable administrative unit and set the stage for a rebirth of the Order in those parts.

In 1597, Liège and the Belgian houses in Spanish territory were separated from the province of Francia and constituted the Belgian province. It was allotted nine friaries, Liège, Bruges, Ieperen, Ghent, Valenciennes, Aalst, Arras, Marche, Brugelette, and four nunneries, Namur, Huy, Liège, and Bruges. Liège (with the nunneries in the diocese, Liège and Huy), and Arras afterwards reverted to Francia. The general chapter of 1598 approved the new province of Belgium.

The establishment of the independent Belgian province corresponded to the reign of Archduke Albert and his consort Isabella, daughter of Philip II (1598-1621). This devout and exemplary couple provided witness and initiative in the reform of Catholic life. In spite of widespread disruption and material losses caused by the clash with incipient Calvinism, the old faith in Belgium not only made a rapid recovery, but soon flourished with renewed life, ushering in a brilliant period of Flemish culture, the age of Rubens and Van Dijk.

The Belgian Province, 1597-1663

On April 25, 1603, Henry Silvio convened the chapter of the Belgian province at Ghent, the first such meeting he held on his historic visitation of the ultramontane provinces. He published decrees in four chapters, dealing with community prayer, the vow of poverty, religious dress, and conduct within the monastery. He visited all the houses of the province except Ypres and Marche and did the same in the convents in Brabant of the Lower German province, holding a congregation at Brussels on June 7 of the priors of Brussels, Enghien, Mechelen, Antwerp, Geraardsbergen, Tienen, the prefect of Louvain, and the confessor of the nuns of Vilvoorde. He published the decrees he had made in Flanders with some variations. Similarly the decrees he had made in Paris were applied to Louvain. He also drew up regulations for a novitiate which was to be situated in Mechelen.

At Mechelen, there lived at this time George Peters (d. 1633), the memory of whose holiness passed into the annals of the province. He received from the prior general permission to lead a life of solitude and prayer, leaving his cell only for meals and divine office.

The Beginnings of Reform

The obscure figure of Francis Potel (d. 1613) may after all merit the title of the father of reform in the Belgian province. A native of Arras, he was elected provincial by default at the chapter of 1603, presided over by Silvio and charged with carrying out his decrees. The following chapter of 1608 made Potel prior of his native convent, into which he introduced the reformed life. Aalst followed suit, and the chapter of 1615 ordered the reform maintained in those two houses, while in the others money was to be kept in the community chest with three keys. Thus, in the Belgian province, as in that of Touraine, reform was the direct fruit of Silvio's visit.

Prior at Aalst since 1611 was Michael Beytius, who also held the post afterwards. Native sons of this convent who stood out for their exemplary lives were Josse van Assche, novice-master and prior, and Peter Wasteels (d. 1658). A doctor of Douai (1633), Wasteels spent some time in Touraine to learn the ways of reform and returned to promote it in his own province. He had ample opportunity for this as prior of Aalst and Ghent, and as provincial (1630-1633). He wrote a defense of John XLIV and of the Eucharist against the Protestants.

At Arras, Potel was succeeded as prior by Adrian La Bourse (1611) and Josse van Assche (1618). Michael de Breucq, of the convent of Arras, is described as "very zealous and rigorous" by the provincial of Provence to the prior general, Gregory Canal, seeking information on conditions in Belgium at the beginning of his term of office in 1625. In 1641, Arras reverted to the province of Francia, where it added support to the forces of reform.

The Reform of Valenciennes, 1621

Meanwhile, a beginning at reform was made in Valenciennes. In 1621, five friars of this convent pledged themselves to reform. One of their number, Mark Caffeau, that year became prior; another, John Bavay, succeeded him in 1626. The reformers were supported by the secular and ecclesiastical authorities: Philip, Prince of Aremberg and Duke of Arschott; Herman, bishop of Arras, and the Infanta Isabella, governess of Belgium. A letter from the latter brought action from the prior general. On July 24, 1623, Sebastian Fantoni, in the last months of his life, wrote to the provincial of Touraine, Philip Thibault, instructing him to send two friars from Nantes to assist in the reform of Valenciennes.

Thibault himself, no longer provincial, answered the prior general's call and on August 11, 1624, accompanied by Luke of St. Anthony and Nicholas Chasteau, inaugurated the reform at Valenciennes in classic Touraine style. Three days were devoted to prayer before the Blessed Sacrament with conferences by the three visitors. Thibault frequently moved his audience to tears. On the third day, the aspirants to the reform renewed their vows. Finally, all made a ten-day retreat.

In 1628, Richard of St. Basil (Ruquelot), prior of Valenciennes, travelled to Rome to obtain for his convent the privileges and statutes of Rennes, as well as authorization to erect a novitiate. Canal granted these requests on October 8.

The Reform of Ghent

Another important center of reform was Ghent, reformed by Martin de Hooghe, sometimes considered the father of reform in the Belgian province. Born at Berlaere near Dendermonde, De Hooghe entered the Order at Ghent. The provincial chapter of 1615 assigned him to the reformed convent of Aalst. Three years later, he became prior of Ghent, and forthwith undertook the reform of his native convent. In this, he had the support of the Infanta Isabella and the Jansenist Jacob Boonen, formerly bishop of Ghent, then archbishop of Mechelen. "Finally,"

Boonen wrote to De Hooghe, September 24, 1623, "God has looked with favor on the Order of his Mother in Belgium gradually to recall it to its pristine splendor. Among other public and private causes of great joy, there is this happy thought, that if this reformation succeeds (as I hope it will) I and my fellow bishops will be freed from innumerable annoyances and hatreds which otherwise we would have to undergo, for we were destined to a struggle unto death and to move heaven and earth. I would drag myself on hands and knees to Rome, if that were necessary to bring to a successful conclusion what with the grace of God I see begun."

In 1625, De Hooghe travelled to Rome to recommend his work to Canal. The general chapter of that year, at which the Belgian province was represented by the provincial, Ghislain Lucas, and his *socius*, Livinus d'Hondt, directed Canal to see to it "that the regular and Strict Observance be introduced into the provinces of Narbonne, Francia, Belgium, and others, the provincials of which have shown willingness to implement it." Canal sent letters to this effect to the Belgan provincial chapter, which met in 1626 and elected Michael de Breucq.

Close collaborator of De Hooghe was Livinus Turf, known in the reform as Livinus of the Most Holy Trinity (d. 1641). Turf entered the Order as a laybrother, but was subsequently destined by his superiors to study for the priesthood. As novice master, subprior, and prior at Ghent and other places, Turf supported and consolidated De Hooghe's work of reform. A man of great austerity, Turf's motto was, "*Ubi rigor, ibi vigor*." He was buried in Brussels, side by side with his friend.

De Hooghe had an opponent and rival in Livinus d'Hondt (Latin: Canisius). D'Hondt stood for a less rigorous type of reform and was willing to allow academic degrees and their perquisites. Also a native of Ghent, he had lived for some time in Italy. Canal made him his commissary general in Ghent, and he subsequently became its prior. When De Hooghe became provincial in 1633, he sent d'Hondt to reform Bruges, but actually to get rid of him in Ghent. D'Hondt often pleaded with Straccio to send him back to Ghent, but De Hooghe opposed this step on the grounds that d'Hondt was a destructive influence. After De Hooghe's death in 1637, Straccio was relieved of the need for a decision, when the bishop of Antwerp asked him to send d'Hondt to reform the Carmelite convent there.

D'Hondt founded the hermitage of Termuylen and wrote a commentary on the Rule and an account of the Belgian convents.

At this point, in 1630, the province acquired from the Lower German province its convents in Brabant: Brussels, Arlon, Mechelen, Gelderen, Tienen, Enghien, Geraardsbergen, Antwerp, and Louvain, besides the nunneries, Gelderen and Vilvoorde. The province thus found the number of its houses doubled, its territory greatly enlarged, and its task of reform rendered more complicated.

The subsequent chapter of 1633 listed eighteen houses and a hospice or residence: Brussels, Ieperen, Arlon, Bruges, Mechelen, Ghent, Gelderen, Valenciennes, Tienen, Arras, Enghien, Aalst, Geraardsbergen, Marche, Antwerp, Brugelette, Louvain, and Saint Pol (1616). The residence of St. Leodegare appears only at this chapter, but it turns up again in the province of Francia, where it was suppressed by Orlandi in 1669 and its goods assigned to Arras. It apparently transferred to Francia along with Arras.

Shortly after, foundations were made at Bonne Esperance (1633) and Douai (1636).

De Hooghe immediately extended his solicitude to the newly acquired houses. In 1631, he introduced reform into Louvain. Two years later, he became provincial and reformed Brussels.

Martin de Hooghe, Provincial, 1633-1637

The chapter of 1633, which elected De Hooghe provincial, was presided over by the Carmelite bishop-elect, Jerome Domin, recommended to Straccio by the Infanta Isabella for the visitation of the province. A member of the Aragon province, Domin was no stranger to Straccio, who had appointed him his secretary during a visitation of Andalusia, before he became general. When Domin became preacher of Mary of Austria, later wife of Emperor Ferdinand III, Straccio took advantage of Domin's position at court to name him commissary for Germany and Belgium.

Among other provisions for reform, the chapter enjoined the new provincial, De Hooghe, to put into practice the decrees which Domin had made during his visitation of the houses, especially those regarding poverty. The *depositum* was abolished. No religious was to live outside the cloister; the priests acting as pastors in Bruges were to return to the convent. The novitiate with the black habit was placed in Brugelette. The reformed friars of Ghent, Louvain, Ypres, Brugelette, and St. Leodegar were authorized to wear the brown habit. Although this time they did not elect their own priors, their right to do so according to the indult of Calixtus III remained intact.

De Hooghe had a supporter in Richard Paul Stravius, archdeacon of Arras and pro-nuncio apostolic in Brussels, who took up residence in the Carmelite convent there and showed a sometimes greater than welcome interest in the affairs of the Order. Toward the end of De Hooghe's term of office as provincial, Stravius suggested that the prior general simply reconfirm him in office as the only hope for reform. Straccio with Italian *delicatezza* agreed that this was an excellent idea, but unfortunately unprecedented in the Order. Instead, he suggested a compromise "which under the direction of your most Reverend Lordship can easily have the same effect with greater *soavità*." According to the constitutions, De Hooghe should step down, but Straccio agreed to dispense him with regard to passive voice and thus open the door to his re-election. At the same time, he forwarded patents appointing Stravius president of the coming provincial chapter. Moreover, Straccio took the precaution to obtain from Pope Urban VIII, on January 28, 1636, authorization to restrict the election of provincial to reformed friars. With the smoothness predicted by Straccio, De Hooghe was reelected provincial. Reformed priors were placed in all the houses. After all these elaborate precautions, De Hooghe died, June 12, 1637.

Discord over the Reform

After the death of De Hooghe, Straccio became concerned about the future of the "as yet tender observance," as he called it a year before the Belgian reformer's demise. His concern proved well founded. De Hooghe's death was the signal for d'Hondt to enter the reform and press for his ideas. De Hooghe's disciples (*Martinisti*) put up a stiff resistance, and a battle ensued which lasted throughout the 40's. It is not clear what happened: no acts are to be found in the *liber provinciae* between the chapters of 1638 and 1649, and historians of the period gloss over the whole affair. The *Martinisti* requested a visit by a commissary general, and Straccio sent Matthias de la Couronne, prominent in the reform of Francia (1640), who among other things ordered all the students gathered into the reformed convents of Brussels (novitiate), Ghent (*professatus*), Aalst (philosophy), Louvain (theology). The internunzio, Stravius, appealed to by the *Martinisti*, directed the provincial chapter of 1641 to be postponed, until the general's reaction to the visitation report by the commissary general could be heard. On August 6, 1641, the outgoing provincial, Richard of St. Basil, protested vigorously against this action. The capitulars asked Straccio to name a new provincial, definitors, and other officials from a list they provided. To make sure of his ground, Straccio obtained authorization from Pope Urban VIII to do so. It is not known whom he appointed, if anyone. He may have named Livinus d'Hondt, who was provincial around this time. (At the general chapters of 1645 and 1648, Cyril of St. Ignatius appears as provincial.)

D'Hondt experienced a disturbed reign. The *Martinisti* were in the ascendancy at Brussels and Ghent. "By a stratagem" Gabriel of the Annunciation gained control of Louvain and moved in with his students. D'Hondt imprisoned him, but the king ordered his release. Eventually, at a chapter presided over by Charles of St. Ghislain, the *Martinisti* gained definitive control, and reform in its purest rigor triumphed in the province.

Gabriel of the Annunciation was prominent among the *Martinisti*. He had been received into the Order by D'Hondt, but did not share his ideas of reform. His later activity in trying to unite Liège with the Belgian province has already been mentioned. At this time, he was on the point of beginning his reforming activity in the German provinces.

With the reform of Mechelen in 1652, the renewal of the province was complete. It had not come about without a certain division of minds. After the death of Martin de Hooghe, there was a while when lesser ideals might have prevailed, and as in some French provinces, a division might have arisen between reformed and not-so-reformed. But due to firm leadership and the collaboration of ecclesiastical and secular authorities, more dedicated spirits prevailed. The Belgian province became one of the most flourishing provinces in the Order, producing such outstanding figures of the Order's spirituality as Arnold of St. Charles, Daniel of the Virgin Mary, Michael of St. Augustine, and Maria Petyt.

The Gallo-Belgian Province

Like some other provinces, the province of Belgium suffered from political and cultural differences. The Flemish and French speaking Belgians petitioned the general chapter of 1660 for separation. The matter was referred to the prior general, Jerome Ari, who during his subsequent visitation of the province created the Flandro-Belgian (Flemish) and Gallo-Belgian (French) provinces, April 19,1663.

The first chapter of the Gallo-Belgian province was celebrated in 1667 by the convents of Valenciennes, Arlon, Marche, Brugelette, Bonne Espérance, Douai, Sainte-Anne-sur-Sambre (1667), Wavre (1667), and Mons (1667). An unidentifiable *domus Jamedensis* is also listed, but passed from the records after 1681. In time, the province added houses in Longwy (1670), Williers (1676), Lille (1679), Nivelles (1679), Saint Laurent (1681), Trélon (1706).

The small Gallo-Belgian province found itself further reduced when the Treaty of Nijmegen, 1678, ceded certain Spanish territories to France. At the request of King Louis XIV, the prior general, Ferdinand Tartaglia declared the Gallo-Belgian province to be one of the provinces of France and separate from its houses which lay in the Spanish Netherlands, July 13, 1680. These houses became the Wallo-Belgian (Walloon) vicariate and in 1683 held the first congregation, at which the convents of Brugelette, Mons, Wavre, and Nivelles were represented. Eventually, the vicariate also acquired La Xhavée, Arlon, Marche, Sainte Anne-sur-Sambre, and Williers. It had the care of the nunneries at Namur and Marche. The general chapter of 1698 granted the vicar the right to vote in its sessions, but did not allow him a *socius*.

On the eve of its division, the Belgian province had 540 members, of whom 295 were priests. Afterwards it reached a peak in 1675 with 615 members. The Flandro-Belgian province contributed to the reform of the Upper German province, while the Gallo-Belgian province assisted in the reform of Poland.

The Lower German Province

The general chapter of 1613 consented to the division of the Lower German province. The Belgian houses (*natio Brabantica*) were to retain the name of the province; the German houses were to be called the province of Cologne. The new Lower German province consisted of the convents of Brussels, Arlon, Mechelen, Gelderen, Tienen, Enghien, Mörs, Geraardsbergen, and Antwerp. The province of Cologne retained Cologne, Boppard, Frankfurt, Trier, Mainz, Speyer, Worms, Aachen and Tönisstein. Pope Paul V added his approval, December 30.

The convent in Mörs was sold to Maurice of Nassau in 1614.

But the arrangement did not long give satisfaction. The general chapter of 1620 granted the petition of both provincials, Ferdinand of St. Victor (Lower Germany) and Balthasar Romaya (Cologne) to re-unite the provinces. Ten years later, as we have seen, the houses in Belgium were relinquished to the province of Belgium. Confirmation by Urban VIII followed on March 22, 1630.

Besides the nine houses listed above, the provincial, John Bachhusen, in 1624, was able to repossess the pre-Reformation houses of Weinheim, Kreuznach, and Hirschhorn. Beilstein on the Mosel was founded in 1637. In the 18th century, Adelheid and Leuchterhof (*Villa Lucida*) appear in the acts of the province.

There could be no question of reform in the Lower German province during the Thirty Year's War (1618-1648), when the Order there was struggling for its very survival. In the successive waves of war, few houses escaped the scourge of pillage, destruction, destitution, and pestilence.

Lower Germany During the Thirty Years' War

Only Cologne, Aachen, and Trier remained immune to the consequences of war. When Gustavus Adolphus took Frankfurt in 1633, he bestowed the churches and convents on the magistrates of the city. For a long time, the chronicler of the Carmelite convent wrote, the magistrates "had been snapping at the house with gaping mouth, in order to gulp it down." The prior, John Bachhusen, and his community betook themselves to Cologne. Two years later, the treaty of Prague enabled them to return to a plundered house with no prospect of compensation.

"Fine providers of the monasteries," the waspish chronicler remarks about the city fathers.

During the Swedish occupation, 1631-1636, Mainz suffered the worst period of hunger and pestilence in its history. Due to its strategic position, it was obliged to quarter a large garrison of 16,000 troops and bear a heavy burden of tribute. Already in 1621 and 1622, the bishopric of Speyer suffered heavy losses from the forces of Ernst von Mansfeld. During the Swedish invasion, religious of other places sought refuge in Speyer, the seat of the imperial tribunal, but no house was more severely tried. In the 30's, the city changed hands several times between Swedes, French, and Bavarians. Troops were quartered in the convent; church and convent were stripped of their contents, religious were held for ransom. All woodwork disappeared from the convent, its vineyards destroyed. It was not until 1658 that restoration could be seriously undertaken.

At the approach of the Swedish army, the prior of Tönisstein, Peter Alberts, took the precaution of having the community's possessions sent to Andernach, where they nonetheless fell a prey to the invaders. Whenever danger threatened, Alberts hid in the surrounding woods. The convent suffered a second spoliation at the hands of the French. It was completely plundered, the friars were robbed of the very clothes they wore, the prior and a laybrother injured.

The convent of Worms was torn down by the Swedes for the defense of the town. Previously, it had been emptied of all furnishings by soldiers and citizenry. It was not until 1657 that a house belonging to the cathedral chapter was purchased.

Weinheim had hardly been regained from Protestant hands in 1624, when the city fell to the Swedish army. During the Swedish occupation, the two Carmelite members of the convent took refuge in Speyer.

The Peace of Westphalia (1648) assigned the Palatinate to the Calvinist Karl Ludwig, who outlawed Catholicism. When the Catholic Duke of Neuberg took possession of the Palatinate in 1685, the Carmelites were able to return. In spite of the pleas of the citizens and the Spanish garrison not to abandon them, the Carmelites of Kreuznach ingloriously fled at the approach of Swedish army, thereby laying themselves open to the accusation by a Protestant minister in 1639 of being mercenaries and not shepherds of souls.

The Peace of Westphalia allowed both religions to co-exist in Kreuznach, and the Carmelites were permitted to maintain a community of three friars there.

Although the Carmelites managed to get their convent back from Protestant Frederick of Hirschhorn (1624), this ruler forbade his subjects to frequent their church, which remained without a congregation. During the Swedish occupation, the friars were driven out. At Frederick's death in 1633, Hirschborn reverted to the Elector of Mainz, who suppressed Protestantism, and the Carmelites were able to return.

Under the Swedes, the Carmelites of Boppard found asylum in Cologne. Not long afterwards, the intervention of the French, summoned by the Elector of Trier, enabled the Carmelites to return, but the material state of the convent was pitiful.

As a result of the ravages of war, the number of friars in the Lower German province was greatly reduced. It has been calculated with likelihood that in 1643 the province could muster only about sixty priests with a like total of students, novices, and brothers. Moreover, communities were in such dire financial straits that every extra mouth to feed was an intolerable burden, and superiors had to be commanded to take in novices. Under these circumstances, it is remarkable that any thought at all was given to reform.

In 1603, Henry Silvio visited the Lower German province to impose his decrees of reform. Proceeding from Belgium and moving south along the Rhine, he visited Aachen, Cologne, Boppard, Mainz, and Frankfurt. In the last convent, he held a meeting on August 27 of the priors of Frankfurt, Trier, Mörs, Worms, and Mainz. He did not hold a provincial chapter or intermediate congregation, because he had already convened the houses of the province in Brabant, at which meeting he had published his reforming decrees. Now he republished these decrees and added others as the occasion required. At least the province had been put on notice by the prior general concerning the decrees of the council of Trent and of the reforming popes culminating in Clement VIII.

Early Measures of Reform

In 1628, John Dunwalt was elected provincial. A native of Cologne and doctor of theology, he was provincial three times and did much for the restoration of the province. Under his regime, the province established its first contacts with the reform of Touraine. In 1633, Dunwalt sent John Weiss to Touraine to learn the ways of reform. John Weissenberg, whom the provincial sent to study at Angers lived only to 1639. Weiss returned to the province in 1638 and was put in charge of the novitiate to train the novices in the method of Touraine and thus gradually bring about the reform of the province. However, the hopes placed in Weiss were dashed, when he died in 1642, only 32 years of age. He was succeeded as novice master by Carl Freywilliger, who was instructed to continue along the lines initiated by Weiss. As Charles of St. Anastasius, Freywilliger, a son of converted Jews, became one of the first reformed friars of the province under the Stricter Observance.

The provincial chapter of 1640, which returned Dunwalt for a third term issued several ordinances concerning observance. It prescribed daily meditation, spiritual instruction of the laybrothers, and the reading of the constitutions and ceremonial in the refectory. The following year, the *depositum* was imposed.

However, pressures were building from inside and outside the Order for the radical reform of the German provinces. The Lower German province hoped to carry out its own reform, but its pace was too slow, its attitude overcautious, and its ideals not set sufficiently high.

In 1644, the definitory bowed to pressure from the vicar general of the Order, Leo Bonfigli, and Archbishop Ferdinand of Cologne, and assigned Aachen as a house of perfect observance. Reformed friars from the province of Touraine were to be invited to introduce the reform. As a measure of good will, the definitory agreed that the constitutions would be strictly observed at Trier.

At the general chapter of 1645, which ordained that at least one reformed house be established in each province and canonized the Stricter Observance as the way of reform in the Order, the provincial, Jacob Orsbach, reported that Aachen had been designated for reform and received permission for the continued use of the black habit there. The provincial of Touraine, Leo of St. John, promised to send reformed friars to Germany.

The reform of Aachen failed to come off. Orsbach died on the return journey from Italy, and Jacob Emans, present at the general chapter as *socius*, was appointed provincial by Bonfigli, now elected general. The Touraine friars were not forthcoming. Few candidates for reform presented themselves. In 1646, Trier was designated for reform instead of Aachen, but the following year it was decided to leave the choice of convent to the Frenchmen, when they arrived.

Finally, Emans himself journeyed to Touraine and on September 7, 1647, returned to Cologne with Antonin de la Charité and Theophilus of St. Claude. The French reformers requested a house where the observance could be integrally implemented and were assigned the convent of Trier. There on February 2, 1648, the Stricter Observance was adopted by a community of six priests, eight professed clerics, four novices, and six laybrothers. The prior was Theodore Maurer (*Murarius*).

The general chapter of 1648 created a special committee consisting of John Baptist de Lezana, historian of the Order; Gabriel of the Annunciation, prior of Ghent; and Leo of St. John, commissary general in France, to study the problem of the extension of the Touraine reform to the German provinces and Poland. The definitory decided to send Gabriel of the Annunciation as commissary general to reform two convents in each of the German provinces. He was further authorized to import Belgian friars for this purpose. Friars for the reform of Poland were to be selected by Leo of St. John and the provincial of Touraine, Urban of the Ascension.

The Lower German province had not been able to afford the expense of sending delegates to the general chapter. The only German at the chapter was a *socius* of the Upper German province, Jerome Ernst.

The General Chapters Sponsor Reform

In letters patent of June 18, the newly elected prior general, John Anthony Filippini, provided specific details concerning Gabriel's commission. He was to take as his associate Antonin de la Charité and reform Aachen and Trier in Lower Germany and Straubing and Bamberg in Upper Germany, establishing the novitiate and house of studies in these places.

With Leo of St. John as a member, the committee at the general chapter can hardly have been unaware that the Touraine friar, Antonin la Charité, had initiated the reform at Trier four months previously. As a matter of fact, after Gabriel had fulfilled the letter of his patents, Antonin took over and continued the reform of the Lower German province. This does not mean that the action of the general chapter was not well-timed or even necessary. The spirit of reform in the province now had autonomous leadership and momentum, and the Stricter Observance nowhere else spread more quickly and harmoniously.

Gabriel of the Annunciation began with the reform of Aachen. He summoned Matthias Hunen from Trier to become prior of Aachen and appointed reformed friars he had brought with him from Belgium to the other offices of the convent. He introduced the brown habit and established a novitiate, clothing the candidates he had brought from Belgium. Hunen he also placed in charge of the novices.

At Trier, Gabriel appointed the Belgian, William of St. Basil, prior. He sent the novices and clerics to Aachen. On July 25, 1649, the community with the exception of Theodoric Heintz donned the brown habit.

After reforming Aachen and Trier according to his patents, Gabriel passed on to Upper Germany and had little more to do with its sister province.

The provincial chapter of Lower Germany, held at Boppard in 1650 under the presidency of Gabriel of the Annunciation, elected Antonin de la Charité provincial. Among the definitors were the priors of Aachen and Trier, Matthias Hunen and William of St. Basil. The chapter decreed the reform of Cologne and named Hunen prior.

The reform and the brown habit were solemnly introduced at Cologne on the feast of Our Lady of Mt. Carmel, July 16, 1650. All accepted the reform except the historian Segerus Pauli, who was convinced that black was the original color of the habit. He continued to live piously among the reformed until his death less than a year later. "The convent which formerly turned away our Blessed Soreth, general of the Order, of happy memory, who had come to reform it in person," Antonin wrote on August 7 to Jerome Ari, procurator general of the Order, "accepted the Most Reverend Father Filippini in the person of his commissaries and humbly submitted to reform. 'This is the Lord's doing' (Ps. 118, 23), and no one will doubt that so singular a benefice is to be completely ascribed to the Blessed Virgin, singular patron of the Order. The three most important convents in the province, Cologne, Trier, and Aachen, are now reformed. Others would also willingly join us, but it is not expedient to accept them now, since not enough persons are available. We must proceed gradually; the reform must be well rooted and firm in these three convents before we proceed to others."

On October 29, Filippini declared Aachen officially reformed.

Antonin de la Charité

In 1652, Antonin was unanimously re-elected provincial at the chapter in Mainz presided over by Filippini. As novice-master at Cologne, Antonin imported from Touraine Damasus of St. Louis who served in the important office of instructing novices until the completion of the reform of the province in 1660. After his return to France, as a relic of his sojourn in Cologne, Damasus produced a history of St. Ursula and companions (Paris, D. Thierry, 1666).

The gentle Antonin was well schooled in the Touraine strategy of leisurely and deliberate expansion. Only three years later was the next convent reformed, when at the request of the Baron of Metternich the observance was introduced in Beilstein. Peter of St. Albert (Alberts) became prior. The same year, 1653, Mainz was declared ready for reform. The historian, Jacob Milendunck, laid down his office as prior and joined the observance. William of St. Basil took his place and after completing his term of office returned to his province in 1656.

The provincial chapter of 1656 elected Antonin to a third term of office. The prior general, Mario Venturini, ordered that two members of the definitory be reformed friars. The constitutions of the Stricter Observance were accepted. Tönnisstein was declared ready for reform, and John of the Cross became prior.

In 1657, Antonin died in Paris. This charitable man amply earned his name "of charity," and was beloved by all in the province. He was truly the reformer of the province, which through him imbibed the fervent spirit of Touraine. Thus Touraine, rather than Belgium, proved to be the "nursery" of reform in the Lower German province. Unfortunately, biographical details concerning Antonin are lacking.

Venturini named Jacob Emans vicar-provincial. Emans was duly elected provincial at the next chapter of 1659. One of the most illustrious members of the province, he entered the observance in 1650, when the reform was introduced at Cologne, and underwent the year's trial for the reform with the fervor of a novice. As second reformed provincial, he completed the reform of the province.

On December 8, 1657, the reform was introduced into Frankfurt; John of St. Fulgence became prior. The magistrates of the Protestant city offered resistence, alleging that the change was equivalent to making a new foundation; they relented before the intervention of the reform-minded Elector-Bishop of Mainz, John Philip von Schönborn.

The same year, a house was acquired for the community of Worms, left homeless by the war. At the same time, the Stricter Observance was introduced. The bishop of Worms, Hugh Eberhard von Kratz von Scharffenstein, "unique patron of our burgeoning reform," offered the Carmelites the nearby church of St. Stephen and provided much material help in the reconstruction of the convent. Henry of All Saints became the first reformed prior.

On July 26, 1658, Emans obtained from the newly-elected Emperor Leopold I imperial protection for the observance in the non-Catholic cities of Frankfurt, Speyer, and Worms. Armed with these patents, Emans overcame the initial opposition of the city fathers of Speyer and introduced the reform. The vicar prior, Avertanus of St. John the Baptist, overwhelmed by the difficulties of the material restoration of the convent, resigned after a year and was succeeded by Bernard of the Child Jesus who remained in office ten years.

The Completion of Reform

By 1659, only three houses, Boppard, Kreuznach, and Hirschhorn, remained unreformed. "Since the number of unreformed religious has so sharply declined that only one community is able to be formed," the provincial chapter of that year decreed the reform of Boppard and Kreuznach. George Seltzer became prior at Boppard. He not only restored the convent spiritually, but materially as well, "so that it could rightfully be called a reformed house." At Kreuznach, Adam of St. Mary was made prior. His predecessor, Caspar Echerig, joined the observance at Mainz.

The general chapter of 1660 declared the province reformed, though Hirschhorn remained unreformed. This last bastion fell the same year. Frederick of the Immaculate Conception was the first reformed prior.

The provincial chapter of 1675 for the first time since the reform of the province presented four candidates for the doctorate at the university of Cologne. Privileges attached to degrees were renounced.

The reformed province of Lower Germany also had its special *Decreta et ordinationes*, comprising legislation of the years 1651-1667.

The province had one nunnery in its charge at Cologne. Originally a beguinage, its nine members received permission from John Baptist Rossi in 1565 to don the Carmelite habit; the provincial, John Mayer, received their vows at Pentecost. During his visit in 1603, Henry Silvio noted that the sisters did not wear the veil, did not observe the cloister, and recited the Little Office of Our Lady. (Silvio imposed the recitation in Latin instead of German.) On March 29, 1653, Filippini granted the brown habit and black veil of the observance, so that at this point the community probably became cloistered nuns of the Second Order. When Jerome Ari visited Cologne ten years later, the community numbered 23, including two novices, under the prioress, Mother Agnes Mungersdorff. "The Most Reverend Father," his secretary noted in the visitation book, "greatly rejoiced at their modesty, piety, devotion, and exemplary way of life."

The Upper German Province

Of the extensive Upper German province only 11 houses survived the Protestant Reformation: Würzburg, Bamberg, Rottenburg, Dinkelsbühl, Ravensburg, Lienz (Tirol), Neustadt a. d. Saale, Straubing, Abensberg, Voitsberg (Styria), and Heilbronn. Vogelsburg existed as a filial house of Würzburg.

The drastic reduction in the number of convents tells only half the story. The understaffed communities lived in direst poverty. Daniel of the Virgin Mary places the number of friars in the province at 40. Under these circumstances, the quality of religious life left much to be desired.

The intrepid traveller, Henry Silvio, not only visited Upper Germany, but penetrated to the remote province of Bohemia-Poland. The Upper German provincial, George Sattler, came to Frankfurt to fetch him and his companions and conduct them to Würzburg, where they arrived September 1, 1603. There they found a community of six priests, four professed clerics and one laybrother under the prior, Nicholas Stiffel. At Bamberg, the prior, John Neff, of Rottenburg, lived with eight professed clerics and one laybrother.

After visiting the Bohemian-Polish province, Silvio returned on November 28 to Straubing, at this time the principal house of the province. Here Sattler also acted as prior over the community of seven priests (including himself), three professed clerics and one brother. At Abensberg, where the visitors admired "the most beautiful church," there were three priests, including the prior, Lawrence Seltenreich, and two clerical novices. It took the general seven days to reach Rottenburg on December 11, because of the exceeding cold, wind, and snow. One day they managed to travel only a mile before they were obliged to take refuge in a hospice. Silvio suffered pains in his stomach but insisted on pressing forward. "At Rottenburg," the secretary, Francis Voersio, noted, "We have a most beautiful convent and church overlooking the river." The community numbered three priests, one professed cleric, one brother, and three novices.

At Rottenburg, Silvio convened the provincial chapter on December 15, 1603. Not all the fathers had brought their white cloaks; also, no one had prepared a discourse for the opening of the chapter. The electors were 14: the prior general; his two *socii* taken from the community; Master Dominic Provana, companion of the general; the provincial, George Sattler; seven priors (Sattler was also prior to Straubing); and two *socii* (Straubing and Wurzburg). The *socius* from Ravensburg had been disqualified because he lacked proper credentials. Of the four candidates for provincial presented by the prior general John Sattler was elected.

The prior general ordered that after Easter two or three students should be sent to Italy for the arts or theology. Two "colleges" were instituted: Bamberg (humanities) and Würzburg (arts and theology). The novitiate was placed in Rottenburg, in a section of the convent separated from the rest. "In this chapter were made almost all the decrees made in the chapter of Poland."

After listing the incomes of Heilbronn, Ravensburg, and Neustadt, the general's secretary ends the account of the visitation with the words, "I was unable to obtain information concerning the other convents."

From the correspondence of John Sattler of the following year further statistics are available. At Dinkelsbühl there was one priest, at Lienz three, at Ravensburg three, at Voitsberg two, at Neustadt one priest and one professed cleric, at Heilbronn two priests and two professed clerics. Meanwhile, however, the prior of Würzburg, Nicholas Stiffel, apostasied and married, while the prior of Abensberg had died in some peasant's cottage. This would place the membership of the province in 1604 at 29 priests, 11 professed clerics, 5 novice clerics, and 3 brothers, or 48 members in all.

Sattler sent the three students to Rome, as agreed. One of them, Bartholomew Einselin, served as provincial during the difficult years of the Thirty Years' War.

In an account of his visitation of 1605, Sattler describes his efforts to implement Silvio's decrees. As far as financial accountability is concerned, account books, inventories of sacristies and libraries were non-existent and had to be compiled from the beginning. Reformed Roman breviaries and missals were used, but not all the Carmelite ceremonies were everywhere observed. "To tell the truth," Sattler writes, "I did not make a great effort to introduce these external and unimportant matters." The meditation insisted on by Silvio was made only in Rottenburg and Straubing. Elsewhere it was omitted, either because the brethren meditated in preparing their sermons, or because they had no time left over from study, especially at Würzburg and Bamberg, or because in some houses there were only one or two friars. "Moreover," Sattler concludes, "to speak from personal experience, the bitter and profound cold in winter is often greater than the warmth of meditating. Our strength is not the strength of stones, our flesh is not brass." The weekly conferences and moral cases prescribed by the chapter had not been carried out. As to private ownership, when Sattler had ordered the brethren to turn over to the community their earnings from Masses, confessions, etc., they had rejoined that they would do so and then live in idleness off the community as others did. The provincial had, however, introduced the *depositum*. All the priors complained about the introduction of the *mensa oblonga* for meals. (The nature of this institution is not clear.) It raised costs, as several abbeys had discovered, "and in these dregs of heresy, which is Germany, we can no longer collect the fragments which are placed before the brethren at table, but the slender resources which we still possess through the goodness of God have to be used with ingenuity and economy." A common novitiate had been built at Straubing, but so far Sattler had not been able to get it started: either the novice master or novices had always been lacking. The organization of a provincial archive, involving the copying and notarizing of many documents, would cost at least 500 German florins. Moreover, incomes of the province were such as required constant revising of agreements and contracts. Instead, Sattler had drawn up a *liber rubricalis*, listing in alphabetical order the documents in the conventual archives with a summary of their contents: by this means, future provincials could make a quick survey of the resources of each house and easily discover any fraud or misappropriation of funds. Finally, the provincial reports that he had not succeeded in getting rid of women cooks in houses like Voitsberg, Heilbronn, and Rottenburg, because they also shepherded the convent's flocks, a type of labor done only by women in Germany.

Under the circumstances, the provincial may be pardoned a certain sense of powerlessness; on the other hand, he seems rather too ready to find reasons for his failure to act.

The Thirty Years' War

In this weakened condition, the Upper German province was now called on to bear the scourge of the Thirty Years' War. An anonymous report to the prior general, dated 1634, provides some details of the effect of the war on the Upper German province up to that year.

Only Lienz (Tyrol) and Voitsberg (Styria), remote from the noise of battle, remained unaffected. When Prince Bernard of Weimar took Würzburg in 1631, the Carmelites fled the convent. Albert Heilfinger and a cleric, John Huber, took refuge in the fortress. In the course of the assault, Heilfinger ministered spiritually to the soldiers. He died as a result of his many wounds at the Franciscan convent, where he had been brought after the fighting had ceased. John Huber was killed in the fortress. In 1633, the Carmelites begged the intercession of the auxiliary bishop with Prince Franz von Hatzfeld for help in restoring the convent which had been damaged by shot and was about to collapse.

The Carmelites of Rottenburg suffered no molestation from the Swedes, but when Julius Frederick, the Protestant Duke of Württemberg, acquired the county of Hohenberg in which Rottenburg was situated, he demanded an oath of submission which the Carmelites refused. They were expelled October 2, 1633. They took refuge for a year in the convent of Ravensburg. In 1638, this convent was plundered by the Swedes.

Abensberg was sacked by the Swedes in the course of the attack on Ingolstadt, and the friars were cruelly beaten.

The Carmelites were chronically in strained relationship with the Protestant magistrates of Heilbronn. The city fathers claimed the right to present three candidates for the election of the prior and administered the material affairs of the house through two procurators. In 1632, the city favored the Swedes in spite of the imperial garrison present there. The Carmelites moved to a house in town from their convent and church of the "Nesselmutter," our Lady of the Nettles, which were torn down in March of 1632 for purposes of defense by the Swedish commander von Schmiedberg. The goods of the convent were bestowed on the city by the Swedes, and the friars were given a small pension.

Other houses suffered in lesser degree. Straubing was occupied by Bernard of Weimar, November 23, 1633, to April 1, 1634. Some friars fled to Voitsberg and Lienz, but the community was not expelled, though it was taxed to pay for the damage caused by fire in the city. In the pestilence of 1634, thirty Carmelites died, including the prior, Melchior Fehl, in the course of administering to the sick.

Bernard of Weimar laid a tribute of 200,000 *thaler* on Bamberg, of which the clergy was required to pay half. Two religious of each convent were taken as hostages. Later the tax was reduced; the portion of the Carmelites was about 200 fl. As at Würzburg, the expulsion of the Jesuits deprived the Carmelites of a school for their clerical students.

At Dinkelsbühl, as it turned out, the friars were not expelled during the occupation by Gustavus Adolf in 1632, but in the words of the writer of the report of 1634 of the effects of the war, the prior, "trembling with fear where there was no reason to fear" (Ps. 13, 5), fled to Bavaria. On a corner of the church was a statue of the legendary *Dinkelsbühler Bauerlein*, which the younger Oxenstjerna, Bengt, is said to have shot off.

At Ravensburg, the infelicitous arrangement by which the Carmelite church had been shared with Protestant preachers was terminated in 1628. On January 27, 1634, the Swedish Colonel Horn took Ravensburg. Twenty persons and fourteen hunting dogs were quartered in the convent for eight weeks.

Though Neustadt (Saale) underwent pressure from the Landgrave of Hesse, it continued to survive.

The provincial, Bartholomew Einselin, labored indefatigably for the recovery of convents lost in the course of the Reformation. After the Edict of Restitution of 1629, he appealed to the emperor for the return of the Order's houses in Esslingen, Augsburg, Nürnberg, Vienna, Schweinfurt, and Nordlingen, but the reversal of the imperial fortunes in war closed the door on this prospect.

The author of the report of 1634 ends his account with the words, "How many religious remain and where each and every one of them is to be found, cannot be known and related. However, in these troubled times and severest persecution of religious - the worst ever experienced in Germany - it is unheard of that anyone defected from the Catholic faith and went over to the heretics."

Whether the prior general, Theodore Straccio, received this report is not clear. (Today it is found in the University Library of Genoa). Only two years later, on June 21, 1636, he complains to the prior of Prague, Master Theophilus Paulucci, of a lack of information on the Upper German province, rumors about which are not reassuring: "I have experienced the greatest displeasure at the news you sent me that the Duke of Bavaria wishes to expel our religious from his State because of their scandalous and relaxed lives.... I continue to be amazed that I cannot manage to obtain a report on the state of that province of Upper Germany. I would like to hold a chapter and elect a new provincial, but I do not know a single friar. Master Eiselin would like to be provincial. If your paternity would send me a report, I would be most grateful. If you want the office of convoking that chapter, let me know and I will send you the patents."

On May 8, 1638, Straccio wrote to Cardinal Ginetti in Cologne, asking whether it would be advisable to send three Spanish fathers to reform and restore the Upper German province: one to be general commissary and reformer, one to be prior of one of the principal houses, one to be regent. He asks the cardinal to send him a report on the state of the province.

The following November 27, Straccio wrote to Ginetti: "The provincial of the province of Upper Germany recently informed me of the miserable and deplorable state of that province caused by past wars. He sees no other way of keeping it from being totally destroyed and annihilated than to unite it to the Lower German province. He is willing to renounce his office, as long as the union takes place."

Gabriel of the Annunciation

A decade later, Gabriel of the Annunciation began the arduous task of restoring the spiritual and material prosperity of the province. No adequate biography exists of this important personage in the history of Carmel in Germany. The life by Tilman of St. Elijah is long on moralizing and short on facts. Where Antonin was gentle, Gabriel was iron-fisted. He served a severe God. He did not wait for the moment of reform to ripen, but drove forward roughshod over all opposition. Tenacious and headstrong, he throve on litigation with never a qualm but that his cause was just. Perhaps he was the man the situation required. Certain it is that he gave no thought to self and spent himself utterly for the Order.

Gabriel of the Annunciation (Dumont) was born of parents of middle station at Freture in the Bishopric-Principality of Liège. As a boy, he attended boarding school at Ath, later studied humanities with the Jesuits in Ghent. He also worked as a scribe in a lawyer's office. He made his novitiate under Martin de Hooghe at Louvain and was received into the Order by Livinus d'Hondt. At the house for professed at Ghent he taught his peers chant and the humanities. With Francis of Bonne Espérance, Augustine of St. Monica, and Daniel of the Virgin Mary he studied philosophy and theology at the Jesuit college at Douai. After ordination, Gabriel taught philosophy at Ghent and theology at Louvain. His participation in the controversy over reform in the province has already been described. From 1641 to 1644, he was prior in Louvain and carried out extensive material improvements in convent and church. He did the same at Ghent, where he next became prior. As *socius* to the provincial, he attended the general chapters of 1645 and 1648, at the latter of which he was designated commissary general for the reform of Germany.

The appointment of Gabriel as reformer was by no means fortuitous, though the background is obscure. The initiative seems to have come from the province itself. Centers of the movement were probably Straubing and Bamberg. Certain members of the Upper German province came to the Belgian province to learn the reformed way of life. According to Gabriel, these requested Ippolito Sessoldi, vicar general of the Order after the death of Leo Bonfigli (January 20, 1647), to appoint him reformer. Sessoldi complied, but Gabriel was not satisfied with the patents for his commission and declined. Sessoldi thereupon ordered the Belgian province to elect someone for the job, and the choice fell unanimously on Gabriel.

On November 13, 1648, Gabriel arrived at Würzburg with three professed students, Wolfgang, Brocard, and Spiridion. The provincial, Jerome Ernst, who in Rome had promised full cooperation, now secretly opposed the project. In letters to Bishop Otto of Bamberg and his councilor, John Neudecker, Ernst declares that Gabriel's companions were fugitives from the province, who previously had been guilty of moral excesses. Gabriel he paints as a troublemaker and rebel, who out of ambition to rule misrepresented his own province in Rome.

The Reform of Upper Germany

Nevertheless, Gabriel proceeded to Bamberg, where he intended to initiate the reform. The mayor of Bamberg, with whom Gabriel had been in correspondence the previous year, arranged an audience with the bishop. In spite of Ernst's efforts to discredit the commissary general, Bishop Otto gave his consent. On December 21, the reform was introduced in the convent of Bamberg. A novitiate was erected, to which Ernst was commanded by Filippini to send all novices. As novice-master at Bamberg Gabriel appointed the Fleming, Josse of the Circumcision (1617-1673). Novice master, prior of Bamberg for a total of seventeen years, as well as in other houses in the province, this saintly man did much by word and deed to bring about the renewal of the province.

Würzburg was reformed in July, 1649. Josse of the Circumcision became first reformed prior. To the renewal of this convent, the Lower German province contributed Dionysius of the Cross (Ballex) and Charles of St. Anastasius (Freywilliger), who here published his *Gnaden-Pfennig der Carmeliter* (Würzburg, J. Herter, 1653), which enjoyed four editions. The splendor of the liturgy in this convent attracted the nobility of the city.

On November 21, 1649, Gabriel introduced the reform of the Stricter Observance in Straubing. The first reformed prior was Andrew of the Mother of Jesus.

At the provincial chapter of 1652 under the presidency of the prior general, John Anthony Filippini, Gabriel of the Annunciation was elected provincial. Re-elected in 1656, he was able to oversee the reform of the rest of the province. Rottenburg and Neustadt were reformed in 1652, Lienz and Voitsberg in 1656, Heilbronn and Abensberg in 1658, Dinkelsbühl in 1661. The date of the reform of Ravensburg is not known.

The renewal of religious life regained the support of the people which showed itself in an increase of vocations and generous financial support. Houses and churches damaged by the wars were repaired or rebuilt. Not only were existing houses materially and spiritually improved; a number of houses abandoned during the Protestant Reformation were regained, and new foundations were made.

The Convents in Bohemia and Vienna

Shortly after reforming Straubing, Gabriel set out in December of 1649 for Prague. His original patents as commissary extended only to the German provinces, but on January 30, 1649, Filippini added Bohemia to the area of his jurisdiction. (Venturini's patents of June 10, 1654, include Upper Germany, Bohemia and Poland.)

The convents of the Order in Bohemia, which since 1462 had formed part of the Bohemian-Polish province, had ceased to exist during the Protestant Reformation.

On his return from the Polish provincial chapter at Poznan, Henry Silvio in November, 1603, travelled over Prague. He found that the abandoned Carmelite convent and church had been ceded by Rudolph II to the Friars Minor of the Observance. He tarried a week to petition the emperor for the return of the foundation to the Order, but eventually continued on his way, and the Franciscans remained in peaceful possession.

In 1626, the Polish friar, Sigismund Gdowski, obtained the parish church of St. Gall in Prague for the Order. About the same time, the former convent of the Order at Chiesch was offered to the Carmelites by Baron George Michna. The prior general, Gregory Canal, appointed Gdowski commissary general for Bohemia. From Italy, Canal sent Bonaventure Tanzarella, Theophilus Paulucci, and cursor Albert Piccarini. When Gdowski joined the Discalced Carmelites in 1628, Canal appointed Tanzarella in his place.

The Carmel of Prague suffered during the Thirty Years' War, but managed to survive. Several Polish friars, living outside the community, lost their lives. In 1626, Elijah Hoinowski, chaplain to Archbishop Gramai, titular of Upsula, was shot by drunken men while passing through an Anabaptist village. In 1634, Bartholomew Matha, parish priest at Turnon, was shot to death outside his church by soldiers of the army of Saxony enroute to attack Prague. The subdeacon, Elijah Sikorski, fled Prague before the advance of the army and was never heard from again.

During the Saxon occupation of Prague, only Paulucci, the prior, remained in the convent. In 1638, Straccio named Master Augustine Biscaret his commissary and on March 18, 1639, Master Bartholomew Giorgia, alias Zanettino, prior. The plague resulting from the siege of Prague by the Swedes under John Banner the same year of 1639 claimed the lives of Biscaret, Zanettino, Paulucci, Baccalaureate Hubert of Liège, and four others. Maurice Rosati, appointed prior on September 24, was also dead within a month. In 1640, Straccio reappointed Tanzarella commissary.

Although the Carmelites continued to exist in Prague, the quality of religious life was low. Refugees from justice in the province of Poland found asylum there. A certain Andrew Vislav led a scandalous life. In 1640, a Polish friar named Joseph killed the prior of Chiesch. The Italians Straccio imported were not always top drawer. Master Albert Conti, a notorious womanizer, was said to have taken a wife while in Prague. Master Julius Caesar Medici (later prior of Traspontina) was in the bishop's prison when arrangements were made to send him to Prague. In 1641, when certain gentlemen were asked to contribute alms to repair the church tower, one of them refused, because the friars were drunkards and lived dissolutely.

Gabriel of the Annunciation arrived in the dead of winter, 1649, while the pest was abroad in Prague. He deposed the Italian superior. A few days later, an aged Polish friar died. This left a Bohemian friar and a Pole at Chiesch. The indomitable Gabriel succeeded in implanting the reformed life in Bohemia. This time alms were forthcoming: in 1654 Emperor Ferdinand III himself contributed 8,000 Bohemian florins toward the construction of a new convent in Prague. The general chapter of the same year united Prague and Chiesch to the Upper German province, until such time as enough foundations could be made to constitute a Bohemian province. Subsequently, houses were started at Plan (1666) and Rakonice (residence, 1669-1706), but the Bohemian houses remained attached to the Upper German province.

The convent at Vienna, which at one time had housed one of the general *studia* of the Order, ceased to exist in the 16th century. The last prior was Hans Zink (d. 1558). In 1568, Emperor Maximilian II conferred the house on the Jesuits. Gabriel of the Annunciation now revived this foundation, once so illustrious, acquiring property in 1660 in the suburb "*auf der Laimgrube.*" Not yet completed when it was burned during the Turkish siege of 1683, the convent was restored by Leopold I.

The Convents of Silesia and Hungary

The Upper German province underwent considerable expansion in Silesia. The single Silesian foundation at Striegau had fallen victim to the Reformation. "In 1658," Tilman of St. Elijah writes, "he (Gabriel) restored to the Order our convent at Striegau in Silesia . . . not without great difficulty and danger along the way from Lutherans who were most hostile to Catholics, especially religious, because of the reformation of the faith." That year, Avertanus of St. Elijah was commissioned by the province to restore the ruinous convent. The restoration was made possible by the benefactions of John Adam, baron de Garnier (1613-1680), to whose generosity a foundation at Gross Strenz was also due (1677). This pious layman spent his last years in the convent of Gross Strenz and died clothed in the Carmelite habit. At his death, the general chapter of 1680 publicly acknowledged the baron's remarkable generosity. The same chapter established a novitiate at Gross Strenz for Silesia because of the distance from the province's novitiate at Straubing. Moneys left by Garnier also enabled the Carmelites to make a foundation at Wohlau (1712), which became a large convent and housed the novitiate. In 1685, the Carmelites purchased the former castle of Duke Henry X at Freistadt for a church and convent.

Through the good offices of Emperor Leopold I, the Carmelites were able to return to Budapest after its recapture from the Turks in 1686. At about the same time, a second foundation was made in Hungary at Stuhlweissenburg (1688).

As the Empire continued to disintegrate in the 18th century and its components gained greater political autonomy, the Carmelite Order within its boundaries underwent corresponding partition.

On April 16, 1731, Pope Clement XII constituted a province the convents in Bohemia, Hungary and Austria. The following general chapter of 1738 suppressed the title and restored the real province in the twenty-ninth place in order of precedence. The province of Bohemia-Hungary-Austria is designated variously in the records as the province of Bohemia or of Austria (after the principal political unit involved) or of Bohemia and Austria, but the same entity is intended.

After Frederick II of Prussia annexed Silesia, the convents of that region were at his request separated from the province of Bohemia-Hungary-Austria. The general chapter of 1756 confirmed the decree of separation which the prior general, Aloysius Laghi, had made two years previously. The vicariate would have consisted of the four Silesian houses mentioned above.

Around 1770, the Bohemia-Hungary-Austria province contained convents in Vienna, Prague, Lienz, Budapest, Voitsberg, Chiesch, Zedlitzdorf, Stuhlweissenburg (Szekesfehervar) with 202 members. Plan in Bohemia, it should be noted, does not occur in this list and hence probably no longer existed.

An Old Soldier Fades Away

The general chapter of 1660 declared the Upper German province completely reformed.

At the same time, Gabriel of the Annunciation was elected assistant general for Germany, Poland, and Belgium. The choice was not altogether a happy one, for Gabriel was a controversial figure in the Belgian province, and many at the chapter protested the choice.

As a matter of fact, he was soon up to his ears in trouble. The new prior general, Jerome Ari, was given to understand that the funds of the Belgian province were being maladministered. When he forbade certain expenditures decreed by the provincial, Francis de Bonne Espérance, and his definitory, these had recourse to the internunzio in Flanders, Jerome, abbot of Montréal. Ari appointed Nicholas of the Stigmata his procurator at the Belgian court and Philip of St. Peter Thomas his commissary for the visitation of the province. Soon the air was thick with anathemas. The provincial was deposed, the internunzio defied, Nicholas landed in jail. When Ari arrived in the province in 1663 and had personally interviewed the parties concerned, he came to the conclusion that he had been ill advised. He blamed Gabriel for this and for his unfortunate choice of representatives in

Belgium. Philip was an old veteran of Gabriel's former wars. Nicholas the prior general defined as *"un furioso."* Ari reversed all his decisions. He had been made to make a *brutta figura*. Nevertheless, when the Belgians renewed their request for the deposition of Gabriel as assistant general, the troubleshooting prior general managed to avoid such a drastic confrontation and brought about a reconciliation of all concerned.

At the end of his term as assistant in 1666, Gabriel became prior at Sorbo, a remote convent of the Roman province near Rome (still existing in ruins). When the danger arose that it might be lost, due to complaints concerning the conduct of the friars there, Gabriel persuaded Pope Alexander VII (his friend from the days of his nuntiature in Cologne) to place it in charge of reformed friars. He himself became its "apostolic prior."

In 1669, Gabriel was named procurator general of the Order at the imperial court. At the provincial chapter over which he presided the following year, he was persuaded to take the office of prior of Vienna. There he spent the last years of his life. Inevitably, he quarreled with the provincial, Angelus of the Cross, who sided with certain dissident members of the community, so that in 1674 the convent was withdrawn from the provincial's jurisdiction and placed immediately under the prior general. On August 15, 1679, at 69 years of age, the irascible reformer passed on to a well-earned repose. His portrait preserved in the convent of Straubing depicts a surprisingly mild-featured person.

The general chapter of 1686 gave the convent of Vienna back to the province.

Chapter 6

The Expansion of the Order in Eastern Europe

The province of Poland emerged from the Reformation with seven houses: Danzig, Cracow, Bydgoszcz, Poznan, Jaslo, Plonsk, and Wilno.

The first news to arrive in Rome after a long period of silence was not reassuring. The cardinal secretary of Pope Gregory XIII complained about the Carmelites in Poland to John Baptist Caffardi, who since the death of Rossi ruled the Order as vicar. On instruction from the Pope himself, the secretary ordered Caffardi to take measures against "such great dissolution, which on the testimony of trustworthy witnesses he declares to be most true"; otherwise, the matter will be taken out of his hands. In 1579, the vicar general accordingly directed that the laws of the Order be read Wednesdays and Fridays in the refectory, the vice of ownership be avoided, and "the shameful actions (*turpia*) with which you are foully branded be repelled."

In Poland, Henry Silvio visited only Cracow and Poznan, but his inspection was thorough. He remained in Cracow from September 25 to October 18, 1603, and received audiences with the nunzio, King Sigismund III, and the prince. The church was "quite good and beautiful", but the convent was "small and poor." Both had been destroyed by fire during the interregnum. In the sacristy, Silvio admired twenty silver chalices and other silver vessels and jewels. In the "ornate and elegant" church, he noted a chapel with an image of the Virgin which performed many miracles and was much frequented by the people. The interrogation of the community lasted from September 29 to October 17, but Silvio postponed making regulations until the chapter. The community under Fr. Stanislas numbered 14 priests, four professed clerics, and 11 novices (two of them clerics).

At Poznan, there were 11 priests, eight professed clerics, three novices, and four brothers. The prior was Lawrence Drusin. Silvio visited the convent from October 27 to November 7, when the chapter began, and found all in good order in church and sacristy. The rooms of the friars were well arranged and without superfluities. Much of the general's time here was taken up with settling disputes between the friars and local citizens. At the chapter which elected Lawrence Drusin provincial, the prior general published his usual decrees of reform. Silvio was agreeably surprised at the degree of observance he found in the Polish convents.

Only the seven houses listed above were represented at the chapter - the convent of St. Anne (Sasiadowice) was still only tentative - but the 17th century witnessed a veritable explosion of foundations. By 1625, the province numbered 23 houses; by 1677, the total had reached 25 with 311 members; by 1686, 32 with 367 members. In 1645, Cracow became a *studium generale*.

However, the quality of religious life in the Polish Carmel did not correspond to these external signs of vitality. Of the 25 houses in existence in 1677, only three - Cracow (*in Arenis*), Lwów, and Wilno (All Saints) - counted ten or more members. Many of the new houses, founded for the laudable purpose of satisfying urgent pastoral needs, were little more than parish rectories which presented opportunities for abuses on the part of both superiors and subjects.

Not a few Carmelites lived outside the convent in secular benefices. On March 18,

1631, Gregory Canal, reacting to complaints by the nunzio, ordered the authorities of the province to remedy the abuse of vagrancy. Under the pretense of the quest, friars remain outside the convent for months or a year. Some reside and remain in the courts of princes and lords. Others leave the province without permission of the provincial.

The continuous wars in the history of Poland made a normal religious life difficult to achieve. Particularly the houses in Russia and Lithuania suffered at various times from incursions by Swedes, Turks, Cossacks, Muscovites, and "Scythians." Raids by Turks on the parish of Sasiadowice in the diocese of Przemysl were an annual affair. The Carmelite convent of St. Anne on Mt. Placid was a fortress in which the inhabitants found refuge.

Plagues, the companion of warfare, were a familiar feature of daily life. For instance, in 1677, seventeen friars died of the plague in the convent of Cracow. In the plague of 1708, the reform alone lost almost forty friars.

As a result of the wars, too, many of the houses were in a permanent state of disrepair and dire poverty. Too often superiors only aggravated the situation. The complaint is heard that provincials appropriated the taxes for their personal use, and that priors did the same with community funds. Wars and plagues made it difficult for provincials to visitate the far-flung province. Nevertheless, the Carmelites did not remain insensitive to the breath of the Counter-Reformation abroad in the land.

Early Attempts at Reform

On November 4, 1631, Straccio sent Master Joseph Pandolfo to visitate Poland, but the commission does not seem to have materialized, for on November 16, 1632, he appointed the Neapolitan Master Albert Barra to this charge. Both appointments received apostolic confirmation. At the definitorial congregation, April 16, 1633, Barra published statutes for the province. He also introduced the nuns into Lwów; an account of this event was presented at the provincial chapter of 1636. The province had a second nunnery at Dubno, founded 1702.

In Master Nicholas Dabrowski, the province acquired a reform-minded provincial. At the definitorial congregation of June 14, 1636, he and his definitory decided to introduce the perfect common life into Poznan and Cracow. The project ran into stiff resistance from the prior of Cracow, Alexander Koslinski, a definitor and an eminent member of the province. Straccio enlisted the help of the nuncio of Poland to introduce the reform with "*suovità et dolcezza.*"

"For experience shows that on similar occasions the use of violence gives rise to many bad effects, and it seems that the superiors in those parts proceed in their actions with too much vehemence." As long as the provincial and the prior are at loggerheads, "they will not be able to accomplish any good." Nevertheless, if the prior remains obdurate, it will be necessary to appoint another. This as a matter of fact happened. Koslinski was deposed and took refuge in Prague. On March 11, 1637, Straccio appointed Thomas Romer prior and reformer of Cracow, but Romer died the following year and nothing ever came of the reform of Cracow.

On November 23, 1641, Straccio wrote to Master Bartholomew Golankovic, urging him to support "the collapsed or certainly wavering observance . . . I do not recommend the reform of the convent of Cracow and Poznan, lest, as the Greeks say, I seem to spur the horse on the plain." Golankovic, who had previously been provincial, is to root out every vestige of ownership and scandal.

The organization of the Stricter Observance by the general chapter of 1645 here as elsewhere in the Order gave new impetus and a point of focus to efforts at reform.

The Reform of Poznan, 1652

The date sometimes given for the definitive reform of Poznan is 1652, during Dabrowski's third term. Promotor of the reform is said to have been a certain Father Andrew who had done his theology in Touraine. In 1660, the bishop of Poznan and certain nobles appealed through Gabriel of the Annunciation to the general chapter, requesting a commissary general to investigate conditions in the province.

Whatever is to be said about efforts at reform up to this point, the movement took definite shape due to Francis of St. Casimir Powzinski. He had studied at Angers with Seraphinus of Jesus and Mary, at various times procurator general, secretary to the general, etc., and Francis used this association to obtain favor for the reform, though for that matter Seraphinus needed no encouragement along that line. Under several generals, this Belgian friar supported reform in many provinces throughout the Order.

During Powzinski's priorate at Poznan, 1659-1664, the community formally embraced the Stricter Observance and requested the protection of the prior general. Ari reminded them that only the prior general could declare a convent reformed, after it had observed the constitutions of the Stricter Observance for a year. The community grew to such an extent that the novice master, Florian of the Mother of God, requested that Bydgoszcz be given to the reform as a novitiate.

In spite of the desire of many of its members to live according to the Stricter Observance, Poznan had no privileged status; its members could be transferred to other houses according to need. Thus, in 1664, Powzinski left Poznan. The new provincial, Serapion Knyper, had little love for the experiment going on there. In a short time, by accident or design, little was left of the reform.

The wind changed again in 1671, when Powzinski became provincial. "The convent of the Stricter Observance, Poznan," he wrote to Orlandi, "is under my special protection." One of his first acts was to send two young priests, Ignatius of St. Joseph and Andrew of the Purification, to Rome, to be assigned a place of study in Lower Germany by the prior general. Ignatius ended up in Louvain, Andrew in Cologne.

On November 5, 1672, Powzinski recommended that the prior general cede Bydgoszcz and Danzig to the reform, so that reformed friars scattered throughout the province could be gathered there. He acknowledged that progress in observance was uneven at Poznan, but urged Orlandi not to heed its detractors. On February 23, 1673, Powzinski was able to write to the general, thanking him for acceding to his request and ordering reformed friars to the two new houses. He also asked Orlandi to recall reformed friars from Germany.

At Danzig, Powzinski published the general's decree of reform and transferred the friars who did not choose that form of life. The prior, Cyprian of St. John the

Baptist, and nine others accepted the observance. At Bydgoszcz, matters did not go so smoothly.

The provincial chapter convened at Poznan, April 15, 1674, elected Nicholas Stoinski provincial. The difference in attitude toward the reform was immediately apparent. After declaring their willingness to support the reform of Poznan, provided the community observed its statutes faithfully, Stoinski and his definitory asked that only Bydgoszcz be added to the reform. More houses were not needed, since few candidates presented themselves to the reform.

Trouble soon broke out at Poznan. Ignatius of St. Joseph and Andrew of the Purification, returned from their studies abroad, became respectively lector in philosophy and novice master. The youthful and not very prudent Ignatius soon emerged as the leader of the reform movement. On the grounds that he did not implement the usages of the reform and had mismanaged funds, the community first imprisoned then forced the resignation of the prior, Angelus of the Visitation Smuczewicz. Appealed to by the litigants, the new prior general, Francis Scannapieco, on March 16, 1675, ordered them to present their cases formally, but meanwhile, on April 26, the provincial, Nicholas Stoinski, summoned by some members of the community, conducted a visitation and concluded (rightly) that Smuczewicz had been wronged, but he took no steps, since the case had been appealed to Rome.

The Reformed Vicariate

Without waiting for the case to be settled, Scannapieco in May, 1675, named Ignatius of St. Joseph vicar provincial for the reformed houses and designated Poznan as the only novitiate of the province. On July 28, 1675, Ignatius and forty members of the Poznan community after a six-day retreat solemnly renewed their vows according to the constitutions of the Stricter Observance. Thereafter, Ignatius set out for Danzig and Bydgoszcz; in the former he planned to allocate the *studium* for philosophy, in the latter the seminary of the reform.

The province was reluctant to lose the important convent of Bydgoszcz. When Ignatius appeared with eighteen priests and students, he was at first not admitted. It was only after the proconsul's men had gotten into the convent by another entrance and opened the main gate that Ignatius was able to take possession on the Feast of the Assumption, 1675. Three days later, Florian of the Cross, prior, and six others renewed their vows according to the reform, August 18, 1675.

At Danzig, the same ceremony was performed on September 3 by Cyprian of St. John the Baptist and the fifteen members of his community.

On October 14, 1675, the Polish reform held its first congregation at Poznan.

Thus, all the formalities prescribed by the articles of Filippini for the introduction of reform into a province were carried out, and the reform finally achieved the independent status necessary for its survival. Unfortunately, it was only skin deep in many members, as appears from occasional serious lapses in conduct on their part. This gave their enemies occasion to refer to the "pseudo-reform," and provided provincials with an excuse for opposing its further extension. The levity with which some took their vows in the reform is shown by the impunity with which they slipped over to the old observance, if the austere life proved too burdensome. Provincials only too readily admitted such renegades to the convents of the province. More than once, reformed superiors asked the prior general to remedy the situation. On

November 2, 1676, Scannapieco declared fugitives from the reform perpetually ineligible for office in the province.

On May 8, 1676, Scannapieco lifted the restriction of the novitiate to Poznan. It was certainly impracticable, if not impossible, to collect the novices of the vast province in one center, but unless the candidates were trained in the observance, it had no future in the province.

Scannapieco generally favored the reform in spite of its weaknesses, and Stoinski and his definitory were preparing to appeal against him to the Holy See, when he died, August 30, 1676. During his two brief years as prior general, he had rendered signal service to the reform, and the Poles were duly grateful. After listing the priors general to whom the reform in Touraine, Belgium, and Germany was indebted, the Polish reformers hailed "Francis Scannapieco alone as the restorer of the Polish province."

At the definitorial meeting of July, 1676, it was decided to offer the reformers the convents of Keyna, Markowa, and Klodawa. The six houses were to become an independent province and renounce all efforts at reforming the other houses of the province. Masters Cyprian Dolezynski and Albert Pacrosa were dispatched to Rome to obtain the approval of the new prior general, Emilio Giacomelli, who granted it, February 1, 1677.

At the provincial chapter which convened, June 20, 1677, the reformed friars present under the leadership of Ignatius of St. Joseph were presented with this *fait accomplit*. Ignatius, who professed to be ignorant of the general's consent, produced instead patents of Giacomelli, dated April 3, 1677, which commissioned Tilman of St. Elijah, subprior of Vienna, and Master Elijah Szablowski, prior of Gulowska Wola, to settle the differences between Stoinski and Ignatius and thereafter to proceed to the separation of certain houses from the province and the erection of an independent reformed province. (Giacomelli had issued patents to this effect with names of mediators left blank, January 8, 1677.) Ignatius and his supporters withdrew from the chapter and protested its acts. The chapter, on the other hand, declared for the implementation of Giacomelli's patents of February 1.

The Visitation by Tilman of St. Elijah, 1677

The meeting with Szablowski never came off, nor did the erection of a reformed province, but Tilman made a visitation of the three reformed convents. This Belgian friar, who had transferred to the Upper German province to help in its reform, had already assisted the Polish reformers with encouragement and advice. His report to Giacomelli on the reform was unfavorable.

Materially and spiritually the situation at Poznan was bad. The vicar was "a young and audacious spirit, who in many matters preferred his own wisdom to the justice of God and who did not know how to obey." The education of the novices was neglected, because for weeks at a time their master was away on the farm amidst servants, serving girls, horses, and cattle. The sacred vessels had been pawned.

At Danzig, Tilman replaced the prior as unsuitable, but the new one proved to be no better.

The commissary was unable to visit Bydgoszcz because the plague was raging there. The prior and subprior died while administering to the sick. They were much lamented by the people they had served and were a loss to the reform because they were among the better members. The plague in Poland, Tilman observed, is worse than elsewhere, since only in the larger cities are there doctors and pharmacists. Those who contract the disease die; those who do not are ostracized and perish of hunger. The provincial had written Tilman that at Cracow seventeen friars had succumbed, among them the ex-provincial, Francis Powzinski, and Angelus Smuczewicz, the controversial prior of Poznan. Another victim, the lector Wladislav, a young man of learning and virtue, had contracted the disease in his zeal for the sick and had infected the others.

Tilman warned those concerned to administer community moneys more carefully, abstain from excess in drinking, avoid conversation with women in the sacristy and elsewhere.

The commissary had also been commissioned to adjudicate the deposition of the prior of Poznan and the seizure of Bydgoszcz by the reformers. He suggested tabling both matters. Both litigants had been wrong: Ignatius in deposing his prior, Stoinski in obstructing the reform at Bydgoszcz. "I see that in this province the stronger conquers the weaker not by reason, nor right, nor rule, nor statute, but by force."

Tilman accused Ignatius of ruling the reform with the aid of a clique at Poznan, consisting of Andrew of the Purification (bursar), Florian of the Holy Cross (prior), Paul of St. Peter (subprior), Theophilus of the Bl. Sacrament (sacristan), and John of the Passion (*socius* of the vicar). He recommended that the general not continue Ignatius in office at the end of his term in July, 1678. He suggested as next vicar Telesphorus of St. Teresa, who would be acceptable to the non-reformed and likely to bring about a measure of peace. He also urged the addition of more houses to the reform, as the existing three were overcrowded.

Disaster overtook the convent at Danzig on May 3, 1678. When the community sallied forth on the Feast of the Finding of the Cross in this predominantly Protestant city, a mob of Lutherans and Calvinists not only broke up the procession but proceeded to pillage the Carmelite church and convent. Sacred vessels were smashed, vestments torn to shreds, the Blessed Sacrament trodden underfoot. The rabble drank to the pope's health from sacred chalices, men and women danced and sang profane songs to the accompaniment of the organ. In the convent, the cells were plundered, the friars severely beaten. There were those who wasted little sympathy on the friars, claiming they had been warned not to undertake so unprecedented a demonstration of the Catholic faith, but upon the command of King John III Sobieski a number of arrests were made, and one person was executed. The city was ordered to pay the Carmelites an indemnity of 25,000 Polish florins.

Telesphorus of St. Teresa, Second Vicar

Evidently, Giacomelli took Tilman's advice, for Telesphorus of St. Teresa (Niklakowicz) became the next vicar provincial of the reform.

The unfortunate reform received a heavy blow in the Fall of 1679, when Ignatius of St. Joseph, who had come to be considered the father of the reform, absconded with a merchant's wife. Later he was captured and fetched back to Poznan. Eventually, he transferred to the Franciscans.

Ignatius' downfall brought a rash of defections to the province. The congregation of the reform of 1680 requested a commissary general to distinguish the reformed from the crypto-reformed. Fortunately, this can of worms never got to be opened. The general chapter of 1681 forbade the provincial to admit refugees from the reform.

Telesphorus presided harmoniously at the provincial chapter of 1681. Telesphorus had studied in Belgium, but he had been obliged to teach theology five years at Cracow before he was released to the reform. He was on good terms with the province and his triennium was more peaceful than his predecessor's. This was due in part also to the fact that Telesphorus was not very exacting. His personal life was far from austere, and he was remiss in eliminating abuses and correcting faults.

Belgian friars were imported in an effort to raise the level of observance: Maurice of St. Francis, of the Gallo-Belgian province, who became subprior at Poznan; and two brothers, Casimir of the Mother Most Amiable and Wolfgang of St. Anne, of the Flemish province, who filled the post of lectors in the same place. The Belgians were in constant friction with the prior, Joseph of St. Michael, a Pole who had been trained in the reform in Germany. He was an exemplary religious, but rigid and severe. The lectors soon made up their minds to return to their province, though at Gross Strenz Tilman of St. Elijah managed to persuade Wolfgang to remain.

Nevertheless, it was Joseph of St. Michael who in 1682 managed to complete the restoration of church and convent of Poznan, damaged by fire twenty-eight years previously. The ruinous state of the principal house of the reform may have been one of the causes of slovenly observance.

Tilman of St. Elijah, Third Vicar

Monsignani looked outside Poland for the third vicar provincial of the reform. On June 6, 1682, he appointed Tilman of St. Elijah to the post. The following October 10, the general added Obory to the reform. Angelus of St. Gregory was placed in charge as vicar prior until elections. Tilman was experienced in the ways of the province and knew how to make necessary allowances for the difficult circumstances of poverty, pestilence, and warfare under which the reform had to grow.

More Belgians were imported: Charles of St. Joseph, Elijah of St. Henry, Ildephonse of St. Frances, and Anastasius of St. Andrew Corsini. Placed in positions of authority, they brought a tradition of well-tried structures and a spirit of prayer and common sharing. However, they sometimes found it difficult to adjust to rugged conditions in Poland. When one of them complained that the friars did not use forks, Tilman had to remind him that even the nobles did not use them in Poland. The Poles felt that the "missionaries" disdained them and considered their ways to be lax.

In a letter to Monsignani of May 20, 1683, Tilman enumerates the drawbacks and advantages of promoting the reform of the province. The Poles are very inconstant; one day they swear to live in the reform, the next they abjure it. The most influential masters of the province are contrary to reform. Filippini's articles for introducing the reform are not observed in points of utmost consequence. Almost all the convents are in a ruinous state —one eats and sleeps without a roof overhead - and the means of restoration are lacking. Nevertheless, the statutes of reform are observed to the letter. In his visitations, he found little worthy of punishment *gravis poenae*. The

Poles "are quick to be upset and disquieted; when burdened, they complain about their superiors, then they soon change and contentedly go about their affairs. They have the faults of their homeland like any others." In appointments of the sacristy, in devout celebration of Mass, in preparation for it and thanksgiving afterwards, in the recitation of the *cursus* of Our Lady and other vocal prayers as well as in the recitation of the divine office they excel the Germans and perhaps all other nations.

All things considered, Tilman's triennium must be rated a period of progress on the painful road of reform in Poland. His capitular conferences, two volumes in manuscript, are still extant in Antwerp.

In 1685, Florence of St. Henry, of the Gallo-Belgian province, was named vicar provincial by Monsignani.

Florence of St. Henry, Fourth Vicar

The general chapter which convened May 23, 1686, elected prior general the Piedmontese reformed friar, Paul of St. Ignatius, who was not present at the chapter. In his absence, the chapter elected vicar general Seraphinus of Jesus and Mary. The only official Polish delegate at the chapter was Joseph of St. Michael. Florence of St. Henry, also present, was given voice. The Polish King John III Sobieski had written to Pope Innocent XI urging the reform of the Carmelites, who, he said, of all religious in his realm had most need of it. Seraphinus, who during many years in various offices of the curia of the Order had been an influential patron of reform and had constantly befriended the movement in Poland, made sure the chapter attended to the King's request. The chapter decreed that the articles of Filippini should be observed in the Polish province, including the restriction of the novitiate to the reform. Moreover, all professions made in unreformed convents since Monsignani had forbidden them in 1684, were declared null and void. Finally, since the provincial and his definitory had requested the division of the province, comprising Greater and Lesser Poland, Russia and Lithuania, the chapter entrusted the division to the commissary general, Florence of St. Henry, who was to visitate all non-reformed convents before and after the division. He should also establish the reform in another convent as soon as possible. In the letters patent which Seraphinus issued to Florence, June 7, 1686, the observance of the decrees which the cardinal protector, Paluzzi Altieri, had drawn up for the reform of Piedmont was also imposed on Poland. In effect, these decrees were only the confirmation of some of the most important articles of Filippini. Florence took care to obtain papal confirmation of his commission, July 4, 1686.

The provincial, Serapion Knyper, was no lover of the reform, and Seraphinus' high-handed action only rubbed salt in his wounds. He went into action at once and succeeded in thwarting the chapter's wishes. In an appeal to the pope of September 9,1686, Knyper claimed Florence had obtained his papal brief *obreptitie et subreptitie*. The reformed friar had misinformed the pontiff about conditions in the province, which did not need reform, since the essentials of religious and common life were observed as faithfully as possible under the circumstances of continual wars and pestilence. In a letter, to Altieri he accused Seraphinus of political motives in importing his fellow-countrymen into Poland. By the same suggestion of political interference, King John was prevailed on to issue a second letter, November 8, 1686, to Altieri against the invasion by Belgian friars. To prove his point that the reform was no improvement over existing observance Knyper sent a list of scandals its members had committed in the past.

In Poland, Florence was politely received, but his commission as visitator was not recognized by the non-reformed. Knyper studiously kept out of sight.

The Provinces of Poland and Russia, 1687

Meanwhile, the provincial directly approached Innocent XI to divide the province. The pope turned the matter over to Altieri, who after consultations with the province's agent, Master Nicholas Czeski, on June 6, 1687, decreed the division of the province. The Polish province, including Cracow and the other houses in Poland, was to retain the name and precedence of the old province. The other province, which was to go by the name of St. Joseph, comprised Lwów and the houses in Black Russia. The cardinal appointed Francis Ciecierski vicar provincial until a chapter the following year. The allocation of Warsaw, Lublin, and the houses in Lithuania was to be determined in a meeting between the Polish provincial, the Russian vicar provincial, and their delegates under the presidency of the nunzio. In the Russian province, Russians and Lithuanians were to alternate in the office of provincial and share the other important offices. On June 27, 1687, Innocent confirmed Altieri's settlement.

The prescribed meeting over the assignment of houses and personnel took place at Warsaw, July 6, 1688, under the presidency of the nunzio to Poland, Cardinal Opizio Pallavicini. Each province received 17 houses. The religious were left free to choose their province: 220 friars (127 priests, 36 clerics and 57 brothers) opted for the Polish province; 109 (65 priests, 28 clerics and 16 brothers) for the Russian province. Lublin stayed with Poland, Warsaw went to Russia.

The province of Poland: Cracow (*in Arenis*), Cracow (St. Thomas), Jaslo, Lublin, Gulowska Wola, Bielsk, Wonsosz, Plonsk, Lipiny, Klodawa, Markowa, Kcyna. In Lithuania: Wilno (All Saints), Lida, Vladislav (alias, Wloclawek), Linkow, Pompiany.

The Russian province of St. Joseph: Lwów (Major convent), Lwów (St. Martin), Sasiadowice (St. Anne on Mt. Placid), Husaków, Trembowla, Rozdól, Horodyszcz, Boszowce, Dorohostaj, Olesko, Warsaw. In Lithuania: Wilno (St. George), Zoludek, Bialynicze, Mohilew, Mscislaw, Csausy.

The division of the Carmelite province only followed an evolution already undergone by the other mendicant orders in Poland. The vast extent of the province, the continuous wars and plagues made it impossible for the provincial to visit the houses regularly. Moreover, the province was split by friction between the Russians and Poles and by the rivalry of the *studia* of Cracow and Lwów. In 1710, Lwów achieved the status of a general *studium* already enjoyed by Cracow.

Among the reasons for dividing the province adduced in 1687 to Pope Innocent XI was that this would facilitate the introduction of the Stricter Observance. At the division of the province, no provision was made for its vicariate of four reformed houses, Poznan, Danzig, Bydgozcz, and Obory. Logically, the vicariate belonged to the Polish province, which theoretically it was meant to absorb and reform according to the Stricter Observance, but the province persisted in its boycott. The provincial chapter held at Gulowska Wola, June 20, 1687, failed to implement the articles of Filippini as directed by the general chapter, thus in effect disowning the reformed houses.

Between 1701 and 1704, the Polish reform made its first foundation at Drohobycz.

The Concord of 1713

The boycott of the reformed by the Polish province continued. The general chapter of 1710, on appeal from Fulgentius Miedzinski, provincial of Poland, ordained that the status of the reformed friars was to remain unchanged, namely, they were allowed two definitors and *socii* to the provincial and general chapters and were not to demand more from the province, until peace had returned to the kingdom and a commissary could be sent to inform the general and his council.

The provincial chapter of Cracow, 1713, subsequent to the general chapter, honored the rights of the reformed friars, and significant progress was made toward harmony. A 15-point Concord was signed, and Kcyna was ceded to the reform. A revision of the Concord at the definitorial congregation of Gulowska Wola, 1715, was approved by the Sacred Congregation, 1716, and by the provincial chapter of Wilno, 1719. Finally, the Concord was given apostolic confirmation by Clement XI, September 25, 1719.

Had this agreement, wholly in the spirit of the articles of Filippini, been put into effect, the reform of the Polish province, if not also of the Russian province, would have been accomplished. However, the Concord ran up against the perennial opposition of the province to the extension of the reform. The brief of Clement XI was challenged on the grounds that the revised text of Gulowska Wola had been substituted for the Concord of Cracow which the pope had meant to confirm. The matter was finally decided in favor of the province. The Congregation for Bishops and Religious, on June 22, 1725, declared the brief of Clement XI *subreptitie et obreptitie* and not to be executed. The following July 21 Pope Benedict XIII confirmed this decision.

The Provinces of Greater and Lesser Poland, 1728

The inevitable finally happened. The reformed houses were separated from the Polish province and made an independent province. Both groups appeared at the general chapter of May, 1728, with the proposal that Lipiny, Plonsk, and Klodawa be attached to the reform, which should then be made an independent province. It was in substance the old suggestion of 1676. The general chapter gave its approval, followed by that of the Congregation for Bishops and Religious on June 20 and of Benedict XIII on June 26.

The reformed province of Greater Poland under the title of Corpus Christi comprised Poznan, Danzig, Bydgoszcz, Obory, Warsaw, Drohobycz, Kcyna, Markowa, Plonsk, Lipiny, Klodawa. It numbered 164 members, not counting novices. Markowa must have been reformed some time previous to 1713, when Kcyna was given to the reform. Trutowo and Zakrzew were founded after 1728.

The original province of Lesser Poland retained Cracow (*in Arenis*), Wilno (All Saints), Cracow (St. Thomas), Gulowska Wola, Jaslo, Lublin, Bielsk, Lida, Wonsonsz, Linkow, Vladislav (Wloclawek), Pompiany, Krupczyce, Zaswierz, Kolesniki, Minsk, Kiejdany, Rosienie. The province had 216 members, not counting novices.

The segregation of the reform from the province, as in all previous cases, beginning with the Mantuan Reform, meant the end to efforts within the province to realize the ideals of the Stricter Observance. In almost a century of struggle, only a half dozen houses had been reformed. The reform failed to permeate Poland as it had France, Belgium, and Germany. Seventeenth century Poland with its history of continuous warfare, destruction, poverty, and plagues was not ready for the tranquil evolution of a profound religious ideal. The desire for a better life was not sufficiently felt in the province: the unreformed friars were right when they claimed that few wanted reform. Those who joined the reform were often not sufficiently prepared or committed. Perhaps the most radical reason for the failure of reform - apart from conditions in the country - was the unrelenting opposition of provincials and definitors to the gradual expansion of reform throughout the province according to the plan of Filippini. What might have been accomplished in the way of reform even under unfavorable conditions can be seen from provincials like Nicholas Dabrowski and Francis Powsinski. Writing around the year 1725, a friar of the reform put the matter briefly: "The past warfare, which has been going on for so many years, consists only in this: that the reform has demanded from the Ancient Observance the rights granted it by the whole Order and by the popes, while the Ancient Observance has refused to grant them to it."

The Provinces of Lithuania, 1756, 1766

In the second half of the 18th century, the convents in the Grand Duchy of Lithuania separated from the provinces of Russia and Lesser Poland. The division was advisable because of differences between Russians and Lithuanians and because of the vast extent of the province.

The Russian province of St. Joseph retained the convents of Lwów (Major), Lwów (St. Martin), Sasiadowice, Husaków, Rozdól, Kochawina, Botszowce, Trembowla, Horodyszcz, Labun, Hlinsk, Dorohostaj, Luck, Kisielin, Olesko, Monasterek (residence).

The Lithuanian province of St. George was allotted Wilno (St. George), Zoludek, Bialynicze, Kniazyce, Mohilew, Csausy, Radomel, Mscislaw, Mazykin, Brest-Litowsk (residence). Master Felician Ciapinski became the first provincial.

Mohilew was designated a *studium generale* in 1782.

A decade later, the Lithuanian houses in the province of Lesser Poland followed suit. The same problems – national antagonisms and the extent of the province – were operative here.

The province of Lesser Poland, reduced to its original size of a century and a half previously, now consisted of Cracow (*in Arenis*), Cracow (St. Thomas), Jaslo, Gulowska Wola, Bielsk, Lublin, Wonsosz, Krupczyce. The condition of the province remained static for the rest of the century until the suppressions.

The Lithuanian province of All Saints comprised the convents of Wilno (All Saints), Lida, Zaswierz, Kolesniki, Minsk, Vladislav (Wloclawek), Linków, Pompiany, Rosienie, Kiejdany, Chwalojnie (residence). Subsequently, foundations were made at Sloboda, Taboryszki, Szematowce, Czerykowice, and Toporzyszcze.

The extraordinary expansion of the Order in Eastern Europe led to the request for a special assistant general for those parts. The general chapter of 1750 granted its consent, confirmed by Benedict XIV, May 15, 1756. The first Polish assistant was Angelus Postepski, provincial of Russia at the time.

Chapter 7

Carmel in Baroque Italy

To speak of Carmel in Italy in the 17th and 18th century is to speak of Carmel in a number of different countries.

The center of Italy was occupied by the Papal States, south of which lay the Kingdom of Naples and Sicily. To the North was situated a number of duchies and republics, Savoy, Milan, Genoa, Venice, Florence, Parma, Mantua, Lucca, Modena, Sardegna. These various political units were actually dependent on the superpowers of Europe, Spain, France, and the Empire. Some were claimed as possessions by virtue of immemorial feudal rights, such as Naples, Sicily, and Sardegna by Spain; others were attached to the great powers by diplomatic marriages or dependency on their help for survival, as Mantua on France. During the 17th century, Spain maintained its existing hegemony over Italy, but in the 18th century, after the extinction of the Hapsburg line uniting Spain and the Empire, France and Austria increasingly extended their influence and power. Italy, especially in the North, was constantly affected by the power plays of the great nations, either directly by invasion or indirectly because of their involvement with these countries in their warfare elsewhere.

The Mantuan Congregation embraced more than one state, but such political pluralism did not also divide the brethren.

Recurrent plagues were by no means confined to the Middle Ages. Besides local outbreaks, the pestilence of 1630 was particularly widespread and destructive of life. A special curse on Italy were the constant raids by Turkish pirates who wreaked destruction and carried off captives into slavery. Many a Carmelite languished in durance vile under the banner of the sickle moon. Such slavery, however, was really not meant to last; it was actually a kidnapping racket, the purpose of which was the ransom.

At the beginning of the 17th century, Italy counted eleven provinces. These were, in order of precedence or foundation: St. Albert in Sicily, Rome, Lombardy, Tuscany, Venice, Terra di Lavoro, Romagna, St. Angelus in Sicily, Puglia, Calabria (1575), Abruzzo (1598).

The establishment of the Carmelites on Sardinia dates from the 16th century. On May 26, 1506, the prior general, Peter Terrasse, authorized the provincial, Silvester de Stobl, to accept a foundation in Sardinia. In 1562, there is a vicar general for Sardinia, Vincent Andrew Galçeran, who requests a foundation in Cagliari, since the Order had lost twelve convents to the Lutherans in Provence and Languedoc. In 1569, James Montañés was named prior of Cagliari and vicar general of Sardinia. The general chapter of 1593 made Sardinia an "absolute" vicariate and gave its vicar voice in general chapters. In 1601, the prior general, Henry Silvio, notes that the vicariate of Sardinia comprised four convents and that two had been abandoned for lack of members. "He did not visit the island of Sardinia," his biographer, Francis Voersio, explains, "because it was a most comfortless (*disaggiosa*) place, and there were only five middling convents." Voersio lists Cagliari, Bosa, Sassari, Mogoro, Chiaramonte, and another unspecified place. The vicariate numbered eighty religious. Oristano (1636) and Alghero (1644) complete the roster of Carmelite houses in Sardinia. In the 18th century there is mention of a hospice at Nurame.

In 1641, Sardinia became a province under the patronage of St. Teresa with Master Gavino Cattayna as first provincial. Rivalry between the principal houses of Cagliari and Sassari led the general chapter of 1648 to ordain that the provincial and officials be elected alternately from these respective regions. The arrangement was confirmed by Pope Clement IX, February 15, 1669.

The reform movement in Italy added five provinces: the First Institute, or Monte Santo, in Sicily (1645), Santa Maria della Vita (1660), Piedmont (1671), the First Institute in the Ecclesiastical States (1705), Santa Maria della Scala del Paradiso (1725). Last but not least, there was the Mantuan Congregation in Northern and Central Italy.

According to a census taken in 1650 there were in round numbers 500 Carmelite friaries with 4,400 members in Italy. (This figure includes novices.)

Convents of the Priors General

Five houses in Italy were under the immediate jurisdiction of the priors general. A sixth house, Palestrina, placed under the prior general by Urban VIII in 1640, was returned to the Roman province in 1759.

The convent of Santa Maria in Traspontina, seat of the general curia and a *studium generale*, was completed in 1615. The embellishment of its church continued throughout the century. In 1650, the community numbered forty-four members. As befitted the residence of the prior general, the constitutions, including the article concerning the deposit box, were carefully observed.

In 1650, the community of San Martino ai Monti comprised twenty friars, including one novice. During his priorate, Filippini restored the church and published a description (1639). On April 12, 1680, Giacomelli introduced the perfect common life and drew up statutes to this effect. Whatever effect these measures may have had, it became necessary a score of years later to make a new attempt at betterment. In 1698, the council of the Order commanded the common life to be introduced. The community was to number nineteen members. Paul of St. Ignatius was to be asked to take up residence as an example of regular life.

Another example of regular life surely was Angelus Paoli (1642-1720), a member of the Tuscan province who spent his life in the convent of San Martino ai Monti in Rome. Although he was strongly drawn to solitary prayer and practised the most harrowing penance, Angelus was particularly devoted to the poor. Daily, he fed hundreds of Rome's teeming beggars in the courtyard of the monastery and sought out the sick in the hospitals, especially that of nearby St. John Lateran. He founded a sanatorium for the convalescent poor, situated between St. Clement's and the Colosseum. At the same time, his spiritual counsel was sought by the rich and noble.

Towards the end of Paoli's life, a report by the prior general, Caspar Pizzolanti, to the Congregation for Religious Discipline in 1722 disclosed that the community had not been visited for many years, the prior did not keep the accounts as required, the *depositum* was not observed. Most of the inmates were old, the convent had become "a hospital for invalids." Among the younger members, only one was capable of carrying out religious functions in the church. For a solemn High Mass, ministers had to be brought from St. Julian's.

In 1759, Clement XIII gave the convent to the Roman province.

The Carmine Maggiore of Naples

Founded before 1268, when it received the body of the ill-fated Conradin from the hands of the executioner, the Carmine became a *studium generale* in 1333. At the general chapter of 1524, "the convent of Naples, which heads all the others in Italy" was placed under the direct jurisdiction of the prior general. In 1593, the prior of Naples was given *de iure* voice in general chapters. Like the other convents dependent on the general, Naples was obliged to provide him with bread (or grain) and wine from its *grancie* located in the region. These *grancie*, or farms, developed into communities with their own priors, appointed, like the prior of the Carmine, by the prior general. In 1650, there were 14 *grancie* with 63 friars.

The Carmine absorbed much of the general's attention. In the course of countless visitations, innumerable decrees were made for the spiritual and material improvement of the convent. Moreover, in the 17th century generals were often represented by a commissary general, distinct from the prior, whose duty it was to watch over observance. Yet the priors general never managed to bring about the perfect common life in the large unwieldy community, which in 1650 numbered 88 members (counting four novices). Writing to his commissary general at Naples on February 3, 1640, Straccio complains: "To my greatest displeasure, I hear from an unbiased person in that convent, who has not and cannot have particular reasons, that the convent is reduced to such a state, particularly in spiritual matters, that of its religious character there remain only the name and the habit, because in effect the friars live worse than seculars, going out alone without their mantles, wearing gloves and fancy cuffs, engaging in commerce and other unlawful legal practices, and having relationships with God knows whom. (I further hear) that the divine services in choir are carried out very poorly, that only with the greatest difficulty are priests persuaded to offer Mass and brothers to serve; there is great freedom in the way of living, idleness on the part of the young. The convent is a constant marketplace without silence, with continual murmuring and unfitting language, continual betrayals of one another, so that in the past few years conditions are as changed and different as heaven is from earth."

If this outburst reflects a moment of discouragement on the part of the aging general, the faults enumerated represent a constantly recurring theme in the visitations of the convent. Later, Straccio declared that of the approximately 150 friars of the Carmine only 11 (including six brothers) kept their money in the deposit box. (The number 150 apparently includes the communities of the *grancie*.)

Even when the *depositum* was observed, the vow of poverty was interpreted in a rather broad sense. During his visitation in 1662, Jerome Ari required that a record of "immobile goods, property and houses which are possessed *ad usum*" be kept in the deposit box.

The plague of 1656 did not spare the Carmine. Of 100 friars only 30 survived.

Not all is shadow in the Neapolitan sky. For centuries, the distinguished Carmine intimately shared the colorful lives of the people in the port area in which it is located. Many friars, outstanding for piety and learning, lived in the Carmine. The priors general sent excellent subjects as priors, regents and commissaries, men who often later became generals themselves. Straccio had been regent of studies there. Among those remembered for their holy lives mention might be made of Julius Castaldi, Salvatore Pasquale, and Anastasius González.

In 1705, the common life was introduced into Capo di Chino, one of the *grancie* of the Carmine. Four years later, the novitiate was transferred there. Another *grancia*, Gragnano, undertook the common life in 1717.

In 1725, the Carmine of Naples and its ten *grancie* (Capo di Chino, Chiaia, Somma, Nola, Posilippo, Lacco Ameno, Pozzuoli, Ottaiano, Gragnano, Arienzo) were joined to five convents separated from the province of Terra di Lavoro (Pomigliano, Castellamare, Nocera de' Pagani, Sant'Elia, Sessa) to form the province of Naples. To these was added the convent of Monte Santo in Naples, which for the occasion abandoned its reformed status. The Carmine, however, failed to become part of the new province and remained subject to the prior general. Monte Santo became the principal house of the province of Naples.

Another Neapolitan convent, Santa Maria del Buon Soccorso, was founded in 1638 for Spanish friars and placed under the jurisdiction of the prior general.

The Convent of Monte Oliveto

From the end of the 16th century, the convent engaged in a continual tug of war with major superiors over the matter of union with the Lombardy province. Even Silvio, writing on November 7, 1598, failed to convince the community: "Since religious Orders were founded so that those who wish to serve God more freely may be united together, there is no doubt that the greater the union, the more perfectly one can attend to the service of God. And because there sometimes arise disturbances between those who live in the same house, provinces were founded, so that one who cannot live peacefully in one place may go to another. Those who have only one house have difficulty serving God with peace and quiet. If some unpleasantness arises, there being no way to remove it, it sometimes grows to such an extent that a religious house becomes a hell." The understanding and loving spirit manifested in this letter - one of the few informal letters of Silvio to come down to us - teaches us a great deal about his character and style of reforming.

Straccio put his finger on a weak spot when he noted the lack of proper legislation: "I continue to be surprised that those friars who profess the primitive Rule do not have some particular constitutions other than the Rule. Certainly in these times, the Rule is not enough to regulate religious observance in all its particulars. That is why the Discalced Fathers and our Fathers of the First Institute, although they profess the primitive Rule, nevertheless have particular constitutions. Although I do not intend to oblige those Fathers to the observance of our constitutions, I would like to find out whether they have constitutions or statutes and ordinances, and have them send me a copy." The general never managed to run to ground the chimerical statutes of Monte Oliveto.

Visitation reports vary from the very negative to the very positive. In the 17th century and subsequently, the life style of Monte Oliveto does not seem to have differed greatly from the rest of the Order, though it would perhaps be unfair to say that the observance eventually reduced itself to the mere practice of abstinence.

The friars were committed to the perfect common life, in spite of the evidence to the contrary in some visitations. It is difficult to judge how deeply they were dedicated to the contemplative life. In that remote house, given the ideal of the primitive Rule, no doubt many were devoted to prayer in their cells.

Nevertheless, the autonomous character of the house, its remoteness, cut it off from the intellectual formation in the Order, and most of its members seem to have been simple friars without great pretension to learning. Troublemakers had greater resonance in the single foundation of Monte Oliveto and had nowhere to go. The lack of specific legislation other than the Rule caused life at times to be somewhat anarchic. It would have helped immensely, if at some time early in its history a member of Monte Oliveto had had the genius to enshrine its spirit in a brief body of laws for the guidance of its members over the years.

The Holy See and the Italian Provinces

The initial formation of candidates for religious life was an area of special concern to the Holy See in its efforts to renew the religious orders. On July 3, 1599, Clement VIII restricted novitiates and *professoria* to reformed convents designated by the Holy See. By his brief of December 17, 1649, Innocent X required permission of the pertinent Roman Congregation for the reception and profession of novices. This requirement was somewhat attenuated on July 18, 1695, by Innocent XII, who allowed houses of formation to be located in any convent which observed the common life.

Such restrictions proved to be an embarrassment for the Carmelite provinces in Italy, where convents observing the common life were conspicuous by their absence. In 1651, the Order's procurator general complained to the Holy See that the thirteen Italian provinces had been diminished by 300 friars. Even after Innocent's legislation, the general chapter of 1698 noted that almost all Italian provinces were destitute of candidates during the past four years due to a lack of convents observing the common life.

Another preoccupation of the Holy See were the numerous small convents of religious orders in Italy. This situation was regarded by Innocent X as the principal cause for the failure of the efforts of the popes to reform the religious orders. In his bull *Instaurandae*, October 15,1652, he ordered the summary suppression of all religious houses, "in which, because of the small number of religious, regular discipline cannot be observed according to the peculiar institutes of each order," relegating to the Congregation for the Religious State the task of working out details.

On October 24, the latter body declared non-existent 212 Carmelite convents, or almost half the houses of the Order in Italy. The Roman province lost 21 out of 32, Romagna 13 out of 26, Tuscany seven out of 14, Lombardy 11 out of 37, Venice 15 out of 27, Abruzzo six out of 13, Terra di Lavoro 43 out of 54, Puglia 11 out of 31, Calabria 24 out of 40, St. Albert 36 out of 70, St. Angelus 22 out of 56, Monte Santo three out of 14.

The decision of the Congregation was subject to appeal and in fact on February 26, 1654, twenty suppressed Carmelite convents were suffered to survive.

In the *arenga* of *Instaurandae*, the pontiff points out the disadvantages of small convents. The divine office in choir, meditation, and other spiritual exercises, silence, cloister, common life, "without which the basis and foundation of religious life can scarcely stand," cannot be carried out in such houses. "Immersed in ease, (religious) give no example of religious life: they go about alone in cities and towns, wander about with seculars, and become involved in mundane affairs." Good religious are unwilling to lead such a life, so that superiors are obliged to send lax ones, who only become worse and incapable thereafter of living a regular cloistered life, which they corrupt. Small convents, especially in remote places, give asylum to wanted criminals, who become more brazen in security to the scandal of the people. When such convents become numerous, it is not surprising that effort at reform remains without fruit, until they are cut off and removed."

The pope, however, fails to record some of the uses of small convents, which to a certain extent justified their existence. They offered convenient stages for friars on begging tours or otherwise travelling. In the *grancie*, one or two priests and brothers supervised the work of laborers. Most of all, small convents were a means of evangelizing isolated and neglected villages, an urgently needed apostolate, for which St. Alphonsus Liguori was to found an order.

All these features, favorable and unfavorable, can be found in the Carmelite experience, and not only in Italy. The superiors of the Order themselves bear out the criticism of Pope Innocent. In 1592, Chizzola obtained faculties from Clement VIII to suppress small houses, "in which formal observance can in no way be introduced." It would seem that he tried to put his powers into practice in both Sicilian provinces. Straccio acquired the same faculties in 1633.

In 1629, the Congregation for Bishops and Religious considered placing under the bishops all religious houses not able to support at least four priests. The superiors in Rome joined forces and managed to scotch this dangerous serpent. Imparting the good news to the Italian provincials on July 28, Canal admits that "unfortunately it is true that in these small places there is very little religious life, and some of them serve as refuges for fugitives from justice, whence arise the most serious consequences, besides the misconduct of some religious, the scandals which often offend the ears of His Holiness and the illustrious Lord Cardinals of the Congregation, to our great detriment." Canal has been placed under obligation to instruct the provincials to keep a sharp eye on their small houses and to punish without mercy any wrongdoing. Canal requests a report on small houses, the superiors in charge, and the friars who inhabit them. In the future, if any grave scandal occurs in such houses, they will be taken away.

Even after the suppression of the small convents, Tartaglia complained in 1681, "In some convents, especially small ones, on the pretext of an insufficient number of religious needed for exact regularity (the brethren) are wont to excuse themselves from observing it. Hence, it comes about that the friars living in them gradually and without realizing it languish and become lax in the way of their profession."

The general chapter of 1625 urged civil authorities to assist small convents in remote places, otherwise they would be closed. It was no idle threat, for rural communities, especially, prized their local friary. When Lady Feliana Spinelli of Collostorto, province of Terra di Lavoro, complained about the Carmelite community (one priest and one brother in 1650) and threatened to turn the convent over to the Capuchins, Straccio replied that he had no objection to giving up the place, but in similar cases the magistrates of the town (*università*) had objected so strongly that the houses had to be taken back. On the other hand, the general chapter of 1613 reported that the Cardinal of Savoy had requested that the convent of Pino (*Alpinum*) be incorporated into that of Turin, "to avoid many scandals which recurrently arise in the aforementioned convent, because it is situated in a mountainous place greatly distant from human concourse and (the supervision of) superiors. Pino survived and was eventually reformed.

The Priors General and the Italian Provinces

Silvio's first concern after election was the material and spiritual condition of the Italian provinces and he spent the first four years of his generalate in their visitation (1598-1601). With the exception possibly of the province of St. Albert his exhortations fell on deaf ears.

Besides the Roman province, Fantoni seems only to have visited the provinces of the south. In his visitations, he did not inquire into the matter of daily meditation. As to the common life, he directed that the "priors or provincials may permit (religious) the use of mobile goods in such a way that their things (*suppellex*) are in keeping with the state of poverty they have professed, so that the other convents may learn from their example how to live in common." At the beginning of the year, all were to make a *sproprio*, a declaration to the superior of all the movable goods they had been given permission to use. He attempted to establish houses in which the common life could be observed: thus, in the province of Naples he designated Aversa, Caserta, and Lucera for the common life; in his own province, Perugia, Orvieto, and Palestrina. In 1619, Pope Paul V authorized him to set aside convents for this purpose.

Canal does not seem to have left Rome during his six year term of office; he conducted his visitations through commissaries. In 1628, he sent Theodore Straccio to visitate Sicily; his *socius* was Master Alfio Licandro. At the chapter of the province of St. Angelus, June 11, Straccio designated six houses for the Stricter Observance: Palermo (Santa Maria de Succurso), Caltanisetta, Monreale, Castelvetrano, Recalmuto, Salemi. On October 8, he wrote to the community of Palermo, announcing his coming and suggesting that meanwhile a beginning be made at observing the perfect common life. If any members of the community did not wish to observe it, he would find them another convent. "All except officials should be content with one room, and the furnishings of the room should conform to the religious poverty they profess, without vanity or any superfluity. In the refectory, the religious should ordinarily be given a portion sufficient to satisfy them and enable them to keep the fasts. It should not be necessary for them to buy special things to eat or to bring baskets, *bozze*, or other things into the refectory."

In the province of St. Albert, Straccio destined Catania for "perfect observance." However, this observance did not exclude the *depositum*.

In a letter of July 7, 1629, to the provincials of Italy, Canal calls attention to matters that particularly require betterment. The ruin of religion rises mostly from avarice and ambition. The provincials should punish wrongdoers and test virtue and merit. Their subjects should be faithful in the service of God, attending choir and making all exercises of virtue. They should be given to the education of youth and novices, none should be admitted who have not had grammar. All, even the simple friars, should apply themselves to study of some sort, especially cases of conscience, so that they can procure their own salvation and that of their neighbor, for such is the proper duty of religious. Each one should be provided with the usual *vestiarium*, the old and infirm should be well cared for. All sorts of games, especially card-playing, should be forbidden under the gravest penalties. All vanity in dress should be eliminated: the use of silk garments, gold or silver rings. Misdeeds should be sternly punished. The decree of the general chapter about the reception of laybrothers should be observed and no one should be accepted without the required qualifications. Relations with seculars should be above exception. Bandits should not be given asylum in the convents.

Theodore Straccio, the last of the great reforming generals, not only encouraged and aided the reform movements, but sought to raise the level of religious commitment in the provinces not yet ripe for radical change.

The education of the laybrothers was often neglected, with the result that ignorance and misconduct was particularly rife in the ranks of these Carmelites. Straccio moved to restrict the novitiates to at least the four or five larger houses in each province. This was not yet up to the standards required by Clement VIII, but it was an improvement over the previous custom by which brothers were received in any house no matter how small. On August 12, 1634, Urban VIII assigned the novitiates for brothers in each province. Another area of concern for Straccio was the condition of studies in Italy. More than once, the prior general complained that regents were recommending candidates for degrees who were not prepared, with the result that Italy abounded in doctors distinguished more for ignorance than learning. He finally took the step of requiring that all Italian candidates for degrees appear in Rome to submit to an examination in the presence of the cardinal protector. On October 8, 1639, Urban VIII confirmed this arrangement, but the general chapter of 1645 petitioned for its suppression.

Straccio and the Reform of the Province of St. Albert

Straccio tried to reform at least one or two houses in each unreformed province.

In 1650, the two Sicilian provinces, the largest in Italy, numbered 126 houses with 944 members. The province of St. Albert had 70 convents with 477 members. That of St. Angelus comprised 56 houses with 467 members. Straccio calls the Sicilian provinces "the principal provinces of our Order," and perhaps for that reason concentrated on them his greatest efforts at renewal. The reformed province of Monte Santo (the First Institute) will be considered in a later chapter. It had 11 houses with 146 members in Sicily, thus bringing the total of Sicilian Carmelites to 1,090 in 137 convents.

On March 8, 1632, as vicar general, Straccio sent an open letter to the provincial chapter of St. Albert which was about to convene. While he was on visitation in Sicily in 1628, many lords and magistrates had asked him to introduce friars of the First Institute into the convents in their lands. Since he has become vicar general, the requests have continued. He urges the fathers gathered for the chapter to make an efficacious resolution to live more religiously than they have in the past and to introduce into at least some houses the perfect common life they vowed to observe. If they continue in their lax ways as they have for so long to the peril of their souls and the complaints of the people, they should not be surprised if they are driven from their convents and that these are taken over by the First Institute. Nor should they allege "the excuse commonly adduced by friars of little spirit who do not know what religious life is in practice," that our houses are too poor to live in observance. St. Bernard's dictum is most true: "*Devotio ponit divitias.*" God is the diligent and solicitous procurator of those who live faithfully in perfect observance, "as experience has shown in other reformed orders poorer than ours, and has been proved by our Father in France. Where before eight or ten religious barely managed to exist with a lack of everything, there now live large numbers with abundance of every good." Straccio lays the responsibility for reform on the provincial and threatens to appoint commissaries for reform if no action is taken.

Shortly after, it looked as though the zealous prior general's wish was about to be realized. From Messina, Master Anthony Adorno wrote that with some volunteers he wished to introduce reform in some convent. On June 19, 1636, Straccio instructed the provincial, John Baptist Lagnuso, to find a house. He would make Adorno prior, even if he had to depose the existing prior, since this was permitted in the interest of reform. Yet on July 3, we find Straccio confiding to Master Deodato Lombardo, prior of the reformed convent of Santa Maria della Concordia in Naples, his conviction that Adorno "is not motivated by the spirit of the more perfect life, but by displeasure at not being able to obtain what he wants." Nevertheless, at the death of Lagnuso, Straccio made Adorno vicar provincial. On December 6, he writes Adorno that he has sent the patents for this office. "Now you will have a chance to put into execution the good intention you have so many times claimed you possess of introducing perfect observance into this province. If in spite of this you disappoint me, I'll never again believe another provincial."

On January 22, Straccio reminds Adorno that during his visitation in 1628 he had warned the brethren that unless they improved their lives, the First Institute would usurp their convents. The *signori giurati* of Noto have asked that the First Institute be given the Carmelite convent which has been mismanaged for years. Straccio instructs Adorno to replace the present community with friars desirous of observance, especially since the local vicar prior is most willing to have this happen and is even willing to introduce the First Institute. The same day, Straccio informed the vicar prior, Albert Aquiliaro, that he had ordered Adorno to introduce the perfect common life; failing this, the convent will be given to the First Institute.

By March 19, Straccio had come to the conclusion that the convent of Noto was not suited for reform. Instead, he suggested to Adorno, in a letter of that date, the convent at Licodia, which in any case should be reformed, since it was the novitiate. He also wanted Milazzo reformed under its prior, Master Francis Polizzi. On March 26, Straccio adds that at the coming chapter besides the novitiate another house will have to be reformed for the professed.

In the provincial chapter of May, 1637, Anthony Adorno was elected provincial. Licodia (novitiate) and Milazzo were designated for reform. Reform failed to come off at Licodia under Anthony Ferraci. The general chapter of 1648 again ordered the reform of Licodia.

As prior of Milazzo to introduce the reform the chapter named Adorno's protegé, Vincent Bottiglieri, still a *cursor*, who had to be dispensed for lack of age. Adorno managed to introduce reform at Milazzo. Straccio had had his doubts about the suitability of Bottiglieri, because of his youth, and as a matter of fact complaints soon arose about his excessive rigidity. Adorno turned against his protegé, but Straccio supported him. When Bottiglieri resigned because of opposition to reform, Straccio had some dark moments. "Truly in the depths of my heart I feel his decision, especially its motive, and I completely lose hope that reform will ever be introduced into any convent of this province... I do not know whom to blame for this, if not my sins, because of which I do not merit that under my government so great a good be done to this province." Straccio refused to accept Bottiglieri's resignation. The young prior survived his troubles and the reform endured. In 1639, he was replaced by Master Placid Galletti.

The cardinal protector insisted that the chapter of 1640 elect a provincial who had spent some time in a reformed house. The choice was Master Andrew Lao, who carried forward the reform of the province under the general's constant advice and encouragement.

When Ignatius Faraci (alias, Facci, Fazzi) became prior of Messina in 1638, Straccio had hopes he would reform the convent, which was also a house of studies, because Faraci had resolved to live in observance, but nothing came of it. In 1640, the provincial made Anthony Adorno prior and introduced reform. Straccio was not impressed: Adorno had made too many vain promises in the past and moreover refused to place his "many hundreds of ducats" in the deposit box. Lao replaced Adorno with Bottiglieri. On October 17, the general was able to communicate to Lao his satisfaction that the reform was going well at Messina. Only ten priests remained, but Straccio was not discouraged. In a letter of August 15, 1641, Straccio observes that "in Messina, Catania, and Milazzo there is some good observance, but not the perfect common life. Since the convents do not provide the necessities to the brethren, the latter possess money and provide for themselves. God grant that they keep it in the deposit box."

In 1638, the prior of Catania, Baccalaureate Jerome Buffone, had written that he was introducing reform into his convent. Straccio had his doubts, because Buffone was not known for religious observance, and inquiry proved his suspicions only too well grounded. In an effort to ameliorate the condition of the convent, reduced to dire poverty by maladministration, the provincial, Anthony Adorno, suspended the *studium* there, transferred the students to other houses and reduced the number of priests from 40 to 16.

On March 25, 1641, Straccio congratulated the provincial, Andrew Lao on the progress of reform at Catania and Messina.

In 1640, Lao made Master Eliodoro Leva prior of Scicli, who successfully introduced reform. A college was instituted there, and Leva was made rector. Due to this circumstance, Straccio on January 31, 1641, expressed to Leva his doubts that the perfect common life could be maintained. "Since those religious are mostly students and are transferred from one day to the next, God knows whether they will have the spirit of reform, because ordinarily students crave liberty." The general's prognosis proved only too true.

On November 21, 1640, Straccio imparted to Mario of Siracusa, president of the First Institute, his great satisfaction that the observance had been introduced into so many houses in the province of St. Albert: Messina, Catania, Milazzo, Licodia and Scicli. However, his happiness was of short duration. Six months later we find him asking the same correspondent to make discreet inquiries as to whether "perfect reform of life" had in fact been introduced into these houses.

Straccio and the Reform of the Province of St. Angelus

In the other Sicilian province of St. Angelus, Straccio on January 15, 1632, authorized the vicar provincial, Master Stephen Cuculla, to set aside certain convents for strict observance and to remove all friars who were unwilling to accept it. On April 1, he named Cuculla provincial.

During his visitation in 1628, Straccio had designated the convent of San Nicolò Bologni in Palermo for reform. On October 25, 1635, he named Peter Di Leonardo prior and reformer. The brethren turned a "merchant's ear" to Di Leonardo's exhortations to observance, and Straccio was obliged to write a stiff letter, threatening to close the novitiate, if the community did not improve.

On December 17, Straccio expressed his satisfaction to Di Leonardo on his progress. The provincial would support him. To the provincial Straccio wrote, "I am utterly disgusted as well as scandalized that in a province with 800 religious, there are not to be found 20 who are willing to live in the observance to which they are bound. The main reason for this is the lack of spirit among the masters and other important fathers. My conscience is clear before God, because I do what I can. Let me only add in conclusion that in France two masters who began to reform themselves were the cause for the eventual reformation of whole provinces."

On November 20, 1636, Straccio reminded Di Leonardo that he should "take care that your religious do not lose the fervor of spirit with which they came to the observance, but rather that they increase it by means of the spiritual exercises in which they should occupy themselves." There are now more volunteers than San Nicolò can accommodate, and Straccio asks Di Leonardo to suggest another house for reform.

Di Leonardo chose Naro, but Straccio favored Bisaquino, which Master Modesto Giaratana, prior of Girgente, who had embraced observance, volunteered to reform but ended by conceding to Di Leonardo's insistence. On January 19, 1640, he transferred Giaratana to the priorship of Bisacquino for its reform. With prompting from the prior general, the provincial chapter of 1639 designated Naro for reform with Peter Di Leonardo as prior. Prior of San Nicolò was Elijah Adornetti. Master Eliodoro Stremola became provincial. None of the friars of Naro wanted reform, and the provincial cleaned out the whole convent. "As if the reform of our mitigated Rule were an unsupportable yoke," Straccio wrote the provincial, June 30, "and they were not obliged to bear it."

Reform received a hard blow when Elijah Adornetti, travelling with William Blasio between Sicily and the mainland, was captured by Turks on the beach in Calabria. Straccio instructed Stremola to collect the ransom with all dispatch from the province and the relatives of the friars. He himself contributed the 100 *scudi* owed by Trapani for his *vestiarium*.

In 1640, some members of the community of Sciacca expressed their desire to live in observance. On January 17, 1641, Straccio sent Di Leonardo patents as prior to introduce reform, but as he declined, Master Alexander Lo Cascio was made prior.

In 1641, the prior general received the welcome news that the provincial hoped to reform the convents of Monreale and Our Lady of Good Help in Palermo. Again Di Leonardo declined becoming prior, but when the brethren kicked against the goad and to Straccio's great mortification appealed to the Sacred Congregation against the reform, the reformer of the province was pressed into service. Straccio was indignant at the cheek of these fathers, "as if observance were contrary to their profession, and the superior could not reform a convent against their will. In short, I am very scandalized at those fathers, and as far as I am concerned, I am determined that the observance continue in that convent."

Other houses of the province of St. Angelus were considered for reform or briefly underwent the influence of the observance of San Nicolò: Salemi, Termini, Caltanisetta, Marsala, Modica, Alessandra, Girgente, Alcamo, Recalmuto, Prizzi, Licata, and Heraclea.

The reform of San Nicolò in Palermo had no special legislation. As to Straccio's constitutions for reform, "the very fact that they were printed in France makes them odious in that kingdom (Sicily)." Neither were the statutes of Santa Maria della Vita or of Turin acceptable. Straccio was quite content if the friars scrupulously observed the constitutions of the Order.

The reform of San Nicolò had the formula for success: a dedicated leader and a provincial sympathetic to reform. The provincial, Eliodoro Stremola, died in office in 1641. As to Peter Di Leonardo, no biography of this unsung hero exists.

Straccio and the Provinces of the Mainland

In 1650, the province of Calabria consisted of 40 houses with 201 members. No house numbered more than a dozen members.

Initiative in reform came from Master Sebastian D'Alessandro, who was also one of the outstanding members of the province. Born at Motta San Giovanni, he made his novitiate at Cosenza and his profession at Catanzaro, 1619. He received his doctorate in theology at Padua and became regent there as well as at Messina and Naples. He was provincial, 1640-1643, 1648-1652. The general chapter of 1654 granted his petition for affiliation with the Carmine of Naples in view of the 14 years or more he had dedicated to that convent. The following general chapter of 1660 made him assistant general for Italy. In 1672, Clement X placed him over the see of Ruvo di Puglia, but he died the same year of an illness contracted while visiting the sick. He published a number of works.

While prefect of the college at the Carmine of Naples, D'Alessandro in 1637 urged Straccio to send a prior and friars of the First Institute to reform Catanzaro. They would receive cooperation from John Matteo. Straccio preferred to send friars of the reform of Santa Maria della Vita of Naples. He made Jerome Monteleone prior, Albert Scaglione preacher, and Philip Finizio subprior. The same year, Monteleone died and was replaced by Finizio. Finizio, however, also fell ill and on recovery could not be induced to return. D'Alessandro, now provincial, returned to his idea of introducing the First Institute. These friars were imported (1641) with Alfio di Jaci as prior. The plan was to keep the convent under the province, but the mixture of two observances did not work and the First Institute withdrew. D'Alessandro, spurred by the danger that the Discalced might be given the convent, now undertook to reform Catanzaro on his own, with what success is not known.

Arnone also wanted to introduce observance in the convents of Cosenza and

Belmonte. In 1638, D'Alessandro returned to his province from Naples, and Straccio made him prior of Belmonte to effect reform. The same year, he made *cursor* Albert Scaglione, of the Della Vita reform, prior of Cosenza for the same purpose. Scaglione, however, lacked the patience of Job required of a reformer, for he was soon in trouble for allegedly striking a friar. He returned to Naples. No more is heard of reform in these houses.

In 1638, an earthquake shook Calabria, bringing ruin and death to a number of Carmelite houses there. On April 29, Straccio wrote anxiously to Arnone for particulars of the disaster.

The general chapter of 1648 ordered San Biase and Belmonte reformed. The prior general, Mario Venturini, named Master Charles M. Rota his commissary to introduce reform into two houses of the Calabrian province.

Cosenza became a *studium generale* in 1762.

The province of Puglia comprised 31 convents with 264 members.

In 1632, Straccio as vicar general commissioned Master Peter Del Frate to reform Bari, but nothing seems to have come of the effort. In 1635, Del Frate became provincial.

Eventually it was at Lecce, the largest house in the province, that an attempt was made to establish a beachhead for reform. Late in 1635, Del Frate imported as prior Peter Briglia, a friar of the Della Vita reform, though a native of Puglia, known to many in the province as their novice master. The problem was to disembarass themselves of the present prior of Lecce, Master Peter Baldassari, a religious esteemed for his accomplishments in the past, but too old and infirm to bring about reform. In the end, Straccio made him his commissary in the convent, an unsatisfactory solution, for the former prior put himself at the head of the opposition to the reformer. Briglia and three other friars imported for reform were awarded priorates elsewhere, Baldassari was re-installed, and life went on as usual.

The general chapter of 1654 declared Lecce a *studium generale.*

When the reform failed at Lecce, some thought was given in 1636 to transporting it to Grottaglie, where the community was reported to be better disposed, but no action was taken. Grottaglie was the novitiate. In 1640, the definitory again resolved, ineffectually it would seem, to reform Grottaglie.

Although Puglia failed to establish a reformed convent, a number of Pugliesi were to be found in the reform of Santa Maria della Vita in Naples. On April 27, 1641, Straccio suggested that *cursor* Lawrence Roppo, then in the reformed convent of Aversa, take some students in the reform from Puglia to reform Barletta. The general also thought of sending the Scaglione brothers, Albert and Carminio. This project also failed. The provincial chapter of 1641 named Baccalaureate Hyacinth Giacobani prior of Barletta.

Other houses of the province which were at one time or other considered for reform were Torre di Paduli (1636-1637) and Monopoli (1639-1640).

The province of Naples, or Terra di Lavoro (to be distinguished from the Carmine of Naples and its dependent *grancie*), in 1650 numbered 54 houses with 280 friars.

From a report of the provincial to Straccio in 1638, it appears that the material condition of the province was satisfactory. "May it please the Lord," the general comments, "that the spiritual state is as good." Here, too, Straccio attempted to initiate reform, at least in one or two houses.

On December 8, 1640, he sent patents as reformer to the prior of Benevento, Master Cyril Misso. On December 22, Straccio wrote that because he did not mean Misso to be a reformer in name only, Misso should initiate the perfect observance of poverty, "the principal basis of reform." It is not known whether Misso actually managed to realize the common life.

In 1641, at the insistence of the Duchess of Laurenzana, Straccio directed the Della Vita Observance to reform the convent of Piedmonte, but the plan had to be abandoned for lack of suitable personnel.

In the provinces of central and northern Italy, Straccio's efforts at reform met with even more meagre results.

The province of Abruzzo was the most insignificant of the Italian provinces. In 1650, it numbered 13 houses with 81 friars. In 1638, Straccio turned over to the First Institute the convent of Billante. Later, Billante reverted to the province.

The Roman province in mid-century numbered 32 houses with 189 members. In 1636, Master John Baptist Boni talked of reforming the novitiate at Velletri, but without result.

From a reference in a letter of Straccio to the prior of Siena, Master Angelus Croce, May 8, 1638, it would appear that this convent of the Tuscan province was "a house of observance." Tuscany was the second smallest province in Italy, numbering in 1650, 14 houses and 179 friars.

The province of Romagna (1650) comprised 26 houses with 180 professed and 11 novices. On April 25, 1637, Straccio called certain matters requiring improvement to the attention of the provincial of Romagna, Master Dominic Calderini. The provincial should make sure that all the friars take the discipline and that the cases of conscience are regularly held. The *depositum* should be observed. The provincial should be particularly vigilant over the observance in the novitiate at Ravenna. The novices should be reared in the fear of God, should frequent spiritual exercises and be instructed in the Rule, which they should learn by heart, the ceremonial, *canto fermo*, and grammar. As he found out when he was in the province, Straccio avers, the religious had not the slightest knowledge of the ceremonial and *canto fermo*. The master of grammar should diligently perform his task, "because, alas, ignorance, the mother of all vices, abounds."

A year and a half later Straccio is still complaining about the relaxed state of the province. It is the fault of the priors, who allow their subjects every liberty. "I can say with truth," Straccio declares to Calderini on November 27, 1638, "that in a few months greater scandals have occurred in that small province than in other Italian provinces which are quite a bit larger." In 1639, Master Albert Massari, Straccio's candidate, became provincial. Under this distinguished Carmelite, who later headed the Order, conditions in the Romagna province may have bettered.

To Master Bernardine Eredi, regent at Ravenna, Straccio wrote in 1637 that Msgr. Ingoli, secretary of the Congregation of Propaganda Fide (Propagation of the Faith), had urged him to reform a convent of the Venetian province, in which young friars could be trained for the mission in Cyprus, to which the prior general had obtained permission to send Carmelites. No prior for such a convent was forthcoming.

The province of Venice in 1650 had 27 houses with 207 members.

Straccio never managed to initiate reform in the Venetian province. Commenting on the provincial chapter of 1641, he urges that the priors insist that all take their meals in the refectory and that they themselves do so too. At Padua, the prior seldom eats in the refectory or attends choir. The masters ordinarily eat in their rooms with their servants or disciples, so that the refectory is abandoned. Many of the students should be withdrawn from studies because of their ignorance and dissolute lives.

Straccio's own province of Lombardy extended through Piedmont, Lombardy, and Liguria and was the most populous province on the Italian mainland. In 1650, it contained 37 houses with 427 friars. A vigorous reform rose in the Piedmontese convents, but did not extend beyond that kingdom and eventually became a separate province. "With time," Straccio wrote hopefully to the provincial in 1638, "this reform should make great progress. I recommend it to Your Paternity as the pupil of my eye. I am greatly pained that in no convent of Lombardy is there a beginning or thought of reform - a sign of poor spirit on the part of the Lombard friars." Straccio had ordered that novices at profession should agree that they would not refuse reform. But normal religious life was difficult in this region which was especially subject to the wars between Spain and France. Thus, in 1638, Straccio was obliged to obtain authorization from Urban VIII to appoint provincial officers, because the chapter could not be held on account of the wars and the resultant poverty of the convents.

According to the definitorial acts of 1714 of the province of Sardinia, Oristano was a reformed convent. In 1852, the common life was finally introduced into all the houses of the province.

Straccio was the last prior general to make a concerted effort to reform the Order. His successors regularly made their visitations, encouraging their subjects to live up to their obligations, but they seem to have come to the conclusion that the perfect common life was an impossible ideal. Individual convents sometimes made application for official recognition as reformed convents. Their number at any particular time is difficult to determine.

The Mantuan Congregation

After Caffardi, Chizzola for obvious reasons did not visitate the Mantuan Congregation. Silvio, like all the reforming generals, could not overlook this important body within the Carmelite Order.

On May 13, 1599, Silvio began the visitation of the Mantuan Congregation at Bologna. The warm feelings between the Congregation and the Order under Caffardi had again cooled. The vicar general of the Congregation, Gabriel Ravasino, sent a protest, claiming that Silvio could not visit the Congregation until he had celebrated a general chapter. Silvio obtained a papal brief confirming his authority and was able to proceed. As he reported to the pope, he found that the members of the Congregation did not know how to meditate, did not possess in common, did not turn over stipends received for preaching, hearing confessions, etc. Once again, the vicar general was found to have violated the cloister, when he conducted the election of the prioress of Brescia in the refectory. Ravasino was declared deposed from office, excommunicated, and irregular, but upon evidence of repentance was duly absolved by the prior general.

After the Brescia incident, the vicars general of the Congregation were deprived of jurisdiction over their nuns, who were placed under that of the bishops, January 4, 1600.

At this time, the second and final edition of the Mantuan constitutions appeared (Bologna, 1602).

Albert Leoni and the Reform of the Congregation

The Carmelites of the Ancient Observance constantly claimed that the Mantuan Congregation was no more observant than they were. Whatever is to be said about the general level of religious fervor, it is certainly true that the Congregation did not profess the perfect common life. Now, like the rest of the Order, the Congregation felt the stirrings of the Counter-Reformational renewal through the agency of Albert Leoni, to be ranked with Peter Behourt, Philip Thibault, John Tuaut, and Desiderio Placa among the pioneers of reform, though his influence was less diffuse.

Albert Leoni (d. 1642), of Revere in the Duchy of Mantua, entered the Order there in the convent of the Congregation of Mantua. After brief assignments in Macerata, Monterubiano, and Rome, he was appointed around 1594 to Florence, where he spent the rest of his life. Albert had not been destined for studies and so was excluded from higher offices and a preaching career. His personal holiness recommended him as a confessor and spiritual guide, and his penitents included some illustrious names. For many years, he was confessor of Bl. Hippolytus Galantini, lay catechist and founder of the Congregation of St. Francis of Christian Doctrine, and witnessed to his penitent's virtue at the process of his beatification. He served as vicar of the monastery of St. Barnabas of the nuns of the Mantuan Congregation. It is not known whether Leoni ever met his sister in Carmel, Mary Magdalen de' Pazzi: relations between the friars and nuns of the monastery of St. Mary of the Angels were far from cordial. In any case, it was that monastery that was chosen by another of his penitents, Camilla Strozzi. As Sister Minima of St. Philip Neri, Camilla distinguished herself for virtue and ability as novice mistress and prioress of the community.

Leoni's spiritual influence included the archducal family, who contributed generously to his projects of reform and charity. He assisted Cosimo II at his death in 1621 and was the spiritual director of the unfortunate Princess Mary Magdalen (d. 1633) in her retreat in the Dominican monastery of the Crocetta.

It was with the consent and support of the reigning family that Albert was able to open his "House of Catechumens" (1636) for the conversion and material assistance of Jews and other non-Christians. Among the warm supporters of this work was the bishop of Fermo, John Baptist Rinuccini, remembered in history for his mission to Ireland in 1645.

In the last year of his life, Leoni undertook the foundation of a mental institution.

Leoni was probably unaware of other early initiatives of reform in course in other parts of the Order. His inspiration to lead the perfect common life came from the reading of Serafino Razzi's biography of St. Catherine de' Ricci (Lucca, 1594). There he found exemplified the peace of mind that comes from truly having all things in common and the destructive effect on community of individual responsibility for one's maintenance.

With others of a like mind and with the promise of financial support by Archduchess Christina, Leoni chose as the site of his experiment the remote house of Castellina, which was only a vicariate and not even a formal convent with a prior. The chapter of the Congregation of 1618 appointed Castellina as a house of perfect common life with Albert as "perpetual vicar." He continued to reside in the convent of St. Mary Major, the Congregation's house in Florence, for Madama Christina would not hear of being deprived of his spiritual ministrations. Mark Giusti was named his representative or associate vicar. Other members of the first community were Faustino Cattani, Alexis Pizzotini, Angelus Camisani, and the laybrothers Bartholomew of Pisa and John Valentini. That same year, Leoni was encouraged in his enterprise by the famous Discalced friar, Dominic of Jesus and Mary, during a visit to Florence.

On June 11, 1620, the community met and promised to observe thirteen *ordini*, or decrees, compiled by Gian Garzia Millini, cardinal protector of the Order, and Valentine Manduli, vicar general of the Congregation. These imposed the perfect common life and specified the relationship of Castellina to the Congregation. Leoni added further regulations particularizing the observances of the reformed way of life. On July 5, 1622, Gregory XV granted approval to the *ordini*.

The edifying lives of its members attracted generous alms from the faithful and aspirants to the community, which around 1630 numbered eighteen friars. The convent was enlarged, and a new church, begun in 1624, was completed five years later. In 1645, Castellina was declared a priory with Fr. John Paul of Rome as first prior.

"I pray the Lord," Leoni wrote, "to enlighten the superiors to maintain this family (of Castellina) and to introduce this paradisaical life in all the convents of our Congregation." This pious wish was for the most part to remain unfulfilled. Leoni failed in an attempt to reform Mary Major of Florence but succeeded in the case of Le Selve. This bucolic foundation, cradle of the Mantuan Reform, was associated to Castellina at the chapter of 1632, presided over by Theodore Straccio. Faustino Cattani was appointed prior.

In 1637, a young cleric, John Anthony Diciotto (1614-1688) entered the reform and became Leoni's favorite son and successor in its leadership.

Viterbo joined the reform through the efforts of Master Bernardine Paoli of Lucca. In 1721, the Congregation for Religious Discipline ordered that the prior be of the common life, as had been the case for the past forty years.

In Viterbo, lived one of the most illustrious sons of the Congregation and of Carmel in Italy. John Dominic Lucchesi (1652-1714), born at Pescaglia near Lucca of peasant folk, entered the Mantuan Congregation at Ferrara. After ordination in 1676, he was assigned to Viterbo, where he spent the remainder of his days, leaving only once to visit his parents before they died. Like many of the persons considered above who were noteworthy for holy lives or for their writings on the spiritual life, John Dominic was a "simple" priest and never had the advantage of graduate education. He functioned in the offices open to this class within the Order: sacristan, novice master, subprior and confessor.

As novice master, he provided a rare example in Carmelite annals of a proper Christian attitude toward the Jews. When the novices, during a walk, failed to return civilly a greeting given them by some passing Jews, they were taken to task by their master on their return.

For his holy life and experience of prayer he was much sought after. His literary remains consist mainly of his letters of spiritual direction to his penitents who seem to have been predominantly nuns. He also had the habit of copying passages from scripture or the spiritual masters on certain themes for the edification of his penitents. These reveal his wide reading and the source of his own spirituality. Some of these little tracts, today preserved in manuscript, on examination may prove to be of his own making. Muratori took time out from his vast scholarly labors to pen a sonnet in honor of the saintly Carmelite, whom he evidently admired.

The Priors General and the Congregation

The running battle between the Congregation and the Order continued during the 17th century. Gregory Canal began the visitation of the Congregation around 1626 in the convent of St. Chrysogonus in Rome. He had betaken himself to the Republic of Venice to visit there the convents of the province and those of the Congregation, when he was recalled to Rome on urgent business of the Holy See. He never resumed the visitation because of his age.

Straccio, who liked to keep all reform movements firmly in hand, did what little he could to intrude on the affairs of the Congregation. On behalf of the Congregation for Bishops and Religious he inquired of Dominic Mary Pulzoni on October 1, 1631, by what authority he remained in office as vicar general after the allotted two years of his term. As a matter of fact, Pulzoni, due to lapse from office in 1630, had had his term prolonged by the Holy See because of the plague of that year.

Straccio's inquiry of Mons. Marc'Aurelio Maraldo, secretary of briefs, whether the Mantuan vicars general had the power to accept novices in places not designated by the Holy See may have had the effect of making the Mantuans more canonically alert. In any case, in 1634, they took pains to obtain apostolic approval for their six novitiates in Bologna, Ferrara, Mantua, Milan, Parma, and Brescia.

The Mantuans scored a point, when on July 29, 1633, the Congregation for Religious denied the right of appeal from the vicar general to the prior general.

Straccio also received patents to visitate the Congregation, but seems only to have visited St. Chrysogonus, to do which he had only to cross the Tiber.

To the 42 convents, which existed in Rossi's time were added during this period 15 new foundations, most of them of little account: Valentano (1580), Ripa Transona (1580), Gonzaga (1580), Sabionetta (1580), Vetralla (1583), Pontremoli (1606), Correggio (1616), Rossignano (1617), Fubino (1625), Caneto (1627), Santa Caterina (1645), Olginate (1647), Casterno (1650), Pavia (1670), San Donato (1674).

Some of the older convents acquired *grancie*, ten in all: Bondeno (1589), Bottrighe (1602), Figarolo were dependent on Ferrara; Soragna (1640), on Parma; Borgognano, on Bologna; Piscaglia, on Lucca; San Pietro in Ongaria (1453) and Campagna (1579), on Mantua; Pischisolido, on Sora; Parodi, on Genoa.

With time, Bondeno, Botttrighe, and Soragna achieved the status of convents. Viconovo (alias Vinovo) reverted to the Lombardy province in 1616 as a consequence of political differences between Savoy and Mantua.

No more foundations were made after the third quarter of the 17th century. In 1650, the 53 convents then existing numbered 706 friars.

The papal suppression of 1652 eliminated Monterubiano, Valentano, Acquapendente, Fermo, and Rossignano.

Venturini obtained faculties to visitate the Congregation from Pope Alexander VII, May 10, 1656, but he never put them to use.

Jerome Ari and the Mantuan Congregation

A crisis within the Congregation became the occasion for a prior general to exercise unprecedented powers. When a dispute arose between two candidates for the vicar generalship, Dominic Muggiani and Bartholomew Mozzoni, Alexander VII on September 3, 1660, temporarily placed the prior general, Jerome Ari, in charge of the Congregation. On October 29, 1660, at Bologna, Ari convoked the diet which elected a procurator general, definitors, and priors. The election of a vicar waited upon the coming chapter.

Immediately after the diet, Ari personally visited 21 of the Congregation's 53 convents, besides 18 others about which he was informed by appointment with their priors.

No doubt Ari's smooth and diplomatic manner contributed much to whatever success his visit enjoyed. Noticing how little effect Silvio's severe measures had had, he did not greatly move the waters. In this, for that matter, he was only following the recommendation of the pope. "If you can't make four, make three," Alexander had advised him. This did not mean that the amiable prior general did not keep his eyes open.

The churches of the Congregation, Ari reported on June 4, 1661, at the end of his visit, are on the whole well appointed, but services leave much to be desired, due to the lack of ceremonials. The Mantuans do not follow the Carmelite Rite as they are obliged to do. Their style of life does not fit their profession of reform, their rooms are well appointed, their dress frivolous, they are little given to silence and retirement.

There are not lacking acts of violence. At Parma, some years ago, a brother murdered the prior, and last Lent the prior was painfully slashed with a razor. Worse perhaps was the lack of truly spiritual men. Ari found only one, Fr. Anthony Asolari, in Bergamo.

In the whole Congregation, there is only one small reformed convent in Castellina, and even there the common life is not perfectly practised. As a matter of fact, disorders have even occurred. The seven members of the community are united against the prior, last August gravely threatened by one of the priests, who at the same time wounded a laybrother. Service in the church is poor, due to the small community; the accounts were in a state of incomprehensible confusion.

In the other houses there is not even the beginning of the common life. The deposit box in Bologna, the most illustrious convent of the Congregation with a community of fifty-six, contains only 50 *scudi* deposited by three or four friars. The *vestiarium* is given in money, preachers keep their earnings. On the whole, the Mantuans maintain themselves at the same economical level as they had before they entered the Order. Even the non-reformed provinces of the Order are more observant in the matter of the *peculium*.

The Congregation is despotically governed by the vicars general and the priors. The former allow the latter to do as they please, in order to win their support for continuance in office. For years now, recourse to the prior general has been abusively prohibited. Knowing what a restraint the authority of the priors general would be upon them, the vicars have always sought to maintain their complete independence from the Order. The visitations of the priors general, infrequent and lacking the needed freedom, have little effect. The brethren join in a conspiracy of silence. Once the prior general closes the visitation, his authority ceases, and his measures for betterment are forgotten. Such, the general concludes, will probably be the fate of the present visitation.

Undoubtedly an excessively dark picture, as the reports of the priors general about the Mantuan Congregation tend to be. However, it is also undoubtedly true that the Mantuan way of life hardly deserved to be called reformed. This had led Ari to set afoot a drive to unite the Congregation to the Order, but he abandoned his plan, when he had been appointed visitator.

When Matthew Orlandi attempted to visitate the Congregation, he met with the usual barrage of legal flak. Appeal to Clement X resulted in the *Ex injuncto nobis*, dated July 12, 1672, a new milestone after Gregory XIII's *Quaecumque* of 1574 on the rocky road of relationships between the Order and the Congregation. The prior general was authorized to visitate the Congregation alone and in person once in the course of his six year term, but only after the lapse of three years. He was also entitled to preside at chapters, not diets, and cast his vote. Finally, the Congregation was liable for his food and travel expenses and for those of his servants incurred during the visitation.

Under these conditions, Orlandi's successor, Francis Scannapieco, presided at the chapter of 1676. Joachim Pontalti, prior general from 1756 to 1762, is said to have visitated the Congregation, but otherwise the Mantuans seem to have been suffered to go their separate ways in peace.

Chapter 8

Movements of Reform in Italy

Although it was intended that all reformed convents in the Order should conform to the constitutions of the Stricter Observance, this legislation, based on the statutes of the province of Touraine, found less favor south of the Alps and the Pyrenees. The spirituality of Italy and Spain tended to be more traditional. Also, it would seem, the urge for renewal was less universally felt. But perhaps the most cogent reason was a political one: Italians and Spaniards were not about to be told by the ultramontane provinces, especially the French, how to live their lives. Nevertheless, a few of the numerous Italian provinces undertook reform in Sicily, Naples and Piedmont. Unfortunately, these efforts failed to renew the provinces concerned, but instead issued in the formation of new provinces, leaving the original provinces unaffected.

The Reform of Monte Santo

The province of St. Albert of Sicily was one of the first in the Order to feel the stirrings of reform. Originator of the reform was Desiderio Placa, doctor of theology, for many years professor at the university of Catania, where he had among his pupils Rocco Pirri, historian of Sicily. Elected provincial in 1592, he attended the general chapter the following year and there met the Discalced friars of Spain who had come to obtain their freedom from the Order. Did he then conceive the idea of an observance of the primitive Rule which would remain attached to the Order? Placa again served as provincial in 1601 and 1609. The prior general, Henry Silvio, visited the province through a vicar, Benedict Faletti, who accepted Placa as his *socius* for the visitation. Placa would thus have assisted at the implementation of Silvio's reforming efforts. He met him personally at the general chapter of 1609. In 1611, Silvio appointed Placa his commissary for Catania, which he took under his own jurisdiction. Perhaps the reform of Monte Santo, like that of Touraine, is to be considered the fruit of a seed planted by the great reformer, Henry Silvio.

Master Desiderio was filled with the desire to lead the perfect life. The university professor began to apply himself to the assiduous practice of prayer, penance, and good works. His corpulent body so shrank from fasting that his skin lay in folds over his belly. He did not disdain manual labor and was to be seen not only sweeping the corridors of the convent but the street outside, conduct for a doctor of theology that caused no little amazement in those times.

Others associated themselves to him, chief among them Alfio Licandro, born in Pèzzolo near Messina, where he entered the Order. He acquired the doctorate in theology and no doubt lectured in the principal houses of the province, especially Catania, but his career cannot be traced, as the provincial acts for this period have seemingly been lost. In 1613, he was elected definitor. More than for his learning Licandro is remembered for his piety and exemplary life.

Other early companions of Master Desiderio were Dionysius of Scicli, Dominic of Castroreale, Dominic of Turino (or, of Naples), Paul of the Cross (or, of Synagra), John Mary of Petralia, Mario of Siracusa, Timothy of Termini. Like the Capuchins, the reformed friars were designated by their given name and their place of birth or profession.

On January 13, 1615, Fantoni authorized the group to begin living the common life and regular observance according to the primitive Rule; this occurred in the convent of Acireale (Jaci). On March 20, 1618, Bishop Bonaventure Secusio of Catania granted Placa the church of Santa Maria dell'Indirizzo with permission to add a convent, where he and his followers might lead a reformed life in common. The church with the unusual title of "St. Mary of Direction," had just been completed to commemorate the rescue in 1610 of Don Peter Giron, Duke of Osuna and Viceroy of Sicily, whose ship was believed to have been miraculously directed into port by rays emanating from a statue of the Virgin.

The manner of life which the reformed friars proposed to lead is laid down in *Decrees for the Institution, Preservation, and Increase of Regular Observance in the Carmelite Convents of Acireale and of St. Mary of Direction in Catania and in the Other Convents to be Built in the Future.* The Rule to be professed is that of St. Albert as mitigated by Pope Innocent IV.

The prayer in solitude inculcated by the Rule is a primary concern of the new reform. This was the means adopted by the first Carmelites to renew the interior man. Unless necessity requires otherwise, the Carmelite should remain in his room like a prisoner in his cell. Mental prayer should be added to vocal; two hours of meditation daily are prescribed. Before retiring, each friar is to make a general examination of conscience lasting fifteen minutes. Twice a year a ten-day retreat should be made. The canonical hours should be celebrated at the proper hour and devoutly. In particular, Matins should be held at midnight. The chant of the hours is to be muted (*cantu demissa*) and in one tone, "lest from its violent protraction the spirit should grow dull, but rather by its means the mind may be prepared for contemplation."

Twice a week there should be a spiritual conference; the same number of times, cases of conscience, after the example of Elijah and Elisha, the fathers of the Order, "who by austerity of life, candor of soul, and untiring service to God and His most blessed Mother, the Order's singular patroness, sought not only their own salvation and perfection but their neighbor's as well."

On Sundays, non-clerics should confer with a designated priest concerning spiritual matters, on Thursdays concerning material needs. On Fridays, faults are to be publicly corrected.

"The members of this family desire most of all the things that concern the glory of God, the sanctification of his most august Name, the propagation of devotion to His holy Mother and the salvation of souls, not only among the faithful but also among peoples in distant lands, who are not of the faith, particularly in that region trod by the feet of Christ, where our Order had its origin and our fathers dwelt with great benefit to souls and in the odor of sanctity, even during the time of the apostles whose coadjutors in the preaching of the gospel they became." Consequently, members of the Institute renounce their wills and are ready to be sent to any mission, especially where there is greatest need.

To carry out this exacting apostolate clerics should not be ordained until they have studied theology for three years after completing the course of philosophy. This is the first time a formal theology course is prescribed for all priests, not only for those destined for graduate study.

All friars not yet fifty years of age are to undergo a year of renewal every seven years. For this purpose, a special house and prior are to be designated.

The brethren are not to seek material gain from spiritual ministrations, but only the reward in heaven which is God.

All titles of honor are renounced. Within the community members should be called Brothers; outside the community, Fathers. Exceptions are titles referring to the ministry, such as lectors, preachers, etc. Those who have positions of honor should sometimes share in menial tasks.

Great care should be exercised in the examination of candidates. Only those should be accepted who are apt for the form of life professed and who are motivated by a desire for perfection.

With regard to poverty, "Our brethren should not be ashamed to practice apostolic begging." Although it should generally be left to non-choir members, others should occasionally engage in it for the sake of mortification. Frugality not opulence should be loved, "not only lest we be burdensome to good people, but that the other poor of Christ might have part of our share." Perfect common life is professed; all things, even the most insignificant, are incorporated into the community to be shared by all.

Finally, the *Decrees* describe the reformed habit which does not differ from that of the rest of the Order except in the roughness of its material.

Although the *Decrees* do not specifically say so, doctorates and their privileges were renounced. In 1815, Pius VII granted permission for graduate degrees and their perquisites, but at the request of the reformed friars retracted his permission in 1821.

Besides the *Decrees*, the reform, known as the First Institute because it followed the Rule of 1247, observed the constitutions of the Order, which also were "salutary and conducive to perfection."

Alfio Licandro, Commissary General

On February 5, 1621, Fantoni approved the reform and lost no time reporting this new missionary enterprise to the Congregation for the Propagation of the Faith.

Desiderio Placa died August 3, 1624, aged 70, and Gregory Canal, vicar general after Fantoni's death, on August 29 appointed Alfio Licandro commissary general over Acireale and St. Mary dell'Indirizzo.

Canal's commissary for the visitation of Sicily, Theodore Straccio, took Licandro for his *socius*. In 1628, the chapter of the province of St. Angelus agreed that the reformed friars might accept a convent at Gibilrossa offered by the Duke of Misilmeri. Straccio confirmed the foundation on July 28. In the subsequent chapter of the province of St. Albert, which convened May 6, 1629, Licandro was elected provincial. At the same time, the convent of St. John Chrysostom (San Giovannello) in Messina, founded a century previously but never able to support more than one or two friars, was confided to the reform "in the hope and wish for betterment." The betterment was in fact forthcoming, for the poverty-stricken little house, title changed to Santa Maria di Monte Santo, proved an attraction to the faithful by the edifying lives of its new tenants and became the principal convent of the reform, eventually giving it its name.

Already in 1607, Master Alfio had acquired for the province of St. Albert the church of St. Mary of the Little Pillar (*del Pilirello*). It is not certain when it passed over to the Institute, probably shortly after Santa Maria di Monte Santo. In 1641, Straccio joined this house and that of Monte Santo to the Institute "*quatenus opus est*," declaring that he had found friars of the First Institute in both of them when he visited Sicily in 1628. The general chapter of 1654 granted the convent of Monte Santo precedence over Del Pilirello.

The friars of the First Institute, or Monte Santo, impressed the people by their fervent and exemplary lives. From everywhere came requests by local authorities for these religious. Reforming generals like Theodore Straccio threatened lax communities that he would consign their convents to Monte Santo. The reform did in fact take over some houses, but not always permanently. Enduring foundations were made at Curinga (1632), Siracusa (1635), Palermo (1636), and Monforte (1636). Monforte near Messina was the ninth house to be founded, before Ascoli on the mainland.

Straccio took advantage of a visit of Licandro to Rome to name him, first, prior of San Martino; then, of Traspontina. Mario of Siracusa became the third commissary general of the Institute.

Rome was the place for a college where foreign languages could be learned and missionaries trained. Mario failed at first to find a site in Rome and instead settled in Ascoli Piceno (1636). In 1639, he managed to buy a house in the Via del Babuino in Rome, and a start could be made with a missionary college.

Missionary Efforts of Monte Santo

The efforts of the friars of Monte Santo in the missionary field resulted in a very meager harvest. One of the goals of the First Institute was to return to Palestine, the cradle of the Order, but here it ran afoul of the Discalced. One of the Discalced missioners in Persia, Prosper of the Holy Spirit, who founded a house in Aleppo, Syria (1627), also made plans to recover the foundation on Mount Carmel. On January 30, 1627, the Congregation for the Propagation of the Faith authorized the Discalced Carmelites to establish a mission on Mount Carmel. But Prosper at first was not able to come to a satisfactory agreement with the local emir, and the opportunity was seized by Gregory Canal and later Theodore Straccio to try to obtain authorization for the Fathers of Monte Santo, but without result. On December 3, 1633, Urban VIII bestowed papal confirmation on the presence of the Discalced on Carmel. In spite of many hardships over the centuries, they managed to remain the envied sole inhabitants of this most treasured of all Carmelite foundations.

When Urban VIII made the Discalced missionary, John Thaddeus of St. Elisha, bishop of Ispahan in Persia, he gave him as his auxiliary the Carmelite Timothy Pérez, of the province of St. Angelus in Sicily. John Thaddeus also asked for Carmelite missioners, and Straccio turned to Monte Santo, appointing on April 1, 1633, Stephen of Acireale, Dominic of Castroreale, and Pacificus of Catania. But John Thaddeus died in Spain in September of the same year. Pérez, who succeeded him as bishop of Ispahan, showed little inclination to leave Spain for his see. The friars of Monte Santo too remained at home.

On July 16, 1629, the Venetian Carmelite, Peter Vespa, was named bishop of Paphos on Cyprus, but it was not until 1636 that the Sublime Porte granted him permission to proceed to his field of labors. At his request for missionaries, Straccio appointed friars of the First Institute, Marius of Siracusa and Smaragdus of Acireale, who on November 14, 1637, obtained papal permission to depart. Meanwhile, Vespa had landed in prison and was only released on payment of 400 *scudi*. On March 16, 1638, the Congregation of the Propagation of the Faith ordered his return. Vespa lingered on, but his freedom was chancy, and he obeyed a second order to return, issued the following February 19. Thus, another mission of Monte Santo died aborning.

The Institute had better luck in Dalmatia, a possession of Venice under constant pressure from the Turks. At the request of the governor of Sebenico, Straccio sent Dominic of Castroreale and Thomas of Milazzo. Permission to work in Sebenico was granted by Propaganda, November 8, 1642. After vain attempts to find a convent there, Dominic and Thomas were given the hermitage of St. Anthony in the diocese of Sebenico as a hospice for working among the refugees of Morlachia. Innocent X granted papal approval on July 13, 1646. The early years of the mission were marked by pestilence and the siege of Sebenico by the Turks. Thomas returned to Sicily and was replaced by the laybrother, Benignus of Ascoli. With better times, Dominic opened a school for the profane sciences and Christian doctrine. He died March 19, 1655.

On May 1, the prior general, Marius Venturini, sent Gregory of Sebenico, a Dalmation but a member of the province of Venice. For a while, Gregory continued Dominic's apostolate, but in 1658, he left Sebenico, where he claimed he could be of no further use, and took up residence in La Maddalena nearby, working among a group of three hundred Morlacchians who had settled there. But Gregory had little faith in the Dalmatian mission and at the end of the year returned to Venice.

Nothing further is known about "Fra. Hubert of Rupe, of the Carmelite Order, superior of the missions of the same Order in the whole diocese of Andros in the Aegean Sea," to whom Innocent XI granted faculties, July 1, 1683. His companion was Jerome of Tivoli.

The friars of Monte Santo were given some very stony soil to till, and the meagre results of their husbandry were often due to circumstances beyond their control. Yet the fact remains that they achieved little in the mission field. Real interest seems to have been lacking. Initiative came mostly from the priors general, especially the energetic Theodore Straccio.

The Provinces of Monte Santo

Meanwhile, the First Institute continued to grow. The general chapter of 1645 commissioned the provincials of Aquitaine and Touraine, Andrew of St. Francis and Leo of St. John, to examine its statutes, at the same time raising its convents to the status of an independent province. The Congregation for Bishops and Religious added its approval February 16, 1646. Licandro became the first provincial of the province of Monte Santo, named by the prior general, Leo Bonfigli, at the first provincial chapter, held in the convent of Santa Maria del Pilirello in Messina, June 6. The general chapter had left the naming of the new province to the prior general.

On May 17, 1647, the intermediate congregation of the province accepted the constitutions of the Stricter Observance with an appendix of its special statutes. On November 19, 1650, the prior general, John Anthony Filippini, approved the appendix to the constitutions. They were published under the title, *Appendices ad Constitutiones reformatas pro fratribus Carmelitis Primi Instituti provinciae Montis Sancti, confectae in comitiis provincialibus anno jubilae 1650* (Romae, typis Francisci Monetae, 1650).

After the foundation in Rome, the Institute developed mostly on the continent. Convents were acquired in Naples (1646), and Porchia in the diocese of Montalto (1646). A couple of Carmelite convents suppressed by Innocent X in 1652 were revived by the Institute: Cantalupo of the Roman province and Polizzi of the Sicilian province of St. Angelus. Cantalupo was acquired for the Institute by Celestine of Sampiero in 1662. Polizzi was granted to the reformed friars by Alexander VII, September 21, 1665. The provincial chapter of 1676 named Bernard of Ascoli, second definitor, procurator for the foundation of a convent in San Vito in Sabina.

The purchase of new property enabled the foundation of the Institute in Rome to expand. The cornerstone for a new church was laid in 1662. Pope Alexander VII had entrusted Carlo Rainaldi with the execution of a plan for two churches flanking the Via del Corso at the point where it runs into the Piazza del Popolo. The twin churches of Our Lady of Monte Santo and Our Lady of the Miracles, begun by Rainaldi, were brought to completion by Gian Lorenzo Bernini and Carlo Fontana.

In 1680, the province of Monte Santo numbered 16 convents with 84 priests, 70 brothers, 30 professed clerics, 5 novice clerics and 5 novice brothers.

Straddling the continent and the island of Sicily and encompassing the Papal States and the kingdoms of Naples and Sicily, the province was cumbersome to administer. Not lacking either was a certain reluctance of the continental Italians to be ruled from Spanish-dominated Sicily. The Sicilians resisted any suggestion of a division of the province, but in the end the continental houses were constituted the province of Monte Santo in the Papal States by decree of the Congregation for Bishops and Religious, June 19, 1705. Litigation dragged on throughout the generalate of the Frenchman, Angelus de Cambolas, whom the Sicilians blamed for their woes, and was only settled by another decree of the Congregation, November 29, 1709.

The province of Sicily included Acireale, Catania, Messina (Monte Santo), Messina (Pilirello), Gibilrossa, Palermo, Siracusa, Monforte, and Polizzi.

The province of the Papal States comprised Curinga, Ascoli, Rome, Naples, Porchia, Cantalupo, and San Vito.

During the rest of its existence the reform added no other permanent foundations.

The reform of Monte Santo produced a number of noteworthy Carmelites. An early member, Gesualdo of Catania (d. 1649) wrote *Sacred Lamentations of the Penitent Soul* (Rome, 1643). A noted preacher, Felix Bonafede occupied some of the principal pulpits of Palermo, Naples, Rome, Bologna, Florence, and Venice. Elected provincial in 1679, he died the same year. Some of his sermons achieved print. Among historians might be mentioned Timothy Fulco of Termini (1608-1680). He founded the convent in Naples and headed the province from 1666 to 1669. His *Breve et universale cronistoria del mondo creato* underwent two editions (Naples, 1669 and 1677). Philip of Sampiero wrote *The Trump of Fame, Sounding Things Human and Divine* (Naples, 1678) "for anyone who desires to know in brief the whole world." He managed to complete only one of four prospective volumes. Elected provincial in 1682, he died the following year. Andrew of Castroreale (1610-1685), perhaps the most prolific writer of the reform, was twice provincial (1658-1662, 1679-1682) and is remembered for his zeal for observance and talents as a peacemaker. He, too, was an active preacher in Sicily and on the continent, besides leaving a number of works on Mary Magdalene de' Pazzi, canonized in 1666. Bernard of Ascoli (1613-1688), of the noble family of the Cruciani, founded the convent of San Vito. For a while, he functioned as confessor to the newly founded *Teresine* of Venice. His *Alphabet of the Prophet Jeremiah* was designed to awaken penitence and contrition in the hearts of the faithful. Joseph Parascandalo, of Naples, published at the end of the 17th and beginning of the 18th century a number of interesting little volumes of verse which might bear looking into. Ignatius Bagnati (1659-1728) entered the reform of Monte Santo in Naples, but for motives of health transferred to the less severe reform of Santa Maria della Vita. In his *Vera mundi aetas* (Naples, 1742) he establishes the date of Christ's birth and of the creation of the world!

The Observance of Santa Maria della Vita

The constant efforts of the priors general to raise the level of observance in the Carmine Maggiore in Naples eventually produced results. Although seemingly irradicable abuses continued to flourish, the community came to count many dedicated religious of the highest ideals. Some of these in 1631 requested permission of the prior general, Gregory Canal, to retire to the convent of Santa Maria della Vita, one of the *grancie* or dependencies of the Carmine situated in the countryside outside the city. There, on February 2, Feast of the Purification of Our Lady, twenty-six friars, mostly from the Carmine, renewed their vows, promising to live according to a strict observance of their obligations. The ritual of the renewal of vows thereafter became an annual occurrence.

The identity of these twenty-six friars is not known, but no doubt they include some of those who immediately afterwards appear in important roles in the movement. Straccio once referred to Fra. Cyril Giaimi as the "first founder of the observance della Vita." Ventimiglia, the historian of Carmel in Italy, calls Master Cyril Candido *"il motore e primo capo."* Candido certainly was the first superior of the reform. Straccio himself should be given as much credit as anyone for the movement. It was he who wrote its special laws and followed its early steps with a concerned and practical eye.

By the end of the following year, the community had grown to such an extent that on November 13, 1632, Straccio granted it the convent of Santa Maria della Concordia, another *grancia* of the Carmine located in a less populous area of Naples. On December 20, he named Master Avertanus Crivelli his commissary for the Concordia.

On January 15, 1633, Straccio made Master Cyril Candido his commissary general over both reformed convents. Candido, who lived on only until October 14, 1634, was already commissary general over the Della Vita convent and so was the first superior general of the reform. He had formerly been prior of the

Carmine and superintendent of its *grancie*. A poet, he composed a hymn to St. Andrew Corsini, which was displayed on a placard during the celebrations for the saint's canonization held in Traspontina in 1629.

Candido's successor as commissary general of the Observance was Master Deodato Lombardo. No biographical information is available on him. He was French, or a French subject, and on this account sometimes experienced difficulty in Spanish Sicily. On Lombardo's resignation, Straccio on July 19, 1636, named Fra. Cyril Giaimi head of the reform with the title of "president." Giaimi was born in San Lorenzello and entered the Order in the Carmine Maggiore of Naples, whose prior he became.

The title of commissary general returned in use with the designation of Master John Michael Cocozza to that office, May 16, 1637. He was given as assistants with consultative vote Masters John Baptist Petronio and Deodato Lombardo. Cocozza, or de Curtis, a native of Naples, entered the novitiate there in 1622. A doctor of theology, he was versed in oriental languages, especially Hebrew. In 1647, Innocent X made him bishop of Syros in the Aegean. He resigned his see in 1655 and the following year became one of the many victims of the great plague in Naples.

When Cocozza became provincial of Naples (or Terra di Lavoro), in May of 1639, the prior general recalled Lombardo as commissary general of the Observance.

After Straccio's death in 1642, there is a gap in our information regarding the superiors of the Neapolitan observance until 1648, when Daniel Scoppa was appointed commissary general, succeeded in 1651 by Onofrio Sorrentino, who was confirmed in office for another year in 1654. In 1656 the durable Deodato is again in office, replaced in 1659 by Daniel Scoppa.

By 1635, Aversa and Cilento had accepted the observance, though the latter did not persevere. On April 16, 1636, Straccio appointed Master John Michael Cocozza prior and reformer of Sorrento. By 1661, San Lorenzello and Forino had been acquired in that order. Torre del Greco appears for the first time in the acts of the chapter of 1673. The chapter of 1712 appointed Fra. Angelico de Bernardis procurator for a new foundation at Faicchio. He was to reside at San Lorenzello until a proper convent could be built. This foundation marks the term of the growth of the reform.

In 1686, the seven convents of the Observance (Santa Maria della Vita in Naples, Santa Maria della Concordia in Naples, Aversa, Sorrento, San Lorenzello, Forino, Torre del Greco) numbered 111 friars.

The Observance showed little inclination to reform the rest of the Order. It did not welcome members of other provinces. In 1641, the Prince of Torrella offered a church and convent on his land, but the reformed friars did not wish to stray too far from Naples. "I am quite disappointed," Straccio wrote to the prince on September 28, "because I find myself cheated of the purpose for which I have so far favored this Observance, namely that it should gradually spread throughout the province." One can hardly blame the brethren for being reluctant to leave the enchanted shore of the Bay of Naples.

The reformed convents carried on their business in annual congregations, but the minutes of these meetings seem to be lost. In 1639, Straccio decreed that priors be elected there rather than in their local communities.

The Province of Santa Maria della Vita

At the general chapter of 1660, with the authorization of Pope Alexander VII the reformed convents in the Kingdom of Naples were erected into a new province under the patronage of St. Raphael. Daniel Scoppa became the first provincial. Scoppa was born in Naples, 1619. He became procurator of the Order and bishop of Nola, 1695-1703.

The general chapter of 1654 had already constituted a general *studium* of the Order the college of St. Cyril, which Straccio had erected in 1635 in the convent of Santa Maria della Vita.

Already on June 12, 1636, Straccio speaks of "decrees which I made for the good governance of this Observance." But some of the brethren were less than enthusiastic, deeming it sufficient to follow the Constitutions, "a sure sign," the prior general wrote to Giaimi on September 25, "that their spirit has grown cold, and that they do not know or do not take into account what our Rule says about works of supererogation."

"I am in doubt," he concludes, "whether the Observance is already growing old in its infancy. God grant that I am wrong." Such gloomy thoughts notwithstanding, Straccio prepared his decrees which were discussed at a congregation in May, 1637. Its observations were incorporated in a final draft. The general chapter of 1645 imposed their observance after examination by the Order's canonist, John Baptist Lezana.

The reformed houses in the kingdom of Naples had no distinctive observances; they simply set out to live the perfect common life and to devote themselves to a life of greater retirement and prayer. "The principal end," the prior general, Jerome Ari, wrote in 1662, "of our province of the Strict Observance of Santa Maria della Vita is the perfect common life." Prayer and seclusion were also stressed. The convent of Santa Maria della Vita, where all members of the reform had their initiation, featured "The Solitude," a structure with four rooms situated in a garden apart from the convent, where the friars could make ten-day retreats or otherwise retire in solitude.

Graduate degrees, the *pons asinorum* of reform, were admitted, but their privileges were curtailed. Graduates enjoyed precedence over simple friars. Masters also had *de iure* place and voice in chapters and immunity from the *tabella*, or list of weekly household tasks.

Among the members of the reformed province of Santa Maria della Vita, two laybrothers are remembered for their holy lives. Their biographer, Andrew Mastelloni, compares to the apostles John and Peter the serene and angelic Paulinus Zabatta (1606-1656) and the fiery Peter of the Cross (d. 1656).

Among spiritual writers of the reform, Cyril Giaimi (d. 1652) wrote a *Compendium of Meditations* in four parts with a discourse on the usefulness of prayer, which saw two editions (Naples, 1640 and 1643). Elisha Vasallo, active as a confessor and spiritual director at the convent of Santa Maria della Vita, wrote *The Christian Invited to Paradise* (Naples, 1643), treating the three ways (purgative, illuminative, unitive), and *The Shining Lily, Symbol of Virginity* (Naples, 1647). Lawrence Mary Brancacci (d. 1652), of the noble Neapolitan family, who had previously been a Discalced, produced an early edition of the works of St. Mary Magdalen de' Pazzi (Naples, 1643) and *Scriptural Exercises and Meditations for the Nativity of Our Lady* (Naples, 1640). Raphael Bavaro's *History of St. Joseph* (Naples, 1723) has a place in the Order's devotion to St. Joseph.

Reform in Piedmont

In 1650, the Carmelite province of Lombardy, which included the political areas of Piedmont, Lombardy, and Liguria, numbered 37 houses with 427 professed religious.

During the 17th century, the Spanish ascendency in Italy was disputed more or less effectively by France. Both powers orchestrated the rivalry of the political divisions of Italy to their own advantage, and the peninsula was in a continual state of turmoil. Piedmont and Savoy, which under its dukes was beginning to emerge as a power in Italy, was strategically located between France and Spain, besides having dynastic ambitions of its own.

In 1629, the army of Emperor Ferdinand II descended into Italy to take a hand in the question of the succession in the Duchy of Mantua. Lombardy suffered all the hardships of a foraging army portrayed by Manzoni in his *Promessi Sposi*. Pestilence followed in 1630. In establishing the novitiate of the Lombardy province in Piacenza, September 6, 1631, Straccio calls attention to the need of replacing "so many honored Masters and Fathers extinguished in the recent pestilence." In 1637, he extended the term as provincial of John Anthony Olivazzi for a year. No chapter could be held because of the poverty of the convents due to pestilence and continual war. The following year, the prior general had to appoint a provincial, John Anthony Glussiano, for the same reason.

One would think, Straccio wrote to the provincial and community of Milan, September 18, 1631, that according to the saying of St. Bernard, "*Multi cum sentiunt poenam, corrigunt culpam*," the religious would lead the laity in showing repentance as a consequence of the terrible pestilence of recent months, which removed thousands of persons. On the contrary, "instead of returning to the observance required of them, (the friars) have become more hardened in their lax way of living."

To better religious observance in Lombardy, Straccio on September 6, 1631, named Master Albert Zacchino commissary general and reformer with the task of introducing the common life at Piacenza. This house was to become a house of perfect observance, where according to papal requirements a novitiate could be established. On March 20, 1633, the prior general made Zacchino prior.

Master Louis Bolla

Reform, when it came, began in Turin, the result of the zeal of Louis Bolla. He was born in the town of Bibiana and entered the Order in Turin. When or where he acquired the doctorate is not known. He twice became prior of Turin: 1620-1624 and 1628-1635. During a visitation by the provincial, Chrysostom Marascha, September 25, 1632, the common life was introduced, "not without effort and difficulty." On May 20, 1633, Bolla was commissioned by the prior general to reform the convent. One of the earliest members of the reform was Michael of St. Joseph (1610-1680), who entered on April 8, 1635. A doctor of the university of Turin and provincial, he wrote a life of Bl. Francis, the Carmelite (Turin, 1675). Friars from outside Piedmont joined the reform, among them a Fleming, Ursmannus of St. Rocco, whom Straccio affiliated with Turin on May 26, 1636. Ursmannus (d. 1666, aged 78), who had come "to help with the observance," was subprior and heard confessions of foreigners. During the civil war under the minority of Charles

Emmanuel II and the regency of Madama Christine, Ursmannus was chaplain to the garrison. For twenty years, he functioned as pastor of the conventual church, Santa Maria della Piazza. He was also active as an exorcist.

Dominic of St. Mary

Most important of those who came to Turin to join the reform was Dominic Virano, destined to replace Bolla at its head. Born in Cherasco in 1605, Virano took the habit there in 1620. After profession, he was sent to study at Milan and Asti. He was ordained in 1629. Two years later, he began graduate studies in theology at Pavia. At the provincial chapter of 1632, Dominic was awarded the baccalaureate by the prior general, Theodore Straccio.

The young friar had already been preaching and writing for some time. After ordination, Dominic began a long and fruitful career as a confessor and spiritual director. At Pavia, he was confessor to the Carmelite monastery of the Holy Angels. Among his penitents was the mystic, Anna Pellino, on whom Dominic conferred the Third Order habit on May 20, 1632. His counsel was also sought by members of distinguished families of the nobility.

Desirous of a more committed way of life, Dominic considered entering the reform of Santa Maria della Vita in Naples or affiliating himself with the reformed convent of Piacenza, when nomination as regent in Turin by Straccio brought him into contact with Bolla's observance. He arrived in Turin on April 23, 1633, and on September 21 renewed his vows according to the reform, taking the name by which he is commonly known, Dominic of St. Mary. On September 2, 1634, Straccio appointed him master of novices in Turin. One of his novices was Paul of St. Ignatius, known for his piety and destined to become prior general of the Order.

Louis Bolla died on November 26, 1635. At the recommendation of the Infantas Christine and Mary, Straccio named Dominic prior of Turin, thus in effect placing in his hand the tiller of the reform.

The Infantas of Savoy took an active interest in the promotion of the reform; its success among the Carmelites owes much to their concern. Princess Mary lent the weight of her authority to bringing the reformed novitiate to Turin in 1634. The royal sisters were quick to recognize the spiritual worth of the novice master and to enlist his services as confessor and director. On March 27, 1635, Straccio named Mary and Christine "protectors" of the province of Lombardy, albeit he was careful to note in his register that this honorific title bestowed no jurisdiction.

On October 12, 1638, Straccio named Dominic commissary general for the reform of Dogliani, having previously confirmed him as prior of Turin. On November 21, the Observance was introduced, friars who were unwilling to accept it were referred to the provincial for placement, and Paul of St. Ignatius was made master of professed and lector in the seminary established there. "Divine service flourished once more," writes Bonaventure Blanciotti, Dominic's biographer, "religious poverty was observed as it should be, mental prayer resumed, and many other religious virtues completely restored."

Writing to Dominic on December 14, 1638, to congratulate him on the reform of Dogliani, Straccio received under his jurisdiction Turin, Dogliani, and other convents to which the reform might spread, at the same time making Dominic his commissary general for their administration. Although the reformed houses were withdrawn from the authority of the provincial, they remained part of the province of Lombardy, should be represented at the chapters, and should pay taxes.

The reform of Dominic's native convent of Cherasco proved more difficult. The community appealed to the French governor, Jauly. In spite of resistance also on the part of the citizens, reform was introduced April 11, 1641, with Paul of St. Ignatius as prior.

Colletto was reformed September 26, 1642, but only after repeated visits to overcome the objections of the community and townspeople. On February 22, 1646, Dominic introduced the reform into Asti, again placing in charge his trusted Paul of St. Ignatius. After Turin, Asti became the principal convent of the reform, but only after many years of controversy, due to the fact that not all members of the community were reformed. The reform of Vinovo came about in 1649 through the intervention of Jerome Ari, then procurator general, later prior general, himself a Piedmontese. That same year, Vinovo became a seminary of professed.

Nature and Legislation of the Reform

The scope of the reform of Turin was simply to observe the constitutions of the Order and the decrees of Clement VIII; in other words, to live the perfect common life with the prayer and recollection imposed by Clement's legislation. Dominic consistently resisted Straccio's efforts to impose other obligations.

Blanciotti states that in 1633 Straccio sent to Bolla "certain handwritten laws which other reformed Carmelites were already using." These apparently constituted the early legislation of the reform. On March 9, 1637, Straccio sent Dominic "a few decrees which I have made for the preservation of this reform," subject to the approval of the Infantas. Shortly after, on June 27, he forwarded Tuaut's Constitutions, published that year, earnestly hoping they would be kindly received. In spite of French influence in Piedmont at the time, the Aquitaine legislation proved unacceptable. A particular stumbling block was the renunciation of academic degrees and their privileges. In the end, the prior general surrendered and agreed that the Turin reform might confine itself to observing the constitutions of the Order and the decrees of Clement VIII. Nevertheless, he could not resist the temptation of a parting shot. "I must warn Your Paternity," Straccio wrote to Dominic on December 7, 1641, "that while you are doing your best to introduce academic degrees into the observance, even beforehand, you are at the same time procuring its downfall, as in fact I have experienced in the case of the observance of Naples. With time, you will repent, as did the Fathers Della Vita."

One supereragatory practice Straccio managed to impose on the reform was abstinence from meat on Monday. His purpose, the prior general explained to the members of the reform on February 10, 1639, was to take the wind out of the sails of the Mantuan Congregation, which was no better than the rest of the Order, but its members abstained from meat on Monday, and he did not want them to boast of this accomplishment over the reformed friars of the Order, who in fact led much more rigorous lives than they. Straccio's decree prescribing this practice is dated April 15, 1639. Subsequent efforts by the reformed friars to be excused from this obligation notwithstanding, the prior general remained firm.

Ultimately, Dominic himself submitted statutes which were approved July 10, 1642, by the vicar general, Albert Massari, Straccio having meanwhile died. They were again approved by the general chapter of 1645. The statutes, or *leges municipales*, like those of other reforms, modified the constitutions in points of minor importance according to the particular needs of the observance.

The same general chapter adopted the Constitutions of the Stricter Observance and ordered them observed by all reformed houses in the Order. But the Turin reform raised the same objections to these laws as they had to Straccio's. On August 25, 1647, the reformed convents of Piedmont convened their first triennial congregation at Asti under the presidency of Dominic of St. Mary. The assembled Fathers voted to reject the Constitutions of the Stricter Observance, but the vicar general, Ippolito Sessoldi, on September 23, vetoed their decision. The following general chapter of 1648 directed the Turin reform to accept the Constitutions of the Stricter Observance. Its members might acquire academic degrees, but these involved no other privilege than that of voting in the provincial chapters of Lombardy. Dominic himself had no objection to academic degrees; in fact, the previous general chapter of 1645 had granted him the doctorate.

On the Feast of the Immaculate Conception, December 8, 1648, Dominic set the example by renewing his vows according to the new constitutions. Thereafter resistance lessened; the unwanted legislation was accepted at the second triennial congregation of 1650, which also produced new municipal laws.

Last Years of Dominic of St. Mary

Due to political conditions, the convents of the Lombardy province which lay in Piedmont were governed by a vicar provincial. Dominic received this office, May 15, 1649; on May 18, 1653, he was elected provincial. In these positions, he became increasingly involved in the visitation and administration of the Lombardy province. His influence in the other political divisions of the province was less; his reform remained confined to Piedmont. Dominic did succeed in introducing the perfect common life in Genoa (novitiate), Melzi, Gavi, Novi, Cremolino, and Piacenza (novitiate). At Genoa he left Andrew Lao as commissary general.

Elected prior of Turin in 1665, Dominic survived only a few months. He died April 27.

Dominic of St. Mary was a gentle person, not given to the fierce asceticism of the times. Like that of other Italian reformers, his vision did not include a return to the contemplative ideal of the primitive Order and was confined to the restoration of regular observance.

The Reformed Province of Piedmont, 1671

Even before Dominic's death observance had fallen off. Admonitions by Jerome Ari to his native province had little or no effect. The same fate was suffered by his successor, Matthew Orlandi.

In an effort to better observance, Orlandi separated the reformed houses of Piedmont from the rest of the province. On March 18, 1671, he instituted the province of Piedmont, consisting of 11 houses: Turin, Dogliani, Cherasco, Coletto, Asti, Vinovo, Pino, Racconigi, Moncalieri, Vercelli, and Rivoli. (Nice, of the province of Provence, was allotted to Piedmont in 1674, after it opted for reform.) The first provincial chapter, convened April 23, elected Charles Mary of the Trinity provincial.

Separation from the province of Lombardy failed to improve observance in the Piedmontese reformed convents. In 1682, Anthony of the Most Holy Trinity, supported by "a good part of the religious of this province," requested the Congregation of Religious to remedy abuses and to restore the exact observance of the reformed constitutions. He suggested that the pope make a Belgian provincial, "because the Piedmontese character corresponds more closely to the Flemish." The request ended up on the desk of the prior general, Angelus Monsignani, whose indifferent health kept him close to Rome, and who contented himself with penning an exhortation to the reformed way of life. In most of the Piedmontese convents, he states in his letter of January 3, 1683, there is scarcely a sign of the Stricter Observance or of the common life. The prior general goes on to list forty-three points from the reformed constitutions which have suffered neglect.

Valentine of St. John, 1631-1691

Complaints about the state of the province and requests for an investigation continued to come. Joseph Mary of St. Berthold, prior of Turin, and Albert Miriale appealed to Innocent XI, who turned the case over to Cardinal Paluzzi degli Altieri, protector of the Order. On February 20, 1685, this prelate appointed apostolic commissary for the visitation of Piedmont a friar from the reformed province of Aquitaine, Valentine of St. John.

Valentine was accompanied on his visitation by Damascene of the Nativity of the Virgin, also of the province of Aquitaine. On December 4, 1685, he made his report. The vice of ownership has permeated the whole province. The common life is professed but not observed; all as a rule have money. The interior life is entirely lacking. Those who wish to live in recollection are held up to scorn. Mental prayer is either completely neglected or only perfunctorily performed. Silence, solitude, religious modesty, renewal of vows, the annual retreat are quite unknown. Conversation, loud talking are heard everywhere. The friars wander about the house, the town, the province. Ambition, factions divide the province. These are the cause of proprietorship, the callousness of superiors, and temerity of subjects who bear arms, go hunting, strike their superiors, leave the convent without permission. The administration of the province is corrupt. Clothing is luxurious and scandalous in form, with colored garments showing through open tunics. The careful selection and training of candidates in the novitiate, *professorium*, and houses of study are neglected. Of the 84 priests in the province only 44 are confessors, some of them quite ignorant of doctrine. Idleness is rampant. In the small houses there is hardly a sign of religious life.

The province, Valentine concludes, badly needs reform. There are about fifteen friars willing to observe the reformed constitutions without any restrictions. Among them, the means can be found to educate the young and restore regular discipline. For this purpose, the large convent of Asti and the small convent of Cherasco are sufficient.

The visitator sent his report both to the prior general and the cardinal protector. Monsignani's reaction was to compose, January 15, 1686, some decrees of reform to be published at the coming provincial chapter. Altieri, on the other hand, authorized by the Congregation for Bishops and Religious, published on January 28, eleven decrees embracing Valentine's plan of reform and adding in modified form some of Filippini's articles for its realization. Those judged suitable by the visitator are to be gathered in the convents of Asti, Dogliani, and Cherasco, where after a retreat of ten days they are to renew their profession before the Blessed Sacrament and promise the literal observance of the Constitutions of the Stricter Observance without obligation to municipal laws or other legislation. Privileges attached to academic degrees are to be renounced. The three convents will house a novitiate, seminary (house of professed), and a house of studies, and will be governed by a vicar provincial immediately under the jurisdiction of the prior general. The office of the vicar, who enjoys the usual powers of the provincial over his own subjects, is to remain until the province is entirely converted to the Stricter Observance, even though the provincial is a member of the reform (a problem occasioned by the articles of Filippini). Every three years another house of the province may be added to the reform. The definitors and the provincial's *socius* must be elected from the reform. Reformed friars may not be sent to unreformed convents, and vice versa.

Valentine presided at the provincial chapter convened on February 15, 1686. Joseph Mary of St. Berthold, the instigator of the visitation, emerged as provincial by a large majority. At the fourth session, Valentine published the cardinal's letter and another of the prior general appointing him vicar provincial. The definitory received these decisions with due reverence, but reserved the right of recourse to the cardinal and prior general "for a more genuine (*synceriori*) explanation of the statements and presuppositions in the aforementioned decree." The chapter made no decrees for the reform of the province as a whole.

Joseph Mary and others like him who saw the need for the improvement of religious observance in the province opposed Valentine's plan from the start. They thought the establishment of a vicariate divisive. Still less did they care to embrace the Stricter Observance. The old battle cry went up in favor of the municipal laws and the observance of the Order's unreformed constitutions with the decrees of Clement VIII.

At the general chapter which met on May 23, 1686, a committee composed of representatives from reformed provinces indeed commented on Altieri's directives and ended by being "unanimously agreed that (the cardinal's decrees) can be confirmed by His Most Holy Lord." On July 4, 1686, the pope's coveted confirmation was forthcoming.

Altieri's reform was off to a shaky start.

The Second Reform of Piedmont

Twelve friars had volunteered to live according to the Stricter Observance. The provincial placed Asti at their disposal, and Valentine took over the formation of novices. He himself set the example in everything, performing even the most humble tasks in the community.

In August, 1687, Valentine appointed Louis of St. Mary Magdalen de' Pazzi vicar provincial and Simon of St. Gerard prior of Asti. Simon was to prove a durable warrior in the battles of the vicariate with the province, but Louis showed rather less than adequate interest in the affairs of the reform. He was frequently to be found at Carignano as spiritual director of the *pinzochera*, Frances Pellianda, a mystic and seer of dubious pedigree. He himself began to show suspicious signs of supernatural favors. Obviously, Valentine's presence still could not be dispensed with. After several shorter extensions, Altieri prolonged his faculties as commissary for two years.

Dogliani was conveyed to the reform without opposition, September 26, 1686, but the community of Cherasco held out against all appeals, until they capitulated in June, 1687, on instructions from the nunzio at Turin.

Valentine convened the first triennial congregation of the vicariate at Cherasco, July 27, 1687.

On May 8, 1688, Cardinal Altieri appointed Elisha of Mount Carmel vicar, and Damascene of the Nativity his assistant. The following June, Valentine returned to Aquitaine, where he became prior of Mortemart before his death in October, 1691.

Valentine seems to have been a retiring, unassuming person, thoughtful of others, and prayerful. "Whenever he could legitimately show someone a favor," Blanciotti writes, "to do so was one of his greatest delights. To speak to him once was to remain a captive of his affectionate nature. Were it not that his office (of commissary general) brought on him many trials, all, moved by his gentle countenance, would have embraced him as a loving father, a most prudent pastor." He performed a thankless task in a spirit of lively faith.

The reform movement lost its initiator and constant supporter in 1698, when death claimed Cardinal Altieri.

The province had always claimed that observance in the reform was no better than its own. The Oratorian, John Dominic of St. Philip Perardo, appointed visitator of Piedmont by the prior general, Caspar Pizzolanti, in 1728, declared this to be so. He further discovered that the members of the province were willing to observe the Constitutions of the Stricter Observance. Nothing lay in the way of the unification of the province. This Pope Benedict XIII decreed on March 26, 1729. For the first time, the province styled itself "of the Stricter Observance." Thus, ironically the goal of all Valentine's labors and trials was realized by the stroke of a pen. One may hope that, if not at first, at least with time, the lives of the Piedmont friars would have met the approval of their zealous reformer.

The reformed province of Piedmont produced many men of virtue and learning. During the century, it gave three priors general to the Order: Jerome Ari (1603-1667), Paul of St. Ignatius (1614-1704), Charles Philibert Barberi (1652-1722). Notable writers include Jerome of St. Clement Aimo who composed a philosophy course according to John Baconthorpe (Turin, 1667, 8 v.) and performed a signal service to the Italian provinces by translating Mark of the Nativity's *Directory for Novices* (Venice, 1686, 2d ed., Turin, 1757) and *Manual for the Third Order* (Venice, 1686, 2d ed. Nice, 1755). Theobald of the Annunciation Ceva (1697-1744) compiled an anthology of sonnets (Turin, 1735) and a posthumous anthology of poems (Venice, 1756), both of which enjoyed considerable popularity and underwent numerous editions until the middle of the 19th century. Theodore of the Purification, John of St. Joseph (a professed cleric), and Peter Thomas of the Nativity are remembered for their holy lives.

Besides Jerome Aimo, spiritual writers of the province include Stanislaus of St. Anthony, novice master at Turin who died in 1648 at the early age of thirty-six. He was the confessor of the Capuchin nun, Mother Vercellana, and for her composed a poem *Pious Lament in the Dark Night* included in her biography. Pius of John Baptist wrote *The Wise Diana*; or the *Soul Devoted to God through Mental Prayer and Holy Communion* (Caramaniole, 1671). Joseph Anthony of St. Elijah, active as an apostolic missionary throughout Piedmont, published a number of popular books of devotion to Sts. Anne and Joachim.

The Reform of Santa Maria della Scala del Paradiso

At the end of our period there occurred, again in the Sicilian province of St. Albert, a final movement of reform, due to three persons initially external to the Order: Salvatore Statella, Jerome Terzo, and Carmela Montalto.

Andrew Statella (1678-1728) was a cadet son of a noble family of Spaccaforno (modern Ispica). His father, Marchese Francis III, sent him to Rome to seek his fortune after graduation from the University of Catania, but his death in 1710 brought Andrew back to his native hearth. At this crucial moment of his life, he made the acquaintance of a rugged hermit, Fra. Jerome Terzo, who urged him to follow an ecclesiastical career. Andrew took his advice, gave himself up to prayer and penance and the following year, 1711, was ordained to the priesthood.

The twenty-seven year old hermit, five years Andrew's junior, was in every way a contrast to the sophisticated young nobleman and already old in the ways of the spirit. Matthew Terzo (1683-1758), like his father, a cobbler by trade, had from his earliest years been attracted to a celibate life of prayer and solitude. In 1707, he was accepted among the hermits of Sts. Jerome and Conrad, four miles outside his native Noto, by the superior, Alfio of Melilli, and given the name Jerome. However, the neophyte hermit, afflicted by the wanderlust seemingly endemic to the vocation, soon transferred with three companions to the nearby sanctuary of Santa Maria della Scala del Paradiso. After Alfio's death, the archbishop of Siracusa, Asdrubal Termini, named Fra. Jerome superior of all the hermits in the archdiocese. As the community grew, Jerome decided to enlarge the hermitage and sanctuary, and it was in connection with an inheritance left by a certain Francis Randazzo that the hermit found himself in Noto, when he met Statella.

After ordination, Statella does not seem to have been attached to a particular parish. Intensely dedicated to prayer and ministry, he used his private means to construct churches and alleviate the poor. His wish to found a *ritiro*, or house for a community of priests, remained unfulfilled. Among the persons he directed in the spiritual life was a young noblewoman, Carmela Montalto (1688-1780), foundress in 1717 of a *conservatorio* in Siracusa dedicated to Our Lady of Mount Carmel. (Conservatories, or communities of sisters with simple vows, will be discussed in the chapter on Carmelite nuns.) She, too, was a friend of Brother Jerome Terzo, who was credited with the cure in 1715 of her brother, Albert.

Carmela's hope was to convert her conservatory into a cloistered monastery under the direction of the Carmelite Order, but there were no reformed friars at hand. There were not wanting in the province of St. Albert priests and brothers desirous of a more committed religious life, Albert Ragusa, Xavier Materazzo, the provincial himself, Clement Castiglione, and others, but lack of financial means so far had hindered the realization of their ideals. Money was no problem for the wealthy Prince Statella, who offered to provide for the support of two convents of twelve friars each and to enter the reform himself, once it was established, for he had always wanted to be a Carmelite.

Castiglione won the consent of his definitory for the reform of the province's convents in Siracusa and Spaccaforno. The permission of the Sacred Congregation for Religious Discipline, granted December 23, 1723, was confirmed by Pope Benedict XIII, July 27, 1724. According to these authorizations, Siracusa was to be the novitiate, Spaccaforno the house for professed. The two reformed houses were to remain under the jurisdiction of the prior general until a vicariate could be erected, their priors being elected by their respective communities. Every three years, another convent of the province was to be assigned to the reform. Obviously, these conditions derive from the articles of Filippini and Cardinal Altieri.

The reform adopted the Constitutions of the Stricter Observance (Catania, 1750). This may have been the personal choice of the reformers. Statella was not only much given to prayer and solitude but was also an admirer of John of St. Samson, translated several of his works, and would have translated them all, had he not been prevented by death. On the other hand, there was the precedent of Piedmont, where Altieri's offensive on behalf of the Stricter Observance was in full swing.

On November 15, 1724, the prior general, Caspar Pizzolanti, added Scicli to the reform, thus opening the way for the election of a vicar provincial. Albert of the Holy Family Ragusa, elected in 1725, became the first vicar of the reform, followed in 1728 by Xavier of the Blessed Sacrament Materazzo. With the reform thus firmly established, Statella himself donned the Carmelite habit, May 12, 1726, receiving the name Salvatore of the Blessed Trinity.

Differences with the province were not long in coming. Where the desire for reform was not sufficiently widespread, the Articles of Filippini, designed to convert a province by gradual stages, inevitably wreaked havoc. The new provincial, Francis Arena, considered it his bounden duty to protect his province against the inroads of reform. The usual friction areas proved sensitive: restriction of the reception of candidates to the reformed novitiate, the obligation to cede convents regularly to the reform, the mandatory election of certain officials from the reform. The reader need not be burdened with all the details of the quarrel; suffice it to say that on December 15, 1727, Benedict XIII imposed silence on the opponents of the reform. Yet he subsequently gave ear to Arena and on the following March 16 peremptorily ordered the coming general chapter to provide for the harmony of the province.

On hearing rumors of Arena's success, the reformers sent to the general definitory, which was to meet at Ferrara in May of 1728, no less a representative than the father of the reform, Salvatore Statella. His presence at the sessions would no doubt have been to the advantage of the reform, but when he got as far as Rimini, he took to bed "with pulmonary fever and asthma" and in a matter of days was dead. "During the five days in which he was tormented by his infirmity," a witness, Fr. Joseph Caffarelli, attests, "he remained always resigned to the will of God, nor did he ever complain of his discomfort, great though it was." He adds: "He made no *sproprio* (account of his possessions), because he was already deprived of everything and had no money."

With the field left clear to Arena, the definitory settled the problem in favor of the province. The reformed were subjected to the provincial. The reformed rejoined by obtaining from Benedict's successor, Clement XII, a decree dated November 7, 1731, once again imposing silence on the opposition. When the reformers received from the Sacred Congregation for Religious Discipline, on October 2, 1732, the annulment of the decrees of the general definitory of Ferrara, the way was opened for the peaceful pursuit of reform.

The Province of Santa Maria della Scala del Paradiso

Catania was ceded to the reform in 1731, Caltagirone at an unknown date. On May 2, 1741, the Sacred Congregation for Religious Discipline added Noto and Augusta.

In 1723, Brother Jerome Terzo finished the construction of his hermitage of Santa Maria della Scala del Paradiso and with time thought of affiliating it to the growing reform of Siracusa. On February 20, 1741, the Sacred Congregation for Religious Discipline made the hermitage a novitiate and granted permission to receive twelve clerical and twelve lay novices. In May, together with most of the other hermits, Jerome himself donned the Carmelite habit. The novice master was Bernard Mary of St. Joseph. Out of humility, Brother Jerome refused ordination and spent the rest of his long life in his beloved hermitage. It must have been a source of some satisfaction to him that the reformed province was given the name of his Virgin of the Ladder to Heaven.

On July 27, 1741, Benedict XIV raised the reformed vicariate to the status of a province under the title of Santa Maria della Scala del Paradiso, comprising the eight convents of Siracusa, Spaccaforno, Scicli, Catania, Caltagirone, Augusta, Noto, and the hermitage of Santa Maria della Scala del Paradiso. Except for Piazza, reformed in 1767, the province experienced no further growth.

The province did not admit academic degrees.

The province of Santa Maria della Scala del Paradiso is the one example of the fully successful implementation of the Stricter Observance south of the Alps. The convents which embraced the reform experienced a profound renewal of religious life. In spite of their poverty, or rather because of it, the reformed friars raised imposing churches and convents, sometimes on the ruins left by the earthquake of 1693. Often reforms only managed to add more convents to a society already heavily burdened with the support of religious. This reform successfully restricted itself to the renewal of the province of St. Albert. Pity that so few convents accepted its benevolent ministrations.

Sister Carmela long outlived her two friends. In 1738, her dream finally came true, and her conservatory was constituted a cloistered monastery under the constitutions of the Stricter Observance.

Chapter 9

Carmel in Baroque Spain and Portugal

Spain after the death of Philip II had passed the peak of her power, but still remained one of the great forces, political and cultural, of Europe. Our period (1600-1750) is filled with endless and inconclusive wars, particularly with her powerful neighbor, France, as she struggled to protect her possessions in the Netherlands, Franche Comté, and Italy. Even after a French pretender, Philip V, ascended the throne (1701), Spain became embroiled with the other great European nations, concerned about this concentration of strength. Under the Bourbons, however, the disastrous economic condition of the country improved a good deal.

In the seventy-five years from 1575 to 1650 the number of religious in Spain, especially in the South, increased enormously. While we must believe that this phenomenon was a grace and a sign of spiritual vitality, it had its negative aspects economically, which became all the more pertinent as religious fervor declined. Reform had the effect of adding more religious Orders rather than improving existing ones. While country districts were neglected pastorally, religious tended to congregate in the cities and towns, where they constituted a serious drain on the local economy. Established religious houses and the secular clergy saw their means of subsistence further threatened by the arrival of the new Orders. The Cortes and municipal authorities constantly renewed needed legislation regulating new religious foundations, but the prudence of the Spanish kings, especially Philip III (1598-1621), was not equal to their piety, and dispensations continued to flow with royal largesse. Local civil pride and rivalry among the nobles also motivated the founding of monasteries and convents.

For the Carmelite provinces of Spain, the 17th century was their golden era. After a period of expansion in the 16th century, the Order in Spain acquired relatively few foundations, but those already existing were well populated, sometimes more than the individual convent should bear economically. Much care was bestowed on education. Examples of learning and virtue abound.

Spain and Portugal were the only nations in which the Order was represented which did not produce at least one province renewed by the ideals of the Catholic Reformation. One would like to think that the reason for this was that the need for renewal was not so great as in some other countries. The 16th century visitations by Audet's commissaries, Rossi, and Chizzola had not been without effect. While Spain conducted warfare throughout the world, her boundaries remained at peace. The Carmelite Order there had not the desperate motive to improve inspired by utter abasement.

The Province of Andalusia

The populous province of Andalusia, the largest in the Order, counted 25 friaries. The first half of the 17th century added only five of these; after this, growth ceased entirely: Seville (Carmen), Gibraleón, Escacena, Ecija, Jaén, Antequera, Trigueros, San Juan del Puerto, Cordova, Granada, Alcalà de Guadaira, Carmona, Utrera, Castro del Rio, Osuna, Aracena, Alhama, Villalba de Alcor, Murcia, Jerez de la Frontera, Seville (San Alberto, 1602), Cordova (San Roque, 1614), Juncal (1610),

San Lucar de Barrameda (1641), Seville (Santa Teresa, 1641).

Ten monasteries of nuns lay within the confines of the province, two founded in the 17th century: Ecija, Granada, Seville (Incarnation, later Bethlehem), Antequera, Aracena, Osuna, Utrera (1580), Seville (Santa Ana, transferred from Paterno del Campo, 1594), Villalba de Alcor (1619), Cañete La Real (1662). The latter two were founded as reformed monasteries following the constitutions of the Stricter Observance. Villalba also had statutes printed in 1639.

At the intermediate congregation of 1674, the provincial, Joseph de Velasco, was able to report that the province numbered 868 friars and 350 nuns in seven monasteries. Whatever the population of the province before this date (no earlier statistics are available), the figure represents a high point, and membership declined thereafter, though not drastically. In 1729, the province still counted 781 friars, novices not included. Numbers were no problem. The many convents were well stocked with friars; it was a small house that did not count 20 members. In 1686, the two smallest houses, Gibraleón and San Juan del Puerto, had 14 members each. The problem was excess of members whom the incomes of the convents could not support. Every once in a while, a moratorium was called on the reception of novices in an effort to keep numbers down. More effective was the scythe of the grim reaper. Statistics are at hand for the number of deceased between 1679 and 1727, a macabre commentary on life expectancy in those times. Every year, death eased the strain on the community budget by from 20 to 40 mouths.

In 1606, Henry Silvio visited the friaries of Jaén, Granada, Castro del Rio, Cordova, Ecija (also the nunnery), Carmona, Seville (the Casa Grande, St. Albert's College and the two nunneries), Alcalá, Utrera (also the nunnery) and the nunnery of Antequera. He held the provincial chapter on April 30 and published his decrees of reform. His visit raised expectations of reform among the more fervent, but had no immediate effect.

Master Diego de Miranda, d. 1644

A pioneer of reform in Andalusia was Master Diego de Miranda (d. 1644). A native of Seville, he was professed there in 1578. He was a *presentatus* lecturing in theology, when Chizzola visited the Carmen in 1595. Before his election as provincial, he had been prior of Granada and of Antequera, rector of St. Albert's College in Seville and first definitor. Himself an exemplary religious, he tried by every means to promote observance in the province. In this he must have had some support, for he was elected provincial, though not without resistance and recourse to the nunzio on the part of those who did not share his ideals.

As provincial, Master Diego set aside for reform the convents of Jaén, Antequera, Utrera, and St. Albert's College in Seville. On July 3, 1617, Sebastian Fantoni granted his authorization, adding his approval of a "*vivendi formulam.*" At the time, Theodore Straccio, then procurator general, was visiting Spain. It is not unlikely that from him Miranda received the support needed to launch his project. Apparently it met with much opposition, for he resigned as provincial "for the sake of peace." On June 4, 1618, Fantoni appointed Master Francis Noyeda in his place.

Lector at St. Albert's College at this time was Francis de Villalobos (1585-1618). A native of Cordova, where he was professed in the Carmelite convent, September 29, 1602, he was as devoted to prayer and penance as he was to learning.

Among the members of the Jaén community at this time was Diego Granado (1582-1620). Born in Gibraleón, he entered the Order there and made his studies at St. Albert's College, Seville. He lived in great poverty and simplicity. His cell contained only the barest necessities, his garments were rough. He asked to be assigned to the remote convent of El Juncal to devote himself to prayer in solitude. In 1617, Miranda sent him to the reformed convent of Jaén. Here Granado also distinguished himself by his simple but effective preaching.

Joseph Castrillo (1560-1622) belonged to a noble family of Jaén. In 1576, he joined the Discalced Carmelites in Alcalá de Henares, where he was attending the university. At the novitiate in Seville, he received the name Joseph of Jesus and Mary. He served as prior in a number of convents, as vicar of Portugal, and as visitator of Lower Andalusia. In 1600, he was appointed to a committee of seven for the revision of the constitutions. At the chapter of the Spanish Congregation, which followed in 1602, Joseph opposed the amalgamation of the two Andalusian provinces. Perhaps this was the beginning of his disaffection with the Discalced. When the visit of Henry Silvio to Spain in 1606 raised hopes of reform in the Order, Joseph transferred to the observant province of Andalusia, retaining the name Joseph but reverting to his family name (1609). He had to wait almost a decade for the cherished reform to be realized. In 1617, he retired to the reformed convent in his native Jaén, where he died five years later.

Around this time, there was a brisk exchange of members between the Discalced Congregation of Spain and the Old Observance.

On August 15, 1628, Gregory Canal made Diego de Miranda commissary general for the reform of Antequera. But he was not alone in reforming zeal, for the same day the prior general approved statutes for the reform of Escacena submitted by the provincial, John Sobrino. Canal warned him, however, that he did not want the reformation of this convent to interfere with the reform of others. The habit was not to be changed. Likewise, the general rejected certain unspecified censures imposed by the statutes.

On October 15, 1634, Theodore Straccio, now prior general, appointed Miranda, rector of St. Albert's College, Seville, his commissary for reform.

Meanwhile, Jaén had lapsed into the old ways. On July 6, 1636, Straccio wrote a letter of encouragement to its unnamed prior who was considering reviving the reform. He could count, the general promised him, on his support and that of the cardinal and the provincial.

Diego de Miranda died in 1644. Three years previously, advanced in age and blind, he had realized the reformed foundations of San Lucar and the College of St. Teresa outside Seville. On November 21, 1642, Pope Urban VIII approved the conditions laid down in the foundation of St. Teresa's. The general chapter of 1645 ordered the conditions observed, adding that the provincial could not remove reformed friars from the convent or hinder those who wished to enter there.

The Reformed Vicariate of Andalusia

Another center of reform in the province was San Juan del Puerto. There, on August 27, 1637, seven priests and five laybrothers undertook to lead the perfect common life. The prior was Master Christopher Eslava. "Observances," dated July 18, 1639, concern the divine office, mental prayer two hours a day, examination of conscience, use of the discipline, renunciation of possessions, austerity of life, equality of all, silence, solitude, care of the sick, schedule of the day and other practices. Leo Bonfigli added his approval, January 9, 1643.

One of the original members of the community of San Juan was Francis Rodas (1570-1639), a native of Seville. He followed the profession of his father, a merchant engaged in the trade of the Indies. When his ship burned in the harbor of Cadiz, leaving him impoverished, Francis thought he recognized the hand of God and set about fulfilling a neglected vow to become a religious. After trying his vocation with the Discalced in Seville, he entered the old Order, making his profession at Antequera in 1598. A smattering of Latin sufficed for ordination to the priesthood in 1601, after which Francis joined the community of St. Albert's in Seville. The former merchant, to the surprise of all, proved to be a man of simplicity and openness. He insisted on turning over all his earnings, though the common life was not the practice in the convent. Although he had not followed the usual courses in philosophy and theology, he acquired a certain knowledge of moral theology to aid his native good sense and was much sought after as a spiritual guide. When the reform began at San Juan in 1637, he immediately volunteered in spite of his age and infirmities. These shortly forced him to return to St. Albert's College, where he had spent his life and where he died an edifying death in 1639.

The remnants of Miranda's reform rallied around the new observance.

John Anthony Filippini took steps to assure the spread of reform in Andalusia by applying his "Articles." On October 18,1650, he named Fray Christopher Beltrán vicar provincial of the reformed convents of St. Teresa of Seville, San Juan del Puerto, San Lucar del Barrameda, and Castro del Rio. But here, as in some other cases, the acceptance of the constitutions of the Stricter Observance raised difficulties. Also, the reform did not want to sever ties definitely with the province. Quite unexpectedly, in this province with its history of discord, the reform caused no disturbance. This may have been due to the personality of Beltrán, who governed the reform for many years and had no pretensions about his rights. The reform settled down to an easy relationship with the province and made no further progress.

The attitude toward reform of representative members of the province may be gleaned from a letter of Master Peter de Quesada, former Discalced, to Filippini. In the past thirty-six years, he writes on May 10, 1650, eight reforms have failed and the ninth is in the process of following suit. Meanwhile, necessary reform is neglected in the province itself. It would be far better to improve observance in essentials than to waste time on works of supererogation.

The provincial chapter of 1653 permitted the reformed community of Castro del Rio to exchange convents with El Juncal. The general chapter of 1648, desiring "that the reform of convents of our Order by divine favor daily grow and increase," had ordered it perfectly introduced into El Juncal.

At the general chapter of 1660, the provincial, Master Barnabas de Las Ruelas, resigned for reasons of health. The chapter appointed Master Eustace Gutiérrez provincial and also named a new definitory. El Juncal was among nine houses which appealed to the nunzio of Spain against this action of the general chapter. At a chapter held at Ecija, May 6, 1661, Master Alphonse de Figueroa was elected provincial.

A new provincial vicar for reform, Master Roderick Crespo, had been appointed on the retirement or death of Beltrán, who for some time had been asking to be relieved of his duties. When Crespo rallied to the rebels, along with the reformed convent of El Juncal the other three reformed houses refused him obedience.

Jerome Ari and the Reform

The new prior general, Jerome Ari, took in hand the slack Andalusian reform.

He entered the province from Toledo (Castile) at Cordova on May 4, 1664. Besides the two houses in that city he visited Ecija, Carmona, Seville (the three friaries and two monasteries of nuns), Osuna, and Antequera, where he convened the provincial chapter, May 25. After the chapter, he passed through Granada and Murcia to the province of Aragon.

At the chapter, Master Bartholomew de Vivero was elected provincial. The acts reveal no special problems in the province, the usual regulations were made concerning divine office, the practice of mental prayer, chapter of faults, records of Mass offerings, and religious garb. Strikingly, no shortcomings are noted in the observance of poverty.

The prior general gave special consideration to the reform. As in other cases, his concern was to discover to what extent it was real. The provincial was to visit the reformed convents carefully and determine which friars "truly and from the heart profess the common life and observe the decrees for reform made in those convents." Moreover, he should find out whether the communities were large enough to carry out perfect reform. Habits should be of rougher material but not differ much from the habits worn by unreformed friars. The provincial should inquire whether the reformed are willing to follow the constitutions of the Stricter Observance. Fathers Christopher and Clement, of the Gallo-Belgian province, who were in Madrid on business, should be fetched to the convent of St. Teresa in Seville to instruct its members and dispose them to accept the Stricter Observance. The prior general would later decide whether it was feasible to follow the same procedure in other houses. St. Teresa's was to be the novitiate; Fray Peter de Augilar, the novice master. San Juan del Puerto was designated a house of studies for the arts and theology.

No mention is made of a vicar for the reform. An alternative agreement was evidently reached, by which the fourth definitor would instead be chosen from the reform. In 1676, Francis of the Conception, when elected first definitor, on being challenged, spontaneously accepted the fourth place in the definitory.

In 1672, Orlando appointed Master John de Noces to conduct the third visitation of the provincialate of John de Castilla. As a result of his visit, the chapter of the following year reported unfavorably on the reformed convents. Since 1649 (that is, since the institution of the Stricter Observance), the reform, it told the prior general, had been such only in name. "Because of the penury and want of the aforementioned convents, devotion, the common life and spirit (which are the essence of reform) not only have been weakened but have been completely abandoned. St. Teresa's and San Lucar were founded on the condition that they would observe the common life and reform, but because of the deficiency mentioned above, this desire of the pious founders has not been carried out." San Juan del Puerto and Carmel in El Juncal labor under the same difficulty. The former is situated in a poverty-stricken hamlet, the latter in a remote desert. Oppressed by want, the religious are obliged to go about seeking alms and are more interested in their own needs than the community's. The common life has disappeared. No one is willing to be prior. The exhortations of the visitator had fallen on deaf ears. Father General is advised that the reform serves only to divide the province.

Later Projects of Reform

After his election as prior general, Paul of St. Ignatius made another attempt to breathe life into the Andalusian reform, ordering it to be restored to its original fervor. The provincial chapter of 1688 declared this to be impossible "because of the calamities of the times." Instead, it composed a "formulary", outlining a feasible plan of reform. Nevertheless, the provincial by his own account, did not despair of reviving the reform. At the annual meeting of the definitory of 1690, he was happy to report that Master Peter de Villanueva, prior of San Juan del Puerto, where the reform had originated, thought he had a good chance of restoring the common life as it had been first observed.

In 1714, the provincial, Andrew de Rojas, was able to announce to the definitory that some friars wished to live according to the Stricter Observance, and that he had assigned them the convent of Mount Carmel at El Juncal, as apt for this form of life. The definitory gave thanks to almighty God, from whom all good gifts come, and recommended the project to the care of the provincial.

A visitation of the province carried out in 1710 by Master Alphonse Galvez revealed no serious mispractices to be corrected. There is no mention of reform among the friars; the four convents formerly considered reformed differ in no respect from the other houses of the province. In fact, the friars at El Juncal, more than in other places, are obliged to absent themselves from the convent to minister to the abandoned inhabitants of those remote parts.

Among the nuns, Villalba and Cañete are still described as reformed. Concerning the nineteen sisters of Cañete, Galvez wrote: "Not only did we find nothing to emend, but rather much to raise our hearts to God who has given us such a choir of angels in human form to admire, each of them showing forth a compendium of the religious virtues."

On this note, we leave our account of reform in the province of Andalusia.

The Province of Castile

To St. Teresa, meditating her first foundation of Discalced friars in 1567, it seemed that the Castilian province was dying out. Her erroneous impression is sometimes taken for fact. In the second half of the 16th century, the Castilian Carmelites shared in the religious ferment of Spain's golden age, adding nine new houses. Except for the founding of a desert house at Piélago a century later, the Castilian province grew no more thereafter: Toledo, Requena, Avila, San Pablo de la Moraleja, Santa María de los Valles, Salamanca, Medina del Campo (1557), Valladolid (1560), Valderas (1566), Alcalá de Henares (1567), Madrid (1574), La Alberca (1587), Valdeolivas (1588), Valdemoro (1589), Segovia (1593), Piélago (1682).

To the monasteries for women which had been in existence in St. Teresa's time (the Incarnation at Avila, where she entered the Order, Fontiveros in the birthplace of St. John of the Cross and Piedrahita) two were added in Madrid: Las Maravillas and Las Baronesas.

At the time of Silvio's visit in 1606, the province numbered 436 friars and 136 nuns. By 1762, the membership of the province had risen to 617 friars in 15 houses.

The Reformed Houses of Valdemoro and Piélago

Castile was only slightly brushed by the reform movement of the Order.

In 1606, Henry Silvio personally visited Salamanca, Medina, San Pablo, Avila (also the Incarnation), and Madrid. Everywhere, and in the chapter which elected Master Ambrose Vallejo provincial, the prior general promulgated the reform of Clement VIII, prescribing the perfect common life, meditation, and strict observance of the cloister. Silvio's exhortations evoked no observable response in the province; neither did any greater success attend upon the efforts of Theodore Straccio, who during his visitation in 1617 here as elsewhere must have assigned some house or houses for reform.

After the institution of the Stricter Observance and its constitutions, the general chapter of 1648 ordered several provinces to initiate reform. In Castile, Requena and Medina were earmarked for reform. We may believe the Castilian Lezana, writing eight years later, when he states that Requena was among the more observant convents of the province.

In May, 1652, reform was introduced in Valdemoro. Details of this development are lacking, but one of its promoters is known to have been Fray Blas Martin, confessor of the devout *beata*, Maria del Campo. Miguel de la Fuente entered the Order here in 1593, when the convent is described by his biographer, Juan de San Angel, as "of the strictest observance," having been founded only four years earlier according to the reform implanted by John Baptist Rossi. When Jerome Ari visited the province in 1664, he instructed the provincial, John García, to provide apt subjects for the offices of prior, subprior, sacristan, and bursar, endowed the convent with special voting rights, and ordered the continuance of the Arts there. For the first time, there is mention of John Gómez Barrientos, appointed lector of the arts, who became the promoter of reform at Piélago.

A hermit by the name of Francis de San Vincente offered to the Carmelites his hermitage situated at Piélago in the diocese of Avila, but the provincial, Salvador Múndula, rejected his proposal. In 1684, Múndula was succeeded by Gómez Barrientos who immediately accepted the hermit's offer when he repeated it. Located in a charming little valley between the highest peaks of the Sierra de San Vincente, the remote hermitage was ideally suited for the contemplative life. On August 26, 1687, the site was taken over by a community of ten under the prior, Manuel de Paredes, nephew of the famous preacher, Bernard de Paredes (d. 1661). Another member of the pioneer community was John of the Holy Angel Llamas, editor of the work of Michael de la Fuente and author of a commentary on the Rule (Madrid, 1717).

On June 17, 1686, Gómez Barrientos had been made commissary general of Piélago and Requena with the usual status of independence from the provincial. Reform of Requena did not come about.

The provincial chapter of 1688 is known to have made decrees regulating the relationship of the reform and its commissary to the province, which, however, have not come down to us.

During his visitation of the province, 1693-1694, the prior general, John Feijóo de Villalobos, a native son, ordered the "primitive institute," the Rule of St. Albert, and the strict common life introduced at Valderas, "where, though unworthy, we donned the habit," at Medina, "where we made our profession and where the Discalced Carmelite reform of St. Teresa and St. John of the Cross originated," at Requena, and at San Pablo. Within a year, the reform observed at Piélago was to be introduced at Los Valles.

Although no mention is made of Valdemoro, the prior general decreed the restoration of its observance and appointed Marcellinus Fernández de Quiros his commissary over the convent.

The designs of the prior general for the reform of his native province remained unfulfilled.

The Concordat of 1700

In 1696, Feijóo renamed Gómez Barrientos commissary and vicar general for Piélago and Valdemoro. The reform of Valdemoro remained in abeyance, in spite of the fact that in 1697 Gómez Barrientos again became provincial. The provincial chapter of 1700, at which he lapsed from office, drew up a concordat between the province and the reform, ordering the reform of Valdemoro and regulating the rights and obligations of the province and the reform.

John Gómez Barrientos, father of the reform, ended his laborious and fruitful life on March 3, 1703. His successor, Fray Anthony of St. Joseph Cabrera, confirmed in office as commissary general and vicar provincial by Clement XI, was immediately confronted with an attempt on the part of the new provincial, Joseph de La Cuerda, to incorporate the two reformed houses into the province. This maneuver failed, but La Cuerda did manage to have the office of vicar provincial withdrawn.

Thereafter, the reform continued in peaceful possession of its two convents, but it spread no further and experienced only a tenuous existence at Valdemoro.

The general chapter of 1728 granted the request of the reformed friars to be allowed to send their students and lectors to the colleges of the Observants, as well as to acquire degrees according to the laws of the reform.

Brother Francis of The Cross, 1585-1647

A remarkable example of piety in the Castilian province was Brother Francis of the Cross. He was born in Mora in the diocese of Toledo and after several unsuccessful attempts to enter religious life was finally accepted as a brother at La Alberca. He had the good fortune to obtain as his spiritual director John de Herrera, disciple of Michael de la Fuente, who directed him according to the principles he had learned from his master.

Brother Francis felt a special attraction to the cross. But the basic element of his spirituality was faith, its precious gratuitousness, and precarious condition in times when the forces of Catholicism, especially Spain's, were locked in a deadly struggle with Protestantism in all its forms. To zeal for the faith he joined the cross, eloquent symbol of Christian belief. On his begging tours about the remote villages and farms, he taught the catechism and erected the Way of the Cross in churches. He exercised his apostolate through a congregation, the Slaves of the Holy Faith, for which he also composed constitutions. In the churches in which the congregation was erected, a special altar featured a large drawing, designed to illustrate pictorially the elements of the faith in a way easily grasped by the simple people. Brother also prescribed a picture of Our Lady of the Faith, combining his Carmelite devotion to Mary with his own special interest in a surprising anticipation of present day intuition of the mystery of Mary.

But Francis' most audacious gesture on behalf of the faith was his design of carrying a cross to the Holy Land. As can be imagined, he had some difficulty obtaining permission for this plan, but the authorities finally relented at Herrera's assurances, imposing only the condition that the cross should not exceed fifteen pounds. Bearing his precious burden, Francis, on March 16, 1643, set out on foot on his long journey. He was fifty-seven years old and took three years to complete his remarkable Way of the Cross.

Travelling through Southern France, he reached Rome, where he received the approval of the vicar general, Leo Bonfigli, and Pope Urban VIII. Thereafter, he returned north to Venice, his port of embarkation. In the Holy Land, assisted by Prosper of the Holy Spirit, the Discalced Carmelite who had recovered Mount Carmel, Francis was at last able to satisfy his devotion and carry his cross to the places which were the scenes of the earthly existence of the Lord and finally place it in the socket that held the original cross on Golgotha. In March of 1646, after innumerable hardships he concluded his heroic voyage, apparently unique in the history of Christian witness, in the convent of Valderas from which he had set out, having satisfied in a simple direct way his thirst to share the cross and proclaim the faith.

The Province of Aragon

The province of Aragon, comprising the disparate political entities of Aragon, Navarre, and Valencia, managed by means of a system of alternates to maintain a surprising degree of unity and harmony. In 1416, when the province of Spain was separated into the provinces of Castile and Aragon, the latter consisted of the convents of Huesca, Sanguesa, Valencia, Zaragoza, Pamplona, and Calatayud. The division was no signal for expansion. For two centuries after the founding of Calatayud around 1300, no enduring foundation was made. Then, in the second half of the 16th century, Aragon joined the religious boom in Spain and eventually added 16 houses: Onda (1566), Játiva (1570), Sadava (1580), Orihuela (1585), Caudete (1585), Alicante (1586), Santa Barbara (1587), Tudela (1597), Villareal (1593), Jaca (1597), Alcañiz (1603), Rubielos (1608), Cox (1611), Aren (1612), Zaragoza (St. Joseph's, 1658), Egea (1675).

The monasteries of sisters also more than doubled. To the 16th century houses – Valencia (Incarnation, 1507), Valencia (St. Anne, 1567), and Onteniente (1575) – Sariñena was added in 1612, giving rise to the monasteries in Huesca (Incarnation, 1622; Assumption, 1656). The illustrious monastery of Zaragoza, home of a number of outstanding religious, dated from 1615.

During his visitation in 1606, Henry Silvio visited only Calatayud and Zaragoza, in which latter place he convened the provincial chapter, August 27. He annulled all previous provincial legislation, imposing instead his own reforming decrees. The province was no stranger to the practice of mental prayer, introduced twenty years previously by Angel de Salazar, vicar general for Spain, and the reforming Michael Carranza, but the prior general did not succeed in imposing the perfect common life prescribed by Clement VIII.

In 1664, there were 486 friars and 352 nuns in its 21 friaries and 6 nunneries.

In 1617, Sebastian Fantoni sent his able procurator general, Theodore Straccio, to visit Spain. At the chapter of Aragon, which he opened at Valencia on October 29, he proposed the introduction of "perfect, exact reform" in a few convents. Rubielos and Aren in Aragon and Onda in Valencia were put forward. The new prior of Rubielos was Jerome Domin, also elected definitor at the chapter and later named bishop of Gaeta, who remained a friend of Straccio throughout his lifetime. Though often nominated for reform, Rubielos always managed to avoid improvement. On the reform of Aren there is no further word, but Onda eventually became a center for reform in the province.

The provincial chapter of 1628, presided over by Master Valerius Jiménez de Embrun, which elected John Pinto de Vitoria provincial, concerned itself at length with reform and study. At the urging of the prior general, Gregory Canal, to assign several convents for "a fuller religious observance," Valencia, Onda, Zaragoza, Calatayud, and Pamplona were designated for this purpose. The definitory also took under advisement the decree of Clement VIII regarding poverty and studied ways and means of implementing it. Evidently its measures (not known) stopped short of the perfect common life, for the chapter went on to define equality in the Order as "proportionate inequality" and decreed extra portions at table for masters, because they "labored more for the honor and growth of the Order." On the other hand, attendance at midnight office was made mandatory on all. Also, because "in smaller convents less care" of novices is possible, novitiates were confined to the three principal houses, Valencia (Valencia), Zaragoza (Aragon), Pamplona (Navarre).

Master Valerius had been provincial since the previous year, when in 1632 "certain graduate fathers from the kingdom of Valencia" requested and were granted permission to initiate "a greater observance and reform" at Onda, as the Vicar General, Theodore Straccio, had recommended.

Villareal, Onda, and Orihuela

After the institution of the Stricter Observance in 1645, successive generals prodded the province to initiate reform. Upon order of Leo Bonfigli "to assign, if possible, a convent for reform," the chapter of 1646 decided that in the whole province none was more suitable than Rubielos. In 1650, the reform-minded Filippini pressed for one reformed house in the Kingdom of Aragon and another in that of Valencia. For the former, the chapter again assigned Rubielos, adding Alcañiz, when it could be readied; for the latter, Villareal. Of these convents, Villareal finally realized reform.

Diego de Tuesta, who should probably be considered the father of reform in the Aragon province, was appointed prior of Villareal; Hyacinth Lizarbe, subprior. The provincial might not send a conventual friar to the reformed convent without the approval of the community; a reformed friar might not be returned to the province without the consent of the provincial.

This year, 1650, was held in the province to be the year of origin of the reform.

On August 21, 1654, the reform of Villareal was introduced into the convent of Onda. By patents of May 5, Filippini appointed the provincial Anastasius Vives de Rocamora, his commissary to bring this about. Diego de Tuesta became the first reformed prior. Tuesta served as prior of Onda, 1656-1663,1667-1670.

Prior of Onda, 1673-1679, was Andrew Caperó. He must have joined the reform around 1668, when the Carmelite bishop of Segorbe, Anastasius Vives de Rocamora, recommends him for his "many gifts of learning and virtue." With him as prior, the community, on May 25, 1673, elected to recite Matins at midnight. The other two reformed houses (Villareal and Orihuela, since 1657) did not share Onda's enthusiasm; in fact, some malcontents complained to the prior general, Matthew Orlandi, that they were forced to rise at midnight for Matins and wear woolen underclothing, and that the teaching of philosophy was neglected. The intermediate congregation of 1674 was obliged to set the record straight: only Onda had undertaken to recite Matins at midnight, only those who wished to do so wore wool, philosophy was well taught in all three houses.

The saintly bishop of Segorbe around the same time resigned his see and retired to Onda, where he died within a year, after giving much edification by his simplicity and humility. Born at Orihuela in 1599, Anastasius Vives de Rocamora was professed in 1615. Elected provincial in 1653, he attended the general chapter of 1654. As bishop of Segorbe, 1661-1673, Vives distinguished himself by his frugal life and concern for the poor.

Provincial from 1686 to 1689, Caperó earned praise for "his religious spirit, understanding, and business acumen" of no less holy a man than Paul Ezquerra.

At Villareal, Sebastian Villanova replaced Tuesta as prior in 1653. Joseph Cleric was named subprior. Filippini was asked to place the convent under the provincial, Master Anastasius Vives, who should also have the power to transfer friars. Villanova was one of the original reformers. He was replaced as prior in 1657 by Joseph Perello, another pioneer, who remained in office until 1663. Other frequently re-elected priors during the rest of the 17th century were John Saura, Michael Seguer, Simon Gargallo, Casimir Piedra.

The provincial chapter of 1657 asked the prior general for permission to replace the prior of Orihuela before his term was up and to proceed with the reform of the convent, a request that Venturini readily granted, December 22. In 1663, Sebastian Villanova, one of the reformers of Villareal, became prior and retained the office for a decade. Other long-term priors were Francis Latorre and Vincent Belengueri.

The reformed convents frequently exchanged members, so that many of the friars mentioned in connection with each house are also to be found serving in the others. Unfortunately, very little information is available on the lives of the early reformed friars of Aragon.

At his visit in 1664, Jerome Ari found three reformed convents: Villareal, Onda, and (though not specified by name) Orihuela. Casimir Piedra was replaced as prior of Villareal by Hyacinth Lizarbe, Joseph Milla as prior of Onda by John Saura. Since the constitutions of the Stricter Observance were deemed unsuitable, a number of special decrees was drawn up to regulate the reform. These in general inculcate the directives of Clement VIII, imposing the perfect common life, daily meditation, austerity of life.

The chapter of 1676 opined that the main cause for the small number of the reformed and the poverty of their houses after twenty-six years of reform was the facility with which they abandoned the reform. The fathers considered (but did not do so) appointing non-reformed priors, because apt subjects for this charge were not to be found in the reform.

When John Feijóo de Villalobos visited the Aragon province in 1693, he apparently saw little evidence of reform, for he ordered the provincial to collect into one house, to be chosen by him, all who professed "our primitive institute" and the common life. The reformed should not be allowed to return to unreformed houses.

The following year, the definitory stated that there were not enough volunteers for the reformed life to be introduced at Rubielos, which presumably was the prior general's choice for the site of reformed living. Evidently, some candidates came forward after all, for in 1695 Villalobos appointed Elisha García vicar and commissary general of the reform "in the Valencian part."

Two years later, there is a complaint from the definitory that the superiors of the reformed houses do not attend to the needs of their subjects. The prior general is asked to permit the provincial to correct such delinquent priors.

The Province of Catalonia

Catalonia, the smallest of the Spanish provinces, grew hardly at all after its heyday in the 14th century, when it had been the focus of the Order's activity. At the time of Silvio's visit in 1606 it numbered thirteen convents: Perpignan, Lérida, Barcelona, Perelada, Gerona, Palma de Mallorca, Manresa, Valls, Campredón, Tàrrega, Salgar (1404), Vich (1406), Olot (1565). To these were added the College of St. Angelus Martyr in Barcelona (1587), Las Borjas (1610), and Ceret (1645). In 1690, it was decided to open a hospice at Mahon on Minorca, preliminary to the convent desired by the inhabitants devoted to the scapular. In 1725, a prior of the "new convent" is first elected.

Ceret and Perpignan were ceded to the province of Toulouse in 1662, as a result of the Treaty of the Pyrenees, 1659, which ended the revolt of the Catalans begun in 1640, and which ceded certain territories to France.

Catalan nationalism and Catalonia's border position in the wars between France and Spain subjected the province to the harassments of war. Lérida, Campredón, Gerona, and Vich are known to have suffered damage and destruction. Between 1705 and 1713, no chapter could be held because of the impoverishment and disruption of the province during the War of the Spanish Succession. Gerona, Lérida, and Perelada lay in the dominion of Philip V, while Olot, Tàrrega, Campredón, and Las Borjas lay in that of Charles III.

Silvio counted 251 friars in the Catalan province, and this number remained more or less constant during the 17th century. In 1768, membership without the community on Minorca stood at 345 friars and 2 semifratres. There were 45 nuns in the monasteries of Barcelona and Valls.

Henry Silvio visited Lérida and Tàrrega, and convened the provincial chapter at Barcelona, September 21, 1606. His decrees for reform left no observable impression.

During his visitation of 1618, when he designated Vich or Gerona as "houses of recollection," Theodore Straccio had no better luck. In 1633, Straccio, now general, repeated his order to establish the perfect common life in one or two houses, "since it is evident, also from the acts of your congregation, that the convents of this province do not observe the common life."

In fact, the following years show a certain concern for observance. After visitation by the Aragonese Master Angelo Palacio, commissary of Straccio, the chapter of 1635 issued a number of decrees, among them one ordering the observance of the deposit box. The congregation of 1641 instituted a house of professed at Barcelona, where clerics would remain until ordination. In 1653, a daily half hour of meditation was introduced.

The general chapter of 1648, which tried to inaugurate the Stricter Observance in provinces where it was lacking, ordered Catalonia to reform Vich.

Valls and Tàrrega

Eventually it was in Valls that reform began. Magin Masso became prior in 1657. His report of the state in which he found the convent reminds one of some of St. Teresa's founding experiences. In the sacristy, corporals and purificators were lacking. Altar cloths were few and in ragged condition. Silver vessels had been pawned for 75 *libras* to pay the *vestiaria* of the brethren. Church and altars were not properly kept, the roof leaked badly. In the larder, only some spoiled turnips were found. Wood destined for making beds had been used for firewood. Hardly a sound bed was at hand, so that the friars had been sleeping together. Bedclothes were wanting. The convent needed extensive repairs, the refectory was in danger of collapse. The convent was 600 *libras* in debt.

At his visit to the reformed convent of Valls on July 16, 1664, Jerome Ari found a community of fourteen. The prior general postponed making decrees until the annual congregation, but he delivered "a devout, severe address on avoiding small faults."

At the congregation, which convened on July 26, Ari urged the provincial, Joseph Métge, to favor the reform and try to open another reformed house. The provincial was not to transfer Angelus Palau, Louis Portet, and others who joined the reform.

In Catalonia, too, the constitutions of the Stricter Observance proved unacceptable, and Ari with some variations issued the same municipal laws as he had in Aragon. Here he legislated an hour's recreation after dinner and supper.

In 1667, Matthew Orlandi appointed Master Angelus Filbet vicar provincial for the reform. At the general's request, the community of Valls elected Magin Masso prior. Angelus Palau succeeded him and remained prior for fourteen years, 1670-1694. During this period, he restored the convent materially and spiritually, and so should probably be considered the moving spirit behind the reform. He was born in Barcelona in 1628 and professed there in 1644.

Carmelus Lusitanus

Portugal, land bound on the east by a frequently hostile Spain and facing westward across the Atlantic, was in reality a remote and *incommunicado* province. It had always enjoyed a reputation for religious observance. Witnesses no less weighty than Nicholas Audet, John Baptist Rossi, and Jerome Gracián left warm encomiums, yet apart from their isolated statements little information on the state of the province during the 16th century has come down to us. From what we know of the province in the 17th century and subsequently, there is no reason to believe that Portugal was better than most provinces. It shared in only a very limited fashion the spiritual renewal that was causing such a remarkable change in other parts of the Order.

By the beginning of the 17th century, the province of Portugal had reached its maximum growth. To the four houses already existing (Moura, Lisbon, Colares, and Vidigueira) were added Beja (1526), Evora (1531), Coimbra (1536), Lagoa (a.k.a. Alagoa, Algarve, 1550), Torres Novas (1558), Setúbal (1598), Alverca (São Romão, 1600), Camarate (1602). The need for a *pied à terre* in the Azores to accommodate friars travelling to and from Brazil led to a foundation at Horta on the island of Fayal (1652). In 1663, a hospice was accepted at Funchal on the island of Madeiros.

In 1697, a group of Carmelite tertiaries of Guimarães made profession as nuns of the Order, thus forming with Beja, Lagos, and Tentúgal the fourth and last of the Carmelite monasteries of nuns in Portugal.

The Visitation of Henry Silvio, 1606

In 1606, Henry Silvio visited the province, stopping at Moura, Vidigueira, Lisbon, Torres Novas, and Coimbra. He did not celebrate a chapter, but on May 18 confirmed Manuel Tavares, elected provincial the previous year.

The *scrutinia*, or interviews, of Silvio's visit have survived. They contain the usual accusations and allegations against subjects and superiors and reveal the general's concern over mental prayer, which was taught to the novices but not always practiced later on. Silvio published his decrees for reform with certain omissions and additions.

Silvio's visitation book lists 253 friars in the dozen convents of the province. The three monasteries included 165 nuns. While the number of houses remained stable, their population increased over the years, with as a result the usual economic crisis.

The "Recollect" House of Colares

In Portugal, Theodore Straccio, the procurator general, sent by Sebastian Fantoni to visitate the Iberian peninsula, registered his one success in attempting to establish houses of perfect common life. The provincial chapter of 1617, at which he presided, designated the convent of St. Ann in Colares as a reformed house and approved its seven statutes. The perfect common life was imposed. Frei Anthony Bautista was elected prior. In 1619, the statutes were confirmed by the nuncio, Ottavio Accaromboni; the following year, by Fantoni.

Straccio's success in this case was probably due to the presence in the province of Frei Stephen of the Purification (1571-1671), after Bl. Nuno Pereira the most notable example of sanctity among men the province produced. He was born in Moura and had a better than usual education, having attended Latin school, when he received the Carmelite habit at Vidigueira. At the college in Coimbra, where he studied theology, were Angelo Pereira, later suffragan of Coimbra, and Amador Arrais, engaged in revising his famous *Dialogues*. At the university he heard, among others, the great Francis Suárez, S.J. However, Stephen never acquired the doctorate.

When he was about 35 years of age, Stephen, who had difficulty hearing, became totally deaf. "When God closed my bodily ears," he told a friend, "he opened those of my soul." For a year, he gave himself up to prayer and penance. The works of Louis of Granada introduced him to mental prayer. Thereafter, he devoted himself wholly to spiritual interests. He was much sought after for direction and advice. Frei Stephen was especially devoted to the Eucharist, to the passion and wounds of Christ, and to the Blessed Virgin, whose slave he professed to be, "not any sort of slave, but one of those little slaves ladies keep as sons." He was also a devotee of St. Teresa, not yet canonized.

At the provincial chapter of 1614, which he attended as *socius* for Vidigueira, Stephen urged the institution of a contemplative house. When Straccio at the following chapter designated Colares for this purpose, Stephen was assigned there. Unfortunately, he lived only a matter of months, and died on November 17, 1617. His last public act had been to preach at a Mass in memory of Blessed Teresa at the invitation of the Discalced Carmelites of Cascais. Louis of the Presentation Mertola has preserved a number of Stephen's letters in his biography written only four years after the holy man's death.

Among the early members of the reformed community of Colares were Francis of the Purification, who in 1624 became the first commissary of the vicariate of Maranhão, and Gonzalo of the Mother of God, a laybrother who accompanied him to Brazil and gave great edification by his holiness of life in São Luis.

During his visit in 1624, the commissary general, Valerio Jiménez de Embun, of the Aragon province, on October 4 drew up 14 statutes for the observance at Colares.

Observance was affected by the poverty of the convent. Noting that Colares had fallen from its pristine observance because of financial straits, the provincial chapter of 1683 arranged for Moura to provide a certain subsistence.

At the request of the provincial, Francis of the Nativity, the general chapter of 1686 ordered statutes drawn up for the betterment of observance at Colares. These may be the statutes which the annual congregation of the province in 1693 required to be observed; anyone who could not do so on account of health should request a transfer.

The following year, the prior general, John Feijóo de Villalobos, visited the province and on his return to Rome drew up an imposing body of statutes for Colares. The perfect common life was no longer observed because of the poverty of the convent. To remedy the situation, the former provincial, Master John Baptist Ruffino, generously offered to assist the impoverished house from his incomes, and Feijóo accepted. The irony of rescuing the common life with the private income of a friar seems to have escaped everyone.

Portugal, 1650-1750

As prior general, Theodore Straccio continued his interest in the Iberian peninsula. On September 10, 1633, he obtained confirmation from Urban VIII for certain decrees he had drawn up for Spain and Portugal. It was not proper for mendicant friars to go about town on horses or mules; these were to be used only on longer trips. Individual friars might not keep personal servants. Urban's brief of June 13, 1625, issued on request of the Spanish king, is renewed; it had recalled all privileges exempting religious from obedience to their superiors.

In a letter to the Infantas of Savoy, May 23, 1640, Straccio announced that he was sending the provincial of Andalusia, John Duran, to visitate Portugal, "since religious discipline had almost completely collapsed there, due to the maladministration of many superiors in the past, particularly of a certain Master Martin Moniz, who for many years held the province in thrall, as it were." One wonders if Straccio was correctly informed in this case, for Moniz is otherwise well spoken of. Opposition to a Spanish visitator in 1640, the year of the revolution, probably had political motivation.

In 1647, the province of Portugal counted 362 friars in 13 convents, and 237 nuns in three monasteries.

The general chapter of 1686 noted about Portugal that "zeal for study is much diminished," and ordered academic chairs to be provided by scholastic disputation (*oppositionem*).

Details of the visitation by John Feijóo de Villalobos are wanting. He celebrated no chapter, but presided over the triennial congregation of 1697.

Beginning with the general chapter of 1728, the Portuguese-speaking provinces were represented by an assistant general.

The Reform of the Vicariate of Brazil

The Stricter Observance fared better in Brazil than in the mother province.

In 1677, Frei John of St. Joseph with four or five others obtained permission to live the perfect common life in the convent of Goiana. Angelus Monsignani took steps to promote the young movement. In letters patent of May 6, 1683, he ordered the reform extended to Rio Real and Recife, and made provisions for the creation of a commissariate on the principles of Filippini's Articles. On December 17, having learned that his predecessor, Matthew Orlandi, had designated Olinda for reform, and urged by the bishop and senate of the city, Monsignani ordered the implementation of this design. He dispatched a copy of the constitutions of the Stricter Observance, which were to be followed in the reformed convents, and appointed John of St. Joseph prior of Olinda and commissary for the reform. Olinda was never won for the reform; the projected commissariate was long in coming. As late as 1692, the reformed friars complained that Monsignani's decrees had never been carried out and requested a commissary who would remove them from the jurisdiction of unsympathetic vicars provincial.

In 1685, the community of Goiana included Christopher of Christ (prior), John of the Incarnation, Manuel of the Assumption, Manuel of St. Joseph, Ferdinand of the Rosary, and Joseph of Jesus and Mary. The latter is especially worth of note. Joseph (1660-1727) was appointed apostolic missionary by the archbishop of Bahia, Emmanuel of the Resurrection O.F.M., in which capacity he travelled more than 900 miles engaged in the work of evangelization. He was the archbishop's confessor and accompanied him on the visitation of his archdiocese. The last part of Joseph's life was spent in Lisbon, where he vigorously promoted the Third Order.

The drowning at sea of the vicar provincial of Brazil and twelve other friars, travelling between Bahia and Rio de Janeiro may have been the spark that finally set the mills of Rome in motion in 1685 to separate the enormous vicariate of Brazil into the vicariate of Rio de Janeiro with convents in Rio de Janeiro, São Paulo, Santos, Angra dos Reis, Mogí das Cruzes, and Vitória do Espírito Santo, and the vicariate of Bahia-Pernambuco with houses in Bahia, Olinda, Sergipe (alias, São Cristóvão), Paraíba, Recife, Goiana, and Rio Real.

In 1686, Francis of the Nativity, provincial of Portugal, backed by King Peter II, required the reformed friars to relinquish Recife and keep Goiana and Paraíba. The reform remained entrenched in these three houses, but retired from Rio Real.

At the request of the prior general, Paul of St. Ignatius, Mark of the Nativity, provincial of Touraine, in 1688, dispatched Alexis of the Assumption and Denis of St. Peter Thomas to Brazil to help the reform take root. Alexis died at Calais, November 17, while waiting to embark, but Denis crossed over and remained for three years, laboring to implant the reformed way of life in the new land.

In 1695, John Feijóo de Villalobos, on visitation in Madrid, was approached by Michael of the Assumption and John of St. Philip Neri, procurators for the reformed convents, with certain complaints about the vicar provincial of Bahia, whom they accused of various transgressions against the rights of the reform. On September 27, the prior general granted all the requests of these friars who "came to us without regard for the long and dangerous inconveniences of the crossing from Pernambuco to Lisbon or for the tiresome journey from Lisbon to Madrid."

He also confirmed Monsignani's decrees of 1683, adding a few of his own. Courses of the Arts and of theology with at least six students each were to be established in two of the reformed convents. One of the definitors of the vicariate should be chosen from among the reformed. The commissary general was granted faculties to accept new foundations for the reform. Finally, because of the great distance between Pernambuco and Rome, the vicar of the province and the commissary general of the reform were to have recourse to the Carmelite bishop of Pernambuco. On their return to Lisbon, Michael and John took care to have Villalobos' patents confirmed by the nuncio of Portugal, George Cornaro, on October 29.

The Carmelite bishop would have been Francis de Lima, since 1691 bishop of São Luis of Maranhão, who only a month previously, on August 22, had been made bishop of Olinda.

On March 22, 1714, the Congregation for Bishops and Religious settled a controversy between the reformed friars and observants of the vicariate of Bahia, decreeing that Goiana, Recife, and Paraíba belonged to the reform, but that it was not to be extended to Olinda. Oddly enough, confirmation of this decree was requested of Clement XI the following June 11 by Joseph of the Nativity, procurator of the reformed friars "of the town of Pernambuco."

In 1716, the "Most Faithful" King John V took the reform under his protection. On April 20, 1720, Pope Clement XI promoted the vicariates of Bahia-Pernambuco and Rio de Janeiro to the status of provinces. Five years later, the reformed convents of Bahia-Pernambuco became a provincial vicariate. Pizzolanti named Michael of the Assumption first vicar.

The Reformed Province of Pernambuco

In 1741, King John V granted the reformed vicariate missions at Baia da Traição and Preguiça in the Captaincy of Paraíba, and Gramació in the Captaincy of Rio

Grande do Norte.

To avoid continual contention with the observants, Pope Benedict XIV, on March 20, 1744, constituted the three convents and six hospices of the reform an independent province, on condition that the six hospices first become formal convents.

At the first chapter of the province of Pernambuco, priors were elected for the convents of Goiana, Paraíba, and Recife and "superiors" for the *aldeias* (*pagi*) of Preguiça, Gramacío, and Baia da Traição. The hospices are shown to be Lisbon, Our Lady da Guia, Our Lady of Mercy, Our Lady of Light, Our Lady of Guadalupe (at Porto Calvo), and Castelho. (A procurator resided at the hospice founded in 1722 in Lisbon, to conduct the affairs of the vicariate with the provincial of Portugal, the king, and the Holy See.) Recife was designated for theology. Permission of the definitory was required for advancing to academic degrees and for other promotions; in fact, no masters appear at the provincial chapters of which there is record.

After the following chapter of 1748, the pope was approached to permit the province to continue, in spite of the fact that the hospices could not then be converted into convents. "As to the number (of friars) there are almost 120; as to their morals and the fulfillment of the duties of their state, with the help of God they live in an exemplary manner, many of them dedicated to studies in the three convents, others, both in the convents and aforementioned regular hospices, zealously serving the spiritual good of the people, now in confessionals and pulpits of the cities and towns, now in continual missionary journeys throughout the whole diocese of Pernambuco." From an appended list, the actual number of friars in the province is seen to be 112: 81 priests, 10 professed clerics, 1 novice cleric, 15 brothers, and 5 novice brothers. The Holy See referred the petition to the decision of the prior general, who gave his consent, March 25, 1749.

It is regrettable that the reform was not extended to the few other remaining convents of the small Bahia province. The modern province of Pernambuco traces its origin to the reformed province of the same name.

Chapter 10

Carmelite Missionary Activity

Carmelite missionary activity in Spanish America, of necessity limited, was carried out despite the Crown. In Portuguese Brazil, on the other hand, the Order flourished, and three provinces and a vicariate came into being. In the present period, the spirited province of Touraine inaugurated a new missionary field in the Caribbean. Post-Catholic Europe itself now came to be regarded as missionary territory into which the renovated Church sent apostles to bring about reconversion to the ancient faith. The Carmelites undertook missions in Ireland, England, the Dutch Republic, and Northern Germany.

The Mission in the Lesser Antilles

The Carmelite missionary effort in the West Indies, or Antilles, was occasioned by a chance meeting on the Loire between a French naval officer, M. de Nuailly, and two Carmelites, Ambrose of St. Anne and the Maurile of St. Michael, en route to preaching a Lenten course. Nuailly was organizing a colony on the island of Grenada in the Lesser Antilles and invited the Carmelites to accompany the expedition. His description of the island paradise in the Caribbean and the rich harvest of pagan souls that awaited the worker fired the two friars with holy desires. The provincial, Leo of St. John, supported this apostolic opportunity for the province. On April 14, 1646, commissioned by the prior general, Leo Bonfigli, he empowered Ambrose to accept foundations for the mission and appointed Maurile his companion. On July 18, 1646, the expedition set out from St. Nazaire. Ambrose and Maurile received the Sacrament for the last time before boarding. "We offered again our lives, our longings, our very blood, affirming that we only sought in such a dangerous and difficult enterprise the honor of God, the conversion of the Indians, the increase of the faith, and the spiritual good of our small colony." After a perilous journey of forty-five days, the travellers went ashore on Martinique on September 1. "We no sooner set foot on land than we fell to our knees and thanked God for our safe arrival, asking that everything be directed for His greater glory."

The development of trade in the islands, principally tobacco and sugar, was in the hands of the Company of the Isles of America, created by Richelieu in 1635 to replace the bankrupt Company of St. Christopher (1626). The Company elected governors for each of the islands, who functioned under a governor-general, representative of the Crown. The Carmelites had been preceded in the islands by Capuchins (1635), Dominicans (1636), and Jesuits (1639).

The new paradise, it turned out, was not without its serpent. The would-be colonists found the islands in a virtual state of civil war. Philippe de Lonvilliers de Poincy, governor of St. Kitt's (St. Christopher's) and governor-general of the Islands, refused to acknowledge the new governor-general, Noel de Thoisy, appointed by the queen regent, Anne of Austria, in 1645, and war was raging between the two parties. Worse still for the Carmelites, Nuailly had second thoughts about founding a colony on Grenada, where the fierce Caribs were notoriously averse to sharing their paradise with anyone. Nuailly returned to France, accompanied by some of the settlers. Others elected to remain on Martinique. This left the Carmelites "with no recommendations, with little knowledge of the islands, without any money or letters of exchange."

At this critical juncture, the misfortune of the Capuchins proved to the benefit of the Carmelites. De Poincy, suspecting the Capuchins of collusion with his enemy Thoisy, expelled them from his island of St. Kitt's. When Maurile presented himself there in mid-September, De Poincy readily accepted the offer of his services. He provided the Carmelite with a lodging near his own chateau and assigned him the care of churches at Montagne and Cayonne as well as the hospital. In November, Maurile was joined by Ambrose, who, however, arrived in a state near to death and took two months to recover.

The pastoral work of the missionaries gradually took the shape it was to retain in the years that followed. The population was composed of the French colonists, negroes, and indians. Of the negroes Maurile wrote: "We can instruct them little by little and eventually baptize them. They have such barbarous and dull intellects that it is almost impossible to teach them to read or write." The indians had some idea of immortality, but it was difficult to convert them because of their libertine and licentious ways. Language, too, formed a barrier. Among the French, a number of conversions from Calvinism was made. Finally, the missioners administered to the English Catholics in the area.

In March of 1647, Maurile returned to France to recruit more missionaries. He presented an account of the mission and its needs to the provincial chapter at Poitiers. In 1649, he travelled to Rome where he reported on the mission to the prior general, John Anthony Filippini. The general invited Maurile to work in Brazil, but he neither undertook that mission nor ever returned to the West Indies. In 1649, he was one of the group of Touraine friars sent to promote reform in the province of Provence. He left a precious account of the beginnings of the mission in the Antilles, *Voyage des Isles Camercanes en l'Amerique, qui font partie des Indes occidentales* (Mans, 1652).

For two years Ambrose of St. Anne labored on alone, redoubling his efforts. In 1649, he was joined on St. Kitts by Innocent of St. Peter, Cosmas of the Presentation, and Brother Leo of St. Joseph, the latter endowed with the useful skills of apothecary and surgeon. Innocent was assigned to Ance Avoigne and Cosmas to Ance a Louve, while Ambrose settled in Montagne near the residence of De Poincy. The same year, the cornerstone was laid for a chapel and convent of the Order at Ance a Louve. Subsequently, other sites for residences were also granted. In each case, the missionaries were allotted a certain share of the tobacco crop for their support. Brother Leo began the construction of a chapel at Pointe de Sable. The reinforced mission, however, received a setback in the death, on July 13, 1650, of Innocent of St. Peter, deeply mourned by the people he served.

In May, 1650, the Carmelite mission received the official recognition of King Louis XIV.

Early in 1651, a third band of missionaries arrived: Athanasius of St. Radegonde, Joseph of St. Claude, James of the Annunciation, and Brother Thomas of the Blessed Sacrament. Their coming was the occasion for opening a mission at Basseterre on the island of Guadeloupe by Joseph of St. Claude, warmly welcomed by the governor of the island, Charles Houel. James only briefly survived the rigors of the long passage. Athanasius labored on St. Kitts, where he won the esteem of

De Poincy and its inhabitants before ill health forced his return to France. Like Maurile, he was active in the reform of Provence, becoming prior of Aix. Not long afterwards, Joseph, too, returned to France and was replaced on Guadeloupe by Cosmas of the Presentation.

In 1651, Brother Leo of St. Joseph returned from France with Albin of the Blessed Sacrament. Leo this time did not survive the hardships of the voyage, and Albin died four days after debarkation on St. Kitts. He joined James of the Annunciation in the cemetery at Montagne. "Charity predominated in these three religious," writes Maurile, "and motivated their whole life. The three of them were about forty years old and all died within three weeks of each other."

Claude of St. John, who brought with him Angelus of St. John, Victorinus of St. Michael, Dosithée of St. James, and Seraphim of St. Peter, replaced Ambrose of St. Anne as provincial vicar of the mission. The new arrivals enabled the Carmelites to open a mission on the island of Marie Galante in 1660. Victorinus, aged 71, was put in charge, but not surprisingly, considering his age, died after a year.

In 1664, Claude of St. John, still in office as vicar, died on St. Kitts. His successor as vicar provincial seems to have been Hyacinth of the Trinity, who died on the missions in 1677. The provincial chapter of 1672 appointed Raphael of St. Agnes.

Around 1660, four more friars joined the mission, only two of whom however, Justus of Jesus and Ferdinand of St. Claude, managed to adjust to the climate. Ferdinand died on the mission in 1677.

The provincial chapter of 1669 drew up *Decreta*, or regulations, for the mission, revised and enlarged by the chapter of 1672.

With the additional personnel, the mission spread to other islands of the Lesser Antilles. In 1650, a contract was made for a convent and chapel on St. Martin's island, but the mission was activated only later. Particulars about the further expansion of the mission are at present not immediately available, but from existing documents it is clear that the Carmelites eventually added missions on Les Saints, St. Dominic, and St. Vincent. There is even mention of a mission on the mainland at Cayenne, Guiana. Besides, the missioners also visited islands where they had no permanent residences. The latter seem to have been modest dwellings for a few missionaries and never became formally erected convents.

The Mission Adopted by the Holy See

A long-standing problem of the Carmelite mission in the Antilles was its ecclesiastical status. At the practical level, the missionaries needed apostolic faculties for pastoral work in those remote regions. From a letter of Jerome Ari to Cardinal Fabio Chigi, March 2, 1663, it appears that the Carmelites in the Antilles had requested of the Propaganda the status of apostolic missionaries with all attendant faculties. From Paris, where he was on visitation, Ari sent his Eminence an account of the mission and his warm endorsement of the request.

The Sacred Congregation of the Propagation of the Faith long deferred recognition of the Carmelite mission. The pleas of the missionaries form a constantly recurring theme in their correspondence with Rome. Finally, in 1712, after the vicar of the mission, Maximin of St. Peter, made a special trip to Rome, the mission was granted apostolic status.

The mission in the Antilles was a credit to the Order and a blessing for the Church during the century and a half of its existence. Volunteers were carefully selected and once on the mission gave edification by their lives and labored heroically to sustain the faith of the Europeans and according to their lights to bring the gospel to the pagans.

The provincial chapter of 1789 ordered the vicar of the islands to send an annual report on the material state of the missions. The conscript fathers evidently did not see the irony of making this decree at so late a date, when the agents of the Revolution would soon be knocking on the door, signalling the end of the province and the mission.

Carmel in Ireland Under the Tudors

It is not at all unlikely that the Order was never lacking in Irish members. In the darkest periods of history, they spring out of the ground like fruit of the proverbial dragon's teeth. Where they were professed and by what right is not always clear. In some cases, they were laymen who joined the Order on the continent, living there and returning to Ireland for longer or shorter periods. There, especially in the Pale, measures against priests could not always be as efficiently enforced as in England. Although there cannot have been many Carmelites in post-Reformation Ireland, there is no reason to believe that their number is limited to the few whose names have actually come down to us.

A number of Irish Carmelites are known to have existed in Tudor times. After the dissolution of the monasteries, the friars sometimes lingered on in the neighborhood, exercising a clandestine apostolate in peril of their lives. Friars Thomas Fleming and Geoffrey Quirk were still in Kinsale in 1557, when they received a legacy. Fleming is again mentioned in a will in the reign of Queen Elizabeth (1559-1603). The missal of the convent of Kilcormac notes the death of Friar Rory O'Morrissey in 1568. A chalice exists which was used in Knocktopher and is dated 1571.

In 1570, four or five convents are said to exist. That year, John Baptist Rossi appointed Mahon McSweeney, of Rathmullen, vicar provincial of Ireland. Concerned as always about observance, the prior general ordered whatever friars remained to gather in these houses to lead a community life. Two years later, Rossi renewed McSweeney's vicarship. Both patents invited the vicar to attend the general chapters, and in fact, he appeared at the chapters of 1575 and 1580, when he was confirmed in office. He was still active in 1600.

In 1596, two Carmelites, Thomas Lynch and Garrot Fitzgerald, accompanied Bishop Malachy O'Malone to Seville.

Carmel in Ireland, 1600-1650

Francis Voersio, faithful secretary of Henry Silvio, made the following entry in his register under the date April 30, 1610: "Fr. John Duane (Odubheamy), an Irishman, was made commissary general of our province of Ireland. A certain Irish Franciscan of the Observance, apostolic commissary of his Order on that island, from which he has just returned, told us that our Order still has many houses and friars on that island, one of whom is the aforementioned Fr. John. For this reason, the Most Reverend Father made him commissary general."

For the next score of years, information on the Carmelites in Ireland is hard to come by. In 1634, Anthony Walsh is known to have been vicar provincial. That year, on behalf of the Congregation of the Propagation of the Faith, Hugh O'Reilly, archbishop of Armagh, arbitrated a dispute between the Carmelites and the Franciscans of Dundalk.

At Christmas time, 1629, the Protestant archbishop of Dublin, Lancelot Bulkeley, headed a raid by soldiery of the Carmelite church in Cook Street. Although the congregation successfully repulsed the intruders, the church was ordered closed, January 31, 1630.

The Carmelites involved in this affair were probably Discalced. As a matter of fact, they had arrived in Ireland in 1625, making their first foundation in Cook Street, Dublin. In 1621, Thomas of Jesus founded a missionary college at Louvain for English, Irish, and Dutch Carmelites, thus insuring a steady source of missionaries for Ireland. In 1638, an Irish province of Discalced Carmelites was erected. By 1643, the province numbered nine foundations: Dublin, Athboy, Drogheda, Ardee, Galway, Limerick, Kilkenny, Kinsale, and Loughrea.

In establishing themselves in Ireland the Discalced made use of the abandoned houses of the old Order. "The religious Orders that were admitted here of old," they reported to their definitory general on September 28, 1625, "may make new foundations without being dependent in any way on the bishop, but religious like ourselves, who never had convents here by order of the Sacred Congregation of the Propagation of the Faith must depend from the bishops and be subject to their jurisdiction. [Hence] we can in no way exist, unless we take over the convents of the Mitigated. . . at least until the mitigated fathers come to Ireland." Propaganda, appealed to by the Discalced in 1629, decided that the consent of the Carmelite prior general was required.

Evidently, this decision failed to settle the matter. The controversy between the two Orders became so heated that the bishops of Down, Connor, and Raphoe, fearing interference from unfriendly authorities, in 1640, appealed to the Congregation of the Propagation of the Faith, which decreed that the Discalced should retain the four convents they had already taken over (apparently Athboy, Drogheda, Ardee, and Kinsale), and that the Carmelites should be left in peaceful possession of the rest of the thirty-two houses of the Order in Ireland. The next two Discalced foundations, Limerick and Kilkenny, were in fact original and independent efforts, though in the case of Loughrea, as will be seen, the Discalced again occupied an existing Carmelite house.

The Belgian province, meanwhile, was educating English and Irish students in their college at Douai. The chapter of 1638 decreed that these students should be carefully examined before being promoted to the novitiate. However, four years later, the Irishman, Robert of the Visitation, who styled himself "provincial pro-vicar of Ireland," wrote to Angelus of St. Agnes, provincial of Touraine, asking him to open a novitiate for the Irish. Since 1635, Robert declared, the Belgian province had admitted Irish postulants to the habit, but could no longer do so because of the wars.

The previous year, 1641, Straccio had made the same proposal. Letters of 1641 to 1643 show that Athanasius of Ste. Radegonde and Matthias of St. Bernard were sent to Ireland. They went first to Dublin, then travelled all over the island and found only two Carmelites. They returned to France after a year.

Twice in 1643, on March 30 and July 7, Albert Massari, vicar general, wrote to Angelus, urging him to send missionaries to Ireland. He in turn had been urged to do so by the secretary of Propaganda. The provincial must have proposed Fulgentius of St. Barbara for the undertaking, for on September 9, Massari appointed this friar commissary general of Ireland, whereupon Pope Urban VIII and the Propaganda added apostolic faculties. The death of the provincial, however, seems to have signalled the end of this project.

Meanwhile, Patrick of St. William had appeared in the province of Touraine and on October 27, 1643, got in touch with Bernard of St. Magdalen, as first definitor in charge of the province after the provincial's death. Patrick had just returned from a year's sojourn in Ireland, where he had found only two Carmelites, Flemings, a priest and a laybrother, living in Waterford. He had attended the Confederation of Kilkenny in 1642 and had defended the rights of the Order against the Dominicans and the Discalced Carmelites. He urged Bernard to follow up on his predecessor's initiative and send friars to Ireland. He volunteered his brother and two or three others as candidates for the Order.

Bernard was already well informed on the subject of Patrick by a youthful Mark of the Nativity, who had been deeply impressed by the Irish missionary and fired with holy zeal by his stories. Patrick, Mark wrote to his superior on September 27, was about forty years old, of a noble family of the County of Monaghan (*Mommonie*). He entered the Order in Bordeaux and had held office in the province of Gascony. In Ireland, he had encountered only three Irish friars and two Flemings, all living apart. He had found twenty-one convents, which Mark enumerated, though there were more. The Dominicans have possessed themselves of Ardfinna, Castlelyons, and Drogheda; the Discalced, of Kinsale. For 200 tournois Patrick can have a roof put on the church of Knocktopher, center of a famous devotion to the Holy Savior, for which people come from all over Ireland. In a part of the country devoted to the Order, he built a chapel to St. Simon Stock, obtained indulgences, and enrolled the faithful in the scapular. Patrick had little use for the Flemish Fathers at Wexford, who do little for the advantage of religion. He preferred to be alone with his two companions, of whom (Mark thinks) Robert (of the Visitation) is one. Mark suggested Fr. Felician for the mission. Mark himself repeatedly but in vain volunteered for the mission, but his time to serve the mission in England and Ireland would come forty years later, when he himself was provincial.

On December 3, Patrick again wrote to Bernard, stressing the need for Touraine to open a mission in Ireland besides that of the Flemish, who are unreformed. To restore an Order without reform is to ruin it. Patrick promised to write instructions to Felician. In whatever port the missioners arrive, they should write to the guardian of the Recollects at Clonmell, and he would come to meet them. Meanwhile, he would ready a house. They should bring altar fittings, chalice, missal, and statues or pictures, especially of the Savior, and books for reading and preaching, for these things cannot be had in Ireland. His name in Ireland is William Hoban.

In an undated letter to Bernard, Mark reiterates his offer to go to Ireland and adds that a certain Lord Lespuis had offered the convent next to his castle at Ballinasmall, thus making two convents ready to receive communities. As a candidate for the mission, Mark presents Fr. Claude, of noble family, who is with the army.

From Mark's letter it further appears that Bernard had agreed to accept four Irish postulants, including Patrick's brother.

Evidently the Carmelite tenure of Knocktopher was not all that secure. In 1646, the Carmelites appealed to Rinuccini to grant them this house, but without result. On the other hand, in 1647, the nuncio bestowed the Carmelite convent at Loughrea on the Discalced. An appeal by the Carmelites to the Holy See two years later was of no avail.

It fell to the next provincial of Touraine, Leo of St. John, to carry forward the project of the Irish mission. The general chapter of 1645 entrusted him with the task of recovering the Order's Irish foundations, and he promised to do all in his power. On January 1, 1646, he could already assure John Anthony Filippini, the prior general elect, that he had sent two friars to explore the ground. He also took the precaution to recommend his missionaries to the nuncio of Ireland, Archbishop John Baptist Rinuccini. The province of Touraine had thus made an official commitment to the Irish mission, and something enduring might have come of it, had the times been propitious.

At the same time, the Belgian province, it would seem, had not abandoned its interest in Ireland. In 1649, two Irishmen, Columban of St. Patrick and Joseph of St. Edmund, on their way from Belgium to Ireland, passed through the province of Touraine and were given certain moneys held in trust by the provincial, Urban of the Ascension.

During the Republican interim and Cromwell's regime (1649-1660) news about Carmelites in Ireland, if there were any, is understandably lacking.

Carmel in Ireland, 1650-1700

The false dawn of the Restoration brought new hope to the Catholics in Ireland; once more the curias of the religious Orders teemed with grandiose plans.

On September 8, 1660, Gabriel of the Annunciation, newly elected assistant general, reported to Jerome Ari from Cologne that while other Orders were recovering their houses in England, Ireland, and Scotland, the Discalced were taking over the Order's. The seven or eight friars of these nationalities who are in Belgium, he advised, should be sent over, with the exception of Fr. Edmund, lector of theology in Louvain, who could remain behind to recruit candidates. The specter of the Discalced possessing themselves of the Order's houses served to spur the brethren to action, but in reality had little substance. After the first raid in pre-Cromwellian times, the Discalced made no further assaults, evidently abiding by the decision of the Propaganda of 1640. Besides, circumstances were now such as to render impossible the foundation of formal religious houses.

During Ari's visitation of Belgium in 1663, Gabriel's plan was carried out, but with a difference. Edmund was put in charge of the mission to Ireland and was given Columban of St. Patrick as a companion. Edmund of the Angels Butler (d. 1668) had been teaching philosophy in the Carmelite *studium* at Louvain for the past ten years. We have seen Columban leaving for Ireland in 1649. He probably sat out part or all of Cromwell's regime in Belgium.

The general chapter of 1666 resolved to request apostolic faculties for the Order's missionaries in England, Ireland, and Scotland, a belated measure. The definitories of the provinces of Francia, Touraine, and Belgium, together with the council of the Order, were to consider ways and means of accepting and educating youths of these nationalities.

The Irish mission was more slippery than a Loughrea eel: the major superiors could never really get their hands on it. Thus, one day early in 1684, the prior general, Angelo Monsignani, sitting in his cell minding his own business, was handed a letter dated from Dublin, December 22, 1683, from one William Shea, claiming to be the only Carmelite in Ireland and asking for faculties to receive and profess four candidates for the Order. In his reply, dated April 8, 1684, the general expressed mild surprise at receiving a missive from Ireland, willingly granted the requested patents, and inquired eagerly for more news. Shea's style was nothing if not laconic. Writing from Dublin, April 1, 1685, he requested patents as commissary and faculties to profess four more youths, but answered none of Monsignani's questions, not even saying whether he had already received any candidates. Complaining about Shea's reticence, the general sent him the faculties he wanted, asking further for particulars about Shea himself: place of birth and profession and how long he had been in Ireland.

Eventually, Shea vouchsafed some information about himself. On August 9, 1687, the next prior general, Paul of St. Ignatius, was able to inform the Flemish provincial, Patrick of St. George, that Shea had been born in 1634, entered the Order at Seville in 1657, and had returned to his native land after profession. On St. Patrick's Day, 1686, he had professed five novices. He was now looking for a place on the continent to educate and profess Irish candidates to the Order.

At the moment, Paul of St. Ignatius was in the process of getting the English mission under way. Cardinal Philip Howard wanted the English mission to be entrusted to the Flemish province; the Irish mission to Touraine. As it turned out, Touraine went to England, and the Flemish provincial, having learned that Shea had been professed in Spain and not in the Stricter Observance, lost interest in the Irish enterprise, which the general thereupon assigned to Touraine.

Fr. Shea's charges accordingly were sent to Touraine. On August 10, 1688, Paul expressed his satisfaction to the provincial, Mark of the Nativity, at the fact that the five clerics professed in Dublin were studying philosophy in Dol, while two other Irishmen and two Englishmen were to be clothed in the habit at La Flèche. Three or four of these Irishmen, as we shall see, ended up on the English mission. Another was Peter Hughes. Yet another, probably Patrick Nicholas, died not long after his arrival in France.

These young men were only the first of Shea's recruits. A letter of the Discalced of Ireland of 1698 to the prior general states that as a consequence of Shea's efforts the Order numbered three times as many members in Ireland as the Discalced. The persecution of Catholics that followed the deposition of James II (1688) drove Shea to France. On October 4, 1689, Paul of St. Ignatius asks Mark of the Nativity to suggest a commissary or coadjutor of Fr. Shea. This is the last mention in the records of this unsung hero who labored so untiringly and effectively for the restoration of the Order in Ireland.

Other Commissaries After Shea

At the end of the 17th and the beginning of the 18th century we find Irish affairs entrusted to the English commissary, Germain of St. James Lebreton. Thus, on January 5, 1697, John Feijóo de Villalobos sent him various decrees for the Carmelites in Ireland. Peter Thomas Sánchez, prior general from 1710 to 1716, formally appointed Germain commissary general of England, Scotland, and Ireland.

On May 1, 1715, Sánchez named Anselm Jackson commissary general of Ireland, again separating the mission from that of England. By that date Germain had apparently died.

In spite of the repressive laws under Hannoverian England, the Carmelites continued to exist in Ireland even increasing in numbers. Peter Hughes, one of Shea's vocations, had been driven back to the continent, but after the death of King William III (1702), he returned to Ireland and recovered Ballinasmall, where he professed candidates to the Order and sent them to France and Spain to study. Fr. T. Dillon after studies in France returned to Ireland in 1697 and took up the ministry in his native Drumraney near Ardnacanny.

One Charles Leary, too, was forced to flee the country and he remained in permanent exile. The prior general assigned him to Provence, where he ended up in Vienne, winning the affection and esteem of his adopted province. In 1699, the provincial, Louis Thomas, asked the general to grant Leary voice and place, since "he is a very good religious, and all the members of the province are very satisfied with him." Subsequently, the provincial chapter of 1701 accorded him filiation, alleging as reasons for this distinction his uprightness and ability and the sufferings he bore for the Faith. Since he was in the province, the capitulars added, he distinguished himself for his unassuming manner and fidelity to the offices confided to him. Leary was stationed in Vienne for about twenty years, holding the offices of sacristan and procurator. In 1718, he was transferred to another house without warning and obeyed without murmuring, refusing all intercession on his behalf.

In 1703, Malachy Stanton appears as chaplain to the Irish soldiers in the bodyguard of the Duke of Parma. He was discharged in 1706.

After the first two decades of the 18th century, the provinces of Flanders and Touraine lose their monopoly over the Irish mission, no doubt because Ireland had its own commissary general. Irish students are found in other provinces, with increasing frequency in Spain.

The general chapter of 1728 considered a petition by the Irish to be allowed after profession to pursue studies in the provinces of the Order and decreed that permission should be sought in each case of the prior general. This wise decision brought a bit of order into Irish affairs and enabled the prior general to offer his services when needed.

In 1729, Matthew of St. Elisha Lyons was named commissary general of Ireland. He had made his studies in the province of Aragon and in the same patents was granted the doctorate in theology.

The Restoration of the Irish Province, 1737

The Irish Fathers petitioned the general chapter of 1731 for the restoration of their province under the constitutions of the Stricter Observance, since there were enough houses and friars to justify this step. Furthermore, they asked for the appointment of a provincial and definitors, besides a vicar general for Scotland who should restore the convent of Edinburgh. Recommendations for these posts could be had from the cardinal protector of Ireland, Joseph Renato Imperiali. The definitors of the chapter referred "this most serious business" to the discretion of the prior general.

At this time the Order counted 12 houses in Ireland and 38 friars.

Louis Benzoni, elected prior general at that chapter of 1731, obtained from Pope Clement XII the brief *Pastoralis officii*, October 10, 1737, erecting the province of Ireland under the Stricter Observance. The convent of Edinburgh was perpetually united to it, and the Irish provincial was given the faculty of naming a vicar for Scotland and a prior of Edinburgh. At the same time, the pope appointed the first provincial in the person of Matthew of St. Elisha Lyons, as well as four definitors, respectively, Simon of St. Simon Stock Burke, Patrick of St. Mary Magdalen Mahoney (*Moans*), James of the Nativity Barnes, and James of St. Teresa Prendergast. *Socii* of the provincial to the general chapter were to be Patrick of St. Mary Magdalene and John of St. Elijah O'Neill. William Fleirr was made vicar of Scotland and prior of Edinburgh; Peter Prendergast, his *socius* and secretary. The erection of the Carmelite province had also been requested by several Irish bishops.

The Irish provincial and his two *socii* dutifully appeared at the general chapter of 1738 and were given their traditional places after Castile.

The first chapter of the restored province of Ireland was held on May 25-31, 1741, under the presidency of Patrick Hughes, eldest in profession. Patrick of St. Mary Magdalen Mahoney was elected provincial; John of St. Mary Magdalen Burke, Raymond of St. Mary Burke, Eugene Sweeney, and Maurice of St. Elisha Stanford definitors. Custos of the province was John of St. Elijah O'Neill; delegates to the general chapter, James Barry and Peter Prendergast. The provincial took Patrick Mahoney as his assistant. Priors of fourteen houses were elected.

With the reorganization of the province, the traffic of students to the continent increased. In 1736, Patrick Hughes, his studies completed, is given his obedience for Ireland. Two years previously, he had obtained the licentiate at the University of Paris, the only Irishman known to have done so. Irishmen are still found in the province of Touraine. In 1736, Henry of St. Mary, a priest, was allowed to transfer from Arras to the province of Gascony. The same year, Luke of St. Mary, a cleric, was also permitted to move from Arras to Piedmont, but for some reason remained in Touraine.

In Gascony, we find James of St. Joseph O'Cain (O'Cahan), to whom the provincial chapter of 1748 granted affiliation. In 1739, he wrote from Toulouse, asking permission to continue his study of theology in Italy or Spain. Many years later (1770-1777) O'Cain is found living as a hermit attached to the chapel of our Lady in Arcachon in the diocese of Bordeaux.

The reformed province of Piedmont was also considered a suitable place for the Irish to study. In 1736, Bernard of St. Albert Feeley (Fily), already a priest, was sent there for theology. He is still there in Turin in 1740, when he receives scapular faculties. In 1738, Patrick of St. Andrew Cummins (Comens) was assigned to Turin for studies. In 1743, Patrick of St. Mary Magdalen Cummins (Comming) wrote to Rome from Turin in a Latin "*satis eloquens.*"

Likewise in Italy, the Carmine in Naples provided opportunity to study to the Irish. John of St. Mary Meaghan was sent there to study theology in 1746. Three years previously, he had been in Asti in the province of Piedmont, probably for study. In 1748, Bartholomew Burke (Burgo) was placed in one of the provinces in the Kingdom of Naples, "*ex arbitrio Sanctissimi.*"

Catholic Spain with its pretensions to the British crown continued to be a logical haven for Irish Carmelites. In 1736, two clerics, Francis of St. Albert and Peter of St. Andrew, were dispatched to Andalusia. Francis Mannin wrote from Barcelona asking to be allowed to study dogmatic theology in France or Germany, but was refused permission after the Catalonian provincial, Angel Horta, reported unfavorably on his conduct. Patrick of St. Albert had obtained the doctorate at the University of Irache in Navarre, but as Joseph of the Virgin Mary Herrera, commissary general for the crown of England, reported from Madrid in 1743, he delayed returning to his province and was misbehaving.

In 1745, Eugene Sweeney was given an obedience for his province. It is not clear where he made his studies. In 1758, Patrick Fitzmaurice was given leave to become an army chaplain.

"The Undoing of the Friars in Ireland"

Decrees by the Congregation of Propagation of the Faith of 1743 and 1751 gave the bishops of Ireland greater control over the mendicant orders and forbade the latter to clothe and profess candidates in Ireland itself. In the future, these should be sent to properly constituted novitiates in Catholic countries and should not return until completion of their theological studies. Behind this action of the Congregation lay rumors and complaints about the friars, their excessive numbers, their idleness, their dissolute lives.

The regulation about novitiates and studies worked a special hardship on the orders. Until then, candidates had been received in more or less makeshift novitiates according to circumstances and had been immediately ordained before being sent abroad to study. Their Mass stipends helped support them during their studies. Against the decree of the Congregation the friars objected that young laymen could not always afford or would not be willing to undertake the expense of an education abroad, and the orders would be undertaking a good deal of trouble and expense over untried vocations. They considered the new regulation their undoing.

The Carmelites joined the other mendicants in seeking the recall of the unpopular decrees. The general chapter of 1756 resolved to request the pope to allow novices to be received in Ireland until a novitiate could be instituted in a Catholic country, but apparently their petition fell on deaf ears.

The formation procedures among the Carmelites evidently did not differ from those of the other mendicants in Ireland. We have seen novices being received in Dublin and Ballinasmall. Likewise, among the students mentioned above as studying on the Continent some were already priests. Complaints were also heard about the conduct of some of the Irish students.

As in the case of the other mendicants, the ban on Irish novitiates seems also to have affected the Carmelites unfavorably. For at least a decade, patents for Irishmen studying on the continent disappear from the registers of the priors general. The Irish provincial, Francis Mannin, unable to attend the general chapter of 1762, appealed to the charity of the capitulars to adopt one or two novices of his province, though, if necessary, he would try to find the means to defray costs. The chapter decided that the Flandro-Belgian province should take in the Irish novices, and that the expenses of their education should be shared by all the provinces of the Order. The buck was all the easier to pass to the Flemings, because they, too, were absent from the chapter. When they were later approached, they politely refused.

The newly elected prior general, Mariano Ventimiglia, bestirred himself on behalf of the Irish province. His correspondence with Mannin shows that in 1762 he found a novitiate for two Irish postulants in Aragon and in 1765 for four aspirants in Catalonia and Castile. The latter year, Mannin had placed two novices in Bordeaux and the following year, 1766, two more in Toulouse. He collected money to acquire a house for Irish students in Spain, but the project never came to term.

Ventimiglia's successor, Joseph Albert Ximénez (1768-1780), likewise had the welfare of the Irish province at heart. In a letter to the Grand Duke of Tuscany, December 8, 1777, he reveals that he had placed fourteen Irish students in the provinces of Spain, two in Siena, three in the Carmine of Naples, and many others in France and Belgium. On September 7, 1778, Ximénez received permission from the Holy See to borrow 20,000 Roman *scudi* for the education of four Irish students in the convent of St. Teresa in Naples. Four more, besides their regent, were ready to set out from Spain. How much of this sum was actually used for the purposes alleged is questionable. It formed part of the enormous debt Ximénez was to leave after him, but that is another story.

Subsequently, John Bourne (Borno) is found studying at the Carmine in Naples, where he made his profession *in articulo mortis*, November 12, 1778. The following January 12, he ratified his vows in St. Teresa's convent, Naples. On March 15, 1779, Bourne received dimissorials for tonsure and orders with a dispensation for age. He returned to his province, his studies finished, in 1781.

In 1779, Anthony Prendergast, member of the community of Traspontina, was granted dimissorials for priesthood. Three years later, he returned to his province from Naples, where he had apparently completed his courses.

In 1781, Patrick Joyce was released to Ireland and the "apostolic mission." The following year, Martin Nolan was sent back to his province "as a missionary."

Around 1780, the Irish province had forty-two members. Thus, it maintained the level of its membership at a time when numbers throughout the Order were decreasing. When all is said and done, the lack of an Irish house of studies was probably adequately compensated by the effective concern of the priors general, and the need to send candidates to proper novitiates can only have improved the quality of religious life of the Irish Carmelites.

Little is known about the lives and deeds of the Irish Carmelites in penal times. They lived, not in stately monastic edifices like their brothers on the continent, but in modest "residences," rarely able to accommodate more than two or three persons, to which were attached primitive chapels. All outward evidence of monastic observance was to be avoided. The priests were often on the road, ministering to the spiritual needs of people in other localities, sometimes settling in a place for years and dying there alone. In bad times, they lived constantly under threat of imprisonment and exile. Their chapels, built at the cost of great sacrifice on the part of their impoverished flocks, might be destroyed by the authorities or by Protestant mobs. Apparently the Irish Carmelites did not consider their heroic lives worth chronicling. For the most part, only oral tradition attests their presence, their sufferings, and their accomplishments.

The English rulers were only too successful in their efforts to stifle the intellectual life of the Catholic population of Ireland. As in the Dark Ages, learning became almost the exclusive prerogative of the clergy, educated on the continent. Not always possessing the leisure and means for original literary creation, they sought to provide reading material for their people by means of translations. One Carmelite who practised this apostolate of the pen was Raymond of St. Patrick O'Connell (1693-1779), prior of Kinsale, who translated into Gaelic Anthony Yvan's *Trumpet of Heaven* (Paris, 1661, etc.). His version which has come down in nine manuscripts has seen a modern edition.

O'Connell was not the first Carmelite to concern himself with Anthony Yvan (1576-1653), writer of spiritual books and founder of the Sisters of Our Lady of Mercy. The ubiquitous Leo of St. John preached his funeral oration, published as *Le vrai serviteur de Dieu, eloge du R. P. Antoine Yvan* (Paris, 1654) and also edited his works, *Le premier recueil des traités spirituels du R. P. Antoine Yvan* (Paris, 1654). O'Connell also translated part of *El Monte Calvario* by Anthony Guevara (1481-1545), but in this case his work remained in manuscript. Guevara's book, as we have seen, was an early favorite of Brother John of St. Samson.

The Irish province chose as its principal patroness the Blessed Virgin Mary Immaculate and St. Patrick as its secondary patron. The choice was approved and confirmed by the Congregation of Rites on May 11, 1754.

The Province of Scotland

The brief of Clement XII, which restored the Irish province in 1737, perpetually united the convent of Edinburgh to it and granted the Irish provincial the faculty of naming a vicar provincial of Scotland and a prior for Edinburgh. Clement himself made the first provision, naming William Fleirr (Flynn?) vicar of Scotland and prior of Edinburgh, with Peter Prendergast as his *socius* and secretary. It is not known whether these officials ever assumed their duties.

Nevertheless, in subsequent general chapters, the office of titular provincial of Scotland was mostly bestowed on candidates other than the Irish provincial.

The English Mission

The restoration of the monarchy under Charles II again offered an opportunity for Catholicism in England. The general chapter of 1666 resolved to seek authorization from the Holy See to send missionaries to England, Ireland, and Scotland. Meanwhile, the provinces of Francia, Touraine, and Belgium, together with the general council of the Order, were to study means of receiving novices from those countries. In fact, it was these provinces, especially Touraine, which were later active in England.

Ironically, it was Thomas Fullwood, who was to prove a broken reed, who got the mission under way. He was an Englishman, only son of parents living in London. Converted to Catholicism in Brussels, he entered the Order in the province of Francia, no doubt in the reformed convent of Caen, where we find him in 1680 participating in the controversy over the novitiate under the name, Damasus of St. Mary. In 1686, he is stated to be 32 years of age and professed 12 years.

On January 29, 1687, Damasus wrote to the prior general, Paul of St. Ignatius, stating his desire to go to London to confirm his family in the faith and enclosing a letter he had written to Philip Howard, O.P., cardinal protector of England. Paul seized the chance to re-establish the Order in England. He approached the English ambassador in Rome, the Earl of Castlemaine, who proved amenable and agreed to carry a letter to King James.

In a "long and serious" interview on September 22, Cardinal Howard thought it best not to send Frenchmen at first, but only Damasus and Henry of St. Teresa, who had a relation influential at the court, as a sort of *avant garde* of the mission. He warned prophetically of the danger of apostasy from the faith in the relaxed atmosphere of heretical England. The provincial of Touraine, Mark of the Nativity, agreed to this plan, as the prior general wrote to the Belgian provincial, Patrick of St. George, suggesting he get in touch with Mark in Paris.

The Arrival of the Missionaries, 1688

At last, on January 12, 1688, Paul was able to send Mark the desired letter of recommendation, dated January 9, from Cardinal Howard to Bishop John Leyburn, vicar apostolic of London. Mark had his little band ready to depart: James Fortin, superior, Germain of St. James Lebreton and Henry of St. Teresa Trent (which the French spelled Trant). Damasus Fullwood preceded them on his own. Since the Frenchmen were ready, they were sent, though it had been agreed that the Belgians should undertake the care of the English mission. Of James Fortin, unfortunately, nothing further is known. Germain of St. James Lebreton was born in 1645 and professed at Tours in 1664. In 1669, he was a student at Nantes. Henry of St. Teresa Trent, the son of an Irishman, was professed at Tours in 1669. In 1685, he is a member of the community of Poitiers, aged 33, professed 16 years, confessor, preacher, and professor of philosophy and theology for five years. The three friars left Paris on November 21, according to the recollection of Germain, and arrived in London twelve days later. In June, Germain obtained a post as one of the chaplains of Sig. Ferrieri, legate of Tuscany.

From Mark of the Nativity, the prior general received news that was not all good. Disagreement had arisen between Henry Trent and his superior, and Damasus, who had preceded the others, had not yet appeared on the scene. Both of them, Paul wrote to Mark on March 30, 1688, should be sent back to their province. They could be replaced by others from the Flemish province, if Fortin, who is on the spot, judges it opportune. "There should be no respect for diversity of province or nationality, but only for Jesus Christ, in whom we all exist."

Henry Trent finally got in touch with the prior general with letters of April 26 and May 4, 1688, explaining his differences with Fortin and asking for separate patents for himself. Paul answered by exhorting him to charity and obedience and referring his request to his provincial, "for I should not blindly make decisions from so far away about matters not familiar to me." Mark later decided not to recall Trent for fear of creating a scandal and sought to bring him to a better frame of mind by gentle persuasion.

In spite of this inauspicious beginning, Mark of the Nativity went ahead with his program for supplying missionaries to England. Through the mediation of Paul of St. Ignatius he had agreed to provide a novitiate and course of studies for the candidates William Shea had assembled in Dublin. Some of these were destined for England. On June 22, 1688, Paul wrote to Mark expressing his satisfaction at the arrival in Touraine of Shea's students, three of them earmarked for England. These were apparently the James and Thomas Fitzmorris and Patrick Nicholas, for whom Paul enclosed dimissorials for orders. Since he does not subsequently appear in England, Nicholas may be the student the prior general reports to Shea on February 15, 1689, as having died.

But by now the "Glorious" Revolution of November, 1688, had taken place, and the chance for a revival of Catholicism in England had passed. With the Act of Toleration of 1689 of William III, repressive measures against Catholics were restored. Bishops and priests were banished. The outbreak of William's War (1689-1697) can hardly have enhanced the welcome of Frenchmen on Albion's shores.

The modest Carmelite enterprise was severely shaken, but survived. The superior, James Fortin, returned to France. Henry Trent abandoned the Catholic faith and settled down in the countryside as a minister. Germain Lebreton lost his patron and took to living as a private citizen, earning his bread through the ministry and his musical skill. Later, he regained his refuge at the Tuscan embassy. When his patron, Sig. Ferrieri, left London, he arranged a place for Germain in the chapel of the Portuguese embassy.

It is interesting to note that Germain supported the liceity for Catholics of the oath of allegiance.

In 1690, the luckless Damasus of St. Mary ended up in jail, not as a martyr for the faith, but for some imprudence. Upon his release, Germain arranged for him to join him at the Portuguese embassy. The prior general, who had little faith in Damasus, urged him to return to his own province or to Belgium.

Nothing daunted by the disastrous course of Catholic affairs, Germain not only stayed at his post but requested reinforcements.

Around Lent of 1693, James of St. Mary Magdalen de' Pazzi Mandin appeared in London. He was a Parisian, professed at Poitiers in 1674. In 1686, he was living at Les Billettes in Paris and said to be about 30 years old. He was to prove a reliable and durable member of the mission.

In 1691 and 1692, the English mission lost two interested friends, when Mark of the Nativity and Paul of St. Ignatius lapsed from office respectively as provincial of Touraine and prior general of the Order. Their dealings with the English mission and each other are marked with prudence, charity, and patient dedication, and reveal two eminent religious motivated by the highest and most disinterested ideals.

The Mission Under Germain Lebreton

In 1695, Germain and Mandin were joined by Theodoric of St. René Devois and James of Jesus and Mary Finn (or O'Finn), who brought patents dated May 1, 1695, from the prior general, John Feijóo de Villalobos, making Germain commissary general. Theodoric was born at Poitiers in 1665 and professed there in 1681. Five years later, he is found among the student clerics at Nantes. He relates about himself that he taught philosophy and theology at the University of Poitiers from his twenty-third to his thirtieth year (1688-1695). Before coming to England, he had also had experience as a missionary in the Poitou. James Finn was an Irishman educated in the Touraine province, apparently one of Williams Shea's vocations.

In 1693, he requested to be affiliated in the Touraine province.

Thus, the little Carmelite band, buffeted by the Revolution, reformed its ranks under the leadership of Germain, durable pioneer, and with sounder members.

Not all the Carmelites in England were included among them. About the same time as Mandin (1693), Elijah of Mount Carmel van de Steen arrived in England as the chaplain of the Count of Aversberg. A member of the Flemish province, Van de Steen was born in Bruges in 1656, professed in 1674 and ordained a priest in 1680. He summoned to join him an Irishman reared in the Flemish province with the unlikely surname of Vanderberg, about whose antecedents or sojourn in England nothing further is known.

In 1696, Germain and Mandin spent eleven days in jail. The same fate was suffered by Theodoric, and his patron was imprisoned in the Tower. On their release, the three friars returned or were deported to France, where Germain attended the provincial chapter in Nantes. Towards the end of the year, Mandin returned to England with a new recruit, Thomas of St. Elias Fitzmorris, both of them being immediately apprehended on arrival. Germain lingered on in France for almost a year. On January 5, 1697, he was commissioned by Villalóbos to execute various decrees regarding Ireland. He returned to England in the fall of 1697 with the other Fitzmorris, James of St. Joseph. Germain left the Portuguese embassy for the country house of a friendly nobleman, where he remained for several years.

The reason for this move by Germain was "persecution" by his "enemies." In fact, a rift quickly occurred between the commissary and the Irish in the mission. Germain accused them of slandering him and suspected that they were the reason for his removal from the Portuguese embassy. Their unconventional conduct scandalized him, but the Irish, used to living under the sword of Damocles, were probably wiser in the ways of survival in penal England. They considered him too inflexible and timid and wanted to depend on a commissary from Ireland. Much of the problem probably lay in the temperament and attitude of Germain, for Theodoric had no trouble getting along with the Irish. It was he whom the prior general, Charles Philibert Barberi, on January 6, 1699, appointed to mediate the dispute. Only on June 20, 1701, did Theodoric send his report, in which he gave a favorable account of all parties concerned, but recommended that the Irish and English missions be separated, and that control of finances should not rest exclusively in the hands of the commissary. Rome does not seem to have taken any further steps in the matter.

The fourth Irishman who besides the two Fitzmorris' and Finn constituted the bane of Germain's life was Anselm of St. Simon Stock, about whom further information is lacking, unless he be the Anselm Jackson named commissary in Ireland in 1715.

In 1698, the Englishman, Stephen of St. Augustine Mason, arrived from Touraine. To Germain he appeared "exceedingly young." Three years later, Theodoric says about Mason that he gives satisfaction to the Catholics among whom he works and could learn, if he applied himself.

The apostolate of a certain Damian, of the Touraine province, was of short duration. In 1700, Germain, who since the death of his patron the previous year had resumed his post in the Portuguese embassy, summoned Damian to join him there. When after almost a year Damian had not appeared, Theodoric joined

Germain. Damian was eventually located in a jail fifty miles from London. After being brought to London, he was deported aboard a ship bound for Ostend.

Damasus Fullwood meanwhile had abandoned the faith and become a minister in London under the name of Dubois. On August 8, 1701, Germain reports to the assistant general, Francis de Latenay, that Damasus was leaving for Barbados. At the same time, Germain repeats a rumor that Henry Trent had died.

In 1701, Elijah van de Steen died in Holland, where he had accompanied the Count of Aversberg. Not long after, Theodoric, who had often been associated with him in the apostolate, crossed over to France and seems never to have returned. He settled in Les Billettes in Paris and continued his English apostolate by means of the pen. He wrote *Justification of the Roman Church on the Re-ordination of Anglican Bishops* (Paris, 1718, 2 v.) and in 1726 received permission to publish certain "polemical dissertations." He also wrote about the miracle of the Sacrament at Les Billettes (Paris, 1725, 2 v.).

On June 19, 1705, the English missionaries under their commissary wrote to congratulate Angelus Cambolas on his election as prior general and to signify their loyalty and obedience. Besides Germain, six friars added their signatures: James of St. Mary Magdalen (Mandin), James of Jesus and Mary (Finn), James of St. Joseph (Fitzmorris), Thomas of St. Elijah (Fitzmorris), Anselm of St. Simon Stock, and Stephen of St. Augustine (Mason).

On February 10, 1713, Peter Thomas Sanchez granted confirmation to the statutes for the mission composed by Germain, adding ten decrees of his own. At the same time, he approved certain investments Germain had made in Paris on behalf of the mission and again named him commissary for England, Scotland, and Ireland. In case of his illness or death, Athanasius of Jesus, lector of theology in the province of Touraine, was to take his place.

It is not known when in fact Germain passed to his reward. Most likely this good and faithful servant died in the land to which he had devoted his life. He was a sincerely spiritual man with a deep sense of duty which inspired in him a firm consciousness of responsibility but little sympathy with those who seemed neglectful. His faith, courage, and learning inspired esteem in the small Catholic community. He preached regularly in the embassies of Tuscany and Portugal to distinguished congregations. He translated from the French a booklet for the Third Order and contemplated publishing his sermons, but it is not known whether they were ever printed.

The English Mission in Later Years

After the first decade of the 18th century, information on the English mission is less forthcoming, but there is no doubt that it continued to exist.

Germain's or Athanasius' successor as commissary may have been George Walker, who studied in Italy at Piacenza and whom Germain had recommended for superior as early as 1704. On November 1, 1710, Sanchez sent Walker to England, where at an unknown date he was placed in charge of the mission. On January 20, 1720, Athanasius of St. Maurice was named to succeed George Walker, deceased. Either Athanasius did not assume office or else functioned in it only briefly, for on June 15, Victor of St. Cecily was appointed commissary. Victor (d. 1723) was born in Tours and had been confessor of the Ursulines at Orléans, assistant novice master at La Flèche (1692) and Tours (1698), before becoming prior at Hennebont in 1702. He wrote *The Way to Heaven*, practical rules for leading souls to high perfection (Vienne, 1702). His experience as a spiritual director was used to good effect among English Catholics, and he is also credited with a number of conversions. He arrived in London in 1713, to all outward appearances an oculist. In 1719, Charles Cornaccioli, prior general, authorized him to purchase a house in *civitate Salmunea* or *Solmunea*, wherever that might be, where the missionaries might live together in community.

In 1722, Alexis of St. Charles de la Mellière became commissary. In 1731, he reports the arrival in England of Peter Brown. Brown, an English Carmelite, seems to have been educated in Italy. In 1728, he is in Rome, where he befriends an Irishman, Thomas Nugent, who subsequently requested to be received into the Order.

Thereafter, silence descends on the mission in England. This does not necessarily mean that Carmelite activity there came to a stop. At the general chapter of 1762, the provincial of Touraine, Lambert Clerardin, claimed the title of provincial of England, since his province was professing and educating English students.

The correspondence of the Carmelite missionaries bears little resemblance to the *Relations* of the Jesuits. The Carmelites provide few details about their apostolate, but it is clear that it involved tutoring, preaching, convert-making and controversy with persons of other persuasions. The missionaries, who had access to the Continent, were also able to perform useful services for their Catholic patrons and friends. In Paris, in 1696, Germain arranged the return of a nun who had fled to England eight years previously, the last four of which she had spent in London, deprived of all resources. After six months of negotiations, he was able to see the nun to a monastery of her order. At the same time, he helped recover her property a girl converted to Catholicism from Calvinism in London. In 1698, Germain travelled again to Belgium to fetch back the gravely ill eldest son of his patron. In August of the following year, he accompanied the two daughters of his patron from Ghent to a monastery in Paris.

The Mission in the Dutch Republic

The revolt of the seven northern provinces of the Netherlands from Spanish rule led to their independence in 1581 and the establishment of the Republic of the United Provinces with the House of Orange as hereditary *stadtholders*. Calvinism became the state religion. Catholics who continued to form a considerable portion of the population were denied the public practice of their faith. Its practice in private was conditional to the payment of taxes and fines and always subject to new oppressive measures (*plakkaten*). Catholics were excluded from public office, state schools, and all of public life. In short, their condition was similar to that of Irish and English Catholics.

The Catholic communion fell into complete disarray, and at first it seemed that the flock, bereft of its shepherds, would be dispersed. Yet Catholicism rallied under the inspired leadership of Sasbout Vosmeer (1583-1614), named vicar apostolic in 1592 with the powers previously held by the vicar general in Cologne. In Vosmeer's successor, Philip Rovenius (1614-1651), Dutch Catholics had no less able a leader. The Catholic faith suffered a setback in the controversy over Jansenism, which was particularly strong in the Calvinistic Netherlands and ended in a clear-cut schism in Utrecht (1723). The government sided with the Jansenists and put an end to the appointment of vicars apostolic (1727). Deprived of central leadership, the Catholics fell back on a system of local jurisdiction presided over by archpriests.

A new generation of zealous and devout secular priests, educated in Belgium and other Catholic countries, was seconded by religious - Jesuits (1592), Franciscans (1614), Dominicans (1620) and Capuchins (1625). Beginning in 1648, the Discalced Carmelites conducted missions in Leiden, the Hague, and Amsterdam. Religious services were conducted in attics or other rented or purchased premises. But here, too, jurisdictional disputes arose between the vicars apostolic and the religious whom the Holy See liked to keep maneuverable through special faculties. In 1626, an equitable *Concordia* gave the vicars authority over religious with regard to their pastoral activities.

The convents of the Carmelite Order in the northern Netherlands had not constituted a separate province, but had formed part of the provinces of Lower Germany and Francia. There could be no question of recovering pre-Reformation houses, much less of restoring a province. However, the Belgian Carmelites joined the other religious orders in succoring their beleaguered fellow Catholics in the north.

The activity of the Carmelites was confined mainly to the *Generaliteitslanden*, won from Spain by the Dutch Republic only in the middle of the 17th century, where restrictions on Catholics were even more strictly enforced than elsewhere. By the end of the century, however, it was again possible for priests to enter the region and practise a discreet ministry. After 1730, (another effect of the controversy with Jansenism), religious were no longer admitted to the Republic, although those already present were permitted to remain.

Around 1637, Jacob Vivarius and Charles Couvrechef, of the convent of Antwerp, opened a mission in Amsterdam. Martin van den Venne, previously prior of Brugge, commissioned by the Congregation of the Propagation of the Faith, joined them in 1650. Two years later, Vivarius died in the mission, and Martin returned to Antwerp, where he had been elected prior. The vicar apostolic, Jacob de la Torre, attempted to have the Carmelites recalled, but Couvrechef at least remained in Amsterdam until his death in 1661. Himself a poet and painter, Couvrechef became the friend of the noted Dutch poet, Joost van den Vondel.

In 1661, the Flemings, Everard of St. Willibrord Bochel and Timothy of St. Macario opened a mission in Amersfoort in the province of Utrecht. Ten years later, the vicar apostolic challenged the legitimacy of their presence, but Everard, who by that time seems to have been alone, stood firm against every onslaught of ecclesiastical censure. He is still in Amersfoort in 1680, when he requested of the prior general permission to donate to the poor certain of his goods, which by right belonged to the province.

Zeeuws Vlaanderen and Western Brabant

When the people of Hontenisse (Hulst) petitioned the bishop of Ghent, Albert de Hornes de Hautekerke, for a priest, he referred them to the Carmelites. The provincial, Sebastian of St. Paul Petit, agreed to meet their needs and through the Catholic Count Oswald van den Bergh, of Boxmeer, obtained permission of the

States General. The first pastor, Godfried of St. John the Baptist Blommaert arrived in 1692, but remained only long enough to build a church, before moving the same year to Haps in Eastern Brabant, where he again undertook the construction of a church. According to the conditions laid down by the States General, the church had to be a barn church made of wood with no exterior ornamentation or religious symbols. Godfried placed it on a site available to the towns of Hontenisse, Ossenisse, Hengstdijk, and Groenendijk.

The Flemish province supplied two friars to the mission of Hontenisse. Godfried was given as an assistant Caspar of St. Giles Allepas, a native of Zevenbergen, where as we shall see, the Carmelites also had a mission. Caspar remained on during the pastorate of Philibert of St. Lawrence de Vos (1692-1694) and in turn succeeded him in that office. He was assisted by Nicholas of All Saints van Mullen. Two laybrothers, Nicholas of St. Livinus Cockhuyt and Guy of the Ascension Hallemans, are also known to have labored on the mission during these years. Upon his death in 1712, Van Mullen, "a truly worthy missionary," as the provincial necrology styles him, was succeeded as assistant by Matthias of St. Leonard Henquinié, who became pastor in 1720. He was assisted during his long pastorate by Sebastian of St. John the Baptist van der Stelt. In 1751, the wooden thatch-covered church burned down and was replaced by a brick structure with a tile roof. Sebastian died in 1761, aged 72, and was replaced by a secular priest, J. W. Adriaensens, since no more religious were forthcoming after the ban of 1730. Matthias continued to head the mission until his death in 1770 at the age of 89. Though no longer permitted to work, the Carmelites at least were able to hand on to the local clergy a well-appointed church and a loyal flock.

Also in Zeeuws Vlaanderen was the Carmelite mission of Aardenburg.

From 1669 to 1740, Carmelites from Antwerp administered the parish of Zevenbergen, northeast of Breda in Western Brabant. The first Carmelite pastor, Caspar of St. Dominic van den Leemputte, took over from the Franciscans. Upon his death in 1678, Leemputte was followed by Modestus of St. Gudula Schuysmans (1678-1712), Bartholomew of the Assumption Collaert (1712-1713), Ignatius of St. Leo van den Brande (1715?-1721), and Adelbert de Saert (1724-1740). Van den Brande in defiance of the authorities replaced the old barn church with one of brick and as a result spent some weeks in jail in The Hague. His release may have come about through the intervention of the Portuguese ambassador, whose chaplain he became in 1721. After the Carmelites gave up the mission, Anthony of St. Francis Audigier remained as assistant until his death in 1759.

From 1673 to 1785, the Carmelites had the care of Rucphen (Rukven), a town east of Roosendaal. The first Carmelite pastor, Archangel of the Holy Spirit van der Zijpe, inherited from the Cistercians a parish of 600 communicants, a barn church and a house. The Protestants had taken over the Catholic church and rectory, notwithstanding the fact that the town counted only half a dozen members of that persuasion. In 1684, the wooden church and priest's house were destroyed by fire. To obtain the means to replace them Archangel had recourse to the bishop and friends in Antwerp, among them his brother-in-law, John Augustus della Faille, of a well-endowed family of the city. Brother Mark, goldsmith, was dispatched to Rucphen to recover the melted silver from the ruins and purify it. For the new barn church the pastor purchased pictures of St. Martin, Our Lady della Bruna and St. Joseph. Unable at the time to replace his house, Archangel moved into the Catholic rectory, abandoned by the Calvinist minister since 1682, but was ejected by the few Protestants of the town. Only in 1694 was he able to occupy a house through the generosity of Jongheer della Faille.

Fr. Archangel was succeeded as pastor by Apollinaris of St. Gertrude van Hove (1706-1713), Oswald of St. John van Elsen (1713-1725), and Alexander of St. James de Man (1725-1785). All worked in the mission until their deaths. Oswald carried out certain improvements in the rectory and church, himself doing the painting and decoration of the latter. From Oswald's pastorate also dates the statuary group of the bestowal of the scapular on St. Simon Stock, still found in the church. In 1768, Alexander renovated the barn church, which Constantine of St. Peter de Nayer, of the convent of Antwerp and otherwise known as a painter, decorated. Alexander seems to have been a good-natured man, beloved of his people. He apparently did not in the least mind the rustic humor at his expense displayed in a lengthy poem indited on the occasion of his golden jubilee of profession in 1762:

> When Carmel's garb to don he did decide,
> All burst with laughter, fit to be tied.
> "Look, fellows, isn't that a sight,"
> They cried, "John de Man's to be a Carmelite!

In parlous times, the good burghers of Rucphen had evidently preserved their sense of humor as well as their faith.

The Carmelites, as usual, neglected to leave an account of their labors. We know at least that the deans on their regular visitations gave them good marks. The Carmelites also instilled a tender devotion to the Mother of God, as attested by artifacts that remain. Until modern times, Rucphen was a popular place of pilgrimage for the scapular feast.

Other Carmelite missions in the Western parts of the Netherlands were 's-Gravenhage, Gorinchem (Gorkum), Sprundel, Standaardsbuiten, and Hilvarenbeek.

Daniel of St. Peter (Bosch, d. 1719) was attached to the Spanish embassy in 's-Gravenhage. He published sermons on the Hail Mary (Ghent, 1694) and a sermon for Good Friday ('s-Gravenhage, 1692).

Boxmeer and Its Missions

An important development for the Carmelite mission in the Dutch Republic was the founding of a convent in the Catholic enclave of Boxmeer in eastern Brabant. In 1652, Count Albert van den Bergh (1607-1656) concluded an agreement with the noted Daniel of the Virgin Mary, then provincial of the Flemish province, to build a Carmelite convent in his domain. His wife, Magdalen de Cusance, had become acquainted with the Carmelites in Brussels and Gelderen and had been edified by their devout manner of celebrating the liturgy. The convent was erected (1652-1709) next to the parish church, the care of which the Carmelites took over from the pastor, Anthony Peelen. No doubt the greater possibility offered by a religious community of providing spiritual care to the Catholics in the surrounding Protestant regions also constituted a motive for the foundation.

As a matter of fact, the Boxmeer community over the years carried out an extensive apostolate in Eastern Brabant, conducting missions in Vierlingsbeek (1681-1712), Sambeek (1654-1760), Beugen (1663-1731), Haps (1691-1731), Mill (1659-1663), Tongelaar, Cuyk, Beers, Groot Linden (1698-1714), Heumen (1706-1732), Balgoy (with Keent and Nederasselt, 1693-1703).

No less effective ministry on behalf of the Catholic faith was the Latin School conducted by the Boxmeer community from 1658 to 1832.

Boxmeer survived the French Revolution and the secularization of the 19th century to become the seed from which sprang modern Carmel in the Netherlands.

The Carmelites certainly were not guilty of the fault, of which religious were accused, of congregating in the cities, where their services were not needed, and of neglecting the rural regions.

The Mission in Northern Germany

Like the countries already considered, Protestant northern Germany offered promising opportunities for missionary zeal. There the German Carmelites undertook a mission in the Baltic seaport of Stralsund in Pomerania, since the Peace of Westphalia (1648) under Swedish control.

In 1780, Martin Efferts took over the mission established by the ex-Jesuit, Giles Dechene, under the jurisdiction of the bishop of Hildesheim as vicar apostolic. The Swedish authorities had granted permission for two priests to reside and conduct services in private homes or a chapel. Efferts labored in the mission until his death in 1793, having meanwhile managed to build a church. He was succeeded by Raphael D'Ossery, Theodore Becker, Clement Happel, Sylvester Bayerlein, and Wendelin Zink. The latter is especially worthy of notice.

Born in Mangolding near Regensburg in 1777, Zink received the Carmelite habit and the name Wendelin in Abensburg. He studied in Straubing and after ordination in 1801 exercised the ministry there. When a request for missionaries for Stralsund came from the Congregation for the Propagation of the Faith, Zink willingly came forward. His appointment as apostolic missionary followed on March 19, 1803. He was accompanied to Stralsund by Sylvester Bayerlein, twice his age, who died a year later.

The twenty-six year old Wendelin stayed on and for thirty-seven years ministered alone to the sparse Catholic population scattered over a wide area that included, besides Stralsund, cities like Greifswald and Wolgast on the mainland of West Pomerania as well as the island of Rügen. In 1807, Zink received faculties to confer the sacrament of Confirmation. Money was scarce, but he managed to restore the church, provide an organ, and acquire a cemetery. To support himself, he acted as tutor in private families, mostly Protestant. After 1821, he conducted the parish school. He was a gifted teacher and, moreover, had acquired considerable learning. He was held in high regard for this quality and was welcomed to local literary circles. He regularly contributed to the Mainz newspaper, *Katholik*, compiled a hymn book for the parish (Stralsund, 1805), as well as a book of devotions and songs (Stralsund, 1826), taken largely from Bishop Challoner. He left a valuable and interesting diary (Straubing, 1983).

Upon Zink's death in 1840 the Carmelite Basil Lang took over the mission, but returned to Ravensburg after a year. Thereafter, the diocesan clergy were able to undertake the care of the parish. Meanwhile, the Carmelites had filled an urgent pastoral need with dedicated fidelity and solicitude.

In Berlin, capital of the Kingdom of Prussia, Catholic worship was at first limited to the embassies of Austria and France. In 1722, a chapel for the use of the military was permitted, and toward the middle of the century the time was ripe for a proper parish church. On November 22, 1746, the Carmelite Eugene Mecenati, of the Mantuan Congregation, who served the Italian and French Catholics of the city, was authorized by Frederick II to collect alms for the construction of a church. It was probably no coincidence that it was dedicated to St. Hedwig, Duchess of Silesia, which Frederick annexed in 1748. Designed by Jean Legeay and modelled on the Pantheon in the current classical style, the church was consecrated in 1773. It is not known whether Mecenati lived to see the realization of the dream for which he had labored unstintingly. The church was seriously damaged during the Battle of Berlin in 1945.

Chapter 11

The Curriculum of Studies

The important matter of the initial formation of religious was not left to chance by the popes of the Catholic Reformation. Abundance of candidates was no problem in an age when the monastery offered a tempting alternative to a life of grinding poverty, though it should not be forgotten that the age was also one of vigorous religious awakening. Emphasis was on the limitation of candidates, their proper selection and education.

The Initial Formation of Religious

Pope Sixtus V, *Cum de omnibus*, November 26, 1587, specified the impediments to admittance to a religious Order.

More significant were Clement VIII's *Institutions* on the reception and education of novices, March 19, 1603, which in substance fixed the form of the novitiate down to modern times. Novices are to be received only in houses officially approved for this purpose. Candidates for the habit should have a knowledge of letters or offer the hope of acquiring it, so that in due time they may receive minor and major orders. On receiving the habit, novices should make a general confession. The novitiate should be segregated from the convent, have separate rooms for each novice or a dormitory large enough to allow each his own bed. The novitiate should also have cells for the novice master and his *socius* (if one is needed), a chapter room heated in the winter, a chapel and a garden for exercise. No one may enter the novitiate except the master, his *socius*, and the superior, who, however, should be accompanied by one of the older fathers. The novice master and his *socius*, whose qualifications are carefully listed, are to be elected by the provincial chapter. The content of the novitiate instruction and certain religious acts are also laid down. The age of profession for clerics is 16, for brothers 20. A register of professions is to be kept. Novices may be received in the house of their affiliation before being sent to the novitiate.

The newly professed are to continue their formation in a *professorium* distinct from the novitiate itself, living more strictly than the older professed and not taking part in the activities of the community but engaging in the study of letters. They are to observe this regimen until Holy Orders or at least three years.

On September 21, 1624, Urban VIII ordered Clement's *Institutions* read in the refectory at least two times a year, a practice observed in Carmelite houses until the publication of the *Codex Iuris Canonici*.

Except for the addition of certain details from the legislation of Sixtus V and Clement VIII, Canal's constitutions of 1626 do not differ from Caffardi's of 1586 in the matter of the formation of clerics. The novices should be destined for the studies for which the community deems them best suited; the Order needs more than doctors and preachers (pt. 1, ch. 14, no. 7).

The professed are to remain cloistered, in charge of a master of professed in the larger convents, of the subprior in the smaller. "They should study not only letters but also morals, and they should be 'spiritual'." This period of formation lasted until the subdiaconate, which according to the Council of Trent (sess. 23,

Ch. 12) was not to be conferred before the age of 22 (pt. 1, ch. 15, nos. 2 and 8). The minimum age for profession was 16 (pt. 1, ch. 14, no. 1).

In the Stricter Observance, the constitutions (1656) add a chapter on postulants, stressing careful selection of candidates, and prescribe in great detail the manner of conducting the novitiates and *professoria*, there called seminaries (pt. 1, ch. 3-6). Novices are not to study, but should devote themselves to meditation and the reading of spiritual books (ch. 5, no. 3). In the seminaries, studies may be undertaken only after the first year; these are specified as the humanities, languages, especially Latin, and rhetoric (ch. 6, nos. 4 and 7). The time to be spent in the seminary is not laid down, this apparently being left to the needs of each province. During his visitation of the province of Gascony in 1669, Mark of the Nativity ordered the seminary course to last two years. In the second year, when studies were allowed, Latin, geography and chronology were to be taught.

The popes from Clement VIII kept close vigil over the houses of formation of religious orders, setting standards of observance for them and reserving their designation to themselves. The articles of Filippini (1648) forbid the reception of novices in any but reformed houses. In reformed provinces, this caused no difficulty, but in partially reformed provinces, non-reformed provincials often objected to being excluded from control of the novitiate. In Italy, the popes designated the convents where novices and professed might be educated; for instance, Alexander VII in 1657 and Clement XIII in 1759.

Together with the establishment of central novitiates and houses for professed, an important factor in the initial formation of Carmelite religious is found in the many excellent manuals this period produced. The most significant of them will be considered later. Also not to be overlooked in the literature of formation are the many commentaries on the Rule which appeared in this age, so concerned with the Order's primitive spirit.

Studies for the Priesthood

This was the time of the flowering of the diocesan seminary under the influence especially of the Jesuit colleges and their *ratio studiorum*, which also departmentalized modern theology and gave it its predominantly apologetical, casuistical, and canonical orientation. Religious orders such as the Theatines, Vincentians, Eudists, Sulpicians, devoted themselves to the education of priests.

Under the influence of the times, the Carmelite Order bestirred itself to do something about its "simple" priests. The house for professed, introduced by Audet, gathered the clerics from the diaspora of small convents in the provinces and gradually - particularly in the reformed provinces - provided them with more education at the secondary level.

The constitutions of 1626, in force until the 20th century, simply repeat previous legislation and show no progress in the education for the priesthood. Simple priests, as well as graduates, were obliged to attend the daily solution of cases of conscience presented by lectors in convents with at least eight priests. Houses with twelve priests were to be assigned a master regent who lectured daily on Sacred Scripture or solved cases of conscience. If confessors failed to attend, they were to be deprived of faculties. Simple priests, so failing, were to be "punished severely" (*acriter*). Even in the *studia* attached to the universities, there should be daily lectures on Scripture or cases of conscience for non-students. All this instruction outside the degree course could be given in the vernacular and should be adapted to the capacity of the audience (pt. 1, ch. 18, nos. 24).

No doubt lectors availed themselves of the growing genre of moral theology manuals.

Before obtaining faculties, confessors were obliged to undergo an examination. Faculties were granted by the prior general, the provincial chapter, or the prior provincial, and communicated to the local ordinary (pt. 1, ch. 10, no. 2).

This "continuing education" of priests was not always forthcoming, especially in small convents, nor evidently were all scholars sufficiently eager. As late as 1609, the general chapter had to take measures against "priests who are ignorant and unable to perform sacred functions, at least by reading Mass clearly and distinctly."

The constitutions of the Stricter Observance (1656) made no provision for doctoral degrees, though such degrees were allowed and pursued in many reformed provinces. The chapter of each province was to designate houses for philosophy and theology. In the house of philosophy one lector, lecturing for an hour and a half twice a day, covered all of logic, ethics, physics, and metaphysics in two years. Two lectors of theology were assigned to cover the *Summa* of St. Thomas in three years. The fourth year of theology was to be taught in one or two separate houses and consisted in a sort of pastoral course. Four months were devoted to canon law; thereafter followed courses in Scripture, apologetics, languages (especially Greek and Hebrew), and homiletics. During this year, too, spiritual exercises were intensified. In fact, growth in holiness, as well as learning, was evaluated at every stage of the course of studies. Of the two chapters concerning studies (pt. 1, ch. 21-22), one is devoted to the regular life in houses of study. The fourth pastoral year was required for preaching.

An examination at the end of the second year of theology selected the students who were to continue the course and become preachers, teachers, and otherwise specialists in the sacred sciences. The rest were given a six month course in moral theology to prepare them to hear confessions (pt. 1, ch. 23, no. 3). This course of studies was obviously less strenuous than the university course and for that reason could be followed by all up to a certain point. The modern course of studies for the priesthood is already adumbrated here.

In 1617, Thibault obtained permission from Fantoni for the reformed students of the province of Touraine to attend the Jesuit college at La Flèche.

For the 17th century, official documents no longer mirror actual practice; most priests had more education than appears there. A more thorough theological formation was obtained by those who entered the degree course and then either through failure or personal choice did not stand for the lectorate or baccalaureate.

In 1692, the prior general, John Feijóo de Villalobos, ordered the establishment of separate colleges for moral theology, to be taught "methodically" by a lector lecturing morning and evening. These colleges were intended for those judged unsuited for graduate study in theology and were to prepare them to administer the sacraments. Another cut-off point occurred after the four year theology course, when those who failed to qualify for the lectorate course were told to "exercise themselves in preaching, so that they might serve religion in that manner."

When the general chapter of 1704 decided that all priests should proceed as far as the lectorate degree, it was no doubt only canonizing longstanding practice.

The constitutions of 1626 name 37 general *studia* (actually they declare the *studia* to be 38, but list only 37): Rome, Paris, Toulouse, Padua, Pavia, Naples, Florence, Siena, Pisa, Turin, Cremona, Ravenna, Catania, Trapani, Messina, Palermo, Barcelona, Salamanca, Alcalá, Lérida, Coimbra, Toledo, Valladolid, Valencia, Huesca, Granada, Seville, Osuna, Cordova, London, Cologne, Mainz, Louvain, Avignon, Perpignan, Bordeaux, Angers (pt. 1, ch. 17, no. 1).

The dozen houses added to those shown by the constitutions of 1586 are situated mostly in Spain, where Aragon and Andalusia also receive representation: Toledo, Valladolid, Valencia, Huesca, Granada, Seville, Osuna, Cordova. In Sicily, Messina and Palermo become general *studia*; in Lower Germany, Mainz; in Flandro-Belgium, Louvain. Mainz had already been constituted in 1539, but seemingly without permanent results.

The general chapter of 1704 lists eight new general *studia*. Four of them were in the smaller Italian provinces: Lecce, Santa Maria della Vita (Naples), Capua, Bologna. The first two became general *studia* at the general chapter of 1654. The *studium* at Bologna was not that of the Mantuan Congregation; the province of Romagna made a foundation there in 1675.

North of the Alps, the Gallo-Belgian province acquired a *studium* at Douai, founded in 1636. After extinction during the Protestant Reformation, the Carmelites of the Upper German province returned to a new location in Vienna in 1661. The general chapter of 1620 ordered regents of philosophy and theology instituted in the *studium* of Cracow, erected by the previous general chapter of 1613, and authorized the provincial and definitory of the Polish province to appoint regents of logic, philosophy, and theology in other convents. Cracow became a general *studium* in 1645. Wilno seems to have been constituted a general *studium* at this chapter of 1704. The situation in France remained unchanged. London was finally omitted from the list of general *studia*.

Later additions are Lwów (1710), Bitonto in Puglia, Cosenza in Calabria (1762), Mohilew (1782).

All these houses of study are required to maintain a full faculty, beginning with the Arts, and an adequate body of students, as well as to accept students from all provinces. It is not clear how many met these standards of the constitutions, nor for that matter how many remained active.

The constitutions had never specified requirements for degrees, perhaps because these varied in different countries. The constitutions of 1626 add a paragraph treating this matter. The candidate for the degree of *cursoratus*, after completing the philosophy course, was required to hold a public disputation and deliver four lectures. The same conditions were placed on the lectorate after the theology course. To receive the baccalaureate, the lector was to lecture for two years or hold two public disputations. The master's degree demanded the same academic acts (pt. 1, ch. 17, no.9). The length of the *cursoratus* and lectorate courses is not indicated, but the general chapter of 1593 ordained that each should last four years. It also ordered masters to acquire the doctor's *laurea* within a year (*Constitutiones et decreta* 1593, ch. 10, nos. 23, 30).

The *laurea* granted by secular universities was an expensive affair. In 1634, Theodore Straccio, on the plea of the poverty of mendicant orders, obtained authorization from Urban VIII for the Carmelite college of Salamanca to bestow this distinction. In 1668, Matthew Orlandi received the same distinction for Traspontina. Finally in 1672, Clement X bestowed faculties to this effect on Carmelite priors general in any *studium* of the Order.

Revisions of the Curriculum

At the end of the 17th century the graduate curriculum underwent a period of flux. The far-ranging general chapter of 1680 under Emilio Giacomelli also concerned itself with graduate studies. It ordained that the course for the *cursoratus* should last three years; that for the lectorate, seven. The baccalaureate and master's degree required no examination. It was enough in the case of the former for the candidate to lecture three years; in the latter, seven years. The master acquired the *laurea* (granted by the general) by a single lecture on three theological conclusions.

This twenty year doctoral course, needless to say, met with little enthusiasm, and two years later Angelo Monsignani obtained *viva voce* authorization from Innocent XI to suspend action until the next chapter. The general chapter of 1686 referred the matter to the prior general, Paul of St. Ignatius, who in practice followed the constitutions regarding study.

John Feijóo de Villalobos, *quondam* professor at Valladolid, took a lively interest in the problem of study, issuing on August 20, 1692, twelve decrees to cure its ills. In every province there were to be four colleges or *studia*: one for philosophy (arts), two for theology, and one for moral theology. After the three year course in philosophy, those found apt to continue in theology proceeded as *cursores* to the second college for a four year course in scholastic theology according to St. Thomas or John Baconthorpe. The rest were sent to the fourth college for moral theology (length of course not specified), so that they might qualify to administer the sacraments, especially confession. Those who failed to make the grade in the second college "should exercise themselves in preaching, so that they might serve religion in that manner." The third college offered a five year course for the lectorate on the four books of the *Sentences* of Peter Lombard and on the sacraments. The baccalaureate was obtained by lecturing three years in philosophy; the master's degree, conferred by the prior general, by lecturing five years in theology. Feijóo's decrees were confirmed by Innocent XII on October 11.

Feijóo's program, reflecting Spanish practice, proved impracticable elsewhere, especially in Italy, where the provinces were too poor to provide the required colleges. There, according to Clement XI, writing in 1711, studies had practically collapsed, lecturers had come to exceed students in number, and many obtained degrees by illicit means.

The general chapter of 1704 restored law and order to Carmelite studies. In effect, it simply updated ch. 17, pt. 1, of the constitutions. The course of studies (outside of Spain) remained the same: the degree of *cursoratus* after three years of philosophy, four lectures on specified books of Aristotle and public disputations on all of philosophy; the lectorate after four years of theology and public disputations on all of theology (no mention of lectures as a requirement); the baccalaureate after two years of lecturing on philosophy or theology or two public disputations on the *Prima* and *Prima Secundae* of St. Thomas' *Summa* held during the two years the student remains at the college; the master's degree after two years of lecturing on philosophy or theology or two public disputations on the *Secunda Secundae* and *Tertia* of the *Summa* held during another two years' permanence in school. Masters must be at least thirty years old and must come to Rome to be examined. (Poland with its own "municipal laws" was excepted.) The prior general granted all degrees, but only after the required studies and examinations had been completed. He also promoted students to the general *studia* and granted permission to study at a public university.

Lectures were held from the feast of the Nativity of Our Lady (September 8) to Sexagesima Sunday; from Ash Wednesday to June 30.

The new regulations for study added some pedagogical requirements. Lecturers were to read daily. Each day they should explain all that they had dictated for writing. A disputation with the students was to be held daily. Monthly "conclusions" were to be published in print and outsiders were to be invited to attend. Printer's proofs of the aforesaid, when presented at the provincial chapter and approved, entitled lectors to be recommended to the prior general for promotion.

Lecturers in theology should strive after seriousness, brevity, and above all clarity. They should not touch lightly on scholastic problems, but should devote time, not so much to adducing authorities, as to inquiring into solid reasons for things. St. Thomas, interpreted by Carmelite authors, especially John Baconthorpe, is to be followed. Philosophy lectors should adhere to Aristotle insofar as his teachings are compatible with Christianity.

This last paragraph is taken from the constitutions of the Stricter Observance, as is a number of others, mostly relating to the spiritual life of the students. Particularly interesting is the opening paragraph of the regulations taken from this source, with its statement that mystical theology is the "best part" for Carmelites. In this way, the Order at large not only benefitted from the fervor of the reform, but the constitutions were made more available to reformed provinces that permitted academic degrees, if not their privileges.

The articles for study of 1704 were confirmed by Pope Clement XI on November 10, 1711. They remained in force until the dissolution of the Order in the 19th century.

Houses of Study in Spain and Portugal

Studies flourished nowhere more than in the Spanish provinces, heirs to the renaissance of Scholasticism there in the previous century. Their colleges, some of them incorporated in the greatest universities of the Catholic world, produced many learned doctors.

The province of Castile had within its borders the most prestigious of Spain's universities, all of them with a Carmelite presence. The Carmelite convent at Salamanca, destroyed in 1626 by the flood of the River Tormes, the "*avenida de San Policarpo,*" was replaced by a more impressive structure, the "Escorial Salmantino," completed in 1651. Around the same time, possibly when St. Teresa was declared patroness of Spain in 1627, the dedication of the college of St. Andrew was changed to that of St. Teresa. In 1634, Pope Urban VIII granted the college the power to confer the doctorate in theology.

Carmelites also held chairs in the arts and theology at the university, noteworthy among them Martin Peraza (d. 1604), Dionysius Jubero (d. 1612), Peter Cornejo de Pedrosa (d. 1618), Ignatius Ponce Vaca (d. 1707), and bishops Alonso Alvarez Barba (1619-1688), Juan de Bonilla (1636-1696), Matthew Panduro y Villafane (1646-1723), John Ladrón de Guevara (1693-1755).

From its beginning, the Carmelite College at Alcalá de Henares seems to have been incorporated in its famous university. By the end of the 16th century, at the time of the visitation of Chizzola in 1594, the college had reached full development as a theologate. In 1616, the college took as its patron St. Cyril of Alexandria. Among the lecturers at the *studium* were John Baptist Lezana and Louis Pérez de Castro. Lecturers at the university included the scripture scholar Diego Turégano y Beñavides (d. 1655), the theologian Miguel Acero (1730-1795?), and the bishops Bernard Serrada (d. 1733) and Joseph López Gil (d. 1802).

Toledo and Valladolid appear as *studia generalia* in the constitutions of 1626. Both were attached to universities and provided students and professors. Among Carmelite professors at the University of Toledo was Lawrence Diaz Encinas (1599-1660), Bishop of Ugento in the Kingdom of Naples. In 1765, Pope Clement XIII authorized the Carmelite College of Toledo to grant the doctorate. Prominent among the Carmelite *cathedratici* at Valladolid were the future prior general, John Feijóo de Villalobos, and Augustine de Torres (d. 1792), bishop of Albarracín.

The province of Castile had its own curriculum of studies, even more demanding than the other Spanish provinces. For the baccalaureate (the term was not used in Spain) five years of lecturing were required, for the *praesentatura* nine years, for the master's degree twelve years (of theology, or nine of theology and three of philosophy). Candidates for the posts of lecturers were selected, not by age or length of time spent in studies, but by competitive examinations.

In the constitutions of 1626, Valencia and Huesca of the province of Aragon were finally accorded the status of general *studia*. Both were associated with universities. At the university of Valencia, Joseph Blanch (d. 1613) held the chair of metaphysics in the faculty of arts. Julian Castelví y Ladrón, of noble lineage, (d. 1637) taught arts and Sacred Scripture at the university. Louis Sanz taught in both faculties of arts and theology. Elisha García, also a member of the faculty, belonged to the reformed convent of Onda. Ambrose Roca de la Serna (d. 1649) taught philosophy. Three former members of the Valencia community became bishops: Peter Olignat de Medicis (d. 1659), bishop of Orihuela, Anastasius Vives de Rocamora (1599-1674), bishop of Segorbe, and Andrew Caperó (d. 1720), bishop of Lugo.

The *studium* at Huesca in Aragon supplied members to the faculties of the university there throughout the 16th century. The general chapter of 1575 specified that the regent or prior of Huesca should be qualified to teach at the university. In 1594, the Carmelite *studium* was incorporated into the university. Angelus Palacios (d. 1645) taught there as well as at Traspontina and the University of Pavia. A man of many parts, he was also versed in medicine, music, and liturgy. Dionysius Blasco (1610-1683) taught theology for more than thirty years, twelve of them as a *cathedraticus de prima*.

The province of Aragon had an important center of studies at Zaragoza, which, however, was not a general *studium* of the Order. The Carmelites studied at the university there and joined its faculty. Among the Carmelite professors at the university, Augustine Nuñez Delgadillo (d. 1631), a distinguished preacher, held the chair of Durandus. John Anastasius Arana (d. 1663) taught philosophy but is remembered as a moral theologian. Raymond Lumbier (1616-1684), notable among Carmelite theologians, held the *cathedra de prima* for thirty-two years. Louis Pueyo y Abadía (d. 1704), also a prolific preacher, held various chairs. Among the graduates from the university were two very well-known names: Mark Anthony Alegre de Casanate (1590-1658) and Roque Albert Faci (d. 1774).

Lumbier was the founder of St. Joseph's College. The provincial chapter of 1590 had ordered a college founded near the university of Zaragoza, but the college, if it ever was founded, does not seem to have survived Peter Lacosta, appointed its perpetual rector, who died in 1592. Lumbier as prior ensconced himself in a magnificent cell in a complex of rooms which also contained the library left by Masters Valerius and Martin Jiménez de Embun, uncle and nephew, his predecessors at the university. A Dominican nun in the monastery of St. Agnes in the city urged Lumbier to give up his luxurious dwelling and commended him to St. Catherine of Siena. When one morning he got the idea of converting the building into a college, Master Raymond considered it an answer to the holy sister's prayers. The same nun suggested placing the college under the patronage of St. Joseph. Lumbier himself gives this account of the origin of the college in a letter to the viceroy of Peru, Melchor de Navarra.

After he became provincial the first time, Lumbier was able to realize his plan, and the college opened its doors in 1658. Its statutes, which have come down in a version of 1692, provided for a community of 16, including a rector, master of students, 2 lectors and not more than 8 students. Dionysius Blasco collected lectures given in St. Joseph's College by Angelus Palacio, Martin Jiménez de Embrun, Michael Ripol de Atienza and others, in the volume *Theologia abbreviata* (Zaragoza, 1670). Roque Albert Faci composed a catalog of the imposing library (Zaragoza, ca. 1750).

In 1725, Benedict XIV granted faculties to the provincial of Aragon to confer the doctorate on masters in Zaragoza, Valencia, and Pamplona.

Of Catalonia's two *studia*, Barcelona and Lérida, the latter suffered severely during the wars. The convent was twice destroyed: in 1642 during the Catalan revolt and in 1707 during the War of the Spanish Succession.

In 1595, Joseph Serrano (d. 1617) founded the College of St. Angelus in Barcelona with 4,000 gold pieces contributed by his penitent, Jerónima Raphael de Juan. In 1740, the Congregation for Bishops and Religious authorized the college to grant doctorates.

Among Carmelites who held chairs in the faculty of Arts at the University of Barcelona were John Pedrolo (d. 1612), who outlived his nephew Michael (d. 1608), Cyril Jiménez (d. 1618), also rector of St. Angelus College, Francis Serrano (d. 1627). None of these published their lectures.

The house of studies of the Catalan province at Palma on the Balearic Island of Majorca did not have the status of a general *studium* of the Order. The Carmelites there attended and taught at its university, much devoted to the doctrines of Raymond Lull. Among Carmelites who held the chair of Lull were Francis Pou (1573-1630) and Raymond de Zanglada (d. 1657). At the general chapter of 1750, the Catalan provincial, Salvador Gallard, complained about Carmelites who held the chair of Lull at the university "without consideration for the honor of our Order" and succeeded in having an end put to the custom. Not all Majorcan Carmelites were guilty of such treason. Peter Thomas Maltés (1654-1732) was a confirmed

Baconist and left works, apparently unpublished, according to his doctrines. Franco John Serra (1691-1770) held the chair of canon law at the university.

Among non-Catalans who concerned themselves with Lull were Augustine Nuñez Delgadillo, *Breve declaración del arte de Raimundo Lullo* (Granada, 1623) and the Italian, Jerome Aymo, who composed a *Syntaxis artis mirabilis* in the manner of the Catalan philosopher.

In the constitutions of 1626, Andalusia was assigned four general *studia*. The College of St. Albert in Seville (as in Zaragoza distinct from the convent) was founded in 1602, due to the munificence of Doña Bernadina Salgar. Michael de Santiago taught at the University of Seville. The College of St. Roch in Cordova was founded in 1586 by St. John of the Cross and transferred to the Order in 1614. John Salvador (d. 1615) lectured at the university there. In 1726, the College of St. Roch at Cordova as granted the faculty of conferring doctorates by Benedict XIII.

Nicholas Santillán taught at the University of Granada. Silvio made him prior of Seville, where he spent 40,000 ducats on the improvement of church and convent, completing the choir stalls and beginning the cloister. The distinguished preacher, Augustine Nuñez Delgadillo (d. 1631) taught at the university of Osuna.

In the province of Portugal, the definitory reported to the prior general, Paul of St. Ignatius, in 1688, there were no written statutes regulating requirements for degrees, but immemorial custom prescribed seven years of lecturing for the *praesentatura* (baccalaureate) and twelve years of lecturing for the *magisterium*. At Coimbra, the provincial, Gregory of Jesus, wrote to Ferdinand Tartaglia in 1681, "There are many doctors, one *cathedraticus* at the university and other substitutes, or *oppositores*." In 1723, Innocent XIII authorized the Carmelite College to grant doctorates.

Houses of Study in Italy

Almost half the general *studia* of the Order were located in Italy. Some of them, of recent institution, were not very significant, having been erected apparently to encourage study in the smaller provinces.

The general chapter of 1593 ordained that "the colleges of San Martino in Rome, Pavia, Padua, Trapani, and Naples are to be constituted emporia of the good disciplines, to which... students of all provinces can be sent."

The College of Traspontina in Rome had the advantage of the presence of the many able men attached to the general administration of the Order. In 1668, Pope Clement IX authorized the granting of the doctorate there. Traspontina replaced San Martino as the curial *studium*.

Carmelites continued to lecture in metaphysics at the Sapienza in Rome, among them many of the most illustrious members of the Order, future priors general and prelates. After 1660, when they received the right of voice, professors of metaphysics at the Sapienza appear regularly at the general chapters. The same chapter of 1660 resolved to petition the pope to assign the chair of metaphysics to the Order. In 1759, Pope Clement XIII granted the Order the chair of moral theology.

At Naples, the Carmine under the immediate jurisdiction of the prior general, continued to produce learned men. Many also graduated from and taught at the *Collegio di Teologi*. Among them were Filocalo Caputo (1582-1644), Peter Andrew Gauggi (1714-1776), and the prior general, Marianus Ventimiglia (1703-1790), all of them prolific writers.

Some also held chairs in the universities of the North: Prudenzio Verdoliva (d. 1621) at Cremona and Padua and Albert Barra at Padua. The Italian *studia*, some of them affiliated with universities since the Middle Ages, were concentrated in the North. Among Carmelites who taught at the University of Florence mention should be made of Christian Ughelli (d. 1634), brother of the celebrated historian and author of *Italia sacra*, and of John Baptist Ventaja (d. 1700), of the province of Andalusia, who tutored (Spanish and philosophy) the sons of Cosimo III, Ferdinand and Giangastone. Another pupil of his was Luke Joseph Cerracchini who duly included him in his history of the university, *Fasti teologali* (Firenze, 1738). Ventaja's brother Francis was dean of the theological faculty in 1693. The priors general, Leo Bonfigli (d. 1647), Anthony Joseph Aimé Feydeau (1658-1746), Caspar Pizzolanti (1674-1765), formerly graced the faculty.

The *studium* of Padua continued to participate in the academic life of the university. Andrew Lao (1614-1675) taught scripture at the university.

Carmelites who taught at the University of Pavia at this time were Angelus Palacio (d. 1645), who published *Sententiae theologicae* (Roma, 1613); Angelus Merli (d. 1649), a native of Pavia and *primarius* at the university, who translated in Italian St. Teresa's *Conceptos del amor de Dios* (Pavia, 1623); Joseph Mary Fornari (1637-1707), for thirty years *primarius* of rational philosophy (logic) and succeeded as such by his brother Lawrence.

Graduates of the University of Turin, who also taught there, were Jerome of St. Clement (d. 1705) and Florido Ambrosio (1759-1838). As dean, Joseph Mary of St. Berthold (d. 1710) issued new statutes, *Statuta vetera et nova* (Augustae Taurinorum, 1701). Jerome Ari (1603-1667), Paul of St. Ignatius (1614-1704), and Charles Philibert Barberi (1652-1722) became priors general. The prestige of learning in the province of Lombardy led to difficulties when the reform was inaugurated.

According to the constitutions of 1602, the Mantuan Congregation had *studia ordinata* at Bologna, Ferrara, and Mantua (ch. 16, no. 1). At Mantua, the Academia Felicia since 1587 had been licensed to grant doctorates. During the Western Schism, the University of Bologna had replaced Paris as the theological center for the Urbanist world, but just as the Carmelite *studium* in Paris had been taken over by the Reform of Albi, so that of Bologna fell to the Mantuan Congregation. The members of the latter made better use of their booty than did their French confreres. Under the Mantuan Congregation, the *studium* at Bologna continued to flourish, and Carmelites regularly received the doctorate and taught at the university. Noteworthy for achievement were Clement Maria Felina, twice vicar general of the Congregation (1664-1668, 1691-1694) and Anthony Pellegrino Orlandi (1660-1727), historian of the arts. John Ricci (d. 1664) taught mathematics and astronomy at the university. Carmelites who participated in the intellectual life of the university of Ferrara include Albert Massari (d. 1643), prior general; Lawrence Penna (1613-1693), musicologist; Joseph Zagaglia (1619-1711), author of a theology course.

Measures to Improve the Italian *Studia*

In spite of achievements in the more important centers of learning, studies in Italy left something to be desired. Throughout this period, the priors general complain of abuses in conferring degrees and apparently succeeded only partially in finding a remedy.

"To our great displeasure, we find that so far little progress has been made in studies," Henry Silvio wrote in 1609 to the regents of Pavia, Padua, Naples, Catania, and Palermo. "All day long, I am importuned and bothered to grant degrees, but no one, or very few, are willing to make the effort to acquire them." He ordered the regents to examine all students and send him a truthful report of their proficiency or lack of it. "If you deceive me," the desperate general concluded, "I will never trust you again."

The general chapter of 1613, observing with regard to Italy that "our houses of study need some reform," decreed that no one should be promoted without having completed the required courses and urged the newly-elected prior general, Sebastian Fantoni, to enforce the constitutions in this matter. The general chapter of 1625 officially announced that there were only four *magistri de gratia* left in Italy (Gregory Spinola, Caesar Peri, Joseph Caccavelli, and Albert Provana) and forbade any more to be created in the future.

Theodore Straccio applied himself no less vigorously to the reform of studies than to the betterment of observance. "The principal reason why learning is lacking in our Order in Italy," he wrote to Master Antonio Adorno at Messina, November 20, 1636, "is that youths without grammar are admitted to the arts, and degrees are conferred on the ignorant." He appointed Adorno, whom he trusted, his examiner of Sicily.

Straccio took the drastic step of requiring all candidates for the doctorate to appear in Rome to be examined before a board consisting of the cardinal protector, the prior general and examiners deputed by him, obtaining apostolic authority from Urban VIII on October 8, 1639. After Straccio's death, the general chapter of 1645 resolved to have the papal brief revoked, urging that it was "most harmful and prejudicial to the Order." Only in 1655, was a repeal obtained. Thereupon, the general chapter of 1660 laid down rules to insure that degrees would be conferred only on those worthy of them.

In 1673, Matthew Orlandi reiterated the conditions for obtaining degrees, renewing the requirement that the doctorate could only be conferred in Rome. Candidates for the examination should first be examined in their provinces, lest they come unprepared and suffer the humiliation of returning home empty-handed. The general chapter of 1680 placed this condition on candidates for the lectorate.

At the general chapter of 1738, lament is still being raised about the excessive number of masters in Italy (one province was burdened with sixty), "who were created only to add votes to the chapters . . . to diminish attendance in choir and reduce the number of those available for the lesser offices in the community." The harmful effect on community life of the privileged status of doctors had not lessened with time.

The General *Studium* of Paris

North of the Alps, the most famous house of studies, its lustre much dimmed, was the Carmelite *studium* in the Place Maubert in Paris.

After its recovery from the Congregation of Albi the venerable *studium* returned to a more normal system of administration, approved by Gregory XIII in 1584. The prior was elected by the community and confirmed by the prior general. Besides masters, baccalaureates, regents, and officials, all priests professed there had the right to vote. Officials were chosen from the provinces. The college was to provide a full curriculum of grammar, rhetoric, logic, philosophy, and theology.

In 1598 the prior of Paris was given *de iure* voice in general chapters.

Henry Silvio's visit in 1603 sealed the Order's possession of the *studium* of Paris and should have marked the beginning of a new era of prosperity. The community numbered sixty-four, including thirteen novices. The prior general introduced his reform: obligatory attendance in choir even on the part of masters, mental prayer, spiritual reading, and the perfect common life. Unfortunately, after his departure these measures remained a dead letter.

The next serious attempt to improve the quality of religious life in the Place Maubert was made by Theodore Straccio, who hoped to entrust the task of reform to the province of Touraine. The provincial, Leo of St. John, was finally persuaded to make the attempt in 1636. Members of the permanent community in the Paris *studium*, who were unwilling to lead the reformed way of life, were dispatched to the provinces. The province of Touraine imported sixty reformed friars to make up the lack. Thirty articles, duly approved by the royal council, were drawn up for the ordinance of the house. The provincial of Touraine was the prior general's commissary. No more novices would be received in Paris, students sent from the provinces would not become conventuals there. The province of Touraine was responsible for the administration of the college and for assuring an adequate staff and student body. The statutes of the province of Touraine were to be strictly enforced. Students sent from the provinces should have made their novitiate and seminary in a reformed house. No changes were made in requirements for study at the university. Each province in turn was entitled to present two candidates for the doctorate. Within the convent, graduate students enjoyed no privileges. Internal studies were conducted according to the usage of Touraine. Straccio caused these articles to be approved by Urban VIII, January 25, 1637.

The new arrangement lasted about three months. One evening at Vespers, the reformed friars were driven from the choir by the conventuals and students. The *coup d'état* ended the effort at reform. The king, Louis XIII, whose support had been engaged for the reform, was absent at the siege of Corbie, and the Touraine friars, reluctant from the start, were in no hurry to return.

The general chapter of 1645, which instituted dual legislation, reformed and non-reformed, restored the Place Maubert to the observance of the latter, insisting besides on keeping the deposit box until such times as the perfect common life could be realized. Students from reformed provinces should continue faithful to their observance. Twelve elected councilors were to assist the prior in temporal matters. With regard to studies, the laws and statutes as annually reported in the *Remigiales* were to be followed. The general chapter of 1654 confirmed these decrees, at the same time forbidding the reception of novices in the Place Maubert, a wise decision, already made by the Touraine reformers: the affiliates of the convent of Paris, unaccountable to any provincial, had been a constant source of complaint.

The *Studium* of Paris Reformed

By the time Jerome Ari visited Paris a decade later, reform had spread through the French provinces, and there was a better chance of survival for reform measures in the general house of studies. Also, there now existed an acknowledged body of reformed legislation. On his first visit, from February 25 to March 3, 1662, Ari confirmed the election of a reformed prior and officials and imposed the Constitutions of the Stricter Observance. It was no longer necessary to entrust the invidious task of reform to one province: on his second visit, from July 27 to September 27,1663, he named all seven French provincials his commissaries for reform. The results of their deliberations and of the prior general's visitation were eighty-four *Decreta pro reformatione magni conventus ac Collegii Carmelitarum Parisiensium*. No one was exempt from choir, day and night, but students and baccalaureates took turns attending during the week. A spiritual director was to oversee the interior and religious life of the students. A special syndic, or bursar, was entrusted with the monetary needs of the students who were not allowed to have money. The prior was assisted by a house council, consisting of the subprior, spiritual director, regents, *clavarii*, and syndics. Lectures were held from the Feast of St. Remy (October 1) to that of St. Elijah (July 20). Every two years three baccalaureates should be presented to the university for the licentiate. It was Ari's wish that reformed friars also participate in this program; the provincials should therefore report policy with regard to academic degrees in their respective provinces. Ari solemnly declared the Paris *studium* a general and royal *studium* to be governed according to the Constitutions of the Stricter Observance. For the "conventuals," that is, those who had made profession in the convent, Ari made special allowance, permitting them a form of observance according to the unreformed constitutions. The community was reduced to seventy members, the number which predictable incomes could support. The general chapter of 1666 confirmed Ari's decrees for Paris. Thus, the Place Maubert finally came to stand under the sign of reform, a condition which persisted with varying degrees of intensity until the end.

During his visitation in 1669, Matthew Orlandi, recalling that the college had been placed under the Stricter Observance in 1663, made forty nine decrees for its faithful preservation. He limited the community to sixty members. (Among other things, he ordered the chasuble made from the cloak of St. Louis of France withdrawn from common use, and worn only on the feast of the saint or by bishops and prelates requesting this privilege.)

"We believe that studies have often declined because they were removed from piety," wrote Angelus of the Conception Cambolas, provincial of Toulouse, during his visitation of the convent in 1672. "In order that studies may bear greater fruit and zeal may arise in the schools, care must be taken to kindle fervor of the soul toward God." As a matter of fact, most of the visitator's directives concern the spiritual life and impose the most scrupulous adherence to the Stricter Observance. He spent some months in revising the formation of the students in philosophy and theology, who now consisted exclusively of reformed friars. He invited the conventuals, or non-reformed friars, to observe the constitutions to which they were bound or return to their provinces.

Affiliation Restored

At the general chapter of 1680, Felician of St. Mary Magdalen, prior of Paris, urged the need of having affiliated, or permanent members of the college. Tartaglia, whom the chapter entrusted with the task of working out details, sent Cambolas to visitate the Place Maubert and introduce affiliation. On May 24, 1681, twenty-one decrees regarding affiliation were published in the community chapter. There should be eighteen affiliates, two from each of the seven French provinces, four elected from the surviving professed members of the convent. They were withdrawn from the jurisdiction of their provincials and allocated *sine die* to the Paris convent. With the first regent and the *baccalaureus formatus*, the affiliates constituted the council, which also elected from its number the prior and other officials of the convent. The affiliates were to swear to uphold the Stricter Observance. The province of Touraine, which had no desire to lend its members to be affiliated to the convent of Paris, at its chapter in Poitiers in 1681 renounced all its rights in the college.

In spite of the curb placed on academic degrees and their privileges by the Stricter Observance, Carmelite studies in Paris cannot be said to have suffered in the 17th century and afterwards. In the 186 years between 1602 and 1788, 213 Carmelites gained licences, compared to 177 in the 227 years between 1373 and 1600. As might be expected, the most observant provinces are hardly represented. After its reform, Touraine graduated no one until the eve of the Revolution, when two Touraine friars received the licence in 1774 and 1784. Aquitaine finally presented four candidates in the first half of the 18th century. Narbonne obtained the most licences (48), in spite of the fact that for some reason no one graduated between 1682 and 1740. After Francia (38 licences) the other provinces profited equally: Toulouse (30), Gascony (29), Provence (29). The latter got off to a late start, receiving its first licentiate in 1662. In this same period, the convent of Paris acquired four licences, the Mantuan Congregation three, and the provinces of Rome, Ireland, Romagna, and Rio de Janeiro one each.

As already mentioned, the Carmelites were entitled to present three candidates for the licence every two years. Carmelite doctors taught at no other college of the university than the Place Maubert.

In the ultramontane provinces, governed by the constitutions of the Stricter Observance, which discouraged the acquisition of doctoral degrees, the Carmelite presence in the universities was severely curtailed. Nevertheless, the internal *studia* flourished, and the reformed provinces were by no means laggards in the pursuit of learning. Moreover, the reformed constitutions did not entirely exclude doctoral degrees, provided certain conditions were met. Some reformed provinces thus maintained their traditional ties with universities. However, Carmelite activity in the ultramontane universities during this period is another of the many subjects that remain to be investigated.

Thomism and Baconism

Traditionally, Carmelite doctors were not required to follow any particular school, except to favor as much as possible the writers of the Order. This policy was not due to scrupulous concern for academic freedom, but to the fact that the Order had never produced a scholastic of sufficient stature. Paragraph 4 of chapter 18 of Caffardi's constitutions of 1586, passed on through those of Canal of 1626 to modern times, canonized this official position: "All should strive above all to uphold and cite the *determinationes* of the doctors of our Order, especially John Baconthorpe, Michael of Bologna, and Thomas Waldensis" (the only ones in print).

Actually, trends had changed. In its decrees regarding studies, the general chapter of 1593 imposed Thomism: "Regents shall profess the doctrine and method of St. Thomas both in philosophy and theology; they may use whatever commentators they wish... However, when occasion arises the Reverend Regents should not fail to cite and confirm by their own reasons and arguments the opinion of our doctors John Baconthorpe and Michael of Bologna in philosophy and theology; with regard to dogma they should allege the doctrine of Thomas of Walden before all others." The definitive legislation of 1704, borrowing the words of the Constitutions of the Stricter Observance, only adds its confirmation: "With regard to St. Thomas (lectors of theology) should embrace his doctrine with the interpretation of the doctors of our Order ... especially John Baconthorpe, called the *Doctor Resolutus*. Lectors of philosophy should strive to adhere to Aristotle as far as the Catholic faith allows." In officially espousing Thomism, the Order was simply following the trend of the times. At this time, the *Summa* of St. Thomas replaced the *Sentences* of Peter Lombard in the schools (though not entirely).

Nevertheless, the Carmelites of the Ancient Observance never became dedicated Thomists like their Discalced brethren. Baconthorpe, if anyone, at this time emerges as the leader of a Carmelite School. Many of the outstanding Carmelite doctors of the time composed *Summae*, or courses in philosophy or scholastic theology "according to the mind of John Baconthorpe": Jerome Aimo, Dionysius Blasco, Elisha Garcia, Berthold of the Blessed Sacrament Crassous, Diego de Castilla, Emmanuel Ignatius Coutinho, Peter Andrew Gauggi, Joseph Zagaglia, Henry of St. Ignatius.

The province of Castile was committed to the teaching of Thomism because of its connection with the university of Salamanca. The general chapter of 1722 approved this tradition, making exception for professors who might occupy chairs dedicated to other schools. An attempt to break this monopoly in 1728 failed. At the request of the provincial, Urban Zayas, whose zeal was highly commended, the definitory general of that year decreed that the professors of Castile might follow any approved doctor, especially Baconthorpe. Zayas' zeal did not equally recommend itself to other members of the province, for Masters Francis Montiel de Fuentenovilla and John Berocal appealed to Benedict XIII, who on February 14, 1730, ordered the doctrine of St. Thomas maintained. In fact, the general chapter the following year decreed the implementation of the papal brief and the fulfillment of the conditions of the will of the late Carmelite bishop, Matthew Panduro y Villafane, who had endowed a course for the doctorate at the university of Salamanca on the condition that candidates profess the doctrine of St. Thomas.

Stirrings of Baconism continued to be felt. At the general chapter of 1728, Zayas had sanguinely announced a prospective chair of Baconthorpe at the university of Salamanca, but the chair never materialized. In 1752, Philip López Aguirre, procurator general for Spain, in the name of the royal convent of Madrid, petitioned King Ferdinand VI for a chair of Baconthorpe in all the major and minor universities of his realm, "as was already the case in France, Mantua, and other parts of Italy, Flanders, Germany and Portugal." The question is known to have been raised at Alcalá and Salamanca, but answered negatively.

The prior general, Aloysius Laghi, warmly approved a decision of the Castilian definitory in 1747 to teach the Resolute Doctor in its houses of study and urged the publication of his works. In fact, the province sponsored a late and now very rare edition of Baconthorpe (Madrid, 1754). Its editor, Nicholas Echevarría, himself displaying no slight proficiency in dialectics, justifies this lapse from Thomism: "The Carmelites of the province of both Castiles are not obliged to expound this illustrious doctor (Baconthorpe) or publish his commentaries, enlightened as they are by the very worthy source of the Angelic Doctor's most clear and solid doctrine. But those who follow this doctor do not abandon the Angelic one, for whoever adheres to St. Augustine of necessity associates himself with his most faithful disciple St. Thomas."

The prior general, Joachim Maria Pontalti, in 1758 ordered the reinstatement of St. Thomas in the academic chairs of the province. Three years later, he specifically annulled the definitorial decision of 1747.

Ignatius Ponce Vaca, though a *cathedraticus* of St. Thomas at Salamanca, produced a philosophy course according to Baconthorpe, *Artium cursus* (Madrid, 1748). In the same vein, John Jiménez, treated several particular philosophical questions: supernatural beatitude (Madrid, 1752), potency and causality of the prime mover (Toledo, 1758), free will (Madrid, 1764).

The Mantuan Congregation followed the rest of the Order. Its constitutions of 1602 echoed the decrees of the general chapter of 1593 and their Thomistic bent, yet we later find among the Mantuans Joseph Zagaglia (1619-1711), according to Bartolomé Xiberta, outstanding theologian of the Order in modern times, "one of the best commentators on Baconthorpe and theologians of the Order."

In the northern provinces, examples of Carmelites conducting extern schools for boys and youths are not rare. It may seem strange that precisely the reformed provinces which stressed the contemplative life should undertake this apostolate, until one recalls that the formation of an informed laity was one of the cherished goals of the Counter-Reformation.

Chapter 12

The Ecclesiastical Sciences and Theological Questions

After the Protestant Reformation, the unity of medieval theology, like other unities of the Middle Ages, dissolved. To scholastic theology (which also came to be called dogmatic theology) more exclusively fell the task of rationalizing the faith; positive theology sought the sources of doctrine in the Scriptures and the Fathers. At the same time, various aspects of theology assumed autonomous existence and methodologies: exegesis, patrology, spiritual theology, homiletics, liturgy, church history. The new shape of theology is illustrated in the title of one of the works of Henry of St. Ignatius: *Theologia vetus, fundamentalis, speculativa, et moralis* (Liège, 1677).

Scholastic Philosophy and Theology

This period of the Catholic Reformation was the richest in philosophers and theologians of the Order since the Middle Ages. On the whole, they continued to worry the same scholastic bones and paid little heed to such contemporaries as Francis Bacon, Descartes, Herbert, Hobbes, and Locke who were busy changing the mentality of the West. Most of the theologians who taught in the *studia* of the Order and in the universities had done an apprenticeship in philosophy and so produced works in both fields.

Some doctors, however, limited themselves to the study of philosophy. Among those who produced courses of philosophy were Dionysius Jubero (d. 1612), Joseph Blanch (d. 1613), Julian Castelví y Ladrón (d. 1637), Louis Sanz (fl. 1637), Dionysius Blasco (1610-1685), Elisha Garcia (fl. 1700), Jerome Aimo (1625-1705), Ignatius Ponce Vaca (d. 1707), Emmanuel Ignatius Coutinho (fl. 1735).

Of these, Jerome Aimo composed a philosophy course according to Baconthorpe (Turin, 1667-1669, 3 v.) which even before its completion was recommended to the whole Order by the general chapter of 1666. The Fathers greatly praised his efforts and ordered him to be given "every religious convenience in the convents in which he lives."

To name the principal authors of complete courses of dogmatic theology, Christopher Silvestrani Brenzone (d. 1608), of Verona, taught in Venice, Florence, and Pisa. He taught in the old style and published a commentary on the three books of the *Sentences* (Verona, 1591), as well as an *Examen theologicum* on books III and IV (Verona, 1599). An *Examen theologicum* on Book II remained in manuscript.

Perhaps the most significant Carmelite theologian of this period was Peter Cornejo de Pedroso (1566-1618), whom the Discalced Merl calls "in the truest sense of the word a forerunner of the Salmanticenses." A native of Salamanca and a graduate of its university, Cornejo successively held the chairs of Ethics, St. Thomas, and Durandus from 1607 until his death. His commentary on parts 1 and 3 of the *Summa* of St. Thomas was published posthumously (Valladolid, 1628-1629, 2 v.). A second edition by Peter Obladen appeared at Bamberg in 1671.

John Baptist Lezana (1586-1659) reflects the official position of his Order in the title of his *Summa of Sacred Theology Drawn from the Doctrine of the Angelic Doctor and other Principal Doctors of the School Especially the Carmelite Order* (Romae, 1651-1658, 3 v.). After studies at Salamanca and Alcalá, Lezana spent his life teaching theology, first in his native province of Castile, after 1625 in Rome at Traspontina and the Sapienza. A prolific writer, he produced noteworthy works in dogmatic and moral theology, canon law, history, and mariology. His opinion was sought and respected outside the Order, as well as within. Of him the old saw was true that his learning was matched by his piety.

Raymond Lumbier (1616-1684), wrote *Quaestiones theologicae scholasticae in primam partem d. Thomae* (Cesaraugustae, apud haeredem A. Verges, 1689) and a collection of theological treatises entitled simply *Tractatus*, of which there were at least seven volumes published at Zaragoza by A. Vergas in the 1670's.

The province of Touraine, as might be expected, adhered to Aristotelian and Thomistic doctrine prescribed by the constitutions. Augustine of the Virgin Mary (d. 1689) produced a *Theologiae Thomisticae cursus* (Parisis, E. Couterot, 1660, 6 v.) and a *Philosophiae Aristo-Thomisticae cursus* (Lugduni, H. Boissat et G. Remens, 1664, 6 v.). Irenaeus of St. James (d. 1676) taught in Paris as well as in the province. He wrote an *Integra philosophia* (Parisiis, D. Thierry, 1655, etc.), a collection of various theological tracts (Poitiers, J. Fleuriau, 1661,1671, 2 v.), and a *Theologia de Verbo Incarnato* (Parisiis, M. de Beaujeu, 1676).

The schools of the Flandro-Belgian province were dominated by the figure of Francis de Bonne Espérance (1617-1677), lector for many years at Louvain. His doctrines, enshrined in his imposing publications, were officially prescribed. His works include *Commentarii tres in universam Aristotelis philosophiam* (Bruxellis, F. Vivienne, 1652) and *In universam theologiam scholasticam* (Antverpiae, J. Meurs, 1662, 6 v.). In time, his authority came to be challenged by his pupil, Henry of St. Ignatius.

Peter Andrew Gauggi, of the Tuscan province, was born in Genoa, 1714, entered the Order in Florence, and studied in Verona. He taught at the Carmine of Naples, but in 1763 was summoned to Rome to write his anonymous *Enchiridion theologicum scholasticum-dogmaticum iuxta mentem Ioannis de Bachone* (Romae, ex typographia Hermatheniana, 1766 1768, 8 v.). Gauggi, deceased in 1776, was also an accomplished preacher and poet.

In the Mantuan Congregation, Joseph Zagaglia was born in Ferrara and taught at the university there. He also served as procurator general for his Congregation. He died in 1711 at the age of 92, leaving an impressive *Cursus theologicus secundum doctrinam Joannis Bacconii* (Ferrariae, Parmae, J. Bulzone, etc., 1671-1725) in eight folio volumes.

Moral Theology

Since Audet's time, lectors for *casus conscientiae* had been prescribed in at least the larger houses. Clement VIII also made such instruction part of his plan for reform. These lectors provided the education of "simple" priests and confessors and also kept the graduates up to date. When moral theology issued as a separate discipline, the Carmelite *studia* likewise began to offer separate courses in moral theology. Special *studia* were even instituted to teach this discipline, especially to those destined for a pastoral rather than an academic career. Carmelite theologians began to contribute works to the new discipline. From 1759, the Carmelites held the chair of moral theology at the Sapienza in Rome.

Stephen of St. Paul (1625-1694), of the Flandro-Belgian province, pastor of

Boxmeer, composed a *Theologia moralis* (Antverpiae, E. Gymnicus, 1664), which underwent many editions. He also wrote *Alphabetum morale concionatorium* (Coloniae Agrippinae, A. Metternich, 1686. 2 v.) complemented with *Auctuarium et indicem concionatorium* (ibid., 1691), an old style dictionary of moral terms useful for preachers.

Certainly the most controversial moralist of the Order was Henry of St. Ignatius (1630-1719), of noble family, regent of the Carmelite *studium* in Douai, originally of the Flandro-Belgian province, later of the Gallo-Belgian province and the Wallo-Belgian vicariate. A disciple of Francis of Bonne Espérance, he became his rival and severest critic. Besides *Theologia vetus, fundamentalis, speculativa, et moralis according to the mind of Baconthorpe* (Liège, 1677, v. 1 only) and *Theologia sanctorum veterum et novissimorum* (Paris, Liège, 1700, etc.) his principal work is *Ethica amoris* (Liège, 1709, 3 v.). Henry attacked the casuists and, while he denied he was a Jansenist, he favored authors of that stripe. His *Ethica amoris* was condemned by various secular and ecclesiastical authorities, including the Holy Office (1714, 1715, 1722). The 1713 chapter of his own Wallo-Belgian vicariate banned this work from the *studia*. Nevertheless, a visit to Rome early in the pontificate of Clement XI earned him the esteem of that pontiff.

The Jesuits particularly were the target of Henry's attacks, which he published under the pseudonym Aletophilus Christianus in *Artes jesuiticae* (Salzburg, 1700, etc.) placed on the Index, July 19, 1707; *Tuba magna mirum clangens sonum* (Salzburg, 1712), appealing to the pope, emperor, and lesser lights for the reform of the Jesuits; *Tuba altera majorem clangens sonum* (1714, etc.). The noted historian of Jansenism, Lucien Ceyssens, O.F.M., concludes that Henry's Jansenism "should be understood in a benign historical sense as 'counter-anti-Jansenist'."

Brocard of St. Nicholas Brocarts (1687-1760), of the Lower German province, wrote among other works, *Theologia moralis fundamentalis* (Coloniae, S. Noethen, 1735) and *Alphabetum morale* (Ibid., 1739). From the latter which he considered "of very great worth" Migne reproduced the treatise on conscience in his *Theologiae cursus completus*.

Other authors of more notable works on moral theology are John Anastasius de Arana (d. 1663), Raymond Lumbier (1616-1684), Richard of the Heart of Mary (1700-1753), Sebaldus of St. Christopher (1678-1759), Bartholomew del Valle y Saavedra (fl. 1760). From the commentaries of Baconthorpe, Elisha García selected *Quaestiones theologicae morales* (Romae, G. Plachi, 1710, 2 v.).

In the climate of Jansenistic rigorism, the doctrine of probabilism came under attack. Two of the sharpest minds of the age, the Cistercian, John Caramuel (1606-1682), and the curialist Prosper Fagnani (1588-1678), addressed themselves to the problem. Fagnani's critique of probabilism first appeared in his commentary on the *Decretales* (Rome, 1661), later as a separate work (Rome, 1665). Caramuel refuted him in his *Apologema* (Lyon, 1663). This was the work which Francis de Bonne Espérance rebutted in his *Apologema retortum* (Louvaine, 1665). St. Alphonsus de Liguori calls Fagnani "the prince of the rigorists," but he bestows the same rank on Caramuel among the laxists.

Earlier, Francis had crossed swords with Caramuel in his *Noctua Belgica adversus aquilam Germanicam* (Lovanii, 1651); details of the controversy are wanting. Likewise obscure are the reasons why Francis attacked Louis Le Pippre, a diocesan priest who became a Capuchin with the name Bonaventure of La Bassée, author of *Parochophilus* (Antwerp, 1635, Paris 1657), which instructs the pastor in his four basic duties of preaching, offering Mass, and providing confession and communion at Easter time. Francis' book is called *Christifidelium parochiale apologeticum* (Bruxellis, 1667). On the other hand, Caramuel found a supporter in Anthony Marinari (1605-1689), author of an *Opusculum de opinione probabili* (Rome, 1666).

Another Carmelite who concerned himself with the question of probabilism was the Belgian Caspar of St. Mary Magdalen de' Pazzi (d. after 1752), who wrote a *Brief Theological Treatise on the Probable Opinion, its method of administering well the sacrament of penance* (Antwerp, 1716).

In 1665 and 1666, Pope Alexander VII published lists of condemned laxist propositions; Innocent XI followed with a similar list in 1676. Lumbier commented on these propositions in his *Noticias teologicas morales* (Madrid, 1682, etc.), which however, landed on the Roman Index the following year. The Dominican Lawrence Pisani also attacked it in the appendix to his *Gedeonis gladius* (Palermo, 1683).

The question of the adequacy of attrition in confession also arose at this time, specifically in Belgium. When the Jesuits of Ghent propagated a catechism (1661) teaching that attrition sufficed, the diocesan clergy drew up a condemnation which was approved by the University of Louvain. The Augustinians, Christopher Wolf and Francis Farvaques, joined in the fray against the Jesuits. To this controversy Francis of Bonne Espérance contributed his *Christifidelium contritionale* (Mechliniae, 1667) and *Clypeus contritionalis* (Antverpiae, 1670), which he claimed followed a via media. On May 5, 1667, Alexander VII urged moderation on the litigants.

Ignatius Ponce Vaca published *Theologico-dogmatica controversia in Tridentini concilii caput de contritione* (Romae, 1705) about the sorrow for sin requisite for the sacrament of penance.

Canon Law

Lezana's most significant work was done in the field of canon law for religious. His *Summa quaestionum regularium* (Romae, 1637-1647, 5 v.), the fruit of many years as a teacher and consultor for the Roman Congregations, remained an honored work of consultation down to recent times. His *Consulta varia* (Venetiis, 1656) provided solutions to moral and canonical cases.

In the same field, Augustine of the Virgin Mary (d. 1689), of Touraine, wrote *Privilegia omnium religiosorum* (Lugduni, H. Boissart et G. Remens, 1661), long a useful reference work. James of St. Anthony (Olimaert, d. 1703), of the Flandro-Belgian province, wrote *Consultationes canonicae pro regularium exemptione* (Lugduni, H. Boissat, 1680), which saw more than one edition. Among the numerous works of Peter Thomas Pugliesi (d. 1707), of Calabria, there is a *Quaesita promptuaria* (Catania, P. Bisogni, 1707, etc.) for religious superiors and a *Praxis civilis et criminalis canonica* (Neapoli, P. Severino, 1712) for trials of religious, taken from the canonical works of Baconthorpe.

Urban of the Ascension (d. 1664) provided the definitive edition of the constitutions of the Stricter Observance, a task for which his canonical expertise had prepared him well. His works include *Summa casuum conscientiae* (Pictavis, J. Thoreau, 1649) and *Institutiones juris canonici* (Lemovicis, apud viduam A. Barbou, 1659). Also of the province of Touraine, Tiburtius of St. James (d. 1673), wrote

Medulla totius iuris canonici compendiosa (Parisiis, J. Julien, 1660), a list of canonical terms and concepts in alphabetical order. John Augustine of St. Teresa, of the Lower German province, is the author of a *Nomognosticon iuris universi* (Coloniae, J. Kalkoven, 1662). Alexander of the Passion, also of the Touraine province, wrote *Inquisitor canonum* (Rennes, 1712-1726, 3 v.), a collection of cases of conscience involving canon law.

Of the Mantuan Congregation, Peter Thomas Malaguzzi composed a *Manuale parochorum* (Ravennae, J. B. Recurtius, 1757), in the form of colloquies.

Bible, Ancient Languages, Patrology

The Renaissance and especially the Protestant Reformation restored Christianity to its scriptural basis, thereby revolutionizing theological method. Language and existential situation of the Bible engaged attention and led to the formation of a separate discipline.

For some reason, the Carmelites have little to show in biblical study. Although they are sometimes found on the chair of Sacred Scripture at the universities, they engaged in little biblical or patristic study apart from that involved in positive theology. Of some note is John de Sylveira (1592-1687), New Testament scholar. He spent his life teaching at Evora and Lisbon, especially in the latter place. From his sister, Baroness Beatrix da Sylveira, he received an annual pension of 1,000 ducats, with which he was able to make many improvements in the church, convent, and library of Lisbon. He wrote extensive commentaries on the gospels, the Acts of the Apostles, and Revelation. A volume of *Opuscula varia* completes his scholarly output. All these works underwent many editions in Lyon, Venice, and Antwerp. His collected works appeared as *Opera omnia* (Venetiis, ex typographia Balleoniana, 1748-1754, 10 v.)

Other writers on scriptural themes include Silvestrani Brenzoni, who published *Lectures on the Letters of St. Paul* (Verona, 1591), *Lectures on the Magnificat* (Verona, 1593), commentaries on Luke, 1, 46 ff. (Verona, 1595) and Psalm 136 (Verona, 1593; Paris, 1608). Diego de Turégano y Benavides (d. 1655), professor of Sacred Scripture at the University of Alcalá, reputed to have a knowledge of Hebrew, left *Lecturae sacrae scripturae litterales et morales* (Alcalá, 1649). Elijah d'Amato (d. 1748), of Montalto in Calabria, learned member of the Academy of the Inculti, treats Old Testament questions like creation, the flood, etc., in his *De' congressi accademici sullo discettabile storico della Bibbia* (Venezia, 1717-1719, 4 v.). The work of Arsenius of St. Robert, of the Wallo-Belgian province, *Antilogiae, sive contradictiones apparentes S. Scripturae* (2d ed., Louvain, 1751), saw several editions.

John Senier (d. 1636), doctor and professor of the University of Cologne, edited in print for the first time the gospel concordance of Guido Terreni (d. 1342), *Quatuor unum*, together with his commentary on the *Magnificat, Benedictus* and *Nunc Dimittis* (Cologne, 1631). At the same time, he produced a second edition of Terreni's *De haeresibus* (Cologne, 1631).

In 1610, Pope Paul V prescribed courses in Hebrew, Greek, and Latin in all *studia* of religious Orders. In more important houses of study, Aramaic should also be taught. After the establishment of the Congregation for the Propagation of the Faith (1622), Pope Urban VIII returned to the subject of languages in a missionary context. He ordered Hebrew, literary and vulgar Greek, Aramaic, Chaldaic, and

"Illyric" taught in the principal *studia* of religious Orders. Two years of language were to be required for the doctorate. The decree was to be read before every provincial and general chapter. Superiors general who failed to comply were to be suspended from office. The brief for the Carmelites was dated October 16, 1623. The only perceptible effect of all this on the Carmelites was an article added to the Constitutions of 1626 (pt. 1, ch. 18, art. 9).

Still the Order did not remain without some achievement in the study of ancient languages. The single star in that firmament was Jacob Wemmers, born in Antwerp in 1598. It is not known when he came to Rome, but there he established relations with the Ethiopian College. His *Lexicon aethiopicum* (Romae, S. C. de Propaganda Fide, 1638), containing also a short grammar, is the first of its kind. Wemmers subsequently became prefect of the Ethiopian Mission of the Congregation and in 1645, bishop of Cairo, but he died the same year, while waiting to embark from Naples. Wemmers' lexicon was almost immediately overshadowed by Job Ludolf's.

Dionysius Jubero (d. 1612), professor at the University of Salamanca, composed a Hebrew dictionary, which, however, was never published and probably perished in the flood of the Tormes in 1626. Paul Mary Ogeri (d. 1811), professor at the University of Turin, wrote *Graeca et latina lingua hebraizantes* (Venetiis, S. Coletus, 1764, which professes to trace Hebrew affinities in Latin and Greek. Bernard de Zamora's Greek grammar, *Gramatica griega filosofica* (Madrid, A. Pérez de Soto, 1771), enjoyed a certain popularity. Zamora taught Greek at the University of Salamanca.

In the field of patrology and patristics, Peter Thomas Santabarbara (d. 1779), of the Romagna province, wrote a defense of the Fathers as a source of Christian doctrine against the Calvinists, John Daille (1594-1670) and John Leclerc (1657-1736): *Critice apologetica veterum ecclesiae patrum* (Venetiis, A. Bassanesi; Bononiae, F. Pesarri, 1758-1765, 4 v.). Of the same province and professor at the University of Bologna, Peter Thomas Cacciari (1693-1769) edited Ruffinus (Romae, A. de Rubeis, 1740-1741, 2 v.) and St. Leo the Great (Romae, J. Collini, 1753-5).

Alexander of the Passion, of the province of Touraine, published *La théologie des Pères des premiers siècles de l'Eglise* (Rennes, 1728, 3 v.) and *Le disciple pacifique de Saint Augustin* (Paris, 1715-1718, 2 v.).

The controversy with Jansenism inevitably produced works concerning the interpretation of the Fathers, beginning with Augustine. Bonaventure of St. Anne (alias, James Vernant, d. 1667) wrote *The Bad Faith of the Jansenists in Translating Passages of St. Augustine.* Lezin of St. Scholastica (d. 1674) published four letters to an abbess of Citeaux under the similar title, *Proof of the Infidelity of the Jansenists in Translations of the Fathers.* Both treatises appeared without authors' names or imprints.

Apologetics

The rise of Protestantism made the defense of orthodoxy a separate theological science. Authors and preachers in many contexts took a swipe at the enemy; here we can mention only a few Carmelites who specialized in polemics.

As a young priest, Leo of St. John worked a number of conversions in the Poitou. His *Seven Columns of Incarnate Wisdom Sustaining the Seven Principal Truths of the Eucharist* (Poitiers, 1629) was answered by a Calvinist minister, Daniel Couppe, with *Anti-Leo; or, the Philistine Columns Overturned* (Saumur, 1630), which Leo in turn answered with a *Response* (Poitiers, 1630). His method in controversy with Protestants was to confine his arguments to reasons based on the Bible, the Fathers, and the councils of the first four centuries. This strategy is also apparent in his *Catholic Instruction for Distinguishing Infallibly the Truth from Lies in the Matter of Religion* (Poitiers, 1647; Latin ed., 1661).

Leo's most significant work, *L'oeconomie de la vraie religion* (Paris, 1643, 2 v., 1653; Latin ed. 1644), won the approbation of Jacques Forton, *sieur de Saint-Ange*, whom it may have influenced, Jean Pierre Camus, the Sorbonne, and other savants. It was directed to, though it did not always convince, a new class of anti-religionists, the *libertins*. Written with Leo's customary clarity and brevity, though perhaps with excessively rigid logic, it recognized and fitted the new Age of Reason.

The Three Fundamental Truths for Instruction in the Catholic Faith (Paris, 1652) publishes the arguments Leo used to bring into the Church Henriette de Coligny, Countess de la Suze. Her adjuration took place, July 20, 1653, in the convent of Les Billettes, Paris, in the presence of the papal nunzio.

In upper Germany, Sebaldus of St. Christopher (1678-1759), lector of theology in various houses of the province, wrote among many works *Scientia salutis* (Bamberg & Frankfurt, 1758, 2 v.), which promises to confound the errors of all pagans, Jews, and heretics.

Elijah Astorini (1651-1702), of the Calabrian province, is of interest mainly as a scientist (see below), but his brief flirtation with Protestantism resulted in *Prodromus apologeticus* (Siena, 1693) in defense of the prerogatives of the Holy See, and *The True Church of Jesus Christ* (Naples, 1700).

Let these few examples suffice of a genre much favored in those times.

Contemporary Theological Problems: Molinism

One of the critical theological issues of the times was the relation of grace to free will. The occasion of this classic debate between the Dominicans and Jesuits, who stressed the role of grace and free will respectively, was a work published in 1588 by the Jesuit Louis Molina, immediately labelled heretical by the Dominican, Dominic Bañez. The controversy between these two influential Orders, who should instead have been breaking lances with heretics, concerned a matter so important that Clement VIII reserved the solution to himself. To examine Molina's works he established the *Congregatio de Auxiliis*, which met for the first time on January 2, 1598. One of its members was Henry Silvio, who, however, resigned soon after his election as prior general, but not before he had submitted a written judgment favorable to Molina.

Silvio's successor on the Congregation and in the chair of metaphysics at the Sapienza was John Anthony Bovio, of the Lombardy province, regent at Traspontina. With slightly varying membership the Congregation labored nine years under the pontificates of Clement VIII and Paul V, appropriately holding its last session on the feast of St. Augustine, August 28, 1607. In its final report, as it had done in its many sessions and reports over the years, the Congregation expressed itself unfavorable to the doctrine of Molina and listed a number of propositions to be condemned by the pope.

The one dissenting voice throughout was that of Bovio. His steadfast opinion, held against the other committee members, was that Molinism was not heretical and should not be condemned. Bovio advised the pope not to define the manner in which grace operates, but to leave the question open to discussion, which, however, should be carried on with due modesty and without accusations of heresy. This solution was the one which in fact the pope adopted. Bovio was not the only one so to advise the pope; such was the opinion of Bellarmine, St. Francis de Sales, and others outside the Congregation also consulted by Paul V. But Bovio's unvarying opposition to the condemnation of Molina probably caused Clement VIII to defer a decision and favorably impressed Paul V. As Pastor observes of Bovio, "His reply already points to the way that Paul V would later go."

Among Carmelite theologians, Henry of St. Ignatius predictably rejected Jesuit Molinism in his *Molinismus profligatus* (Leodii, 1715). Alexander of the Passion in his *Disciple pacifique de Saint Augustin* (Paris, 1715-1718, 2 v.), mentioned above, addresses himself to the problem of grace and free will - according to C. Toussaint "a remarkable analysis of the works of St. Augustine on this difficult material." Gregory Sebenico (d. 1676), of the Venetian province, rejected both the Dominican and Jesuit theories and proposed a third in his *Nova concordia divinae praedestinationis cum libertate voluntatis creatae* (Venetiis, 1665).

The Theology of the Church, Galicanism

John Anthony Bovio also had a part to play in the clamorous quarrel between the Holy See and the Republic of Venice in 1606. The occasion was the arrest by secular authorities of two priests in violation of clerical immunity acknowledged in Catholic countries, but more important, the promulgation of laws limiting the Church's right to possess property. Such attacks were by no means without precedent in the history of the Church; the novelty in this case was that the Church's right was contested on theological grounds. The theological foundation for the pretensions of the Most Serene Republic was supplied by its official theologian, the Servite, Paul Sarpi. When on April 17, 1606, Pope Paul V excommunicated the senate and declared the Republic under interdict, Sarpi wrote a treatise repudiating the pontiff's action. Cardinals Robert Bellarmine, Boniface Caetani and Caesar Baronio, and the University of Bologna rose to the defense of the Church. By no means insignificant was Bovio's response to Sarpi, which saw a number of editions in the same year of 1606. Couched in restrained and dignified language, it showed impressive learning and mastery of the question at hand. It won the respect of the protagonists of both sides and can only have benefitted the papal cause. Paul showed his appreciation by naming Bovio to the diocese of Molfetta, which he capably administered until his death in 1622.

Bovio defended the traditional temporal claims of the papacy, not all of which modern Catholic theologians would be prepared to acknowledge. On the other hand, Sarpi's teachings should not be confused with present day theory of separation of Church and State. He preached the absolute power of the State. The Servite friar did not reply directly to his Carmelite antagonist; this service was performed by his confrere, Fulgenzio Micanzio, who in turn was answered by the Carmelite, Stephen Barbieri. In 1608, through the mediation of King Henry IV of France, peace of a sort was restored between Venice and Rome.

The Venetian affair is only an isolated incident in the growing tendency of Catholic rulers to subject the Church to the State. This development which would reach its most disastrous consequences in the latter half of the 18th century is best known as Gallicanism from the country where it took its local habitation. It was both a theology which denied the supreme authority of the pope in the Church and a practical policy which restricted his powers outside his own States. Under the circumstances, the study of the nature of the Church received the special attention of theologians, and the tract *De Ecclesia* acquired a separate existence.

It must have taken a bit of courage for Bonaventure of St. Anne (d. 1667), of the province of Touraine, to write his *Defense of our Holy Father and Pope against the Errors of These Times* (Metz, 1658, etc.), prudently issued under the pseudonym Jacques de Vernant. In fact, the University of Paris censured the work, May 24, 1664, but Alexander VII ordered the faithful to ignore the censure, June 25, 1665. Vernant's opponents included Anthony Arnauld, Jacques Boileau, and other lesser lights.

Matthias de la Couronne (d. 1676), of the Francia province, wrote a massive work in 12 folio volumes, *Sanctitas Ecclesiae Romanae* (Liége, 1663-1668).

At the University of Valladolid, safely behind the Pyrenees, Emmanuel Anthony Vidax under the direction of John Feijóo de Villalobos defended a thesis against the Four Gallican Articles, published as *Davidis monomachia* (Valladolid, 1684).

Jansenism

The keen-witted Leo of St. John soon suspected that the two pillars of Jansenistic doctrine, Jansen's *Augustinus* (1640) and Anthony Arnauld's *Frequent Communion* (1643), were founded on sand. His *Sincere and Charitable Sentiments Regarding the Questions of Predestination and Frequent Communion* (n. p., 1643) is an early contribution to the questions. Written under the significant pseudonym of François Irénée, it sounds the conciliatory note that was to be Leo's lifelong attitude. The two sides, he claims, are basically in agreement. The controversy is useless and moreover dangerous, for it can lead to serious division in the Church. To avoid this, Leo does not hesitate to call on the secular arm. (The intimate relation of Church and State, of spiritual and temporal, was another conviction of his.)

In his *Letter of a Doctor of Theology to a Friend Regarding a Book Called "Sentiments"* (n. p., 1644) Arnauld accuses Leo of not having grasped the point at issue and of exaggerating the danger of a schism. Besides, peace should not be bought at the expense of truth. If Leo thinks that abstention from Holy Communion is a great evil, he, Arnauld, considers unworthy reception a greater evil still. Most of all, he deplores Leo's appeal to secular authority to maintain the peace.

In 1653, Innocent X condemned five propositions alleged by the French hierarchy to epitomize Jansen's fundamental errors. One of the fifteen consultors to the commission instituted beforehand to pass judgment on the propositions was the Carmelite Dominic Campanella (1581-1663), who consistently voted to condemn them. A native of Putignano in Puglia, ex-Jesuit and classmate at the Roman College of the historian of Trent, Peter Sforza Pallavicini, Campanella taught at the Order's *studia* in Palermo, Naples, and Rome, as well as at the Sapienza. He also filled the offices of prior of Traspontina and procurator general of the Order. Apparently in recognition of his services on the commission, he was made bishop of Sant'Agata dei Goti in 1654.

The confusion which the five propositions destined to occasion in the Church is already adumbrated in a decree of the general chapter of 1654 ordering lecturers to teach the doctrine of the papal bull without interpretation, evasion, or tergiversation. In 1680, the general chapter again warned teachers and preachers not to teach, preach, or publish anything "in the least redolent of this damnable doctrine (Jansenism)."

Carmelites who later wrote against Jansen and his doctrines include Anthony Marinari (1605-1689), of the province of Puglia, great nephew of the Tridentine theologian of the same name. His professorship at the Sapienza brought him to the notice of Cardinal Francis Barberini, whose suffragan in the diocese of Velletri he became in 1667. There Marinari found time to produce *Verus Augustinus* (Velletri, 1669-1677, 3 v.) against Jansen's work.

Alexander of St. Teresa (Van der Brugghe), of the Flandro-Belgian province, professor in the Order's *studium* at Louvain, produced a number of books against Jansenism. His *Clypeus religionis* (Coloniae, 1679, 2v.) covered the whole range of Jansenistic doctrines. In Flemish, he wrote *The Rule of Faith* (Ypres, 1682) and *Refutation of the Practice of Justification* (Ypres, 1683) against the seven articles of faith allegedly required to be believed *necessitate medii*.

Although not directly involved in the Jansenistic debate over frequent Communion, a work worth mentioning is *Burning Lamps Before the Blessed Sacrament* (Antwerp, 1706, 8 v.) a collection of examples of Eucharistic devotion taken from the lives of saints and devout persons by Timothy of the Presentation (d. 1710), of the Flandro-Belgian province. The author follows a moderate policy in the matter of the frequency of receiving Communion.

While the nature of the sorrow for sin required in confession was also debated among Catholic theologians, it is not difficult to conjecture which side the Jansenists would favor. Some Carmelite authors who treated this question have been mentioned above. To these may be added in the context of Jansenism, *Tempestas Novaturiens novissima* (Coloniae, 1686) of Alexander of St. Teresa against the novel doctrines circulating about confession. His earlier *Hydra prophanarum novitatum* (1685) against the hydra headed beast of heresy had been attacked by the anonymous author of a *Bellum poeticum*. The *Tempestas*, a rebuttal, in turn came under fire from Henry of St. Ignatius. Daniel of the Virgin Mary wrote a Flemish *Introduction to Christian Penitence* (Antwerpen, 1649) and translated into his native language *The Golden Art of Confessing* (2d ed., Brussel, 1649) by the Franciscan Christian Leutbreuer.

In its attitude toward Marian devotion, Jansenism touched a specially sensitive nerve of the Carmelite Order. Its members were not the least active among the opponents of the *Monita salutaria B. V. Mariae ad cultores suos indiscretos*, a work written in 1673 by the German layman, Adam Widenfeld, for the purpose of mitigating excesses in Marian devotion. From Ghent, Gratian of St. Elias and from Mechelen Michael of St. Augustine importuned the assistant general, Seraphim of Jesus and Mary, to have the book condemned. It was in fact placed on the Roman Index, June 19, 1674, with the condition *donec corrigatur*. This repressive measure did not entirely discourage the book's popularity, and controversy continued. Under pseudonyms, James of St. Anthony wrote a *Monitorum salutarium consonantia haereticis* (Mariaeburgi Catholicorum, 1675). Gregory of St. Martin, of the Gallo-Belgian province, published a *Juste apologie du culte de la Mere de Dieu* (Douai, 1674) against Widenfeld's book. Valentine of St. Amandus (d. 1687), of the Flandro-Belgian province, is probably the anonymous author of *Tractatus brevis ad Monita salutaria*

(Gandavi, 1673). While not directed at Widenfeld, Alexander of St. Teresa's *Praeco marianus* (Coloniae, 1681) sought justification for Marian devotion in the Fathers.

Quesnel and the *Unigenitus*

When Pasquier Quesnel revived Jansenistic teachings in his book, *Moral Reflections on the New Testament* (1693), Clement XI's bull, *Unigenitus* (1713), which condemned 101 statements taken from it, created the same sort of underground opposition as had Jansen's *Augustinus*. Again, religious rallied to the papal cause. As to the Carmelites, the prior general, Charles Cornaccioli, in 1718 required written allegiance from the French provinces. Another prior general, the Frenchman, Anthony Joseph Amable Feydeau, wrote *Reasons for Accepting the Constitution "Unigenitus"* (1742). Brocard of St. Nicholas published *The Bull "Unigenitus" and the Nullity of an Appeal to a Future General Council* (Treviris, 1719) and a *Dissertatio bipartita theologicopolemica* (Treviris, 1726) about the controversy on the occasion of the schism of Quesnel.

Part Four

THE CATHOLIC REFORMATION (1600-1750)
(Section 2)

Chapter 1

Prayer and Solitude

Through the Stricter Observance especially, the Carmelites participated in the fervor of the Catholic Reformation at every level. The Order was led back to the source of its being and made consciously aware of its vocation to prayer. It produced abundant and significant spiritual literature, the record of the religious experience of its choicest spirits, among them not a few members of the Third Order, which continued to evolve toward its present form. The Marian element of Carmelite spirituality was stressed, especially through the scapular confraternity. The apostolate became interiorized and charged with new zeal. Even materially, the Order prospered: in spite of wars and pestilence its numbers grew, its convents and churches were embellished or rebuilt in the new style.

Liturgical Prayer

Like other medieval orders, the Carmelites were charged by the Church with the community celebration of the liturgy. The first concern of the constitutions and of canonical visitors was the liturgical prayer of communities. This concern was often directed to externals such as cleanliness and the condition of the vestments and sacred vessels, but at the time such details could not always be taken for granted. After Clement VIII, exemptions from participation in choir were no longer tolerated. However, graduate students, lecturers, and preachers preparing sermons were dispensed from some of the hours or attended by turns. Matins continued to be celebrated at midnight, a heavy burden on communities engaged in the apostolate and often neglected by less fervent ones.

The improvement in the quality of religious life and the promotion of contemplative prayer, wrought especially by the Stricter Observance, had their effect on liturgical prayer as it was celebrated both by the religious and the laity. The divine office, recited or chanted with devotion and solemnity, was also a source of edification for the people, as the choir was normally situated around or behind the high altar. The celebration of the liturgy in the Carmelite churches at Brussels and Guelders so impressed Magdalen de Cusance that she prevailed on her husband, Count Albert van den Bergh, to bring the Carmelites to Boxmeer (1652).

The liturgical books in use were substantially those of the Tridentine reform already described under the 16th century: Caffardi's breviary (1585) and missal (1587), Fantoni's ceremonial (1616). The offices of the Carmelite saints, eliminated from these books but preserved by the Discalced, were finally added, together with feasts meanwhile acquired, to Orlandi's breviary (Antwerp, 1672) and editions by subsequent priors general.

In the renaissance of the liturgy, chant books took on their modern form. Sebastian Fantoni issued a *Directorium chori* (Neapoli, G.G. Carlini, 1614), containing musical texts for Mass and office, as well as a *processionale*, or chants for processions. Reprinted by following priors general, Orlandi (1668), Barberi (1699), Laghi (1755), Ximénez (1774), it remained the official chant book until the reform of Gregorian chant in the 20th century. The composer, or compiler, was Archangelus Paoli (d. 1635), prior and novice master in the Carmine of Florence.

Two provinces produced their own chant books. The Flemish province issued a *Directorium chori* in a beautiful edition by Plantin (Antverpiae 1650). The *Processionale*, published separately, was more comprehensive than the Order's. Processions, inherited from the Rite of the Holy Sepulchre, were a larger feature of the Carmelite than of the Roman rite. The distinguished musician, Benedict of St. Joseph (Buns), revised his province's chant books: the directory with the title *Manuale chori* (Bruxellis, 1721); the processional (Antverpiae, 1711).

It should cause no surprise that the Portuguese province, so devoted to music, sacred and profane, should wish to create its own chant books. Caspar Campello (d. 1622), novice master at the Carmo of Lisbon, composed a *Processionarium* (Ulyssipone, 1610), revised in 1642 by Anthony Segre, director of chant in the same convent. An Italian edition appeared in Venice in 1717. This book seems to be the predecessor of the *Directorium chori* (Lisbonae, 1754), the work of Louis Caesar de Menezes, published posthumously by an anonymous member of the province.

Mental Prayer and Contemplation

Although the reform of the Order brought about a renewal of the liturgy, its most striking feature was its emphasis on the contemplative nature of the Order. "We profess," the constitutions of the Stricter Observance expressly declare, "that the first and foremost part of our institution consists in prayer and contemplation" (pt. 1, ch. 14, no. 1).

The life of prayer of the Order underwent a profound renewal. Mental prayer was assiduously practiced, leading not infrequently to mystical experience. This contemplative renaissance took place, not surprisingly, in terms of contemporary spirituality. Medieval forms gave way to the practice of methodical meditation, examination of conscience, eucharistic adoration, annual retreats.

Mental prayer, imposed on all religious by Clement VIII, was spread through the Order by Henry Silvio and his successors. Silvio not only ordered meditation to be made but, where necessary, taught the brethren a method. He recommended especially Peter of Alcantara and Louis of Granada.

The directory of novices of the Touraine province developed a "Carmelite" method of making mental prayer. Translated into Latin and Italian, it had a widespread influence in the Order until modern times. Five kinds of prayer are distinguished: oral, mental, mixed, aspirative, and unitive or contemplative prayer.

The Touraine method of making mental prayer, or meditation, owes much to the Jesuit School, especially to Francis Arias and Louis de la Puente. To the Dominican, Louis de Granada, the method probably owes its voluntaristic and affective tendencies. More distinctive is the emphasis on aspirative prayer, or the practice of the presence of God, considered to be especially adapted to implementing the injunction of the Carmelite Rule to meditate day and night on the law of the Lord. Here the influence of John of St. Samson and of Dominic of St. Albert is particularly discernible, and through them that of the Franciscan, Henry Herp. The directory stops on the threshold of mystical prayer, as a condition not likely to be found in novices, though it does deal with what it calls the prayer of simple regard. The mystical experience of the Order is recorded in the works of its spiritual writers.

The practice of the prayer of simple regard was widespread, also among the laity, who were guided in every stage of the spiritual life by their directors. Spiritual direction was a favored ministry of the Carmelites.

The Eremitical Life

The return to the primitive ideal of the Order involved, besides the renewal of the spirit of prayer, the practice of solitude distinctive of the hermits of Mount Carmel and the early foundations of the Order in Europe.

It was the Discalced Thomas of Jesus who conceived the idea of establishing hermitages, where the original Carmelite style of life could be observed. He founded the first "desert" at Bolarque in Spain (1592), and it was in that country that most hermitages appeared, but the Italian Congregation issued the earliest legislation regarding this type of foundation.

The Stricter Observance, through Touraine, took over from the Discalced both the idea and the form of hermitages. The chapter which its constitutions devoted to this sort of foundation (pt. 1, ch. 2) is drawn almost literally from the Discalced legislation. An important difference is the requirement that the hermitage be attached to a convent.

"We ordain that in every province there be one eremitical convent, remote from cities and the noise of people, where some of us may live under strict cloister, wholly dedicated to the contemplation of heavenly things and to the practices of holy solitude" (no. 1).

The hermitage, which should accommodate no more than twelve solitaries in separate dwelling places (no. 6), is attached to a regular convent, the prior and officials of which carry out necessary business with the outside world (no. 4). Visiting friars should also be lodged in the convent (no. 7). The provincial's permission is required to enter the area of the hermitage proper (no. 10). The prior must visit each hermit once a week (no. 3).

On Sundays, the hermits join the community in the convent for meditation, chapter of faults, office, Mass, and a spiritual conference (no. 15). On Thursdays, the hermits gather to discuss Sunday's conference (no. 16). Likewise, on the principal feasts and special occasions, the hermits come to the convent for sung Mass and office (no. 17).

In the hermitage, Mass is not sung and the office is recited in a monotone with long pauses (no. 25). Vestments should be made of wool, simple and unadorned, as should be all the appurtenances of the hermitage (no. 26).

The hermits are not to engage in scholarly pursuits (no. 18), preach or hear confessions (no. 19). Continual silence is to be observed "after the example of our Father Elijah, Leader and Prince of Hermits" (no. 22). Besides two hours of meditation in common (no. 21), the hermits should dedicate another hour in their cells "to this truly angelic exercise."

"The rest of the time they should be so occupied with the presence of God and heavenly conversation that they may truly strive to meditate day and night on the law of the Lord" (no. 23).

Every year, the prior should add a few trees, fruit bearing and otherwise, so that the place "may be more apt for prayer and contemplation" (no. 13) - a curiously romantic touch (inherited from the Discalced) well in advance of Rousseau.

The practice of the solitary life was largely confined to France and Belgium, countries in which the Stricter Observance particularly flourished. The earlier Carmelite experiments with the solitary life, undertaken before the Stricter Observance had taken firm root, were less successful. In some cases, it was a question of reviving previously existing hermitages, Carmelite or otherwise. Hermits, often attached to a rustic chapel, to the care of which they were appointed by the bishop, abounded everywhere.

St. Louis in the Forest of Valence (Aquitaine)

In 1491, upon recommendation of Louis d'Amboise, bishop of Albi, King Charles VIII granted a tract of land in his forest in Valence for a hermitage to a certain Pierre Dauzits, apparently a Benedictine monk. After the latter's demise, the reforming bishop granted the hermitage dedicated to St. Louis to the reformed Congregation of Albi, in the founding of which he had played a leading role. Not unlikely, at least in the early fervent days of the Congregation, some Carmelites led the solitary life in the forest of Valence. During the religious wars, especially in 1574, when the Huguenots laid siege to Valence, there would have been little leisure for the contemplative life.

As in the case of other houses of the province of Aquitaine, the reform introduced by John Tuaut brought new life to the hermitage of St. Louis. In 1623, Angelus Bridel, commissioned by the prior of Albi, on which it depended, undertook the restoration of chapel and convent, buried under brambles and thorns, the lair of wild animals. Two years later, the bishop of Albi was able to bless the new chapel.

At the time he began his work of reconstruction, Bridel was a young friar of twenty-four years. In 1669, he is described as being seventy years of age, having lived in the hermitage *cum odore sanctae vitae* for forty-eight years, thirty of them as vicar.

The structure renewed by Bridel faced east and contained the chapel of St. Louis, 27 ft. long, 15 ft. wide, and 15 ft. high, with a single altar, two confessionals and a pulpit. A large porch fronted the chapel. The adjacent sacristy was 12 ft. square. An addition to the chapel in 1630 housed a kitchen and refectory. On the upper story, but not over the chapel, were three rooms, reached by a wooden stair, one each for a guest, the sick and procurator. Around 1653, a wing was added to the north, a barn for storing grain with a wine cellar. The upper story contained eight cells for religious. A third building was situated some distance to the southwest of the monastic structures. It contained a stable for horses, a bakery, and a dining hall for hired laborers. The chapel and cells were enclosed within a fence of wooden stakes.

Since the chapter of 1644, the hermitage of St. Louis had enjoyed the status of a convent independent of Albi. In 1688, the cornerstone of a new church was laid.

In a letter of 1670 to the bishop of Albi, the provincial, Charles of St. Joseph, declared that the community of St. Louis "lived an eremitical life according to their institute." Their life in any case did not exclude a certain amount of assistance in the hamlets round about, as parish registers attest. Although it had no "miraculous" image, the chapel was frequented by large crowds on certain feast days, especially the feast of St. Louis, when twelve confessors were not enough.

Priors were elected to the hermitage down to the Revolution.

Graville (Jurisdiction of the Prior General)

Graville in the diocese of Bazas belonged under the immediate jurisdiction of the prior general. Its founder, Andrew Blanchard, was a member of the province of Narbonne, but Graville itself was situated in the Gironde, territory actually of the province of Gascony. Who the hermits were, or from what provinces they were recruited, is not known. The fact that the hermitage was the responsibility of the faraway prior general augured ill for its efficient administration, but the renaissance of the contemplative life had hardly begun, and there was no experience in the conduct of hermitages. The location of Graville would be explained by the friendship of Blanchard with its lord.

The latter, Count Henry de Gournai, Lord of Marcheville, travelled to Rome to request from the prior general permission to establish a hermitage. The Bishop of Bazas, Henry Listolfe Maroni, added his solicitations. On April 15, 1638, Straccio named Andrew Blanchard his commissary for the new foundation, to be made "in the place which the aforesaid Bishop Henry and Count Henry would assign to him." The hermitage was to be immediately subject to the prior general through his commissary, who had the same powers as a provincial. Its members had no voice in the provincial chapter and could not leave the hermitage without the general's permission. All this is apparent from the brief of Urban VIII, May 4, 1639, confirming Straccio's patents. The prior general had just finished his constitutions for reformed houses with its chapter on hermitages (1637). He must have been gratified by this blossoming of the eremitical spirit. His provisions for Graville are obviously suggested by Monte Oliveto.

A certain M. de Quincarnon donated his domain of Graville, forty *arpents* of woodland in the parish of Bernos, fifteen kilometers from Bazas. Pierre Drilhole, second archdeacon of Bazas, contributed 4,000 *livres* toward the construction of the hermitage. All these persons, including the bishop of Bazas, derived from Jansenist circles.

Little is known about the life and personality of Andrew Blanchard. He obtained the licentiate in theology at the University of Paris in 1628. In 1643, he became the prior of Clermont. At the time of the foundation of the hermitage, he was prior of Mende. His association with some of the reformed houses of the province, as well as his desire to lead the solitary life, suggests that he formed part of the group of reformers in the province.

Blanchard is said to have composed statutes for the hermitage, now lost.

According to an extant list of priors of Clermont, Blanchard was again prior there, 1648-1650. In that case, he would not have been on hand in 1649 to admit the nemesis of the institution, the notorious prophet and mystic, John Labadie. This bizarre character was no stranger to the Bordelais. He had entered the Jesuit Order in Bordeaux and made his studies there. He also spent a year at the Jesuit college in Agen (1634), where he may have made the acquaintance of the eremitical community under the leadership of Anthony Sabré. He impressed all with his oratorical talents and mystical gifts, though not Surin, who detected in him a spirit of overweening pride. Great was the consternation, when in 1638 Labadie requested to be dispensed from his religious vows, later alleging that this step had been necessary to respond to an interior call to restore primitive Christianity. As a secular priest, he had already worn out his welcome in several dioceses by his curious doctrines, when he appeared at Graville.

There he at once summoned Sabré and his companions from their hermitage in Agen; together they made prior a certain Sylvester, probably one of their number. On April 28, 1650, Labadie left Graville, riding a donkey and carrying a large statue of Christ, and so was not there on May 3, when the new bishop of Bazas, Samuel Martineau, arrived to restore order. From Carmel, Labadie that same year turned to Calvinism, which in turn he abandoned after a controversial career, to found his own sect of Labadists. Sabré died on October 5, having seen the error of his ways and written an open letter to Labadie about his conversion to Calvinism (Bazas, 1651). Sabré's companions, however, continued contumacious, encouraged by Labadie's letters to reinstate Sylvester. Finally, Martineau had recourse to the secular arm, invaded Graville by force, jailed seven of the hermits, and sent the others away.

The hermitage did not survive the disturbance. From Clement of St. Bernard, sub-delegated commissary, Blanchard received permission to leave the hermitage and return to his province of Narbonne. He appears a third time as prior of Clermont in 1655. He apparently did not finish his term, for it is certain that he was prior of Dijon in 1658. He died at Besançon, 1661.

Lormont (Gascony)

The hermitage of Lormont had a venerable tradition antedating its occupation by the Carmelites. The chapel of St. Catherine of Lormont, situated on the cliffs above the Garonne at a point near the present railway tunnel to Orléans, was attended by a resident hermit. Earliest references date from 1386. In 1446, the Carmelites of Bordeaux obtained possession of chapel and hermitage from the owners of the property, heirs of the late Peyde Moulon de Camarsac, and thereafter supplied the "hermit" or chaplain for the chapel, which was a popular place of pilgrimage, especially of mariners returning from long sea voyages.

In 1570, the hermitage was destroyed by Huguenots. After the Great Pestilence of 1585, the Carmelites virtually abandoned the ruined hermitage, into which other hermits occasionally settled. In 1614, under the prior of Bordeaux, Raymond Rateguy, the situation was clarified and the exclusive rights of the Carmelites to the site confirmed. Thereafter, the Carmelites continued to inhabit the hermitage and serve the chapel, in spite of its ruinous state. Later practice shows that the Carmelites presented a friar, who was then officially appointed to the office by the archbishop.

A drawing by Hermann van der Hem shows Lormont as it was in 1646.

With the reform of the province of Gascony, Lormont entered a new phase of its history. To Andrew of St. Peter, former provincial and professor at the University of Bordeaux, and Maur of the Child Jesus, the hermitage above the Garonne seemed indicated as the hermitage prescribed for every reformed province by the constitutions of the Stricter Observance. Generous patrons for the renovation of the buildings presented themselves in the persons of the president of the parliament of Bordeaux, Arnaud de Pontac, and his learned and devout spouse, Louise de Thou, penitent of Surin and benefactress of the Discalced nunnery of Bordeaux. The pious couple desired "to contribute to the increase of the cult which the religious of the Order of Our Lady of Mount Carmel render to so glorious a patroness and to augment as much as they can devotion to the adorable mystery of the Infant Jesus." They further considered that "these places of retreat, established in so holy a fashion by the first founders of the said Order, are very efficacious means for preserving the spirit of prayer, which is the soul of religious perfection, and, moreover, these places of solitude are very suitable and conformable to the hidden state of soul characterizing the Holy Child Jesus during his infancy." In the emphasis on the Divine Infancy, it is not difficult to discern the hand of Maur of the Child Jesus.

During his visitation of Gascony, Jerome Ari lent a ready ear to the project. Under his presidency, the chapter held at Agen in 1664 gratefully accepted the generous offer of Arnaud de Pontac. The hermitage of Lormont was to be financially independent of the convent of Bordeaux and to have control of all revenues accruing to it. Andrew of St. Peter was named procurator with powers to negotiate a contract with Pontac, oversee the construction, collect alms, and live on the premises to supervise the work. As soon as the building was far enough advanced, Andrew, Maur, and a lay brother, Roch of the Assumption, were authorized to take up residence at Lormont, after consultation with the provincial and permission from the archbishop.

These arrangements did not affect the service of the chapel of St. Catherine. A chaplain, nominated by the community of Bordeaux and approved by the archbishop, might still offer the foundation Masses, but should have nothing to do with the hermits. If the chaplaincy should become vacant or be renounced, the hermits might assume its duties.

Thus authorized, Andrew proceeded to sign a contract with Arnaud and Louise, December 18, 1665. The hermitage was to be named St. Catherine of the Child Jesus. As soon as conditions permitted, Andrew, Maur, and Roch were to take up residence in Lormont and remain there stably. They or their successors could not be removed except for canonical reasons. The hermitage was to accommodate up to three priests and one brother. Any besides the present occupants were to be chosen by the hermits themselves together with the prior of Bordeaux and the provincial. Every Monday, a Mass was to be offered in honor of the Divine Infancy. Further, the hermits were to remember their benefactors in their prayers and honor them as their patrons and founders. In return, these agreed to contribute 8,000 *livres*: 6,000 *en fonds revenants*, 2,000 for construction.

In 1671, the restoration of Lormont began. According to an 18th century report, the tiny chapel measured six by three meters. The sculptured *retable* of the single altar pictured St. Catherine with her wheel. Before her, appeared Christ and the Virgin; above her, an angel. An arch supported by two panels with floral designs bore the arms of the Carmelite Order in silver and sable. Joined to the chapel was the hermitage, consisting of five cells (two for guests), refectory, and kitchen. Furnishings of the cells were sparse and austere. The library was lodged in the prior's cell, and its catalog has survived.

The hermits were allowed to leave their solitude for considerations of obedience or charity. Maur visited persons he directed in Bordeaux and elsewhere. In 1675 and 1685, he was elected provincial; in 1679, prior of Bordeaux .

Around 1680, the hermits were joined by a layman, Charles de Brion, scion of a noble family, which tried every means to lure him back to the world. At the command of Maur, his spiritual director, he took orders. He stayed on at Lormont after Maur's death in 1690, but in 1701 moved into Bordeaux to the Hôpital de la Manufacture, a sort of refuge for the needy, who were taught trades. There he remained until his family persuaded him to return to Paris.

How long thereafter the solitary life was lived in Lormont, if at all, is not known.

With time, the Bordeaux Carmel even lost interest in the chaplaincy. In 1766, Archbishop Louis Jacques d'Audibert de Lussan on pastoral visitation found the site abandoned, the chapel used as a tool shed, the door to the hermitage missing. He ordered the Carmelites to renovate the chapel and restore it to sacred use.

Basses Loges (Touraine)

Oddly, Touraine did not take steps to fulfill the requirements of the constitutions regarding hermitages until relatively late. Since 1630, through the munificence of Louis XIII, Les Billettes in Paris had possessed a hospice, known as Basses Loges, situated in the Forest of Fontainebleau near the Seine, a mile from the royal castle.

The first steps toward realizing the province's dream of a hermitage were taken by Angélique of St. Francis, subprior of Les Billettes in Paris. He obtained from Monsignani patents dated March 29, 1683, appointing him commissary general, charged with establishing a hermitage of the Order in France. The conditions of his appointment were roughly those laid down by Straccio in 1638 for Graville. On May 9, fourteen friars of the province desirous to lead the solitary life met at Les Billettes and named Angélique their procurator to carry out any necessary negotiations.

Fortunately, the plan of an autonomous foundation under the prior general never materialized. Instead, the province took the matter in hand. On September 11, 1684, the community of Les Billettes, persuaded by the provincial, Stephen of St. Francis Xavier, ceded its rights over Basses Loges to the province, thus eluding by this amicable settlement the quarrels which had been the bane of Lormont. Construction began at once. A report of March 16, 1686, describes the progress of the work. The previously existing cruciform church was dedicated to St. Nicholas with altars to St. Louis and St. Teresa in the transepts. Precious possessions of the sacristy were silver vestments sewn by Queen Anne of Austria and Princess Marie Therese. The royal family had always been generous benefactors of Basses Loges and hopefully would aid with the work of construction. According to Leo of St. John, the altar of St. Teresa was a votive offering for peace by Queen Anne.

Upon completion, the report continues, the hermitage will not be the least of the houses of the province and will be their crown. Part of the church is finished, as well as five of the fourteen cells. The hermitage is in the form of a quadrangular cloister measuring 55 rods (*perticas*) east and west, 40 rods north and south. There are five cells each on the eastern and western sides, none on the northern. On the southern side, are four more cells and the church, extending into the midst of the cells.

The hermitage is situated in a valley, above which the wooded hills rise like so many steps to heaven. There are natural caves no human ingenuity could devise. Only the calls of animals are heard and the sound of water leaping into the air, flowing onto the plain, or murmuring sweetly like the fountain of Elijah.

The general chapter of 1686 expressed warm approval of the enterprise.

The provincial chapter of 1687, which elected Mark of the Nativity provincial, announced the completion of the hermitage and called for volunteers for the solitary life. Hilarion of St. Ursula was to continue as provincial vicar.

On August 14, 1687, the new provincial officially "established" the hermitage of Basses Loges. He composed *Reglemens et éclaircissements*, regulating in minute detail the daily life of the hermits, which he caused to be approved by the annual congregation of May, 1688, and which he promulgated at his visitation of the hermitage in October. Perhaps on that occasion also, the first prior was elected in the person of Angélique of St. Francis, a fitting gesture. He was succeeded at the following chapter of 1690 by Ignatius of St. Henry.

At present, no information is available on the subsequent history of Basses Loges, but it evidently continued to function. Priors of the "solitude" were regularly elected at the provincial chapters down to the Revolution. Around 1710, Noel Laimerie of the province of Toulouse, stated that Basses Loges and Sainte Anne d'Auray were the only surviving Carmelite hermitages in France.

The Carmelite church of Sainte Anne d'Auray, patroness of Brittany, was a much frequented center of devotion. Its convent, which could accommodate forty friars, was no hermitage. Remotely situated, perhaps in the early 18th century it also served as a contemplative house for the Breton half of the province of Touraine.

The national constitutions, imposed on the French provinces in 1772, retained the legislation on hermitages (pt. 1, ch. 9), an unexpected kudos to the contemplative life in the age of Illuminism and a sign, perhaps, that Basses Loges still survived at that date.

Termuylen

The Belgian province conducted a successful experiment in the solitary life, which passed over to the Flemish (Flandro-Belgian) province at the time of the division (1663).

The chapel of Our Lady of the Mule in the forest of Liedekerke traced its origin to the Middle Ages and was the result of a vow made to the Virgin, who appeared astride a white mule to local lords on crusade in Egypt, praying for a safe return from the wars. In the course of time, the chapel came under the care of the Carmelites of Aalst. The attached house was later destroyed.

The chapel of Termuylen seemed the ideal site for the hermitage prescribed by the constitutions of the Stricter Observance. The provincial chapter of 1649 commissioned the prior of Aalst, Livinus D'Hondt to construct the province's hermitage there. Priors were asked to find benefactors for each of the cells of the hermitage. D'Hondt died the following year without being able to complete the task assigned him.

The chapter of 1652 under the presidency of Filippini elected provincial Daniel of the Virgin, who promoted the ideal of the solitary life. On May 17, at the chapter itself, Filippini issued patents declaring Count de Boisson, his wife, and children founders of Termuylen by reason of their benefactions. Before the chapter, on March 21, Daniel, as prior of Brussels, had engaged the services of a surveyor, M. Deblocke, who drew up a blueprint. According to his plan, still extant, twelve cells form a circle around the chapel, the whole complex surrounded by a wall and flanking the chapel of Our Lady of the Mule and attached house.

By the following year the foundation had sufficiently progressed to allow Filippini, on September 6, to make Termuylen a convent independent of Aalst. The general chapter of 1654 declared Termuylen a "*locus eremiticus*" and granted its superior voice in the provincial chapter. On December 23, Daniel promulgated an *Ordo vitae regularis*, consisting of fifteen rules for the conduct of the hermitage.

The first superior of Termuylen, which in the beginning rated only a vicar, was Berthold of St. Joseph, an allusion perhaps to St. Berthold, thought to be the first Latin prior of the hermitage on Mount Carmel. Born in Gelderen in 1624, he died in 1653, only twenty-eight years old. He left a history in Flemish of Termuylen (Gent, 1653). Another vicar of Termuylen, apparently the second, was Francis of the Child Jesus (d. 1667), author of *A Very Profitable Instruction for Using the Holy Sacrament of Penance Well and Piously* (Gent, 1660), which saw several editions. He also published *Albert the Great's Exceedingly Devout Little Book on Forsaking Transitory Things and Cleaving to God Alone*, with reflections from the works of St. Teresa and St. John of the Cross (Ghent, 1663).

After Termuylen was given voice in the provincial chapters, its superiors, beginning with Fulgentius of the Purification in 1656, regularly attended these gatherings, until the suppression of the province. Gratián of St. Elias, elected in 1659, wrote a *Mirror of Good Thoughts for Every Day of the Month* (Ghent, 1665) and *Exercises for Philothea during her Monthly Retreat* (Ghent, 1671). The book-lover will note with delight his gracious little volume, *Beauté de Carmel* (1660), in which twenty-six sonnets recounting legends of Carmel face as many engravings by Peter Clouwet made from drawings by Abraham van Diepenbeke. Among translations Gratián made, should be mentioned his version in Flemish of Boudon's *True Devotion to Mary, the Mother of God* (Ghent, 1697).

In 1659, the construction of the hermitage was still not completed. On March 22, Venturini, noting that its "construction had not been promoted with due diligence because no one person had been put in charge," appointed Michael of St. Augustine his commissioner. Jerome Ari's visit to Termuylen was brief. Arriving around noon of May 19, 1663, he was in Brussels by six o'clock that evening. The community of hermits under Gratián of St. Elias, in the last days of his vicarship, numbered five priests, three brothers, and a *donatus*. "With special joy," the general's secretary wrote, "the Most Reverend Father observed that the eremitical convent is most suited to the Carmelite spirit and to recollection. It is well begun and laid out and with God's help is proceeding favorably. He will take up the matter of enlarging it at the provincial chapter." At that chapter, Matthias Hunen, one of the reformers of Lower Germany, who chose to remain in Belgium at the division of the provinces, was elected vicar of Termuylen.

At the chapter of 1681, Termuylen was raised to the status of a convent with a prior, Augustine of St. Francis Xavier, an indication no doubt that the hermitage had finally reached the full term of its development.

When Munsterbilsen in the Flandro-Belgian province is called a hermitage in official documents, the term refers only to its original condition, before it was acquired by the Carmelites as a hospice for *terminarii*, or questing friars and preachers. Bestowed on the Order by Isabelle Henriette, abbess of Munsterbilsen, in 1672, it was made a vicariate by the chapter of 1674 with Peter Thomas of St. Cyril as its first vicar. Munsterbilsen never became a full-fledged convent with a prior.

The foregoing exhausts the list of known hermitages in the style of the constitutions. Peter Anson, indefatigable student of the solitary life, is a bit hard on Carmelite hermitages, Calced and Discalced, which he characterizes as "period pieces," belonging "to the same social system that created the Palace of Versailles." Nonetheless, the prayer and penance practised in Termuylen was of the same sort as ever hermits practised.

The old Order was not as successful in conducting these hermitages as the Discalced, who after all invented the genre. The old Carmel carried the burden of the ages and continued sometimes to express its contemplative inclination in less organized ways.

Late in the 17th century, George of St. Mary, of the province of Francia, obtained leave to retire to a solitary place, where he eventually died. He was held by all to be "a man of mystical ways, most dedicated to the practice of penance and solitude."

The case has already been noted of the Irishman, James of St. Joseph O'Cain, who from 1770 to 1778 lived as a recluse attached to the Lady chapel in Arcachon in the diocese of Bordeaux. It is thought that Denis O'Mahoney was a Carmelite of the old Observance. He built a hermitage on the site associated with St. Finbar on the island in lake Gougane Barra, West Cork, where he died around the year 1700.

In Sicily, Prosper Giambertoni (d. 1642), of the convent of Piazza in the province of St. Albert, was a doctor of theology and taught in universities of the Italian continent before he received permission to live as a hermit near his native Piazza.

It would be difficult to say how many Carmelites chose this form of life. The perfect solitary, as Dom Paul Ziegler of Quarr Abbey has observed, remains unknown and has no history.

Chapter 2

Spiritual Literature of Carmel

After the separation of the Discalced reform from the Order, St. Teresa and St. John of the Cross became the exclusive reserve of the movement they had initiated and the subject of commentary by Discalced writers who constitute what is now generally known as the "Carmelite School" of spirituality. But the old Order, renewed by the Stricter Observance, also produced an abundant spiritual literature, characteristically eclectic in form, which takes the shape of the time and place in which it originates. These writings hardly constitute a "school", but are no less interesting for their variety.

By the 17th century, in which the renewal of the old Carmel took place, the focus of the Catholic renaissance had shifted from Spain to France, and it is here that we must look for the most significant spiritual literature the Order produced. We have already noted the relationship of the reform of Touraine with the leaders of the French mystical movement through Philip Thibault. The movement strongly marked the spirituality of Touraine and the writers it soon began to produce.

Early Writers of Touraine

With the exception of its saints, Brother John of St. Samson is the greatest mystic the Order produced. His writings, collected after his death by Donatian of St. Nicholas, fill two folio volumes (Rennes, 1658-1659). They are a reflection of John's personal experience and do not present a systematic outline of the spiritual life, though a doctrinal line is discernible. He follows the Rheno-Flemish school, especially Ruysbroeck and Herp. Like Ruysbroeck, Brother John anchors the spiritual life in the mystery of the Trinity. In the eternal procession of the Word all creatures are ideally produced. Creatures live in the divine Wisdom according to an ideal being (exemplar) and aspire to reunion with God. This need for reunion is the basis of the spiritual life as well as the process of introversion by which man in his search for God descends into his own soul to find the point of closest contact with his creator. God is the true Center of the soul. The possibility of union with the Center flows from the doctrine of exemplarism. John's terms, "inmost soul" (*fond de l'âme*), "essence of the soul," correspond to Ruysbroeck's third part of the soul, where the superior faculties inhere in God.

One of the tenets of the abstract school of spirituality is the possibility of a direct relationship of the soul to God. According to John of St. Samson, before the soul can arrive at direct union with God, known as consummation, it must pass through the state of introversion in which all its forces merge into one surge of love. This introversion is the condition of the elevation of the soul properly so-called, which John also calls transformation by which the soul arrives at consummation. This state is characterized by three signs: simple idleness or nudity of the spirit, when the faculties of the soul remain passive; contemplation, or vision of the divine object, accompanied by non-knowing; enjoyment, in which the soul lives the life of the Trinity. The peace which this enjoyment brings is God himself. Brother John expressly excludes surpassing the humanity of Christ. The imitation of Christ, conformity with his humanity (*au dehors*), and divinity (*au dedans*) is one of the essential points of his doctrine.

Suzanne Bouchereaux sums up Brother John's spirituality as reflected in his writings: passionate attachment to Christ and his cross, burning expressions of love of the mystic spouse, overflowing joy in the profound deaths he experiences at sharing the beatitude and glory of the object in which he is consumed. Leonce Reypens, authority on Ruysbroeck, pronounces John of St. Samson "the most profound of the French mystics." For Louis Cognet he is "the most eminent representative" of the French abstract school of mysticism.

Dominic of St. Albert, favorite disciple of Brother John, was born at Fougères in 1596. He was studying at the Jesuit College of St. Thomas in Rennes, when he came to know the Carmelites and felt the call to join them. He made his novitiate under Matthew Pinault and his profession in 1614 in the hands of the prior, Philip Thibault. After his novitiate, Dominic stayed on as assistant to the novice master. Brother John found in him a kindred spirit whom he quickly led along the ways of mystical prayer. Dominic later became master of novices at Angers, lector in theology and regent of studies at Rennes, vicar of the Observance of Rennes (1630), and prior of Nantes (1632), where he died two years later.

Only three years professed, Dominic at the request of his superiors wrote a spiritual guide for the novices and professed students of Rennes, *Exercitatio spiritualis fratrum tam novitiorum quam professorum*, including his *Regulae exteriores; seu, praxis externa praecipuarum virtutum* (Paris, 1650). Showing remarkable balance and prudence, the youthful author writes "for those who converse familiarly, uniquely, and confidently with God," it is not necessary "to try to distinquish the purgative, illuminative, and unitive ways, because where there is love, one always makes progress." In these *Jugendwerke*, the influence of Brother John is very marked, but Dominic's theological formation is evident in the clear and orderly exposition of the topic.

In his more mature works, *Théologie mystique* and *Traité de l'oraison mentale* - for Janssen "by far his most beautiful work" - Dominic shows more independence. Though he uses the terminology of the German mystics, his doctrine is closer to that of Hugh de Balma (pseudo-Bonaventure). Direct contemplation of God is not possible in this life. Love and desire, not knowledge, are the means of direct union with God. They are aroused directly by God in the summit of the soul (*sommet de l'ésprit*). The highest mystical state is not the repose of union but the restlessness, pain, and suffering caused by the insatiable desire to be united more intimately with God.

Another alumnus of the Jesuit College of St. Thomas at Rennes was Bernard of St. Magdalen (1589-1669), born near Saumur. Like Dominic, he was drawn to the Carmelites and was clothed in the habit in 1609, only a year after the reform of Rennes had been consolidated under Thibault as prior, and he lived to the ripe age of 82. Although he held office as prior a number of times and was elected provincial in 1629, most of his religious life was devoted to the formation of the young members of the reform. He spent forty years, though not consecutively, in this work and merited to be called by Mark of the Nativity the spiritual father of the reform. During his term as novice master at Rennes from 1632 to 1647, he gathered material for the important directory of novices, to which Mark of the Nativity gave final form. Other works by Bernard, a directory of novice masters and a life of his close friend, Philip Thibault, remained in manuscript and untraceable to date.

Anthony of St. Martin (de la Porte) came from a titled family in Angers related to Cardinal Armand de Richelieu. After profession in the hands of Thibault at Rennes in 1611, he was one of the first to be sent for theology to the Jesuit college of La Flèche. In 1619, he was appointed to teach philosophy at Rennes. Later, he served as prior in several convents of the province and was elected vicar of the reform in 1626. Assigned to the newly-established convent in the rue des Billettes in Paris in 1631, Anthony remained there, engaged in preaching and writing until his death in 1650. Of his published works, *Présence de Jésus Christ dans les hopitaux et prisons* (Paris, L. Cottereau, 1648) induced many ladies of the court to engage in works of charity. A similar work apparently was his earlier *Tresor des richesses dans le sein des pauvres* (Paris, L. Cottereaux, 1648). His *Conversation interieure avec Jésus Christ dans le tres saint sacrement de l'autel* (Paris, S. Hure, 1644) became a popular manual for visits to the Blessed Sacrament. His most extensive work, the four volume *Conduites de la grâce* (Paris, veuve de J. Petit Pas, 1645-1648), which was anti-Jansenistic only in the sense that it was orthodox - for its author wished to avoid controversy - is said to have brought about many conversions. Anthony left unpublished *Les vacances spirituelles* and *Contemplations amoureuses sur la passion de Jésus Christ*.

Touraine Writers: the Second Generation

The diversified literary output of Leo of St. John (1600-1671) includes much that regards the spiritual life. He concerns himself with mysticism in his sermons and even apologetical works, so there is no point in listing spiritual titles, with the exception perhaps of his most ambitious work of this sort, *La conduite général de la théologie mystique* (Paris, 1654-1656, 2 v.).

Leo shows influences of pseudo-Dionysius, St. Teresa, and Cardinal John Bona (d. 1674). The course of his life was determined to a large extent by his early contact with John of St. Samson, which concentrated his strong apostolic urge into the single-minded purpose of leading men to Christ, who is the Truth. He borrows expressions from the master of his youth, but his style is quite different: clear, sinewy language, ample periods, well-constructed line of thought.

Leo discovers three degrees in man: moral, spiritual, and mystical, to which correspond the virtues of hope, charity, and faith. All baptized persons are called to sanctity, hence should flee multiplicity and enter into themselves to find God, in whose image they have been created. The mystic way of this return comprises renunciation, not-knowing, loving. Thus one arrives at conformity to the will of God, the crown of an asceticism summed up in the Pauline phrase, dear to John of St. Samson, *"Christo confixus sum cruci"* (Gal. 2:19). The science of the saints consists in tasting, in acts of the will, not of the intellect. Love alone makes man abandon creatures for God and, after he has entered into the divine repose, to return to creatures.

Leo greatly admired St. Teresa for the way she reconciled the life of the intellect with that of the will, an unconscious reflection perhaps of his own drives. St. John of the Cross he neglects completely.

Peter of the Resurrection (d. 1673) served for many years as novice master in the province of Touraine. His many works remain to be studied. Those known to exist are *La vie spirituelle déduite avec méthode* (Rennes, 1659-1660, 3 v.), *Le manuel des religieux profez* (Nantes, 1664-1666, 4 pts.), and *De la conversation religieux* (Rennes, 1671).

Maur of the Child Jesus (d. 1690) entered the novitiate at Rennes in 1633, when

Bernard of St. Magdalen was novice master. "For his singular piety," Mark of the Nativity later wrote, "(Maur) was very dear to Brother John of St. Samson, from whom he also seems to have imbibed the spirit of mystical prayer." Around 1648, Maur transferred to the province of Gascony and remained there until his death. His activity on behalf of reform has already been described. He spent the last twenty years of his life in the hermitage of Lormont.

Maur often left his hermit's cell on errands of spiritual direction, to which he devoted much effort. The Visitandines, the Carmelite nuns, Feuillants, and lay persons in Bordeaux, Paris, and elsewhere were among those he counselled. To John Joseph Surin, Jesuit exorcist of Loudun, he was "a close friend." Maur's writings reflect his practical involvement in the spiritual life. He did not intend to expound mystical theology in the sense of a systematization of the data of experience; he defines mystical theology as "the theology of the heart" and writes out of his own experience.

The authors found on Maur's bookshelf in his hermit's cell include, besides the Fathers and St. Thomas (the Touraine reform scrupulously followed the injunction of the constitutions), his master, John of St. Samson, and the writers recommended by him: Tauler and Ruysbroeck. "To present their content," Bouchereaux has written of Maur's works, "is to repeat the doctrine of John of St. Samson." However, also present in Maur's little library was St. John of the Cross, by then available in translation, who added the Carmelite tradition from below the Pyrenees to the influence of the abstract school of the North.

Maur's teaching revolves around the two poles of emptying of self and submission to the Spirit. The former is described as "annihilation (*anéantissement*)," renunciation of every interest which should give way to the divine action in the soul. Prayer is adherence, ever more simple, to the divine presence. It is the prayer of simple regard, found universally in the spirituality of 17th century France.

Maur's principal work, *L'Entree a la divine Sagesse* (Bordeaux, 1652), which also includes his previously published *Théologie chrétienne et mystique* (Bordeaux, 1651) underwent six editions, the last at Soignies, 1921-1933. A Flemish translation saw three editions. *La royaume intérieur de Jésus Christ dans les ames* (Paris, 1664) and *La crèche de l'Enfant Jésus* (Bordeaux, probably after 1664) witness to the author's Christological emphasis. An unpublished *Traité de la vie intérieure* (1673) and a number of letters of spiritual direction complete the corpus of his works.

Contemporary and friend of Maur was Mark of the Nativity (1617-1696). He was a student at the Jesuit College at La Flèche, when he was attracted to the Order by the example of his Carmelite fellow students. He donned the habit in 1631 and received his early formation in the spiritual life from Bernard of St. Magdalen and John of St. Samson, whose amanuensis he became. Mark was among the students sent to Paris in 1636 in the ill-fated attempt to reform the Place Maubert. After its failure, he completed his studies at Angers and Rennes. During his lifetime, he served as prior in various convents, was elected provincial in 1687, and was named novice master four times.

Mark's contribution to the spiritual literature and the life itself of the Order is the directory of novices for the province of Touraine, *La conduite spirituelle des novices* (Paris, 1650-1651, 4 v.). During his long years as novice master, Bernard of St. Magdalen had "adumbrated" - the word is Mark's - such a directory but had never given it final form. The chapter of Poitiers in 1647 entrusted this task to Bernard's disciple, Mark of the Nativity. Mark retired to Aulnay and in two years completed his commission. The four volumes treat respectively the four themes, motives for entering a religious Order, the principal mysteries of the faith, religious life, and the method for making mental prayer. This last volume, which provided instruction on methodical meditation, mixed prayer, and aspirative prayer, influenced the life of prayer of generations of Carmelites everywhere, and of all influences came closest to forming a "Carmelite" way of prayer. It made its way in translation into Germany and Italy and in the *Directorium carmelitanum vitae spiritualis* (Vatican City, 1940) extended its teachings into modern times.

Bernard of St. Magdalen had also prepared material for a directory explaining the manner of performing the external duties of religious life, which he considered of vital importance for the faithful maintenance of observance. Mark also completed and published this directory, now of little or no relevance: *Directoire des petits offices de la religion* (Angers, 1677-1680, 5 v.).

The other French provinces produced no spiritual writers comparable to those of Touraine; in fact, their literary output is remarkably meager.

Benignus of St. Martin (d. 1636), of Dijon, became a Carmelite in the Narbonne province after the death of his wife. He wrote *Sallies of the Lover of Jesus and Mary on the Sacrifice of the Mass* (Dijon, 1634).

Also of Narbonne is Jean Cuissot (d. 1681), doctor of Paris, royal preacher, and author of *The Criminal Soul at the Feet of Jesus* (Lyon, 1651), intended for dying sinners, and *The Clock of the Criminal Soul* (Lyon, date unknown), about the holy names of Jesus, Mary, and Joseph. Cuissot had been designated for a bishopric by Louis XIV and had already acquired his episcopal robes, when he fell into disgrace and was banished to the provinces.

George Cologne (d. 1637), provincial of Toulouse, wrote a *Spiritual Exercise for the Devout Soul* (Toulouse, 1633). In the province of Provence, Simon Guerin published *Ten Day Spiritual Exercises* (Lyon, 1668).

One is hard put to find a Carmelite spiritual writer in 18th century France. For that matter, it was hardly an age of Christian vitality. The quarrels with Jansenism, anti-mysticism - ever present, but brought to a head by Quietism - and the raillery of skeptics and atheists marked the end of the "mystical invasion" of the previous century.

Belgian Spiritual Writers

The flourishing Belgian provinces produced a rich spiritual literature.

Michael of St. Augustine (1621-1684) was born in Brussels. To say that he came of a devout family is no pious platitude: his seven brothers became priests, and of his three sisters two became *beguins*, one a Franciscan tertiary. From his early education with the Augustinians dates his fervent devotion to Mary and the second element of his religious name which he received on entering the Carmelite novitiate at Louvain in 1639. He spent most of his life in Mechelen, where he was prior three times. He also served three terms as provincial.

In spite of his administrative preoccupations, Michael wrote voluminously. His principal works, *Introduction to the Land of Carmel* (Latin and Flemish, 1659), *The Devout Life in Christ* (Flemish, 1661; Latin, 1663), *Temptations of Those Who Wish to Live Devoutly in Christ* (Latin, 1663), *Instruction about a Thorough Mortification of Self*

(Flemish, 1669) he collected under the title, *Institutionum mysticarum libri quatuor* (Antwerp, 1671), adding his famous treatise, *The Mary-Form and Marian Life in Mary*. The work constitutes a doctrinally sound introduction to the whole of the ascetical and mystical life based on the author's personal experience and reflection on the scriptures and the Fathers. "From various angles," writes Fr. Gabriel Wessels, "he approaches the idea of the spiritual life as a fundamental turning away from creatures and a conversion to God. Thus, he seldom goes astray into subtle minutiae and supersedes in clarity many masters of asceticism and mysticism."

Another of Michael's penitents was the young cleric, Arnold of St. Charles (1650-1672). Professed at Mechelen, May 17, 1671, he lived only until September 15 of the following year, yet he left an imperishable memory for holiness of life. Michael of St. Augustine wrote his life in Flemish, *A Mirror of Religious Perfection* (Kortrijk, 1677) and edited his notebook of spiritual reflections under the title in Flemish, *Spiritual Cabinet of Devout Practices* (Ghent, 1677).

Daniel of the Virgin Mary (1616-1678) is chiefly remembered for his historical writings (see below), yet his contribution to spiritual literature is by no means negligible. In his *Speculum carmelitanum* he made available the primitive spiritual documents of the Order, besides lives of saints and holy persons. His spiritual writings, composed in his native language, enjoyed great success. His *Golden Art of Confession* (Brussels, 1647), an adaptation of Leutbreuer's *Miroir des penitents*, underwent at least eight editions and was translated into French. His *Art of Arts* (Antwerp 1646), which also saw eight editions, the last at Bruges in 1938, is a treatise on prayer according to St. Teresa. Other spiritual works were *A Spiritual ABC* (Antwerp, 1669), meditations on the passion of Christ; an *Art of Dying* (Brussels, 1649) and an *Instruction for a Devout Life and a Happy Eternity* (Antwerp, 1668).

German and Polish Spiritual Writers

The German provinces, late in renewal because of the Thirty Years' War, began to produce religious literature only after the bloom was off the Catholic Restoration. Like the Carthusians of Cologne in the previous century, the German Carmelites devoted much effort to the diffusion of spiritual books through translation.

In Lower Germany, John Seiner (d. 1636), lecturer at the University of Cologne, wrote a life of Mary Magdalen de' Pazzi on the occasion of her beatification (Cologne, 1627) and a book, entitled *Homo mortalis* (Frankfurt, 1625). His claim to a defense of the scapular confraternity against Conrad, Dominican prior of Frankfurt, is shared by Matthew Tympius. Seiner also edited for the first time Guido Terreni's gospel concordance, *Quatuor unum* (Cologne, 1635).

Charles of St. Anastasius Freywilliger (d. 1670), active in the reform of the province, was the most prolific German writer, though much of his production was in the way of translation. He completed John Weiss' *Maria Carmelitana* (Cologne, 1643). His *Gnaden Pfennig der Carmeliter* (Würzburg, 1653) saw four editions. His translations were useful additions to German spiritual literature. He put into German Surius' edition of Tauler's sermons (Cologne, 1660), Philip Doutreman's *Paedagogus Christianus* (Cologne, 1664), and Jacob Masen's *Aurum sapientum* (Cologne, 1664). Of Surius' *Lives of the Saints* he produced an enlarged edition (Cologne, 1666). Of Carmelite writers he translated Dominic of St. Albert's *Exercitatio spiritualis* (Rottenburg, 1654) and Daniel of the Virgin Mary's *Art of Arts* (Cologne, 1659).

Henry of Mount Carmel (1615-16780), teacher, prior, and provincial, was another leader in the renewal of the province. He wrote a book about the scapular, *Passport to Heaven*, which appeared in Latin and German (Mainz, 1652). Further, he translated from Italian into Latin the sermons of Alexander de Calamato under the title, *Sylva nova; seu, cithara mystica* (Frankfurt, 1656) and the *Theologia mystica* of Vincent Caraffa, S.J. (Frankfurt, 1658).

George of the Queen of Angels, who received his formation in the province of Touraine and later became provincial (1669), published a book of sermons on the scapular, *Trifoedus marianum* (Cologne, 1660). He also translated Leo of St. John's *Alliance de la Vierge* (Cologne, 1655) about the scapular, and Christopher de Avendaño's sermons with the title, *Aurea corona sanctuarii* (Cologne, 1666). Perhaps his most useful contribution to spiritual literature was his anonymous translation of the fourth volume of the Touraine directory of novices, *Methodus clara et facilis vacandi orationi mentali* (Cologne, 1687).

In the Upper German province, John of St. Bernard (d. 1702), as provincial, wrote *Jesus amabilis xenio datus* (Straubing, 1666) to promote devotion to the Child Jesus among novices and professed clerics. Another provincial, Hyacinth of the Mother of God (d. 1723), is the anonymous author of *Nova schola virtutum* (Vienna, 1707), a digest of volume four of the Touraine directory. The number of its editions is an indication of its effectiveness in propagating the Touraine method of prayer in Germany. An edition in German is also known. Ferdinand of St. Bruno (1668-1733) wrote *The Art of Dying Most Necessary for All Men to Know* (Vienna, 1722). Finally, mention should be made of a manual of asceticism, *Ascetica et moralis doctrinae dives virtutum schola* (Würzburg, 1740), the author of which remains unknown. An unpublished *Theological, Ascetical Treatise on the Preparation for Religious Life* (1775) was in use in the novitiate at Abensberg.

In the Polish province, Adrian Zaremba (fl. 1626), royal preacher and polemicist known as "the scourge of heretics," also wrote *The Art of Dying Well*, which appeared in Latin and Polish versions. Serapion Knyper, opponent of the Stricter Observance, but according to his lights zealous for the good of the province, published *Mensa caelestis* (Cracow, 1665), drawn from the writings of the Fathers. Martin Rubszynski, provincial of the Russian province, wrote the first life of St. Mary Magdalen de' Pazzi in Polish, as well as ascetical works of enduring value. The province of Lesser Poland had a sort of official prayer book, *Paradisus caelestis* (new ed., Cracow, 1749), containing prayers for every act in a friar's day from rising to retiring. It seems to have been replaced by *Ascessus ad paradisum caelestem* (Cracow, 1764), composed by Constantine Strzalkowski.

Spiritual Writers of Spain

Spain ranks with France and Belgium for the number and excellence of spiritual writings produced at this time. Although interest in St. Teresa and St. John of the Cross and influence of their doctrines are not wanting in the old Carmel, its impressive literary production, for the most part overlooked by historians of religious literature, is quite independent in theme and inspiration. This is not to say that it is not regrettable that the Order should have so largely left to others the study and absorption of the teachings of these two great Carmelite Doctors of the Church and masters of the spiritual life.

Michael de la Fuente, 1573-1625

Michael de la Fuente (1573-1625) stands midway between the 16th and 17th centuries, Spain's golden age and era of decline. Depending on the point of departure, opinions on La Fuente have differed widely. For no less an authority than Menéndez Pelayo, his *Three Lives of Man* is "the best treatise of mystical psychology in the Spanish language." The dedicated student of St. Teresa and St. John of the Cross, E. Allison Peers, finds in La Fuente "an advanced stage of decadence." One could perhaps accept the judgement of the Franciscan John Baptist Gomis, that with St. Teresa and St. John of the Cross, Michael de la Fuente represents the best spiritual writing Carmel in Spain has produced.

Michael had already completed grammar and rhetoric at the Jesuit College of St. Isidore at Madrid, when in 1593 he entered the novitiate of the province of Castile at Valdemoro. He had been preceded in the Order by his brother, John, and would be followed by a nephew, also called Michael, who would become a doctor in theology and professor at the University of Toledo.

Fray Michael spent most of his life in Toledo. There he distinguished himself for a life of intense prayer and pastoral ministry. He served as novice master for three terms. He also carried on a far-reaching apostolate of spiritual direction, not only of nuns and *beatas* (among them Blessed Mary of Jesus, Discalced Carmelite nun), but of persons living in the world.

La Fuente's writings were an instrument of his apostolate and reflect practical needs rather than scientific concerns. For the Third Order he wrote a Rule (see below). It was not his intention to make religious of tertiaries, but to form them in the Carmelite spirit of prayer. To this end, he added to the Rule "Exercises in Mental Prayer," which reveal his experiential grasp of prayer even in its mystical states and his masterly methods of instruction. His *Compendio historial de Nuestra Señora del Carmen* (Toledo, Diego Rodriguez, 1619), written for tertiaries and members of Carmelite confraternities, provides an account, in the spirit of the times, of the history of the Order and the graces granted it by the Virgin Mary. No copy of La Fuente's *Ordinances* (Toledo, Juan Ruiz, 1625) for his Congregation of Our Lady of Mount Carmel has so far come to light.

It was also La Fuente's desire to lead the faithful to union with God through prayer and nakedness of spirit that led him to compose his classic *Three Lives of Man* (Toledo, Juan Ruiz, 1623). The three lives of man are corporal, rational, and spiritual, corresponding to the senses, the intellect, and the spirit, or faculty to relate to the divine. The special feature of the book is its psychological approach to the spiritual life. A complete manual of spiritual theology, *Three Lives* is construed according to the structure of the soul. La Fuente has been characterized as a mere compiler of others' ideas. A writer of impressive erudition, La Fuente is the debtor of the whole tradition of Christian spiritual literature, but his synthesis ends by being an original production, enriched by the author's own mystical experiences. In him, the streams of Rhenish and Spanish traditions are fused.

Other Spiritual Writers of Spain

Appalled by the general ignorance of religion, which reached the point "that one might almost say that there are Indies in Spain and mountainous wildernesses in the heart of Castile," Christopher Márquez (1566-1632) wrote *Treasury of the*

Ignorant (Madrid, 1614). A native of Madrid, he spent most of his life there as master of professed (among them John Baptist Lezana) and as a confessor and director with a reputation for virtue and spiritual discernment. A succinct but well-written explanation of the Creed and the commandments of God and of the Church, the Treasury is designed to lead the faithful to the enlightened practice of prayer, on the art of which a "dialog" concludes the work. In distinguishing prayer into reading, meditation, prayer, and contemplation, Márquez follows the *Scala paradisi* of pseudo-Augustine Guigues II.

A native of Toledo, Joseph Maestro (fl. 1720) like Michael de la Fuente passed most of his life there. He taught theology at the Carmelite *studium* but was also in charge of the novices. For them he wrote *A Brief Instruction for Beginners in the Ways of God* (Madrid, 1717), treating mental prayer, the exercise of virtue and the duties of the state of life. The latter consideration leads to a brief explanation of the Carmelite Rule. The author distinguishes two kinds of prayer: natural, which is in our power to practice, though with the grace of God, and supernatural, or infused. Maestro's exposition of natural prayer, consisting of mental prayer and contemplation, is based on the teaching of St. Teresa and emphasizes the role of the will. He only briefly touches on infused prayer, which is taught by God alone; his reserve may be due to fear of the Inquisition or to his own suspicion of mystical states. He is sometimes ranged among Carmelite proponents of acquired contemplation.

Also of the Castilian province is Bartholomew Díaz de Encinas (d. 1642), whose twin, Lawrence, became bishop of Ugento in the Kingdom of Naples, taught in the *studia* of the Order at Toledo and Alcalá. He wrote *An Easy Way to Please God* (Alcalá, 1641). Though a native of Toledo, Diego Ramírez (d. 1650) lived all his life in Italy as a teacher and preacher in the province of Lombardy. He is the author of *The Guard of the Tongue* (Milan, 1602). John of the Holy Angel (Llamas), one of the reformed friars of Piélago, reprinted La Fuente's *Tres vidas*, prefacing it with a sketch of the life of the author (Madrid, 1710), and wrote a commentary on the Carmelite Rule, *Religious Discipline in Spiritual Considerations and Moral Reflections* (Madrid, 1717).

In the Aragon province, Anthony Oliván de Maldonado (d. 1631) entered the Order in his native Zaragoza, making his profession in 1584. The provincial chapter of 1612 pronounced him a master of theology. He wrote *Moral Governance of the Soul* (Barcelona, 1623), an ascetical treatise comprising thirty-seven discourses, the purpose of which was to instruct the soul on how to conduct itself in the service of God, teaching it the virtues and correcting its vices, "so that this moral governance reach its perfection and completion in the divine service." The work displays much erudition but its style is diffuse and overladen.

Ambrose Roca de la Serna (1577-1649), of a noble family of Valencia, acquired the doctorate at the University of Valencia and later taught there. His *Light for the Soul at the Hour of Death* (Valencia, 1634) described the journey of the soul from birth to death in not undistinguished verse. The work also contains "*Abecedarios de amor divino*" in equally tasteful verses, an example of the widespread practice of aspirative prayer among Carmelites. By 1726, Roca's popular book had undergone fifteen editions.

Paul Ezquerra (1626-1697) wrote *Escuela de perfección* (Zaragoza, 1675), the fruit of thirty-three years' experience as novice master at Zaragoza, though he intended his words to reach the laity as well as religious. He was not a professional theologian

- out of humility he had passed up the opportunity of higher studies - and his book is not a systematic exposition of spirituality, yet it bears the mark of years of study and experience. Divided into three parts, it treats respectively the virtues, mental prayer, and the three ways (purgative, illuminative, unitive).

Vincent Olleme (1630-1701) was born in Valencia and received the Carmelite habit there in 1645. The provincial chapter of 1663 declared him a master of theology. His *Treasures of the Liberality of God Lavished on the Center of the Soul Guided by the Light of Faith* (Valencia, 1666) not only describes mystical states but gives evidence of their experience. Of the three books into which the work is divided, the first inquires whether mystical experience is principally a matter of the intellect or the will and proposes the eclectic solution common to Carmelite writers, which gives equal preponderance to both faculties. The other two books describe the various mystical states and show the influence of St. John of the Cross, whom he recognizes as an "admirable contemplative" before his sanctity was officially acknowledged by the Church.

The provinces of Andalusia and Catalonia seemingly produced no writers comparable to the best among those enumerated above, but their literary output in the field of spirituality remains largely to be investigated.

Jerome Gracián, 1545-1614

Jerome Gracián, contemporary of the greatest figures in the golden age of Spanish spiritual writing, may be included here because he ended his life as a member of the old Order of Carmel and as such wrote most of his works. No attempt can be made to examine in detail the flood that issued from his pen. The edition of his collected works by Silverio of St. Teresa (Burgos, 1932-1933, 3 v.), which includes 39 titles, is by no means complete; new manuscripts continue to surface. In spite of his doctorate from Alcalá, Master Gracián was not a professional theologian; all commentators confirm Silverio's judgement that he was a popularizer. His writing, of a strongly autobiographical cast, reflects the successive interests of his apostolate. Every aspect of the ascetical and mystical life is covered, principally from the optic of spiritual discernment, or the discovery of the "true spirit" which produces purity in the soul, enlightenment in the intellect, and love in the will. Suffering is the surest and most direct road to this condition. His books reflect the doctrine of St. Teresa, though not always faithfully, and are meant to propagate it. Zeal for souls, Jerome teaches, is an essential element in the Carmelite spirit. His expositions are marred by excessive fondness for farfetched divisions and bizarre constructions.

Discalced authors have devoted much study to Gracián, though the final word has not yet been spoken. While admitting his limitations, they tend to rate him highly. Outside the Order, Louis Cognet has written, "In spite of all attempts at rehabilitation, Gracián's personal views, as they come to us through his works, remain inconsistent and confused."

Spiritual Writers of Portugal

If information is lacking on Portuguese spiritual literature in general, the reader would be unwise to nurture great expectations of enlightenment on the Carmelites. The following is a list of some writers, authors mostly of works of popular devotion, though these upon examination may sometimes be found to contain surprises of mystical doctrine.

Peter de Mello Fragoso (d. 1635) is remembered especially for his holy life. Of a noble family of Lisbon, he entered the Order there and was professed in 1595. In religious life, he distinguished himself for penance, mental prayer, and the reading of spiritual books, especially St. Teresa. When a sacrilegious theft of the Blessed Sacrament was committed in the cathedral, he betook himself there with a rope around his neck and exhorted bystanders to do penance for their sins. A handsome man, he sought to reduce his body by penance. He was much devoted to the Blessed Virgin and promoted her Third Order, especially among the nobility, his peers. One of his conquests was the future King John IV. Besides a life of St. Charles Borromeo (Lisbon, 1616) and a Rule for the Third Order (Lisbon, 1630), Mello wrote *Prayers to Our Lady according to the Mysteries of the Life and Death of Jesus, Mary, and Joseph*, which appeared posthumously in the lives of Carmelite saints by Emmanuel Ferreira (Lisbon, 1645).

Louis of the Presentation Mertola (d. 1653) had already attended the University of Evora before be entered the Order at Beja in 1559. Nevertheless, he never seems to have acquired the doctorate. He is remembered as novice master in Lisbon, confessor, and spiritual director. The temper of the man is evidenced by his visitation of the vicariate of Brazil (1643-1644), already recounted, when he stressed especially the importance of fostering an interior spirit. Besides a number of religious biographies, he wrote *The Excellencies of Mercy and the Fruits of Almsgiving* (Lisbon, 1625).

Peter of the Cross Juzarte (d. 1678) exemplifies the course of education of the simple priest. After the arts at Coimbra, he did moral theology at Torres Novas to be able to hear confessions and preach. He led a devout life committed to the ministry, especially as commissary of the Third Order at Camarate and Lisbon. Besides books for the Third Order and a life of Stephen of the Purification, he wrote a *Brief Spiritual Exercise for Living Well* (Lisbon, 1659) and a *Spiritual Exercise for Dying Well* (Lisbon, 1659).

The Act of Contrition by Francis de Azevedo (d. 1696) underwent several editions with, added in the later ones, *A Pastoral Staff.* Frei Francis entered the Order at the reformed convent of Collares in 1651. Among the offices he held was that of commissary for the Third Order at Setúbal and Lisbon. He had a sister in the Carmelite monastery of Beja, Marian of the Purification, whose holy life he tried to emulate. Much devoted to St. Teresa, he died on her feast day.

Rocco of St. Teresa (d. 1728), doctor of theology, served as rector at Coimbra, novice master in Lisbon, and apostolic visitator of Bahia and Rio de Janeiro. He published *Faith Based on the Cross of Christ Triumphant* (Lisbon, 1698), excerpted from Savonarola's *Triumph of Christ.*

Stephen of St. Angelus, elected provincial in 1724, attended the meeting of the general definitory at Ferrara in 1728. Apparently unequal to the task of original composition, he published several works of devotion for the benefit of the faithful. He translated from the Italian *Food for the Soul; or the True Practice of Mental Prayer* (Lisbon, 1726), meditations on the Passion of Christ for every day of the year. From the "manuscripts" of St. Francis de Sales he compiled *Devout Exercises for the Preparation and Thanksgiving for Confession and Communion* (Lisbon and Antwerp, 1732). He translated Giles Leoindelicato's *Jardim Carmelitano* (Lisbon, 1741, 2 pts.), making additions of his own. His *Lamp of Truth Newly Lit in the Temple of Carmel* (Lisbon, 1750) is about the Carmelite habit.

Italian Spiritual Writings

The Italian provinces early had a directory of the religious life, provided by Henry Silvio as a tool in the work of his reform. He engaged the services of Jerome Gracián, at the same time equipping him with Soreth's *Expositio regulae* and the *Book of the First Monks*, which Gracián had never seen. *On Regular Discipline* (Venice, 1600) in Italian dress by John Anthony Bovio was distributed throughout Italy at the expense of the prior general, who ordered it read in the refectories. In three parts, the book treats of the religious state and the Carmelite Rule, the three vows, and mental prayer according to the method Gracián had already previously evolved.

It was the reform of Piedmont which late in the century made the Touraine directory available to Italians in a translation by Jerome of St. Clement Aimo (Venice, 1684, 4 v.). *Lo spirito delle azioni religiose* (Turin, 1732) by Theobald of the Annunciation Ceva, of the same reform, is a compendium of the directory's third volume.

Carmel in Italy produced many spiritual writers, mostly of books of popular devotion, none of them seemingly of the stature of the outstanding figures in France, Belgium, and Spain. They remain to be studied; meanwhile, the following is a random selection of names.

In the province of St. Angelus in Sicily, Philip Giordani, of Trapani, wrote *A Method of Reciting the Rosary for the Souls in Purgatory* (Messina, 1691). Ignatius Mary Rossi, provincial, profited by his experience as a superior to write *The Carmelite Novice Instructed by his Master* (Naples, 1764) and *The Carmelite Prior Instructed in His Office* (Palermo, 1767).

At the Carmine of Naples, Joseph Tancredi (d. 1624) wrote *A Flame of Divine Love* (Naples, 1618), a book of verse in the form of a dialog designed to wean readers from the passing things of time to the enduring joys of eternity. Peter Thomas Moscarella, Sr. (1629-1700) served as prior of Calabria. A renowned preacher, he dislocated his arm while preaching the Lenten course at Salerno. He improved his leisure while recuperating by composing *L'orologio concertato* (Naples, 1687), instructing provincials on the proper manner of conducting their ministry. Gennaro Milone published spiritual exercises at Naples in 1708. Cyril Perrone (1655-1737) was known for his love of the poor and devotion to the ministry of the confessional. Among his writings is an *Instruction on Mental Prayer* (Naples, 1716).

In the province of Calabria, Paul Anthony Foscarini (d. 1616), better known for his theories on the heliocentric universe, also wrote *Meditationes, preces. et exercitia quotidiana* (Cosenza, 1615) on the Our Father, disposed according to the days of the week and the three degrees of progress in the spiritual life. Peter Thomas Pugliesi (d. 1707), theologian, canon lawyer, historian, composed a number of spiritual works, among them *Scapularis Partheno-Carmelitici garophilacium* (Naples, date unknown), a *Historical, Ascetical and Moral Explanation of the Carmelite Rule* (Naples, 1707) and a work with the curious title *The Two Noble Twins, Breasts of the Virgin Mary*; that is, the Confraternities of the Rosary and of Carmel (Naples, date unknown).

In the Tuscan province, Archangelus Paoli, of Florence, already mentioned in connection with the liturgical chant of the Order, wrote *Scorta spirituale* (Spiritual Guide), which underwent a fourth edition at Florence in 1617. Cosimo Facelli

(d. 1632), of Pisa, wrote lives of the saints, but is more memorable for his *Facella spirituale* (Spiritual Lamp), which remained in manuscript until recently. It still lies in the tradition of the previous century and in a series of chapters without close sequence calls for solitude, contempt of the world, and divine contemplation. "A last gleam," Fr. Catena writes, "of that humanistic Renaissance light which was gradually fading everywhere."

In the Romagna province, Lawrence Natali (d. 1673), prior of Ancona many years and provincial, wrote *Spiritual Ethics* (Ancona, 1665).

In the province of Lombardy, John Baptist Spinola, of the noble Genoese family, left an unpublished treatise on the manner of making mental prayer (1606). Paul Anthony Monelia (d. 1740), of Milan, did translations out of French and besides composed popular books on St. Teresa, St. John of the Cross, and St. Mary Magdalen de' Pazzi.

Joseph Mary Sardi (d. 1749), regent of studies at Venice, is more notable as a preacher, but he also published *The Young Carmelite Instructed in his Rule, his Obligations, and his Privileges* (Venice, 1737).

The Mantuan Congregation produced proportionately a good number of spiritual writers, a sign perhaps of its religious vitality.

Peter Thomas Sarraceni (1566-1643) was given the task of composing a manual of meditation for the use especially of novices. The result was his *Instruction on Mental Prayer* (Bologna, 1599), which appeared in a revised edition with the title *Mental Prayer* (Bologna, 1636). After a remote, proximate, and immediate preparation, meditation itself is described as imaginative, intellectual, volitional, and memorial. Volitional meditation, or contemplation, is the simple gaze of the intellect accompanied by affections. By memorial meditation is meant aspirative prayer. The constitutions for the nuns of the Congregation (1656) suggest the method of Sarraceni or that of Serafino Giorgi. The latter's method remains to be found.

Among spiritual writers of the Mantuan Congregation note might be taken of Zachary Bergomelli (d. 1626), who wrote *Tears of the Sinner Contained in the Seven Penitential Psalms* (Bergamo, 1620). Cherubino Ferrari, theologian at the ducal court of Mantua, renowned preacher, noticed with favor by St. Charles Borromeo, was a man of many talents. Credited with a knowledge of Hebrew, besides Latin and Greek, he was also regarded as an authority in numismatics and the deciphering of ancient inscriptions. He also composed religious poetry, especially about the Virgin Mary, such as his *Rimes on the Hail Mary* (Parma, 1624) and *Tears of the Blessed Virgin Beneath the Cross* (Milan, 1623). Another Marian poet was Dionysius Solerti, author of *A Ten-Stringed Psalter on the Magnificat* (Bergamo, 1629). Julius Caesar Borghi, who died of the plague at Bologna in 1632, published *Devout Spiritual Exercises* (Bologna, 1620). Anthony di Rovigo composed a treatise on behalf of the novices (Ferrara, 1648).

Preaching in Baroque Carmel

In the second half of the 17th century, sacred oratory entered on a period of unequalled brilliance, featuring the classic names of Jacques Benigne Bossuet, François Fénelon, Louis Bourdeloue, S.J., Paolo Segneri, S.J., St. Leonard of Port Maurice, O.F.M., and many other representatives of the clergy, secular and religious.

For Carmel, too, it was a time rich in examples of excellence in pulpit eloquence.

Many of the Carmelites known for their contribution to theology, spiritual literature, the fine arts and science did not neglect the apostolate of the spoken word. Many others are remembered through the publication of individual occasional sermons, preached before distinguished audiences in royal courts and cathedrals. Here can be considered only a few of the most important figures of Carmelites who may be characterized primarily as preachers.

Perhaps the most illustrious orator the Order produced in this period was Leo of St. John. He owed his early formation as a preacher to Philip Cospéan, preceptor also of Bossuet, and from this source learned to base his content and style on the Scriptures and the Fathers rather than on pagan authors of classic antiquity. To Cospéan especially Leo owed the all-pervading influence of his "divine master," St. Paul.

During his long and fruitful career, Leo came to occupy the most prestigious pulpits of the realm. On December 24, 1638, he preached the funeral sermon of Père Joseph in the Capuchin convent of Paris, while three hundred coaches of his illustrious audience waited outside the church. Patronized by Richelieu, he assisted him on his death bed and preached his eulogy (Paris, 1643). Mazarin continued the patronage of his predecessor; of him, too, Leo preached the eulogy (Paris, 1661). Both these sermons also appeared in Latin, Italian, and Spanish. In 1645, Leo was named ordinary preacher of the King. His *Annee royale* (Paris, 1655, 3 v.) contains the sermons he preached in the royal presences in 1652 and 1653.

Leo was engaged in a collected edition of his many published sermons when be died. The last three of the four volumes of *Somme des sermons* (Paris, 1671-1675) were seen to by Damasus of St. Joseph.

Leo's concept of the office of preacher is found in his *Treatise on Christian Eloquence* (Paris, 1654), "perhaps the most profound analysis of the 'true eloquence' of the Christian preacher in the 17th century" (F. Duine). In St. Paul, he finds support for his enthusiastic description of an apostle. An apostle is called primarily to preach. Preaching is the *"opus evangelistae"* par excellence. The preacher must preach the word of God, the Word made flesh. The preacher himself must excel in holiness of life, austerity, zeal, and knowledge, based especially on the Bible, the Fathers, the most recent theologians, and spiritual writers. Important, too, are prayer and contemplation (for Leo is a protagonist of the "mixed" life). Like St. Paul, the greatest mystics were also the most zealous apostles and preachers. Ambassadors of Christ, preachers receive their instructions from their Lord in the secrecy of prayer.

Under the influence of Bérulle, Leo's sermons are strongly Christocentric. The Carmelite preached Christ and him crucified. He exhorted Christians to crucify the old man, to the perfection required by the Father, to the imitation of Christ, especially by the application of the interior states of the Incarnate Word. Leo also recommends Bérulle's vow of slavery and the way of annihilation.

Another Frenchman, also of the Touraine province, Simon of the Virgin (d. 1728) is known for his polished style and command of the French language in its purest form. Dom Anthony Rivet de la Grange pays him homage in the preface to the first volume of the *Histoire littéraire de la France* (p. 33) and Migne reprinted his sermons. His sermons were published posthumously in 15 volumes under the title, *Actions chrétiennes* (Liège, 1744-1746): two volumes for Advent, six for Lent, six of panegyrics, and one for an octave of the Blessed Sacrament.

In Spain, Carmel produced many distinguished orators, especially in the faculties of universities. Christopher de Avendaño (d. 1628), a native of Valladolid, entered the Order at Medina del Campo and received the doctorate at Valladolid. He served as prior in several convents of the Castilian province; otherwise, his career was undistinguished, except for his prolific activity as a preacher, which also earned him renown outside his native land. He was appointed court preacher by Philip IV. His published sermons exceed in number those of any other Spanish Carmelite and comprise collections of sermons for Advent (Madrid, 1617) and Lent (Madrid, 1622, 2 v.), for feasts of Our Lady (Valladolid, 1620) and the saints (Madrid, 1626, 2 v.), all of which underwent numerous editions and were translated into French and Italian. The sermons for saints were also translated into Latin and published in Cologne, 1660.

Bernard de Paredes (d. 1661), also of the Castilian province, does not seem to have made university studies, yet he became a distinguished preacher. His published sermons, which underwent various editions, comprised sermons for Sundays from the first Sunday of Advent to Quinquagesima (Madrid, 1648), sermons for the Sundays, Wednesdays, and Fridays of Lent and Holy Week (Madrid, 1649), and sermons for the weekdays of Lent (Madrid, 1652).

Augustine Nuñez Delgadillo (d. 1631) entered the Order at Granada and taught in the universities of Osuna and Zaragoza. He preached with great success in Granada, Cordova, Zaragoza, Valencia, and the court, though he published relatively little: *The Victory of the Just Celebrated by David in Psalm XVII* (Granada, 1618) and *Heavenly Mines Discovered in the Gospels of Lent* (Madrid, 1629).

In his funeral eulogy, Master Anthony de Sagrameña recalls four characteristics of Fray Augustine's sermons, in which he excelled most preachers in the Church. The first was originality of ideas. "He studied constantly," Sagramena declares, "yet when he ascended the pulpit, it seemed that he never read books, because the explanation he gave of Scripture was not to be found in them." Secondly, he spoke the truth in the pulpit, "he freely reprehended all the vices to be found in the nation, and this was the reason why he was not invited to preach in certain pulpits." Thirdly, he spoke clearly, "so that all understood him: children and adults, the learned and the ignorant were able to grasp his doctrine. "What use is it," Sagramena adds, "if a preacher discourse subtly and speak with courtly language called cultured, if the audience does not understand him or is not up to the doctrine he teaches?" Fourthly, be preached "solid Scripture without admixture of legendary stories, which is one of the most important conditions a preacher should observe."

Luis Pueyo y Abadía (d. 1704) won a place for himself as a professor of philosophy (1670-1673) and theology (1692-1698) at the University of Zaragoza before being made bishop of Albarracín. He published *Analogías de púlpito y cathedra* (Zaragoza, 1676), *Proporciones predicables* for feasts of Mary and Joseph (Zaragoza, 1694), and two volumes of sermons on St. Thomas Aquinas (Zaragoza, 1695 and 1696).

Also of the Aragon province, Joseph Bardaxi (d. 1626) was born of a noble family of Zaragoza, acquired the doctor's degree, and taught in the cathedral school of Gerona. He published sermons for Advent and the saints (Barcelona, 1613), and *Quaresmal duplicado* (Zaragoza, 1620), which reached only the third Sunday of Lent. Much of his life he spent in the province of Catalonia. He preached the funeral sermon for Joseph Serrano (Barcelona, 1615), provincial of that province and himself a preacher of note, though his sermons remained unpublished.

Hyacinth de Arañaz, master of theology, held a number of important posts in the Order. An accomplished orator and preacher to the king, he published *Quaresma continual* (Pamplona, 1713-1714, 2 v.) and *Various Sermons* (Pamplona, 1712, 2 v.).

Matthew Maya, doctor of the University of Zaragoza, provincial of Aragon, composed an anthology of the sermons of a number of Carmelites, *Jardín de sermones varios* (Zaragoza, 1676).

The Carmo of Lisbon was very much in the eye of the court, and its preachers were no strangers to royal audiences.

A colorful figure among Carmelite preachers in Portugal was Timothy de Cibra e Pimentel (d. 1661). Born in Lisbon, he entered the Carmo there in 1613 and eventually became its prior. It is not clear how he became procurator of the Order in Vienna. Perhaps it was in connection with that office that Urban VIII made him an "apostolic preacher." Before the Portuguese revolution, Cibra was also active in the province of Andalusia. In 1640, he is found in the Spanish house in Naples, where on September 29 Straccio sent him patents as confessor of Don Francis de Melo, Spanish legate to the diet of Ratisbon. There, Cibra's Portuguese blood asserted itself, and he embarrassed Melo by allegedly plotting for the release from prison of the Infante Duarte. Appealed to by Melo, Straccio on May 31, 1640, ordered Cibra to report to the convent of Cremona, at the same time instructing the prior there to lock him up on arrival. Whether this pleasure was ever accorded the prior is not known. The incident certainly did not damage Cibra in the eyes of King John IV, who made him his court preacher, and it was he who was chosen to deliver the eulogy, when death finally released the unfortunate prince (Lisbon, 1650). Cibra's principal published works are *The Sling of David*, five sermons in defense of the Eucharist against heretics and crypto-Jewish Christians, on the occasion of the profanation committed in the Church of St. Engracia in Lisbon (Rome, 1631), and *An Octave in Vindication of the Statue of the Virgin Cast into the Fire preached before the Inquisition* (Granada and Seville, 1638-1639, 2 v.).

Caspar dos Reis (d. 1660), doctor of theology at the University of Coimbra, provincial from 1651 to 1654, confessor of Raymond de Lancastro, Duke of Aveiro, and Duchess Maria Manrique de Lara, published only one volume of *A Lantern for Preachers and Professors of Sacred Scripture* (Lisbon, 1658), intended to comprise three volumes.

Joseph de Souza (1664-1730), prior of Lisbon and provincial, 1721-1724, was one of the most prolific preachers of the province, judging by his published works, which include sermons on the Immaculate Conception (Lisbon, 1721), on feasts of Jesus and Mary (Lisbon, 1722), on the saints (Lisbon, 1723) and sermons for Lent (Lisbon, 1724). A second edition appeared in Lisbon in 1732.

Joseph de Lima (1668-1745), missionary, theologian and director of the Third Order, published a collection of his sermons, *Evangelical Pilgrimage* (Lisbon, 1720-1732, 2 v.).

In Brazil, Emmanuel of the Mother of God Bulhoens, of Bahia, became prior of his native city and provincial. Besides many individual sermons, he had printed *Sermons for various Feasts of Mary* (Lisbon, 1737) and *Various Sermons* (1739).

Eusebius de Mattos (d. 1692), of Bahia, had been a Jesuit for thirty-three years before becoming a Carmelite in 1677. Esteemed by the famous Brazilian Jesuit, Anthony Vieira, he was a gifted orator, poet, musician, mathematician and painter. His printed sermons are *Ecce Homo*, homilies for the Fridays of Lent (Lisbon, 1667) and the posthumous *Sermons, part I* (Lisbon, 1694).

Ignatius Ramos (d. 1731), of Bahia, attended the general chapter of 1692 as representative of his vicariate and was appointed vicar by Feijóo de Villalobos. The general chapter of 1710 allowed him to join the Portuguese province. At the end of his life he collected his sermons into four volumes with the allusive title *Ramos evangelicos* (Lisbon, 1724-1730).

Undoubtedly the most remarkable Carmelite preacher in Italy at this time was Andrew Mastelloni (1641-1722), of Naples. Of his six brothers, Joseph became a Dominican and John bishop of Vieste. Andrew already had minor orders and was studying at the University of Bari, when he received the Carmelite habit in the reformed convent of Santa Maria della Vita in 1657. Called to Rome by Jerome Ari, he obtained the lectorate at Traspontina, where Jerome Aimo was regent (1663). The doctorate followed in 1666, after Andrew had functioned as regent in Asti. During his life he filled many important posts: regent of St. Cyril's College, prior of Santa Maria della Vita and of Traspontina, provincial, assistant general for Italy. Yet these functions do not define the man. Preaching and writing occupied most of his time, until in old age blindness (cataracts) diminished, if it did not entirely cut off the flow of his productivity. Besides biography, history, asceticism, his more than thirty published works include many volumes of sermons, for Mastelloni was above all a preacher, a publicist of Mary. For more than twenty years he preached three days a week in three churches of Naples. The main burden of his discourse, as well as the inspiration of his life, was the Blessed Virgin.

His sermons on the Eucharist, *Four Altars Erected in Four Sermons* (Naples, 1687) touch many Marian themes, especially her priesthood. The *Two Salutations of Mary* (Naples, 1687, 3 v.), on the Hail Mary and the *Salve Regina*, were preached in the church of the Annunciata in Naples. Worthy of note is his discussion in part 1 of the so-called mariological principle of eminence and of Mary's fullness of grace. In part 2, he places the foundation of the Queenship of Mary in her relationship to the divine Persons and calls her "Queen of our Hearts," anticipating the terminology of Grignion de Montfort. The *Litany of Our Lady* (Naples, 1694, 5 v.) is perhaps his most scientific work, in which he skillfully passes in review the main aspects of Mary's role in human redemption, the consequences of this role and her other prerogatives. Here, too, he develops his thought concerning the first principle of Mariology, combining the scholastic principle of the divine maternity with the patristic principle of Mary's association in the redemption as the New Eve. In this theory, Mastelloni is in the vanguard of a tradition since proposed by many reputable theologians. His *Canticle of the Blessed Virgin* (Naples, 1697, 3 v.) expressly states that Mary was not only free of original sin but also free of the proximate debt of contracting it. Mastelloni himself calls volume 1 of this work a little Marian *summa*. In *The Mystery of the Body of Jesus Christ* (Naples, 1710), which treats more extensively Mary's relation to the Eucharist, Mastelloni bestows on her the title of "Saint Mary of the Sacrament," which later St. Peter Julian Eymard was to render popular.

While his style is not entirely free of the defects of the time, and he is sometimes carried away by his love for his Mother, his sermons are solidly doctrinal and his presentation is open and personal. Mastelloni deliberately preferred the pulpit to the cathedra as a means of spreading devotion to Mary. His theology is therefore expressed as oratory, but his oratory is doctrinal and gives evidence of assiduous theological preparation and a firm grasp of Marian doctrine. Mastelloni is an eminent example of the expression in a person of the Marian aspect of the Carmelite vocation.

Filocalo Caputo (1582-1644), of the Carmine of Naples, elected its prior in 1626, was dean of the *Collegio dei Teologi* and theologian of Cardinal Desio Caraffa, archbishop of Naples. A noted preacher, he occupied the pulpits of many of the principal cities of the continent and Sicily. His *Lenten Sermons* (Naples, 1628, 2 v.) and *Panegyrics* (Naples, 1641-1643, 3 v.) were also reprinted.

Andrew of Castroreale Ferraro (d. 1685) was a member of the reform of Monte Santo. He filled all the offices of responsibility in his province, including that of provincial (1658). His collected sermons include *Al'una delle due, discorsi disingannati* (Naples, 1667) and *Sacra novena problematica dell Incarnazione del Verbo* (Naples, 1673).

Charles Sernicola (1659-1721), born in Naples, the son of a physician, received the habit in the Carmine in 1674. As regent of studies in Florence, he won the esteem of the Grand Duke Cosimo III and of Cardinal Francis Maria Medici, whose theologian he became. He was a member of various academies: the Pellegrini of Rome, the Pigri of Bari, the Spensierati of Rossano. At Naples, he taught in the *Collegio dei Teologi* and was prior of the Carmine, 1691-1694. Finally, he served as provincial of his province of Terra di Lavoro. A prolific poet, he also distinguished himself in the pulpit, publishing *Politiche sacre per lo buon governo de' sudditi*, sermons for Wednesdays, Fridays and Sundays of Lent (Naples, 1710); *Sermons for Advent* (Naples, 1712); *Sacred Panegyrics* (Naples, 1705-1714, 3 v.).

Joseph Maria Sardi (d. 1749), of Venice, regent of studies in his native city and provincial, published several collections of sermons: *Sermons on the Commandments and Precepts* (Venice, 1741), *Sermons for Fostering Devotion to Mary* (Venice, 1742), *Sermons for Sacred Missions* (Venice, 1745), *Sacred Lectures on the Rosary* (Venice, 1747).

In the Mantuan Congregation, Vincent Maria Silvani (d. 1729), of Lucca, was made a master of theology in 1703 and became procurator of the Congregation in 1709. His published sermons include *Sacred Panegyrics* (Lucca, 1718, 2 v.) and *Lenten Sermons* (Lucca, 1727).

These few examples from the eighteen provinces of Italy will have to suffice. In Lent, the chairs of the universities and *studia* were emptied, as the more prominent doctors set out on a tour of the great cities. Some priors general assigned the preachers for the various pulpits throughout Italy.

The traditional sermon by the procurator general of the Order in the presence of the pope remained in force. The Carmelite dates were the fourth Sundays of Advent and Lent.

The Belgian Carmelites, creators of an abundant spiritual literature, were less given to printing their sermons. The most prolific preacher among them was Leo of St. Lawrence (d. 1702), born in Brussels, where be entered the Order and was several times prior. His printed sermons include *Sermons for Advent* (Antwerp, 1699) and *Lenten Sermons for Sundays about a Failing Christianity* (Antwerp). Posthumously published were *Sanctoral* (Antwerp, 1722) and *Favus Samsonis ex ore leonis prodiens* (Cologne, 1723). These collections in their Latin form underwent many editions.

Other preachers include Gregory of St. Martin, *The Grandeur of the Eucharist*

(Douai, 1688); Peter of the Guardian Angel (d. 1689), *The Double Spirit of Elias*, sermons for feasts of Jesus and Mary (Cologne, 1684); Isidore of St. Giles (d. 1691), *The Crown of Twelve Stars*, sermons on feasts of Our Lady (Antwerp, 1685); Dominic of the Nativity (d. 1722), *Sermons for Feastdays* (Antwerp, 1722).

Pacificus of the Cross (fl. 1700) belonged to the Wallo-Belgian vicariate, but his mother tongue was German, and it was in that language that he preached the sermons contained in the two folio volumes entitled *Spiritual Woodland of Morals*, sermons for Sundays (Augsburg-Graz, 1719) and *Spiritual Woodland of Flowers*, sermons for feastdays (Augsburg-Graz, 1720). Both these works saw various reprintings. Pacificus is known to have been prior of Arlon and definitor of the vicariate, but his life is best summed up in terms of the apostolate of preaching he carried out between 1674 and 1714 in the surrounding towns and hamlets of Luxemburg. "For more than forty years, in pursuit of my spiritual calling, I crossed many a mountain and deep valley, hedges and bushes and forests, meadows, heaths and fields, for the salvation of my neighbor." Unlike many of the sermon collections so far considered, which were intended for urban audiences or high-born personages on solemn occasions, Pacificus' sermons are addressed to simple farm people. He speaks their language, is familiar with the circumstances of their daily lives, recommends the intercession of their obscure saints, not all of whom would have passed muster with the Bollandists. Nevertheless, Pacificus gives evidence of being well-read in the Scriptures, Fathers, and medieval and contemporary writers. "We have here," writes Emil Donckel, "a source of the first rank for the lives and ways of our farmers, from the end of the 17th to the beginning of the 18th century."

In the Lower German province, George of the Queen of the Angels, professor at the University of Cologne and provincial, preached particularly on the Virgin Mary. His published sermons include *Evening Sacrifice*, Lenten sermons preached in the Carmelite church in Mainz (Cologne, 1683); *Triboedus marianum*, Sunday sermons on the scapular confraternity (Cologne, 1683); *Mariae decus*, sermons for feasts of Our Lady (Cologne, 1683). George also translated Avendaño's sermons for saints (Cologne, 1660).

In the Upper German province, Eusebius of St. Tiburtius (1667-1743) taught in various convents including Straubing, where he published *Amara dulcis evangelica*, sermons for Sundays (Augsburg-Graz, 1736) and *Dulcamara panegyrica*, sermons for saints' feastdays (Augsburg-Graz, 1736).

The constitutions of 1626 reproduced unaltered the legislation about preaching of those of 1586. Preaching was one of the most important apostolic concerns of the Order and absorbed much of its effort and talent. It was an alternative to an academic career, open to those who had not the ability for, or did not wish to pursue graduate studies. Preaching, however, was also assiduously engaged in by doctors of theology. Unfortunately, together with teaching, it often constituted an obstacle to the common life. The pious declaration by the constitutions that the emoluments accruing from preaching belong to the community is to be understood in the light of the practice of the deposit box. The registers of Theodore Straccio show that preachers in Italy at that time were expected to contribute five percent of their earnings to the community, and even this was not always forthcoming.

Chapter 3

Marian Doctrine and Devotion

By its nature, the Carmelite Order is not only contemplative but also Marian. During this period of renewal, the Marian tradition of the Order was reaffirmed and strengthened.

Mariology, like other theological disciplines, at this time established an autonomous identity. Theological reflection concerned especially the Immaculate Conception, co-redemption, and mediation. The Carmelites produced no general works of Mariology, though many wrote treatises on the Immaculate Conception and incidentally treated other Marian themes in their theological writings. Subjects most commonly considered were Mary's predestination, her Immaculate Conception, virginity, marriage with St. Joseph, meriting of the Incarnation and divine maternity, divine maternity itself, vision of the essence of God, cult of hyperdulia. Oddly, although Carmelite devotional books and sermons often treated the co-redemption and the spiritual maternity of Mary, these mysteries were hardly treated in scientific works.

Later writings betray a decline in the quality of theological reflection. While the mediation of Mary is shown from patristic texts, her maternity of people is demonstrated mostly by accounts of her miraculous favors. In the contemporary doctrine on grace, adoptive sonship was too juridically conceived and was not assigned its proper role in participation in the divine nature. Also, Mary's motherhood was too narrowly seen as patronage of the Order, which could not be shown from the sources of revelation.

In their defense of the doctrine of the Immaculate Conception, the Carmelites continued a tradition of the Order going back to earliest times. Then they were motivated mainly by historical reasons, convinced as they were that the Immaculate Conception had been revealed to Elijah in the little cloud, and that the allegedly Carmelite Cyril of Alexandria had defended the doctrine at the Council of Ephesus. Though they continued to believe and defend these legends, the Carmelites of the 17th and 18th centuries also adduced more theological grounds for their convictions.

Two Carmelites contributed to the evolution of the theory of the *debitum peccati* in Mary. The first printed work to treat specifically of this matter was *The Triumphs of the Queen of the Angels* (Seville, 1616) by the Andalusian, Bartholomew de Loaysa, who taught that the Virgin was remotely obliged to the contraction of sin in Adam. In his *Liber apostolicus pro Immaculatae Deiparae Virginis conceptione* (Madrid, 1616) John Baptist Lezana, then a young professor in the Carmelite *studium* of Alcalá, distinguishes the *debitum remotum* and *proximum peccati* in Mary and concludes that she was exempt from the latter. Lezana was the first to employ this terminology. He was indebted to his teacher, Peter Cornejo, who distinguished original sin *in fieri* and *in facto esse*.

In his *Magni prophetae Eliae visio de Immaculata B. V. Conceptione* (Antwerpen, 1665), Francis de Bonne Espérance denies the *debitum* in Mary, declaring that she had only an aptitude for contracting it.

Apart from Carmelite theologians and preachers who treated the Immaculate Conception in general contexts, some of the more significant writers who devoted special books to the question include Bishop Peter de Carranza, Bartholomew de Loaysa, Oliver of St. Anastasius, Alexis of St. Mary, Andrew Barzeski, Stephen Duarte, Charles Sernicola. A manuscript list, now apparently lost, by Louis Jacob supplied the noted bibliographer of the Immaculate Conception, Peter Alba y Astorga, O.F.M., with information on Carmelite writers.

It is on the Iberian peninsula, also, that the vow to espouse the doctrine of the Immaculate Conception is most commonly found. The province of Portugal introduced it around 1617, Aragon in 1624, and Andalusia in 1653. In the latter, after 1758, the vow took the form of a fourth vow of religious profession.

At the universities, too, Carmelites supported proposals to vow to defend the immaculatist doctrine. At the University of Salamanca, the Carmelites, Bartholomew Sánchez, Peter Cornejo, and Diego López are among the doctors who in 1617 declare the immaculatist doctrine more probable. Sánchez and López also favored the view that the university should take an oath to defend the Immaculate Conception.

The vow was sometimes taken with the condition, "to the shedding of blood." The famous historian, Louis Anthony Muratori, who had little faith in the Immaculate Conception, under various pseudonyms attacked the "blood vow" as superstitious. Elijah d'Amato, of the Calabrian province, answered Muratori in a sermon, later published. Joseph Mary of Jesus, of the province of Santa Maria della Vita, under the pseudonym, Joseph Anthony de Vera, indited a two-volume rebuttal, *Deipara eiusque cultores vindicati* (Naples, 1753), which has been called "a fine *summa* of Mariology" (Claudio Catena). Carmel Pafumi, of the Sicilian province of St. Albert, wrote *The Little Ones Undeceived with Regard to the Certainty and Other Merits of the Mystery of the Immaculate Conception* (Catania, 1747), which also defended the vow unto the shedding of blood.

The Carmelite Cult of Mary

In the earlier form of the Order's title, "Order of St. Mary of Mount Carmel," the words "Most Blessed Mother of God" appeared after 1379, though no official decree to this effect is known. The general chapter of 1680 now added the phrase "and ever virgin" to complete the title of the Order which remained official until recently: "Order of the Most Blessed Mother of God and ever Virgin Mary of Mount Carmel."

In spite of what the Order's title might lead one to believe, the Carmelites never developed a devotion to Mary as Mother of God. This element seems to have been added in the 14th century only to strengthen the Order's historical claim to its name.

The same is not true of the other part of the title, "ever Virgin." Here one finds the Marian mystery to which the Carmelites were most characteristically devoted. From the interpretation which the *Institutio primorum monachorum* (once more readily available in the edition of Daniel of the Virgin Mary) gave to Elijah's vision of the little cloud (*nubecula*) rising out of the sea (1 Kgs. 18: 42-44), the Carmelites knew that Elijah and his followers were the first to embrace the state of virginity (which was also the meaning of the word Carmel). When Mary, too, after the example of Elijah undertook to observe virginity, the Carmelites recognized in her their sister and long-awaited mother of the Messiah. From her home in nearby Nazareth, Mary often visited them on Mount Carmel.

This traditional account lived on in the writings of the 17th and 18th century, with the difference that it is now Elijah who imitates Mary's virginity prophetically foreseen in the little cloud, to which the foundation of the Order is traced in the strict order of causality.

A curious example of the Order's emphasis on Mary's virginity is found in the missal of 1584. There, in the rubrics taken from the Roman missal of 1578, the words "*Sancta Maria*" are systematically converted into "*beata Virgo.*"

The concept of Mary's virginity in Carmelite devotion included not so much bodily integrity as purity of heart, by which the soul clings exclusively to God. In this respect especially, the Carmelites were able to imitate Mary.

Another variation traceable to this time is the substitution of the concept of purity for that of virginity used exclusively by 14th century writers. This is noticeable in a striking way in Daniel of the Virgin Mary's commentary on the *Institutio*, in which he invariably uses the term purity to comment on passages referring to Mary's virginity. A strong influence in this development was St. Mary Magdalen de' Pazzi, who, ravished by the beauty of purity, extolled it in her ecstasies and proclaimed its importance for the spiritual life, especially for union with God. It is also this virtue which she emphasizes in her frequent references to Mary. The liturgy in turn praised the purity of St. Mary Magdalen, whose influence was widespread as the saint of the Old Carmel *par excellence*. The white mantle, too, which early writers related to Mary's Immaculate Conception or virginity, was now regarded as the symbol of purity. Matthias of St. John succinctly expresses the conviction of his time: "The Carmelite Order was especially founded to honor the purity of the Blessed Virgin." Fr. Hoppenbrouwers concludes that "the cult of Blessed Mary of Mount Carmel in the period of our investigation (1550-1750) was the cult of the Most Pure Virgin."

Mother and Ornament of Carmel

The devotion of Carmel to Mary as Virgin refers to her relationship to God. In her relation to the human race, Carmelites continued to honor Mary as their patroness, as they had from earliest times. Of two aspects, Mother and Queen, of which patronage is susceptible, the former with time predominated in the Order.

After Clement VIII imposed uniformity on approved litanies in 1601, the invocation, "Mother and Ornament of Carmel," remained in Carmelite litanies. The same title is regularly found in the letters of affiliation of the priors general and on the coat of arms of the Order. Authors who comment on Mary as Mother of Carmel adduce especially the formulas of papal letters and the words of Mary herself to St. Simon Stock. In the 18th century, the Queenship of Mary appears alongside of her Motherhood, a phenomenon no doubt reflecting the changing image of a queen in that period.

The title, "Ornament of Carmel" (*Decor Carmeli*) derives from Scripture (Is 35, 2), and for John Baconthorpe who first applies the title, it meant the Order which was given to Mary for her ornament. In 1479, Arnold Bostius remarks almost as an aside that the patroness of the Order is the ornament of Carmel. Not enough writers have commented on this title to enable us to assign it a traditional meaning. It seems simply to have meant that Mary belonged to the Carmelite Order and was its glory. In any case, "Mother and Ornament of Carmel" aptly describes Mary in her traditional role in Carmel as Patroness (Mother) and most pure Virgin (ornament).

The Scapular Devotion

In the minds of the Carmelites of the 17th and 18th century, no gift of the Mother of Carmel equaled that of the scapular. During this period, the cult of Our Lady of Mount Carmel becomes in effect the cult of Our Lady of the Scapular. This process had already matured in the 16th century.

The preferred account of the vision of St. Simon Stock was that of John Palaeonydorus (d. 1507), who reported our Lady's words as: "Receive, most beloved (son), this scapular of your Order, the sign (*signum*) of my confraternity, a privilege for you and all Carmelites; whoever dies in it will not suffer eternal fire. It is a sign of salvation, a safeguard in danger, a pledge of peace, and eternal covenant." Earlier 17th century writers, more attuned to medieval mentality, brought into greater relief the character of the scapular as a symbol. Thus, Peter Thomas Saraceni calls the scapular "a memorial of devotion, an outstanding gift of love." From the many books of the time, two facets of the scapular emerge: the patronage of Mary and man's service or devotion. Not all authors treat both aspects; Lezana in his book, *Maria patrona* (Romae, 1648), is mainly concerned with the former. With time, probably due to the influence of rationalism, sensitivity to the symbolic value of the scapular diminishes.

The prominence accorded to the promise to St. Simon Stock caused the scapular to be conceived as a symbol of protection rather than of cult. In this way, it complemented the title of the Order which spoke to the faithful of the cult of Mary. There was a certain parallelism between the two, and they were often treated together. Both were symbols of the relationship between the Order and its patroness, both were benefactions from her hands.

The Scapular Confraternity

Confraternities, like much else in the Counter-Reformational Church, were organized by and centered in the Holy See. In his brief, *Quaecumque*, December 7, 1604, Clement VII laid down the rules for forming confraternities. Paul V, *Cum certas*, October 30, 1606, allowed the prior general or his vicar to establish the confraternity of Our Lady of Mount Carmel in non-Carmelite as well as Carmelite churches. While this faculty enormously extended the possibility of propagation of the confraternity, it also loosed the Order's control, and authorities of the Order seem at first to have regarded it with the suspicion accorded the Trojan horse. The constitutions of 1626 allow the erection of confraternities in non-Carmelite churches only if there is no church of the Order in the locality and with the previous condition that such confraternities will cease to be, if a Carmelite foundation is subsequently made (pt. 4, ch. 28, no. 3). The province of Touraine chose not to avail itself of the Pauline faculty (1619). Nevertheless, the extension of the confraternity to non-Carmelite churches proved to be of immense benefit to all concerned, diffusing the Carmelite presence into areas (for instance, Spanish America) where the Carmelite habit would never make its appearance.

Theodore Straccio composed an official *Manner of Instituting the Confraternity of the Carmelite Order* (Rome, 1634), which he distributed to all provincials, ordering them to provide copies in the houses of their jurisdiction. Subsequently, he issued an enlarged *Instruction* (Rome, 1640). Here was clearly and authoritatively set forth all the Carmelite needed to know about indulgences and confraternities, a subject about which previously there had existed considerable confusion. The nature of the Carmelite confraternity appears from the obligations of its members. To enjoy the many indulgences attached to membership, enrollment in the scapular and in the register of the confraternity is required. The scapular must be worn about the neck day and night. Moreover, to obtain the Virgin's help after death (the Sabbatine Privilege) it is necessary to observe chastity according to one's state in life and to recite the Little Office of Our Lady, or alternatively to abstain from meat on Wednesday and Saturday.

The scapular devotion received continual encouragement from the Holy See. During the 17th century Urban VIII (1628), Clement X (1673, 1674, and 1675) and Innocent XI (1678, 1679, 1682, 1684) signified their approval.

Thus organized and propagated by the highest authorities, the scapular confraternity spread through every corner of Christendom and with the rosary represented the most popular devotion in the Church. Art itself offers its own unpremeditated witness to this universality. Goya's man about to be garrotted (the British Museum) and François Rude's Neapolitan fisher boy (the Louvre) have in common their scapular of Our Lady of Mount Carmel.

Scapular Writings

Carmelite Marian writings during this period are practically identical with writings on the scapular. In a list by no means complete, Simon Besalduch mentions over a hundred 17th and 18th century titles.

Noteworthy early works include *L'esguillon des devots à la Vierge Marie du Mont Carmel* (Limoges, 1619) by John Tuaut, *The Fountain of Elijah Watering the Garden of the Church* (Paris, 1624) by Toussaint Foucher, *Thesaurus Carmelitarum* (Cologne, 1625), by Cyprian of St. Mary, which underwent a number of editions, and *Spiritual Instruction for Devotees of the Blessed Virgin Mary of Carmel* (Bologna, 1635) by Peter Thomas Saraceni. *L'Alliance de la Vierge touchant les privileges du s. scapulaire des Carmes*, by Leo of St. John enjoyed a widespread popularity, saw almost forty editions (the 25th at Paris, 1653) and a Latin translation. Its famous author bestowed the scapular on Louis XIV as he had on Louis XIII.

The second half of the century produced the best of scapular writings, in which the Christian and Marian doctrines symbolized by the scapular were consistently brought forward. *The Adoption of the Children of the Virgin into the Order and Confraternity of Our Lady of Mount Carmel* (Paris, 1646) by the Discalced Carmelite Gregory Nazianzen of St. Basil (d. 1677), as its title declares, explains the devotion in terms of filial adoption. In his *Maria patrona* (Rome, 1648), John Baptist Lezana showed the relationship of the scapular devotion to the spirit of the Order and produced the best synthesis of Carmelite Marian devotion since Bostius. The *Theological Treatise on the Protection of the Immaculate Virgin* (Paris, 1650) by Irenaeus of St. James (d. 1676), of the Touraine province, "one of the best of the writers who defended the scapular in the early phases of the controversy" (Bartolomé Xiberta), while polemical in intent, made a greater effort to explain Our Lady's promises theologically. Matthias of St. John (d. 1681), of the Touraine province, in his *True Devotion of the Holy Scapular* (Paris, 1656) emphasized the interior spirit of the scapular devotion and showed how true devotion to Mary can be practiced through its means. The *Clavis aurea thesauri Partheno-Carmelitici* (Vienna, 1669) by the

Discalced Paul of the Saints (d. 1683) provided an inexhaustible source of material on the scapular. His confrere, Raphael of St. Joseph, an accomplished preacher, chose his title from the scapular promise in Palaeonydorus' version for his work, *Signum salutis, salus in periculis* (Linz, 1718), which, Fr. Xiberta concludes, "I would like to call the golden crown of the older literature on the scapular."

Not to be omitted here is Daniel of the Virgin Mary's *Speculum carmelitanum* (Antwerpen,1680, 4 v.), which made available Ribot's collection, not printed since 1507. This collection of primitive writings, particularly the *Institution of the First Monks*, enshrined the legends of the Order, many of them regarding Mary. Also included were 15th century works like Arnold Bostius' *De patronatu Beatae Virginis Mariae* (a summary), hitherto unpublished, as well as essays and commentaries by Daniel himself. This rich deposit of lore, among other things "a veritable *summa* of the scapular" (Xiberta), now became widely available; the general chapter of 1680 ordered it placed in all libraries of the Order.

A special genre was the confraternity handbook or manual, featuring a brief history of the Order, miracles of Our Lady, prayers, privileges, and indulgences of the confraternity and Third Order. This sort of booklet with its stress on indulgence gathering and miracles of a dubious sort was not always conducive to solid devotion and sometimes merited the criticism of those who for various motives sought to mitigate the excesses in Marian devotion. Early specimens of the 16th century have already been noted. Among the practitioners of the genre are found some illustrious names: Francis Potel, Josse van Assche, Michael de la Fuente, William Champcheurieux, Angelus LeBlanc. *The Compendious Narration of the Indulgences, Privileges and Graces Granted to the Order, Confraternities and Churches of the Most Glorious Mother of God, the Virgin Mary of Carmel*, by Simon Grassi (1650-1723), of the Tuscan province, underwent sixty editions.

The Scapular Controversy

While the faithful unreservedly accepted the scapular story and flocked to the confraternity in great numbers, the intellectual world of Descartes was not disposed to admit medieval miracle accounts without question. The peaceful possession of the field by the scapular devotion came to an end in 1642, when John Launoy challenged the historicity of the scapular vision and the Sabbatine bull. The third and final edition of his work had the title *Five Essays Concerning the Vision of Simon Stock, the Privilege of the Sabbatine Bull, and the Confraternity of the Carmelite Scapular* (Paris, 1653).

Launoy (1603-1678), doctor of the College of Navarre, was one of the most learned men of his time, widely travelled, a researcher of libraries. His works especially concerned theology and the constitutional history of the Church, but his approach was mainly polemical, his themes born of occasional circumstances. He denied papal infallibility, the Immaculate Conception, and Mary's bodily Assumption. Launoy was no Jansenist, but his minimalism was in the line of those sectaries and agreeable to them. His criticism of Carmelite traditions was only one of a series of attacks on the pretensions of religious orders, which earned him the sobriquet of *"dénicheur des saints"* (a play on the French word for niche and nest) and destroyer of monastic privileges.

In the face of this attack, Carmelites and their Discalced brothers joined forces against the common enemy. John Cheron, whose stepmother attributed her cure from an illness to St. Simon Stock, immediately replied to Launoy with his *Privilegiati scapularis et visionis S. Simonis Stockii vindiciae* (Bordeaux, 1642). He unblushingly produced out of thin air what purported to be fragments from a biography of St. Simon Stock by his *socius*, Peter Swanyngton, recounting the saint's vision and a subsequent miracle. Thomas Aquinas of St. Joseph (d. 1649), one of the first French Discalced, an able historian esteemed by Launoy himself, wrote *Two Apologetical Dissertations in Favor of the Scapular Confraternity* (Tulle, 1648). Philibert Fezay (d. 1649), provincial of Provence and professor at the University of Aix, like Cheron had personal reasons for entering the fray. His brother, John Anthony, prior of Avignon, owed his miraculous cure to Our Lady of Mount Carmel. Philibert produced *The Double Privilege of the Scapular and Confraternity of the Glorious Virgin Mary of Mount Carmel* (Aix, 1649) in answer to Launoy.

Launoy's reservations about the historical basis of the scapular devotion were well taken, but his criticisms at times were excessive. Thus, he at first claimed that Palaeonydorus, writing in 1495, was the earliest witness to the scapular vision. Such inaccuracy gave the Carmelites an opportunity they were not slow to seize for casting doubt on his reliability.

Later critics of the scapular devotion included such reputable scholars as Noel Alexander (1639-1724), John Baptist Thiers (1636-1703), and John Anthony Muratori (1672-1750). Reservations about the scapular devotion were doctrinal as well as historical. Certainly not all writers and preachers were adequately informed or prudent. In 1610, Silvio called to account Angelo Merli, prior of Pavia, with regard to an anonymous *Raccolta d'alcune gratie fatte dalla Santissima Vergine Maria del Carmine ai suoi devoti* (Pavia, P. Bartoli, 1610), which contained "a few things that are not true and lack foundation." At the provincial chapter of Catalonia in 1618, Straccio complained that many preachers sold scapulars and preached indulgences revoked by Paul V, "which is deceiving the faithful, for they preach matters without truth or value." However, objections were often based on an impoverished concept of Marian doctrine and of the role of Our Lady in the Church. Yet they served to make acceptance of the devotion more balanced and informed, and caused the Carmelites to develop its theology.

It hurt the Carmelites not at all to have the distinguished Jesuit, Theophilus Raynaud, take up the cudgels on their behalf. His *Scapulare Partheno-carmeliticum* (Paris, 1654), was prepared for the printer by Leo of St. John, but not to the satisfaction of the author, who complained bitterly about Leo's editorial hardihood. Leo urged some sort of official recognition for Raynaud, and as a matter of fact the general chapter of 1654 decreed letters of affiliation for him and suffrages throughout the Order at his death. Raynaud's support of the scapular devotion was all the more significant in that he was a professional Mariologist and not given to loose judgements in the matter of Marian doctrine. "The classic treatise on the scapular," in the words of Fr. Esteve, Raynaud's book underwent a number of editions and was included by Jean Jacques Bourassé in his *Summa aurea*.

On the other hand, the Bollandists who were having enough trouble with the Carmelites over the origin of the Order avoided the whole issue of the Scapular in the May volume of the *Acta Sanctorum*, which should have treated the life of St. Simon Stock. In the appendix to the May volume, Daniel Papebroch eventually published the biographical details on St. Simon in John Grossi's *Viridarium*, but omitted the account of the vision, alleging that he could not have included it without certain observations which would have displeased his old antagonists. He could hardly have devised a more damaging strategy to exasperate his antagonists.

Persons whose favor increased the scapular's prestige were Bl. Claude de la Columbière, S.J., René Billuart, O.P., John Crasset, S.J., and St. Alphonsus de Liguori. Most important of all was the warm endorsement of Pope Benedict XIV (1740-1758), who after reviewing all the historical difficulties concluded, "We believe the vision to be authentic and think it should be accepted by all."

The Scapular Feast

In the 17th century, the Order's patronal feast underwent a final evolution. Here, too, the scapular asserted its preeminence and became the exclusive object of the Solemn Commemoration, hereafter simply called the "Scapular Feast." No doubt a contributing factor to this development was the acquisition of the second nocturn lessons beginning, "*Cum sacra Pentecostes die*," which recounted the vision of St. Simon Stock. John of St. Bernard in his *Jesus amabilis* (Straubing, 1666) seems to be the first to attribute the origin of the feast to the gratitude of the Order for the gift of the scapular, an interpretation that subsequently found favor with many writers.

The general chapter of 1609 unanimously decreed that the Commemoration of the Blessed Virgin should be the Order's principal feast. That of 1620 recommended that "since the Feast of the Commemoration of the Blessed Virgin Mary is the titular feast of our Order," permission should be obtained from the Holy See to celebrate it with an octave. The same resolution was repeated in 1625. The desired permission was obtained three years later.

The approval of the scapular feast for the Order prepared the way for its celebration generally in the Church. The feast appeared spontaneously on a number of diocesan calendars with or without the approval of the Congregation of Rites, required since 1628. At the request of Queen Mariana in 1674, the feast was granted to all the Spanish realms. In 1670, Leopold I obtained it for the Empire. Other sovereigns followed suit: Portugal (1679), Tuscany and Genoa (1682), Parma (1683), Savoy and Lucca (1684), Poland (1704), the Papal States (1725). Other rites, Mozarabic, Ambrosian, Chaldaic, Greek (in Calabria), Maronite adopted the feast. Finally, on September 24, 1726, Pope Benedict XIII extended the feast to the universal Church with the rank of *duplex major*. The prior general, Caspar Pizzolanti, in a circular letter of December, gave voice to the joy and gratitude of the whole Order.

"When Benedict XIII in the 18th century," wrote Dom Prosper Guéranger with regard to July 16 in his classic *Année liturgique*, "extended the feast of July 16 to the entire Church, he was, as it were, only officially consecrating the universal acceptance which in fact the cult of the Queen of Carmel had by that time acquired almost everywhere."

Historians of spirituality have not sufficiently brought out the importance of the scapular devotion in Catholic life in the past.

Preaching Our Lady

Many prescriptions of the constitutions, liturgical and otherwise, nourished the Marian life of the Order. The constitutions of 1626 canonized legislation for preachers regarding Our Lady which had been composed by Rossi for Italy in 1568 and extended to the whole Order by the general chapter of 1593. In their sermons on Saturdays of Lent, preachers should always introduce a Marian theme. Also, they should often preach on Carmel's saints, the antiquity and eminence of the Order, the Scapular Confraternity and indulgences. However, the constitutions prudently add, they should avoid "excessive exaggeration" (Pt. 1, ch. 10, no. 9).

Marian Shrines and Images

As befitted a Marian Order, Carmelite churches were often dedicated to Our Lady of Mount Carmel or to Mary under one of her other titles. Even when the patron of a church was a saint, it would contain a Marian shrine which absorbed the attention of the people. The focus of Marian churches and shrines was the image of Our Lady, sculptured or painted, usually of some antiquity, deemed miraculous either because of its origin or of the graces and favors obtained through the intercession of the Blessed Virgin (*Gnadenbilden*).

In the history of the Church, Marian shrines and images have played a significant role as rallying points of popular devotion. For this reason and to illustrate graphically Carmelite devotion to Mary in the 17th century, it seemed justifiable to treat at some length the Order's Marian shrines and images.

Several authors spanning the period under consideration have left lists of the most famous Carmelite Marian shrines of their times: Francis Voersio (1620), John Pinto de Vitoria (1626), John Baptist Lezana (1648), Francis Mary Maggio, C.R. (1677), Daniel of the Virgin Mary (1680), Francis Colmenero (1754), Roque Albert Faci (1759). Voersio writes from personal experience garnered during his extensive travels as secretary to Henry Silvio. Faci's list is the longest, understandably so, since all tend to copy from their predecessors.

Marian Shrines and Images in Italy

No particular image is the official representation of Our Lady of Mount Carmel, but if any were to be considered such, it would be the Madonna called "*La Bruna*" of the Carmine of Naples, unequalled for fame and popularity. In his time, Lezana, long resident in Rome, ranked it second only to Our Lady of Loreto among famous images of Mary in Italy. In the Byzantine style, the life-size painting on wood was claimed to be the work of St. Luke, brought to Naples by the Carmelites emigrating from Palestine, but it probably originated in Tuscany in the 13th century. Our Lady in a blue mantle and reddish brown tunic is pictured from the waist upward, holding the Child Jesus, who presses his cheek to hers. In 1580, the picture was enshrined in a marble altar in the Renaissance style, thought to be the work of the Cimafonti brothers. The painting was restored with indifferent success by, among others, Francesco Solimene (1699).

Dearly beloved by the people of Naples, the *Madonna della Bruna* has also been the object of devotion of rulers, popes, and saints. Wednesday is the day dedicated in her honor.

The choice between *La Bruna* and Our Lady of Trapani for preeminence among Carmel-Madonnas is a difficult one. Not so, however, if artistic quality is the primary consideration. This life-size marble statue of the Blessed Virgin has awakened universal enthusiasm over its beauty. "Most precious pearl of our Order," cries Faci in an apt figure of speech recalling the translucent quality of the marble.

"He who would see her more beautiful must go to heaven to see her," exclaimed the Viceroy of Sicily, Diego Enríquez de Guzmán.

Mary is standing and holding the Child, whose right arm is laid on her breast, his left hand placed in her right. Mother and Child regard each other smilingly. Our Lady's smile is one of those miracles of art that occur only in an occasional Mona Lisa. According to the legendary account of its origin, discounting variant versions, the statue was brought to Trapani in the 13th century by Pisans fleeing from the Saracens. Dr. Maria Pia Sibilia Cosentino rejects such legends and, basing her judgment on stylistic features alone, assigns the statue to Giovanni Pisano (1245-1314). On the other hand, Hanno-Walter Kruft avails himself of the legendary data (even obtaining the services of an expert to decipher the alleged Syrian inscription on the statue) to conclude that the figure did indeed originate in the East in the middle of the 14th century, probably the work of a Pisan sculptor on Cyprus.

In the Carmelite church of the Annunziata, the Madonna of Trapani is enshrined in a richly ornamented chapel which one enters through the fine marble portal of Antonello Gagini. There, writes Cosentino, "the people of Trapani have venerated her for centuries, heaping treasures on her with oriental fanaticism, proud of her, jealous of her, casting at her feet everything good and everything bad." The many copies of the Madonna attest the fact that not only the people of Trapani but persons of all nations have been given an inkling of the beauty of Mary through "this stupendous work of art which providentially found a home in Trapani."

Madonnas in the Byzantine Style

Byzantine madonnas, or in the Byzantine style, held to have been brought by the early Carmelites from the Holy Land, usually represent the longest traditions of Marian devotion in the Order.

The image venerated in Traspontina in Rome was solemnly transferred there in the 15th century from the original foundation in Rome, to be moved again in the relocation of Traspontina nearer the Vatican. At the request of Theodore Straccio, the icon was crowned by the Vatican Chapter in 1641, the first of the Carmelite madonnas to receive this distinction. In 1674, it was enshrined over the main altar under the baldachin of rare marbles designed by Carlo Fontana.

Another Byzantine madonna, allegedly brought by the Carmelites from Palestine, is the *Madonna del Popolo*, a 13th century painting of the Tuscan School venerated in the Carmine of Florence. Only in heaven is Our Lady more gloriously enthroned: the *Madonna del Popolo* is framed by the Brancacci chapel.

Siena in the Tuscan province is not listed by the old authors as a place of particular Marian devotion, but it possessed a genuine Byzantine Virgin, as usual said to have been brought by the Carmelites from the East, besides another 13th century Gothic madonna "of the Little Mantles" (*dei Mantellini*).

Copies of the madonna of Traspontina were venerated in several places. The madonna originally venerated in San Martino ai Monti in Rome since its foundation in 1299 seems to have been the 14th century Byzantine painting of the Sienese School today preserved in the friary there. It was replaced by a work painted by Jerome Massei around 1595 after the Traspontina madonna. Crowned by the Vatican Chapter in 1659, it was transferred in 1793 to the Lady Chapel in the left nave of the church. Not long thereafter occurred the invasion by the French, who walked off with the golden crown affixed to the painting at the time of its coronation.

Marian Shrines in Sicily

Sicily, where countless churches are dedicated to Our Lady of Mount Carmel, may itself be called her shrine. In the Carmine Maggiore of Palermo is the madonna painted around 1492 by Thomas de Vigilia, noted artist of the same city. The life-size figure, shown in the act of suckling the Christ Child, is framed by eight smaller vignettes representing episodes of Carmelite history and the scapular devotion. The historian of Sicilian art, Joachim di Marzio notes "the profound expression of majesty and tenderness" of the Virgin. The picture forms the altarpiece of the altar in the left transept of the church, framed by a grandiose arch supported by four spiral columns in the style of Bernini, the creation of the Serpotta brothers, Joseph and James. An identical madonna by Thomas de Vigilia is found in the Carmelite church of Corleone; it is not clear which is the older.

In the style of the madonna of Palermo is that in Catania painted in 1501 by Antonio di Viterbo, known as *Il Pastura*. Beside Our Lady nursing the Child, stand Sts. Elijah and Berthold. Eight vignettes likewise recount the favors of Mary. The painting remained intact in the rubble of the church after the earthquake of 1693, but only in 1932 was it restored to the present church. This grandiose structure, built under the aegis of the reform of Santa Maria della Scala, which had taken over the convent in 1729, conceded the place of honor in the Lady Chapel to the painting of Our Lady of Mount Carmel by Sebastian Toccarini (1703-1773) reflecting the style of Guido Reni. Crowned by the Vatican Chapter in 1833, this image of Mary attracted the devotion of the faithful in later times.

Contemporaries do not fail to mention the devotion of the people of Messina to the miraculous image of Our Lady of Mount Carmel venerated at the Carmine and reputed to have been brought from Mount Carmel to this very early settlement of the Order in Europe. The painting, in fact of the 15th century and attributed to Polidoro di Caravaggio, is a mantle Virgin, flanked by Elijah and Elisha, who is shielding the Carmelites and their affiliates under her mantle from the wrath of Christ threatening famine, pestilence, and war. Polidoro might have added earthquakes, three of which (in 1693, 1785, and 1906) the painting survived to find refuge in the Museo Nazionale of Messina.

Other Italian Shrines

In the monumental Carmine of Pavia in the Lombardy province, Our Lady of Grace became the subject of devotion after a crippled woman was instantaneously cured in 1597. Faci records the many cures effected during a pestilence around the same time. The fresco in a rich baroque frame represents the Virgin with the Infant on her lap. In her right hand she has a rose. The Child Jesus is holding an open book. Beside them in black habits are Sts. Julius d'Orta and St. Anthony the Abbot. The Lady Chapel contains a lovely marble figure of Our Lady of Mount Carmel by John Angelo Giudici (1699).

Among famous Marian shrines of the Order Lezana rates Padua in the Venetian province second only to Naples and Trapani. The devotion of the people to Our Lady of Lights was stimulated by her miraculous intervention in the pestilence which devastated all of Italy in 1576. At that time the picture was transferred to the Carmelite church. Attributed to Stefano dall'Arzere, disciple of Tiziano, the oval-shaped painting shows Mary holding out her Child for the adoration of the faithful.

At Cervia in the Romagna province, the miraculous image of Our Lady of the Pine, said to have been found affixed to a pine by wood gatherers, is of the Venetian school of the 15th century and shows Mary seated on a throne and nursing the Infant. The painting became the object of special devotion to the lay brother, Jerome Lambertini, who settled down by it to live as a hermit. Before his death (ca. 1515), a church and convent had risen to accommodate the devotion of the people. Suppressed by Innocent X in 1652, the remote convent was subsequently torn down, but the little Romanesque church and its madonna survived to be masterfully restored in 1972.

The Madonna of the Virgins of Macerata is a mantle-virgin shielding young people of both sexes, hence her title. It is said to have been painted in 1533 by a local artist, Lawrence, called Juda, of Matelica. A product of the Renaissance at its height, the work nevertheless breathes an old-fashioned air of the naif. Among the curious favors attributed to the Madonna is the salvation of a child from a crocodile, the skin of which hangs to the left of the Lady Chapel.

The 15th century fresco by an unknown artist of Our Lady of Grace at San Felice del Benaco shows Mary clothed in brown tunic and white mantle, seated on a throne, with Sts. Albert and Angelus at her side. The Child Jesus lies in her lap with a swallow perched on the thumb of his left hand.

The following is a list of places in Italy, some of them already referred to above, with images of Our Lady of Mount Carmel crowned by the Vatican Chapter: Accadia, Ariano Irpino, Avigliano, Bologna (S. Martino), Cagliari, Calvenzano di Vergato, Capannori, Catania, Curinga, Desenzano al Serio, Ferrara, Forlì, Genoa, Iesi, Laurenzana (*santuario diocesana*), Loana, Mesagna, Montefalcone, Valfortore, Naples (Carmine), Noto, Nocera dei Pagani, Palmi, Polla, Randazzo, Riccia, Rionero in Vulture (Collegiata S. Marco), Roma (Monte Santo), Roma (Transpontina), Roma (San Martino), San Felice del Benaco, Scalea, Sorrento, and Trisulti di Collepardo.

Marian Shrines and Images of Castile

The Marian devotion of Spain and Portugal is proverbial; no small share of it relates to Our Lady of Mount Carmel. Unfortunately, in this case time has treated less kindly the objects of popular devotion. Spanish and Portuguese Carmelites, unlike their Italian confreres, have few ancient madonnas about which to center their devotion to Mary. Only their memory remains in the fervent pages of Carmelite chroniclers, especially of that great devotee of Mary, John Baptist Lezana. In many cases, these images seem to have been of great antiquity: their style was Gothic and their legends often tell of discovery underground, where they were allegedly hidden in Moslem times.

In the province of Castile, a relic to survive to modern times is the statue in wood of Our Lady of Mount Carmel in the Carmelite church of Madrid, today the parish church of San Luis. The work of Juan Sánchez Barba (1654), it is enshrined in the *retable* of the main altar, executed by Sebastian Benavente. Originally, the Virgin was shown bestowing the scapular on St. Simon Stock, but the figure of the latter was subsequently destroyed. The noble ladies of the court vied with each other in providing rich garments for the image.

The church of Alcalà de Henares had a statue of Our Lady of Mount Carmel of medium height, "very miraculous and devotional," the gift of Doña Isabel Gutiérrez, wife of a secretary of Charles V in Flanders. It was venerated in a special chapel of the church and had its own confraternity. In 1604, Antonio Navarro placed it among the most popular and famous in the kingdom and archbishopric of Toledo.

The Carmen of Toledo was originally the site of the oratory of Our Lady *de Alficen*, previously in the care of other religious. The situation of the chapel under the choir of the church, reminiscent of clandestine devotion of Moorish times, also gave to this Virgin the appellation, *Soterraña*. The convent of San Pablo de la Moraleja had been transferred to the Order in 1315 by Ferdinand Velásquez, archdeacon of Avila, who with eight other priests had lived by the shrine of Our Lady *Soterraña*. The icon of the Virgin in the subterranean chapel became the object of renewed devotion after 1436, when a widely publicized miracle occurred. Perhaps an even greater attraction was the fabulous treasury of relics renowned throughout Castile, whose kings showered privileges and gifts on the chapel. Requena honored still another Virgin *Soterraña*, hidden during the Moslem Conquest and later discovered by an humble shepherd. Today, Our Lady as represented by this statue, is the patroness of the town. The rustic chapel of Our Lady of the Valley at Los Valles was a popular place of pilgrimage before the coming of the Carmelites. "Within the memory of man it has never been heard said that this holy image left its house and convent in procession to seek water, as is the custom of the inhabitants of that region, and did not find it in abundance."

Valderas (1597), Valdeolivas (1612), and La Alberca (1613) in turn became centers of devotion to three statues of Mary found in a trunk which a soldier left in the safekeeping of the friars and failed to claim. They were about a yard in length and had features "somewhat swarthy, devout and gracious." That of La Alberca occurs in the life of Brother Francis of the Cross who was greatly devoted to it. The Confraternity of Our Lady of Succor of Valderas exists today.

Shrines and Images of Aragon and Catalonia

In the Carmelite church of Valencia in the province of Aragon, Our Lady *la Morenica* was venerated in the Blessed Sacrament chapel, consecrated in 1343. A much treasured relic was the slipper of the Virgin, encased in gold-plated silver, which in his times, Pinto de Vitoria assures us, had been opened only once at the request of King Philip III and his fiancee, present in the city to celebrate their engagement.

Zaragoza prized its ancient Madonna *de la Candelaria* preserved in the chapel of its confraternity in the church. Mary was the principal figure of the *retable* also picturing the Presentation, St. Jerome, various prophets with texts from their writings. The Virgin, painted on wood, was about six feet in height. Seated on a throne, she was clothed in a blue mantle and wore an imperial crown. With her left hand she supported the Child, who regarded not his mother but the instruments of the passion offered by an angel. One foot was suspended in air, as though the Infant were eager to embrace his destiny of suffering. "I have heard of no particular miracles," Faci concludes, "but I presume they are exceptional."

In the Carmelite church of Onda was the image of Our Lady of Hope, or

Expectancy, reputed to antedate Moorish times. In 1561, the pestilence suddenly ceased at Our Lady's intercession. In 1751, a new and sumptuous *camarín* was inaugurated, on which occasion Master Peter Nicholau preached the sermon (Valencia, 1751). Jerome Caset, known for his piety and close friend of John Sanz, attributed to this madonna of Onda his escape unharmed after a fall from a great height onto a stone pavement. Spared from the fire that destroyed the church in 1835, the statue was restored in 1887 to the new church constructed by the Carmelites after their return in 1880.

Elsewhere in the province, Aren (1610) enshrined an ancient image of Our Lady de Piedrahita, first venerated in a remote oratory in the mountains. Made of hardest stone, the figure was six palms in height. Mary wore a blue mantle spangled with stars, "as the Queen of Heaven," and held the Infant who had a small bird in his hands.

In 1597, the Carmelites were given charge of the shrine and ancient image of Our Lady of Victory which commemorated the liberation of Jaca from the Moors. Though they moved inside the town in 1614, they continued to administer the sanctuary.

Huesca honored a statue of Mary reputed to antedate the establishment of the Carmelite convent, possibly the oldest foundation of the Order in Spain. The statue, enshrined in the chapel of the confraternity of Our Lady of Mount Carmel, was of wood, about three feet tall. The Virgin supported the Child with her right hand and with her left showed him an apple.

Rubielos, founded in 1608, cherished an image of Our Lady of Mount Carmel donated by the Discalced Carmelite nuns of Zaragoza, "always well inclined toward our province," Faci observes.

The sanctuary of Our Lady of the Fount, or Well, in Sanguesa was given in charge of the Carmelites in the 13th century and after their transfer within the city in 1380 they continued its care. Votive plaques witnessed to the favors granted to the faithful who had recourse to this madonna in their hour of need. Cases of safety from drowning in the Aragon River were especially commemorated.

In the province of Catalonia the faithful of Lérida found comfort during years of war and destruction in recourse to Our Lady of Mount Carmel. The Gothic image, which had formed the principal feature of the stone *retable* of the main altar in the original church, showed the Virgin and Child characteristically wearing crowns. On visits to Lérida, St. Vincent Ferrer never failed to show reverence to this image. In the third church of the Carmelites, completed in 1766, the statue was placed over the main portal.

The miraculous image of the Virgin in Manresa was discovered during excavations in the church in the 14th century. In Lezana's time, it was over the main altar (*capella maior*). This is no doubt the statue preserved today in the Museo Municipal of Manresa.

A Gothic Virgin and Child from the Carmen of Barcelona, the early object of Carmelite devotion, is in the Museo Provincial of Barcelona.

No Carmelite was more devoted to Our Lady of Mount Carmel than the diocesan priest, Francis Colmenero, author of *El Carmelo ilustrado* (Valladolid, 1754). During parish missions conducted in a dozen dioceses of Castile, Galicia, Asturias, Aragon, and Portugal, he caused 760 images of the Mother of Carmel to be placed in the parishes in which he preached.

Marian Shrines of Andalusia

Jerez de la Frontera in the province of Andalusia treasures an historic image of Our Lady, today the most famous Carmelite Virgin in Spain. This lovely 16th century statue, measuring 1.75 meters, probably arrived with the Carmelites from Seville in 1586. In her right hand, the Virgin holds a scepter, in her left the Infant. The latter, added to the figure a century later, is attributed to Luisa Roldán (La Roldana). "In this statue," writes Fr. Barbero Moreno, "antiquity, art, beauty, devotion, and charm form a combination so happy, so harmonious, so perfect as to cry out for crowning by the Holy See," a distinction conferred in 1925.

During the renovation in 1428 of the sanctuary of the church of the Carmen of Seville, an ancient statue of the Virgin was unearthed. Measuring about four and a half feet, the figure, stated by Faci to be of white marble, represented the Virgin at full length, her features and those of the Child of a swarthy hue. On the pedestal were the figures of a kneeling religious and an *Ecce homo*. The ladies of Seville clothed the statue in rich garments and a large scapular. The statue, actually of alabaster, in modern times found its way to the church of St. Laurence.

The feast of the Immaculate Conception was celebrated with special solemnity at the Carmen of Seville, thanks to a legacy of John Ponce, Count of Medellín. In this connection, Faci mentions a "most beautiful" picture venerated by the faithful, which however he admits not having seen. It would indeed have been beautiful, if it is the painting of Mary Immaculate by Velásquez, formerly of the Carmen of Seville, now in the National Gallery in London.

A painting of Our Lady of Mount Carmel with St. Simon Stock and St. Teresa (School of Seville), now in the Church of St. Stephen, may be provenant from one of the Order's convents in Seville, possibly the reformed College of St. Teresa. That it is not of Discalced origin is evident from Our Lady's brooch.

The statue of Our Lady of Mount Carmel in the Carmelite church in Granada was located on the right side altar. Noble ladies of the Third Order adorned it with elaborate clothing studded with precious stones of great value. The many votive tablets attesting to favors received were removed in 1740, when church and chapel were renovated. Today the statue is found in the cathedral.

Marian Shrines of Portugal and Brazil

No contemporary Carmelite author fails to mention Nossa Senhora das Reliquias at Vidigueira in the province of Portugal. The authoritative Luis de Granada, moreover, witnesses to the miraculous cure there of Caterina de Taide, known personally to him. Until the last century, the Carmelite church also held the tomb of the great navigator, Vasco da Gama, made Count of Vidigueira by King Manuel I.

The Madonna which graced the main altar of the royal Carmo of Lisbon was thought to date from the time of the founder, St. Nuno Alvares Pereira, Our Lady's own knight. It once held a candle, a relic of its original dedication to the mystery of the Purification. The statue was held in great veneration by the Court. King John V (1706-1750) had it fetched to the palace on the occasion of an illness and caused it to be richly clothed. In 1722, Master Louis Caesar de Menezes instituted an annual novena, himself bearing the expense of the first celebration, aided by Manuel de Sá.

The statue evidently survived the earthquake of 1755, as Faci writing four years later speaks of it as existing.

More fortunate than the mother province of Portugal, Carmel in Brazil today cherishes its three centuries-old statue of Our Lady of Mount Carmel at Recife (Pernambuco). The Virgin, larger than life size, holds the Child in her left hand, a scepter in her right. The statue is exquisitely carved of cedar wood and is thought to have been imported from Portugal before the occupation of Recife by the Dutch, when it was kept carefully hidden. In 1908, Our Lady of Mount Carmel was declared patroness of the city; in 1919 the image was canonically crowned, the fourth on the American continent to receive this honor after those of Guadalupe (Mexico), Lujan (Argentina), Sao Paulo (Brazil).

In the Carmelite church of Bahia in the province of Bahia-Pernambuco, authors record a phenomenon similar to that at present occurring at the mission of San Juan Capistrano in California. Every year on the feast of Our Lady of Mount Carmel (July 16), a dove was said to return and fly about the church for three days and "no one ever saw it eat anything."

Marian Shrines and Images in France

The absence of Carmelites in France since the Revolution makes it difficult to trace evidences of Carmelite Marian cult in that country. Also, the authors who concerned themselves with the subject of Marian shrines are Italians and Spaniards, who had only vague ideas about what went on in the North. Nevertheless, devotion to Mary flourished in the eldest daughter of the Church.

In the province of Touraine, Angers was the center of devotion to Our Lady of Recovery (*Notre Dame de la Recouvrance*). Her statue measured four feet and was preserved in a chapel on the left side of the church, lined with votive tablets of grateful suppliants. In 1562, the Calvinists dragged the statue by a rope around its neck to the bridge and threw it into the Maine. In 1646, after a triumphal procession, it was placed on a new altar, where it remained until the Revolution.

The Lady Chapel in the right nave of the Carmelite church at Loudun contained a painting of Virgin and Child, "represented with unusual skill." Richelieu had caused the chapel to be entirely renovated.

Germane to its devotion to Mary is the Order's devotion to St. Anne. In 1627, the Carmelites were summoned to Auray to take charge of the cult which arose when a simple laborer discovered in a field a statue of St. Anne. Seraphinus of Jesus and three others formed the first community. Hugh of St. Francis wrote the first history of the cult of St. Anne d'Auray; Benedict of St. Peter was the architect of the chapel which formed the focus of the devotion until 1866, when the cornerstone was placed on the present grandiose basilica, which the Bretons built for their beloved patroness.

Limoges in the province of Aquitaine fostered a fervent devotion to Our Lady of Mount Carmel. The confraternity attached to the Carmelite church numbered 9,000 members, inspired no doubt by the presence of a relic of St. Simon Stock. Yet it was Aurillac, according to a report of the provincial to the historian, Lezana, that distinguished itself most for the scapular devotion.

The miraculous image of the Weeping Virgin (*Notre Dame des Plaintes*) at La Rochette in the province of Provence happily still exists. The statue was said to have been found by a shepherd who was alerted by the sound of weeping coming from a thorn bush. "There," writes Lezana, "he saw the statue of the Most Blessed Virgin like a lily among thorns." In his time, the statue was over the main altar of the 15th century church.

The devotion to Our Lady of Light (*Notre Dames des Lumières*) arose from the miraculous cure of Anthony Denante, who in 1661 saw a marvelous light issuing from the ruins of a chapel of the Virgin near the village of Goult. Michael of the Holy Spirit, of the province of Touraine, but present in Provence as commissary general, obtained for the Order the restored chapel and erected a convent capable of lodging eight to ten religious (1664). He also wrote *The Pilgrimage of Our Lady of Light* (Lyon, 1666).

Bordeaux in Gascony had the unique privilege of harboring the mortal remains of the saint of the scapular, Simon Stock. Next to his chapel in the Carmelite church was that of Our Lady of Recovery, built by the English during their reign in France. There King Edward III, wounded in the arm, is said to have knelt to impetrate recovery. "Formerly God worked miracles there," Lezana remarks, "but now more rarely, as the devotion of the people has cooled."

Toulouse itself had, according to the legend, been founded on land provided by a Jew, converted by a vision of the Virgin. In any case, since the 13th century, devotion to Our Lady flourished there and many favors were recorded. In 1982, a pilgrim's badge of Our Lady of Mount Carmel in Toulouse, now in the Museum of London, was found during excavations for the Swan Lane Car Park, Upper Thames Street, London.

Marian Shrines and Images in Belgium

The Flemish province vied with Naples in devotion to their madonna. The provincial, Michael of St. Augustine, carried a picture of *La Bruna* with him everywhere and placed it before him wherever he stayed. At his insistence, the annual congregation of 1657 urged superiors to provide their churches and convents with copies of this painting which had come from Mount Carmel. The same year, Brussels set the example, followed by the other houses of the province. The prior of Aalst, Isidore of St. Giles, himself cured of an illness by the *Madonna della Bruna*, not only enshrined her picture in the conventual church but wrote *Enkindling of Devotion to the Miraculous Image of our Blessed Virgin of Naples* (Ghent, 1670). At Ieperen, attendance at the Wednesday devotions was so great that the crowd overflowed into the street. At Bruges many priests were required to hear confessions from five until noon. At the evening devotions, crowds were so dense one could walk over the heads, to use Isidore's picturesque expression. At Antwerp, the chapel of Our Lady of Naples in the conventual church was enriched with silver candlesticks and a silver arch over the picture.

La Bruna penetrated even into the inhospitable regions of the Calvinistic North, where Belgian Carmelites were active in the Mission of Holland. When the church of Rukven burned down in 1684, Archangelus of the Holy Spirit, in charge as pastor, installed a *Madonna della Bruna* in the new building.

Arlon in the Walloon vicariate also venerated *La Bruna*. Philip of the Visitation (Vizquin) wrote the history of her picture (Bruxelles, 1661).

The shrine of Our Lady of Sorrows, *Aan de Esche*, was served by the Carmelites of Gelderen and was credited with many miraculous cures, especially from hernia.

In the Gallo-Belgian province, the statue of Our Lady of Good Hope, which Jesuit scholastics had placed in a hollow tree in the forest near Valenciennes, became the object of popular devotion and the site of a church consecrated in 1629. Four years later, the Carmelites took charge and erected the convent of Bonne Espérance, which became the novitiate of the province.

Marian Shrines and Images in Germany

During the visitation of Germany in 1603, Voersio, secretary of the prior general, Henry Silvio, was particularly impressed by the devotion of the people to the statue in the Lady Chapel of the Carmelite church in Cologne. The statue was of glided stucco and "of such beauty that many who have knowledge of this sort of image say that its equal cannot be found."

Thönisstein in the same Lower German province venerated an ancient statue of Our Lady of Sorrows, said to have been miraculously found in a thicket (1388). In 1465, the Carmelites took over the shrine erected in her honor. A history of the devotion appeared in Cologne in 1665.

Undoubtedly one of the most famous Marian shrines of the Order north of the Alps was that of Our Lady of the Nettles (*Nesselmutter*) located at Heilbronn in the Upper German province. It was found in 1442 by a devout couple, Albert and Kunigunda, in a niche in a wall overgrown by nettles. Pilgrimages began to the spot (since it proved mysteriously impossible to move the statue), and in 1448 a Carmelite convent was founded there. The noted Benedictine polymath, John Trithemius (1462-1516), wrote the first history of the devotion, *De laudibus et miraculis B. Mariae in urticeto factis*. During the Reformation, the statue fell into Protestant hands and was lost; the present statue is a copy made in 1550. After various peregrinations, in 1661, it found a final resting-place in the scapular chapel in the Carmelite church of Straubing, where it has since been cherished with uninterrupted devotion.

Our Lady of the Nettles is a wooden *pietà* or *Vesperbild*, showing the Virgin holding the body of her Son after his crucifixion. "Artistically it is of mediocre quality," writes Fr. Hatzold, "but so much the greater is its value for the veneration of the faithful."

Straubing had, possibly from the time of its foundation from Regensburg in 1367, its own *Gnadenbild*, today preserved on the altar of St. Sebastian. The statue, popularly called "The Growing Virgin," shows Mary seated on a throne and smiling at her Child, whom she supports with her left hand and who is holding a round object. Both figures are crowned. That of the Virgin is lacking its right arm. The title alludes to the legend that the figure of the Infant grew on the arm of its mother. The other name for this image, "Our Lady of the Snow," refers to the snowy landscape on the *retable* of the altar on which it stands.

Marian Shrines and Images of Eastern Europe

Carmel in Eastern Europe, appropriately enough, possessed a number of famous Marian shrines. Cracow's Virgin *in Arenis* attracted the devotion of the faithful in 1587, when the image was found intact among the ashes, after the suburb was put to the torch for the defense of the city. The wall to which the painting was attached also outlasted the destruction wreaked on the church by the Swedes in 1655. With the establishment of peace in 1657, the church was rebuilt, and devotion to Our

Lady *in Arenis* resumed, all the more fervently for the trials of the past.

The Virgin, shown in half figure, wears an expression rather of concern and sadness. The child on her arm holds a book in his left hand, while his right rests on a round object offered by his mother. The picture was crowned by the Vatican Chapter in 1883.

When Obory was founded from Bygoszcz in 1605, the friars brought with them a miraculous statue, a *pietà*, one of two statues which the mother house possessed, the other being of Our Lady of the Scapular. Already the source of many miracles, Our Lady of Sorrows continued her benevolent ministry in this new location, as many votive tablets attested.

The miraculous image of Our Lady in the Carmelite church in Kochawina (Russia) is a painting showing Mary at half figure, holding the Child Jesus. Both have haloes and are richly clothed in damask garments. The Infant is holding a book. On May 26, 1755, after due investigation, the Archbishop of Lwow, Nicholas Ignatius Wyzycki, declared the picture thaumaturgic.

The Carmelite Virgin of Wola Gulowska is pictured offering an apple to her child, who raises his right hand in blessing. In this attractive picture, Mary's veil and mantle and the Child's tunic are of a dusky color with gilt borders.

Other Carmelite images of Mary crowned by the Vatican Chapter are those of Bialynicze and Botszowce in the Russian province, crowned in 1761 and 1777 respectively. In the Lithuanian province of St. George, Our Lady *Ostra Brama* of Wilno was crowned in 1927. The miraculous image of Bialynicze is a picture showing the half figure of Mary with the divine Child. Both are wearing crowns. Mary holds a scepter, the Child a globe. Wilno is remembered by Faci after Lezana.

The older authors also notice Jaslo (Lesser Poland), Poznan (Greater Poland) and Sasiadowice (Russia). Jaslo was saved from financial ruin by the fact that her statue over the main altar began to work miracles, attracting many suppliants and their generous alms. The miraculous image of Poznan is in the style of an icon, the half figure of the Virgin and the Child encased in silver. Mary is holding the scapular, and she and the Child are crowned.

Marian Shines and Images in Monasteries of Women

The nuns, too, were the privileged custodians of Marian images. Famous is that of Our Lady of Consolation at Vilvoorde. This statue had been venerated in the beguinage of Our Lady of Consolation and was the gift in 1247 of Sophia, Duchess of Brabant, who had received four statues from her mother, St. Elizabeth of Hungary. The other three Sophia gave to her sister-in-law, Mechtilda, who in turn bestowed one on the Carmelites of Haarlem. "The fair Order of Carmel should rejoice," writes Lezana, "that of four most precious jewels it should have two." When the Carmelite nuns took over the beguinage of Vilvoorde in 1469, they also took charge of its miraculous Virgin. In 1579, during the Calvinist reign of terror the statue was saved by a lay sister, Catherine Vayems, who, dressed as a peasant, smuggled it out of the city in a swath of hay on her head. At Mechelen, where the nuns fled, the statue escaped unharmed in the seizure of the city by Olivier van den Tempel in 1580. In 1587, when the *gueux* again sacked Vilvoorde, the statue once more remained intact. During the continual wars of the 17th century, the nuns several times carried their precious treasure to safety in other cities, Brussels,

Antwerp, Mechelen.

The statue consists of a bust of the Virgin holding the Infant on her left arm, is carved from oak and 63 cm. in height. "The features, appropriately colored," writes H. P. Vanderspeeten, "have a remarkable expression of tenderness, which reassures and consoles."

Treasured in the monastery of Sion in Bruges was the Virgin painted by Gerard David in 1509, today in the Museum of Rouen.

The history of the monastery of Madrid is closely bound up with its miraculous image of Our Lady of the Marigolds (*de las Maravillas*); in fact, the building was the gift of Philip IV in gratitude to this Virgin for recovery from illness (1646). The figure was about four and a half feet high. Mary supported the Child and held a flower in her hand. The nuns managed to safeguard their treasure during the vicissitudes of the 19th century, but in the civil war (1936-1939) the Reds discovered it in the patio of the monastery and burned it.

This lengthy but inadequate account of the Marian shrines of the Order in the 17th and 18th centuries is most fittingly closed with the words of Francis Voersio, who visited many Carmelite centers of Marian devotion throughout the world: "Because the Order bears the title and name of our Lady, all Carmelite churches are frequented by the people with great devotion in every part of the world; nor is there a church of the Order in which there is not a chapel or altar of this Mother of God, cared for with great reverence."

Chapter 4

The Carmelite Nuns, 1600-1750

In 1600, there existed less than fifty cloistered Carmelite monasteries, not as many as there are today. By 1750, the Order numbered over a hundred.

The monasteries catered to the nobility and the rising wealthy bourgeois class. Girls of humble social origins tended to become lay sisters. Recruitment often took place at a very early age and by fiat of the head of the household, who for that matter had no less authority in arranging marriages. It should not be imagined that all girls were regimented into the convent; oftentimes parental opposition had to be overcome before a girl could realize her dream of becoming a nun.

The fervid Baroque spirituality, its penances, its mysticism, is nowhere more evident than in the monasteries. New foundations were generally made under the aegis of reform. The effect of the Stricter Observance on existing monasteries remains to be investigated.

In 1653, the prior general, John Anthony Filippini, drew up constitutions for Carmelite nuns, which were approved by the general chapter of 1680 and published the same year in Venice. Few monasteries, however, showed any inclination to adopt them.

In Italy, growth was particularly marked in the Kingdom of Naples, where Carmelite nunneries had been few, and in the Venetian Republic, where they had been wholly lacking. In many cases, monasteries grew out of that peculiarly Italian institution, the *conservatorio*. Of various kinds, the conservatories that concern us here were houses of religious women without cloister or vows, which provided an education for girls, especially with a view to recruitment for religious life. Such conservatories corresponded to the needs of the upper middle class, which aspired to a good education but was not always eligible for admission to the monasteries reserved for the nobility. Conservatories were easier to found, because the lack of cloister and solemn vows made the sisters' commitment less irrevocable and consequently eased the economic requirements for papal cloister and the consent of the municipality for foundation. As a rule, Carmelite conservatories were intended for the contemplative life, kept a cloister as a private commitment, admitted children and young girls principally as candidates for the Order, and applied for papal enclosure as soon as feasible.

St. Mary of the Angels, Florence

St. Mary of the Angels in Florence, which attracted the daughters of the leading families of that great city, was the Order's most important nunnery in Italy, although it had passed under the jurisdiction of the archbishop in 1520 and had little to do with the superiors of the Order. Made illustrious by the presence of St. Mary Magdalen de' Pazzi, the monastery greatly influenced the other Carmelite nunneries of Italy. Its constitutions, revised in accordance with the saint's suggestions (Florence, 1611), were accepted or imitated in other Carmels.

By 1624, the old and decrepit premises no longer sufficed for the eighty nuns who composed the community. That year, Pope Urban VIII gave them the imposing Cistercian abbey in the Piazza Savonarola, Borgo Pinti, with its beautiful church adorned with paintings by Botticelli, Perugino, Ghirlandaio, and other masters.

The interest in the monastery of Urban VIII, formerly Maffei Barberini, of Florence, may be explained in part by the presence there of his nieces, Innocenza of the Incarnation (1559-1666) and Grace of the Blessed Sacrament (1607-1665). It was this pope who on May 8, 1626, beatified Sr. Mary Magdalen de' Pazzi.

After the death of St. Mary Magdalen, religious fervor continued unabated. Of the saint's contemporaries, her novice mistress and prioress, Evangelista Del Giocondo (1534-1625) and her girlhood companion and tireless amanuensis, Pacifica del Tovaglia (1566-1627), long outlived her and carried forward the memory and reality of her holiness. Many of the saint's novices, it need hardly be said, did honor to her training: Mary Sommai (1580-1615), Catherine Angelica Ximénez (d. 1627), Mary Grace Pazzi (1587-1656).

Among the outstanding figures of our period was Sr. Minima of St. Philip Neri Strozzi (1617-1672). Left an orphan at nine years of age, she was reared by her maternal grandmother Ginevra Martellini in the house of her uncles. Another uncle, the Oratorian, Peter Bini, directed her youthful piety, but when her family objected to the public practices of penance he imposed, the archbishop of Florence, Peter Niccolini, substituted him with the Carmelite, Albert Leoni. It was no doubt due to his influence that she decided to enter the monastery of St. Mary of the Angels (1634). Much of her life was occupied with the responsible offices of prioress and novice mistress. Besides maxims, conferences, and letters published in her biographies she wrote *Istruttioni spirituali* (Perugia, 1671).

One of Sr. Minima's notable subjects and her biographer was Serafica Orlandini (1650-1727). She was greatly attached to her only brother, more so after the death of her parents, but when he also died, she took it as a sign that God was calling her to himself. Lives of St. Teresa and Mary Magdalen de' Pazzi inclined her to Carmel, but left her undecided which Order to choose. Eventually, she entered the monastery of St. Mary of the Angels (1667), renouncing without a qualm the wealth to which she was sole heiress. By her holiness of life, practical sense and qualities of leadership, she contributed as few others to the spiritual and material welfare of the community. For many years, she served as *camerlenga*, or bursar, and placed the monastery on a secure financial basis, in spite of the frequently difficult times. Grand Duke Cosimo III learned to appreciate her qualities in the course of the building of a chapel in honor of St. Mary Magdalen de' Pazzi, which he commissioned in the monastery church. Elected prioress eight times, she served in this capacity for twenty-one years. She reintroduced perpetual adoration of the Blessed Sacrament, for some reason discontinued since the days of the saint, and added a year of novitiate to the period of formation of candidates. In times when the most ferocious penances were practised, she advised mortification of the will. Prayer for her was above all doing the will of the Father as expressed in the Lord's Prayer. She stressed the essential Christian qualities of meekness and charity.

Among Sr. Orlandini's literary remains are a revised edition of Puccini's life of St. Mary Magdalen de' Pazzi (Lucca, 1716) and of Strozzi's life of Sr. Minima (Florence, 1737). She had previously written a *Brief Sketch of the Life of Sr. M. Minima* (Lucca, 1717) with an appendix of Minima's spiritual maxims. She also wrote a volume of collected lives of the sisters of St. Mary's monastery and a life of Gesualda of St. Joseph Gianni (1654-1725) which remained unpublished.

Biographer in turn of Serafica Orlandini and of her eight companions in the novitiate was Sr. Teresa Mary Magdalen Trenta (1670-1740). Daughter of a distinguished family of Lucca, she is the subject of an interesting romantic story. When King Frederick IV of Denmark, then heir apparent, visited Lucca in 1692, he met Mary Magdalen at a ball in his honor and was evidently much taken with her. After his return to Denmark and her entry into the monastery of St. Mary's in Florence, he sent her royal gifts and on his second visit to Italy in 1708 did not fail to visit her on March 21. One would like to think that their long conversation concerned something other than an attempt on the part of the nun to convert the king to Catholicism, as pious biographers assert. In the course of her long life, Teresa served as novice mistress and prioress. She is credited with an anonymous *Ristretto della vita di Santa Maria Maddalena de' Pazzi*, printed in Lucca by Salvatore and Giovanni Domenico Marascandoli. Her lives of Serafica Orlandini and companions remained unpublished.

Rome, Monterotondo, Vetralla

St. Mary's gave rise to the illustrious monastery of the Incarnation in Rome, requested, or ordered, by Urban VIII. The prioress of St. Mary's, Mary Grace Pazzi, niece of the Florentine saint, was chosen to head the new community which included, besides the two papal nieces, Innocenza and Grace, six other nuns, among them the newly professed Minima of St. Philip Neri. The pope settled the Carmelites near at hand to the Quirinal, at Quattro Fontane in the Strada Pia. The brief of foundation is dated August 1, 1639. When Mary Grace and three others returned to Florence, Sr. Innocenza became prioress. Urban's sister-in-law, mother of his two nieces, Donna Constance Barberini (1575-1644), also joined the community, but was allowed to make profession only on her deathbed. By 1654, the community numbered twenty-four. Urban had expressly specified that only daughters of nobility be admitted. Innocenza drew up *Constitutions* (Rome, 1658), using as her sources the constitutions of the Carmelites, Jesuits and Visitandines. At the same time, *Essercitii spirituali* (Rome, 1658) practised in the monastery were published. For obvious reasons, the monastery and its nuns were called "*Le Barberine.*"

Sr. Innocenza absented herself briefly from Rome in order to found the monastery of Mount Tabor in nearby Monterotondo. *Instruttioni* published for this monastery in Rome, 1668, followed the general lines of the constitutions of the Roman motherhouse.

The Barberine also founded the monastery of Mount Carmel in Vetralla in the diocese of Viterbo. It was a devout and zealous parish priest, Benedict Baldi (1632-1694), a model of Counter-Reformation priesthood, who conceived the idea of enriching his native town with a monastery of contemplative nuns. Through his efforts, the ancient fortress of Vetralla was converted into a monastery. There he gathered eight young women to form a conservatory, until contemplative nuns could be found to instruct them in cloistered living. The prioress of the Incarnation, Teresa of the Mother of God Rasponi, offered to provide assistance. Authorization was granted by Clement IX in February of 1669, and three Carmelites were dispatched to Vetralla: Minima of St. Mary Magdalen de' Pazzi (Anguillara), her sister Angela Catherine of Jesus, and Angela Teresa of Jesus in Glory (Corsini). They returned to Rome in 1674, after the Vetralla community was well established and Sr. Mary Magdalen of the Blessed Sacrament had been elected prioress. In 1695, the cornerstone was laid of a church, blessed in 1711. The benefactor of the monastery in this undertaking was Prince Livio Odescalchi, nephew of Innocent XI. The architect was Carlo Buratti, who also added a wing to the monastery, completed around 1732.

The monastery of Mount Carmel in Vetralla was blessed to have for a while the spiritual ministrations of the founder of the Passionists, St. Paul of the Cross (1694-1775).

The Venetian Monasteries

In the North, an unusual development took place in the Republic of Venice, where no Carmelite nunneries had yet been founded. Responsible for this growth was Marietta Ferrazzi, known in religion as Angela Ventura of the Blessed Sacrament (1623-1688).

Luigi Ferrazzi, a weaver of Venice, and his wife, Magdalen Poli, produced no fewer than twenty-three offspring. Lest environmentalists become needlessly alarmed, let it be said at once that all, except Cecily and Marietta, perished in the disastrous plague of 1630. The two surviving orphans were placed, first with an uncle, later with a devout lady, Modesta Salandi, living near the Carmelite monastery. Her spiritual director, Master Bonaventure Pinzoni, took a special interest in Marietta, struck by her intelligence and piety. She became proficient not only in all the feminine arts, so that she took over the management of Modesta's household, but under Master Pinzoni's tutelage learned reading, writing, and other scholarly attainments.

Marietta was undoubtedly a young woman of strong character and unusual intelligence and piety. She was soon attracting other girls to her ideals of religious dedication and making practical plans for obtaining a house where they might live together. In 1643, at twenty years of age she signed a contract to purchase an abandoned Franciscan monastery for 3,000 ducats. Fifteen women joined Marietta in the conservatory dedicated to St. Teresa. They wore modest secular dress and recited the divine office according to the Carmelite rite, taught them by Master Bonaventure. The prudent virgin further guaranteed the stability of her house by placing it under the *ius patronato* of the Republic (1648). At the same time, the restored church was declared fit for sacred functions. The sisters also adopted the habit of Carmel. Their original design was to follow the constitutions of St. Teresa, but eventually they accepted those composed by Filippini. In 1667, the monastery was declared cloistered and immediately subject to the general of the Order. Pinzoni was appointed commissary or delegate. The community had grown to thirty-seven, a new church had been built, the monastery enlarged. Before the death of the foundress, the monastery included almost a hundred nuns. Among its chaplains or commissaries was Jerome Aimo.

Besides this impressive achievement, Sr. Mary Angela also has to her credit foundations at Verona (1654), Padua (1662), and Vicenza (1670).

The Mantuan Congregation

For the nuns under its care, the Mantuan Congregation published constitutions composed by John Baptist Guarguanti (Bergamo, 1656). The *"Convertite"* of Bologna also issued their own legislation (Bologna, 1738), as did the nuns of Sutri (Ronciglione, 1743).

The thirteen monasteries of the Congregation - Parma, Reggio Emilia, Brescia, Ferrara (San Gabriele), Mantua, Trino, Florence (San Barnaba), Sutri, Vinovo, Alhino, Ferrara (*"Convertite"*), Ferrara (Santa Lucia), Bologna (*"Convertite"*) - experienced a modest increment.

The monastery of St. Ursula in Bergamo had been founded in 1573. There, thirty sisters followed a Rule composed by St. Charles Borromeo. The Congregation undertook their direction in 1609. In 1656, they adopted the Carmelite habit and cloister. Two nuns, Michela Caria and Anne Felicity Marina, came from Albino to initiate them into the Carmelite way of life. The former became "abbess," the latter prioress. The monastery remained under the jurisdiction of the bishop.

In Camaiore, the Congregation took over a pre-existing conservatory, founded in 1590 by Mary Magdalen Buonucelli. Leading spirit in the change which took place in 1634 was Jacinta Ricci, known in religion as Cherubina of the Lamb of God (1601-1663). An orphan, Jacinta at twelve years of age ended up in the care of her two paternal aunts. When one of these died, the other placed her niece, aged fifteen, in the conservatory of Camaiore. The *Spiritual Exercises* of St. Ignatius convinced her that she should embrace the religious life. She made her simple vows in 1634. Under the direction of Fr. John Baptist Cioni, she made rapid progress in prayer, in time being favored even with mystical experiences. In 1628, she was made mistress of novices. When the conservatory adopted the Carmelite Rule and cloister, Sr. Cherubina was elected subprioress. Also due to her influence were a number of particular customs thenceforth observed in the monastery. The foundress, Sr. Mary Magdalen, lived under cloister for two years before her death in 1636, aged 62. From 1643, Cherubina served two terms as prioress. The last three years of her life were consumed by her last illness. Her confessor, Fr. Jerome Fiorentini, assisted her in her last moments.

The monastery of Novellara was founded in 1668 at the request of Alphonse Gonzaga II, Count of Novellara and Bagnoli, and dedicated to his favorite saint, Teresa of Avila. Three tertiaries were fetched from Reggio to make the foundation: Ursula Vecchi Mellari, Mary Magdalen Asassia, and Angela Catherine Mellari, Ursula's daughter. They became respectively Ursula Mary of St. Joseph, Mary Magdalen of the Cross, and Angela Catherine of St. Joseph. They lodged in a house near the Carmelite church belonging to the confraternity of Our Lady of Mount Carmel. By 1674, six other women had joined the community. A monastery was begun in 1679; the church of St. Teresa was blessed in 1684.

Holy Name monastery in Velletri was founded through the beneficence of Fulvio Mariola. On May 12, 1641, the first twelve nuns were given the Carmelite habit in a solemn ceremony in the cathedral. Among them was the widow of the founder, Lucile Assalonne, who took the name Anne in religion. A nun from the monastery of Sutri, Clara Androsilla, initiated the community into the Carmelite way of life.

On the other hand, in 1616, Vinovo ceased to exist due to political conditions.

In 1661, Jerome Ari visited the monasteries of Brescia, Albino, Trino, Reggio, and Florence. He would have liked to introduce the perfect common life, he told the 59 nuns in Brescia, but since the poverty of the community did not permit it, he contented himself with urging them to do so at the earliest possible opportunity. Meanwhile, they should make the *sproprio*, or declaration of their possessions, at least once a year. He was happy to find that the community of Albino (38 nuns) observed the perfect common life. "The state of the monastery," he noted about Trino with its community of 31, "although without the common life," otherwise did not require special decrees. The 73 nuns at Reggio Emilia, he decided, "needed rather to be encouraged in their life of virtue, since they are excellent religious, than to be corrected for defects." In the monastery of St. Barnabas in Florence with 69 nuns, Ari considered it sufficient to make, in the words of his secretary, Sebastian Fantoni Castrucci, "a pious and efficacious sermon."

Other Italian Monasteries

About a dozen other monasteries appeared in other parts of Italy.

Little is known besides the name of the Retreat of the Presentation and the monastery of the Holy Family which existed at Asti (Piedmont) during the 18th century.

Pescia in the Republic of Lucca was founded in 1634 by the Carmelite, Joseph Bonetti.

Pisa in the Archduchy of Tuscany, where the Carmelites had been present since 1249, finally received a monastery of nuns in 1630 through the initiative of John Baptist Petroni, later provincial of Tuscany. The foundation was affiliated to the Order in 1633. Here, Margaret Columba Lanfranchi (d. 1649) is remembered for holiness.

In the Papal States, the bishop of Iesi, Peter Matthew Petrucci (d. 1701) in 1684 made Carmelite the Franciscan conservatory founded in 1660. The still existing monastery received papal cloister in 1697. There the famous Franciscan preacher, St. Leonard of Port Maurice (1676-1751), erected one of his innumerable stations of the cross. Also in the diocese of Iesi, Montecarotto was founded in 1671 by the tertiary, Frances of Jesus, with the encouragement of the bishop, later Cardinal Alderano Cybo. Papal cloister was introduced in 1737.

Orvieto was founded in 1662 by Sr. Teresa Magdalen of the Conception (d. 1683), formerly of a non-Carmelite conservatory.

In the Kingdom of the Two Sicilies, the illustrious monastery of the Holy Cross of Lucca in Naples in 1637 made a second foundation in the same city, the monastery of the Blessed Sacrament, which followed the reform of St. Mary della Vita. In 1627, Srs. Faustina Giscale and Felicity Bonelli, of the same monastery of the Holy Cross, had founded Somma. Castellamare, which already had a monastery founded from the Holy Cross in 1560 in the 18th century seems also to have had a second monastery dedicated to St. Teresa.

Little is known of the Carmelite monasteries in Avellino (1623), Montecorvino (1766), and Solofra (1697).

In spite of its numerous friaries, Sicily for some reason never had many nunneries. To Messina and Palermo was added Siracusa, founded in 1717 as a conservatory by Sr. Carmela of the Blessed Trinity Montalto (d. 1780), assisted by Srs. Anna Maria and Felicity Gargallo. It received cloister in 1738 and followed the reform of Santa Maria della Scala, initiated by her friend, Jerome Terzo.

Monasteries of Spain: Castile

Spain added another dozen to its fourteen existing monasteries of cloistered nuns.

In the Castilian province, a monastery of the old Carmel finally came into existence in Madrid, the nation's capital. A devout lady, Joan de Baraona, obtained permission from Pope Paul V to found a *beaterio*. In 1613, the provincial, Anthony Pérez, advised her with regard to the purchase of a house and provided the first six candidates from among his penitents, clothing them in the tertiary habit of Carmel. When Doña Baraona ill-advisedly admitted two married women, separated from their husbands, as members of the community, religious observance began to suffer, due to the resulting distractions and lack of peace. The friars advised the sisters to move to another site (1617). It would seem that the foundress did not accompany them. In their new location, the sisters acquired the chapel of St. Anthony the Abbot, where through a grill they recited the divine office according to the Carmelite rite. They followed the constitutions for nuns issued by Ferdinand Suárez (Seville, 1603), a translation from the Latin of John Stephen Chizzola's decrees of 1595. In 1627, the community passed under the jurisdiction of the ordinary as a step toward obtaining cloister. This consummation was achieved in 1630. On that occasion, too, new constitutions were composed (Madrid, 1630, reprinted 1757). In 1644, three Discalced nuns from the monastery of La Imagen in Alcalá de Henares took over the offices of prioress, subprioress, and mistress of novices, "in order to instruct them (the nuns) in the manner and form of recollection." It was at this time, it would seem, that the monastery adopted the Roman rite.

The Madrid monastery, still in existence, takes its name from the miraculous image of Our Lady of the Marigolds (*de las Maravillas*), which the community acquired in 1627. King Philip IV was much devoted to this statue and, in consequence of a miraculous cure he attributed to it, built a new church for the monastery (1646).

Some confusion exists about another monastery in Madrid, sometimes listed as Discalced. Popularly known as "*Las Baronesas*," the monastery owed its existence to the generosity of Baroness Beatrix de Sylveira, sister of the Carmelite scripture scholar. Fray Francisco Majuelo turned over to her royal patents, which he had obtained for a monastery of Recollect Carmelite nuns, and which she lacked for the monastery of forty nuns she was willing to provide. On August 15, 1651, six young noblewomen took possession of the premises and two days later received the Carmelite habit according to the mitigated Rule. Four Discalced Trinitarian nuns filled the offices of authority until the neophytes learned the ways of contemplative life. The monastery, dedicated to the Nativity and St. Joseph, was placed under the jurisdiction of Archbishop Baltasar de Moscoso y Sandoval, who also wrote its constitutions (Madrid, 1662). Construction of a church and convent was undertaken by the architect John de Lobera in 1675, but took half a century to complete. The sisters lived the perfect common life. Well endowed, the monastery was intended for noblewomen of modest means, and no dowry was required.

The third volume of his commentary on the Gospels (bk. 6, qu. 8) John de Sylveira pays his sister the compliment of applying to her the passage in Proverbs 31 about the "good wife," exemplifying every detail of scripture from her foundation in the *calle Alcalá* in Madrid.

The Incarnation of Avila

After the death of St. Teresa (1582), the Incarnation of Avila was dominated by the personality of this great saint and dedicated to the perpetuation and imitation of her spirit and to the propagation of devotion to her. This direction was already indicated by the vicar general for Spain, Michael de Carranza, during a visit in 1588. On the occasion of the beatification of Teresa in 1614, the Carmelite friars and nuns vied with their Discalced brothers and sisters in the celebration of the event. No less a person than the learned Peter Cornejo de Pedrosa, professor at Salamanca, arrived to preach at the friary and the Incarnation. The canonization of the saint followed in 1622. When St. Teresa was declared patron of Spain, one of Carmel's most eloquent preachers, Christopher de Avendaño, delivered four sermons in Avila, one of them in the Incarnation.

Nevertheless, relations between the friars and sisters at times were less than cordial. The chapter of 1624 discussed resigning the direction of the Incarnation as burdensome to the superiors of the province and moreover ineffective, because the nuns appealed from their decisions to other tribunals. In the end, it was the nuns themselves who obtained from Pope Urban VIII a brief signed May 8, 1631, exempting them from the jurisdiction of the Order and placing them under that of the bishop. The prior of Avila, Diego Sánchez, protested and earned a rebuke from the definitory. The bishop, Francis Márquez de Gaceta, forbade the nuns under censure to have any communication with their Carmelite brothers. The thirteen nuns of the community of forty-three who wished to remain under the obedience of the Order were refused permission to transfer to another monastery.

Although Urban's brief adduces no reasons for the final break, it was apparently occasioned by an incident of a serious nature. In 1629, the prior of Avila, Celedón de los Santos, and a lay brother, Francis Ortiz, were found guilty of violating the cloister of the monastery by night and were condemned to the galleys. It was a dreadful scandal, for Celedón was a man of standing in the province, twice elected provincial. He lasted two years at his new occupation before being released to die. New constitutions were published for the monastery (Salamanca, 1662).

The separation from the Order's jurisdiction of the Incarnation put an end to recurring family squabbles but also isolated it from the mainstream of the Carmelite tradition in which it had grown.

Mary of Jesus, 1589-1662

Piedrahita at this time produced a famous sister, who, however, was sixty-two when she entered the monastery and already renowned as a visionary and holy person. Mary Muñoz was born of humble folk at Hoyos del Espino, a mountain village in the township of Piedrahita. Hoyos venerated Our Lady of the Hawthorn (*del Espino*), and Mary added this element to her surname. From childhood, Mary was given to spiritual things and was gifted with rare mystical endowments. The Carmel of Piedrahita preserves a pall she made at the age of six with a painting of the Virgin, "as I saw her in heaven." The cattle she was set to watch used to wait patiently outside the church without straying, while she assisted at Mass and made her devotions. Poor as she was, she managed by dint of extra work to buy a silver lamp in Salamanca for the Virgin of the Hawthorn, which was used in the church until 1735, when it was melted down to make a larger one. Mary was one of the witnesses who testified to miracles wrought in her favor by her beloved Virgin of the Hawthorn.

Her confessor, Andrew Sánchez Tejado (1569-1635) ordered her to write - or rather, to dictate, for she could not write - the first account of her life.

Mary had already tried in vain to enter the Discalced monastery at Alba de Tormes. In 1651, she attempted again to become a religious, this time at Piedrahita. The provincial of Castile, Diego de Viña, gave his consent, but when she appeared on the scene, the vicar of the monastery, Francis de La Concha, would not accept this old and unlettered woman, who moreover had no dowry. Doña Elizabeth Calderón, who favored her candidacy, took her into her cell as her maid. After he had heard Mary's confession, the vicar changed his mind as to her suitability for the religious life, and she was admitted as a lay sister. Her profession as Mary of Jesus del Espino, May 5, 1652, turned out to be a splendid occasion, on which her admirer, the mayor of Piedrahita, Diego Gómez, treated her and her family to a lavish banquet complete with musicians.

The nuns did not regret having admitted Sister Mary. She even managed to accumulate a dowry. At times they must have been amused at this simple peasant woman who stepped so unaffectedly over the threshold of the other world and who referred to the Lord as her "little Lamb." Through Doña Elizabeth's brother, Antonio Calderón, prior of the cathedral of Granada, Mary arranged to have the famous painter, Alonso Cano, reproduce her vision of Christ at the pillar of scourging, a painting still treasured by the nuns of Piedrahita. In 1675, at the behest of her superiors she dictated a second account of her life and spiritual itinerary. In the last four years of her life she became blind.

The general chapter of 1680 ordered Master Matthew Panduro y Villafañe to compile lives of Sister Mary of Jesus and of Sister Agnes and to send them to Master John Gómez Barrientos in Brussels, presumably to be printed there. Forty years elapsed before the appearance of Louis of St. Teresa's (d. 1714) posthumous life of Mary of Jesus, based on materials gathered by Master Matthew Grogero (Salamanca, 1720).

The other nun referred to by the general chapter, Sister Agnes, of Fontiveros, never found her Boswell. She seems to have been the Agnes de Castellanos briefly mentioned by Lezana.

The Catalan Monasteries

The most remarkable development in the situation of the nuns in Spain was their growth in Catalonia, where they had been entirely lacking. These foundations are specifically stated in the sources to observe the perfect common life.

Founder of the monastery of Villafranca del Panadés was Master Martin Román, authorized to this end by Theodore Straccio, on February 20, 1640. He would have looked to the province of Aragon for sisters to people his monastery, but Catalonia, overrun by the French, was cut off from the rest of Spain. Nothing daunted, he gathered six tertiaries into his monastery, blessed on April 22, 1643, and himself instructed them in the ways of Carmel according to the constitutions of St. Mary's in Florence. The first prioress was Mary Magdalen of St. Jerome. In 1647, the province accepted responsibility for the nuns, but in 1740 they passed under the jurisdiction of the bishop.

Master Román's makeshift community at Villafranca not only turned out to be excellent in itself but fruitful with life for others. Not long afterwards, he called on it to provide the membership for a monastery he planned to found in Barcelona. For this purpose he obtained letters patent from Leo Bonfigli on August 19, 1645.

The new monastery of the Incarnation was inaugurated on May 12, 1649, with two nuns from Villafranca, Gertrude of the Child Jesus (prioress) and Teresa of Jesus, and three novices, soon joined by five others. Master Román again undertook the direction of the sisters, living in a nearby house, and again introduced the Florentine constitutions. In 1674, a new chapel was inaugurated, the work of the master builder, John Termens. There Martin Román, who had died in 1663, found his last resting place.

The prior of the reformed convent of Valls, Master Angelus Palau, whose sister, Engracia of the Holy Spirit, was a nun in Villafranca, in 1676 obtained a commission from Emile Giacomelli to bring Carmelite sisters to Valls. One of his penitents, a wealthy widow, Frances Saperas y Vidal, provided the financial means, to which Palau added an inheritance of his own. Doña Frances, moreover, with two cousins requested admission to the new foundation; with a candidate for the lay sisterhood they were sent to Barcelona to try their vocation. There, on December 5, 1680, the four aspirants were given the habit, Doña Frances receiving the name Frances of the Presentation. Two days later, headed by the prospective prioress, Margaret of St. Elijah, they set out for Valls, passing through Villafranca, where they were joined by Engracia of the Holy Spirit and Anna Maria of Christ. The new monastery of the Presentation was inaugurated on December 15. Two years later, the nuns from Barcelona and Villafranca returned to their original monasteries, and Sister Frances took over the reins. During her long term of office, 1682-1717, she placed the monastery on a firm foundation of fervent observance, becoming in effect its spiritual as well as its material foundress. In 1719, religious services were begun in the new chapel, to which the finishing touches were added only in 1781.

"That now makes three monasteries of reformed Carmelite nuns that Your Reverence has in this your province," the provincial, John de Cancer, wrote to the prior general, Ferdinand Tartaglia, January 4, 1681. "They shed much luster and esteem on our holy habit for the great virtue and perfection with which they live, observing with all rigor the common life." On July 24, 1683, Cancer was able to report to Tartaglia the foundation of another reformed monastery earlier that month in Vich.

In spite of the fact that Vich already had a Discalced Carmelite monastery, municipal authorities in 1663 authorized putting into effect a legacy left in 1660 by Francis Llucía de Codina y de Pons, canon of the cathedral of Vich, benefactor also of the Incarnation of Barcelona. The Discalced, Joseph of the Conception (d. 1689), was the architect of the monastery, which, however, suffered many delays in its construction. Conventual life was finally initiated on July 1, 1693, by Sister Mary of the Cross, of Villafranca, and by four professed nuns and three novices of Barcelona. The benefactor, Canon Codina, fortunate heir to the sisters' prayers and sacrifices, was entombed in the chapel constructed between 1731 and 1741. The *retable* of the main altar picturing the Presentation, title of the foundation, was the work of Mariano Colomer.

Eulalia of the Cross, 1669-1725

Among the dedicated women who peopled the Catalan monasteries, Eulalia of the Cross (1669-1725) is especially remembered and revered. Her parents, John Mora and Magdalen Xammar, united two noble families of Corbera and Gerona respectively. In their case, the old hagiographers' chestnut, that they were as noble for virtue as for blood, is no cliché, at least if the fruit of their union is any indication. Of their ten children, all girls, three became Cistercians, three Jeronymites, and three Carmelites. Of two boys by John's previous marriage, Francis became a Jesuit and eloquent orator. Clementia, Ignatia and Eulalia entered the Incarnation of Barcelona.

As a child of nine, Clementia accompanied the foundresses to Vich, was professed as Clementia of Jesus and Mary (1689) and in time became prioress. Eulalia was seven when she entered the Incarnation and was professed in 1685 at the canonical age of sixteen. She became a religious of outstanding virtue and exalted prayer. Her writings in two volumes are preserved in a copy made by her spiritual director, Joseph Cabrer (d. 1769).

The Monasteries of the Province of Aragon

At the beginning of the 17th century, the province of Aragon counted three cloistered monasteries: the Incarnation and St. Anne's in Valencia, and Onteniente.

Foundress of the monastery of St. Michael in Sariñena in 1612 was Sr. Frances Pérez de Botanos, who subsequently became the first prioress of the monastery of the Incarnation and St. Michael in Huesca. This foundation was made in 1622 by the local prior, Peter Jerome Sobrino, with moneys donated by Doña Anne de Santa-pau, who herself received the habit there. In 1623, the Confraternity of St. Michael turned over its church to the nuns. In 1656, a second Carmelite monastery, dedicated to the Assumption, rose in Huesca when eleven nuns under Sr. Beatrix Pastor opted to live under episcopal jurisdiction.

With the foundation of the Incarnation of Zaragoza the province acquired a monastery in this important center. Doña Anne de Carrillo, widow of Peter García and penitent of Fray Anthony Oliván y Maldonado, desired to donate her house for a monastery which she herself could afterwards enter. Her brother, Don Martin de Carrillo, canon of the cathedral, whom she consulted, at first attempted to dissuade her. Later he reconsidered, and on July 11, 1615, the new monastery opened with nuns fetched from the Incarnation of Valencia: Seraphina Andrea Bonastre, prioress; Agnes de Ariño, subprioress and novice mistress; Catherine de Horto, bursar; Magdalen Sanz, portress. Besides Doña Anne and two nieces, three other young women entered the cloister that day. The monastery of the Incarnation of Zaragoza in time came to number about one hundred nuns and ran into serious financial difficulties, requiring constant financial assistance from the province.

The Escobar Sisters

"He would do a distinctive service," Fr. Valerius Hoppenbrouwers, O. Carm., writes of this monastery, "who would dedicate a monograph to this Carmelite community and its more important members, among them the three Escobar sisters," Mary, Margaret, and Marianne. Their mother, Marianne Villalba y Vincente (1565-1623), was herself a person of no mediocre piety. She was a tertiary of the Order of Minims, and her spiritual director was John Pérez of the same Order. The link between Carmel and her daughters seems to have been Fray Anthony Oliván who knew Caspar Escobar and often spoke to him in enthusiastic terms of the religious fervor of the newly founded monastery of Carmelite nuns.

Of the three sisters, the eldest, Mary (1599-1654), entered the Incarnation at the relatively mature age of seventeen and was professed the following year, 1618. Of a serene character, instinctively inclined to contemplation, Mary was a pillar of strength to her younger sisters. Her account of her interior trials and graces of prayer has been published. Marianne (1603-1660) was professed the year after Mary, but had been living in the monastery from the age of fourteen. She long survived her short-lived sisters. At the age of nine, Margaret (1608-1641) was admitted to Holy Communion by the famous Carmelite preacher, Christopher de Avendaño, in Zaragoza to preach for the Confraternity of the Blessed Sacrament in the parish of St. Paul, to which the Escobars belonged. The next year, as an *educanda*, she followed her older sisters into Carmel and was given the habit in 1620. Entrusted with the delicate task of guiding these sisters, all gifted with mystical graces, was Bartholomew Viota (d. 1641). To his suggestion we owe their accounts of their interior life.

Seraphina Bonastre, 1571-1649

Seraphina Bonastre, first prioress of Zaragoza, was born in Valencia, the youngest of three daughters of Peter Bonastre and Magdalen Sistero. Her first guides in the spiritual life were an aunt and Jerome de Mur, S.J. Feeling called to the religious life, she entered the Incarnation of Valencia and in 1588 made her profession in the hands of Michael Carranza, then provincial. Spiritual directors in these first years of her religious life were John Sanz and, in his absence, Angelus Palacios. Such was her progress in religious perfection that she was chosen to head the sisters selected to make the foundation in Zaragoza. She established the new community in great fervor of spirit, herself providing the lead in all things. She indicated her readiness to comply with the request of Doña Anna de Carrillo that the monastery be modelled on the usages of the Discalced, "since we are all shoots springing from the same tree, the roots and foundation of which is the continual meditation on the most holy life of Christ Our Lord. It is to this that we are principally obliged by the Rule under which we all strive and which in this matter has not been mitigated for the Observants." Seraphina's autobiography and story of her soul, edited by Peter de Oxea, S.J., and preceded by a brief account of her life by Joseph Andres, S.J., was published by Raymund Lumbier (Zaragoza, 1675).

Francis Pastor, of the province of Aragon, published constitutions for Carmelite nuns based on those of Ferdinand Suárez (see below) and the decrees of Chizzola (Valencia, 1731).

The Andalusian Monasteries

In 1600, Andalusia had more Carmelite monasteries than all the other Spanish provinces put together. By the end of the century, this could no longer be said, though it still had the most monasteries of any single province, in spite of only a modest growth. Three nunneries were added to those already existing in Ecija, Granada, Seville (Incarnation), Antequera, Aracena, Osuna, Utrera, Seville (St. Anne's).

The provincial, Ferdinand Suárez, published *Constitutions of the Carmelite Nuns of the Regular Observance, Composed by Apostolic Authority* (Seville, 1603), which made available in Spanish Chizzola's decrees of 1595.

The Incarnation of Granada published its own *Perpetual Constitutions* (Granada, 1735).

Villalba del Alcor was founded from St. Anne's, Seville, in 1619. There, Sr. Beatrix Jinoco (1577-1622) had long desired to live in a monastery where the perfect common life was observed. When she learned from her sister Agnes that their uncle, Franco García Jiménez, planned to subsidize the founding of a monastery in Villalba del Alcor near her native Mancanilla, she convinced him that it should be Carmelite. The contract agreed to by the provincial, Diego de Miranda, stipulated that Beatrix should be prioress for life and that the special statutes she had drawn up for perfect observance be enforced, together with the constitutions of the Order. Three professed nuns, one novice and two postulants accompanied Sr. Beatrix from Seville to form the new community.

Providence arranged that Sr. Beatrix' lifelong priorate should be of short duration. When she died after three years in office, the provincial, Alphonsus Sobrino, deemed it advisable to import Elizabeth de Vargas (1572-1627) to head the young community. A native of Carmona, Elisabeth was professed in the monastery of Our Lady *de los Remedios* in Ecija (1588). There she had already lived for many years according to the primitive Rule and so was fully qualified to fill the office of superior in a reformed monastery.

From Villalla a foundation was made in 1662 at Cañete la Real through the generosity of Melchor de Rojas y Saaverda, former rector of the University of Osuna and native of Cañete, who contributed buildings which had been a tavern. The provincial, Estacio Gutierrez, summoned four nuns from Villalba under Sr. Catherine of Jesus. Another, Jerónima Román, who aspired to live the reformed life, came from Antequera and took the name Jerónima of St. Elisha. The new reformed monastery was dedicated to the Blessed Sacrament.

Sr. Catherine of Jesus (1598-1676) was born in Seville of the noble Viscayan family of the Zabaletos. After the death of her parents, she was reared by an aunt, a devout woman who brought her niece with her into a *beaterio*. A Dominican confessor encouraged Catherine's desire to enter a cloistered monastery. She would no longer have been a child but a mature person when she entered the monastery of Villalba, which, however, probably had not been long founded, for the common and recollected life had still not been firmly established. Catherine labored so efficaciously to bring this about that the provincial was able to apply there confidently for the foundresses of a reformed monastery in Cañete. This monastery, too, Catherine, several times elected prioress and novice mistress, confirmed in the same tradition of reform.

St. Joseph's in Puerto Rico

In spite of the fact that the Order counted many friaries in the New World, the sisters had never set foot there. The Carmelites of Spain had not been allowed to make permanent foundations in the colonies, and Portugal, which might have provided sisters for Brazil, had few monasteries. There was also the practical difficulty of supporting cloistered monasteries in a society still struggling to establish itself.

The foundation of a cloistered Carmelite monastery in America came about somewhat after the manner of Las Baronesas in Madrid, which however it preceded.

In 1642, the noble lady, Anna de Lanzós, donated her palace for a monastery in San Juan de Puerto Rico. Royal permission was obtained in 1646. When efforts to import Carmelite nuns from Seville proved unavailing, three Dominicans, Louise de Valdelomar, Mary de Ayala, and Jerónima de Otañes, were fetched from Queen of Angels monastery in Santo Domingo to initiate religious life according to the Carmelite Rule (1651). Doña Anna entered the monastery as Anna of Jesus, together with her sister, Antonia of the Incarnation. After the Dominicans returned to their monastery, Anna of Jesus took over as prioress. The monastery, dedicated to St. Joseph, does not seem to have had cloister. The Dominicans laid a firm foundation of Carmelite life, for the monastery of St. Joseph, isolated, unaided, flourished as none other until the present day.

The Carmelite Sisters in Portugal

A fourth monastery, Guimarães, was added to Beja, Lagos, and Tentúgal to complete the growth of the Order's nunneries in Portugal.

In 1685, a conservatory for needy girls was founded in Guimarães under the patronage of Francis Antuñes Torres. Two years later, the inmates received the Carmelite tertiary habit. In time, a church was built and cloisters added, so that in 1704 the conservatory became a cloistered monastery. The nuns made solemn profession in the name of the vicar general for Portugal, Master Anthony of the Incarnation. When the archbishop of Braga understandably challenged this informal arrangement, Benedict XIII sanated the situation, August 3, 1726. In 1745, the monastery passed under the jurisdiction of the bishop.

The Portuguese nunneries seem to have been affected even less than the friaries by the winds of reform abroad in other parts of the Order. In Beja, which was probably only a mirror of religious life as found in the other nunneries, the common life was not observed. Noble and wealthy nuns still had their own "houses," or living quarters, where they lived with their maids and infant candidates to religious life, often their nieces. Yet this monastery produced two of the most famous Carmelite nuns of the century.

Marianne of the Purification, 1623-1695

Marianne of the Purification Azevedo was born in Lisbon, the daughter of a wealthy goldsmith. The eldest of eleven children of Antonio Azevedo by his second wife, Maria da Cruz, Marianne remained at home until she was forty years old, living a life of retirement and prayer. For a while (1661), she wore the Theatine habit, until Rome forbade the practice. When her brother, Francis Azevedo, who was a Carmelite, became chaplain of the monastery of Our Lady of Hope (*Esperança*) in Beja, he persuaded her to enter it. She was professed in November 29, 1664, a mature woman with long experience of prayer and penance. In Carmel, Marianne did not find the opportunity for the prayer and solitude she longed for. The Esperança was a sprawling complex of "houses," or living quarters, containing over a hundred nuns. Together with another young nun, she was designated to share the house of Sister Brites da Graça and her maid. The continual visits and gossip sessions were a distraction to Marianne, who longed only to be alone with her Divine Spouse.

In Frei Anthony de Escobar (1618-1681), named confessor of the Esperança in 1667, she found a sympathetic friend, who unfortunately proved to be her worst enemy. Instead of making little of her visions, ecstacies, and locutions, he encouraged them, even publicized them, putting them to the test in public. Inevitably, the Inquisition turned its attention to this visionary nun who was causing such an uproar. The investigation, initiated in October, 1668, ended with a whimper. Its final stage began in February of 1670, when the Inquisitor, John da Costa Pimenta, appeared at the monastery door to question Marianne and its inmates. He found that the culprit herself had been made mistress of novices. Contrary to previous evidence, the sisters had nothing but praise for Marianne. Close investigation into an alleged fast by Marianne showed that in fact she had had absolutely nothing to eat the whole of the previous November. The dry well of the monastery, too, proved to contain water as a result of her prayers. After seven weeks of questioning, of which no written record remains, the Inquisitor with a word of assurance to the nuns returned to Evora, and nothing further was heard of the matter. Her contemporaries took this as a victory for Marianne. Recently it has been conjectured that Pimenta, experienced in the matter of visions, genuine or otherwise, concluded that Marianne was deluded but sincere and virtuous (the two conditions are not necessarily mutually exclusive) and persuaded the mesa of the Inquisition of Evora to bury the process in the archive. "In our case," Mauricio Bruni concludes, "the tribunal of the Holy Office is in no way the horrible monster it is usually pictured to be."

Marianne continued her life as before without interference from the Inquisition, and her reputation for sanctity grew with the years. After two terms as novice mistress, she served as prioress from 1680 to 1683. Marianne was by nature gentle and affable, in spite of her implacable asceticism, but she proved an effective leader, who brought greater calm and recollection to the monastery. Her most distinctive achievement was the establishment of a "desert," or area within the monastery precinct with cells to which the sisters could retire at will for solitude, prayer, and penance. There, Marianne spent the last twelve years of her life, finally in possession of the precious pearl of contemplation for which she had exchanged her all. There, too, she was visited in 1695 by the prior general, John Feijóo de Villalobos, who spent a long time in conversation with her and on leaving assured the sisters that he had been rewarded for all the fatigues of the visitation. The decrees of the subsequent provincial chapter under his presidency, treating at length the spiritual care of the nuns, may perhaps be traced to this conversation.

Marianne left a spiritual diary begun in 1668 at the insistence of Escobar and ending with the year 1675. In her last years, her mystical seizures seem to have decreased. Frei John da Luz had inherited the difficult task of directing this extraordinary woman.

Perpetua da Luz, 1684-1736

Perpetua da Luz was a native of Beja itself. Her parents, Manuel da Costa Diniz and Leonor de Jesus, were Carmelite tertiaries and reared their daughter in religious ways. It was only after the death of her father, to whom she was greatly devoted, that Perpetua at the relatively mature age of twenty entered the Esperança. With the reception of the habit on October 22, 1704, she began a comfortable and undistinguished religious life, until August 23, 1719, when she heard a sermon which proved a turning point in her life. She exchanged her elegant habit for one of rough wool, emptied her cell of its luxuries, and by a public act of renunciation surrendered her possessions to the monastery. Two nuns were assigned by the prioress, Ursula Teresa of St. Anthony, to see to her wants, since there was no provision for the common life. She also undertook a regime of fierce penitential practices which ruined her health and probably occasioned a seven year period (1722-1729) of hallucinations ascribed to the devil. Like many another holy but overzealous person she came to the belated conclusion that "great penances are only great illusions."

Meanwhile, however, she had experienced her first ecstasy in 1721, which initiated a series of supernatural phenomena ending only with her death. Her account of her spiritual experiences, written at the command of her spiritual directors, John de Souza and Joseph de Aguiar, perished in the earthquake of 1755, not, however, until part of it had been included in her biography by Joseph Pereira. "The writings of the Carmelite nun," writes Pablo Garrido, "despite their tormented psychology, strike one by their perfect orthodoxy, lived during difficult times. Unconsciously, she contributed to dissipating the fog of Quietism and specifically the doctrine of pure love. She makes a plea for loving God because he is he who is, but also for loving the virtues because they are the work of God."

The French Monasteries

Beyond the Italian and Iberian peninsulas, Carmelite nunneries remained few and far between. The marvelous renascence of Carmelite life there that expressed itself, among other ways, in the multiplication of friaries, had little similar resonance in terms of monasteries of nuns. The presence of the feminine branch of Carmel remained restricted mainly to the provinces in which John Soreth had erected the first cloistered monasteries: Belgium, Francia, and Touraine. The spread of Carmelite nunneries in France was hardly favored by the monopoly the influential Discalced nuns claimed to have for making Carmelite foundations outside Brittany.

At the beginning of the 17th century, the province of Francia counted monasteries at Liège and Huy. The latter became the seedbed of a luxuriant growth. From Huy, Dinant was founded in 1605. It was only poetic justice. Dinant had been established in 1455, but when it was sacked and burned by the troops of Charles, Count of Charolais, in 1466, part of the community took refuge in Huy. Other foundations from Huy were Rochefort (1626), Ciney (1630) and Fumay (1633). Ciney became Discalced in 1649. All these houses lay in the Belgian diocese of Namur, with the exception of Fumay in the diocese of Reims.

In Reims, too, was situated Charleville, founded in 1620 through the munificence of Charles I Gonzaga, Duke of Mantua.

In the territory of the province of Touraine, lay the monasteries of Nantes and Vannes, venerable foundations of Bl. Frances d'Amboise, who had been at pains to secure the right for her sisters to choose their confessors from any province. Such confessors were thereby absolved from obedience to their provincials. The privilege had made sense in previous centuries, but became an anachronism and a source of endless controversy after the French provinces were reformed.

As provincial, Philip Thibault was himself responsible for the foundation in 1622 of the monastery of the Holy Sepulchre at Rennes. It had the benefit of the spiritual ministrations of the exemplary members of the nearby friary, cradle of the reform of the Order. Not the least solicitous was Brother John of St. Samson, whom Thibault often led to the monastery. Two of John's spiritual daughters, foundresses who had come from Vannes, were Valence of St. Clare (1601-1628) and Gilette of St. Francis (1600-1647). Under the direction of Brother John, Valence made great progress in the interior life. Such was her love of God that she could not hear it spoken of without falling into ecstasy. One of these occasions was witnessed by Dominic of St. Albert. She filled a number of offices in the community and in spite of her youth became prioress.

Even before she had entered the monastery of Nazareth at Vannes, 1617, Gilette had dedicated herself to a life of prayer and penance. At Rennes, she, too, came under the influence of Brother John and other early figures in the Observance of Rennes. "The axis of her spiritual life was Christ," writes Fr. Wilderink. "It was her union to Christ that determined her relation to the eternal Father and the Virgin Mary. The Holy Spirit was her friend, her intimate. She felt herself raised by the Word and the Holy Spirit before the majesty of God the Father and in a special manner presented to him for adoption as his child." Her mystical union with God did not lessen her concern for her fellow man. She wrote a *Treatise* on the State and Union of the Church, which brought upon her the disapproval of her superiors and sisters. This tract and other spiritual writings have apparently been lost.

It may have been either to Valence or to Gilette that John of St. Samson wrote "one of his most beautiful letters of direction" (Suzanne Bouchereaux).

In 1627, Thibault became vicar of Nazareth in Vannes. That same year, he arranged for the monastery to make a second foundation at Ploërmel under the title of Bethlehem. It became Thibault's favorite monastery, "his beloved Bethlehem," to which he often returned.

Leader of the little band of four foundresses was Joan of the Assumption (d. 1645). She was greatly devoted to the Passion, and while meditating on this mystery, experienced in her body the sufferings of Christ. She is also remembered for her serene and imperturbable spirit.

Biographical sketches of a few of the sisters in this fervent community have come down to us. When the sisters enroute to found their monastery in Ploërmel stayed in the house of her father, Joan of the Child Jesus (d. 1670) was so impressed by their conversation and conduct that she followed in their footsteps.

On her way to arrange the contract of her betrothal to the nobleman, John Hallon de Lestriagat, Marie Therese of St. Stephen (d. 1673) stopped in at the monastery of Ploërmel to visit relatives of her fiancé. Later, a messenger met her underway with the news that John was gravely ill. She arrived in Rennes in time to have him die in her arms. After this, she decided to enter the monastery of Ploërmel. She was guided in this decision by Stephen of St. Francis Xavier, who had assisted her lover in his last hours.

Perrine of St. Teresa (d. 1673), of noble family, was devoted to the poor. At times, her generosity was such that it was to be feared that the sisters would go hungry, but the larder (miraculously, the sisters said) always contained enough for the needs of all. Marie of the Child Jesus (d. 1683) served as novice mistress and prioress. In keeping with her name, she was especially devoted to the Infant Jesus, a devotion the Touraine friars imported into the monasteries under their care, and had a confraternity erected in the church. Calliope of St. Francis (d. 1706) was so attracted to solitude that she made a vow not to leave her cell except for community acts and the claims of charity. This did not hinder her from being elected novice mistress and prioress.

For the nuns of Rennes and Ploërmel Stephen of St. Francis Xavier composed his *Exhortations monastiques* (Rennes, 1687).

In 1600, the sisters of Vannes elected John de Launay, ex-provincial, their confessor. He became their vicar in 1607 and served in that capacity until his death twenty years later. Launay did much to raise the spiritual level of the monastery, introducing many of the principles and practices of the Observance of Rennes. This process was continued and perfected by Thibault.

In true style of the Touraine reform, he set about providing structures apt for religious life. Nazareth was poorly arranged and unhealthy. Two or three sisters shared the same small cell. Thibault erected adequate buildings and separated the novitiate from the quarters of the professed. Needless to say, he stressed the interior life and the practice of prayer. He recommended the *Spiritual Combat* and commented on it often. Unfortunately, these conferences seem to have been lost. On his death in 1638, Thibault was interred under the main altar of the monastery church.

The monasteries in the province of Touraine, contemporary to the spiritual renewal of France and beneficiaries of the ministrations of their brothers in the initial fervor of reform, were unequalled in the quality of their religious life.

The Monasteries in Belgium, Germany, and Poland

In the territory of the Flandro-Belgian province, venerable nunneries existed in Bruges, Gelderen and Vilvoorde. When the Wallo-Belgian Vicariate was erected in 1681, Namur fell within its ambit.

Margaret of the Mother of God, of Sion monastery in Bruges, died in 1647, only twenty-eight years old, but the memory of her holy life remained green. Joan of the Cross gave Margaret her spiritual formation. She was long prioress and died with a reputation for holiness in 1653. The catalog of the Sion library, dated 1723, has survived and may provide an indication of the spirituality of the monastery.

It was from Bruges that Daniel of the Virgin Mary in 1663 obtained sisters for a foundation in Louvain.

During the wars between the Spanish Netherlands and Holland and France, Vilvoorde often lay in the path of the contending armies. The Carmelite sisters were forced to flee to Brussels, Antwerp, and Mechelen in 1621, 1635, 1667, 1695, 1702. In spite of these peregrinations, they managed to build a new church, consecrated in 1671. During the 18th century, the sisters enjoyed a well-earned peace and twice – in 1728 and 1778 – celebrated anniversaries of their miraculous statue of Our Lady of Consolation, acquired (it was thought) in 1228.

Two sisters of Vilvoorde whose fame for sanctity lived after them were Mary of St. Joseph (d. 1660), of noble parentage, who became prioress, and Petronella van der Elst (d. 1674), a lay sister whose brother Josse was abbot of Grimberg in Brabant.

Vilvoorde provided the sisters for a new foundation in Boxmeer. In 1666, the pastor of that town, Anthony Peelen, noted for zeal and charity, had bequeathed his property, "Elzendaal," for a monastery of nuns, and the provincial, Francis of Bonne Espérance, had no difficulty in obtaining it for the Order from Countess

Magdalen van den Bergh, who admitted to "a particular inclination and affection for the sisters of the Order of Mount Carmel" (1671). On September 1, 1672, Michael of St. Augustine, named vicar by Francis, appointed four sisters under Petronilla of St. Joseph for the proposed foundation. The roads between Vilvoorde and Boxmeer were beset with roving bands of marauding soldiers, but from her anchorhold in Mechelen Maria Petyt assured the sisters that they would arrive safely, as indeed happened on September 9. In that Catholic island of the Protestant North, the sisters undertook the education of girls. Cloister was imposed in 1678. In 1682, the cornerstone of a new monastery and chapel was blessed. Several times in the course of the 18th century, Boxmeer provided asylum for the community of Gelderen, fleeing before the disturbances of war.

A sister of the monastery of Namur noted for holiness was Sr. Anne Loison (1552-1631). From Namur, Marche was founded in 1620. Of the nuns of this monastery, Celestine of St. Simon Stock composed a biography (1678) of Scholastica of St. Elijah (1613-1650), in which he also provided a brief sketch of the life of Catherine of St. Paul.

In Germany, the Stricter Observance produced no monastery of nuns, and the house in Cologne of tertiary sisters with simple vows remained the only Carmelite establishment for women in Germany. In 1653, Filippini authorized the sisters to adopt the habit of the Touraine nuns and to wear the black veil, hence from that point onward they were probably cloistered contemplative nuns.

On the other hand, the Polish Carmelites introduced their sisters to their native country. As early as 1632, Bartholomew Golankovic, requested authorization of the prior general to found a monastery in Lwów, in which he proposed to enclose a group of noble young ladies, tertiaries of the Order. Straccio actually accorded the permission to Nicholas Dabrowski three years later, but the project does not seem to have been realized until 1677.

A Carmelite monastery was established in Dubno in 1702 through the munificence of Theophila Ludovica, Countess of Ostrog and Zastaw.

Chapter 5

The Third Order of Carmel

The *Cum nulla* of Nicholas V (1452) had granted apostolic approval to the various types of religious women in the Carmelite Order, "lest they seem to live without the protection of apostolic authority." Among the many privileges granted to the Carmelites by the *Mare magnum* of Sixtus IV (1476) is that of having a Third Order like the other mendicants, that is, a Third Order in the modern sense, as an association of both men and women, married and single, living in the world. The granting of such approval does not seem to have corresponded to an actual need, but simply formed part of the package of privileges which was the *Mare magnum*. The development of the Third Order in its present form lay only in our period. Lay persons living as Carmelites in the world are clearly distinguished from the friars and nuns and are given their own Rule applicable throughout the Order, their vows and obligations are clarified, they are organized into groups with external activities. This development in the Carmelite Order appeared to other Orders with tertiaries to be an unwarranted novelty.

Juridical Evolution of the Third Order

The *Manual de las beatas y hermanos terceros* (Sevilla, 1592) by Diego Martínez de Coria Maldonado already distinguishes three Orders of Carmelites: friars and nuns, *pinzochere, mantellates,* and *beatas,* and finally tertiaries. The latter comprise not only women but also men, not only celibates but all persons, married or unmarried. Tertiaries profess the two simple vows of chastity and obedience according to their state in life, which they are free to change. The distinction between tertiaries and confraternity members, however, is not yet clear. This distinction is made in the *Regla y modo de vida de los hermanos terceros y beatas de N. S. del Carmen* (Toledo, 1615), which Miguel de la Fuente composed for his tertiaries and which presents the Third Order fully developed in its modern form.

Authors who closely follow Miguel's *Regla* include John Tuaut and John Bonet. Others such as Peter of the Cross Juzarte, Rocco Albert Faci, show its influence.

Quite independent and important in its own right is the *Spiritual Treasure* (Catania, 1624) of Elijah Maruggi. Purported to be only a translation of the work by the same name of Mark de Guadalajara y Xavier (Zaragoza, 1616), it becomes an original work through Maruggi's additions, especially his Rule and statutes. Limited to unmarried women and widows bound by a vow of perfect chastity, the text is outstanding for clarity and order, clearly distinguishing, as none of its predecessors had, the Rule from explanatory statutes. "This body of laws of the Third Order," writes Tomás Motta, historian of the Third Order, "is far superior to all previous Rules, both as to its juridical character and its spiritual doctrine, so that it may be said that Elijah Maruggi produced a work in every way admirable."

The heir to some extent of La Fuente and Maruggi, Straccio's *Opusculum regularum et constitutionum pro tertiariis utriusque sexus* (Roncilione, 1637) is important as the first attempt to provide an official Third Order Rule for the whole Order. Its true author is probably the canonist, John Baptist Lezana, the second volume of whose *Summa quaestionum regularium*, printed the same year of 1637, contained an excellent tract on the Third Orders. Straccio would have availed himself of his services, as he had of those of Tuaut to compose his constitutions for the Stricter Observance. Like Straccio's *Instruction* for the confraternity, the *Opusculum* is intended to provide information for the directors of the Third Order. The sixth chapter contains the brief Rule based on that of St. Albert. The vows, with the exception of the obligation of poverty, are those professed by the friars and nuns. They are simple in nature and oblige under pain of serious sin, though Straccio later seems to contradict himself, making the obligation depend on the intention of the one making profession. The Rule is directed to men as well as women, married as well as single persons, though in fact Straccio has in mind principally unmarried women.

Emilio Giacomelli issued a new and revised Rule (Rome, 1676), to which his successor as prior general, Ferdinand Tartaglia, added statutes (1679). This legislation, which clarifies and perfects Straccio's and which applies equally to men as well as women, is intended to replace all other Rules and "marks the end of the first period of the juridical evolution of the Carmelite Third Order" (Tomás Motta).

The Giacomelli-Tartaglia Rule and statutes came down to modern times in John Baptist Bettini's *Compendio e dichiarazione della regola del Terz'Ordine* (Firenze, 1849), the many editions of which eventually achieved official status.

For some reason, the Rule and statutes of Giacomelli and Tartaglia were never accepted in the flourishing Third Order of Spain and Portugal. There Straccio's Rule continued in vogue with the important difference that Third Order members were not required to make vows but only proposals or resolutions without obligation in conscience. Such was the concept of the Third Order propounded by John Bonet, Peter of the Cross Juzarte, Joseph of Jesus and Mary, Roque Albert Faci, and Michael de Azevedo, the latter two providing its theory.

The Rule of the Third Order is simply the Rule of St. Albert adapted to the lives of laymen and laywomen. Its purpose is accordingly the same: to lead a committed Christian life in the Carmelite spirit of prayer and service. "The purpose of the Carmelite Order," Tartaglia wrote, "as well as the Rule of the tertiaries taken from it, is to adhere to God by a continual and loving presence, and to serve him faithfully with a pure heart and a good conscience in honor of, and out of love for the Blessed Virgin." It is safe to say that the Carmelites of the 17th and 18th century exercised no more effective apostolate than the fostering of Christian life in the members of the Third Order individually or in organized chapters. The flowering of the Third Order, moreover, coincided with the heydey of spiritual direction. This apostolate attracted some of the most dedicated spirits of the Order and produced choicest fruits of Christian living.

The Third Order in Spain

In the countries of the Iberian peninsula and their dependencies, the Carmelite Third Order flourished as nowhere else.

In the province of Castile, the Third Order in Toledo had the benefit of the ministrations of Michael de la Fuente in its early stages. He was led to compose his Rule precisely because of the constantly growing number of tertiaries and *beatas*. In the surrounding towns, also, Fray Michael clothed hundreds of persons in the tertiary habit. The town of Almonacid counted five or six hundred tertiaries. The sight of them proceeding devoutly in pairs to Holy Communion on the second

Sunday of the month gave great edification. To lead his tertiaries into the ways of prayer La Fuente composed his *Exercises in Mental Prayer*. Among the *beatas* he directed, Agnes of Jesus and Mary del Aguila y Canales are remembered for holiness of life. The biography of the latter was told in a sermon by Francis López Terán published in Madrid in 1634. La Fuente's work in Toledo lived on in such figures as Elisabeth of Jesus, author of a diffuse account of her spiritual experiences, *Tesoro del Carmelo* (Madrid, 1685), the *beata* Mary Encinas, whose life and virtues were described by Gabriel Cabrera, La Fuente's successor as director of the Third Order in Toledo, and Mary Magdalen of the Incarnation Sánchez (1650-1704), likewise the author of a spiritual autobiography.

During his brief sojourn in Segovia, Fray Miguel introduced into the ways of the spirit tertiaries like Luke de Aguilar y Silleras, "the holy silversmith," and Joan of Jesus and Juliana Rodríguez, the two sisters of the noted Jesuit writer, Alphonsus Rodríguez.

Salamanca boasted one of the most flourishing chapters in Spain. In 1731, it numbered 800 members, among them persons of social distinction, members of the clergy and of the university. For this chapter, Joseph Zaragoza y Parada wrote his *Espejo carmelitano* (Salamanca, 1742). Chapters such as Avila (1729), Valladolid (1754), Valderas (1756), and Badajoz (1795) sought affiliation (*hermandad*) with Salamanca. Others like the Discalced chapter of Palencia took Salamanca as their model. The Third Order chapel in Salamanca survived the friars' convent there.

The Third Order of Madrid received official recognition from the prior general, Joachim Pontalti, in 1759 and was subjected to the superiors of the Order in 1763. Its statutes appeared in 1765. The chapter published the Rule of Straccio in 1797. An illustrious *beata*, or tertiary, of Madrid was Mary of the Ascension del Campo (d. 1670), who left a spiritual autobiography at the command of her confessor, Bartholomew Comugnas. Her funeral oration by Louis de Ibarra was published at Madrid in 1680.

The Third Order of Medina del Campo deserves mention if only on account of its most illustrious member, Francis de Yepes, brother of St. John of the Cross. Francis' life, virtues, and edifying death were described by Joseph de Velasco in a book published at Barcelona in 1624. Other tertiaries of Medina were Elisabeth Cortés (1554-1633), whose life was written by her confessor, Jerome Olmos, and Joan Mary de Quintas (d. 1698). At the command of her confessor, Philip Ruiz de Montemayor, she wrote *Seven Petitions on the Our Father*.

The Third Order of Valladolid was founded by Fray John Andrew Espirdo (d. 1773). One of its first members was Francis Muñoz (1668-1738), chaplain to the Oratory of Valladolid, an exemplary priest wholly given to the sacred ministry. Another dedicated priest was Francis Colmenero, devotee of Mary and indefatigable preacher of missions in neglected areas, who wrote *El Carmelo ilustrado con favores de la Reyna de los Angeles* (Valladolid, 1754). As mentioned above, the Valladolid chapter sought affiliation with Salamanca in 1754. In 1790, it received approbation from the prior general, Peter Thomas Marocchi, and published an edition of the Rule of Straccio (Valladolid. 1796), reprinted various times during the 19th century.

The Third Order of Granada in the province of Andalusia was founded in 1648 by decree of the provincial, John Duran, an act which aroused the opposition of the Franciscans, who claimed that such a thing as a Carmelite Third Order did not exist. The case was solved in favor of the Carmelites in 1651. For the Third Order of Granada Joseph de Montesinos composed his *Camino de la gloria por el Monte Carmelo* (2d ed., Granada, 1711).

In the province of Aragon, Valencia had been the scene of the apostolate of John Sanz, as Toledo had been that of Michael de la Fuente. Among the *beatas* Sanz directed, the memory has endured of the penitential Raphaela Ibarra, Euphemia Sanz, the young and wealthy Paula de Villafranca (d. 1605), and Theodora Piquera (d. 1610). For the latter, Sanz composed a *Rule and Way of Life* (1591), an early attempt to supply the lack of legislation for lay persons interested in living according to the spirit of Carmel. Theodora died with sayings from Sanz' Abecedario on her lips.

Other tertiaries of Valencia were the visionary, Louise Zaragoza (1647-1727), whose spirit was examined and approved by the prior general, John Feijóo de Villalobos, during his visitation of Spain, and Josepha Siguenza, greatly devoted to the Holy Childhood. She was assisted on her deathbed by her inseparable companion, Vicenta of the Blessed Sacrament (1677-1751). Roque Albert Faci published lives of Josepha and Vicenta (Zaragoza, 1751).

In 1743, the Third Order of Zaragoza is declared to have been in existence only a few years. This statement is made by Dr. Francis Lorieri, diocesan censor of Roque Alberto Faci's *Carmelo esmaltado con tantas brillantes estrellas quantas flores terceras* (Zaragoza, 1743), a work which Higinio Gandarias, O.C.D., declares to be "the best book written on the Third Order up to the time in which we are writing (1954)."

The founding of the Third Order in Onda also awakened controversy with a religious order which authors do not identify. The Capuchin, Fr. Torrecilla published a defense of the Carmelite Third Order on the occasion.

The Third Order enjoyed a vigorous life in the province of Catalonia. The historic chapter of Barcelona was founded in 1662 by John Bonet, who wrote his *Espejo de vida y exercicios de virtud* (Barcelona, 1664) for the edification of its members. In its preface, he testifies to the existence of numerous tertiaries in Vich, Mallorca, Manresa, Olot, and Villafranca de Panadés. The general chapter of 1666 declared Bonet perpetual commissary general of the Third Order in Barcelona. Upon his death, the general chapter of 1698 appointed Master Angelus Feliú, provincial of Catalonia, as his successor.

The Third Order of Olot was organized in 1673. Its chapel, situated within the cloister of the Carmelite convent, was completed in 1733. The memory has lasted of the tertiary, Catharine Bovera, born in 1623, the daughter of a carpenter. She lived alone in her house in great recollection and prayer. The sight of her in her tertiary habit, her features always alight with peace and cheerfulness, was a comfort to all who beheld her. She died at an early age in the plague of 1650.

Palma de Mallorca produced a number of tertiaries noted for sanctity of life. Joan Oliver (1554-1614) was born of wealthy parents, but when the family fortunes failed, she set about earning her living by embroidering, a skill at which she became quite proficient. She was favored by mystical experiences at prayer, once remaining seventy days in ecstasy. Joan Borrás y Noguera (1582-1637) was the mother of five children, all of whom died in infancy. She also survived her husband, from whom she had suffered lifelong mistreatment. Eleanor Ortiz (1570-1650) was one of those mystics who manage to live without eating. In this manner, she passed six years. At the order of King Philip III, the bishop of Mallorca, Simon Bauza, investigated this phenomenon and reported favorably (1614).

The Third Order in Lisbon

There is little or no evidence before the middle of the 17th century for a Carmelite Third Order as an externally organized group with elected officials, public religious acts such as processions, community works of charity, even separate churches. Granada (1649) provides an early example, perhaps the first, and seemed a novelty at the time. This development of the Carmelite Third Order into an externally visible body occurred early in Portugal, specifically in Lisbon, and may even be the source of the form which the Third Order was to take in the future.

One of the most notable tertiary chapters in the Order, which has enjoyed a continuous existence to the present day, Lisbon owed its foundation to the initiative of Antonia of the Holy Spirit (d. 1637), a devout matron who subsequently became a tertiary in the new chapter. At her instigation, her confessor, Frei Peter de Mello Fragoso, with the collaboration of Frei Clement of the Holy Angel and the lay brother Simon of St. Mary, founded the Lisbon chapter of the Third Order. According to a plaque in the Third Order chapel, the date of foundation was 1629. Mello became the first commissary and composed a Rule (Lisbon, 1630).

The initiative, challenged by the Franciscans, was successfully defended by the learned John de Sylveira. On August 31, 1630, the Apostolic Collector, Lawrence Tramallo, issued a verdict favorable to the Carmelites, confirmed against appeal on May 6, 1631. Sylveira's treatise on the Third Order, of which the defense of the Lisbon chapter was a part, was known to Lezana in Rome and hence also to Straccio. The Lisbon controversy may have determined the prior general to favor the organization and spread of the Third Order by providing legislation applicable throughout the Order. His *Opusculum regularum* in fact contributed greatly to this end, especially on the Iberian peninsula and its dependencies.

After Mello Fragoso, the Third Order of Lisbon was blessed by a succession of able commissaries, or directors, whose influence was felt throughout Portuguese-speaking Carmel. Peter of the Cross Juzarte's *Regra e constituiçoens* (Lisbon, 1644) was reprinted in 1670 and edited with a supplement on indulgences in 1685 by Emmanuel of the Incarnation. Juzarte (d. 1678) also wrote *The Garden of Varied and Choice Flowers* (Lisbon, 1671), lives of tertiaries distinguished for holiness. Joseph of Jesus and Mary (1660-1727) was active as a missionary in Brazil before becoming commissary of the Third Order, first in Villafranca and then in Lisbon. During his term as commissary, a sumptuous hospital for ailing tertiaries was begun in 1703. His *Thesouro carmelitano* (Lisbon, 1705) enjoyed printings into the 19th century. Michael de Azevedo (d. 1811) composed a commentary on the Third Order Rule (Lisbon, 1778), often published in Portugal and Brazil into the 20th century.

These authors reproduced the Rule of Straccio, but in a much attenuated form with regard to the nature of the obligations assumed by Carmelite tertiaries. In 1665, a committee of three tertiaries composed statutes or rules of procedure for the chapter, approved by the prior general, Matthew Orlandi (1667), and John Feijóo de Villalobos (1694), and finally published by Jorge de Britto (Lisbon, 1715). The tertiaries' chapel (1638) was situated in the main cloister of the convent.

Manuel de Sá states that in his day the Third Order of Lisbon numbered 25,000 members. Its glory, however, lay not in large numbers and external pomp but in the fruits of Christian living it produced. Mariana das Candeas, companion to Antonia of the Holy Spirit in a life of prayer and good works, died as she had lived in her little house near the bridge of Alcantara. She was accompanied to her final resting place in the friary burial plot not only by the other tertiaries but by a throng of the poor, now bereft of her support. Elizabeth of Jesus was led to undertake a life of penance through a vision in which she beheld Christ threatening to castigate the city. She shared her experiences in prayer with the commissary, Clement of the Angel, and the learned and virtuous Louis of the Presentation (of Mertola). Mary of Jesus, gifted with prophecy, was directed by the Dominican John de Vasconcellos. The pious Doña Louise Cabral, mother of the Count of Faro, included among the objects of her benefactions the novices of the Carmo, a not superfluous charity in times when candidates for the Order were dependent on the chancy contents of the community chest. Vincent Pereira, priest, never accepted the charge of a church or parish and lived alone in extreme poverty, the better to be able to help the poor. Greatly devoted to the souls in Purgatory, he could be seen by night walking barefooted through the streets, asking for prayer on their behalf. Magdalen of Christ, unmarried, was in charge of the charitable institution de Santa Misericordia.

Emmanuel de Casta (1666-1697) was a young shoemaker who supported his sister and her daughter. The former was "of such a harsh nature as to be a source of much merit for me in the sight of the Lord God." When he was not working, he devoted his time to prayer, penance, and the care of the sick in hospitals. He left a brief account of his life and way of prayer.

Anna Emmanuel of the Conception (d. 1646) joined the company of the Collector General on a visit to the tomb of the apostles in Rome. There in 1625, she obtained permission from Pope Urban VIII to proceed to the Holy Land. The tireless pilgrim journeyed another time to the Holy House of Loreto, armed with patents from the commissary of the Third Order, which Straccio confirmed on her passage through Rome. She brought back to Lisbon two paintings of Italian madonnas, *Our Lady de Pedrada* and *Our Lady das Punhaladas*, which became the objects of veneration in the chapel of the Captive Christ in the Carmo. Anna's life was written by Emmanuel Ferreira (d. 1654).

Among others, mention might be made of the Third Order chapters at Beja, Camarate, Evora, Faro, Moura, Setúbal, Vidigueira, and Torres Novas. The names of a number of tertiaries of these chapters, remembered for holiness of life are known today.

The Third Order also thrived on the Portugese islands of the Azores and Madeira. In the course of time, the confraternity and Third Order of Carmel spread throughout the Azores.

The direction of the Third Order in Funchal occasioned the foundation of a Carmelite friary there in 1663. The tertiaries donated their chapel and a piece of ground for a convent. However, the foundation never developed beyond the status of a hospice, or residence for a few friars, charged with the care of the Third Order.

The Third Order in Brazil

The Third Order on the model of Lisbon travelled early to Brazil and became no less popular than in the mother country.

The chapter of Bahia (modern Salvador) with the title of St. Teresa dates from October 19, 1636, and was granted papal confirmation, December 21, 1695. In 1644, permission was requested of the friars to build a tertiary church, completely destroyed by fire in 1788. The same year, under the priorate of Innocent Joseph da Costa, merchant, construction began on a new church, blessed in 1803. In 1819, the cornerstone was laid of a hospital destined to serve the tertiaries. The care of ill members seems to be a distinctive feature of the Third Order in Portugal.

The tertiary church of Cachoeira, today an artistic monument, was begun in 1691 on land donated by the friars.

During his visitation of Spain in 1695, John Feijóo de Villalobos signed patents for the foundation of the Third Order in Recife, at the same time naming Emmanuel of the Assumption commissary. The following year, the vicar provincial of Bahia and Pernambuco, Emmanuel of the Nativity Ferreira, drew up statutes, which remained in force until the second half of the 19th century. Straccio's Rule in the edition of Michael de Azevedo provided the necessary legislation. The cornerstone of a tertiary church was laid in 1700. In 1757, the tertiaries numbered 2,000. A hospital for tertiaries was begun in 1868.

The tertiary chapter of Olinda preceded that of Recife; the request for the foundation of the latter adduces the motive that the only other chapter in Olinda is too far away. The chapter of Paraíba already existed in 1752, the date of an agreement with the friars. The chapter of Goiana was established in 1753.

In 1648, a group of tertiaries professed in Portugal met to found a chapter in Rio de Janeiro. Ignatius of the Purification became their first commissary. The prior of the convent, Anthony of the Angels, composed statutes which guided the chapter until they were replaced in 1697 by those composed by Emmanuel of the Nativity Ferreira. By way of a Rule, the tertiaries were regulated by Joseph of Jesus and Mary's *Thesouro carmelitano* (Lisbon, 1705) and Azevedo's *Regra* (Lisbon, 1778). In 1661, construction was begun on a chapel within the conventual precincts, completed in 1669. In 1755, the foundations were laid for the new tertiary church, blessed in 1770. A hospital for indigent tertiaries was begun in 1733. In 1785, a burial place was completed on the site of the old chapel and served the tertiaries until 1850, when an imperial decree forbade interment inside the city.

The earliest surviving acts of the meetings of the Third Order of São Paulo date from 1674. The statutes of Emmanuel Ferreira were put in force in 1697, revised in 1743. The beautiful tertiary church attached to that of the friars was decorated with the paintings of Pedro Alexandrino (1760) and Frei Jesuino of Mount Carmel (1798).

Other historic Third Order chapters of which the churches still exist are Mogí das Cruces, Angra dos Reis, and Santos (1752).

The Third Order in Italy

Italy with its hundreds of Carmelite convents and monasteries, with its centuries' old tradition of confraternities and *pinzochere*, offered fertile soil for the development of the Third Order in its modern form. There, too, the legislation composed by the priors general - to a large extent with an eye to conditions in Italy - received its most widespread acceptance.

The *Manuale del Terz'Ordine* (Venice, 1686), compiled by Jerome Aimo at the behest of the prior general, Angelo Monsignani, contained, besides the Rule, statutes and ceremonial, a "spiritual directory," taken from Mark of the Nativity's directory for novices, which Aimo had also translated. Its wide use is attested to by its many editions, especially that arranged in the 19th century by John Baptist Bettini.

With its strong tradition of *pinzochere* wearing the Carmelite habit and living like religious in the bosom of their family, the Italian tertiary movement in our period (1600-1750) does not give the impression of an externally organized institution as in Portugal. An idea of the Third Order in Italy can best be had through the lives of individual tertiaries, who - given the background of the movement - were predominantly women. Here only a few can be remembered.

Several tertiaries of Monte San Giuliano in the Sicilian province of St. Angelus are memorable for holiness of life. Leonarda Surdo (1606-1638) was early influenced by the devout habits of an elder sister, who was wont to frequent the local circle of Carmelite tertiaries. At her sister's death, Leonarda was clothed in the Carmelite habit. The same year, 1625, pestilence broke out in the town. After two of Leonarda's sisters died, her mother was carried off to the pesthouse, and the girl was left alone in the house under guard. During the months she was thus confined, Carmelite friars, one is pleased to relate, making the rounds of their tertiaries, regularly brought her food. When her father died and her mother remarried, Leonarda found her stepfather's household unsympathetic to her way of life, and a small house was found, where she could be near her sister tertiaries and her spiritual director. There she led a life of prayer and penance until her early death at twenty-nine years of age. Her spiritual director collected two volumes, still extant in manuscript, of her mystical experiences.

Matthia Labita (1612-1649) was converted as a result of a grace received in church on the Feast of the Epiphany, 1628. She was vested with the tertiary habit by Master Timothy Teodori, prior of the Carmelite convent of Monte San Giuliano, thus initiating a life of prayer and contemplation marked by frequent mystical phenomena. During a pastoral visit in 1640, Cardinal John Louis Spinola commissioned his vicar general, Fabrizio del Nobile, to examine her spirit. The examination, carried out with the aid of Jerome del Finale, the vicar's confessor, and James of Genoa, Capuchin, was wholly favorable. Two volumes of her spiritual experiences remain, of which Vito Calvini evidently availed himself to write Matthia's biography (Palermo, 1675).

On the continent, the church of Our Lady of Grace in Bologna, of the Romagna province, harbored a fervent group of tertiaries, especially under the zealous guidance of Ferdinand Salvi (1694-1765). One of his penitents was Ursula Righi (1644-1724), the mother of numerous daughters, whom she reared in Christian piety and eventually settled in marriage. Her other interest beside her family was the spiritual life. Unlettered, she had others read to her from spiritual books and was able to retain whatever she thus heard. The last two years of her life were spent in bed in a state of complete paralysis, a condition she bore with cheerfulness and patience. Her confessors were Aloysius Albicini, S.J., and later Ferdinand Salvi, who chronicled her life.

Joan Mary Magdalen Guerini (1683-1754), of Lugo, like St. Teresa, as a child wanted to live as a hermit in the desert. When her father understandably refused his consent, she contented herself with living in as retired a manner as possible at home. After the death of her parents, she joined a Carmelite tertiary, Mary Magdalen Teresia Musi, received the tertiary habit in 1725. A diary of her spiritual life up to the year 1732 was kept by her director, Fr. Horace Buora. That year, Joan applied for entrance to the Carmelite Sisters delle Grazie in Bologna.

Anna Pellino (1586-1656), of Pavia, was left an orphan at three or four years of age. Obliged to marry to obtain support, she obeyed her husband, who did not favor her frequent visits to church. She worked as a servant in the Benedictine nunnery of St. Helen. After a day of hard work, she did not omit her many devotions. Her confessor ordered her not to exceed an hour, but since she became too absorbed to notice the time, an angel, the story goes, was commissioned from on high to take charge of the hour glass. This humble woman was granted many mystical gifts. Among her confessors was the reformer of the Lombardy province, Dominic of St. Mary, who admitted her to the Third Order in 1632 and wrote an account of her spiritual itinerary.

Among his many activities on behalf of religion, Dominic of St. Mary promoted the Third Order among persons of both sexes and all social conditions.

Angela Victoria Turelli, 1710-1733

Angela Victoria Turelli (1710-1733) was born in Palliano in the Papal States into a family of nine children. As soon as she was old enough, she joined the others in the fields, but the work proved beyond her strength and she was assigned the care of the house. She preferred the solitude of the home during the day, for she felt drawn to prayer. In the Capuchin, Francis of Ceccano, she found a skilled spiritual director, who immediately perceived her rare promise and quickly and easily sped her along the path of Christian perfection. He is the author of her biography (Roma, 1765), the first of a number of studies. In 1732, Angela made the trip to Palestrina to be clothed in the tertiary habit by Master Eugene Ghisi, authorized for this office by the prior general, Louis Benzoni. To complete her renunciation of the world, she left home for a room in the house of a charitable woman willing to receive her. This simple unlettered peasant girl puts one in mind of St. Thérèse of Lisieux by her total abandonment to God, her outspoken determination to be a saint, her early death from lung disease (*idropsia di petto*), brought on by grinding poverty and voluntary austerities.

Lucretia Michelini, 1636-1662

Lucretia Michelini, of Crevalcore in the territory of Bologna, was one of those persons converted by a book, in her case, a devout treatise entitled *School of Divine Love*. (Sometimes spiritual books of very indifferent quality produce the most astonishing effects.) Lucretia's father, Geminiano, was a carpenter, her mother a school teacher, and in time she was able to help her mother conduct her classes. Her conversion inclined Lucretia to a life of retirement and the following of Christ, especially in his Passion. Unable to enter a monastery, apparently because the family could not afford a dowry, in 1657 she obtained her father's reluctant consent to become a Carmelite tertiary. In her new vocation, Lucretia was able to devote herself wholeheartedly to solitude and contemplation, achieving the heights of mystical prayer. In 1661, while in the parish church of St. Silvester, she felt the first symptoms of the sickness which took her life the following year at the age of twenty-six. Her biography was written by Giuseppe Maria Graziani, O.F.M.Cap. (Modena, 1726).

Mariangela Virgili, 1661-1734

No doubt the most noteworthy of Italian tertiaries is Mariangela Virgili, whose fellow townspeople of Ronciglione are enthusiastically promoting her cause of beatification. Her family, formerly well-to-do, had latterly fallen on evil days. Serafino, her father, a shoemaker augmented his meager earnings by work in the fields. At six years of age, the little girl had already made her life's decision, resolving to dedicate herself entirely to God through the three vows. This vocation she realized in her poverty-stricken home, earning her bread by work in the fields, washing laundry, doing household chores. In spite of heavy work and chronic illness, she practiced a rigorous fast and total abstinence from meat. Her life was marked with many mystical experiences, described with delightful candor and simplicity in her autobiography. Her spiritual director, the Capuchin, Francis of Ceccano put into writing the story of her life, which at his request she dictated to him (Roma, 1765). At thirty-nine years of age, Mariangela received the Carmelite habit as a tertiary. In that capacity, she could exert an influence in the town not possible as a private individual. From that time forward, she devoted her time to apostolic works, visiting the sick and those in prison, relieving the poor, converting and helping women of ill fame.

The Carmelite Sisters "delle Grazie"

Sometimes tertiaries came together to form communities for mutual support. In at least one case, such a community grew into a religious institute, the first of the modern Congregations of Sisters, new branches of the tree of Carmel.

Mary Magdalen Mazzoni Sangiorgi (1683-1749), of Bologna, mother of six children, three of whom died in infancy, was in turn widowed at the age of 32. She determined to remain single, in order to devote herself to religious interests. A decisive moment in her life was the acquaintance with Ferdinand Salvi, who became her spiritual director and received her into the Third Order in 1723. It as not long before she was joined in the works of charity, to which she now increasingly devoted herself, by six other women, including probably one of her daughters, Mary Angela. In 1724, the community acquired a house in the Via Solferino. Fr. Salvi formulated a Rule according to the ideals of the foundress, who insisted above all on the perfect common life. The special apostolate of the new institute was the education of needy girls, but the sisters also undertook the care of aged persons. The sisters adopted the habit of the nuns of the monastery of Our Lady of the Angels in Florence, a consequence of Mother Mazzoni's devotion to St. Mary Magdalen de' Pazzi. The community was called Carmelite Tertiaries of St. Mary Magdalen de' Pazzi, or *delle Grazie*, after the nearby Carmelite church. The new institute received the approval of the prior general, Louis Benzoni, on February 8, 1735. In 1744, cloister was imposed, a measure which conformed to the foundress' spirit of prayer and retirement. The first superior after her death was Sr. Catherine Pilati, who in 1754 founded a house of the institute in Rovereto.

The 20th century saw the foundation of a number of other houses by the Carmelite Sisters *delle Grazie*.

The "Viperesche"

In other cases, communities of tertiaries remained limited to one foundation.

Among the many works of charity of the Roman noblewoman Livia Vipereschi (1606-1675) was the Conservatory of the Immaculate Conception, a home for lodging and educating girls for the married or religious state (1668). Signora Vipereschi herself ended her days there, after having endowed it with her fortune. Some of the girls elected to remain in the Conservatory, forming a religious community dedicated to its care. Two cloistered Carmelite nuns from Messina, Antonia Orechia, and her sister, Anne Catherine, became the first and second prioress respectively. Jerome Serafini (d. 1688), of the nearby convent of San Martino ai Monti, was followed as chaplain by Angelo Paoli and Anthony Pennazzi, the former, however, soon renouncing this activity in favor of his apostolate in the hospital of St. John Lateran. Pennazzi introduced the Office of the Blessed Virgin according to the Carmelite Rite.

The "Viperesche" were oblates wearing the Carmelite habit without vows, cloister, or Rule. Pope Clement X granted them all the spiritual privileges of Carmelite nuns.

Other single communities are found at Lucca (1645), Medicina (1688), Desenzaano del Garda (ca. 1706), Serravalle (1726).

The Third Order in France

The French provinces produced some of the best tertiary literature, but little is known at present about the external life of the Third Order or its members. In Aquitaine, Jean Tuaut early published his *Esquillon des devots à la Vierge du Mont Carmel* (Limoges, 1619) and was no doubt personally responsible for the spread of the Third Order in his province. Andrew of St. Nicholas, of the province of Narbonne, wrote *Antiquity, Privileges, and Duties of the Third Order of the Blessed Virgin Mary* (Lyon, 1666), but Louis Jacob thought he had rather overreached himself in ascribing tertiaries to the Old Testament.

The province of Touraine could be trusted to issue books for tertiaries of high caliber. Stephen of St. Francis Xavier's manual, *The Third Order of Our Lady of Mount Carmel* (Paris, 1672), places the Carmelite Third Order in the framework of Third Orders in general and presents it as an effective way of fulfilling the universal Christian duty to be perfect. He contents himself with tracing the Third Order to the briefs of Nicholas V and Sixtus IV, without pausing "to stir the ashes of our ancient patriarchs and prophets to find the origin of our Third Order and demonstrate its nobility by its antiquity." He omits the ritual and text of the Rule, confining himself to a commentary on the Rule. As special features of the Carmelite Third Order he singles out devotion to Mary and contemplation. He devotes considerable space to a treatment of prayer, including its mystical stages.

The *Manual of the Third Order of Our Lady of Mount Carmel* (Angers, 1681) by Mark of the Nativity reproduces the Rule and statutes of Jacomelli and Tartaglia in French, but is taken up mostly by a "spiritual directory," which thoroughly instructs the tertiaries in the ways of prayer, especially meditation and the practice of the presence of God. A final section treats of indulgences. Parts of the book, principally the Rule and statutes, were reprinted many times down to the middle of the 19th century.

Curiously, these authors make no mention of French tertiaries of exemplary lives. They are satisfied to propose as models a few famous tertiaries of other countries.

The Third Order in Belgium

In Belgium, Daniel of the Virgin Mary wrote his *Description of the Third Order of Mount Carmel* (Antwerp, 1646), which underwent several editions. He provides a commentary on Straccio's Rule with many beautiful Marian considerations.

Daniel's book was replaced at the end of the century by James of St. Anthony's useful *Original, Actual and Practical Description of the Third Order of Our Lady of Mount Carmel* (Antwerp, 1691), which remained the tertiary manual of the Flemish-speaking tertiaries until modern times. Three parts recount the origin of the Third Order, reproduce the text of the Rule and provide a commentary. A ritual or ceremonial completes the volume. With Andrew of St. Nicholas, James traces the origin of the Third Order to the Old Testament. The Rule, confirmed by the prior general, Paul of St. Ignatius, in 1691, was "almost in the same form and expressed in the same terms as approved by the superiors of our province and for many years prescribed for the brothers and sisters of our Third Rule to their great spiritual profit." In effect, it is the Rule of St. Albert applied to secular living. Christian virtues, especially those practiced in Carmel, the reception of the sacraments, and daily devotions are severally enlarged on. Instruction on prayer in its higher stages, found in the French manuals, is lacking.

The Gallo-Belgian province probably availed itself of the French manuals. Philip of the Visitation was the zealous director of the Third Order in Valenciennes. He celebrated in Latin verses the history of the Third Order in his *Anastasis Tertii Carmelitarum Ordinis* (Valenciennes, 1670) and illustrious tertiaries in French verse in his *Genealogy and Praise of the Third Order of Our Lady of Mount Carmel* (Valenciennes, 1671).

Philip also wrote the life of Pauline Lepetit (d. 1641), a devout anchoress affiliated with the Order. Her parents having succumbed to the pestilence in 1575, Pauline was reared in Mons by her maternal uncle, Arnold Leclercq. A Lenten sermon by Francis Durin, of the Carmelite convent of Valenciennes, caused her to renounce the world. She followed Durin to Valenciennes and joined a group of devout women whose director he was. In 1585, she received the Carmelite habit at the hands of the prior of Valenciennes and shortly thereafter retired to a hermitage attached to the parish church of Bellioël, a town between Brugelette and Ath. There, as in "a most delightful paradise" she spent her long life in prayer and penance. A touching *fioretto* has her summoning the birds from the surrounding forest to join her in singing the praises of the Lord. Among her favorite books was the *Imitation of Christ*. At the advice of the prior of Brugelette, she placed the statue of the Child Jesus on the altar of her oratory, as a protection against the assaults of the evil one. She did not remain aloof from the life of the Church and the advance of Protestanism and envied the fate of her confrere, John Vanegas, burned alive by the Moors. Many persons came for counsel to the grille of her hermitage, among them the noble lady, Margaret Philippa de Gauche, Countess of Masting, whom she advised to become a canoness in Mons and who was also enrolled in the Carmelite Third Order. When the convent of Valenciennes accepted reform, she, too, undertook the new way of life, making a general confession to the prior, John Baptist Bavay, and submitting an inventory of her few poor possessions. She was assisted in her last hours by the prior of Brugelette, her superior in matters of the spirit.

Among other Belgian tertiaries, Maria Ock (1622-1685), of Liège, professed in the Third Order by Matthew de la Couronne, local prior, later became a nun. In 1648, she was cured, miraculously it was thought, after drinking St. Albert's water.

In the Flemish province, Barbara van Berchem (1648-1701), the daughter of wealthy parents of Brugge, took the name in the Third Order of Barbara Teresa of St. Joseph. She was joined in her life of prayer and penance by her sisters, Anne and Mary. Her confessor, the poet, Augustine of St. Gummarus (d. 1703), left an account of her life.

Maria Petyt, 1623-1677

Belgium was the homeland of the one who must be ranked as the most illustrious product of the tertiary movement, one of the most interesting mystics of the Low Countries and of the Carmelite Order.

Maria was born in Hazebrouck of a well-to-do merchant family. She felt attracted to religious life and tried her vocation with the Canonesses of St. Augustine in Ghent (1641), but was rejected during her novitiate, when eye trouble made it seem likely that she would not be able to follow the choir. She joined the settlement of beguines in Ghent, for she began to feel a need for solitude and prayer. She made the acquaintance of Gabriel of the Annunciation, who undertook her direction. Later, she went to live with another devout woman and her mother, both of whom had a similar desire to lead a contemplative life. Such *pinzochere* or *beatas* were called "spiritual daughters" in the Low Countries. When Gabriel left Ghent in 1646, Maria had the good fortune or providential grace to come under the direction of the twenty year-old Michael of St. Augustine, only two years her senior and at the time lecturing in philosophy in the Carmelite *studium*. He remained Maria's director for the rest of her life and led her along the way of mystical prayer, which was God's design for her. In 1657, she moved with her two companions into an anchorhold attached to the Carmelite church in Mechelen, from which the sacred functions could be followed through a small window. Fr. Michael composed a way of life approved by the prior general, John Anthony Filippini, and confirmed by Jerome Ari during his visitation, and received the three vows of his spiritual daughters. In time, Maria was joined by other companions who continued their way of life after her death. James of St. Anthony succeeded Michael as their director (1684).

At Michael's behest, Maria wrote an account of her life and kept a record of her spiritual experiences, which he published in a final edition of four volumes (Ghent, 1683-1684). She hearkens back directly to the characteristic medieval spirituality of the Netherlands with little trace of Baroque devotion, an unusual if not unique phenomenon in 17th century Flemish spiritual literature. She belongs to the spirituality of annihilation: the quieting of all the faculties, in order to experience God directly in the center of the soul. Since she was not writing for publication, she could express herself frankly without fear of being tarred with the brush of Quietism. Like many great mystics, Maria was also a talented writer, comparable with the best spiritual authors of the Low Countries. Her style is straightforward, picturesque, and flavored with humor. Engrossed in the difficult task of describing her mystical experiences, she has no time for artificiality. One of the most refreshing aspects of Maria's writings, Albert Deblaere, S.J., declares, is their unfailing directness: "In the midst of the most sublime mystical reflections, she retains her attention fixed on the concrete details of life, the spontaneous reactions of a very simple woman."

A special feature of Maria's spirituality is the perseverance in her of Marian devotion in mystical states. Of her description of her contemplative experience of union with Mary, Deblaere writes: "We are faced with a description of an original and new experience in our (Flemish) literature and, as far as we know, in European literature." Maria Petyt anticipates the Marian spirituality of which Grignion de Montfort is generally considered the originator, though this does not mean that the saint owes his doctrine to the Carmelite tertiary.

The Lower German province used the manual of Daniel of the Virgin Mary in a version by that indefatigable translator, Charles of St. Anastasius: *Short Description and Rule of the Third Order* (Cologne, 1658; 2d ed., 1721). This translation appeared in abbreviated form for use in the Upper German province with the title, *Short Treatise on the Third Order* (Bamberg, 1719).

Further information on the Third Order in the provinces of Germany and Eastern Europe is not at hand.

Chapter 6

The Fine Arts in Italy and Spain

The vigorous renewal of Catholic life found expression in the arts in the triumphant and exuberant style known as baroque, continuing in its later form of rococo even through the first half of the Age of Reason. Today, the face of historic Carmel is baroque. Man's inhumanity, natural calamities, changing taste, for the most part erased the features of the Middle Ages.

In this period, Carmel produced no figure of stature in the arts. In the massive effort of constructing or restoring their buildings, the Carmelites, like other religious, called on the services of contemporary artists, creating a pictorial record of the Order's ideals and achievements to which some of the greatest masters of the age contributed.

The constitutions of the Stricter Observance enter into some detail with regard to the plan of churches and convents and, moreover, require before undertaking construction consultation with the "prefect of building." There should be one or two such prefects in each province, sufficiently knowledgeable about architecture, to be appointed by the provincial chapter (pt. 1, ch. 1, no. 12).

Nowhere more than in the arts does the changed tone of Carmelite spirituality become evident. The artistic ornamentation of Carmelite churches in the Middle Ages and Renaissance shows little that is specific to the Order. The Virgin and saints are invoked under titles of universal or local interest. At most, the figure of a Carmelite will appear on the fringes of a scene. Mantle Virgins and an occasional Albert or Angelus only confirm the Rule. With the Counter-Reformation, however, the Order's new sense of identity filled Carmelite churches with a gallery of saints and depictions of miracles proper to the Order. The Virgin appears clothed in the Carmelite habit and by preference is shown bestowing the scapular. Not only the first canonized saints, Teresa, John of the Cross, Andrew Corsini, Mary Magdalen de' Pazzi, but a whole crowd of other holy Carmelites, real and imaginary, fill the niches and adorn the altars of the Order's churches. The phenomenon is closely dependent on literary sources, on the Order's awakened awareness of its history and traditions, as published especially in Lezana's *Annales* (1645-1656) and Daniel of the Virgin Mary's *Speculum carmelitanum* (1680).

It makes little sense to consider the fine arts only in reference to the old Carmel, as distinct from the Discalced, for artistic themes and iconography of the two Orders are identical. It is frequently difficult or impossible to determine the provenance, Calced or Discalced, of works of art of Carmelite inspiration at present preserved in galleries and museums. Yet considerations of space and lack of competence on the part of the writer make it advisable to maintain the distinction. Excellent iconographical studies exist of works of art concerning St. Teresa and St. John of the Cross.

In what follows it should be noted that information sometimes antedates one or both World Wars, which notoriously had a way of altering the skylines of cities and towns.

The Great Italian Masters

In the *belle arti*, Italy maintained its position of preeminence and tradition of papal patronage established in the Renaissance.

Among Baroque masters, Il Guercino (1591-1666) left in his native Cento a painting of Our Lady of Mount Carmel bestowing the scapular on St. Simon Stock accompanied by two Franciscans (Museo Civico). In his canvas in the Church of San Gregorio in Messina, Our Lady is shown handing the scapular to a Carmelite nun (St. Teresa?), flanked by St. Joseph, an infant St. John the Baptist, and St. Albert. A painting differing strikingly from those of the same subject by Guercino's compatriot and rival, Guido Reni, pictures a bald St. Andrew Corsini tearfully contemplating a crucifix (Florence, Galleria Corsini). Guercino depicted the Glorification of St. Chrysogonus on the ceiling of the nave of the Carmelite church in Rome dedicated to that saint (now in the collection of the Duke of Sutherland, Stafford House, London). The artist, in fact, lived not far from the Carmelite church in Bologna. On his knees, he polychromed its miraculous statue of Our Lady of Mount Carmel (1644).

Guido Reni (1575-1642) twice painted St. Andrew Corsini, canonized in 1629 (Bologna, Pinacoteca; Roma, Palazzo Barberini). St. Andrew also appears in a beautiful picture of Our Lady of Mount Carmel by Caravaggio (Messina, Museo Nazionale).

In the Rococo period, Giambattista Tiepolo (1696-1770) touches some characteristic features of Carmelite devotion in his painting of the scapular vision, in which St. Simon Stock is accompanied by St. Andrew Corsini and St. Mary Magdalen de' Pazzi (Milano, Brera Museum). But the great Venetian artist's masterpiece was done for the Scuola Grande dei Carmini in Venice, where on the ceiling of the *salone grande* Our Lady in the act of bestowing the scapular on St. Simon soars in a lambent sky amid a throng of joyful angels. It was probably for the *scuola* or confraternity that Tiepolo designed the processional banner picturing Our Lady of the Scapular, now in the possession of a private collector in London.

For his work in the Scuola Grande, Tiepolo was enrolled in the Confraternity of Our Lady of Mount Carmel. He concerned himself with Carmelite themes on other occasions. Not yet twenty years old, he had portrayed the apotheosis of St. Teresa on the ceiling of her chapel in the Discalced Carmelite church in Venice (1715). Later, he returned to fill the ceiling of the nave with a grandiose Flight of the Holy House of Loreto, unfortunately destroyed in a bombardment of the First World War.

In Mary Magdalen de' Pazzi, we have the other example, besides Teresa, of a Carmelite saint who sat for a portrait before the invention of the daguerro-type. Santi di Tito, no more than Juan de la Miseria, was a great artist, but we must be grateful for his portrait of the seventeen year-old Lucrezia Pazzi, painted on the eve of her entrance into the novitiate (1583). Lucrezia in a brocade gown, a garland of flowers in her hair, was no great beauty, though she was not exactly ill-favored either, with large dark eyes and abundant black hair. One would expect this ecstatic mystic, descendant of a noble Florentine family, to provide the ideal subject of Baroque art. The saint has indeed been often depicted in paintings, engravings, and statuary, but apart from Tiepolo (if it is indeed Mary Magdalen in the painting in the Brera Museum of Milano) no great master was inspired by the colorful episodes of her spiritual itinerary. Francesco Curradi confessed to having done more than eighty portraits of her, as had other Florentine painters like Nicodemo and one of the Casini. One searches in vain for these names in reference works of art. Among rather more reputable Italian artists who portrayed St. Mary Magdalen mention may be made of Guido Cagnacci (1601-1681), Pier Francesco Silvani (1620-1681), Cesare Gennari (1637-1688), Ciro Fern (1634-1689), Ludovico Gemignani (1643-1697), Luca Giordano (1632-1705), Antonio Franchi (1634-1709).

Carmelite Churches of Rome

It is hardly practicable to describe here the hundreds of Carmelite churches and convents in Italy, many of them for that matter are still here to be seen and admired at first hand. At the risk of turning this account into something resembling a guidebook of the Touring Club Italiano a few of the more significant churches and their artistic contents may be passed in review.

The Church of Santa Maria in Traspontina in Rome is advantageously situated on the spacious Via della Conciliazione between Castel Sant'Angelo and the Basilica of St. Peter. The cornerstone of this church, for centuries the seat of the central administration of the Order, was laid in 1566, and more than a century elapsed before its completion. The architects, Sallustio Peruzzi (d. 1573), Ottavio Mascherino, and Francesco Peperello were responsible for its construction. The facade by Peruzzi, built partly with stone from the Colosseum, was the first to be designed in two orders, or storeys, though it was actually preceded in execution by that of the Gesù by Vignola. The belfry by Peperello (1637) contains a 14th century English bell, refounded and enlarged to weigh 3,300 lbs. (1761). The church consists of a single nave with lateral chapels, transept and apse, surmounted at the juncture of transept and nave by a cupola (Mascherino), deliberately curtailed so as not to interfere with the artillery range of the Castel Sant'Angelo. In the sanctuary is the elegant altar by Carlo Fontana with its baldacchino in the form of a crown supported by columns and its singular globe-shaped tabernacle. The altarpiece is the miraculous image of the Virgin mentioned above.

The Basilica of San Martino ai Monti on the Esquiline Hill near St. Mary Major is of great archeological interest. It arose in connection with the third century *titulus Equitii* and has fundamentally retained the form given it by Pope Sergius II (844-847). It received its present baroque veneer from the architect, Filippo Gagliardi, in the years 1635-1664. Gagliardi opened six large windows with balconies in the clerestory, the central ones with simulated perspectives - a device typical of him, which earned him the nickname "*delle prospettive.*" He further lowered the floor level by almost a meter and redesigned the confession with its sarcophagus of historic relics. One of the most striking additions is Gaspard Dughet's cycle of frescoes depicting the life of Elijah.

From the end of the 18th century date the main altar by Francesco Belli and the redecoration of the chapel of Our Lady of Mount Carmel to the left of the apse by A. de Dominicis.

Likewise of archeological interest is the 12th century Basilica of San Crisogono in Trastevere, one of the titular churches of Rome dating from Constantinian times. Although Mesnard declares the church to have been "profoundly modified" by the architect J. B. Soria in 1623, this is not immediately evident to the unpracticed eye, at least in the interior, which gives the impression of antiquity with its simple central nave bounded by ancient columns deriving from classical Roman ruins. The magnificent lacunar ceiling, according to Apollonj Ghetti "one of the most beautiful ceilings in the basilicas of Rome," is an addition by Soria. The central panel formerly held a Glorification of St. Chrysogonus by Guercino. Large windows were opened in the clerestory, the medieval altar was retained, but the confession was removed and a new baldacchino constructed. A 14th century mosaic of the Virgin with Sts. Chrysogonus and James, probably the work of Pietro Cavallini, was placed in the apse.

Little evidence remains of the Carmelite occupancy of the church, since 1847 in the possession of the Trinitarians. The 15th century fresco of Our Lady of Grace, the object of great popular devotion, framed by a painting representing Sts. Francis and Teresa in ecstatic prayer by the French Carmelite, Jacques Povillard (1751-1818), no longer exists.

In 1661, Pope Alexander VII, to provide a fitting entrance into Rome from the Porta del Popolo commissioned Carlo Rainaldi to design twin churches to frame the three streets leading into the square. Of the two churches, Santa Maria dei Miracoli (1678) and Santa Maria in Monte Santo, the latter was entrusted to the friars of the reform of Monte Santo. Begun by Rainaldi in 1662, it was continued after his death in 1667 by Carlo Fontana and Mattia de Rossi, supervised by Gian Lorenzo Bernini (1675). The church, oval in form, has a porch with four columns in classic style. The cupola is surrounded externally by a balustrade and eight statues of Carmelite saints by pupils of Bernini, working probably from his designs. In four niches in the arch of the apse are statues of the popes by Filippo Cercani. The main altar by Mattia de Rossi, holds the miraculous image of Our Lady of Monte Santo. Busts of popes in the sanctuary are chalk forms of bronze originals, now lost, by Girolamo Lucenti (d. 1698) who cast Bernini's bronze pillars of the baldacchino in St. Peter's.

In this church Pope Pius XII, as a child, was enrolled in the scapular confraternity, and Pope John XXIII was ordained a priest.

Of Carmelite interest in Rome is the Corsini chapel erected in the Lateran Basilica by the Corsini pope Clement XII (1730-1740), distinguished patron of the arts. The work of Clement's favorite architect, Alessandro Galilei, the chapel like the basilica itself is in Pastor's phrase "a little museum of the Roman sculpture of the time."

"It would perhaps be saying too much," the same author continues, "to aver that the sepulchre of the Corsini is one of the most beautiful chapels not only in Rome but in the whole world, but it is undoubtedly a masterpiece of elegance, harmony and magnificence."

Of the 140 saints represented on Bernini's colonnade before St. Peter's Basilica in Rome four are Carmelites: St. Albert, St. Mary Magdalen de' Pazzi, St. Teresa, St. Andrew Corsini.

Within St. Peter's itself, the statue which "the whole Order erected to its founder, the prophet Elijah," to quote the *cartella* at its base, occupies a place of honor on the right side of the apse between the confession and the cathedra. The figure is the work of Agostino Cornacchini, author also of the equestrian statue of Charlemagne in the atrium of the basilica. Its cost (4,000 *scudi*) was shared by the Order (half) and by the two Discalced Congregations of Spain and Italy (a quarter each). Completed in 1726 and set in its niche the following year, the statue seemed to the Carmelites a confirmation by the Holy See of their claims to their prophetic origin. It is indeed fortunate that the ill-conceived historical controversy at the time did not prove an obstacle to the realization of this unique witness of a religious Order to its spirit.

Other Carmelite Churches in Italy

From an embarrassment of riches, we select a few examples of Carmelite churches from various regions of Italy.

No church, surely, is more "Carmelite" than the Carmini of Venice, crowded during the 17th and 18th centuries with representations of Carmelite saints and events of the Order's history, but otherwise structurally unaltered since the 14th century.

In the polygonal apse, lighted by two orders of large windows, the main altar formerly held the Scapular Vision with Sts. Angelus and Mary Magdalen de' Pazzi by Stroiffi, now lost. On the walls of the sanctuary are painted eucharistic themes by Jacopo Palma the Younger, Gaspare Diziani, and Marco Vincentino. The beautifully carved choir stalls contain representations of Carmelite saints, executed between 1663 and 1688, possibly by Andrea Brustolon.

The chapel of Our Lady of Mount Carmel, which continued to be the object of the solicitude of the Confraternity after its transfer to the Scuola Grande in 1599, contained an altarpiece by Pace Pace depicting Our Lady with Carmelites. The vault was frescoed by Sebastiano Ricci in 1708. The statues of Humility by Giuseppe Torretto (1721) and of Virginity by Antonio Corradini (1721) are among the best works of these sculptors. The stalls of the small choir are adorned with carvings representing miracles of Our Lady of Mount Carmel attributed to Antonio Gay (1686-1769).

Other works of Carmelite interest in the chapels and on the altars include the *Deposition from the Cross with St. Albert* by Alvise Dal Friso, *St. Teresa and the Trinity* by Bernardino Prudenti, *The Child Mary Instructed by Anne with Sts. Joachim and Peter* (the keys embellished with the Carmelite coat of arms) by Gaspare Diziani, *St. Albert Blessing a Child* by Pietro Liberi, *The Trinity with Sts. Mary Magdalen de' Pazzi, and Aloysius Gonzaga* by Bernardino Liberale.

Noteworthy masterpieces not of Carmelite inspiration are a *Nativity with Sts. Helen and Catherine of Alexandria* by Cima da Conegliano (1509), a *St. Nicholas with Sts. John the Baptist and Lucy* by Lorenzo Lotto (1527-1529), *St. Liberale Freeing Two Prisoners* by Alessandro Varotari, called *il Padovanino. The Circumcision* on the fourth altar in the right nave was assigned to Tintoretto by Vasari, but it is now considered to be by Polidoro Lanzani. (A genuine Tintoretto, an Epiphany, is preserved in the artistic Carmelite church of Santa Maria delle Vergini in Macerata.)

Two organs in the nave near the main altar are modern. The 15th century organ, replaced in 1653, was used by Claudio Monteverdi. The lofts are frescoed by Andrea Vincentino (1542-1615), Andrea Schiavone (1522-1563) and Giuseppe Heintz (1653, 1664).

The nave is occupied by a grandiose glorification of Carmel in its saints and history. Between the arches, on pedestals above the pillars, are statues of Carmelite saints by unknown 17th century sculptors, among them possibly Francesco Pianta the Younger and Pietro Morando. In the clerestory above are twenty-four large paintings depicting episodes in the history of the Order, by Giovanni Carboncini, Gaspare Diziani, Giovanni Battista Lambranzi, Pietro Liberi, Sebastiano Mazzoni, Girolamo Brusaferro, Andrea Celesti, Nicolo' Bambini, Ludovico David, Vincenzo da Canal, Gregorio Lazzarini and other unidentified artists. Until the last century, the whole dialogue between paintings and sculpture was crowned and interpreted by the paintings of Lambranzi on the vaulted ceiling of the nave, showing the deeds of Elijah, the prophet, and the glory of the Virgin. Without these transcendent themes, the beholder is introduced rather too abruptly to the particular events of Carmelite history represented in the clerestory. On the other hand, one finds here paintings by reputable artists - for instance, Lazzarini's freeing of Valenciennes through the intercession of the Virgin Mary - not attempted before or since.

The church of San Martino Maggiore, Bologna, given its present form by Giovanni da Brensa, 1491-1496, retained its Gothic look, and while each century added its works of art, this was not done at the expense of what went before, "as a result making of this monumental church an interesting art gallery."

The sanctuary received its octagonal form in 1669 during the priorate of Clemente Felina, noted author of the Mantuan Congregation. The rich *retable* of gilded wood by Andrea da Formigine and his son Giacomo (16th century) contains the painting by Girolamo Sicciolante of the Virgin with John the Baptist, Catherine, and other saints, among them Albert of Sicily (1548). On the walls are an Annunciation attributed to Bartolomeo Passaroti and a Death of St. Joseph by Giacinto Giglioli (1594-1665). The choir stalls are of the 17th century. The organ by Giovanni Cipri (1556) is housed in a beautiful gilt wooded cabinet attributed to Giacomo Marcoaldi.

The chapel of Our Lady of Mount Carmel at the head of the right nave was designed by Alfonso Torreggiani (1753) and frescoed by Vittono Bigari (1696-1776), who did the Scapular Vision in the cupola. The venerable statue of Our Lady of Mount Carmel is by Guglielmo Borgognone (1644), polychromed by Guercino. On the walls are paintings of the martyrdom of St. Ursula by Giovanni Giacomo Sementi, pupil of Guido Reni, and of St. Charles Borromeo with Sts. Andrew Corsini and Teresa, by Alessandro Tiarini (1577-1668). A rich wrought-iron chancel closes off from its austere environment "a distinct jewel of baroque art."

The side naves each contain five chapels. In the right nave, the stone *retable* in pure Renaissance style designed by Bartolomeo Ramenghi, called *il Bagnavacallo*, contains the *Adoration of the Magi* by Girolamo da Carpi (1592), considered his masterpiece. In the chapel of St. Mary Magdalen de' Pazzi, the painting by Cesare Gennari (1637-1688), shows the saint with Andrew Corsini and Albert of Sicily. She is also represented by a beautiful polychrome statue by Angelo Pié in the chapel of the Guardian Angels, as well as by a painting by Domenico Rizzi (1494-1567). The chapel of Joachim and Anne with its painting of the saints by Giulio Taraschi (1558) contains the fresco of the Virgin and Child, much restored, which recalls the style of Lippo Dalmasio (1352-1410). In the adjoining chapel is the painting by Amico Aspertini (1474-1532) of St. Nicholas, accompanied by Sts. Lucy and Augustine, granting a dowry to destitute young women, "a singular composition."

In the left nave are an Assumption by Lorenzo Costa (1506), long attributed to Perugino because of its Umbrian style, a St. Jerome by Lodovico Carracci (1591) and a Crucifixion with St. Peter Thomas and the apostles, Andrew and Bartholomew, by Bartolomeo Cesi (1556-1629).

Francesco Francia's painting of the Virgin is enshrined in a chapel "of Bramantesque solemnity," "the jewel of the church." The painting in a gilt wood *retable* shows the Virgin enthroned and holding the Child. At her feet are Sts. Rocco, Bernardine of Siena, Anthony the Abbot, and Sebastian. Through an arch in the throne, characteristic of the Ferrarese style, is a landscape with Carmelites.

The Carmine Maggiore in Naples, the most prestigious foundation of the Order in Italy, originally was a Gothic church of a single nave with frescoes depicting the life of Christ by Luigi Siciliano, later touched up by Francesco Solimene, who also executed other works in the church. All this disappeared when the church was given its present form by the architect Tagliacozzi-Canale (1753-1766). The marble decoration is due to the brothers Giuseppe and Gennaro Cimafonte, the stucco work to Francesco Gargiulo. The choir at the rear of the church originally had walnut stalls carved by Francesco Zucca (1536). These were lost when lightning struck the tower in 1762, taking the lives of several friars engaged in the recitation of the office. The twelve side chapels, separated by double Corinthian pilasters, are enclosed by inlaid marble railings supporting iron grills. The nave is divided from the transept by a high rood screen bearing the famous miraculous crucifix. The present lacunar ceiling is a faithful copy of that by the Cistercian Bonaventura Presti (1659), destroyed during an aerial bombardment in 1943. In the center was the magnificent figure of *La Bruna* by Giovanni Conte, called the Dwarf.

The miraculous image of *La Bruna* is enshrined in an exquisite marble *retable* attributed to Tommaso Malvita (1500), who executed the altar of St. Barbara in the atrium of the church. The five-sided apse (1670), of varied and precious inlaid marbles, has in its four lateral sides huge alabaster urns, hollow and with removable covers, which compare favorably with anything similar found in Versailles. The main altar with its *antependium* of rare marbles and precious stone, is one of the most beautiful in Naples.

In the chapels of transept and nave are works of art by such artists as Solimene, Matthia Preti, Sarnelli, Francesco de Mura, Andrea d'Asti, Cavalliere Viola.

In 1847, Maximilian of Bavaria commissioned the statue by Albert Thorwaldsen of Conradin, Duke of Swabia, executed in the square outside the Carmine in 1268. The 13th century statue of Elisabeth of Bavaria, mother of Conradin, formerly in the Carmine, is now in the Museo Nazionale di San Martino.

The familiar belfry of the Carmine is composed of a quadrangular base in three orders (1615-1620), surmounted by two octagonal sections (1622) by Giangiacomo Conforto. The curvilinear spire was added in 1631 by the Dominican Giuseppe Nuvolo.

The Gothic church of Trapani (1332) was transformed into a baroque structure by Giovanni Amico, 1760. A reminder of the medieval church is the Sailors' Chapel, constructed in 1476. Here was placed the baptismal font (1486), now in the Museum of Trapani, upon which Gagini modelled his holy water fonts in the Duomo of Palermo. Also in the Museum of Trapani is the Carmine's bronze lecturn by Annibale Scudaniglio (1582).

The two chapels beside the sanctuary contain an antique wooden crucifix by Orlando and a statue of Elijah by Nolfo Trapanese. In the chapel of St. Albert is the celebrated silver statue of the saint, attributed to V. Bonaiuto.

Most of the artistic skill was expended on the lavish chapel of Our Lady of Trapani, itself a church, entered from behind the main altar. The beautiful marble arch at the entrance to the chapel is the work of Antonello Gagini. The bronze grating was cast by Guglielmo Musarra.

The grandiose Carmelite convent of Trapani has become the Museo Pepoli.

Before leaving the subject of the fine arts in Italy, mention should be made of the list of painters, sculptors, and architects by Pellegrino Antonio Orlandi (1660-1727), *Abecedario pittorico* (Bologna, 1704), which underwent many editions and is still useful.

The Great Spanish Masters

In Spain, the great masters of the age concerned themselves with Carmelite themes. Murillo, painter of Our Lady *par excellence*, is credited with at least three portraits of Our Lady of Mount Carmel, today in the Louvre (Paris), the Heinemann Galery (Munich) and the University of Southern California (Los Angeles). At the time of his death, he was working on the Virgin of Carmel in the Women's Hospital in Cádiz.

Velázquez' Immmaculate Conception, now in the National Gallery, London, was painted for the Casa Grande in Seville. A relation has been seen between this painting and the book by the Sevillian friar, John de las Ruelas, *Hermosura corporal de la Madre de Dios* (Sevilla, 1621), devoted to a description of every aspect of the Virgin's physical beauty, surely a unique contribution to Marian literature.

Zurbaran's Cyril of Constantinople and Peter Thomas (both in the Museum of Fine Arts, Boston) are as unconventional iconographically as his other saints. In the case of Peter Thomas, the Spanish master must have known the biography by Philippe de Mézières, contemporary of the saint, for instead of being shown with his conventional iconographical symbols Peter Thomas is seen with the hat he wore on his incessant travels, wearing the habit of the humble Carmelite friar in spite of his patriarchal dignity, and reciting his breviary, which he never neglected on land or sea - all details carefully pointed out by his devoted friend, Philippe.

Carmelite Churches in Spain

After various wars and suppressions, not much remains of Carmelite artifacts and buildings in Spain.

Carmelite churches, for the most part despoiled of their original contents and not always still in Carmelite hands, survive in Madrid, Valderas, Cordova, Ecija, Antequera, Jerez de la Frontera, Osuna, Murcia, Triguera, Utrera, Alhama, Granada, Valencia, Orihuela, Manresa, Olot, Perelada, Valls, Vich. In respect of surviving structures, Andalusia is the most fortunate.

The church of the Order in Madrid (1611-1640), the work of the architect, Miguel de Soria (d. 1638), may be seen today as the church of the Carmen y San Luis. Its original contents are known from the account of Antonio Palomino. The *retable* of the main altar, designed by Sebastian de Benavente, featured a statuary group representing the scapular vision, carved by Juan Sanchez Barba, who also executed the other figures of the *retable*. Paintings in the church included a "very famous" baptism of St. John by Diego Polo the Younger, a picture of the Guardian Angel attached to the pulpit by Angelo Nardi, a "famous" Elijah, an Elisha and a Trinity by Antonio Pereda, a Conception in the chapel of the Santo Cristo by Antonio Castrejon.

Palomino tells a delightful tale about a painting made for the cloister by Sebastian Muñoz, of the death in 1689 of the twenty-six year old Queen María Luisa, who had been buried in the Carmelite habit. The friars stoutly held that the picture did not resemble the Queen nor were they to be dissuaded by a group of the artist's friends.

"You know more about art than I, but everyone is an authority on what the Queen looked like," declared the prior, Juan Barrientos.

"That's just the perfection of the picture," he was told, "because the dead Queen did not resemble the Queen alive."

"That's all very well," the prior rejoined, smiling, "if you'll stand here all day long and explain that to everyone who comes along and sees the picture."

His riposte suggested the solution. Muñoz added a medallion held by two mournful cupids, who showed the Queen as she was in life. A legend, perfectly suiting the lugubrious taste of the age, read: *Nec semper lilia florent* (Lilies do not bloom forever). The scene in the cloister, which adds an insight into the character of the reformer, Juan Barrientos, would itself have provided a fit subject for a painting.

The church in Cordova was recovered by the Order in 1916 and contains what is perhaps the single most striking work of Carmelite art extant in Spain: Juan Valdés Leal's paintings for the monumental *retable* of the main altar, depicting scenes from the life of Elijah and containing portraits of various other saints.

The Salesians occupy the site of the former Carmelite convent in Ecija, but the church with its lovely tower, characteristic of the town, still exists. Of a restrained baroque, the church consists of two naves, transept and cupola. The baroque *retable* of the main altar is in Fr. Martínez Grande's opinion "without question one of the most beautiful examples to be found of this architectural style." It holds an image of the Virgin, "a graceful statue, but without great merit." Lateral panels display two large paintings depicting episodes in the history of the Rule. The second nave contains the remarkable chapel of Our Lady *de la Soledad,* her statue said to be the work of Tamariz Martel. Other statues worthy of note are an Elijah, "a most beautiful and exceptional sculpture (which) compares favorably with the best in the museums and expositions of Spain." A Gothic Christ is in all likelihood the work of Montes de Oca. The choir stalls, "of a very chaste baroque", have been moved to the Carmelite church of Osuna.

In 1939, the Carmelites repossessed their original church in Antequera. A new convent was added in 1949. Compared to the church of Ecija, Fr. Martínez Grande finds "the monumental church of Antequera of a decidedly overloaded style, decadent baroque, so opulent and unrestrained as to sin by affectation." In the choir are three 17th century canvases of the Andalusian School, depicting the profession, death, and burial of St. Albert.

In 1880, the Carmelites returned to their church in Jerez de la Frontera (1727), despoiled of its contents. The 16th century image of Our Lady of Mount Carmel, however, was saved, and today reigns from its *camarín* behind the main altar. Art work, statues, and paintings in the church are of the 19th and 20th century.

Church and convent of Osuna reverted to the Order in 1891. The expressive Virgin in her *camarín* above the main altar (17th century) has won the hearts of many. Other altars and *retables* are dedicated to Bl. Francus, Elijah, Teresa. Carmelite themes are also reflected in the 17th century paintings which adorn the church.

The important convent of Valencia today is the Museo Provincial de Valencia. In 1842, the church returned to service as the parish church of the Holy Cross, but it had already suffered much under the French (1812) and after the exclaustration (1835), when it served as a place of storage. In the description by the Marqués de Cruilles (1876), the large church "of Corinthian architecture" was composed of a single nave with nine chapels on each side. The chapel of the Third Order by the Valencian architect, Vicente Gascó (1780), situated to the right of the entrance, contained paintings by Luis de Sotomayor, depicting the history of the miraculous image of Our Lady "*La Morenita*." The *sagrario* of this chapel (1783) was surmounted by a painting attributed to Jerónimo Espinosa. Luis Martín Malo celebrated the chapel in a long poem, *La capille de N. S. del Carmen de Valencia* (Valencia, 1784). All these artifacts were destroyed in the Civil War, 1936-1939. Ponz noticed a number of paintings he assigned to Jerónimo Espinosa: a Transfiguration over the main altar (later in the Museo Provincial), an Ascension of Elijah, a Mantle Virgin, a Death of St. Albert, and an Andrew Corsini on an altar near the entrance to the church. A catalog of 1850 of 586 paintings in Museo Provincial contains canvases of indubitably Carmelite inspiration (as far as can be identified from the sparse data the catalog provides) by José Zapata, Luis Planes, Bautista Suñer, Francisco Brú, Gaspar de la Huerta, Vicente Salvador, Estévan March, some of them probably from the Carmen of Valencia.

The Carmelite church of Olot, of Gothic style, was completed in 1572 or shortly thereafter. The beautiful cloister by Lazaro Cisterna, architect of Geronda, was built, 1600-1611, "perhaps the best architectural work today in the city of Olot." The *retable* of the main altar (1623) was burned during the Seven Years' War. The present *camarín* dates from 1720. During the Seven Years' War, the convent became a fort, and the church suffered much damage. After the expulsion of the friars (1835), the church was reopened for cult in 1843. The Carmelites returned in 1892. During the Civil War convent and church again suffered deterioration.

The beautiful 14th century Gothic church of Perelada, saved from destruction in 1854-1855, when it reverted to the original donors, the Counts of Perelada, who tastefully restored it, today shows no evidence of the baroque period of its existence. No doubt it was then that the main altar of the Virgin was embellished with statues of Sts. Telesphorus and Andrew Corsini, and chapels were dedicated to Albert, Mary Magdalen de' Pazzi, and the Holy Sepulchre. In 1446, six altar stones were consecrated, of Anthony and Catherine, James, Blaise and Anne, the Holy Cross, Sebastian and Paul, the Trinity and Michael and finally the 11,000 Virgins. The *retable* of the latter was fetched from Mallorca in 1383. The convent with its lovely 14th century cloister houses a library and museum.

No longer existing are the original churches and convents in Salamanca ("the Escorial of Salamanca"), Valladolid, Segovia, Toledo, Medina del Campo, Seville, Zaragoza, Villarreal, Caudete, Barcelona, Palma de Mallorca, Lérida. Some fragments of their furnishings survive in other churches and museums.

Carmelite Art in Portugal

The earthquake of 1755 caused extensive damage throughout the province of Portugal. Most of the convents survived to be suppressed in 1834, but in what state is at present not known. A few examples of their condition may be listed.

The ruins of the great Gothic church of the Carmo of Lisbon, the fragment of its rose window standing against the sky like a sickle moon, still dominates the modern city from the heights reached by the elevator constructed by the creator of the Eiffel tower. Ancient authors are extravagant in their praise of this structure, the opulent gift of the wealthy Constable, St. Nuno Alvares Pereira, before his entry into the Order. Constructed by the master builders, Alfonso, Rodrigo, and Gonçalo Anes, it consists of three naves and a transept, the naves divided by five Gothic arches.

Eighteenth century descriptions of the church abound in detail and reveal the fact that its interior was thoroughly transformed in baroque times. The *capela-mor*, or sanctuary, reputed the richest in the court, was provided with a new *retable* commissioned by the distinguished scripture scholar, John de Sylveira. At the summit was the figure of the Savior. At the second level was the tribune of the Blessed Sacrament containing the silver, gem-studded tabernacle, surmounted by a tall monstrance (1693) and backed by a canopy in the form of a burst of rays (1700). The tribune was flanked by life-size statues of Elijah and Elisha, the former bearing the sword of Nuno himself. Also alleged to derive from the Holy Constable was the statue of Our Lady of Mount Carmel standing on the lower level of the *retable* on a silver base provided by Frei José de Sousa with income from his published sermons (1722). The Virgin held the Child on her left arm, the scapular in her right hand. Her rich garments were provided by King John V, among others (1709). Costly crowns of gold and diamonds for Virgin and Child were the pious gift of Frei Cajetano de Santo Alberto, distinguished musician and cantor in the royal chapel. The altar, too, was richly furnished with candlesticks by the noted João Frederico Passos. Above two windows beside the Virgin's throne were figures of St. Teresa and St. Mary Magdalen de' Pazzi. A triumphal arch bearing two huge angels with spears and shields enclosed the structure and terminated in two pulpits (1717, 1718) from which the Word was proclaimed on solemn occasions. Above the choir stalls, the work of Diogo de Carta, were paintings of the saints of the Order, below which were seventeen reliquaries (1690). On the left side of the sanctuary was the tomb of St. Nuno, on the right the small organ.

The elaborate furnishings of the other chapels of the church are described by contemporaries with equal abundance of detail.

The harsh hand of time has swept away this splendor of precious metals, gems, marble, and glided wood and has drastically restored the simplicity of Gothic line to the broken walls that remain.

In the 18th century, the church at Vidigueira had been in existence since 1593. Its elegant facade with window and "eye," or small, round aperture, was flanked by two towers. On the main altar above the tabernacle was the popular Virgin of the Relics. The gilded *retable*, "of excellent architecture," (M. de Sá) had five panels showing the Birth of Mary, Annunciation, Presentation, Adoration of the Magi, and Assumption. The altar held statues of Our Lady granting the scapular to St. Simon and of the prophet Elijah. On the left wall of the sanctuary was a Transfiguration, "a singular painting." There, too, in a niche were the mortal remains of the famous "Argonaut," Vasco da Gama.

The original Carmelite church of Évora, described by contemporaries as "very majestic," had a single nave with six chapels, besides two in the transept and the sanctuary with its altar. The monastery with spacious cloister and extensive gardens was large enough to accommodate King Philip III of Spain and his retinue during his journey in 1619, celebrated by the poet Francisco Rodríguez Lobo. Convent and church were destroyed in the siege of Evora by Don Juan of Austria in 1663, though some of the furnishings of the church must have been salvaged, judging by descriptions of the succeeding church.

Begun in 1669, the new church, "one of the most singular in the province of Alentejo," took twenty-one years to complete and was the work of "the two best architects at that time in Lisbon." The wooden *retable* with its pillars was painted to look like stone. It held the miraculous image of Our Lady of Light from the original church and statues of Elijah and Elisha.

Unfortunately, authors fail to identify all but a few of the artists responsible for the works of art in all these churches. No doubt the list would include, at least in the case of Lisbon, some of the outstanding masters of Portugal.

One would expect the "Holy Constable," St. Nuno Alvares Pereira, to have been more frequently portrayed in the arts. Today his statue is found on the colonnade of the Praça do Mercado in Lisbon and on the square of the basilica of Fatima.

Baroque Churches in Brazil

Brazil by no means lagged behind the mother country in the splendor of its buildings and their furnishings.

The present church of Bahia (modern Salvador), begun in 1602, has a single ponderous tower and a facade in two orders, the lower with three portals, matched above by three windows, the whole crowned with a typical voluted pediment. Within, the ornate *retable* of gilded wood enshrines the statue of Our Lady of Mount Carmel, said to have been brought from Lisbon by the original community in 1585. On each side, are statues of Elijah and Elisha. The precious tabernacle and antependium of wrought silver are the work of Caetano Mendes Costa (1732). Beside the altar are two silver candelabra weighing eighty kilos each. The sanctuary is set off from the nave by a railing of hand carved jacaranda of singular beauty. The equally striking choir stalls in the sanctuary are of the same rare wood. In the ceiling over the choir is a painting representing the apotheosis of Carmel. Chapels are dedicated to the Blessed Sacrament, St. Anne, St. Joseph, and Our Lady of Mercy (*Piedade*). The elaborate *retable* of the Blessed Sacrament chapel is the gift of Bernardo Vieira Ravasco, poet-soldier and brother of the Carmelite, Antonio Vieira, and was gilded by Frei Serafim de Santa Teresa Pontes in 1755. The chapel of St. Joseph also contains a statue of Our Lady of a Happy Death, placed there in 1685. The object of great veneration is an ancient crucifix called *Santo Cristo do Monte*.

The Carmo was the center of resistance during the attack of the Dutch on Bahia. There in the "*sala histórica*", as it is now called, the enemy signed the act of capitulation on April 30, 1625. In the same room was held the First Legislative Assembly of Bahia, December 1, 1828.

The church of Recife was begun in 1663 and completed in 1767. Its ornamental facade filigreed with stuccos is flanked by two towers, one lacking belfry and steeple. Above three portals are corresponding windows, between which are statues of Elijah and Elisha and small round apertures. The entablature of florid rococo lines contains an ancient stone statue of the Virgin.

The three naves of the church have thirteen chapels and twelve altars. The main chapel, or sanctuary, was the gift (1658) of Captain Diogo Cavalcanti de Vasconcellos, wealthy landowner of Goyana, who lies buried there. On the *retable* in a burst of golden rays and surrounded by jubilant angels stands the miraculous image of Our Lady of Mount Carmel. In niches in the pilasters of the *retable* are statues of Elijah and Elisha. The sanctuary also contains the hand carved jacaranda choir stalls and on the walls between balconies are paintings of the saints of the Order.

The *retable* of the Blessed Sacrament altar, completed in 1696 and gilded in 1738, had a life-size crucifix, now in the choir loft. The chapel of *Senhor Bom Jesus dos Passos* was begun in 1696. Its embellishment and gilding which occupied the years 1785-1797 was paid for by Frei Manoel de Monte Carmelo, scion of a wealthy family, who also is interred there. The altar of Our Lady of the Conception chapel dates from 1708. The other altars are of cedar wood in the same florid style, each one different from the other.

Descriptions of other important churches, such as Rio de Janeiro, Olinda, Santos, and Goyana, are not at hand.

Chapter 7

The Fine Arts in the Ultramontane Provinces

With Italy, France was a center of Baroque art, and under the reign of the Sun King became the arbiter of artistic taste throughout Europe.

Little remains of the artistic patrimony of the Order in France. Almost completely rebuilt after the wars of religion, Carmel there would have been baroque in form. At the time of the Revolution, not only the enemies of the Republic were put on the block and horribly mutilated. Churches and monastic establishments and their contents were similarly dismantled and dispersed. Silver objects - chalices, candlesticks, thuribles, crosses, monstrances, even statues - were often packed off to the Mint. In some instances, a purpose, sacred or profane, was found for convents and churches, which were consequently saved.

In the province of Provence, the Carmelite churches of Avignon, Marseille, Le Luc, and La Rochette continued as parish churches. The church of Pertuis became a theatre. The convent of Vienne was converted into a textile factory.

The 14th century church of Avignon, become the parish church of St. Symphorien, was saved together with its cloister, recently restored. Among its furnishings are paintings by Nicolas Mignard, Guillaume Grève, Guillaume Ernest Grève, Pierre Parrocel, Philippe Sauvan.

In the attractive 17th century church of Our Lady of Mount Carmel in Marseilles, the main altar of gilded wood is the work of Antoine Duparc (1733), completed by the Polish artist, Johann Gottlieb Courlaffski, "a very beautiful ensemble." The walnut choir stalls in the style of Louis XIV are in the Musée du Vieux Marseille. The pulpit, "of great purity of line," is attributed to Pierre Puget (André Bouyala d'Arnaud). In the side chapels are sculptures representing the Adoration of the Magi, the Crucifixion and the Baptism of Christ.

The famous triptych of the Burning Bush by Nicolas Froment (1476), now in the Cathedral of St. Sauveur at Aix, formerly graced the chapel of King René, "the Good," of Provence (1434-1480) in the Carmelite church, which must have been a veritable museum of art. The Revolutionary agent, who in 1790 inventoried the contents of the church, fortunately showed an unusual sensitivity in describing them, listing not only the names of the chapels, but objects of art and their creators. In the chapel of King René, he notes, besides the triptych, "*ouvrage très estimé*," a painting of St. Mire (Nicholas of Myra?) by one of the Darets. For various chapels the same masters made paintings of Christ, the Holy Family, St. Anne, Our Lady of Victory, St. Albert, and St. Andrew Corsini. The altarpiece of the Scapular chapel was by the "famous Mignard." This may be the painting now in the Church of St. Jean de Malte in Aix. The altar piece of the chapel of St. Sebastian was by Michel Serre. The painting over the altar of St. Thomas, the perceptive agent remarks, was "*fort bon*." Under the windows at the end of the choir were three statues of the Virgin of painted and gilded stone, "which are said to be very ancient."

Churches of the Narbonne province to survive were Clermont-Ferrand (St. Genès-les-Carmes), Moulins (St. Pierre), Le Puy (St. Pierre), Nimes (St. Baudile), Bagnols (Chapelle des Pénitents), Mende (St. Dominique). The convents of Chalon and Mende became city halls, Dijon a Visitation monastery.

The 14th century church of Le Puy formerly contained four large Aubusson tapestries representing scenes from the life of the prophet Elijah (since 1869 in the Musée Crozatier). Among the paintings of the church are a Virgin placing the Child Jesus in the arms of St. Felix of Cantalice by Guy François, a subject also attempted by other and more prestigious masters. Guy's son, Jean, painted a Nativity of the Virgin and a Christ on the Cross. A *pietà* and an excellent copy of Murillo's Virgin and St. Elizabeth are by Chaminade. One of the most prized possessions of the Musée Crozatier is the 15th century Mantle Virgin painted on silk, transferred from the Carmelite church in 1852, probably the banner of one of its confraternities. "It is a painting universally admired, a pure marvel of composition and coloring" (André Chanal).

The church at Castelsarrasin in the province of Toulouse was converted into a prison, but its "charming ogival belfry" remained standing (M. Pottier). The convent of Carcassonne became a post office. The convent of Pamiers was occupied by the Discalced Carmelites from 1854 to 1901.

The cloister of the convent of Trie in Gascony found its way to the Metropolitan Museum of New York. Its church became a garage. The church in Lectoure survived as the parish church of St. Esprit. The church of Jonzac became the court house, its convent a prison.

In the province of Touraine, the Carmelite church of Loudun became the parish church of St. Hilaire. In 1867, what was left of the church of La Flocellière was restored and put to use as the church of Our Lady of Loreto.

The main altar of the church of Angers was dedicated to St. Joseph. In the choir was a beautiful tapestry representing the life of the Virgin with figures of Carmelites. The chapels were dedicated to Our Lady of Recovery, the *Ecce Homo* (with a statue of St. Symphorien), St. Anne (with a statue of St. Barbara), St. Joachim, St. Martha, St. Rocco, Job. On the right was an altar with a sculpted group, the Flight into Egypt, which even the Huguenots did not have the heart to destroy.

Brother Sebastian of St. Aniane (d. 1669), of the province of Touraine, was skilled in poetry, physics, and history, but he was mainly active as an architect. The convents of Les Billettes, Orléans, and Nantes were the particular beneficiaries of his expertise. He left manuscript works on painting and architecture, preserved in the conventual archive of Orléans, where they were consulted by students of the arts.

The Carmelite convent of Aurillac in the Aquitaine province became a lycée for girls. The main altar of the church and a sarcophagus of St. Pamphilius were removed to the church of Notre Dame aux Neiges. In 1872, the *baldacchino* was sent to the church of St. Nicholas-des-Champs in Paris. The church in Pléaux was restored in 1896; the convent had been a minor seminary since 1820. The church of Lauzerte survived the Revolution as an *eglise succursale* with the title Notre Dame des Carmes. The convent at La Châtre became the city hall, in which the chapel with its paintings was retained.

Some of the paintings in the church of Limoges were by a certain Brother Luke who also executed an altarpiece for the church of the hermitage of St. Sever at Vire.

The inventory of 1790 of the church of La Rochefoucauld listed an Assumption over the main altar and paintings in the chapels of St. Anne, St. Paul, St. Joseph ("*tableau assez grand*"), St. Anthony, a Christ. In the Lady Chapel was a "judgement of Sts. Crispin and Crispinian." In the sacristy, the agent of the Republic noted among other things a silver Virgin on an oak pedestal, 10-1/2". She wore a crown, *"qui est faussée,"* held a palm in her right hand and the Child Jesus in her left. The Infant had a globe in his hand. In a cabinet were three paintings of 4', 5' and 6' representing the Virgin, Elijah, and Elisha respectively. In the refectory, he found "a large painting representing Mount Carmel (and) another which is very ancient, painted on wood and encased in a gilded frame." The church was put to profane uses, the convent became a school.

In the province of Francia, the Order's beautiful 14th century church in Metz was the work of Pierre Perrat, architect of the cathedral. In a dilapidated state, it was barbarously torn down in 1826. Its exquisite stone altar, however, had been acquired by the Empress Josephine for the chapel at Malmaison, but her divorce from Napoleon put an end to her plans. The altar, still in the fourteen crates in which it had been shipped from Metz, fell into private hands. Once it narrowly escaped being used for paving blocks. Eventually, the upper half was purchased by the Marquis of Pontalba for the chapel of his castle of Mont l'Evêque near Senlis, the lower part became a gallery in the castle of Gueulzion of Baron d'Hurzel near Douai.

The Carmelite church of St. Amand is today the city hall. Melun became a theatre. The convent of Liège was converted into a hotel. The altarpiece of the main altar of its church held a painting of the scapular vision by Walter Damery (Museum of Mainz). Over the entrance to the cloister was a statue of Elijah by Jean del Cour.

The Carmelite Churches of Paris

Of the Order's church and convent in the Place Maubert only a few remnants of the convent are recognizable in an apartment building. The main altar by Jacquin (1683), known from an engraving, featured a sculptured group of the Transfiguration. The church also had statues of Elijah and Elisha and pictures of St. Anthony and St. Paul the Hermit. A group, larger than life, described by Joan Evans as the Virgin giving a rosary to a kneeling Carmelite accompanied by Sts. Joseph, Joachim, Teresa, and Laura, is more likely a representation of the scapular vision. A 15th century processional cross is in the Musée de Cluny. A series of frescoes traced the life of St. Louis.

The church of Les Billettes, the Paris house of the province of Touraine, is since 1812 a Lutheran church, rue des Archives 24. Its 15th century cloister, which antedates the coming of the Carmelites, is the only remaining medieval cloister in Paris.

Carmelite Art in the Low Countries

In this land that produced the *Speculum Carmelitanum*, the legendary past of the Order is displayed in every detail in Carmelite churches. In this task, the greatest Flemish masters collaborated.

Rubens, to begin with, painted many masterpieces for both Orders of Carmelites. For the Carmelites of Antwerp, he portrayed the Death of Christ and Mary taught by her parents (both in the Museum voor Schone Kunsten) and the Adoration of the Magi. He designed the main altar dedicated to the Blessed Sacrament and its altar piece, the Glorification of the Eucharist (sketch in the Metropolitan Museum, New York), but the latter, now lost, was actually painted by Gerard Zeghers. The altar was built by Rubens' friend, Hans van Mildert. Rubens also painted the portrait of John de la Court, prior of Antwerp, 1610-1622, (Collection of Lord Plunket, London) and of another unidentified Carmelite (Rotterdam, Museum Boymans).

In the Flandro-Belgian province, the Carmelite church of Antwerp, no longer in existence, was a treasury of art, setting forth the twin themes of the Elian and Marian character of the Order. Twenty windows designed by Jacob Floris and executed by Abraham van Diepenbeke depicted the lives of Elijah and Elisha. Another dozen told the life of Mary, scriptural and legendary. For the richly decorated chapel of the Mystical Rose, Rubens designed embroideries (now in the Church of St. Charles Borromeo, Antwerp). At the entrance to the chapel stood statues of Joachim and Anne attributed to Joris van Horenbeke. Mention has already been made of the chapel of *La Bruna*; its altar was by Moons or Erasmus Quellin. Besides, the church contained a wealth of paintings. Pierre Franchois painted Elijah's vision of the cloud; P. Eyckens the Elder, Elias fed by the raven and his ascent into heaven; Peter Theys, St. Emerentia consulting the prophets about her marriage; P. van Lint, a visit of Mary to Mount Carmel; François Goubeau, Mary appearing to her former suitor, St. Agabus; H. Sporckman, Mary appearing to Pope Honorius III (Museum Plantin-Moretus, Antwerp); J. Jordaens, the emigration of the Carmelites to the West; J. Coetsiers, the apparition of Mary to St. Peter Thomas. Van Lint depicted the delightful legend of the appearance of Mary to the Carmelites of Mechelen, when she distributed to each member of the community a gift corresponding to his particular virtue (Museo Lázaro Galdiano, Madrid). Other paintings in this church were a communion of St. Teresa by Gerard Zeghers, St. Charles Borromeo by H. Sporckmans, the Burial of Christ by Abraham Janssens, and a Last Judgment with a scandalous abundance of nudes by J. de Backer (Koninklijk Museum voor Schone Kunsten, Antwerp). Thomas Willeborts, called Bosschaert, who did a painting of St. Catherine's mystical marriage, also chose to be buried in the church. The statuary of the church included figures of Mary Magdalen de' Pazzi and Charles Borromeo by Moons and Elias fed by the raven by H. Verbruggen.

The altarpiece of the main altar of the church in Brussels held a reproduction of *La Bruna*, supported by two cherubim. The altar also displayed statues of Elijah and Enoch. In the choir were paintings by Victor Janssens showing the life of Elijah and one by J. van Helmont on the sacrifice of the prophet. Bernard van Orley's painting of Elijah fed by the raven probably originally belonged to this cycle but was moved to the nave to make way for Duplici's Last Judgment. For the wainscoting above the choir stalls Victor Janssens had painted pictures of unspecified saints. The nave developed the Marian theme: the *Annunciation* by M. van der Voort, the *Marriage of Our Lady and her Purification* by M. de Haese (now in St. Catherine's Church, Brussels), the *Holy Family* by Victor Janssens. Joined to the transept was a Scapular Chapel with a painting by Jan van Orley of the vision of St. Simon Stock. There, too, may have hung Victor Janssens' picture of the scapular vision including Mary Magdalen de' Pazzi, now in the Carmelite convent of Boxmeer. Beside the chapel were a "Virgin with Carmelites" by Erasmus Quellin the Younger and what seems to have been a picture about the Sabbatine privilege by J. van Helmont. The church also had a chapel dedicated to St. Anne with an altarpiece showing the saint instructing Mary (a copy of Rubens?) and an altar of St. Catherine. Among the paintings were one by Victor Janssens of St. Charles Borromeo and another by G.

de Crayer of St. Dorothy. The beautiful pulpit with Elias comforted by the angel and six confessionals by Edmond Plumier are in the church of Notre Dame de la Chapelle, Brussels.

For the Carmelite church in Brussels, Brother Macarius Berlere (d. 1666) designed the "pleasing" bell tower. Contemporary authors praise the "perfect taste" of the main altar in the Minims' church in Brussels, the work of a Carmelite brother, possibly Macarius. He designed the church of the Carmelite nuns at Vilvoorde.

Witness to the Carmelite presence in Mechelen is the admirable painting by Lucas Franchois of Mary with the Child in intimate conversation with a file of accompanying Carmelites. The church is also known to have had a landscape by the noted local painter, Berincx, and statues of St. Joseph and St. Mary Magdalen de' Pazzi by Nicholas Vanderveken.

Although the composition of the furnishings of the church in Brugge is not known, a number of art works illustrating the nature and history of the Order have been preserved, scattered to the four winds. On the Elian theme is a painting by De Deyster of Elijah comforted by the angel (1680), now in the Cathedral of the Heilige Verlosser. D. Nollet, a local artist, in a work now in the church of Notre Dame, pictured Elijah and the ambassadors of Ochosias, "a painting," writes Cécile Edmond, "which charms by the richness of its coloring and the correctness of composition." The striking pulpit now in St. Martin's Church, Rousselaer, featured Elijah rebuking Achab (1603). With regard to the Virgin Mary, De Deyster painted an Assumption (north aisle of the deanery church of Gistel), Mary appearing to Andrew Corsini at his first Mass (Church of St. Gilles, Brugge) and Mary offering the Infant to St. Albert (now lost). Erasmus Quellin the Younger painted the scapular vision (Cathedral of the H. Verlosser) and D. Nollet pictured St. Louis saved by the Virgin from the peril of the sea (Musée de la Poterie, Brugge).

Of the saints, Bakereel portrayed Charles Borromeo (H. Verlosser Cathedral); De Deyster, Mary Magdalen receiving the stigmata (St. Martin's Church, Kortrijk) and Angelus in the desert (deanery church, Gistel). This last painting is rated by Edmond as the artist's greatest work. "Design and coloring are excellent and the scene with only two figures in a woody landscape is in the grand style." A painting by J.B. Herregouts the Younger, apparently of St. Cyril of Alexandria, no longer exists.

The church and convent of Ghent, another important house of the Flemish province, exist today and are included in a plan to restore the surrounding historic area known as "*Het Patershol.*" The main altar (now in the Church of the Recollects) had held a copy of the *Madonna della Bruna*. Eight confessionals, "rightly famous in the history of art," with joining wainscoting are in the Augustinian *Sint Stephanuskerk*. The Augustinians also bought the pulpit, organ and choir stalls. By some quirk of fate, portions of the wainscoting found their way to Hazelwood Castle, Tadcaster, Yorkshire.

Among paintings that have survived, three by G. de Crayer are concerned with the scapular: the scapular vision, the granting of the Sabbatine bull, and Our Lady freeing souls from Purgatory (at present all in the Discalced church, Ghent). T. Boeyermans painted the mystical marriage of St. Mary Magdalen de' Pazzi (Discalced church) and St. Charles Borromeo administering to the sick (Museum voor Schone Kunsten). Finally, there is a 16th century triptych about the Beatitudes, a Crowning with Thorns attributed to Jan Janssens, and a Crucifixion by J. van

Helmont (all in the Museum voor Schone Kunsten). T. Boeyermans is also known to have done a cycle of nine paintings depicting episodes of Carmelite history.

The interesting anonymous painting, which Edmond styles "the Master of the Carmelite Order," today in the Discalced convent of Ghent, is oblong in shape to represent a panoramic landscape. The picture of which the outstanding feature is the figure of the Virgin leading the Child and followed by Carmelite saints, pictorially unfolds the Elian and Marian character of the Order.

Of the Gallo-Belgian province, the Church of St. Andrew in Lille still exists and contains three paintings by J. van Oost the Younger, showing Mary and Joseph jointly holding the Child Jesus (an iconographical rarity), the scapular vision (side altar) and Mary Magdalen de' Pazzi entering into glory. There is also a Teresa transfixed, "a beautiful statue, of which the flowing drapery recalls the manner of Bernini."

Of the Wallo-Belgian Vicariate, the Carmelite church in La Xhavée is today the parish church. Over the main altar is a painting of the scapular vision. The church in Wavre became the city hall and has been tastefully restored after serious damage during the war in 1940. Its four confessionals, carved by Brother Arnold of St. Francis, are in the village church of Vieux Sart, near Corroy-Le-Grand. The choir stalls are the work of Brothers Albert of St. Joseph and Angelus of St. Mary. Laurent Delvaux, of Ghent, moved to Nivelles, and for the Carmelite church there carved the tabernacle, confessionals (St. Gertrude Church), and "admirable" pulpit depicting Elijah comforted by an angel (Church of the Holy Sepulchre). By his own wish, he was buried in the Carmelite church at the foot of his pulpit. Four confessionals and wainscoting by his hand ended up in St. Nicholas Church in Nivelles, but were destroyed during the war in 1940.

Both at Wavre and Nivelles, brothers are seen wielding a trowel, cutting stone or wood, placing windows. At other times, they direct the work - whether as architects or builders is not certain.

In Boxmeer in the Netherlands, the Carmelites took over the 14th century Gothic style church with its sturdy tower. Around 1430, the nave had been enlarged and during the rest of the century embellished with wall paintings discovered during restorations in 1885. The new main altar, dedicated to St. Peter, patron of the church, dated from 1562. Ornamented with gilded figures, it occupied the whole rear wall of the sanctuary. Side altars dedicated to St. Barbara, the Holy Spirit, the Blessed Virgin, and the miraculous relic of the precious blood, to which there was great popular devotion, were added during the 15th century. In 1700, the image of the *Madonna della Bruna* was given pride of place in the Mary chapel. Other works of art in the church were the organ cabinet built by Jan Werkens of Venraij (1637) and the tomb in black, white, and red marble of Count Oswald van den Bergh and his wife (1741).

The church was dynamited in the Second World War, but the convent and its artifacts remained intact. The latter include the eighteen stained glass windows in the cloister made on designs by Abraham van Diepenbeke (d. 1675) and portraits of the noble ruling family of Boxmeer.

Carmelite Art in Germany

In the war torn German nations, the Baroque style got off to a late but glorious explosion of airy and fantastic form, by no means the least significant artistic phenomenon of the age. The Stricter Observance revived Carmelite life in the German provinces, recovering and restoring its convents and churches.

In the Lower German province, of the imposing convent and church in Cologne, the most important Carmelite foundation in Germany, intellectual center during the Middle Ages, focus of Counter-Reformational activity, where papal legates with their numerous entourage found ample accommodations during diplomatic missions, only an insignificant fraction of conventual buildings and a few scattered artifacts remain.

An altarpiece, painted around 1510 and showing St. Angelus the Martyr, is today in the treasury of the cathedral of Aachen.

The Carmelite church in Boppard, "Pearl of the Rhine," has maintained its Gothic characteristics to the present day. Its richly carved oaken choir stalls A. Reichensperger reckoned "among the most elegant and noble to come down from the prolific 15th century." Six of its stained glass windows today form the most striking feature of the Boppard Room in The Cloisters in Fort Tyron Park, New York.

Beilstein, to which the Carmelites returned in 1948, was founded under the Stricter Observance. The church, built 1691-1738, is the work of David Wynant, a lay brother of the Augustinian Canons of Springiersbach. The baroque *retable* of walnut, flanked by two pairs of smooth and convoluted pillars, holds a statue of the patron, St. Joseph. Side altars are dedicated to St. Anne and the scapular vision. The former also has a painting of St. Mary Magdalen de' Pazzi being granted the veil of virginity; the latter, the appearance of the Virgin to St. Albert of Sicily, all *comme il faut* according to 17th century Carmelite devotion. The paintings were the work of the Carmelite Andrew Corsini of St. Henry. A 13th century "Black Madonna," brought by a Spaniard to Beilstein during the Thirty Years' War, was honored in a special chapel. In modern times, the statue passed through private hands to the Diözesanmuseum of Trier, whence it was restored to its original site (1950).

The 15th century Carmelite church and convent of Frankfurt are remarkable for the frescoes of Jerg Ratgeb. This artist hardly finds a mention in histories of art, and only belatedly has been ranked with Dürer and Grünewald among the great German masters. Ratgeb's tempera frescoes, covering three sides of the cloister, consisted of a continuous band of images of miniaturistic detail, 4.5 m. high and 120 m. long - a total of 550 sq. m. - picturing the life of Christ, each mystery matched by its prophetic antecedant in the Old Testament, "a mighty symphony such as no one before or after him created, completed in the almost inconceivable period of one hundred weeks, for it bears the date 1517." Fried Lübbecke does not hesitate to add that it is "one of the greatest masterpieces of all time." Whatever is to be said of this opinion, one has to think of the Brancaccio chapel to challenge it, as far as art related to Carmel is concerned. Ratgeb covered the smaller area of the refectory with the story of Elias and the history of the monks on Mount Carmel - after the symphony of the cloister, "a sort of piece of chamber music." These great masterpieces suffered severely after the premises served as a warehouse during the 19th century and were bombarded in World War II.

The 14th century Carmelite church in Mainz has remained structurally unchanged, in spite of its disastrous past. The church suffered extensive damage from use as a warehouse during the 19th century. It was restored, when the Carmelites returned in 1924, but once more reduced to ruins during a bombardment in 1942. The church was again renovated in 1954.

Furnishings of the past include the *retable* of the former high altar, a triptych in bas-relief, showing the crowning of the Virgin with Sts. Albert of Jerusalem and Angelus the Martyr. The twelve apostles are pictured on the wings (1517). A 15th century statue of unusual iconographic style represents the Virgin holding the Child, who is writing the names of the just on a scroll. In her right hand, Mary holds a crucifix surrounded by angels catching the precious blood in chalices. She wears a high, foliated crown (Blätterkrone). The tombstone of Margaret of Rodewachern, Grafin of Nassau-Saarbrücken (d. 1490), is the worse for wear, but of such high quality as to recall the art of Hans von Düren.

In the Upper German province, the Carmelite convent in Vienna, "am Hof," suppressed in 1784, was demolished in 1905. The 15th century *retable* of the main altar of the first Carmelite church "am Hof" with some unusual iconographical representations of Our Lady is preserved in the Augustiner-Chorherrenstift, Klosterneuburg.

Straubing is the only German foundation to enjoy a continuous Carmelite presence since its foundation in 1367 and with Bamberg is the most imposing foundation of the Order, North of the Alps. Its late Gothic church was given a Baroque face-lifting by architect Wolfgang Dientzenhofer (1700). The main altar and its statues were created by the sculptor Joseph Matthias Götz (1741). The larger-than-life statues represent the prophet Elijah, Pope Telesphorus, St. Angelus (right side), the prophet Elisha, Pope Dionysius, St. Albert (left side). Fifty-six *putti* swarm about the structure. The altarpiece, the Descent of the Holy Spirit on the Apostles, was painted by Michael Unterberger. Of the other altars, that of the scapular with statues of St. Cyril of Alexandria and Andrew Corsini, is also the creation of Götz. Brother Modestus of St. Stephen, joiner, helped with its construction. The altarpiece, depicting the scapular vision, was painted by Alphonsus of St. Angelus, of the Gallo-Belgian province (1646). The same artists are responsible for altar and statues of Sts. Peter Thomas and Brocard in the chapel of St. Sebastian (1740). The altarpiece, showing the martyrdom of Sebastian against a wintry background, was painted by Johann Kroner in 1660. The flamboyant rococo pulpit was carved by Anton Keller (1756).

In 1589, the Carmelites moved from their original Carmelite church and convent *"in der Au,"* in Bamberg, founded in 1273, to St. Theodore's, an abandoned abbey of Cistercian nuns (12th century), after their original site was requisitioned by the archbishop for that new-fangled Tridentine institution, a seminary. In 1611, the seminary was entrusted to the Jesuits, who built a new St. Martin's church (1686-1691).

With Justus Heinrich Dientzenhofer as architect, the Carmelites proceeded to turn Romanesque St. Theodore's into a stylish contemporary structure (1692-1707). The church was turned around with an attractive baroque facade at its eastern end. Within, a festive space was created, framed by graceful pilasters and gently vaulted roof. A pleasant contrast with the white walls was formed by the splendid brown and gold altars and pulpit, the work of Brother Leopold of St. Albert. The altarpieces were painted by the court painter, Sebastian Reinhard, the statues apparently carved by Leonhard Goldwitzer, assisted by the sons of Johann Georg Götz. The main altar was dedicated to the Virgin and St. Theodore; the other altars to Our Lady of Loreto, the Scapular, St. Joseph, St. Barbara, St. John Nepomucene, St. Teresa, St. Albert, St. Anne, and the Holy Cross.

The cloister garth of the original Cistercian abbey (1392) with its interesting capitals, a fairy land of plants, animals, friezes, and fantastic symbols, is today an enduring tourist attraction.

In some cases, structures survived after they had been emptied of their intended occupants as long ago as the Reformation. After serving various profane purposes, the erstwhile Carmelite church in Nördlingen was reopened to Catholic worship in 1829. The conventual buildings with their late Gothic cloister became the rectory and teachers' living quarters.

Augsburg and Weissenburg lived on as Protestant churches, their convents as schools. In Dinkelsbühl, where the Carmelites lived until 1803, the church exists, its convent torn down. After 1869, the Carmelite convent in Ravensburg served as a court house.

The artistic patrimony of the more than sixty Carmelite foundations in Eastern Europe (Poland, Lithuania, Russia), many of them founded in this period, remains to be studied.

Chapter 8

Literature, History, Science, Music

In this era, when everywhere great classic figures of the national literatures emerged, the Order produced no writers of importance comparable to some in its past. Not that the Carmelites did not indulge the Muse, particularly of poetry. Closer scrutiny may reveal some mute inglorious Milton, but so far no one has been found to pass under review all the inflated rhetoric produced by the Order at this time. With the mention of the following names, the list of more noteworthy writers will not be far from complete.

Belles Lettres

In France, Nicholas Dadier (1553-1628), pupil of Ronsard, enjoyed a certain reputation as a popular religious poet. A member of the province of Touraine and prior in several of its convents, he is not known to have embraced the reform which originated and matured during his lifetime. Among his works is a translation into French of Mantuan's *Parthenice mariana* (Rennes, 1613), an authentic poetic creation on its own. "The author is a true artist of verse," writes Jean Marmier, "even a great artist, in spite of his lapses. Among the versifiers of his time, innumerable in the province (of Brittany), there are few who possess to an equal degree his sense of verbal harmony, of the fluid and expressive movement of the poetic phrase; even fewer are those who sustain in an almost continuous fashion an ease of style which becomes truly musical, transcending mere facility."

Peter of St. Louis (1626-1709) wrote *Magdalen in the Desert of Sainte Baume* (Lyon, 1668, 1694, 1700), a poem of about 7000 lines. It was included by Bernard de la Monnoye in his *Pièces choisies*. In spite of this enviable printing record, it is to be feared that the quality of Peter's verse does not equal their quantity. He won the dubious distinction of being included in Théophile Gautier's *Grotesques*. Peter also wrote *La Muse, bouquetière de Notre Dame de Laurette*, which was published in Italy, at Viterbo, 1672. His *Eliade* remained unprinted until edited by Abbé Follard (Aix, 1827). Besides, Peter was an indefatigable maker of anagrams.

Louis of St. Peter, of the Francia province, wrote in French *Sacred Pictures of the Temple of Mount Carmel* (Liège, 1659), and *Miscellany of Poems* (Liège, 1660).

Peter Matthieu (d. 1620), formerly of the Albi Congregation, is the author of *L'histoire d'Aelius Sejanus* (1617) and other historical and romantic tales.

In Belgium, Charles Couvrechef (1588-1661?), painter and poet, was one of the clerical friends of the noted Dutch poet, Joost van den Vondel. Couvrechef served as sacristan, subprior, and prior (1634) of his native convent in Antwerp, as well as confessor to the nuns of Vilvoorde. During the "Croatian" pestilence of 1622, the Carmelites of Antwerp undertook the care of 1,400 stricken soldiers in their large church, and Couvrechef was one of three to survive of the twenty who ministered to the sick. He joined the reform when it was introduced in Antwerp, taking the name, Charles of St. Teresa. He spent many years, possibly dying there, in the mission initiated around 1637 by the convent of Antwerp among the Catholics of Amsterdam. In a historical *novella* published in the *Volks-Almanak* of 1857, Pauwels Foreestier relates a visit of the two friends, Vondel and Couvrechef, to the "spiritual daughter," Dina Noortdijck, in the beguinage of Amsterdam. In the same sketch, the Carmelite is also pictured as a friend of Abraham van Diepenbeke.

In typical Flemish style, Charles specialized in still life paintings of flowers, fruit, and ears of corn, with which he embellished other pictures, especially of the Virgin. He also painted miniature portraits of the twenty-five priors of Antwerp up to and including himself. To these, he added laudatory verses much as Vondel did for his friends. Vondel, as a matter of fact, provided a sonnet for Couvrechef's self-portrait, praising his "true hand" in painting floral wreaths, his devotion to Carmel and Mary. The Dutch poet also penned lines for his friend's fiftieth anniversary of profession (1658). Couvrechef's miniatures and all but a few of his poems seem to be lost, but his paintings may have provided the model for the existing series of miniatures of the priors of Antwerp by Constantius of St. Peter (d. 1768).

Oliver of St. Anastasius (d. 1674) wrote quite a bit of verse, not all of it negligible. By way of example, his *Carmelite Garden of Spiritual Delights* (2 v., Antwerp, 1659-1661), illustrated with engravings by Clouwet and Diepenbeke, celebrates the saints of the Order, each symbolized by a flower. Before Bobbie Burns saw the flea on the lady's bonnet or rendered the mouse homeless with his plow, Oliver soliloquized in similar fashion in "A Little Song About a Fly that Flew into the Candle," which still appears in anthologies. It occurs in his translation from the Latin of *Apology for the Virtues* attributed to St. Cyril of Alexandria (Antwerp, 1666).

Similarly, the writings of Gabriel of St. John the Baptist, subprior of Gelderen, are a mixture of prose and poetry. Most poetic of all are the fanciful titles of his books; *Christina, Bride of Christ, Clothed According to the Style of Paris and Paradise* (Antwerp, 1690). Gabriel still appears in anthologies.

In Spain, Carmel engaged the pens of some of the most illustrious writers of Spain. Lope de Vega composed a play, *The Life and Death of St. Teresa of Jesus* (Firenze, 1970), besides sonnets in her honor. Calderón, too, wrote a poem, *La primer flor del Carmelo*. The popular Bl. Franco of Siena was the subject of a swashbuckling play by Augustine Moreto (1618-1699), *El lego del Carmen*.

Among Carmelites, the often reprinted poem, *Light of the Soul*, by Ambrose Roca de la Serna (1597-1649), which combines depth of religious feeling with felicity of expression, is undoubtedly the most significant literary work produced by the Order in Spain at this time.

Left out of consideration here is Spain's greatest religious poet, Saint John of the Cross, about whom a whole literature exists.

In Portugal, Thomas de Faria (d. 1628), provincial and coadjutor bishop of Lisbon, translated Camoes' *Lusiades* into Latin (Lisbon, 1622). The fourth canto celebrates the valorous deeds of Nuno Alvares de Pereira.

Manuel das Chagas (d. 1666) wrote *Teresa militante*, "an heroic poem in thirteen cantos" (Lisbon, 1630). He also celebrated in verse the king's escape from an assassination attempt (Lisbon, 1644) and the birth of the Infante Peter (Lisbon, 1648).

Anthony de Escobar (d. 1681) composed *novelas* under the name of Gerard, possibly because their content was not religious. *Crystaes de alma* (Lisbon, 1690), addressed to Margaret Juliana de Tavora, daughter of the Count of São Miguel, has the subtitle, "phrases from the heart, rhetoric of feeling, loving disarray." *Doze novelas* (Lisbon, 1674), like the foregoing a combination of prose and verse, was written for the count's eldest son, Alvaro Joseph Botelho de Tavora.

Congratulating the Carmelite, Theobald Ceva, on his anthology *Scelta di sonetti* (Turin, 1735), Muratori wrote, "Pardon me for saying so, but I was no little surprised to find a religious of your Order endowed with such nice discernment in poetic matters." After such an unkindly cut from one of Italy's most learned spirits, the reader can hardly nourish very sanguine hope with regard to the Order's poetic production in Italy.

Theobald of the Annunciation Ceva (1697-1746), of the reformed province of Piedmont, compiled another anthology, *Scelta di canzoni*, which appeared posthumously (Venice, 1756). Both collections intended for use in the schools underwent many editions into the 19th century.

Also of the Piedmont province, Athanasius Cavalli (1731-1797), scientist and mathematician, composed a "physico-historical" poem on Vesuvius (Milan, 1769). Carlambrogio Vioglieri, of the Romagna province, published a small volume of occasional verse in various classic meters, *Poesie sacre* (Ancona, 1768).

In the Mantuan Congregation, Cherubino Ferrari (d. ca. 1625) published, besides many prose works, *Poetic Compositions on Divers Beautiful Subjects* (Milan, 1617), *Rhymes on the Hail Mary* (Parma, 1624), *Tears of the Blessed Virgin Beneath the Cross* (Milan, 1623). Dionysius Solerti (d. 1633) also wrote copiously, but burned his manuscripts to avoid contagion during the plague of 1630. Spared from the holocaust was his poetic commentary on the canticle of Mary, *Magnificat, psalterium decachordum* (Bergamo, 1629).

A number of members of the Carmine Maggiore of Naples published books of verse. Joseph Tancredi (d. 1624) wrote *Flame of Divine Love* (Naples, 1618), nine dialogues concerning good and evil. Filocalo Caputo (1582-1644) composed *Parnassus Transferred to Mount Carmel* (Naples, 1624). His *Poesie* (Roma, 1698) was published posthumously. *Elia rivelante* (Naples, 1653) by Lucantonio Rossi (1606-1664) is, as the title hints, a life of the prophet Elijah told by himself. The poem is not without its "felicitous passages" according to Fr. Anastasius Cuschieri, himself a poet. Most prolific of all was Charles Sernicola (1659-1721) who published about a dozen books of verse, the merit of which remains to be determined.

Equally productive, Joseph Parascandolo, of the convent of Monte Santo in Naples, wrote *La colomba ambasciatrice* (Naples, 1701), "sacred letters" exchanged between various personages, historic, and legendary. *Il Museo antico del Carmelo* (Naples, 1729), "placed in the perspective of the Muses," celebrates those "valiant women of the Old Testament, Susanna and Esther, "both pertaining in some way to Carmel." An unabashed supporter of the brief Austrian hegemony over Naples, Parascandolo included among his poetic effusions *Triumphus Parthenopaeus* (Naples, 1707), epigrams on the entry of the Austrian army into the kingdom; *Mars germanicus* (Naples, 1712) and *Austriadum duplex hymnaeus* (Naples, 1714) to celebrate the weddings of Emperor Charles VI with Elizabeth Christina, princess of Wolfenbüttel, and of King John of Portugal with Marianne of Austria. These works, probably out of consideration for his Austrian readers, were composed in Latin.

Though no author of original works, the Venetian Archangelus Agostini made an appreciable cultural contribution through his translations. Under the pseudonym Selvaggio Canturani, he translated an impressive array of French works. One source credits him with translating 47 works of 28 authors to the total of 127 volumes. Not a few of these translations underwent a number of editions. His *opus* ranged through the fields of scripture, apologetics, devotion, sacred oratory, history, literature, and medicine, and included such authors as Bourdaloue, Bossuet, Boileau, Calmet, Fleury, Crasset, Croiset. He had already completed eight volumes of Calmet's *Universal History* when he passed to his reward in 1746, aged 85.

Carmelite Historiography, 1600-1700

The renewal of the spirit of the Order brought in its train an interest in Carmelite origins and traditions, imparting to that concern a religious and evangelizing fervor not always compatible with objective historical research. Likewise, the historiography of the Order is one of the areas in which the Baroque manifests itself with characteristic abandon. Legends of Carmelite origins, which in the Middle Ages were recounted with relative sobriety, now balloon into the most grotesque shapes of fantasy. With learned display of references and abundance of imaginative detail, the Order is shown to derive historically from the prophet Elijah, counting among its members, if only of the Third Order, prominent figures of the Old Testament and just about any saint connected with Palestine and the beginnings of the eremitical life. That this baseless fabric, this insubstantial pageant convinced some of the people all of the time and all of the people some of the time is not entirely surprising, for this style of historical writing was widespread. No historian of a city or a family worth his salt was content to stay his researches short of Troy at least. By the end of our period, however, some Carmelite historians were showing the influence of the critical spirit of the Enlightenment.

The appearance of Baronius' pathfinding *Annales ecclesiastici* (12 v., Rome, 1588-1607), a creditable response to the Protestant Centuriators of Magdeburg, prompted a number of the older religious Orders to compile annals of their own institutions. The Carmelites had an added motive in the fact that the learned Oratorian had summarily dismissed their pretensions to antiquity. He denied that St. Cyril of Alexandria and John XLIV were Carmelites, or that the Order existed in the 5th century. "The burning thirst after ancestral nobility sometimes causes men to rave," he commented laconically. From this authoritative snub Carmelite claims to antiquity never fully recovered.

The versatile John Baptist de Lezana, already often referred to, undertook the task of compiling the annals of Carmel. His *Annales sacri, prophetici, et Eliani Ordinis B. V. M. de Monte Carmeli* (4 v., Rome, 1645-1656) remained incomplete at his death. The title of the work already betrays its contents. The first three volumes are devoted to the "history" of the Order from the time of the prophet Elijah (930 B. C.) to the year 1141 A. D. The last volume carries the Order's history forward to 1515. However, the earlier volumes also treat matters which fall into this last period, due to the author's habit of antedating events. Although not to be compared with the Franciscan Wadding's homonymous work, Lezana's *Annales* continue to be useful to the student of Carmelite history.

Daniel of the Virgin Mary's monumental *Speculum carmelitanum* (4 pts. in 2 v., Antwerp, 1680) appeared posthumously, but he first conceived the idea for it in 1641. It was intended to be a library or collection of source materials on the Carmelite Order. Part 1 of volume 1 contains, besides the four works presented by Philip Ribot (the *Institutio primorum monachorum*, the *Letter* of Cyril, the *Chronicle* of Sanvico, and

Sibert de Beka's *Considerationes super regulam*), twelve chronicles or histories by John Grossi, John Hildesheim, John Baconthorpe, Bernard Oler, Thomas Bradley, Baptist Mantuanus, John de Veneta, Peter Bruijn, John of Mechelen, John Palaeonydorus, Arnold Bostius, John Trithemius, O.S.B. Part 2 of volume 1, devoted to the Virgin Mary, patroness of the Order, reproduces Baldwin Leers' *Collectanea*, Arnold Bostius' *De patronatu* (in part), John Baptist Lezana's *Maria patrona* and Theodore Straccio's *Instructio* on scapular confraternities, followed by the commentaries on the Rule by John Baconthorpe and Bl. John Soreth. The volume closes with the second volume of *Carmeli Armentarium* by Francis of Bonne Esperance, an afterthought of Daniel's editors. The two parts of volume 2 contain collected lives of Carmelite saints arranged according to the calendar and conclude with a section on illustrious persons. Like volume 1, this volume includes occasional works by other authors which enhance its value.

Daniel was no professional historian, as he was the first to admit, and he lacked critical sense. Nevertheless, the *Speculum* retains its interest because of the source materials and other works it reproduces.

While awaiting the appearance of the *Speculum*, ten years in the printing, Daniel issued its copy in miniature, *Vinea Carmeli* (Antwerp, 1662). He adds, however, a section on the history of the Order down to his own time and a description of the existing provinces.

Carmelites and Bollandists

Contemporaneously with the *Speculum*, the printer, Michael Knobbaert of Antwerp was issuing the *Acta Sanctorum*, a horse of a different color. This famous work, compiled by a team of Jesuits in Antwerp called Bollandists after John Bollandus (1596-1665), originator of the enterprise, undertook a scientific study of the lives of the saints with critical editions of the sources and other materials. The first volumes which appeared in 1643 caused no stir among the Carmelites, but subsequent volumes with the lives of St. Berthold (March 29), St. Albert of Jerusalem (April 7) and St. Angelus (May 5) abundantly showed that the learned editors of the *Acta* were not about to accept the Carmelites' version of the origin of monasticism and of their Order; neither would they fill their volumes with imaginary saints nor enlist the Desert Fathers and early monks among the Carmelites. The cloud-capp'd towers of Carmelite hagiography melted into thin air.

The Carmelites of the Flemish province, in the bosom of which the viper had reared its ugly head, sprang to the defense of the Order. Francis of Bonne-Espérance, ex-provincial and professor emeritus of Louvain University, published *Historico-theologicum Carmeli Armamentarium* (Antwerp, 1669) defending the traditional thesis that Elijah was the founder of religious life with its three vows and that the Carmelites were his successors in an unbroken line. For him, the Bollandist silence on these points was as bad as a denial. A second volume, printed at Cologne in 1677, replied to specific points made by Godfried Henschen and Daniel Papebroch concerning St. Albert of Jerusalem and the foundation dates of the convents of Florence and Boppard. The provincial, Sebastian of St. Paul, directed a *Libellus supplex* (Frankfurt, 1683) to Pope Innocent XI, requesting the supreme authority of the Church to decide the issue between the Carmelites and the Bollandists. He followed this with a full-scale attack, *Exhibitio errorum* (Cologne, 1693), in which he accused Papebroch of doctrinal errors against scripture, papal and conciliar decisions, and approved liturgical texts.

On February 14, 1691, the Spanish Calced and Discalced procurators, John Gómez Barrientos and Peter of the Conception, denounced the *Propylaeum* of the May volume of the *Acta* to the Spanish Inquisition. In fact, on November 14, 1695, that august body, never loath to hurl the ban, placed on its *Index* the fourteen volumes for March, April and May of the *Acta sanctorum*. This measure, which called into question the purity of his faith, stung Papebroch into replying to Sebastian's allegations with his *Responsio ad Exhibitionem errorum* (3 v., Antwerp, 1696-1698), otherwise a waste of his precious time, for as he had said about Francis de Bonne Espérance, "a theologian, no matter how profound, who has not learned to treat historical matters with specialized study, is no more apt to draw the right conclusions than to teach the art of poetry." The Bollandist, Conrad Janninck, dispatched to the eternal city, managed to keep the *Acta* off the Roman *Index* but failed to win the influence of the Roman authorities against the Spanish Inquisition. His efforts to soften this rigid body only had effect in 1715, but Papebroch had gone down to his grave under censure the previous year.

John Feijóo de Villalobos, elected general in 1692, pursued the policy of a diplomatic solution, seeking direct adjudication by the Holy See. His efforts met with success, when Innocent XII on November 20, 1698, imposed perpetual silence on both parties to the controversy. It was a victory for the Carmelites, for they posed no threat to the Jesuits in academic debate and they were left in peaceful possession of their traditions, which had not been unfavorably judged. Feijóo himself had set the example in two works about the antiquities of the Order, *Brevis chronologia religionis perfectae* (Lyon, 1696) and *Historico-sacra et theologica dissertatio de vera origine et progressu monastices* (Nola, 1697), across which the shadow of Papebroch never falls.

Not all Carmelites arose in arms against the Bollandists; in fact, outside Belgium, and in Rome itself, the reaction was more restrained. Papebroch himself mentions a couple of Carmelite "Nicodemuses," one of them the bibliographer, Louis Jacob, who congratulated him on his courageous pursuit of truth. The humble Daniel of the Virgin Mary, "blessed soul, who always loved me, and whom I always loved," as Papebroch proclaimed, was another friend, and although relations were strained after the publication of the April *Acta*, the two never engaged in public polemics. The anti-Bollandist features of the *Speculum* were additions by its editors Valentine of St. Amandus and Gratian of St. Elijah. Daniel received good critical advice - not always followed - from the regent of studies in Traspontina, Louis Pérez de Castro, and the Belgian, Seraphinus of Jesus and Mary, procurator general, both admirers of Papebroch. They warned him about the unreliability of Lezana's dates, which Papebroach later exposed.

The reception of the *Speculum* in Rome was markedly cool. While the general chapter of 1680 ordered all provincials to acquire copies of the *Speculum*, it also required that in the future any book concerning the history, privileges, and indulgences of the Order be sent to Rome for examination before publication, "lest anything contrary to historical truth be published." In fact, the *Speculum* which the prior general had approved was not that which was published. In Belgium, it was feared that Papebroch would see in the decree of the chapter a tacit approval of his views.

Daniel's adviser, Louis Pérez de Castro (1635-1689), belied Papebroch's remark about theologian-historians. A member of the convent of Toledo, he taught theology at Salamanca and Alcalá and at Traspontina and the Sapienza in Rome, where he remained behind after representing his province of Castile at the general chapter of 1666. He was hardly less able in history, which he studied with a keen critical eye for sources. He corresponded widely over historical matters. Nicholas Antonio acknowledged his collaboration on the *Bibliotheca hispana*. He left among other writings six unpublished volumes of miscellaneous notes.

The controversy with the Bollandists is not one of the more glorious pages of the Order's history. The Carmelites almost managed to destroy one of the great undertakings of Catholic scholarship. However, there are mitigating circumstances which have not always been sufficiently averted to. The assailants of Papebroch, however faulty their historical methodology, were sincere men, firmly convinced of the reality of the Carmelite legend, which they believed confirmed by the highest teaching authority of the Church. To characterize them as calumniators is simplistic. Equally simplistic is to treat the question exclusively as an academic issue involving only historical accuracy. At stake was the Carmelite charism as conceived at that time, and the revelations of the Bollandists profoundly affected the spiritual lives of thousands of religious and laypersons affiliated with the Order.

Carmelite Historiography, 1700-1800

Although the Carmelites did not officially relinquish their belief in the continuous descent of the Order from the prophet Elijah, the Battle of the Bollandists had a sobering effect, and they began to apply themselves to less ethereal historical interests. Several useful works were produced.

Elisha Monsignano edited the *Bullarium carmelitanum* (2 v., Rome, 1715-1718), continued by Joseph Albert Ximénez (2 v., Rome, 1768), still an indispensable tool. The *Historia chronologica priorum generalium* (Naples, 1773) by Marianus Ventimiglia provides a history of the Order through the lives of its priors general, beginning with the "Latin Era," a handy distinction for avoiding the thorny problem of the alleged history of the Order before 1200. Charles Vaghi wrote the history of the Mantuan Congregation, *Commentaria* (Parma, 1725). Its continuation to 1782 by Jerome Vigo remained unpublished and is housed in the general archive of the Order in Rome.

A comprehensive bibliography, listing the works of about 2,500 Calced and Discalced authors, *Bibliotheca carmelitana* (2 v., Orléans, 1752) was compiled by Cosmas of St. Stephen de Villiers (1683-1758) and was immediately hailed by savants as a remarkable monument of learning. Although it suffers from the usual shortcomings of bibliographical efforts of the time, it is the most ambitious project of the sort ever published and remains indispensable. Helpful, too, are the biographies presented of each author. The anonymous *Bibliotheca carmelitana lusitana* (Rome, 1754) undertook to supply omissions of Portuguese writers.

Villiers had a precedent in a work which remained unpublished, the *Bibliotheca carmelitana* of Louis of St. Charles Jacob (1608-1670), a much more important figure in the field of bibliography. Jacob entered the Order at Châlon-sur-Saône in 1625 and received the name Louis of St. Charles in the reform recently introduced there. His interests were antiquarian and in 1639 he travelled to Italy examining famous libraries. Fruit of his studies were *Bibliotheca pontificia* (Lyon, 1643), compiled at the suggestion of Gabriel Naudé, noted bibliographer and librarian, and *Traicté des plus belles bibliothèques dans le monde* (Paris, 1644). But of Jacob's many other bibliographical undertakings most important were the annual lists of books published in Paris and in France, *Bibliographia parisina* and *Bibliographia gallica universalis*, forerunners of the national bibliography of France. He became librarian of John de Gondi, Cardinal de Retz, and lived in the house of Achille de Harlay, where he died.

Although born in Genoa, Seraphinus Potenza (1697-1763) was the son of Neapolitan parents and entered the Order at Chiaia in the province of Naples (1714). His early interest in the Order's past received added stimulus after his transfer to Rome in 1723. There he made himself useful as sacristan of Traspontina, but except for the office of prior (1756) he remained free of more absorbing responsibilities and so could devote himself to his beloved studies. He planned to publish the collected lives of Carmelite saints and servants of God and gathered fourteen volumes of materials, which unfortunately were never given final form. What these biographies would have been like can be gathered from his letter to a conferre, Ferdinand Salvi, January 8, 1731: "We have made ourselves so ridiculous with these stories of ours that it is high time that we undertook a bit of revision and showed the world that we have finally arrived at writing the truth." On April 25, he wrote to the same correspondent: "Our forefathers have left our most beautiful memoirs in oblivion by their neglect, in order to devote themselves to supporting and defending fables." Potenza's researches made him eminently suited for the office of postulator general, and he ably directed the processes of several causes. He shared his learning with many correspondents within and outside the Order. He collaborated with John Mazzucchelli on his *Scrittori d'Italia* (Brescia, 1753-1763, 2 v. in 7 pts.) and supplied information to Mariano Ruele, who edited *scanzie* 21-23 (Rovereto, 1733, 1736 and Rome, 1739) of the *Biblioteca volante* of John Cinelli and Dionysius Sangassani.

The general chapter of 1660 instituted the office of Historian of the Order. Its incumbent was to be appointed by the prior general and should reside in Rome. The following chapter of 1666 repeated the decree, this time ordaining that the council of the Order should name the historian and determine the tax to be levied for his support. In fact, on September 25, Daniel of the Virgin Mary received the nomination. Two years later, Valentine of St. Amandus was named his associate. Thereafter, provision for the office seems to have been only sporadically made. In 1698, Archangelus Michael Gervasi, of the province of Santa Maria della Vita, was appointed; in 1733, Theobald Ceva.

The establishment in Rome of a general archive of the Order had been decreed in 1593 by John Stephen Chizzola. His successor, Henry Silvio, also concerned himself with the proper maintenance of the archive. Those who are known to have functioned as archivists are Augustine Biscaret (d. 1638/9), who left there his unfinished bibliographical work *Palmites Vineae Carmeli*, Marianus Ruele and John Anthony Petrignani (1713-1782).

The Exact Sciences and Medicine

The developing exact sciences found an echo in the Order. No scientists are to be found among the Carmelites; their interest lay principally in the study and teaching of science and in its relation to religion.

Certainly the most outstanding figure among Carmelites interested in science and natural philosophy at this time was Elijah Astorini (1651-1702). The son of a physician in Albidona, he entered the Order at Cosenza (1667), studied philosophy in the Carmine Maggiore of Naples, where he became a member of the Academy of the Incauti, and theology in Rome. In Naples, he was taught by Anello Rossi; in Rome, by Louis Pérez de Castro. As regent of studies at Cosenza (1680), he ended up in the archbishop's prison for his teachings, which rejected Aristotle and followed the natural philosophy of such thinkers as Marcus Aurelius Severino, Charles Musitano, and especially of Thomas Cornelio, whose nephew Astorini later professed to be. In 1683, he was in Bari, where he became associated with G. Tremigliozzi, protagonist of anti-galenian doctrines in medicine. Shortly after, he followed the example of the prior, Angelo Rocco, and fled to friendlier climes in Switzerland.

At Basle, Astorini observed the medical experiments of J. J. Herder (1684) and for a year followed the theology courses of J. R. Wettstein. After a brief sojourn in the Palatinate under the patronage of the Prince Elector, Charles (d. May 26, 1686), he followed the lectures of J. J. Waldschmiedt at Marburg and received the doctorate in medicine at Groningen with the dissertation, *De vitali oeconomia foetus in utero* (Groningen, 1686). In the Netherlands, he got into difficulty for his defense of Catholicism, which he had never rejected. Absolved by the bishop of Münster in 1688, he was back in Rome and in the Order two years later.

From 1691 to 1694, he lived in Tuscany, where he established relationships with such intellectuals as Alexander Marchetti, Anthony Magliabechi (his letters to whom are still extant), Francis Redi, Vincent Viviani. Through Astorini, the philosophical scientific tradition of the South was put into contact with the experimental theory of Tuscany. In 1691, Prince Gian Gastone de' Medici bestowed on the Carmelite the chair of mathematics at the *Nuova Accademia dei Nobili Senesi*. In this connection, he produced *Elementa Euclidis nova methodo et succincta demonstrata* (Siena, 1691; 2d ed., Naples, 1701). Through Redi, he acquired the special chair of Natural Philosophy at the University of Siena (1692-1694). Astorini was also one of the founders of the *Accademia dei Fisiocritici* and became its "perpetual prince." He used his experience in Protestant countries to write *Prodromus apologeticus de potestate Sanctae Sedis Apostolicae* (Siena, 1693).

Back in his province in 1694, Astorini again became regent at Cosenza and resident or prior in various other convents. Opposition stirred up by his scientific and philosophical ideas was offset by the protection of Ferdinand Vincent Spinelli, Prince of Tarsia, whose library he undertook to set in order, and of the archbishop of Benevento, Vincent Mary Orsini, later Benedict XIII. In his final years, he produced another polemical work, *De vera ecclesia Iesu Christi* (Naples, 1700), in which he professed to show that Catholicism was not inseparably wedded to Aristotelianism; an edition of the *Conics* of Apollonius of Perga (Naples, 1698, 1702); and *Ars magna Pythagorica*, which remained unpublished. Other works seem to be lost.

Among other Neapolitan Carmelites who published works, Ignatius Bagnati (1659-1730) made his profession in the convent of the reform of Monte Santo (1676) but later transferred to the less severe reform of Santa Maria della Vita (1686). He taught mathematics at the *Collegio dei Cinesi*. Andrew M. Coscioni posthumously edited his *Vera mundi aetas* (Naples, 1742), which professed to establish the dates of the birth of Christ and of the creation of the world.

Elijah Del Re (d. 1733) belonged to the Puglia province, but became affiliated with the Carmine of Naples. He was "primary mathematician" of King Philip V of Spain, an academy member of Frankfurt, and of the *Spensierati* of Rossano. He produced annual *Discorsi astronomici*, a sort of Farmers' Almanac, the predictions of which were so uncanny that he came under suspicion in Rome. His other works include *Aritmetica e geometrica prattica* (Naples, 1697; 2d ed. 1733) and *Vaticinio delle stelle*, "an astrological-philosophical discourse" (Venice, 1702).

In the Mantuan Congregation, John Cicci (1607-1664) taught mathematics and astronomy at the university of his native Bologna from 1642 until his death. He published an Italian translation of Euclid's *Elements* which enjoyed two editions (Bologna, 1651, 1686), but his other works remained in manuscript.

Felix Pellegrino Carisi (1675-1733) was official mathematician of Duke Rinaldo I of Modena. His *Scuola dell' aritmatica pratica* (Parma, 1707-1726, 5 v.) was highly reputed and saw several editions.

Perhaps the most prolific mathematician among the Carmelites in Spain was Michael of Jesus and Mary Hualde, of the Audalusian province. Of his many published works the best is *Arithmetica demonstrada* (Pamplona, 1776). Much of his output is concerned with his controversy with the Trinitarian, Peter of St. Martin.

In the field of mechanics, Sebastian Truchet (1657-1729), of the Narbonne province, early acquired remarkable skill in constructing mechanical devices. In Paris, where he had been sent for theological studies, he attracted the attention of Colbert, when without knowing that it belonged to the king, he set aright a clock sent to Louis XIV by Charles II of England, which had baffled the royal watchmaker, Henry Martinot (1676). The king endowed the friar with a pension to continue his studies and experiments. In 1699, Truchet was nominated by the king to the Academy of Sciences and made contributions to its acts in 1699 and 1705. Skilled in hydraulics, Sebastian engaged in the building of numerous canals, including one in Orléans, commissioned by Duke Philip I. He was also involved in the installation of the irrigation system in the gardens of Versailles. His less grandiose achievements included making a pair of articulated hands for a Swedish official named Gunterfeld, whose own had been removed by cannon shot, and two cleverly devised landscapes with moving figures, which delighted the king, who kept them in his castle of Marly.

Around this time, cases begin to occur of religious possessing clocks (*horologia rotata*), though in the beginning permission of the prior general seems to have been required for this novelty.

Traditionally, the medical profession was not incompatible with the clerical and religious state. In the Middle Ages, the only condition laid down by the Carmelite constitutions for the practice of medicine is adequate proficiency. The constitutions of Bl. John Soreth add the requirement of permission from the Holy See, legislation which remained in force in modern times.

Mention has already been made of Astorini's interest in medical theory and his competence as a graduate in medicine of Groningen University.

Undoubtedly the most eminent representative of the medical profession among the Carmelites of the 17th and 18th centuries was Emmanuel de Azevedo (d.

1672), already before entering the Order at Lisbon in 1648 a physician whose skill had ten years previously won for him from King Philip II of Spain the position of *protomedico* of the ocean-going fleet. As a Carmelite, Azevedo continued to practice medicine and wrote a work, *Correction of the Abuses Introduced Against True Medical Method* (Lisbon, 1668; 2d ed., 1690). He is no theoretical innovator, but evinces sound notions, due to his long and varied career, of the best therapeutic practice of the time. His book also provides autobiographical details concerning his experiences with the Spanish fleet in every corner of the known world.

Azevedo was not the only Portuguese Carmelite skilled in medical science. The contemporary acts of the chapter of 1671 speak of a Brother Anthony of the Conception, "approved in the art of surgery."

As already recounted on occasion, the Carmelites did not limit their services to spiritual ministrations during the many plagues that continued to ravish Europe. Thus, in the terrible Italian pestilence of 1630, Clement Perruzzola (1588-1659), of the Lombardy province, devoted himself generously to the care of the sick. The following year, he published *Apparato a conservatori della sanità* (Turin, 1631), describing the causes, symptoms, and remedies of contagion.

Besides his spiritual ministrations, Alberto Leoni undertook the foundation of a house for the care of the insane. In antiquity, mentally disturbed persons were considered incurable, and the worst cases were confined in chains and beaten to subdue them. Only in the 15th century, was some thought given to a more humane treatment of these unfortunates.

The first hospital or institute for the insane in Italy was founded in Rome in 1548 in the pontificate of Paul III. In 1642, Leoni had received Archbishop Niccolini's approval for such an institution in Florence - the second in Italy - and had acquired an anonymous donation for buying a house, when death overtook him at the age of 79. The project was carried forward by his confrere, John Anthony Diciotto. A congregation of twelve Florentine noblemen administered the pious undertaking. The hospital itself was in charge of a secular priest as chaplain. Called the hospital of St. Dorothy, it underwent several changes of name and site to become the modern Psychiatric Hospital of Florence at San Salvi.

A less exacting profession which religious practised more frequently and with greater chance of success was that of pharmacist or herbalist. It was an art especially practiced, it would seem, by lay brothers, useful also for the infirmarian in charge of the sick within the convent. Thus, during his visitation of the Place Maubert in 1663, Orlandi recommended that a lay brother be trained in the pharmaceutical art, in order to care of the sick. According to the decree of the Sacred Congregation of the Council, 1632, religious were allowed to operate pharmacies only for the poor and their own infirm, not for the general public. Inevitably, difficulties with professional pharmacists arose, as in Rome with the College of Herbalists in 1695, and with the same body in Barcelona in 1746. The pharmacy inaugurated in 1750 by the Discalced Carmelites of the convent of La Scala in Rome is still in operation.

Music in Baroque Carmel

This was the period when the artists familiar to the average listener today, Corelli, Purcell, Rameau, Bach, Handel, Scarlatti, and others, made their appearance. It was also the last time the Catholic Church, if no longer a leader in the art of music, continued to express its religious sentiments in the contemporary musical idiom. Polyphony, which had reached its perfection in Palestrina (d. 1594) was on the decline and gave way to new forms of monody with *basso continuo* accompaniment.

In the 17th and 18th centuries, the Order made its most abundant and final contribution to musical production, though its activity was largely confined to Portugal and Italy. In Portugal, polyphony remained in vogue, while in Italy the new forms were often favored. The Carmelites naturally confined their interest mostly to sacred music: "sacred songs" (*cantiones sacrae*), litanies, and Masses almost always furnished with organ or other instrumental accompaniment. Theoretical works and textbooks were also produced.

Apart from the Order's interest in music, there is a unique instance of a great master's concern for a Carmelite theme. On January 14, 1707, F. Valesio's *Diario di Roma* noted: "There has arrived in this city a Saxon, an excellent player on the harpsichord and a composer of music, who has today displayed his ability in playing the organ in the Church of St. John (Lateran) to the amazement of everyone." It was not the only performance of religious music the twenty-two year old Lutheran, Georg Friedrich Handel, executed in the papist capital. A group of manuscript scores by Handel, until recently a mystifying jigsaw puzzle, turned out to constitute a *Vespers for the Feast of Our Lady of Mount Carmel* (July 16) performed in the Carmelite Church of Santa Maria in Monte Santo. How the composer came to choose that particular theme to be presented in that particular church remains a mystery.

In Italy, music was particularly cultivated in the Mantuan Congregation and the northeastern provinces located near the important centers of musical culture, Bologna, Modena, and Venice.

The Mantuan Congregation with its principal house in Bologna produced one of the notable Carmelite musicians of this epoch, Lawrence Penna (1631-1693), of Bologna, where he became a member of the prestigious *Accademia Filarmonica* and the *Accademia dei Filaschi* with the name *l'Indefesso*. Choir master in the Carmelite churches of Casal Monferrato and Parma, and in the cathedral of Imola, he was both a theoretician and a composer. His *Primi albori musicali per li principianti della musica figurata distinti in tre libri* (Bologna, 1672) underwent many editions in the 17th century and was recently reprinted. Book 2 was also issued by G. Sala in Venice, 1678. His *Direttorio del canto fermo* (Modena, 1689) proved less popular. His numerous published compositions included Masses and psalms for voices with instrument accompaniment. An exception to Penna's exclusively religious inspiration is *Correnti francesi a quattro* (Modena, 1689), a work for stringed instruments written for the wedding of Alexander Sanvitali, Count of Fontanelato.

Also of the Mantuan Congregation, Zaccharias Zanetti, of Bologna, appears in 1594 as chaplain of the imperial choir of Rudolph II. He compiled an anthology of sacred songs for two and three voices and organ, *Sacrae et divinae cantiones* (Venice, 1619). John Mary Verrato, of Ferrara (not to be confused with the 16th century theologian of the same name), organist and music teacher, published a book guaranteed to impart the art of singing in two weeks or a fortnight (Venice, 1623). Francis Mary Vallara (1687-ca. 1740), of Parma, concerned himself especially with the teaching of Gregorian chant, publishing *Scuola corale* (Modena, 1700, 1707), *Teorico-prattico del canto gregoriano* (Parma, 1721) and *Primizie di canto fermo* (2d ed., Parma, 1724). His compositions, *Selva di varie composizioni ecclesiastiche in canto fermo*

(Parma, 1733) for one choir or two in counterpoint, have been judged "not very interesting" (Prudentius Mirck, O. Carm.).

In the Romagna province, Elijah Vannini (1644-1709) entered the Carmelite convent in his native Medicina and was professed in 1662. It is not known where or by whom he obtained his musical formation. He soon acquired a reputation as an organist, playing on solemn occasions in the church of his province in Bologna, Our Lady of Grace. In 1677, he was invited by Cardinal Paluzzo Altieri to become choir master in the cathedral of Ravenna, a post he held with distinction for a quarter of a century. On retirement, he returned to Medicina, acting during his last years as chaplain to the Carmelite tertiary sisters. Besides manuscript works seemingly lost, he published *Symphonies, opus 1* (Bologna, 1691), for three stringed instruments and *basso continuo*. Other works, *Litanies of the Blessed Virgin Mary, opus 2* (Bologna, 1692), *Psalms for Vespers, opus 3* (Bologna, 1693), *Litanies, opus 4* (Bologna, 1698), *Psalms for Complin, opus 5* (Bologna, 1699), were designed for various voices with instrumental accompaniment. Vannini's work lies in the evolving stream of the Bolognese school, which will lead to Corelli. Interest in his compositions has recently revived, and concerts of his compositions have been presented.

Alexander Tadei (d. 1667) joined the Venetian province, but his family was domiciled at Gandria in the Ticino canton of Switzerland, and he himself may have been born in Graz. He received his musical education from John Gabrieli in Venice. Archduke Ferdinand appointed Tadei organist of the cathedral of Graz (1607), and when his patron became Holy Roman Emperor (1619), Tadei followed him to Vienna as *Hoforganist*, an appointment he retained until 1628. In 1617, Tadei had married Delfina Datili, widow, and her death in 1628 may have been the signal for his entering the Carmelite Order the following year. The monk's cowl at first seems to have sat uneasily on his shoulders, and difficulties with his superiors developed (1636), but matters were smoothed out, and the musician persevered in the Order. Only a fraction of what must have been Tadei's production remains. G. B. Bonometti included a motet (three voices with *basso continuo*) of Tadei in his *Parnassus musicus Ferdinandaeus* (Venice, 1615). Tadei's psalms for Vespers (eight voices with bass for organ) were published at Venice in 1628, and in modern times his *Missa sine nomine* for sixteen voices (ed. by W. Jensinghaus, Lugano, 1937).

Also of the Venetian province, Peter Columbina, member of the choir of San Marco, in 1681 was awarded a gold medal by the *procuratori* of Venice for his compositions, which, however, seem to be lost. His authoritative recommendation was sought by Jerome Filago Casati (1598-1677), of the Lombardy province. At the age of thirteen, Casati had been named organist of the cathedral of his native Novara and he later became choir master there (1635). Of his published works are known *Sacrae cantiones, opus 1* (Venice, 1625), *Numeri musicali, opus 2* (Milano, 1624), *Armonicae cantiones, opus 3* (Milano, 1635), *Messa e salmi, opus 5* (Milano, 1646), *Liber quintus mottectorum, opus 7* (Milano, 1637), arrangements for voices, some with accompaniment, of Masses, litanies, and motets.

Mention has already been made of Archangelus Paoli's *Directorium chori* (Naples, 1614). He also wrote *A Brief Introduction to Plain Chant* (Florence, 1623) and *Cantio sacra et plena in Missa decantanda* (Florence, 1624).

In the Roman province, Albert Lazzari (d. 1675), choir master and composer, was a member of the *Accademia degli Spennati* of Faenza with the name *il Vigilante* (1635) and of the *Accademia degli Offuscati* of Cesena with the name *il Appannato* (1636). He published two volumes of *Armonie spirituali* (Venice, 1635, 1647), comprising a Mass, litanies, and motets for various voices. "Lazzari was a minor figure of the Venetian School," writes Claudio Sartori, "a careful craftsman of concerted polyphony."

In the south of Italy, Anello Antignani (d. 1639), prior of the Carmine of Naples, published madrigals for four voices (Naples, 1610) and *Sacred Songs, Book 3* (Naples, 1620) for various voices with basso for organ. Also intended for various voices with bass for organ was *Sacred Songs, Book 1* (Naples, 1618) by Anthony Summonzi (d. 1673), likewise prior of the Carmine. Anthony Ferrari, organist of the Carmine of Catania, wrote *Sacred Songs, Book 1* (Rome, 1617) for one or more voices with bass for organ, and a *Garland of Sacred Flowers* (Rome, 1617).

The province of Portugal placed much emphasis on sacred music and produced one of the notable musicians of the Order, Manuel Cardoso (1570-1650). He studied music under the noted Manuel Mendes, choir master of the cathedral of Evora, one of the important musical centers of Portugal. Cardoso entered the Order in Lisbon, making his profession in 1589. He soon distinguished himself as choir master and composer. His works at this time include *Canticles of Our Lady* (Lisbon, 1613), *Masses* (Lisbon, 1625) and *Book of Various Motets* (Lisbon, 1628). In 1631, King Philip IV invited him to Madrid, where he wrote his *Messa felipina* on a theme proposed by Matthew Romero, choir master of the royal chapel. This composition was included in his *Masses of Our Lady* (Lisbon, 1636). The Carmelite *mestre* found no less favor with the music-loving King John IV, once the Portuguese crown was restored (1640). Cardoso did not take advantage of his privileged position and observed a very simple lifestyle. He served as definitor (1638) and vicar provincial (1644).

All Cardoso's compositions are in the polyphonic tradition still current in Portugal. This style seems also to have been his personal preference for expressing his religious sentiments. "Not originality alone," concludes Fr. Mirck, "but musical validity determines whether a composition is a work of art, and we believe that the musical validity of Cardoso's Masses is such that they still merit attention." As a matter of fact, some of Cardoso's work has recently been published.

Manuscript works of a number of other Portuguese composers noted by musicologists have remained dormant in archives.

In the 17th and 18th century, Spain is singularly lacking in Carmelite musicians who achieved publication. Only at the end of this period, we find Peter Carrera Lanchares, student of José Lidón and organist of the Carmen of Madrid, who wrote *Salmodia organica* (1792; *Addiciones*, 1814). *Rudimentos de musica* (2 pts., Madrid, 1815) was intended for the students of the *Real Seminario de Nobles*, in which institution he consequently seems to have been teaching.

France was no more lucky in wooing Euterpe. The single name that can be mentioned here, too, is that of Barnabas of St. Cecilia, a native of Nantes. He served as organist in the convents of Orléans and Rennes and died in 1747 at the early age of thirty-eight. He left *Missae suavissimo ac facillimo modulamine musico pro nuda voce compositae instar plani simplicique cantus* (Nantes, 1739) for untrained voices.

On the other hand, the Netherlands and Germany produced composers who continue to attract attention.

Benedict of St. Joseph (Buns, 1642-1716) spent most of his life in the isolated convent of Boxmeer, yet he achieved a reputation in wide circles. Besides serving as organist, he was repeatedly elected subprior and delegate to the provincial chapter. From his prayerful retreat, Buns issued a steady stream of musical creations: *Masses, Litanies and Motets, opus 1* (Antwerp, 1656); *Corona stellarum duodecim serta, opus 2* (2d ed., Antwerp, 1673); *Flosculi musici, opus 3* (Antwerp, 1672); *Musica montana in Monte Carmelo composita, opus 4* (Antwerp, 1677); *Completoriale melos musicum, opus 5* (Antwerp, 1677); *Encomia sacra, opus 6* (Utrecht, 1683); *Orpheus gaudens ac lugens, opus 7* (Antwerp, 1693); *Orpheus Elianus e Carmelo in Orbem editus, opus 8* (Amsterdam, 1699?). Of a ninth work, published in 1701 and consisting of a Mass and motets for one to three voices with instrument accompaniment, no copy has been found. Buns' processional and choir manual have already been noticed above.

Buns is no innovator, he has not yet adopted chromatic variation, his style is still predominantly homophonic, his sonatas have not achieved the stability of form found in his contemporary, Corelli. He is a talented and skilled craftsman, who achieved distinction among his contemporaries.

A typical example of Carmelite musical production in the Baroque period is Spiridion of Mount Carmel (1615-1685), of the Upper German province, author of concerted Masses and a textbook on musical technique. Born John Nenning in Bad Neustadt a. d. Saale, he donned the Carmelite habit at Bamberg in 1637. Nenning himself attributes his musical formation to the Cistercian Abbot, Francis of Schöntal (*Spezia*), whom he calls his twin (*uterinus frater*). In 1643, he is in Rome, no doubt to study theology, but he found time to play the organ for Matthew Orlandi, himself skilled in the art, who that year was free of his duties as regent. Nenning was one of those interested in reform, who travelled to Belgium to learn its ways. In 1648, he returned with Gabriel of the Annunciation to initiate the reform of the province in Bamberg and three years later renewed his vows as Spiridion of Mount Carmel. In 1653, he is in Turin, possibly in connection with the acceptance of the constitutions of the Stricter Observance by the Piedmont Reform. He is still there in 1655, when Venturini authorizes him to act as chaplain to the German soldiers in Savoy. Back in Germany, he was soon in trouble and moved from assignment to assignment. He was accused of being a *proprietarius* and a troublemaker and even underwent a prison sentence. Gabriel now declared his former protegé to be a troublesome person, who became more stubborn as time went on - a classic case of the pot calling the kettle black. Spiridion's difficulty was that the severe demands of the reformed way of life conflicted with his need as a musician to move about and personally dispose of money. Eventually he settled down peaceably enough in Bamberg, winning the esteem of secular and ecclesiastical authorities and busying himself with the publication of his music.

Spiridion's first published work was *Musica Romana* (Nürnberg, 1665), an anthology of thirteen pieces by Boniface Graziani, Francis Foggia, and G. G. Carissimi with a *Salve Regina* of his own, obviously a souvenir of his Roman sojourn. In his *Musica theo-liturgica* (Würzburg, 1668), four Masses with optional violin accompaniment, "Spiridion, like G. Arnold," writes A. Scharnagl, "at the same time active as *Hoforganist* in Bamberg, represents the Baroque concerted style." His *Nova instructio* (4 v., Bamberg/Würzburg, 1669-1675/1677), claiming to be a new way of learning organ and instrument playing and the art of composition, "is of importance as a textbook for the technique of playing and composing in the second half of the 17th century."

Justin of the Espousals (1675-1747) succeeded Spiridon as the representative of the musical tradition in the Upper German province. Born in Bamberg, he entered the Order there in 1690 and was professed the following year. During his lifetime, Justin was stationed in many different houses of the province. He styled himself an "organist and preacher," appellations which fittingly describe his peripatetic existence. He also appears as a military chaplain (1709). He wrote *Cembalum pro duobus* (Lienz, 1703), songs and dances for keyboard instruments, and two textbooks: *Chirologia organico-musica* (Nürnberg, 1711) and *Musicalische Arbeit- und Kurz-Weil* (Augsburg, 1723). "Fr. Justin's publications," writes F. W. Riedel, "were meant in the first place for didactic purposes. They belong to the genre of 'methods', dear to the 17th and 18th centuries, which sought to offer the beginning organ or choir master, as well as the amateur music lover, a compendium of the art of playing the clavichord.... The *Schlag-Stücke* which accompany the theoretic execution are worthwhile and characteristic examples of the then usual kinds of music for keyboard instruments.... His textbooks offer a clear picture of the practice of keyboard technique in the first half of the 18th century."

In Poland, Andrew Paskiwics, who lived in the second half of the 17th century, left manuscript compositions, among them a Mass for four voices. Two *Agnus Dei* for four voices were published in modern times. Since his compositions are preserved in the cathedral archive of Cracow, Paskiwics probably belonged to the province of Lesser Poland.

An area still largely to be investigated is that of folk music. The widespread devotion to Our Lady of Mount Carmel led to the creation of many songs and ballads in her honor.

Part Five

THE MODERN PERIOD (1750-1950)

Chapter 1

Carmel Under Absolutism

In the 18th century, the Age of Enlightenment ushered in the de-Christianization of Europe. The flaccid Catholic and Protestant Churches were no match for the fashionable Deism, rationalism, and Freemasonry which reasoned against and railed against a supernatural, revealed religion. The reaction of the Church to its first contact with atheism in its own backyard was abhorrence and disapproval.

The reaction of the Church to another aspect of the new age - its aspirations to political freedom and democracy - was to cling more desperately to the *Ancien Regime*, which was at least nominally Catholic. Monarchism, in itself not a bad form of government, by the second half of the century had become as grotesque as the Hapsburg chin. In the form of Gallicanism, Febronianism, and Josephinism, monarchy, deeply imbued with Illuminism and often only vaguely Christian, sought the nationalization of the Church and its complete subjection to the State. The blissful union of altar and throne, so enthusiastically extolled by Bossuet in the previous century, had turned hopelessly sour. In destroying the old Catholic States, Republicanism only saved the Church from an impossible marriage.

If absolute monarchism had become only a caricature of government, the Church as an element of society was not much better. Its privileged status, fitting in a Christian social system, was becoming more and more anachronistic. Its traditional social roles of education, care of the sick and the poor, arbiter of morals, were increasingly absorbed by the state. The absolute monarchs, for all their worldliness, still conceived of society as religious and were content to take over the management of the Church. It was left to the liberal governments of the 19th century to banish the Church entirely from public life and to create a secular state. Thus, the Church was no longer harassed by sacristan kings; it was simply ignored.

No more glaring witness to the old order of things was there than the ubiquitous religious orders. Reduced in numbers, discredited by the intelligentsia, for the most part intellectually and spiritually stagnant, they were in no condition to meet the onslaught of secular reformers and abolitionists. Long before the 19th century anti-clericalism gave them the *coup de grace*, the orders were subjected to various forms of interference by Catholic rulers, intent on sometimes well-meant but always ill-conceived attempts at reform. It should be added, however, that there was a long precedent for secular meddling in their affairs, occasioned by the religious themselves, who had been in the habit of appealing to the crown from unwelcome decisions of their legitimate superiors.

The *Commission des Reguliers*

As in so many other areas of life, France, homeland of Gallicanism, set the fashion in reform of religious life.

Subsequent to complaints about the decline of religious observance voiced in the Assembly of the Clergy in 1765, a royal *Commission des Reguliers* was created the following year. Composed of members of the hierarchy and of the royal council, it was actually steered by its reporter, Stephen Charles Loménie de Brienne, archbishop of Toulouse. A royal edict of 1768 set the age of religious profession at twenty-one for men and eighteen for women, forbade the acceptance of candidates not of French citizenship, required a minimum of nine members in a convent and limited each order to one house in any place, two in Paris. National chapters under royal commissaries were to revise the legislation of religious institutions. A decree of 1773 practically eliminated religious exemption.

In all this, the pope had nothing to say. Clement XIII protested in vain.

The commission was disbanded in 1780, but continued to function another four years. In all, it suppressed 426 religious houses, involving several entire orders, among them Grandmont. Brienne, a worldly prelate, "who spent more time leaning on his billiard cue than in saying Masses" (John McManners), had little sympathy for religious orders. While not all their ills should be ascribed to him, his ministrations only hastened their demise. Between 1768 and 1790, the number of French religious fell from 22,499 to 14,868. As d'Alembert observed, raising the required age of profession was a painless way of suppressing the religious orders.

The records of Brienne's commission provide, among other things, statistical data on the Order in France in 1768. The eight Carmelite provinces numbered 129 houses with 1199 members: Narbonne had 20 convents and 150 friars; Francia, 18 convents, 223 friars; Provence, 18 convents, 86 friars; Aquitaine, 13 convents, 104 friars; Touraine, 25 convents, 199 friars; Gascony, 17 convents, 117 friars; Toulouse, 10 convents, 68 friars; Gallo-Belgium, 7 convents, 191 friars. Twenty-one houses were marked for suppression, but they remained in existence.

Particularly dramatic is the decline in membership of the great province of Touraine, which in 1669 had 569 friars. Only seven of its convents included ten or more members. Seven others were adjudged useless - the largest number of any province. The small Gallo-Belgian province was the most flourishing. None of its seven houses counted less than ten friars. Except for the general *studium* of Paris (61 members), Lille (55), Valenciennes (40), and Douai (38) were the most populous Carmelite convents in France. Francia, too, was in good condition. All its houses, except Bourges (nine friars) and Saint-Amand (eight friars) counted at least ten members. Only these two provinces were not required to relinquish foundations.

The prescribed national chapter of the French provinces opened at the Place Maubert on July 10, 1770. Each provincial was accompanied by two delegates, one representing the priors; the other, the conventuals. The purpose of the meeting was to update the constitutions of the Order. It need hardly be said that the delegates were far from happy with this high-handed interference, however salutary, in their internal affairs. "It is not due to any lack of will on my part," the provincial of Narbonne, Louis Pernet, wrote to a confrere, Aimable Chazottier, on July 30, "that I have not been able to give you any definite news of our activity. What we agree upon unanimously is only too often not to the taste of the Office General of the Commission, of which the archbishop of Toulouse is the soul, and who seems to oppose whatever we decide as soon as it does not suit his taste .... I will simply say that no one in our assembly is satisfied with the results."

The constitutions drawn up by the national chapter appeared under the title, *Constitutiones Fratrum Beatissimae Dei Genitricis et Virginis Mariae de Monte Carmelo Antiquae Oservantiae regularis in congregatione nationali Parisiis habita 1770 recognitae et emendatae* (Paris, 1772). At Ximénez' request, Pope Clement XIV accorded his approval, May 30, 1772. The introduction to the constitutions is signed by Pacifique

Macarten, of the Touraine province, who seems also to be responsible for their final form.

Four parts treat of religious observance and the government of the whole Order, the provinces, and individual convents. The brief Part 2 on the general governance of the Order concedes the prior general "true and real power in our whole Order, but only according to the norm and tenure of these statutes and not otherwise" (*Caput unicum*, par. 2, no. 1). How the French government could limit a power admitted to be universal is one of the mysteries of Gallicanism.

Part 1 on religious observance, it must be admitted, is altogether a creditable piece of work. The law is briefly expressed in a simple, straightforward way without the legalistic *detritus* accumulated by centuries of living. The existence of the Stricter Observance in France is ignored, but the life prescribed for all French Carmelites is basically that of the reform. The important elements of Carmelite life, prayer, solitude, poverty, are given their due emphasis. All incomes, even from individual effort such as preaching, are to be consigned to the procurator, although the superior may allow money for reasons of health or studies (ch. 1, par. 1, no. 3). Black is prescribed for the habit, which should be of cheap woolen cloth (ch. 3, par. 1, no. 1). Certain sensible relaxations are allowed, which bring the law closer to actual living conditions of the time. Matins are set at five o'clock in the morning rather than midnight (ch. 2, par. 2, no. 2). Although religious are forbidden to possess costly objects, the use of a watch (*horologium portatile*) is permitted with due authorization (ch. 1, par. 1, no. 2). The spirit of the Enlightment appears in the more humane sanctions for misdeeds. Crimes that would involve capital punishment in civil law are punished with life imprisonment, but the cell should be healthful and open to the light. The prisoner should be supplied with spiritual books and even allowed to study, "lest the punishment ... turn to the detriment of the whole life." The superior should visit him daily (ch. 10, par. 5). Torture, still allowed in the Order's constitutions of 1626 (pt. 4, ch. 21, no. 11), is eliminated.

Under this law, the French Carmelites could have lived according to their vocation. The only ominous note was that their life was no longer their own, and in fact this precious commodity would soon be required of them in a more drastic manner.

Josephinism in Germany and Belgium

Although he did much to improve the condition of the secular clergy, Emperor Joseph II (1780-1790) had no use for religious, whom he considered a blight on society. On November 29, 1781, a stroke of his pen suppressed all establishments of religious men and women not dedicated to teaching, care of the sick, or scholarship.

The emperor's edict eliminated the province of Bohemia-Hungary-Austria and its 202 members. This province, as we have seen, comprised Vienna, Lienz, Voitsberg, and Zedlitzdorf in Austria; Prague and Chiesch in Bohemia; and Buda and Szekesfehervar (Fünfkirchen) in Hungary. All these houses had been inherited from the Upper German province in 1731, except Zedlitzdorf, which consequently had been founded after that date.

After Austria lost Silesia to Frederick II of Prussia in 1740, the Carmelite convents situated in that duchy (Striegau, Gross Strenz, Freistadt and Wohlau) in 1754 were constituted a vicariate independent of the province of Bohemia-

Hungary- Austria. The vicariate numbered 69 professed members (41 priests, 9 clerics, 19 brothers) and 3 novices. In 1762, the membership of the vicariate had decreased to 47 members (34 priests, 13 brothers).

After the creation of the Bohemia-Hungary-Austria province in 1731, the Upper German province counted the convents of Würzburg, Bamberg, Rottenburg, Dinkelsbühl, Neustadt a. d. Saale, Ravensburg, Straubing, Abensberg, and Heilbronn with 240 members.

The province was further reduced when Rottenburg was assigned to the Bohemia-Hungary-Austria province (1775), and the Bavarian government insisted on the separation of Straubing and Abensberg, which became the Vicariate of Bavaria (1771).

The Bavarian rulers were not to be outdone in zeal for reform by their Catholic brothers in other lands. Among the laws affecting the Church promulgated by King Maximilian III Joseph, that of November 2, 1769, set the age for profession at twenty-one, abolished monastic prisons, and forbade questing. In the case of crimes liable to capital punishment, religious delinquents were to be expelled from their Order and handed over to the secular authorities. The law of December 30, 1769, decreed that all orders with at least three houses in Bavaria should be constituted independent provinces. Bavarian religious could not attend general chapters, receive commands from superiors outside the kingdom, nor make contributions to them. Elections were to be presided over by a commissioner selected from the Ecclesiastical Council, which granted authorization to hold the chapter in the first place. A decree of August 1, 1701, forbade monasteries and convents to acquire land, houses, and other property of the sort. On September 16, 1730, the sale of real estate to the clergy was forbidden.

In spite of the ban on foreign travel, the Vicariate of Bavaria was represented at all the general chapters held during this period (1775, 1782, 1788).

The Lower German province, situated mainly in the ecclesiastical states in and around the Rhineland, had less interference from its rulers, though the prince bishops of that region were not untouched by Illuminism and Febronianism, as witness the Punctuation of Ems (1786).

In 1768, the province numbered 15 well-staffed convents and 2 residences with 363 members: Cologne, Boppard, Frankfurt, Kreuznach, Trier, Mainz, Speyer, Worms, Aachen, Weinheim, Hirschhorn, Thönisstein, Beilstein, Adelheid, Leuchterhof, Hesloch (res.) and Simmer (res.). "Almost all the convents of the province have been rebuilt in the past fifty years," a report of 1763 reads. "Recently, the greatly enlarged novitiate in Cologne was erected from the foundations. The treasury of the province still owes 9,000 Rhenish florins for it. Moreover, all the convents of the province have suffered much from excessive taxes levied in the wars." The same report shows that, at the time, Frankfurt and Aachen were serving as hospitals for French soldiers.

The Treaty of Rastadt, ending the War of the Spanish Succession (1701-1713), ceded the Spanish Netherlands to Austria; thus, Belgium also fell under mantle of the benevolent absolutism of the Hapsburgs. With edicts of May 13, 1771, and April 18, 1772, Maria Teresa set the age of religious profession at 25 years. In 1779, Joseph II required female religious to be 21 before profession and restored the dowry for candidates to poor monasteries. On November 28, 1781, Belgian religious were declared independent of foreign superiors and in 1782 dependent on the bishops. A decree of November 13 of the latter year suspended recruitment to the religious life. On March 13, 1783, "useless" convents, especially of contemplatives, were suppressed.

As a result of the emperor's decree forbidding contacts outside the realm, Boxmeer and Geldern disappeared from the roster of the province. Boxmeer was placed under the prior general. A decree of Joseph II of November 18, 1785, agreed to by the prior general, placed Geldern under the Lower German province.

With Boxmeer and Geldern went their respective nunneries, which were thus spared from the emperor's aversion to the contemplative life. Not so Brugge and Louvain, which were in the care of the Flemish province. Vilvoorde continued to exist, perhaps because the nuns also undertook the education of girls.

In 1786, the Flandro-Belgian province comprised 13 houses: Mechelen, Brussels, Ieperen, Brugge, Gent, Tienen, Aalst, Enghien, Geraardsbergen, Antwerp, Louvain, Termuylen, Bottelaer (vic.).

The Wallo-Belgian vicariate remained unchanged: Arlon, Marche, Brugelette, Sainte Anne-sur-Sambre, Wavre, Mons, Nivelles, Williers, La Xhavée.

The general congregation of 1786 assigned a confessor only to Vilvoorde; hence it may be assumed that the two Walloon nunneries, Namur and Marche, had undergone the fate of their Flemish counterparts.

The First Partition of Poland, 1772

In the First Partition of Poland, a number of Carmelite houses, mostly of the Russian province, fell under Austrian rule in Galicia: Lwów (Major Carmel), Lwów (St. Martin), Jaslo (province of Lesser Poland), Husaków, Kochawina, Drohobycz (province of Greater Poland), Trembowla, Botszowce, Rozdól, Sasiadowice. In 1792, half of these were suppressed. The remainder, separated from the Order and placed under episcopal jurisdiction, constituted what was now called the province of Galicia in Austria: Lwów (Major Carmel), Trembowla, Botszowce, Rozdól, Sasiadowice.

At this time, the Carmelite nunnery of Lwów fell a victim to the Emperor's myopia with regard to contemplative life.

The other Carmelite provinces remained unaffected by the gains of Russia and Prussia. The Russian province, shorn of its Galician houses, now consisted of Horodyszcze, Olewsk, Dorohostaj, Kisielin, Luck, Labún, and Annapol. Residences were opened at Monsterek and Toporzyszcze. Bonsterek was later voluntarily abandoned, and its community moved to Ostróg, to the former college of the Jesuits, who had been ousted in 1772. That same year, a residence was opened in Uszomierz and another in Bar in 1759, but the latter was abandoned in 1792.

During its brief existence, the convent of Bar experienced a moment of glory. Its founder, Mark Jandowicz (1713-1799), was an ardent supporter of the Confederation of Bar (1768), which nourished the hopeless dream of driving the Russians from Poland. During the unsuccessful defense of Bar, Jandowicz circulated among the Polish troops, encouraging them with his fiery words and prayers. A romantic painting by G. Styka immortalizes this occasion. For his patriotism, Fr. Jandowicz spent eight years in a Russian prison. In the revolt of the Poles previous to the Third Partition, the aged Carmelite played the same role for the troops of

Kosciusko. His final testament, entitled *Wieszczba*, predicted the restoration of Poland. The Carmelite patriot is also the subject of a play by one of Poland's greatest poets, Julius Slowack (1809-1849).

The two Lithuanian provinces of St. George and All Saints remained as they had been at the time of their institution in 1756 and 1766 respectively, except that Pompiany, of the province of All Saints, seems to have been suppressed at this time. On the other hand, Sloboda was founded between 1778 and 1783. After 1786, the convent of St. George in Wilno and that of Zoludek, of the province of St. George, are listed in the chapter acts of All Saints.

The provinces of Greater and Lesser Poland fell mainly under Prussian rule. They, too, remained substantially as they had been at the time of their division in 1728. Only their convents which had fallen to Austria were suppressed. Drohobycz in Greater Poland was suppressed in 1789. Jaslo in Lesser Poland was also extinguished at this time. Its miraculous image eventually found asylum in the parish church of Tarnowiec.

Absolutism in Northern Italy

The Treaty of Rastadt (1714) also conferred on Austria certain territories in Italy, where as a consequence the imperial policies regarding relations of Church and state prevailed. In 1765, Leopold II of Austria, brother of Joseph II and his successor in 1790, took charge of the Duchy of Milan and initiated a series of provisions regarding religious. A *Giunta Economale* regulated mixed affairs between Church and state. The pragmatic of September 5, 1767, required royal consent for the erection of churches and convents and possession by *mortmain*, and furthermore required such corporations to submit title of their possessions. Religious communities had to submit an annual *tabella*, or report, listing the names of the members of each house, together with its incomes and debts. The year 1769 brought decrees abolishing conventual prisons (March 9), closing *grancie* and hospices (April 15), and suppressing small convents (April 27). An edict of 1774 confined the conferral of the doctorate to the University of Pavia, (where, incidentally, ecclesiastical students might be properly inoculated with the principles of Gallicanism, Febronianism, and Jansenism). A circular of January 18, 1776, forbade candidates to be received into religious Orders without the royal *beneplacitum*. The following year, superiors general were limited to one visit during their term of office.

The Carmelite province of Lombardy extended through the duchies of Milan, Mantua, Parma, and the Republic of Genoa. In 1767, the province numbered eighteen houses: Genoa, Pavia, Milan, Cremona, Piacenza, Novara, Alessandria, Novi, Incisa, Lodi, Bassignano, Melegnano, Monte Oliveto, Gavi, Cremolino, Luino, Como and Melzi.

In 1771, Lodi, Melegnano, Como, Melzi and Carnate succumbed to the ban of 1769 on small houses. Luino was apparently suppressed for the same reason (1778).

The reorganization and reduction of the number of parishes, another concern of the sacristan emperor, in 1783 eliminated the important convents of Milan and Cremona. On the other hand, in 1788, the Carmelite church of Pavia was made a parish, into which several others were incorporated. The Carmelite, Joseph Agradi, remained in charge of the parish until his death in 1811, but the community seems to have been disbanded in 1788.

Other houses were lost to the province through the trend of absolutist States to cut off religious houses in their territories from outside relationships. By imperial decree of April 11, 1781, the province was separated from its houses in the Republic of Genoa. These would have been Genoa and its *grancie* Lavagna, Novi, Gavi, and Monte Oliveto.

On August 31, 1784, Ximénez named a Father Ripetti his commissary for the vicariate of Genoa, and on his resignation replaced him on December 3 with Brocard Boccardi, prior of Novi. Boccardi was again named commissary in 1793. On May 6, 1797, Cyril Capozza was given the office at the discretion of the prior general.

In 1733, the Congregation for Bishops and Religious had definitively attached Monte Oliveto to the Lombardy province, thus terminating its long history as an independent contemplative convent.

On August 1, 1785, Pius VI at the request of Ferdinand, Duke of Parma, transferred Piacenza to the Romagna province.

On the other hand, Lombardy was assigned Rovereto, when the Republic of Venice in 1769 disembarrassed itself of foreign houses, but this convent was in turn suppressed in 1785.

Thus perished from the face of the earth the once flourishing Lombardy province, which had extended over the whole of northern Italy.

The Serenissima, never a very submissive daughter of the Church, during these years of general revolt against papal ties showed little inclination to mend her ways. An edict of September 7, 1768, placed religious under the jurisdiction of the bishops, abolished conventual prisons, and established the age of twenty-one for entering the novitiate and twenty-five for profession. The decree of the Republic of February 23, 1770, forbade religious to leave the convent without a companion and set a curfew for them of eleven o'clock at night. On August 2, 1770, the Republic suppressed all religious houses with less than twelve members.

As a result of these laws, especially the latter, the Carmelite province of Venice lost its houses in Desenzano del Garda, Cerea, Gottolengo, Udine, and Strada. In 1782, there remained only the convents of Venice, Padua, Verona, Vicenza, Crema, and Pontaglio.

For their sins, the religious of the Grand Duchy of Tuscany were given the long-lived Peter Leopold II, brother of Emperor Joseph II and architect of the Synod of Pistoia (1786), aided and abetted by the notorious Scipio de Ricci. A steady stream of decrees emanating from the *Segretaria del Regio Diritto* progressively separated the Carmelites from Rome and subjected them to the State.

On May 4, 1775, the archduke set the age for entering the novitiate at eighteen years; for profession, twenty-one years completed. To anticipate any monkish skulduggery, candidates were required to show proof of age in Florence or Siena.

A decree of January 10, 1778, admitted the usage already introduced, permitting bishops and religious superiors to avail themselves of royal ministers in proceeding against persons enjoying the *privilegium fori*. Censures involving temporal punishment required the royal *exsequatur*. In circular of January 8, 1780, the archduke again offered the secular arm to superiors in maintaining observance and furthermore threatened them with perpetual ineligibility for office in the Grand Duchy, if they tried to cover up abuses.

On January 12, 1778, religious superiors were ordered to send full information regarding 1) taxes regularly sent to Rome, 2) incomes of each house and the number of religious thus able to be supported without begging and individual incomes, 3) houses incapable of maintaining more than five members, 4) the number of religious, Tuscan and foreign, in the province and the number of Tuscans within and outside the Grand Duchy, 5) all legacies and dowries. Superiors were further requested to suggest which small houses might be suppressed and how their incomes might best be disposed of, and further how the remaining convents might make themselves more useful by supporting poor youths, conducting free schools, hospitals, etc. The Carmelite provincial, Peter Paul Pagni obediently supplied the desired information, but answered in reply to the last two questions that his small convents were needed for the spiritual care of the locality and that elsewhere his seventy-six priests, of whom seventeen were studying, others elderly, were already working to full capacity.

A decree of June 15, 1782, forbade sending taxes to Rome; these were to be given to the Tuscan bishops. Another circular of the following July 10, beginning, "It is the mind of His Royal Highness that the religious Orders should be recalled to serving the only purpose for which they have been admitted to the state, which is to cooperate in helping the secular clergy in spiritual assistance to the people," annulled all privileges of religious and placed them under the jurisdiction of the bishops. If religious were only an aid to the diocesan clergy, it followed that the bishop, not the religious superior granted dimissorials for orders.

Religious from other provinces were not given residence in Tuscany. Those on a visit were not permitted to preach.

The decree of October 23, 1787, forbade the reception of any more novices and ordered novices to be dismissed without profession.

Religious had been forbidden to alienate immobile property without the sovereign's permission. A decree of April 18, 1789, extended this prohibition to contracting debts on the goods of the convent.

A law of October 2,1788, prescribed the form for holding chapters.

Of the ten convents comprising the Carmelite province of Tuscany, Montepulciano was suppressed in 1774, Fivizzano and Roccastrada in 1782, Prato and Montecatini in 1785. Carrara, in the Duchy of Modena, was cut loose from Tuscany. In 1789, the prior general accepted it under his immediate jurisdiction. At the provincial chapter of 1789, held according to the form prescribed by His Royal Highness and presided over by his representative, only the priors of Florence, Siena, Pisa, and Corniola (alias Empoli) answered the roll call.

As if all this were not enough, a fire which began during the night preceding January 29, 1771, laid in ruins the monumental Carmine of Florence. The nave with its works of art was totally destroyed. Fortunately, the Brancacci and Corsini chapels in the transepts were spared - the Corsini chapel less so. The friars refused to give in to discouragement and the very next day started to collect alms for the restoration of the church. All of Florence, beginning with Archduke Peter Leopold himself, generously answered their appeal.

Carmel in Southern Italy Under the Bourbons

The Treaty of Vienna, which concluded the War of the Polish Succession (1738), recognized Charles IV of Bourbon as King of Naples and Sicily. The Bourbons, especially through their regent Bernard Tanucci (1759-1764) adopted the usual policy of enlightened monarchs toward religious orders.

On December 17, 1768, a royal dispatch ordered small convents suppressed. The administration of their goods was entrusted to a council (*giunta*), composed of the *Giudice della Regia Monarchia* and the *Regio Segreto*. In these realms, lay the Carmelite provinces of St. Albert, St. Angelo, Monte Santo, Santa Maria Della Scala, Terra di Lavoro, Puglia, Calabria, Abruzzo, Santa Maria della Vita, and Naples.

The Sicilian provinces seem to have been little affected by the legislation regarding religious. Only a few insignificant convents were closed.

Thirty-two convents are represented in the acts of 1786 of the province of St. Albert, a number that remains constant into the 19th century: Messina, Gualtieri, Milazzo, Pozzo di Gotto, Furnari, Tripi, San Pietro Patti, Raccuja, Sinagra, Librizzi, Francavilla, Castiglione, Linguaglossa, Randazzo, Cerami, Nicosia, Petralia, Calascibetta, Enna (alias Castrogiovanni), Mazzarino, Eraclea (alias Terranova, Gela), Licodia, Chiaramonte, Ragusa, Modica, Buscemi, Sortino, Lentini, Francofonte, Paterno, Regalbuto, Troina.

Nature seemed allied to the unsympathetic government. In the disastrous earthquake of 1785, seventeen convents and churches of the province were damaged or destroyed.

In the 19th century, without the two Maltese convents, Valletta and Notabile, the province of St. Angelus still counted thirty-three houses: Palermo, Trapani, Marsala, Sciacca, Agrigenti, Licata, Caltanisetta, Sutera, Caltabellotta, Salemi, Alcarno, Corleone, Monte S. Giuliano, Mazzara, Bivona, Partanna, Sambuca, Monreale, Racalmuto, Naro, Burgio, Bisacquino, Castelvetrano, Prizzi, Gibellina, Carini, Favara, Termini, Canicatti, Palermo (S. Nicolo), Alessandria, Licata (Sant'Angelo), Partinico.

Of the nine houses of the Monte Santo province in Sicily, the convent in Siracusa was torn down with its church in 1735 during the defense of the city in the war between Austrians and Spaniards under Charles VI. The Carmelites were given the church of St. Catherine, which in turn was suppressed by royal decree as a small convent (1786). The convent of Santa Maria del Pilirello in Messina was suppressed by the government in 1784. The church was entrusted to the care of the Carmelite Gabriel Alagona, but after being damaged by earthquake in 1786 it was ordered demolished the following year.

The nine convents of the province of Santa Maria della Scala all survived into the nineteenth century.

On the mainland, the province of Calabria was the hardest hit by decrees of suppression. As late as 1763, the province numbered twenty convents. The chapter of 1786 mustered only eight convents: Corigliano, Carolei, Cosenza, Belmonte, Montalto, Cassano, Lungro, Mongrassano.

In spite of its poverty, one is pleased to report, the province in 1763 voted to contribute twenty ducats annually to the support of Irish students "beyond the seas."

On the other hand, neighboring Puglia kept its numerous brood intact. As late as 1776 at least, it still counted twenty-seven convents: Presicce, Nardò (Neretum), Lecce, Mesagne, Carovigno (Santa Maria del Soccorso), Monopoli, Trani, Cerignola, Canosa, Gensano, Noia, Conversano (*Cupersanum*), Putignano, Martina, Taranto,

Grottaglie, Torre Palude, San Pietro in Galatina, Brindisi, Carovigno (Carmine), Ostuni, Bari, Baruli, Andria, Bitonto, Francavilla, and Murciano.

The other Carmelite provinces in the Kingdom of Naples also show little change. The few houses that cease to exist at this time may have simply been spontaneously abandoned.

In 1781, the province of Terra di Lavoro still numbered its nineteen convents: Capua, Caserta, Cervinara, Benevento, Grottaminarda, Melfi, Salerno, Rocca degl'Aspidi, Cilento, Piedimonte d'Alife, Venafro, Bocino, Bovino, Lucera, Torre Maggiore, Tricarico, Monte Sant'Angelo, Campolieto, Barile.

In 1786, the Neapolitan province consisted of thirteen houses: Naples (Monte Santo), Chiaia, Nocera dei Pagani, Sessa, Capo di Chino, Gragnano, Ottaiano, Somma, Lacco, Nola, Pomigliano, Posilippo, Arienzo.

In 1786, only the two Neapolitan convents (Della Vita and Della Concordia), San Lorenzello, Torre del Greco, and Faicchio occur in the chapter acts of the province of Santa Maria della Vita.

The membership of the province of Abruzzo was largely composed of friars from the Republic of Lucca. A royal decree of 1769 banished all "foreign" religious. The resulting void in the ranks was filled with "nationals" of the Kingdom of Naples. In 1784, the province still maintained its eight convents: Bellanti, Penne, Pianella, Ortona, Aquila, Teramo, Campli, and Atessa.

The three provinces in the Papal States, Rome, Romagna, and Monte Santo remained immune from interference by civil authorities; at least here the government had the competence to legislate religious reform.

In 1781, the Roman province counted seventeen houses: San Martino in Rome (ceded to the province in 1759), Perugia, Orvieto, Cellere, Viterbo, Canepina, Viano, Ronciglione, Sorbo, Albano, Velletri, Palestrina (under the jurisdiction of the prior general from 1640 to 1759), Tivoli, Celano, Sulmona, Leonessa, Pettorana.

In 1785, the four last houses, situated in the Kingdom of Naples, were detached from the province and made a vicariate, no doubt at the request of the sovereign. Also Sorbo, perhaps too insignificant to warrant a prior, disappears from the acts of the provincial chapters after 1781.

St. Julian's, the Order's oldest foundation in Rome, had ceased to be an autonomous convent in 1581, when it was subjected to the prior of nearby St. Martin's. In 1783, St. Julian's was sold to the Redemptorists, who evidently were not happy with the agreement, for in 1791 they complained to the Holy See that the sale had been usurious. Church and convent have since made way for other buildings.

In 1760, the province of Romagna elected priors of seventeen convents. Of the latter, Sabbiosa, Corso, and Guiglia disappeared in the course of the century. The remaining houses were: Forlì, Ravenna, Imola, Lugo, Massalombarda, Medicina, Bologna (Santa Maria delle Grazie), Cesena, Rimini, Pesaro, Senigallia, Ancona, Iesi, Bagnacavallo.

Curinga of the province of Monte Santo was transferred to the Calabrian province, where it succumbed to the royal reforms. In 1738, a hospice had been accepted in Nereto, which lay in the Kingdom of Naples and which consequently fell a victim to the ban on small houses (1768).

The island of Sardinia, for centuries the possession of Spain, in 1714 was placed under Austrian rule. The Treaty of London of 1720 in turn ceded the island to Savoy. The House of Savoy undertook to set matters right in the Carmelite province of Sardinia, which for that matter was in a deplorable financial, if not spiritual state. At the intermediate congregation of 1765 the provincial, Cyril Bo, reported on an interview with the viceroy. There was to be only one house of theology (Cagliari) and one of philosophy (Sassari). The number of lectors was to be reduced, as well as the number of laybrothers. Likewise, there was to be only one novitiate. Sassari-outside-the-Walls was suppressed. About the same time, the hospice at Nurame was abandoned.

The distressful economic condition of the province was due in part to over population of the convents, which could not supply the needs of their communities. Hence the reduction of the non-productive elements, laybrothers, and non-ordained clerics. Hence, too, the prohibition to receive more novices. On the other hand, a sufficient number of priests had to be maintained to satisfy Mass obligations.

The chapter of 1766 applied itself to the reduction of the communities. The number of friars in each of the seven convents was specified by law. The total membership of the province was set at 108 friars: 68 priests, 28 brothers, 8 clerics, 4 novices.

The same chapter promulgated new statutes for studies "according to the mind of his Royal Majesty of this Kingdom of Sardinia."

At the repeated request of the King of Savoy, the general chapter of 1768 removed the province from the jurisdiction of the assistant general for Spain and placed it under the Italian assistancy.

The limitation of candidates did not improve the material condition of the province and in time proved counter-productive. A request made to the Congregation of Religious Discipline in 1777 to open a second novitiate at Sassari noted that by that time the province had fallen thirty priests short of the number stipulated by royal decree.

At that time (1777), the Carmelite convents in Sardinia were: Cagliari, Sassari-Within-the-Walls, Mogoro, Alghero, Bosa, Oristani, Chiaramonte.

Chapter 2

The Brink of Bankruptcy

Unhappy witness to this early distintegration of the Order and himself an unwitting contributor to it was Joseph Albert Ximénez, prior general from 1768 to 1780, successor to Marianus Ventimiglia. A Spanish *hidalgo*, Ximénez entered the Order at Zaragoza, making his profession in 1735. He obtained the doctorate in the Order (1760), not, it would seem, at a university, and he was not destined for a teaching career. Instead, he distinguished himself as a preacher in important pulpits of Spain, as well as before the royal council. He functioned as a synodal examiner in various dioceses and as theologian of the nuncio of Spain. He attended the general chapter held in Venice in 1762, afterwards continuing on to Rome, where he was destined to remain. After one Spanish assistant died and another resigned, Ximénez took over the office. Similarly, he became procurator general in 1765, after the death of Christopher Alvarez de Palma. The general chapter of 1768 unanimously elected him prior general.

Ximénez in Spain

The prior general requested and received from the general chapter special powers for himself and his council to deal with certain problems relating to the Spanish provinces, "both with regard to the number of religious in each convent and other matters concerning their more felicitous and holy governance."

In fact, the royal council had requested a financial account of the Spanish provincials - an ominous sign of suppressions to come. It would seem that this action had been triggered by the appeals to the council of certain "grave fathers," especially of the Castilian province, about the excessive number of religious without incomes. On January 2, 1769, the council wrote to the prior general about the question, strongly urging the desirability of his presence in Spain. Ximénez lost no time in making an appearance in Madrid, where he was received by King Charles III with all honor due his rank. Using the figures the provincials had previously submitted to the royal council, he found that the province of Andalusia counted 25 houses and 651 members, Aragon 22 houses with 745 members, Castile 16 houses with 573 members, Catalonia 14 houses (omitting Mahon) with 363 members. He calculated the number of friars each convent could support from its incomes, eliminated superfluous expenditures, ordered each friar to return to his own convent, and forbade the reception of novices. Finally, he suppressed a few small houses: Tàrrega and Salgar in Catalonia, Seville (St. Teresa), Cordova (Carmen), Trigueros, Escacena, Alcalá de Guadaira, and Priego in Andalusia.

Ximénez projected a rather drastic reduction in the membership of the Spanish provinces. He estimated viable membership at 1,328 friars as against the actual population of 2,332 - a cut of almost fifty percent.

The prior general also issued a series of decrees designed to improve the quality of Carmelite life in Spain. They concerned the limitation and formation of novices, updating of the curriculum of studies, training of preachers, faithful attendance in choir, accurate records of Mass intentions, scrupulous administration of community goods, and other aspects of religious observance. His concern was mainly for those externals that would present the Order to the 18th century layman as a credible and efficient organization.

Ximénez' reduction for the most part remained a dead letter, at least as far as the diminution of the number of convents was concerned. However, his prompt action showed his willingness to cooperate in the solution of the problems of the civil government, and the regime which had expelled the Jesuits from Spain and in general had little sympathy for religious commended him and gave the Carmelites no further trouble.

The condition of the Order in Portugal during the second half of the 18th century had greatly deteriorated, mainly due, however, to an act of God beyond human control.

The Lisbon Earthquake, 1755

On the morning of All Saints, 1755, when the churches were crowded with the faithful fulfilling their holy day obligation, occurred the horrendous earthquake of Lisbon, a disaster that filled all Europe with fear and foreboding. Three heavy shocks over a period of five or six minutes reduced the city to a ruin under a thick cloud of dust. Shortly thereafter, the sea rose in a great tidal wave, and the Tagus broke its banks, enveloping buildings and drowning their occupants. Even so, much might have been saved from the rubble, but a fierce fire broke out and utterly consumed the contents of public buildings, churches, palaces, libraries, and archives of this wealthy and cultured city. It has been estimated that about ten to fifteen thousand persons were drowned, crushed, burnt, and otherwise killed in the catastrophe.

Lisbon was only the epicenter of the quake. It caused extensive damage throughout southwest Portugal and northern Africa and was also felt in southern Spain and France.

Of the many contemporary accounts of the disaster the Carmelites possess one which describes its effects on the Order's province of Portugal. It was written on January 29, 1756, three months after the quake by none other than the historian, Joseph of St. Anne Pereira, at the time provincial, reporting on the event to Rome. More details were added by the provincial definitory in a letter dated the day after Christmas, 1757.

At the time, the provincial was visiting the nunnery at Lagos in Algave, one of the areas hardest hit by the quake. The monastery, "a noble edifice," came crashing down, killing twenty-two nuns and severely injuring forty-three more, out of a community of one hundred and twenty-five, besides boarders and servants, three hundred persons in all. Pereira was saved by a wall left partially standing. Here as in Lisbon, the sea rose to add to the damage and toll in lives. With his companions and the domestics, the provincial set about extracting the nuns trapped in the ruins, saw to the burial of the dead, and the care of the injured, and foraged for food, which was also shared with the poor. He managed to rescue the Blessed Sacrament buried under heaps of plaster and stone. For a week, the friars and sisters had "no other shelter than a field under the open sky." Later, Pereira was able to obtain shelter for the nuns. Meanwhile, news began to trickle in, bringing information on the national scope of the calamity. The Carmels of Lagoa and Setúbal had been levelled to the ground "in such a way that none of the material could be used again." When the news arrived of the destruction of "our beloved Carmo and the whole city of Lisbon,"

Pereira recounts, "unable to resist my feelings, I was seized by a mortal dizziness accompanied by fever," a condition that lasted from noon to midnight, nor were thirty cuppings sufficient to restore him to consciousness. Soon thereafter, his veins still open from the bleedings inflicted on him by the doctors, he set out for Lisbon.

"Our incomparable Carmo," convent and church, lay in ruins. The main altar and six chapels of the transept extending beyond the roof had remained upright, but the following fire consumed everything. The Blessed Sacrament and images of the Virgin and of Christ, the latter in bas-relief, known as the "Ricattato," were spared. "Our precious archive" and library were destroyed. Pereira also lamented the loss of the books and manuscripts in his cell, which, being on the top floor, was the first to come tumbling down. A large number of persons perished in the church, including entire families who had come for confession. Fourteen friars died, three of them in the confessional.

Setúbal had not only been damaged by the earthquake; the following tidal wave swept away a large part of the building. Francis of the Conception died. At Lagoa, now a heap of stones, Emmanuel of the Nativity, making his thanksgiving in the sanctuary, was killed; the prior and subprior, extracted from the ruins, came close to death. Collares, Torres Novas, Vidigueira, and Beja were no longer habitable and would require large sums to repair. Alverca with its church collapsed totally. The damage to the college in Coimbra amounted to 5,000 *cruceiros*. Only Evora and Moura with the nunneries of Beja and Tentúgal remained unscathed. (Although not mentioned by the provincial, Camarate, too, suffered unspecified damage).

Historians have noticed the prompt and courageous efforts at recovery of the Portuguese people under the able and efficient leadership of the Marquis de Pombal. The same spirit was evinced by the Carmelites, as appears from the letter of the definitory of Christmas, 1757. Pereira's influence at the court, where he was confessor of the Princess of Brazil and of the Infantas, proved of great help. By royal mandate, roads leading to the Carmo were cleared for the transport of building materials, the Carmelites were supplied with wood from the royal forest, and fifty workers were provided to clear the ruins. On July 2, 1758, the community returned to the convent in solemn procession, bearing the Blessed Sacrament and the image of the Virgin. The reconstruction of the other convents was also carried forward, but costs were enormous and progress was slow, especially after the death of the energetic and courageous Joseph Pereira. The province never fully recovered from the havoc wreaked by the earthquake. The church of the Carmo of Lisbon was never rebuilt, and today its gaunt and fragmentary walls, become a national monument, lower down on the city, a witness to a glorious past and its fiery ending.

Information is lacking on Carmel in Portugal between the year of the earthquake and the suppression of the province. Acts of chapters were not sent to Rome, nor did the Portuguese attend the general chapters after 1756. Perhaps the Pombal regime discouraged relations with Rome. The rupture of Portugal with Rome in 1760 is given as the reason for the absence of the Portuguese from the general chapter of 1762.

The Curia in Financial Straits

The general chapter of 1775 was presided over by the pope himself, Pius VI, who honored the assembly with a brief discourse, later printed, and dispensed the prior general from ineligibility for re-election. This sign of papal favor did not harm the chances of the incumbent, and as a matter of fact Ximénez was re-elected by an overwhelming majority, though he did not live to complete his second term, dying in Naples on December 13, 1780.

At the prior general's unexpected death, the committee designed in 1648 to meet this emergency convened in Traspontina the following December 21 to elect his successor. The French assistant, Andrew Audras, was chosen.

Andrew Audras (1720-1784), a member of the convent of Lyon in the province of Narbonne, studied at the Place Maubert and became a doctor of the Sorbonne. He attended the general chapter of 1762 as prior of Paris. In 1768, he was made assistant general for France, a post he retained until his election as prior general.

If the Jesuits had their Lavallette, the Carmelites had their Ximénez. Great had been the consternation in Rome at the sudden death of the prior general in Naples; greater still was the consternation, when it was discovered that, unbeknownst to all, he had involved the Order, and specifically the convent of Traspontina, in a staggering debt.

Upon investigation, it transpired that Ximénez had six times obtained from the Holy See authorization to make loans on the property of Traspontina and the Order: on January 23, 1777, for 24,000 *scudi*; on March 26, for 6,000; on November 2, for 12,000; on September 7, 1778, for 35,000; on July 11, 1779, for 22,000; on March 16, 1780, for 20,000. In all, he had obtained permission to borrow 119,000 *scudi*. As a motive for raising this sum, he alleged various needs of the Spanish convent in Naples, Santa Maria del Soccorso. He lost no time in mortgaging various holdings of the Order in Rome.

At an audience on September 18, 1781, the pope was intransigent, ordering the debt to be paid even at the expedient of selling the Order's convents. "If within a certain time the convents are not sold," Audras quotes him as saying, "We will see that they are, beginning in Rome with San Martino and Traspontina and in Romagna with Cesena (Pius' birthplace)." Audras had come to request that the innumerable suits be cited to one court, preferably the Rota or one of the Congregations.

The general chapter of 1782 agreed that the debt was the responsibility of the convents in the Papal States. The prior general and his council were authorized to sell the mountain villas of Traspontina and San Martino and to take further measures to liquidate the rest of the debt.

Over the next five years, the debt was gradually paid off. On August 2, 1787, a papal rescript was obtained to borrow 1,500 *scudi* to satisfy the last two creditors of Fr. Ximénez. Palestrina assumed a mortgage of 1,000 *scudi*; Medicina, of 500.

As always happens in these cases, the question afterwards arises: "How was it possible?" Certainly, there seems to have been a remarkable indifference to precautionary measures. The Holy See seemingly made no attempt to ascertain whether the canonical conditions were being observed in these repeated requests to borrow large sums of money. The banks never verified whether Traspontina actually consented to the heavy liens on its property. Most mystifying of all, what happened to the money? "He dissipated it all in gifts," Audras told the pope in answer to the same question - a statement repeated by others in similar terms. But why should Ximénez, who seems always to have conducted his affairs with prudence, suddenly become a prodigal spendthrift in the last three years of his life?

A clue to the mystery may perhaps be found in far-off Mexico. In 1769, the Carmelite, Joseph Vincent Díaz Bravo, had been appointed bishop of Durango in those parts, and previous to departure for the New World had contracted a debt of 120,000 *pesos fuertes*. By good fortune, he had met Ximénez, present at the time in Madrid, who had generously undertaken to assume the debt. The two Carmelites were from the same province of Aragon, and so no doubt knew each other. Before a notary on December 8, 1769, Díaz promised to redeem the debt in six annual payments of 20,000 *pesos*. In case of his death, this debt was to be given preference over all others, in payment of which he pledged all his possessions present and future. Díaz, in fact, died in Madrid in 1772, leaving all or part of his debt unredeemed.

By 1775, the term for the full payment of the debt, we find Ximénez taking steps for its remittance. On August 14, he had his contract with Díaz again notarized in Madrid. At a meeting of the council of the Order on September 26,1776, he told its members about a Carmelite bishop who had died, leaving a great debt, to which the episcopal *mensa* was unequal, and gave it as his opinion that "the glory and good name" (*decor et estimatio*) of the Order required that it satisfy the creditors. If Ximénez revealed to the council that he was already responsible for the debt, this does not appear from the copy of the minutes of the meeting, made by the secretary, Master Joseph M. Spinedi, which has come down to us. In fact, the meeting was never entered into the register of the council. A copy of the minutes of the council meeting, which specified the bishop's debt to be 120,000 *scudi* - the amount ultimately borrowed by the prior general - was attached to Ximénez' request to the Holy See to make the first loan of 24,000 *scudi*. A fortnight thereafter, on February 13, 1777, Ximénez had an Italian translation of his agreement with Díaz made by Emmanuel Mendizabal, archivist of the Ministry of Spain in Rome, witnessed by a notary of the Roman curia. This translation was again notarized on October 7, 1780.

The prior general now proceeded to borrow money on the Order's property in Rome. On September 7, 1778, the date of the fourth loan, John Baptist Sisco, the Order's procurator at the Spanish court, obtained from the Holy See authorization for the Spanish provinces to apply incomes from the suppressed convent of Priego and other convents eliminated by Ximénez to the sum already paid, because of the "misfortune well-known to His Holiness." On October 9, 1780, a notarized copy of this rescript was made (on behalf of Ximénez?). Whatever the result of this maneuver, the prior general continued borrowing money in Rome.

On October 7, 1780, two days before the notarization of his rescript, Pius VI confirmed the decree of the general chapter of 1680 to the effect that the prior general could do anything able to be done by any member of the Order, individually or in chapter general or otherwise. Ximénez was evidently preparing to give an account of his stewardship, when death spared him this embarrassment.

Thus, rather than wasting money in vain prodigality, Ximénez seems to have been trying to pay off a debt about which there were circumstances derogatory to the Order that demanded secrecy. The locale of the debt would have been Spain (hence the use of Santa Maria del Soccorso), its object the indebtedness of the bishop of Durango. Was Pope Pius aware of the real destination of the large sums the Carmelite general was continually borrowing? Was any Carmelite in Rome in Ximénez' confidence? It should not surprise us if not everyone was telling everything he knew.

The generally debilitated economic condition of religious orders in the late 18th century formed part of their image of declining powers and gave the state an excuse for interfering in their affairs. Among Carmelites at this time, there are signs of increasing economic weakness: requests for reductions of Mass obligations, permissions not to hold chapters and intermediate congregations because of expense, elimination of *socii* to provincial chapters requested for the same reason. Ximénez' legacy of financial chaos at the center of the Order added impetus to the downward trend in religious vitality of the Carmelites.

The Suppression of the Mantuan Congregation and Other Reforms

Related in part to the Ximénez fiasco was the suppression of the Mantuan Congregation and of the reformed province of Monte Santo in the Papal States, which Audras now asked of the pope. He gave as his reason that the houses of these reforms were few, sparsely populated and impoverished, but no doubt motives of strengthening the Order through these increments influenced his petition. At the same time, King Victor Amadeus of Savoy, whose practical lay mind could make little sense out of the different sorts of Carmelites in his realms, asked that they all be reduced to one entity. Pope Pius VI acceded to both these requests in his bull "*Exigit apostolici*," March 21, 1783, uniting to the Order the Mantuan Congregation and the reformed provinces of Monte Santo and Piedmont. All Carmelite convents in the Papal States were to be aggregated either to the Roman or the Romagna provinces. In Savoy, there was to be only the province of Piedmont, to which the Mantuan nunneries were subjected. The vicar general of the Mantuan Congregation, whose office ceased to exist, was to be accorded the privileges of an ex-general. Similarly Mantuan procurators general retained the privileges of their former offices. Doctorates, baccalaureates, and other academic degrees legitimately acquired were to remain intact. Controversy over precedence among doctors as a result of this academic injection forms a conspicuous if inglorious feature of these declining years.

On September 30, 1785, Pius added a rider to his decree, declaring it to have been his intention to include the Sicilian reformed provinces of Monte Santo and Santa Maria della Scala. He does not say how these provinces are to be incorporated into the others in Sicily, and in fact both retained their identity. No provision was made concerning the reformed province of Santa Maria della Vita in the Kingdom of Naples. It, too, continued its existence as a province of the Order. The Holy See does not seem to have been very well informed regarding the reform movements in the Order.

Thus ended with a whimper the Mantuan Congregation which for four centuries had brightened the pages of Carmelite history with many moments of religious fervor and examples of learning and virtue.

As to the reformed provinces, which in fact formed part of the Order like the other provinces, the pope's decision in practice could only mean that they were dispensed from their reformed observances and were henceforth obligated to follow the general constitutions of 1626. What profit there was in this is not clear.

North of the Alps, the Stricter Observance had not been abolished, but the

French provinces had been given new constitutions through the magnanimity of King Louis XV.

In mid-18th century the Mantuan Congregation still numbered 53 convents, but by the year of its suppression, like the rest of the Order, it had suffered some hard knocks from absolutist regimes.

On September 7, 1768, the Venetian Republic insisted on the separation from the Congregation of the convents within its boundaries. The resultant Venetian Congregation comprised the convents of Brescia, Bergamo, Venice, Salò, Gorlago, Collalto, Bariano, San Felice, Rai, Bottrighe, and Desenzano al Serio. All of these, with the exception of Brescia, Bergamo, Salò, and Desenzano al Serio, succumbed almost immediately to the law of the suppression of small convents (1770). In most cases, the manner of their extinction was particularly brutal. The friars were given short notice to vacate the premises and were escorted on their way by soldiery.

The four remaining convents continued an independent existence, segregated from the Order. Salò disappeared between the chapters of 1780 and 1784. Desenzano was suppressed in 1788. On May 28, 1790, the council of the Order, "for the sake of peace and quiet," approved the acts of the Venetian chapter, held apparently by only Brescia and Bergamo. Presumably, they regularly held chapters until the French invasion at the end of the century, but the acts have so far not been found.

In the Duchy of Milan under Austrian rule, the Mantuan Congregation suffered the same fate as the Lombardy province. All its houses were suppressed, its religious pensioned off. Where the conventual church survived as a parish church, a Carmelite remained briefly as pastor. The rest of the community found refuge in other convents or among their families; others, finally, became secular priests. Santa Caterina was suppressed in 1770, Soncino in 1772, San Giacomo and Casterno in 1780, Olginate, Pavia, and Milan in 1782.

In the Duchy of Mantua, the long reign of the Gonzagas, loyal supporters and patrons of the Mantuan Congregation, came to an end in 1707, when their territories passed under Austrian control. By 1783, most of the nine convents of the Congregation in the duchy had been eliminated. Frassino was suppressed in 1772, Gonzaga, Cannetto, Sabbionetta, and Revere in 1780. The papal bull of suppression, March 21, 1783, was not recognized in the duchy, but what the pope was powerless to bring about, the emperor accomplished without effort, and the historic convent of Mantua, which had given the reform its name, was extinguished on May 5. Fubino, Casal Monferrato, and Trino survived.

In the duchies of Parma and Modena, the traditional rulers remained in power. In the Duchy of Parma, Soragna was suppressed in 1769 by Marquis William du Tillot during the minority of Duke Ferdinand, Infante of Spain. The convent of Parma itself continued to exist.

The dukes of Modena were less favorably inclined toward religious than the pious Ferdinand of Parma. On short notice, the Carmelites were evicted from Camurana, Correggio, and Novellara in 1768 and from Modena in 1783. Only Reggio remained in these realms.

In the Republic of Genoa, the Congregation had convents in the capital (Our Lady of the Angels) and in Pontremoli. The latter was suppressed in 1783.

In the Grand Duchy of Tuscany, the Mantuan Congregation was represented in Florence, Pistoia, Morrocco, Castellina, Le Selve, Anghiari, Lucca. The latter, actually located in the Republic of Lucca, was probably set adrift from the other convents by the *Segretaria del Regio Diritto*. Otherwise, with the exception of Anghiari, suppressed late in 1783, the other houses were allowed to exist.

In the Papal States, the Mantuan Congregation had a safe haven: Rome (San Crisogono), Ferrara, Bologna, Viterbo, Macerata, Sora, Vetralla, San Donato. Sutri had become a grancia of San Crisogono. Ferrara possessed a *grancia* in Bondeno.

Hence, the Mantuan Congregation suppressed by Pope Pius VI was a mere shadow of its former self. By the time the Catholic rulers finished their work, it consisted of only twenty-seven convents, four of which (Salò, Mantua, Pontremoli, Anghiari), as we have seen, for other reasons did not survive the year of the papal ban.

Consequent on the bull of Pope Pius VI, Viterbo, Vetralla and Macerata went to the Roman province; Rome (San Crisogono), Bologna, Ferrara, Reggio, Parma, and Lucca to Romagna; Sora and San Donato, to Terra di Lavoro; Our Lady of the Angels in Genoa, to the vicariate of Genoa; Fubino, Trino, and Casal Monferrato, to the Piedmont province.

The five Mantuan convents in Tuscany (Florence, Pistoia, Morrocco, Castellina, Le Selve) obtained leave from the Grand Duke to establish a vicariate. They held their first chapter on August 11, 1783. In 1794, a ducal decree united them to the Tuscan province.

Desenzano al Serio (suppressed in 1788), Brescia, and Bergamo, we saw, led an independent life in the Republic of Venice. Thus, the Serenissima was able once more to manifest its disdain for papal decrees, and the Mantuan Congregation could continue to cling tenuously and hopelessly to a thread of life.

The five convents of the province of Monte Santo in the Papal States - Rome (Monte Santo), Cantalupo, Porchia, San Vito, Ascoli - were bestowed on the Roman province. Cantalupo and Porchia never appear in the provincial chapters, hence were either abandoned or too small to merit representation. The Roman province gave up its own convent in Viterbo and retained that of the Congregation.

Besides the three Mantuan houses, the Piedmont province, now released from its allegiance to the Stricter Observance, inherited Alessandria, Bassignano, Incisa, Cremolino, and Novara from the erstwhile Lombardy province. These, added to the province's own houses in Turin, Asti, Vercelli, Nice, Moncalieri, Dogliani, Pino, Racconigi, Vinovo, Coletto, Rivoli, and Cherasco, brought the total of its houses to twenty.

The General Chapter of 1788

In the general chapter of 1788, John Tufano, former procurator general, who also enjoyed the title of ex-prior general by papal favor, was elected prior general in a tight race, 45 to 42, with the actual procurator general, Francis Torricelli.

John Tufano (1724-1790) was born at Saviniano near Nola and entered the Order in the Carmine Maggiore of Naples. He obtained his master's degree in Rome and functioned as regent there. In Naples, he also held important positions: dean of the *Collegio dei Teologi*, and novice master and prior of the Carmine, appointed by the king in 1772. In 1765, he was elected provincial of the Neapolitan province; in 1776, assistant general for Italy. He survived his election as prior general only two years. A trip to his native Saviniano to recover his health proved ineffective.

The general chapter of 1788, which for that matter accomplished nothing of significance except pathetically to appeal a final time for the introduction of the common life, was the last to be held until 1838. In between, lay the turbulent years from the French Revolution to the Council of Vienna and its aftermath.

Chapter 3

The French Revolution

In 1789, the hour had struck for the eldest daughter of the Church to do penance for her sins, and if the severity of the retribution is any indication, those sins were scarlet indeed.

Initially, the French Revolution was a sort genetic cleansing; had it taken place today, its leaders would have found themselves haled before the court in The Hague, to be tried for their crimes.

The Church, which constituted the influential First Estate of the land, was swept from its pedestal along with the monarchy, to which it was inseparably bound. Its hierarchy constituted to a large degree a group of worldly careerists, comparable to those in politics and the army, and was the exclusive terrain of the nobility, separated by an impassable gulf from the underpaid lower clergy, who had nothing whatever to say in the conduct of ecclesiastical affairs. The aristocratic hierarchy and French theologians had made every effort to divorce the Gallican Church from Rome and strengthen its ties to the crown. They were now to experience the disadvantages of their situation as an isolated, national Church.

The Convocation of the Estates General, 1789

No need to trace in great detail the familiar course of the French Revolution. Driven by the desperate financial situation of the country, King Louis XVI in 1789 summoned the Estates General for the first time since 1614, in order to ponder the problem and suggest remedies. This body, to the surprise of all, perhaps even of itself, proceeded to sweep away the entire social structure of the country, probably the only cure for its ills. This action was made possible in the first instance by the successful manoeuvre on the part of the Third Estate, by which it was decided that the three Estates should vote as one body. Critical in this decision in turn was the support of the lower clergy, who thus won a voice with their ecclesiastical overlords and incidentally sealed the doom of the Church. The combined Estates, forthwith baptized the National Assembly, thus fell under the power of its most numerous and radical element.

It was Talleyrand, bishop of Autun, who proposed the nationalization of church property and the support of the clergy by the state. Decreed on November 2, 1789, this act in effect eliminated the social function of the Church in France. The First Estate in the *ancien regime* had been a virtual state within the State, immune from taxation on its extensive properties, except for the contributions it voluntarily voted to the crown. Education, care of the sick, registration of births and marriages, censorship, vigilance over public morals were its exclusive prerogative. Together with the seizure of ecclesiastical property and as a consequence thereof, all these functions became the competence of the state. As the Enlightenment saw no use in religion but its social service, the Church was in fact set adrift, a useless and foreign body in the mainstream of a secular society.

Included in the sequestered ecclesiastical property, of course, were monasteries, friaries, nunneries, and other houses of religious. Besides, on February 13, 1790, taking an illogical and wholly unwarranted leap into the private realm of conscience, the Assembly declared all vows abolished and graciously invited religious to avail themselves of the freedom and the pension granted them by the state. Those who refused the offer were to be banded together in central houses regardless of the order to which they had originally belonged. The prospect of so dismal a future led not a few to opt for the pension and private life.

The Civil Constitution of the Clergy, 1790

On July 12, 1790, the Civil Constitution of the Clergy was promulgated, devising a new structure for the French Church. Besides praiseworthy features, which eliminated many abuses and injustices, the Constitution contained others more questionable, particularly the method of ecclesiastical appointment. Bishops were to be chosen by the Assembly of each Department, pastors by the district assemblies, in which all citizens, Catholic or not, had the right to vote. More serious yet, the Church had not been consulted with regard to any of these changes. The Assembly would not consent to a national synod, so we have the spectacle of the Gallican Church at last seeking the approbation of the pope.

Pius VI, appealed to by the king, delayed his reply, and so the National Assembly on November 27 imposed the Constitution on the clergy under oath. The verdict of history has been that, apart from the violation of conscience, this act of the Assembly was a mistake, because for the first time it split the nation internally and gave opponents of the revolution inside and outside France a valid grievance. The burden on the consciences of the priests was aggravated when Pius VI condemned the Civil Constitution on May 4, 1791. Of 160 bishops only seven took the oath; about half of the parish priests became "jurors." The question of the liceity of taking the oath is extremely complicated and individual juror priests are not to be condemned out of hand. Nevertheless, the faithful have always held in special veneration those confessors, who sometimes at the cost of their lives, refused to yield to the tyrant. Strictly speaking, the oath was required only of public officials, but if they wanted to carry out parochial duties or collect their pensions, religious were liable to the same condition. Eventually, the oath became the touchstone of patriotism for any priest. In practice, non-juring priests encountered much hostility and were frequently hindered from offering Mass publicly and ministering to their loyal flocks.

The Legislative Assembly and the National Convention, 1791-1795

On September 30, 1791, the Assembly, which had come to be styled "Constituent," voluntarily ceded its place to the Legislative Assembly, a more radical body with less clerical representation, and the situation of the non-juring clergy rapidly deteriorated. A decree of the Assembly of November 29 declared them "suspect," that is, liable to expulsion from the commune. With the declaration of war against Austria, April 20, 1792, and the initial French setbacks, they became even more suspect as collaborators with the enemy and the scheming *émigrés*. A law of May 26 rendered refractory priests subject to deportation on cognizance of twenty "active" citizens. On August 14, this penalty could be inflicted by denunciation of only six citizens. By the end of the month, a new oath was devised, the vague "oath of Liberty and Equality," which said nothing of the Civil Constitution of the Clergy, but required fidelity unto death to "Liberty, equality, the security of persons and property."

At the news of the fall of Verdun on September 2, 1792, panic seized the populace of Paris, which invaded the prisons and massacred 1,400 persons, among them 3 bishops and 220 priests.

In the elections of the same month, the Legislative Assembly gave way to the National Convention, under which the worst excesses of the Revolution occurred. As ever more radical extremists succeeded each other in the Convention, a madness, known as the "Terror," seized the French people, when throughout the land thousands of innocent victims under the flimsiest pretexts were conveyed to the guillotine or otherwise slaughtered as traitors to their country. In the general bloodletting, priests and religious were not overlooked. Not only deportation but death now became the penalty for refusing the oath. In fact, any priest, non-juring or constitutional, could be deported at the request of six citizens. Estimates of the number of priests killed ranged from 2,000 to 5,000. Deportation, which in reality involved imprisonment aboard overcrowded slavers waiting in the harbors to slip past the British blockade, was continued even under the Directory (1795-1799). Of 850 priests imprisoned on the three ships at Rochefort, 274 survived.

Not satisfied with the oath, the authorities encouraged priests to abjure their vocation. Forty-seven of 85 constitutional bishops and about 20,000 priests, most of them induced by fear and other constraints, publicly apostasized. Another way for a priest to prove his patriotism was to marry. By a decree of November 13, 1793, this expedient exempted him from deportation or imprisonment. By Napoleon's time, 3,224 requests for marriage had been made, 911 by religious.

Many members of the clergy, however, avoided these alarums. Between 30,000 to 40,000 non-juring priests, a tenth of them religious, managed to escape from France, principally to England, Spain, and the Papal States.

But by now the masters of France had renounced Christianity, constitutional or otherwise, and the de-Christianization of the country was actively promoted. Churches were desecrated by sacrilegious ceremonies. The goddess of Reason became the object of the new cult. Her enthronement in the cathedral of Notre Dame in Paris on November 10, 1793, is the most famous example of many similar festivals held all over France. All vestiges of religion were removed from the calendar. The years were reckoned, not from the birth of the Savior, but from the declaration of the Republic, September 22, 1792. A ten-day week replaced the traditional one. The *decadi* were observed with patriotic celebrations. Robespierre believed that the revolution needed religion and on May 7, 1794, decreed the existence of a Supreme Being and the immortality of the soul. His religion, however, fell with his head under the guillotine, July 28, 1794. Thereafter, Theophilanthropy enjoyed a brief vogue. Whatever benefits the Revolution brought the nation, the reform of religion was not one of them.

On February 21, 1795, the National Convention decreed the separation of Church and state. The latter recognized no religion and forbade its external signs but guaranteed its free exercise. The Church, constitutional and refractory, emerged cautiously from the catacombs. However, peace, fragile as it was, proved of short duration. On September 14, 1797, three members of the Directory, which had succeeded the Convention in 1795, staged a coup and took over power. They imposed an oath of "hatred of royalty" and invested themselves with the arbitrary right to deport recalcitrants. Thousands of priests were deported to Cayenne or imprisoned at Rochefort and on the islands of Re and Oleron. From this purgatory, the Church was finally rescued by Napoleon.

The End of Carmel in France, 1790

In the Spring of 1790, municipal authorities all over France betook themselves to the convents located in the areas of their jurisdiction to carry out the prescriptions of the National Assembly regarding the sequestration of ecclesiastical property. Inventories were drawn up, and the religious were assembled in each convent and given the alternative of remaining in religious life or departing with a pension.

The choice of liberty, we have seen, did not necessarily mean the renunciation of the religious vocation. To end one's life in a catchall community held few charms, and no doubt many thought they had a better chance to lead a spiritual life in private. Yet, as in the case of the constitutional oath, one admires, even if one were not prepared to imitate, the religious who were not intimidated by force and, casting all their hope on divine Providence, chose the uncertain state of religious poverty. One may safely gage the fervor of a community by the number of its members who made this choice.

The community of Lyon in the province of Narbonne may serve as an example. Of thirteen friars, two elected to remain *tout court*. Three said they would stay, if there were no change in their way of life. One deferred an answer until he knew where he would be assigned, if he decided to remain a religious. Seven chose liberty and a pension.

The twenty-five members of the convent of Bordeaux in the province of Gascony, with one notable exception, chose the religious state and refused the liberty extended by the State. The exception was Pierre Mamousse, subprior, aged thirty-four, who on April 27, 1790, declared: "Sirs, the most grave motives move me to profit from this day forward by the beneficent views of the nation. This illustrious Assembly, in decreeing liberty for the monasteries, was no doubt aware that it would find among religious, victims of coercion, who bear their chains with sorrow and despair. I was not wrong. I accept with joy and appreciation the precious gift of liberty which it deigns to confer on me. I am ready to depart as soon as the first quarter of my pension is paid me. My one ambition on quitting the cloister will be to serve my country, to labor and cooperate with all my strength for its glory and prosperity. I swear to be faithful to the nation, to the law, and to the king, and to uphold the new constitution to the best of my ability."

It is notorious that some of the most enthusiastic apostles of the Revolution were former religious. Among Carmelites, too, patriots are to be found, though not all perhaps as obsequious as Père Mamousse. In 1794, Pierre Peyronnet, formerly of the convent of Notre Dame des Lumières (Provence), is found living in Vaugines. There the municipality attests about him, on the 22 thermidor, year IV, that "since he has been living among us, he has had ties of friendship and particular relationships with no one but good *sans-culottes* farmers, to whom he has always spoken the language of virtue. His habits are simple, and he shows himself on every occasion the true friend of patriots, whom he has taken into his house, when they were persecuted." The municipality, however, notes with regret that citizen Peyronnet, age 55, is still unmarried.

Amable Choury, of the convent of Nîmes (Narbonne), stayed on as the vicar of the parish of St. Baudile, so he must have taken the constitutional oath. Applying for a supplementary pension on February 12, 1791, he attests about himself that he has "several times made an apology for the Revolution from the pulpit (and) constantly preached to the people confidence in the justice of the National Assembly and its decrees."

In Paris, the ten friars of Les Billettes, who with their superior, Charles Peter Nicolle, chose to remain in religious life, were moved in with the Discalced in the rue Vaugirard. They complained to the department of Paris that the cells in the Discalced convent were too small to contain all their furniture. Moreover, they were used to having a fire in their rooms, and those same cells had no stoves. Philip Thibault must have turned over in his grave.

Ironically, the "Massacre at the Carmelites'," which took place there during the panic of September 2, 1790, involved no Carmelites. "It seems certain," writes Jean-Marie de l'Enfant-Jésus, "that some Discalced were still present in the convent," which on August 17 had been ordered vacated by October 14. Lodged in the upper storey of the monastery, they would have been overlooked by the mob that slaughtered 115 bishops, priests, and religious imprisoned in the church. It is not known at present whether any of the Carmelites of Les Billettes were also there. Likewise unknown is the fate of the community in the Place Maubert, no doubt opportunely emptied of its students from the provinces.

After the suppression of the religious Orders, Carmelite convents, churches, and their contents were sold at public auction. Most of the churches were torn down for their building material or to make way for new edifices, thoroughfares or squares. A few remained as parish churches. Convents, too, were sometimes converted into public buildings or private dwellings. A few artifacts survive in museums and in private collections.

By 1790, membership in the eight French provinces of the Order had shrunk to 721. From the acts of the provincial chapters on the eve of the Revolution it would appear that the number of convents remained constant, except in Provence, where only fourteen of twenty convents were left. Pertuis, Estoublon, Saint Hilaire, Manosque, Pinet, and Le Luc were already abandoned, Saint Marcellin, Pont Beauvoisin, and La Rochette, located in the Kingdom of Savoy, briefly outlived the Revolution, until French troops also invaded that realm.

As to the fate of the French Carmelites, some returned to their families or to private life. It was easier for religious to fade into the landscape than for diocesan priests, engaged in the public administration of parishes. This ministry was also open to religious willing to take the oath; Amable Choury undoubtedly was not the only Carmelite to avail himself of this opportunity. Some Carmelites embraced the Revolution, others joined the ranks of the *emigrés*. Finally, some gave their lives for the faith.

Carmelites Under the Guillotine

Thirty-four members of the Order are known to have suffered death or imprisonment, but the last word has by no means been spoken on the Carmelites during the Revolution.

Best known is Martinien Pannetier (1718-1794), a native of Bordeaux, where he pronounced his vows in 1738 and where he spent his long life. Besides filling other offices, he taught theology in the University of Bordeaux. This institution held its general assemblies in one of the halls of the Carmelite convent. There, too, the theology faculty held its courses, taught by a diocesan priest, an Augustinian, a Dominican, and a Carmelite. But Martinien also engaged in pastoral work, in spiritual guidance, and in the direction of the Third Order, for which he wrote *Instruction à l'usage des confrères de Notre-Dame du Mont Carmel* and *La vie de Saint-Simon Stock*, both of which underwent numerous editions.

When the convent was suppressed, Martinien, on April 27, 1790, declared to the municipal authorities that "he had been in religion fifty-three years in the house of Bordeaux, that he loved his estate too much to abandon it, and that he hoped and desired to finish his days there."

Fr. Martinien, who had taken up residence with a friend in the rue Sainte Eulalie, no. 14, only a few steps from the convent, gave thought to the relics of St. Simon Stock, hidden in a casket behind one of the altars in the church. He enlisted the help of Dominic Soupre, aged 26, youngest member of the community, who gained entrance to the church through the convent. In the street below, Martinien, his ancient bones unequal to the scaling of walls, awaited the descent of the casket at the end of a rope of sheets.

Meantime, the situation of the refractory priests worsened, and Fr. Martinien deemed it wise to move out to the country house of Dufaure de Lajarthe, former secretary of the king. There he was joined in July of 1792 by his friend, Abbé Langoiran, vicar general of the diocese, and Abbé Dupuy, vicar of St. Michel. Their presence was betrayed by the housekeeper, whose husband was a member of the revolutionary club of Cauderan, and at 4 o'clock of the morning of July 13, the National Guard surprised and arrested the three priests. Langoiran and Dupuy were slaughtered by a mob in Bordeaux, but Martinien escaped and lived to fight another day. Dufaure de Laparthe paid with his life for harboring the priests.

The murder of Langoiran and Dupuy had been an isolated case of mob violence, but with the institution on October 23, 1793, of the Military Commission with the notorious revolutionary, Jean Baptiste Lacombe at its head, the Terror had come to Bordeaux. During the ten months of its existence, this frightful tribunal managed to execute 314 victims. Pannetier did not long evade its clutches. He was arrested on July 20, 1794, by agents of the Comité de Surveillance and brought before Lacombe. The verdict on the feisty old Carmelite, full of the spirit of Eleazar Maccabee, was a foregone conclusion. On July 21, his head fell under the guillotine. Thérèse Thiac and Anne Bernard, both members of the Third Order who had harbored Martinien, were also executed.

Two other Carmelite victims of the guillotine seem to have been also involved in counter-revolutionary activities.

Michael (Louis) Barrot (alias, Berraud, 1727-1793) was born in Villefranche and made his profession in 1744. He was not present when the inventories were made in the Carmelite convent of Lyon. When the inventory of 1790 was taken, he was living with his parents in Neuville-sur-Saone. In September of 1791, we find him petitioning the municipal officers of Lyon for his pension, which was accordingly granted him. He resided in the rue Saint-Côme and carried on his ministry in spite of the adverse laws. During the revolt of Lyon against the Convention, he acted as secretary of one of the sections. After the siege, the revolutionary commission arrested Louis Barrot, "quondam Carmelite, counter-revolutionary, secretary of the *permanance.*" For the rest, he steadfastly refused to take the oath *Liberté-Egalité* or to renounce his priesthood. He was executed on December 18, 1793.

John Baptist Bedouin (1762-1794) was born at Sorgues and made his profession in the convent of Avignon. On June 10, 1790, the County revolted against papal rule and requested to be incorporated into France. During the insurrection against the Convention, he was appointed a secretary for the federalists, but never served as such. With the return of the revolutionaries to power, he was imprisoned at Avignon on April 4, 1794. On June 5, his case was referred to Orange, where he was guillotined, June 26.

Imprisoned at Agen as refractory priests, their ultimate fate unknown, were Francis Labrunie and Louis Lamothe. At the chapter of Gascony of 1789, Labrunie was re-elected prior of Bergérac, an office he had held since 1779. Previously, he had been prior of Condom. In 1789, Lamothe became prior of Lectoure. He had also served as prior of Marmande, Rabastens, Bergérac, and Agen.

The Deportations at Rochefort, 1794

A decree of August 26, 1792, had specified that non-juring priests should be deported to French Guiana, but the war with England, which began on February 1, 1793, prevented French ships from navigating at will, and the prisoners were kept waiting on board unwholesome craft off the coast of Brittany. Priests from southern and central France were sent to Bordeaux for deportation; those from the North and East to Rochefort at the mouth of the Charente. The prisoners were sent off for these destinations in open carts, chained two by two, or sometimes seven by seven. Everywhere they were exposed to the vilification of the rabble, though they often met with touching testimonies of loyalty and sympathy.

In March, 1794, the vessel, "Les Deux Associés," was consigned by the Convention as a prison ship to house the prisoners of Rochefort. On June 27, this ship was joined by the "Washington," which anchored nearby and in turn began to take over the inmates of the jails of Rochefort.

Four hundred prisoners were confined on board the "Deux Associés," a ship 90' x 30' in size. During the day, they suffered an intolerable restraint and were obliged to stand most of the time. The food was of a most unappetizing sort and was served without table utensils, except for a bowl supplied to each prisoner. The nights were even a greater torture. Crammed into the unventilated holds, the prisoners sprawled next to each other in every available inch of room. It was impossible to change one's position without disturbing those round about. A few open buckets placed at the end of the hold provided the only and inadequate means of easing nature. Sleep amid the stench and jostling of the crowded holds was possible only in the advanced stages of exhaustion.

That disease should be rampant aboard the ships was inevitable. It was finally decided to evacuate the sick to the nearby isle of Madame. A report of August, 1794, reveals that of 497 deportees aboard the "Deux Associés," 245 had died, 144 had been hospitalized. Only 108 remained on board. These were later evacuated on to the "Washington," while a third ship, "L'Indien," was reserved for convalescents.

Though conditions on the island were far from ideal, they presented a blessed respite for the distressed prisoners. They were not given the run of the island, but were allowed to walk up and down in front of the tents which were their abodes. Still, the disease and exhaustion caused on the prison ships continued to take their toll. During the first few weeks, seven or eight priests died each day.

On October 30, 1794, the deportees were ordered back to the ships. The sick were put on the "Indien," the convalescents on the "Deux Associés," and the sound on the "Washington." Only 274 survivors were held on these three ships, of the 800 priests who came aboard them during the months of imprisonment. The island of Madame held 275 graves, that of Aix 210. Other bodies were buried along the shores of the Charente to the number of 100.

Carmelites at Rochefort

Notable among the Carmelites destined for deportation from Rochefort for refusing the oath was James Retouret (1746-1794), the son of a merchant of Limoges. He made his studies in the Jesuit College of Limoges and joined the Carmelites in the convent of the Order in the same city, making his profession in 1762. He was followed into the Order two years later by a younger brother, Stephen, and had been preceded by an uncle. He never made graduate studies, and his career is characteristic of the "simple" priest. A Tiburtius Retouret, who may have been he, was elected subprior and director of professed in Limoges, 1779. He distinguished himself for his piety and spirit of prayer. Besides being a much sought-after spiritual director, he was an excellent preacher. His health was very indifferent, and he was afflicted with a chronic liver complaint. During the Revolution, he took the *liberté-égalité* oath, but he failed to qualify for a *certificat de civisme* and was put in jail. There he retracted his oath, first before another priest, then before William Imbert, commissary of the municipality of Limoges, on February 22, 1794. Sentenced to deportation, he was imprisoned on the "Deux Associés," and died on Madame Island in the night of August 25, 1794.

In 1925, the bishop of La Rochelle et Saintes forwarded to Rome the completed informative process in the cause of beatification of James Retouret. He was beatified on October 1, 1995.

Of the same community as Retouret and professed a year after him was Isidore (John) Dupont (1746-1822). He was subprior and master of novices in Limoges, when the authorities took up inventory in 1790. On March 26, 1794, a decree of the directory of the district of Limoges ordered his deportation, but where he was imprisoned is not clear. He survived the Revolution and died in his native Chabanais.

Another native of Limoges, Severinus of St. Valentine (Francis Rouffle, ca. 1739-1794), held offices in a number of convents in the province of Aquitaine. When the Revolution broke out, he was prior of Mortemart. Upon its suppression, he returned to Limoges, where he was jailed for refusing the oath. He was among the first convoy of priests to leave Limoges, February 25, 1794, among whom was the historian of this deportation, Abbé Labiche de Reignefort. At Rochefort, Severinus was embarked on the "Deux Associés" and died on July 16, 1794. He was buried on the island of Aix.

Like all the foregoing, a member of the province of Aquitaine, Anthony (Joseph) Savary (1744-1794) was born in Mortemart, the son of an advocate in the local parliament. He entered the Carmelite convent in his native town and remained there after the suppression of the convent. He took the *liberté-egalité* oath but failed to merit a *certificat de civisme*, and thus became suspect. On September 28, 1793, he was imprisoned at Limoges, where he retracted his oath before an ecclesiastical superior and publicly before Imbert. Deported as a consequence, he was confined on the "Deux Associés" and died there on May 5, 1794. He was buried on the island of Aix.

In this theatre are found two friars of the province of Touraine. Gatien of St. Maurille (Michael Le Lièvre, 1734-1794) was professed at Rennes in 1752. He served as prior of Le Guildo (1773) and Loudun (1776), but thereafter he is found as a member of the community of Pont l'Abbé. He refused the oath and carried on his ministry clandestinely among the faithful of the diocese of Quimper. Condemned to be deported on July 2, 1794, he was sent to Rochefort and died aboard the "Washington," October 11. He was buried on Madame Island.

John Baptist Peter Letourneau (1752-1794), a native of Angers, lived in the convent of Vivonne. He refused the constitutional oath but took that of *liberté-egalité*. This did not spare him imprisonment in the department of Vienne and deportation in February of 1794. Aboard the "Deux Associés," he retracted his oath and died during the night of September 9. He was buried on Madame Island.

Carmelites Deported from Bordeaux, 1793-1794

A decree of the *Comité de Salut Public*, of January 25,1794, specified Bordeaux as a depot of deportation, but already in the early months of 1793 numerous convoys of priests had arrived in the city. The last contingent of deportees arrived in August of 1794. In November, they were embarked on three ancient slavers, the "Jeanty," the "Dunkerque," and the "Républicain." They were capable of holding 50 slaves each, but 250 priests were herded aboard the "Jeanty" and 350 aboard the other two vessels.

Two hundred and fifty priests had already died in prisons ashore. The original intention had been to land the priests on the coasts of Africa, but due to the English blockade the ships were unable to sail. Instead, they slipped up the coast, entered the Charente River, and cast anchor besides the prison ships at Rochefort. From then on, the history of the Bordeaux captives is identical with that of their confreres in Rochefort.

Among Carmelites who suffered in this theatre, Ambrose (John Francis) Brustier (1735-1794) pronounced his vows in 1761 in the convent of Toulouse. In 1774, he appears as procurator of the community. At the suppression of the convent, Brustier chose to remain in the religious life, as did twenty of the community of twenty-four. In 1793, he went into hiding, but was apprehended on April 17 of that year and incarcerated in St. Catherine prison. Sent to Bordeaux for deportation in the convoy of March 10, 1794, he was imprisoned in the Minor Seminary, where he soon fell seriously ill. Transferred to the hospital of St. André on August 19, 1794, he died four days later.

It is not known where Cyril (John) Bessières (1734-1794), of the province of Aquitaine, was professed, unless it was in Cahors, where he was arrested as a refractory priest. He arrived in Bordeaux on April 30, 1793, and was imprisoned successively in the fortress of Ha and the convent of the Catharinettes. When his health failed, he was taken to the hospital of St. André, where he expired on

November 15, 1794.

John Peter Lefebvre, a native of Orléans, seems to have been called in religion Theophilus. A friar by that name was elected prior of St. Pol de Léon in the Touraine provincial chapter of 1789. He had just finished a term of office as prior of Hennebont. At Bordeaux, he was imprisoned in the Fort du Ha, then in the citadel of Blaye, and finally died aboard the "Jeanty".

Deportations Under the Directory, 1795-1799

The Directory at first had some success in deporting non-juring priests to the penal colony of Cayenne in French Guiana. During 1798, about 300 victims were thus disposed of, but the great distance to be traversed and the blockade of the British constrained the Directory to abandon the plan and to resort to the old policy of imprisonment, this time on the islands of Re and Oléron off the coast of Brittany.

It is not known how many Carmelites were deported to Cayenne. Marie-Pierre Imbault was aboard "La Vaillante," when she was taken by the British, and so he joined the emigrés in England. He was born in 1738 in Orléans and entered the Order there. Before deportation, he had been imprisoned on Ile de Re, June 18, 1798.

There Claude Francis Dourlot, of the Millau convent, landed on August 12, 1799. He had evidently been picked up in Paris, for some sources give this city as his point of origin. Four months later, this young priest died in the hospital.

Another member of the Narbonne province, but interned on Oléron, was Peter John Mathey, born in Gray in the diocese of Besançon. In the chapter of 1786, he was elected prior of Mende. He was imprisoned on the island on March 27, 1799.

A number of Touraine Carmelites are also known to have been imprisoned on Ile de Re but were eventually freed.

Carmelite *Emigrés*

Less religious fled the land than diocesan priests, no doubt because the parochial activities of the latter made them more vulnerable to the consequences of refusing the oath. While at first glance it would seem that the situation of religious was more favorable, in that they could find asylum in another house of their Order abroad, in reality the prospects were not so rosy. Many houses were overcrowded or financially unviable, and religious knew from experience that outsiders were not always welcome.

Statistics on the clergy who escaped from France are fragmentary; those concerning the Carmelites are nonexistent. Twelve Carmelites from Sainte Anne d'Auray (probably the whole community, which in 1768 counted seventeen members) landed in Bilbao. A Carmelite from Agen and another from Toulouse are listed as present in the diocese of Cartagena, where the Order had a convent in Murcia. The Carmelite community of Huesca offered asylum to eight diocesan priests.

The odyssey is known of Dominic Soupre (1766-1853), the young priest who burgled the relics of St. Simon Stock. After the assassination of Abbés Langoiran and Dupuy and the narrow escape of Fr. Martinien, in January of 1793, with two confreres, Nicholas Crozilhac and Daniel Dumeau, Dominic found a path through the Pyrenees to Spain. His companions were burdened with dignity and years. The former, aged 63, was an ex-provincial; the latter, aged 51, was novice master in Bordeaux at the time the convent was suppressed. The young Frenchman found asylum at Pamplona and Zaragoza, presumably in the Carmelite convents of those cities. Eventually Cardinal Francis Anthony Lorenzana, archbishop of Toledo, who had been given charge of the emigrants, secured a post for the Carmelite as a tutor of the Prince of the Asturias, the future Ferdinand VII, (a post he filled with indifferent success, to judge by the result) until his return to France after the concordate of 1801.

Back in Bordeaux, Soupre, like many other religious, placed himself at the disposal of Archbishop Charles Francis d' Aviau as a member of his clergy, since religious orders were still proscribed. After serving in a number of parishes of the city, he became pastor in 1816 of Holy Cross parish, where he remained for the rest of his active priestly life. He is especially notable for his collaboration with his parishioner, Catherine Grenier, in the foundation of a congregation of sisters dedicated to social work, the "Doctrine Chrétienne," still flourishing. Upon his retirement from active duty in 1830, Archbishop John Louis de Cheverus, former bishop of Boston, "one of the most beautiful spirits of the American Church" (Theodore Maynard), took him into the episcopal palace and made him an honorary canon. From these last years, date a number of works composed for his spiritual daughters.

On his return to Bordeaux, Soupre had recovered the relics of St. Simon Stock and sent them to be preserved in the cathedral. On November 7, 1816, Archbishop d'Aviau conducted an official inquiry into their authenticity. Cited to give testimony, the former Carmelite declared that the casket, bearing the seal of the Bordeaux Carmel, was indeed the one he had rescued from the revolutionaries. The archbishop confirmed the authenticity of the relics and ordered them enclosed in a suitable reliquary with his seal and deposited in the pedestal of the statue of Our Lady of Mount Carmel in the cathedral.

Fr. Soupre had been reunited to four other Carmelites in Bordeaux. Daniel (John Baptist) Dumeau, his fellow-exile, became vicar of St. Eulalie Church, until his death in 1814. John Cazabonet, who had taught philosophy as a Carmelite, was placed in charge of Villenave-d'Ornon. Severinus (Bernard) Poumicon had been provincial at the outbreak of the Revolution, a doctor of Paris and royal professor. In 1807, he was made curé of the important parish of Blanquefort on the outskirts of Bordeaux. With Brother Honoré (James) Minvielle he also testified to the authenticity of the relics of St. Simon Stock. A fourth ex-Carmelite, Father Bardinet, is not found in the Bordeaux community at the time of its dissolution and so must have come from a convent in another place. His assignment as a diocesan priest is not known.

At Abensberg, we find five French refugees: Bruno Bernard, Firmin Regnault, Pierre Raoult, Ghislain Dhuin, Louis Joseph Bracq. Other German convents no doubt offered asylum to the French fugitives. The latter would have returned home after the Concordat, just previous to the dissolution of the German houses themselves.

The Papal States constituted a natural haven for those fleeing before the enemies of the Church. It was no doubt this consideration that brought Gabriel (James) Pouillard to Rome. His exile, however, can hardly be considered a hardship, for the city of the Caesars and the popes afforded him a greater opportunity to indulge his passion for antiquarian research and to form an acquaintance with other savants. His activity in the field of the fine arts will be considered below. Born in Aix in 1751, he entered the Carmelite convent there and was one of its eleven members at the time of its suppression. In Rome, he stayed first at San Crisogono, then at San Martino, where he acted as sacristan. In 1799, he undertook the spiritual care of the French soldiers in Santo Spirito hospital. In 1807, he returned to France. For a brief period, he served in the chapter of the cathedral of Lyon and taught in the seminary of Belley. There he also undertook the direction of a girl's school conducted by ex-Cistercian nuns. In Paris, he became the curator of the famous collection of Cardinal Joseph Fesch, Napoleon's uncle and ambassador to the Holy See. In 1814, Talleyrand appointed him sacristan of the royal chapel in the Tuilleries. It was in front of this august edifice that he was run over by a cabriolet, December 29, 1818. He succumbed to his injuries the following August 8, not the first or last victim of the hectic traffic of Paris.

The French Revolution in Belgium, 1792

Alarmed at the turn of events in France, European rulers organized an offensive aimed at restoring the monarchy there, but the French armies, especially under the leadership of Napoleon Bonaparte, were everywhere victorious. And where the tri-color flew, religious orders disappeared.

The first to be overrun by the armies of the Revolution was Belgium (1792), annexed to France in 1795. The suppression of religious orders (1796) and oath imposed on the clergy (1797) followed. At this time, the Flandro-Belgian province, as we have seen, numbered thirteen convents; the Wallo-Belgian vicariate, nine.

After the extinction of the province of Francia, its three convents situated in Belgian territory, Liège, Verviers, Wégimont, had been constituted the vicariate of Liège, with Sebastian Fonsay its vicar (1791). The following year, it held what was no doubt its only chapter.

After the tragic "Peasants' War" of 1798, the Directory enforced the oath of the clergy with imprisonment and deportation. A number of Belgian Carmelites are known to have been deported to the islands of Re and Oléron but survived long enough to be eventually released.

The decisive victory of Waterloo on Belgian soil (1815) brought no change in the fortunes of religious. The Council of Vienna (1815) united Belgium to the Netherlands under Protestant William I. Only after the establishment of the independence of Belgium in 1831 were religious orders there able to regroup, but the Carmelites were not among them.

The End of the Carmelite Nuns in France

One of the most dramatic incidents during the Terror, celebrated in music, drama, and fiction, is the martyrdom by the guillotine in Paris of the sixteen Discalced Carmelite nuns of Compiègne. No nuns of the old Carmel are known to have been guillotined. They counted only six monasteries in the territory of France, but if one were to trace the history of their disappearance, one would no doubt encounter many examples of courageous Christian witness.

On June 1, 1790, the thirty-two nuns of "Les Couets" in Nantes were expelled from their monastery by a crowd of men and women, among whom the president of the "Society of Patriotic Women" distinguished herself. The nuns are said to have been beaten on the occasion and one of them thrown into a pond. They were able to return in December, but definitively left on August 26, 1792. The prioress, Jeanne de la Roussière and another nun were banished from the Republic. Another sister later died in the drownings at Nantes.

The monasteries of Nantes, Vannes, Rennes, and Ploermel were in the care of the province of Touraine. Francia had six monasteries under its jurisdiction, but only Charleville and Fumay, in the dioceses of Reims, lay within the boundaries of France. After the suppression of the monasteries there, the vicariate of Liège took under its wing the four remaining monasteries of Liège, Huy, Dinant, and Rochefort, which thus received a brief reprieve before being suppressed.

At the dissolution of their monasteries, women religious had no other alternative than to return to their families. Some contemplative communities remained in existence by opening a school.

Chapter 4

Carmel Under Napoleon

The sacristan monarchs of the 18th century, who still saw a limited use for religious life as a social service, were succeeded by Napoleon and the later liberal governments, for whom the elimination of the religious orders was a *conditio sine qua non* of the new society.

The *Reichsdeputationshauptschluss*

The separate Peace of Lunéville, February 8, 1801, between France and Austria during the Second War of Coalition (1799-1802) confirmed the seizure by the French of the left bank of the Rhine and compensated the losses of German princes with the ecclesiastical states and free imperial cities on the right bank. The *Reichsdeputationshauptschluss* (the world's longest word for a simple act of thievery), of February 25, 1803, extended the terms of Lunéville to include a general secularization. Article 25 decreed the seizure of the property of religious orders. The fall of Napoleon made no difference, at least in this matter of the spoliation of the Church, to the enlightened princes and monarchs.

These years saw the extinction of what was left of the Order in Germany: the sixteen convents of the Lower German province (Gelderen, it will be remembered, was added in 1785), the six convents of the Upper German province, and the two convents of the Bavarian vicariate. The nunnery of Gelderen was suppressed with the friary.

Of the Lower German province, churches, and in some cases convents converted to other uses, survived in Gelderen, Beilstein, Boppard, Kreuznach, Mainz, Weinheim, and Hirschhorn.

At Trier, the last Carmelite to offer Mass on July 26,1802, had not yet made the final genuflection before the impatient commissar swept everything off the altar onto the floor. At Weinheim, one regrets to report, the brethren showed less Christian forbearance. When the sergeant-major of cavalry arrived at two o'clock in the morning, he was told by the bursar, Norbert Haas, (more keenly sensitive to financial loss than the others), to come back later. Haas' door had to be broken down, and he had to be forcibly loaded onto the coach which would take him as far as the first post station. Brother Wendelin wanted to ring the tocsin, and another friar declared that if he had 100,000 men and enough money, he would declare war. The troublesome Haas also threw a number of documents down the privy, but after they had been retrieved by a luckless corporal, they were found to have no value.

Of the six Upper German convents and churches, those in Bamberg and Neustadt exist today. The convent in Neustadt became an *Aussterbekloster*, where the religious were allowed to remain until their death. The last Carmelite obligingly passed away in 1848.

On March 29, 1802, the Carmelites of Abensberg were given one day's notice to move in with the community of Straubing, the other convent constituting the Bavarian Vicariate. Straubing, too, had been sequestered by the state, but the religious were allowed to occupy the premises as long as they lived.

The Order in Eastern Europe

The second and third partitions of Poland (1792, 1795) and the brief hegemony of Napoleon entailed few if any losses for the Order in Eastern Europe. The treaty of Vienna (1815) canonized the tri-partite division of Poland.

In Russian Poland, under Alexander I (1801-1825) the Carmelite provinces of Russia, Lithuania (St. George), and Lithuania (All Saints) remained intact. With the names of Volhynia, White Russia, and Lithuania, they still totalled more than thirty houses. The oppressive reign of Nicholas I (1825-1855) occasioned the insurrection of 1830-1831, punished with, among other measures, the extinction of many Roman Catholic religious houses. After 1832, there remained of the three provinces only Wilno, Mohilew, Luck, Sloboda, Zaswierz, and Krupczyce. These, too, disappeared after the revolt of 1863 under Alexander II (1855-1881).

It was no doubt at this time that the nunnery of Dubno ceased to be.

The province of Southern Prussia (formerly Lesser and Greater Poland) comprised nineteen convents. These in the course of the 19th century dwindled to twelve: Cracow (in Arenis), Warsaw, Lipiny, Klodawa, Zakrzew, Trutowa, Plonsk, Obory, Gulowska Wola, Kcyna, Danzig, Poznan, and finally to two. Cracow came under the rule of Austria in 1846, when that country absorbed the Republic of Cracow, established by the treaty of Vienna (1815). Obory escaped extinction by being named a depot where religious from suppressed houses could live out the remainder of their lives.

The convents of the Silesian vicariate (Freistadt, Gross Strenz, Striegau, Wohlau) in the Kingdom of Prussia seem to have fallen victim to Napoleon's brief conquest. Gross Strenz (modern Alteichenau) was suppressed in 1810. The convent serves secular purposes, the church became the parish.

After all the Carmelite convents Austria closed in its far-flung realm, it is ironic that the last remnant of the Order's Eastern European houses should find shelter under its wing. The province of Galicia (Cracow, Lwów, Trembowla, Botszowce, Rozdól, Sasiadowice, Pilzno) passed unscathed through all the troubles of the times. Cracow was added to the province in 1852. Pilzno, a former Augustinian convent, was acquired in 1842. We have already told how Obory in Russian Poland survived.

The Carmelite convent in the Catholic Sovereignty of Boxmeer remained intact during the French revolutionary occupation (1795-1798), the brief Batavia Republic (1798-1806), and the equally short-lived reign of Louis Bonaparte (1806-1810), but, when Napoleon incorporated the Netherlands into the French Empire, Boxmeer was included in the decree of January 3, 1812, which dissolved the few existing religious houses. On August 20, G. L. Bonnechose, sub-prefect of the *arrondissement* of Nijmegen, went through the usual ceremony of dispossession. The friars found refuge with members of the flock or their families, leaving behind one of their number to care for the parish. After Napoleon's defeat, they drifted back, and by April 20, 1814, the whole community was reinstated. However, their satisfaction at once more picking up the thread of their religious life was abruptly extinguished, when King William I on the following September 2 announced that the decree of 1812 was to remain in force, though he graciously allowed the friars to occupy the convent until death.

Italy Under Napoleon

Named general-in-chief of the army in Italy (1796), Napoleon quickly overran the northern part of the peninsula. The Treaty of Campo Formio with Austria (1797) set up the Cisalpine Republic, comprising Lombardy, Parma, Modena, the part of the Venetian Republic west of the Adige, and the Papal States of Bologna, Ferrara, and Romagna. The remainder of Venice was bestowed on Austria. The following year, the French annexed Piedmont and Savoy, and the Kingdom of Naples became the Parthenopean Republic.

After Napoleon had himself elected emperor (1804), the republics became kingdoms. The Cisalpine Republic, to which Genoa and the rest of Venice were added, was now called the Kingdom of Italy with Prince Eugene de Beauharnais as viceroy. In 1806, Napoleon's brother, Joseph, was placed on the throne of the Kingdom of Naples, succeeded in 1808 by General Joachim Murat. The Papal States themselves, after the emperor lost patience with Pius VII, were annexed to France (1809).

The fate of the religious orders in these territories followed their respective political fortunes. The general law of June 2, 1810, suppressed religious orders throughout Italy.

Occupation by the French marked the end of the northern provinces of the Order. Churches and community properties were sold or turned to secular uses. Even after the Council of Vienna (1815) restored the old Order, the new owners of ecclesiastical property, mostly the monied middle class, which was to become the backbone of anticlerical liberal society, were not about to relinquish their ill-gotten gains. Carmelite churches which became parish churches were saved and in some cases exist today, as do the convents turned into public buildings. Furnishings of demolished Carmelite churches were sometimes transferred to other parish churches.

The twenty convents of the extensive Piedmont province were all suppressed by the Napoleonic regime. Fortunately, the monumental Carmelite church of Turin, dedicated to Our Lady of Mount Carmel and Bl. Amedeo IX of Savoy, was designated a parish and escaped demolition. The friars were expelled in 1801, but a Carmelite remained in charge of the parish until 1842. The extensive convent was transformed into a school. Churches also outlived the departure of the Carmelites at Casal Monferrato, Dogliani (replaced by a new structure in 1859), Pino, and Incisa. In yet other cases, venerated images of Our Lady survived, as at Trino, Novara, Vercelli, and Racconigi.

The once proud Republic of Genoa in 1805 was unceremoniously annexed to France. Even the fall of Napoleon brought no betterment in her condition. From 1815, she became part of the Kingdom of Sardegna. Of the six foundations in the Carmelite vicariate of Genoa, the churches of Genoa (Carmine), Lavagna, and Monte Oliveto survived as parishes. The convent of Lavagna became the city hall. In 1803, the Carmelites of Monte Oliveto turned over their parish to the diocese. The last member of the former community, Joseph Casaccia, died in 1812.

On the other hand, the seven houses of the Sardinian province remained intact for the time being. English dominion of the seas spared the island occupation by the French.

The six houses of the Carmelite province of Venice, besides Brescia and

Bergamo of the Mantuan Congregation, at this time ceased to be. However, the most important Carmelite churches in the Venetian territory, Brescia, Padua, Verona, and Venice, remained open to cult, passed into the hands of the diocesan clergy, and together with their treasures of art were saved for posterity.

Although at first the hereditary archdukes were suffered to rule Tuscany, the Treaty of Fontainebleau, October 29, 1807, united it to France with Napoleon's sister, Elisa, as archduchess (1809). On March 24, 1808, the property of religious orders was declared the patrimony of the state; although not abolished, they were forbidden to admit novices. On September 13, 1810, religious houses were closed and the religious habit ostracized.

By these laws, the Carmelite province of Tuscany, consisting of nine convents, ceased to be. However, all or most of the churches escaped destruction. Moreover, after Waterloo, the Carmine of Florence and Pisa managed to gather communities, and when Grand Duke Leopold II, on February 5, 1843, graciously allowed Castellina to be reopened, the Holy See, the following June 3, declared the Tuscan province reconstituted. That year and thereafter, provincial chapters were regularly held.

Of the score of convents of the Romagna province (see above), only six appeared at the first chapter held in the aftermath of the storm (1823): Lugo, Forlì, Senigallia, Ancona, Iesi, and Ascoli Piceno. The last four lay in the Marches, safely within the Papal States, had been suppressed only in 1810, and their restoration was welcomed by the authorities. The rest of the province's houses were situated in Romagna (except Lucca in the principality of Lucca), had been incorporated into the Cisalpine Republic early in the French occupation, and later were given less encouragement to reconstitute themselves.

Ascoli had been acquired in exchange for San Crisogono, Rome, in a trade with the Roman province (1820). Lucca, too, was recovered, but was placed, first under the prior general, later under Tuscany.

Many of the churches of the suppressed communities are still in use, though not always for sacred purposes, as in the case of the Carmine of Parma, which became a warehouse of the State Archive. In some instances, where one or two friars had been left in charge of the parish after the suppression of the Order, the Carmelites outlived their persecutors and reorganized communities, at least until 1866. This happened in Forlì, Lugo, and Senigallia.

The reign of Napoleon over the Papal States left the Roman province in possession of only half its houses. The provincial chapter of 1807 still elected eighteen priors; after a decade, that of 1817 elected only nine priors to Perugia, Rome (San Martino), Viterbo, Albano, Velletri, Palestrina, Canepina, San Vito Romano, Cantalupo.

Thus, the passing of the Napoleonic era left in Northern and Central Italy only the shattered remnants of the provinces of Tuscany, Romagna, and Rome.

The Suppression of the Order in the Kingdom of Naples

Although with the exception of the province of Calabria the Order in the south of Italy had remained relatively intact under the Bourbons, during the brief Napoleonic hegemony (1806-1815) it came down like a house of cards.

The invasion of the French and the constitution of the Parthenopean Republic

(1799) already occasioned damage to churches and convents, including those of the Carmelites. In 1809, religious orders were suppressed by Murat and their property incorporated into the state. This act wiped out six Carmelite provinces, comprising eighty-three convents.

The Carmine Maggiore of Naples was one of the houses that survived. When the Bourbons restored the religious orders in 1820, the Carmelites returned, but severely reduced in numbers. The prior general, Aloysius Anthony Faro, was obliged to import about ten friars from Puglia to bring the membership of the community up to the required number of twenty-four. He appointed Elias Angelus Scialpi, of the province of Monte Santo, commissary general for the restoration of the Order in the Kingdom.

The convent of Our Lady of Good Help (*Santa Maria del Buon Soccorso*), the house for Spanish friars under the jurisdiction of the prior general, can hardly have been looked upon with a kindly eye by the French and does not seem to have been subsequently revived.

Little or nothing is known at present of the individual fate of the convents of the provinces in the Kingdom of Naples: Puglia (27 convents in 1776), Calabria (eight convents in 1786), Terra di Lavoro (21 convents in 1785), Naples (13 convents in 1786), Santa Maria della Vita (six convents in 1786), and Abruzzo (eight convents in 1784).

After the hurricane had passed, some flotsam and jetsam surfaced. Decrees of the Sacred Congregation for Bishops and Religious of December 10 and 17, 1847, ordained that the Carmelite convents then existing in the Kingdom of Naples *citra pharum* should constitute the province of Naples, at the same time appointing four definitors and a provincial in the person of Elisha Romanazzi. When the royal *exequatur* was given on August 10, 1850, it became possible that same year to hold a definitorial meeting and elect the priors of San Giovanni a Teduccio, Ostuni, Sulmona, Penne, Francavilla Fontana, Mesagne, and Conversano.

The provincial chapter of 1855 confirmed Romanazzi in office and in addition elected priors to the newly restored convents of Noicattaro and Nardò. A report made the following year showed that the nine houses of the province contained 81 friars: 47 priests, 7 novices, 6 professed clerics, and 21 brothers. The convents were well staffed, though in financial straits, due to the alienation of much of their property.

Neither were they able to accept most of the invitations by bishops, municipalities, and influential laymen to reoccupy abandoned convents and churches. For the most part, willing Carmelites were not to be found. Some had become secular priests or in other ways had settled into a new way of life. Others, elderly and comfortably ensconced in the bosoms of their families, were disinclined to try the uncertain future in a religious community. Also, the sense of conventuality was still strong in these parts; religious felt little responsibility to rescue any convent not their own. Moreover, no one dreamt of establishing a convent without a stable income from property and other assets (a condition, for that matter, also insisted upon by the crown), and it was precisely this commodity which was in particular demand. It was a time that called for heroes, and heroes were as scarce then as they are now. All the more credit to those who clung tenaciously to their vocation and with an optimism not justified by reality strove to pass on to posterity the gift of Carmel's way of life.

In 1858, the province drew support and strength from a visitation by the prior general, Jerome Priori.

The provincial chapter of 1859 elected Aloysius Fusco provincial, as well as a prior of a tenth convent, Oria. This foundation is generally overlooked because of its brief existence.

In Sicily, shielded by the British fleet, the four provinces with their eighty-one convents remained for the time being intact.

The French briefly held Malta in 1798, but that was long enough to end forever the tenure of the Knights. The Treaty of Amiens of 1802, restoring the Knights to power, was never implemented. Instead, the Treaty of Paris of 1814 bestowed the island on the English. As a result, the two Carmelite convents existing on Malta in 1819 were separated from the Sicilian province of St. Angelus and placed under a vicar provincial appointed by the prior general. The Maltese Carmelites themselves had long desired this arrangement.

The first Carmelite foundation in Malta was in a place called San Leonardo, about a mile or so outside Mdina, then the capital of Malta. There, the friars took possession of the church of the Annunciation, left in 1418 by the will of Lady Margaret d'Aragona di Pellegrino. In 1659, the community moved inside Mdina, but continued to offer Mass weekly at the Annunciation. Valletta was founded in 1570. The still existing convent, founded in 1611 at Vittoriosa (*Il Birgu*), in 1652 succumbed to the suppression of Innocent X.

To sum up, in the middle of the 19th century, there existed in Italy, besides Lucca, the Carmine Maggiore of Naples, and Traspontina, all subject to the prior general, 9 provinces: Sardinia (7 convents), Tuscany (3), Romagna (6), Rome (9), Naples (10), St. Angelus (33), St. Albert (32), Monte Santo (7), and Santa Maria della Scala (9)– a total of 119 convents, two thirds of them in Sicily, where the French had not set foot.

The Suppression of the Italian Monasteries

The French occupation of Italy had the same deleterious effect on the Carmelite nunneries. Few of the thirty-odd foundations on the peninsula saw the second decade of the 19th century.

The nuns of St. Mary of the Angels in Florence were ejected from their home by the French, but were able to return afterwards. Already in 1786, they had provided asylum for their sisters of the Annunciation monastery, suppressed by Archduke Peter Leopold. Pisa, also in Tuscany, and Pescia in Lucca probably were extinguished at this time.

The monasteries in the north were all lost: Asti (the Presentation and the Holy Family) in Piedmont, Pontecurone in Lombardy, and the four nunneries of the Venetian group: Venice (St. Teresa), Padua, Verona, and Vicenza. A community of *pinzocchere* in Venice, the conservatory of Our Lady of Hope, ended its three hundred-year existence.

In the Papal States, the Barberine of Rome outlived the troubles of the 19th century, but subsequently left the Eternal City to return to their mother house in Florence (1907). Of the two foundations made from this monastery, Vetralla and Monterotonda, the former flourishes today. Iesi in the Marches also defied all attempts on its life and in 1822 welcomed the refugees from Montecarotto. Orvieto in Umbria fell victim to the war on nuns.

Of ten monasteries in the Kingdom of Naples, that of the Holy Cross in Naples, which provided a home for their sisters of the monastery of the Blessed Sacrament, Castellamare (Holy Cross), and Solofra, remained intact. Avellino, Castellamare (St. Teresa), Caulonia, Montecorvino, Putignano, and Somma succumbed to the pressure of the times.

The Sicilian nunneries, like the friaries, for the time being were safe.

The bull of suppression of 1783, as we have seen, placed the nuns of the Mantuan Congregation in the care of the Piedmont province. Girolamo Vigo, writing not long after 1783, lists only six nunneries: Albino, Brescia, Florence (St. Barnabas), Novellara, Reggio, and Trino. He also includes Mantua, but himself chronicles its suppression, June 29, 1782. The other seven monasteries – Parma, Bologna (*"Convertite"*), Bergamo, Camaiore, and the three foundations of the Congregation in Ferrara - had evidently already undergone the fate of the friaries. In any case, there is no evidence that they survived the French occupation. In the Papal States, Sutri and Velletri, not mentioned by Vigo, staunchly resisted extinction – Velletri until 1921, Sutri until the present day.

Thus, in the end, the numerous nunneries of Italy had been reduced to thirteen: Florence, Rome (-1907), Velletri (-1921), Sutri, Vetralla, Iesi, Naples, Castellamare (-1952), Solofra (-1939), Fisciano, Messina, Palermo, Siracusa.

Oddly enough, in these calamitous years the Order actually acquired a monastery. Anna of St. Teresa, a Carmelite tertiary of Molinella (Bologna) under the direction of Fr. Peter Tombi, had for years lived in retirement, dedicated to prayer and good works. By 1773, others had joined her, and a community was formed, which that same year transferred to Ravenna. The sisters devoted themselves to the education of girls and the care of the aged. In 1782, according to the new disposition of the Congregation for Bishops and Religious, the community as a diocesan congregation passed under the jurisdiction of the bishop. After dispersal by the French, the community regrouped, but the Carmelite friary of Ravenna did not revive, and the sisters lost contact with the Order. In 1840, they undertook papal cloister and solemn vows. They professed the Carmelite rule as mitigated by Pope Eugene IV and followed constitutions revised by their ecclesiastical superior, Cardinal Chiarissimo Confalieri.

The General Curia, 1790-1808

The central administration of the Order, as well as individual provinces and convents, was disrupted by the anti-religious legislation of the times. For one thing, there was little left of the Order to administer. The jealous nationalism of the Catholic kings and rulers cut the curia off from the provinces outside the Papal States and incidentally also cut off a necessary source of income to conduct the affairs of the Order.

There could be no question of convoking a general chapter; instead, Pius VI on November 6, 1790, named Peter Thomas Marrocchi prior general with powers to appoint his council. A native of Lugo, Marrocchi had been elected assistant general for Italy at the chapter of 1788. With the exception of Simon Pomponi, whom he named to fill his own post of Italian assistant, he simply confirmed the existing council: Louis Leroy, procurator general; Brocard of St. George Koeniger, Germany; Roque Melchor, Spain; Andrew Rodziewicz, Poland. The services of a French assistant were no longer required. Although Martial Vroblasci had been named assistant for Poland at the chapter of 1788, he does not seem to have functioned as such, as he never signed the register of the general council. Similarly, instead of Angelus Perramon, made assistant for Spain at the chapter of 1788, we find Roque Melchor signing the register of the council beginning June 27, 1789. On August 5, 1793, Francis de Paul Greindl appears as successor of Koeniger.

In 1794, Pius VI named Roque Melchor prior general, together with John Baptist Onesti procurator and John Baptist Comandini assistant for Italy. Marianus Poradowski became assistant for Poland, John Battl for Spain. Greindl remained in office.

However, the arrival of the French in Rome signalled the dispersal of the curia in March of 1798. Judging by the signatures in the register of the council, its non-Italian members, including the prior general himself, had already prudently betaken themselves to their native *lares et penates*. On October 5, 1798, the procurator general, John Baptist Onesti, who was also commissary general in the prior general's absence from Italy, was granted faculties by Pius VI to compose a council from among the elder members of whatever convent he happened to be living in. By 1800, he was back in Traspontina, where on December 21 he made up a council of the prior of Traspontina, the ex-provincial of Rome, and the pastor of Traspontina, respectively Peter Thomas Fantozzi, Anastasius Pomponi, and Camillus Bartolucci. To these was added John Baptist Comandini, actual assistant general for Italy. Pomponi does not seem to have functioned very long.

Meanwhile, the absent Melchor's term as prior general having expired, Pius VII on January 14, 1803, confirmed him in office *ad beneplacitum S. Sedis.*

In 1804, Comandini was named to succeed Onesti as commissary general in Italy. Joseph Bartoli, the secretary of the council, became procurator general. Fantozzi and Bartolucci retained their offices. For that matter, they had little opportunity to exercise their powers. Until the fall of Napoleon, the council met three times in 1804, once in 1805, and once in 1808. Besides steps to alleviate the debt of the church of Monte Santo in Rome, the confirmation of four provincial chapters constituted the sum of their accomplishments during this period.

The Bull *Inter Graviores*, 1804

At the insistence of his prime minister, Emmanuel Godoy, King Charles IV of Spain obtained from Pius VII the bull "*Inter graviores*," May 15, 1804, which established an alternative in the election of superiors general of religious orders. The superiors general should be alternatively Spanish and reside in Spain and non-Spanish and reside outside the realms of His Catholic Majesty. The part of an order not represented by the superior general should be governed by a vicar with his full powers. The idea of the alternative was the pope's, a palliation of a more radical form of control suggested by Godoy. The latter, knowing he could exercise control over candidates through the *patronato regio* was satisfied to agree. Godoy's goal, of course, was the isolation of the religious orders, a Spanish dream since Philip II, long ago accomplished in France and the Empire, but without the promised beneficent results.

Given the troubled condition of the times, the pope's complicated plan proved difficult to realize. The orderly alternation of general chapters in Spain and elsewhere with the respective elections of superiors and vicars general never took place, at least among the Carmelites. Although at the appearance of *"Inter graviores,"* the Carmelite prior general was actually a Spaniard, Roque Melchor, resident in Spain and confirmed in office only the previous year, the ex-provincial of Aragon, Santiago Huarte, was appointed vicar general of Spain, April 15, 1805. After the Peninsular War, he was followed by Emmanuel Regidor, formerly procurator at the Spanish court, appointed on July 1, 1815, by the papal nuncio, Peter Gravina, who also confirmed him in office on October 4, 1824. The following year, Regidor managed to convoke a "general" chapter at Madrid, which reelected him. As a result of this election, Regidor assumed the title of prior general, on the basis of *"Inter graviores."* His Italian equivalent, Aloysius Scalabrini (1825-1832), received from Leo XII only the title of vicar general. Emmanuel Regidor should be given a place among the priors general of the Order.

Regidor's most significant accomplishment was to obtain the approval of the Holy See for the proper office of the Solemn Commemoration of Our Lady of Mount Carmel, granted in 1828 and extended to the Discalced Carmelites the following year. "What the sacred Order of Carmel has long and persistently desired ... we have finally had the happiness to obtain," he wrote with joy in his circular letter presenting the liturgical text.

The Spanish chapter of 1832 elected the Castilian provincial Felix García vicar general. On August 19, 1838, Gregory XVI appointed an apostolic commissary for the Carmelites on the Spanish peninsula in the person of Edward Comas, who enjoyed all the rights and prerogatives of the former vicars general. The purpose of this office was to provide some sort of shepherd for the scattered flock of Spanish Carmelites, homeless since 1836.

The General Curia, 1808-1838

In Rome, Pius VII appointed Timothy Ascensi prior general on January 9, 1807. Some time previously, Ascensi had become assistant general. On July 19, 1808, the pope granted him powers to choose his council from the community of San Martino, where he was staying. To Aloysius Quartaroli, procurator general; Joseph Bartoli, assistant for Italy; Paul Barsotti, assistant for Germany, he added on August 1 John Baptist Comandini, ex-vicar general; Aloysius Carlini, ex-provincial; John Anthony Gregori, regent. The following day, the group held its only meeting of which there is record and approved with sanations the chapter acts of Greater Poland.

Silence descends on the curia for the period of Napoleon's annexation of the Papal States (1809-1814). With other major superiors, the Carmelite prior general was deported to France. The suppression of 1810 would have emptied the Roman convents of their contents.

The pope's first consideration upon his restoration was the revival of the religious orders, who were also responsible for the education of the young and the care of the sick. On July 1, 1814, Pius VII announced the creation of a Congregation for Reform under Cardinal Anthony Sala. The pontiff's aim was not only to restore religious to their homes but above all to reform religious life. On August 22, 1814, the Congregation for Bishops and Religious issued a decree providing for the restoration of at least one convent of the orders in Rome, in which their respective rules could be perfectly observed.

On October 7, the same congregation appointed vicar general Joseph Bartoli, of the Roman province. His council, which met six times from 1816 to 1819, consisted for the most part of Aloysius Quartaroli, procurator general; Serafino Confini, Joseph M. Mazzetti, and Aloysius M. Carlini. In the single meeting of 1819, held on June 4, Antoninus Ragusa appears as assistant for Italy.

In Aloysius Anthony Faro (1755-1832), of the province of Santa Maria della Scala Paradiso, the Order again had a prior general, appointed by Pius VII on September 25, 1819. This nomination may be related to Pius' policy of religious reform, for Faro had run no Roman career and was probably summoned from Sicily on his reputation alone. Known for his piety and learning, he had refuted the theory that the goods of the Church were the property of the state in two tracts addressed in 1812 to the Parliament of Sicily, of which a second edition received the warm approval of Mauro Capellari, vicar general of the Camaldolese and later Pope Gregory XVI (*Opuscoli catolico-politici*, Roma, 1824). As general, in fact, Faro successfully promoted the restoration of Carmelite convents, especially in Lucca, Romagna, and Naples. Born at Pedara near Mount Etna, he entered the Order at Siracusa. He taught philosophy and theology in the *studium* of the province and canon law at the University of Catania. He served as prior in a number of convents and was twice elected provincial.

Faro was succeeded by another Sicilian, Aloysius Scalabrini (1767), of Trapani, on May 19, 1825, appointed vicar general by Leo XII. In the 20's, the general council met regularly, though infrequently – two to four times a year – to treat the affairs of the Order, mostly of the Italian provinces.

At the end of his term of office, 1832, Scalabrini was able to conduct an election by mail to choose a prior general. Besides the Roman curia, Naples (Carmine) and Trapani, ten provinces and vicariates sent votes: St. Albert, St. Angelus, Rome, Romagna, Ireland, Monte Santo, Santa Maria della Scala del Paradiso, Poland (vicariate of Prussia), Malta (vicariate), Tuscany (vicariate). The perennial titular provinces of the Holy Land, England, Saxony, and Denmark, were allowed one vote between them. The result of the votation favored Aloysius Calamata (1784-1848), of the convent of Lucca.

For some reason, no meetings are entered into the register of the general council between 1826 and 1839.

Chapter 5

The Suppression of the Order in Spain and Portugal

The Spanish people did not behead their king, but not a few of them had become dissatisfied with his performance; the French invader was summarily driven out, but his ideals of democratic liberty lingered on. The nineteenth century in Spain is filled with the see-saw struggle between monarchism and republicanism. As in other Catholic countries, the preliminary to political change was the destruction of the religious orders, in Spain part of the social fabric as nowhere else.

The Suppression of the Order in Spain, 1836

Many convents and churches suffered damage during the Peninsular War (1808-1813). They were occupied by troops, despoiled of their contents, and left in a ruinous state. At least two Carmelite convents were actually the focus of fighting. The Carmelite convent in Zaragoza near the *Puerta del Carmen* was one of the points of resistance to the French during the sieges of 1808 and 1809. From the pulpit, the prior of the Carmen fired the populace to resistance. At Toledo, the French made a stand in the Carmen against the Spaniards advancing from Andalusia by the bridge of Alcantara (1809).

With the restoration of Ferdinand VII in 1813, the religious returned to their convents, but the work of reconstruction had hardly begun before the *"decreto de los monacales"* of October 25, 1820, which eliminated major superiors, suppressed convents with less than twenty-four members, and forbade the reception of novices, again emptied many Carmelite convents. The abolition of the constitution of 1823 once more permitted the re-establishment of the religious orders.

In comparison to members of the Order in other countries, the Spanish Carmelites were most persistent in their vocation. Neither the reign of Joseph Bonaparte (1808-1813) nor the constitutional triennium (1820-1823) eliminated a single Carmelite community. Each time, the friars returned to their ruined homes to resume their lives as religious. Naturally, this persistent persecution took its toll in numbers. Between 1808 and 1835, membership of the Order in Spain fell from 1,689 to 1,078.

The chaotic political and economic condition of Spain was exacerbated by the question of the succession, issuing in the Carlist War (1834-1840). To ease the financial problems of the nation and as a sop to the liberals, the prime minister, the Conde de Toreno, had recourse to the threadbare and ineffective expedient of sequestering religious property. The decree of July 25, 1835, closed all religious houses with less than twelve members. Thirty-three Carmelite convents were suppressed, leaving 227 friars homeless: the Aragon province lost 11 houses involving 88 members; Catalonia, 6 houses with 37 members; Castile, 5 houses with 26 members; Andalusia, 11 houses with 76 members.

The closure of the religious houses was accompanied throughout Spain by scenes of mob violence, the murder of religious, and the destruction of historic buildings and works of art - the *"degüelle de los frailes."* The very day of the decree, July 25, 1835, violence broke out against the twenty-six religious houses of Barcelona. Among others, the Carmen was reduced to a heap of cinders. Too late, the friars gave thought to their safety. The vice provincial, Francis Cells, was hacked to pieces in the street. Louis Nadal was discovered hiding in the garden and was dispatched with repeated blows of a knife. The professed cleric, Ramón Bruguera, was found dying in the street by a group of women who forthwith finished him off, flaying his head and back with sewing awls and combs. The next day, soldiers were able to collect religious and conduct them to safety in the fortresses of the city. Only on July 29 was a commission formed to see to their food and other needs. Eventually they were given passports to leave the city. A police report reveals that, of the 75 inmates of the Carmen, 4 had died, 58 had found asylum in the forts, and 13 were in hiding or otherwise unaccounted for.

On August 2 of that year of violence, the Carmelite church of Onda was burned to the ground.

The Carmelites had had better luck the previous year during the "*matanza de los frailes*" in Madrid, July 17, 1834, in which a number of Jesuits, Dominicans, Mercedarians, and Franciscans lost their lives. Two groups set off to attack the convents of the Carmelites and the Franciscans, but the determined stand taken by Don José Paulin, a brigadier of the artillery, accompanied by eleven volunteers, saved the Carmen.

The violence shown religious at this time did not reflect the attitude of the Spanish people at large, but was the work of gangs of organized extremists.

Toreno was succeeded by the more radical Juan Alvarez Mendizábal, whose decree of March 8, 1836, extinguished all religious orders in Spain, except those engaged in teaching or nursing. Thus ended the long and glorious history of Carmel in Spain, parent of St. John of the Cross and St. Teresa of Avila, the Discalced Reform, and many learned and saintly men and women. The ex-Carmelites returned to their families or became diocesan priests. Few are known to have emigrated. There was no place to go.

Of the more than seventy historic churches a few remain; in Andalusia: Ecija, Antequera, Cordova, Utrera, Osuna, Alhama, Jerez de la Frontera, Seville (College of St. Albert); in Aragon: Valencia, Alicante, Tudela; in Castile: Valderas, Madrid; in Catalonia: Perelada, Manresa, Valls, Vich, Olot, Mahon.

The Law of 1836 and the Nuns

Hitherto, the anti-clericals had not presumed to act against the respected nuns of Spain. This forebearance came to an end in 1836, though the law treated them more leniently than the male religious. Leaving unaffected the sisters engaged in teaching and nursing, the law suppressed all monasteries of cloistered nuns with less than twenty members. However, these smaller communities were allowed to join those which qualified for continued existence. Only one monastery of an order was allowed in each town. The sisters were forbidden to accept novices, and their property was sequestered, thus withdrawing their means of support. The law of exclaustration, or the so-called right of religious to secularize, was also affirmed. Much to the disappointment of the liberals, the nuns showed no great inclination to avail themselves of the proffered freedom. Quite the contrary. They raised such a holy dust with the queen that their affairs were conducted with considerable leniency by diocesan committees and other authorities.

The seizure of their property worked great hardship on cloistered women, but they asked only to be allowed to die in peace in their beloved cloisters. It should have occurred to the apostles of liberty that in denying these women their desire to live their own innocent lives, they were trampling on some rather fundamental human rights.

As a result of the stiff resistance of the nuns, only about 150 to 200 of 1000 to 1070 monasteries underwent amalgamation. When the ban on novices was lifted in 1851, the nuns were back in business.

The story of the Carmelite nuns in Spain corresponds to the general situation.

On the eve of the exclaustration, the Order in Spain still had its full complement of twenty-six monasteries; in the province of Castile: Madrid (Las Maravillas), Madrid (La Baronesa), Avila, Fontiveros, Piedrahita; in Catalonia: Barcelona, Villafranca del Panadés, Valls, Vich; in Aragon: Valencia (Incarnation), Valencia (St. Anne), Onteniente, Sariñena, Huesca (Incarnation), Huesca (Assumption), Zaragoza; in Andalusia: Ecija, Granada, Seville (Incarnation), Seville (St. Anne), Antequera, Aracena, Osuna, Utrera, Villalba del Alcor, Cañete La Real.

In most cities, with two Carmelite monasteries, one was eliminated. In Madrid, the nuns of La Baronesa joined their sisters in Las Maravillas, bringing with them their precious autograph of St. Teresa and other articles of devotion, including busts of Christ crowned with thorns and of the Sorrowful Mother, attributed to Pedro de Mena and José de Mora. In 1869, this community was also turned out of doors to find shelter with the Mercedarians until 1891, when it once again acquired its old home.

The monastery of Las Maravillas lay in the center of the fighting during the insurrection against the French, on May 2, 1808. The nuns were frightened out of their wits by the rain of cannon shot that fell on their monastery, but one courageous novice, Edwarda of St. Bonaventure, crawled out a window and with crucifix in hand went about among the soldiers to raise their spirits, an incident remembered by more than one historian. After the chaplain calmed their fears, the sisters took on the care of the wounded without regard to friend or foe. One young French officer had the consolation of hearing his native tongue spoken by the nun who assisted him at his last moments on earth. She was Sister Pelagia Revult, who entered the monastery in 1794, possibly an emigrée during the Revolution.

In Valencia, the monastery of St. Anne was amalgamated to the Incarnation, in Seville the monastery of St. Anne took in the Incarnation. In 1852, Ecija was united to Osuna. Sariñena seems to have been simply suppressed outright. In 1842, the Assumption in Huesca was united to the Incarnation, but the nuns were able to return to their original home in 1852. Again, in 1868, they were expelled, only to return once more. By 1888, there were only three nuns left in Utrera, but reinforcements from Granada gave them a new lease on life.

Thus, in spite of bullying and force, the Carmelite nuns persevered in their hidden life of prayer, though in slightly fewer monasteries. They may be confidently included in the praise which Revuelta González, sober historian of the exclaustration, lavishes on all Spanish nuns: "the protagonists in one of the most admirable and unheralded demonstrations of faith in contemporary history."

The Suppression of the Order in Portugal and Brazil

The extinction of religious orders in Portugal parallels that in Spain; in fact, anticipates it. A decree of May 30, 1834, sponsored by King Peter IV and his minister of justice, Joachim Anthony de Aguiar, abolished religious orders, confiscated their properties and pensioned off the religious. The measure was in part a sop to the liberal elements of his government who had supported him in his successful war against his brother, the reactionary Michael.

Before his victory on the mainland, Peter had seized the Azores and introduced anti-religious measures in May, 1832. Thus, the convent of Horta on the island of Faial and its fifteen inmates was the first house of the province to go. In 1834, the other twelve convents and one hospice followed suit: Lisbon, Moura, Colares, Vidigueira, Beja, Evora, Coimbra, Alagoa, Torres Novas, Setúbal, Alverca, Camarate, and the hospice of Funchal on Madeira Island.

The picturesque ruin of the Carmo of Lisbon has been preserved as the seat of the Association of Portuguese Archeologists. The convent built after the earthquake of 1755 became a barracks.

The bankrupt government of Portugal was in no position nor mood to lavish generous pensions on the dispossessed religious. Their plight in Portugal seems to have been more critical than elsewhere. In 1842, a visiting prince was struck by "the thousands of friars, suddenly cast upon the world with such meager means of subsistence that an ex-religious and a beggar appear to be almost synonymous."

The nuns were allowed to remain in their monasteries as long as they lived, but were forbidden to accept novices. The Order had four nunneries in Portugal: Beja, Lagos, Tentúgal, and Guimarâes. In 1846, the Carmelites of Beja took in the Poor Clares. In 1894, the last prioress, María José Segurado, was elected for the ninth time. After her death, the church was torn down by the Viscount of Ribeira Brava, who transported certain of its furnishings to his property of Vidigueira. A modern building, completed in 1940, replaces the monastery.

The last surviving sister in Tentúgal, the *Revista carmelitana* reports under the date line, July 23, 1889, is seventy-seven years old and ill. When she dies, the government will impound church and monastery.

At the invasion by the French in 1807, King John VI fled to Brazil. Afterwards, he was in no hurry to return, for the political situation at home was not promising, but he finally went back in 1821, leaving his son Peter as regent. The following year, the regent was declared Emperor Peter I of an independent Brazil. In 1831, Peter abdicated in favor of his son Peter, still in his minority, and returned to Portugal to claim his title of King Peter IV. In 1841, on reaching the proper age, his son was crowned Emperor Peter II of Brazil. The country, meanwhile, had acquired a constitution (1821). The anti-clerical Masonic Lodge, influential in the governments of all the Latin countries, was especially active in South America.

Under the empire, religious were subjected to a number of bothersome laws in the best style of European absolutism. A specific act of the provincial assemblies was required for the admission of novices. Profession was to be made in the presence of a justice of the peace, who should also sign the act (1828). An attempt to make the presence of the justice a requirement for the validity of profession failed. Permission to accept novices was very sparingly given, at a rate calculated to empty the convents and missions. A decree of July 10, 1828, banned non-Brazilian religious. Another, of December 9, 1830, forbade the alienation of religious property, mobile and immobile, without the authorization of the government. The patent purpose of this law was to assure the government of its ultimate booty.

On December 3, 1831, the minister of justice, Diego Antonio Feijó, announced to the papal nuncio, Peter Ostini, probably to the latter's surprise, that he might proceed to the reform of the religious of Brazil. The religious regarded this maneuver of Feijó, otherwise notorious for his illuminist and Febronian leanings, as an exercise of black humor in poor taste, especially as the ban on novices and non-Brazilians, two obvious sources of renewal, continued in force. The reform only added another vexation to the troubled existence of religious. Their thinning ranks were further reduced by transfers to the less embattled diocesan clergy. Religious observance, in Brazil no less than in Europe, was at a low ebb by the latter half of the 18th century, but this state of affairs was in no small part due to continued interference by secular authorities in spiritual matters concerning religious.

Finally, the decree of May 19, 1855, issued by the minister of justice, Nabuco de Araujo, forbade the reception of novices outright. The religious were not dispossessed, but remained proprietors as long as they lived.

The first result of the apostolic visitation of 1785 was the suppression of Santos. Its community of twelve and its movable goods were incorporated into the Carmo of Rio de Janeiro. Frei Luis Monteiro was left in charge of the empty premises.

It says much for the magnificence of the Carmo of Rio de Janeiro that King Pedro on his arrival in Brazil should choose it for the royal palace and chapel (1808). As their abode, the Carmelites were assigned the former diocesan seminary and its church of *Nossa Senhora de Lapa*, built in 1751. Subsequently, the original Carmelite church became the cathedral.

After 1855, most of the other convents of the province were also gradually left tenantless. Michael of the Conception Gomes, the last surviving Carmelite in Itú (founded 1719), died in 1872. The last Carmelite in São Paulo died in 1877. At Angra dos Reis and Mogí das Cruzes, the Carmelites showed a most unpatriotic disinclination to shuffle off the mortal coil, and these houses remained in the possession of the Order. Vitória was the only convent not later repossessed by the Carmelites. In 1860, they consented to its use as a military barracks. Anthony das Neves, the last prior, died on April 5, 1871. In 1897, the bishop claimed the property for a diocesan seminary, but the project proved impractical, and in 1900, the Sisters of Charity of St. Vincent de Paul opened there the College of Our Lady of Help.

After the secession of the reformed convents in Pernambuco (1744), the Bahia-Pernambuco province tended to designate itself by the first element in its title. It was composed of six convents: Olinda, Bahia, Sergipe, Rio Real, Cabo de Santo Agostinho (founded 1687), and Cachoeira (founded 1688). The reformed province of Pernambuco remained confined to Recife, Goiana, Paraiba, and several hospices and missions.

As the grim reaper thinned the ranks of the Carmelites, the survivors gradually fell back on the principal convents of their respective provinces, Bahia and Recife, which eventually won the race with death. In 1871, Frei Innocent of Mount Carmel Sena, last prior of Olinda, cradle of the Order in Brazil, closed the door on the empty convent and set out for Bahia. In 1866, the internuncio of Brazil named the bishop of Bahia apostolic visitator of what was left of the Carmelite province of Bahia. Pernambuco seems to have maintained an independent existence.

Perhaps the Order's most regrettable casualty of the war on religious was its mission in the Amazon region. In their heydey in 1751, the Carmelites administered eighteen *aldeias* in those remote parts. In 1755, the Marquis de Pombal took the material care of the *aldeias* out of the hands of the religious, who thereafter were only to concern themselves with spiritual matters. The segregation of religious from their superiors abroad and the banishment of non-Brazilian religious (1828) worked a special hardship on the Maranhâo vicariate, which depended on the province of Portugal. After 1828, the vicariate, cut adrift from its base, disintegrated rapidly. In 1841, the Holy See joined the convents of the vicariate situated in Para to the province of Rio de Janeiro. These would have been Belém and Vigia, which at the time housed only five or six friars. The secession left the vicariate the convents of São Luis, Tapuitapera (alias, Alcantara), and Ponta da Bonfim (hospice). The last prior of Tapuitapera, John of St. Philomena Bastos, became a diocesan priest in 1876. With the death of Cajetan of St. Rita Serejo in São Luis, May 8, 1891, the Maranhâo vicariate ceased to exist, and the secular labors of the Carmelite missionaries along the inhospitable Amazon became the heritage of dusty archives.

Carmelites in the Revolutions of 1817 and 1824

The flight of the Portuguese court to its colony in South America kindled the passion for independence in the hearts of many Brazilians and led to uprisings in the northeastern provinces, notably Pernambuco. After independence, dissatisfaction with the imperial constitution again sparked insurrection in that region. The clergy, including the Carmelites, played a notable role in the revolutions of 1817 and 1824. They did not limit themselves to patriotic exhortations, but often stood at the head of the troops or fought in the ranks. Carmelites afterwards executed for their part in the revolutions included Joachim of the Divine Love Rabelo, Joseph Ignatius Ribeiro de Abreu e Lima, Michael Joachim d'Almeida e Castro, Francis of St. Peter, Francis of St. Mary, Alexander of the Purification, Joseph of St. Hyacinth, Francis of St. Anne Brito, and the three Brayner brothers, Joseph dos Prazeres, Emmanuel of Mount Carmel, Joseph Mary of the Sacrament.

Of these patriots, the most noteworthy is Joachim of the Divine Love Rabelo, nicknamed Frei Caneca (1779-1825), still remembered as an important figure in Brazil's past.

The General Chapter of 1838

In 1838, Calamata convened a general chapter, the first in half a century. The chapter attempted to revive studies in the Order, establishing a new roster of general *studia* and other houses of theology and philosophy. Nine provinces and vicariates sent delegates. Ireland, Poland and Tuscany, which had mailed ballots in 1832, failed to appear. On the other hand, Sardinia and Portugal were this time represented, the latter by one Joseph Joachim Rodríguez. The Neapolitan Joseph Cataldi (1769-1841), of the Monte Santo province, was elected prior general *in absentia*. It was clearly specified that his jurisdiction did not extend to the Spanish peninsula.

Sixty-nine at the time of his election, Cataldi survived this distinction only three years. Though a Neapolitan by birth, he entered the Order at Siracusa, a convent of the reformed province of Monte Santo. He was the son of a physician who destined him to follow in his footsteps but who died when Joseph was only fifteen. Left without resources to continue his studies, Joseph took up the military profession. While stationed in Sicily, he came to know the Carmelites of Siracusa and there sought admission to the community. At an unknown date, he transferred to the Romagna province and was prior of Ascoli when elected prior general, an honor he seems to have owed not to a distinguished career in high office but to personal merit alone. He was in fact distinguished for his austere and prayerful life, skill as a spiritual director, and sacred orator.

Joseph Palma (1775-1843), of the Sicilian province of St. Angelus, also had only a brief term in office. Elected prior general in 1841 by the committee designated for this purpose in 1648 and now resurrected for the occasion, he became bishop of Avellino in 1843 and died the same year.

His removal from the scene occasioned another election in 1843 by the aforementioned committee, which chose Augustine Maria Ferrara (1775-1851), of the province of Santa Maria della Scala del Paradiso. His generalate corresponded to the early years of the pontificate of Pius IX, who shared with Pius VII a concern for the reform of religious.

In his encyclical, *Ubi primum*, June 17, 1847, to the major superiors of religious orders, the pope announced the creation of the special Congregation of the State of Religious Orders, dedicated to the improvement of religious life. In this context is to be placed the decree of the Congregation for Bishops and Religious, November 6, 1847, for the reform of the general council of the Carmelites. With the dismantling of the Order in so many countries, the membership and activity of the council had become rather haphazard. Ferrara had contented himself with two assistants, Simon Spilotros and Lawrence Piccioni. His procurator general was John Chrysostom Schiró. The Sacred Congregation declared these officials honorably retired and nominated Joseph Raymond Lobina procurator general and Elisha Romanazzi, Jerome Priori, Albert Angelus Ricciardi, and Elias Alberani assistants in that order. They were to meet once a week and enjoyed decisive voice in the affairs of the Order, whereas previously their vote had been only consultative. Lobina was also named postulator of causes for life.

The requirement of weekly meetings was rather unrealistic, at least in the case of the Carmelites, and Ferrara's council was only slightly more active than previous ones.

In most religious orders, the office of postulator of causes of the saints emerged only in the 18th century, though the Dominicans created this official as early as 1629, at the time that Urban VIII was establishing the canonical procedure. Among the Carmelites, the general chapter of 1762 determined that "there should be only one postulator in Rome, who can represent the Order with the Holy See" and appointed Master Jerome Pasquini to the office. Earlier in the century, Serafino Potenza (1697-1763) had ably conducted a number of causes and was certainly responsible for organizing the archive of the postulator. Postulators, especially in this troubled period, do not seem to have been regularly appointed. In 1794, Master Hyacinth Terzi stated that he had been postulator for twenty years. Not long before Lobina, Joseph Palma had filled the office.

At their meeting of November 12, 1847, to implement the instructions of the Sacred Congregation, the council of the Order fixed the community of Traspontina at eighteen members: the prior general, the procurator general, four assistants general, the lecturer at the Sapienza, the regent of studies, the postulator general, the pastor, the assistant pastor, and seven laybrothers.

On November 14, 1849, Lobina was named prior general by Pius IX. Born in Cagliari, Sardinia, in 1788, Lobina had been assistant general before becoming procurator of the Order. He visited the provinces of Sicily and Rome and sent Jerome Priori, procurator general, to the Netherlands.

The General Chapter of 1856

When Lobina died on February 23, 1854, Priori, appointed vicar general by Pius IX on September 22, summoned a general chapter in 1856, which elected him prior general. Besides eight Italian provinces, Ireland, Malta (vicariate), and Galicia were at hand. The chapter noted the absence of representatives from the provinces of Monte Santo, Russian Poland, and Brazil. (It makes no mention of Prussian Poland and Silesia.) The provincial of Ireland, Albert Bennett, added a note of distinction: a baccalaureate of the University of Louvain, he was also the vice-rector of All Hallows College, Dublin. The convent of Straubing, through the title of Provincial of Scotland, was able to be represented in the person of its prior, Cyril Knoll.

Among other decisions, the chapter rejected a proposal for abolishing *socii* of priors to provincial chapters, but allowed priors of small houses voice in such chapters, even though the election of *socii* (requiring at least five voters) had proved impossible. Since the Order no longer had provinces in France, Portugal, and Germany, the number of assistants general was reduced to two (without geographical specification). Finally, at the insistence also of Pius IX, the introduction of the common life, at least in the novitiates, is warmly inculcated. The chapter added that its decision did not apply to the reformed provinces, which by their apostolically approved constitutions observed the common life.

No other general chapter was held until 1889. The Carmelites had not yet reached the nadir of their fortunes.

Chapter 6

The *Risorgimento*

Nineteenth century Europe produced an anti-Catholicism that would make American Know Nothingism look like the Knights of Columbus.

The third quarter of the nineteenth century saw the dissolution of what little was left of the Carmelites in Italy after Napoleon got through with them. In Sicily and the Papal States, the last considerable concentration of Carmelites was disbanded, the central administration was disrupted, and the Order teetered on the brink of extinction. On the other hand, outside Italy its comatose body began to show faint signs of revival, and beginnings of life stirred on the continents beyond the seas. During these critical years, the Order was blessed with a prior general endowed with qualities suited to the times: tenacious endurance and alertness to emerging opportunity.

Angelo Savini, Vicar General, 1863-1889

In November, 1861, the prior general, Jerome Priori, explained to the Holy See the impossibility of holding a general chapter and asked for instructions. (Those were the troubled times of the Savoyan invasion of the peninsula of Italy and Sicily.) Priori's term was extended for a year, after which he was told to hold an election by mail. The balloting favored the incumbent in office, who, however, understandably declined the burdensome honor. Thereupon, the Holy See, on June 26, 1863, named Angelo Savini vicar general *ad nutum Sanctae Sedis*.

Savini was born in 1816 at Forlì, entered the novitiate at Iesi, and made his profession there in 1835. Ordination followed in 1839, and the doctorate in 1844.

From 1848 to 1851, Savini served as provincial of his province of Romagna. Thereafter, he dedicated himself to the teaching of theology in the convent of Forlì and in the diocesan seminary. He acted as the theologian of Bishop Vincent Tomba at the Synod of Ravenna, when he impressed Cardinal Gaetano Baluffi with his theological knowledge.

In Rome, Savini filled a number of offices in the service of the Church: confessor of the Vatican Chapter (1859), consultor of the Congregation of Indulgences (1861) and of the Congregation for Bishops and Religious (1864), examiner of the Roman clergy (1867), professor of moral theology at the Sapienza. He sat at the helm of the Order for a quarter of a century, acquitting himself admirably under very trying circumstances, but he was never given the title of prior general. It proved impossible to convene a general chapter; for that matter, there was very little of the Order left to convene. In 1866, he was confirmed in office for another six years; thereafter, in 1873, his vicarship was extended indefinitely.

It was Savini's painful duty to witness the general suppression of the Order in Italy in 1866. He encouraged the scattered flock by letter, at times augmenting meager incomes with the slender means at his disposal. In times of bleak despair, he clung to hope, collecting candidates for the Order, even from countries outside Italy, at Traspontina, Canepina, Palestrina, Viterbo, or wherever he could provide a refuge.

In 1873, the shepherd himself was struck down, when the Italian government seized Traspontina. A few friars were allowed to remain to care for the church, and Savini was given the use of his chambers during his lifetime. Eventually, enough of one wing of the convent was made available, and Savini was able to gather around him a small group of aspirants, the pathetic hope for the future.

The *Risorgimento*

The time had come for Italy to gather its traditional political units into one national fold, as was occurring in Germany. This development in modern nations greatly simplified government and public services, but it also involved the easier manipulation of large population masses by public and private interests and, as we have learned, the ability to wage bigger and better wars.

The role of Prussia was undertaken in Italy by the Kingdom of Piedmont-Sardinia. With the aid of Napoleon III, Victor Emmanuel II, guided by his able president of the council, Count Camillo Cavour, in 1859, drove the Austrians out of Lombardy. In March of the following year, Central Italy (Tuscany, Parma, Modena and Romagna) opted for union with Piedmont. With the connivance of Cavour, the Piedmontese general, Giuseppe Garibaldi, and his famous "Thousand" set sail from Quarto near Genoa and on May 11, 1860, landed at Marsala to wrest the Kingdom of the Two Sicilies from the Bourbons. On August 12, with Sicily already in his power, Garibaldi disembarked in Calabria to complete the conquest of the South before proceeding to settle accounts with the pope, for whom he nurtured an implacable hatred. Cavour decided it was time to contain this unpredictable force. Victor Emmanuel marched south at the head of a Piedmontese army, on the way gathering into the fold Papal Umbria and Ancona. On November 7, the King and Garibaldi entered Naples in triumph. On March 14, 1861, Victor Emmanuel was proclaimed king of Italy in Turin. This left the remnant of the Papal States, protected by Napoleon III, who had no reason to desire a powerful united Italy south of his realm. Even this support of the pope failed when the Franco-Prussian War claimed the French garrison of Rome. On September 20, 1870, after meeting a token resistance by the papal forces, the Italian *bersaglieri* breached the Porta Pia of Rome, Pope Pius IX retreated to the Vatican palace, and the Roman Question replaced the Papal States.

Once again the creation of a modern secular State required the expulsion of the Church from the traditional public functions it had exercised in Catholic society. Cavour's shibboleth, "A free Church in a free state," meant a Church in a State without religion. The freedom of the Church in such a country, of course, is always dependent on the good will of the state. Moreover, in Italy, as in other formerly Catholic countries, the removal of the Church from public life was often motivated, not only by the good of the state but also by hatred of religion. The forces of nationalism were sometimes identical with those of atheism.

The fate of the Church, and of religious orders in particular, in the rest of the peninsula, as the armies of Piedmont advanced, could be guessed from the laws already passed in that kingdom. In 1850, the Siccardi laws abolished the privilege of the canon, the right of sanctuary, and the right of the Church to acquire property without the consent of the state. In 1855, Cavour abolished the religious orders and sequestered their property. After the establishment of the Kingdom of Italy, this law was applied in 1866 to the rest of the peninsula except the Papal States.

There it was put into force on June 19, 1873. Religious habits vanished even from the streets of Rome. So much for Cavour's free Church.

The Suppression of 1866 in Sardinia and Sicily

The seven convents of the Sardinian province, which had outlived the Napoleonic menace, were now extinguished. In September, 1863, the community of Sassari was told to vacate the premises and betake themselves to a hospice of the Friars Minor. The following December, the provincial, Carmelo Rau, was ordered to withdraw the brethren from Bosa. The law of 1866 suppressed the rest of the convents, but in all cases one or two Carmelites remained in charge of the church.

A report by Rau of 1872 reveals that there were two priests and two laybrothers in Sassari and five priests and one lay brother in Cagliari. These led a community life as far as circumstances permitted. One priest was in charge of each of the Carmelite churches of Bosa, Alghero, and Chiaramonte. Oristano and Mogoro had been abandoned and were in the care of the diocesan clergy. Twenty-two Carmelites were living on their own.

Bosa was given up that same year of 1872. Fr. Stephen Pezzi held on to the Order's church in Chiaramonte until 1903. The Carmelites remained in charge of the churches in Sassari and Cagliari until the reconstitution of their communities in recent times.

The law of 1866 worked its most spectacular effect among the 81 convents in Sicily, the last bastion of the Order in Europe, as it was the first. In 1862, the last chapter of the province of St. Angelus still elected thirty-three priors. Here, too, the Carmelites remained for a time in charge of many of their churches after the communities were dispersed in 1866. The important foundations in Trapani and Palermo maintained a continuous Carmelite presence until their restoration.

Although the Carmelites by *fiat* of the Italian government had ceased to be, they left behind them many churches, erected with painstaking labor and sacrifice on the part of the faithful, a ponderable contribution to the life of the Church in the region. Former Carmelite churches remained open for cult in Marsala, Sciacca, Agrigento, Licata (Carmine), Sutera, Caltabellotta, Corleone, Bivona, Partanna, Sambuca, Monreale, Racalmuto, Bisaquino, Castelvetrano, Carini, Termini, Canicatti, Licata (S. Angelo), and Partinico.

The rest of the province's churches no longer exist or are in a ruinous state: Caltanisetta, Salemi, Alcamo, Monte San Giuliano, Mazara, Naro, Burgio, Prizzi, Gibellina, Favara, Palermo (S. Nicolò), and Alessandria.

After the island was taken by Garibaldi, the provincial, Master Angelo Amoroso, was arrested as a sympathizer of the Bourbon monarchy.

The last chapter of the province of St. Albert in 1862 shows thirty-two convents still at hand. The Order's churches in Messina and Pozzo di Gotto remained in the care of the Carmelites until the present day. Most of the other thirty continued to be of use to the faithful after the friars' departure: Buscemi, Calascibetta, Castiglione, Castrogiovanni (alias, Enna), Cerami, Chiaramonte, Terranova (alias, Eraclea), Erancavilla, Furnari, Gualtieri, Lentini, Licodia, Linguaglossa, Mazarino, Milazzo, Modica, Nicosia, Paternò, Ragusa, Randazzo, Regalbuto, Sinagra, Troina, San Piero Patti.

No longer in use or in existence are Francofonte, Petralia Soprana, Raccuja, Sortino, Tripi, Librizzi.

A report on the state of the province of Monte Santo, dating from the years 1855-1859, shows that the province numbered 66 friars, distributed through the 7 convents as follows: Catania 14, Palermo 14, Monforte 16, Acireale 8, Gibilrossa 4, Messina 6, and Polizzi 4.

With the exception of Gibilrossa, Palermo, and Monforte, the former Carmelite churches of this province are still in use, officiated now by diocesan priests.

In 1859, on the eve of the suppression, the province of Santa Maria della Scala numbered 92 members (seven not yet in vows). Siracusa housed 14 members, Spaccaforno (modern Ispica) 12, Scicli 9, Catania 14, Caltagirone 14, Noto 7, the desert house of Santa Maria della Scala 6, Augusta 5, Piazza 5. Six friars were living outside their convents with or without benefit of a papal brief.

The province held its last chapter the very year of the suppression, 1866. Only in Catania did the Carmelites manage to outlive the decree of extinction. All its churches are in use today at the service of their respective dioceses.

The three Sicilian nunneries in Messina, Palermo, and Siracusa also ceased to exist in the course of the century. The monastery of Santa Lucia di Valverde in Palermo was still at hand in 1892, when the sisters begged the prior general for financial assistance. Its beautiful church remains today.

The Suppression of 1866 in the Kingdom of Naples

After conquering the Kingdom of Naples, the Piedmontese lost no time in disposing of the religious orders. However, the law of suppression of February 17, 1861, was not everywhere immediately effective; only the general suppression of 1866 made a clean sweep of the religious houses.

A report by the provincial of Naples, Luigi Fusco, of March 6, 1872, reveals that only San Giovanni a Teduccio then boasted what might be called a community. The friars had been expelled on December 18, 1866, two priests and a lay brother being left in charge of the church. Later, at the request of the municipality, five priests, one of them the provincial, and three lay brothers were allowed to occupy part of the convent, to serve not only the church but other pastoral needs of the region. Five churches of the province were still cared for by Carmelites: at Penne, Noicattaro, and Ostuni, a priest was assisted by a brother; at Conversano and Nardò, a priest labored single-handed.

At this time, the province counted 79 members, seven of whom no longer acknowledged any relation to the Order.

Mesagna, not mentioned by Fusco, was later regained and survived into modern times. Fr. Angelo Deflorio arrived on April 28, 1875, to begin the ministry, which with the assistance of sundry other Carmelites he was to continue for the rest of the century.

By 1885, the number of priests living privately or in the two existing communities of San Giovanni a Teduccio and Mesagne had dwindled to thirty-five. The brothers, about whom statistics are lacking, labored no less tirelessly to keep alive the flickering flame of Carmelite existence.

The Suppression of 1866 in Central Italy

In 1865, the Tuscan province numbered 38 members: 19 in Florence, 14 in Pisa, 5 in Castellina. The suppression of the following year scattered the flock, leaving as usual only a skeleton staff for religious services in the churches. However, in each of the three houses, the Carmelites managed to maintain their presence and eventually to reconstitute communities. In December of 1874, the community of Florence regrouped. The following February, the provincial, John Baptist Bettini, held a visitation of the nine priests and five brothers. In 1878, a novitiate was opened. In 1884, Castellina became a novitiate.

Lucca was restored after the Napoleonic suppression and placed under the prior general. The general chapter of 1838 granted voice in general chapters and their definitories to Caesar Pera, "national" prior of Lucca. In 1838, the community consisted of 11 priests, 4 lay brothers, and 4 novices. After the annexation of Lucca by Tuscany in 1847, the Minister of Ecclesiastical Affairs on October 26, 1849, notified the Carmelite provincial that the convent of the Order in Lucca now pertained to his jurisdiction, but religious by now had a way of dealing with that sort of impertinence, and Lucca remained under the general. In 1863, the community numbered 11 priests and three brothers. After the general suppression of 1866, all that remained in 1884, in the words of the vicar general, Angelo Savini, to the Congregation for Bishops and Religious, were "a few individuals gathered in a house they had acquired." Specifically they were four priests and a lay brother. Much credit goes to this isolated community for its courageous resistance to all attempts to eliminate it.

The annexation of Romagna and the Marches by Piedmont proved permanently fatal to two Carmelite convents in that territory. The decree sponsored by Lorenzo Valerio, of March 3, 1861, signaled a new suppression, from which Ancona and Iesi did not recover.

In 1859, the Romagna province had been assigned by Pius IX the convent of Macerata, empty of Carmelites since the rule of Napoleon. Two years later, they were again dislodged. Only a priest and a brother remained to care for the church. Here as well as at Lugo, Forlì, Senigallia, and Ascoli Piceno, the Carmelites managed to hang on until better times.

The Romagna province held its last chapter in 1855, its last definitorial meeting the following year. In 1889, its five convents were inhabited by seventeen friars.

The Roman province was severely hit by the suppressions, leaving behind half its ten houses: Viterbo, Canepina, Velletri, San Vito, and Cantalupo. The latter and Perugia, situated in Umbria, did not await the fall of the Papal States, but succumbed to the suppression of 1861. Perugia, however, lived to fight another day, as did San Martino in Rome, Albano, and Palestrina.

To this remnant should be added the convent of San Nicolò ai Cesarini in Rome, former church of the Somaschi Fathers, which Pius IX in 1847 bestowed on the Carmelites in exchange for San Crisogono, given to the Trinitarians.

Carmelite Revolutionaries and Liberals

It should not be supposed that all Carmelites were opposed to political change. During the brief Parthenopean Republic, Francis Xavier Granata (1748-1799) welcomed republican ideas and the overthrow of the monarchy and oppressive feudal structures. Born in Rionero in Vulture, Michael Granata entered the Carmelite Order, receiving the name Francis Xavier. He was particularly partial to the study of mathematics and philosophy, subjects he taught in the Royal Military Academy of Naples from 1778 until his election as provincial of Terra di Lavoro in 1795. During the Republic, he became commissary of the canton of Sannazzaro. Arrested upon the restoration of the Bourbons, he was executed on December 12, 1779, in the Piazza Mercato in front of the Carmine Maggiore.

The prior of Martina Franca in the Puglia province, Peter Thomas Carucci (1752-1834), was also converted to the ideals of liberty of the French Revolution. At the restoration, he was arrested in Naples and condemned to death, but with the help of a former pupil was able to escape. In 1817, he returned to Martina Franca, where he taught philosophy and law, dying an octogenarian. The Carmelite convent had been suppressed by the French in 1806.

John Calcagni, of Mesagne in the same province, was a protagonist of Italian unity, though no hero to be proposed to the adulation of school children. Arrested on July 22, 1837, as a member of *La Giovane Italia*, he was condemned to nineteen years imprisonment in chains. He had previously been sentenced to death for poisoning his superior, but had been released on cognizance of the Order. In 1841, the prior general, Joseph Cataldi, fearful lest Calcagni be granted amnesty and return to his convent, requested the Holy See to expel him from the Order, since such an act by the prior general would probably not be recognized by the secular authorities. Whether the wretched man was in fact freed of his chains is not known.

In Sicily, the province of St. Albert counted a number of alleged Carbonari among its members. A governmental *ministeriale* deprived ten friars of active and passive voice and expelled them from the provincial chapter of 1823; further ordering them transferred from their convents of Cerami, Troina, Petralia, Castrogiovanni, Francofonte, and Francavilla.

The neglect of the church in Nicosia after the suppression of 1866 was attributed to "the religious themselves, contaminated by the pestilence of liberalism."

After the expulsion of the Carmelites from their convent in Messina in 1871, a certain Fr. Dominic Abate, "revolutionary," did all in his power to have turned out of doors the three friars who remained to care for the church.

In the province of St. Angelus, Luigi Domingo in 1860 provided asylum in the convent of Carini to the revoluntionary, Rosolino Pilo, wounded in an encounter with the police. At his death, Pilo was granted absolution by a Carmelite. Domingo had already been active in the revolution of 1848 and as a result had been imprisoned on an island off Palermo. For his adherence to Garibaldi's cause, he was deprived on March 5, 1860, of the lectorate bestowed on him in 1847 by the prior general, Augustine Ferrara.

1876

Looking back over the disastrous 19th century, we may take the year 1876 as the low tide in the Order's fortunes since its initiation. The last wave of suppressions had taken place in Prussia and Italy, and revival had not yet definitely set in. From what remains to be said, it will be seen that in 1876 there remained 58 Carmelite convents in the world: under the prior general 3 (Traspontina, Naples, Lucca), the Roman province 5, Sardegna 2, the Tuscan province 3, the Romagna province 5, Southern Italy 2, Sicily 5, Malta 2, Germany 2, The Netherlands 2, the Polish province (Galicia) 8, the Irish province 8, England 1 (Merthyr Tydfil), Brazil 5. To these must be added eight convents in North America, yet to be considered.

In terms of number of houses, the nuns returned to their status in the 16th century and lost two centuries of growth. Forty monasteries remained: in the Low Countries 2 (Boxmeer, Vilvoorde), Italy 13, Spain 21, Portugal 4. The four Portuguese nunneries, forbidden to receive novices, did not survive the 19th century. The constancy of the Spanish nuns has already been noted. In Spain, the war on the nuns resulted in only five casualties: Madrid (La Baronesa), Valencia (St. Anne), Ecija, Sariñena, Seville (Incarnation).

Chapter 7

Revival in Europe Outside Italy

"The top of Carmel withers, the flower of your Majorcan sons falls, time and again death has gloried in victory over us, and hardly any of your exclaustrated Carmelites remain. You would perform an office of solace, you would heal us, you would dry our tears with a paternal hand, if you would hear the plea of the Majorcan Carmelites, of whom I am the unworthy head, who ask of you to admit as novices pious and sufficiently lettered youths."

These florid phrases, penned in Palma on November 18, 1858, announced to the prior general, Jerome Priori, that Carmel in Spain was about to lift its head.

Carmel on Majorca

Their writer, John Angelus Torrents, describes himself as head of the Carmelites on Majorca. In dimissorial letters of October 20, 1864, he signs himself "vicar provincial of Majorca and vicegerent general of all Spain." The same dimissorials are also signed by James Albert Gomila, Michael Moranta, and Francis Angelus Vidal, possibly the only other Carmelites on the island. As a subdeacon, Gomila had published theses, defended in the Carmelite church in Palma (Palmae Balearum, B. Villalonga, 1827).

John Angelus Torrents (1804-1885), father of the revival of the Order in Spain, was born in Palma de Mallorca and studied in the Jesuit college there before taking the Carmelite habit in 1824. Upon ordination in 1828, he became regent of studies in the convent of Palma and *super-numeriano* on the faculty of philosophy of the Royal University of Majorca. He also functioned as commissary of the local Third Order and director of the Carmelite confraternity. After the suppression of the convent in 1835, Torrents remained in his native city, zealously dedicating himself to the work of the confessional and the pulpit. He became chaplain of the Discalced Carmelite nuns; in their chapel he preached many of his innumerable sermons, for which he was famous on the island, and from the same chapel he was buried. During his busy lifetime, he found time to translate from the Latin the three volumes of the *Glorias del Carmelo* of the Jesuit, José Andrés, adding a fourth volume on the Carmelite Order in Majorca (Palma, 1860-1861). His *Recreaciones marianas*, a work of 800 pages in four volumes, presenting two meditations for every day of the year, remained in manuscript.

In 1864, Savini opened a novitiate in Traspontina, to which Torrents was at last able to send his pious and sufficiently lettered youths. At least sixteen Majorcans are known to have been dispatched to Rome; their names are worth remembering: Francis Angelus Bennazar, Francis Canals, Luke Anthony Pons (1864); Peter Thomas Amorós (1865), Leonard Grimaldi (1866); Anastasius Borrás, Cyril Ramis, Andrew Serra, John of the Cross Tomás (1868), Mariano Nadal, Simon Vicens (1869); Joseph Belaguer, Albert Cirer, Elisha Durán, Brocard Sastre, Angelus Vidal (1872). (The dates refer to the year in which the young men began their novitiate.) The suppression of 1873 put an end to Savini's novitiate.

The Concordat of 1851 of Spain with the Holy See had opened the door to the re-establishment of religious orders. If Savini planned to revive the Carmelite

Order with his Majorcan recruits, his hopes were dashed. On their return to the island, the young Carmelites showed little inclination to form communities and chose instead to carry on the priestly ministry from private homes on the plea that their families needed their support. Torrents himself, long unused to community life and comfortably ensconced in his chaplaincy of the Carmelite nuns, was not the first to set the example. For him, it was enough that there were once more Carmelites on the island to promote devotion to Our Lady.

A formal order of Savini to Torrents on September 18, 1875, to gather four or five young priests in a suitable house, in order to live in community, fell on deaf ears. In spite of Torrents' recalcitrance, one young priest at least was disposed to carry out the prior general's command. Anastasius Borrás (1850-1908), a native of Palma, was sent by Torrents to Rome, where he entered the novitiate in 1868 and was ordained a priest in 1872. On returning to Palma in 1875, Borrás at first had difficulty finding a site for a foundation, but a letter to Savini of April 25, 1876, finds him settled in a house with the professed cleric, Elisha Durán, on temporary leave from his studies in Rome for reasons of health. After completing his studies, Durán, together with Albert Cirer, was given an obedience on August 15, 1877, for the newly founded hospice. The following year, on August 2, 1878, Joseph Belaguer and Brocard Sastre were allotted the same destination. On July 16, 1877, Savini had appointed Borrás superior of the hospice.

The risky existence of the Palma residence was brief, but some of its inmates were to play a fundamental role in the ultimate restoration of the Order in Spain.

Montpellier, 1876-1880

In January of 1876, we find the Catalan Carmelite, Joseph Barcons, in Montpellier, whence he wrote to the vicar general, Angelo Savini, on the 29th: "God knows how long I, too, have been thinking of founding a hospice, now in Africa, now in America, now in France. The first time I set foot in France, my heart told me, 'Here a Carmelite hospice must be founded!' And lo, you write your first letter to corroborate my insignificant thoughts. With the help of Your Reverence they will become great thoughts."

Perhaps the bishop of Montpellier had offered a foundation to the Carmelite vicar general; or, hearing of Barcons' presence in France, Savini suggested he look into the possibility of founding a house there.

Undoubtedly, the two were acquainted. Joseph Barcons (1810-1884) was born in Olot and in 1829 entered the Order as a member of the Catalan province. After the suppression of 1835, he found asylum in Italy. In 1843, he wrote from Ponzano to the Spanish commissary general, Edward Comas, resident in Traspontina, reporting his success in finding a house for Spanish Carmelites. His sojourn in Italy was probably not lengthy, judging by the grievous injury he inflicts on Dante's idiom in his letters. He returned to Spain, seemingly to lead the life of an exclaustrated religious in or near his family, for in 1865 he is found in his native town.

Savini answered his communication with letters patent, dated February 2, 1876, constituting him commissary general for founding a convent in France. After investigating possibilities in Ginac and Cette, Barcons bought a house in Montpellier. The bishop assigned him the care of the church or chapel of Saint León with land adjoining for the construction of a convent. On December 11, there arrived from Boxmeer, summoned by Savini, the pioneer community: Gabriel Marini (alias, Wilson, Italian), Anastasius Kreidt (American), Alphonsus Hartmann (Dutch), and Bro. Aloysius Sentis (Dutch). On December 31, they settled in their house. The same day, Barcons blessed the church.

The faithful welcomed the young community and showed its appreciation by generous support. On their side, the Carmelites responded by the witness of their prayerful life and by the spiritual assistance they provided, not only in their little church of Saint Léon, but also in surrounding parishes and towns.

In Gabriel Marini, whom he appointed on June 22, 1877, the vicar general found a steady and able superior. Marini had entered the Order in Palestrina and had left Italy under the name Wilson to avoid military service.

Others, who for longer or shorter periods served in Montpellier, were Brother Thomas Serrat (Catalan), Alphonsus Koene (Dutch), Peter Thomas Foglietta (Italian), Felix Cullen (Irish), Bro. Martin van Rijk (Dutch). The founder himself, Joseph Barcons, was absent much of the time in Spain in search of money and candidates. After February 6, 1878, when he was charged with founding a convent in Jérez de la Frontera, he appeared no more in France.

The March Laws of the Third Republic

In any case, the days of the Carmelite convent of Montpellier were numbered. In 1880, it fell victim to the March Laws suppressing all convents not approved by the government and deporting foreign religious. When the commissary made his appearance on October 16, accompanied by soldiers and gendarmes, the prior, Gabriel Wilson, refused to admit them, claiming that the house was his property and that he had committed no crime. Accordingly, the authorities broke down the door of the house as well as those of the rooms, behind which the friars had barricaded themselves. Challenged to produce proof of ownership, Gabriel was acknowledged as proprietor, but told he would have to leave France nevertheless. Outside, a crowd had gathered, which cheered the Carmelites when they emerged and hung garlands on the doors of the convent and church. The bishop and his vicars visited the fathers in the homes where they had been accorded hospitality. Fifteen hundred francs were speedily collected to pay for their voyage, which began amid the well-wishing of a crowd come to see them safely on their way.

Alphonse Koene was on vacation when the expulsion took place, Felix Cullen returned to Ireland, Alphonse Hartmann and the two laybrothers (Aloysius Sentis and Martin van Rijk) to Holland.

Hartmann's story has a tragic ending. On November 5, 1880, Savini had given him leave to remain outside the cloister as long as necessary. January 2, 1881, found him in a hotel in Brussels. He had been mortally ill, was in financial straits, and had applied to Louis Veuillot's *Comité de l'oeuvre du Denier des Expulsés* for relief. On March 6, he wrote to Savini from his native Rotterdam, whither he had gone to assist at the deathbed of his mother. He asked the vicar general to assign him to Rome, America, or Ireland. Savini summoned him to Rome, whither he shipped his baggage on May 11. He himself never appeared. Instead, there came an inquiry from Mr. Rudolph de Good, consul in the Netherlands, as to the identity of a body which had been found in a Rotterdam hotel and which indeed proved to be that of Alphonse Hartmann, "aged about 31 years."

Gabriel Wilson followed his superior, Joseph Barcons, to Jérez de la Frontera, whence on November 27, 1880, he reported progress in learning the Spanish language. "Almost all the time I have been in religious life, I have spent in learning foreign languages," wrote this Italian with an English name, who had come to France from Holland; "perhaps after I have learned Spanish I shall have to acquire other languages."

The Montpellier convent was a promising beginning, and there is no reason to believe that, were it not for the tyrannical laws of the Third Republic, Carmel of the Ancient Observance would not have continued in France until today.

The Restoration of the Order in Spain

Meanwhile, an opportunity had presented itself to the vigilant Savini to revive the Order on the Spanish mainland, specifically in Jérez de la Frontera near Cádiz on the southern coast of Spain.

After the suppression of 1835, Joseph Anthony Briosso had remained in charge of the Carmelite church in Jérez until the September Revolution of 1868, when it was converted into a military storehouse. Briosso moved to the Church of St. Dionysius, bringing with him the statues and scapular confraternity of the Carmen. After the restoration of Alfonsus XII (1875), we find Ildefonso Carvallo, Joseph Metendez, and Joseph Infante living with Briosso. The first of these wrote to the vicar general on May 26, 1877, announcing among other business of the parish that he had applied to the government for authorization to reopen the Order's church. Savini lost no time in forwarding to Carvallo on October 1, 1877, patents as commissary general to recuperate the Order's former convent in Jerez. Carvallo's reply of October 17 was cautious. He doubted whether any Carmelite could be found in Spain willing to return to the cloister. He suggested applying for volunteers to the young Spaniards living in Rome or in Palma. The bishop gave him full support, but "the Father General of this Spanish realm" wanted everything to proceed under his control. What was he to do, Carvallo wanted to know.

This last ominous note refers to the peculiar situation of the Carmelites in Spain, still subject to the provisions of *Inter graviores*. On June 2, 1865, Pius IX had named Michael Pérez y Valls apostolic commissary general for Spain, the successor apparently of Edward Comas - at least no other such commissary is known to have existed. As such, Pérez ruled over the Carmelite Order in Spain, present not in convents but in scattered individuals, each absorbed in his pastoral ministry. Pérez himself was a canon of the cathedral of Zaragoza. Even the office of provincial was continued, these officials being especially necessary for the direction of the nuns.

The exclaustrated Carmelite, as we have seen in other contexts, had in common a touching loyalty to the Order, generous response to the monetary appeals of the priors general, and an unconquerable aversion to returning to the cloister.

In a subsequent letter, Carvallo told Savini that the archbishop had suggested that "the way to escape the yoke of the Father General of this Spanish realm was to request the extinction and abolition of all the dispositions of the bull *Inter graviores* relating to the Spanish Carmelites," as the Discalced and the Dominicans had already done.

"As to myself," Pérez had written to Savini on October 9, 1865, "I have said again and again that I want to resign from an office to which I am not equal, and that anyone who would remove me from it would do me a favor." In spite of this affirmation, repeated on other occasions, Pérez proved reluctant to lay down the *fasces*. Appeals by the vicar general, the cardinal archbishop of Zaragoza, and the cardinal protector of the Order failed to dislodge him. The Holy See showed characteristic forbearance toward any appointee not actually guilty of wrongdoing. The news of Pérez' demise on August 8, 1886, can hardly have been wholly unwelcome in Rome. No successor was ever named.

It soon became evident that no action would be forthcoming from Carvallo, who was not as disloyal to Pérez as he seemed to profess. The vicar general took his advice and looked outside the Spanish mainland for subjects for Carmelite life. He summoned Joseph Barcons from Montpellier, appointing him on February 6, 1878, "commissary for founding convents in the Spanish realms." Pérez protested to the cardinal protector against this duplication of jurisdiction about which he had not been informed, but the procurator general of the Order, Elisha Giordano, explained to the Congregation for Bishops and Religious that Barcons had no jurisdiction over exclaustrated Carmelites and was empowered only to found new houses subject to the vicar general, a bit of casuistry that seemed to satisfy the Sacred Congregation, which, for that matter, was not about to impede the formation of proper religious houses. Thus unceremoniously set aside, Carvallo showed no further interest in the business of reopening the Carmelite church of Jérez, in fact, was quite hostile to his usurper.

The Carmelite archbishop of Seville, Joachim Lluch y Garriga, in whose jurisdiction Jérez lay, granted Barcons the cure of the former Servite church, *Las Angustias*. Meanwhile, the commissary pursued the business of acquiring the Carmelite church, left pending by Ildephonse Carvallo. On April 15, 1878, he was able to inform Savini that Madrid had ceded the church together with 10,000 *scudi* for its restoration. Coal, wood and straw were removed against the terminal date of July 1. Quarters for eight religious were also provided. On April 10, 1880, occurred the solemn repossession of the church with the transfer of the statues of the Virgin, Elijah, and Teresa.

For his community, Barcons, besides accepting new candidates, enticed Anastasius Borrás and Joseph Belaguer from Palma, and from Montpellier Gabriel Marini. The arrival of Elisha Durán from Palma marked the end of the residence there. Evidently, Savini had decided that Jérez on the mainland was the more promising enterprise and was willing to sacrifice the hospice of Palma. On July 12, 1880, he appointed Borrás vicar prior of Jérez.

The Carmelites had their eye on their former convent. "Our actual domicile, though capacious, lacks the form of a regular convent," Borrás told Savini. The death of her husband placed a large fortune at the disposition of his pious widow, Doña Elena de Paramo y del Corro, and enabled her to realize a long cherished wish to restore the Carmelites to their ancient home. This generous woman not only purchased the convent at an exorbitant price, but after the Carmelites had taken possession on November 19, 1884, paid for its restoration.

On the very day of the return to the convent, Borrás sat down to pen a letter to the vicar general, announcing the death of the man who had made it possible. Acceding to Barcons' request to be relieved of office, Savini on August 26,

1884, appointed Anastasius Borrás his successor as commissary general for new foundations. Barcons lived only until the following November 17.

With John Torrents, Joseph Barcons shares credit for reviving the Order in Spain. A typical exclaustrate, Torrents had little interest in founding communities, but he fostered the young vocations of those who did, especially Anastasius Borrás, Elisha Duran, and Cyril Ramis. These found in Barcons the leader who enabled them to realize their aspirations after Carmelite life.

The Province of Spain

Contemporaneously, negotiations were in course to recover the Carmen of Onda, formerly of the Aragon province. Church and convent lay in ruins, the statue of the Virgin was preserved in the parish church. The exclaustrated Carmelite, Vincent Peydro, conceived the idea of restoring this foundation of his Order. With royal authorization of February 26, 1879, and the consent of the proprietor, Don Emmanuel Pastor y Lazaro, granted on May 19, he proceeded with the reconstruction, himself collecting the necessary funds. In the Spring of 1880, the church was completed. Since the previous October, Peydro had already occupied the premises, joined by Francis Sola and Brother Joseph Guillot, the latter, however, dying soon afterwards.

In all this, Peydro was in correspondence with the Spanish commissary, Pérez. Nevertheless, in May of 1881, he invited Barcons to visit Onda. Savini admitted the new foundation under his jurisdiction. Candidates were received and a novitiate was opened with the permission of Rome.

On August 6, 1883, Barcons returned with some professed clerics. The community was strengthened by the advent of Maurice Balduz, former companion of Barcons in Italy, and by Simon María Scarano, summoned by Savini from Malta. As was only proper, Peydro was placed in charge of the convent he founded. Onda, remotely situated in the hills, became a large and flourishing community, the novitiate of the restored Carmel in Spain.

Before the last decade of the century, a third convent of the Order was restored. The Carmelite sisters in nearby Onteniente continually urged the commissary general, Anastasius Borrás, to recover the Order's convent in Caudete, formerly of the Aragon province. Sister Rosalia Algarra, a native of Caudete, had received word from a nephew there that the municipality and clergy were favorably inclined, and that the people eagerly awaited the return of the friars. Her cousin, Don José Requena y Requena, undertook the restoration of the local hospital and moved there the few patients who remained in the convent, which was being used for the care of the sick. He also donated a house to accommodate the Guardia Civil who occupied part of the convent. Finally, Requena collected the monies needed to make church and convent once more fit for use.

On August 20, 1888, the Carmelites travelled from Onda to repossess their house in Caudete. They were Albert Gutiérrez, José Gomis, Salvador Barri, Bro. Angelo Fuster, and seven professed clerics.

The stage was thus set for the formation of a province. On January 26, 1890, the prior general, Aloysius Galli, established the Spanish province of the Most Holy Name of Mary, appointing Anastasius Borrás provincial and Elisha Durán, Albert Gutiérrez, Elias Roselló, and Peter Thomas Frias definitors.

Before the end of the century, foundations followed in Hinojosa del Duque (1890), Osuna (1891), Olot (1892), Seville (Buen Suceso, 1896).

The restoration of the Order in Spain was eminently successful. Under dedicated leaders like Barcons and Borrás, exemplary communities were established, solid foundation stones for future growth. With the Netherlands, Spain spearheaded the revival of the Order in other parts of the world.

The Province of Galicia in Austria

In the middle of the nineteenth century, Carmel north of the Alps boasted, besides the Polish provinces in Austrian Galicia and Prussia (the latter suppressed in 1875), two convents, Straubing and Boxmeer, graveyards for whatever Carmelites remained after their governments had forbidden the reception of novices. Yet, in spite of thinning ranks in choir and refectory, these old friars never lost hope, and in the end their perseverance was rewarded.

After the partitions of Poland, the Carmelites in Austrian Galicia were placed under the jurisdiction of the bishops, who performed all the functions of the prior general, but around the middle of the century, regular contact with Rome was again resumed. Beginning with 1852, the acts of the provincial chapters were regularly dispatched to the curia for approval.

Around 1870, the seven convents of the province of Galicia numbered 30 priests, 14 brothers, and three professed clerics.

Noteworthy figures in the province at this time include Alphonse Jakiel, who, except for the years 1855-1859, headed the province from 1846 to 1870. In 1866, he was accorded the honorary title of ex-procurator general with its prerogatives because "he had restored regular observance, removed abuses, increased the number of religious, and what is more, by his prudent administration saved a number of convents from total ruin." At the same time, Carl Milanyak, who for many years had taught all the religious in Lwów church history and sacred scripture, was granted the doctorate by Savini. He subsequently headed the province in 1874-1883 and 1889-1893.

The Germano-Holland Province, 1879

At the end of the long reign of William I, only three old friars remained in the Carmel of Boxmeer, when his successor, William II, lifted the ban on novices, November 28, 1840. Within a few months four diocesan priests and three brothers had taken the habit; in ten years, the community counted twenty-four members. In 1855, Boxmeer was able to spare six priests, five brothers, and four professed clerics for a new foundation in Zenderen. In the Netherlands, Savini at his accession to office found ready at hand a dependable source for his projects of expansion outside Italy. In 1866, he named Augustine van Uden commissary general of the Netherlands.

Merthyr Tydfil

Two years previously, he had asked him to open a mission in the Beverley diocese in England. Early in 1864, Van Uden sent Elias van der Velden, who, when he found no suitable opening in the Beverley diocese, on August 29, 1865, took possession of the parish of Merthyr Tydfil, Wales, which served a congregation of poverty-stricken Irish iron workers and coal miners. The parish also conducted a school. Later, Boxmeer sent Anastasius Smits and Hilarion Driessen, deacons who were soon ordained, and Brother Berthold Landers.

Late in 1867, the Irish province sent Martin Angelus Bruton, who took charge of the mission, for Van de Velden had meanwhile, without permission it would seem, crossed to America, where he left the Order. The following year, Smits and Landers left for America to collect badly needed funds for the mission and never returned to England. Driessen followed them the same year, 1868, but without authorization, and he eventually became a diocesan priest. Thus, although under the jurisdiction of the vicar general, Merthyr Tydfil became the responsibility of the Irish province. Bruton was assisted by various Irish Carmelites until his premature death from overwork and privation (1875). The mission was abandoned four years later.

Straubing

The concordat which Bavaria concluded with the Holy See on June 5, 1817, allowed for the revival of some religious houses for teaching, the care of the sick, or assistance to pastors. By that time, only about twenty religious houses remained in the kingdom. At first, the government was by no means precipitous in licensing foundations. Up to 1832, only fourteen permissions had been accorded. By 1841, the number of religious houses had reached one hundred and sixty-one.

By that date, there remained in Straubing only the prior, Peter Heitzer. A request for restoration made in 1826 to King Louis I, who had ascended the throne the previous year, was rejected on the grounds that the financial stability of the convent was not guaranteed. This obstacle was unexpectedly removed in 1840, when the pastor of Geltolfing, Joseph Angermuller, granted the Carmelites a sum he had set aside for founding a Capuchin convent. Thereupon, on June 19, 1841, the king gave his consent to reopening the Carmel of Straubing. There was no time to be lost, for Heitzer was advanced in years; preference was given to ordained candidates. This was by no means a bad policy, for there were then many diocesan priests whose first choice in ordinary times would have been the cloistered life. When Heitzer died, a community had been established, comprising Albert Weiss (prior), Elisha Primbs, Louis Fritz, and Xavier Huber.

Under Cyril Knoll, prior from 1851 to 1857, Straubing in 1854 accepted the care of the Marian shrine at Sossau. Gerard Wieslhuber labored in this pilgrimage place for thirty years and was widely known and loved.

In 1857, Knoll personally headed a group of Carmelites to found a house in Pest, Hungary, but various reasons, chief among them nationalist feelings against Germans, caused the hospice to be abandoned in 1861.

On July 15, 1879, Straubing was joined to Boxmeer and Zenderen to become the Germano-Holland province. Van Uden was named its head. This union allowed for the interchange of personnel and the pooling of resources.

The Restoration of the Monasteries in the Low Countries

During the regime of the French, the nunnery of Elzendaal in Boxmeer was suppressed the same day as the friary, August 20, 1812. Like their Carmelite brothers, the sisters returned to their cloister on April 20, 1814, also under the condition that they receive no novices. When this ban was lifted, November 28, 1840, new candidates quickly presented themselves. With the arrival of the Sisters of Charity in 1865, the Carmelites were able to discontinue teaching, a task formerly imposed on them by the exigencies of the times.

On May 23, 1889, twelve nuns began a new Carmel in Zenderen.

In Belgium, the French, on November 5, 1796, expelled the nuns from their monastery in Vilvoorde. Two weeks previously, however, Sister Petronilla of St. Mary had smuggled out the cherished statue of Our Lady of Consolation in a bale of hay, as one of her sisters had once done before her. Most of the nuns with the confessors of the monastery took refuge in the beguinage of the city, until the times permitted them to return on November 8, 1802. Their confessors were the exclaustrated Carmelites, Cornelius Claes and Dionysius de Roey. With the establishment of modern Belgium in 1830, the nuns were once more free to take novices. After thirty-four years, only six nuns remained. The prioress was Joan Frances of St. Mary Vereecken.

The Irish Province in the Nineteenth Century

While the remainder of the Order in Europe and Brazil suffered drastic diminution at the hands of secular authorities, the province of Ireland, no less harassed but inured to persecution, made painful progress toward revival.

The first provincial chapter after the restoration of the province (1741) elected priors to fourteen houses: Dublin, Ballinasmale, Caltranapallice, Horton, Knocktopher, Cork, Leighlinbridge, Crevaghbane, Kinsale, Thurles, Ballinveillin (Milltown), Knockmore, Ballynahinch, Castleyons.

Some of these convents were a hope rather than a reality. The re-occupation of Cork, for instance, failed to materialize at this time. Moreover, other convents not included in this list later briefly appear as houses of the Order. Evidently, the situation was one of flux, with attempts, variously successful, to reoccupy pre-Reformation houses with a mere handful of friars. In 1801, the province is said to have ten convents (unspecified) with twenty-eight priests. The provincial chapter of 1819 no longer mentions Horton, Ballynahinch, Crevaghbane, Knockmore, Castlelyons, Cork, but includes Cloncurry, Athboy, Loughrea, Galway, and Moate. By the chapter of 1823, the situation begins to firm. At that meeting were represented Dublin, Kildare, Moate, Kinsale, Knocktopher, Tohergar (alias) Ballinamore, whither Caltranapallice had transferred, Leighlin, Crevaghbane, and Ballinasmale. By 1840, Leighlin and Crevaghbane are no longer spoken of. The province numbered twenty-six priests. In 1870, the province, consisting of forty-one priests, had reached its modern shape: Dublin (19 priests, 11 professed clerics), Knocktopher (4 priests), Moate (3 priests), Kinsale (2 priests), Kildare (2 priests).

Administration at the provincial level was difficult to maintain. Between 1804 and 1816, no chapters were held. Chapters were held in 1819 and 1823, but the Holy See appointed William Kinsela provincial in 1826. In 1829, Rome allowed Thomas Coleman to be re-elected, extending his term at its lapse in 1832 to a fourth year. The council of the Order approved acts of chapters in 1843 and 1846, but Thomas Bennett was designated provincial by Pius IX in 1852 and confirmed in office by the prior general for another three years.

In spite of limited resources, the spirit of the province was one of progress, and the Carmelites carried on a brisk apostolate among the downtrodden Catholics of Ireland, ministering to their spiritual needs, conducting schools for their children, and providing material succor to the poor.

Whitefriars Street and Father Spratt

Dublin was the center of Carmelite life, somewhat to the neglect of the country houses. Carmelite presence in Dublin during the 17th century was probably only intermittent. We have seen William Shea receiving candidates in the 80's. In 1697, the friars seem to have settled in Cornmarket. From 1728, when Francis Leahy acquired a house and chapel in Ashe Street, historical continuity can be traced. Here the Carmelites conducted a flourishing scapular confraternity throughout the city and environs, and opened a school for boys. When the lease lapsed in 1806, the community moved to French Street with a modest chapel in Cuffe Lane. Here, too, in 1822 they opened a school in Longford Street.

In 1825, the site of the original Dublin foundation was purchased in Whitefriar Street. The following year, saw the laying of the cornerstone of a church, completed in 1827. It was the creditable work of George Papworth, a noted architect of the city, and cost 4,000 pounds, "and proves," a contemporary adds, "how much can be done with small means, when taste and judgement are combined." Here was enshrined a Gothic statue of the Virgin in wood, discovered in an ordinary sale shop, now popularly known as Our Lady of Dublin.

The French Street school also accompanied the Fathers to the new site in Whitefriar Street. The National Education Act of 1831 brought a measure of financial relief. In 1850, the former Methodist meeting house north of the church provided larger quarters until 1895, when a proper school building was erected.

Author of this development of the Dublin Carmel was the indefatigable apostle, John Spratt. He was born in 1796 in Cork Street, Dublin, and as a young man decided to become a Carmelite. For his novitiate and studies, he was sent in 1816 to St. Albert's College, Cordova. After his return to French Street, he immediately distinguished himself for his apostolic zeal, establishing in 1822 his school for poor children. The chapter of 1823 returned him as prior, in which capacity he engineered the transfer to Whitefriar Street, built its church, and endowed it with the statue of Our Lady which he had discovered.

Here one can only list the many philanthropic works undertaken by Spratt on behalf of the desperately impoverished Catholics of Dublin. From 1834, until his death he acted as honorary secretary of the Sick and Indigent Room Keepers Society, devoting much time to this activity. Charitable institutions due to him were a Magdalen Asylum and St. Joseph's Night Refuge. In 1856, he founded the Catholic Young Men's Society, which offered instructive lectures by qualified speakers. Perhaps he is best remembered as a temperance crusader. He converted the chapel in Cuffe Lane into a temperance hall. He was signing a deed for the purchase of a refuge for poor women and children, when he died, Whit Sunday, May 27, 1871.

Thomas Albert Bennett, 1801-1897

Another eminent figure of the time, active especially in the field of education, was Thomas Albert Bennett, "possibly the ablest member of the Irish province in the nineteenth century" (Peter O'Dwyer). Born in Arles, Co. Leix, Bennett lived as a young man with his uncle, a goldsmith in Dame Street, Dublin. After profession and ordination, he was sent to Louvain and obtained the bachelor's degree, 1841. On his return to the province, he was assigned to Whitefriar Street. Through his fellow Carmelite, John Colgan, secretary of the newly-founded All Hallows College, Bennett was engaged to teach scripture and church history. In 1861, he became president of the college. Through his association with All Hallows, he made many friends of eminent standing among the clergy, not the least of them Cardinal Paul Cullen, who is said to have had him as his theologian at the Synod of Thurles (1850). As a result of the appeal of this synod to religious to undertake primary and secondary education, Carmelite convents featured a secondary school.

In 1852, Pope Pius IX appointed Bennett provincial, and in 1855, he was confirmed in office for another *triennium*. That same year, the vicar general, Jerome Priori, granted him the doctorate.

As provincial, Bennett opened a classical and commercial school in Dominick Street (1854), which continued to exist until 1902. In 1860, Terenure College opened its doors. Enlarged in 1878 and 1894, it still flourishes today, the oldest existing educational institution of the Order.

Bennett likewise enlarged the Whitefriar Street church (thereby destroying its original symmetry) and built a new convent to include novices and students.

The formation program of the Irish province only gradually emerged from the restrictions imposed by penal laws. The profession book of the Casa Grande of Seville includes the names of a score of Irish students during the first three decades of the 19th century. Catholic Emancipation in 1829 and the suppression of the Order in Spain, favorite training ground of Irish students, created conditions favorable to developing a domestic program of formation. The annexation of the Papal States closed another avenue outside the province. The provincial chapter of 1871 decreed the establishment of a novitiate at Terenure with Michael Gilligan as novice master.

In 1843, the community of Whitefriar Street (hence practically the province) at the urging of Fr. Withers undertook the observance of the common life, possible now since Emancipation.

The Country Houses

During the 1798 Rising, the prior of Kildare was hanged by the soldiery, but a certain Mrs. Kennedy and others cut him down and revived him. A Fr. Farrell was killed in the massacre of Gibbet Rath on the Curragh. During the nineteenth century, the Carmelites conducted a flourishing school in Kildare. The present church, a pleasing example of 19th century Gothic, was built from 1884 to 1887.

In the Tithe War of 1830, Fr. O'Keefe organized resistance to the tax in the Knocktopher area. In 1843, the existing church replaced the thatched cottage which for a century had served as a place of worship. In 1851, Fr. Scally opened a school, which functioned until the end of the century.

At Kinsale, Fr. Lulem in 1837 undertook the construction of a new church, which was completed in 1850. A convent was built in 1854.

The church at Moate, due to the initiative of Fr. McDonnell, was completed in 1868. The convent was built two years later.

The provincial chapter of 1871 was an historic event: it was presided over by Angelo Savini, the first superior general ever known to have set foot on the Emerald Isle. His visit had been preceded by a long and wearisome voyage through Italy, Germany, Belgium, and England. On the continent, he and his companion, Aloysius Galli, had allowed themselves overnight stops only in Florence, Padua, Verona, Munich, and Brussels. Of Italy's formerly numerous convents, only Florence remained available for hospitality, though in Verona he admired the Order's former church. In England, he journeyed to Merthyr Tydfil, whence he crossed over to Ireland. There he went to all the houses. On his way back to Rome, he travelled over Boxmeer, at which point his diary is suspended. It was thereafter that he must have visited the new monastery at Xanten. Oddly enough, he does not seem to have visited Straubing.

An Attempt to Return to Mount Carmel

Savini's generalate, spanning the years that saw the collapse of the Order in Italy, even the alienation of the curial convent, Traspontina, was oriented toward the support of efforts to restore or implant the Order in other countries that allowed, no matter how grudgingly, the necessary freedom. No project of his was more dearly cherished or more bitterly disillusioning than his attempt to recover and restore the hermitage near the fountain of Elijah on Mount Carmel.

In his appeal to the pope, the vicar general states that the desire of the Order to recuperate the original foundation on Mount Carmel had become so urgent that he felt obliged to secure its fulfillment. His first step seems to have been to sound out the attitude of the Latin patriarch of Jerusalem, Joseph Valerga. This prelate, appointed by Pius IX in 1847, was the first Latin patriarch to take up residence in the Holy City since the Crusades. He was no doubt well acquainted with the Discalced Carmelites on Mount Carmel; a brother, Charles Hyacinth of St. Elias, vicar apostolic of Quilon, and a sister, Seraphina Teresa, a nun in the monastery of Parma, were members of their Order. Savini may have made Valerga's acquaintance at the Vatican Council; the patriarch, in any case, visited the convent of the Order in Albano.

In his reply of July 17, 1872, Valerga stated that he not only had no objection to Savini's plan but wished it every success. He reminded the vicar general, however, of the need to obtain the permission of the Holy See, which in turn would probably consult the Discalced Carmelites already settled on Carmel. He urged Savini to come to some understanding with the preposite general.

In fact, the Congregation of the Propagation of the Faith turned over Savini's request, seemingly made in November, 1872, to the Discalced Carmelites. Their preposite general, Luke of St. John of the Cross, replied on December 9, firmly rejecting the proposal and adducing as his reasons the bull of Urban VIII, 1633, which forbade any other Order to make a foundation on Mount Carmel, and the fact that the Discalced in the person of Prosper of the Holy Spirit had purchased the property from Emir Trarabeo. Finally, Fr. Luke declared that it would be impossible to keep peace between the two neighboring communities, who indeed professed the same rule but with notable differences. The audience of the Propaganda held on April 28, 1873, resulted in the decision, "not expedient" (*non expedit*).

Before this crushing defeat, Savini had written to Patriarch Vincent Bracco, successor to Valerga, who meanwhile had died, asking whether it were true that the latter had placed as a condition to his consent that of the Discalced. The patriarch assured Savini that his predecessor had made no such condition, but had merely pointed out in common prudence that the new foundation should be financially self-supporting and enjoy peace with its neighbor on the mountain. Though written on April 18, Bracco's reply did not reach Rome until after the meeting of the Congregation. It immediately revived Savini's spirits and prompted him to pursue his cause, this time with the aid of a lawyer, Francis Cerasi.

Early in 1875, a hopeful Savini returned to the lists. Cerasi's brief before the Propaganda concentrated on proving that all canonical requirements for the foundation of a religious house were satisfied and addressed itself particularly to the objections of the Discalced preposite general. The lawyer had no difficulty in showing that Pope Urban's prohibition to found on Mount Carmel was conditional on permission of the Holy See, which was what the plaintiff was asking. As to rights over the property, the Emir had not sold the whole mountain range to Fr. Prosper but only the part occupied by the convent of the Discalced. Finally, the Carmelite brief assured the Congregation that there would be perpetual brotherly love between the two Carmelite communities. These considerations this time had their weight with their eminences. The audience of the Congregation of February 26, 1875, allowed the Carmelite vicar general to proceed with his plan. "Truly a miracle of the most holy Virgin, considering the hostility of so many persons disaffected with our Order," Savini wrote on his copy of the brief. In an audience of April 12, Pius IX received him with enthusiasm and encouraged him "in his difficult but not impossible task."

A letter from John Baptist Agnozzi, pro-secretary of the Propaganda, May 4, 1875, formally authorized the vicar general to proceed with the restoration of the hermitage near the fountain of Elijah on Mount Carmel, at the same time reminding him of Valerga's two recommendations: financial soundness of the enterprise and steps to secure the peace with the Discalced. On June 4, Agnozzi further required proof by authentic documents that Savini in fact had at hand money enough to buy the land, restore the convent, and maintain a community, specifying the sum saved for each of these purposes.

With a circular, dated October 15, 1875, and opening with the ringing words, "The time has come to gather the scattered stones of Mount Carmel," the vicar general set out to fire the generosity of all members of the Order, its affiliates and friends. He had hardly begun his campaign before he received news that the Discalced had surreptitiously purchased the desired site. This information was subsequently shown to be untrue, but not before the two superiors general had exchanged some very acerb missives.

On November 7, 1876, Savini reported to the Congregation that he had amassed 110,000 in specie for the purchase of the land and construction of the convent. Furthermore, the provinces of Malta, Galicia, Holland, Germany, Ireland, and America had pledged 1,000 *francs* annually for the support of each future member of the community on Carmel.

In May of 1878, the Congregation met to decide whether the return of the Carmelites to Mount Carmel would disturb the peace and whether the sum collected by the vicar general was sufficient for his purpose. Here the matter ended, at least according to information currently at hand. Obviously, the Congregation concluded that either one or both of the conditions of their assent had not been met.

The stones remained scattered over Carmel.

Chapter 8

Carmel Beyond the Seas

The destruction of the religious orders struck a mortal blow at the Church, which thus lost one of its arms, together with the diocesan clergy indispensable to the work of ministry and evangelization. One of the first concerns of the popes, particularly of Pius IX, was not only the restoration but also the renewal of religious life. This latter consummation, however devoutly to be desired, was difficult to bring about. The remnants of the orders, reeling from the blows dealt them, were decimated, lacking the means of leading a tranquil life and of properly educating and forming its aspirants. On the other hand, the needs of the Church, deprived of so great a portion of its clergy, were most pressing, and bishops no more than religious superiors could afford to examine very closely the qualifications of the shepherds placed in charge of the flocks.

The restoration of the Carmelite Order reflects these conditions and is marked by hasty, often ineffective expansion and perfunctory examination and training of candidates. Concern for interior growth and the charism of the Order was a luxury the crying needs of the Church did not permit. New foundations were made in places lacking the tradition of a Carmelite presence by persons who had little idea of the history and spirit of the institution. Yet these defects do not wholly mar the picture of a halcyon time of frequent journeys, danger from rivers, danger at sea, in toil and hardship, in hunger and thirst, endured by selfless men unconcerned for their greatness.

The Order in the United States of America

As prior of Straubing, Cyril Knoll adopted a policy of expansion, even though, as he must have realized, the original community had not achieved stability. He no doubt felt that the times did not permit a leisurely growth and looked to new foundations for an increase of members and economic resources. We have already noticed his settlement in Sossau and unsuccessful effort at a foundation in Pest. He had better luck in America.

Cyril Knoll (1813-1900) was born in Schellenberg, Bavaria, and was ordained for the diocese of Regensberg in 1838. A first attempt to try the Carmelite life in Straubing in 1846 lasted only two months, but a second experiment three years later proved enduring, and Knoll made his vows on July 9, 1850. In a matter of months, on March 4, 1851, he was named prior of Straubing.

Even before he was back from the short-lived venture in Pest, Knoll had plans for a new swarming from the hive of Straubing. During his absence, Leander Streber, O.F.M., pastor of St. Martin's parish in Louisville, Kentucky, had arrived in Straubing in 1858, looking for priests and religious to work in the diocese. He succeeded in recruiting three Ursuline sisters, who immediately opened a school in his parish. They also kept their friend and confessor, Cyril Knoll, informed of their progress in the new land, and when they heard that he was negotiating with the pastor, who needed an assistant, they urged him to come and be their spiritual guide. Armed with letters patent as commissary general in America, dated February 8, 1864, Knoll set out for Louisville, accompanied by Xavier Huber

(1819-1888).

Huber's role as co-founder of Carmel in America was secondary, though important. He spent most of his life outside his community, questing for funds.

Upon the Carmelites' arrival on June 8, 1864, it turned out that Streber did not need their help after all, but the bishop of Vincennes, Maurice de St. Palais, was happy to entrust to their care the church in St. Joseph's Hill, Indiana., thirteen miles north of Louisville.

St. Joseph's, however, failed to meet Knoll's idea of the cradle of Carmel in America. On the way to Louisville, Knoll and Huber had visited Abbot Boniface Wimmer of St. Vincent's, doyen of German Catholicism in America, who was keenly aware of the need of priests to serve the concentration of German nationals in the mid-West. They had also met Kilian Guenther, of the vicariate apostolic of Kansas, a student at St. Vincent's, who likewise recommended that territory as a field of labor.

The Jesuit vicar apostolic of Kansas, John Baptist Miège, welcomed the Carmelites and on October 9, 1864, two days after their arrival in Leavenworth, turned over to them the German parish of St. Joseph. Moreover, Guenther, renamed Louis, took the habit, as did Albert Heimann, pastor of the cathedral. Early in 1865, the Carmelites took charge of St. Boniface Church of the Catholic settlement on Pottawatomie Creek, later called Scipio, which in turn served a number of missions in the vicinity. When a theological student, Angelus Kempen, and a laybrother, Joseph Eschrich, took the habit, and Brother Simon Stock Edenhofer came from Straubing, the community in 1866 counted six members.

Cumberland, Maryland, 1866-1875

At this point, Knoll put into operation his dubious strategy of strengthening one foundation by starting another, though in this case it must be admitted that a house in the more populous East was desirable from every point of view. A visit to Leavenworth by Joseph Helmprecht, boyhood friend of Cyril and provincial of the Redemptorists, led to the purchase of their convent in Cumberland, Maryland. The commissary general and Brother Simon arrived there on September 21, 1866. Huber and Guenther were to follow. In Leavenworth, Knoll left Albert Heimann and Brother Joseph Eschrich; in Scipio, Angelus Kempen.

The Redemptorist convent, to which was attached the German parish of Sts. Peter and Paul, was extensive and designed as a novitiate. Faced with a lack of priests (who were also a source of income), Knoll set about immediately to fill his novitiate. His requirements for acceptance were modest, or rather non-existent, and he netted mostly burnt offerings, leftovers from other orders and fugitives from irate bishops, who soon departed, not always without a trail of scandal. Candidates moved in and out of Knoll's novitiate like figures on a mechanical clock; nevertheless, over the years, Cumberland produced its share of exemplary religious like Elias Meyer, Bernard Fink, Anselm Duell, Anastasius Kreidt, and Alphonse Brandstaetter.

The Kentucky Commissariate, 1874-1881

The care of the missions attached to Cumberland required English speaking priests. Savini again answered the need. On September 19, 1867, two young Irish priests, who had recently completed their studies in Rome, Peter Thomas Meagher and Theodoric McDonald, arrived in Cumberland. From England, the vicar general provided Anastasius Smits and Brother Berthold Landers, Dutchmen, who arrived on July 15, 1868. This international mixture proved highly explosive, and once again the exiguous forces of the Order were dissipated. To Smits, for one, educated as he had been in the severe observance of the Netherlands, Knoll's version of the Carmelite charism was a scandal. He and Brother Berthold ended up in New Jersey, where on February 1, 1869, the parish in Fort Lee was given into his charge.

About the same time, Meagher and McDonald, nominally still subject to Knoll, took over the parish of Upper Marlboro, MD., to which were attached several missions and the spiritual care of the newly emancipated blacks. Foundations followed in Paducah, KY (1870), and Louisville, KY (1873). For these houses, Savini eventually sent a group of Irish youths he had brought from the Carmelite college in Knocktopher to be educated in Rome: Angelus Forristal, the Murphy brothers (Brocard and Albert), the Walsh brothers (Frank and Joseph), and Cyril Feehan. The Commissariate of Kentucky was erected on September 8, 1874, with Peter Thomas Meagher as commissary.

The Separate Jurisdiction of Kansas, 1869-1878

The two Kansas houses considered themselves ill-used by Father Knoll, who had not only deserted them but constantly called upon them for men and money. On May 23, 1869, Savini took the Kansas houses under his direct jurisdiction with Albert Heimann as superior. Kansas affairs immediately began to look up. Heimann built the imposing neo-Gothic church of St. Joseph in Leavenworth (1871). In Scipio, he acquired land for a farm to support the community, built a stone church and convent, and opened a school for boys. Disaster struck in 1874 with the failure of crops and nationwide economic depression. Heimann took a leaf from Knoll's book and opened a foundation in the East at Niagara Falls, Ontario (1875). This foundation prospered and eased the financial strain on Kansas. Much credit accrues to Pius Mayer, admitted to the habit in Scipio in 1875 and sent to Niagara immediately after profession.

The American Commissariate Reunited, 1881-1890

Meanwhile, Knoll was showing unmistakable symptoms of his old malady of wanderlust. In 1873, he accepted the care of St. Peter's parish in Butler, PA. He had no sooner liquidated the debt owing the Redemptorists, when typically without consulting anyone, least of all the prior general, he sold Cumberland to the Capuchins, seeking refuge from the *Kulturkampf*, and moved to Holy Trinity parish in Pittsburgh (1875). After the general indignation had died down, the move, which finally gave the Order a foundation in a large city, was seen to be wise.

In 1878, Knoll and Heimann agreed to unite their jurisdictions. Three years later, Knoll resigned as commissary of the German houses. His reason for doing this is not clear, unless it be that the old battler was weary at last. His decision opened the way for uniting all the American houses under one hand. This Savini did on September 24, 1881.

For commissary, to the surprise and dismay of many, the vicar general chose Anastasius Smits, whose existence was virtually unnoticed. After his flight from

Cumberland, Smits had been ordered by Savini to report to Straubing. This he promised to do in a few months, as soon as he could pay a few debts. Instead, he applied for secularization, but seems to have been refused. Thereafter, he abandoned all contact with the Order, of which he professed to be ashamed, until 1874, when he made his peace with Savini. The latter's orders to proceed to Cumberland again fell on deaf ears. It is a measure of Knoll's disinterestedness that when Savini contemplated uniting the English-speaking houses, he should suggest as commissary the man who despised him. This solution was actually adopted on January 8, 1881.

Cyril Knoll spent the last eighteen years of his life in retirement in Scipio. The diminutive Father of Carmel in America (he was only five feet tall) had gone about his task the hard way. He tried to expand the Order too rapidly, with the result that he was chronically short of men and money. To supply both these critical needs, he did not inquire very closely into the qualifications of candidates to the Order. His communities remained spiritually immature. Knoll lacked the gift of leadership, was hasty in his judgments, and neither sought nor accepted advice. Yet he himself was a man of unimpeachable morals, on fire with zeal for the Order and the Church. Perpetually in search of money, he sought no gain for himself. He performed the labors of Hercules and suffered grinding poverty without complaint.

Smits's administration was as different from Knoll's as were the two men. He placed the novitiate in Niagara Falls, or rather confirmed it in that role. He relinquished Paducah in 1881; Louisville and Upper Marlboro had already been abandoned in 1875. But his main concern was to improve, or rather introduce religious observance. His efforts, however, met with little success, for apart from the fact that he had some hard nuts to crack, he was too severe and unbending. He was one of those people who affects to be scandalized at the human reality of religious life; moreover, he had the unpleasant habit of gossiping with bishops about the sins of the brethren.

Savini must have realized that Smits was not the one to carry forward Carmel in America. In 1886, he replaced him with Pius Mayer, a man for whom Smits also had little regard. The gifted and energetic future prior general, in fact, led the commissariate into quieter waters. He enlarged the convent of New Baltimore and placed there the novitiate and well-staffed house of studies. Pittsburgh became the provincial house and focus of importance. Periodical meetings of priors were held, decisions were made in concert. Knoll's motley collection of far-flung houses began to look like a province.

When the American province was constituted on February 20, 1890, Mayer became the first provincial. The definitors appointed by Rome were Cyril Knoll, Albert Heimann, Leo van der Heuvel, and Dominic O'Malley. The convents that remained after the tumult and the shouting had died were Scipio, Pittsburgh, Niagara Falls, Englewood, Leavenworth, and New Baltimore, with 28 priests, 14 brothers, and 2 clerics.

If the American province survived its hectic beginnings, it is due in no small measure to Angelo Savini, who, while his own house was coming down about his ears, kept a sharp eye on events beyond the seas, made peace among his quarrelsome sons, gathered indispensable recruits from his badly battered Order, promptly granted requested authorizations, and provided the jurisdictional structures required for each stage of the province's growth.

The Commissariate of the South

Another group distinct from the American province was the Commissariate of the South, located in Texas and Louisiana. It was not only distinct but antagonistic. Its history is at once splendid and inglorious. The reunion of all American houses into one commissariate in 1881 roused little enthusiasm in the Scipio community, especially since a member of the "Irish" region had been placed in charge. The German houses wanted to retain their ethnic identity. Scipio, moreover, was in a phase of expansion, and its members looked forward to a promising future. They were outraged at Smits's plan of closing their novitiate in favor of a single novitiate at Niagara and of syphoning off their hard-earned savings on behalf of the general needs of the commissariate.

Backbone of the resistance in Scipio were the three Peters brothers, Anastasius, Boniface, and Hubert. Born in Breberen near Aachen, all three had successively entered the Order in Boxmeer, and after having been briefly stationed in Straubing, had emigrated to America and to Scipio. Anastasius had been previously assigned to New Baltimore, Butler, and Beaver Falls in Pennsylvania, where according to Smits he had worn out his welcome by scandalous behavior. In Scipio, Anastasius acted as prior, Boniface as novice master. A nephew, Berthold Ohlenforst, set for the fall of many in Israel, was in the novitiate during the year, 1881/1882. Two other nephews, Angelus and Basil, subsequently followed their uncles into the Order.

A protest from the Germans to Savini at Smits's appointment included the names of the Peters brothers, Elias Meyer, Alphonsus Brandstaeter, Norbert Bausch, Anselm Duell, and Bernard Fink. Cyril Knoll, Louis Guenther, and John Verheyen, prior of Pittsburgh, also added their assent.

Smits did nothing to mollify their aggrieved feelings, reasonable or not; in fact, he exacerbated them. During a visitation of Scipio, he deposed the prior, Anastasius Peters, whom he accused of scandalous conduct and ordered back to Europe. Hubert transferred to the Capuchins; Anastasius's reaction was more drastic. If he could not remain a German in the American commissariate, he would found a community in which he could. One night in mid-August of 1882, accompanied by Brother Anton Keber and two novices, Albert Wagner and Andrew Führwerk, he secretly left Scipio, taking with him necessary supplies and (it was later alleged) part of the community funds.

Marienfeld, Texas

Anastasius's venture was by no means haphazard. He was joining a Scipio resident, Adam Konz, who was emigrating to West Texas on land offered for settlement by the Texas and Pacific Railroad. The group descended from the coaches at Grelton Station, midway between Fort Worth and El Paso, as far as the tracks were laid. With two tents to serve as convent and chapel, Anastasius offered the first Mass on August 27, 1882. A frame church and convent, dedicated respectively to St. Joseph and the Most Pure Heart of Mary, were soon erected and in turn replaced by an adobe and frame convent (1884) and a stone church (1888). A school for boys was begun in 1883. The Daughters of Divine Providence came from San Antonio to take charge of the school for girls (1886).

Catholic families arrived, and the town grew and prospered. In its growth and

606   *Part V: The Modern Period, 1750-1950*

development Anastasius played a prominent role. Shortly upon arrival, he had the settlement's name changed to Marienfeld.

The Carmelite community also grew. In October of 1882, Boniface had arrived with his nephew and novice Berthold Ohlenforst. Other candidates presented themselves, and by the summer of 1885 the community numbered 4 priests, 3 professed clerics, and 4 brothers. The following year, Boniface travelled to Germany in search of money and volunteers. Chanceries had been duly informed by American and German Carmelites about the surreptitious origin of Marienfeld. Nevertheless, Boniface's expedition proved a success; he returned with a satisfactory sum of money and, more important still, with seventeen candidates.

Meantime, the canonical status of the Texas Carmelites had been regularized. The bishop of San Antonio, John Neraz, sorely in need of priests, interceded on their behalf, and on April 18, 1885, Angelo Savini, overriding Smits's furious protests, officially recognized the foundation and confirmed Anastasius and Boniface in their respective offices of prior and novice master.

If no one else, Bishop Neraz valued the hard-working Marienfeld community for its dedication to the spiritual needs of the settlements scattered over a vast area of Texas and New Mexico. The conveyance of the missionaries here was the iron horse. Over a distance of more than two hundred miles along the Texas and Pacific Railroad, the Carmelites regularly visited Big Spring, Colorado City, Pecos, Toyah, Midland, Odessa, Barston, Jatan, and Van Horn. During the Carmelites' ministry, churches were built at Big Spring, Pecos, Toyah, and Midland.

Branching northwards at Pecos, the Pecos Valley Railroad brought the missionaries to Eddy, Malaga, Red Bluff, Loving, Roswell, and Weed in southeast New Mexico. Simon Weeg completed the Church of St. Edward the Confessor at Eddy, renamed Carlsbad in 1899, where the famous caverns were subsequently discovered.

Thirty miles south of Toyah, the Carmelites visited farming communities along Toyah Creek at La Meta, Santa Isabel, Saragosa, Lindio, Brogado, Ojo, and Victoria.

Most of these settlements were remote and primitive - even, as in the case of Pecos and Toyah, lawless, which it would have taken a Wyatt Earp to tame. The congregations were mainly Irish, German, and Mexican, too poor to support the missionaries, who depended for their needs on German mission societies and other benefactors. Among the missionaries in this area, Albert Wagner and Simon Weeg deserve special mention.

But tragic hours awaited the Marienfeld community. In 1886, drought and sandstorms - the dreaded scourge of West Texas - descended on the farms and would not go away. Many farmers abandoned the area, and the town lost its Catholic aura. But drought is an act of God; the trial that man laid on the community was crueller yet.

On October 11, 1889, a sensational news report released nationwide told of an alleged murder of a student by the priests of the Marienfeld convent. Behind the accusation made by a former student, Gerard Mayer, lay the fact that Francis Esser, who had been waiting for a dispensation from his vows, on August 23 had hanged himself in his room. Andrew Führwerk, in charge during the absence of the prior, Anastasius Peters, reported the tragedy to Adam Konz, justice of the peace, and asked that the matter be kept secret to avoid scandal. Konz made out the necessary papers, and the body was quietly laid to rest the following day.

The scandal that might have arisen over the suicide was nothing compared to that which now ensued. Consequent on Gerard Mayer's allegations, Konz and Führwerk were arrested in September, 1889. Tried on October 8, they were found innocent. Führwerk received permission to withdraw to Castroville as chaplain of the Sisters of Divine Providence. But the anti-Catholic sentiment in the town was not appeased. A group of bigots broke into the church, removed the statue of St. Joseph, and burned it in the town square. The atmosphere continued so heated that Konz and Führwerk were recalled to Marienfeld to stand trial before a superior judge. On February 14, 1890, the new trial began before a grand jury. The members of the convent, called upon to testify individually, unanimously declared the innocence of the accused. When his turn came, Mayer withdrew his accusation. The whole absurd affair cost the Carmelites $500 and their good name. Shattered by the experience, poor Führwerk sought a dispensation and was incardinated in the San Antonio diocese, where he labored as an exemplary priest until his death in 1916.

In 1890, the Protestant majority of the town managed to have the name of the town changed to Stanton.

The iniquitous newspaper account did not fail to make its way to Rome, due no doubt to the solicitude of certain implacable members of the American province. This thunderbolt, together with complaints about Anastasius Peters' excessive drinking, led the new prior general, Aloysius Galli, to entrust Pius Mayer with the visitation of the Southern Carmelites. Mayer reported favorably on the religious spirit of these Carmelites living in extreme poverty. Vows had to be sanated, because profession had hitherto been made in the name of Anastasius Peters, who had cavalierly appropriated to himself the role of prior general. The visitator ended by recommending the institution of a commissariate of the South. Anastasius' drinking could not have been that abusive, for Mayer presented him for commissary. These arrangements were ratified by Galli on June 16, 1890.

Carmel, Louisiana

A commissariate was a possibility because a second foundation had meanwhile been made. The unrelenting Texas drought had driven the Carmelites to the aqueous confines of neighboring Louisiana.

On April 19, 1888, Anthony Durier, bishop of Natchitoches, entrusted the Carmelites with the parish of Bayou Pierre and its missions. Berthold Ohlenforst was named the first pastor. Early in 1889, the first Carmelites appeared; by June, the community comprised ten members. A two-story convent of logs, stone and mud was erected, and land for farming was cleared. The regular life with daily conventual Mass and Matins at midnight was initiated. After the establishment of the commissariate, it was decided to transfer the novices and students to Bayou Pierre, and for this purpose the convent was enlarged. Boniface performed his usual role of novice master and lecturer. By July of 1891, twenty-six friars were living in the convent of St. Joseph. Nevertheless, the climate of this swampy region was unhealthy, and the community was no stranger to sickness and death.

Anastasius took over the care of the post office and here, too, changed the name of the town, calling it Carmel, this time with permanent results. He established a school for boys, as well as one for girls in the care of a community of women, whom he invested in the Third Order habit.

De Soto parish was the territory assigned to the Carmelites. It included missions in Bayou Dole, Oxford, Mansfield, Spanish Town, Grandcane, Prairie River, Kingston, Bayou Walter, Bayou Gloster, Côte d'Afrique, and De Point. Later, stations were opened at Grevelpoint, Bayou Bourbeaux, Clarence, Stonewall, Rosalina, and Gloster. About 1,500 Catholics, most of them Creoles and blacks, lived in these settlements scattered over an area of thirty miles. The missionaries visited them on horseback.

An interesting aspect of the Carmelites' activity in De Soto parish was their apostolate among the blacks. For their use, a small stone chapel was built at Carmel. Dedicated to the Immaculate Conception and today popularly known as the "Rock Chapel," it was decorated with paintings by Marianus Nyssen and Angelus Ohlenforst. Similar chapels were built at Rambin, Bayou Gloster, and Bayou Walter. In the latter place and at Carmel, schools for blacks were opened. In support of this apostolate, the missionaries published a periodical, *Das Marienkind*. The education of the blacks was not gratifying to certain elements in the white population and contributed to the ill feeling against the Carmelites in their coming hour of trial.

Fort Davis, Texas

In 1892, at the request of Bishop Neraz, the Marienfeld community accepted another mission territory running south to the Mexican border, a vast area of about 17,000 sq. mi., comprising the Big Bend of the Rio Grande River. In the fall of that year, Albert Wagner and Brocard Ecken took over the partially built church and rectory in Fort Davis, which was to be their headquarters. In time, they were joined by Telesphorus Hardt, Elisha Rick, Angelus Ohlenforst, Frank Maas, and Brother Angelus Augustine Maurer.

The mission circuit from Fort Davis was an arduous one, accomplished in a rig drawn by mules with a Mexican driver at the reins. The entire tour of the mission stations took about three or four weeks. The missionaries travelled some 500 mi. to minister to about 800 families, most of them Mexican. At the end of each tour, the missionaries rested a few weeks in Fort Davis.

Fort Stockton had already been visited from the Toya Creek missions, 57 miles to the west. Brocard Ecken literally helped the Mexican community rebuild its church, working as a carpenter for six weeks. From this place, Hermosa was attended.

Alpine, Marathon, Marfa, and Valentine lay along the Texas and New Orleans Railroad. None of these settlements had churches, Mass being offered in homes. Marathon was the point of departure for three remote missions, the road leading 105 miles through the mountains south to the Rio Grande. At Boracho Rancho, the priest served cattlemen; at Boquillas, miners. San Vicente on the Rio Grande boasted a church for the Mexicans.

The tour to Presidio and its stations was the longest and, starting south from Marfa, took three or four weeks. After ministering to farmers at San Esteban, the missionary visited ranches at Alamito, Casa Piedra, and Alamito Rancho. Pulvo and Lajitas were towns, the former with a chapel. From Lajitas, the priest moved into the Chisos Mountains to seek out the miners at Terlinqua Abaja, Terlinqua, Study Butte, and Chisos. In these places, the priest at times felt called upon to protest the unfair working conditions of the miners. At Castalon, a town on the Rio Grande, there were only ten Mexican families. Proceeding up the river, the missionary came to Presidio, where the church lacked a roof, so he offered Mass in the rectory. At Rancho de los Indios, Rancho de la Cruz, San José, Ruidosa, Candelaria, and Favor Ranch the congregations consisted of farmers and ranch workers. In some of these places, chapels were available for worship. Shafter, the last stop of the tour, was a violent mining town, where about 150 Mexican Catholics were to be found.

The Carmelites of the Commissariate of the South may truly be said to have carried out the Messianic function of bringing the gospel to the poor. Unfortunately, the meritorious work of the commissariate has been swallowed up by its sensational end.

The End of the Commissariate of the South

In August of 1889, contemporary to the scandal of Marienfeld, another occurred in Louisiana, which oddly did not create a sensation. There shame was brought on the community by one of its own members.

The Peters brothers' nephew, Berthold Ohlenforst, absconded with the wife of the Catholic community's leading citizen, Simon Lafitte. The dishonorable deed had been forgiven and all but forgotten, when four years later the prodigal son returned. His uncles not only readmitted him to the community but after a token penance placed him in charge of the black apostolate. The reaction of the community, lay and religious, was predictably that of the elder son. Latent discontent with the Peters-Ohlenforst dynasty found a focus. Complaints were made to the prior general, not only about Berthold's blatant reinstatement, but about mismanagement of finances, and Anastasius' frequent intoxication. Students had been kept against their will and forced to take Orders. Certain laymen complained to the bishop that the Carmelites, especially Anastasius, frequented saloons.

Berthold was sent to Fort Davis, and the storm might have blown over, but unfortunately appeal had also been made to the Holy See, which as a matter of course demanded clarification of the prior general. Unsatisfied with his reply, the Congregation for the Propagation of the Faith on December 22, 1894, ordered an apostolic visitation. Bishop Durier, appointed to carry it out, among other measures replaced Anastasius Peters by Albert Wagner, forbade frequenting saloons, and ordered the Third Order sisters to be affiliated with the Order or disbanded. (The sisters were subsequently disbanded.)

The arrangements for the improvement of the commissariate rang the knell of its demise. Anastasius, whatever his faults, was in fact the only one able to head the commissariate. Wagner could not cope with the split allegiance which now developed and which Anastasius, in fact, fomented. He took over the new foundation in Thurber, TX (1895), and ignored Wagner's authority. Even after Anastasius' departure for Europe, whither he had been preceded by Boniface, the membership of the commissariate continued to dwindle, until only eleven priests were left. At this point the Propaganda, on June 8, 1896, dissolved the Commissariate of the South. Of its remaining members, some were incorporated in the American province, where they met with a cold welcome, some chose to remain in the missions as diocesan priests.

Thus, by a combination of bad judgment, bad will, and human weakness on the part of a few came to an end an impressive missionary effort, which might have developed into a flourishing province and immeasurably enriched the Carmelite presence in America. In the marble halls of the Vatican, the Carmelite life-style in the Wild West occasioned excessive alarm. The allegedly scandalous lives of the Southern Carmelites would have been less widely known, and hence less scandalous, were it not for the righteous blathering of members of the American province.

But when all is said and done, the worst enemy of the commissariate was the one on whom it depended for its existence. Anastasius Peters was ahead of his time in his dedication to the need of the moment and disregard for proper procedure. A man of demonic but undisciplined energies, like a gunman of the West, he was at last disarmed and rendered ineffectual by the law he had elected to ignore.

The Mission to the Choctaw Indians, 1899-1904

The German Carmelites were immediately replaced in the Southwest by others, this time from the Netherlands.

In 1898, the Rev. Bartholomew J. Bekkers appeared in the Netherlands looking for a religious order to take over the mission he had established fifteen years previously among the Choctaw Indians of Mississippi. The central mission was located at Tucker and boasted a church, a school, a rectory, and a convent for the three Sisters of Mercy who taught in the school.

The Carmelites responded favorably to his appeal. The provincial, Joseph Kersten, on February 18, 1899, signed a contract with Thomas Heslin, bishop of Natchez, and selected volunteers. On March 20, Augustine Breek (superior), Herman Joseph Hamers, Leopold Wijsbeck, Brothers Alexander Donkers and Lebuinus Klunder arrived at Tucker. (The name must have occasioned considerable mirth among Carmelites who originated in Twente; *tukker* was the nickname of persons coming from Twente.)

The missionaries were appalled at the primitive condition of the buildings and the poverty and ignorance of the Indians who lived scattered about in the woods, after having been driven from their land by the whites. Food was monotonous and poor, the heat unbearable.

Nevertheless, the friars went to work courageously. Brother Lebuinus developed the garden and farm. Alexander, a skilled carpenter, was responsible for improving the buildings. After enlarging the existing structures, he eventually built a two-story convent (1901) and a new church (1903). In 1900, the community received a cook in the person of Brother Jacob Spruit, thereby relieving the sisters of this task.

The mission extended over six counties of Eastern Mississippi and included white communities at Damascus, Holy Cross, Louisville, and Ackerman. The Indians were mainly concentrated around Tucker and in Scott County, about thirty miles to the southwest. The missionaries travelled on horseback or by buggy over poor roads, impassable in the rainy season. The Indians would arrive in family groups on Saturday, attend Sunday High Mass, visit, dance, and play ball until evening benediction, after which they set out for their homes. They were poorly instructed and considered it better to receive than to give. The missionaries, struggling with the Choctaw language, insisted on adequate instruction before baptism and tried to interest the Indians in supporting their church. The latter showed little interest in settling on the land the diocese had acquired for this purpose and preferred living in the woods. There the missionaries penetrated to visit the sick. Progress in conversion was slow but perceptible, and the bishop was satisfied with the work accomplished. Breek and Hamers took care of the mission. Wijsbeck was mostly used by the bishop to supply in parishes where there was need.

Communication with the province was difficult, and the provincial, Lambert Smeets, and his definitory, elected in 1900, showed less interest in and understanding of the mission, insisting that no detail of religious observance be omitted, even to the constant wearing of the habit. Breek urged the expansion of the mission beyond Mississippi to white parishes, which could help support the Indian interest. To the prior general, he suggested creating a commissariate under a superior authorized to make independent decisions.

Breek's proposal regarding expansion was accepted, and a foundation was made in New Athens, Illinois, in the diocese of Belleville. In November, 1901, Macarius Walterbosch and Brother Pancratius Helmich arrived from the Netherlands to take over the German parish in New Athens, IL. Smeets soon transferred Wijsbeck from Tucker. The parish, saddled with a debt for a new school, failed to be a source of economic assistance to the Indian mission.

Antler, Indian Territory

At this point, the American government decided to move the Mississippi Indians into Indian territory, an area roughly corresponding to the present State of Oklahoma. Ecclesiastically, the territory was a vicariate apostolic (1891) under Bishop Theophile Meerschaert. The Tucker Carmelites were willing to follow the Choctaws to their new home in Antler, I. T., but the provincial chapter of the Netherlands of 1903 determined to abandon the mission and suggested to the prior general, Pius Mayer, that any missionaries who wished to remain at their post be joined to the American province or to the New York Carmelites. The chapter of the American province, meeting under Mayer's presidency the same year, expressed willingness to adopt the Dutch mission.

Late in 1903 Augustine Breek, Herman Joseph Hamers, Lebuinus Klunder, and Jacob Spruit left Tucker for Antler, a town of 2,000 inhabitants, mostly whites and blacks. There, the Carmelites had a church, rectory, and school for Indians. Mission centers to serve the Choctaws and Chickasaws were situated at Ardmore, Durant, McAlester, and Poteau, a territory of 12,000 sq. mi. to be covered on horseback. At the centers, the missionaries were expected to gather the Indians in churches for whites, already administered by diocesan clergy, without disturbing the services. As Bishop Meerschaert had warned, no money was available for the Indian mission. This lack and the great distances to be covered led Breek, in August of 1904, to recommend to the American provincial, Ambrose Bruder, the closing of the Indian mission, a step Bruder took in December.

During their short-lived missionary effort, the Carmelites worked unselfishly and effectively to preserve in the faith the Catholic tribes of the Choctaws and Chickasaws in a hostile Protestant environment. Their failure was not due to lack of good will and self-sacrificing labor.

Carmel in New York, 1889

A number of Irish Carmelites, dispatched by the prior general, had contributed to the founding of the American province. Now the Irish province undertook to establish its own foundations in the United States of America. Its apostolate was not among the Mexicans of the Southwest nor among the Indians of Mississippi but among the Irish emigrants of New York City.

Monsignor James McMahon, pastor of St. Andrew's Church and benefactor of the Catholic University of America, after whom a hall was named, offered the Irish Carmelites a generous sum of money for a church to be built on a site specified by him. The offer was made to Michael A. Moore, who happened to be in New York at the time. McMahon was a lifelong devotee of Carmel. Archbishop Michael Corrigan upon advisement rejected McMahon's site and instead proposed to the Carmelites a slice of St. Stephen's parish with the care of Bellevue Hospital. After prolonged and complicated negotiations, involving the denunciation of the archbishop to the Congregation for the Propagation of the Faith, the Carmelites decided that it was the better part of valor to accept the archbishop's proposal and renounce McMahon's gift, relying on the generosity of the poor to finance the projected parish.

In 1889, the provincial, John Bartley, led a group consisting of Edward Southwell, Michael Daly, and Philip McDonnell to New York to initiate the foundation. The church was built and ready for use within the same year. When Bartley returned to Ireland, he left Southwell as vicar prior, Daly as pastor, and McDonnell as treasurer. They were joined by Thomas Feehan and John Whitley, Irish Carmelites on loan to the American commissariate.

Within the century, in 1897, a second foundation was made at Tarrytown, NY. Both houses remained subject to the province of Ireland.

The Carmelites' service over the years to the poor and sick in Bellevue Hospital can only be termed heroic and is one of the bright pages of the Order's history in the United States.

Carmel in Australia, 1881

The American foundations of the Irish province had been preceded by others in the farthest corners of the earth.

In 1881, at the invitation of the bishop of Adelaide, the Carmelites settled in Gawler, about twenty-five miles north of Adelaide. The original community consisted of Joseph Butler (prior), Brocard Leybourne, Ignatius Carr, Patrick Shaffrey, and Hilarion Byrne. The parish covered 700 miles and included ten towns, four of which had churches.

Joseph Butler particularly was an accomplished orator and was much in demand for lectures, missions, and retreats. His mission tours together with Patrick Shaffrey led to a second foundation in 1882 at Sandridge parish, Victoria, an area that included centers which became Port Melbourne and Middle Park. In the former place, there was a church, St. Joseph's; in Middle Park, a church was completed in 1891. When these two places became parishes, the Carmelites in 1909 moved from their original convent, completed in 1886, to separate priories in each place. In 1902, Gawler was abandoned in favor of Port Adelaide, a less extensive but more populous parish. Everywhere schools were founded or developed.

The Irish province regularly sent able and dedicated missionaries, among whom – besides Joseph Butler – Robert Power, Thomas Kelly, Joseph Kindelan, John Scanlon, Elias Magennis, and John Cogan may be singled out for special mention.

The Revival of the Order in Brazil, 1894

Evidently, by the end of the nineteenth century the Order was capable of organized and sustained efforts at expansion. While the Germans and the Irish set out for fabled lands as yet untrodden by Carmelite feet, the Spaniards turned to their America and the provinces founded centuries ago by their sister province of Portugal.

Already in 1886, the vicar provincial, Albert of St. Augusta Cabral de Vasconcelos, writing from Recife, begged Savini to send religious to restore the Pernambuco province. The surviving friars of the province, he stated, were all in one convent (Recife). The other four houses were in the hands of secular priests. These were old and infirm, and some of the younger ones did not have a good reputation. Savini managed to scrape together an international brigade in the persons of Angelus Mallia, Andrew Montebello, and Joseph Gregory Geoghegan. However, this first attempt to restore Carmel in Brazil was unsuccessful; early in 1889, Cabral and the newcomers parted company amid mutual recriminations.

With the election of a new prior general, Cabral in 1894 renewed his insistent appeals for reinforcements. By this date, a more serious and sustained effort could be made; the Spanish province was on the road to recovery and was able to respond to the need. On July 7, 1894, a group of four priests and two brothers set out for Recife: Joachim Guarch (commissary general), Elisha Gómez, Cyril Font, Marianus Gordon, and two brothers: Angelus Irigoyen and Elisha Gómez.

In 1895, a second group of two priests, three clerics, and two brothers was dispatched from Spain. The same year, the council of the Order authorized the provincial of Spain to name a vicar provincial for Brazil. It also appointed Cyril Font commissary general. In practice, the two offices were combined into one.

The Spaniards undertook to restore not only the Pernambuco province but the Order in Brazil generally. Cabral's urgency was not shared with equal warmth in Rio de Janeiro and Bahia. The few surviving Brazilian friars in these places refused to recognize the commissary general and to subject themselves to the Spanish province. Moreover, they would not turn over the Order's property to the Spaniards, nor was this permitted by law. The Brazilians were loath to correct their free and easy ways and to submit to religious discipline. Under these circumstances, the Spaniards found the restoration of Brazilian Carmel a discouraging task.

Actually, Leo XIII had previously, on September 3, 1891, placed the religious of Brazil under the jurisdiction of the bishops. These, in turn, delegated their faculties to an episcopal "visitator." Into this situation, a commissary appointed by the prior general in Rome fitted like a square peg in a round hole. With time, things sorted themselves out, but at first, conflicts could not be entirely avoided.

In letters to Rome, dated August 23, and October 22, 1900, the provincial, Elisha Durán, reported on the situation in Brazil. Of the vicariate of Maranhão nothing remained. The Pernambuco province counted three convents and one hospice. In Recife, there were five Spanish friars. Two years after the arrival of the newcomers in 1894, the two Brazilians at hand had died, leaving the former in command of the situation. Of the Bahia province, there existed only the convent of Bahia with two Spaniards and the Brazilian, Innocent of Mount Carmel Sena. Another Brazilian priest was living outside the convent in concubinage. The Rio de Janeiro province counted six houses, two of them, Rio and Angra dos Reis, inhabited. São Paulo and Santos could be renovated without great expense. In Rio, there were seven Spaniards; in Angra, two Spaniards and the Brazilian, Ignatius of the Conception Silva, who boasted the title of provincial. The other Brazilian in the province, Anthony Muniz, lived outside the convent and in the public press carried on guerrilla warfare with ecclesiastical authorities and his Spanish confreres.

Originally, there had been in Rio Fathers Frubão and Manuel da Ascensão Franco, the administrator of the convent's vast patrimony. When Frubão died in 1896, Marian Gordon and Carmel Pastor took up residence. Upon Manuel's death in 1899, the archbishop appointed a lay administrator of the convent's possessions. At the request of the internunzio, six friars were dispatched to Angra dos Reis, destined to be a novitiate. The Spanish had little faith in the feasibility of a novitiate in Brazil. Novices were few (in seven years, Recife had received only one) and there was little chance of their being properly initiated into religious life. Durán preferred establishing a missionary college for Brazil in Spain.

The general chapter of 1902 instructed the procurator general to obtain from the Holy See a mandate assigning the possessions of the Order in Brazil to the Spanish province, an arrangement which had little likelihood of success.

Chapter 9

Carmelites at the First Vatican Council

The opening session of the First Vatican Council took place on a rainy December 8, 1869. "Such an assembly of prelates," William Ullathorne, Benedictine bishop of Birmingham, wrote the following day, "whether you consider numbers, or the character of their training and breadth of experience, was never witnessed in this world before." At hand from every corner of the globe were 48 cardinals, 9 patriarchs, 7 primates, 117 archbishops, 479 bishops, 14 abbots, and 25 superiors of orders and congregations - in all, 699 council fathers. Lost in the sea of silver copes and white mitres were three of the four bishops the Carmelite Order boasted at the time, and its vicar general.

The Carmelite Bishops at the Council

The council fathers were seated according to rank and, in the case of those endowed with episcopal orders, by the date of their promotion. Eldest of the Carmelite bishops was Elias Anthony Alberani (1812-1876), promoted to the see of Montefeltro on June 16, 1856. He was born in Fusignano (Ravenna), his mother, Domenica Monti, being the niece of the poet, Vincenzo Monti. He entered the Order in Ascoli Piceno, where he was professed in 1822. Ordination to the priesthood followed, and degrees in theology and canon law. In the Order, he served as provincial of Romagna, assistant general, and procurator general.

As bishop of Imola, Pius IX had come to know and esteem the Carmelite friar and insisted on personally consecrating him bishop in the chapel of the Quirinale. In 1860, Alberani was transferred to the see of Ascoli. It was the year Garibaldi landed in Sicily. "He found the *mensa* burdened with debt," writes Bruno Bellone, "the cathedral dilapidated, Piedmontese troops billetted in the seminary, the religious orders suppressed, pastors killed or arrested, guerillas in the mountains of the diocese. He confronted the situation with goodness and gentleness, imposing himself by virtue and doctrine. The sixteen years of his pontificate were characterized by continual charity of the poor, extensive restoration of the cathedral, and constant zeal for the spiritual welfare of clergy and laypeople, as witness his pastoral letters which are simple and touching."

At the council, Alberani was one of the silent majority who stood by and did not plunge into the tide of theological debate conducted by the great theologians and leaders of the council. His name first appears in the acts at the third session of the council. His silence, however, did not necessarily indicate a lack of appreciation for the issues. In spite of his personal attachment to Pius IX, he did not clamor for a definition of infallibility; in fact, he signed a petition of thirteen bishops of the Marches protesting its debate out of due order.

Salvatore Angelo Demartis (1817-1901) was the most vocal Carmelite in the council. He was born in Sassari and had begun the study of theology at the university there, when he took the Carmelite habit in 1835. After ordination in 1840, he continued his studies at the university, receiving the doctorate in 1843. For four years, he taught theology in the Carmelite convent in Sassari before being called to Rome as regent of studies in Traspontina. He was not left without other offices: penitentiary (confessor) in St. Peter's Basilica (1851), consultant to the Congregation of the Index (1854) and to the Congregation of Extraordinary Ecclesiastical Affairs (1866). From 1859 to 1867, he taught moral theology at the Sapienza (two manuscript volumes of his lectures are preserved in the private library of the bishop of Nuoro). Pius IX, who occasionally dropped in on the community of Traspontina, honored him with his friendship and wanted him at his side when he came to die. On February 22, 1867, he created Demartis bishop of Galtelli-Nuoro.

The appointment was by no means a *sinecure*. The diocese had been vacant for fifteen years (only three Sardinian bishops attended the council; the other eight sees were vacant). Demartis's first task was to win back the bishop's house in Nuoro, which had been seized by the municipality. This was only the opening skirmish of a lifelong war with the influential liberals and Masons in his diocese.

Of the Carmelites present at the council, Simon Spilotros (1806-1877) held the most important position as a member of one of the influential deputations, a role he probably owed to his friendship with Sixtus Riario Sforza, archbishop of Naples and leader of the southern Italians. Born in Putignano in the diocese of Bari, Spilotros joined the Roman province, no doubt for lack of Carmelites in Puglia after the Napoleonic suppressions. He donned the habit in San Martino ai Monti in Rome, 1822, and was ordained seven years later. He became provincial of the Roman province (1840-1847) and pastor of San Martino (1850-1858). Besides being regent of studies in Traspontina and professor of moral theology at the Sapienza, he functioned as theologian of the Apostolic *Dataria*, examiner of the clergy, penitentiary in St. Peter's, censor of the Academy of the Liturgy, secretary of the Theological College. In 1859, Pius IX made him bishop of Tricarico.

Joachim Lluch y Garriga, 1816-1882

Certainly the most eminent of the Carmelites at the council was Joachim Lluch y Garriga (1816-1882), at the time bishop of Salamanca. He was born in Manresa, one of thirteen children of Anthony and Mariana Garriga. The family soon moved to Barcelona, probably because of the political troubles in Manresa in 1822. In spite of the family's limited resources, Joachim was given a good education before he entered the Carmen of Barcelona in 1830. He escaped the massacre of 1835, but since the Carmen had been destroyed and he wished to continue his religious vocation after the suppression of 1836, he emigrated to Rome. The prior general, Aloysius Calamata, assigned him to Lucca, where he remained until 1847. Lluch finished his studies at the University of Lucca and was ordained in 1838, not yet twenty-three years of age.

The young Spanish exile, who on his arrival in Italy already had a knowledge of Italian, quickly gave proof of ability and talent. He was appointed novice master and regent of studies and was assiduous in the pulpit and confessional. He contributed to the journal *Progmalogia Cattolica* and was active in local literary circles. The prominence he had achieved among the clergy of Lucca is evident from the fact that on May 27, 1847, Duke Charles Louis submitted his name for the vacant see of Lucca. But in a matter of months, Charles Louis was dead, Lucca was annexed to Tuscany, and Joachim was back in Barcelona. The archduchy did not welcome foreign religious within its borders, and the Papal States did not promise a very secure asylum. In fact, the following year Pio Nono was a fugitive in Gaeta.

In Barcelona, Lluch lived as an exclaustrated Carmelite under the apostolic commissary, Edward Comas. He was appointed pastor of St. Michael's Church, professor of moral theology in the diocesan seminary, examiner of the clergy, and prior of Holy Cross Hospital. During the cholera epidemic of 1854, he devoted himself to the sick without consideration of consequences to himself. Once again, he came to the attention of authorities as a candidate for episcopal promotion, this time with results, for in 1858 Pius IX named him bishop of the Canary Islands. Again during an epidemic in Santa Cruz, Tenerife, he showed a dedication which won him the first class cross of the *Orden Civil de Beneficencia*. In 1859, he inaugurated an official diocesan bulletin, one of the earliest of its kind.

On March 13, 1868, Bishop Lluch was transferred to the see of Salamanca. He was hardly installed, when the revolution which dethroned Isabella II broke out (1868-1875). These were chancy years for the Church, when it was extremely inconvenient for the bishop to be absent at the Vatican Council. As much as possible, Lluch kept in the good graces of the current regime, even when Salamanca was declared a federal canton at the end of the brief reign of King Amadeo (1871-1873), with the result that the diocese was spared the more extreme measures of the governments before the restoration. His pastoral on the separation of Church and state and articles on the civil and religious aspects of marriage attracted wide notice.

On January 16, 1874, Bishop Lluch was made bishop of Barcelona, but it was not until the accession of Alphonse XII that the nomination took effect. Of his activities in his new see, special mention should be made of his Catalan *Institute of Artisans and Workers*, an ambitious program on behalf of the worker, which envisioned night schools for adults, popular libraries, pawn-broking shops (*montepios*), and cooperatives. Only the schools and libraries seem to some extent to have gotten off the drawing board.

When the important see of Seville fell vacant in May of 1875, the Spanish government and the Holy See took two years to agree on a prelate to fill the office. Finally, both parties agreed on Pius IX's choice, the bishop of Barcelona, whom he pronounced archbishop of Seville in the consistory of June 22, 1877. A final honor was conferred on the distinguished Carmelite on March 27, 1882, when Leo XIII made him a cardinal, but he did not live to receive the hat.

During the council, the Carmelite bishops lodged in Traspontina, conveniently located near the Vatican. Lluch also obtained quarters there for his fellow Catalan and friend, Constantine Bonet, bishop of Gerona - no small convenience, for the Spanish bishops were too poor to afford their own carriages and had to walk to and from St. Peter's in all sorts of weather.

The Preliminaries

No need to recapitulate here the well-known background of the controversial council: the conviction on the part of the majority of the need for a confrontation of Catholic doctrine with modern philosophies and theories and for a clarification of papal primacy; the concern of the liberal minority lest the council canonize the *status quo* and further ostracize the Church from the contemporary scene; and the worry of secular powers, for the first time without representation at a council, about the effect of conciliar prescriptions on their citizens.

The Carmelite conciliar fathers, Italian and Spanish, were predictably conservative and infallibilist. By pastoral experience and theological knowledge they were well fitted to participate in the council.

The procedure of the council was laid down by the brief of Pius IX, *Multiplices inter.* The council fathers met for discussions and decisions in general congregations, of which eighty-nine were actually held. Formal public sessions marked the end of each stage of the proceedings. *Schemata*, or the matter for discussion, had been prepared beforehand by theologians and canonists. The criticisms and changes suggested in the general congregations were applied to the *schemata* by deputations, or commissions of twenty-four council fathers.

These deputations were four: on Faith, Discipline, Religious Orders, and Eastern Churches. Of these, the most important was the deputation on Faith, which, it was certain, would treat the primacy and infallibility of the pope, and which the redoubtable Manning took care to pack with infallibilists (including himself). Lluch came briefly under consideration as a Spanish possibility, but failed to make the final list. The labors of the other three deputations resulted in no conciliar constitutions, though their efforts were not wholly in vain, proving useful later in compiling the code of canon law. In the sixth general congregation on January 3, 1870, Simon Spilotros was elected thirteenth member of the deputation on religious.

After the election of the deputations, the actual work of the council had gotten under way in the fourth general congregation, December 28, with the discussion of the *schema* on Faith. The debate lasted until the ninth general congregation on January 10, when Spilotros spoke to the issue. He wanted a reference made to the infallibility of the pope in the chapters dealing with faith and the grounds of faith. This ticklish issue, the hidden agenda of the council, was too important to be introduced *per transennam* at this point. In fact, the whole *schema*, principally the work of the eminent Jesuit theologian, J.B. Franzelin, was unacceptable to the fathers. It was found to be too lengthy, schoolish, and irrelevant to the actual problems of the day, and was remanded to its deputation, "mangled and pulled to pieces, bleeding in every limb," as Ullathorne remarked. "It is not the first time," he observed, "that I have seen the work of the ablest theologians, when the episcopate bring their deeper instinct and keener experience upon it, go to pieces like chaff and consigned to reconstruction." The *schema* did not return to the general congregation until March 18.

The *Schemata* on Bishops and on Vacant Sees

Meanwhile, the council fathers turned to a consideration of matters of discipline, involving the reform of canon law. Discussion of the *schemata* on Bishops and on Vacant Sees lasted from January 14 to January 25. The emended texts never reappeared, due to the untimely prorogation of the council, but Demartis and Lluch made interventions in the eleventh general congregation on January 15.

Demartis wanted the ancient custom restored by which the neighboring bishop ruled a diocese *sede vacante*. The rule introduced by the Council of Trent and confirmed in the present *schema*, that a vicar be elected by the chapter, notoriously led to scandalous quarrels, "sometimes even besmirched with the stain of simony." In any case, Demartis wanted the requirement of the doctorate lifted. This suggestion was seconded by the following speaker, Bishop Ferdinand Ramírez y Vázquez, of Badajoz, and by many other bishops, but was never accepted by the deputation. The Carmelite's reference to capitular vicars of Paris as an example of the ill effects of their ruling a diocese *sede vacante* elicited a rebuttal on January 19 by the archbishop of Paris, George Darboy. Demartis' interest in the problem is understandable in the light of the situation in Sardinia with its many vacant sees.

Demartis was preceded by his brother Carmelite, Joachim Lluch, who approved both *schemata*, especially the requirement of the triennial visitation of the diocese by the bishop, the quinquennial visit to Rome, and the regular holding of synods. The effectiveness of the latter in recent times was especially evident in France, Germany, and America. He hoped the council would soon be over, to allow the bishops to get back to their duties. He approved the exclusion of brothers and nephews of the bishop from the office of vicar general. The latter ought to be required to be "a licentiate in canon law and expert in theology," rather than a doctor in theology. He anticipated that mention of the rights of bishops, missing from the *schemata*, would be added in others (perhaps a veiled reference to the imminent constitution on the primacy of the pope). He, too, wanted the requirement of the doctorate lifted from the office of capitular vicar and an admonition added about dissensions concerning the elections by the chapter. Where the neighboring bishop by custom ruled the vacant diocese, the metropolitan should decide in cases in which several neighbors were involved. The prerequisites of capitular vicars should be specified, to place some restraint on human cupidity.

"Next came the bishop of Salamanca," Julius Arrigoni, archbishop of Lucca, wrote in his diary, "speaking in unctuous and whining tones and with affected gestures. He found the ordinations and prescriptions of the *schema* excellent, the fathers most wise, the orators most eloquent. He alone was weak and ignorant. Such was the sum and total of what he said." Whoever has read Salamanca's speech will wonder whether the good archbishop was not nodding during its delivery. Lluch's speech was succinct and to the point, incorporating a number of specific suggestions based on experience and a knowledge of the historical background of the issues. Arrigoni, himself an accomplished preacher, was drawn to notice especially the oratorical style of the conciliar addresses. Of those he was highly critical and sarcastic, though he did not honor the assembly with a sample of his own eloquence.

The bishop of Salamanca made a different impression on another diarist, Leo Dehon, stenographer of the council, founder of the Priests of the Sacred Heart, pioneer of Catholic social action. He includes him among the most eloquent of the Spanish orators. "These bishops," he adds, "are truly theologians. In Spain, distinctions are won by competition. At the council, the fruits of this ancient canonical rule are evident. The Spanish bishops seem to surpass all the others."

In urging a quick end to the council, Lluch was simply voicing the attitude of the other Spanish bishops, who had left behind them revolutionary Spain. "They were at the council," writes Martin Tejedor, "with the intention of getting out as soon as possible without theological niceties or radical revisions in the Church. The one result they wanted was papal infallibility."

Some of Demartis' observations appear in the synopsis of the discussion on the four *schemata* concerning discipline.

The *Schema* on Clerical Life and Conduct

Discussion on the *schema* on Clerical Life and Conduct began in the sixteenth general congregation on January 25 and lasted through eight congregations until February 8, when the text was remanded to the deputation on discipline. Among the thirty-eight speakers Demartis and Lluch again appeared.

Demartis was the first speaker in the twentieth congregation on February 3, confining his remarks to three points. With regard to ecclesiastical goods, he wanted a distinction made between funds destined for the upkeep of churches and sacred services and personal incomes deriving from benefices. Since the question was disputed among authorities, the latter type of income should not be forbidden to be willed to relatives. "Rather than warning the clergy not to abuse church incomes and benefices," he wryly remarks, "they should be exhorted to bear with good will the lack of many necessities." Secondly, he pointed out that it was not clear whether the bishop's prerogatives in judging clerics guilty of incontinence extended to members of his chapter, with regard to whom the law had placed certain restrictions. Demartis wanted these privileges abolished. Finally he thought that the *schema* left too much to the judgement of the bishop and wanted the grounds for suspicion of incontinence clearly specified. "Nothing is more deplorable (*miserius*) in a society," he added, "than that the judges rule the laws, rather than that the laws rule the judges."

Speaking in the twenty-second congregation on February 7, the bishop of Salamanca approved the first chapter of the *schema*. With regard to the reform of the breviary proposed in the second, he urged prudence in correcting alleged historical errors and defended the simple Latin style of prose and verse. Further, Lluch wanted chapter three to describe less graphically the sins of the clergy and objected to the use of the word "concubinage." It is no use urging parents to supervise their children's reading, he said, if they find offensive words in religious literature. Finally, he wanted no changes made in the existing law concerning extrajudiciary sentences by bishops *ex informata conscientia* in cases of grave and secret clerical offenses.

Lluch's prudery with regard to the *schema*'s description of clerical sins provoked hilarity in the solemn assemblage. "He lacks common sense," was the comment of his fellow bishop, Roderick Ysuto, of Burgos. Arrigoni, strangely enough, does not allude to this gaffe, but does not fail to observe, "Msgr. Lluch, bishop of Salamanca, finished (the congregation) with wheedling and syrupy words, saying he found the *schema* opportune and wise."

The Revised *Schema* on Faith

After a month's adjournment, to give the deputations a chance to catch up on their work of revision, the council fathers gathered in the thirtieth general congregation on March 18 to consider the revised *schema* on Faith, now reduced to its present form of four chapters and a preface (*proemium*), the work largely of Bishop Conrad Martin of Paderborn. First, the text as a whole was discussed, then the preface and each of the chapters in turn.

In the thirty-fifth general congregation on March 28, Demartis spoke on the second chapter. In the course of the debate, various speakers had alluded to the doctrine of Traditionalism, which denied that God could be known by unaided reason and which "gave rise to keen debates of a high order." Bishop John Joseph Faict, of Bruges, who preceded Demartis condemned Traditionalism in any form. The Carmelite bishop, replying to his arguments, defended mitigated Traditionalism which presupposed some sort of education or preparation of reason. Accordingly, he wanted the phrase, "able to use his reason," added to the *schema* and "enjoying the use of" reason added to canon one. The council vindicated the powers of human reason without entering into the quarrels of the schools.

Arrigoni, who seemingly agreed with Faict, noted about Demartis that he "rose in a fury to refute the preceding bishop of Bruges; he repeated the history of Traditionalism with hard, bitter, and passionate words and defended mitigated Traditionalism *ad nauseam*. He ended amid general boredom and impatience." The written text at least of Demartis' address betrays little sign of his alleged anger.

At the forty-fifth general congregation on April 19, a straw vote was taken on the whole document. The five Carmelites were at hand and joined the majority in voting *placet*, except Demartis who with eighty-two others voted *placet iuxta modum*. There were no negative votes. Those whose vote was conditional were required to submit their suggestions in writing. Demartis wanted the first two canons in chapter one eliminated, because implicitly included in canon five. In chapter four, he wanted the words "*omnes officii monemus*" changed to "*stricte praecipimus*."

At the third public session on April 24, the constitution "on Catholic Faith" was unanimously decreed by the council fathers and confirmed by Pope Pius IX. All five Carmelite council fathers gave their assent.

The *Schema* on the Church

It was now the turn of the *schema* on the Church, in the minds of many the *raison d'etre* of the council. The document consisted of fifteen chapters and twenty-one canons. The latter, leaked to the German press, caused a sensation in diplomatic circles, and for a while it looked as though England, Austria, and Bavaria might try to block discussion of the relation of Church and state. The whole thing turned out to be a tempest in a teapot, for only chapter eleven, on the primacy of the pope, came before the council.

The first ten chapters dealt with undisputed Catholic doctrine on the Church, but the more impatient infallibilists, seeing no end to the discussions that would ensue, urged the immediate introduction of chapters eleven and twelve on the Roman pontiff. Petitions to this effect began to pour into the committee on suggestions for topics of debate (*de postulatis*) countered by others of the minority requesting that the agenda of the council be respected. Finally, appealed to personally by a petition of about one hundred bishops, Pius ordered the debate on the Roman pontiff to proceed at once. An announcement of his decision was made in the forty-seventh congregation on April 29. On May 13, at the fiftieth congregation, this important matter began to be considered.

Although the bishops of some religious orders signed petitions as a group, the Carmelites showed no such coherence. The names of Savini and Lluch are found appended to petitions to define papal infallibility. On the other hand, Alberani joined thirteen bishops of the Marches to request that this question be treated in its proper sequence within the *schema*. These prelates wished to abide by the originally announced business of the council, namely to confront the principal religious problems of the day. Spilotros and Demartis likewise were in no hurry to define infallibility, at least they made no petition to this effect.

The *Schema* on the Roman Pontiff

The new *schema* on the pope, like that on Faith, consisted of a *proemium* and four chapters. Alike, too, was the procedure of debate, which first considered the document as a whole, then each of its parts. The discussion of the *schema* as a whole, "the crucial debate," in the phrase of Butler, raged from May 13 to June 3, when it was closured by the presidents of the sessions, much to the indignation of the minority. (Lluch was one of the more than one hundred and fifty bishops who requested closure.) The debate, in effect, concerned the advisability of defining papal infallibility and engaged the great minds of the council in a mordant duel. There followed the discussion of the parts of the *schema*: the *proemium*, three chapters on the primacy (institution, perpetuation, and nature), and the fourth on infallibility.

One of the grievances of the minority was the restraint put on their liberty to speak. The council fathers were not loath on occasion to make their feelings known, when the speaker was too long-winded, strayed from the subject, or expressed a sentiment which scandalized them. The unfortunate Demartis was shot down in this fashion, called to order by the president of the session, Cardinal Hannibal Capalti, during the debate on the third chapter (seventy first general congregation, June 14). The incident cannot be better told than in the words of Dom Cuthbert Butler:

"A bishop from the Island of Sardinia spoke on appeals from Pope to General Council, and urged that the decrees of Popes are irreformable, whence may be argued their infallibility.

"Capalti: The question before us is not the infallibility but the primacy.

"The Bishop: I am not speaking of infallibility; I am speaking of inerrancy (laughter); and he went on.

"Cardinal de Luca: We read in the Book of Proverbs, 'Rebuke a wise man, and he will love you.' As you, Rt. Rev. Father, are a wise man, you will not be displeased at my reminding you we are not talking of the infallibility of the Roman Pontiff, but of his ordinary, direct episcopal power over the whole Church. Therefore, we all ask you to come back to the point.

"The Bishop: But I have to show from the practice of the Church that the decrees of the Roman Pontiff are irreformable.

"Many Fathers: That belongs to chapter IV.

"The Bishop: It is in chapter III, chapter III, chapter III.

"The Fathers: Chapter IV, chapter IV.

"The Bishop: Good, thanks very much ('*Bene! gratias ago*') and down he came."

Two Carmelites were scheduled to comment on the important chapter four on infallibility, but they never ascended the *ambo*. Lluch waived his right to speak in the eightieth congregation, held on July 1. Savini, who finally would have made his voice heard in the assembly, also renounced his turn in the eighty-second congregation of July 4, but submitted his emendations privately.

These show that, with many, he was most emphatic in insisting that the infallibility of the pope was not contingent on the consent of the Church. In fact, the phrase, "not from the consent of the Church" (*non autem ex consensu Ecclesiae*), was added to the text in the eighty-sixth congregation on July 16 and appears in the constitution *Pastor aeternus*. Other emendations concern parts of the text which were subsequently dropped. He wanted the phrase, "as soon as they become known to him" (*ut primum ei innotuerint*) more sharply defined, to include the idea of sufficient knowledge. He agreed with Bishop Joseph Caixal y Estrade, of Urgel, and with Archbishop Paul Cullen, of Dublin, that the last part of the text, beginning "And because" (*Et quoniam*) should be omitted (as in fact it was); he also seconded Cullen's version of the canon.

The Carmelites all registered their *placet* at the trial vote on the schema taken at the eighty-fifth general congregation on July 13.

Finally, at the fourth public session on July 18, amid a violent thunderstorm that all but drowned out the voices of the council fathers, the constitution, *Pastor aeternus*, was formally defined and confirmed by the pope. "Nothing approaching to the solemn splendor of that storm could have been prepared," wrote the Rev. T. Mozley, special correspondent to the London *Times*, "and never will those who saw it and felt it forget the promulgation of the Constitution on the Church."

The five Carmelite council fathers were among the five hundred and thirty-three who cast affirmative votes. Those who would have voted negatively (about sixty fathers) preferred to absent themselves, except Edward Fitzgerald, of Little Rock, Arkansas, and Aloysius Riccio, of Caiazzo, whose *non placet*, heard above the storm, continues to echo down the years.

The Carmelites made no outstanding contributions to the council, but they shared in the painstaking daily labor of hammering out the verbal expression of the conciliar documents. They had the privilege of joining in the definition of Catholic doctrine, particularly the dogma of papal infallibility.

Carmelite Bishops in the Nineteenth Century

It may not be without interest to consider briefly the Carmelite bishops of the nineteenth century. In the course of its history to the twentieth century, the Carmelite Order contributed about three hundred members to the hierarchy. In round numbers, 150 are of the 14th and 15th centuries, 50 of the 16th century, 80 of the 17th and 18th centuries, and 20 of the 19th century. For the most part, Carmelite bishops were hewers of wood and drawers of water, occupying the more insignificant sees, or serving in the missions, or as auxiliaries. It is a wonder that nineteenth century Carmel was able to contribute anyone to this exacting and exalted ministry, considering the fewness of its members. More of a wonder still, is the fact that the only two cardinals Carmel ever produced are found in this unlucky century.

Placid Tadini (1759-1847), with Joachim Lluch y Garriga one of the two Carmelite cardinals, lacks an adequate biography. He was born in Moncorvo and entered the Order in the Piedmont province, living for a time in the convent of Turin. A doctor of theology, he taught at the universities of Alessandria and Padua. No doubt it was the dissolution by Napoleon of the Order in Piedmont that brought Tadini to Rome, where he spent twenty years. He followed Timothy Ascensi at the Sapienza in 1824 and also taught in Traspontina. He filled the offices of assistant general and penitentiary of St. Peter's. Appointed bishop of Biella in 1829, he was transferred to the important see of Genoa three years later. Pope Gregory XVI made him a cardinal in 1835. King Charles Albert of Sardegna appointed him his counselor and conferred on him the Order of Sts. Maurice and Lazarus. Tadini held a synod, of which the acts were printed (Genoa, 1838). He consecrated St. Anthony Gianelli bishop of Bobbio in 1839. As we have seen, Tadini issued his sermons and pastorals in two volumes (Genoa, 1840-1841). Augustine Molin states that Tadini published his dissertation on prophecy in Padua at the end of the 18th century and in Piedmont printed a work on the Jewish sanhedrin.

Chapter 10

The Spiritual Life and Devotion, 1750-1900

In view of what has been recounted so far, the gentle reader will foster no great expectations about the interior life of the Order during this period. The continual meddling of the Catholic monarchs in the internal affairs of religious orders, the nationalization and isolation of the latter, rendered impossible proper communication and administration. The frontal attack by the French Revolution, Napoleon, and the liberal governments left only ruins.

The enemies of the Church failed to realize that they were robbing religious not only of their material possessions but also of that pearl of great price for which they had sold their all: a life of intimacy with God in prayer in the goodly company of brothers. The destruction of their life of prayer in community was the severest deprivation religious suffered (though they also raised no little stir over the loss of their properties). Also, by being unjustly deprived of their right to exist as corporate bodies, religious could no longer live the life of evangelical poverty to which they were committed in conscience by the most solemn promises (not always very faithfully kept, it is true). The law forced them to appear as private individuals and to own possessions in their own name. Little wonder that, as we have seen, after living for years in the world, few Carmelites, given the chance, showed much inclination to return to the cloister.

The Holy See and the Reform of Religious

Mons. Andrew Bizzarri, secretary of the Congregation of the State of Religious Orders, in a preliminary report to Pius IX (1847) painted a dark picture of the state to which religious life had been reduced by the middle of the 19th century: general neglect of the vow of poverty, murmuring against superiors, idleness during the greater part of the day, widespread ignorance of most religious, carelessness in the selection of candidates, haphazard training of novices, inept novice masters, neglect of canonical visitation, chapters the prey of partisanship and ambition. The secretary makes no allusion to the prayer life of religious.

To what extent these strictures applied to the Carmelite Order is a matter that awaits investigation. The common life was observed in the reformed convents; in the others, the deposit box was imposed, not always successfully. The general chapter of 1856, we have seen, at the behest of Pius IX urged the observance of the common life, at least in the novitiates. These often left much to be desired, though an effort seems to have been made to assign exemplary religious to the office of novice master. Due to a lack of membership, the standard of selection of candidates was no doubt lowered, but the same fewness of numbers made idleness less of a problem to Carmelites with fewer hands to do the work. With regard to clerical ignorance, more will be said below about the intellectual life of the Order.

Pius' reform addressed itself to two problems: the proper formation of a new generation of religious and the observance of the common life. On January 25, 1848, the decree *Romani pontifices* required candidates for religious orders to obtain testimonial letters from their bishops. The same day, *Regulari disciplinae* established some norms for admission to the habit and profession applicable in Italy. These matters were taken out of the hands of the local superior and entrusted to committees of provincial and general examiners. The most significant innovation was introduced in the encyclical, *Neminem latet*, March 19, 1857, by which Pius IX required a three-year period of simple vows before the final commitment of solemn vows. These he declared necessary for the validity of solemn vows in his apostolic letter, *Ad universalis*, February 7, 1862. The new law kept the canon lawyers hustling for a while, but it was largely to determine the quality of religious life in modern times. The three year interval enabled young religious to try their vocation and to leave or be rejected, if unsuited. Hitherto, the one profession of vows, taken as early as the age of sixteen, immovably fixed the novice in the religious state, from which in Catholic society there was no return.

With regard to the common life, the approach was gradual. The decree of the Congregation for Bishops and Religious of April 22, 1851, ordered the common life observed in novitiates. The constitutions were to be carefully carried out in houses of study, especially in the matter of poverty, and every house was to have a deposit box. These mandates had a familiar ring to Carmelite ears, but times had changed. In the new reality of increasing ecclesiastical centralization, the arm of Rome had lengthened. In fact, in the phoenix of religious life, which rose from the ashes of the nineteenth century, the common life finally prevailed.

The Liturgy

The suppression of the convents put an end to the choral recitation of the divine office. In such communities as remained, its maintenance was an obligation, often carried out under unfavorable circumstances due to reduced numbers and consequent increased burden of apostolic activities. Daily Mass for the people, of course, was offered in the churches of the Order.

There was a notable falling-off in the production of liturgical books. Although the Flemish province produced a breviary with the approval of Ximénez (Antwerp, 1769), no breviary appeared after Ventimiglia's of Venice in 1764, until Priori's (Rome 1855). Ximénez' *Diurnum* (Venice, 1771) was succeeded only by Priori's (Rome, 1856). Over a century elapsed between Pontalti's missal (Venice, 1760) and Savini's (Rome, 1866). As the members, churches, and convents of the Order ominously diminished, printing liturgical books according to the Carmelite rite was an act of the purest faith.

At this time, the liturgical calendar was enriched with a number of new Carmelite *beati*. In fact, at no other period was the work of beatification so assiduously plied as during these years, when the Order was on the point of extinction. Blesseds Angelus Augustine Mazzinghi (1761), Joan Scopelli (1771), Aloysius Rabata (1841), Avertanus and Romaeus (1842), Louis Morbioli (1843), Jacobinus (1845), Frances d'Amboise (1863), Archangela Girlani (1864), John Soreth (1866), Baptist of Mantua (1885) were successively raised to the altar. No prior general was more active in promoting causes than Angelo Savini. Subsequently, the beatification of Joan of Toulouse (1895), Bartholomew Fanti (1909), and Nun' Alvares Pereira (1918) completed the roster of Carmelites accorded liturgical honors, until very recent times.

Marian Devotion

With the almost total destruction of the Order and its theological tradition, Carmelite spirituality during the 19th century narrowed down to its Marian element. If not theoretically, at least concretely the Order's function in the Church was seen to be the promotion of devotion to Mary, specifically to Our Lady of Mount Carmel and her scapular. In many instances, after the sequestration of their convents, Carmelites clung to their churches for the sake of the scapular confraternity or the Third Order. In fact, in the century that witnessed the proclamation of the dogma of the Immaculate Conception (1854) and the visions of St. Bernadette of Lourdes (1858) Catholic devotion itself was markedly Marian, partly, too, in reaction to the criticism of rationalists, Protestants, and a minority Catholic element which regarded the cult of Mary as unevangelical, superstitious, or at best supererogatory.

"Before the pilgrimage to Lourdes was instituted and the invocation of Our Lady of Lourdes became widespread," writes the Dominican, Henri Petitot, "there was no more honored name in Christendom than that of Our Lady of Mount Carmel. In Bernadette's time, most of the children in all Christian families wore the brown scapular on their breasts." This popularity was due not so much to the Carmelites, become a vanishing species, than to the diocesan priests and religious men and women, especially of the new orders, who recommended the brown scapular in their schools, parishes, mission sermons, and books.

Preeminent among them were not a few saints, who may be credited with a certain surety of instinct in matters spiritual, some of them also outstanding preachers and apostles of the age.

Such were St. Pompilio Pirotti (1710-1766), Scolopian and apostle of the Abruzzi, devotee of Our Lady, who everywhere preached the scapular; St. Alphonsus Liguori (1696-1787), founder of the Redemptorists, remembered for his popular *Glories of Mary*, who himself wore the scapular, found intact at the exhumation of his body, recommended it to priests, and defended it against critics; St. Anthony Claret (1807-1870), founder of the Claretians and "Apostle of Spain," who brought it about that hardly a person was to be found in Catalonia without his rosary and scapular; St. John Bosco (1815-1888), founder of the Salesians and faithful wearer of the scapular, which was also found incorrupt at the opening of his tomb in 1929; St. Leonard Murialdo (1828-1900), founder of the Josephites, a fervent devotee of Mary, who wore the scapular and recommended wearing it to the young.

By no means all Catholic historians and theologians accepted the scapular vision or approved the devotion, but no clamorous controversies occurred, and on the whole devotion to Our Lady of Mount Carmel enjoyed a peaceful lot in the 19th century. Some scapular booklets appeared by non-Carmelite as well as Carmelite authors, none of them notable for theological content.

A decree of the Sacred Congregation of Indulgences and Relics, issued on March 26, 1887, and confirmed by Pope Leo XIII on April 27, prescribed that the scapular of Our Lady of Mount Carmel should be imposed separately from the other scapulars.

The Immaculate Conception

The Revolution of 1848 did not distract Pio Nono from his concern over the definition of the Immaculate Conception. From exile in Gaeta, he instructed

Cardinal Aloysius Lambruschini to gather a few cardinals who had fled to Naples and some consultors into an ante-preparatory congregation and decide whether the Immaculate Conception of the Virgin Mary should be defined, and if so, the manner of doing it. Among the consultors of the Congregation which met in Naples on December 22, 1848, was the Carmelite, Joseph Mazzetti, titular bishop of Centuria, who was alone in his opinion that the question should be further studied. When it was agreed that the time was ripe for definition, he suggested that the bishops of the Church be gathered together, or at least that the procedures of canonizations be followed. The Congregation ended by advising the pope to canvass the episcopacy with an encyclical, and the result, of course, was the *Ubi primum* of February 2, 1849.

To answer the encyclical, there were in the Carmelite Order, besides Mazzetti, only the Souza brothers in far-off Brazil: Charles of St. Joseph, bishop of São Luis do Maranhão, and Peter of St. Marianna, titular bishop of Chrysopolis. The latter's episcopal character was simply an honor conferred on him due to his role as tutor of the future Pedro II.

The Carmelites enthusiastically greeted the declaration of the dogma of the Immaculate Conception in 1854. Not the least impressive of the celebrations held in Rome for the occasion was the triduum observed in Traspontina, February 23-25, 1855. "One should not overlook the fact," the reporter of the *Giornale di Roma* wrote on March 1, "that the festivity had a particular character of its own, inasmuch as it was the people of Rome, that is, the inhabitants of Rione 14 (Borgo), who joined the family of the Carmelite Fathers in honoring the great Virgin Mother of God."

Some Examples of Saintly Carmelites

Not all saints are canonized. To say nothing of those who suffered and died for the faith in revolutionary France, other Carmelites in these parlous times managed to live their vocation to the full and reached the maturity of the Christian life. Although naturally fewer than in the heyday of the Order, saintly Carmelites undoubtedly existed in greater numbers than the scanty records reveal.

The delegates of the province of Santa Maria della Vita requested the general chapter of 1768 to enforce the raising of funds for the cause of Brother Stephen Pelosio and to appoint a postulator. Stephen Pelosio (1689-1763) was dead only five years at this time. He was born at Sondrio in the Valtellina. As a young man, he devoted himself to prayer and the apostolate of catechizing in those remote mountain regions. He was engaged to Martha Strangone, of the village of Triasso, when both young people agreed to enter religious life. Martha became a Benedictine nun in the monastery of San Lorenzo near Sondrio, where she died in 1758 after an exemplary life. In 1716, Stephen applied for admittance into the Order at the Carmine of Milan. The prior general, Charles Cornaccioli, on a visit to the convent, was impressed by the piety of the young man and advised him to enter the reformed convent of Santa Maria della Vita in Naples. In 1720, Stephen made profession as a laybrother. Brother Stephen did not belie the early promise of his youth, but through his long life persevered earnestly in the highest ideals of religious life. His love for the poor and profound experience of prayer made a lasting impression on the people. His crucifix, still preserved in the Carmine Maggiore of Naples, is reputed to have spoken to him. After his death, many favors were attributed to his intercession, among them, the cure from a long-standing illness of his contemporary, Fr. Peter Thomas Musco, who became his first biographer. The cause of his beatification was introduced, but somewhere in the course of several transferrals during the hectic years of religious suppressions, his body was lost track of, and today the site of his tomb is unknown.

Salvatore Pagnani (1685-1771) was born in Crispano near Capua and took the habit at Caserta in 1703. Ordained five years later, he served as prior in a number of convents and finally as provincial of the province of Terra di Lavoro. He spent the last thirty-five years of his life in Capua. A man of prayer and penitence, he was much sought after as a spiritual director. Much of his attention was absorbed by the monastery, which with Mariangela of Divine Love he founded in 1734. Mariangela had been a penitent of St. Alphonsus Liguori, and both she and Pagnani appear in his correspondence, which betrays a warm regard and affection for the Carmelite friar. Pagnani's direction of the nuns was simple and unaffected. "God has been and will be your director," he told them. The sisters introduced the cause of his beatification in the dioceses of Aversa and Melfi and asked the general chapter of 1775 for funds to introduce it in Capua. "This important request was referred to the decision and zeal of the Most Reverend Father General," the fathers decided. The zeal of the prior general, Joseph Albert Ximénez, was evidently equal to the occasion, for the manuscript of the process, completed in 1782, is today found in the archiepiscopal archive of Capua.

Mariano Cacace, of the convent of Monte Santo in Naples, was the tutor and spiritual director of Bl. Justin de Jacobis, future vicar apostolic of Abissinia and apostle of Ethiopia, during the latter's formative years from fifteen to eighteen. He discovered the young man's vocation as a missionary and encouraged him to join the Vincentians. After the suppression of his convent in 1809, Fr. Mariano moved to the Carmine Maggiore, where he served as novice master from 1825 to 1835. He died a holy death on March 9, 1845.

Anthony da Fonseca (1697-1755), the son of laborers, entered the Carmelite Order after his ordination at the age of twenty-five. He was stationed at Faya, two leagues from Guarda, which was probably a hospice, for no convent of the Portuguese province is known by that name. He was an object of wonder to the simple folk of the place for the many hours he spent in prayer, oblivious to his surroundings, and he gained a reputation as a thaumaturge. He died on August 8, 1755, only two months before the great earthquake. His memory was buried with much else in that traumatic occurrence.

On the other hand, Joseph of St. Barbara (1698-1785) came of noble stock, though like St. Teresa he made little of the fact. Born of the Ortiz and La Estrella families in Huelva, he entered the Order at San Juan del Puerto in 1714. He made his studies at the Casa Grande in Seville, where he spent the rest of his long life. Before entering, he had received a good education, including Latin School, but he never completed higher studies, remaining a *presentado*, or bachelor, all his life. This may have been due to personal choice; in any case, his career was concerned with pastoral ministry. He spent long hours in the confessional and in spiritual direction. In the community, he served as sacristan, sub-prior, and prior. Whether as superior or subject, he was remarkably faithful to the duties of his state. He devoted many hours to prayer; indeed, his spiritual director later testified that Fray José lived in a state of continual prayer. He observed the rule without its mitigations. When he came to die, told to make a list of his belongings, he could write nothing on the paper, because he owned nothing. He died with the reputation of being a saint, and miracles were soon attributed to his intercession.

John Soreth Brunner (1842-1901) was born in the village of Oberhaid (Ostmark) and was baptised Michael. When he was eleven, his parents moved to Gossersdorf and apprenticed him to a shoemaker. In 1864, he experienced the grace of conversion and withdrew from society. Until he was thirty, he lived a celibate life in the home of his parents, devoting himself to prayer and penance. In the 70's he settled in Straubing as a journeyman in his trade. He was the master's most prized worker and was also well-liked by his fellows. "He was no crapehanger," one of them testified; "he was always cheerful and enjoyed a good laugh." Eventually, he entered the Carmelite convent in Straubing, making his simple profession in 1885 with the name John Soreth. He was given the job of porter, and of course with him at hand the community was well shod. In these tasks and in a life of hidden prayer, Brother John spent the last six years of his life. "No one remembers ever having heard an improper or unkind word from his mouth," a witness states. His reputation for sanctity lived after him. In 1947, his body was exhumed in connection with his process of beatification.

Another laybrother of the Upper German province, known for his sanctity, was Brother Aloysius Ehrlich (1868-1945), a carpenter, who exercised his prayerful trade, not only in his own province but also in Rome and Palestine. The informative process of his cause was begun in Bamberg, on September 24, 1953.

Some Lives of Holy Carmelite Nuns

In spite of the weight of public opinion against them and of active persecution by governments, women with a contemplative vocation quietly continued to follow their bent. If in the best of times they are not given to vaunting their accomplishments, it need hardly be said that information regarding the period under consideration is of the scantiest. A few examples of cloistered Carmelite nuns may be offered here.

From the monastery of St. Mary of the Angels in Florence was Mary Magdalen Constance of the Blessed Sacrament Picchi (1839-1895). She came from a well-to-do Florentine family, her father being a music master. Her mother, née Virginia Bargigli, died in 1854. Her father was not opposed to her religious vocation, but would not hear of her entering a strict contemplative community. After his death, however, being free to follow her natural inclination, she chose the Carmelite monastery of St. Mary of the Angels in Florence, where she entered the novitiate on February 15, 1859. She had to wait ten years to pronounce her vows, because the Tuscan government had decided that nuns should not make profession until they were thirty years of age. With the suppression of 1866, their future became even more uncertain, their monastery being sequestered and available for their use only for their lifetime. Under the circumstances, the archbishop of Florence, Joachim Limberti, permitted the nuns to make only simple profession, which Mary Magdalen Constance finally made on May 13, 1872.

Upon the accession of Archbishop Eugene Cesconi and better times, she was allowed to make solemn profession on June 4, 1876. Mary Magdalen Constance served in all the offices of the monastery: assistant novice mistress, bursar (during the move to the Piazza Savonarola in 1888), novice mistress, prioress. In all these capacities, she comported herself with a perfection which convinced her sisters of her extraordinary virtue. She left a spiritual diary published after her death by her director, Alexander Gallerani, S. J., as well as biographies of several sisters who had been under her care in the novitiate.

Sister Mary Minima Louise of Jesus of Nazareth Salvatori (1730-1831) was one of those persons who from infancy show an inclination to prayer and an aptitude for mystical gifts. She was born in Caprarola near Rome of a family that seems to have been well provided with this world's goods. From the ages of eight to twelve, she attended the school of St. John in Zoccoli in Viterbo, conducted by the *Maestre Pie*, one of whom was the inevitable aunt. In what she later considered a lapse from grace, she began a courtship with a young man, but her celibate calling reasserted itself, and she entered the Carmelite monastery in Vetralla, pronouncing her vows on June 7, 1804. The suppression of the monasteries in 1810 found her back in her family. There, as much as possible, she led the life of a cloistered nun. The sisters had been instructed to apply to their confessors for the permissions they would normally seek from the prioress. She had the good fortune to find an excellent spiritual director in the Discalced Carmelite, Paul of St. Joseph, who was her guide in the ways of the spirit for the rest of her days.

After the return of Pius VII, Vetralla was not immediately ready to receive its inmates, but Mary Minima, in November of 1814, was taken in by the Barberine in Rome, until she was able to return to her own monastery on September 29, 1819. From 1822 until her death, she was prioress, being re-elected to that office three times. Her special effort was to repair the spiritual and material damage done by the suppression. Fr. Paul had ordered Sister Mary Minima to record her spiritual itinerary in writing, and this document at once served him in composing her biography (Roma, 1833) and also shows her to have practiced the most heroic virtues and to have reached the most exalted mystical states.

At the age of twelve, Sister Mary Emilia Guttadauro (1829-1877) entered the monastery of the Holy Cross in Naples as an *educanda*. Her religious life was characterized by obedience. She accepted with serenity whatever her superiors or divine Providence had in store for her. No doubt this attitude had its origin in her relation to her aunt, Sister Mary Rosa Ricciardi, to whom as a child she was wholly submissive; yet her conformity took the form of a loving attachment rather than a grovelling servitude. Sister Mary Emilia made her profession on October 25, 1853. During her religious life she held only the humbler offices, such as assistant sacristan, portress, baker, assistant directress of the *educande*. Only months before her death, she became sub-prioress. A striking feature of her life were the amazing mystical phenomena, which together with continual illness occurred therein. On April 26, 1856, she was cured of total paralysis and blindness through a vision of Our Lady of Good Counsel. This event was the prelude to a lifetime of visions and raptures. Of these sensational manifestations it may at least be said that they left behind in her solid fruits of virtue. "Her virtue," wrote Sister Mary Matilda Buonanno, her companion and biographer, "was a lovable and tender virtue.... It was a happy virtue, not narrow-minded, always in good taste, compliant."

If the Carmelite monastery of Osuna exists today, it is due in no slight measure to Sister Mary Josefa of the Incarnation Amarillo (1811-1891). Born in the town of Arahal, she early manifested a desire to become a religious, but she lacked the means to provide her dowry. Since she could play the organ, the sisters waived this condition, and Sister Mary Josefa received the habit on July 1, 1827. At the time, the community counted only seven nuns, but this number must have soon increased, for the monastery survived the suppression of small communities in 1836. In 1852, as we have seen, the community was joined by that of Ecija. For thirty-three years until her death, Sister Mary Josefa headed the monastery as prioress and brought about its spiritual and material renewal. A new church, blessed on April 29, 1883, replaced the old structure, which threatened ruin. She also renovated the monastery. More important than these material improvements, necessary though they were, she reinstated the common life. Shortly before her death, she had the consolation of seeing her brothers in Carmel return to Osuna, consequent on her effective intervention and fervent prayers.

The Carmelite Third Order

The dissolution of most of the Carmelite friaries and their churches, of course, adversely affected the chapters of the Third Order connected with them. Yet, in many cases the Third Order (as well as the scapular confraternities) survived under the direction of diocesan priests, themselves often tertiaries. Not infrequently, these zealous persons were the means of restoring the friars to their former churches, which they had saved from destruction.

The official Third Order rule, as promulgated by Emilio Giacomelli in 1678 and explained by his successor Ferdinand Tartaglia in his *Statuta* of the following year, had long ago gone out of print. In order to minister to the needs of the tertiaries of Florence, John Baptist Bettini compiled his *Compendio e dichiarazione della regola del Terz'Ordine* (Firenze, 1849), in which he presented the tertiary rule and statutes in an abridged and, he evidently thought, a more convenient form. This rule received a semi-official status, when it was included in a manual intended for tertiaries and confraternity members and approved by Angelo Savini, *Offizio parvo della B. Vergine Maria* (Roma, 1869). Its official status became definite in the next edition of the *Compendio e dichiarazione* (Firenze, 1896), printed "by order of" Aloysius Galli and in the final reprint sanctioned by John Lorenzoni (Roma, 1915). Translations appeared in Dutch (Handboek, Boxmeer, 1877) and in German (Regel-Buchlein, Straubing, 1907). Bettini's manual substantially reproduced Giacomelli's rule, but in a form less apt for a legislative text.

We have seen that Giacomelli's rule was either unknown or unrecognized on the Iberian peninsula, where the earlier rule of Theodore Straccio, interpreted in a wide sense to exclude vows, remained in vogue. In our period, this viewpoint was still exposed by Michael de Azeveda in his *Regra da ordem terceira* (Lisboa, 1778), but was vigorously attacked by Joseph Eloi do Rego in his *Manual da veneravel ordem terceira* (Ponta Delgado, 1881), written under the aegis of Angelo Savini in defense of the tertiary vows.

Two figures stand out among Carmelite tertiaries of the 19th century. Librada Ferrarons (1803-1842) resembles earlier tertiaries in the extraordinary and mystical aspects of her life. She was the daughter of a poor weaver of Olot, a town in

Catalonia which had had a Carmelite convent since 1565. The family was devout and closely united in the bonds of parental and filial love. John Ferarrons was barely able to provide it support, and when he fell ill and died, no other remedy remained than to send the six-year old Librada, eldest of three girls, into the streets to beg. For two years the child supported the family in this way, until she was able to go to work in a textile factory. She spent the next nineteen years, the extent of her active life, in this work and developed a high degree of skill, which together with her diligence and honesty made her a very desirable employee. She rose to a position which placed her in charge of other women workers.

In 1819, she made her vows in the Third Order of Carmel. This act marked a further step in the life of prayer and solitude to which she was dedicated. At work, her expert fingers flying over the loom left her thoughts free to dwell with God. Her supervision of the girls included tactful encouragement to do good. She organized the recitation of the rosary during work - a pious practice for that matter not unusual in the factories of Catholic Spain in those days.

Librada was a handsome girl with attractive features, tall and robust. Yet her health was not good, due no doubt to her undernourished and overworked childhood. Less and less able to work, in 1830 she took to her bed, where she remained until her death. Her sickness baffled the doctors both in its symptoms and in its intensity, and they could only conclude that it was beyond nature that she could remain alive and support such agonies. In her last years, she experienced visions and other mystical graces, as attested by her confessors. These were the Carmelite Antonio Bonavia, until with the suppression of the convent he left Olot, and the diocesan priests Aloysius Vila, Peter Rovira, and Dr. Joachim Masmitjá. Librada's virtuous life, patiently borne sufferings, and mystical prayer were not lost on the people, who to this day keep alive her cult in the hope of her canonization.

As Librada Ferrarons has been proposed as an ideal Christian worker, so Carmen de Sojo (1856-1890) may serve as a model of a Christian mother. Her father was a businessman in the town of Reus, and both he and his wife were given to practices of piety and works of charity. At the age of fifteen, Carmen (her mother was much devoted to Our Lady of Mount Carmel) was given in marriage to a friend of the family, George Anguera, a physician of Barcelona. Thus, a mere child with no experience of the world was called on to be a wife and head the household of a city doctor, who, moreover, was deeply involved in the Carlist war then in progress. Suspected partisans of Don Carlos received asylum in Dr. Anguera's house, the wounded were treated there. The doctor was often absent on secret missions and neglected to leave behind or lacked the means to pay the bills. By June of 1878, his exhausted wife was at death's door and had been given the last rites, but she recovered. Carmen was convinced, that this had come about through the intercession of Blessed Joseph Oriol, whose cause of canonization was being promoted by her spiritual director, Salvador Casanas. Carmen not only regained her health but also acquired the ability, which had previously eluded her, to bear children, of which she had five. Her spiritual director, the future cardinal, led her by the stony way of Calvary, and though some of his methods seem strange today, they produced a hardy and virile spirit in his penitent.

Carmen was in every way a typical upper middle class wife and mother, devoted to her husband, her children, her household, her charities, her guests. No one suspected the penances she practiced, not even her physician husband, who unbelievably did not realize until it was too late that she was dying of tuberculosis. The recognition of her merits came after death, and the cause of her beatification is being actively pursued. With her husband, Carmen had entered the Third Order of Carmel, and both faithfully followed its way. Born on the feast of St. Teresa of Avila, Carmen was also devoted to St. Mary Magdalen de' Pazzi.

Among tertiaries of the latter half of the 18th century mention may be made of Lucia Casanova of Castelbolognese, Anna Tassinari of Forlì (d. 1759), Olimpia Giacomelli of Bologna (d. 1760), Gertrude Picca, mystic and stigmatic of Velletri (1763-after 1799), Euphemia Pellegrini also of Velletri (1737-1806).

Spiritual Writings

Nothing illustrates more graphically the reduced condition of the Order at this time than the dwindling trickle of its spiritual writings. The difficulty of tracing the slender literary output of the Order is increased by the want of bibliographical aids after Cosmas de Villiers' *Bibliotheca carmelitana* (1752).

The period opens with one of the Order's most prolific writers, Roque Alberto Faci (d. 1774), of the province of Aragon, author of more than fifty works. His *Aragon, Kingdom of Christ and Dowry of Mary Most Holy* (2v., Zaragoza, 1739-1750), illustrative of a particular interest of his, describes thousands of images, crucifixes, and relics venerated in the cities and towns of Aragon and often no longer existent, "a work" in the words of the editors of the facsimile edition of 1979, "of capital importance to the historiography of Aragon." Of similar nature is his *Carmel Consecrated with Holy Images of Christ and Mary* (Zaragoza, 1759), levied upon more than once above.

To an unfortunately skimpy literature on St. Teresa of Avila by Carmelite authors Faci contributed three titles: *Life of our Holy Mother St. Teresa of Jesus* (Zaragoza, 1744), *The Admirable Days and Works of St. Teresa of Jesus* (Pamplona, 1764), and the untranslatable *Gracias de la gracia de S. Teresa de Jesús*, or the lighter side of St. Teresa (Zaragoza, 1757). This last work is a complement to the homonymous *Gracias de la gracia, saladas agudezas de los santos* (salty witticisms of the saints) by the priest humorist, Joseph Boneta. His brother, Fray Anthony Albert Boneta, was Faci's novice master in 1698, and according to Faci supplied his brother with the material for his book. Fray Anthony Albert was also much devoted to St. Teresa "and always carried her books about with him and at recreation time recounted to us many sallies of the saint."

Other writings of Faci concern hagiography, the Virgin Mary, the Third Order, and bibliography. Among his hagiographical works, one might notice his edition of the life of St. Albert of Sicily, written by Diego Yanguas, O.P., at the request of St. Teresa (Zaragoza, 1754).

For the benefit of the sisters, Edward Comas, apostolic commissary for Spain, collected into one volume several treatises by the 18th century writer, Francis Pastor. Besides his commentary on the Carmelite rule and his treatises on the vows and indulgences, this useful little book contained Chizzola's decrees for nuns (1595) and *Avisos* of St. John of the Cross and St. Teresa of Avila (Zaragoza 1856).

In Portugal, Cajetan do Vencimento's *Directory of Meditations* was issued in an edition by Alphonse Francis de Carvalho (Lisbon, 1763). Cajetan is also the author of a biography of Marianna of the Purification (Lisbon, 1747).

In Italy, an anonymous Carmelite, presumably of the Venetian province, wrote a little book on the virtues, *The Tree of the Virtues, Called the Tree of Life in the Apocalypse* (Venice, 1753; 2d ed., 1758). Boniface of St. Paul Giardi, of the reformed province of Piedmont, translated St. Augustine's exposition of Psalm 118, adding a commentary of spiritual reflections (Turin, 1775-1777, 2 v.).

For the edification of his subjects, Ignatius Maria Rossi, provincial of the St. Angelus province, wrote *The Carmelite Novice Instructed by His Master in the Religious State* (Naples, 1764) and *The Carmelite Prior Instructed in His Office* (Palermo, 1767).

The prior general, Joseph Cataldi, published *Paraphrases and Reflections on the Our Father and Elijah, Prodigy of Nature and Grace*, which constitute the first two volumes of his collected works (4 v., Naples, 1839-1840). With regard to the second title, the author apologizes for his failure to indicate his sources, since he composed the book in two months in a place where he could not have recourse to them.

In France, bereft of Carmelites for half a century, appeared a mysterious reprint of the 17th century *Exhortations mystiques*, by Stephen of St. Francis Xavier (Avignon, 1836) without any indication of the one responsible or the motive for the reproduction.

The exclaustrated Carmelite, Thomas Chais, wrote *The Excellence of the Devotion of the Holy Scapular*, which underwent at least three editions (Lyon, 1824, 1835; Paris, 1838). The scapular devotion, it would seem, was still alive and well.

Perhaps the most notable Carmelite contribution to spiritual literature of these years was the translation into German of the works of St. John of the Cross (Sulzbach, 1830, 2 v.) and St. Teresa of Avila (Sulzbach, 1831-1832, 5 v.) by Gallus Schwab (1779-1837). Born in Staffelstein (Oberfranken), he was stationed in the Carmelite convent of Bamberg at the time of its suppression. He joined the diocesan clergy and, after serving in a number of parishes, was appointed in 1833 regent of the diocesan seminary of Regensburg and member of the bishop's council.

Preaching

Preaching may be said to have continued to flourish, considering the drastically reduced membership of the Order. Although preaching in Italy was limited by Napoleon to parish priests in their own churches, and for special occasions, such as Advent and Lenten courses, required imperial authorization, preachers otherwise were free to ply their trade. Religious continued to preach as secular priests, after their order had been disbanded. This period produced Carmelite preachers comparable to any the Order had previously seen.

Evasio Leone (1765-1821), primarily a literary figure, also distinguished himself in the pulpit and was much sought after for special occasions. His sermons, characterized more by rhetorical elegance than plain evangelical fervor, comprise a large part of his collected works (4 v., Ancona, 1853-1854).

Of Joseph Cataldi's collected works mentioned above, volume three contains panegyrics, volume four sermons on Our Lady of Mount Carmel, by no means exhaustive of the thirty-seven Lenten courses, besides missions and occasional sermons he preached. "The word issued from his lips," wrote Joachim Ventura, former general of the Theatines, "simply and alive, popular and serious, learned and touching, full of spirit and fire. His sermons were not marked by learning and artifice, but had all the ardor of zeal and force of truth."

Cardinal Placid Tadini published a selection of fifteen homilies and seventeen pastoral letters (2 v., Genoa, 1840-1841).

Joseph Sbisà gathered his panegyrics on feasts of the saints and the Virgin Mary (Siena, 1894), as well as sermons for liturgical seasons, Advent, Christmas, etc. (Siena, 1895).

Among preachers of the second half of the 18th century are Joseph Anthony Santini, of Iesi (*Lenten sermons*, Venice, 1775), Gregory Seratrice, of the Piedmont province (*Panegyrics*, Vercelli, 1777), Albert Marchi, of the Sardegna province (*Panegyrics*, vol. 1, Cagliari, 1784). Marchi was professor of experimental physics at the Royal University of Cagliari, later of dogmatic theology at the same institution. Evidently in the good graces of the ruling family, he preached the funeral oration of Maria Antonia Ferdinanda, Queen of Sardegna, in the cathedral of Cagliari (Cagliari, 1785). Bishop Joseph Maria Pilo, bishop of Ales and Terralba in Sardegna, published his homilies (Cagliari, 1781-1785, 4 v.), which he directed to his people after he was too old and infirm to visit them personally, as had been his wont.

Italy, where religious enjoyed freedom until 1866, naturally produced the most preachers, but it was Spain that gave birth to the most illustrious representative of sacred oratory at this time and perhaps in the Order's history, Juan González (1812-1883), of the province of Castile. Since he is also noteworthy on other accounts, let it suffice here to call attention to his *Catholicism and Society Defended from the Pulpit* (11 v., Madrid, 1866-1867), a massive collection that enjoyed a wide vogue and was familiarly known to clerical users as "The González."

Carlos Morata, of the province of Aragon, collected the sermons he preached in the cathedral of Valencia, adding an interesting prefix on the state of preaching in Spain (*Panegyrical and Moral Sermons*, pt. 1, Valencia, 1802).

In Straubing, Germany, Ludwig Fritz (1812-1896) is worthy of note. His impressive homiletic production includes Marian sermons (2 v., Schaffhausen, 1856-1857), sermons on the office for the Dead (new ed., 2 v., Regensburg, 1895), and sermons on the Little Office of Our Lady (2 v., Regensburg, 1895).

Chapter 11

The Intellectual Life, 1750-1900

The general chapter of 1838 was the first opportunity since the French Revolution given the Carmelites to gather and consider general concerns of the Order. One of these was the pursuit of learning, since the Middle Ages a private concern of the old orders.

The Curriculum of Studies

The chapter made a valiant effort to shore up the sadly sagging academic structure. A new roster of ten general *studia* was drawn up: Messina, Dublin, Coimbra, Forlì, Palermo (S. Nicolò), Trapani, Florence, Pisa, Naples (Carmine Maggiore), and Lucca. Coimbra, it should be noted, had by this time been suppressed.

Provincial *studia* were also designated: in the province of St. Albert, Modica for philosophy and theology, Calascibetta for theology; Petralia Soprana and Linguaglossa for philosophy; in the Roman province, Velletri for theology, Palestrina for philosophy; in the province of Romagna, Iesi for philosophy and theology; in the province of Sardegna, Cagliari and Sassari, both for philosophy and theology; in the province of Monte Santo, Palermo and Monforte for philosophy and theology, Catania for philosophy; in the province of Santa Maria della Scala, Catania for philosophy and theology, Caltagirone for philosophy, Scicli for theology; in the province of Malta, Notabile for philosophy and theology. In the Kingdom of Naples, Ostuni, Francavilla, Penne, and Sulmona were declared *studia* for philosophy and theology. At the time, these four convents in Puglia and Abruzzo were floating in a void and were temporarily governed by a commissary of the prior general. In 1850, they would become part of the new Neapolitan province.

With regard to the course of studies, the chapter confirmed the decrees of 1704, approved by Pope Clement XI in 1711. However, the course content was revised: for theology the text of Anthony Gauggi was to be followed; for philosophy that of "the recent author Fractamaiori." Oddly enough, the chapter makes no reference to the *Decreta gradus ac studia respicientia* (Velletri, 1836) of the prior general, Aloysius Calamata, approved by the Congregation for Bishops and Religious, August 23, 1836.

Thus, while Catholic thinkers, especially in Germany, were beginning to develop a positive-historical methodology in step with the advancement of knowledge, the chapter officially affirmed its loyalty to scholasticism. The reduction of the course content to a single manual was a policy which unfortunately was to prevail in modern theological schools.

The Church itself opted for scholasticism, which in the form of Neo-Thomism underwent a phoenix-like transformation and in all countries attracted the support of outstanding Catholic thinkers, especially after Leo XIII in his encyclical, *Aeterni patris*, August 4, 1879, recommended the doctrine of the Angelic Doctor as the vehicle for restoring Catholic philosophy. On the occasion, Angelo Savini wrote to the pope, thanking him for this document, at the same time passing in review the Carmelite contribution to theology.

The New Theology

Nevertheless, there had been signs that Carmelites were beginning to move away from scholasticism toward positive historical theology. Authorities never had much luck legislating Carmelite doctrine. In 1760, Joachim Pontalti had found it necessary to call regents to order. He bewailed their excessive freedom of opinion and itch to follow the new proponents of modern philosophy. Lecturers were too prolix: they inserted extraneous historical facts into their lectures and heaped up texts of the councils and the Fathers. The prior general did not deny probability to the doctrines of the moderns, but deemed them less apt for elucidating revelation and confuting heretics. Recommending the systems of Thomism and Baconism, he went on to describe the streamlined logically reasoned manner in which lectures should be presented.

Deserving of Pontalti's censure, if not its actual provocation, was John Philibert Periconi (1707-1797), credited with having introduced Cartesianism into the *studia* of the Order in Sicily and Rome. A native of Palermo, he became affiliated to the province of Venice, where he functioned as regent in Padua. His published works include an *Apology for the Conjugal State* (Padua, 1796) in reply to an anonymous French work, and a defense of the Christian faith, *Reason of the Gospel* (2 v., Venice, 1777), both of them innocent of scholastic reasoning. Pericone is Molin's Socrates in his *Philibert, or Dialogues on Theology*, from which the master's ideas on theological methodology may be gleaned.

Augustine Molin (1775-1840), a convert from Jewry in childhood, was born in Venice and entered the Order there in 1796. He made his studies in the *studium* of Padua and was lecturing there at the time of its suppression in 1810. As a diocesan priest, he continued his pedagogical career. A distinguished and fruitful career in academe was cut short, when he was accused of an act of homosexuality with a seminarian, while conducting a retreat for clerics in Verona in 1821. He never ceased to protest his innocence and demand a fair trial. Molin had by no means lost the confidence of many estimable persons and was able to continue, though in a muted measure, his life of study, preaching, and teaching until his death in 1840.

Molin wrote extensively but published little. His former pupil, who became custodian of the Barberini library, Sante Pieralisi, incorporated the sixty manuscript volumes of his works into this collection, whence they found their way in 1902 into the Vatican Library. They comprise sacred scripture, philosophy, theology, sermons, ascetics, biography, literature, fine arts, and science. His paraphrase of the psalms in Italian (Padua, 1845) and life of St. Mark (Rome, 1864) were published posthumously. His works witness to an unusual breadth of mind and learning and place Molin in the first ranks of the savants of his time.

Of particular interest is his *Philibert, or Dialogues on Theology* (Barb. Lat. 3417), in which in the form of a dialogue with Periconi in the role of Plato, he proposes the reform of theological studies. He rejects the notion of theology proposed by late scholastics, which would exclude the content of revelation from theological science and reduce its role to drawing conclusions from revelation. Theology, he contends, should concern itself principally with the sources of revelation, scripture and tradition, bringing to bear on them all the linguistic and scientific disciplines developed in modern times. Philosophy he considers a polemical function of theology. While Molin's methodology is in some respects a salutary reaction to the abuses of scholasticism, his exclusion of all deduction from theology is excessive and his inclusion of philosophy in a subordinate role in theology confuses two sciences. The range of skills he requires of the perfect theologian is unrealistic and causes him to conclude that such a paragon has never existed and perhaps never will.

During Molin's lifetime, dedication to contemporary thinking is to be found in the very person of a prior general, Aloysius Anthony Faro (1755-1832), in praise of whom it was said that "disdaining the jargon of the peripatetics and the much admired subtleties of the scholastics, he learned through the philosophical writings of Bacon and Locke the interesting art of guiding the spirit carefully along the difficult path of truth and then of reasoning according to a conclusive and precise method" (L.B. Corvaja). His well-furnished library, which among other works contained those of Lamennais, Barruel, and De Maistre, shows that he was well acquainted with contemporary French thinking.

In Portugal, Pombal's reform of studies revolutionized Carmelite thinking in philosophy and theology. To correspond to the new statutes of the University of Coimbra, the provincial, Francis Ferreira da Graça, issued *Estatutos literarios* (Lisboa, 1776), which replaced Balthasar Limpo's statutes of 1555. Two types of institution were prescribed: a college of the arts (Collegio da Bella Instrucção), which would offer Greek, Hebrew, Arabic, and rhetoric (part 2) and a "College of Major Sciences" with chairs of philosophy, church history, dogmatic or polemical theology, canon law, and sacred scripture (part 3). Philosophy was not to be rated a mere handmaid of theology, but was to be placed among the major disciplines (pt. 3, ch. 1, no. 1). The professor of theology should treat the two principal *loci*, scripture and tradition, and confute errors in their regard. He should not treat hypothetical questions, "all sophistical questions whatsoever, useless and unimportant for dogma and only introduced by men who, with the erroneous maxims of their scholastic doctrine, distort and confuse the proper order of letters" (pt. 3, ch. 4, no. 4). It is to be hoped that Pombal had better luck than Urban VIII in making the Carmelites learn oriental languages.

The decadence of studies, the provincial states, set in with the *Additamentos* of 1620, which eliminated the *biblici* and enforced speculative theology. On entering the college, students would be required to swear to observe its statutes, being given to understand that by their oath they agreed not to follow nor defend "those pernicious doctrines and erroneous maxims of the Jesuits, which have been proscribed and condemned by the laws of his majesty" (pt. 1, ch. 2, no. 4).

Anselm Erlacher, who taught philosophy and theology in the *studia* of the Upper German province, was a follower of Kant. His works, all published at Würzburg, comprise *Philosophical Theses* (1794), *The Religion Founded by Jesus of Nazareth* (1796), and *Aphorisms Taken from the Whole of Philosophy* (1798). He was prior of Bamberg, when the convent was suppressed in 1802 and thereafter exchanged the academic chair for a chaplaincy in an insane asylum.

The Carmelite program of internal studies failed to outride the storms of the 19th century. Academic degrees (lectorate, baccalaureate, magisterium) continued to be conferred by the priors general, but were not recognized outside the Order and within it amounted to little more than honorary degrees, bestowing certain privileges of precedence and suffrage, which had better been left buried in the ruins of the past. Henceforth, minor and major seminaries of the Order were regulated by the prescriptions of canon law and the Holy See. Such studies, preparatory to the priesthood, were generally recognized by secular and ecclesiastical institutions of learning as valid for further study.

The long line of Carmelite professors at the Sapienza in Rome terminated in the year 1871 and in the person of Angelo Savini. This rupture was hardly a matter of free choice after the fall of the Papal States and the nationalization of the university. On February 10, 1872, C. Carlucci, rector of the Royal University of Rome, announced that Angelo Savini had ceased to be a professor of moral theology as of November 1, 1871, since he had not resumed teaching in the new scholastic year and had declared that he would also abstain in the future.

Theological Writings

The work of Peter Andrew Gauggi (1714-1776) recommended by the general chapter of 1838 was entitled *Enchiridion theologicum scholasticum dogmaticum iuxta mentem Ioannis de Bacone* (8 v., Romae, 1766-1768) and was the last of the *summae*, or comprehensive summaries of all theology, in Carmelite theological writings. The beggarly production of the century and a half that followed treats only individual aspects or topics of theology. Works of moral theology and apologetics predominate.

Peter Thomas Malaguzzi, member of the Mantuan congregation and professor at the University of Ferrara, published *A Manual for Parish Priests* (2 v., Ravenna, 1757) in the form of questions and answers. Peter Reyneri, former provincial of Piedmont, composed *The Truly Learned Christian* (4 v., Turin, 1772-1776), a sort of popular *summa* for the laity, also in question and answer form. An admirer, who also remained anonymous, published a series of lectures by an anonymous Carmelite in the cathedral of Iesi on the first three chapters of Genesis: *Saggio di alcune lezioni della sacra scrittura* (Iesi, 1777). While Camillo Carmignani (1803-1867), professor in the University of Florence and its dean, 1863-1864, spent his life in study and teaching, little of his labor saw print. His *Treatise on Human Acts* appeared posthumously (Florence, 1898).

An impressive work, composed in the twilight of Carmel in Portugal, was the ten-volume *Minister of Jesus Christ in the Tribunal of Penance* (Lisbon, 1797-1802) by Michael d'Azevedo. Also worthy of notice are the (Seventeen) *Moral Dissertations* (3 v., 1814-1815) by Joseph of St. Cyril Carneiro, doctor of the University of Coimbra and royal censor of the Holy Office. He got a taste of his own medicine, when his work fell under censure for its "absurd propositions contrary to the laws of the kingdom." Target of official displeasure was dissertation sixteen, "That the government of the Church is monarchical and that its monarch is the Pope" (III, 275-302).

Joseph Vincent Díaz Bravo, prior and regent of Tudela in the province of Aragon, addressed himself to a very particular problem in two books, *The Confessor Instructed in What Concerns his Accomplice in the Heinous Sin Against the Sixth Commandment* (Pamplona, 1751; Madrid, 1756) and *The Penitent Improperly Questioned About the Name and Habitation of his Accomplice* (Madrid, 1768). In the area of commutative justice, Martin Benessat, of the convent of Vich, wrote an *Aviso caritativo* (Vich, 1790) against Joseph Maria de Uria Nafarrando, author of *Increasing Business with a Clear*

Conscience.

Walbertus of St. Aldegunde (1687-1751), quondam provincial of Wallo-Belgium, produced a *Moral Theology, or Solution of Cases of Conscience* (4 t. in 8 v., Mons, 1738-1739). The *Summa of the Cavillings of Heretics* by Angelus Postepski (1704-1767), former assistant general for the Polish provinces, was published in Venice in 1768, after his death in Lwów. The most recent heretics treated are Spinoza and Quesnel. The author refutes every one of the 101 alleged errors of the latter, who is the only 18th century figure considered.

In the fields of catechetics and apologetics the *Explicación y comento de las preguntas y respuestas de la declaración de la doctrina cristiana* of Francis Xavier Arribas, first published in 1732, continued to be of use (Salamanca, 1746; Almería, 1826). Francis Mary Soldini published *Apologetical Thoughts on the Christian Religion* (Siena, 1792); Joseph Angelo Chercher issued *Conferences on Science, Faith, and Church in Relation to Man and Society* (Caltagirone, 1889). John Caspar Hoepffner (1681-1765) wrote an explanation of the catechism of Canisius in five volumes. Gallus Schab, whose translations of spiritual works were noted above, also produced apologetical and catechetical books: *The Riches, Beauty, and Power of the Christian Faith* (Sulzbach, 1827, 2 v.), *Elucidation of Apologetics*, (Sulzbach, 1832), and *Handbook of the Regensburg Catechism* (Sulzbach, 1836).

Historical Works

Mariano Ventimiglia (1703-1790) was the most important Carmelite historian of the second half of the 18th century. Mention has already been made of his *Chronological History of the Priors General of the Carmelite Order* (Naples, 1773), often consulted in the course of the present work. He also wrote a history of the Order in Italy, *Il sacro Carmelo italiano* (Naples, 1779), featuring lists of convents in each province as they are found in the 18th century; and a work devoted to illustrious sons of the Carmine Maggiore of Naples (Naples, 1756). His writings, though not above reproach from a critical point of view, remain useful.

Engelbert of St. Frances (1701-1779), assistant general for Germany, performed a signal service with his *Brief Series of the General Chapters*, 1318-1762 (Rome, 1765). The *Liber ordinis*, containing the acts of the general chapters, remained buried in the archive of the Order, and Engelbert's calendar of the principal decrees of each chapter was for most Carmelites long the only source of information about these important assemblies.

The *Short Compendium of the Origin and Antiquity of the Holy Order of Carmel* (Madrid, 1766) by Emmanuel García Calahorra fortunately does not confine itself to the theme announced in the title, but also provides data on the provinces up to the middle of the 18th century.

Histories of individual provinces are regrettably a rarity in Carmelite historiography. On the eve of the suppression of the Venetian province Valerius Anthony Zarrabini composed his *Historical Series of Carmelites* (Venice, 1779), little more than a pamphlet but a welcome contribution to the scanty knowledge about this province. Earlier in the 18th century Eusebio Blasco y Llorente published *Historical and Apologetical Ratiocinations for the Adornment of Carmel in Aragon* (Zaragoza, 1726), in spite of its bombastic title still a source of useful information.

A unique item of Carmelite historiography is the anonymous *History of the*

Order of Our Lady of Mount Carmel in the Holy Land Under its First Nine Priors General (Maastricht, 1798), actually written by the Discalced Carmelite, John Nepomucene of the Holy Family, the first and for at least another century, the last attempt at a critical appraisal of the Order's origins and early years. Not all the author's conclusions have stood the test of time, but the book is a surprising phenomenon of critical method, which found no echo in Carmelite circles. The time and place of its production, Belgium under revolutionary France, may explain its critical tone and the scarcity of its remaining copies.

Remarkable about the 19th century, otherwise undistinguished for Carmelite historiography, is the brisk production of hagiographical works. In the troubled years of Lucca's tenuous existence, Joseph Fanucci managed to write biographies of St. Angelus the Martyr (Lucca, 1870; Monza, 1883), Bl. Baptist of Mantua (Lucca, 1887), Elijah the prophet (Lucca, 1888), Bl. Bartholomew Fanti (Lucca, 1891), Ven. John Dominic Lucchesi (Lucca, 1892), St. Avertanus (Lucca, 1895). In Florence, the learned Santi Mattei (1816-1887) wrote lives of St. Andrew Corsini (Florence, 1872), St. Simon Stock (Rome, 1873), and Bl. John Soreth (Rome, 1874), besides translating and condensing F. Richard's life of Bl. Frances d'Amboise (Rome, 1869).

Andrew Elias Farrington (1840-1922) has to his credit a score of spiritual works, among them lives of St. Mary Magdalen de' Pazzi (Dublin, 1889) and St. Simon Stock (Dublin, 1892). His *St. Elias and the Carmelites* (Dublin, 1890) tells the story of Carmel through the lives of its saints.

These works incorporate all the worst features of 19th century popular hagiography; nevertheless they struck a sympathetic cord in a large circle of readers at a time when the Order was prostrate. During the worst years, the prior general, Angelo Savini, took consolation from distributing these little books among his scattered flock.

Linus of Mount Carmel Melo Luna (1821-1874), of the Pernambuco province, was director of the provincial public library in Recife (1860) and one of the founders of the Archeological Society of Pernambuco (1862). He served as provincial from 1850 to 1853, but after the law of 1855, he applied for secularization. In 1872, he was named canon of the cathedral of Olinda. Besides articles in the *Revista do Instituto Arquelógico de Pernambuco* and other reviews, he wrote *An Historical and Biographical Memorial of the Clergy of Pernambuco* (Recife, 1857). A preacher of the Royal Chapel, he published a number of sermons delivered on special occasions. As a Carmelite he wrote several devotional treatises: *An Exposition of the Excellent Devotion of the Holy Scapular of Our Lady of Mount Carmel* (Recife, 1852), *A Brief Notice of the Most Important Facts in the Life of St. Teresa of Jesus* (Recife, 1852, 1912) and *A Brief Notice of the Excellent Cult of the Immaculate Conception of Mary* (Recife, 1855), composed on the occasion of the declaration of the dogma.

Belles Lettres: J. M. Pagnini

Indicative of the temper of the times, while theology languished, some figures of eminence emerge in the fields of letters, arts, and science.

Joseph Maria Pagnini (1737-1814) was the son of Francesco, gardener of the Carmine of Pistoia. The friars noticed the precocious intelligence of the boy and encouraged his father to have him educated. In 1753, Pagnini took the Carmelite habit in Florence in the convent of the Mantuan Congregation and made his novitiate in Parma. In 1759, he offered his first Mass in his native Pistoia. Joseph had for his first teacher the priest, Joseph Borelli, a man of some culture with a special interest in Latin, but his particular mentor in the classics was Caesar Franchini Taviani (1700-1780), professor of rhetoric in the public schools, who over the years monitored not only his scholarly but his spiritual progress as well. Pagnini was capable of verse of some quality, but as Franchini realized, his genius lay in translating, in transmuting the linguistic vesture of a work of art.

Some of Pagnini's compositions came to the attention of Carlo Frugoni, celebrated poet of the court of Parma, and whether or not it was due to his interest, the fact remains that in 1764 Duke Philip invited the Carmelite to teach in the academy of his pages. On Philip's death in 1769 and the succession of Ferdinand, the *Paggeria* was joined to the College of Nobles to form the new university, in which Pagnini was given the chair of rhetoric and Greek. But teaching to him was only a routine chore, perfunctorily performed. His real life lay among his literary friends in this "Athens of Italy" and in the study and translation of his beloved classics. His translation of the *Odes of Anacreon* appeared in Venice in 1766, thought to be the first translation from the Greek to be printed. At the time, he was working on the Greek bucolics, Theocritus, Moschus, Bion, and Simmia. Theocritus was a favorite of William Du Tillot, who urged him to finish his translation and promised to pay for its printing, but the French minister had already been driven from the duchy of Parma (1771), when the work finally appeared (Parma, 1780). In the course of time, there followed italianizations of Terence (*Phormia*, 1783), Callimachus (1792), Epictetus (1793), Cebete (1793), Sappho (1794), Hesiod (1797). His translation of the satires and letters of Horace, published posthumously (Pisa, 1814), had been crowned by the Academy of the Crusca three years previously. He used the pseudonym Pistogene Eleuterio, or his name in the Arcadia of Rome, Eritisco Pilenejo. His friend, Giambattista Bodoni added to his compositions elegance of printed form.

Pagnini did not confine his translating skill to the ancient classical languages. He had for his tutor in English the learned Minim, Francis Jacquier, and translated Pope's *Four Seasons* (Parma, 1780) and *Ode to St. Cecilia* (Parma 1800), as well as *Dinarbas* (Pistoia, 1791) by Cornelia Knight, a lady poetess in vogue at the time.

Other learned women of Pagnini's acquaintance were Mary Magdalen Morelli (in Arcadia, Corilla Olimpica), poetess crowned on the Campidoglio in 1776, and Fortuna Sulgher Fantastici Marchesini (Arcadian name, Temira Parasside), skilled in languages and the natural sciences. Pagnini translated Voltaire's *Alzire* (Parma, 1797). His French friends were Du Tillot and the Abbé de Condillac.

Pagnini kept aloof from politics and learned to live under whatever regime was in power, a studious objectivity, which might not find favor in more patriotic breasts. When Duke Ferdinand died in 1802, the friar thought of returning to Florence, to his convent by affiliation; instead he accepted the offer of the chair of the humanities at the University of Pisa. Under the French, he was assigned the chair of Latin literature and was elected dean of the faculty of letters.

One might easily form the impression that for Pagnini his religious vocation was a poor second to classical scholarship. There can be little doubt that the cloister attracted him as a refuge for study, yet through the unsettled times, the suppression of the Mantuan Congregation, the annexation of Parma by the French, he remained loyal to the Order. Only at the general secularization of 1810, which ejected him from his convent, did he take up residence in private as a secular priest, in which capacity the bishop of Pistoia thoughtfully made him a canon of his cathedral. His funeral was held in the Carmine of Pisa, and he was buried in the suburban church of San Jacobo degli Scalzi, where his nephew Joseph Cucchi erected his tomb. "Many are the examples of his Christian virtues that might be adduced, especially his charity toward the poor," his biographer, Sebastian Ciampi, concludes.

Evasio Leone, 1765-1820

Evasio Leone was born in Casal Monferrato, and entered the Order in Asti of the Piedmont province. He made his studies in Turin and upon their completion began lecturing there. He was still a student, when he produced a translation in Italian verse of the *Song of Solomon* (Turin, 1787), which like the Mantuan's precocious *Eclogues* remained his most successful work. It won him immediate recognition, was set to music by Giuseppe Pietro Bagetti, and saw many printings. His later versification of the *Lamentations of Jeremiah* (Turin, 1798) was less successful.

Leone soon became intensely active in literary circles. The newly founded academy of the *Unanimi* wanted him as a member with the name *Sollecito*. He contributed articles to the *Giornale Scientifico Letterario*. In 1790, the king appointed him doctor of the College of Fine Arts in the University of Turin. In token of gratitude, Leone composed *The Princes of the Royal House of Savoy* (Turin, 1792), in which the achievements of each of the dukes from the year 1000 are described in a sonnet, but which remained incomplete due to the French invasion.

Under the French, Leone published a sonnet, *On the Inauguration of the Tree of Liberty in the Square of the Commune in Turin*, in the newspaper *Il Repubblicano Piemontese*, January 5, 1799, a composition which would hardly have endeared him to the Austrians, who occupied Savoy the following June. In any case, the Carmine of Turin was suppressed in April of that year, and Leone sought asylum in Parma, even more alluring to a votary of the Muses.

There, too, he was soon much in demand as an occasional preacher and as a poet at the social events of the nobility. The *Accademia Italiana* received him into its membership. He lived in the same convent as Pagnini and cultivated the same learned friends. His relationship to Bodoni seems to have been even closer, and a number of his books were issued by the famous printer. In 1802, the bishop of Orvieto, Caesar Brancadoro, the same year obtained for him the chair of eloquence and poetry at the University of Fermo. The following year, Brancadoro succeeded to the archbishopric of Fermo. After the French in 1808 annexed the Marches, Leone's academic career survived. He served as regent of the new University of Fermo from 1809 to 1813, as well as lecturer in the fine arts and ancient and modern history. He was the first editor of the *Giornale del Tronto* established in 1813. His star fell with Napoleon's. His precipitous exit from Fermo in May of 1814 suggests that his relations with the French invader had been rather warmer than would commend him to the restored papacy. Brancadora, one of the black cardinals deported to Paris, on his return showed no inclination to recall the Carmelite. Repeated appeals to friends in Parma such as Giambattista Bodoni and Angelo Pezzana, learned curator of the library of Parma, also failed to bear fruit.

Leone spent his last years as a wanderer on the face of the earth, in perpetual search of gainful employment to replenish his dwindling funds, without a thought, it would seem, of returning to the convent. After his disappearance from Fermo, he embarked from Naples on a ship which met with a storm and had to run for port at Monopoli on the Adriatic. The bishop, Lawrence Villani, welcomed the famous poet and orator, and placed him in charge of studies in his seminary and *liceo*. Leone's Mecenas, however, died soon afterwards. His next asylum was Corfù, where the Count of Grattagliano, consul for Naples and Austria, took him under his patronage. The island had only just become a British protectorate, and the High Commissioner, Sir Thomas Maitland, entrusted the famous man of letters with the task of tidying up the literary style of the constitutions. On his *Vision on the Tomb of the Princess of Wales* (Corfù, 1818), which he considered his *chef d'oeuvre*, Leone pinned his hopes for a professorship of Italian and Latin literature in a proposed University of the Ionian Islands, but this institution never materialized. In fact, the *Vision* was posthumously censured by the Sacred Congregation of the Index, August 26, 1822.

At this time, too, Leone busied himself with the edition of a manuscript of the *De consolatione*, by Nicholas, 15th century bishop of Modrussa, which he had rescued on the point of being shredded by a grocer in Fermo, and concerning which he carried on a learned correspondence with his librarian friend, Angelo Pezzana. Leone's transcript of the manuscript, forwarded to his brother, William, professor in the University of Turin, has been lost sight of.

In 1818, Leone undertook a Byronic trip to Greece and communicated his romantic ruminations to his friend, Thomas Salvadori, in letters of September 5 and November 18. On his return to Corfù, he decided on a second voyage of literary exploration with a view to publishing an account of his travels. Thereafter, Leone is heard of no more. One rumor had him dead on the Greek island of Cerigo, but all inquiries by his brother were in vain. There is reason to believe that, at the end, Evasio, subject to fits of profound depression, had become mentally unbalanced. His writings, occasional sermons, eulogies, and poems, underwent many editions, some by Bodoni. Today, the once lionized Carmelite's works are as unknown as his grave.

Another Italian poet was Felix Zampi, a native of Ascoli and member of the reformed province of Monte Santo, who anticipated Leone by two score years with his verse paraphrase of the *Lamentations of Jeremiah* (Venice, 1756). Carlambrogio Vioglieri, of Ravenna, published *Sacred Poetry* (Ancona, 1760). His name in the Arcadia of Rome was Cratone Ismenio. Cyril Bellotti, of the Carmel of Lucca, produced *La Partenepanagia* (Camajore, 1887), a life of the Virgin Mary in seventeen cantos comprising around 6,000 lines.

John González, 1812-1883

John González, whose sermons have already been noticed, might equally be ranked among polemicist theologians, but the vehicle of his thought, journalism, concerned with particular political circumstances, would rather place him among men of letters. Born in Romanones in the province of Guadalajara, he entered the Order in the Carmen of Madrid, pronouncing his vows in 1831. Studying in Toledo, when the suppression of 1836 occurred, he continued his courses for the licentiate at the university.

During these years González's vocation as a defender of the faith of Spain was shaped through acquaintance with a number of young men, who would constitute the nucleus of Catholic journalism in the years to come. The principal contributors to *El Católico*, founded in 1840 after Baldomero Espartero wrested the regency from Queen Maria Cristina. In Madrid, González joined the staff of *La Cruz*, founded in 1842 by his Toledo classmate, Luis Carbonero y Sol. Juan Donoso Cortés sought his collaboration, and he also contributed to Balmes' *Pensamiento de la Nación*, which promoted the marriage of Isabella II to the eldest son of Don Carlos (V) as a way of solving the Carlist dilemma.

This was also the hope nourished by *La Esperanza*, founded in 1844 by Pedro La Hoz, of which González became editor and to which he contributed regularly for seven years and intermittently for a total of two more. In 1848, he founded *La Iglesia* and assumed its direction. In 1847, González obtained the doctorate at the University of Madrid and three years later was named court preacher.

In 1853, González moved to Valladolid, where for the next fifteen years he taught dogmatic theology in the seminary. At the same time, he was named a canon of the cathedral, a distinction by which he became nationally known as "The Canon." Besides articles in newspapers, he wrote *A New Manual for Curates* (Madrid, 1849), *The Papacy, Especially in the 19th Century* (Madrid, 1850), also translated into French and Italian, *The Catechism of the Virgin* (1870), a defense of the Virgin Mary, which the Discalced Carmelites of London were said to have translated into English, and *The Future of the Catholic Nations* (1877), translated into French as well. His monumental *Sermons* (Madrid, 1853-1866, 10 v.) was an arsenal of apologetic material for 19th century Catholic Spain. González collaborated with Monescillo and Carbonero y Sol in the production of the *Colección de Autores Clásicos*. After the chaotic years of the maladroit republic (1873-1875), Spain again had a king, Alfonso XII, and a well-earned peace. The ex-Carmelite's political thought, though predictable, would be interesting to investigate.

Frei Caneca's political and journalistic writings have already been noticed.

The Fine Arts

While the fine arts of secular inspiration advanced with giant strides into the modern period, religious art and art by religious, it need hardly be said, suffered a severe decline, from which it has not yet recovered. Still, some Carmelites in a modest way practised the arts as well as letters.

In the field of architecture, the Order is worthily represented by Brother Joseph Albert Pina, (1693-1773). He was born in Moyuela and made his profession in Zaragoza (1719). In the region of Aragon, he constructed twenty-four churches, among them the Carmelite church of Játiva (no longer in existence), the church of the Carmelite nuns of Onteniente, the chapel of Our Lady of Grace in Caudete, and the deanery church of Villarreal de los Infantes. He was directing the construction of the collegiate church as well as the Carmelite church of Játiva when death overtook him. Balbino Velasco judges him "one of the most important baroque architects of Aragon and Valencia. We are led to this conclusion," he comments, "by the grandeur, elegance, and sense of proportion and order of the deanery church of Villarreal." Pina left an influence on his nephew, the Hieronymite monk and architect, Francis of St. Barbara.

Michael of the Angels Menchaca, of the Castilian province, followed Bishop Bernard Serrada (1672-1733) to South America and built his cathedral in Cuzco. In the Romagna province, Brother Joachim Pronti, of Rimini, constructed the vaulted ceiling of the Carmine of Florence after the fire of 1771. In the same city, he designed the Church of St. Mark (1777). His master in the art was Brother Dionysius Pagnini, of Pesaro, who died in 1767 at the premature age of thirty-two.

In spite of his name, the mulatto primitive, Jesuino of Mount Carmel Gusmão (1764-1819) was not a Carmelite - his mixed blood barred him even from becoming a tertiary - but, greatly devoted to Carmel, he filled the Order's church in Itù with his interesting naive paintings, of which the ceiling of the sanctuary, a medallion representing St. Teresa on the ceiling of the nave, and a medallion of the Infant of Prague have survived. In São Paulo, he painted the ceiling of the Carmelite church, since demolished, with the exception of a medallion from the ceiling of one of the chapels; also the ceiling of the church of the Carmelite Third Order and eighteen oil paintings on wood in the corridor leading from the sacristy to the street. Ten oil paintings on wood, executed for the convent of St. Teresa, now in the museum of the Metropolitan Curia, cannot with certainty be attributed to him.

In the Romagna province, Melchior Oltremari, born in Bergantino (Mantua), painted a number of Carmelite saints for the convent of Lugo. Joachim Poggi (d. 1796) was a joiner who built the night choir in the Church of Our Lady of Graces in Bologna. Elias Facchini (d. 1874), a woodcarver, made sets of candelabra in Forlì.

In Upper Germany, the lay brothers, Thaddaeus of St. Serapion (1694-1768) and Paul of St. John Evangelist (1734-1773) were goldsmiths. In 1765, the latter made four silver chandeliers for the St. Joseph's chapel in the church of Abensberg on the occasion of the centenary of the confraternity. In Straubing, for the confraternity of bakers' helpers he made the poles for the processional canopy of the Blessed Sacrament out of gilded copper with silver figures. The material for the canopy was selected by Brother Nicholas of St. Barbara (1713-1768), by profession a vestment maker. In the same province, Brother Gregory of St. Matthew (1735-1784) illuminated a number of liturgical books in Straubing and Abensberg.

The Natural Sciences

In this period, the Brazilian provinces distinguished themselves in the natural sciences. Pedro de Santa Marianna Souza (1782-1864), of the Pernambuco province, studied mathematics at the Royal Marine Academy in Lisbon. From 1813 to 1833, he taught that subject at the Military Academy in Rio de Janeiro, having many illustrious persons among his pupils. In 1833, he became the tutor of Peter II and took up residence in the imperial palace. In 1841, he was named titular bishop of Chrysopolis. Five years later, he was granted an honorary doctorate in mathematics. His *Memorial on the Identity of the Product of Imaginary Factors With the Same Factors Multiplied by Each Other* (Rio de Janeiro, 1824) is preserved in the National Library in Rio de Janeiro.

Custodio Alves Serrão (1799-1873), a native of Maranhão, taught science (botany, zoology, chemistry, and mineralogy) in the Military Academy of Rio de Janeiro, 1825-1847. He was also the director of the National Museum and Botanical Gardens. In the interest of his specialty, he led an expedition of exploration into

Northern Brazil. Besides articles for periodicals, he wrote *Lectures on Chemistry and Mineralogy* (Rio de Janeiro, 1833) and *A Brief Notice on a Collection of Types of Brazilian Wood* (n. p., 1867).

Leander of the Blessed Sacrament (1780-1829), of the Pernambuco province, lectured on botany at the Academy of Medicine and Surgery in Rio de Janeiro, and from 1824 directed the Botanical Gardens. His writings include *Instructions on Collecting, Preserving, and Shipping Objects of Brazilian Natural History and the Founding of the Museum and Botanical Gardens of Rio de Janeiro* (1819) and *An Economical Memorial on the Planting, Culture, and Preparation of Tea* (1825).

In Italy, we find a number of Carmelites teaching science in the universities. John Anthony Serrani (1706-1760), provincial of the Romagna province from 1757 to 1760, taught mathematics at Verona and was otherwise devoted to the arts and sciences. He was interested in archeology and corresponded with the poet, Scipio Maffei, and Joseph Bianchini, continuator of Baronius. Albert Marchi (d. 1794) was appointed professor of experimental physics at the University of Cagliari by Charles Emmanuel I, a post he held for fourteen years. Likewise in Sardinia, Joseph Albert Sircana (d. after 1820) taught physics at the University of Sassari. Francis Piacentini (1743-1827) lectured on physics and mathematics in the diocesan seminary of Pisa. Athanasius Cavalli (1731-1797) was a professor of experimental physics in the Gregorian University of Rome.

Chapter 12

Carmelus Redivivus, 1889-1919

In the last quarter of the nineteenth century, corresponding to the long reign of the more liberal Leo XIII, religious orders, like the Church itself, having been stripped of their civil role in society, were allowed by the governments to revive. The Church was freed from the interference which it had suffered from absolutist Catholic regimes and from material cares, and was able to devote itself exclusively to spiritual concerns. However, it should not be forgotten that the price paid was the end of Christian society. We leave to other admirers the warmest praise of the nineteenth century anti-clerical liberals. Whatever noble motives lay behind their actions, the welfare of the Church and the religious interests of the people were not among them. The world they were building had no place for God, as we have come to know.

For the Carmelites, the years 1889 to 1930 saw the consummation of the restoration of the Order. These years may be divided into three periods, corresponding to the terms of office of three outstanding priors general: Aloysius Galli (1889-1900), Pius Mayer (1902-1918), and Peter Elias Magennis (1919-1931).

The General Chapter of 1889

By 1889, the Order was sufficiently revived to permit the convocation of a general chapter, the first since 1856. The years between had been catastrophic, but now the worst was over and the Order could raise its eyes to the future. At hand in Traspontina on October 14, besides two commissaries and the priors of Naples and Trapani, were the representatives of ten provinces, or remnants thereof: St. Albert, Rome, Ireland, Tuscany, Germano-Holland, Naples, Romagna, St. Angelus, Galicia, Malta (vicariate). The Italian provinces were headed by vicar provincials appointed by the vicar general due to the impossibility of holding chapters. In recent years, the prior general had managed with only two assistants, the actual ones being Albert Caruso (first) and Aloysius Galli (second). The latter was elected prior general by a comfortable majority.

The outgoing general, Angelo Savini, lacked a month until his seventy-third birthday and lived only three more months until January 17, 1890. For a quarter of a century, he had provided alert and balanced leadership during the worst period in the Order's history.

Aloysius Galli (1842-1900) was born in Poggio in the diocese of Rieti and took the Carmelite habit in Palestrina, June 12, 1859. After studies in Traspontina, he was ordained to the priesthood in 1864. Galli spent the rest of his life in Rome. He served first as assistant novice master in Traspontina (1865), then as novice master (1872). Concurrently, he was a consultor of the Congregation of Rites and a Lenten preacher in various Carmelite churches in Italy. In 1872, he was granted the master's degree in philosophy and theology. In 1884, he became pastor of San Nicolò ai Cesarini in the Largo Argentina, and in 1887 assistant general.

The chapter was presided over by the cardinal protector, John Simeoni, the first protector since 1593 to occupy himself exclusively with the Order's affairs. Since the division from the Discalced, one cardinal had overseen both orders, but in 1881 the

Discalced had requested and obtained a separate protector of their own. Six years previously, they had achieved unity through the fusion of the Spanish and Italian Congregations (the Portuguese Congregation had remained defunct). Perhaps the move toward a separate protector was precipitated by the difference over Mount Carmel, when a common protector would have constituted a conflict of interests.

Cardinal protectors of the Order after John Simeoni (1881-1892) were Vincent Vannutelli (1892-1930), Bonaventure Cerretti (1930-1933), Francis Marchetti Selvaggiani (1934-1951), Adeodato Piazza, O.C.D. (1951-1957), Dominic Tardini (1959-1961). In a letter of April 28, 1964, the Vatican Secretariate of State advised the dean of the Sacred College that cardinal protectors of religious orders would no longer be named.

The general chapter of 1889 is one of the important chapters in the history of the Order. Although not all its decisions were immediately implemented, it sketched out the form of Carmelite life, which, in common with other religious orders, was to be obtained in modern times. New constitutions were to be drawn up, based on the principles of the Stricter Observance, especially with regard to the common life. While the chapter notes that it cannot countermand the reformed constitutions, approved by the popes, its decision to accept them in principle in effect did away with any distinction of observance in the Order. The designation "reformed" became anachronistic. The chapter also abolished conventuality; individual religious were to belong to a province rather than a convent.

The storms of the suppressions had swept away the whole clutter of abusive customs and privileges. Landed property, the main source of income for communities, had been sequestered by the state, and they were now forced to share in common the offerings of the faithful, which became their only means of support. The secular state had unwittingly achieved overnight what no pope or superior had been able to bring about with centuries of effort.

It was agreed that the assistants should again number four.

In view of the "deplorable lack of space in Traspontina" a new house should be built to contain the general council and students of various provinces destined for higher studies and to provide lodging for the brethren visiting Rome.

The two commissaries present at the chapter were those of Spain and the United States of America. The chapter erected both commissariates into provinces.

The color of the habit should be brown (*griseus*), that of the reform. In Spain, the friars were to wear the rosary, an item of apparel also recommended to the rest of the Order, and in fact the Netherlands adopted it.

The General Chapter of 1896

The general chapter of 1896 returned Galli to office. The representation was that of 1889, except for the absence of the prior of Trapani and the presence of the prior of Traspontina. For some reason, too, the province of Monte Santo was at hand in the person of its provincial, Carmel Pagano; there can hardly have been much left of the province. There were still only two assistants general. The assembled fathers again urged the issue of new constitutions.

It was also proposed to separate the Bavarian convents from the Netherlands and constitute them a vicariate. To Straubing and Sossau, Mainburg and Habsberg had been added in 1892 and 1893 respectively. On December 8, 1896, the general council implemented the proposal, later appointing Anton Seidl vicar provincial of Bavaria.

In the Netherlands, convents were founded at Oss (1890) and Hoogeveen (1905). The Dutch houses were distinguished for a most exact religious observance. In 1880, they had issued a new edition of the constitutions of the Stricter Observance, which they followed most faithfully.

The vicariate of Malta also became a province. In 1892, the convent of San Giljan (St. Julian's) was added to those of Mdina (Notabile) and Valletta, thus fulfilling the requirements for the erection of a province. On May 31, 1892, the council of the Order, implementing the rescript of the Congregation for Bishops and Religious of May 7, formally instituted the Maltese province of St. Elias. In the 20th century, convents were established at Santa Venera (1912), Fgura (1945), and Fleur-de-Lys (1947).

The International College of St. Albert, Rome

The chapter did not refer to the new general *studium* the previous chapter had ordered erected in Rome, but the prior general had not been idle. Galli had been collecting money throughout the Order, when circumstances brought matters to a head. Late in 1893, Galli was notified by the Italian government that the part of Traspontina still occupied by the religious was needed for a barracks and would have to be vacated by January 2. Only a few rooms would be available for the pastor and curates. Up to that time, the front wing of the monastery had been taken over by the Order.

Galli leased the second and third floors of the Palazzo dei Convertendi in the nearby Piazza Scossacavalli, until then occupied by the Benedictines, who were moving to their new college on the Aventine. To these quarters, the prior general moved the curia and the students who attended the Pontificio Seminario Vaticano. Meanwhile, plans went ahead for a new college in the adjacent Prati section of the city.

On July 20, feast of St. Elijah the prophet, 1899, the cardinal protector of the Order, Vincent Vannutelli, laid the cornerstone of the new college, dedicated to St. Albert of Sicily, patron of the *studium*, when it was still located in Traspontina. The building was ready by the fall of 1901, in time for the opening of the school year. The modest faculty consisted of Francis Raiti (assistant general and first prior of the college), dogma; Anastasius Ronci (provincial of Rome), moral; Aloysius Malfatti (procurator general), philosophy. Aloysius Galli did not live to see the opening of his college; he died unexpectedly on May 2, 1900.

Galli's generalate still lay within the period of the Order's first awakening from the disorder wrought by the suppressions and continued with accelerated pace the revival fostered by Savini. He encouraged the recruitment and education of candidates, especially in Italy, where seminaries were established in Nocera Umbra, Montecatini, and Albano. More than once, he made the rounds of the provinces, visiting Spain, Germany, the Netherlands, and Ireland, to encourage the Order's growth in those places.

Galli was the last Italian up to the present to be elected by a general chapter. Control of affairs was slipping from the hands of the Italians, who had kept the Order alive during its almost mortal illness, and passing to the young provinces and to the old ones showing growth. The council of the Order, made up entirely of Italian members, met on May 8, 1900, six days after Galli's death, and elected Simon Bernardini (1838-1919) prior general. Born in Castelplanio in the diocese of Iesi, he entered the Carmelite convent in the latter city. He obtained the doctorate in 1872 and the following year was elected provincial of Romagna, an office he held for ten years. At the same time, he functioned as pastor in Macerata. In 1883, Savini called him to Rome to be procurator general of the Order and pastor of Traspontina. The general chapter of 1889 elected him first assistant general. As we have seen, it was Bernardini who completed St. Albert's College.

The General Chapter of 1902

Oddly enough, the general chapter convoked by Bernardini in 1902 did not elect him prior general. Instead, the American provincial, Pius Mayer, handily prevailed over him with 38 votes to 28.

Pius Mayer (1848-1918) was born in Riedlingen, Swabia, of a family with a tradition of civil service. He received his secondary education at the Jesuit college in Feldkirch. Thereafter, he attended business college and worked in the city hall with his father. After he had opted for the priesthood and emigrated to America, he made his studies at St. Francis Seminary in Milwaukee and was ordained for the diocese of Leavenworth in 1871. He was assistant at the cathedral, when he decided to become a Carmelite. Professed at Scipio in 1876, he functioned as prior in various convents before his appointment as commissary in 1886 and first American provincial in 1890.

Pius Mayer was an unusually talented man, gifted with artistic as well as practical, organizational ability. Under Pius Mayer, the Order entered into the modern era of its history, passed from mere survival to autonomous if tenuous existence. It acquired modern legislation, a realistic educational program, and the tools of prayer. It established contact with its intellectual and spiritual past.

Besides the curia (prior general, procurator general, and four assistants general) and the prior of the Carmine of Naples, representatives of eleven provinces were present at the chapter: Ireland, Tuscany, Germano-Holland, Naples, Romagna, St. Angelus, Poland, Malta, Spain, the United States of America, and Bavaria.

The most important achievement of the chapter was the drafting of new constitutions. The Order may be said to have been virtually without legislation, for the current constitutions of 1626, last reprinted in 1756, even if copies could be found, no longer corresponded to the situation in which the Order found itself at the beginning of the twentieth century. To provide the new legislation, Mayer suggested to the chapter the formation of a commission, which turned out to be composed of the three provincials, Elisha Duran (Spain), Richard Colfer (Ireland), Aloysius Malfatti (Roma), and the assistant general leaving office, Albert Pulen (Germano-Holland). During the two weeks' duration of the chapter, the commission produced a text which was discussed at every stage by the assembly. In the end, the commission was authorized to produce the final draft and after approval by the Holy See to consign it to the printer.

The Constitutions of 1904

The new constitutions (Rome, 1904), sealed with the approval of Pius X, February 20, 1904, are divided into three parts, dealing with religious life, the government of convents, and, thirdly, of provinces and the Order.

A preliminary chapter is devoted to the Virgin Mary, special patroness of the Order. In the future, all Carmelite churches are to be dedicated to Our Lady, though her parents and spouse are also admitted as patrons. Churches of the Order must have a chapel of Our Lady of Mount Carmel and her statue should be placed above the main altar. The feast of the Solemn Commemoration is to be celebrated with special pomp, preceded and followed by octaves of prayer. Marian devotions are prescribed for Wednesdays and Saturdays. Once a year an instruction should be given on the scapular. The brethren should call themselves not simply Carmelites, but Brothers of the Virgin Mary of Mount Carmel. All public rooms of the convents are to be adorned with an image of Our Lady.

These not entirely novel prescriptions, placed at the head of the constitutions in lieu of the traditional first chapter on the nature of the Order, reflect the strong Marian emphasis which Carmelite spirituality had acquired in recent centuries.

The commission for drafting the constitutions followed the simple procedure of summarizing and adapting the constitutions of the Stricter Observance. Recent papal legislation and the drastically altered condition of the Order, of course, also influenced the text. The result of the commission's labors was a modest booklet of less than 200 pages, in which the law is expressed in 454 short paragraphs, a striking contrast to the complicated legal texts which had preceded it.

The most original sections deal with the formation of candidates, studies, and the government of the Order.

In these constitutions, the minor seminary has its origin. It insured that candidates receiving the habit would have an adequate education in the humanities, often prescribed in the past but too seldom realized. A five year course is decreed. With time, entrance to the Order in most provinces was through the minor seminary. "Late" vocations were the exception. It was this institution that peopled the convents, and accounts for the expansion of the Order during the first half of the century.

The preliminary three-year simple vows are, of course, found there; their dispensation is reserved to the Holy See, but the prior general and his council may dismiss religious from the Order. Those professed with simple vows retain radical dominion of their goods, but not their administration nor usufruct. Upon profession, clerics are to be immediately sent to a house of studies, and may no longer live scattered about in the convents. This ancient decree was now to find general realization in the modern major seminary, but it still often failed to take hold where it had always been neglected. Two months before solemn profession, religious are to renounce all dominion. For solemn profession, the approval of the conventual chapter is required.

The creaky engine of internal graduate studies was once more set in motion. Only the prior general can promote to academic degrees those who are recommended by the definitory of their province. The degree of *cursoratus* crowns the completion of the philosophy course and an examination before the provincial and examiners appointed by him. The lectorate is conferred only on solemnly professed priests after finishing ecclesiastical studies and undergoing an examination as above in logic, metaphysics, and dogmatic theology. The baccalaureate is bestowed on lectors after three years of teaching. The *magisterium* requires another four years of teaching and an examination on all of philosophy and on forty theses covering dogmatic theology. The examining board is comprised of the prior general and his council and the regent of Traspontina or the college of St. Albert.

Few were to follow this curriculum beyond the lectorate, and certainly the Order's seminaries were not dependent on it for their teachers, who preferred recognized academic degrees, if they had any at all.

Lay brothers should live in a convent, preferably the novitiate, for at least three years before admission into the novitiate. These candidates were called postulants (in Italy, *terzini*). The function of the lay brotherhood continued to be regarded in terms of domestic service and material upkeep of the convents.

With regard to the governance of the Order, two kinds of houses are distinguished: convents with at least five members having active and passive voice, and residences with less. Convents are governed by a prior, residences by a *praeses*. Local officials are a prior, subprior, councilors (two in a convent, one in a residence), sacristan, procurator, and secretary.

Preliminary to the founding of a province, the prior general appoints his commissary general, who eventually establishes a commissariate. When three convents (with five voting members) have been founded, a province may be erected. Provincial officials include the provincial, assistant provincial, four definitors, and the *custos*. Between the provincial chapters, which occur every three years, an annual congregation is held.

The council of the Order consists of the prior general, procurator general, and four assistants general (from Italy, Spain, Ireland, and the Netherlands). All these officials are elected by the general chapter held every six years. The prior general may name five titular provincials for the Holy Land, England, Scotland, Saxony, and Denmark.

An innovation was the office of bursar general (*oeconomus Ordinis*), who was to be elected from among the assistants general.

The constitutions of 1904 provided an indispensable aid to the restoration of the Order. Through the constitutions of 1930, which were based on them, they continued to regulate Carmelite life until recently.

Carmel in Europe, 1902-1919

For Italy, the first decades of the 20th century were marked not so much by expansion as by reorganization of the scattered remnants of the former provinces.

In 1890, the province of Romagna numbered only fifteen members, mostly elderly, in five convents. The foundation of a house in Esanatoglia in 1907 failed to stem the slide into oblivion. Two years later, the Congregation of Religious assigned Forlì and Lugo to the Tuscan province; Macerata, Senigallia, Ascoli, and Esanatoglia to that of Rome, thus writing finis to the Romagna province. The latter two convents were abandoned in 1912.

At the same time, in 1909, the Roman province incorporated the remains of the Sardinian province, Cagliari and Sassari. In 1907, Rome celebrated its first provincial chapter since 1870. In that year, the province consisted of the convent of San Martino ai Monti and the residences of Perugia, Palestrina, Albano, Nocera Umbra, and San Nicolò ai Cesarini (Rome).

The general chapter of 1902 added Lucca, recently under the jurisdiction of the prior general, to the three houses of the Tuscan province (Florence, Pisa, and Castellina). The following year, this province held its first chapter since 1862.

Of the four Sicilian provinces, peopled at one time by over a thousand members, there remained at the beginning of the 20th century only about twenty or thirty friars in Messina (St. Albert), Pozzo di Gotto (St. Albert), Palermo (St. Angelus), Trapani (St. Angelus), and Catania (Santa Maria della Scala). This miscellany Pius Mayer collected into a commissariate in 1910.

Only shortly before, this little flock had been further reduced by the earthquake of 1908. Early in the morning of December 28, the island had been rocked by quakes which leveled towns and cities, principal among them Messina. There, the Carmelite convent was totally destroyed, and of the church only part of the side walls and apse remained standing. Brother Joseph Cannizzaro was buried alive under the ruins of the *campanile*. Frs. Anselm Alessi, Augustine Tornatore, and Giles Lo Giudice, though injured themselves, distinguished themselves in rescuing others. Pozzo di Gotto and Milazzo were also seriously damaged. The Carmelites returned to Milazzo for a few years after 1911, but it was only in 1954 that they re-established themselves definitely.

The problem of vocations was perhaps more acute than elsewhere in the scattered, understaffed provinces of Italy. Aloysius Galli opened a minor seminary for all Italy at Montecatini, which the Carmelites had repossessed in 1888, but which was again abandoned in 1902. Meanwhile in 1894, the seminary had been transferred to Castellina, to be in turn moved in 1909 to Nocera Umbra. The decree of the general chapter of 1919, ordering each province to establish its own minor seminary, was implemented the same year by the provinces of Rome and Naples.

In 1905, the province of Spain was divided into the provinces of Andalusia and Arago-Valentina. To the latter were allotted the convents of Caudete, Onda, and Olot; to the former, Jerez de la Frontera, Osuna, Seville, and Hinojosa del Duque.

North of the Alps, the province of Poland (Austrian Galicia), augmented by the addition of Obory of the former reformed province of the Blessed Sacrament (Greater Poland), in 1919 counted seven other houses in Cracow, Sasiadowice, Lwów, Trembowla, Botszowce, Rozdól, Pilzno. With only 22 priests, seven brothers, and one cleric, the province was very scantily populated. Only Cracow qualified as a convent. Mayer imported several Dutch friars to fill posts of responsibility. Brocard de Vlieger and Leonard Stumpel served as novice master and master of students respectively. Angelus Wijtenburg taught philosophy at Cracow during the academic year 1905-1906. In 1913, Anastasius ter Haar was named commissary general of the province, Plechelmus Croonen prior of Cracow. The possibly beneficent effect of these reinforcements, however, was blunted by the First World War.

In the Bavarian vicariate, the historic convent in Bamberg was repossessed in 1902, but Habsberg and Mainburg were abandoned in 1913 and 1918 respectively.

Meanwhile, the Peters brothers, Anastasius and Boniface, and a number of their followers from the former Texas commissariate, showing little inclination to return either to the Netherlands or Bavaria, acquired the care of the Marian shrine of Maria Taferl in Austria (1895). In 1900, a foundation was made in Zedlitzdorf, which with Maria Taferl the general chapter of 1902 considered uniting to the hard-pressed Bavarian vicariate. Instead, the commissariate of Austria was erected in 1903. Other foundations were made in Vienna (1906), Kirchwiedern (Kostelní

Vydrí, 1908), Sitzgras (1911). Zedlitsdorf was abandoned, when Kirchwiedern was accepted.

In 1917, the Germano-Holland province, which eventually became known as the province of the Netherlands, made a fifth foundation at Aalsmeer. After a rather shaky start in Merthyr Tydfil, Pudsey, and Tucker, the Dutch province, which was to become the Order's most successful missionary, finally struck its stride in Brazil.

Carmel in Brazil, 1904-1919

The restoration of the three Brazilian provinces in the end proved a task beyond the resources of the province of Spain. The provincial chapter of 1900 accordingly notified the nunzio of Brazil that it would like to confine its efforts to the North, leaving to some other province the restoration of Rio de Janeiro. In 1916, it was settled that Andalusia should have the care of Bahia; Arago-Valentina, of Pernambuco. In 1906, Pius Mayer decreed that the provincial of Pernambuco should also be his commissary for Bahia, and in fact, from that year until 1923, a vicar for Bahia was regularly appointed by the provincial of Pernambuco. In 1919, the province of Bahia counted four priests, one deacon, and two brothers, all Spaniards, living in Bahia and Cachoeira. São Cristovão was unoccupied. That same year, the province of Pernambuco numbered ten priests and three brothers, all concentrated in Recife.

On June 23, 1904, Pius Mayer approached the provincial of the Dutch province, Lambert Smeets, to take in hand the abandoned Rio de Janeiro province. The task was accepted on condition that the administration of its properties should devolve on the Order. On November 27, 1904, 6 priests and 2 brothers arrived in Rio de Janeiro: Frs. Cyril Thewes (superior), Athanasius Ryswijk, William Meijer, Serapion de Lange, Gregory Meijer, Constance Lokkers, and Brothers Simon Jans and Anastasius Korterik. The Spanish friars under Andrew Prat handed over the convent da Lapa. In December, William Meijer and Constance Lokkers proceeded to Angra dos Reis, where they found the faithful Ignatius of the Conception Silva. In 1906, the bishop of Petrópolis, John Braga, granted the Carmelites the parishes of Angra dos Reis, Mambucaba, Ribeira, Jacuacanga, Ilha Grande, and Jacarei. This long neglected region offered the missionaries plentiful opportunity for the exercise of apostolic zeal.

On May 16, 1905, Frs. Cyril Thewes, William Meijer, and Brother Simon Jans arrived to take over the convent of São Paulo. Here they ran afoul of the redoubtable Anthony of the Blessed Virgin Muniz Barreto, prior of Mogi das Cruces, who was engaged in a legal fracas with the bishop of São Paulo. In 1877, Muniz had been named *praeses* of the convents of São Paulo, Santos, and Mogi das Cruces by the vicar general of Rio, Felix M. de Freitas Albuquerque, and confirmed in that office in 1883 by the apostolic visitator, Edward Duarte e Silva. When Ignatius of the Conception Silva was appointed provincial in 1900, he named the bishop of São Paulo, Anthony Alvarenga, and his vicar general, Manuel Vicente, administrators of the Order's property in São Paulo and Santos, an arrangement with which Muniz did not agree. Finally, on June 22, 1906, the case was settled in favor of the bishop, and Muniz was consoled with the perpetual priorship of Mogi das Cruces. When he died in 1919, his brothers were free to enter into possession of their convent.

Santos was recovered in 1906, Itú in 1917.

Everywhere the Dutch Carmelites, who have distinguished themselves as educators, opened schools or continued those already in existence: Rio de Janeiro (1908), Itú (1908), São Paulo (1911), Santos (1917). The schools in Mogi das Cruzes and Angra dos Reis proved to be short-lived.

The Dutch Fathers took in hand the Third Order, which had survived the suppression of religious. In Angra dos Reis and Mogi das Cruces, Ignatius Silva and Anthony Muniz had kept alive the local Third Order. In Rio, the chapter had degenerated into superstition and fetishism and was disbanded by the director, Thomas Jansen, who inaugurated a new chapter on December 8, 1910, with the profession of 32 novices, 16 women and 16 men. This chapter was the nucleus from which others arose.

In 1919, the province had 22 members: 18 priests and four brothers. Only Rio and São Paulo rated as convents.

The springtime of Carmel suffered a blight by the illness and death of the prior general, April 28, 1918. Pius Mayer was one of the great generals of the Order, though there were some who did not think so: the general chapter of 1908 had barely returned him to office on the second ballot.

On April 20, 1913, the cardinal protector, Vincent Vannutelli, named John Lorenzoni pro-vicar and pro-procurator general; a year later, Pius X authorized him to use the title vicar general. John Lorenzoni (1850-1941) was born in San Felice Circeo in the diocese of Terracina and pronounced his vows in Palestrina. Due to the suppressions, he made his studies in Malta and was ordained in 1874. His early years in the priesthood were spent in the formation of candidates as novice master and lector in Malta and Castellina near Florence. Thereafter, he filled the important posts of vicar provincial of Tuscany (1897), prior of the Carmine of Naples and vicar provincial of Naples (1900), assistant general (1903), and provincial of Rome (1909).

Lorenzoni did not convoke a general chapter until a year after his appointment as vicar; by that time, the First World War had broken out and extended his term of office another five years.

World War I

The First World War was mainly fought in countries in which the Order no longer had foundations, and so material damage was minimal. The exception was the Polish province with convents in belligerent Russia and Austria.

At Botszowcc, church and convent were reduced to a heap of ruins during a bombardment. The pastor, Theodore Bajorek, with seven hundred parishioners escaped death in the subterranean vaults of the convent. The church at Lwów was damaged by shells, which also wounded the provincial, Martin Maciak. The roof was destroyed during hostilities between Poland and the Ukraine in 1920. The church and convent of Sasiadowice were also deprived of their roofs, the library and convent sacked. Rozdól and Trembowla likewise underwent damage. In 1915, twelve members (a third) of the province were reported under arms.

The other provinces situated in countries involved in the war were affected only by the military draft. In 1915, the commissariate of Austria had four members in the army: Augustine Scharrenberg, Brocard Morak (novice), and Spiridion Schaf and a certain John (lay brothers).

The Bavarian province had under arms Simon Schmitt, Anastasius Ottenweller, and the laybrothers, Ecardus, Justin, and Henry Treundorfer, Casimir Winterl, Stephen Troppmann, Theodore Kuffner, Alphonse Fendt. Simon Schmitt, ironically, was a member of the American province, called up while on vacation in his native Germany. Fendt was one of nine members of the Straubing community summoned to military duty. Seven were sent to the front, two served in hospitals. All returned alive, but Fendt, Willibald Brunner, Theresius Lang, and Berthold Hutler did not long outlive the experience.

The American province volunteered a chaplain to the American army in the person of Urban Lager.

The Irish province contributed chaplains Joseph Hastings and Alphonse McDermott to the English army.

Toward the end of the war, the Italian provinces counted ninety friars in the armed services, "all the youth the Order has in Italy." During an aerial bombardment on December 28, 1917, the cupola of the Carmine of Padua, no longer in the Order's possession, was destroyed.

The Internal Life of the Order, 1902-1919

With Savini's missal (1866) and breviary (1886) and Galli's diurnum (1898), the brethren were adequately equipped with liturgical books. However, as to the manner of praying they remained considerably in the dark, the *Ceremoniale* not having been printed since 1616. The text in a revised edition by Gabriel Wessels (Rome, 1906) served the Order until the Carmelite rite was abandoned in 1972.

The ceremonial, however, was intended for liturgical functions within the Order and was not suited for the administration of the sacraments to the laity in the parishes which the Carmelites now increasingly administered. In these circumstances, Carmelite pastors were wont to use the Roman ritual. Mayer's ritual (Rome, 1903) adapted the Carmelite rite to parochial needs, adding from the Roman rite only what was not accounted for in the Order's ceremonial. The edition was immediately challenged by Mayer's predecessor in office, Simon Bernardini, at the time pastor of Traspontina, who brought the case before the Congregation of Rites. This body vindicated Mayer, and the ritual according to the Carmelite Rite, the first in the history of the Order, passed into use - though probably not immediately at Traspontina. Mayer also obtained from the Holy See a much needed updating of Carmelite indulgences. New lists were published of indulgences granted to the Third Order (1903), to the Order itself (1907), and to the scapular confraternity (1908).

Likewise, he appointed Gabriel Wessels postulator of causes (1905) and established a permanent fund for beatifications. Wessels proved an active postulator, proposing to the general chapter of 1908 a lengthy, if uncritical, list of Carmelite candidates for beatification. Of these, Bartholomew Fanti (1909) and Nun'Alvares Pereira (1918) were actually raised to the altars.

The Scapular Controversy

The relatively peaceful possession of the field by the scapular devotion came to an end at the beginning of the 20th century. The innocent cause of the controversy was the Discalced Carmelite, Benedict Mary of the Holy Cross Zimmerman (1859-

1937). A Swiss convert from Zwinglianism, he brought to the Order a fresh critical approach to its historiography. One of his first concerns was to provide a sound documentary basis for the scapular vision. As his researches progressed, however, he was forced to discard some of the time-honored texts adduced to document the vision. Reflecting on Zimmerman's studies, the Jesuit, Herbert Thurston, famous student of popular devotions, concluded that the Carmelite had only succeeded in showing that the scapular vision lacked adequate historical grounds. The learned canonist, Augustine Boudinhon, repeated Thurston's conclusions in the *Revue du clergé français*. On the part of the Order, Gabriel Wessels replied to Zimmerman in the *Analecta*; Elias Magennis wrote *The Scapular and Some Critics* (Rome, 1914) and *Scapulare Beatae Virginis Mariae, Ioannes Cheron et fragmentum Petri Swanyngton* (Rome, 1915).

In effect, writing about the scapular, favorable or adverse, continued to revolve around these scholars' hypotheses, especially Zimmerman's, until recent times, when the question became a dead issue. The debate had the good effect of stilling the quarrel over primary documentary evidence for the scapular vision, shown to be lacking. The tone of the discussion, however, was too narrowly hermeneutic.

In 1892, Galli had obtained the *toties quoties* indulgence for the feast of Our Lady of Mount Carmel. In 1903, Mayer acquired from the Holy See confirmation of the ancient Carmelite custom of singing the votive Mass of Our Lady of Mount Carmel on Saturdays.

Study and Writing, 1902-1919

Although Mayer's constitutions retain the structures for internal graduate studies, he himself preferred the Order's students to frequent the universities, an attitude no doubt prompted by his experience before he became a Carmelite and by the Order's *de facto* inadequate educational facilities. The general chapter of 1902 actually approved the education of Carmelites at universities.

Mayer certainly had little faith in St. Albert's College as an educational institution. The general chapter which elected him decreed measures for alleviating "the enormous debts with which our International College of St. Albert in Rome is burdened." The measures evidently proved inadequate, for on December 8, 1903, the council of the Order decided to sell the college and to rent a house for itself and the students, a decision fortunately revoked two years later. After the second scholastic year, the faculty of the College was retired, and the students were sent to the Apollinaris. The College had never been canonically erected and was considered one community with Traspontina, but in 1907 the council decided to request separation from the Holy See.

An important event for the intellectual and spiritual life of the Order was the founding in 1909 of the *Analecta Ordinis Carmelitarum*, which provided the few scattered Carmelites of the time with worldwide news of the Order and opened up to them the treasures of its spirit and tradition. It would be difficult to overestimate the role of this periodical publication as a bond of fraternity and an instrument of instruction in the evolution of the 20th century Carmelite.

Editor of the *Analecta* was Gabriel Wessels (1861-1944), former prior of Boxmeer and assistant general since 1902. Besides his contributions to the *Analecta* - a lengthy study of the Carmelite Rite, editions of early texts, biographies of illustrious and saintly Carmelites - early products in his long career - were the Order's ceremonial (Rome, 1906) and the edition of the acts of the general chapters, 1318-1593 (Rome, 1912). In the matter of the antiquity of the Order, Wessels' attachment to traditional historiographical *schemata* blunted his critical sense, yet he provided the Order with many significant works, even though some were only reprints of earlier but rare publications, and it would be a long time before Carmelite historiography advanced significantly beyond the point at which he left it.

Linked with Wessels' name is that of the Discalced historian, Benedict Zimmerman, already alluded to above, who occupied himself extensively with the pre-Teresian history of the Carmelites. His *Monumenta historica carmelitana* (Lérins, 1905-1907) reproduced important sources from manuscripts. He brought to bear on Carmelite studies especially the information contained in the notebooks of John Bale (1495-1563), which he found in the British Museum. Zimmerman's pioneer work, unfortunately, raised such a storm that his superiors felt constrained to forbid him to write about early Carmelite history and the scapular. His sharp critical approach shocked and outraged the brethren, sometimes, it must be admitted with some reason, for Zimmerman, despite the novelty of critical methodology he brought to Carmelite studies, was not without his shortcomings as an historian, and it would have behooved him to be more cautious in his deductions from scanty sources. Nevertheless, even though he himself did not always succeed in discovering the truth, he taught the Carmelites that they had nothing to fear from it. Among his important historical contributions are his editions of the *Ordinale* of Sibert de Beka (Paris, 1910) and of the registers of Peter Terrasse (Rome, 1931) and John Baptist Rossi (Rome, 1936).

In its first four volumes, the *Analecta* noticed 126 titles by Carmelite authors, translators, and editors for the period 1900-1919. Among the more noteworthy, mention may be made of Angelicus Koenders, whose solid works on the liturgy include *A Handbook of the Liturgy* (Nijmegen, 1914-1915, 2 v.), *A Catechism of the Liturgy* (Nijmegen, 1915; 2d ed., 's-Hertogenbosch, 1926); *A Popular Handbook of the Liturgy* (Nijmegen, 1916; 2d ed., Turnhout, 1939).

Eugene Driessen obtained a doctorate in sacred scripture in 1913, and although he published no books in his specialty, he wrote extensively in periodicals. With his brother, Hubert, Titus Brandsma, and Athanasius van Rijswijck, he collaborated on a translation into Dutch of the works of St. Teresa of Avila (Bussum, 1918-1926, 4 v.).

Joseph Llovera's *Elementary Treatise of Christian Sociology* (Barcelona, 1909) saw an 8th edition in 1953 and a translation into Dutch by Hubert Driessen ('s-Hertogenbosch, 1912) and may be considered a classic work.

Among popular writers, the more prolific may be named. Basil van Kesteren performed a service to his beleaguered fellow Catholics in the Netherlands by his numerous translations and original works of a popular polemical and instructive character. In Caudete, Simon Besalduch established a Center for the Propagation of Devotion to the Virgin of Carmel, which dispensed information, scapulars, and medals, and offered other aids to those interested in the confraternity and the Third Order. In connection with this work, he published many pamphlets and books, principal among them his *Manual of Devotion to the Virgin of Carmel* (Barcelona, 1916), *Before the Altar of the Virgin of Carmel* (Barcelona, 1919), *The Pulpit of the Virgin of*

Carmel (Barcelona, 1926), *Encyclopedia of the Scapular of Carmel* (Barcelona, 1926). Luis Llop, poet and novelist, under the pseudonym "Azael" wrote edifying books which, it is said, are not all without literary merit.

All these writers were young men who continued their activity into the post-war period.

A new phenomenon in the Carmelite literary world was the adoption of journalism to spread Carmelite spirituality and publicize the Order. Between 1876 and 1892, Linus Soler y Garrigosa, a Barcelona lawyer and Carmelite tertiary, published the *Revista Carmelitana* (13 v.), which provided spiritual reading and news of both Carmelite Orders throughout the world. It remains a unique source of information about the Carmelites at a time when they were not even officially recognized as existing in many countries. The young American province predictably was the first to try this new-fangled way of bringing the Carmelite message to the public. *The Carmelite Review* (13 v.), founded in 1893, unfortunately lasted only until 1906. Its German language complement, *Rundschau vom Berge Karmel* (2 v.) was even more short-lived, running only from 1897 to 1899. The honor of being the oldest continuous Carmelite periodical belongs to *El Santo Escapulario*, initiated in 1904 by the Spanish province. At the division of the province in 1906, the Andalusian province took the publication in hand. The Dutch Carmelites launched *Carmelrozen* in 1912, and their confreres in Brazil responded the same year with *O Mensageiro do Carmelo*. The excellent *Il Monte Carmelo*, founded in 1915 at St. Albert's College, benefitted by its presence at the center of the Order and by the rich spiritual and artistic heritage of Italian Carmel. The skillful editing of the review from its inception until his death in 1944 was only one of the many accomplishments of the universally loved Antoninus Franco, of the Sicilian province, who spent his life as a religious in St. Albert's College, where he functioned as professor of theology, master of students, prior, secretary to the prior general, procurator general, and vicar general during the second World War.

Chapter 13

Revival Continued, 1919-1931

The war was only an unpleasant memory, when the general chapter convened on October 12, 1919. The vicar general, John Lorenzoni, was eligible for election, but in a tight race was edged out on the third ballot by the assistant general for the English-speaking provinces.

Elias Magennis, 1919-1931

Born in Tanderagee, Co. Mayo, Ireland, Elias Magennis (1868-1937) entered the novitiate at Terenure in 1887, a mature young man, who had already studied for the diocesan priesthood. After obtaining an A.B. degree at the Royal University of Dublin and a licentiate in theology at the Jesuit College of Milltown Park, he was ordained a priest in 1894.

Magennis' early years as a priest were spent in the Carmelite secondary school in Dominick St., Dublin, and in Knocktopher. From 1898 to 1906, he worked in Australia in the original foundation at Gawler, later moving with the community to Port Adelaide. During these pioneer years in Australia, he already showed the characteristics that were to mark his lifelong career: winning ways, dedicated zeal for the faith, loyalty to his Irish origins, practical organizational ability, interest in learning and culture. As novice master in Ireland, 1906 to 1909, he revealed another aspect of his nature: a strict insistence on religious observance.

In many areas, the Carmelites still showed the effects of the dissolution of religious orders in the previous century, and Magennis was to do a great deal toward fostering awareness of their religious as well as their sacerdotal vocation. He spent much of his term as assistant general, 1908-1919, in the United States, where he busied himself with promoting the cause of Irish freedom. He was on intimate terms with leading Irish patriots and played no small role in political events during the critical war years, but this aspect of his activity, perhaps its principal feature, must be left to other bards to sing.

The Restoration Completed, 1919-1931

In the years after the war, Magennis resumed the restoration of the Order and carried it to its completion. The Order by no means ceased to grow thereafter, but by the third decade of the twentieth century its body was complete in every limb and ready to mature.

On July 19, 1922, the Bavarian province and Austrian vicariate were joined to re-establish the Upper German province. Albert Sauerer was appointed provincial. The restored province, dedicated to the prophet Elias, consisted of the convents of Straubing (with Sossau), Bamberg, and Vienna, and of the residences of Maria Taferl, Springiersbach, Sitzgras, and Kirchwiedern. Springiersbach, a former monastery of Augustinian canons, was acquired by the Carmelites on September 7 of the same year, 1922. Maria Taferl was abandoned on October 19. In 1927, at the request of the Czechoslovakian government, Kirchwiedern (Kostelní Vydří) was placed under the jurisdiction of the prior general. Sossau and Sitzgras were relinquished in 1926.

At this time, the province of the Netherlands doubled its foundations, opening houses in Merkelbeek (1923), Oldenzaal (1927), and Nijmegen (1929). Merkelbeek, a large former Benedictine abbey, became the provincial house of studies. The house in Nijmegen was destined for students at the Catholic University. In 1923, the Dutch fathers also reoccupied and reconstructed the former convent and church of the Order in Mainz, a step toward rebuilding the Lower German province, which historically had included convents in the Netherlands, Germany, Belgium, and France. Architects of this expansion were the energetic threesome, Cyprian Verbeek, provincial; Titus Brandsma, definitor; and Hubert Driessen, procurator general of the Order. They also launched the province on its career of secondary education.

In 1922, the convents of the Irish province in the United States were declared a commissariate with Finbar O'Connor as first commissary, and comprising houses in New York (28th Street), Tarrytown, Middletown (1917), and New York (Bronx, 1920). In 1931, the commissariate became a province dedicated to St. Elias. The first provincial was Dionysius Flanagan.

Magennis took a personal interest in the growth of Carmel in his beloved Australia. With the establishment in Albert Park of a novitiate (1928), the way was opened for the erection of the commissariate of Australia, March 22, 1930. Francis Power was named the first commissary. Middle Park, Port Melbourne, and Adelaide were the other houses constituting the new commissariate.

Carmel in Spain continued to prosper. New foundations permitted the separation in 1932 of Catalonia from the Arago-Valentina province. Elias Sendra was named commissary over the convents in Barcelona (1924), Olot, Tàrrega (original church repossessed in 1926), and Tarrasa (1928).

The Arago-Valentina province retained the convents of Onda, Onda (residence), Cueva Santa (1922), Villareal (1923), Cuellar (El Henar, 1924), Madrid (1924). The friars were expelled from their convent in Caudete during the revolution, which unseated the monarchy in 1931. A regular community was not reconstituted until 1954.

At this time, the Carmelites were also able to return to several countries from which persecution had driven them.

"The Most Reverend Father General himself explained his plan of restoring Carmel in England," the secretary of the general council noted on December 3, 1925. Consequent to this concern of Fr. Magennis, the Irish province once more attempted to re-establish the Order in England, this time with success. On July 31, 1926, John Cogan, accompanied by Brother Francus Hicks, took over the parish of Faversham in Kent. Fr. Carmel Tabone and Brother Joseph Caruana arrived from Rome in the parish of Sittingbourne, which had a church, rectory, and school. Fr. Cogan and Brother Joseph settled in on November 30, 1926. The following July, they were joined by Laurence Hunt. Elias Lynch replaced Cogan in 1931.

Another project of Magennis' administration was the return of the Carmelites to Portugal. Negotiations were opened with the cardinal patriarch of Lisbon and Andalusia was prevailed upon to undertake the work. On August 7, 1930, Elisha Rúbio Maia arrived in Lisbon and established residence in a rented apartment. The Carmelites had no church nor parish and simply provided assistance in the parish of Santa Isabel, in which their apartment was situated.

In Poland, however, recovery still lay beyond the horizon. A visitation in 1926 by the assistant general, John Brenninger, resulted in the naming of Elisha Sánchez Paredes vicar provincial. He labored fruitfully for the upbuilding of the province until 1940, when he returned to his own province of Andalusia. Franco Bueno Carrizo, of the same province, functioned for a time as novice master. Both were religious of the highest quality, representative of the sort of assistance Spain could provide in the years before the civil war.

Renewed Missionary Activity

The growing vitality of the Order is seen in its renewed missionary activity. In these years, the Carmelites resumed their ecclesial missionary role, interrupted by the religious suppressions. The Spanish provinces, after assisting with the revival of Carmel in Brazil, finally succeeded in putting down roots in their own America. Under the mission-minded Elias Sendra, (1881-1946), provincial of the Arago-Valentina province, the Carmelites returned to the Antilles, this time to the Greater Antilles. In 1920, William Jones, O.S.A., bishop of Puerto Rico, entrusted to the Carmelites the island of Vieques with the neighboring island of Culebres. The same year, the Order was given a parish in Ciales on the main island of Puerto Rico. Foundations followed in Fajardo (1923), Morovis (1925), and Santurce (1931), which also conducted an academy (1949) and a high school (1958). Vieques and Fajardo were returned to the bishop in 1940, in the wake of the Spanish Civil War.

These extra-provincial activities, regarded by European Carmelites as missionary, in reality concerned mainly peoples of European extraction with a long, if sometimes rudimentary, Christian tradition. Now, however, the Dutch province felt ready to undertake an apostolate involving the evangelization of non-Christian peoples.

From the Congregation of the Propagation of the Faith, headed by Cardinal William van Rossum, the Netherlands province received the care of the eastern end of the island of Java and the island of Madura. In 1923, Clement van der Pas (superior), Paschal Breukel, and Linus Henckens arrived to take over from the Jesuits, active in the area since 1859, the districts of Pasueruan, Bezuki, and Madura, a territory covering 24,409 sq. km. with about 6,500,000 inhabitants. Of these, 2,691 Europeans and less than 200 Javanese were Catholics. Three churches served the Europeans in Malang (Sacred Heart), Pasueruan, and Lawang. The Ursulines conducted six schools with 500 pupils.

The Church had to be materially as well as spiritually constructed. Emphasis was laid on the apostolate to the Javanese people, especially through schools. To the existing churches with resident pastors, were added Probolingo (1924) and Djember (1928). Churches were built for the Javanese in Baleardjosari (1925) and Malang (1929). To aid the Ursulines, other teaching and nursing congregations, of brothers as well as sisters, were imported from the Netherlands. To stimulate interest in the mission, a magazine, *Vox*, was founded in Malang (1929). On April 27, 1927, with only seven priests active on the mission, it was declared an apostolic prefecture with Clement van der Pas as prefect.

On March 1,1929, the Congregation of the Consistory assigned to the Carmelites of the Rio de Janeiro province the prelature of Paracatú in northwestern Minas

Geraes. The territory covered 69,382 sq. km. with 71,000 inhabitants (in 1920) and comprised the municipalities of Paracatú, San Romão, and João Pinheiro. The apostolic administrator of the prelature, Elisha van der Weijer, appointed on April 27, 1929, was accompanied by Carmel Lambooij, Michael Jonkers, and Brother Romeo Areanjo to initiate the work. The prelature contained six parishes; eventually residences were established in the principal towns of Paracatú, San Romão, and João Pinheiro. The many chapels attached to the parishes were served only with the greatest difficulty, for roads were nonexistent.

The Carmelite dream of returning to the Holy Land was finally realized by the American province of the Most Pure Heart of Mary. It was not to Mount Carmel, however, that the friars returned. They purchased from the Latin patriarch of Jerusalem the Catholic hospice for pilgrims in Nablus near biblical Sichem. The project was the particular darling of Hilary Doswald, elected assistant general in the chapter of 1925. With Columba Downey, he arrived in Nablus on January 5, 1929, to take over the hospice. Canonical erection followed on February 11. After the brief term as superior of Urban Lager, Simon Schmitt became prior, to remain so for the rest of the life of the foundation.

During the first years of its existence, the convent was a house of studies, attended by students of the Irish and the American province of St. Elias, as well as by those of the province of the Most Pure Heart of Mary, but Nablus was a hotbed of Arab resistance to British rule, and hardly a haven for quiet study, so the *studium* was suspended. More successful was a small school for Arab boys, mostly Moslem. Besides, the Carmelites had the spiritual care of the English-speaking Catholics of the town and environs and acted as chaplains to the Sisters of St. Joseph of the Apparition and to the English garrison. Proselytizing among the fanatical Moslems was next to impossible. "Our aim in acquiring this mission," Fr. Simon wrote, "was to contribute our share in assisting the Church in her great missionary endeavors to gain souls for Christ. Whether and in how far this lofty purpose can be successfully carried out in Nablus is a question of no importance, as long as missionary work is done." After describing the Carmelite apostolate in Nablus, he concludes, "our mission house is like a small oasis in the desert."

During World War II, the mission was kept open by Brother Aloysius Scafidi, when Fr. Simon, a German citizen, was interned by the British. After the war, Fr. Simon returned to America in poor health, and the province abandoned the mission. The soil of this vineyard was of the stoniest, and his brothers, lacking Fr. Simon's austere faith, had little stomach for its culture. Yet the decision to withdraw is to be regretted. An oasis in the desert dried up and a tangible contact of the Carmelites with their origins was lost. Perhaps, too, Nablus might have proved a stepping stone to that Mount of their desire.

The Constitutions of 1930

The general chapter of 1925 re-elected Magennis by an overwhelming majority. The main topic of discussion there was the text of new constitutions. The publication of the *Codex Iuris Canonici* in 1917 rendered imperative the revision of the constitutions of the Order. For this purpose, the council of the Order on October 23, 1919, had appointed a commission consisting of Gabriel Wessels, Samuel Vanni, and Manuel Barranera. After making a number of amendments, the general chapter of 1925 authorized the commission to give the finishing touches to the text before publication. The constitutions finally appeared in 1930.

The revisors closely followed the structure and wording of the preceding constitutions of 1904, making changes and additions to suit the requirements of the code of canon law. Thus, the influence of the Stricter Observance continued to make itself felt in the new legislation.

The opening chapter defines the Carmelite Order as an exempt clerical order with solemn vows (art. 1) and describes it as dedicated to the contemplative life as a basis for the active, and having a special devotion to the Blessed Virgin (art. 2). The Marian cult is delineated in considerable detail, as in the previous constitutions (art. 3-17).

To the minor seminary, now called the Marianate, to be established in every province and commissariate, is reserved a special chapter which minutely regulates its administration (pt. 1, ch. 2). For that matter, the code of canon law had prescribed the minor seminary in every diocese (can. 1354). Novitiate and profession are carefully accommodated to the new code, but the chapter on laybrothers with its antiquated prescriptions is incorporated intact (pt. 1, ch. 3-5).

In the chapter on studies (pt. 1, ch. 19), an article is dedicated to the International College of St. Albert, which is declared "the scholastic center of the whole Order" (art. 199). Each province or commissariate should have its own college or major seminary (art 201). The philosophy course is to last at least two years, the theology course at least four (art. 210). The doctrine of St. Thomas is to be followed, according to the instructions of the Holy See (art. 206, 210). Besides these internal studies, the constitutions recommend that provincials with the permission of the prior general send certain select students to universities approved by the Holy See in order to obtain academic degrees (art. 216). After these provisions of chapter 19 for the intellectual training of the members of the Order, chapter 20 on the academic degrees conferred by the Order, repeated from other constitutions and other times, is an anachronism.

Special chapters are added concerning parishes and missions (pt. 1, ch. 23 and 24), though these apostolates are by no means novelties in the experience of the Order.

With regard to local administration, a convent is defined as any canonically erected religious house, whether formed or not. Its superior is called a prior. Houses of studies may be designated as colleges (art. 302). A "formed house" in canonical parlance was a religious house with six professed members, of whom four were priests (can. 488, no. 5). Besides the prior, local officials are the subprior, master of novices, prefect of studies, sacristan, councillors (one in small convents, two in convents having eight electors, three in convents having twelve), bursar, secretary (pt. 2, ch. 28-35). The chapter on the care of the sick, omitted in the constitutions of 1904, is restored (pt. 2, ch. 37).

Elections are no longer regulated according to the Council of Trent, as the constitutions of 1904 required (n. 308), but according to the code of canon law (pt. 2, ch. 40). The same is to be observed with regard to the general administration of the Order. To have voice in the general chapter, a commissariate must have at least one formed house and two non-formed houses (art 402). A province must contain at least three formed houses (art. 403, 404).

The Third Order Regular, 1902-1913

The nineteenth century particularly saw the rise of active sisterhoods with simple vows. During the Enlightenment, absolute monarchs had banned cloistered contemplative life as unenlightened and unproductive. The liberal governments were no less illiberal with regard to cloistered nuns, but suffered religious women to engage in such useful occupations as the care of the sick and the education of children.

Mention has already been made of the Carmelite Sisters delle Grazie (1725). Pius Mayer affiliated two modern congregations to the Order.

Rita Rodrigues das Neves (1859-1906) was born in Fazenda do Bom Retiro (São Paulo). A widow, she dedicated herself to works of charity, especially the care of the poor and the infirm. In 1897, she undertook the direction of the hospital *Nossa Senhora de Nazare* in Saquarema (Rio). Feeling the need of belonging to the religious state, on December 2, 1899, in the Carmo of Rio de Janeiro, Rita made her profession in the Third Order of Carmel, taking the name Maria das Neves. The Spanish friars had only recently arrived to restore this foundation, and Frei Carmel Pastor received her vows. At hand also was her friend, Bishop Francis do Rego Maia, who is considered the canonical founder of the congregation. Back in Saquarema, Maria was joined by three other companions. However, the hospital of Saquarema was forced to close due to lack of funds, and the sisters moved to Campos (Rio) in 1902. But Maria's health was fragile, and four years later the infant institution was deprived of its foundress, a victim of tuberculosis.

On September 9, 1913, the Carmelite Sisters of Divine Providence, as the sisters were called, were affiliated to the Order. Constitutions, arranged by Canon Joseph Cota, of Mariana (MG), were approved by the Holy See in 1925. On December 7, 1954, the sisters obtained the *decretum laudis*. In 1979, the congregation numbered 49 houses with 343 professed members.

The Sisters of the Virgin Mary of Mount Carmel (*Hermanas de la Virgen María del Monte Carmelo*) came into being in Spain through the intervention of the Carmelite Fathers in the incipient development of a congregation of sisters. Tomasa Ortiz Real felt called to found a teaching and nursing congregation. With the approval of the diocesan authority of Murcia, Tomasa and three companions established a foundation in Pueblo de Soto (1884). They followed the constitutions of the *Carmelitas de la Caridad*. Tomasa took the religious name Piedad of the Cross. In late 1887 or early 1888, the community moved to a better location in the more populous Alcantarilla. In 1888, a second foundation had been made in Caudete, in the Calle Santa Barbara. The two communities, Caudete and Alcantarilla, eventually drifted apart. The Carmelite friars of Caudete provided the tertiaries there with the opportunity for guidance, and the prior, Cyril Font, took up their cause, determined to attach them to the Order. The bishop of Orihuela, John Maura Gelabert, appointed him spiritual director and on February 26, 1891, named Sister Aguasvivas Vives Pla "head of the family" of the Carmelite tertiaries of Caudete. After this, the two groups went their separate ways, and Mother Piedad's evolved into the Salesian Sisters of the Sacred Heart of Jesus (*Hermanas Salesianas del Sagrado Corazon de Jesús*).

On March 6, 1891, Font, authorized by the bishop, clothed in the habit the eight tertiaries who comprised the community of Caudete. The following March 3, they pronounced their perpetual vows in the hands of the spiritual director, Aguasvivas on the occasion changing her name to Teresa. The congregation moved its mother house to Orihuela in 1899. Meanwhile, in 1896, a second foundation had been made in Santa Pola (Alicante).

The bishop on October 15, 1899, named Elisea Oliver Molina superior. She ruled the congregation as mother general for twenty-seven years, led the institute from its infancy to mature security, and consequently is to be considered its real foundress.

In 1905, Pius Mayer aggregated the congregation to the Carmelite Order. Two years later, new constitutions were composed by Elias Ortiz, which remained in force until 1942, the date of the *decretum laudis*. In 1950, Pius XII definitively approved the congregation. In 1979, it counted 60 houses and 445 professed sisters in Spain, Italy, Portugal, Puerto Rico, the Dominican Republic, Indonesia, and Rwanda.

The Third Order Regular, 1919-1931

Under Elias Magennis, a number of congregations of sisters found a hospitable welcome to Carmel's family.

The Carmelite Missionary Sisters of St. Therese of the Child Jesus (*Suore Carmelitane Missionarie di S. Teresa del Bambino Gesù*) were founded by Mother Maria Crocifissa Curcio. Born of noble parents in 1877 in Ispica, Sicily, Rose Curcio early felt the call to serve the gospel. She gathered several girls of like aspirations in a house in Modica and began the work to which she was to dedicate her future institute: the education of girls, particularly orphans and the poor. During a visit to Catania, Rose was clothed in the tertiary habit in the Carmelite church of that city and took the name Maria Crocifissa. She established correspondence with Albert Grammatico, provincial of the Sicilian province. When he later joined the faculty of St. Albert's College in Rome, he spoke about Mother Crocifissa's work to a young confrere, Lawrence van den Eerenbeemt (1886-1977), born in Rome of a Dutch father, Peter, who had served in the papal army in 1870 and married Joan Negri, of a well-to-do Roman family.

Lawrence recommended that Crocifissa move her headquarters near Rome in seaside Santa Marinella, where he ministered during the summers. In 1925, the prior general, Elias Magennis, affiliated the new institute with the Order. In order to dedicate himself completely to the affairs of the sisters, Lawrence abandoned the habit in 1930, was incardinated in the diocese of Porto and St. Rufina and named "ecclesiastical assistant" of the Carmelite sisters. The same year, the institute was constituted a congregation of diocesan right.

The Carmelite Missionary Sisters had already taken firm root in Italy, when in 1947 they were able to establish their first mission in Paracatú, Brazil. In 1979, the congregation numbered 210 professed sisters in 30 houses in Italy, Malta, and Brazil.

In 1969, the prior general, Kilian Healy, readmitted Fr. Lawrence to the Order which he had never left in spirit.

Susanna Paz Castillo Ramírez (1863-1940) was born in Altagracia de Orituco (Est. Guárico). Her paternal grandmother was the sister of the Liberator, Simon Bolivar; political events also played a role in shaping her vocation. The revolution of 1901, called "*La Libertadora*," was centered in Altagracia and on the victory of the governmental forces left behind the usual detritus of wounded, sick, and destitute. To remedy the situation in some measure, the local pastor, Sixtus Sosa Díaz, founded a hospital. Susanna with a few companions undertook to staff Sosa's St. Anthony's Hospital.

It was only a matter of time before these devout women would seek to consecrate their service by religious vows. In 1910, the bishop of the diocese of Calabozo, Philip Neri Sendrea, received the profession of Susanna and five companions, thereby constituting the congregation of the Little Sisters of the Poor of Altagracia de Orituco. Susanna took the name Candelaria of St. Joseph from her devotion to the Presentation of Our Lady (Candlemas). When Fr. Sosa became bishop of Guayana in 1915, the new institute acquired an influential as well as an interested patron. Hospitals were founded in Upata (1916), Porlamar (1918), Barcelona (1921), Cumaná (1922). With time, the sisters also began to conduct schools.

The coming of the Carmelites to Porlamar in 1922 presented Mother Candelaria with an opportunity that seemed providential. On March 25, 1925, the congregation was aggregated to the Carmelite Order with the title of Third Order Regular Carmelite Sisters of Venezuela (*Hermanas Terciarias Regulares Carmelitas Venezolanas*). In 1979, the Carmelite Sisters of Venezuela counted 13 houses and 75 professed sisters.

The Corpus Christi Carmelites started out as Dominican tertiaries. Clara Perrins (1876-1949) was born in Handsworth, Birmingham, of Protestant parents. A chance remark heard as a child that Catholics believed in the Real Presence led to her conversion at sixteen years of age. She legally changed her surname to Ellerker after a Catholic ancestor, who had taken part in the Pilgrimage of Grace. The banner he had borne depicting the Blessed Sacrament and the wounds of Christ was to become the emblem of the congregation she came to found, which like its foundress was specially devoted to the Eucharist, the inspiration of her conversion. On the death of Clara's father, her mother and two sisters followed her into the Church.

Clara received a good education, graduating from St. Andrew's University in Edinburgh. At the suggestion of the bishop of Nottingham, she decided to dedicate herself to social work. A community, of which her mother and sister Ethel formed a part, gathered in Leicester under the direction of the famous Dominican, Vincent McNabb, superior of the nearby priory. In 1908, Clara, her mother, and two companions made their profession as Dominican tertiaries, Clara taking the name Mary of the Blessed Sacrament. Corpus Christi House, as the community was called, carried on a varied apostolate: teaching, counselling, publishing pamphlets (the Corpus Christi Books), dialoguing with non-Catholics. It also became a center for retreats, the famous Dominican, Bede Jarrett, being one of the retreat masters.

The Dominican connection led to other foundations. In 1920, at the invitation of the Dominican archbishop of Port-of-Spain in Trinidad, B.W.I., the Corpus Christi Sisters undertook the care of the home for the aged. The same year, they answered the call of the Dominican Bishop McNicholas to open a house in Duluth, MN. Their work there included an apostolate among the Indians. In 1925, the sisters settled in Scottsbluff, NE., to work among the Mexicans.

In spite of the help and encouragement of the Dominican Fathers, the Corpus Christi Sisters were not destined to become part of that Order. The group had from the beginning been attracted by the spirituality of St. Thérèse of Lisieux. Visits to Canon Taylor's shrine to the saint in Carfin, Glasgow, and to the Carmel of Lisieux confirmed Mother Mary in her leaning toward the Carmelite Order. An interview in Chicago with the provincial, Lawrence Diether, led to the aggregation of the Corpus Christi Sisters to Carmel, February 7, 1927.

Port-of-Spain became the mother house of the new congregation. In 1946, it received its *decretum laudis*, the approval of the Holy See, and new constitutions. The congregation has flourished especially in the Carribbean area. In 1979, the Corpus Christi Carmelites had 20 foundations and 133 professed sisters.

The Institute of Our Lady of Carmel (*Istituto di Nostra Signora del Carmelo*) is actually the oldest of the congregations at present affiliated to the Carmelite Order. In 1852, Maria Scrilli (1825-1889) with a few companions opened a school for girls in her native Montevarchi, in the Archduchy of Tuscany. The enterprise was so successful that a royal decree two years later entrusted to them the Leopoldine normal schools, at the same time allowing them to become religious.

On October 15,1854, Maria and three companions were clothed in the tertiary habit of Carmel by the *proposto* of Montevarchi, James Gabellini. Maria took the name Maria Teresa of Jesus. In 1855, the community, called Poor Sisters of the Heart of Mary (*Poverine del Cuore di Maria*), received the approval of the bishop of Fiesole, Joachim Antonelli. The following year, a second house was opened in Foiano (Arezzo), and arrangements had been undertaken with the provincial of Tuscany to affiliate the group with the Carmelite Order, when the suppression of 1860 disbanded the sisters.

For fifteen years, the sisters lived with their families in secular dress, until they managed to open another school in Florence. At Maria's death in 1889, the institute numbered three members, one of them paralyzed, and was on the point of being merged with another sisterhood by Cardinal Augustine Bausa, when Maria Mosca (1862-1934) joined it.

Under the dynamic leadership of this second foundress, the institute took on new life, grew in membership, and multiplied its foundations, undertaking, besides teaching, the care of the sick and other works of charity. She elaborated constitutions and in 1929 obtained for her institute recognition from Cardinal Alphonse Mistrangelo as a diocesan congregation. The same year, Elias Magennis affiliated it to the Order as the Institute of Our Lady of Mount Carmel. The *decretum laudis* followed in 1933. By 1979, the Institute numbered 212 members in 36 houses in Italy, Poland, the United States, and India.

The Sisters of Our Lady of Mount Carmel trace their origin to France. Since 1702, the parish of St. Francis de Paula in Tours had its Carmelite tertiaries, approved as such twenty years later. In 1824, Charles Boutelou, assistant pastor, conceived the idea of joining them into a religious community for the education of working-class girls and the care of the sick. The same year, he obtained episcopal approval of the community and its statutes, composed by himself. In 1826, the sisters adopted a religious habit. Superior of the community was Sister St. Paul Bazire, one of its members was Therese Chevrel, who was to become foundress of the American congregation.

The sisterhood had grown to fifty members, had moved to a more favorable location in Vouvray and had acquired the former Benedictine abbey in Bougueil, when the July Revolution of 1830 erupted, driving King Charles X from the throne of France. Boutelou, suspect of royalist leanings, emigrated to America, where Bishop Leo de Neckere of New Orleans assigned him to Assumption parish in Plattenville, LA. Thither in 1833 he summoned Therese Chevrel and a companion, Sister Augustine Clerc. The sisters who remained in France survived the crisis, but abandoned their Carmelite affiliation and exist today as the Sisters of St. Martin of Tours.

After preliminary assignment to Plattenville, Sisters Therese and Augustine in March, 1838, were asked by Bishop Anthony Blanc, successor to the deceased De Neckere, to take charge of a school for free black girls in St. Claude Street, New Orleans. Bishop Blanc accorded the Sisters of Mount Carmel recognition as a religious community and appointed Stephen Rousselon their superior. For almost three decades, this priest was to be their wise and kindly support. In 1840, on the same property in St. Claude Street the sisters opened a school for white girls. With the access of more candidates, schools were opened in Lafayette (1846), Thibodaux (1855), and Algiers (1857, abandoned in 1888).

In 1859, the "Sisters of the Third Order of Mount Carmel of the Archdiocese of New Orleans" numbered twenty-three professed members who conducted five schools. That year, too, Archbishop Blanc gave approval to new constitutions. Based on Boutelou's statutes, they comprise thirteen articles and declare that "for the time being" the community's "principal work" is "the Christian education of young girls, boarders or day students, of the middle and lower classes of society."

This promising beginning received a check through the Civil War (1861-1865), which cut off communication with France and brought beggary to the South. Nevertheless, the Carmelites managed to keep open all their schools and provided nursing care during the war and yellow fever epidemics.

With the signing of the peace, the rhythm of growth of the institute was restored. Of the other schools opened during the 19th century, New Iberia (1870), Paincourtville (1876), Abbeville (1885), and Rayne (1891) remain today. The school for black girls in New Orleans and one which had been opened in New Iberia were closed around the turn of the century for want of students. Except for recent foundations in the Philippine Islands the sisters have confined their efforts to the State of Louisiana, where they have pioneered Catholic education.

The first general chapter was held in 1891; it elected Sister Therese superior general and approved revised constitutions printed the following year. On May 28, 1930, the sisters were affiliated with the Order. In 1979, the Sisters of Our Lady of Mount Carmel counted 142 members in 16 houses.

The last congregation founded in this period, the Carmelite Sisters for the Aged and Infirm, was aggregated to the Order in its very origins. As a Little Sister of the Poor since 1914, Mother Angeline Teresa McCrory (1894-1984) noticed the need for the care of aged persons, who had means, yet lacked a proper home and care. Encouraged in her ideas by Cardinal Patrick Hayes of New York, she and six other sisters obtained permission in 1929 to leave their institute in order to dedicate themselves to their new apostolate. Through the mediacy of Dionysius Flanagan, provincial of the province of St. Elias and friend of the community, affiliation with the Order was granted by Elias Magennis on August 24, 1931, one of his last official acts. Patrick Russell assisted the foundress in drawing up the first constitutions, published in 1934. The congregation received the *decretum laudis* in 1957.

On September 29, 1931, the sisters opened St. Patrick's Home in the Bronx, already characterized by the distinctive features which Mother Angeline incorporated in all her foundations. She pioneered in personalized care for the aged, which emphasized the privacy, dignity, and independence of the individual. Persons with means, as well as the poor, were admitted. They enjoyed privacy, freedom to come and go, make purchases, etc. Married couples were able to spend their last years together. For her creative ideas, Mother Angeline received many tokens of public recognition during her lifetime, among them the National Award of Honor of the American Association of Homes for the Aging (1969).

In 1979, the congregation had 350 professed sisters and 34 institutions in the United States and Ireland.

The Third Order Secular, 1919-1931

After the publication of the new code of canon law in 1917, religious institutions with Third Orders undertook the revision of their constitutions. The Carmelite tertiary Rule in the form given it by Bettini particularly needed restatement in proper legal form. The prior general, Elias Magennis, himself "under our personal care" supervised the revision of the Carmelite tertiary Rule. He did not confine himself to changes in sentence structure and terminology. Vows, he felt, were too much to expect of the 20th century tertiary and were the reason why few lay persons enrolled in the Third Order. Vows were therefore no longer required, but could be pronounced by the individual tertiary on the advice of a spiritual director. Magennis' Rule was undoubtedly impoverished by the elimination of this distinctive and traditional element of tertiary spirituality. It further lost its individuality by extensive borrowings from the Dominican tertiary Rule.

The new Rule was published in the *Manuale del Terz' Ordine della Beata Vergine Maria del Monte Carmelo*, Roma, 1925. The English edition had the title *Carmelite Devotional Handbook for the Use of Tertians and Other Clients of Our Lady of Mount Carmel*, Rome, 1925. A version for the Spanish-speaking countries by Simon Besalduch, *Manual del terciario carmelita*, Barcelona, 1930, had little success in Spanish America. In Brazil, Straccio's Rule in the edition by Michael de Azevedo was by no means eliminated by the new Rule.

By relaxing the Rule of the Third Order, Magennis evidently hoped to increase its membership. In fact, he organized several public celebrations designed to publicize and animate Carmel in all its branches. Such occasions were the sixth centenary of the granting of the Sabbatine Privilege, for which Pius XI wrote a letter, March 18, 1922, and the seventh centenary of the approval of the Carmelite Rule, which coincided with the canonization of St. Therese of the Child Jesus, May 17, 1925. For this event, Pius likewise issued a letter, November 15, 1925.

In the person of Spiridion Varsallo, Magennis on November 19, 1925, appointed the first commissary for the Second and Third Orders.

Among tertiaries who distinguished themselves for their dedicated Christian lives in these years are Maria Concetta Todaro (1858-1923), of Palermo, who led a celibate life devoted to works of charity; Wiera Francia (1898-1928), of Forli, Catholic Action member and diocesan president of the Union of Catholic Women;

Wilhelmina Ronconi (1864-1936), of Pesaro, social worker, educator, lecturer, author; Rita Pagni (1910-1938), young wife who offered up her brief existence in a spirit of heroic sacrifice; Anna Zelikova (1924-1941), daughter of Czechoslovakian farmers, who modelled her life and sufferings on the spirituality of St. Therese; Marian Laguens Pellicer (1905-1947), Aragonese diocesan priest, invalided for thirteen years; George Preca (1880-1962), diocesan priest of Malta, founder of the Society of Christian Doctrine and author of numerous books and pamphlets of instruction.

The Intellectual Life, 1919-1931

Magennis did not share Mayer's reservations with regard to internal studies; besides, the Order was now much better situated for educating its own, and with his customary vigor immediately set about reviving the international college in Rome.

The first academic year began in October, 1920, under the regency of Hubert Driessen. Two years later, the college could no longer accommodate the students Magennis collected from every corner of the Carmelite world. Late in 1922, work began on a fourth storey to the building; by July of 1923, it was completed. The academic program of 1923-1924 presented a complete curriculum for four years of theology and three years of philosophy with a faculty of twelve professors, with few exceptions doctors. Besides music and archeology, Italian, Latin, Greek, and Hebrew were also taught.

On March 26, 1924, the Congregation of Seminaries and Universities recognized the lectorate of St. Albert's as qualifying the student for admission to the Gregorian University, the Biblicum or any other ecclesiastical institute requiring the laurea.

The college chapel proving no longer adequate, a new chapel, actually a church, was constructed next to the college. The cornerstone was laid in May of 1925, but it was not until January 6, 1928, that the completed structure was inaugurated.

In 1926, the philosophy course was suspended, it being Magennis' intention to build another college to house that branch of learning. On March 19, 1930, Cardinal Basil Pompili laid the cornerstone of Pius XI College on land adjacent to San Martino ai Monti Basilica, but Magennis had already lapsed from office, when it opened its doors to the students of the first academic year, November, 1932.

Carmelite Writing, 1919-1931

A number of the writers active in the first two decades of the century continued their activity into this period. At this time, Gabriel Wessels published facsimile editions of Cosmas de Villiers' *Bibliotheca carmelitana* (Rome, 1927) and Mariano Ventimiglia's lives of the priors general. Interest in the mystical literature of the Order was carried forward by a new writer, John Brenninger (1890-1945), assistant for Germany and Holland since 1925. His studies of the spiritual writers of Carmel, particularly of the Touraine province, and more so his original writings, to be mentioned below, did much to awaken the awareness of the Order to its special charism.

It is to Magennis' credit to have fostered the talent of the most significant theologian the Order produced in modern times. The first published work of Bartholomew Xiberta (1897-1967), *Clavis Ecclesiae* (Rome, 1922), his doctoral dissertation at the Gregorian University in Rome, made history as an exposition of the doctrine of the ecclesial dimension of the sacrament of penance. His early attention was devoted to the medieval theologians and philosophers of the Order: his *Carmelite Scholastics of the 14th Century* (Louvain, 1931). Another notable production of these years was his *Guiu Terrena, Carmelita de Perpinya* (Barcelona, 1932). These studies won him the esteem of Cardinal Franz Ehrle, Martin Grabmann, and other scholars in the field.

The bulk of Xiberta's literary production, however, lay in the post-war years and concerned systematic theology. His numerous published works, the fruit of a lifelong teaching career in St. Albert's College, Rome, include his *Introductio in sacram theologiam* (Madrid, 1949; 2d ed., 1964), *Tractatus de Verbo Incarnato* (Madrid, 1954, 2 v.), *El Yo de Jesucristo* (Barcelona, 1954), *Enchiridion de Verbo Incarnato* (Madrid, 1957), *La tradición y su problemática actual* (Barcelona, 1964). These earned him an honored place among theologians of the time. An eclectic, though an admirer especially of Matthias Scheeben, Xiberta stressed the unity of theology and deplored its departmentalization in modern times. Many of his insights, regarding for instance the Church, penance, grace, have since become current coin of the realm.

Titus Brandsma (1881-1942) earned his doctorate in philosophy at the Gregorian University of Rome in 1909. When the Catholic University of Nijmegen was founded in 1923, Titus was invited to join the faculty. Besides teaching his subject, he also lectured on mysticism, especially of the Low Countries. In 1932, Titus became *rector magnificus* of the university. His inaugural address, *"Godsbegrip"* (The Concept of God), struck his audience as an experienced insight rather than a mere academic exercise, and continues to appeal today.

Brandsma wrote extensively in newspapers and popular magazines as well as in learned journals. Worthy of note is a series of articles on medieval mystics of the Low Countries written for *De Gelderlander*. A lecture tour in the United States resulted in a modest volume of no scholarly pretensions, *Carmelite Mysticism, Historical Sketches* (Chicago, 1936), which nevertheless was the first attempt at a historical synthesis of Carmelite spirituality. Titus' interests were many and included Marian devotion, ecumenism, Frisian culture, and journalism. This last preoccupation was to prove the occasion of his death.

Not to be overlooked among Carmelite scholars of this period is Albert Grammatico (1884-1960), professor in St. Albert's College. A man of wide culture, his particular interest was philosophy. His literary production was confined to articles in learned journals; he published no monographs.

Three histories may be mentioned here, not so much for their intrinsic merit as for their timeliness: *Der deutsche Carmel*, by Clement Martini (Bamberg, 1922-1926, 2 v.); *The White Friars*, a history of Carmel in Great Britain and Ireland, by Romaeus Patrick McCaffrey (Dublin, 1926); *Le Carmel en France* (Toulouse, 1936-1939, 7 v.), by Antoine de la Présentation, O.C.D., the pre-Teresian history of three of the seven Carmelite provinces in France. Although the work of amateurs, betraying the failings of their kind, these works were the first histories in their respective fields and appeared at a time when they were sorely needed.

A promising historian was Paul Caioli (1887-1962), of the Tuscan province, founder and editor of the excellent but short-lived *Rivista storica carmelitana* (1929-1932). His biography of St. Andrew Corsini (Florence, 1929) remains definitive.

Apart from these initial efforts, however, he prepared for publication little of his considerable store of historical knowledge, especially of the Renaissance and the city of Florence.

In the field of popular instructive literature, the Australian John Gearon (1890-1970) wrote *Scruples, Words of Consolation* (Dublin, 1925) and *Catholicism, a Religion of Common Sense* (London, 1930), books which saw more than one printing and translation.

Another popularizer and pamphleteer, Albert Dolan (1892-1951), of the American province of the Most Pure Heart of Mary, early sensed the appeal of St. Thérèse of Lisieux for the modern person. His principal writings were gathered in *Collected Little Flower Works* (Chicago, 1929). More effective yet for spreading the message of the saint was the Society of the Little Flower, established by him in 1923, the year of Thérèse's beatification, and still in existence. Fr. Dolan was also the author of a number of popular apologetical and religious books.

Chapter 14

The War Years, 1931-1947

The three decades before the Second Vatican Council were occupied by the generalates of Hilary Doswald (1931-1947) and Kilian Lynch (1947-1959) and were characterized by continued material growth and a deepening of the interior life of the Order. These trends experienced a check during Doswald's term of office from the Spanish Civil War and the Second World War, nor were the regimes of Nazism in Germany and of Fascism in Italy conducive to the weal of religion in those countries. The high point of the Order's condition in modern times was reached in the generalate of Kilian Lynch.

The general chapter of 1931 elected Hilary Doswald prior general. He was born in 1877 in Saulgau, Würtemberg, where his parents were living temporarily. He responded to the appeal of Pius Mayer, on a visit in Germany, and with Sebastian Urnauer emigrated to America, where both young men entered the novitiate of the Carmelites in New Baltimore, PA., making their profession on December 26, 1894. After ordination in 1900, Fr. Hilary filled various posts in the province, until his election as assistant general in 1925. Re-elected prior general in 1937, he remained in office another decade due to the World War. He died in Rome, while on a visit to celebrate his golden jubilee of ordination, and was buried in Campo Verano.

Shaping the Spirit of Carmel

Hilary Doswald's generalate, in spite of adverse political conditions, was marked by concern for the interior life of the Order and by a search for the spirit of Carmel. In those years was shaped, especially under the stern tutelage of John Brenninger, the spirituality that was to permeate Carmel until Vatican II. Between 1908 and 1938, the Order had more than doubled its membership, which rose from 757 to 1607 friars. Awareness of the spiritual heritage of Carmel had sharpened, especially through the pages of the *Analecta* and the classic works edited by Gabriel Wessels. The 20th century Carmelite, particularly in the new provinces, was beginning to show an interest in his roots and his identity.

The general chapter of 1931 called for a convention of novice masters, "that we may have a life that is truly common and the same in all novitiates." The meeting took place in St. Albert's College, Rome, October 3-8, 1932. At hand were novice masters from the provinces of Rome, the Netherlands, Upper Germany, Andalusia, the Most Pure Heart of Mary (U.S.A.), Arago-Valencia, Tuscany, St. Elias (U.S.A.), Malta, Ireland , Sicily, and Rio de Janeiro. Others, like the novice master of Australia, Francis Bartolo, mailed papers. The papers read in the eleven sessions were not published as such, but were reduced by John Brenninger to an organic unity, defining Carmelite life and how it was to be implemented. Published with the title *Vita Carmelitana* (Rome, 1933), it was translated into various languages, and became an important factor in shaping Carmelite life in modern times.

One of the resolutions of the meeting urged the composition of a manual for the formation of novices. The task was eventually accomplished by John Brenninger and appeared with the title *Directorium carmelitanum vitae spiritualis, praesertim novitiis instruendis compilatum* (Rome, 1940). Likewise translated into other languages, this voluminous work was recognized also outside the Order as an important statement of the spiritual and religious life and became the keystone of Carmelite formation in the decades to come.

Immersed as its author was in the spirituality of Touraine, it was inevitable that this school should become the source for the doctrine expounded in the new *Directorium*. At the time, this was considered its most laudable feature. Unfortunately, whatever the excellence of that spirituality, it had the disadvantage of being ill-suited to the needs of the 20th century Carmelite. As a result, it invested the ideal of Carmel, particularly its immemorial vocation to prayer, with a certain aura of unreality. Nevertheless, the action of the Holy Spirit was not wanting; earnest religious equally found their way to spiritual maturity along this stony path. Some might even look back nostalgically upon its steep and misty reaches. Carmel was only reflecting the Catholic climate of the time. The Church which emerged from the storms of revolution and political liberalism into a changed world also reverted to Baroque spirituality.

The time had come again to reprint the liturgical books of the Order. This involved a certain amount of revision, for Magennis in 1930 had introduced a new calendary, and in the Roman rite Pius X had in 1911 decreed a reformed distribution of the psalms through the hours to permit the recitation of the entire psalter in the course of each week. The general chapter of 1931 kept in mind these necessary modifications in ordering the re-issue of the Order's liturgical books. The Carmelite psalter appeared in 1933, followed two years later by the *Missal* and in 1938 by the *Breviary*. The recitation of the Hours had been facilitated by the publication in 1935 of a *Diurnum*. The preparation of these liturgical books was the work of Bartholomew Xiberta.

The Scapular Medal

The scapular devotion enjoyed a continuing if diminishing vogue. Here, too, the changing times made themselves felt. In 1910, the Holy Office had granted permission to substitute the medal for the cloth scapular. The medal should have on one side the image of our Lady, on the other that of the Sacred Heart. This concession to modernity was received with mixed feelings by the Carmelites, for whom the scapular was a garment, a symbol of the habit. No less an authority than Bartholomew Xiberta claimed that the decree of 1910 actually confirmed the use of the cloth scapular and permitted the medal only where the cloth scapular was "a notable inconvenience." The cloth scapular remained the "perfect form" of the devotion. Some doubted whether our Lady's promise was attached to the medal. On the other hand, Albert Dolan made a spirited "Appeal for a Scapular Medal Crusade." Its extreme expressions provoked a statement by the curias of both Orders, Calced and Discalced, of the *sensus communis* of Carmel, endorsing Xiberta's point of view.

The Spanish Civil War, 1936-1939

At this time, Carmel had no more promising provinces than those of Spain, characterized by fervent religious observance and zealous missionary spirit. During his visitation in 1923, Elias Magennis was struck by "the excellent religious state of the friars and nuns living in Spain." In 1932, the Catalan houses (Barcelona, Olot Tàrrega, Tarrasa) were separated from the Arago-Valentine province to constitute an autonomous commissariate. In 1938, Carmel in Spain numbered 245 friars.

The flourishing state of Carmel in Spain received a rude shock from the Civil War (1936-1939). In 1931, King Alphonse XIII retired into exile to make way for the Second Republic. The new constitution (art. 26), reflecting the influence of the Socialist component of the coalition government, disestablished the Church, nationalized Church property, outlawed teaching by religious orders, which it subjected to the arbitrary surveillance of the State.

The revolution did not occur without violence against religious, perpetrated by extremist elements of the left. In the outburst of convent burning which occurred in Madrid and Andalusia in May, 1931, the convent and church in Jerez de la Frontera were sacked, the library burned, the press of *El Santo Escapulario* destroyed. In Seville, the church was damaged and the statue of Our Lady of Mount Carmel broken to pieces. Grave damage was also suffered in Cordova. At Caudete (Arago-Valentina), the convent was sequestered by the civil authorities. In Rome, the council of the Order met to consider what measures should be taken in view of the political situation in Spain.

In 1934, the Carmelite nunnery in Villafranca del Pañadés was partially reduced to ruins.

Spain was still too Catholic on the one hand and too infiltrated with extreme Socialist elements on the other to take kindly to the condition of a liberal secular State. Between the jaws of this pincer the Republic quickly crumbled. The crunch began in 1936 with the revolt of the army under General Francisco Franco in Morocco (Nationalists) and ended with his victory in 1939 over the government troops (Loyalists), which often seemed more Communist or Socialist than liberal Republican. World sentiment on behalf of Democracy, Communism, or Fascism became involved to the extent of providing military assistance to the side of its preference. To most Catholics, especially religious, living in areas dominated by Communist and anarchist elements, the struggle seemed to involve the survival of religion and their very lives. They may be forgiven if they greeted perhaps a little too warmly the victory of the *Generalísimo*, savior of the faith.

After the smoke of battle had cleared, it was found that the holocaust had cost the Church, besides incalculable material loss in the destruction of ecclesiastical property, the lives of 4,184 diocesan priests, 2,365 religious men, and 283 religious women. Among these were 57 Carmelite friars (counting three missing after the war) and two Carmelite nuns.

Most of the atrocities occurred at the outbreak of the war in the patriotic reaction against the revolt of the army and were perpetrated by Communists and anarchists, who identified the Church with oppression of the poor, though unalloyed hatred of religion is probably not to be eliminated from their motives. The instinctive reaction of the religious on being driven out of their convents was to head for home, but no course could have been more disastrous. In the small towns where they were well known, they stood little chance of remaining unnoticed. In any case, an able-bodied man not under arms was sure to attract attention. Most of those who survived made their way to the nationalist zone, buried themselves in some city, or never left a secret hiding-place, like an Elizabethan priest hole, until the end of hostilities. Nuns had a better chance of camouflaging themselves.

Most of the Carmelite foundations lay in the eastern or loyalist zone.

The Catalan Province, 1936-1939

With Elias Sendra at its head, the Catalan commissariate immediately undertook the renewal of the missions in Porlamar and La Asunción in Venezuela (1933). To these were added Aimores (1933) and Resplendor (1936) in Minas Geraes, Brazil. In 1934, the commissariate numbered 44 friars: 28 priests, eight brothers, six professed clerics, and two novices. It could ill afford the murder of 16 of its members and the ruination of all its Catalan convents.

The entire community of Tárrega, consisting of 12 members (four priests, five clerics, and three brothers) under the prior, Angel Prat Hostench, was exterminated. They had decided to abandon the convent and were waiting for a train, when they were arrested by members of the local revolutionary committee. They were taken to Cervera and in the cemetery were shot on July 28, 1936. Their bodies were then soaked with gasoline and burned.

The church in Olot was plundered and the statue of Our Lady shattered, though it was later able to be restored. The convent in which the air force had established its headquarters, was correspondingly spared. The members of the Olot community who perished included the prior, Ferdinand Llovera Puigsech. The commissary general, Elias Sendra, was accidently present in Olot, but he left for Barcelona, where he intended to embark for Venezuela. His Venezuelan passport gave him immunity, and he thought it might be made to include Fr. Llovera. All went well, until they were actually boarding the ship for Marseilles, when Llovera was held back. He was confined for twelve days in the palace of justice before being condemned to death by a "popular tribunal." While awaiting execution, he heard the confessions of his twelve companions and comforted them in their last hour. The group was shot in the moat of the castle of Monjuich, November 22.

Anastasius Dorca Coromina was one of those killed in Tárraga, where he was present to preach the octave of the feast of Our Lady of Mount Carmel. The subdeacon, Eufrosion Raga Nadal, was captured in Barcelona and was shot on Oct. 6.

In Tarrasa, the war interrupted the construction of a convent and devastated the half completed structure. Brothers Louis Ayet Canós and Angel Presta Battle were apprehended in the act of leaving the premises. On October 12, they were loaded onto a truck together with others and were never heard from again.

Since 1922, the Carmelites in Barcelona were living in the Avenida de la Virgen de Monserrat, 36. This convent was now also destroyed, but its inhabitants, permanent and transitory, escaped with their lives. The commissary, as we have seen, escaped to Venezuela. Bishop Frederick Costa, Carmel Estorch, Augustine Forcadell, Louis Codinach (later a missionary in Brazil), Henry Pujolrás, and Brother Franco Bassols by various routes and fortunes made their way to Rome.

The Arago-Valentina Province, 1936-1939

In spite of two amputations, the Arago-Valentine province remained the largest province in Spain. In 1935, it comprised the convents of Onda (residence, 1895), Cueva Santa (1922), Segorbe (1923), El Henar (1924), Madrid (1924), Villarreal (1925). The same year, the Carmelites made a foundation in Zaragoza. In 1938, the province counted 137 members. With the exception of El Henar and Zaragoza, all these houses suffered from the war either materially or in personnel. Twenty-eight members of the province underwent violent deaths.

The Carmen of Onda was situated outside the town and served as a house of studies and novitiate. In 1936, the community consisted of four priests, 20 professed clerics, one professed brother, and three postulant lay-brothers. In the town itself was a "residence" with three priests and three brothers.

In spite of the expressed wish of the socialist mayor that law and order be maintained, a band of revolutionaries early on July 27 appeared at the door of the Carmen and ordered all its inmates to vacate the premises in an hour. The community met at the residence in town, where they were given safe-conducts and told to leave town by nine in the morning. It was agreed that each one should set out for his native town. Of those who travelled singly, Benjamin Sanchiz Moliner and Louis Mollá Grifo, clerics; Dionysius Bonfil Taday and Joseph Plana Puig, priests, were later captured and shot.

Twenty-one friars of the two Onda communities boarded the train for Villarreal, setting off on a macabre odyssey that ended in death for most of them.

At Villarreal, Anastasius Ballester Nebot, sub-prior of the Carmen, was detained and ended his journey in the cemetery of Cuevas de Vinroma. At El Cabãnal, the cleric, Thomas González Bañez and Brother Peter Thomas Iglesias de Frutas were taken from the train by a revolutionary armed with a pistol, but both survived the war. The other eighteen were questioned in one of the Communist committees and in the police headquarters in Valencia. John of the Cross and Philip García García, brothers by blood, were detained but later released. The others were given safe-conducts for Madrid and breathed more easily. The provincial, Raphael Sarría Colomer, and Brother Florence Marquínez Sampedro left the group destined for Algemesí. The provincial met his death in Alcira. Brother Florence was among the missing after the war, as was Brother Angelo Martín de la Fuente, who set off by himself before the others boarded the train. John Evangelist Muñoz Tornero alighted at Albacete and after a period of hiding was apprehended and shot in Almusafes. During the trip to Madrid, the remaining travellers were guarded by a group of anarchists, whose leader treated them with kindness and consideration. On arrival, the cleric, Isidore Garrido Muñoz, managed to slip away from the guards. Since no trains were leaving for the north, where the war was in progress, the eleven Carmelites were lodged in a home for the poor. In the course of the next fortnight, Brother Franco Arranz de la Fuente and the cleric, Albert García Melero, were allowed to join their families living in Madrid. On August 14, the nine Carmelites, all clerics, were removed to St. Catherine's Home for the Blind. They were there only three days, when at midnight of August 17 they were awakened by a group of soldiers from the nearby *Casa del Pueblo* (formerly the novitiate and sanatorium of the Carmelite Sisters of Charity). The youngest, Richard Román Blanco, and two young Augustinians were spared. The rest were loaded onto a truck, driven to the cemetery in the suburb Carabanchel and shot. They were Daniel García Anton, Aurelio García Antón, Francis Pérez Pérez, Adalbert Vicente Vicente, Silvan Villanueva González, Angel Sánchez Rodrígues, Angel Reguillón Lobato, Bartholomew Fanti Andres Vecilla. "In this instance," writes Antonio Montera, "the bureaucracy of the cemetery functioned efficiently and left a thorough record of the deceased, adding in each case the clinical and telegraphic note, 'Death due to a trauma caused by a firearm'."

In 1922, at the request of the bishop of Segorbe, Louis Amígo, the Carmelites had taken charge of the shrine of Our Lady of the Holy Cave (*Cueva Santa*). In July of 1936, the community consisted of three priests and three brothers under the prior Elias Requena Muñoz. Besides, two priests and a brother were present on a visit. At the outbreak of the war, on July 23, representatives of the municipality and the local Communist committee presented themselves and summarily closed the shrine and its hospice. The Carmelites first found asylum with friends in nearby Altura before dispersing to the homes of their families. All but two of them survived the war. Brother Manuel Gumbau Doñate was taken prisoner on his way to Segorbe. He seems to have been executed on August 14 at the gate of the cemetery of Segorbe. John Baptist Ferre Vaño and Brother Joseph Pascual Beneyto, both natives of Bocairente, found refuge with their families until their capture. On September 29, they were removed to La Cañada and there by a roadside shrine of Our Lady of Mount Carmel near the cemetery were shot to death.

Since 1923, the Carmelites had a residence in Segorbe as a support for the *Cueva Santa*. The community of one priest and four brothers, expelled from their house on July 21, were given asylum by friends. All except Brother Elias Asensi, who never moved from his refuge in Segorbe in the home of the tertiary, Doña Carmen Clemente, were eventually killed. Gerard Requena Agarra was seized in the home of his sister Mariana in his native Caudete. Later his body was found in a pool of blood on the road to Ocaña-Alicante. Brother Gerard Beti Bonfill, being paralytic, was removed to the hospital. On August 16, armed Communists presented themselves and announced that his bed and that of an octogenarian Franciscan, Brother Emilio Belda, were needed for the wounded in war. The two friars were loaded into a car, driven to Navajas and shot. Brother Vincent Saúch Brusca was captured in a private home in Segorbe. In jail, he found among the prisoners the bishop of Segorbe, Michael Serra Sucarrats, the bishop's brother, the vicar general, and two Franciscan lay brothers, who were to be his companions in death. On August 9, this group was dispatched by rifle fire in Vall de Uxo on the road to Algar, but not before the executioners had received the blessing and forgiveness of the bishop and his companions. Brother Jacobino Arranz de la Fuente had found shelter with a family in Segorbe, but out of consideration for his hosts, who he feared might suffer reprisals on his behalf, left on August 20 without a word to anyone. Later, in a field in Altura, was found the body of a man who had been assassinated, which proved to be that of Brother Jacobino.

In the Calle Ayala in Madrid, the community, including the provincial who had his residence there, in 1936 numbered eight priests and three brothers. Bands of extremists roved the city, burning churches and convents and hunting down priests and religious. On July 20, feast of the prophet Elijah, the community, following the example of the prophet fleeing before Jezabel, dispersed among the homes of friends in the city. Five of them did not see the end of the war. The provincial, Raphael Sarría Colomer, was absent in Onda and was killed, as we have seen, in his native Algemesí. The prior, Albert Marco Alemán, found a home with the Aguilar sisters, Margaret and Henrietta. A maid servant in another apartment reported them reciting the rosary. Arrested on August 31, he was taken with thirty others to Paracuellos del Jarama for execution. Thousands found their death there, machine-gunned on the edge of trenches ready to receive their bodies. Redemptus Julve

Ortells was held back in the Atocha Station in Madrid, as he was about to board the train for Villarreal and, it would seem, never left the station alive. His place of burial is unknown. Peter Thomas Carbó Adell was captured in Forcall and was one of seventy machine-gunned in Castellon de la Plana on October 3. Brother Simeon Manrique Rubio was taken from his mother's home and with others shot in the town of Moncófar, October 22.

The convent of Villarreal, founded in 1925, housed the Mariani (minor seminarians) of the province. On July 22, the community left the convent, having already dismissed the seminarians. Joseph Plana Puig took refuge in the home of his brother, Joachim, in San Mateo. On August 13, he was taken to the barracks of the Civil Guard and the same day executed. Eliseus Almela Clausell, on leaving the convent, stayed with two young women, María Alayrach and María Gracia Vidal, who were caring for his aged father. On August 15, he was taken to the casa consistorial, seat of the revolutionary committee, for questioning before being loaded into a car and taken to Arta, where he was shot. Stephen Bordás Querol was ordained hardly a month and a half, when the war broke out and the persecution of religious began. He made his way to Forcall. Detained on August 29, he was removed first to Morella then to Castellón de la Plana. During the night of October 2-3, he became one of the seventy victims shot in the cemetery there. Peter Thomas Carbó of the convent of Madrid, as already mentioned, was his companion in death. Two other members of the convent of Villarreal, John Baptist Muñoz Tornero and John Baptist Ferre Vaño, we saw, met their fate elsewhere.

The Andalusian Province, 1936-1939

To the four convents, of which it was composed at the time of its separation from the Arago-Valentina province in 1906 (Jerez de la Frontera, Seville, Osuna, Hinojosa del Duque), Andalusia had added Cordova (1916), Carmona (1928), Lisbon (1932), and Montoro (1935). At Cordova, the Carmelites recovered their original church with its reredos by Juan Valdés Leal, but not their convent. The church was vandalized in 1931. The original foundation in Carmona having been destroyed, the friars returned to a new location. The convent served as a marianate from 1944, but was again abandoned in 1959. In 1938, the province numbered 89 friars.

Two convents were affected by the war with ten casualties. In July of 1936, the town of Hinojosa del Duque was held alternately by rightist and leftist troops, ending up in the hands of the latter. The convent was the residence of the provincial and the marianate. At the time, it comprised 22 members: 11 priests, four professed clerics, and seven lay brothers. The provincial, Raphael Rangel Castellano, and three other priests were absent when disaster struck. During a raid of a motorized column of communists from Pueblo Nuevo del Terrible on July 27, the community, with the exception of Brothers Joseph Ruiz Cardeñosa and Anthony Martín Povea, left the convent. Later the same day, a force of the Civil Guard from Pozoblanco repossessed the town and the red forces retreated, taking with them a number of prisoners, among them José Gonzáles Delgado, rector of the marianate, and Brother Joachim Romero Olmos. The former, after questioning in the town hall of Pueblo Nuevo del Terrible was sentenced and shot. Brother Joachim, who had spent most of his life in Brazil, was mistaken for a Portuguese and released to travel to Lisbon.

After the war, it was discovered that he had never reached Portugal.

Another raid on the convent by leftist extremists occurred on August 14. The inevitable pillage of the church followed. Brother Peter Velasco Narbona had meanwhile joined the other two brothers. He and Brother Antonio Martín were gunned down at the door of the choir. Brother Joseph Ruiz was taken to prison, where he was joined by Brother Eliseo Camargo Montes, who had been apprehended in a private home. On August 18, the two brothers with eighteen other prisoners were driven out of town in a truck and shot.

Carmel Moyano Linares, ex-provincial, was discovered in hiding by a former pupil of the convent school, now a Communist soldier. After undergoing imprisonment and many humiliations, Carmel was marched out of town with twenty others and shot. Still alive, he was beaten to death with a stone.

In the new foundation of Montoro, the community consisted of two priests, two clerics, and two brothers. At the outbreak of the war, the prior, Joseph Mateos Carballido, with Elisha Durán Cintas, the cleric James Carretero Rojas, and Brother Ramón Pérez Sousa were imprisoned with sixty rightists. On July 22, at the approach of the Nationalist troops a mob broke into the prison. Most of its inmates, including the four Carmelites, who were not backward in declaring themselves willing to die, were dispatched with hatchets, knives, and explosives. Brother Franco Jiménez Márquez and the cleric, Romeo Perea Cortés, had previously managed to escape. The latter had been inducted into the Loyalist army, but with the help of injections by a sympathetic doctor successfully counterfeited illness. He made his way into the Nationalist zone and from there to the Grande Seminaire of Bayonne. He ended up in St. Albert's College in Rome, where he was ordained. He lived to carry on a long and fruitful apostolate, especially as a writer, in the province of Pernambuco.

The Carmelite Nuns in the Spanish Civil War

The Spanish nunneries in the loyalist zone, where extreme leftists were in control, were likewise not spared, although information about their fate is at present rather fragmentary. In most cases, the sisters were probably forced to abandon their monasteries and seek shelter among families, friends, other monasteries, or even foreign countries.

The four Catalan monasteries (Barcelona, Villafranca del Pañadés, Vich, and Valls) suffered complete or partial destruction. Two nuns from Villafranca found a temporary home in Heerlen in the Netherlands, others returned to their families or friends and were sometimes able to be of assistance to priests in hiding.

The Barcelona nuns had already seen their monastery devastated during the anarchist revolt in July, 1909, known as the "Tragic Week." Now again on July 19, 1936, the twenty-seven nuns were forced to abandon their cloister and seek shelter in private homes. Fifteen of them were aboard the "Sicilia," which sailed for Italy on September 10 with a thousand other nuns. Fr. Albert Grammatico was on hand in Genoa to conduct the sisters to Rome. They were welcomed in monasteries in Florence, Jesi, Vetralla, and Rome, until they were able to return to Barcelona in 1939. The monastery had been used as a prison and was substantially intact, though in need of extensive repairs. The furnishings of the church had been burned.

In Catalonia, there was also a community of tertiary sisters in Bañoles. Founded in 1858 by Carmen of St. John of the Cross, a refugee from the 1848 revolution in

Rome, it was affiliated with the Order in 1907. Only in 1951 did the sisters obtain the status of cloistered nuns of the Order. Their monastery was spared destruction in 1936, but required renovation before it was again habitable.

Elsewhere, in Caudete (founded in 1915) the nuns had already been expelled in the revolution of 1931. During the Civil War, they were again made to abandon their monastery, which with the church they found in ruins on their return. The church of the Incarnation monastery in Huesca was hit by an incendiary bomb. The nuns were reciting the liturgical hours, but escaped without injury. The monastery of the Assumption in the same town was also destroyed, as was Onteniente.

The monastery and church of Cañete la Real were sacked and their furnishings burned or stolen. The nuns at first were taken in by friends but were later expelled from the town. They took refuge in the monasteries of Osuna, Jerez de la Frontera, and Seville (S. Ana). Toward the end of their exile, they were able to gather together as a community.

In Utrera, Sister Natividad Aranda, who lay dying at thirty-five years of age, offered her life for the safety of her sisters. She died on July 14, and in fact the sisters remained unharmed.

The community of Madrid (Las Maravillas) was also forced to leave the monastery briefly in the revolution of 1931. In the Civil War, church and convent were damaged by fire, the nuns dispersed. Afterwards, they gathered in an apartment in the Calle Ayala, until their monastery could be restored. The church was finished in 1942.

Three Carmelite nuns lost their lives. Mary of the Patronage of St. Joseph Badía Flaquer (1903-1936), of the monastery of Vich, on an errand to neighbors unfortunately arrived while a search of the premises was in progress. With the others in the house, she was taken to the town hall for questioning. About 11 o'clock at night on August 13, she was driven in a car with four soldiers to San Martín de Ruideperas. A second car held the eighty-nine year-old vicar general of the diocese, James Serra Jordi, and the pastor of Artés, Joseph Bisbal. The cars stopped at the parish church and the priests were taken out and shot. Sister Mary tried to run away, but was brought down with machine gun fire.

Sister Trinity Martínez Gil (1893-1936), sub-prioress of the Incarnation in Valencia, went into hiding in her native Alcudia de Carlet. She was taken into custody with another woman, whom she never ceased to comfort as they were taken to the place of their execution on the road to Sueca, September 24.

Sister Josepha Ricard Casabant (1889-1936), of the same monastery, was executed in her native Albal on the road to Silla, September 8. She was killed together with the parish priest of the town, whose death she was forced to witness before being told that her turn was next.

Of the sisterhoods affiliated with the Order no members seem to have suffered a violent death. They lived, however, in the shadow of death, expelled from their convents and institutions, which they often found much the worse for wear on their return after the war.

The Second World War, 1939-1945

In the Second World War, the Order in Europe felt the full force of modern world conflict. In terms of material loss, Carmel in Italy was affected the most, when the allies fought their way up the peninsula.

The earliest loss was the church and convent in Cagliari, Sardinia, destroyed during an air raid on February 28, 1943. Pisa was hit three times: on September 24, 1943, and on January 18 and June 20, 1944. The convent was levelled to the ground, the ancient church seriously damaged.

On September 25, 1943, the concussion from a hit on the *campanile* of the historic Carmine of Bologna caused part of the roof to collapse and shattered most of the stained glass windows.

The convent and a good part of the Carmelite church in Ravenna were also demolished.

The bombardment of February 2, 1944, caused fissures in the walls of "La Stella" church and convent in Albano. Eight days later, Anselm Reali was killed in an air raid. Upon the evacuation of the town, he had taken refuge in the Propaganda College in Castel Gondolfo. Reali was the author of a popular booklet, *Così parlò la Madonna* (Cagliari, 1938), which saw many reprints.

The oratory of the Carmelite confraternity across from the church in Palestrina was razed by a bomb on January 22,1944.

In the South, the Carmine Maggiore of Naples, situated in the harbor area, was particularly vulnerable. From bombardments on March 28,1943, and subsequently in April the ceiling of the church collapsed and the tiles of the roof were broken. Apart from this damage and the collapse of some interior walls of the convent, quickly repaired by the Allies even before the end of the war, the Carmine emerged unscathed, its familiar belfry towering over ruins all around.

Constant bombarding forced the friars to leave their convent in San Giovanni a Teduccio and seek asylum with their Discalced brothers in Torre del Greco, bringing with them as much of the furnishings of church and convent as possible. Their church suffered only minor damage, but the furnishings were lost, when the Germans dynamited the Discalced convent upon retreating. The Germans also set mines in the convent of Caivano, but fortunately neglected to detonate them.

During a bombardment on December 2,1943, part of the roof, the rose window in the facade, as well as all the other windows in the new church in Bari were destroyed.

The church in Palmi suffered only minor damage.

In Sicily, the Carmelite church in Catania was hit by a bomb, which demolished the chapel of St. Spiridion and damaged the rest of the nave. The Carmine of Messina (1908) miraculously suffered no direct hit from the bombs which rained around it. These, however, shattered doors and windows, and several ceilings in the convent came down. Trapani and Palermo had the same good fortune and minor damage.

To the Carmelite victims of the war should be added, in fine, Raphael Saler, curate of Santa Giustina in Vittorio Veneto, who, while administering to his flock during an air raid, was himself buried under falling walls. The death of Mario Ruggeri was no accident. Removed from his convent in Ravenna, he was assigned to enforced labor. Though only thirty years old, Fr. Mario was delicate in health, and when he proved unable to work, he was simply shot out of hand.

Casualties among Italian nunneries were the monasteries of Ravenna and Vetralla, January 20-22, 1944. Even when monasteries were spared material loss, religious routine was disrupted, when the sisters had to leave the cloister in areas under continual fire.

Institutions in Sant'Angelo del Pesco, Castiglione Messer Marino (Campobasso), Lanciano (Chieti), and Ancona, cared for by the sisters of the Institute of Our Lady of Mount Carmel, were either destroyed or damaged. At Ancona, on November 7, 1943, Sister Joan Ricci was buried under the ruins of the prison in which she was serving the inmates. Her wish expressed at the 25th anniversary of her profession was fulfilled: "Jesus, grant that I may truly serve you in the exercise of charity until the end of my life."

The four convents of the province of Malta (a fifth house, in Fgura, was added in 1945) escaped harm during the intensive bombing carried out by the *Luftwaffe* especially, with the exception of the church in Valletta, which suffered damage to the choir. On February 15, 1942, the prior of Valletta, Gerard Pace, surprised in the street by an air raid, was killed by falling masonry.

At present, the attitude of Italian Carmelites to Fascism is difficult to assess. Unlike the situation in occupied countries, in Italy, patriotism, especially in time of war, worked in favor of the regime. As in other orders and among the secular clergy, allegiances were no doubt divided. For that matter, the Congregation of Religious, on February 10, 1924, had instructed religious to stay out of politics. Heroic protest was no more welcome than lyric sycophancy.

By the Lateran Pact, which he concluded with Benito Mussolini, on February 11, 1929, Pius XI believed that he had "given God back to Italy and Italy to God." The agreement certainly solved the anomalous position in which the Church had found itself since 1870. A similar service was performed for religious by art. 29b of the concordat appended to the pact, which recognized religious associations as juridical entities. The last obstacle to the normal existence and growth of religious orders in Italy had been removed.

The Province of the Netherlands During the War

Only three of the nine European foundations of the province experienced destruction of buildings, but all of them at one time or another were requisitioned as barracks or hospitals with notable damage to interiors and loss of furnishings, and community life suffered from the dispersal of the religious. The Carmelites, too, shared with the populace the deprivations of war and occupation: scarcity of food and fuel, tension created by the continual bombings and rocket attacks, fear of deportation and imprisonment.

On February 22, 1944, the convent in Nijmegen was hit during the air raid on the city of that day. Miraculously, the community of twenty-two friars, who happened to be together in the refectory, was unharmed. Amid the dust and shock of the explosion the prior, Raphael Gooijer, called out, "Are you people still alive?" - a question which became famous in the province and for which he suffered a great deal of teasing. The convent still allowed for a certain Spartan existence, but the church of St. Augustine, situated at some distance from the convent and served by the Carmelites, was totally destroyed. On retreating during the battle of Arnhem, the Germans in turn set fire to what remained of the convent (September 18).

During the night of October 19-20, 1944, the 15th century church of Boxmeer was reduced to ruins, when the Germans dynamited its tower, as they did the towers of all the churches along the River Meuse, which had become the front line of battle between the advancing Allies and retreating Germans. Fortunately, the historic convent remained substantially intact and exists today.

The convents suffered not only at the hands of the Germans. During an Allied air raid on Mainz, in the night of August 11-12, 1942, fire from neighboring houses engulfed the medieval church and convent, which the province had recovered and restored as recently as 1924.

Of the attitude of the Dutch Carmelites to Nazism and its local variety, the *Nationaal Socialistische Beweging* (NSB), there remains no doubt. All equally rejected the political tenets of the oppressors, and some paid for their convictions with imprisonment and death.

Fabian Kluessjen was imprisoned for seven months in Arnhem and Utrecht for alleged political statements in his religion classes. Fridolinus Meenhuis, ordained only two years, was betrayed by an informer and dragged out of bed on Christmas night, 1944. At the liberation, he exchanged the concentration camp of Neuengamme for a hospital in Groningen, where he died on June 21, 1945, a victim of malnutrition and mistreatment.

Before the war, Amandus van der Weij, professor of philosophy, had already exposed the evils of National Socialism by the spoken and written word. He outlived four years of imprisonment in Buchenwald and other places of detention to record his experiences in his book, *In het voorgeborchte der Hel* - in the Limbo of Hell (Heemstede, 1946).

Another inmate of Buchenwald was Elias Wouters, on leave from the mission in the East Indies, but he was soon released, when it was discovered that he had contracted leprosy.

Two assistants in the Carmelite parish of Boxmeer, Xavier Lutz and Sylvester van Geffen, were denounced by a member of the NSB in October of 1942 and spent a year in the concentration camp of Vucht.

The Dutch Carmelites in general reacted to the rigors of the occupation and war with humor and courage. In Titus Brandsma, suffering blossomed into the perfection of Christian love. Among his Carmelite brothers, Titus was universally admired for his tireless and varied activities, but even more he was loved for his cheerful spirit, willing helpfulness, and unassuming charity. That these qualities were evidence of a profound Christian maturity was proven by the dramatic ending of his life.

After the invasion of the Netherlands by the Germans on May 10, 1940, the Dutch hierarchy under Archbishop John de Jong soon came into open conflict with National Socialism. Catholics were forbidden under pain of excommunication to participate in party activities which violated Catholic principles. When the Catholic press was ordered to publish news releases and advertisements emanating from the Nazi public relations bureau, De Jong moved to counteract the directive. He asked Titus as spiritual director of the Catholic press to visit editors with instructions to resist Nazi propaganda. In making his request, the archbishop made no secret of the danger of the mission, which Titus equally understood. Shadowed by the Gestapo, he had visited fourteen newspapers, before he was taken into custody on January 19,1942. In prison at Scheveningen he replied to questioning candidly and calmly, openly admitting that he opposed National Socialism, because it was irreconcilable with his Catholic faith. As a result of his questioning, Hardegen reported to his superiors that Brandsma was dangerous to the cause and should be confined for the duration of the war.

At Scheveningen, Brandsma's contemplative spirit turned his solitary cell into a haven of peace and joy. Happy to be alone with Christ, he spent the time praying and writing. To the long tradition of prison literature he contributed *Mijn cel en dagorde van een gevangene* (Tilburg, 1944) and even began a biography of St. Teresa of Avila, writing between the lines of a book. His often printed and translated *Lines to a Crucifix in Prison* speaks the simple and humble language of a lover:

> O Jesus, when I look on you,
> My love for you starts up anew,
> And tells me that your heart loves me,
> And you my special friend would be.
>
> More courage I will need for sure,
> But any pain will I endure,
> Because it makes me like to you
> And leads unto your kingdom too.
>
> In sorrow do I find my bliss,
> For sorrow now no more is this
> Rather the path that must be trod
> That makes me one with you, my God.
>
> Oh, leave me here alone and still,
> And all round, the cold and chill.
> To enter here I will have none;
> I weary not when I'm alone,
>
> For, Jesus, you are at my side;
> Never so close did we abide.
> Stay with me, Jesus, my delight,
> Your presence near makes all things right.

On March 12, 1942, Titus was transferred out of Scheveningen, ending on June 19 in the dreaded concentration camp of Dachau. In that hell, the frail sixty-one year old Carmelite lasted little more than a month, being dispatched with a mortal injection on July 26. This is not the place to describe his heroic suffering; suffice it to record his prayerful calm, his cheerful optimism, his support of his fellow sufferers, his genuine love of his hateful tormentors.

At Dachau, Titus found Brother Raphael Tijhuis who survived four brutal years there and lived to witness to his confrere's heroic virtue.

The four nunneries in the province - "Elzendaal" and St. Joseph's in Boxmeer, Zenderen, and Heerlen - remained structurally intact, but the two Boxmeer monasteries were occupied by troops between November 1944 and March 1945, while the nuns were dispersed.

The extra-provincial activities of the Dutch province naturally suffered from the war - Brazil, if only because the source of personnel had dried up. When on December 8, 1941, Japan declared war, the Netherlands, invaded by Germany, was in no position to defend its colony in Indonesia (then, the Dutch East Indies). The

Japanese invaded the islands and on March 9, 1942, took Malang. All European influence on the inhabitants was to end: schools were closed, European civil servants, teachers, clergy, and religious were interned. Among these were the thirty or so Carmelites, including Bishop Avertanus Albers. Although conditions in the camps were far from comfortable, and crowding, lack of food, and sickness were common, they were bearable to the courageous. A few Carmelites suffered actual mistreatment. Romualdus Bijlhout and Willebrord Ardts, military chaplains, were questioned by the secret police, the Kem-Pé-Tai, by their usual methods. Marius Blijdenstein was beaten about the face with a stick, kicked, and confined in cramped quarters for two weeks, because he inadvertently violated the blackout.

Chaplain Xavier Vloet was being transferred to Thailand with 1,200 soldier prisoners, when their transport was torpedoed. He stayed with the ship to the last to offer assistance to those who remained. On August 3, 1944, he had been selected from among other priests in the prison in Batavia to accompany the transport, because he looked the healthiest.

The Javanese Carmelite, Albert Gondowardaja, was arrested by the Kem-Pé-Tai for some unknown reason and died of hunger and exhaustion in prison in Bandoeng.

On August 15, 1945, Japan capitulated. The Europeans had hardly been freed, when they landed back in the camps and prisons, this time confined by the Indonesian Nationalists, making a bid for independence. By August, 1947, the Dutch were once more in control. The interim brought additional destruction and pillage, but the fidelity of the missionaries to their task throughout all political change convinced the Indonesian people of their disinterestedness, and the mission, if somewhat tattered, came out of the trial with increased prestige.

Both the Japanese occupation and the subsequent revolution indeed entailed much damage to churches, schools, and other buildings belonging to the Carmelites and other religious active in the mission.

One benefit derived from the disruption of the mission by the Japanese occupation. Before the war, aspirants to the Order were sent to the Netherlands for higher studies. This system yielded two Javanese priests in ten years: Gerard Singgih and Albert Gondowardaja. When three candidates, who had presented themselves shortly before the war were unable to leave for the Netherlands, their further education was undertaken in Malang by the Carmelites, until these were interned. After the liberation, it was found that the three candidates had not only persevered under the tutelage of Fr. Singgih, but had been joined by five others. Clearly a formation program in Indonesia was indicated. A beginning was made on February 2, 1947, when a novitiate was established in Malang with Alexis van Wanrooij as first novice master.

The War in Germany and Poland

The six convents of the Upper German province - Straubing, Bamberg, Vienna, Springiersbach, Bad Reichenhall (1934), Kirchwiedern - lay outside the immediate theatre of war, yet did not wholly escape its consequences. On February 21, 1945, the Carmelite church in Vienna was destroyed by an air raid, and Gabriel Koeser lost his life in the ruins. The church, which since 1929 had consisted of the crypt only, had been completed and consecrated by Cardinal Theodore Innitzer as recently as August 30, 1942. The previous church had burned down in 1928.

Straubing and Springiersbach were occupied by troops. The historic church and convent of Springiersbach were destroyed by fire occasioned by carelessness (1940). The National Socialist regime closed the seminary of the Order in Bamberg (1941).

In Germany, as in Italy, the clergy were not exempt from military duty: priests were enrolled in the medical corps, brothers and seminarians in the armed forces. At the outbreak of the war, 12 priests, five professed clerics, and 17 lay brothers were inducted - almost half the province, numbering 86 professed members. Of these, Engelbert Jakob was declared missing in action at the end of the war. Remigius Ostler, a professed cleric of twenty-two years of age, was killed on the Eastern front, June 22, 1941. Another cleric, Ubaldus Vetter, lost his life during the Italian campaign, December 11, 1943. Brother Anscar Renker was left dead on the battlefield of Vitebsk on November 27, 1943. Thaddaeus Karpinski, a native of Berlin, was a member of the Dutch province stationed in Mainz. He was not heard from again after he wrote a letter from the front at Tschigirin, December 6, 1943.

The reaction of Carmelites to Nazism remains to be looked into, if such an inquiry be possible. Certainly, the Church had not the reasons to be grateful to Nazism that it did to Fascism.

Among Carmelites, examples of resistance to the regime are found. Angelus Wielhaller was accused of insulting Nazism and the Führer, Adolf Hitler, and was banished from Straubing (1934). The Nazis accused Norbert Stahlhofen of misuse of the pulpit in Pfaffmunster. Tried in Nürnberg, he was imprisoned in Regensburg from August 11 to November 11, 1937.

With the establishment of the Popular Democracy of Czechoslovakia in 1949, religious orders were suppressed, and the convent of the Upper German province in Kostelní Vydří (formerly Kirchwiedern) ceased to be. At the time, the community consisted of Procopius Valena, prior since 1931; Methodius Minarik, assigned there upon completion of his studies in 1939; and Melchior Karasek. The latter remained as pastor of the parish. During their two score years occupancy of the place, the Carmelites had promoted devotion to the Virgin through her centuries-old image in the church.

Germany occupied Poland in 1936 and ceded certain Eastern territories to Russia. In this way, the historic convents of Lwów, Rozdól, Botszowce, Trembowla, and Sasiadowice, situated in that region, were definitively lost to the Order. Casimir Maciejewsky was taken from the convent of Trembowla by the Soviets and afterwards shot.

There remained of the province in German-occupied Poland: Cracow, Pilzno, Lipiny, Obory, and Wola Gulowska. Lipiny does not appear in the catalogs of the province previous to the war, probably because it was considered one with Pilzno. Wola Gulowska had been repossessed in 1924. Shortly after the war it was possible to make foundations in Chyzne (1946), Trutowo (1946), Baborów (1947), and Danzig (1947).

In occupied countries, Nazi authorities were less inhibited in their attitude to the Catholic Church than they were on their native soil. In Poland, the mask was dropped without further ado. Churches, seminaries, and religious houses were closed. Of 7,000 priests, half were killed. In Dachau, alone 2,800 were interned, of whom only 816 survived.

Carmelite victims of Dachau were the prior of Obory, Simon Buszla, Bruno Makowski, and Leo Koza. Hilary Januszewski, prior of Cracow, died there of typhus, while serving fellow prisoners infected with it. Albert Urbanski lived through it all and wrote *Duchowni w Dachau* (Cracow, 1945). Brother Gerard Kowalski died in Auschwitz. Boleslaus Huczynski, chaplain, rests in the Polish cemetery at Monte Cassino.

The English-speaking provinces of the Order shared in the war mainly by contributing voluntary chaplains to the armed forces of their respective countries. Chaplains of the American province of the Most Pure Heart of Mary were: Theodore Hatton, Walter Poynton, Victor Schwar, Reginald Madren, Gilbert Burns, Edmund Welsh, Alfred Gilligan, Aquinas Colgan, Justin O'Connell, Raymond Huttner, Henry Goodwin, Roderick Hurley, Hubert McCarren, Peter Thomas Sherry, Neal O'Connor. Aquinas Colgan was killed on Mindanao Island, May 6, 1945, while attempting to minister to a dying soldier. Roderick Hurley was awarded the Bronz Star.

The American province of St. Elias sent Simon Vital, Finbar Lynn, Alphonsus Galligan, and John McGrath. Finbar Lynn also won the Bronze Star. Ailbe McNamee, Cyril Murphy, and Telesphorus Bulbert, of the Irish province, served as chaplains in the British armed forces, as did Joe Philipps, Walter Bridger, David de Laughrey, Robert Frizzell, Charles Haughey, and Kevin McMahon, of the Australian commissariate.

Chapter 15

The Good Years, 1947-1959

The general chapter finally convened on May 16, 1947, after an interval of almost a decade. The provincial of the American province of St. Elias was handily elected prior general.

Born in Ballymanus, Co. Wicklow, in 1902, Kilian Lynch was one of three brothers, who each in his own way was to distinguish himself in the service of the Order. On making his profession in 1922, he was sent to St. Albert's College in Rome, where he crowned with the lectorate *summa cum laude* three years of philosophy (1922-1925) and four years of theology (1925-1929). Meanwhile, he also acquired doctorates at the Roman Academy of St. Thomas (1926) and the Vatican College (1929). He was ordained to the priesthood on June 17,1928. His brilliant scholastic record led his superiors to promote him to further study at the Pontifical Gregorian University, from which he emerged with a doctorate and the title "*magister aggregatus*." Upon completion of his studies in 1931, he did not return to Ireland, but instead was sent to the Irish commissariate in the United States, which early that year had become a province. There, he took over the post of dean of philosophy at Marymount College, Tarrytown, NY, and in 1934 became prior of the Carmelite convent in Tarrytown and first definitor of the province. After two terms as prior, he was made pastor of Tarrytown. The provincial chapter of 1943 elected him provincial, and he had been reelected in 1946, when the general chapter of the following year called him to head the Order.

The General Chapter of 1947

The chapter was concerned about the Order's vocation to prayer and decreed that the interior life should not be engulfed by activity. Meditation should be made daily without fail. Pastors should not consider themselves exempt from community life. The prior general was to establish a hermitage and provide statutes for it. The need for a manual of the history of the Order was recognized. Unity between the provinces was to be fostered by a news bulletin, of which Albert Groeneveld should be editor. (*The Vinculum* [1948-1953] resulted from this decree.)

The proper spiritual and material care of the nuns was again recommended. A new rule of the Third Order Secular should be composed, which would restore the vows and receive the approbation of the Holy See. Hilary Doswald was praised for his firm stand on the question of the scapular medal, and the general curia was ordered to arrange the celebration of the scapular centenary "with the utmost solemnity."

With regard to the administration of the Order, the chapter granted a third delegate to provinces with more than one hundred members entitled to vote. The prior general was given the authority to name the commissary and two definitors. Missions with at least three priests were entitled to a representative with the right to vote in the provincial chapter. Decrees of a general chapter had to be confirmed by the subsequent chapter in order to be permanently binding.

The Western world recovered remarkably soon from the material consequences of the war, and a period of well-being and optimism replaced the destitution and despair of the years of conflict. For the Church under Pope Pius XII, the 50s were also a time of outward growth and confident self-assurance. Under the dynamic leadership of Kilian Lynch, the Carmelite Order shared abundantly the spirit and accomplishments of the time. Damaged churches and religious houses and institutions were restored, vocations abounded, marianates sprang up like mushrooms, convents multiplied, studies flourished, public manifestations of the faith were organized, the Third Order and scapular confraternity grew apace. Whereas in the decade 1938-1948 membership in the Order increased by only 219 religious, during the years 1948-1959 membership rose by 767. This growth continued through the following years before the Second Vatican Council to reach a high point in 1963 of 2,760 members in the Order.

The re-election of the incumbent prior general by the general chapter of 1953 was a matter of course.

The Internal Life of the Order

With the Order adequately supplied with liturgical texts, this period is marked by a concern for the chant of the Order. It was in the area of the liturgy of the Church that the winds of change first made themselves felt. With the Roman rite in a state of flux, the Order's liturgists were put to some pains to keep the Carmelite rite apace of the times. Nevertheless, after the "*Maxima redemptionis nostrae mysteria,*" of November 16, 1955, Angelo Coan, Master of Music and the Order's expert on liturgical music, managed to have in the choir stalls in time for the Holy Week of 1956 the *Ordo Sacri Tridui* (Paris, 1956), in which the Carmelite rite, supplied with reformed chants, was adapted to the new order of ceremonies. Actually, Fr. Coan was at work on a *chorale*, which would provide chant for all the liturgical needs of the Order, a task complicated by the lack of a consistent musical tradition. In 1957, he produced the first volume of the *Chorale*, presenting the chant for compline, *Officium completorii* (Paris, 1957). The second volume, *Antiphonale missarum* (Paris, 1960), appeared under the prior general, Kilian Healy. In preparing the Carmelite musical texts, Fr. Coan did not have recourse simply to the Roman *Liber usualis* but was graciously given access to their manuscript collection by the monks of Solesmes.

Mayer's embattled ritual (1903) being long out of print, Fr. Kilian issued a new one (Città del Vaticano, 1952), this time without opposition. Prepared by Angelo Coan, it featured a number of useful additions besides musical notation.

Three foundations, due largely to the initiative of Fr. Kilian, were important for the spiritual life of the Order. In 1949, the Carmelites recovered their ancient convent at Aylesford, one of the Order's first foundations in Europe. Aylesford under Kilian's brother, Malachy, became a frequented Marian shrine and spiritual center, a rallying point for the restoration of the Order in England, and in general a spiritual return to their origins for all Carmelites.

The foundation in Wölfnitz, Austria, restored the eremitical ideal of Carmelite life. The community inaugurated its life of prayer on September 14, 1956, under Philip van Duynhoven, prior. The statutes decreed by the general chapter had been supplied by Fr. Kilian the previous March 19.

A foundation at the site of the apparitions of Our Lady at Fatima corresponded to the Order's Marian aspirations. In an interview with the visionary of Fatima on October 13, 1951, Sister Lucy had asked the prior general to do something at Fatima to reanimate the ancient devotion of the Portuguese to Our Lady of Mount Carmel. Her words were a sacred trust and Fr. Kilian set out to implement them. The Casa Beato Nuno, appropriately named after the national hero of Portugal, was inaugurated on August 14, 1947, during the triennial congregation convened there for that purpose. This assembly constituted the new foundation the International Center of the Third Order Secular with Nuno Alves Corrêa as director general.

The faculty and students of St. Albert's College, Rome, had been scattered by the war, and it remained the task of the newly elected prior general to rebuild it. This he not only accomplished, but brought the College to an unparalleled degree of prosperity. In the peak year of 1958-1959 the student body numbered 58 with a faculty of 16, besides 16 graduate students attending the universities of Rome.

Fr. Kilian crowned his efforts on behalf of Carmelite studies by publishing in his final year in office the *Ratio studiorum generalis* (Rome, 1959), which specified Carmelite priestly studies in detail, bringing these into line with the recent general legislation of the Holy See.

Not the least of Fr. Kilian's accomplishments for the internal life of the Order was the establishment in 1951 of the *Institutum Carmelitanum*. In 1945, immediately after the war, the *Nederlands Carmelitaans Historisch Instituut* had been erected in Boxmeer under the able leadership of Victor Roefs, but the focus of its interest was Carmel in the Netherlands. Otherwise, the investigation of the Order's general history and spirituality, past and present, was the unique responsibility of the current editor of the *Analecta Ordinis Carmelitarum*, which tended to appear rather sporadically. In the *Institutum Carmelitanum*, embodied in a permanent staff of scholars, Carmelite studies achieved stability and continuity. Through its review, *Carmelus*, and its series of regularly published monographs the learned world in general as well as the Carmelite community have been provided with a fund of information that has proven of critical value for the building of the Order's future in changing times.

Three Public Celebrations

In the spirit of the times, the Order gave expression to its devotion through impressive public celebrations. The seventh centenary of the granting of the scapular, celebrated from July 16, 1950, to July 16, 1951, was commemorated on a grandiose scale, as the general chapter had ordained. Early in 1948, the prior general already announced the proposed celebration. Together with the Discalced Carmelites a program, projecting scientific studies, publicity, local congresses, lectures, and novenas was drawn up. A listing of all scapular confraternities erected from 1604 to 1948 was composed from archival and other sources. From August 5th to the 9th, fifteen thousand devotees met in Rome in an International Marian Congress to initiate the centenary. Pope Pius XII honored the occasion with his letter on the scapular devotion, *Neminem profecto latet*, February 11, 1950. Similar meetings were held in the provinces, and bishops sent pastoral letters. The centennial year concluded at Aylesford, July 14-16, 1951, with the solemn return of the relics of St. Simon Stock from Bordeaux. The Discalced Carmelite, Cardinal Adeodato Piazza, presided over the ceremony attended by bishops, civil authorities, including

Eamon de Valera, president of Ireland, and 25,000 faithful. This occasion also elicited a letter of Pius XII.

The Marian Year, 1954, commemorating the declaration of the dogma of the Immaculate Conception, was likewise celebrated by the Carmelites with proper dedication. On November 21, 1953, Kilian Lynch issued a circular letter, urging the participation of the whole Order in the celebration. On November 10, 1954, almost 400 members of both Orders paid their pilgrimage visit to the Basilica of Mary Major in Rome. At the Mariological Congress, held at the Lateran University, Bartholomew Xiberta spoke at one of the plenary sessions, while the Carmelites held their own particular session, at which papers were presented by Bishop Gabriel Couto, Eamon Carroll, Kilian Healy, Irenaeus Rosier, Claude Catena, and Bruno Borchert.

The fifth centenary of the bull, *Cum nulla*, of Nicholas V, October 7, 1452, confirming the membership of women in the Order, was commemorated by a letter of Pius XII, *Quinque abhinc saeculis*, July 25, 1952. At the same time, Kilian Lynch communicated to the Order his intention of erecting at Fatima, where Our Lady had appeared in the Carmelite habit, an international center for the Third Order and scapular confraternity. Five years later, the building was completed, and its inauguration was the occasion for holding an International Congress of the Third Order, August 13-15, 1957. For this event, too, the pope wrote a letter, *Ex obsequentissimis litteris*, dated April 3, 1957. Two thousand tertiaries attended the congress, presided over by Cardinal Piazza, who, besides officiating at the liturgy, delivered a notable address on the spirituality of the Third Order and its purpose in the modern world. In separate sessions, according to language, the tertiaries heard papers read by experts from each nation.

The Second and Third Orders

Already in Hilary Doswald's time, the shortcomings of Magennis's tertiary rule were felt. John Brenninger was given the task of composing a new Rule. His familiarity with the spiritual doctrine of Carmel and practical experience (he had been named secretary general of the Third Order in 1939) eminently fitted him for the undertaking. Keeping in view the preceding legislation of Soreth, Strazio, Jacomelli, and Tartaglia, Brenninger's Rule, as is to be expected of its author, proposes a high ideal of holiness to the tertiary, who is expected to assist daily at Mass and receive Holy Communion, make a half hour meditation, do spiritual reading and an examination of conscience. Once a month, the tertiary should make a day of recollection and every year a retreat of at least three days. Most important of all, Brenninger's Rule restored the vows of obedience and chastity which had traditionally characterized the Carmelite Third Order. "We do not hesitate to affirm," Tomás Motta concludes in his canonical study of the evolution of the Third Order of Carmel, "that (this Rule) is the best of its kind in comparison with preceding rules of the Carmelite Third Order and one of the better rules among those of other orders." This Rule Kilian Lynch promulgated, having first obtained the approval of the Holy See, on July 16, 1948.

The scorn of the Enlightenment and the open hostility of 19th century Liberalism brought about a blight on cloistered Carmelite life which lasted two and a half centuries. The active sisterhoods were found socially useful, and this was the period of their origin and growth, but the 18th century witnessed cloistered foundations only at Ostuni (1730) and Siracusa (cloister, 1738). In the 19th century, St. Joseph's in Boxmeer was founded by refugees from Xanten (1876) and in turn gave rise to the Carmel of Zenderen (1889).

During the first decades of the 20th century, too, growth remained practically at a standstill. Father John Baptist Felíu founded the Carmel of Caudete with nuns from Onteniente, headed by his sister, Joachima of Jesus (1914). "Elzendaal" in Boxmeer gave rise to Heerlen in 1928. Sister Teresa of Jesus crossed the seas from Naples to found the monastery of Allentown, PA. (1931).

In the generalate of Kilian Lynch, and due largely to his interest, cloistered Carmel came to life again. In 1948 "Elzendaal" in Boxmeer joined Heerlen to form a community in Jaboticabal, Brazil. Eight years later, "Elzendaal" founded the first monastery of the old Carmel in England at Blackburn, Lancashire (1956). Not to be outdone, St. Joseph's in Boxmeer in 1948 established at Schlüsselau the first German cloistered Carmel since that of Cologne (1565-1802). In 1958, it also made a foundation in Oss.

In Spain, *Las Maravillas* of Madrid founded the Carmel of San José de las Matas, Dominican Republic (1954). Four years later, it established the first cloistered Carmel in the Far East at Dumaguete in the Philippine Islands. Seville undertook the return of the Carmelite nuns to Portugal, making foundations at Moncorvo (1949) and Beja (1954). In 1955, Utrera and Villalba joined forces to found the first African Carmelite monastery at Kakamega, Kenya. Barcelona and Villafranca del Pañadés together added a sixth Catalan monastery in Tàrrega (1953). In 1951, the sisters of Bañolas had accepted cloister, to become the fifth Catalan monastery. The same year, the Third Order sisters of Camerino in Italy had become cloistered nuns.

In the United States, Allentown gave rise to Wahpeton, ND (1954) and Asheville, NC (1956). The first Carmelite monastery in the New World, San Juan in Puerto Rico, which at the time had moved to Santurce, PR, established another Caribbean Carmel at Ciudad Trujillo in the Dominican Republic (1957).

Among sisters remarkable for their holy lives might be noted Josephine Koning (1863-1931), of St. Joseph's, Boxmeer; Elia of the Mother of God (1906-1934), of Vilvoorde; Rosaria of St. Philomena (1865-1935), of Ostuni; Mary Lourdes of the Most Blessed Sacrament (1916-1948), of Piedrahita, Mary Magdalen de' Pazzi Sanz Perea (1876-1953), of Utrera.

At this time, another tertiary sisterhood was affiliated to the Order. At the general chapter of 1922 of the Sisters of the Virgin Mary of Mount Carmel (of Orihuela), a difference arose which resulted in the withdrawal of a group of sisters headed by Sister Asunción Soler Gimeno. The bone of contention seems to have been policies concerning the congregation of the Carmelite Sisters of St. John of God, founded in 1882, which the Sacred Heart Carmelites had been requested to reform. In any case, the dissidents returned to Limonar, Malaga, to the house of the St. John of God Sisters they had previously reformed, and on May 13, 1924, received recognition from the bishop of Malaga, Manuel González García. Like the parent branch, the new sisterhood flourished. In 1939, it absorbed the Sisters of the Sacred Heart and Mary Immaculate (of Almogia, Malaga); in 1951, the Carmelite Third Order Sisters of Charity (of Palma de Mallorca). In 1947, Kilian Lynch aggregated the sisters to the Order. When they received approval for seven years from the Holy See in 1955, they were given the present form of their name, the Carmelite Sisters of the Sacred Heart of Jesus. On June 13,1965, Pope Paul VI granted definitive approval. In 1979, the congregation comprised 39 houses and 229 professed sisters in Spain, England, Mozambique, Portugal, the Dominican Republic, and Venezuela. The sisters dedicate themselves to any social and educational need.

The apostolic constitution, *Provida mater*, of February 2, 1947, recognized the secular institute as a new and efficacious way of pursuing Christian perfection in the world. The Secular Institute of Our Lady of Mount Carmel was founded by Winifred and Joan Swingler under the direction of Malachy Lynch. It was initiated on November 1, 1949, upon the return of the Carmelites to Aylesford. The foundresses had been joined by a third member, Elizabeth Young. In 1958, the Institute received the more expressive title, "The Leaven." Members undergo a probationary period of six months, three years as a student member, six years of commitment to *The Leaven*, after which they make an act of consecration for life. The constitutions were approved by the archbishop of Southwark. In 1979, *The Leaven* counted five student members, four committed members, and nine members consecrated for life.

Further Development of the Order

The Carmine of Naples had remained, as always, directly under the jurisdiction of the priors general. When the friars of the Carmine returned to Vico Equense (1932) and Sorrento (1936), though in the case of the former not to the original location, these filial houses were also taken under the general's protection. On January 4, 1947, Hilary Doswald gave them their independence by the creation of the *La Bruna* commissariate with Albert Salzano as first commissary.

During his visitation in 1948, Kilian Lynch raised the commissariate of Australia to the status of a province with the title "Our Lady Help of Christians." Joseph Nugent was named first provincial. The new province numbered 41 members in 7 convents at Middle Park, Port Melbourne, Adelaide, Brisbane, Mitcham, Wahroonga, and Meadowbank, NZ.

In Spain, the commissariate of Castile was separated from the Arago-Valentine province with the title, "Mother of Carmel," November 3, 1948. The new commissariate, headed by Alphonsus M. López, was assigned the convents of El Henar, the newly founded Salamanca, and Lomas de Zamora, Argentina, in the process of being founded, besides the care of the nuns of *Las Maravillas*, Madrid, and of Fontiveros. It numbered 24 members. In 1951, foundations were made in Santander and Viernoles.

In 1950, Catalonia was restored as a province with Pablo Casadevall as first provincial. Besides Barcelona, Olot, Tarrasa, and Tárrega, the province had houses in Porlamar and La Asunción in Venezuela and Aimores and Resplendor in Brazil. Calixto in the latter country was added around this time.

The previous year, on February 9, 1949, Pernambuco also became once more a province. Sebastian Boerkamp was named provincial. The new province counted houses in Recife, Goiana, Princesa Isabel (1938), and Gamelleira (1921). By 1957, Campina Grande and Camocim had been added.

In 1933, at the request of Hilary Doswald, Aloysius Gonzaga Oliveira took over the directorship of the historic Third Order of Lisbon, which through all the vicissitudes of time had maintained its vigil beside the ruins of the Carmo, tomb of St. Nuno Alvares Pereira. (The prior general would have known Aloysius from the latter's years of study in St. Cyril's College, Chicago.)

In 1941, Nuno of St. Mary Gomes Vaz de Castro was ordained, the first Portuguese Carmelite to receive orders in two centuries. He joined Fr. Rubio in the parish of Santa Isabel. Otherwise, Carmel in Portugal showed little signs of life.

Kilian Lynch now undertook to awaken the dormant enterprise. In 1948, the annual congregation of the Andalusian province named Raphael M. Rangel vicar provincial of Portugal. In 1949, he accepted a parish in Mirando do Douro, which the prior general designated as a marianate. It actually opened in October, but accommodations proved inadequate and a new site was acquired in Braga (1951). Meanwhile, Portugal, always a burden to the Andalusian province, was becoming unbearable. The prior general was showing interest in a foundation in Fatima, and in 1953 insisted that the rented house in Lisbon be purchased. At the general chapter of 1953, the Andalusians requested to be relieved of their responsibility in Portugal. At its chapter in 1954, Rio de Janeiro agreed to continue the restoration of the mother province, begun by Andalusia, and appointed Cyril Alleman commissary general. At Braga, the first group of seminarians was ready for the novitiate, so a seminary was opened in Falperra near Braga (1954), while Braga itself was designated the novitiate. It continued as such until 1959, when the novitiate moved to Longra (Douro). The foundation of the Casa Beato Nuno at Fatima provided, like Aylesford in England, wider perspectives and ministry for Carmel in Portugal. The houses of formation gave hope for its future.

On January 1, 1952, Kilian Lynch erected the houses of the Irish province in England into a commissariate general, the first step in restoring the second oldest province in the Order. At the first definitorial meeting on January 8, Laserian Geary was appointed commissary general. In the prewar years, Carmel in England had made good progress. In 1938, a third foundation was made in Kent at Hartley. Meanwhile, the Carmelites had undertaken an apostolate in Wales. At the invitation of the bishop of Cardiff, Michael McGrath, they took charge of the diocesan seminary, St. Mary's College in Aberystwyth (1936). At the same time, they were entrusted with the parish of Our Lady of the Angels and St. Winifred, of which Malachy Lynch took charge in January, 1936. Fr. Malachy also built a little jewel of a church at Lampeter, blessed on July 16, 1940, to care for the Catholics of the district. When a house was added, Bellarmine O'Neill took up residence. In 1947, the seminary was transferred to Llandeilo. St. Mary's of Aberystwyth remained in use for late vocations. The mission in non-Catholic Wales was a difficult one, carried out in a spirit of faith without regard for tangible results or rewards.

The recovery of historic Aylesford, recounted above, was a milestone in the history of the English Carmel in modern times, providing the Carmelites with a mission of more than local significance. In 1951, the Carmelites also acquired Allington Castle, a medieval castle once the home of the poet, Thomas Wyatt (1503-1541), and made of it a retreat center. In 1958, the school at Llandeilo was moved to Cheltenham, Glo., and given the name Whitefriars School.

On September 12, 1969, the ancient province of England and Wales, suppressed in 1538, again became a reality.

Carmel in Asia and Africa

The mission of the Dutch province in Indonesia continued to prosper. On March 15, 1939, Pius XII had made Malang an apostolic vicariate. Its vicar, Avertanus Albers, received episcopal consecration the following August 10. In 1958, the vicariate counted 67 Carmelites: 50 priests (14 of them Indonesian), five brothers, and 12 Indonesian professed clerics. In 1960, Indonesia was made a commissariate general with Martin Sarka Dipojudo as commissary. In 1967, it became a province; Andrew Harjaka was named provincial. When Bishop Albers resigned as ordinary of Malang (1972), Dionysius Hadisumarta was appointed his successor and given episcopal consecration on July 16, 1973.

With the increase in native vocations and the lessening of Dutch influence in Indonesia in the postwar years, the Dutch Carmelites looked for other mission fields in which to labor and ended by choosing the Philippine Islands. In 1958, they settled in Escalante and Toboso on Negros Island. It was the beginning of an extensive missionary effort that was to spread to other of the Philippine Islands.

The Irish Carmelites, too, were ready to take on new commitments. Their American and Australian fledglings had waxed strong and become provinces; England as a commissariate was also weaned from the mother province. This time, the Irish Carmelites chose to work in Africa, the only continent on which Carmel was not yet present. On July 22, 1946, the Sacred Congregation for the Propagation of the Faith granted the Carmelites permission to work in the vicariate apostolic of Salisbury, in what was then Southern Rhodesia (modern Zimbabwe). The Carmelites were to work side by side with the Jesuits, pioneers in the area, who were to teach them their trade. The first Carmelites, Donal Raymond Lamont (superior), Anselm Corbett, and Luke Flynn, left Ireland on October 7, 1946. A year later, they were reinforced by A. Eugene Wright, J. Ambrose Roche, J. Mel Hill, and Brothers Bernard Clinch and Angelus Kinsella. On January 1, 1948, Triashill Mission was entrusted to the Carmelites; later the same year, St. Kilian's. To help with these responsibilities John Baptist Sharkey and Matthew Ahern arrived in 1949. Other Jesuit missions were taken over: St. Robert's and St. Barbara's in 1949, the parish in Umtali (modern Mutare), and Mount Melleray in 1950. The new mission of St. Anne's was founded in 1951.

On March 23, 1950, the Sacred Congregation for the Propagation of the Faith canonically erected Triashill, St. Barbara's, St. Kilian's, and Umtali. Three years later, on February 6, 1953, the same Congregation erected the Prefecture Apostolic of Umtali with Donal Lamont as prefect apostolic. At the time, 22 Carmelites were active in the mission. Other missions were taken over or founded: St. Benedict's (1953), Regina Coeli (1955), St. Therese's (1956). On February 1, 1957, the prefecture was made a diocese with Donal Lamont as its first bishop. The Carmelites built well on the foundations laid by their Jesuit predecessors, adding churches, schools, and hospitals, teaching, catechizing, visiting outlying stations in the native reserve. In a decade, they had created a diocese.

The German Mission in Brazil

The German Carmelites, who hitherto had shown little inclination to stray far from their historic convents in Bavaria and the Rhineland (and who can blame them?), were now also smitten with missionary fever.

In the 30s, the province had sent several members to help the Pernambuco province and at the same time to prepare themselves for a mission of the German province: Ulrich Gövert in 1936 and Alphonse Ballsieper with the postulant Andrew Hillebrand in 1937. The war put the quietus on these plans, but after the cessation of hostilities, the prior general urged the provincial to reanimate the project. Gövert, who had served as novice master and definitor of the Pernambuco province, was the indicated man for the job. By the bishop of Jacarezinho, Gerardo Sigaud, he was assigned the parish of Paranavaí (Paraná), and on September 2, 1951, took possession of a small rectory and a roofless church in a remote village of about sixty houses. The parish, however, was not lacking in members, counting 50,000 persons scattered over an area of 130 sq. mi. In October, Brother Stanislaus arrived from Recife and proved a great help as a catechist and jack-of-all trades. Fr. Ulrich immediately undertook the construction of a large new church and the establishment of a school. When Hartwig Wunderlich, an experienced carpenter and cabinet maker as well as a priest, came in September, 1952, the church building was already complete, and he was able to start on the altars and other furnishings. After the new church was built, the school was moved into the old structure, making available room for 300 pupils. In 1956, the school of Our Lady of Mount Carmel of Paranavaí won first place among the schools of Paraná.

In 1953, Bonaventure Einberger appeared and took charge of the German settlement of Graciosa, where he began to build a marianate (seminary). By 1959, the seminary housed twenty boys and was already too small. More help presented itself in 1954 in the persons of Albert Först and Burkhard Lippert, though ill health obliged the latter to return to Germany the following year. A welcome addition to the mission staff were four Carmelite Missionary Sisters of St. Therese of the Child Jesus (*Suore Missionarie di Santa Teresa del Bambino Gesù*): Sisters Canisia Popp (superior), Tomassina Draisma, Gabriella Scodina, and Grazia Cavalla, who debarked at Santos in June, 1955. The group had been picked with a view also to language skills: Sister Canisia was Austrian; Tomassina, Dutch. Bernard Rech was a Brazilian of German descent, who had studied for the diocesan priesthood, but later applied for admission to the Carmelite Order. Ordained in the parish church of Paranavaí in 1955, he returned to the mission two years later, after receiving the name Athanasius in the novitiate of Straubing.

The provincial chapter of 1955 separated the offices of prior and pastor, allotting the former to Albert Först, the latter to the father of the mission, Ulrich Gövert. In only five years, he had carved a Christian community from the wilderness.

The American Mission in Peru

The American province of the Most Pure Heart of Mary, second only to the Netherlands in strength of membership and means, in no way equalled the latter's missionary record. The most fertile soil for the missions were provinces in small countries with an abundance of vocations. The widespread American province had always found more to do than it could handle within its native shores. Now, however, the provincial chapter of 1948 resolved to answer the call of Pius XII to North America to send laborers to its southern neighbors. The same year found the former provincial, Matthew O'Neill, and Howard Rafferty enroute to South America to explore possibilities for missionary activity. The result of their investigation was the decision to found houses in Lima, Peru, and Santiago, Chile - not exactly jungle territory but promising bases for future expansion in each country.

On August 4, 1949, the archbishop of Lima, Cardinal John Gualbert Guevara, turned over to Fr. Matthew O'Neill and Leon Battle the parish of Our Lady of Mount Carmel. Fr. Matthew was named first pastor, but his parish was a phantasm. It remained to gather the faithful, buy land, and construct buildings. Until 1952, parish activities centered in a house in the Calle Arias Aragüez, 659, which served as rectory and chapel. Between 1950 and 1953, land was acquired with funds from the province. In March, 1953, a structure was completed, which was to serve as church and parish hall. In May of the following year, a new convent was occupied by the community, to which had been added Alban Quinn (1950), Nevin Hayes (1951), and Jeffry Fairfield (1952). In 1952, the parish was dealt a hard blow, when Fr. Matthew suffered a stroke and had to return to the United States, where he lived an invalid until his death in 1961. Nevin Hayes took his place as pastor. Jeffry Fairfield was named prior.

It was decided to concentrate the parish's resources on building a school rather than a church. Kindergarten was initiated in the storey over the church in 1956, while construction on an elementary school was begun. The structure was continued year by year as classes were added. American Sister Servants of the Immaculate Heart of Mary took charge of instruction. In 1961, construction began on a secondary school in charge of the Carmelites, which grew in the same manner as the elementary school. When Nevin Hayes was called to head the prelature of Sicuani in 1959, Jeffry took charge of the parish, succeeded in turn by Alban Quinn in 1961. Besides the schools, the parish developed a *Club Carmelitas*, for social events, a credit cooperative, a service providing food, clothing, and medical aid to the poor, evening classes for children. In the course of a decade, a vibrant Christian community had been created from what was an anomalous fringe of an expanding modern metropolis.

Contemporaneously with the Lima project, Sylvester Snee (superior) and Pierce Gilmartin took possession of the parish of the Curé d'Ars in Santiago, Chile in 1949. In 1958, an enlarged community was able to take charge of the parish of San Miguel, of which Fr. Pierce was named pastor. In these parishes, too, were introduced social services, medical aid, credit cooperatives, and schools. The two parishes embraced a population of 100,000. The burden, however, proved more than the province could bear, and the Santiago parishes were regretfully returned to the archbishop in 1970.

The provincial chapter of 1966 named Alban Quinn provincial commissary for Chile and Peru.

An opportunity to do something more closely approaching missionary work was offered to the American Carmelites, when Pope John XXIII assigned them the prelature *nullius* of Sicuani, separated from the archdiocese of Cuzco, January 10, 1959, at the same time naming Nevin Hayes prelate ordinary. Situated 3,500 meters above sea level, the prelature embraced the provinces of Canchis, Canas, Chumibilcas, and Espinar. The new prelate's flock consisted mainly of poor Indians speaking Quechua and scattered about in inaccessible villages. On March 11, Msgr. Hayes took possession of his see in the adobe cathedral of Sicuani. The immediate problem was the scarcity of priests; only 11 priests were at hand to staff the 21 parishes inhabited by about 300,000 persons, most of them nominally Catholic. Beginning in 1960, Carmelites arrived to lend a hand: Bertrand Malone, Aquinas Houle, Earl Corkery, Dudley O'Keefe, Blaise McInerney.

Two native Discalced sisterhoods, the Carmelite Nazarene Sisters and the Carmelite Nazarene Sisters of San Blas, had been conducting the State secondary school and the hospital respectively. Since they were greatly reduced in numbers with little prospect of reviving, the prelate absorbed them with the Discalced Carmelite Missionaries (*Carmelitas Misioneras*), whom he fetched from Barcelona. He also imported the Sisters of Mercy of the Chicago province, who staffed the hospital as well as a high school for girls. With time, there were added a training program for catechists, a credit cooperative, and a retreat center. In 1967, Msgr. Hayes moved to a new house in Tinaya, constructed large enough to provide lodging and rest for his priests who came to Sicuani from the outlying villages.

On August 5, 1965, in the cathedral of Chicago, Msgr. Hayes was consecrated titular bishop of *Novasinnensis*. When he was forced to retire for reasons of health, he was succeeded in the prelature by Alban Quinn (1971).

The altitude of Sicuani, added to the usual inconveniences of missionary work, make of this mission one of the most difficult Carmelites are called upon to cultivate.

The Maltese Mission in Bolivia and Peru

For the past century or so, Maltese Carmelites are to be found quietly providing needed assistance in many provinces during their restoration or foundation. Not until this time, however, did they attempt to establish foundations of their own outside the island. In 1949, Redemptus Gauci and Ignatius Axisa took over the parish of Our Lady of Mount Carmel in Tingo in the diocese of Arequipa, Peru. The parish included four villages, one of which, Bellavista, was accessible only on horseback. The parishioners in this widespread area numbered 11,000, many of them poor Indios living in the mountains. The two pioneers were soon joined by other missionaries: Edward Vella and Carmel Cassar in 1950, Hilary Camilleri in 1952, Anthony Vidal, Seraphim Abela, and Emygdius Fiorini in 1955, Gregory Grima in 1957.

These added forces enabled the Maltese to think of expanding their activities. Their choice fell on Bolivia, a country in which the Carmelites had never been represented. In 1956, Edward Vella and Seraphim Abela accepted the parish of Our Lady of Fatima in La Paz. Later the same year, Ignatius Axisa joined them. At the same time, Bartholomew Attard and Emygdius Fiornini took over the parish of St. Rocco in Tarija. The Bolivian foundations were reinforced by the arrival of Paulinus Cremona and Philip Briffa in 1957 and Salvatore Bartolo and Francis Xavier Caruana in 1958.

The provincial chapter of 1958 appointed Edward Vella commissary general of the houses in Bolivia and Peru, thus completing the administrative structure of the Maltese missions.

On June 5, 1962, Pope John XXIII created the prelature of Chuquibamba in Southern Peru and named Redemptus Gauci first prelate ordinary. The prelature, embracing the provinces of Condesuyas, Camaná, Castilla, and La Union, ranged from sea level at Camaná to 5,500 meters. In the altitude, the same poverty and ignorance prevailed as elsewhere in Peru under similar conditions. The Cathedral of St. Anne in Chuquibamba having been destroyed by an earthquake, use was made of the Church of the Immaculate Conception. The 15 parishes of the prelature were administered by eight diocesan priests. To these, four others were soon added, three Peruvians and one North American. Msgr. Gauci brought Gregory Grima and Francis Xavier Caruana with him to man the chancery, but when diocesan priests became available, the Carmelites in October moved to a location in Camaná. On September 8, 1963, work was begun on a seminary to house the seminarians studying in other places. In Chuquibamba, six Sisters of St. Dorothy administered the public school; in Camaná, seven Franciscan Tertiaries of Our Lady of Fatima performed a like service. Msgr. Gauci lost no time in obtaining the spiritual assistance of his sisters in Carmel, and in 1966 established a cloistered Carmel in Camaná with eight nuns from Onteniente.

On April 13, 1967, Pope Paul VI named Msgr. Gauci titular bishop of Idensis in Mauretania. Upon the bishop's untimely death in 1978, the prelature passed from Carmelite hands.

In the present century, the Carmelites have heavily invested their modest resources in the South American continent, traditional site of their missionary efforts and the densest concentration of Catholics in the world. In 1957, there were 23 Carmelite foundations, many of them centers for mission stations, representing eight provinces in Brazil, Peru, Chile, Argentina, Venezuela, Bolivia, and Puerto Rico.

Conclusion

The general chapter of 1959 elected as prior general Kilian Healy, of the American province of the Most Pure Heart of Mary, since 1953 assistant general for the English-speaking provinces. He was born in 1912 in Worcester, Mass., and entered the Order at Niagara Falls, making his profession in 1931. Ordination followed in 1937, after studies at Mount Carmel College, Niagara Falls, and St. Albert's College, Rome. He taught systematic theology at Whitefriars Hall, Washington, DC, of which he was elected prior in 1945. Recalled to Rome for doctoral studies, he obtained his degree at the Pontifical Gregorian University in 1952.

Before the general chapter, Kilian Healy's name had not featured prominently among likely candidates, yet he issued from the assembly as prior general, the man of prayerful patience and serenity, suited to the troubled times that awaited the Order and the Church. He was re-elected in 1965. In his first term of office lay the Pied Piper - Vatican II; in his second term, payment of the aforementioned musician. Kilian Healy may be classed with Nicholas Audet and Angelo Savini among priors general who ruled the Order during its most difficult years.

The death of Pius XII on October 9, 1958, marked the end of the Tridentine Church. During his reign the world and the Church seemed to have made a complete recovery from the shambles of the war, yet men and women were never the same after that experience. Also, the secular state was not proving to be the paradise its architects had planned. With time, malaise set in, disillusionment with the status quo, loss of faith and hope. And if the secular structures no longer seemed adequate, the alienation of the Church from its environment, always present to a certain extent since the secularization of society, was sensed by the faithful with ever growing urgency. This feeling found voice at the Second Vatican Council and launched the Church on new unchartered seas. If the bark of Peter suffered notable buffetings, the tiny craft of Carmel shipped no less water. Good judgement did not always mark the post-conciliar years, but revolutions are not known for their prudence. The change had to come, and Carmel, finding itself at the crossroads as so many times in the past, had no doubt which way to go.

Certainly Carmel has come a long way from its desert homeland. The Order of today would be difficult to identify with the unpretentious group of hermits come together for the purpose of following Christ on his native soil. Yet the modern Carmelite has been drawn by the same vision as his spiritual ancestors. Carmel's itinerary through time and space has been traced above. It has not always been an edifying spectacle, because it is a human story. Still, the Carmelites were men and women informed by the spirit of Christ and shielded by the mantle of his Mother and to that extent consistent with their ideal. They were never a very important Order in the Church: the title, friars minor, suits them better than the Franciscans. Nevertheless, we find Carmel at hand to share the vicissitudes of the Church throughout the last eight hundred years of its existence, at times making a humble but distinctive contribution. Is it presumptuous to say, as can safely be asserted of the great religious orders, that without Carmel the story of the Church would not be quite the same?

Some Carmelite Websites

**For more information about the Carmelites today
and our ministries worldwide, visit:**
http://carmelites.info

**For more information about other publications from
Carmelite Media, visit:**
http://carmelites.info/publications

Index

Index

www.ingramcontent.com/pod-product-compliance
Lightning Source LLC
Chambersburg PA
CBHW030938150426
42812CB00064B/3042/J